COLCHESTER UNITED
FROM GRAHAM TO WHITTON
– A Complete Record –

Colchester Utd: Graham to Whitton – A Complete Record	1-874287-27-9
Portsmouth: From Tindall to Ball – A Complete Record	1-874287-25-2
Halifax Town: From Ball to Lillis – A Complete Record	1-874287-26-0
Bristol City: The Modern Era – A Complete Record	1-874287-28-7
Coventry City: The Elite Era – A Complete Record	1-874287-03-1
Luton Town: The Modern Era – A Complete Record	1-874287-05-8
Hereford United: The League Era – A Complete Record	1-874287-18-X
West Ham: From Greenwood to Redknapp – Match by Match	1-874287-19-8
Wimbledon: From Southern League to Premiership	1-874287-09-0
Wimbledon: From Wembley to Selhurst	1-874287-20-1
Aberdeen: The European Era – A Complete Record	1-874287-11-2
The Story of the Rangers 1873-1923	1-874287-16-3
The Story of the Celtic 1888-1938	1-874287-15-5
History of the Everton Football Club 1878-1928	1-874287-14-7
The Romance of the Wednesday 1867-1926	1-874287-17-1
Red Dragons in Europe – A Complete Record	1-874287-01-5
The Book of Football: A History to 1905-06	1-874287-13-9
England: The Quest for the World Cup – A Complete Record	1-897850-40-9
Scotland: The Quest for the World Cup – A Complete Record	1-897850-50-6
Ireland: The Quest for the World Cup – A Complete Record	1-897850-80-8

COLCHESTER UNITED
FROM GRAHAM TO WHITTON
— A Complete Record —

Series Editor: Clive Leatherdale
Series Consultant: Leigh Edwards

Jeff Whitehead

DESERT ISLAND BOOKS LIMITED

First Published in 1999

DESERT ISLAND BOOKS LIMITED
89 Park Street, Westcliff-on-Sea, Essex SS0 7PD
United Kingdom
www.desertislandbooks.com

British Library Cataloguing-in-Publication Data
A catalogue record for this book is available from the British Library

ISBN   1-874287-27-9

Printed in Great Britain
by
Biddles Ltd, Guildford

Photographs in this book are reproduced by kind permission of
The *East Anglian Daily Times*: sponsors for the Millennium season:
pages 68 (top), 69 (top), 75 (bottom), 152 (top), 153 (top), 154, 156.
Newsquest (Essex) owner of 'Colchester's truly local papers'
the Essex *County Standard* and *Evening Gazette*:
pages 65, 66 (top), 67, 77 (bottom), 149 (top), 151 (top), 157.
EJ Keegan, Chairman and Managing Director, St Catherine's Group Ltd,
and David Keegan:
pages 72 (bottom), 73 (top), 74 (bottom), 75 (top), 76 (top).
Mrs Val Tasker and Andrew Tasker, in memory of Tony Tasker:
pages 68 (bottom), 70, 71 (top), 72 (top), 73 (bottom).
Brian Wheeler on behalf of Colchester United FC:
pages 74 (top), 77 (top), 149 (bottom), 150, 152 (bottom), 153 (bottom), 155,
158 (top), 159 (top), 160.

CONTENTS

3. SO NEAR, SO FAR – 1981-1988

4. HEADING FOR THE ABYSS – 1988-1990

5. THE VAUXHALL CONFERENCE – 1990-1992

6. BACK TO THE LEAGUE – 1992-1999

PREFACE

It is easy for someone to say that they 'support' Manchester United or one of the other so-called glamour clubs, but it is only those of us who follow our home town clubs through good times and bad who really know what it means to be a 'true' supporter!

Colchester United have had many highs and lows over the years. Three Wembley appearances in six years is an achievement which few clubs, at any level, can claim in their roll of honour. Our lowest point, of course, was relegation from the Football League. That we bounced back so quickly is a tribute to all involved with the Club – and the fantastic backing of supporters during that period was vital.

I have been watching the U's now for more than forty years. I recall my first game. Myland Primary School football team was treated by one of the parents to see a match at Layer Road in 1957. It was against Newport County. We won 1-0. I was hooked!

Although I became the town's MP in 1997 I have declined the Club's offer to sit in the stand – I prefer to be on the terraces. I don't know the names of all those regulars around me, but I know their faces. Whatever our backgrounds, we have one common interest – supporting Colchester United. 'Our' team!

The Club is in effect the town's ambassador because nationwide more people know of Colchester through football connections than in other ways. I do my bit; I often wear a U's tie in the House of Commons.

I am honoured to be given the opportunity to write this preface. I congratulate Jeff Whitehead for writing this magnificent book about 'our' Club. It will be a source of great interest to all genuine U's supporters.

BOB RUSSELL
MP for Colchester

AUTHOR'S NOTE

I was first encouraged to collect U's home match programmes by my father, and soon I was hooked. Away programmes followed via 'Layer Road Lil', a fellow passenger on Cedric's Coaches matchday 'special' from Wivenhoe to Layer Road, and one of U's 'Supremo's' away supporters. To accompany my growing programme collection, I began to keep scrapbooks of U's newspaper clippings. It was not until twelve years later in 1984 that their potential use became apparent. As a Technician Apprentice at Woods of Colchester, I spent time as a trainee draughtsman with, amongst others, Albert 'Digger' Kettle. 'Digger' had been a swashbuckling full-back during the late 1940s when non-league U's had reached the FA Cup fifth round.

It was 'Digger', armed with his own scrapbooks, who first suggested that I should attempt a book on the U's. I proceeded with vigour, albeit without a publisher nor journalistic training, until it emerged that Hal Mason was preparing his book *The Official History of the U's*. Bowing to his superior 'internal' knowledge, I laid my work to rest.

Imagine my delight when in late 1998 I was commissioned by Clive Leatherdale to write this book on the U's to complement his excellent Desert Island Football History series. Countless hours later, though stifled by the mysterious disappearance from the local press filing cabinets of most early U's photographs, the unique format of this book was complete.

I am indebted to the unflinching assistance given by Kevin Drury during the compilation of this book and for cross-checking the statistics and proof-reading the text. I would also like to record my thanks for the cooperation of Brian Wheeler and staff at Colchester United, Francis Ponder of the Colchester *Evening Gazette*, Scott Dolling and Sharon Boswell at the *East Anglian Daily Times*, Jenny Wilson of Queensway Publishing and Robert Jeckells.

Finally to my wife Marilyn, and my entire family, thank you for your encouragement and understanding in what has been a marathon research project.

JEFF WHITEHEAD, September 1999

INTRODUCTION

Despite carrying the mantle of Britain's oldest recorded town, Colchester, or Camulodunum, as the Romans named it back in AD 49, embraced professional football only in 1937. In their short history, the club have battled against lack of finance, support and, until recently, success. Optimism is forged by the prospect of a new stadium at the beginning of the new Millennium, the present ground at Layer Road being well past its use-by date. When the fans of the new century sit, cramped in their plastic seats, eating their plastic fast-food and watching play-backs on the big screen, will they spare a thought for homely Layer Road?

Remember the timber terracing at the Layer Road End that flexed under foot as excited fans bounced up and down; the smell of lineament wafting from the changing room mixing uninvitingly with the burger bar next door; running for cover from the open Clock End as the heavens opened; the choke of cigarette smoke on a calm chill night; brushing rust particles from your hair as another stray pass hits the Barside roof; and the Post Horn Gallop; the grace of Arsenal, Leeds, Manchester United and others; Cup glory; relegation sorrow; championship joy and promotion dreams. Packed to the rafters or bare to the bones; Layer Road has witnessed it all. We fans may be few, but it is, for the moment, home. As a new era dawns at that new home, how did it all begin?

In October 1873 the amateur club Colchester Town was born. Playing on various sites around the town, they moved in 1909 to what is now the home of Colchester United in Layer Road. After spending their early years in local Essex leagues, Town joined the Spartan League in 1925 and were elected direct into its First Division. After ten nondescript seasons Town join the newly formed Eastern Counties League. In March 1937 the professional club Colchester United was formed. As the Essex FA would not allow both a professional and an amateur club to be administered by the same body, Town, whom many wanted to run side by side with United, folded in December of the same year.

It was hoped that professionalism would catapult the new Colchester United into the Football League. The 'U's' as they quickly became known, as opposed to 'The Oysters' of Town, kicked off their Southern League status at Yeovil and Petters United on 28 August 1937, losing 0-3. It was not long before U's won their first trophy, picking up the Southern League Cup at the end of that season beating their opening day opponents 4-3 on aggregate.

With neighbours Ipswich gaining election to the League in 1938, time was ripe for U's to follow. U's first application at the end of 1938-39 returned no votes, whereupon World War II intervened. A series of representative matches were staged during those years, with a number of Football League stars who were serving their military service at Colchester Garrison gracing Layer Road.

When competitive football recommenced in 1945-46, new player-manager Syd Fieldus was given this ultimatum: 'there must be no wasteful spending'. This principal would govern the U's to the present day, as they rarely had cash to throw around. When they ignored this edict in the late 1980s, the money was poorly spent and resulted in relegation out of the League.

Fieldus soon handed over to player-manager Ted Fenton and in little over a year United enjoyed a sparkling FA Cup run. Wins over Chelmsford, Banbury Spencer and Third Division (North) Wrexham set up a home tie with First Division Huddersfield. Bob Curry's goal brought Bradford PA to town in the fourth round and U's won 3-2. In the fifth round Blackpool's maestros Stanley Matthews and Stan Mortensen put paid to United's dream in front of 30,000 at Bloomfield Road. Fenton's reward was to be appointed assistant manager at West Ham.

Despite finishing second on goal-average to Merthyr, in 1950 U's, under Jimmy Allen, were elected to the Football League when it expanded to 92 clubs.

Confounding those critics who doubted whether the town could sustain a League side, U's boasted a five-figure average attendance in their first season. However, they found the going tough for the next few years, successfully applying for re-election in 1953-54 and 1954-55. Ted Fenton's brother, Benny, took charge in early 1955 and two years later almost led U's to the Second Division. Though U's were relegated to the new Fourth Division in 1960-61, Fenton's side were promoted as runners-up the following season, with Bobby Hunt setting the club record goalscoring total of 37 goals. U's could not build on this success and Fenton moved to Millwall frustrated by the characteristic financial restraints that beset U's. New boss, former England centre-half Neil Franklin, shuttled U's between Third and Fourth Divisions via promotion and relegations in the mid-1960s. This book picks up the baton at the end of Franklin's reign with the introduction of a new manager – Dick Graham.

## 1

GRANDAD'S ARMY
1968-1973

LEAGUE DIVISION 4	**1968-69**
Division 4	6th
League Cup	2nd Round
FA Cup	2nd Round

The reign of Neil Franklin had ended ignominiously following relegation to the Fourth Division at the end of 1967-68. That season had started well enough, but a disastrous run of just one win after the turn of the New Year culminated in a humiliating 1-5 home thrashing by Peterborough on the last day of the season. He was shown the door two days later. Franklin had been a key member of the England international defence, having partnered Billy Wright in 27 internationals immediately after the War. He had been expected to join up with England for the 1950 World Cup finals in Brazil, but to escape the stranglehold imposed by the minimum wage had opted instead to ply his trade in Colombia, where his talents were more generously appreciated. The FA condemned his decision – partly because Colombia was not affiliated with FIFA – and upon his disillusioned return he found himself banned. This effectively black-balled him to the lower echelons of the Football League. He passed away in 1992, aged 74.

Dick Graham arrived from a humbler and less controversial background. After the War he had protected Crystal Palace's goal on over 250 occasions as they hovered in the nether reaches of the old Third Division (South). He was forced to retire when only 29 because of back trouble, and was out of the game for five years before returning to football with a coaching job at West Brom. When Crystal Palace's Arthur Rowe fell ill, Graham at last became a league manager. He guided Palace from Division Four to Division Two and to the quarter-finals of the FA Cup, before taking over the hot seat at Walsall and later Orient. His mandate, on his 1 June 1968 appointment at Layer Road, was to emulate his success at Selhurst Park and hoist Colchester United into the Second Division.

Did You Know?

U's lost the final of the same cup to two different opponents in two months in 1949. The final of the 1947-48 Southern League Cup had been delayed a year.

The squad that Graham inherited – minus its two chief goalscorers, Reg Stratton and Peter Bullock – appeared unable to lift the gloom. Not until he had seen the side in action a few times was Graham able to see what was needed to set them on the winning trail. Six players – Adams, Barlow, Alan Buck, Mansfield, Moughton and Perryman – never wore a U's shirt again, following an awful start when only one point was gained from the first five fixtures. Graham's answer was to plunge into the transfer market. Within two months he signed seven new players, recouping most of his outlay by selling centre-half Duncan Forbes to Norwich and half-back Derek Trevis to Walsall for a combined fee of £19,000.

The tide began to turn in the next ten games, with six wins and just one defeat. Three of those wins came on opposition territory at Chesterfield, Scunthorpe and Lincoln. Much of this upturn in fortune was due to the experience brought by goalkeeper Tony Macedo. In the late 1950s, Macedo shared the Fulham limelight with Haynes, Cohen and Robson. He represented England at Under-23 level and, but for the fact that he was born in Gibraltar, might even have gained full international recognition. Macedo's arrival sparked a new-found confidence in the defence, which helped the team to a club-record seven successive victories. Indeed, in his first twelve games Macedo conceded just seven goals. At the end of the season he was rewarded with a testimonial match against Ipswich, when an audience of 4,515 recorded their appreciation.

That seven-match record was established at the end of a prolific run of 33 points from a possible 42, the only defeats coming at the hands of Bradford, Newport and Swansea. After 26 games U's stood fourth and were the highest away goalscorers in the division. United won four away games in a row: Aldershot (2-1), Workington (1-0), Wrexham (3-0) and Grimsby (4-2). Three of Graham's signings – Danny Light (twelve goals), Brian Gibbs (eight), along with Owen Simpson (also with eight) – topped the U's scoring chart. Twenty-year-old Light had been an apprentice at Palace under Graham, and followed his former boss to Layer Road for a £4,000 fee. He had scored twice on his Palace debut, and netted another after three minutes of his second match. As for Gibbs, he was born in Gillingham (Dorset) and signed from Gillingham (Kent). The £6,000 fee was a bargain: in the three seasons from 1965-66 he had been Gills' top scorer with 23, fifteen, and fifteen goals respectively.

Did You Know?

Defender Ray Price became United's first playing substitute when coming on against Rochdale on 19 September 1965.

The FA Cup brought a visit from Athenian Leaguers Chesham United, who had enjoyed a bye into the first round, owing to their FA Amateur Cup Final appearance at Wembley the previous season, which they had lost 0-1 to Leytonstone in front of 52,000 spectators. Colchester brushed Chesham aside to set up a home tie with Exeter City in the second round. Dreams of reaching the third round and emulating the previous season's battles with the likes of West Bromwich Albion were dashed by Alan Banks' breakaway goal. Exeter hosted Manchester United in the third round, but were beaten 1-3.

All good things come to an end, and it was at Roots Hall in February that the U's league record was halted. The defeat knocked the wind out of the U's sails, for they secured only two more wins in the next nine games. An Easter mini-revival brought victories over Chesterfield, Exeter and Peterborough in the space of four days, each by a solitary goal. Micky Brown's winner at London Road, two minutes from time, signalled the U's first-ever six-point haul from an Easter programme. Hopes were high, therefore, that promotion would be their reward, with four successive home fixtures to come, two of them involving clashes with promotion rivals – Bradford City and Halifax. Sadly, three of the matches were drawn, and Swansea became only the third side to escape Layer Road with both points when they completed U's home campaign. Other teams chasing promotion capitalised on their games in hand – caused by the inclement month of December – and Colchester slipped out of the top four.

Although Doncaster Rovers had opened up an uncatchable gap at the top, the fixture backlog helped produce a grandstand finish. Aldershot, Darlington, Halifax, Rochdale, Bradford City, Lincoln, U's and Southend indulged in a frantic sprint for the line, with the northern clubs keeping their noses in front. For the city of Bradford, one club had gained elevation, whilst the other had amassed a miserly 20 points at the bottom.

Daily Telegraph columnist Robert Oxby wrote these words about the Manager of the Year award: 'The test surely is not whether a man can manage the gifted players of the First Division but whether he can conjure wonder out of emptiness in the Fourth. In the past weeks seven managers out of eight have told me that Dick Graham is their man of the year. He is also mine.'

Match of the Season 1968-69
Colchester 4 Southend 0

Division 4, 29 November 1968

Shrewd Shrimpers' boss Ernie Shepherd had, like Dick Graham, been active in the transfer market, signing Gary Moore from Grimsby for £8,000 and David Chambers for £4,000 from Southern League Cambridge United. Both had scored early in their Roots Hall career, and indeed Moore had netted at Layer Road for Grimsby as recently as 4 October. Southend also had in their ranks Chico Hamilton, who had been subject of a £25,000 bid by West Brom and who would shortly sign for Aston Villa.

The U's were without the inspirational Tony Macedo, giving Ron Willis a second opportunity between the sticks, following his debut the previous week, for this, the 29th Essex derby. The attendance of 10,604 was Layer Road's first five-figure gate since April 1966, when 10,200 watched the promotion clash with Luton, and was swelled by a large contingent from the Thames estuary.

The game produced one of Colchester's greatest league performances thus far. Southend, in fairness, played their part, but by the end the U's could have won by six or seven as they hit the woodwork three times. It was Jim Oliver's night, a night when he was irresistible. He scored the first when it looked odds against him doing so. Brian Gibbs also scored, and Terry Dyson notched one from the spot. The other goal was a 25-yard beauty from Owen Simpson, who would ironically join the Shrimpers at the end of the season. Oliver would also spark interest from Roots Hall, but like many of his U's colleagues he lived well away from Colchester, Norwich in fact, and refused to uproot to the seaside town.

Little did the crowd know, as they buzzed away from Layer Road afterwards, that U's would win their next seven league games to create a club record. Ironically it was Southend, some ten weeks later, who ended the run at their Roots Hall ground. The Shrimpers' fate that season was similar to Colchester's, losing games in hand and ending up one place and one point below the U's. This was all the more galling for Southend, whose home attendances had been the highest in the division, averaging 10,381 compared to U's 6,109.

LEAGUE DIVISION 4   **1969-70**
Division 4   10th
League Cup   2nd Round
FA Cup   1st Round

Graham spent the close season raiding the transfer market for a further seven new players. Goalkeeper Graham Smith would prove to be a notable capture; he had impressed as a stand-in stopper for Notts County against U's in February, while a student at Loughborough University. Graham also returned to one of his former clubs to bring in Orient players Bert Howe and Roy Massey, both of whom he had recruited at Brisbane Road when he was the O's boss. Youngster Micky Cook had also been released by Orient. Bobby Howlett, Steve Pitt and Ray Whittaker completed the list of new faces.

The new season kicked off with a number of incentive schemes in operation; cash prizes for the highest scoring team in each division, Sportsman of the Month awards and a gallon bottle of whiskey for the Manager of the Month. At Layer Road, match officials would enjoy their modernised dressing room. The downside was that the League had banned Friday night football, to satisfy the demands of the Pools companies.

For Graham, the first-day trip to Lincoln City had its worries. As most of his squad lived well away from Colchester, it was not until the players met up at Grantham for lunch that Graham and new trainer Dennis Mochan knew they had a full squad from which to pick a team.

By October, Massey led the Fourth Division goal-charts with an impressive return of eleven goals. The team sat in sixth place, two points off a top-four spot, and a further two points behind unbeaten leaders Port Vale. An injury crisis, however, sparked a poor run of one win in eight, and that was at the expense of struggling Bradford Park Avenue. By early November, the U's had only one ever-present – Ray Whittaker. The injury problem was so acute that 18-year-old Micky Cook was drafted in to make his full debut in a 1-1 draw at Aldershot. Also in the line-up was reserve-team manager Terry Dyson, and trainer Dennis Mochan occupied the substitute's bench.

Interest in an FA Cup run ended where it started, in deepest South Wales at the Somerton Park, home of Newport County. U's solitary goal in that 1-2 defeat came off the boot of County player-manager Bobby Ferguson. Ferguson would later take over from Bobby Robson at Ipswich when the latter was installed as England manager in 1982.

Did You Know?

In 1953 United appointed a new manager, only to discover his credentials were less than accurate. The board had to re-advertise the vacancy.

In the longer term, in the light of Massey's injuries Graham signed Yorkshireman Ken Jones from Millwall. A £5,000 fee secured the six-foot wing-half, although during Neil Franklin's reign he might well have joined the U's from Southend, prior to his arrival at the Den. Indeed, Jones had been part of the record-breaking Lions side that went 59 home games unbeaten. Jones netted his first goal for Colchester in his third appearance, at Gresty Road, Crewe, and by his ninth game had plundered four more.

A boardroom change saw Bill Graver taking over as chairman, after Arthur Neville resigned due to business commitments. Graver would oversee the dawning of the new decade and all that it might hold. At about the same time, secretary Claude Orrin retired after 21 years service. Orrin had groomed his successor, David Havell for two years. Havell, 23, became the League's youngest club secretary. Graham, meanwhile, was absent for much of December. Back pain, a legacy of his curtailed playing career, confined him to bed.

Brian Hall picked up one of the aforementioned awards when he was named November Sportsman of the Month for Division Four by the Football League *Review* magazine. Older supporters will remember that the *Review* was inserted in most clubs programmes during the late 1960s and early 70s.

By the turn of the New Year, early league leaders Port Vale's bubble had finally burst, allowing Chesterfield and Wrexham to vie with Vale for top slot. U's were sitting mid-table, seven points off both the promotion and relegation packs.

Graham welcomed in the new decade with an ageist philosophy: 'I believe in signing players who have done something big, and giving them a new lease of life.' The latest of his veteran intake was Bobby Cram, aged thirty, who had been playing in Canada with Vancouver Royals. Cram had played for West Brom in the First Division for the four seasons preceding 1967, at a time when Graham was trainer at the Hawthorns.

Massey's attempted return, after a couple of reserve outings, was delayed when he was injured in a clash with Mel Nurse at Swansea. After 28 games Aldershot's Jack Howarth led the division's scoring charts with eighteen goals, just seven ahead of Massey who had missed half of those games. How many might Massey have had at the same stage if he had played and continued his scoring prowess?

One of the most vital 'signings' of this or any other season was not made by Dick Graham. Assisted by a cheque for £5,800 from Vic Keeble's thriving Development Association, plus a low interest loan from the Football Association, the board concluded the purchase of Layer Road from Colchester Borough Council. The foresight of this purchase did not bear fruition until 23 years later, when the ground was sold back to the Council to stave off what would have been the club's extinction through mounting debts.

League leaders Chesterfield, who were suffering a bout of promotion jitters, were faced twice in nineteen days during another Jones scoring spree. Indeed, following the derby defeat at Southend, he found the net on ten occasions. U's proud eleven-game unbeaten home record was brought abruptly to an end at the beginning of April by Dixie McNeil's hat-trick for Northampton. McNeil would become one of a handful of lower division journeymen to hold a goalscoring 'Indian sign' over United. The loss of Massey, Cook and Oliver at this stage of the season left U's with insufficient ammunition to mount a late challenge.

Questions remained: What if Massey had not been injured? What if Jones and Cram had been signed earlier? The feeling was that the U's had the basis of a good side, and so the new season was anticipated with great expectations. As a measure of the club's forward planning, youngsters John McLaughlin and Lindsay Smith were both signed as apprentices as the season drew to a close.

Match of the Season 1969-70

Ipswich 4 Colchester 0

League Cup, 2nd Round, 3 September 1969

U's had qualified for the second round by winning at Reading in a first-round replay. Having contested a 1-1 draw at Layer Road, where first-choice keeper Ron Willis sustained a serious eye injury, U's travelled to Elm Park knowing that a plum draw at neighbours Ipswich awaited the victors. New signing Roy Massey responded with a hat-trick to send U's to Portman Road.

The two clubs had not met competitively since 1956-57, in the old Third Division (South), when U's nearly reached the Second Division, only to be pipped for promotion by the Suffolk side. In the league clash that season at Layer Road, before a record home league attendance of 18,559, U's were awarded a penalty. Up stepped player-manager Benny Fenton, but the diving Roy Bailey saved. The game ended 0-0, and Colchester, to date, have never again come so close to (old) Second Division status. For Ipswich, under Alf Ramsey, promotion formed the springboard for untold success.

The League Cup-tie was U's first against a First Division side since West Brom in 1968. United started well against Ipswich, but lost their foot-hold in midfield and conceded two late penalties within sixty seconds of each other – one needless and the other somewhat harsh – which made the score look worse than it really was. For the record, Tommy Carroll, Mick Mills and Frank Brogan's two penalties accounted for the goals. For Brogan they were his sixteenth and seventeenth successful spot-kicks.

In the succeeding years, both clubs have enjoyed their ups and downs – albeit at different levels. A steady procession of players, both young and old, has left Portman Road for the short trek down the A12. However, probably the most notable switch of allegiance was the departure of the then U's manager George Burley up the A12 at Christmas 1994. The manner of his departure forged a huge rift between the clubs and fans alike, with the wounds still not completely healed.

LEAGUE DIVISION 4   **1970-71**
Division 4   6th
League Cup   2nd Round
FA Cup   Quarter-finals

While England were suffering disappointment in the 1970 Mexico World Cup, Graham was pondering how to improve his side's goal-power. To this end, he revealed another large batch of summer signings. One of these was Ray Crawford, who had been capped twice for England in the early 1960s during the ascendant years of his then club, Ipswich. Only Jimmy Greaves, of players still playing in 1970, had scored more than Crawford's career haul of 264. Another new recruit also had England connections – Brian Owen, who was trainer to the Young England squad. Graham's now customary close-season shopping spree was completed by the capture of Brian Garvey, Mick Mahon and John Kurila.

This was the eleventh season of the League Cup's existence, and U's kicked off with a home tie against new-boys Cambridge. The visitors had been elected to the League after winning the Southern League championship in successive seasons. They were no match for U's, who ran out 5-0 winners. The next round saw a first-ever meeting with Birmingham City. The first game was drawn, and United led 1-0 in the St Andrews replay with just seven minutes remaining, but two goals by the Midlanders ended U's cup hopes. Maybe they would reach the FA Cup third round and have another pot at the big boys.

Peter Hills, Sports Editor of the *Essex County Standard*, noted that the sponsored competitions that Watney's, Texaco and Ford had introduced into the professional game could only have beneficial effects. Hills personally proposed a pre-season tournament involving East Anglia's premier clubs. An embryonic idea was formulating, and his newspaper would become pioneers in club sponsorship. A sponsored East Anglian (professional) Cup would also be introduced, briefly, towards the end of the decade.

In the League, U's followed up the Birmingham replay with a trip to Bournemouth. Colchester-born John Bond was manager of the Cherries, and he plotted a 4-1 win. Ted MacDougall scored all four and would add a further 45 in a memorable goalscoring season. Bond, MacDougall and four other members of the Bournemouth side that day would all re-convene at Norwich in the late 1970s.

The fixture computer had done U's no favours, financially, as seven of the first eleven league fixtures were away from Layer Road, but at least the League had backtracked from its decision to ban Friday night football, allowing U's to arrange ten such fixtures.

The October win at Peterborough was marked by Roy Massey's first goal for over a year. He had been cruelly dogged by injuries and deserved that goal more than most. Ironic, then, that he made a 50-yard run to score it. Crawford's hat-trick against Crewe brought about the usual presentation of the match ball. The snag was that cost-conscious chairman Bill Graver asked Crawford to go and find the ball himself – it nestled in one of the neighbouring gardens!

By the time Sussex County League side Ringmer visited in the first round of the FA Cup, United had embarked on a seven-match unbeaten run that had hoisted them up to seventh place, eight points behind leaders Notts Co, four points behind fourth-placed Northampton. The FA Cup, however, would put promotion on the back burner for the next four months. Ringmer were disposed of via Crawford's second hat-trick of the term. The second round brought about a rare double: having seen off Cambridge in the League Cup; U's did likewise in the FA Cup.

Whilst the chrysalis of what was to be a momentous cup run was still unravelling, Graham faced another injury crisis: Massey had broken down yet again and Owen had fractured his kneecap. This necessitated another foray into the transfer market, as a result of which Graham made two noteworthy signings – Dave Simmons and Brian Lewis. Simmons arrived from Aston Villa, who had bought him from Arsenal for £20,000. Lewis boasted Palace, Portsmouth, Coventry and Luton as his previous clubs and a £6,000 fee to Oxford secured his move to Layer Road. When the pair both scored on their debuts at Sincil Bank, the *Sun* wrote 'Dick Graham has a habit of overcoming crisis situations with the greatest of ease, and he proved it again at Lincoln.'

The third round draw was awaited with baited breath. How anticlimactic then, ears pinned to transistor radios, when U's came out of the hat away to Southern League Barnet. The Bees had produced a 6-1 win over Fourth Division Newport in the first round, establishing a post-war record victory for a non-league side over a senior club. Their sloping Underhill pitch would also prove a stern test. As it was, the original Saturday tie was iced-off, with many United fans already having descended on the fog-bound north London suburb. The following Tuesday, with conditions hardly any better, Mick Mahon's goal secured a 1-0 victory.

If the third round draw had proved disappointing, then a fourth-round trip to the winners of the Rochdale v Coventry tie looked sure to result in a long-awaited trip to a First Division side. But Rochdale shocked the Sky Blues with a 2-1 win before a 13,011 crowd. For Rochdale's tie with United, the local police decided not to make the match all-ticket but to put an ambitious ground limit of

30,000 on the tie. It was Rochdale's first ever appearance in the fourth round, and a creditable 12,321 spectators watched an enthralling cup-tie. Indeed, in later years one-tenth of that attendance would be the norm for league games between the sides at Spotland. All looked lost when U's trailed 1-3, Bobby Cram having missed a penalty. But in the closing minutes Graham's latest additions turned up trumps to earn a Layer Road replay.

Chairman Graver wrote of the experience: 'Sitting in the directors' box at Rochdale at 4.30pm on Saturday last, I certainly did not believe in fairies. Ten minutes later I knew all the fairies who support the U's descended on Spotland and Rochdale all of a sudden were playing eleven of our lads with a fairy on each shoulder. Thank you lads for a memorable match and thank you fairies for your kindness.'

The fairies were in evidence again when U's beat Rochdale 5-0 to set up a home tie with Leeds (see Match of the Season). The Wembley dream ended 0-5 in front of a packed Goodison Park in the quarter-finals, but U's had made an indelible mark on FA Cup history. Roger Heywood of the *Sun* wrote about the Everton defeat: 'Little Colchester's cup death took place exactly the way Dick Graham decreed it – which isn't really surprising, because he wrote the script. It was dramatic, extravagant, exaggerated beyond all proportion – but always entertaining. So typical of the man.'

After the hectic spell of cup-ties, during which they had clung onto seventh spot in the League, U's had to squeeze in a backlog of fixtures. Tired legs and just one point over Easter put paid to their promotion ambitions. In March Graham actually offered his resignation, following a clash with chairman Bill Graver, but withdrew it when the chairman stood down himself. The U's consolation was that – as one of highest scoring sides not to achieve promotion – they qualified for the Watney Cup competition that would provide the curtain-raiser for the following season.

Notts County won the title with a record number of points, and were followed up by Bournemouth, Oldham and York. For Barrow it was the end of the road. Hereford were elected in their place.

Match of the Season 1970-71
Colchester 3 Leeds 2

FA Cup, 5th Round, 13 February 1971

The enormity of Colchester's task was put into perspective by the achievements of their visitors since gaining promotion to the top division in 1963-64. Leeds had won the League Championship once

---

Did You Know?

The day after England won the World Cup in 1966, Colchester United played Southport in an evening friendly in Buncrana in the Republic of Ireland.

---

and been runners-up three times; they had reached the FA Cup final twice and the semi-final on two other occasions; had won the League Cup, the Fairs Cup (and been beaten finalists), and had reached the semi-finals of the European Cup.

Graham's retort was: 'They're only eleven men, same as us.' His philosophy of bringing in experienced campaigners meant that six of his team were over thirty. Because of this, the press dubbed them 'Grandad's Army'. Graham pledged only that his players would be fit and would verbally bully each other into performing. Ray Crawford was the only one to offer a direct promise, recalling his days at Ipswich when he 'always scored against Jack Charlton'.

The clamour that surrounded the tie meant that 2,400 – ten times the norm – turned up at a midweek reserve game with Brighton to claim tickets. United hiked their admission charge from six shillings to twelve shillings and sixpence (62p) for standing, and from nine shillings to 25 shillings for seating. 16,000 tickets were sold, including 4,000 to the Yorkshire side.

Sensationally, U's raced into a 2-0 half-time lead. David Coleman's interval report for BBC Grandstand pricked the ears of the nation's football lovers. Crawford had carried out his promise, twice, harassing Charlton for the first and swivelling to turn in the second whilst grounded. When Dave Simmons nodded in the third a couple of minutes after the break, it appeared to shake Leeds into the realisation that they had a game on. Norman Hunter and Johnny Giles pulled goals back, and only a super save from Graham Smith prevented a Mick Jones equaliser three minutes from time.

Before the game, Graham had jested that if U's won he would scale the walls of Colchester Castle. The press made sure he lived up to that promise. But the fun was not to last. In the next round Colchester travelled to Goodison Park, amid great expectation, and were thumped by Everton 0-5.

The Leeds game had a bearing on the fortunes of both participants, for neither achieved their objective that season. Leeds lost the title to double winners Arsenal by just one point, whilst the U's, with new-found world-wide fame, missed out on promotion to Division Three by two points. That failure, however, was to lead to another chapter in the club's history the following season, a reward for the number of league goals they had plundered.

LEAGUE DIVISION 4   **1971-72**
Division 4   11th
League Cup   3rd Round
FA Cup   1st Round

Season 1971-72 was unusual for Colchester United in that its climax came at the beginning rather than at the end. Having qualified for the Watney Cup, by virtue of their goalscoring feats, U's surprised everyone by winning it (see Match of the Season).

Infused with the confidence that stemmed from this unexpected triumph, U's players and supporters alike seemed justified in thinking that promotion was within the team's grasp. The bookies backed the U's for instant promotion. Yet, ever since Benny Fenton had been, harshly, blamed for *that* penalty miss against Ipswich in 1957, a school of thought maintained that Colchester United neither wanted, nor could afford, Second Division football. Chairman Roy Chapman assured fans that the club did want promotion, wanted it badly, and that the Third Division was the objective above all others for the coming season.

Ray Crawford's decision, taken after the first tie in the Watney Cup, to try his luck playing in South Africa was the first step in the break-up of 'Grandad's Army'. One beneficiary was young Steve Leslie, who had picked up three Amateur England Youth caps the previous season, and who now quickly cracked in his first senior goal. Once again, the fixture computer had been unkind to the U's, asking them to meander the country in six of their opening nine games. Not surprisingly, with their mantle of cast-iron promotion favourites, everyone was determined to beat them. As a result, United dropped all but one point from those early travels, and at one time U's sat just two places off the bottom.

Misery in the League was temporarily offset by success in the League Cup. Brentford were swept aside 3-1 before the U's were paired with Dave Mackay's Swindon from the Second Division. Swindon, like the U's, were doughty cup-fighters and had caused a sensation whilst still a Third Division club in beating Arsenal 3-1 in the 1969 Wembley League Cup Final. But on this occasion they had no answer to Brian Lewis's hat-trick.

The third round draw rekindled nostalgic memories of United's 1948 cup run, reacquainting the U's with Blackpool. There was to be no revenge: even without the artistry of Stanley Matthews and the finishing of Stan Mortenson in their armoury, the Tangerines, relegated from Division One, hit the U's for four without reply.

Another of Graham's protégés, 16-year-old Lindsay Smith, received an October call-up to the England Youth team trials, accompanying Brian Owen to Bisham Abbey. As one professional career was taking shape, another was forcibly ended. With his knees unable to stand the rigours of the professional game, Roy Massey enjoyed a November testimonial against Ipswich. A crowd of 4,849 gave the likeable Yorkshireman a triumphant send-off into his new career of teaching and youth football.

All eyes were on the FA Cup, but after the U's magnificent exploits the previous term it was a major disappointment that fewer than 6,000 turned up for the first round home tie with Third Division Shrewsbury. Perhaps the fans knew that U's had consumed all their FA Cup luck in one season. The Shropshire side were in no mood to become whipping boys and a George Andrews hat-trick meant that they became the first higher division club ever to win an FA Cup-tie at Layer Road since U's were elected to the League.

The next youth product to grab the headlines was 18-year-old Clacton lad Steve Foley, a regular in the Midweek League reserve team, who enjoyed a cracking Layer Road debut with two goals in a 3-0 victory over Exeter. Unfortunately, in his next match he suffered a tendon injury. In a month of departures and new faces, one of the heroes of the Leeds, Everton and West Brom matches, keeper Graham Smith, was sold to West Brom for £10,000. Don Revie's side must have been sick of the sight of Smith, for he lined up for his Albion debut against Leeds! Curiously, the U's team-sheet remained unchanged – youngster *Barry* Smith would take the place of his namesake in goal. John Kurila became another 'Grandad' to depart, when moving to Lincoln.

1971 was without question the most memorable calendar year in United's history. As 1971 slipped into 1972, Brentford led the table with thirty points from 22 games with U's eight points behind with a game in hand. More importantly, United were only five points off fourth place and were ready to launch a concerted effort for a coveted spot in Division Three. Graham kicked-off the New Year by fielding Colchester's youngest-ever side. At Crewe, U's fielded five teenagers, and 16-year-old John McLaughlin was named as substitute. Cook and Leslie both scored in a 4-2 win. Two weeks later, at Doncaster, United had no fewer than four goals ruled out, and went down 0-2.

By now, the club had other worries. The publication of United's balance sheet prompted an emergency meeting to consider the £21,000 loss in the previous financial year. Graham concluded that his hands were tied and that youth was the key to the future. The youngsters had received harsh criticism from some of the success-hungry United fans, which prompted the following appeal: 'The club are going through a period when the younger element are being

Did You Know?

United's Bobby Blackwood broke his jaw twice in collisions with QPR's Les Allen – first in August 1966, then five months later in the return fixture.

blooded, when tolerance and understanding from supporters is of prime importance.' When it was reported that the floodlights would need restoration work in the close season, an appeal fund was set up with the aim of raising £10,000. The first fund-raising event was a film shown at the Cameo Cinema in Colchester, namely the Watney Mann commissioned footage of the U's summer triumph 'World At Their Feet: Watney Cup 1971.' A showing of the Henry Cooper v Cassius Clay Heavyweight Boxing bout preceded the football.

Graham was quoted as saying that the best way to resolve his and a host of other clubs' finances would be a return to regionalised leagues. However, northern clubs were likely to object, as they relied on their share of gate money from their sorties down south. Regionalisation would also leave U's with long hauls to the south-west. To add to United's woes, power strikes that crippled the country ruled out floodlight matches at Layer Road between 21 January and 13 March.

By the time normality returned, Graham was ready to pitch yet more youngsters into his side. At Hartlepool in March he intro-duced two further 16-year-olds, John McLaughlin and Tony Wingate. Richard Bourne became the season's final fledgling when he came on as a substitute at Chester. Among those making way for the new intake was John Gilchrist, whose departure into non-league management further weakened the 'Leeds legacy' at Layer Road. United's wage bill was being systematically slashed to reduce the club's outgoings.

Despite a strong run-in, U's did not have enough to challenge in what had been a season of major transition. They finished nine points off promotion and fifteen points behind champions Grimsby, who had been involved in a mini-promotion tussle with neighbours Lincoln and Scunthorpe all season. Ken Jones, Brian Lewis and Bobby Cram (who returned to Canada) all bid farewell by the end of the campaign. The future lay in the hands of Graham's maturing youngsters. It was hoped that they would come more and more into prominence in the following season.

To round off the season, a second money-raising event was staged to fund the work on the stadium's lighting when U's faced Blackpool in a challenge match based on the Watney Cup's experi-mental offside and penalty shoot-out rules.

Match of the Season 1971-72

West Brom 4   Colchester 4

Watney Cup final, 7 August 1971

The Watney Cup had been introduced at the start of the 1970-71 season with Derby emerging as the inaugural winners, beating Manchester United 4-1 in front of 32,049. The two highest scoring teams in each division who did not gain promotion qualified for the competition. The First Division sides would be drawn against the Third Division teams, and the Second Division would encounter the Fourth Division pair. For 1971-72, the competing teams were Manchester United, West Brom, Carlisle, Luton, Halifax, Wrexham, Colchester and Crewe. The competition would also experiment with a variation of the offside rule. Players would not be adjudged offside in the other team's half, but only once they crossed the 18-yard line. The upshot was that once teams realised they were likely to miss out on promotion, they were handed an incentive to go all out for goals, for they had little to lose.

United's opening Watney Cup game against Luton provided the last game in a U's shirt for Ray Crawford, before he moved to South Africa to play for Durban City. When United then overcame Carlisle, they qualified for the final at the Hawthorns. West Brom had dispatched Halifax, surprise conquerors of Manchester United.

A magnificent final vindicated those who had conceived the competition, for it produced eight goals and a nail-biting penalty decider. If only the simultaneous pre-season friendly between Birmingham and Aston Villa at St Andrews, which attracted 36,000, had been rescheduled, the Hawthorns attendance of 18,487 would surely have been exceeded.

The game went to penalties when Jeff Astle mis-hit Albion's fourth goal in the dying moments. It was left to one of Graham's fledglings, 18-year-old Phil Bloss, to calmly stroke home United's fourth, and winning, penalty-kick. Bloss, making only his second senior appearance, revealed that it was between himself and Dave Simmons as to who would take it. Experienced Simmons 'allowed' Bloss the privilege, 'because he was the younger!'

Philips Osborn of the *Sunday Express* reported: 'There was no question about the Essex men deserving the trophy. They used a fluid 4-4-2 line up, they chased and they harried Albion at every turn, never allowing the difference in status to become apparent.'

For Graham and Cram – lifting the trophy in U's red change strip – it was a wonderful return to one of their former grounds. For U's fans, the exploits of 1971 would often be toasted.

LEAGUE DIVISION 4   1972-73

Division 4   22nd (sought re-election)
League Cup   1st Round
FA Cup   2nd Round

The new floodlight fund bore fruit, as dazzling U's took on St Mirren in a pre-season friendly to mark the switch-on by the Mayor. Not only were the new lights bright, but United sported an all-white kit, new club badge, and wore red boots! Fans were a little downhearted that Graham did not sign any big names in the close season. His latest additions fitted in well with the boardroom-backed youth policy. Three of them came from the Brisbane Road 'nursery', namely Bobby Moss, Martin Binks and John South. Of the others, Steve Wooldridge had played a handful of games for Plymouth, whilst Phil Thomas and Des Kelly had been kept out of their respective Bournemouth and Norwich sides by the performances of their seniors.

The enthusiasm and unchecked optimism of youth combined to see the season off to a good start, with victory over new-boys Hereford. But that win was followed by a demoralising four league defeats, not to mention a first-round exit in the League Cup, which sparked a stormy shareholders meeting. The outcome was the resignation of Dick Graham, after a shareholder had publicly questioned Graham's on-field strategy. The shareholder in question was attending his first such meeting, and was reported to have 'won his five shares in a raffle'.

The managerless team responded by thrashing Crewe 5-1 the following night, with Dave Simmons claiming the match ball after his hat-trick. Despite attempts to coax Graham back, his mind was made up. Graham explained how a strict economic policy had been laid down, and that it was his job to enforce it. In place of tried and tested experienced players, he had been forced to play teenagers knowing full well that should they fail to produce results he would be sacrificing his own professional integrity. Graham was pleased that the youngsters he had introduced had contributed much to the team's mid-table position the previous season. He added that his resignation was not a snub to the Colchester board, but a protest against that minority of supporters who demanded miracles without thought to the club's professional and financial limitations. In Graham's absence, the club's Scottish coach, Denis Mochan, took temporary charge of team affairs, having been signed as a player by Franklin back in 1966-67. The upheavals resulted in U's worst start in their history, with just six points earned from the first thirteen matches.

> **Did You Know?**
>
> **United's first ever Friday night home game was v Port Vale on 20 September 1968. The gate was 6,441, an increase of 2,500 on the previous home match.**

There were few glimmers of light at this time, though Lindsay Smith and John McLaughlin were both invited back for a second trial with the England Youth squad. With U's at the bottom of the table, Mochan's reign came to an end following a draw at Peterborough. New Posh manager Noel Cantwell had boasted in the local paper that his side would 'steamroller this one [versus Colchester]'. Some measure of U's loss of faith came with the announcement that Supporters Club membership had plummeted from over 3,000 to less than 1,000.

The new manager was unveiled as Jim Smith, the wing-half player-manager of Northern Premier League Boston United. A Sheffield lad, he had joined the Blades from school and then played for Aldershot. Four years later he returned north to Halifax, before joining Lincoln in 1968. His first U's game in charge was against Mansfield (coincidentally the home 'debut' on the terraces of the author). Smith's first task was to find a replacement keeper for Barry Smith, who, following the Mansfield game, was discovered to have been playing with a broken wrist for several weeks. The new manager's immediate impression of his team was not lacking in candour; he felt that the team needed strengthening in every department!

The FA Cup brought some relief from the basement struggle when Bognor Regis from the Southern League First Division (South) were thumped 6-0. In the second round, U's put up a brave fight before losing to Bournemouth in a Layer Road replay. Bournemouth had sold their prolific scorer Ted MacDougall to Manchester United for an astronomic fee of £200,000. But Smith had done enough in his first weeks to earn the Manager of the Month award. His achievement? U's had climbed off the bottom!

Jim Smith's first transfer buy would be the most inspired purchase he ever made for the U's. He returned to his old club Boston to sign Bobby Svarc for £6,000. Svarc had notched 52 goals in eighteen months at York Street, had featured against United in his days at Sincil Bank, and boasted First Division experience as an 18-year-old Leicester apprentice. Injury, however, would prevent Svarc from having a major impact in what remained of his first season.

Smith also called on another of his ex-Lincoln colleagues in Ray Harford. Both men would go on to become top-flight managers. By

---

Did You Know?

**In the late 1960s and early 1970s, season tickets at Layer Road
were cheaper for women than for men.**

---

the turn of the year United had only sixteen points, seven points
from safety, and with only Darlington beneath them. Injury problems were not limited to Svarc. Three days after John McLaughlin
made his debut in the England Youth team in Naples, he dislocated
his shoulder in the League game at Hereford.

By March, Smith had seen enough to know that his side's fate
was effectively sealed. Accepting the inevitable, he called instead
for a massive turnout of supporters through the turnstiles, aware
that gate-size was often taken into consideration when matters of
re-election were being decided.

The visit of Lincoln City, managed by 28-year-old Graham
Taylor, saw Dixie McNeil – so often the curse of the U's – grab both
goals in a 2-0 win. With 21 points from 32 games, U's were truly up
against it. Another of Smith's captures at this stage would prove
significant in U's history. Bobby Roberts was enticed to become his
right-hand man. Roberts had played for Motherwell, Leicester and
Mansfield. While at Filbert Street he had played in the 1968-69 FA
Cup Final defeat at the hands of Manchester City. He moved to
Layer Road from Coventry, where he had been instrumental in the
Sky Blues' thriving youth set-up.

The irony of Reading's equaliser in their March visit to Layer
Road was that it was ex-U's forward Bobby Hunt who scored it.
Hunt had come close to rejoining the U's earlier in the season, and
had also scored for Northampton against U's on Boxing Day, but
that goal for Reading virtually sealed re-election for his former club.
U's last fleeting hopes of avoiding that sorry outcome disappeared
with a home defeat by Exeter. Smith summed up the season as one
of stop-go performances. Failure to pull away from safety was a
result of inconsistency, he maintained.

For some weeks, chairman Roy Chapman had been trying to
canvass support from the League chairman who would vote at the
League AGM. United, after a difficult first few years had enjoyed a
reasonably stable record since joining the League, but nothing could
be left to chance. In the event, U's safely negotiated the ballot box,
earning Jim Smith the benefit of a summer of reassessment.

Graham's fledglings had come of age the hard way. His endeavours would lead to four of them – Micky Cook, Steve Foley, Steve
Leslie and Lindsay Smith – playing a large part in the future ups
and downs of the club.

Match of the Season 1972-73

Colchester 1 Hereford 0

Division 4, 12 August 1972

The election of Hereford United to the exclusive 92-club member-ship of the Football League mirrored the path Colchester had taken in securing their own League status back in 1950. Like the U's in 1948, Hereford had drawn the nation's admiration with a giant-killing FA Cup run. In the third round of the 1971-72 competition, Hereford had earned a 2-2 draw at St James' Park, Newcastle. The TV cameras homed in on Edgar Street for the replay, where Ronnie Radford scored what was adjudged Goal of the Season. West Ham required two games to overcome Hereford in the next stage, by which time Hereford had staked a mighty claim for admission to the Football League, even though they would finish second to Chelmsford in the Southern League. Barrow made way for the West Country club.

It was ironic, therefore, that Layer Road would host the Bulls' first game in Division Four. A commemorative timepiece was the only thing U's presented to their opponents that day. Dick Graham had turned full circle in his team selection: Mick Mahon, at 24, was the oldest player in the side. Only Stuart Morgan and Bobby Noble had much in the way of league experience, with the other eight players all under 21 years of age. 19-year-old Steve Foley's goal two minutes after the interval gave the U's both points, but it was to prove a false dawn for both clubs. Come the end of the campaign the youthful U's had to seek re-election, while Hereford were promoted as runners-up to Southport.

## 2

THE YO-YO YEARS
1973-1981

LEAGUE DIVISION 4	1973-74
Division 4	3rd (Promoted)
League Cup	1st Round
FA Cup	1st Round

During the close season Jim Smith sought to resolve the defensive inadequacies that had led to re-election the previous season. To this end, he signed the Watford pair Mike Walker and Mick Packer, acquired Barry Dyson from Orient, and broke the club transfer record to bring Paul Aimson in from Bournemouth for £11,000. U's also had a new chairman, Robert Jackson.

The new campaign began well on a dustbowl at Barnsley. Bobby Svarc showed his intentions for the coming season when he scored the quickest goal of the day in just 45 seconds. Already, the memory of possibly United's worst-ever season was fading, though the League Cup did not detain U's long: they bowed out at Gillingham.

Evening Gazette Sports Editor Peter Hills had predicted back in 1970 that sponsorship would be the saving grace of many clubs. The first home game against Crewe was a mould-breaking occasion when the *Evening Gazette* became the first-ever commercial sponsor of an English football match. Before kick-off the crowd were entertained by displays of archery, judo and basketball. Music was performed by the Colchester Air Training Corps. The *piece de resistance* was reserved for Editor John Gerard, who collected the match ball from an Army helicopter hovering over the pitch before presenting it to the match officials. It was fitting that United should win the match 3-2, to go joint top, but there was a price to pay: Paul Aimson's sustained a knee injury that all but ended his career.

United went top following a stormy Layer Road clash with fellow challengers Exeter. A bad tackle by a City player on Stuart Morgan caused the Welshman to be stretchered off, and so enraged Smith that he strode onto the pitch to confront referee Brian Homewood. That outburst earned the U's boss an FA fine.

> **Did You Know?**
>
> **Many of Dick Graham's signings lived nowhere near Colchester, which meant the club's expenses soared.**

That Exeter clash sparked a run of twelve league games unbeaten. In that run, Svarc equalled the club's individual match scoring record by cracking in four goals at Chester. Originally, the Chester press covering the game for their Colchester counterparts reported that Micky Cook and Steve Foley had scored the second-half goals, but U's officially confirmed that Svarc had got them all. By mid-November, three Division Four strikers – Svarc (fourteen), Exeter's Fred Binney (sixteen) and Gillingham's Brian Yeo (eighteen) – topped the scoring charts of the entire Football league, and were fast gaining a reputation as fearsome sharpshooters.

As with the League Cup, U's exited the FA Cup at the first stage. The scene had been set for the two pacemakers in the Fourth Division to provide an enthralling FA Cup spectacle, but the performance of U's and Peterborough in front of a near 10,000 tension-packed Layer Road crowd proved to be a let-down. Posh won 3-2 to march on – eventually losing 1-4 at home to Leeds in a fourth round that attracted 28,000 spectators.

December brought the first eagerly awaited 'four-pointers' of the campaign. Leading Peterborough on goal-average, U's travelled to third-placed Gillingham, only to be thumped 1-4. It was only U's second league defeat in twenty outings. Seven days later the damage was repaired with a 3-0 win at Stockport. The next vital clash came on Boxing Day, with Posh making a quick return after their FA Cup victory. The clubs had since swapped positions in the table and so the 1-1 draw suited the visitors more. The two four-pointers, in other words, yielded just one point for United.

1973 had begun with the objective of getting out of the bottom four, and closed with a 1-0 win over Northampton and the aim to stay in the top four. U's occupied pole position, three points ahead of nearest challengers Posh and Gills. Jim Smith and coach Bobby Roberts had performed a remarkable turnaround in U's fortunes. Chairman Robert Jackson's New Year message read: 'Neither I, nor any of my fellow directors, are unapproachable, impersonal, business tycoons. We all live in Colchester, our telephone numbers are in the directory. Any of us will go anywhere, meet anyone, and do anything to ensure the survival and success of this club.'

The power crisis that dogged the country meant that matches had to kick-off early to avoid using floodlights, and the match programme for the Lincoln home game in January was reduced to just four pages by power restrictions at the printers. The departure of Mick Mahon to Wimbledon in that opening week of 1974 meant that in three years the entire team that had disposed of mighty Leeds had departed to pastures new.

Failure to reach the purported break-even attendance figure of 7,000 meant that the board denied Smith the money needed to sign Southend full-back Alex Smith. The power crisis and subsequent switch from Friday to Saturday football did not help United's finances, which was a pity, as the team were playing their most attractive football for some time and had already overtaken the 50-goal mark.

In an attempt to find ways to ease the financial burden on clubs, the Football League sanctioned the playing of matches on Sundays. U's first exposure to Sunday football was at Belle Vue, Doncaster, in January, and a week later they also played at Bury. Both Sunday games ended in 0-2 defeats, denting United's championship aspirations. Eight years would pass before Layer Road would host its first Sunday football. The results of the other January games, however, were so favourable that they earned Smith the Manager of the Month award.

All eyes were looking ahead to March, when United faced their crunch match at London Road. Peterborough's feisty cup run had played havoc with their league programme, so that they went into the U's match with four games in hand. Posh's 2-0 victory went a long way to denying United the title. Colchester appeared to have shot themselves in the foot. They won only one match in five, and were not helped by Svarc's goals drying up. As a stop-gap measure, Smith swooped on deadline day to 'borrow' 6ft 2in forward Gary Moore from Southend, who would turn out to be one of the most productive short-term signings ever made by the club. Moore's seven goals in eleven matches did much to ensure U's promotion, although both Posh and Gills leapfrogged above them in the final standings. The attendance of 10,007 for the visit of Gillingham would prove to be the last five-figure league attendance recorded at Layer Road.

Having spent six seasons in Division Four, in what had been one of the most turbulent periods in the club's history, United had at last secured promotion to the Third Division. The fans had flocked back to Layer Road to produce an average gate of just under 6,000. Although not enough to break even, it had been a remarkable jump from the 3,200 average of the previous season. The U's fans had gone from despair to exhilaration in just twelve short months, and the prospect of facing up to fallen giants and celebrity managers in the Third Division would ensure a spirited challenge ahead.

Match of the Season 1973-74

Colchester 2 Brentford 1

Division 4, 12 April 1974

Good Friday visitors Brentford, under Clacton-born manager Mike Everett, occupied a safe mid-table position. They had been relegated from the Third Division and for a while re-election loomed. A good run of results since transfer deadline day had, however, removed those fears. Brentford's upturn had coincided with the £12,000 signing of ex-Everton and Scotland Jimmy Gabriel from Bournemouth. Gabriel, indeed, had once been a U's target. As for United, a run of six games, yielded ten points and eleven goals, had taken them to the brink of the Third Division.

Gary Moore, who had arrived from Southend on deadline day, scored two crucial goals, one in each half, sandwiching a Simmons header, against the run of play, on the hour. Moore struck first on 37 minutes, after Stuart Morgan pressurised Bees' keeper Steve Sherwood at a corner. Former U's striker Dave Simmons, who had been involved in a ding-dong battle with Morgan, stunned the 8,154 Layer Road crowd when he escaped his shadow to nod in Dave Metchick's cross. The equaliser spurred U's to their best football of the match. Alex Smith intercepted a poor pass on the right and crossed to the far post, where Moore sent a blinding header past Sherwood. Only a brilliant one-handed save from Sherwood prevented the blond loan star from completing his hat-trick.

Without a game on Easter Saturday it appeared that U's would travel to Griffin Park four days later to rubber-stamp promotion. As it transpired, Northampton drew 1-1 with Crewe on the Sunday, ensuring that the Cobblers could not overhaul U's points tally.

A jubilant Jim Smith said: 'We are delighted, but it is a little disappointing to have to depend on someone else's results to put us in the Third Division. As far as the championship goes, Peterborough must obviously be the favourites. We are confident we can win our last three games to give us a good chance. I don't think anybody has had the injury problems that have hit us this season. I'm sure that without them we would have clinched the championship a fortnight ago.'

Those last three games yielded just two more points, bringing the club a record haul of sixty. Peterborough's games in hand saw them crowned champions, and Gills' 2-0 win at Layer Road made them runners-up. Svarc, with 26 goals, finished as the division's fourth highest scorer behind Brian Yeo (32), Fred Binney (31) and Reading's Les Chappell (28).

LEAGUE DIVISION 3   **1974-75**
Division 3   11th
League Cup   Quarter-finals
FA Cup   2nd Round

The forerunners of Colchester United had been formed in 1873. One hundred years later it was deemed fit to stage a Centenary Challenge between U's and Ipswich. This match was the highpoint of the summer's pre-season friendlies, the U's losing 2-3 before a crowd of 5,236. Promotion had done little to appease U's accountants: chairman Jackson revealed that the break-even attendance figure had risen to an unfeasible 9,200. Jackson assured supporters that if crowds reached 7,500, no players would be sold. Smith's only close-season signings were Jimmy Lindsay, a ball-playing midfielder from Watford, and John Froggatt, three times a 20-goal-a-season partner to Bobby Svarc in Jim Smith's successful Boston United side.

The league season started well enough, with just two defeats in the first thirteen games – at home to Walsall and away at Blackburn. This sterling form lifted the U's into third place, keeping company with such illustrious names as Preston, Blackburn and Crystal Palace.

While U's were carving their niche in the new division, a League Cup run was gathering momentum. Having disposed of Second Division Oxford and fellow Third Division pacesetters Southend, United prepared to meet First Division opponents in the third round. There was to be no sell-out crowd, however, as those opponents were Carlisle, experiencing their one and only season in the big time. The Cumbrian side had won their first three Division One games and briefly topped the league. By the time they visited Layer Road they had slipped to thirteenth, and were dispatched by the same 2-0 score-line that they had suffered on their last visit, in the Watney Cup three years previously. United wore the mantle of giant-killers once again – helped by a freakish burst of penalties. Four of U's five goals scored in the League Cup thus far had been from the penalty spot.

Postponement of the Essex derby with Southend – Layer Road was waterlogged – denied Colchester the chance of hitting top spot. But by now the league was playing second fiddle to the League Cup. Only three points were harvested from a possible twelve. The Svarc-Froggatt combination took a long time to get going, but did when Grimsby came to town. At a time when the club was reeling from the shock resignation of chairman Jackson, Froggatt notched his first league hat-trick and Svarc weighed in with a brace. Froggatt was on a roll, and eight days later he grabbed the crucial goal at Vicarage Road in the FA Cup. United now had two cup-runs to contend with, not to mention a push for the Second Division.

It was not long before the U's cup dreams were over for another season. First, Aston Villa ended the League Cup run at the quarter-final stage with a 2-1 win at Layer Road. Then, sensationally, Isthmian League Leatherhead outplayed the U's at their tiny Fetcham Grove ground and won 1-0. United had hoped to persuade Leatherhead to switch the tie to Layer Road, and when they failed they appealed to the FA on the grounds of Fetcham's feeble floodlights. Instead of sanctioning the change, the FA instructed that the kick-off be brought forward to 2.15pm. The Colchester press slated U's performance: 'This was the worst display I have ever seen from a Colchester United team'; 'United had no pride and precious little determination. They certainly could have no complaints about the result'; 'U's resembled a Border League side in the opening twenty minutes'.

The performance left Jim Smith squirming in his seat, and at the final whistle he conceded: 'Frankly this defeat brought shame on all connected with the club, especially having come so close to the League Cup semi-finals just over a week ago.' The giant-killers had been slayed themselves, and boy, did it hurt. Leatherhead would go on to create their own slice of FA Cup history, and one of their players, the outspoken Chris Kelly, became dubbed the 'Leatherhead Lip'. Leatherhead's subsequent win over Brighton and gallant defeat at Leicester did much to ease Colchester's embarrassment.

League fixtures came thick and fast as normal service was resumed. Christmas provided a double-header against Peterborough and Malcolm Allison's Crystal Palace – whose players included Terry Venables and England Under-23 winger Peter Taylor. (Palace that season returned an average home attendance of 17,824 and had topped 20,000 on three occasions. United, in comparison, averaged 5,122 at Layer Road). A three-point haul was enough to keep U's in the promotion reckoning. United ushered in 1975 in fifth place, only two points behind leaders Blackburn. But Wrexham trailed United by only two points, and were eleventh, which showed how congested the division was.

Sadly, it was not until February that United chalked up another win. Their victims, Huddersfield, were making their first visit since U's unceremoniously dumped them out of the 1947-48 FA Cup. The previous week that persistent tormentor of the U's, Fred Binney, had popped up again, this time in a Brighton shirt, to sting United with two more goals. United's stuttering performances early in 1975 persuaded Smith to bring in two loan signings – full-back Danny

Cameron of Sheffield Wednesday and striker Ian McDonald from Liverpool. McDonald's two goals in five matches convinced himself, if no one else, that he might soon follow in the footsteps of Kevin Keegan and challenge for a place in Anfield's first team. Cameron wanted to stay at Layer Road, but U's could not afford the £10,000 fee demanded.

The season's run-in was tinged with sadness when Paul Aimson, U's record purchase, revealed that he would have to quit playing. He had notched 141 Football League goals in his career, but made only four starts for U's, scoring twice. United's promotion challenge was ebbing away: the U's had led Swindon 3-0 in January when a waterlogged pitch caused an abandonment, but at least they had the satisfaction of winning the re-match 2-0. The crowd-pulling power of the bigger city clubs – Palace, Plymouth, Preston, and Charlton – dwarfed that of the U's. Indeed, when United visited Home Park only 23,500 turned up to see the Pilgrims gain certain promotion! Two months earlier, 38,000 had watched Argyle host Everton in the FA Cup. U's midweek trip to Selhurst Park realised almost 17,000, but United could only dream of competing financially with their much bigger brothers. Although they had fallen out of the promotion race, they would still have a say in the outcome, frustrating the challenge of Bobby Charlton's Preston and their Lancashire neighbours Blackburn.

United's rewards for 1974-75 came from other sources. The night before the home fixture with Plymouth, U's reserve team clinched the London Midweek League title. Before the Preston game, Bobby Charlton presented the U's Young Player of the Year award to 17-year-old Ian Allinson. United had achieved what they had set out to do – consolidated their Third Division place – and once again embarked on a memorable cup run.

Jim Smith's Layer Road reign effectively came to an end on 12 June, when Gordon Lee, manager of champions Blackburn, took over the hot seat at Newcastle. Eight days later the U's boss was installed as the chief at Ewood Park. When the dust from the managerial merry-go-round had settled, Bobby Roberts found himself promoted in Smith's wake.

Match of the Season 1974-75

Southampton 0   Colchester 1

League Cup, 4th Round replay, 25 November 1974

Lawrie McMenemy's Southampton had been finding the Second Division hard going, having a string of indifferent results. Up front,

---

Did You Know?

In 1970-71, Brentford keeper Chic Brodie was injured by a dog, as shown on Anglia TV. Brodie missed most of the season as a result of the injury.

---

though, they paraded two strikers valued at £300,000 each – 20-cap England international Mick Channon and the once-brilliant Peter Osgood, who had claimed four England caps during his Chelsea career. Saints' ranks also included a former U's adversary in ex-Gills full-back David Peach.

Southampton had been expected to bounce straight back to the top division after being relegated the previous season. In round three of the League Cup they had slammed Derby 5-0 at the Dell, and had also reached the (Anglo-Scottish) Texaco Cup Final, beating Glasgow Rangers and Oldham on the way.

McMenemy appeared so worried by United that he personally 'spied' on five U's fixtures leading up to the tie. Jim Smith had similarly watched Saints in action and thought he had identified a weakness in the middle of their defence. The original tie, at Layer Road, ended goal-less. U's thought they were worth a win, having forced thirteen corners to Saints' two. The group of Chelsea fans who turned up to cheer on U's left disappointed that Southampton's cup exit – which would signal the return of their hero Osgood to Stamford Bridge – had not materialised.

The Monday night replay at the Dell was sandwiched between U's FA Cup win at Watford and Saints 0-1 Texaco Cup Final first-leg defeat to Newcastle. Barry Dominey, an 18-year-old with only six appearances under his belt, headed United's winner from Steve Leslie's free-kick. Mick Walker's 80th-minute one-handed save from Mick Channon sealed United's latest memorable giant-killing act. Smith quipped afterwards: 'It was a wonderful feeling when we won two cup-ties in little more than 48 hours. On that kind of form we've honestly got a good chance against anybody.'

The quarter-finals brought Ron Saunders' Aston Villa to Layer Road. Villa would finish the season as runners-up to Manchester United and their 2-1 win over U's earned them an apparently 'easy' two-leg semi-final with Fourth Division Chester. In fact, they scraped through 5-4 on aggregate to reach the Wembley final, where they beat Norwich 1-0.

LEAGUE DIVISION 3   **1975-76**
Division 3   22nd (relegated)
League Cup   1st Round
FA Cup   1st Round

New boss Bobby Roberts, who had guided the reserves to their League championship the previous season, inherited virtually all of the previous season's squad. To it, he added the experienced John Williams from Watford, Torquay centre-half Derek Harrison and Paul Dyer from Notts County. Harrison, to be precise, although at Leicester during Roberts' playing career, was actually signed by Smith after impressing in Paul Aimson's testimonial. Leaving Layer Road was Jimmy Lindsay, who moved to Hereford for a profitable fee of £15,000. On the eve of the season Roberts was forced to sign John O'Donnell on loan from Cambridge as a stop-gap defender. Indeed, Roberts had to play himself in the League Cup-tie with Palace, when his managerial career got off to an unpromising start. Four of the first five league games ended in defeat, although U's almost retrieved a three-goal Selhurst Park deficit in the League Cup.

Roberts' first league win came at the expense of Brighton, leaving only Chester and Peterborough without any league points. The following Wednesday, Chester inflicted what was to be the U's only defeat in ten games, a run which saw only three goals conceded and which lifted U's to the comparative luxury of fourteenth. This upturn in form coincided with the return of Ray Harford to the club as coach. Harford had been released by Smith in the summer and had been playing at Southern League Romford.

The improvement was tempered by the enforced sale of Bobby Svarc to Blackburn Rovers, where he linked up with his former boss Jim Smith. Roberts, in fact, was to be continually frustrated in his efforts to bolster his squad. Despite the fact that he quickly netted United £35,000 in transfer fees, little of this appears to have been made available to him.

United's winning run was brought to an abrupt end at Saltergate, where they were hammered 1-6 by Chesterfield. Worse was to follow eleven days later, when Southern League Dover extinguished United's FA Cup dreams, 4-1 in a replay at their Crabble Athletic ground. The Kent side included one of Dick Graham's signings in their side, Danny Light, though he did not score any of Dover's seven goals over the two matches. Having become renowned for their giant-killing exploits, United had, for the second season in succession, sunk to the depths with a humiliating elimination by a non-league side.

Did You Know?
Three fathers and sons have played for United's first team – Peter and Steve Wright, Bert and Peter Barlow, and Allan and Lee Hunter.

U's problems were clear: the loss of Svarc had contributed to the fact that just six goals had been scored at home – the lowest in the Football League, whilst the eight-goal away tally was also equal-lowest, shared with Chester. Roberts' ill luck in the transfer market was demonstrated by the protracted wrangling over 13-goal striker Bobby Mountford. Rochdale demanded a lump sum, U's insisted on instalments. After three weeks' negotiations, a deal was struck for the player to become Colchester's record purchase at £17,500. Mountford travelled to Layer Road, only to fail his medical. In the meantime, U's three December matches had produced just one point and one goal. One of those defeats was to Wrexham, who had astonishingly reached the quarter-finals of the European Cup-Winners' Cup.

The New Year started disastrously for United, as they piled up seven consecutive defeats. For the second time on their travels they were hit for six. This time Brighton were the executioners, and the division's leading marksman Fred Binney grabbed a pair to take his tally to nineteen, three ahead of ex-U's loanee Peter Silvester of Southend. Roberts made wholesale changes for the visit of Hereford, dropping goalkeeper Mike Walker in favour of Bristol City loanee Len Bond, and including local lad Stewart Bright for only the second time. The hunt for goals was entrusted to the inexperienced Billy Telford, on loan from Peterborough, and when he came up trumps in only the third minute, the manager's bold move appeared to have paid off. Alas, promotion-chasing Hereford were too strong and ran in four goals of their own.

Impatient U's supporters voted with their feet at the next home game, when only 2,245 turned up to see Chesterfield complete a league double at United's expense. The attendance was the lowest in Colchester's league history. Defensive inadequacies were so marked that fans called for coach Ray Harford to be recalled to steady the sinking ship. Roberts resisted the temptation to do so, and to general bafflement signed a striker instead. Much rested on the shoulders of Colin Garwood, for by this time U's had slipped to second from bottom. In only his second game, Garwood notched a brace and, and in the next match, against Chester, inspired fellow new boy Bobby Gough to open his United account. The pair would form a potent strike force, but unfortunately not until the following season.

Did You Know?

**United's Eric Burgess had a famous sister – Anthea Redfern, hostess of TV's
The Generation Game and one-time wife of Bruce Forsyth.**

Sheffield's vast Hillsborough stadium echoed to the tiny 6,905 crowd who saw Wednesday beat United 1-0. It was U's first visit to Sheffield, and the Owls' lowest-ever attendance. Seven days later 55,000 would watch as Manchester United beat Derby in the FA Cup semi-final at the same stadium.

Ironically, U's hit their best form for the final six matches of the term, but the damage had been done. Those two wins and four draws left them three points short of safety. Hereford, who had only been in the Football league four seasons, won the championship, whilst Essex rivals Southend accompanied Colchester back to the basement.

Defender Micky Cook was awarded a testimonial match against Ipswich, with Roberts heaping praise on United's 'Mr Consistency'. 'I cannot think of a player with more enthusiasm than Micky Cook. He is a model professional who always gives ninety minutes' endeavour.' For Roberts, his first season of league management had been a trying time, hindered by injuries and financial restraint. He would spend the summer preparing for a rapid return to the Third Division, pinning his hopes on the 'G-force' of his new strike partnership of Gough and Garwood.

Match of the Season 1975-76

Colchester 0 Crystal Palace 3

Division 3, 10 January 1976

On paper, January looked a difficult month for United. They would host Malcolm Allison's runaway leaders Crystal Palace, and visit Brighton and Hereford, who were tucked in behind Palace in second and third spot. Roberts had captured a striker in time for the Palace match, when Bobby Gough made his first start. Terry Venables had hung up his playing boots to become coach at Selhurst, and Roberts commented that Venables was 'a first-rate manager in the making'.

United had beaten Palace at Layer Road in the League Cup first-round, second leg, but narrowly bowed out on the aggregate score. The Eagles were reported to be in debt to the tune of over £1 million, but everything about them was big – from Malcolm Allison's Fedora hat, to his cigar and their 20,000 average crowds. Palace could also boast the most talked about player of the season in England Under-23 winger Peter Taylor. Even their surnames were 'big'. Dave Swindlehurst would end his career at Layer Road in the late 1980s, as would Martin Hinshelwood's younger brother Paul, and midfielder Nick Chatterton.

The match, in front of Layer Road's biggest crowd of the season, 6,240, proved to be a canter for Palace from the moment Barry Dominey handed Alan Whittle's lob onto the bar. Taylor slammed in the resultant spot-kick and Swindlehurst and Whittle added two more goals. Roberts was critical of Mike Walker and moaned: 'our keeper gave them all three'. Roberts, in fact, would be the only manager ever to drop Walker from U's Number 1 jersey in the Welshman's distinguished Layer Road career. Walker would miss a handful of other games, but only because of injury.

Defeat by Palace heralded a disastrous run of seven straight losses for United, in which they conceded 22 goals. Palace were also suffering hiccups: their win at Colchester would be their only success in twelve league games. Distracted by an FA Cup run that carried them to the semi-finals, they eventually missed out on promotion.

LEAGUE DIVISION 4   1976-77

Division 4   3rd (promoted)
League Cup   1st Round
FA Cup   4th Round

U's pre-season build-up, curiously, included several cricket matches against local opposition. On the soccer pitch, Roberts pinned his faith in the squad that had been relegated, the only addition to it being Ian Cranstone, a young keeper from Spurs, as understudy to Mike Walker. Roberts' plan for the new season centred on John Froggatt, aided by winter signing Bobby Gough and newer recruit Colin Garwood. Roberts demanded goals, goals, goals and had set each striker a scoring target to aim at. Asked if he would settle for twenty goals apiece, Roberts replied: 'I'm looking for better than that.'

U's first competitive match was at the Den in the League Cup. In a bid to bolster flagging spectator interest, the competition had been brought forward to the first Saturday of the season. United's 1-2 first-leg deficit was cancelled out in the return at Layer Road, forcing an early-season replay. It was drawn 4-4, the first time in their history that U's had recorded such a score. Garwood scored three of the goals, but the aftermath was to be less memorable, as United fell to the Lions in their second senior penalty shoot-out. The first, of course, had been on that joyous Watney Cup-winning day in 1971.

There was better news in the league: United's first four home games saw twelve U's goals, but the Colchester public was still reluctant to leave the comfort of their armchairs. Average attendances hovered below the 3,000 mark. All the endeavour spent in winning three straight home league games was negated by three away defeats, but a 0-0 draw at Bournemouth marked a temporary turning point in United's travels. The previous season it had been that wretched haul of just sixteen away goals that made relegation all but inevitable, and Roberts knew this weakness had to be redressed if U's were to bounce back at the first attempt. Young centre-half Steve Dowman served notice of his arrival in league football by scoring with his first touch at Watford, after coming on as sub. For such an inexperienced player, Dowman would enjoy an astonishingly productive season.

Garwood, who had been dropped for the visit to Dean Court for 'not performing' in away games, answered his manager in the best possible way when he cracked his second hat-trick of the season in a 6-2 demolition of winless Hartlepool. In eleven full appearances, Garwood found the net on eleven occasions. Only Barney Daniels, of early pacesetters Stockport County, with twelve goals, had scored more.

United's fragility away from home resurfaced with defeats at Scunthorpe and Doncaster in the space of three days. In fact, U's had taken just two points from seven away games. If only a few of those games had been won, then, coupled with their formidable home record, U's would have raced away at the top. In a bid to bolster his defence, Roberts tried to lure ex-U's favourite Duncan Forbes from Norwich. Nearing the end of a distinguished career, Forbes had played 278 league games for the Canaries since his £10,000 transfer from Layer Road in September 1968. This was eight games more than he had played for U's. Ironically, he played at Layer Road when loaned to Torquay in the midst of his transfer negotiations with U's. United hammered Torquay 4-0 and among the scorers was Colin Garwood, who notched his fourteenth goal of the season, all of them having been scored at Layer Road.

Forbes shortly agreed personal terms with United, only for Norwich boss John Bond to veto the move. But the very fact that such a high-profile player was prepared to come to a 'backwater' like Layer Road might make others think likewise. In little over a year, Roberts had dramatically changed U's fortunes. From suffering from a shortage of points, goals and confidence, they now stood on the verge of the top four, and boasted the highest scoring rate in the country. It was therefore fitting that Roberts picked up the November Manager of the Month award, after that month had produced four wins, ten goals and none conceded. U's had also progressed in the FA Cup at the expense of Ron Atkinson's divisional leaders Cambridge, and earned their first away win of the season, at Barnsley.

As the festive season approached, U's had eased their way into the third round of the FA Cup to face Southern League Kettering and sat fourth in the table – three points behind leaders Bradford City, but with a game in hand. They had already played six of the top eight sides away from home, and so were rightly confident of launching a sustained promotion bid. Rampant U's crashed in nine goals in their first two league games of 1977, ideal preparation for what might have been a tricky trip to Derek Dougan's Kettering. Considering that United had fallen to non-league opposition in both the previous campaigns, it was a relief that on this occasion they gave a nerveless display. When another big goal-haul overwhelmed Southport, talk turned to the record books, in particular to Brentford's 1929-30 season when the Bees won all 21 home fixtures. Bobby Hunt's 1961-62 club record goalscoring haul for U's was also under threat.

Unfortunately, leaders Cambridge spoilt U's 100 per cent home record in the unlucky thirteenth game. But the Colchester public had finally woken up to U's entertaining style, with gates rising to almost 5,000. The success also brought the scouts flocking to Layer Road, with Dowman, Lindsay Smith, Steve Leslie and Micky Cook under the spotlight. Speculation mounted that massive £50,000 transfer fees would be flooding into the Layer Road coffers. The FA Cup duel with Derby provided the perfect shop window for the quartet, so much so that County boss Colin Murphy tried to capture Cook, after the full-back had stitched up Leighton James in the first game and in the replay. January had been a fine month for United and Roberts picked up his second Manager of the Month award. February saw the team finally click away from home, collecting wins at lowly cash-strapped Newport, Workington and Halifax. The only blemish came in a tense Essex derby at Layer Road, when Southend snatched an 87th-minute winner.

U's destiny was clearly in their own hands, four of the last six home games being against fellow promotion chasers. But six successive draws in March and April heaped the pressure back on as rivals played catch-up, and when United contrived to lose their penultimate game at Darlington, promotion hung on a knife-edge. Swansea had staged a tremendous late season run, with seven wins and a draw, to pose a serious threat. Both Swansea and United had difficult last day fixtures: U's would host already-promoted Bradford City, needing a point to go up, whilst the Welshmen travelled to champions Cambridge. Fortunately U's did enough with a 2-1 win, despite Swansea's 3-2 victory at the Abbey.

Those same U's fans who had called for Roberts' head twelve months previously mobbed him during frenzied scenes at the final whistle. U's were back in the Third Division. Chairman Rippingale forecast: 'there is no way we will be back in the Fourth Division again,' as he handed out glasses of champagne in the players' lounge. Roberts confessed that he had kept news of Swansea's 3-0 half-time lead from his players at the interval, sensing that 'they were under enough pressure as it was'.

Match of the Season 1976-77

Colchester 1 Derby 1

FA Cup, 5th Round, 29 February 1977

United's home league record had been hitherto impeccable, but after twelve straight wins, U's had fallen to leaders Cambridge, whom they now trailed by three points, with a game in hand.

Did You Know?

Ray Crawford was England's first full international to play for United, but Jackie Robinson of England and Sheff Wed guested for U's during 1945-46.

Seven days later, Colchester's home record looked under threat again, this time by Derby County in the FA Cup. Derby were labouring in fifteenth place in the old First Division with just four wins, and this despite heavy investment in new players. Their strike-force of Derek Hales, Charlie George and Leighton James was one of the most costly in the country. The Rams had previously been managed by Brian Clough and Dave Mackay. Both had secured the League championship, but Mackay then found himself sacked in favour of the little known Colin Murphy.

At a packed Layer Road, Murphy's side took the lead through Derek Hales. Hales had taken time to settle in the Rams side following his £280,000 move from Charlton, but took his half-chance well, after John Froggatt had played him onside. County appeared content to sit back, allowing U's in the second half to pummel Colin Boulton's goal, but without creating clear-cut openings. As the game wore on, Derby must have hoped that their time-wasting antics would not cost them dearly. Referee Crabbe, a prison officer from Exeter, saw fit to sentence the tie to five minutes and 51 seconds injury-time. It was in the fifth minute of added time that Colin Garwood preserved U's unbeaten home cup record against First Division sides. He met Bobby Gough's knockdown to spark scenes at Layer Road of pure bedlam.

Even then the excitement was not finished. U's full-back Micky Cook had snuffed Welsh international wing-wizard Leighton James out of the game. James had had his nose put out of joint, and in the tunnel afterwards jostled with Cook and Garwood. To the national press James claimed that U's were 'kickers', to which Garwood retorted through the same channel: 'at least I *scored* a goal' to 'cry baby' James.

The replay, in front of the BBC Sportsnight cameras, saw a 1-0 win for Derby. This time, James allowed his feet to do the talking, but not before Bobby Gough had struck the post with a late half-volley. U's would have deserved extra-time against their nervy hosts, who won through to face Blackburn. A familiar 'spy' in the crowd heaped praise on U's, saying, 'I'd much rather face Derby than Colchester'. That face belonged to ex-United boss Jim Smith, boss of Blackburn Rovers.

LEAGUE DIVISION 3   **1977-1978**
Division 3   8th
League Cup   3rd Round
FA Cup   2nd round

With time to reflect on the coming season, manager Roberts opted for a change of style, vowing to build attacks more patiently instead of using frenzied long balls. This, he felt, was better suited to the Third Division. With virtually the same squad that had gained promotion, he felt there was no reason why U's could not mount a serious challenge for the Second Division.

U's kicked off their 27th league campaign at the same venue that they had started their very first, Gillingham's Priestfield Stadium, and this time enjoyed a 3-1 win. Subsequent victories over Bradford City and Chester saw U's lead the table, having already stated their intentions by demolishing Aldershot 5-2 over two legs in the League Cup, and secured a 1-1 draw at Jim Smith's Blackburn in the second round. When the third round draw was made, U's incentive for the Blackburn replay was a trip to Elland Road, Leeds. But Colchester needed no additional motivation: they demolished previously unbeaten Rovers to the tune of 4-0. It was rumoured around this time that Everton were preparing to bid for Steve Dowman, but Roberts dismissed this as newspaper talk. Elland Road, though, would be a fine stage for U's potential stars to display their wares.

U's early success in 1977-78 was achieved against a mounting backdrop of injuries. After just six league games, Roberts was down to the bare bones with just eleven fit professionals, but his team still topped the division. A bruising 'battle of the Alamo' at Portsmouth further depleted the ranks, even though Roberts had swooped to sign Doncaster's Liverpudlian centre-half Steve Wignall for £5,000.

A three-match goal-drought and a home defeat by Port Vale finally knocked U's off their lofty perch, which they never regained. It is not unusual for promoted clubs to start well; the measure is whether they are able to sustain the challenge. New signing Wignall already looked a bargain buy, matching his clean-cut appearance off the field with equally groomed football skills on it. Young Ian Allinson, twenty, was already tipped for First Division stardom: his contribution in the 15-goal haul of the 'G-force', Bobby Gough and Colin Garwood, did not go unnoticed by admiring observers.

September was a month which saw United's inability to turn chances into goals make the heady days of league leadership seem light years away. Perhaps the distraction of the Leeds tie was partly responsible for a dismal return of just one win in nine league games. The team boarded the coach for South Yorkshire in the knowledge that Saturday's defeat by Cambridge had seen them plummet seven places to tenth. United also had to contend with the distraction caused by contract rebel Lindsay Smith, who finally signed for Cambridge for £12,000 just days before the league game at the Abbey. Smith had been in protracted dispute with the U's board over his wages, had demanded to leave, and early in the season had been loaned to both Charlton and Millwall. On the question of Smith's 'outrageous' pay demands, Roberts ruefully proclaimed: 'I closed my eyes and thought I was talking to Pele.'

Lightning did not strike twice. Leeds comprehensively dumped U's out of the Cup, but no amount of wins over United would extinguish the ghost of 1971 and Grandad's Army.

The league table was tight enough for United to fancy they could bridge the gap with the leading teams, but two home wins were effectively cancelled out by away defeats at Walsall and leaders Wrexham. The Wrexham match marked the first occasion a U's league match had been featured on BBC's Match of the Day. There was no 'Saturday Night Fever' back in Essex, however, as the Welsh team ran out 2-1 winners.

Bobby Roberts' success with the U's was by this time being noticed far and wide, even as far away as the United States. Tampa Bay Rowdies, in Florida, one of the United States' leading clubs at that time, approached Bobby Roberts with an offer to become their manager. More and more British players and senior coaches were choosing to join the exodus to 'Stateside Soccer' but, fortunately for United, Roberts decided to stay put.

The FA Cup brought a long-drawn-out tie against Bournemouth, which was settled at the third attempt by a Colin Garwood hat-trick at neutral Watford. This was only the second occasion that United had played on a neutral ground since their arrival in the league – the first being an FA Cup first round second replay against Peterborough in 1961-62, when 12,000 saw Posh win 3-0 at Norwich. Unfortunately, only 2,230 hardy souls braved the chill conditions at Vicarage Road. Ironically, it was Watford who awaited the winners in the next round. Having done their spying from the comfort of their own surroundings, the Hornets duly put paid to U's Cup hopes for another year.

Approaching the festive season, U's striking rate was sinking to such an alarming low that Roberts delved into the transfer market to capture Darlington's top scorer Eddie Rowles for a club record £15,000. It proved to be no quick fix, as Rowles took a month to score his first U's goal. By then the rot had set in, with just one win to show in ten fixtures, and that win – at home to Portsmouth –

Did You Know?

The final count of United fans at the FA Cup-tie at Everton in 1971 was three charter planes, four trains, over 50 coaches and countless private cars.

---

was achieved at huge cost. Rowles broke his ankle seven minutes after notching his first goal at Layer Road, and was sidelined for the rest of the season. That blow, coupled with striker Garwood joining Pompey for £25,000 and John Froggatt moving to Port Vale for £10,000, meant that United had effectively sold off their slim promotion hopes. The lack of depth in the squad forced Roberts to experiment with youth-teamers Tony Evans, Steve Wright and Russell Cotton, who each showed promise in fleeting appearances towards the end of the campaign. If one discounts Rowles and the inexperienced young threesome, Roberts was left with a basic squad of just fourteen players to choose from.

Overall, though there seemed little doubt that United could put out a useful team, it was never more evident that the club's hand-to-mouth existence would deny the manager a large enough squad to sustain a concerted challenge for the Second Division. Cambridge, however, had shown the way to a brighter future. They had been promoted along with the U's the previous season, and, like Hereford before them, had gained rapid promotion straight to the Second Division soon after being admitted to the Football League. Of the newly elected 'class of 1950', only Scunthorpe had reached that elevated status (1958-64). The others – Gillingham, Shrewsbury and Colchester – were still trying.

Elsewhere, both John Froggatt (with just three goals) and Colin Garwood (two) failed to fire their new clubs to safety. Both Vale and Pompey sunk into the basement division.

Colchester's season ended on a nostalgic, rain-drenched, night when Smith, Hall, Wood, Garvey, Kurila, Gibbs, Simmons and Mahon – along with guests Trevor Francis and Keith Bertschin – took on Millwall in a benefit match for John Gilchrist, who had recently undergone kidney treatment. Grandad's Army was, temporarily, back on parade.

Match of the Season 1977-78

Leeds 4   Colchester 0

League Cup, 3rd Round, 26 October 1977

A headline-grabbing 4-0 win over Jim Smith's Second Division Blackburn set up an intriguing third round tie at Elland Road. It was only six and a half years since U's had stunned the football world with *that* win over Leeds at Layer Road. Jimmy Armfield's current Leeds side were languishing in mid-table in the First Division, but had disposed of Rochdale 3-0 at Spotland in the previous round.

Since that 1971 tie, Leeds had won the championship in 1973-74, been runners-up in 1970-71 and 1971-72 (when they also won the FA Cup), won the Fairs Cup in 1970-71 and been beaten in the European Cup final in 1974-75. Such was their success that its architect, Don Revie, had been chosen to lead England's 1978 World Cup qualifying campaign. England gained the wrong man and Leeds lost the right one. Revie's successor, Brian Clough, had been sacked after 44 days in charge, leaving Armfield to try to steady a rocking ship.

The contrasting status of the two sides was highlighted in the weekend fixtures prior to the League Cup-tie. Liverpool attracted 45,500 to Elland Road, whilst just 5,423 paid to watch the East Anglian derby at Cambridge, where U's contract rebel Lindsay Smith made his Cambridge debut.

Though none of U's famous 'Grandad's Army' still wore a Colchester shirt, Paul Madeley and Peter Lorimer remained from the 1971 Leeds side. Such was Leeds' decline, however, that none of their Scottish internationals (David Harvey, Frank Gray, Peter Lorimer, Arthur Graham, Eddie Gray) would take part in World Cup 78. When one adds England caps Trevor Cherry and Paul Madeley, and Wales' Carl Harris, the current Leeds side boasted one less international player than that in 1971.

Leeds could never, *will* never, bury the ghost of that defeat but their 4-0 victory at least saved them further embarrassment. Their wingers, Harris and Graham, were in devastating form. Though U's defence found no answer to the aerial power of Jordan, they were not disgraced and Steve Dowman did his growing reputation no harm at all.

Leeds went on to beat Bolton and Everton before losing the two-legged semi-final to Nottingham Forest, whilst U's returned to their ultimate objective of achieving Second Division status.

LEAGUE DIVISION 3   **1978-79**
Division 3   7th
League Cup   1st Round
FA Cup   5th Round

U's suffered a pre-season dent to their confidence when they finished wooden-spoonists in the inaugural Willhire Cup four-team tournament. A creditable 0-0 draw against an Ipswich side parading the FA Cup that they had won at Wembley in May, preceded 1-2 defeats against Norwich and Cambridge.

Bobby Roberts introduced just one summer signing – Mansfield's Northern Ireland-capped Pat Sharkey, a former Portman Road apprentice. Sharkey was soon in action – missing a penalty on his home debut against Charlton in the season's League Cup curtain raiser. The £10,000 Irishman proved to have 'off-the-field' problems, however, which meant the U's were effectively back to the same squad as the previous season. To make matters worse, midfielder Steve Leslie broke his leg at Hillsborough in only the third league outing of the campaign. Four consecutive goalless returns saw U's sink into the bottom four, but a late Micky Cook winner against Chester finally kick-started United's push. Last-gasp goals would become a feature of U's season as Roberts drove home the message that games lasted ninety minutes – or more.

To overcome the loss of Leslie, the U's signed Exeter's Bobby Hodge for £15,000. Following 120 games in a Grecian shirt, his first for U's was ironically in a 1-2 defeat against his former chums at St James' Park. A dramatic 3-2 win over Swindon at Layer Road enabled United to claw their way into the top half of the table, trailing star-studded Watford in second place by two points with eleven games played. Leaders Shrewsbury were a further three points to the good.

That Swindon game provided a clear demonstration of the spirit instilled into the team. U's turned around a 0-2 half-time deficit into a 3-2 victory, with 18-year-old Tony Evans staking his claim for a permanent place with his first league goal. It was not long before he grabbed his second, salvaging a point in the derby with Southend at Layer Road. Though U's remained unbeaten at home, hopes of joining the promotion-chasing pack were stymied by the fact that they had yet to win away from Layer Road.

Roberts, in fact, had little choice but to delve into the transfer market when Eddie Rowles, having recovered from his broken ankle, suffered Achilles problems. The U's transfer record of £15,000 was equalled yet again when Trevor Lee signed from Millwall. In doing so, the 24-year-old striker became the first senior coloured player to don a U's shirt. He had formed a potent strike-force at the Den with Phil Walker, as, indeed, the pair had at non-league Epsom and Ewell prior to their move into league football.

Considering the apathetic support at the gate, Trevor Lee's fee constituted 'splashing out', leaving chairman Jack Rippingale to bemoan: 'I just can't understand the crowds for football that is as entertaining as you could have. It seems to me the only time we get any peak enthusiasm is when a cup run comes along.' Prophetic words, as U's embarked on the FA Cup trail with a home tie against Oxford. Bobby Gough's hat-trick in a 4-2 win secured the match ball.

The second round draw, by one of those quirks, paired U's with their surprise vanquishers of four seasons earlier – Leatherhead. Surely lightening would not strike twice? Since that fateful day at Fetcham Grove, Leatherhead had enhanced their giant-killing repu-tation with wins over Brighton, Cambridge and Northampton, and been beaten FA Trophy finalists at Wembley. Bobby Gough contin-ued his FA Cup scoring spree to put U's 1-0 up, but 'Leatherhead Lip' Chris Kelly equalised late on. Mercifully, U's skated past their non-league opponents in the ice-bound replay. Lee started the 4-0 demolition with his first goal for United. The win earned a costly long-haul trek to Darlington in the third round.

Pre-Christmas visitors Watford had stunned the lower echelons of the Football League by spending £200,000 – a veritable fortune in those days – on Leicester centre-half Steve Sims. But Watford could afford it: they topped the table and had reached the League Cup semi-final, beating Manchester United at Old Trafford. They also boasted the league's leading scorer in Ross Jenkins, and, most important of all, could call upon the bottomless pockets of chairman Elton John. How could the likes of Colchester compete? Well, compete they did and Watford were fortunate to escape with a 1-0 victory that signalled U's first home league defeat of the season.

Following the Watford game the harsh winter put Layer Road out of action for a financially crippling five weeks. United played five away games in that period and it took a Bobby Hodge goal to finally secure the elusive first away win of the season. Crucially, it came at Feethams, as Jack Rippingale's cherished Cup run gathered momentum. Once again, however, the subsequent draw was unkind, as travel-weary U's faced a visit to giant-killers Newport. 'Match of the Season' takes up the story.

Back in the league, U's strung together a run of eleven points from a possible sixteen to dispel relegation fears. If only U's had picked up more on their travels, they might even have challenged Watford, Swansea and Shrewsbury at the top. As it was, the elusive

---

Did You Know?

Tony Wingate had United's shortest ever career – two touches after coming on as an 88th-minute sub at Hartlepool in 1971-72. Injury ended his career.

---

first away League win came as late as match 32 at the County Ground, Swindon, when a Trevor Lee brace earned a 2-1 victory.

In an unprecedented gesture, the Football League awarded all clubs £10,000 as 'compensation' for the gate revenues lost through inclement weather. The gate receipts from the Manchester United FA Cup-tie had kept U's afloat, just as Rippingale had predicted. The coffers were further boosted when Sharkey was off-loaded to Peterborough for £8,000, but deadline day came and went further comings and goings.

United reserved their most sparkling performance for the Good Friday visit to Graham Taylor's champions-elect Watford. In front of almost 18,000 spectators, U's turned the form-book upside down with a breathtaking 3-0 win. Such were Watford's exploits, that this improbable result attracted national press attention. The *Daily Mirror* wrote: 'Elton John must have thought he was watching Top of the Flops, but Colchester were so impressive on the break.' The *Daily Mail* reported: 'The league leaders were humiliated for 90 minutes,' whilst The *Sun* bannered: 'Lee Finds A Watford Gap' – referring to the forward's double strike.

Sadly, United could not carry the result into the remainder of the Easter programme and despite being undefeated in the last six games with three wins and three draws, fell short of third-placed Swansea by nine points. What better way to round off the season than by securing a club record away win? U's journeyed to the Wirral and thumped relegated Tranmere 5-1. One defeat in the last twelve games would be a rock onto which to build for yet another assault on the Second Division prize.

Match of the Season 1978-79

Colchester 0 Manchester United 1

FA Cup, 5th Round, 20 February 1979

U's travelled to South Wales for the re-arranged fourth round tie with Newport in the knowledge that the victors would host either Manchester United or Fulham in the next round. Ninety goal-less minutes brought the Welsh team back to Colchester, whilst Fulham held the Red Devils to a 1-1 draw at Craven Cottage. Because of international call-ups, the Old Trafford replay was put back a week, leaving U's, 1-0 replay winners over Newport, with an anxious wait to hear who their opponents would be.

When Manchester United won through, the national press reported Colchester chairman Jack Rippingale as saying, 'we don't want to host Manchester United fans'. Man U laboured at the time under a stigma, with a hardcore of their so-called 'fans' wreaking havoc and destruction on many of the towns and cities where their idols performed. Colchester offered a 'policeable' 300 tickets, but the FA insisted on Man U receiving their full allocation of 4,000.

The northern giants were trying to emulate their former glory days. They had sunk into the Second Division, but under Tommy Docherty had returned at the first attempt and reached two successive FA Cup finals – winning the second, against Liverpool. Docherty was sacked after becoming involved with the wife of a staff colleague. Dave Sexton took over the helm, and had spent over £1 million on ex-Leeds pair Joe Jordan and Gordon McQueen, and Mickey Thomas from Wrexham. For all that, the Red Devils were playing inconsistently, languishing in First Division mid-table.

The arctic conditions put paid to the original Saturday tie, with six inches of snow covering the pitch. Over 150 volunteers helped to clear the grass of its white blanket, but the re-arranged midweek tie hit the attendance – Man U returned over 1,000 tickets. Colchester fans, fearful of the Red Army reputation, also stayed indoors in worrying numbers. The route from the railway station to the stadium was a temporary wasteland of boarded up shop-fronts as proprietors sought to protect their premises. Mindful of the need for crowd control, Colchester had enlisted the help of the Army, who provided 150 soldiers from the local garrison as extra stewards.

The game itself was settled with just four minutes remaining on the clock. Jimmy Greenhoff popped in his fourteenth goal of the season after Thomas's corner had skidded off Andy Ritchie's head. Only five minutes earlier, Colchester had sprung Man Utd's shaky offside trap. Keeper Gary Bailey raced to the edge of his box to deny Steve Foley, but was helpless as the loose ball spun to Trevor Lee. Lee's shot zipped past two defenders but was cleared off the line by the outstretched boot of left-back Arthur Albiston.

Dave Sexton commented afterwards: 'I would have settled for a draw, Colchester deserved a game at Old Trafford, as did their fans, whose work on the pitch produced a perfect playing surface.' Man U marched onwards to the final, when they lost to a last-gasp Alan Sunderland goal for Arsenal.

LEAGUE DIVISION 3   **1979-80**
Division 3   5th
League Cup   2nd Round
FA Cup   3rd Round

Bobby Roberts opted to start the new season with the same squad that had fared well at the back end of 1978-79. The consistency shown in those last dozen matches needed to be reproduced all season, otherwise Colchester would be once again a club nibbling at the bait of the Second Division, with the occasional scrap of a cup run thrown in. Roberts' 19-man squad, already hit by injuries to Paul Dyer, Eddie Rowles, Mick Packer and Bobby Hodge, was further depleted when Ray Bunkell and Steve Foley took heavy knocks on the club's pre-season tour of West Germany. Once again, the Willhire Cup produced a competitive edge to the build-up, but once again U's fared poorly, losing to Ipswich (0-2), and drawing with Norwich (2-2) and Cambridge (1-1).

U's progressed into the second round of the League Cup before a Division Three ball had been kicked. Second Division new-boys Watford, still scarred by the 3-0 mauling by U's that in effect denied them the previous season's championship by just one point to Shrewsbury, were on the receiving end again. United won 3-2 over two legs to set up a two-legged tie with Ron Saunders' Aston Villa.

The first league opponents to visit Layer Road were Sheffield United, who had sought to emulate the success of Argentinians Osvaldo Ardiles and Ricky Villa at Spurs by signing the 'Gaucho' pair of Alex Sabella and Pedro Verde. A third Argentinian, Diego Maradona had reportedly been 'not up to much!' Micky Cook, for so long a near-permanent fixture on U's team-sheet, finally broke Peter Wright's club-record 452 appearances when he turned out against Jack Charlton's Sheffield Wednesday in September.

Fresh from the League Cup defeat at Villa Park, U's began a run of ten games undefeated. These included four away wins at Grimsby, Mansfield, Sheffield United and Southend. Roberts had already redressed the previous season's wretched away form by steering his side to five league wins from seven away fixtures. U's sat second in the table after fifteen matches, level on points with big-city side Sheffield United, which was a fine testament to the coaching ability of Roberts and his right-hand man Ray Harford. The U's displays had not gone unnoticed, with eight-goal Trevor Lee being wooed by a number of suitors, including Aston Villa.

Early November, following a 0-3 setback at Blackburn, saw United stutter. They collected just two points from the next three games, slipping down to fourth. But a 5-2 hammering of Plymouth set things up nicely for an FA Cup clash between the same sides eight days later. The Devon side were not going to succumb so easily second time round, securing a home replay thanks to a late equaliser. The stalemate at Home Park was finally broken only after Ian Allinson netted in extra-time. A second round home tie with Bournemouth would present an ideal opportunity for U's to get amongst the third round big boys.

Meanwhile, in the league, U's had to travel to Millwall's Den, an intimidating place at the best of times, but U's passed their sternest test yet when they beat the league leaders 2-1. Trevor Lee, returning to his former club, opened the scoring. The nation was by this time beginning to sit up and take notice of the so-called backwater club from north Essex, so much so that BBC Radio's Sport on Two took in the match as one of it's featured games. For the first time, U's fans were able to keep tabs on their heroes as Ipswich-based Radio Orwell provided quarter-hour updates on their matchday sports programme. The 1980s arrived with U's occupying their highest position for 23 years, and through to the third round of the FA Cup, thanks to Eddie Rowles' goal against Bournemouth.

Defeat in the third round by Third Division Reading set the alarm bells ringing. With no lucrative Cup run to fall back on, in the event of United gaining promotion to the Second Division their ramshackle Layer Road ground could not hope to meet the conditions laid down in the Safety at Sports Ground Act 1975. Director Maurice Cadman warned that the cost of refurbishing Layer Road would be £280,000. The land it occupied was assessed as being worth £150,000 to a property developer, and, with Football Grounds Improvement Trust money available, that figure was not unobtainable. The sticking point dated back to when the club had purchased the ground from the local council in 1971. One of the conditions of sale was that the land could not be sold for housing – and on this point the Council would not budge.

The proposed development of Layer Road involved shifting the pitch 23 feet towards the Clock End, leaving space for a 5,000 capacity terrace behind the Layer Road goal. Opposite the main stand would be an all-seater stand with executive boxes. With only a few standing terraces behind the Clock End goal, the capacity would be an adequate 18,000. There was considerable bite-your-tongue friction between the club and the Council, especially as the many corporate events organised by the thriving Commercial Department often saw the principal protagonists sitting around the same function table.

On the pitch, United's outstanding away form was for a while being undermined by a loss of confidence – and points – at home.

Did You Know?

Dick Graham thought United's all-blue strip 'disappeared' under the floodlights, and in 1972-73 switched the kit to all-white.

Expectant U's fans repeatedly turned up at Layer Road buoyed by the thought: 'we can go top today if we win.' But a succession of draws meant that United were always in the slipstream of the red half of Sheffield. The tide appeared to have turned with three successive 2-1 victories, including a four-pointer against new leaders Grimsby, but the good work was undone with three goal-shy defeats on the trot. The result that finally knocked the stuffing out of U's was surely the second of those defeats, when Blackburn's Duncan MacKenzie appeared to impede keeper Mike Walker, allowing his team-mate, Andy Crawford, to net the only goal of the game at Layer Road.

Many of the other teams had also caught up with United, partly due to capitalising on their games in hand, partly due to United's woeful form *chez nous*. Roberts demanded one last promotion push. The response was a 6-1 thumping of Brentford at Layer Road, but at a cost, as Steve Foley and Bobby Gough picked up injuries. It was no surprise, then, that U's challenge petered out as the walking-wounded 13-man squad limped through their remaining fixtures. Youngsters Tony Evans, Russell Cotton and Gary Harvey all sampled first-team action, with Harvey netting an eye-catching brace at Swindon.

United's end-of-season tour took them to the USA, where they were set to play Miami Dolphins. The U's party arrived just as race riots exploded in the City's ghetto. The riots caused the match to be moved to a junior grid-iron pitch. In these farcical conditions the ball rebounded into play off the existing 'American' goalposts, and Micky Cook, Trevor Lee and two American players were sent off. Oh, and Eddie Rowles secured a 1-0 victory.

Compared with their some-time illustrious and big-spending Third Division counterparts, U's had been the surprise team to most unbiased observers. United occupied one of the top four berths for much of the campaign, largely thanks to an impressive return of ten away wins, and yet the Colchester public failed to respond to the stimulus of a winning team. Only Wimbledon and Chester averaged lower home attendances. Roberts braced himself for a summer exodus: many players' contracts were up and others were eager to play regularly on the lofty stages on which U's had performed during the season. Would U's have the stamina to sustain another promotion drive?

Match of the Season 1979-80

Aston Villa 0 Colchester 2

League Cup, 2nd Round, 2nd leg, 5 September 1979

The visit of Villa in the first leg rekindled memories of the quarter-final defeat in the same competition five years earlier, when U's had come so close to a first-ever trip to Wembley. Since that tie, Villa had climbed into the First Division. The beauty of the League Cup draw was that for the first time lower division clubs who made it past the first round were guaranteed a tie against a First or Second Division club. The second round had been rearranged on a seeding basis, and would be played over two legs. United would therefore be making a first appearance at Villa Park.

The first leg belonged to Villa's 18-year-old England Youth international Gary Shaw. He was only called up because regular forward Andy Gray was in contract dispute and about to join Wolves for more than £1 milion, whilst Gray's partner, Brian Little, was injured. With only a handful of appearances under his belt, Shaw struck in each half to seemingly put Villa in command.

The second leg was played out in front of a near-20,000 crowd. It was Villa who spent the opening minutes demonstrating the difference in skill between the respective divisions. But despite their possession, Villa could not find the target, and when Steve Foley hit a long cross to the far side of the box, Steve Wignall nodded back into Trevor Lee's path for the big coloured striker to stoop and head past Jimmy Rimmer's left hand.

Villa looked more threatening in the second half as skipper Dennis Mortimer drove them forward, but it was Bobby Gough who levelled on aggregate with a 20-yard volley into the roof of the net. Colchester had sensationally salvaged the tie, and with no further scoring in extra-time, it was left to a penalty shoot-out to decide the outcome. Incredibly, each of the first sixteen penalties was scored. The score stood 8-8, and with both sides rapidly running out of bodies to take the kicks, up stepped U's keeper Mike Walker. Sadly, he blasted U's ninth kick over the bar. It was left to Villa's £220,000 signing from Burnley, Tony Morley, to scrape the Midlanders through to the next round, by nine penalties to eight.

Strictly speaking, United had won for the first time ever at the ground of a First Division side in normal time. League Cup specialists Aston Villa – they had won the trophy in 1961, 1975 and 1977, and been beaten finalists in 1963 and 1971 – were knocked out in a third round replay at Everton. For Colchester, their magnificent performance would act as a springboard for a promotion bid.

LEAGUE DIVISION 3   **1980-81**
Division 3   22nd (relegated)
League Cup   1st Round
FA Cup   3rd Round

The feared break-up of the U's squad failed to materialise in the close season, with Steve Dowman the only player to say farewell, joining Wrexham for £75,000. Pre-season results were not encouraging. In what would be the last of the Willhire Cup competitions U's lost 1-4 at Ipswich, drew 1-1 at Norwich and lost 0-1 at home to Cambridge. Despite these results, Roberts optimistically declared his squad to be stronger in depth than at any time he had been with the club. He conceded that he might have been overprotective in not fielding his younger players, when some of the more seasoned campaigners were off-colour during the previous season. Roberts vowed to keep faith with his 4-4-2 formation that had resulted in promotion from the Fourth Division and successive Third Division placings of eighth, seventh and fifth.

U's biggest 'signing' of the summer was their first-ever shirt sponsorship deal with Royal London Mutual Insurance. The company was in the process of building a new headquarters in the town and was keen to be seen to contribute to local life. On the pitch, midfielder Dennis Longhorn joined on a free from Aldershot, whilst Steve Foley's brother-in-law, Nigel Crouch, had formerly been an Ipswich apprentice. The young full-back suffered a fiery debut, as he was sent-off for retaliation on Gillingham's Steve Bruce in the opening League Cup-tie. The blend of the team was not right and as early as the second home fixture fans voted with their feet. A new record low home attendance of 1,979 was established in the 1-1 draw with Walsall. The counter-attraction of Essex county cricket at the Castle Park did not help matters.

United's long-awaited first win did not come until the eighth attempt, when U's mauled Millwall's young Lions 3-0. The game was overshadowed by a bizarre incident. Sgt Frank Ruggles of Essex constabulary, who was one of a number of boys in blue keeping an eye on the London side's rowdier element, strode onto the pitch at the Layer Road end while U's were preparing to take a corner. Ruggles warned the visitors' Mel Blyth for bad language. The incident made the national evening news and even reached Governmental level as the debate raged as to who had jurisdiction on the field of play – the referee or the Police. Home Secretary William Whitelaw said, in defence of the Police: 'we have a right to expect these highly-paid young men to set an example to those who go to watch them.' Blyth later received an official Police caution.

Did You Know?

Steve Leslie was United's lowest-ever top scorer. In 1975-76 he topped the scoring charts with just 6 goals.

Despite four games unbeaten, U's form was indifferent, with many fans labelling their style of play 'boring'. Goals were needed – fast, whereupon chairman Jack Rippingale forked out a club record £25,000 on Scot Kevin Bremner. Bremner, brother of Villa's Des, was the leading scorer of Scotland's Highland League side Keith, with thirteen goals in fourteen starts. The tigerish striker came off the bench and almost snatched a dramatic late debut winner against Barnsley. Bremner had bite and passion for the game, qualities that had seemed to drain away from the rest of the squad. His never-say-die, chase everything attitude was just the fillip U's ailing season needed.

Bremner's arrival sparked a more attacking policy. This appeased the fans, as Layer Road was turned into a virtual fortress. Six consecutive league wins to the end of the year saw the club move into a safe mid-table spot. Victories over Portsmouth and Yeovil carried United into the FA Cup third round yet again. The battle with Yeovil, between two of the country's most famous Cup giant-killers, was featured on the BBC's Nine O'clock News, but Lee and Bremner denied the media 'vultures' the outcome they sought, as U's ran out 2-0 replay winners on the famed Huish slope.

To bolster a late push for promotion, Roberts signed, or so he thought, Nuneaton centre-half John Glover for £30,000. The non-leaguer resigned from his well-paid full-time computer job, but then, after weeks of dallying, got cold feet and called off the deal. Gillingham, who had made a tentative approach at the beginning of December for Lee, returned with £90,000 for the striker whom they considered would save them from relegation. Ironically, it was Lee who had plunged his new team-mates into the drop zone with a last-minute U's winner against the Gills over Christmas.

An unlucky loss to Second Division Watford in the FA Cup preceded four defeats on the trot as United's League form nose-dived. Faced now with a looming relegation battle, and the cash from the sake of Lee burning holes in his pocket, Roberts splashed out £25,000 on Ipswich midfielder Roger Osborne and £15,000 on young Chelsea's young Roy McDonough, who had made a name for himself with Walsall. McDonough boasted that he would win ninety per cent of aerial duels. He almost lived up to that claim on his debut against Burnley with an 88 per cent return, and also bagged United's opening goal. But the transfer spree was not yet finished. Roberts laid out a further £15,000 on Millwall defender Phil Coleman.

Amid a blaze of publicity at the end of January, United had announced a £5 million stadium plan. Sandwiched between Colne Bank Avenue and North Station, the project would see the construction of a 25,000-seater stadium. The Colne River Centre, as it was to be known, would provide 3,500 parking spaces, sports halls, a showground, a 175-bed hotel and 200,000 square feet of retail development. The retail was needed to fund the project, but it proved to be the sticking point, as it opposed the Borough policy on such developments.

The Borough Council's response to the Stadium plans was that it was 'an excuse to build a hypermarket, with a stadium thrown in as a token gesture'. In short, there was little chance of the project ever getting off the ground, as environmental issues could also be used to scupper the ambitious plans – the site formed part of a flood meadow. Stadium setbacks were followed by a disastrous attempt to stage Sunday football. The 1-2 home defeat by Reading, although showing an increase of 1,000 at the gate, was hampered by strict rules governing Sunday events of any kind. Colchester clergyman Reg Bedford even threatened to report the club under the 200-year-old Sunday Observance Act.

The club was now in turmoil. From the relative safety of fourteenth place, just two points from the ensuing eight games saw U's plunge into the drop zone. A goal from up-and-coming striker John Aldridge at Newport County's Somerton Park ensured United would face the stark reality of Fourth Division football again. United's new players had failed to settle into the side quickly enough, and the team's fall from mid-table had been nothing short of catastrophic. A new record low attendance of 1,430 was set for the last home fixture of the season, by which time U's fate had already been sealed. Those who bothered to turn out saw 18-year-old Tony Adcock – whose performances in the reserves had earned this, his league debut, and of whom much was expected next season.

Having come so close to promotion to the Second Division, everything had been thrown to the winds as yo-yo United slipped into the basement for the second time in six years. Questions surfaced again as to whether the town would ever be able to sustain a Second Division club, or indeed wanted the status anyway. The new stadium was a must if United were ever to unlock the financially restrictive chains that tied them to Layer Road, and consequently prevented them from mounting a serious cash-backed challenge.

Match of the Season 1980-81

Colchester 2   Charlton 0

Division 3, 28 February 1981

Mike Bailey's Charlton visited Layer Road boasting a five-point cushion over fourth-placed Barnsley. Charlton were most people's favourites to win the championship and bounce back to the division from which they had been relegated the previous season. United had stunned the Charlton faithful in September, when a late Bobby Hodge goal had shattered their 100 per cent record at the Valley and earned United what was to be only one of two away victories all season.

Coach Ray Harford warned U's about Charlton's prolific strike-force. 21-goal Derek Hales had last scored at Layer Road in the 1-1 FA Cup draw with Derby in 1976-77, and Hales was now aided and abetted by 18-year-old Paul Walsh. Walsh had already picked up England Youth honours and Harford rated his display in that match at the Valley as a 'half a million pound showing'. Roberts' reshuffled side included just six names from the earlier fixture.

Before the biggest Layer Road league attendance of the season, U's £80,000 combined captures – Kevin Bremner, Roy McDonough, Roger Osborne and Phil Coleman – helped to catch Charlton cold in the first ten minutes. The rain-lashed pitch helped Steve Foley's 35-yard sixth-minute shot to skid off Peter Shaw and past keeper Nicky Johns. Four minutes later pandemonium broke out as Johns rugby-tackled Bremner to the ground and Mick Packer coolly slotted the spot-kick home. Charlton had the ball in the net on three offside occasions in the second period, but United adapted to the treacherous conditions much better than did their high-flying opponents.

Packer, who received a silver salver in recognition of his 300 U's appearances before kick-off, accepted the adulation of his ecstatic boss afterwards when Roberts proclaimed: 'Mick was brilliant, and he was largely responsible for seeing that young Walsh didn't get a look in all afternoon.'

For Charlton the result was but a blip on their record, as they secured promotion in third place, just two points behind champions Rotherham. Colchester would not put on another committed display all season. Such was the work-rate of Bremner that the *East Anglian Daily Times* declared: 'if ever there was a human equivalent of the Grand National, then Bremner would be red-hot favourite.' As the Valiants moved up a Division, the U's would slide in the opposite direction.

## 3

SO NEAR, SO FAR
1981-1988

LEAGUE DIVISION 4   **1981-82**
Division 4   6th
League Cup   3rd Round
FA Cup   3rd Round

Despite the disappointment of relegation, U's chairman Jack Rippingale gave Bobby Roberts the dreaded vote of confidence – and then promptly resigned himself in June – disillusioned with lack of local support and with what he considered a general deterioration in footballing standards. U's bank balance, boosted by Roberts' transfer dealings, realised a year-end profit of £8,742. This was just as well, as belts would need to be tightened in the Fourth Division, which this season harboured a distinct northern bias in its composition. This would require costly overnight stays and probably reduce home attendances through lower away support.

Ray Harford's pre-season move to Fulham proved to be a major setback. Harford had formed a useful coaching partnership with Roberts, but said he felt stale. Malcolm MacDonald's Cottagers offered him a chance to step up the managerial ladder, a chance he would grab with both hands. In time he would manage Fulham, Luton and Premiership Blackburn.

The league kicked-off with the first long haul north. Hartlepool were thumped 3-1 and the goals fiesta continued when Tranmere were crushed 4-0 at Layer Road. Buoyed by the explosive start, and with the proposed new stadium hanging in the balance, new chairman Maurice Cadman pleaded for the fans' support through the turnstiles. A floodlit cricket match was staged at Layer Road between Essex and a Colchester & Ipswich Town XI, though this did not stop the Council knocking for six the ambitious plans for the Colne River Centre. The Council claimed that the development would affect the proposed Culver Precinct in the town centre, and warned of the danger that while the stadium might never be built, the shops would.

Did You Know?

The home game with Cambridge in 1977-78 was held up for seven minutes. Police had removed the corner flags to prevent fans using them as weapons.

The rejection of the plan prompted Cadman to warn that United were losing £2,000 a week and that in view of the nationwide recession the club was finding difficulty attracting sponsors. The Council's decision, he feared, could signal the beginning of the end for League football in the town. Cadman cited the example of the opening-day fixture at Hartlepool. The Football League stipulated that home clubs paid the visitors a minimum of £600 in expenses, but the paltry attendance of 2,007 meant that U's could only pocket the said minimum. United's travelling and accommodation costs had amounted to £450. The £150 left to cover the weekly wage bill clearly highlighted that commercial activities outside of football were essential to survival, but the Council Covenant on Layer Road, forbidding anything but football at the ground, was looking like an ever-tightening noose.

On a brighter note, U's progressed into the League Cup second round at the expense of regular adversaries Gillingham and faced Second Division Cambridge in the second round. Roy McDonough, Kevin Bremner and Ian Allinson were forming a potent strike-force. The trio, ably aided by the exciting Tony Adcock, contributed to U's healthy tally of 28 goals from the first eleven league games. High-scoring U's, with five successive league and cup successes, finally woke the slumbering Colchester public, as gates broke through the 3,000 barrier. The anticipation of the League Cup draw, after U's had disposed of Cambridge, was deflated by the news that United faced a 500-mile round trip to face fellow Fourth Division Tranmere.

A first-minute goal at Prenton Park, from which United never recovered, and a 1-2 home setback to league 'babes' Wigan were the only blemishes on an otherwise steady first quarter of the season. U's hovered around the top six, benefiting from the new 'three points for a win' before hitting top spot at the end of November. U's, the Football League's 43-goal top scorers, led Sheffield United on goal-difference, and as the month's top marksmen won the monthly £1,000 prize in a Pepsi-sponsored competition. Liquid recognition ensured that Roberts' Christmas drink cabinet would be well stocked, as he picked up the divisional Manager of the Month awards for both November and December.

The FA Cup visit of Newport, who were seen off 2-0, heralded a harsh winter that saw U's stay top throughout December, despite playing only two league games. The twice-postponed second round

Ray Crawford waits for the loose ball as Brian Gibbs challenges the keeper (1970-71)

Raw Crawford heads U's first goal in the FA Cup-tie with Leeds (February 1971)

A pressman snaps Dave Simmons, who has scored for U's v Leeds (February 1971)

Match programme for Colchester's FA Cup-tie with Leeds (February 1971)

Dick Graham climbs Colchester Castle, as he had promised if Colchester beat Leeds

Graham Smith saves from Everton's Henry Newton in the FA Cup (March 1971)

Shrewsbury keeper Mulhearn thwarts U's Ken Jones in the FA Cup (November 1971)

Record appearance holder Micky Cook, in the early stages of his career (March 1972)

Chairman Roy Chapman welcomes new manager Jim Smith (October 1972)

The cover of this match programme shows John Froggatt scoring against Gillingham

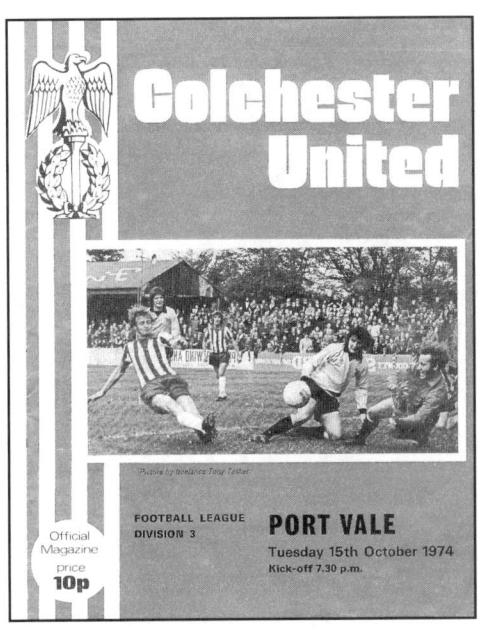

Steve Dowman fails to score from this corner against Chester (August 1977)

Ray Harford and Bobby Roberts watch pensively from the dug-out (1977-78)

Steve Leslie jumps highest in this defeat at Cambridge (October 1977)

The author, aged 12, raises the Cup during a Junior U's Wembley tour (April 1978)

Ipswich's John Wark is transfixed by Steve Foley in the Willhire Cup (July 1978)

Lee, Hodge and Gough prepare for Man Utd in the FA Cup by visiting the dairy

United cheerleaders drum up support in the late 1970s

Future U's bosses Steve Wignall and Mike Walker are in the back row (August 1979)

High-kicking Mick McCarthy (Barnsley) clears from Trevor Lee (September 1979)

Cyril Lea's 1983-84 squad face the cameras (August 1983)

Adam Nichols climbs highest during the 6-0 thrashing of Hartlepool (December 1983)

Groundsman Alan Powers tries in vain to get Layer Road playable (Winter 1985)

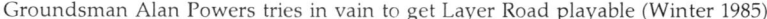

Steve Leslie, Jim Smith, comedian George Roper and Bobby Roberts (April 1985)

This style of programme cover was used throughout the 1985-1986 season

Comedian and U's director Frank Carson shows where his loyalties lie (1986-87)

One great name greets another – Jock Wallace and Alan Ball (April 1989)

tie at Brentford was finally staged – and drawn, throwing United's fixture-list into chaos. U's had to pull out the stops to stage the replay. The now customary army of snow-clearing fans, armed with all manner of implements, were rewarded for their exertions when a bizarre own-goal by Bees' Jim McNichol presented U's with a third round trip to Geordieland to face Newcastle. U's lost after a replay.

The Council, meanwhile, refused the club's request to lift the Covenant on Layer Road. The Council backed the arguments of local residents opposed to the football ground becoming a seven-day-a-week social and conference facility. United were curtly reminded that they had purchased the ground for a bargain price in the early 1970s, and that the Covenant formed part of that bargain.

Inactivity, due to the inclement conditions, affected the rhythm of the side, who welcomed in the New Year with three draws and a defeat at Torquay. Aided by 'the financial assistance' of sponsors Royal London, Roberts bought £25,000 striker John Lyons, whose CV showed 49 goals from 161 appearances for Wrexham, Millwall and Cambridge. Lyons responded to his new environment, scoring a fourth-minute goal in the vital BBC Match of the Day clash with Sheffield United. U's 5-2 victory was ample advertisement for the town's apathetic armchair fans. But what followed was a disastrous run of injuries and suspensions that saw the crippled U's claim only two wins in the next eleven games, as a result of which they slipped to seventh. Roberts pleaded for his players to display the character that had punished so many defences earlier in the season, but unbeknown to manager, fans and press, changes were afoot in the boardroom.

With eight games remaining, Bobby Roberts was asked to quit. Dwindling interest on the terraces, as promotion faded, prompted Cadman to ask the U's boss to relinquish the remainder of his five-year contract. Eighteen months earlier Roberts had steered U's to the brink of the Second Division. He had wheeled and dealed in the transfer market and had developed the potential of Kevin Bremner, Tony Adcock and Ian Allinson, all of whom were gold bars in United's vaults. Roberts, however, refused to go, demanded compensation, and six games (and only one defeat) later he was sacked. As a parting shot, Roberts blooded youngsters Perry Groves and Wayne Ward, as proof that the future bode well. Amid cries of foul play by supporters and local press, Cadman countered: 'The loss of support and the financial situation is grim. We are looking for someone to put confidence and interest back into the club. Our situation is more or less that overnight our gates have halved, and we are in a major loss situation. We can only hope that the Council and the townspeople support us in the future.'

When the dust had settled, Allan Hunter, the former Ipswich and Northern Ireland international was named as the new manager. United had finished a disappointing sixth, sixteen points off fourth spot. The 50-goal pairing of Allinson and Bremner had seen their efforts come to nothing.

Match of the Season 1981-82

Colchester 3 Newcastle 4

FA Cup, 3rd Round replay, 18 January 1982

Two days after their second round replay victory over Brentford, U's were scheduled to travel to St James' Park, Newcastle. The Magpies were in something of a slump. The nationwide recession had bitten hard in the north east, whose industrial prospects were mirrored on the football field. Arthur Cox's side was wallowing in second division mid-table, averaging attendances of just 16,000.

The tie was scheduled for Saturday, but frost necessitated a postponement. As a result, United's travelling army of supporters was badly depleted. U's first ever visit to Newcastle ended 1-1, when Steve Wignall's header cancelled out Imre Varadi's strike.

The replay twice fell victim to the weather, with the Newcastle party already ensconced in the Marks Tey Hotel when the news broke of the second postponement. The wait by the match-starved Colchester fans was worth it, as a marvellously entertaining game ebbed and flowed. Twice U's hauled themselves back from two-goal deficits. Exciting starlet Chris Waddle fired Newcastle into the lead as the 7,505 crowd, which might even have been an underestimate, jostled for favourable vantage points. Then Wes Saunders drove in a long-range effort that threatened to bring U's to their knees. With just seconds remaining in the first period, up popped Micky Cook, who had celebrated 500 U's appearances in October, to reduce the arrears. Spurred on by that timely goal, U's tore into their opponents and were rewarded when Steve Carney's needless handball gave Ian Allinson's the chance to take the tie into extra-time. Four minutes into the extra period, John Brownlie put the Geordies in front again, and when Imre Varadi stretched the lead with just five minute left, Colchester looked down and out. But within sixty seconds Allinson struck again from twelve yards. This time there was to be no reprieve. Referee Trelford Mills' shrill whistle signalled the end of an enthralling tie. The blue and white mud-stained shirts left the field to the raucous refrain of 'we'll support you evermore'. In defeat the U's had won, won the respect of the Colchester public. Newcastle fell to Grimsby in the next round.

LEAGUE DIVISION 4   **1982-83**
League Division 4   6th
Milk Cup   2nd Round
FA Cup   1st Round
Football League Trophy   1st Round

A virgin football manager, Allan Hunter, U's new player-boss, had been presented with the opportunity to prove he had what was necessary. As a player he had represented Coleraine, Oldham and Blackburn before becoming a defensive rock in the successful Ipswich side of the late 1970s. He had worn the green shirt of Northern Ireland in 53 internationals.

Hunter was not Colchester's first dual-role player-manager. That role had been previously filled by Syd Fieldus and the Fenton brothers, Ted and Benny, in the late 1940s and 1950s. Hunter cemented the Ipswich connection with his first signing – that other staunch Ipswich defender, Kevin Beattie. Released from Portman Road, the 28-year-old injury-plagued Beattie had been expected to quit football altogether, but the call from his former team-mate proved too tempting. The episode angered Ipswich manager Bobby Robson, who blasted 'if we had known that he [Beattie] was going to continue playing, then we would have asked a fee for him.'

Completing the influx of Portman Road old boys was coach Cyril Lea – who, after leaving Suffolk, had occupied the same role at Stoke and Hull – and young goalkeeper Alec Chamberlain. United fans expected the Beattie-Hunter defensive partnership to form the rock on which their promotion fight would begin.

A conflict of a different nature emphasised what a liability under-used, covenant-restricted Layer Road had become. A Wrestling circus, with Dangerous Danny Lynch topping the bill against the Kansas City Striker, drew a midweek crowd of over 200. This demonstrated to the Borough Council the direction in which the club should be allowed to diversify in its search for additional revenue.

U's own strikers had been doing their part, scoring enough goals to take the club to the top of the table after six games. The defence, as optimistically predicted, had also remained resolute, going five games without conceding from the start of the season. Beattie, however, had yet to play: he had aggravated the very injury that had supposedly, in Bobby Robson's eyes, ended his career, and he had suffered a broken nose to boot.

The icing on the cake for U's workmanlike performances thus far was a Milk Cup-tie with First Division Southampton. But this double-header with the Saints, described in Match of the Season, coincided with a dramatic loss of league form. Two points from six games plunged United to thirteenth, though a three-game winning run restored the status quo. Few, if anyone at the club, recognised the troubled mind of striker John Lyons as he poached a brace in the second of those wins, against Mansfield. Lyons spent his 26th birthday preparing for what turned out to be his last appearance for United, against Chester. He took his own life 24 hours later. The Football League, insensitively, refused U's leave to postpone their fixture at Tranmere. This was particularly galling as Rovers looked set to be wound up by the High Court, in which case the result would be expunged from the records.

Driven by their sense of emotional loss, U's trounced their hosts 4-2, with Roy McDonough dedicating his first-minute goal to Lyons' memory. The tragedy of Lyons' death threatened to derail U's season, and would leave an indelible mark on manager Hunter. The inquest suggested that Lyons had been barracked by a section of the home crowd, which, allied to personal problems, had resulted in his depressive state.

It was not long before the vaunted Hunter-Beattie partnership was consigned to memory. Flamboyant Middlesbrough manager Malcolm Allison took the injury-prone Beattie back to his native north for a brief spell. As for Hunter, he was forced to quit playing when an old knee injury flared up. Hanging up his boots sowed the first seeds of self-doubt in the Irishman's mind, as he struggled to come to terms with the rigours of management. Although U's were comfortably placed by the turn of the year, following a 0-4 thrashing at Halifax Hunter decided to call it a day. Still deeply moved by Lyon's death, he explained: 'As a player, I always tried to be honest, but as a manager there are times when you have to be less than honest. I don't like the hassle that goes with being a football manager. I enjoyed parts of it, but the parts I did not like outweighed them. I never fell in love with the job, and once I stopped playing it just finished it [the job] off for me.' First-team coach Cyril Lea stepped in as caretaker whilst the U's board set about finding a new permanent replacement.

Lea initially fared well, with five wins in his first six games, which hoisted his name to the forefront of applicants for the job. He also offloaded pay rebel Kevin Bremner, who had spent much of the season trying to leave Layer Road. The nomadic Scotsman spent loan periods at Birmingham, Wrexham and Plymouth before joining George Graham's Millwall for £25,000. Bremner's absence created an opportunity for Tony Adcock, which the home-grown talent seized with both hands. In the first game under Lea's charge, the flame-haired striker cracked a hat-trick in a 4-3 victory over Crewe.

Did You Know?

In 1978-79, Man Utd became the first top division club to win at Layer Road. Eight others had tried and failed in the FA Cup and League Cup.

The main external candidate for the manager's position was Arsenal's John Hollins, but he opted to stay with the Gunners, no doubt hoping that an FA Cup final would provide a fitting finalé to his illustrious career. In the event, Arsenal lost to Manchester United in the semi-finals.

The U's needed stability in the run-in, with the team hauling itself into contention for promotion. By transfer deadline day United lay fifth, which impressed the board sufficiently to extend Lea's caretakership until the end of the season.

Bolstering his forward line for the home straight, Lea signed Brentford's Keith Bowen, son of former Wales manager Dave, initially on loan and then permanently for £10,000. Bowen scored on his debut as U's saw off rivals Bury 2-1, but a costly home defeat against second-placed Port Vale after Easter spelt disaster for U's aspirations. Five points behind fourth-placed Bury, United thrashed fellow challengers Scunthorpe 5-1, only for flickering hopes to be extinguished in a disastrous four days in Greater Manchester. First Stockport, and then Rochdale, left U's pointless. Winning their last three games meant United missed promotion by just two points. Wimbledon, Hull and Port Vale had long-since achieved elevation, leaving Scunthorpe to leapfrog U's and Bury to claim fourth spot.

Media tycoon Robert Maxwell's proposed merger of Oxford and Reading to form Thames Valley Royals briefly raised the prospect of an additional promotion slot being made available for the fifth-placed club. But fans of the two clubs concerned poured scorn on the merger idea. In any case, U's had finished sixth, not fifth. Failure to secure promotion was estimated to have denied the club a £100,000 bounty in terms of increased sponsorship, larger crowds and a £30,000 insurance pay-out for finishing in the top four. The previous campaign, the rot had set in before the run-in, this time U's had come from behind, only to stumble at the last hurdle.

As the season closed, so did the playing career of 37-year-old goalkeeper Mike Walker. The former Welsh Under-23 international had donned the No 1 jersey in a U's-record 310 consecutive games between 1977 and January 1983. He had missed only nine games in ten seasons of sterling service. Walker was one of two players to refuse to sign a new contract. Ian Allinson, who had blazed a goal-trail across the country in recent seasons, was the other. The Allinson saga was set to leave a bitter taste in U's mouths.

Did You Know?

**Future Essex and England cricketer Neil Foster was a member
of Colchester United's 1979-80 youth team.**

Match of the Season 1982-83

Southampton 4 Colchester 2

Milk Cup, 2nd Round, 2nd leg, 26 October 1982

Having seen off Aldershot 3-0 on aggregate in the first round, U's drew Hampshire opposition again in the second round. First Division Southampton boasted England keeper Peter Shilton, Alan Ball and David Armstrong, who had just been called up by England manager Booby Robson. However, Kevin Keegan, Saints' other big name, had left the Dell to join up with Second Division Newcastle.

Saints players Steve Moran and Mark Wright had courted controversy when detained in a Swedish jail following an alleged incident after the team's UEFA Cup defeat in Norkopping, which forced them to miss the first leg at Layer Road. There, Saints were indebted to the peerless Shilton, as the sides fought out a 0-0 stalemate, just as they had done eight years earlier in the same competition. Visiting boss Lawrie McMenemy fended off all questions afterwards, as press 'hounds' sought exclusives on the jailing of two players rather than the cup-tie itself.

U's fans travelling to the second leg anticipated a repeat of the 1974 glory night, when Barry Dominey's header gave United a famous 1-0 win. But lightning did not strike twice. United took a first-half lead via an Ian Allinson penalty after Mark Wright upended John Lyons. Tricky winger Danny Wallace, well policed by Micky Cook, broke clear to level. Five minutes before the break, ex-England midfielder Alan Ball threaded the ball to Nick Holmes, whose pinpoint cross was guided home by Keith Cassells. Five minutes into the second period United's fans were in full voice when John Lyons fired a great goal past Shilton. At this stage, with the scores level, U's two away goals would have seen them through, only for Armstrong to tee himself up for a stunning volley. In the dying seconds, Steve Moran flattered Saints when he stabbed home from a seemingly offside position.

McMenemy failed to offer any public praise for U's battling performance, though Shilton told Mike Walker that he thought Colchester would be worthy winners of the Fourth Division. Southampton saw off Manchester City next before succumbing to Manchester United in the fourth round.

LEAGUE DIVISION 4   **1983-84**
Canon Division 4   8th
Milk Cup   3rd Round
FA Cup   3rd Round
Associate Members Cup   2nd Round

Four months after being installed as caretaker manager, Cyril Lea was appointed U's new boss. Knowing that his first priority was to acquire a player-coach, Lea sought to fill that position from outside the club, see below, then turn his attention to strengthening his squad. Lea's plans were dealt a massive blow when Ian Allinson, scorer of fifty goals in the previous two seasons, disputed the new contract on offer and demanded a free transfer. Backed by the Professional Footballers Association, Allinson took U's to a tribunal, where United Secretary Martin Bennett claimed that the new contract was equal or better than the old one. The tribunal ruled in favour of Allinson on a technicality, which meant the player was entitled to a free transfer.

It was not just United who were enraged by £100,000-rated Allinson's actions. The winger had supposedly shaken hands with Fulham manager Malcolm MacDonald, where the player hoped to resume his career. But sitting on the appeal panel happened to be a representative of Arsenal, who soon alerted his masters. MacDonald was none too chuffed when Allinson shrugged off their alleged gentleman's agreement and plumped for Highbury instead. Allinson countered: 'I feel sorry for Malcolm, but I couldn't turn down the chance of First Division football.' Once again a small fry, Colchester, had been 'shafted' by a big boy. Would Arsenal ever have signed Allinson, but for that unfortunate contractual dispute?

Lea seemed unperturbed by the Allinson fiasco, having speedy youngster Perry Groves waiting in the wings to take over. Up front, Tony Adcock and Keith Bowen had struck up a fine understanding in the closing weeks of the previous campaign. Former Manchester United and Scotland international Stewart Houston arrived as player-coach to join up with Tony Hadley, signed from Southend, and U's new first-choice goalkeeper, Alec Chamberlain. When, in September, left-back Ian Phillips signed from Northampton, U's defence had been completely re-modelled. Only Micky Cook and Steve Wignall remained from the previous season's back line.

Lea's plans bore fruit when the team conceded a miserly four goals in the opening eight league games. It took runaway leaders York to pierce the otherwise exemplary goals-against column with a 3-0 win at Bootham Crescent. At the other end of the pitch, Adcock was attracting rave reviews. He had already notched eleven goals by the time United lined up in the Milk Cup second round, second leg, against Swansea. Chairman Cadman pledged that if the attendance for the Swansea tie exceeded 5,000, then Lea would be given funds to buy two new players. Both Adcock, with a 40th-minute winner, and the paying public, all 5,204 of them, came up trumps. U's secured another money-spinning crack at Manchester United in the third round, four and a half years since the clubs' first encounter. Cadman promised: 'I won't welch on my promise,' but he could afford to be self-assured with record gate receipts anticipated from the Red Devils' visit.

As Layer Road prepared itself to burst at the seams, yet another new stadium plan surfaced. The site, bordered by Turner Road and the town's mainline North Station, proposed a 15,000 capacity stadium with other sporting and retail outlets. The stadium would boast an all-weather surface that would be more resilient and 'football-friendly' than the springy astro-turf at QPR's Loftus Road. Talks would be held with a variety of landowners, including British Rail and North-East Essex Health Authority. Colchester decided, ill-advisedly, to put cup-tie tickets on sale prior to the league meeting with Crewe, an exercise that backfired disastrously. Many fans were still queuing for their precious tickets behind the main stand as the game kicked-off. If those U's fans felt aggrieved, as tempers frayed, then spare a thought for Jeff Hull, who was stretchered off after a heavy tackle and missed the Man Utd tie as a result.

Manchester United came and conquered, Lea picked up the October Manager of the Month award, and the club continued its quest for promotion. Goalscoring was no problem: indeed, in thrashing Hartlepool 6-0, United defenders accounted for five of the goals. A week later, in the FA Cup, Wealdstone escaped lightly, conceding only four goals, all in the first half. Seven days later it was Halifax's turn to be hit by four United goals. It was in that game that Micky Cook was sent off for retaliation.

U's longest-serving player made headlines for better reasons in February, when he made his 600th league appearance for the club. Cook was a model of consistency; his career averaged 41 games per season over his fifteen years at Layer Road. Tony Adcock had some way to go to match those figures, but his goal-getting exploits had stirred the attention of Liverpool. Following exploratory talks, the Anfield club pulled out of negotiations. Adcock's goals, however, were unable to prevent Charlton dumping U's out of the FA Cup, though an unbeaten run after Boxing Day maintained sixth place in the table. Mindful of the looming transfer deadline, with speculation mounting that Adcock's days at Layer Road were numbered, Lea introduced £10,000 striker Les Mutrie from his former club Hull.

The consistency of York, Doncaster, Reading and Bristol City prevented U's from climbing into the top four. When the Minstermen became the first league victors at Layer Road in almost twelve months, U's season inexplicably disintegrated. Lea, perhaps a little selfishly, dropped Adcock in favour of *his* signing Mutrie, at a time when the teenage striker had taken his season's tally to 28 goals. Adcock responded when inevitably recalled by netting five further goals by the end of the campaign.

By this time, U's fans had had enough of their team promising so much, but never delivering. Having gone seven games without a win, just 1,226 (a new record low) turned up to see that run ended by a 3-0 win over Torquay. Irreparable damage had already been inflicted on hopes of promotion. For the final four fixtures only pride was at stake.

Failure yet again to earn promotion had put the very future of the club at stake. Season after season the U's board had budgeted for success and each time the team had fallen short. The culmination of all those 'maybe next years' had caught up on the club. Chairman Cadman announced radical plans to recoup the £250,000 splashed out since relegation in 1981. Players would no longer be paid bonuses, but if promotion were attained then an insurance policy would ensure that overall they would be better off. One player immediately dissented, and for his pains Steve Wignall asked to be placed on the transfer list. Cadman closed the Commercial Department and offered his chair to anybody prepared to inject a 'substantial amount of money' into the club. This substantial amount, it appeared, equated to about £150,000.

For Colchester's longest serving pair, Micky Cook and Steve Leslie, injuries put paid to their sparkling Layer Road careers after fifteen and thirteen years' service respectively. Both had been one-club men, both had resisted the temptation to move on to bigger clubs in the mid-1970s, epitomising the loyalty that is so sadly lacking in the game today. As the 'old heads' stepped down, Lea looked to have a youthful squad at his disposal come the start of the new season.

Match of the Season 1983-84

Colchester 0 Manchester United 2

Milk Cup, 3rd Round, 8 November 1983

The third round draw brought *the* tie, the one that every minnow dreamed of. Almost greedily, Colchester would welcome the Red Devils of Manchester for the second time in four and a half years.

Did You Know?

Six months after being released by United, Steve Wright and Jeff Wood played for HJK Helsinki against Liverpool in the 1981-82 European Cup.

In 1979, U's had missed out on an FA Cup replay at Old Trafford by just four minutes. This time, chairman Cadman jested 'we've got a score to settle [referring to Jimmy Greenhoff's 86th-minute winner] and we might just turn the tables this time.' The club bungled ticket sales by offering the first batch on the day U's hosted Crewe. The queues were so long that it was almost half-time before they disappeared. As in the previous encounter, Manchester United were unable to sell their full allocation of 3,500 tickets and returned 2,000 – most of which were snapped up by eager local fans.

On the field, Ron Atkinson's Manchester United were fast becoming a millionaires' club, with a squad costing a combined £6 million. Pulling the strings on the park was Britain's most costly footballer, £1.5 million Bryan Robson. U's also had to contend with Robson's midfield partners, Ray Wilkins and Dutchman Arnold Muhren. U's side had been assembled for no more than £50,000, and so it was that the princes took on the paupers.

The match went to form, the League leaders taking an early lead through giant centre-half Gordon McQueen. Only seconds earlier McQueen had desperately hacked a Roger Osborne effort off the line. What might have been 1-0 was now 0-1. Manchester United doubled their lead on 23 minutes, when Remi Moses made space and with a classy drag-back slotted past Alec Chamberlain. U's battled well in the second period but lacked the guile to trouble their illustrious opponents. Unlike the previous encounter, this time there was no doubting the justice of the outcome. Lea conceded: 'we didn't have the pace to get round the back of them – the two full-backs are very quick.' For his part, Atkinson was pleased that his side had 'battled it out'.

One crumb of comfort for U's was record gate receipts, to the tune of £22,745.50. The 13,031 attendance would prove to be the last ever five-figure attendance at Layer Road, a consequence of the Taylor Report. Atkinson's side went on to finish fourth behind Liverpool, Southampton and Nottingham Forest. Oxford, in the Milk Cup, and Bournemouth, in the FA Cup, ended their domestic trophy aspirations, whilst Juventus halted their European Cup-Winners' Cup hopes in the semi-finals.

LEAGUE DIVISION 4   **1984-85**
Canon Division 4   7th
Milk Cup   1st Round
FA Cup   2nd Round
Freight Rover Trophy   2nd Round

Having slashed players' wages by thirty percent in favour of an insurance-backed promotion bonus, cost-cutting chairman Cadman waited for a summer exodus from Layer Road. Remarkably, five of the eight players due for contract renewal elected to stay. The main dissenter, Steve Wignall, buzzed off to join the Bees of Brentford. Les Mutrie, an expensive £10,000 misfit with just seventeen appearances, returned to his native north-east, and Tony Hadley simply failed to show up for pre-season training. He was later discovered alive and well in the Southend side that came to town on the opening day of the season. Sharpshooter Tony Adcock proved that the summer had not diminished his appetite for goals, netting a 35-minute hat-trick. But the Shrimpers fought back to earn a 3-3 draw. Fighting between fans marred what was a thrilling curtain-raiser. Eighteen Southend 'followers', many of whom spent the ninety minutes 'eyeing' U's fans rather than the match, were arrested.

U's fans had their eyes on the big boys, particularly as the team came away with only a 2-3 deficit from the Milk Cup first round, first leg at Gillingham. If the 'un-weighted' National Lottery balls had been used in the Milk Cup draw, then perhaps United would have avoided being paired with the Gills for the third time in five seasons. Gills' 2-0 second leg win would not be the last time the two teams would clash this season. Nor was it free from violence. The thuggery associated with Millwall, Chelsea and Manchester United, in the main, had arrived in Colchester as a small group sought to emulate their 'heroes'. Media coverage of disturbances at matches up and down the country only served to fuel the hatred between rival fans. Minnows like Colchester suffered most. If fathers were afraid to take sons to matches, where would the next generation of supporters come from?

Or younger players, for that matter. The new team had an average age of 23, even allowing for Roger Osborne and Stewart Houston celebrating 35 birthdays apiece. Cyril Lea's 14-man squad, containing nine under-21s, displayed understandable naivety in defence, but as the highest scorers collected the division's Canon award for the first two months of the season. Ten games and a goals column of twenty scored, twenty conceded, underlined United's shortcomings. To shore up the defence, ex-apprentice Andy Farrell (Colchester born and bred) and Keith Day, a non-contract signing from non-league Aveley, stepped into the breach and performed admirably. Day did enough to earn a full contract. With U's strapped for cash, non-contract players were considered. Transfer fees were out of the question, without selling first, as Cadman's belt-tightening scheme took effect.

United soon closed the gap on the early pace-setters, six wins from eight games in September and October hoisted them into sixth place, but an equally poor spell saw them slip back to tenth by the time the FA Cup arrived. U's cup campaigns have a habit of stirring up memories of their former glories, but this season's draw had also thrown up the added ingredient of an Essex derby at Roots Hall. A blood and thunder cup-tie ended in a draw, but jubilant U's marched into the second round when Perry Groves bagged the all-important replay winner, fourteen minutes into extra-time. After-wards, referring to his simple tap-in, Groves quipped 'I'm deadly from two yards.' Groves would develop a liking for matches against Southend, against whom he always seemed to score.

As for bogey teams, or rather bogey cup draws, there were no prizes for guessing who were paired with U's in the second round. Gillingham, riding high in the Third Division, ruthlessly and pro-fessionally massacred U's 5-0 to dish out United's biggest-ever hiding on home soil. Nor was that the last U's would see of Gillingham this season, as the two teams came out of the hat together in the draw for the Freight Rover Trophy.

U's were in no mood to celebrate Christmas in the traditional giving way. Liverpool had resurrected their interest in Adcock. Fourteen goals in sixteen league games warranted a hefty price tag. Just 21, Adcock had time on his side to make it in the big time. West Ham, Ipswich and Southampton all declared an interest in the £100,000-rated striker. Cadman admitted that because ice-bound Layer Road could stage no matches and earn no income for most of January, he was open to big offers for the jewel in U's crown.

With finances, as usual, in disarray, the last thing Cadman needed was a call from a 'local businessman' who expressed inter-est in buying the club. It turned out to be a hoax, but one that was gleefully reported in the national press. Fortunately for U's, they were not the only ones taken in by the prankster. A local high-performance car dealer had loaned him an expensive sports car on the basis of his 'lottery win', and Cambridge United wined and dined him in another 'take-over' bid.

United's annual promotion bid finally began to take shape, built on the back of ten unbeaten games up to 1 March. They had also achieved the near impossible, knocking Gillingham, at the third attempt, out of a cup competition (the Freight Rover). It was at this time of upturn in U's fortunes that two major blows struck the club in the space of three weeks. First, sponsors Royal London pulled the plug on their five-year shirt-sponsorship deal; second, following his second hat-trick of the season, versus Chesterfield, Adcock twisted his knee in training. The ginger-haired striker, with 28 goals now to his credit, was only a signature away from leaving the club in exchange for a massive transfer fee. Cruelly, the twisted knee exposed a cartilage problem and surgery was the only solution. In the blink of an eye, United lost their major benefactor and potential pot of gold.

Stung by the double loss, Lea turned to young Russell Irving to fill Adcock's boots. Irving returned a respectable seven goals in U's last fifteen matches. His two at Exeter helped United equal their 5-1 record away victory, set at Tranmere in 1979. Another club record – Bobby Hunt's 1961-62 total of 37 league goals in a season – would surely have been under threat from Adcock but for his injury. Accustomed now to seasonal tail-end collapses, United went to form. Good enough to claim sixth or seventh place, they did not possess that extra gear needed to impose themselves at the very top. Perhaps that extra gear would be found by the cash injection offered by a mysterious 'sugar daddy'.

At an extraordinary shareholder meeting, Jonathan Crisp emerged as the mystery buyer. Crisp seized control of the club by virtue of his £150,000 take-over. Shares to the value of £75,000 gave him overall charge, whilst another £75,000 took the form of a six-year mortgage on Layer Road. Crisp planned to use his experience as head of Marketing Solutions to sell United to the stay-away Colchester public, and vowed to have the club gracing the Second Division in a state-of-the-art stadium within five years. Crisp's prospectus would in time catastrophically backfire. But for the moment, the pain of yet another promotion failure was eased as U's fans eagerly anticipated the dawning of a new era. In the light of the Bradford City fire, which claimed 56 lives, that era ought to have accelerated United's move to a super modern stadium.

Match of the Season 1984-85
Southend 2 Colchester 5

Division 4, 29 January 1985

U's renewed their rivalry with Essex neighbours Southend, seeking to close the gap on the Fourth Division's leading pack. Meeting for the fourth time this season, having faced each other once in the league and twice in the FA Cup, U's were buoyed by memories of

---
Did You Know?

In 1984-85 United faced Gillingham in all three cups – losing in the Milk Cup and FA Cup, but triumphing in the Freight Rover Trophy.

---

their extra-time Cup replay victory at Layer Road. The Shrimpers, managed by England World Cup-winning skipper Booby Moore, had lost the mantle of Essex's top team by virtue of relegation in 1983-84. The apathetic Essex football public, at both extremities of the county, meant that average attendances at both clubs failed to exceed 2,100. Indeed, the 2,401 that bothered to assemble at Roots Hall for this particular fixture accounted for the lowest-ever league gate for an Essex derby. Previous outbreaks of violence at the fixture also deterred many from attending.

Torn apart by U's three-goal salvo in fifteen first-half minutes, Southend appeared to be still shell-shocked by their 1-5 hammering at Chester three days previously. But U's turned the screw, pushing Southend nearer re-election. Only eight minutes had passed when Adcock started the rout – Noel Parkinson's cross was flicked on by Keith Day for top-scorer Tony Adcock to pierce the Shrimpers' defence for the fifth time this season. Two great solo goals by Perry Groves then gave Colchester an unassailable lead. U's spent the remainder of the first half playing exhibition football. Parkinson, Roger Osborne and Groves should have added to the first-half total as the home side looked at sixes and sevens.

Bobby Moore's half-time roasting helped to stabilise a previously one-sided encounter until Keith Bowen planted a powerful header that would have escaped the stadium were it not for the back of the net. To be fair to the demoralised home side, they plugged away and Tony Hadley, once of Colchester, reduced the arrears. But not for long. Bowen raced away to add his second and U's fifth. Ten minutes from time Glenn Pennyfather caught Colchester's defence cold, but Southend's two goals were minor blemishes on an all-round classy performance by Colchester.

The win kept U's in the hunt for promotion, although their challenge would peter out as the season reached its home straight. Southend escaped re-election by virtue of a last-day victory over Torquay. Following two wretched seasons, Moore's days in the Roots Hall hot seat were numbered. World-class players do not necessarily make good managers. Staying put in the Fourth Division would give U's flying winger Perry Groves the chance to torment his 'favourite' team again.

LEAGUE DIVISION 4   **1985-86**
Canon Division 4   6th
Milk Cup   1st Round
FA Cup   1st Round
Freight Rover Trophy   1st Round

In the wake of the fire at Valley Parade and the hideous climax to a night of rioting by Liverpool and Juventus fans at the Heysel Stadium in Brussels, spectator safety at Layer Road topped the list of close-season priorities. The predominantly timber main stand and Layer Road End terracing posed potential fire hazards. For the first time, visiting supporters would be penned into a specifically designated 'away section'. Hooligans convicted of offences in and around the ground would receive stadium bans of varying lengths. Yet endless years of waiting to move to a new stadium had resulted in a reluctance to carry out maintenance at Layer Road. Now the club faced a potential bill of £500,000, just to comply with new safety legislation. Millwall's notorious following would provide as good a test as any for the Layer Road improvements, for U's had been drawn to face the Lions in the Milk Cup. United followers stayed indoors as the police-enforced, 6.30pm all-ticket tie saw just 1,430 at the gate, and passed off relatively peacefully.

Football's tarnished image meant sponsorship was hard to come by. U's shirts were unadorned by any logo when the Canon League opener against Stockport kicked off at 11.30am, in an attempt to reduce drunkenness. By mid-September, attendances were so low – despite U's winning ways that saw the team in fourth place – that Lea issued a public appeal. He urged: 'If you want to see goals, then come to Layer Road.' His words had some effect: the gate for the visit of Cambridge rose by 500 to 2,500. Those new faces seemed sure to be disappointed, since U's invariably turned in a stinker whenever they most needed to impress, but this time the returning 'stay-aways' were rewarded by a Tony Adcock hat-trick in a 4-1 win. Victories at Orient and Burnley, and over table-topping Port Vale at Layer Road, ensured that Lea's Manager of the Month award for September would be presented to a near-capacity crowd. No, United had not suddenly acquired 16,000 fans. Lacking a ground safety certificate, the capacity had been temporarily reduced to 4,900. Moves to increase the safe capacity, in the event of further success, were put on hold by the ever-cautious, cash-conscious U's board. For once, their prudence was justified as the 3,927 gate for the Exeter game proved to be the highest of the season. Besides, the Turner Rise stadium project was resurfacing, two years after it was first announced, and the club did not want to spend unnecessarily.

Did You Know?

At Crewe in April 1986, the team-coach broke down, Hal Mason hitched a lift with the team-sheet and two players found their hotel had only a double bed.

By now United had other worries to contend with. Second Division Grimsby revealed that Lea had been short-listed for their vacant manager's post. Despite living in nearby Hull, the U's boss surprisingly ruled himself out of contention.

Lea's thin squad was made thinner when striker Keith Bowen crashed his car, hours after the home game with Northampton. Driving back, ironically, to his Northampton home, the eight-goal forward sustained head injuries and a broken leg. Added to which, chairman Cadman admitted that summer safety work on the stadium had swallowed the £80,000 budgeted for team strengthening. Failure to find an adequate partner for lively Adcock effectively put paid to United's brief flirtation with the summit of the division. Ex-Ipswich veterans Trevor Whymark and Robin Turner failed dismally to fill the breach. Six successive league defeats, four of them bereft of U's goals, meant United sunk to twelfth. In the FA Cup, Gola League Wycombe booted U's into touch at their sloping Loakes Park, whereupon U's owner, Crisp, made a rare public comment on *his* team. Sadly for Lea it comprised just one word – 'gutless'.

Pessimistic Lea could offer no solace: 'People think we will just snap out of it [the goalless, winless run], but I think we're in for a hard time of it.' This was hardly the glint of steel that his inexperienced troops needed. Behind the scenes, former U's goalkeeper Mike Walker had been cutting his teeth in management, steering United's reserves into the top four of the Eastern Counties League. Walker's popularity with fans was demonstrated when 2,853 turned out for his December testimonial 2-1 win against an Arsenal side that included former U's winger Ian Allinson. Walker's successes were duly noted for future reference.

New Year's Day was no happy occasion for defender Keith Day, who dislocated his shoulder against leaders Swindon for the fourth time since August. The fifth came two days later, prompting Lea, in desperation, to demand cash for new players. Crisp's priority, however, was to improve facilities: in his Appeal '86 he promised to match pound for pound all monies raised by local businessmen and individuals alike. Instead of money for players, Lea had to rely on ex-West Ham teenager Terry Baker and home-grown Kirk Game to cover for the duration of Day's recuperation from surgery.

Marooned in mid-table, United were now as likely to be sucked into the re-election mire as to mount a fresh assault on promotion.

The fires of early season were extinguished. A new record-low derby crowd of 1,915 watched the game with Southend, following which severe weather cocooned Layer Road for five weeks. The interlude did nothing to restore the passions of North Essex football fans. Lea, in the last throes of his United career, attempted to sign yet another Ipswich cast-off – Kevin Steggles. The sparse, disgruntled crowd witnessed Crewe's first victory at Layer Road in 25 years and finally lost patience with the manager.

The fact that Lea had been unable to replace October car-crash victim Bowen until deadline day was a major factor in U's demise. That replacement was Mike Ferguson, once of Coventry and Everton, who now teamed up with another ex-Sky Blue in Colchester lad Tommy English. Three weeks from the end of a torrid season, Lea, along with coach Stewart Houston, was shown the door. Lea had been in situ for three years and overseen a period of great changes. His playing budget had been cut, forcing him to operate a wafer-thin squad, yet U's had challenged for promotion in each season under his care. Replacing Lea as caretaker for the final eight games was the aforementioned Mike Walker. Chairman Cadman said the manager's position would not be advertised until Walker had had his chance. Speculation mounted that one of Crisp's football friends, such as Tony Woodcock, Paul Mariner or Brian Talbot, might be in line for the job.

Walker's intervention brought a breath of fresh air. Five wins, three draws, and no losses hoisted U's from thirteenth to sixth. U's fans mused whether, had he been appointed earlier, Walker might have steered the division's 88-goal top scorers to promotion. As it was, they were denied by just nine points. The closing games were eventful for the English brothers. First Tommy scored a hat-trick against Preston, only for Tony to net a treble four days later against Peterborough. Before the week was out both were sent off at Crewe for brawling with Gary Blissett.

Walker delivered fighting talk upon being named as U's fourth manager of the 1980s. 'This club is going places next season.'

Match of the Season 1985-86
Southend 2   Colchester 4

Division 4, 22 October 1985

The previous season, Southend had rattled in nine goals against Colchester in four clashes – but did not win any, on account of U's scoring thirteen, including five at Roots Hall in the corresponding league fixture. Eight months on and the two Essex clubs sat proudly side by side at the top of the table, U's with their noses in front by a point. Colchester, however, like Southend, had suffered a few hiccups leading up to this derby clash. Home draws against Exeter and Scunthorpe, and a defeat at Mansfield, had set U's back slightly. Two players were in action against their former clubs – the Shrimpers' striker Roy McDonough, later to have a second spell at Layer Road, and U's former Roots Hall youngster Jeff Hull. Southend boss Bobby Moore said of McDonough: 'I am hoping that playing against his old club will bring the best out of Roy.'

8,120 fans from all over Essex flocked to Roots Hall to see the clash of the early season titans. It proved to be Perry Groves' night, as his explosive pace ripped the home side's defence to shreds. After last season's humiliation, one would have expected Southend to be better prepared to counter Groves' searing spurts. Yet his 60-yard run set up Keith Bowen for a 16th-minute tap-in opener. The other 'highlight' of the first half – according to the national press – was a pitch invasion by Colchester fans. In fact, knife-wielding Southend thugs had infiltrated U's allocated South Bank section, forcing fans to flee in the only direction available.

Four minutes after the break, Southend's former West Ham star Frank Lampard played Groves onside as the youngster raced onto Alec Chamberlain's long punt. Fumbling a back-pass, Steve Hatter, then presented the 20-year-old Groves with the chance to round Jim Stannard in the home goal for his second goal. Leading 3-0, U's were rocked by headers from John Gymer and, inevitably, big Roy McDonough. But with five minutes remaining, and Southend pressing forward for an equaliser, Groves once again exposed their snail-like defence to cap his first-ever professional hat-trick.

Unfortunately for Southend, 'Champagne Perry' hadn't finished with them yet this season. The draw for the Freight Rover Trophy draw summoned Southend to Layer Road. Perry sparkled again, blasting a first-half treble, this time from the centre-forward role as Colchester emerged 4-1 winners. Perry was substituted on 55 minutes, probably to spare Southend's blushes. Three weeks later, in the league encounter at Layer Road, Groves was well-shackled by McDonough, who had been handed the task of man-marking Southend's living nightmare. Seven clashes between the sides in two seasons had realised an incredible 23-12 goal margin in favour of U's.

Both clubs failed to sustain their early season promise and both would start the new season with a new man in charge. Dave Webb moved into Roots Hall and Mike Walker took hold of the Layer Road reigns.

LEAGUE DIVISION 4   **1986-87**
Today Division 4   5th (play-offs)
Littlewoods Cup   1st Round
FA Cup   2nd Round
Sherpa Van Trophy   1st Round

Returning to the traditional blue and white striped shirts, albeit sky blue, United unveiled a new sponsor in British Telecom's free '0800 Link-line' service. The team photo-call, with logo-adorned shirts, proved premature, as the small print for the deal had not been finalised. Trade Union intervention at BT resulted in the sponsors pulling out of the deal, leaving no time for U's to find another backer. Another reputed millionaire, David Johnson, joined the board and former Arsenal double-winning manager Bertie Mee was appointed part-time football consultant. Everything in U's garden seemed rosy. Crisp pledged: 'This is just the beginning.' It certainly was. On the pitch, new full-time boss Mike Walker declared himself happy with the eight-game unbeaten squad that had earned him the post following his temporary stewardship at the tail end of the previous season.

An air of optimism pervaded Layer Road, as even the bookies made United favourites for the title. Hampered by injuries and suspensions, U's kicked off the season with a 1-3 setback at Lincoln and a Littlewoods Cup exit to Peterborough. Walker's honeymoon was over before it had begun. Stung by the effect of a couple of key absentees, Walker exploited the club's hitherto unknown wealth to capture Millwall and Crystal Palace old boys Nick Chatterton and Paul Hinshelwood. Making way was Perry Groves, who had hankered after a shot at the big time and put in a transfer request. George Graham agreed a fee of £70,000 and took Groves to Highbury. Such was Groves' joy at joining the Gunners that before the ink was dry on his contract he was seen sporting his Arsenal tracksuit in a Colchester supermarket. Blessed with lightening pace and a long throw-in to boot, Groves teamed up with another former U's man in Ian Allinson. In fact, the duo would only start one First Division game together, though they would combine on several occasions when one or the other came off the bench.

Boardroom activities continued to overshadow U's injury-hit early season progress. Comedian Frank Carson, a friend of Crisp, joined the board and humoured the inquisitive press with 'I deny I have bought myself another joke'. Chairman Cadman added, 'I have always been in favour of a two-tier board of local people, and fund-raising celebrities. Expect to see a couple more "stars" join the board in the near future.' Pop star David Essex, seen in the Layer

Road directors' box, was rumoured to be the next recruit. One face returning to Layer Road, after a spell in local non-league, was former player Steve Foley, who was appointed Youth Team coach. Bereft of four of his five possible strikers, including hotshot broken-arm victim Tony Adcock, Walker shuffled his pack to produce a side that lay fourth after ten matches, testament to his ability to get the best from the players at his disposal.

Re-enforcements were needed as the treatment room swelled to overflowing. Midfielder Steve Grenfell was recruited from Spurs' reserves in time for the first ever league meeting with once-mighty Wolves. A 3-0 win in front of 4,741, the biggest crowd since the visit of Sheffield United in 1982, stirred calls for the 4,900 capacity to be increased. But as had happened the previous season, the club appeared to have peaked in terms of paying spectators, as a result of which expenditure for ground improvements was cautiously put on hold.

Whilst always keen to attract paying customers, the club read the riot act to U's yobs who ran amok in Bishops Stortford town centre prior to the FA Cup-tie between the two sides. Crisp snarled a curt 'Go away and stay away', for these undesirables threatened to disrupt the friendly family environment taking shape at the club. The Mayor of Colchester, Bob Russell, sent a public apology to his Bishop Stortford counterpart. The replay victory over Stortford earned a trip to Aldershot in the next round. United grew sick of the mention of their fellow garrison town's name, as thrice in December U's travelled to the Recreation Ground, only to be beaten each time. Defeats in the FA Cup (2-3), Freight Rover Trophy (2-4) and Division Four (0-1) meant that U's slipped to eighth place, but still qualified for the next round of the Freight Rover Trophy in the New Year.

The year 1986 ended with Cadman handing over the chairman-ship to owner Crisp. Cadman felt that he had fulfilled his task in bringing a 'rich uncle' (Crisp) to the club, and had held the fort whilst Crisp attended to overseas business commitments. David Essex announced on a radio chat show that he was 'about to become director of a football club' as Crisp set about replacing the old guard with his own men. Cadman had steered United from impoverished relegation fodder to a situation of relative financial stability. As reward for his efforts he was made the club's first ever honorary life president.

Every season since dropping into the Fourth Division in 1981, U's had shown promise, only to falter at the final hurdle. Were they to suffer the same fate again? Returning from injury, Tony Adcock had not yet gelled with Tommy English, and Mike Ferguson had failed to live up to expectations. Walker introduced Simon Lowe from Hartlepool in a bid to bolster his attack, promising U's fans that, with a full-strength side, the team would blaze a trail to promotion. But to achieve that end, Walker needed to redress the abysmal away form that had seen twelve defeats in fourteen trips between November and March.

What Walker did not need was the leak of a confidential circular to all league clubs detailing the availability of all the club's players. The *Yellow Advertiser* free-sheet headlines screamed: 'All on the list.' Reporter Robert Jobson happened to be the son of Southend United chairman Vic Jobson, but both Essex clubs closed ranks as to the source of the leak. Walker defended himself by saying it was customary prior to deadline day to circularise names, and with a number of contracts about to expire it was only right and proper for U's to listen to offers. As for Mr Jobson Jnr, rightly or wrongly, he found himself for a time no longer welcome at Layer Road.

A couple of Colchester players around this time must have felt equally unwelcome. Mike Walker went public in his efforts to inject zest into the talented, but sometimes lazy Tommy English. But the manager's methods backfired. The striker countered that as a result of Walker's slur in the local press he could no longer play under the U's boss. English also demanded a public apology. Another forward, Keith Bowen, having been out recuperating for sixteen months following his car crash, was finally forced to quit the game on medical advice.

To kick-start the run in, Walker adopted more direct tactics, with shoot-on-sight instructions to his forwards. He brought in winger Winston White from Bury to fill the cavernous gap vacated by the early season departure of wide-man Groves. The change in style suited Simon Lowe, who struck five goals in two games, including a hat-trick against Stockport. Brimming with new-found confidence, U's accumulated eighteen points from eight undefeated matches to put themselves in with a shout of claiming the third promotion place. Fourth spot, which previously would have ensured promotion, had been swallowed up by the inaugural play-off competition. Two one-goal defeats and a goalless draw meant that U's hopes hinged on the results of others. The 'others' duly obliged. Wolves, in the play-offs, did not.

Promotion bridesmaids once again, club secretary Martin Bennett fielded questions about why a number of Layer Road games had inconveniently been made all-ticket. Explaining the need for controlled segregation, he reiterated that the club had no intention of following Luton's lead and introducing a 100 per cent members-only scheme. Time would, unfortunately, tell.

Did You Know?

United's English brothers – Tom and Tony – were both sent off in the same game, at Crewe in April 1986. Tony was kicked and Tom rushed to 'help' him.

Match of the Season 1986-87

Colchester 0 Wolves 2

Division 4, play-off, 1st leg, 14 May 1987

Despite losing in the final minute at Preston on the last day of the season, U's secured a promotion play-off spot when rivals Orient lost at Turf Moor, a result which saved Burnley from the drop to the GM Vauxhall Conference. Accompanying United into the play-offs were Graham Turner's Wolves and Aldershot, who had left U's chances on a knife-edge with their 1-0 win at Layer Road in the penultimate game of the season. The play-off format pitched the clubs finishing fourth, fifth and sixth in Division Four with the side that had finished 21st in the Division Three – Bolton Wanderers. Bolton thereby took on sixth-placed Shots, whilst U's faced the fourth-placed men from Molineux.

An increased 5,200 ground capacity housed a 4,829 crowd for the first leg at Layer Road. United started well, but two goals in the space of four minutes gave the Black Country side a commanding first-leg lead. First, Robert Kelly looped a header over Alec Chamberlain. Incessant rain contrived to assist Wolves' second goal; Tony English slipped, allowing Andy Thompson a cross-shot that smacked against the inside of the post. Live-wire Steve Bull, in his first season in the Old Gold, reacted first to slot in the loose ball. The visitors had keeper Mark Kendall to thank for a string of fine saves to leave United with a mountain to climb in the second leg.

The kick-off for the return was delayed as Molineux's biggest crowd for almost three seasons, 16,330, took their places. Kendall was again the busier keeper, but goal-shy U's failed to find the net for the fifth game in succession. Andy Mutch did force the ball over the line in the opening period but was ruled offside. Wolves defended stoutly after half-time, as did U's Terry Baker, who kept a tight reign on hit-man Bull. The damage had been done in that four-minute spell at Layer Road, presenting Wolves with a two-legged final against Aldershot. Wolves lost 0-3 on aggregate.

U's had come as close as ever in recent seasons to achieving promotion. Some fans were now convinced it was never to be.

LEAGUE DIVISION 4   **1987-88**
Barclays Division 4   9th
Littlewoods Cup   1st Round
FA Cup   3rd Round
Sherpa Van Trophy   Quarter-finals (South)

Mike Walker's second full season in charge started with a bomb-shell. Ace striker Tony Adcock, 24, felt the time was right to try his luck on a bigger stage. Second Division Manchester City paid £80,000 for him and bagged themselves a bargain. In only his third full appearance, Adcock grabbed a hat-trick in City's 10-1 massacre of Huddersfield. However, the big city life did not suit Adcock, and before the season was out he moved on to Northampton. Walker had lost a striker but found a coach in Allan Hunter, four and a half years after he had quit as manager.

The second bombshell of the summer took everyone by surprise. Chairman Crisp revoked the words of his club secretary and introduced a 100 per cent ground membership scheme, effectively a ban on away supporters. U's fans would have to pay £5 to become a club member, although cup-ties would be exempt. Crisp explained that as only Wolves among Division Four clubs enjoyed a large following, only a few dozen die-hard followers of other clubs would be affected.

In these circumstances Crisp felt he should concentrate on providing facilities for the people who mattered – U's fans. Critics replied that Crisp was being naïve. Football fans are passionate people, whether they supported Manchester United or Rochdale, and Crisp was merely exposing his lack of terrace knowledge. Quite simply, those dozen or so die-hards are the life-blood of any club marooned in the lower reaches of the league. Lose them and a club slowly dies. Crisp cited the success of a similar scheme at Luton that had resulted in zero arrests the previous season. He also had in mind complaints from U's fans who had to sacrifice their favourite Layer Road End terracing every time the away support threatened to exceed 400 or so. Tradition had it that home fans changed ends at half-time, to enable them to stand behind the goal under attack. Over the years, the 'Layer Road Roar' had been responsible for many a passion-induced late win. For the 'big' matches of the previous season, this tradition had been done away with, simply to accommodate away fans. To side-step the mounting resentment to the scheme, by U's fans, opponents, and most importantly casual supporters who wanted to turn up as and when they chose, United disclosed a Council report on the Turner Rise Stadium project. No one was persuaded by this attempt to deflect attention from the real issue, and a number of fans vowed never again to set foot inside Layer Road whilst the members scheme was in operation.

Although the Football League had insisted on 50 per cent membership at *all* grounds, Layer Road's entrances were all at one end of the stadium, which, Crisp pointed out, made it impractical – hence the 100 per cent scheme. Though Crisp was a top marketing consultant, he appeared to have been ill-advised. The reaction of those who mattered, the fans themselves, was exemplified by one of tens of letters to the Colchester *Evening Gazette*, which began 'When will this man admit he is wrong?'

Amid all this controversy, Walker's team was breaking up. Following Adcock out of the club were Keith Day to Orient, keeper Alec Chamberlain to league champions Everton, and Andy Farrell to Burnley. With Tommy English and Mike Ferguson falling foul of Walker, they too were soon packing their bags. If he were not careful, Walker would have to kick off this, the U's jubilee season without a team.

In fact, United started in fine style with a 3-0 win at Burnley. But the off-field shenanigans overshadowed anything that the players could achieve. The club was negotiating with property developers regarding the new stadium, which had now been given the green light by council planners. As a result, Reading-based 'Norcross Estates' was soon to appear emblazoned on the players' shirts. The first game under the new members-only scheme attracted just 1,372, a drop of 1,400 on the average gate the previous season. U's did not have a large enough fan base to operate an exclusive membership system. Only 1,600 had signed up, and it would shortly become clear that some of them were Wolves and Orient supporters trying to beat the ban.

Using money from transfers, not gate receipts, Walker splashed out a club record £40,000 on Englishman Dale Tempest from Belgian club Lokeren to partner his summer £15,000 signing, Mario Walsh. But when just 1,164 paid to watch U's thrash Peterborough 4-1, questions were raised as to whether the club could see out the season. Determined to see the scheme through, Crisp replied that low crowds did not matter, as the club's finances were stronger than they had ever been. It was not long before the 1,140 gate for the visit of Swansea established a new record-low league gate.

Walker, meanwhile, was slowly lifting his side off the floor. He introduced his second 'international' signing when former Arsenal youngster Colin Hill signed from Portuguese side Maritimo. The October home game with Darlington had a sensational aftermath, when the manager's seat became vacant. Match of the Season takes up the story.

Did You Know?

When Jock Wallace became manager in 1988-89, he became the third former goalkeeper to hold the job – following Dick Graham and Mike Walker.

Walker's successor, Roger Brown, must have thought it was his birthday and Christmas all rolled into one as he slipped nicely into the hot seat of a winning side. He even picked up the December manager of the month award. However, with aggrieved supporters still boycotting home matches, Brown would have to achieve something spectacular to repair the hurt United fans felt at the enforced loss of Walker, one of U's great sons.

The first big test for both Brown and the members scheme came when leaders Wolves came to town. Trailing the visitors by a point at kick-off, U's lost to an Andy Thompson penalty. Hundreds of Wolves fans 'swelled' the gate to 2,413. The members scheme – 'it was only an experiment' – had backfired, and chief executive David Barnard announced its cessation.

Top spot on New Year's Day proved to be the pinnacle for Roger Brown's team. Having brought in his own players, his reshaped side won just five games in the second half of the season and finished ninth, 77th in the Football League, U's lowest position for fifteen years. Nineteen debutants in one season tells its own story.

Crisp had plenty to ponder upon during the summer break. U's were reputed to be losing £6,000 per week and needed 14,000 crowds to break even. The Turner Rise Stadium plan was on the drawing board, and in the interim he had to consider ground-sharing, probably with Ipswich Town. Layer Road had a market value of up to £2.8m for housing development, and if sold that sum would help pay off Crisp's underwriting of the club.

Not before time, the chairman admitted the members scheme had been ill-conceived. He was roundly booed whenever the home crowd caught sight of his bearded figure. Moreover, final placings in recent years of sixth, sixth, eighth, seventh, sixth, fifth and ninth had taken United so near, yet so far from the Third Division. Now the very future of the club was shrouded in doubt.

Match of the Season 1987-88

Colchester 2 Darlington 1

Division 4, 30 October 1988

U's could go top should they conjure up a six-goal winning margin against Darlington. Richard Wilkins' seemingly offside opener drew surprisingly little complaint from the Quakers' defence. The penalty award, however, from which Nick Chatterton scored U's second, was vehemently denounced, so much so that the visitors' Phil Bonnyman was ordered off. Keeper Jerry Roberts saved the kick, but Chatterton reacted quickest to the loose ball. With time running out, U's defence could boast having gone seven and a half hours without conceding a goal. Alas, three minutes from time, Gary Worthington broke through to score for Darlington. The 2-1 win carried Colchester to third spot overnight.

Few could have anticipated what was to happen 48 hours later. Following a late-night meeting with Crisp, both Walker and coach Allan Hunter were reported as having quit 'over a matter of principle'. Neither of them was under contract. Crisp declared: 'It should be perfectly clear that after seven wins this is not about results. I want someone who will want to win for Colchester as much as I do, who will be tough and set the right standards, and who will not tolerate people who do not want to win. The people of Colchester will think that I have had another brainstorm, but it is an issue we have been debating for months.' U's fans did indeed think their wealthy benefactor had had a brainstorm.

Furious Walker retorted: 'There is no way we would have quit United in their present position. We were sacked.' Convinced that Crisp had already lined up a replacement, Walker added, 'He appears to have decided weeks ago to get rid of us, but the upturn in form has been an embarrassment to him. He wanted us to resign, but we wouldn't. If there was any disagreement it was that the chairman wanted us to kick our way out of the division.'

Steve Foley was appointed caretaker for Tuesday's 4-1 win at Rochdale, but, confirming Walker's fears, the new man was in place by the Wednesday. Roger Brown, former Fulham and Norwich centre-half and currently manager of Poole Town, was introduced by Crisp in these glowing terms: 'Brown was a manager in industry before he started at a late age in professional football. He has proven management skills outside the game. He is a strong, tough, hard man.' Wary of his *faux pas* over the membership scheme, Crisp added, 'It wasn't just my decision to bring him here. I had professional advice.'

This momentous change in the affairs of Colchester United can be seen with hindsight to have triggered the decline that would culminate with demotion from the League. Walker would land on his feet at Norwich and enjoy Premiership and European glory. The question: 'Was he sacked or was he pushed?' seems likely to go to the grave. The final embarrassment for Crisp was when Walker was 'posthumously' awarded the October Manager of the Month award.

## 4

HEADING FOR THE ABYSS
1988-1990

LEAGUE DIVISION 4	**1988-89**
Division 4	22nd
Littlewoods Cup	4th Round
FA Cup	3rd Round
Sherpa Van Trophy	Quarter-finals (South)

It was a relief for everyone when U's reassembled at Layer Road for the new season. It had been expected that United would be ground-sharing with Ipswich, Chelmsford, Wivenhoe or Braintree. The folly of selling Layer Road, before a new stadium had been built, was made clear to Crisp by a delegation of ex-U's board members.

Manager Brown, meanwhile, had no centre-forward. Ex-England international Paul Mariner joined the commercial department rather than donning the No 9 shirt. Brown turned instead to veteran Dave Swindlehurst, and introduced the untried trio of Kevin Bedford, Dave Barnett and Steve Cartwright. Barnett made an immediate impact, being sent off on his debut against York. 'Psycho', as he was dubbed by the dwindling Layer Road faithful, had another early bath eight games later against Scunthorpe. By then, goals had proved hard to come by, and in consequence U's had crashed out of the Littlewoods Cup to Tony Adcock's Northampton, and had amassed just twelve points and ten goals.

For Leyton Orient, goals were no problem, particularly against the U's. Having already inflicted U's joint-record 0-7 defeat in 1952, the O's now went one better and humiliated United 0-8 at Brisbane Road. The body language of the players, and sardonic cheers by U's fans as each Orient goal hit the net, suggested that if it took an 0-8 mauling to remove their managerial misfit, then so be it. Brown's time was unquestionably up, and again Crisp would have to brace himself for the flak. Having been given three months to prove himself, Brown resigned. Forty-seven games under his command had realised just fifteen wins. U's had slipped into the bottom four, with relegation to the GM Vauxhall Conference a real possibility.

Gates were at an all-time low, and a farmer from Great Horkesley laid claim to a plot of land within the proposed Turner Rise development, scuppering U's stadium plans.

On Brown's resignation, Crisp admitted: 'Brown was relatively untried. I had not met him until his interview, where he impressed me immensely. We will not make a half-cock decision next time. I think we will trust our own judgement (rather than that of so-called professional advisors). The fans deserve better.'

Steve Foley, for the second time, was charged with temporarily administering the first team while a new leader was sought. Blue and white through and through, Foley as a U's old boy immediately instilled a sense of passion in the townsfolk. Following that 0-8 horror show, his verve put 900 on the attendance for the next home game. The battle had commenced. Foley discarded the misfits Brown had introduced, but could do little to repair the shattered confidence of those that remained. Indeed, United did not win a league match in the twelve games under Foley's charge.

The FA Cup was a different matter. Foley, strangely, was able to fire up his troops for cup-ties. Bottom of the table U's stunned four higher division sides, each on their own patch: Fulham (1-0), Swansea (3-1), Shrewsbury (3-0) and Sheffield United (3-3). The Blades finally ended the cup run at Layer Road 2-0 in a replay.

Crisp's search for the right man ended when former Glasgow Rangers manager Jock Wallace was appointed. Wallace, 53, had been living in Spain, where he had managed Seville, after leaving Leicester City. His physical presence and clenched-fist determination stirred a rallying cry from the Colchester *Evening Gazette*, which launched an SOS campaign, Save Our Soccer. Trailing third from bottom Hereford by ten points, it was likely that U's or Darlington, who were one point better off than United, would drop to the GMVC. This was no time for behind-the-scenes bickering. Colchester United's proud 39-year League membership was under serious threat.

Having overseen two league games and two defeats, Wallace identified a weak link. Young keeper Mark Walton had performed well enough, but it was time to make way for former West Ham goalie Tom McAlister. Wallace then brought in Bohemian's young winger Paul McGee for £35,000. First Division Wimbledon were so impressed by the tiny Irishman's performances that after only four appearances they splashed out a package amounting to £150,000 for his services. Still more players arrived: Ian Allinson returned after spells with Arsenal, Luton and Stoke, and Les Taylor cost £20,000 from Reading. It was a goal by part-timer John Warner, a Ford security guard, that afforded Wallace his first league victory, at

Scunthorpe's new Glandford Park. It was Colchester's first win in nineteen games. Crisp issued a heartfelt plea, recognising that the team needed support to survive: 'Let's forget all our differences for now, we can sort them out when the League future of Colchester United is secure,' he said. Attendances soared to the 4,000 mark as the quest for U's survival reached fever pitch.

Results picked up. The U's drew level on points with Darlington, but more importantly had two games in hand with seventeen still to play. They had also narrowed the gap separating them from the other strugglers. The more clubs that were dragged into the mire, the easier U's escape would become. Wallace now signed left-back Clive Stafford from Diss Town, plus a real gem from his native Scotland in rugged striker Robert Scott.

For a while it seemed that whatever U's did, Darlington either equalled or bettered. United stayed rooted to the bottom. Wallace had one more trump card up his sleeve, appointing England World Cup-winner Alan Ball as his coach until the end of the season. Foley agreed to step aside to return to his post as youth team boss. Ball arrived in the middle of a five-match winless run, which used up one of United's precious games in hand and allowed Darlington to creep four points ahead.

As the half-time scores were announced during the fixture at Lincoln, it was revealed that the Liverpool v Nottingham Forest FA Cup semi-final had been delayed. It was not until the U's match was over that news filtered through of the enormity of the tragedy at Hillsborough. It is said that everyone remembers where they were when John F Kennedy was assassinated: football fans remember likewise how they heard of the tragedies of Bradford City, Heysel and now Hillsborough.

A spine-tingling silence observed the memory of those who had died as U's lined up to face Carlisle. Six games remained, four of them at home, and United still had to go to Darlington.

Match of the Season 1988-89

Darlington 1 Colchester 2

Division 4, 29 April 1989

Still languishing at the foot of the table, a midweek victory over Wrexham moved U's to within one point of Darlington with four games each to play. United had suffered only one defeat in their last seven and were unbeaten at Layer Road since January. Manager Jock Wallace boosted morale at the club by agreeing to stay on for another season.

Did You Know?

In 1990-91, United's youth team scored 199 goals. One of their only two
defeats came in the second leg of a cup-tie, having won the first leg 10-0.

Hundreds of U's fans made the trip to the north-east and were
in full voice long before the match got under way. Crowd congestion meant that the kick-off was delayed. Hearts sank as a hopeful
punt by home defender Paul Dyson evaded the U's offside trap,
leaving Gary MacDonald one on one with Tom McAlister. The burly
U's custodian clipped MacDonald's heels, leaving FIFA referee
Keith Hackett with no option but to point to the spot. Cool as you
like, Phil Bonnyman converted the penalty to put Quakers 1-0 up.
U's players, like their vociferous army of supporters, never flagged,
but it took a mistake by home keeper Mark Prudhoe to bring about
the equaliser. Mark Radford challenged Prudhoe for Les Taylor's
cross. The ball fell to Radford, who found Mario Walsh, who netted. U's fans continued in fine voice throughout the interval. Eight
minutes into the second half the match was won. Steve Hetzke
headed on a right-wing corner for Robert Scott to turn and fire
home. It was fitting for Wallace that a fellow Scot had won the
three crucial points. Three games to go and U's were off the bottom
for the first time since November. Darlington Manager Brian Little,
like Wallace, refused to accept that the battle was over.

The 'cup finals' came thick and fast. Being a Bank Holiday
weekend, U's lined up against Halifax on the Monday. United went
0-2 behind, but in eighteen second-half minutes turned the game
around to win 3-2. The cat and mouse chase continued when
Darlington went to Cambridge the next day and won 3-1. And so to
Friday. Play-off hopefuls Exeter visited Layer Road and were
thumped 4-0. United were five points clear of Darlington and fans
invaded the pitch. Safety was ensured the next afternoon, when
Scunthorpe trounced the Quakers 5-1. By virtue of their last day
win at Torquay, audacious U's even climbed above Doncaster to
finish 22nd. Panic? What panic?

It had been an agonising, nerve-jangling battle that had captured
the imagination of the Colchester public. Extraordinary attendances,
rising from 1,200 to over 5,000, were visible proof that support
existed in the town. If a team at the bottom could transfix so many,
then how many could a side at the top attract? Crisp's courage in
waiting for the right man had been vindicated. For once, chairman
and supporters shared the same opinion; Colchester United must
never, ever be allowed to get in this situation again.

LEAGUE DIVISION 4   **1989-90**
Barclays Division 4   24th (relegated)
Littlewoods Cup   1st Round
FA Cup   2nd Round
Leyland Daf Trophy   1st Round

Boosted by Jock Wallace's decision to stay, U's received a further fillip when coach Alan Ball signed a three-year deal, albeit with a get-out clause that allowed him to take up any position offered to him by a First or Second Division club. If he stayed, he could expect to be appointed manager upon Wallace's retirement. On the player-front, want-aways Mark Walton and Colin Hill were valued much higher, but a transfer tribunal did U's no favours, Hill fetching £85,000 from Sheffield United and keeper Walton £75,000 from Norwich. Wallace, an ex-goalie himself, brought in 25-year-old Irishman John Grace. Grace's nervy start necessitated the arrival of experienced Roger Hansbury on loan. Goalkeeping used to be the least of Colchester's worries. From having Mike Walker and Alec Chamberlain virtually unchallenged in goal for nigh on ten years, U's now had a steady flow of short-term fixes between the sticks. Wallace's quest for Irishmen and Scotsmen – 'they don't know how to lose' – continued apace, with the arrival from Ireland of half a dozen trainees including 17-year-old Mark Kinsella.

Hansbury did not stem the tide of goals against. Thirteen goals shipped in five league and cup games warranted fresh defensive ballast. Southampton defender Mark Blake joined on loan, and United responded with three draws and a 4-1 win over new boys Maidstone. Saints' asking price of £150,000 heralded Blake's swift return to the Dell. Next to pull on the centre-half's shirt was Billy Gilbert, who had played under Ball at Pompey in a team saddled with a horrendous disciplinary record.

Wallace's young team were sliding down the table at an alarm-ing rate. The pruning of the playing squad was starting to backfire on the manager. Following a 0-4 defeat at Aldershot that left United just three points off the bottom, Wallace fumed: 'I'm absolutely disillusioned with their performance. It was the worst by any team of mine in 25 years of management.' This was not the same Jock Wallace who had inspired salvation only months earlier. Something was amiss. Alan Ball was not going to stay around to find out, exercising the get-out clause in his contract to become Mick Mills' first-team coach at Stoke City. Mills must have wished Ball had stayed in Essex, as he himself was soon sacked and replaced by Ball. There was no doubt that Ball's enthusiasm and coaching skills had been of considerable benefit to Wallace during the dark days of the previous term. It was therefore less than tactful of Ball to reveal that Colchester had been merely a 'hospital' to cure the hurt of his sacking at Pompey.

Two points from ten games proved to be the final straw for everyone. The crippling £750,000 debt prevented most of the £200,000 transfer takings from being spent. The players joining the club were no better than those already on the books. The return of Tommy English and the signing of Trevor Morgan did little to stir the attack. Wallace's mix of youth and has-beens failed to gel. Just 1,720 saw woeful Torquay murder United at Layer Road 3-0. A week previously, following the 0-2 home FA Cup defeat by Birmingham, Wallace had been appointed a U's director, in recognition, said Crisp, that such a great man had come to Colchester. There was no argument over that, but what did it mean? In the aftermath of the Torquay debacle, Wallace stepped down. Steve Foley took temporary charge for the third time in as many years. Foley immediately inspired his players to only their second victory of the season in the Boxing Day clash at Roots Hall.

1990 dawned just as 1989 had done: United were 92nd in the league. It was a sad sign of the times when John Warner, re-engaged by Foley, found it more rewarding to play for Dagenham part-time, than join the U's full-time. Wallace's replacement was none other than former Ipswich and England defender Mick Mills, who had been sacked by Stoke and replaced by Alan Ball back in October. Monotone of voice and uninspiring to the fans, Mills exuded none of the exuberance of Jock Wallace. This time around U's did not seem able to sustain enough impetus to haul themselves off the bottom.

Mill's appointed his ex-Stoke coach, Sammy Chung, and must take credit for two players he brought in. Scott Barrett, a goalkeeper loaned from Stoke, and Neale Marmon, an Englishman playing in West Germany, looked good enough to help escape the clutches of the GMVC. Mills installed Billy Gilbert as a sweeper and the tactics reaped dividends. Both Gillingham and Grimsby were beaten at Layer Road in the space of four days, moving U's five points above Wrexham, but having played a game more. The upturn was tinged with shock, when Jock Wallace revealed that he was suffering from Parkinson's Disease. A chance discussion with physio Charlie Simpson over his symptoms had prompted the diagnosis. Wallace returned home to Spain, and would seek treatment in the USA.

United's finances were also ailing. Figures for the financial year ending May 1989 revealed a loss of £316,719. This put the club over £1 million in the red. U's fans were entitled to demand what they had got for their money.

Did You Know?

In August 1991 at Slough, When Roy McDonough scored 4 goals to equal U's individual scoring record, his wife bought the match ball from the host club.

A 4-0 win over Carlisle seemed to suggest that U's had turned the corner. It was the team's fifth home win in seven under Mills. Unfortunately, home wins were countered by away defeats. The crunch game came at Wrexham's Racecourse Ground in late March. Boosted by the unveiling of another stadium plan, this time next to the A12 at Ardleigh, U's introduced Nottingham Forest youngster Andrew Marriott to replace Barrett in goal, whose loan spell had expired. Marriott was pitched straight into the relegation cauldron. United felt they were desperately unlucky to lose to the Welsh team. They were twice in front, but the five-minute cloudburst that swamped the Racecourse seemed a harbinger from the gods. Wrexham scored two late goals to earn a crucial victory.

One ray of hope remained. U's still had to face two fellow strugglers, Doncaster and Hartlepool. Both games were won 2-0, but were sandwiched between 0-2 and 1-4 defeats by Southend and Torquay respectively. Fixture-less on the penultimate Saturday of the season, owing to the East Anglian derby with Cambridge being switched to Sunday, U's were left twiddling their thumbs, hoping against hope that their rivals would lose.

Match of the Season 1989-90

Cambridge 4 Colchester 0

Division 4, 29 April 1990

Colchester's second consecutive fight against demotion to the backwaters of the Vauxhall Conference was borne by a side robbed of its backbone. Keeper Mark Walton, centre-half Colin Hill and striker Mario Walsh had been sold during the summer. None had been adequately replaced. Soaring debts had restricted major forays into the transfer market, necessitating a reliance on young players who would normally have been tried and rested. U's plight was such that these youngsters had to carry the burden of premature regular first-team football. Six consecutive home defeats before Christmas had plunged United into desperate trouble. Tactically, new manager Mick Mills manufactured an upturn in home form. But without the calibre of player he needed, he was destined to be associated with two relegated clubs in the same season – his first, Stoke, propped up the Second Division.

By a quirk of fixture planning, Colchester travelled to the Abbey Stadium already knowing their fate. Less than 24 hours earlier, wins by Hartlepool (2-0 v Aldershot) and Doncaster (4-0 v Rochdale) had carried both clubs beyond the reach of United. Come August, U's would be playing in the GM Vauxhall Conference. Cambridge merely drove the final nail in the coffin. For future Colchester player Michael Cheetham, it proved an auspicious occasion as he notched the first hat-trick of his professional career. Cheetham opened Cambridge's account on 25 minutes, racing on to Chris Leadbitter's pass. That was followed ten minutes later by a Steve Claridge turn and shot. A second-half double substitution seemed to disrupt U's formation. Tony English tripped Cheetham, and three minutes later Scott Daniels felled John Taylor, giving Cheetham two spot-kicks to complete his treble. Further joy awaited Cambridge in the Wembley play-off final, where Dion Dublin secured a 1-0 win over Stockport.

Colchester's season had one more act to run. The final curtain fell a week later, following a 2-2 home draw with Burnley. With the Monty Python song 'Always Look On The Bright Side Of Life' echoing from the terraces, an impromptu conga commenced on the Barside of the ground. U's, and their fans, might be down but they certainly weren't out.

For Colchester United, it was farewell to the League after 40 seasons of limited success. Both Lincoln and Darlington, previously relegated to the GM Vauxhall Conference, had returned to the Fourth Division at the first attempt, fitter and leaner for the experience. U's, however, had other problems. They were seriously in debt and had suffered yet another setback in their long search for a modern new home. The Parish Council of Ardleigh had objected to plans to build a stadium at Wick Lane, on the extreme outskirts of the village. Ground-sharing with neighbours Wivenhoe appeared the only option. Fears were expressed that U's might follow the example of Newport County, the other side to have suffered demotion to the GMVC, who folded completely.

U's fans, although devastated, urged one another to believe that the drop into non-league would signal a re-birth of the club. Crisp, humbler than in his early days, had to face up to the fact that he had promised Second Division football in a new stadium within five years. Time had expired on that promise and it appeared that U's would be playing *second-rate* football in a *shared* stadium. Money had not brought success; the harsh lesson was that that right had to be earned.

## 5

THE VAUXHALL CONFERENCE 1990-92

VAUXHALL CONFERENCE	1990-91
GMVC	2nd
FA Cup	2nd Round
FA Trophy	Quarter-finals
Bob Lord Trophy	2nd Round

The dark clouds of relegation had hardly blown over when Mick Mills quit as U's manager. He had tried in vain to prevent U's fall and might well have succeeded given an earlier engagement. Without a contract, his departure was no real surprise. Next to try his luck would be Ian Atkins, ex-Ipswich and Everton and latterly skipper of Third Division Birmingham City. Turning down a two-year deal as Birmingham player-coach, Atkins accepted the player-manager position at Layer Road for the same duration. Meanwhile, those clutching at straws were yet hoping that League status might be restored. But when ailing Aldershot survived a winding up order in the High Court, U's fate was sealed. Atkins therefore had the task of preparing his new club-mates, including six fresh faces to Layer Road, for pastures new.

United were, of course, the GMVC's big draw. They were given the honour of being the first ever league visitors to Yeovil's new £3.2m Huish Park stadium. It was ironic that Yeovil had succeeded in building a new stadium, whilst United's plans were still on the drawing board. The west country men, by winning 2-0, gave fair warning to the only full-time professional club in the Conference that they would have to fight every inch of the way. Crisp had boasted to the GMVC committee that his club was the Liverpool of their league. Such inflammatory words served only to fuel opponents' hunger, and begin United's alienation by the non-league set. One thing to please U's fans was to discover that after the furore of crowd segregation in the 'big' league, none existed in the Conference. By the second game at Welling, it was clear that supporters could wander around picturesque little grounds and be welcomed into the social clubs of their hosts. Civility was the order of the day. Perhaps the drop was not so bad after all.

Initially, attendances seemed to be holding up too, with 2,000 fans retaining their allegiance. The vagary of non-league fixtures gave an untidy look to the GMVC table after seven matches, or was it five or even four? Some clubs had already been involved in the FA Cup preliminary rounds, but in the league Kettering set the early pace, dropping only two points from their seven fixtures. United, still finding their feet, trailed the Poppies by ten points. The GMVC fixture computer must have calculated that the Colchester players enjoyed motorways, for United were given seven excursions in the first eleven fixtures.

Chairman Crisp demonstrated his intentions by dipping into his own pocket. A £30,000 transfer of Mario Walsh to Southend, fourteen months previously, had not worked out. Crisp bought him back for £25,000 and Walsh fired U's up amongst the early season leaders with seven goals in his first five outings. Another significant capture was that of keeper Scott Barrett, who had had a spell on loan at Layer Road during Mick Mills' reign. A transfer tribunal set his fee at £25,000. Atkins' next move was to bring back former favourite Roy McDonough, now 32, from Southend. He, too, would prove to be an important capture.

Equally significant had been the Mowat Group's decision at the end of the previous season to release details of the proposed Stadium Park development at Ardleigh to the *Mail on Sunday*. In the pages of the *Mail*'s Money Section, Mowat spilled the beans on the proposed location of the new stadium, giving 'Nimby's'(Not-In-My-Back-Yarders) ample time to plan, consider and raise objections. On the drawing board and in the distributed literature the plans looked grandiose. But their premature release meant that they were now almost dead in the water. Mowat, however, went ahead with the planning application.

U's enjoyed an easy ride in the first three months of the season, boasting a 100 per cent home record from six games and third spot behind Barnet and leaders Kettering. November would test United's mettle. The Poppies' 15-match unbeaten start was shattered by Wycombe, 1-5, a week before U's visited Rockingham Road. United still trailed Kettering by nine points, but now had the opportunity to close it to six. It was not to be. Dougie Keast's screamer won the day for the leaders in what was an action-packed thriller.

Some measure of United's overall form was evident a week later when Third Division Reading were beaten 2-1 in the FA Cup. The decision by British Sky Broadcasting to screen live the second round tie with Leyton Orient was the forerunner of the 'play any time, any day' nonsense that satellite media now dictates. BSB opted to transmit the game at 8pm on a Sunday, in return for a U's bounty of £30,000. Snow eventually put paid to what would have been the first-ever Sunday night fixture in Britain. The rescheduled game was in due course shown, but as few people in those days had the proper aerial, U's reaped two rewards – first, BSB's fee; second, a gate of more than 6,000 to watch a 0-0 stalemate. Some of that money, at BSB's insistence, went on improving Layer Road's feeble floodlights. United lost the replay 1-4.

Atkins now brought in ex-Sunderland centre-half Shaun Elliott and experimented with American triallist Mike Masters. The big games were coming thick and fast, capped by a festive season double-header against Barry Fry's second-placed Barnet. The Boxing Day clash at Layer Road ended 0-0, but on New Year's Day United went to Underhill and secured a vital 3-1 win, thereby leapfrogging the Bees. Kettering were still blazing a trail at the top, ten points ahead of United, but they remained within catching distance and, more importantly, eleven of United's nineteen remaining games were at their impregnable Layer Road fortress.

As one stadium – the proposed Stadium Park – took a buffeting from objectors at its official launch, U's set their sights on another – Wembley. The FA Trophy, the FA Cup of non-league football, offered United a realistic chance of reaching the Twin Towers and gracing the hallowed turf for the first time in their history. In these propitious circumstances it was unthinkable that Atkins might wish to leave. But his former club, Birmingham City, having sacked Dave Mackay, approached Atkins with an offer to succeed him. To the relief of everyone, the Midlands club appointed Lou Macari instead. While Atkins was reaffirming his commitment to U's cause, the club committed themselves to finding a new stadium, selling the ground back to the Council for £1.2m, thereby erasing the club's debts. United would rent the ground back, but there was a strict time limit – three years.

A new threat now identified itself. While U's were engaged in FA Trophy duties, Altrincham had struck a winning run to increase the runaway three to four. Coincidentally, Kettering's early season bubble had burst. For them, January and February were dreadful months. Barnet now led Kettering on goal-difference with 61 points, followed by U's on 60 and Altrincham, with a game in hand, on 58. Battle for the one coveted Football League place now commenced in earnest. Defeats at home to Yeovil and at Wycombe, prevented U's from assuming the leadership. Atkins' decision to bolster his squad with the signings of David Leworthy, ex-U's Rudi Hedman, Steve McGavin and Garry Osbourne seemed to disrupt momentum.

> **Did You Know?**
>
> In September 1991, Scott Barrett became United's only goalkeeper to score in open play, scoring the last-minute winner at Wycombe Wanderers.

United's full-time squad should have been equal to the demands imposed by the two-games-a-week run-in. But the intervention of another satellite TV company threw a spanner in the works. Keen though they were for British Aerospace Sportscast's money, United did not need the consequent run of evening fixtures. Opponents played up for the cameras, U's fans were deterred from travelling, and their rivals were advantaged by playing later, by which time they knew United's score.

United went top in the second week of April, just in time for the most critical four-day period of the season. U's overcame faltering Kettering 3-1, with Warren Donald scoring his first ever U's goal. The Colchester *Evening Gazette* headlined 'Donald Breaks His Duck'. This sub-editor's gem had no doubt been penned well in advance, waiting for the moment to be unleashed. Next up were Altrincham, who had two games in hand and whose unashamed intention at Layer Road was not to lose. Watched by the highest GMVC crowd of the season, a capacity 7,221, Altrincham achieved their draw.

The pressure finally told on Altrincham and Colchester. Fixture congestion suffocated Altrincham's League dreams, while United went camera shy. Satellite-covered games at Kidderminster and Telford realised one point and no goals. The failings of those around them enabled Barry Fry's Barnet to wrestle top spot. On the last Saturday of the season, United had to beat Kidderminster and hope that the GMVC's whipping boys Fisher Athletic could somehow defeat Barnet. Sensationally, the Docklands outfit took a 2-1 lead, to the delight of those at Layer Road, ears pinned to tiny radios. United were already 2-0 up. When a rumour circulated that Fisher had added a third, Layer Road erupted. But in fact Barnet had equalised. Ecstasy turned to stunned silence as Barnet added two further goals to clinch the title.

Ian Atkins grudgingly accepted the runners-up trophy, admitting 'I've never wanted anything for coming second'. Crisp, having decided to withdraw his £10,000-a-week funding, offered his assessment: 'Everyone talks about how well Ian Atkins did. But to come second with a fully professional team in a part-time league is a bloody disgrace.' Crisp warned that it was time to sell or go bust. £250,000 was needed for the club to survive. The entire squad was put up for sale. For Atkins, the lure of a return to his hometown club, Birmingham, as coach proved too tempting to refuse.

Match of the Season 1990-91

Colchester 3   Wivenhoe 0

FA Trophy, 3rd Round, 23 February 1991

U's kicked off their first-ever FA Trophy campaign in sub-zero temperatures in the flight-path of Heathrow Airport. Gary Bennett's solitary goal saw off the challenge of Vauxhall Premier side Windsor and Eton. Next, Merseysiders Runcorn visited Layer Road. Runcorn were in the chasing pack in the Conference. Robust and uncompromising, they made U's labour for their 2-0 win. The third round draw paired U's with their neighbours Wivenhoe Town. U's fall from grace, coupled with the Dragons' promotion as champions to the Vauxhall Premier League, meant that the two clubs were now just one division, as well as just a few miles, apart. Many United fans, disgruntled by the Crisp era, had adopted Wivenhoe as their second team (or first, in some cases). Twenty-odd years previously, Wivenhoe had been playing Essex and Suffolk Border League football on the town's recreation ground. Now ensconced in their homely Broad Lane ground, previously a carrot field, Wivenhoe had invested heavily to attract a string of ex-League players to fuel their rise through various divisions of non-league football. Three of those players – Steve Leslie, Lee Hunter and Steve Wright – had worn U's colours at one time or another, as had Phil Coleman, who found himself suspended for this clash. The Dragons' manager also needed no introduction. Micky Cook held U's appearance record of 613 league games.

The tie was watched by a crowd of 4,923, a record for the competition, short of the semi-finals, United dominated from start to finish. Bennett's cross eluded ex-Luton man Lil Fuccillo for Roy McDonough to steer a diving header past Tony Godden. Wivenhoe's hotshot strikers Steve Clark and Martin Gittings each wasted half-chances before United wrapped up the tie. McDonough set up Bennett, and Bennett added a second when Wright deflected Tony English's cross into his path. In the circumstances, everyone was happy. Trophy favourites U's had avoided a possible humiliation, whilst injury-hit Dragons had done themselves proud.

In the quarter-finals, HFS Loans leaders Witton Albion grabbed two late Layer Road goals to earn a two-legged semi-final with Wycombe. As for Wivenhoe, they would in time be hit hard by the Inland Revenue over alleged irregularities, and slither down the divisions. It is doubtful that these friendly neighbours will ever again come as close in status.

VAUXHALL CONFERENCE   **1991-92**
GMVC   1st (champions)
FA Cup   2nd Round
FA Trophy   Winners
Bob Lord Trophy   1st Round

Worldly-wise from their first exposure to the GMVC, U's were entering a new era. Chairman Crisp had called it a day after a five-year reign. His legacy was a disastrous members scheme, the dismissal of a successful manager at a time when United were joint top of the Fourth Division, and leaving the club on the brink of extinction with debts approaching £1.5m. One of his few pluses was the appointment of Jock Wallace, who, along with Alan Ball, fended off demotion to the GMVC. This 'success' was muted by the fact that Crisp had promised Second Division football within five years and a new stadium. He had failed on both counts and at consider-able cost to his pride and personal wealth. Launching a new campaign 'United behind United', new chairman James Bowdidge, a Colchester man and U's fan, pledged to give the club back to the people of the town.

Bowdidge appointed Roy McDonough as United's player-coach. McDonough vowed to abandon the sweeper system favoured by Ian Atkins and press forward in search of goals. Too often during the previous season, U's had gone a goal up and sat on the lead, only to succumb to late goals. True to his word, McDonough found the net four times himself at Slough, and rampant U's hit Bath for five without reply in the next game. Gary Bennett, with three in that game, and Steve McGavin, with two, were set to form a potent partnership with their player-coach.

Less harmonious, was the relationship between Colchester United and the Mowat Group. Shirt-sponsors Holimarine, part of the Mowat Group, had apparently failed to deliver £20,000 owed to the club, as a result of which U's pulled the plug on the deal, and also severed any hopes of Stadium Park ever getting off the ground. Instead, U's decided to go it alone and search for a site within the borough of Colchester. There were, apparently, around ten such sites to consider.

McDonough brought in his old Southend mates Paul Roberts – to replace Scott Daniels – and Jason Cook in time for the top-of-the-table clash at Wycombe's Adams Park. No scriptwriter could have penned the dramatic last-minute events that the 5,186 crowd wit-nessed. It was 1-1 when goalkeeper Scott Barrett drop-kicked a clearance. The ball pinged off the saturated pitch and sailed over home keeper Paul Hyde's head. The result took U's to within three points of leaders Wycombe and would have a major bearing on the season's outcome. With Farnborough now taking over at the top, U's visit to the John Roberts Ground took on added significance. The Hampshire side had inflicted U's only home defeat thus far. Backed by almost 1,500 fans, U's gained their revenge, a 2-0 victory taking them top for the first time. However, the realities of being non-league were driven home when United had to qualify for the first round proper of the FA Cup. Defeating Burton 5-0, U's were paired with Alan Ball's Exeter, who paraded in their ranks £50,000 ex-U's Scott Daniels. Two 0-0 draws paved the way for a 2-4 penalty shoot-out defeat, leaving United eliminated from a competition in which they failed to concede a goal from open play. Although the FA had opted to do away with second replays, it was still a cruel way to exit the most famous cup competition in the world.

U's would also, it appeared, have to quit Layer Road in a year and a half when their lease expired. With no new stadium on the horizon, talks resurfaced with Wivenhoe about a possible ground-share. Such problems did not apply to Wycombe, who already had a neat, modern stadium. Under Martin O'Neill, Wycombe were no less desperate to capture League status, but it appeared that U's had the Indian sign on them. United's 3-0 home trouncing of the Buckinghamshire outfit completed a notable double and opened up a four-point gap at the top. Wycombe keeper Paul Hyde was also confronted with an unwelcome double. Not content with having permitted Scott Barrett's downfield punt to bounce over his head, he now found himself unnerved by the Layer Road taunts, gifting United two further goals.

At the final whistle McDonough turned the knife: 'If Wycombe think they are the best team in the GMVC, then they had better think again. We beat them in style in the end.' O'Neill remained tight-lipped. Nine days later Wycombe returned to Layer Road in the meaningless Bob Lord Trophy. This time they thrashed a mixed U's team of triallists and youngsters 6-2. McDonough's public retort that he was glad that U's were out of the competition did not impress the GMVC hierarchy. McDonough added: 'We proved what we can do in the games that mattered.'

What did matter was Scott Barrett's bombshell that he wanted a transfer and Birmingham City's reported interest in Steve McGavin. Ex-U's Mario Walsh also scored a Boxing Day winner for Redbridge Forest, which constituted United's first away defeat of the season. As 1992 dawned, United led Wycombe by seven and third-placed Farnborough by an unbridgable sixteen points. With half a season still to go, it was clear that Wycombe alone stood between United and a return to the League.

Did You Know?

United's visit to Farnborough in September 1991 in the Vauxhall Conference created a then record home crowd for the Hampshire club of 3,069.

Or rather, Wycombe and the bureaucrats of the Football League, who now ruled that member clubs should have a minimum ten-year tenure on their ground. United had less than two. Cap in hand, Colchester United returned to the Council to plead for an extension on their lease.

Wycombe, meanwhile, had nibbled away at U's lead, and with games in hand had the capacity to overtake them. It was therefore an unwelcome distraction when satellite broadcasters Sportscast started rewriting the fixture list once again. Supporters packed the Hippodrome Nightclub to watch transmitted pictures of United's 2-2 draw at Kettering. The frozen pitch would surely have led to a postponement but for the presence of the cameras. News that Aldershot were about to be declared bankrupt fuelled rumours that the Conference champions *and* runners-up would both be promoted to the League. The uncertainty ushered in a poor spell for both Wycombe and Colchester, who were whacked 1-4 by Welling.

McDonough rallied his troops to such an extent that they conceded just one goal in eight games, a run which culminated in a 4-0 win at Boston. By this time, however, U's onward march in the FA Trophy meant they had Wembley in their sights. Macclesfield were still smarting from their elimination at United's hands when the teams met again in the Conference. United fought back from a dodgy start to earn a 4-4 draw, and that point would prove vital. Wycombe's win at Gateshead left the two title-chasers separated only by goal-difference, in which U's held a decisive advantage.

United's penultimate game, in front of 6,303, brought a 3-1 midweek win over Kettering. Two days later hundreds of U's fans swelled the gate at Redbridge's Dagenham home for the visit of Wycombe. Needing eight goals to equal United's goal-difference, Wycombe stunned the noisy Colchester/Redbridge alliance by racing into a five-goal lead. Mercifully, Redbridge kept a clean-sheet for the remaining forty minutes.

So to the last day. Wycombe needed to beat Witton by a huge margin to keep the pressure on United. Wycombe did their bit by beating Witton 4-0, but United had the final say. A hat-trick by American Mike Masters was the highlight of their 5-0 home romp over already-relegated Barrow. Fans streamed onto the pitch in celebration, not yet sure whether ground regulations would allow United back into the League. An end-of-season snub awaited U's in the shape of the otherwise excellent *Non-League Directory*. Colchester United's details were mysteriously absent.

The Council extended the lease on Layer Road to the mandatory ten years, and even pledged an annual grant of the kind afforded to other arts and recreation facilities in the town. The planned new stadium was unveiled as a computer-generated image.

Chairman Bowdidge launched a 'Back to the League' appeal in the Colchester *Evening Gazette* with a view to raising £100,000. This would fund the League's demands for higher safety standards. New crash barriers would be erected and wooden terraces replaced by concrete. Fans chipped in with an assortment of DIY skills. Following a Football League inspection, the green light was given; U's were back in the League. Rising like a phoenix from the flames, the only way was up.

Match of the Season 1991-92

Colchester 3 Witton 1

FA Trophy Final, 10 May 1992

The previous season, U's had been knocked out of the FA Trophy in the quarter-finals by HFS Loans League champions-to-be Witton. U's embarked on their second tilt at the FA Trophy with a first round tie against Kingstonian. United were seconds from elimination when keeper Scott Barrett raced upfield at a corner-kick and set up Tony English's equaliser. Barrett thus earned himself another appearance on BBC's 'A Question of Sport' in the 'What happened next' section, following his goal at Wycombe.

United survived the replay, but also needed two games to dispose of their GMVC bogey team Merthyr in the next round. Morecambe and Telford were then swept aside to set up a two-legged semi-final with Macclesfield. Roared on by nearly 1,000 fans at Moss Rose, United's 3-0 first-leg lead was severely tested, and Jason Cook's volley to level on the night is treasured by all who saw it.

Crucially, Wembley did not distract United from their GMVC title aspirations. Fans queued to buy tickets. Why? Wembley held 76,000; it was never going to sell out. But it is in a true fan's psyche that he must have that precious ticket in his grasp, to feel it, stroke it, then hide it.

More than 23,000 Colchestrians, plus curious outsiders, clutched precious vouchers. Hats, scarves and banners were frantically produced. Going to Wembley proved to be a major merchandising opportunity. The *Sun*, via the intervention of an employee who happened to be a fan, sponsored United's shirts.

The blue and white convoy that had turned the A12 into a mobile street party settled in their seats on a gloriously sunny day. Witton, the 'other' team from Northwich, were also making their Wembley debuts. The Cheshire side were rocked as early as the fifth minute when Mike Masters became the first American to score at the stadium. Nicky Smith's sliding finish to put U's 2-0 up would surely be decisive. But no. The balding Mike Lutkevitch netted to set up a nerve-racking finale. When, with nine minutes left, Jason Cook was sent off by referee Kieron Barratt, Essex finger-nails were being gnawed to the bone. As Witton surged forward, Steve McGavin plundered one of his typically 'silky' goals to ensure that blue and white ribbons would be tied around the trophy. The expelled Cook was barred from receiving a winners medal, but substitute Eamonn Collins magnanimously presented the youngster with his own.

The Wembley lap of honour continued all the way back up the A12. The win, coupled with the Conference title gained eight days previously, meant that U's followed in the footsteps of Wealdstone, the only other club to have won the coveted non-league double. Two days later United boarded an open-top bus to parade their silverware to 10,000 flag-waving fans outside the town hall.

## 6

BACK TO THE LEAGUE
1992-1999

LEAGUE DIVISION 3	**1992-93**
Barclays Division 3	10th
Coca-Cola Cup	1st Round
FA Cup	2nd Round
Autoglass Trophy	1st Round

Down-payment of a £150,000 bond to the Football League, to cover players' wages, rubber-stamped United's return to the League following their memorable non-league double season. Their return coincided with the advent of the FA Premier League, and the nominal upgrading of the three remaining divisions. Hey presto, U's leaped two divisions, albeit in name only. The demise of Aldershot and Maidstone United left the new Division Three with just 22 clubs. In other circumstances, Wycombe Wanderers might have been invited to fill one of those spare places, but the FA were intent on reducing the Premier League from 22 to twenty clubs. The third division was to be restocked by tinkering with promotion and relegation.

Player-manager McDonough spent much of the summer trying unavailingly to persuade 'the goalie', as he called Scott Barrett, to stay. Barrett's defection to Gillingham proved costly to United, who, try as they might, could not find a competent successor. Five No 1s would be employed during 1992-93, seven if we include friendlies. One player who *did* want to play for United was Mike Masters. League regulations stipulated that non-EEC players must be full internationals to play first-team football. Masters' summer appearance for the USA against the Ukraine was deemed insufficient for the Professional Footballers Association to recommend that the Home Office grant him a work permit. With 350 UK professional footballers seeking clubs, the PFA insisted that United find a British alternative to Masters. 'Where do we find a 6ft 4in, 20-goal-a-season man who is likely to represent his country in the 1994 World Cup?' enquired chairman Parker. Some statisticians claim

Masters to be U's most (full) capped player, though strictly speaking he was not contracted to the U's at the time.

Time, or lack of it, obliged chairman James Bowdidge to step down to concentrate on his business interests. He had chaired U's in their best ever season and enjoyed the unusual distinction, for a chairman, of having the crowd chant his name on one occasion. When local businessman Gordon Parker, who had been on the clubs books as an amateur in the early 1950s, assumed the chair, he was making United a truly family-run club. His daughter Jackie was U's lottery manager and her husband Roy was U's player-manager. But family ties would in due course present difficulties for all concerned.

Oddly, the opening three fixtures brought together a quartet of successive GMVC champions: U's hosted Lincoln and Darlington and travelled to Barnet. Both Quakers and Barnet had climbed two rungs up the ladder after rising from the GMVC, only to drop back to the League basement. U's, too, were confident that the impetus of the previous season would carry them into (the new) Division Two. The expanded fan-base generated by the Wembley excitement was waiting to be tapped on a longer basis.

But United came down to earth with a bump. Four defeats in the first five games, bottom of the league, and a Coca-Cola Cup exit to Brighton, was hardly going to convert occasionals to regulars. McDonough's regular brushes with the FA Disciplinary Committee, Masters' work-permit refusal, and Steve McGavin's holiday injury combined to leave United short on goal-power. Various centre-forwards were invited to sign for U's, but none did. United could not pay bumper wages, and McDonough's only successes were in attracting former team-mates. This method of recruitment was nothing new at Layer Road. The 1980s, for example, had seen a flood of former Ipswich youths, rejects and has-beens, but few real gems.

The return of Steve McGavin lifted U's, but the striker found it difficult to shed the pounds accumulated during his lay-off. His 26 goals the previous season promised an equally prolific return in the League, but for one reason or another he failed to make double figures. The new emerging talent was 19-year-old Mark Kinsella, capped at Under-21 level by the Republic of Ireland. Dynamic from box to box, 'Sheedy' – so called after former Republic international Kevin Sheedy – had a knack for long-range goals. Reports that a host of European clubs were interested in his services proved unfounded, a blow to the player and cash-strapped U's alike.

Still without a full-time goalkeeper, McDonough brought in ex-Walsall team-mate Ron Green from Kidderminster. Green, however, had long since seen the best days of his League career. Defensive frailties continued to cost U's dear. The arrival on loan of Millwall's 19-year-old keeper Carl Emberson at last sparked a run of decent form which by the turn of the year hoisted United into a play-off berth. More worryingly, McDonough's brash style was rubbing off on his team, and United's disciplinary record threatened a heavy end-of-season fine.

Hopes of a play-off place subsided as quickly as they had materialised. Hungry for success, United fans began to turn against McDonough, especially when he sacked fiery recruit Tony Sorrell. Sorrell had won the admiration of United followers with three man-of-the-match performances in seven appearances. His accumulation of cards – two yellow and one red – coupled with a training ground 'incident', prompted skipper Tony English to come out in defence of his beleaguered boss. The players, too, were not altogether happy with Sorrell's disruptive influence. Discipline was, of course, at the top of U's agenda, so much so that individual club fines were trebled.

Slated for dismantling the GMVC winning side, despite tightened purse-strings, McDonough recruited his fourth keeper for the remainder of the season. Fred Barber quickly became a crowd favourite with his trademark 'Old Man' mask and habit of kneeling to pay homage to United's fans. Apart from two horror-shows at Rochdale (2-5) and Crewe (1-7), Barber helped U's claw their way back into play-off contention. McDonough, meanwhile, announced he was hanging up his boots. Ageing legs, abuse from fans, and a second red card of the season, at Rochdale, had taken its toll. Another of Steve Foley's youth team prospects, Paul Abrahams, filled the gap vacated by McDonough's retirement. Seizing his chance, Abrahams' six goals re-fuelled U's play-off hopes, only for defeats in the last two games to deprive them by four points.

Memories are short. Twelve months earlier U's had basked in the glory of the double. Now McDonough was villain. Conceding a 'seven', a 'five', and six 'fours' was the root of goal-shy United's problems.

Match of the Season 1992-93
Crewe 7 Colchester 1

Division 3, 24 March 1993

Having quit playing only three weeks earlier, Roy McDonough looked forward to contesting the play-offs. 'I honestly feel we will be too strong for them,' he warned, as United prepared for their visit

---

Did You Know?

When groundsman David Blacknell had trouble with foxes in 1991-92, the ground was dubbed 'Lair Road'.

---

to sixth-placed Crewe. But Dario Gradi's side, renowned for neat football, de-railed U's hopes with a scintillating display. U's defence was at sixes and sevens (pun intended) all afternoon, even though three of United's players needed pain-killing injections before they took the field. One of that trio, Paul Roberts, was clearly hampered by his knock but had his own motive in playing: 'I've never completed a full season of League appearances before. A little ankle injury is not going to stop me this time.' By the end of ninety minutes he would wish it had.

Roberts had sold Fred Barber short with a second-minute backpass that Tony Naylor tucked away with ease. Twenty minutes later Tony English levelled with his first league goal of the season. U's threatened to take command, with Steve McGavin going close, only for Crewe's Dave McKearney to volley home from ten yards. Naylor then showed Roberts a clean pair of heels to add his second, and the contest was effectively over when Phil Clarkson left U's defence spread-eagled on the turf to make it 4-1 to the Railwaymen on the stroke of half-time.

Ears burning from a McDonough tongue-lashing, U's improved early in the second half. Steve Ball engineered no fewer than six chances. However, the half belonged to Naylor. He completed his hat-trick when U's failed to clear McKearney's cross, and added a header for Crewe's sixth. Naylor's fifth goal came the same way as his first, via the unfortunate Roberts, whom he turned inside out. Remarkably, Naylor had only scored once in the previous sixteen games.

U's fans who had cheered when Leyton Orient stuck eight goals past Roger Browns' U's five and a half years earlier were not so jocular this time. As for Crewe, they reached the Wembley play-off final but lost to York on penalties.

LEAGUE DIVISION 3	**1993-94**
Endsleigh Division 3	17th
Coca-Cola Cup	1st Round
FA Cup	1st Round
Autoglass Trophy	Quarter-finals (South)

Following 79 cautions and three dismissals in 1992-93, United were summoned by the FA to explain their shocking disciplinary record. A suspended fine of £7,500 was an ample rap on the knuckles. It was apt, thought some, that United's poorly received new playing kit resembled a prison uniform. The non-traditional blue shirts with upwardly pointing white arrows had been roundly booed when unveiled to supporters at the end of the previous season.

Player-manager McDonough, chief source of United's discipline problems, looked to have solved his goalkeeping problems by signing Premier League Oldham's John Keeley. Keeley's nickname 'Lucky' would not stand the test of time. Equally inappropriate was Barry Fry's £150,000 bid to lure Steve McGavin to Southend. Fry needed to replace Nottingham Forest-bound Stan Collymore, although Fry's interest in McGavin would not be easily deterred.

McDonough continued to utter rash statements, many of which backfired on him. He 'guaranteed' promotion, provided the team could win most of its home games. McDonough's cavalier tactics saw Torquay and Shrewsbury recover from 0-3 and 1-3 down respectively to earn 3-3-draws. When Rochdale won 5-2 at Layer Road, both goalkeeper – with an unnecessary gesture to the home crowd – and manager faced the wrath of the fans. U's were jeered off the pitch. Sloppy defending overshadowed the introduction of Steve Brown, a young striker signed from Scunthorpe. Brown notched three goals in three games and looked a real find, whilst another signing, Alan Dickens, once of West Ham, was asked to provide the 'old head' needed in midfield. Typically erratic, United won the next two games by an aggregate score of 9-3. Brown's hat-trick against Bury helped U's into fifth place.

United's first eight fixtures had seen forty goals, but eighteen of these had been in their own net. No sooner had McDonough signed another ex-Southend man, Adam Locke, than history was made in U's 0-5 thrashing at Hereford. Trailing to a Chris Pike's opener, U's had two keepers sent off, first Keeley, then substitute keeper Nathan Munson (this season permitted substitute goalkeepers for the first time). McDonough himself took over between the sticks. U's thereby became the first team to have two keepers sent off in one match, a statistical oddity that paved the way for another – Chris Pike had scored three goals past three different goalkeepers.

Did You Know?

United's five draws in 1992-93 was the lowest they have ever recorded in a season. They included no 1-1 draws either, the commonest score of all.

McDonough's goalkeeping problems returned. Both offenders received concurrent bans, which necessitated yet another search for goalkeeping cover. At Gillingham, neither the Priestfield programme editor nor the Colchester manager knew who would occupy U's green jersey. United's line-up showed: '1. To be announced.' Chelmsford reserve Mickey Desborough filled the void at the eleventh hour and was not to blame for United's 0-3 defeat. Neither was Keeley three days later when United were crushed 3-7 at Darlington. The beleaguered McDonough confessed: 'I haven't thought about the sack. Until we get some new faces here I don't have any options.' The crisis raised the question: 'Who sacks the manager?' United's chairman, Gordon Parker, was McDonough's father-in-law. Instead of the sack, McDonough received a vote of confidence plus limited funds to buy players – Martin Grainger having been sold to Brentford £60,000.

Home defeat by non-league Sutton in the FA Cup was the first such loss in United's history. Predictably, this season, U's did not lose 0-1 but 3-4. McDonough's kamikaze insistence on piling forward at all times cost them dear. Having fought back to 3-3, U's defence was threadbare for Sutton to exploit for the fourth time.

McDonough tried in vain to bring in new blood, offering Steve McGavin to Barry Fry in return for £50,000 and Southend players John Cornwell and Steve Tilson. Cornwell refused the deal, but Fry hadn't given up, and McDonough was further rocked when 'Lucky' Keeley fell down the stairs at home and broke a bone in his foot. In four months at Layer Road, Keeley had already suffered a minor car accident and six stitches in an eye injury sustained on a squash-court. Now he faced a long lay-off. Fortunately for McDonough, John Sheffield proved a competent stand-in. Nothing McDonough did, though, could appease the hyper-critical fans. Bowing to their demands, he tightened the defence – only for the goals to dry up.

Reflecting on a torrid year McDonough vowed 'Give me £100,000 and I'll guarantee promotion.' Barry Fry must have heard his call: the new Birmingham boss finally got his man McGavin for £150,000. As McGavin had hardly set the League alight since his prolific time in the Vauxhall Conference, the deal was a good one for U's who were now loosing £3,000 per week. The small-print of the transfer, however, was not so favourable: the money would arrive from St Andrews in dribs and drabs, and in any case was subject to the number of appearances made. The upshot was that none of the money was made available to McDonough.

Enter U's fifth keeper of the season – John Cheesewright. Playing Mark Kinsella at sweeper stiffened the defence, but with Brown forgetting how to score and McDonough (having donned his boots again) struggling, the versatile Kinsella was needed all over the pitch. McDonough raided Roots Hall yet again, this time to sign Christian Hyslop. The 21-year-old defender became the third, and quickest, U's player ever to be sent off on his debut. This was at Northampton, though in fairness to Hyslop his seventh-minute red card was reduced on appeal to yellow.

And to be fair to McDonough, he was operating on a miserly budget. Seven of his team that lost at home to Torquay were free transfers and the remainder cost £10,000 between them. Desperately short of goals, he attempted to bring in Ipswich's Steve Whitton, but chairman Parker refused the necessary funds, saying, 'Performances on the pitch equals people through the gate.'

Patience snapped when Wycombe, of all teams (they had been promoted to the League twelve months after United), inflicted on U's a fourth successive home defeat. Fans called for McDonough's head and that of the spendthrift board. In a blunt statement, the board spelled out the economic realities of life at Layer Road in terms that brooked no argument.

Transfer deadline-day arrived, whereupon Whitton was at last snared, funded by supporters and local businessmen. Also joining United were six teenage cast-offs from higher division clubs and an American goalkeeper, Taylor Barada. U's avoided the threat of a second demotion to the Conference with a shock win at Walsall, as did eventual wooden-spoonists Northampton Town, when the ground of Conference champions Kidderminster ground was ruled sub-standard. Northampton's soon-to-be-completed Sixfields Stadium might have swung the decision against Kidderminster. So might the mismanagement of League newcomers Maidstone and Barnet, who had done the integrity of the GMVC few favours.

McDonough, celebrated his 500th league game as a player on the final day of the season, at Carlisle, but was destined to be denied the prized target of 100 league goals. Three short of that target, and facing a players' revolt over reduced wages, McDonough was sacked. Chairman Parker himself broke the news to his son-in-law, and set in train the search for a 'more experienced man'.

McDonough oozed commitment and had steered U's to the finest eight days in their history with the non-league double. Heart always on his sleeve, he had been a victim of financial restraints, and a tendency to overstate his well-meant ambitions for the club.

Match of the Season 1993-94
Wycombe 2   Colchester 5

Division 3, 18 September 1993

Having been denied by United on goal-difference in 1992, Martin O'Neill's Wycombe as expected breezed their way to the GMVC title a year later. Like United, Wycombe completed the double when trouncing Runcorn 4-1 in the FA Trophy final. O'Neill had turned down summer offers to take over from Brian Clough at Nottingham Forest. Undefeated Wycombe entered the first ever League meeting with United in fourth place whilst U's were still smarting from a 2-5 home defeat by Rochdale. Speaking in the *Bucks Free Press*, O'Neill said of McDonough: 'I cannot say that he is my best friend. He made a lot of nonsensical remarks in his local paper a couple of seasons ago. I would not go out of my way to speak to him.' In the Wycombe match programme, director and TV commentator Alan Parry reminded Wycombe fans to 'remember their natural modesty and dignity when United pipped us on goal-difference for the GMVC title. Martin won't need any motivational talk today.' Parry was wrong.

Stung by a week of criticism, U's stormed to victory, their first five-goal haul on the road since March 1985 at Exeter. Wycombe had taken the lead via a penalty from Keith Scott after Paul Roberts scythed Tim Langford. The game turned on a controversial sending off. Home defender Jason Cousins slipped and handled the ball while tackling Mark Kinsella, for which referee Clive Wilkes produced his red card. On the stroke of half-time Kinsella levelled with a rasping 20-yard drive.

Four minutes after the break Wycombe regained the lead through Langford's rising shot. Wycombe faded, and it was no surprise when Steve McGavin capped a silky run to equalise. What was not expected was U's three goals in fifteen minutes. First, McDonough grabbed his third of the season, rejoicing from one end of the pitch to the other. Substitute Martin Grainger made it four with a left-footed screamer, and new boy Steve Brown netted his fourth goal in four games. The 1,500 U's fans in the 6,025 crowd celebrated long after the final whistle. How fickle they had been, seven days previously, when castigating their manager and players. The fickleness was two-way, however; McDonough had slammed the fans and now milked their adulation. Neither cared about last week now: this annihilation of the holier than thou Buckinghamshire upstarts was poetic justice.

LEAGUE DIVISION 3	**1994-95**
Endsleigh Division 3	10th
Coca-Cola Cup	1st Round
FA Cup	3rd Round
Autowindscreen Shield	Quarter-finals (South)

A summer of speculation as to the identity of U's latest manager ended when former Ipswich and Scotland full-back George Burley was unveiled. Burley had spent the previous season as player-coach at Scottish Premier League side Motherwell. Unlike McDonough, Burley had no intention of performing both functions for United, announcing that he was coming purely as a manager. Another change was to revert to U's familiar blue and white stripes, following the eyesores inflicted on supporters the previous term.

Burley's first appointment was ex-Ipswich boss Bobby Ferguson, who arrived as part-time coach. Pre-season preparations got off to a bad start when local non-leaguers Sudbury thrashed a full-strength U's team 5-0. Burley replied to his critics that he had inherited the previous season's squad and that fans should be patient. Strangely, Burley declined to play Carl Emberson, U's new £20,000 keeper. Emberson had been signed prior to Burley's arrival and did not figure in the Scotsman's plans. This was a bizarre situation for cash-strapped U's, especially when Burley publicly pursued ex-U's keeper Mark Walton.

Six straight defeats, including a Coca-Cola Cup exit to Brentford, rang the alarm bells loud and clear. Such was the crisis that Burley went back on his pledge and decided to play himself. Hindered by injuries and the lack of depth to his squad, Burley brought in ex-Portman Road boys Dale Roberts, to be his assistant, and midfielder Trevor Putney. United prospered immediately. In the next fifteen league matches U's were beaten once, won nine, and soared from rock bottom to fifth by Christmas. U's had also progressed to the third round of the FA Cup, where they were paired with Premiership Wimbledon. Burley's explanation for the dramatic upturn was simple: the players had responded to his call for high standards and they had discovered a new hunger for the game. The 4-2 win over Scunthorpe, transmitted on Anglia TV's Kick-Off programme, gave Burley the opportunity to purr, 'It was good to show the television viewers of East Anglia just how well we are playing.'

Eighteen miles up the A12, someone *was* watching. Speculation that Ipswich were set to pounce for Burley to replace sacked John Lyall was scotched by U's chairman Gordon Parker. 'I know the Ipswich directors very well, and if they were going to make an approach they would have done so by now. George is a very good young manager but this position has probably come around a little early for him. That can only be good news for Colchester United.' U's fans had little idea of the Christmas bombshell that was set to explode as they ventured out of doors to see their heroes in action against Northampton.

Shorn of regional and local news programmes over the festive period, many of the 5,064 assembled for the noon kick-off with the Cobblers were blissfully unaware that Burley had resigned two days previously.

Burley's top-flight managerial ambitions seemed to have been dashed when Ipswich refused to meet the compensation demand. He responded by resigning from United instead, which meant he was free to talk to any club he wished, and before 1994 was out he had been installed as boss at Portman Road. Parker fumed, 'We had given Ipswich permission to speak to George, subject to a compensation package being agreed.'

The Cobbald family tradition at Ipswich had earned the club the tag of being the 'Gentleman's Club' of English football. The current regime, however, by appearing to poach Burley, had fallen short of the high standards of their predecessors. Similar criticism might be levelled at Burley himself, who left Parker to tell the stunned players of his departure. Burley, so keen to instil loyalty in his U's players, had not led by example. U's fans would never forget what had been done to them by their near neighbours. Justice would be done, financially, once the FA tribunal wheels eventually rolled into motion.

Burley's assistant, Dale Roberts, took charge for the next five matches, while the names of ex-Liverpool Mark Lawrenson and ex-Bournemouth boss Tony Pulis were bandied about as potential replacements. It was, however, a late contender who was given the job. Steve Wignall, a one-time rock in the heart of U's defence, was introduced as United's twentieth manager. Wignall had spent the latter years leading re-born Aldershot Town through the Diadora Leagues. He now set himself the task of turning Layer Road into a fortress, saying: 'Other teams used to dread coming here when I was a player and together we have got to make it that kind of place again.'

The U's new boss walked straight into an injury crisis. This included the loss of keeper Cheesewright to a mystery virus that rendered him dizzy, and which opened the door for forgotten man Carl Emberson. Wignall presided over what was probably United's greatest comeback in their history. Trailing at Scunthorpe 0-3 after eighteen minutes the U's boss inspired his side to a stunning 4-3 win. Canadian triallist Niall Thompson came off the bench to grab two goals in three minutes to register the new manager's first victory. Thompson was not the only player signing on the dotted line. Brentford's 22-year-old reserve striker Carl Asaba arrived on loan and scored on his debut at Barnet to put U's fifth. Asaba was clearly a talent, and was so enthused by the prospect of his debut that he had turned up at Underhill two hours early. The articulate Asaba declared: 'If Steve Wignall wants me and Dave Webb (Brentford's boss) is prepared to release me, I will be very happy to stay.' Webb would eventually recall him to reinforce Brentford's promotion quest, as U's could not raise the asking price. Later in his career, Asaba would attract much larger fees and come back to haunt United more than once. His next U's goal, however, formed part of an historic occasion.

For United's home match with Darlington in March, the U's hosted the 'Great Give-away'. In conjunction with local businesses, fans were admitted free of charge, exchanging a voucher printed in the Colchester *Evening Gazette* for a match ticket. This made it the first ever Football League match where all spectators were (legally) admitted free. Supporters were able to take advantage of shuttle bus services from the town centre. Once in the ground they had a cup of tea waiting for them and a subsidised programme. As kick-off approached, the Red Devils parachute display team delivered the match ball from the sky. In all, 6,055 took advantage of the offer. They were rewarded by Asaba's solitary goal, which kept U's in the leading pack.

When Paul Abrahams moved to Griffin Park, it seemed odds on that Asaba would become a United player. At the same time, Wignall was systematically dismantling the squad he had inherited from Burley. In came Paul Gibbs, loanee Martin Williams, Tony McCarthy, Michael Cheetham and Robbie Reinelt. The extent of the changes proved unsettling at a critical time. Three defeats followed. The final four games yielded just two points as United finished a disappointing tenth, seven points short of a play-off berth.

Looking back, Wignall declared, ' I said when I came here that it would take two years to get the team I wanted.' He would not be far wrong.

Match of the Season 1994-95

Wimbledon 1   Colchester 0

FA Cup, 3rd Round, 7 January 1995

United's first ever clash with opponents from the recently formed FA Carling Premiership had been earned in some style. A tricky trip

Did You Know?

Mark Kinsella was the first United player to win Under-21 caps when selected to play for the Republic of Ireland in 1992-93.

to Middlesex to take on Diadora Premier side Yeading was made more difficult by the pouring rain and uneven playing surface. Twice in front, U's had to settle for a 2-2 draw, but they proved irresistible in the replay, crashing in seven goals. The second-round haul to Exeter also courted controversy, when City keeper Andy Woodman was sent off for handball with his side 1-0 up. Relentless United pressure saw Tony English grab a late winner, after Steve Whitton had levelled early in the second period.

George Burley's resignation gave his assistant Dale Roberts the chance, as caretaker, to pit his wits against the Wimbledon 'Crazy Gang'. Homeless Dons, tenants of Crystal Palace at Selhurst Park, occupied a mid-table spot, some twenty points behind Kenny Dalglish's table-topping Blackburn. Every club of Colchester's size had ambitions to 'do a Wimbledon' and climb through the divisions. The Dons, under Joe Kinnear, had developed a resilience that time and again silenced the critics who regularly condemned their so-called long-ball tactics.

Backed by almost half of the near 7,000 crowd, U's were caught cold on nine minutes. Keeper John Cheesewright failed to collect an Alan Kimble cross, and Andy Clarke won the ball in the air to leave Mick Harford with a simple header. The threatened goal avalanche never materialised as U's grew in confidence. Mark Kinsella tested Hans Segers with a blistering 20-yard drive that the keeper tipped over. Steve Whitton unleashed an effort that flashed narrowly wide. Yet for all their possession United could not break down the Dons, nor get enough bodies forward into the box. U's received a standing ovation at the end for a brave performance, whilst Wimbledon faced the wrath of the relieved Kinnear.

Afterwards Kinnear admitted, 'This game was always a potential banana skin and Colchester made it very difficult for us by working their socks off. Their whole team deserves the Man of the Match award.' Indeed, Kinsella and Adam Locke both proved that they could play on a higher stage, and Locke had made lionhearted Vinnie Jones look like a pussycat on more than one occasion.

Wimbledon bowed out to Liverpool in a fifth round replay and finished a creditable ninth in the Premiership.

LEAGUE DIVISION 3	**1995-96**
Endsleigh Division 3	7th (play-offs)
Coca-Cola Cup	1st Round
FA Cup	1st Round
Autowindscreen Shield	Quarter-finals (South)

Midfield maestro Mark Kinsella announced his desire to move on, to further his career and enhance his chances of representing the full Republic of Ireland side. Initially rejecting a new contract, he looked set to join First Division Southend for a fee that would smash U's £150,000 record, paid by Wimbledon for fellow Irishman Paul McGee. Wignall countered the expected loss by recruiting ex-U's favourite Tony Adcock, who had been freed by Luton. Adcock was seen as the lethal striker needed to capitalise on the supply-line provided by Michael Cheetham and assistant-manager Steve Whitton. Kinsella, meanwhile, having played in a friendly for Southend, was subject to dilly-dallying by Shrimpers' boss Ronnie Whelan. This obliged Kinsella to sign a week-to-week contract with U's in order to be eligible for the opening game against Plymouth. Whelan's indecision eventually resulted in Kinsella signing a new 12-month deal to stay at Layer Road. Great news for Wignall and United fans alike.

What did not go down well with Wignall was the clampdown by referees, which threatened to decimate his thin squad through suspensions. United's first eight games witnessed, in total for both sides, three red cards and 22 yellows. Wignall's biggest blow, however, came at Darlington, when Sean Gregan's knee-high chop looked to have ended Whitton's playing career. Diagnosed as cruciate ligament damage, Whitton, like Alan Shearer before him, vowed to prove the experts wrong and play again.

Whitton's misfortune opened the door for Robbie Reinelt, who responded with a double in the 2-0 win over Hereford. Adcock also grabbed a brace in a 2-1 win at Cardiff that took U's to fourth place, three points behind leaders Gillingham. The next game at Fulham drew a paltry Craven Cottage crowd of 2,870.

Four league games without a win, coupled with humiliation in the FA Cup, prompted Wignall to bring in Luton's young centre-half David Greene on loan. Another Republic of Ireland Under-21 international, Greene looked a useful find, slotting in with elegant Tony McCarthy and man-mountain Peter Cawley. The defeat by Mansfield was noteworthy, not least because of its bruising confrontation between U's indomitable back three and Mansfield's huge centre-forward Mark Sale. Sale performed so well that United made a number of bids for him.

Did You Know?

In 1993-94, when United experimented with squad numbering, YTS striker Justin Booty was given shirt No 29 – the highest number to represent the U's.

The aforementioned cup humiliation came at Beazer Homes League Gravesend & Northfleet. U's were shamed both on and off the pitch. Following major disturbances during the home game with Exeter, when U's followers invaded the away end, stole a flag and set fire to it, the cup-tie in Kent was made all-ticket. U's received only 610 of these, a quantity they could have sold three times over. Many fans travelled ticketless, but following outbreaks of trouble – some involving day-tripping Gillingham fans – the local Police advised that entry also be allowed through the turnstiles.

So much for what happened off the field. On it, Wignall branded his side 'moral cowards'. He added: 'They were a disgrace – they bottled it.' This would not be the last time a Wignall team would demonstrate its ineptitude against a minnow. But as one cup run came to an end, another was gathering momentum. U's travelled to Second Division Oxford in the Autowindscreen Shield and won 2-1. They did not need the new FIFA-sanctioned 'Golden Goal' rule as Simon Betts' penalty in normal time took U's through to face Peterborough with a Wembley final now in their sights. Pleasure at the win was dampened when it was leaned that Hal Mason, former programme editor, radio reporter, author and doyen of the press box had passed away.

A landmark case in the European Court of Justices brought by Belgian player Jean-Marc Bosman was set to change the entire face of football economics. The ECJ ruled that players out of contract would now be able to sign for whomever they wished. For small clubs like Colchester, the prospect of loosing the likes of Kinsella, whom they had nurtured, for nothing was a bitter pill. Meanwhile, Wignall signed Peterborough's ex-Ipswich midfielder David Gregory, whilst Sale's broken toe put his arrival on hold. Returning to Layer Road on loan was Brentford's Paul Abrahams.

U's welcomed in the New Year at Torquay with Kinsella scoring after just fifteen seconds. Fifth-placed U's trailed leaders Gillingham by ten points, tucked in behind moneybags Preston and Plymouth with half the season completed. Preparing for the match at Wigan, an unguarded remark by skipper Cawley, which was intended to gee up his side, backfired. Cawley declared it was time for United to rid themselves of the tag of 'southern softies' and battle their way to the top. Cawley added: 'Wigan is one of the dustbins of the world and I never want to play there again.' Cawley's words found their way to Wigan boss John Deehan, who pinned them up in the home dressing room. It was ample motivation for the Latics, who cruised to a 2-0 win. Six further winless games followed for United, making eight in all.

Behind the scenes, U's board were trying to resolve the issue of George Burley's compensation from Ipswich. The matter was set to go to a football tribunal, having been refused time in the civil courts. These were unsettling times for Colchester United. Mark Sale turned down U's persistent advances and Abrahams returned to Brentford. Peterborough's Scott McGleish, who had scored for Posh in U's Autowindscreen exit at London Road, took his place. McGleish scored a number of important goals and celebrated each with a spectacular somersault. U's, now boosted by the surprisingly early return of Whitton, lost just twice in the fourteen matches prior to the penultimate day of the season. That was not enough to claim automatic promotion, but an injury-time winner at Mansfield by full-back Joe Dunne – signed on a short-term contract from Gillingham – pushed open the play-off door.

On the last day, U's had to beat Doncaster and hope that either Hereford or Wigan slipped up. On the stroke of half-time, Layer Road's biggest crowd of the season, 5,083, saw Paul Gibb's cross from inside Rover's half sail into the Doncaster net. United held on to win, and when it was announced that Wigan had lost 1-2 at Northampton, Layer Road erupted in frenzy. Wignall could not constrain his delight, saying: 'Right now I'm so high, I need a pair of diving boots to keep my feet on the ground.' Goalscorer Gibbs joked, 'I'd like to be able to say that I spotted the keeper off his line'. Now only big-spending Neil Warnock's Plymouth stood in the way of a second trip to Wembley.

Match of the Season 1995-96

Plymouth 3 Colchester 1

Division 3, Play-offs, 2nd leg, 15 May 1996

A measure of manager Steve Wignall's relative success could be gauged from the sum available to him for team-building, compared with that for his counterpart at Argyle, Neil Warnock. The Pilgrims had spent over £1m in an effort to escape the soccer basement, whilst Wignall had been restricted to £2,000. Warnock had earlier inflamed United with his remarks that 'little teams like Colchester shouldn't even be on the same pitch as [big city] clubs such as ours.' He was, however, rightly wary of United, who had taken four league points off Argyle this season.

The first-leg all-ticket 6,511 Layer Road crowd was treated to a stunning goal from Mark Kinsella, who received the ball 35-yards out, waltzed past Martin Barlow, and shot into the goal populated by dumbstruck Argyle fans. In the second half, Robbie Reinelt hit a post before Plymouth threw caution to the wind in their search of an away goal. First, Micky Heathcote flashed a header wide; then Chris Billy missed a simple tap-in. The agonising groans of Plymouth fans watching on a huge screen back at Home Park could surely be heard all over Devon and Cornwall. U's held on. They were halfway to Wembley and had kept a clean sheet.

Warnock, like ex-U's boss Roy McDonough, savoured the reputation of a rude tongue. He complained that U's fans had thrown objects at his players, even though the 'missiles' had come from the Layer Road end, where Argyle fans had been housed. Warnock urged Argyle supporters to provide a hostile reception, 'throwing abuse, not missiles' at the visitors.

Inside three minutes Mickey Evans erased United's advantage, capitalising on Chris Leadbitter's knock-on. Shortly before half-time Paul Gibbs conceded a free-kick, and Leadbitter curled in a great free-kick to put Argyle ahead on aggregate. Tony Adcock replaced Robbie Reinelt at the interval and Adam Locke came on for the limping Gus Caesar. The second half saw plenty of needle, especially when Warnock was technically 'sent off' from the dug-out after demanding that U's Tony McCarthy be sent off. Warnock had a point. The United defender had scythed Adrian Littlejohn and deserved to walk, but somehow escaped punishment. Out of the blue, Kinsella uncorked another screamer, which with away goals counting double meant U's now had their noses in front.

Warnock's rantings were now conducted from the Mayflower Terrace behind the dug-outs. With extra-time looming, Barlow escaped down the right and crossed for Paul Williams to clinch a first-ever trip to Wembley for Argyle.

U's skipper Peter Cawley admitted: 'We lost the game in the first three minutes. Some of our lads must go home and ask themselves why they did not compete. In a couple of weeks they will realise how close they were to promotion.' Warnock incensed chairman Gordon Parker both by his antics over the McCarthy incident and his insensitive remark: 'When you reach the play-offs and only bring 100 fans with you, you don't deserve to go to Wembley.' In fact, over 500 United fans had made the 700-mile, fourteen-hour midweek round-trek. Plymouth beat Darlington 2-1 in the Wembley final in front of 43,000. U's fans could be forgiven for thinking that any big city club who could only half-fill Wembley did not deserve to be in the Second Division.

LEAGUE DIVISION 3   **1996-97**
Nationwide Division 3   8th
Coca-Cola Cup   2nd Round
FA Cup   1st Round
Autowindscreen Shield   Losing finalists

After the summer euphoria of the Euro 96, U's boss Steve Wignall prepared his team to go one better this time round. Promotion was one of the few cards he could play in his attempts to keep highly valued Mark Kinsella at Layer Road, and that card had been snatched away. Inevitably, Kinsella would leave. 'Sheedy' deserved the chance to perform on a higher stage, and no Colchester supporter disagreed with that. Kinsella might have gone a year earlier, but had stayed with the U's and inspired their assault on the play-offs. In preparation for his departure, Wignall captured ex-U's Richard Wilkins from Hereford and signed David Greene following the player's successful loan spell in the last campaign. Both cost £30,000, whilst Wignall's former Aldershot team-mate David Barnes arrived on a free.

The new Clock End all-seater stand gave Layer Road a more complete look. The Clock, or Open End, had remained three-quarters derelict ever since U's regained League status in 1992. The £85,000 needed at the time to bring it up to safety standard was not available, and there had been few occasions when that extra capacity was needed. What was needed was a decision from Charlton's Alan Curbishley. The Addicks' boss appeared to have been impressed by Kinsella in two trial games, and with Charlton having earned £3 million from the sale of Lee Bowyer to Leeds, he could certainly afford him.

Kinsella eventually joined Charlton seven games into the season. U's had collected only one win by then, but had advanced in the Coca-Cola Cup in dramatic circumstances. Trailing First Division West Brom 2-3 from the first leg, many U's fans travelled to the Hawthorns just to tick off another ground on the list of those visited. Robbie Reinelt levelled the aggregate scores in the first half, but when injured Canadian keeper Garrett Caldwell failed to appear for the second half, all looked lost. U's had no substitute keeper on the bench. Steve Whitton went in goal, and there was some suggestion that the Baggies' did not recognise him. Either way, they failed to put him under any pressure. Further goals by Reinelt and Joe Dunne saw United through to the second round for the first time since 1983. U's held another First Division side, Huddersfield, to a 1-1 draw in the first leg at the futuristic McAlpine Stadium, but minus Kinsella bowed out in extra-time at Layer Road.

U's league season finally sparked into life in mid-October, from when they lost just twice in fourteen games to the end of the year. Paul Abrahams returned from Brentford for £20,000, and Wignall signed former U's apprentice John Taylor on loan from Luton. Having been released by United, Taylor had drifted into non-league before playing for Cambridge United, Bradford City and Bristol Rovers. He looked an ideally tall, athletic target-man. Four goals, including a brace in the seven-goal mauling of John Beck's Lincoln, appeared to book Taylor's permanent move to Layer Road, only for Cambridge to step in, as U's dallied over contracts, to offer a post as player-coach. U's loss was Cambridge's gain. Following a Boxing Day draw at Brighton's Goldstone Ground, U's trailed runaway leaders Fulham by nineteen points, but were only two points adrift of a play-off place. Wignall set a target of forty points from the remaining 21 games to reach the play-offs, but admitted that the loss of Kinsella was a major handicap. 'Sheedy's' midfield industry, he felt, would have turned some of the thirteen draws thus far into wins.

Victory over Fulham and a draw against second-placed Carlisle showed U's had the appetite for success. Four successive wins in the league were boosted by a welcome run in the Autowindscreen Shield. United advanced to the quarter-finals for the second year running, courtesy of three away wins, but this cup excitement was to savage United's promotion hopes.

As Wembley loomed larger on United's horizons, league form dived. Fifteen months after first being approached, Mark Sale finally signed from Mansfield for £25,000, but neither his introduction nor that of Torquay full-back Scott Stamps could halt a run of six defeats from eight games. U's plummeted from third to thirteenth, following the conclusion of the Easter programme. Sale insisted that he was a target man not a goalscorer, which was not what U's fans wanted to hear. The club had been crying out for a 20-goal a season man since the mid-1980s, during Adcock's first spell.

Suspensions for Tony McCarthy and Paul Buckle, that forced the pair to miss United's visit to Wembley in the Autowindrscreen Shield, served as a late-season motivator for a second Wembley trip. Skipper Cawley led the battle-cry: 'We want to get in the play-offs so that Macca and Bucks can get to play at Wembley.' But three wins and a draw meant that United missed out by just one point, despite the Wembley-inflicted collapse over the Easter period. Wembley was not solely to blame; nine home draws told its own story.

A week is a long time in football. From being oh-so-near Wembley heroes, U's had lost everything. The final nail was driven in by

Northampton in the final home game of the season. Wignall reflected afterward: 'The trouble comes when you give the fans a taste of success. They come to expect it and want more. I think the pressure of that got to the players and they became a little impatient. We tried route-one football to Mark Sale too much, instead of the football we know we can play.'

Many fans felt that this missed the point, which was that fielding a tall striker inevitably converted U's to a long-ball game. Players such as Chris Fry and Adam Locke, who had played a big part in United's earlier successes, found themselves on the fringes.

At the conclusion of an exciting but empty-handed season, Wignall offered final words of defiance: 'I won't be happy until I have guided this club to promotion. All I ask of the fans is trust me with your team.' They did, and Wignall would deliver.

Match of the Season 1996-97

Colchester 3 Peterborough 0

Autowindscreen Shield, 18 March 1997

Often labelled the 'Mickey Mouse' Cup because of its intrusion into the fixture-congested winter and pathetic support at the turnstiles, the Associate Members Cup had been repackaged over the years as sponsors came and went. Some clubs used the competition as a chance to blood youngsters; others saw it as their only realistic chance of reaching Wembley.

United's path to the Southern area final had been arduous, having been drawn away for the first three rounds. At Millwall, U's secured their first ever 'Golden Goal' win when Paul Buckle scored in the third minute of extra-time.

Barry Fry's struggling Second Division Peterborough barred U's path to a second trip to Wembley. Posh's two first-leg goals threatened to derail Colchester's hopes. Dazzling winger Ricky Otto beat Emberson with a low drive and Ken Charlery crashed an unstoppable shot into the roof of the net.

U's produced a storming display in the second leg to take the tie into extra-time. Andy Edwards failed to clear a David Gregory free-kick, leaving Chris Fry to halve the deficit. When Posh's Charlery was sent off for a needless second booking, U's scented blood and

Paul Buckle levelled the aggregate scores with a rasping drive. It was left to sub Paul Abrahams to clinch a Wembley spot with a truly golden 'Golden Goal'.

In view of United's last visit to the Twin towers, the merchandising bandwagon rolled into action. A CD of the U's theme song 'Up the U's' was made by local punk band Special Duties. Over 20,000 Colchester folk once again trod the path up Wembley Way to see their heroes take on Carlisle. Particularly galling was the fact that Buckle and McCarthy were suspended, whilst Carlisle used video evidence to ensure that the influential Warren Aspinall had a booking, and thus a suspension, rescinded.

The match was a tense affair with few chances and after 120 minutes the scoreline was still blank. A penalty shoot-out ensued. Carlisle's Owen Archdeacon and United's Peter Cawley both failed from the spot, as did U's Karl Duguid. The Cumbrian team's skipper, Steve Hayward, had only to convert his kick to lift the Shield. He obliged on both counts. Young Duguid was inconsolable, but hoped via the play-offs to have the chance to enjoy Wembley a second time. It did not happen.

LEAGUE DIVISION 3   **1997-98**
Nationwide Division 3   4th (play-offs, promoted)
Coca-Cola Cup   1st Round
FA Cup   2nd Round
Autowindscreen Shield   1st Round

A £55,000 shirt sponsorship deal followed on the heels of a three-year £100,000 kit deal with kit manufacturers Patrick. Uniquely, U's would bear the name of Guardian Direct on their home kit and Ashby's when on their travels. Manager Wignall, after coming close the previous season, demanded funds for squad strengthening. Paul Gibbs, Adam Locke, Chris Fry and Tony McCarthy had all left during the summer. Even though Fry had been voted supporters' Player of the Year, he did not figure in Wignall's plans. McCarthy, still smarting from the suspension that cost him his Wembley place, returned to Ireland to continue his studies and play part-time for Shelbourne.

More money rolled into Layer Road with the belated settlement of the George Burley saga. Ipswich Town had been ordered to pay £135,000 plus interest, and almost £100,000 in costs, two and a half years after Burley had walked out on United. Scorned once, chairman Parker refused managerless Brentford permission to speak to Wignall without a £300,000 compensation package being agreed beforehand. That figure was sufficient to make the Bees' buzz off, though Wignall was angered that he had not at least been able to speak to his former club. Normally mild-mannered, Wignall seethed even more following U's defeat at Hartlepool. This particular fixture had developed into something of a grudge, provoked by dismissals for Locke and McCarthy in recent meetings. 'Teams like Hartlepool shouldn't be above us in the table,' insisted Wignall. But above them they were, as U's close-season optimism waned. They were dumped out of the Coca-Cola Cup by Luton, and a 1-4 thrashing at Cambridge left them languishing in seventeenth place.

Centre-half David Greene proved himself an unlikely goalscoring spearhead in U's revival: his four goals in five games helped secure ten points. Arsenal youngster Isaiah Rankin arrived on loan and roasted ten Third Division defences with his pace and eye for goal. Wignall tried unsuccessfully to secure his loan services for the entire season. On Rankin's return to Highbury he made a brief substitute appearance in the North London derby with Spurs before eventually joining Bradford City for £1.3 million, which was a little out of United's price range. U's inability to hold onto a lead started to cost them dear, but despite only two wins in eight games leading up to Christmas, which included an FA Cup exit at the hands of Vauxhall

Conference side Hereford, U's were still only seven points off the play-off positions.

Notwithstanding the fact that they reached the previous year's final, United were not too aggrieved when Leyton Orient knocked them out of the Autowindscreen Shield. They could now, as they say, concentrate on the league. A bizarre Boxing Day match at Gillingham against tenants Brighton finished 4-4. U's led 3-0 at the break, only to be pegged back by Paul Emblem's hat-trick. Scott Stamps netted a fourth for United, only for Peter Cawley to concede a penalty four minutes from time.

U's failure to stamp themselves on the division prompted the first murmurings of discontent against Wignall, who assured fans he was no quitter and set about signing a new striker. The New Year heralded the arrival of Neil Gregory on loan from Ipswich, a player whom Wignall had pursued for two years. Brother of U's midfielder David, Neil looked a class act, scoring two gems at Darlington, only for United to suffer a late collapse and lose 2-4.

Wignall acknowledged U's frailties by signing young Leicester defender Guy Branston. The 19-year-old belied his tender years to block up the previously sieve-like defence. It was no coincidence that in his first five games Branston's ox-like strength inspired U's to four wins and a draw, without the loss of a goal. Wignall had successfully plugged United's weak spot and from then on they never looked back. A clear indication of their promotion credentials came at Meadow Lane in late March. All-conquering Notts County were set to clinch the title with eight games still remaining. United's 0-0 draw, allied with their earlier 2-0 win at Layer Road, made them the only side to prevent champions-elect Notts from scoring against them.

Neil Gregory finally signed for a club record £50,000. U's fans had questioned the board's ambition when its initial offer of £10,000 was peremptorily rejected. The gulf between the haves and the have-nots of English football was widening, as evidenced when Leicester City quoted £500,000 for Branston's services.

On the pitch the team was gelling nicely; off it, the club and the council jointly commissioned a feasibility report into a new stadium. The designers and builders of Huddersfield Town's McAlpine Stadium were invited to consider every aspect of the matter. It appeared that club and the council were now in harmony over the question of a new home for Colchester United. U's lease on Layer Road would expire in 2002, and no one could lose sight of the fact that the existing ground occupied prime housing land.

Four wins on the trot carried United into fourth place with three games left. Each of those games left an indelible memory. Chester

---

Did You Know?

United's record reserve-team win is 19-0 over St Albans in 1994 in the Capital League. United's youth team also won 19-0 against Whatfield in 1948.

---

centre-half Spencer Whelan scored with an enormous punt from the halfway line, whereupon United fell apart and lost 1-3. The penultimate game was soured by the fact that play-off rivals Leyton Orient had had three points deducted for fielding suspended players, and rightly or wrongly they blamed Colchester United for whipping up the campaign that led to that outcome. Orient sought to rectify the injustice on the pitch, though the 1-1 outcome was enough to guarantee U's a play-off place – at the very least. The last game was just that for Doncaster Rovers, who had already finished miles adrift and were bound for the Vauxhall Conference. A mock funeral preceded the kick-off, and orchestrated pitch invasions thereafter threatened to disrupt United's quest for the win that might just secure the third automatic promotion spot. Neil Gregory's winning goal for United was not enough, as Lincoln beat Brighton 2-1.

A two-legged play-off semi-final with Barnet beckoned. Greg Heald's goal gave Barnet the advantage at Underhill, but the loss of ace striker Shaun Devine, who along with Branston was sent off, proved a major handicap for the Bees. Branston's loan was up, and as it could not be extended he would in any case have missed the second leg. Barnet sorely missed Devine in the return leg, and David Gregory levelled the aggregate scores as early as the twelfth minute. Warren Goodhind grabbed a crucial away goal just before the break, but the game turned on the hour when Barnet's Lee Howarth was sent off. Five minutes later Greene put United in front and in extra-time Gregory lashed in his second to send U's and their magnificently raucous fans back to what was fast becoming their second home – Wembley.

Match of the Season 1997-98

Colchester 1 Torquay 0

Division 3, Play-offs, final, 22 May 1998

The Football Association slashed the potential attendance for the play-off final by staging a meaningless friendly between England and Saudi Arabia on the scheduled Saturday. The switch to Friday night caused problems for the travelling fans of both clubs – Torquay, because of the distance involved and the need for a full day off work; and Colchester, because coaches were booked else-where for their usual school runs. As a result, the 19,486 crowd was the lowest ever recorded for a Wembley play-off final.

Both teams were making their third visit to Wembley. Torquay had lost to Bolton Wanderers in the 1989 Sherpa Van final, but beaten Blackpool on penalties in the 1991 Third Division play-off final. Such was U's familiarity with the national stadium that when one young fan, studying the stadium seating on the back of her ticket, asked her father where they were going to sit, the answer came quickly: 'where we usually sit!'

The pre-match entertainment included a smoky pyrotechnic display and the sound of Robbie Williams' hit song 'Let Me Enter-tain You'. Elevation to the Second Division would greet the winners of this match with a chance to pit their wits against the likes of Manchester City, Stoke and Al-Fayed's money-no-object Fulham. In United's first real attack, Steve Forbes flicked the ball onto the trailing hand of Jon Gittens and referee Mick Fletcher gave a conten-tious penalty which David Gregory converted off the inside of a post. It was Gregory's tenth penalty of the season and third goal in the play-offs, though, sadly for Gregory, play-off goals and appear-ances do not count in Football League records.

Torquay's frustration resulted in a succession of yellow cards, and after half-time U's were denied a second penalty when former Layer Road favourite Paul Gibbs hauled down Neil Gregory. Torquay pressed forward, Gibbs saw a long-range shot fly over, and Carl Emberson turned Andy Gurney's drive around the post. That was Torquay's swansong. The final whistle blew; skipper Richard Wilkins climbed the 39 steps; hoisted the silver and gold trophy and United basked in the glory of regaining the status they had lost eighteen years previously.

Tearful Torquay players remained dumbstruck on the turf. There was no prize for the losers, not even a medal, and worse still they had only needed a draw on the last day at Leyton Orient to have had secured automatic promotion.

LEAGUE DIVISION 2   **1998-99**
Nationwide Division 2   18th
Worthington Cup   1st Round
FA Cup   1st Round
Autowindscreen Shield   1st Round

United's pre-season was soured when play-off Man-of-the-Match Carl Emberson said he wanted away. But when no bigger club came in for him, the goalkeeper agreed to sign a twelve-month contract. Wignall tried to re-capture Leicester's Guy Branston by the same means in which he had pursued Arsenal's Isaiah Rankin the previous season. Football League clubs were allowed to take Premiership youngsters on loan for a whole season, but neither Arsenal nor Leicester were prepared to go along with the idea. Ipswich's experienced Welsh International Geraint Williams joined United, as did young Dutchman Arafath Heuval. U's line-up would become increasingly cosmopolitan as the season wore on, but Heuval spent his entire time nursing injuries. Two play-off trophies were paraded in U's pre-season friendly with Charlton. The Addicks, skippered by ex-U's Mark Kinsella, had won their play-off final – thanks to a penalty shoot-out – to reach the Premiership.

Wignall set himself three targets for the coming season: a top six spot, to pit his wits against the host of big-name managers, and to keep U's and their supporters flushed with success. The pundits, however, predicted a quick return to the basement for United. Manchester City, Stoke and Fulham were, unsurprisingly, the bookies' favourites for promotion. U's mettle would be tested as the latter pair visited Layer Road in the first weeks of the season and both gained 1-0 wins. Kevin Keegan, the Fulham boss, admitted afterwards 'Colchester deserved something out of the game; we were fortunate to get all the points.' Stoke boss Brian Little also praised United, saying, 'Colchester ran us ragged in the second half.'

Reading's Madejski Stadium was anything but ragged. United gained a 1-1 draw in the £37 million 25,000-seater arena, whose futuristic wonders revived thoughts of U's own pressing need for a new home. The preferred site was revealed as Cuckoo Farm, adjacent to the A12, and which happened to be council-owned. The success of the scheme hinged, first, on the provision of a new access road to connect with the A12 and, second, on obtaining the necessary private finance.

The timing of United's 'Quid-a-kid' entrance price for the visit of Burnley coincided with the beginning of Steve Wignall's problems. The rain-soaked 0-4 defeat failed to impress the 5,500 crowd. Many of the players appeared unmotivated, and the euphoria of Wembley had been quickly replaced by the sober realisation that U's were the paupers in a division of comparatively wealthy clubs. Defeat at Manchester City left United hovering just above the relegation line. Fortunately, they kept their noses above that line throughout the season.

The straw that broke the camel's back came at the unlikely outpost of Bedlington, twelve miles north of Newcastle. It was the first time that the early rounds of the FA Cup had not been regionalised into north and south. The Northern League side showed scant respect for U's seasoned professionals and romped to a 4-1 FA Cup knockout. The result was the most humiliating in U's history, eclipsing the 0-8 defeat at Leyton Orient and any previous cup defeats by non-league clubs. Wignall admitted, 'This defeat will scar me for a long time – I hope it will for my players too'. It did: they only won one of the next nine league games and crashed out of the Autowindscreen Shield at home to Gillingham by another humiliating 1-5 scoreline.

Despite mounting criticism on the terraces and in the local press, there seemed no immediate threat to Wignall's position. The U's boss was having a torrid time in the transfer market as a string of would-be signings shunned Layer Road. In desperation he unveiled the jewel in the crown of United's Youth policy. Lomana Tresor Lua Lua, a French-Zairean, became a scoring substitute in the 1-3 defeat at Chesterfield. Seven days later, following yet another home battering, 1-3 by Wrexham, Wignall threw in the towel. He had been undoubtedly the most successful manager in United's history, and he confessed, 'I cannot take this squad any further.' Frustrated by the wage demands of players and in particular their agents who he felt were undermining the transfer market, he was probably right.

If the views of the players counted for anything, Steve Whitton would have been offered the job, but Second Division status had been long in coming and now was no time to gamble with the inexperienced. Whitton took caretaker charge for two games, helped by backroom staff Micky Cook and Paul Dyer, but United already knew who they wanted. Scarborough boss and former Carlisle manager Mick Wadsworth became U's 21st manager. Wadsworth had a good track record with both his former clubs, winning the Third Division championship at Carlisle, coupled with a Wembley appearance in the Autowindscreen final, and taking Scarborough to the play-off semi-finals the previous season, where they fell to Torquay. Wadsworth had also been part of Bobby Robson's 1990 World Cup backroom team.

Did You Know?

Up to 1998-99, United have never faced Chelsea, Leicester, Liverpool, Sunderland, Tottenham or West Ham in a first-team fixture.

Two quick wins pinpointed those positions which Wadsworth felt needed strengthening. The new manager signed Frenchman Stephane Pounewatchy and midfield terrier Warren Aspinall, both of whom had played under him at Brunton Park. Wadsworth was not finished there. In came Charlton striker Bradley Allen and another Frenchman in Fabrice Richard. U's fans had never seen such an influx, but still Wadsworth had a major coup up his sleeve. United's most colourful signing was unveiled during the return match with Manchester City, which had been chosen by Sky television to be only the second £7.95 pay-per-view football match ever broadcast, following the Oxford versus Sunderland clash some weeks earlier.

Wadsworth had augmented U's foreign legion by the signing of a Brazilian. Jose Antunes Fumaca, from Italian Serie C club Catuense, had been trying to fix up a loan spell with an English club. Wadsworth spotted him playing for Grimsby reserves. Fumaca was destined to play just fourteen minutes against Manchester City, as he sustained a serious head injury in a sickening clash with City's Andy Morrison. Fumaca then joined Barnsley, where he spent the rest of the season wallowing in the Tykes' reserves. Of all the players to pull on a U's shirt, Fumaca had excited as much as any, with a short–lived display of Brazilian flair and nonchalance.

Much work still had to be done to consolidate United's status, but Wadsworth's tactical acumen guided United through to safety. A 3-3 draw at relegation rivals Northampton and a 2-1 win over play-off chasing Bournemouth saw U's finish eighteenth, despite losing their final two games. Wadsworth started preparing for the new season early, axing nine players from his squad before the final game at Blackpool.

Match of the Season 1998-99

Manchester City 2 Colchester 1

Division 2, 31 October 1998

When the final whistle had blown at Wembley in the play-off final, this was *the* fixture that made U's fans drool in anticipation. In just three seasons Manchester City had fallen from the Premiership to the nether regions of the Second Division. As recently as 1992 City

Skipper Tony English waves farewell to the Football League at Cambridge (April 1990)

Artists impression of the proposed Stadium Park development (January 1991)

Jimmy King (Wivenhoe) fails to prevent Gary Bennett's cross (February 1991)

Keeper Scott Barrett will bear any burden after scoring at Wycombe (January 1992)

Dick Graham celebrates the 21st anniversary of U's famous Cup win over Leeds

Programme of FA Trophy final v Witton Albion (May 1992)

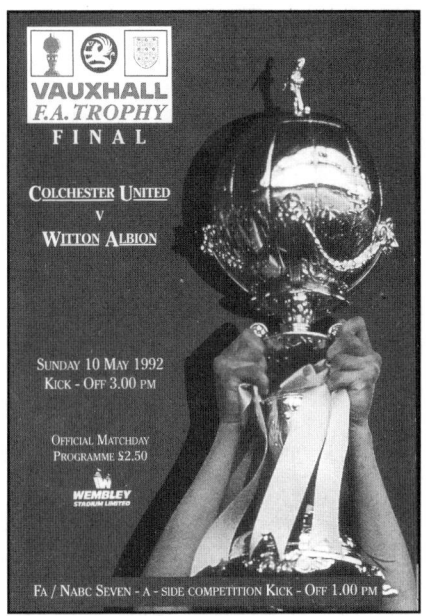

Coach Phillips, player-manager McDonough, and Gary Bennett with GMVC trophy

Mark Kinsella with the GMVC trophy and FA Trophy (August 1992)

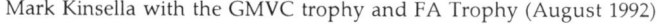

Paul Abrahams' diving headed goal against Scunthorpe (May 1993)

Gary Bennett shoots, despite this tackle by a Northampton defender (September 1993)

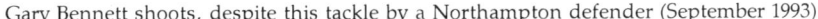

Stand-in keeper McDonough can't keep out Pike's penalty for Hereford (October 1993)

Mark Kinsella fires this thunderbolt at Wimbledon in the FA Cup (January 1995)

Loanee striker Carl Asaba wins this aerial duel against Scarborough (March 1995)

The Red Devils Parachute team entertain before kick-off v Darlington (March 1995)

Tony McCarthy tugs Mansfield's Mark Sale, who later joined U's (November 1995)

U's celebrate reaching the play-offs following their win over Doncaster (May 1996)

Dennis, Locke and McGleish acknowledge the crowd after reaching the play-offs

Scott McGleish gets stuck in at Plymouth, as U's lose the play-off (May 1996)

Adam Locke in action v Northampton, who ended U's play-off hopes (April 1997)

Programme for Autowindscreen Shield final v Carlisle (April 1997)

David Gregory celebrates levelling in the play-offs against Barnet (May 1998)

Programme for Division Three play-off final at Wembley v Torquay (May 1998)

D Gregory fends off Torquay's Steve McCall in the Wembley play-off final (May 1998)

Manager Steve Wignall hoists the play-off trophy outside the Town Hall (July 1998)

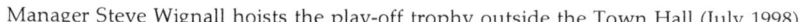

had finished fifth in the top division, at a time when U's were languishing in the Vauxhall Conference. Although both clubs were competing on the same playing field, City and United were in other respects light years apart. Steeped in history, City boasted 27,000 average gates and a worldwide loyal fan-base, whereas U's could count on a hardcore of perhaps 3,500 fans.

In the week preceding the fixture with United at Maine Road, City brought in loanees Andy Morrison from Huddersfield and Michael Branch from Everton. The two played a pivotal role on their City debuts.

With 1,600 fans making the journey from Essex, U's were not without support in the vast arena. United's best chance of the opening half came in the tenth minute, when Tony Lock's header spun away from goal. U's left the field at the interval to a standing ovation from their fans, whereas City were roundly booed, and not for the first time that season. The expectant, and increasingly impatient loyal fans had witnessed too many of these performances. City boss Joe Royle obviously fired his team for the second period, and it was a little piece of Premiership kidology that led to City's opener. Branch fell as if pole-axed by the slightest of nudges from David Greene, and referee Mr Pike gave a penalty, scored by Northern Ireland international Kevin Horlock. Three minutes later, with U's still fuming, City stretched their lead. Carl Emberson tipped Shaun Goater's header over the bar but, from the resulting Horlock corner, Morrison powered a header into the net. City seemed set to steamroller U's, but they had not reckoned with Jason Dozzell's first goal for United. U's then pushed forward in search of the equaliser, and Greene, Scott Stamps and Mark Sale all came close. This left U's exposed at the back, but Emberson stood firm, making five significant saves.

Relieved City boss Royle said afterwards: 'We improved after the first half, but in true City style almost threw it away.' Proud U's boss Steve Wignall concluded: 'They knew it wasn't a penalty, but my players showed great character. No one could have complained if we had nicked a point.'

Manchester City picked themselves up in the second half of the season and reached the Wembley play-off final, where they got the better of Gillingham on penalties, having scored twice in injury-time to invoke the extra thirty minutes.

Postscript: Mick Wadsworth's reign proved to be short-lived as just two weeks into the 1999-2000 season he quit, blaming the burden of travelling from his Yorkshire home. On the eve of the season managing director Steve Gage had also resigned, and U's fans could be forgiven for thinking that there was perhaps more to this double departure than met the eye. Wadsworth had engineered a massive clear-out of players before the end of the season and brought in a number of potentially exciting prospects to form an inexperienced but better-paid smaller squad. Steve Whitton, U's assistant manager and supposed preferred candidate ahead of Wadsworth when Steve Wignall resigned, was charged with leading United into the new millennium with little or nothing to spend.

A fair wind and tide should shortly see United cosseted in a new stadium, a fitting springboard for future prosperity and success. U's die-hard fans deserve it.

GUIDE TO SEASONAL SUMMARIES

Col 1:   Match number (for league fixtures); Round (for cup-ties).
   e.g. 2:1 means 'Second round; first leg.'
   e.g. 4R means 'Fourth round replay.'

Col 2:   Date of the fixture and whether Home (H), Away (A), or Neutral (N).

Col 3:   Opposition.

Col 4:   Attendances. Home gates appear in roman; Away gates in *italics*.
   Figures in **bold** indicate the largest and smallest gates, at home and away.
   Average home and away attendances appear after the final league match.

Col 5:   Respective league positions of Colchester and their opponents after the match.
   Colchester's position appears on the top line in roman.
   Their opponents' position appears on the second line in *italics*.
   For cup-ties, the division and position of opponents is provided.
    e.g. 2:12 means the opposition are twelfth in Division 2.

Col 6:   The top line shows the result: W(in), D(raw), or L(ose).
   The second line shows Colchester's cumulative points total.

Col 7:   The match score, Colchester's given first.
   Scores in **bold** indicate Colchester's biggest league win and heaviest defeat.

Col 8:   The half-time score, Colchester's given first.

Col 9:   The top lines shows Colchester's scorers and times of goals in roman.
   The second line shows opponents' scorers and times of goals in *italics*.
   A 'p' after the time of a goal denotes a penalty; 'og' an own-goal.
   The third line gives the name of the match referee.

Team line-ups: Colchester line-ups appear on the top line, irrespective of whether
   they are home or away. Opposition teams appear on the second line in *italics*.
   Players of either side who are sent off are marked !
   Colchester players making their league debuts are displayed in **bold**.

Substitutes: Names of substitutes appear only if they actually took the field.
   A player substituted is marked *
   A second player substituted is marked ˆ
   A third player substituted is marked "
   These marks do not necessarily indicate the sequence of substitutions.

N.B.   For clarity, all information appearing in *italics* relates to opposing teams.

LEAGUE DIVISION 4 — Manager: Dick Graham — SEASON 1968-69

Results summary

No	Date	V	Opponent	Att	Pos	Pt	Res	F–A	H–T
1	10/8	A	Brentford	7,580	—	0	L	0–4	0–1
2	17/8	H	Rochdale	3,969	23 / 7	—	D	0–0	0–0
3	24/8	A	Chester	5,813	23 / 4	—	L	1–5	1–2
4	26/8	H	Scunthorpe	3,771	16 / 24	—	L	0–4	0–1
5	31/8	H	Doncaster	3,199	24 / 8	—	L	1–2	0–0
6	7/9	H	York	3,756	22 / 17	3	W	1–0	0–0
7	14/9	A	Bradford C	6,879	23 / 21	4	D	1–1	1–0
8	16/9	A	Chesterfield	4,693	22 / 20	6	W	2–0	1–0
9	20/9	H	Port Vale	6,441	15 / 23	8	W	1–0	1–0
10	28/9	A	Exeter	5,146	14 / 18	9	D	1–1	1–1
11	4/10	H	Grimsby	7,543	13 / 21	11	W	2–1	1–1

Match details

1. BRENTFORD (A) — 10/8
Scorers/Times: [Ross 81] — Deakin 3, Moughton 60 (og), Terry 73. Ref: H New
United: Adams, Honeywood, Moughton, Forbes, Hall, Simpson, Trevis, Oliver, Joslyn, Martin*, Price, 12 Mansfield
Brentford: Phillips, Jones, Hunt, Higginson, Gelson, Nelmes, Dobson, Deakin, Terry, Ross, Mansley
Graham, 48, takes over from Neil Franklin after relegation last season. A season ticket in the standing area will cost £5. The match kicks off at 7.15 pm to avoid clashing with QPR v Leicester. Moughton own-goals in attempting to clear Ross's effort which rebounds off the woodwork.

2. ROCHDALE (H) — 17/8
Ref: T Reynolds
United: Adams, Moughton, Hall, Joslyn, Forbes, Honeywood, Price, Oliver, Oliver, Mansfield*, Martin, 12 Simpson
Rochdale: Harker, Radcliffe, Ryder, Leech, Parry, Ashworth, Whitehead*, Melledew, Jenkins, Jenkins, Butler, Fletcher
Poor finishing leads to stalemate. U's are looking for the right blend. Ryder's shot on 22 minutes is deflected into the path of Butler, whose shot rebounds off the post into Adams' arms. Jenkins has a 40th-minute goal ruled out from an indirect free-kick as the ref hadn't blown his whistle.

3. CHESTER (A) — 24/8
Scorers: Simpson 23 [Sutton 72] — Jones L 6, 34, Dearden 50, Talbot 62. Ref: C Thomas
United: Adams, Mochan*, Hall, Joslyn, Forbes, Honeywood, Light, Moughton, Oliver, Simpson, Dyson, 12 Perryman
Chester: Carling, Jones R, Sear, Ashworth, Turner, Brodie, Dearden, Metcalfe, Talbot, Sutton, Jones L
Jones robs Hall to open for Chester. United level against the run of play, when Simpson takes on Light's through ball. Dearden strikes a daisy-cutter. At 1-3, Oliver hits the post, only for Talbot to net a loose ball and then find Sutton unmarked. Light is booked for a foul on Brodie (72).

4. SCUNTHORPE (H) — 26/8
Scorers: Kerr 24, 68, Heath 63, Deere 88. Ref: B Homewood
United: Buck A, Perryman, Hall, Moughton*, Forbes, Trevis, Price, Light, Mansfield, Simpson, Barlow, 12 Dyson
Scunthorpe: Barnard, Hemstead, Barker, Lindsey, Holt, Welbourne, Colquhoun, Kerr, Deere, Heath, Punton
Graham circulates the names of five players. Moughton is released after a two-month trial. U's new striped kit is on show for the first time. Light's shot goes through Barnard's hands, but Derek Hemstead clears off the line. United have an abysmal goal record of one for, 13 against.

5. DONCASTER (H) — 31/8
Scorers: Simpson 90p [Webber 52, Johnson 90] Ref: K Markham
United: Adams, Forbes, Simpson, Joslyn, Wood, Honeywood*, Martin, Hall, Trevis, Light, Dyson, 12 Oliver
Doncaster: Ogston, Wilcockson, Clish, Gray, Robertson, Flowers, Rabjohn, Jeffrey, Webber, Johnson, Usher
Wood loans from Orient. Wilcockson handles Dyson's shot (34), but Ogston saves Light's penalty. Minutes later Dyson has a goal ruled out for offside. Webber flicks Usher's free-kick wide of Adams. Johnson lashes home a late loose ball. In injury-time Robertson trips Brian Hall.

6. YORK (H) — 7/9
Scorers: Light 68 Ref: M Sinclair
United: Macedo, Mochan, Hall, Trevis, Joslyn, Wood, Oliver, Forbes, Light, Simpson, Price, 12 Honeywood
York: Widdowson, Baker, Kelly, Carr, Jackson, Coleman, Boyer, Shepherd, MacDougall, Spratt, Hodgson
Gibbs (£6k Gills) awaits FL clearance, but Macedo (Fulham) joins on loan. Carr's foul on Light earns a booking. Forbes flicks on Oliver's corner, for Light to nod past Widdowson. Hall grazes the bar (28). Phil Boyer cracks the angle of bar and post (76). U's first win in 20 games.

7. BRADFORD C (A) — 14/9
Scorers: Light 32 [Bannister 66] Ref: V Batty
United: Macedo, Mochan, Hall*, Trevis, Joslyn, Wood, Simpson, Oliver, Light, Gibbs, Dyson, 12 Honeywood
Bradford C: Roberts, Bayliss, Cooper, Stowell, Hallett, Middleton*, Hall, Ham, Leighton, Rackstraw, Waker, Bannister
Forbes joins Norwich (£10k), and Wood signs (£3k). Dyson and Gibbs both have shots blocked before the linesman confirms Light's effort is in. Gibbs outpaces two defenders (47), but hits the post. Bannister heads City level after Hall departs (65), injured. Light hits the bar late on.

8. CHESTERFIELD (A) — 16/9
Scorers: Gibbs 11, Trevis 58 Ref: V James
United: Macedo, Mochan, Hall, Trevis, Joslyn, Wood, Simpson, Oliver, Trevis, Gibbs, Dyson*, 12 Honeywood
Chesterfield: Humphreys, Holmes, Lumsden, Kettleborough, Phelan, Hughes, Warnock, Randall, Webber, Moore, Martin*, Pugh
U's best performance since the cup-tie with WBA, eight months ago. Gibbs turns smartly on the greasy surface to slip under Alan Humphreys. Kevin Randall rattles the bar, and Macedo saves one-handed from Mick Hughes. Trevis nets, in acres of space, to continue United's revival.

9. PORT VALE (H) — 20/9
Scorers: Joslyn 39 Ref: G Hill
United: Macedo, Mochan, Hall, Trevis, Joslyn, Wood, Simpson, Forbes, Light, Simpson, Price, 12 Dyson
Port Vale: Hickson, Boulton, Wilson, James*, Sproson, King, Mahon, Cullerton, Chapman, Gough, Williams, Asprey
The Friday kick-off adds 2,500 at the gate. Joslyn's stunning goal, his first for U's, is a 35-yarder that beats Hickson for pace, from Simpson's pass. Hall hacks Cullerton's shot off the line (76), and Mick Mahon and Bobby Gough, booked for kicking Light, come close for Vale late on.

10. EXETER (A) — 28/9
Scorers: Gibbs 2 [Banks 40] Ref: T Reynolds
United: Macedo, Mochan, Hall, Joslyn, Bickles, Wood, Simpson, Light, Gibbs, Oliver, Dyson, 12 Curtis
Exeter: Shearing, Smyth, Blain, Kirkham*, Harvey, Newman, Corr, Banks, Bullock, Mitten, Pleat, Curtis
The players choose Wood to take over the captaincy when Trevis joins Walsall (£11k). West Ham's Bickles signs (free). Gibbs gets a head to Simpson's early cross, but Banks' diving header from David Pleat's cross earns the Grecians a point. Ex-U's Peter Bullock turns out for City.

11. GRIMSBY (H) — 4/10
Scorers: Gibbs 8, 77 [Housley 29] Ref: K Walker
United: Macedo, Mochan, Hall, Joslyn, Bickles, Wood, Simpson, Oliver, Light, Gibbs, Dyson, 12 Dyson
Grimsby: Macey, Worthington, Duncliffe, Ross, Rathbone, Jobling, Housley, Hickman, Moore, Boylen, Davidson
Dyson signs (free), after two months trial. Hall swings a free-kick to unmarked Gibbs. Stuart Housley levels from Mariners' first attack, via a corner. Gibbs seals the win, heading in Bickles' free-kick. Worthington (42), Ross (44) and Rathbone (83) (Town), and Oliver (78) and Rathbone are booked.

League Match Records (Matches 12–23)

#	Date	V	Opponent	Att			Res	Pts	Score	HT	Our scorers	Opp scorers	Referee
12	8/10	A	SCUNTHORPE	2,748	12	20	W	13	3-2	0-1	Gibbs 46, 64, Bickles 83	Kerr 22, Heath 86p	G Kew
13	12/10	A	NEWPORT	3,262	15	13	L	13	0-1	0-0	—	McClelland 56	D Counsel
14	19/10	H	DARLINGTON	6,323	14	1	D	14	0-0	0-0	—	—	R Challis
15	26/10	A	LINCOLN	6,833	13	8	W	16	3-0	2-0	Peden 36 (og), Hall 44, Oliver 65	—	H Williams
16	2/11	H	WREXHAM	5,806	10	15	W	18	2-1	0-0	Price 68, Oliver 90	Smith 73	R Paine
17	4/11	H	WORKINGTON	6,702	6	8	W	20	3-0	1-0	Light 36, Oliver 57, Price 71	—	E Wallace
18	9/11	A	BRADFORD PA	2,011	9	24	L	20	1-2	1-1	Oliver 5	Brannan 39, Gould 67	N Graham
19	23/11	A	SWANSEA	5,080	12	10	L	20	0-2	0-0	—	Gwyther 72, Hall 85 (og)	D Smith
20	29/11	H	SOUTHEND	10,604	11	9	W	22	4-0	1-0	Oliver 12, Simpson 56, Gibbs 87, [Dyson 90p]	—	R Barker
21	14/12	H	NEWPORT	3,532	9	17	W	24	2-1	1-1	Light 23, Wood 80	Deacy 27	J Yates
22	26/12	A	GRIMSBY	5,559	9	21	W	26	4-2	1-1	Oliver 31, Bickles 63, Light 71, 81	Oates 20, Hickman 80	H Davey
23	11/1	A	WREXHAM	7,471	6	14	W	28	3-0	2-0	Gibbs 20, Light 29, 88	—	R Matthewson

Line-ups (our players, top; opponents, below)

12. SCUNTHORPE (A) — Macedo, Mochan, Hall, Joslyn, Bickles, Wood, Simpson, Oliver, Light, Gibbs, Dyson
Barnard, Hemstead, Foxton, Davidson, Holt, Welbourne, Wilson, Heath, Deere, Kerr, Punton

O'Rourke trials from Ipswich. Scribes covering U's games complain that overhanging trees obscure a floodlight, casting a shadow. Barnards' kick hits Gibbs' back and flies in. Bickles grabs the winner, via Foxton's header onto his own bar, after conceding a dubious penalty to Heath.

13. NEWPORT (A) — Macedo, Mochan, Hall, Joslyn, Bickles, Wood, Simpson, Oliver, Light, Gibbs, Dyson
Weare, Williams, McLoughlin, Jones, Wood, Rowland, Robinson, Hill, Buck, Wookey, McClelland / Cooper*

Oliver is fouled by Mike McLoughlin (6), but blasts wide. Wood heads David Williams' first-half header off the line, via the underside of the bar. Williams provides the free-kick from which John McClelland scores past the unsighted Macedo, ending the seven-match unbeaten run.

14. DARLINGTON (H) — Macedo, Mochan, Hall, Joslyn, Bickles, Wood, Simpson, Oliver, Light, Gibbs, Dyson
Moor, Peverell, Keeble, Sproates, Abelson, Atkinson, Gauden, Felton, Robson, Hale, Morton

Quakers are the only unbeaten side left in the country. Their rugged defence and cool keeper Moor keep United at bay. Play is stopped, for the fourth time in seven home games, owing to coins being thrown at visiting players from the Layer Road End. Gauden hits the bar in injury-time.

15. LINCOLN (A) — Macedo, Mochan, Hall, Joslyn, Bickles, Wood, Simpson, Oliver, Light, Gibbs, Brown
Kennedy, Taylor, Peden, Smith J, Harford, Grummett, Hughes, Kearns, Corner, Lewis, Smith D

Willis (Charlton £2k), and Brown (Luton) sign. Gibbs shoulder-charges Kennedy over the line (23), but the goal is disallowed. George Peden deflects Simpson's shot into his own net, and Hall strikes twice from an acute angle before the break. Oliver nets the third, outpacing Ray Harford.

16. WREXHAM (H) — Macedo, Mochan, Hall, Price, Bickles, Wood, Brown, Oliver, Light, Gibbs*, Dyson
Livsey, Ingle, Bermingham, Davis, May, Bradbury, Beanland, Moir, Smith, Purdie, Kinsey

Macedo completes a £6k move, whilst Mansfield joins Brentwood. Gibbs is taken to hospital after a sickening clash with Eddie May (4), for an op to straighten his cheekbone. Livsey tips Hall's effort onto the bar, for Price to net the rebound. Simpson's winner comes in the 93rd minute.

17. WORKINGTON (H) — Macedo, Mochan, Hall, Price, Bickles, Honeywood, Brown, Oliver, Light, Simpson, Dyson
Rogan, Ogivie, Butler, Geidmintis, Spencer, Middlemass, Holliday, Griffin, Tyrer, Tinnion, McGettigan

Light's 25-yarder gives U's the lead, but Macedo has to make fine saves from John Ogilvie and Eddie Holliday. Oliver nets his third goal in three games, and there are bookings for both Dyson and Simpson. Referee Mr Wallace punishes verbal, rather than physical, challenges.

18. BRADFORD PA (A) — Macedo, Mochan, Hall, Price, Bickles, Wood, Brown*, Oliver, Light, Simpson, Dyson / Honeywood
Hardie, Singleton, Gibson, Drury, Tanner, Robinson, Gould, Clancy, Draper, Brannan, Cockburn

Avenue are in danger of extinction, as well as re-election. Hardie gets a hand to Oliver's header, from Bickles' cross, but can't keep it out. A 30-yarder by Brannan surprises Macedo. Simpson is booked for a foul on Brannan. Gould snatches the winner, heading in from close range.

19. SWANSEA (A) — Willis, Mochan, Hall, Honeywood, Wood, Joslyn, Brown, O'Rourke*, Light, Rowan, Dyson
John, Lawrence, Gomersall, Williams A, Nurse, Slee, Evans, Williams H, Biggs, Gwyther / Screen, Simpson

Rowan trials from Detroit Cougars. The incessant morning rain dampens U's all-yellow kit. Rowan's cross goes into the net, out of reach of John, but is ruled out for offside (46). David Gwyther nets for Swans, their lead is doubled when Hall deflects Brian Evans' shot past Willis.

20. SOUTHEND (H) — Willis, Mochan, Hall, Price, Bickles, Wood, Rowan, Oliver, Light, Gibbs, Dyson
Roberts, Beesley, Stone, Kurila, McMillan, Chisnall, Clayton, Chambers, Moore, Best, Hamilton / Slack

U's are set to buy Layer Rd for £12k, with conditional use. Oliver latches onto McMillan's poor back-pass, then pulls back for Simpson's 25-yarder. Dyson helps on Oliver's cross to Gibbs. The linesman spots Roberts taking a swipe at Rowan, giving Dyson a birthday penalty-kick.

21. NEWPORT (H) — Willis, Mochan, Hall, Price, Bickles, Wood, Rowan, Oliver, Light, Gibbs, Dyson
Weare, Williams, McLoughlin, Cooper, Deacy, Rowland, King, Buck, Hill, Young, McClelland

Rowan signs a deal, replacing O'Rourke, who is released. Price is recalled after netting four for the reserves in midweek. Good work by Hall sets up Light. McLoughlin's free-kick is headed in by Mike Deacy, with Willis struggling to reach. Wood wins it, heading in Dyson's corner.

22. GRIMSBY (A) — Macedo, Mochan, Hall, Joslyn, Bickles, Wood, Simpson, Oliver, Light, Gibbs, Dyson
Macey, Worthington, Duncliffe, Davidson, Rathbone, Ross, Brace, Hickman, Walter, Boylen, Oates

Graham scotches rumours that he is wanted by Ipswich to replace Wolves-bound Bill McGarry. Accounts to May 1968 show a loss of £11k, but the Dev. Assoc. and Supporters Club's efforts realise a £2k profit. Rathbone is booked for fouling Gibbs, which leads to Bickles' goal.

23. WREXHAM (A) — Macedo, Mochan, Hall, Joslyn, Bickles, Wood, Simpson, Oliver, Light, Gibbs, Dyson
Reeves, Ingle, Bermingham, Davis, May, Bradbury, Moir, Beanland, Tinnion, Kinsey, Griffiths

Wrexham field new boy Brian Tinnion (£13k Workington). Simpson goes in goal for five minutes after the break, whilst Macedo has stitches. Gibbs heads in Mochan's right-wing cross. Light's 20-yard deflected shot leaves Reeves stranded. The last goal is the best from 30 yards out.

LEAGUE DIVISION 4   Manager: Dick Graham   SEASON 1968-69

Results

No	Date	H/A	Opponents	Att	Pos	Res	Pt	F-A	H-T	Scorers, Times, and Referees
24	18/1	H	BRADFORD PA	5,914	7 / 24	W	30	3-0	1-0	Hall 16, Dyson 50p, Oliver 53 — Ref: M Sinclair
25	24/1	A	WORKINGTON	2,584	5 / 6	W	32	1-0	1-0	Oliver 31 — Ref: J Hill
26	1/2	A	ALDERSHOT	8,383	4 / 2	W	34	2-1	1-1	Gibbs 42, Dyson 88 / *Howarth 4* — Ref: R Challis
27	14/2	A	SOUTHEND	12,681	4 / 11	L	34	1-3	0-1	Light 84 / *Moore 38, Best 54, 78* — Ref: K Walker
28	22/2	H	NOTTS CO	6,612	5 / 20	D	35	1-1	0-0	Gibbs 67 / *Butlin 53* — Ref: R Johnson
29	28/2	H	BRENTFORD	7,268	3 / 12	W	37	2-1	1-1	Joslyn 38, Light 84 / *Neilson 15* — Ref: T Dawes
30	4/3	H	HALIFAX	3,400	4 / 11	L	37	1-2	1-2	Shawcross 16 (og) / *Pearson 25, Massie 31* — Ref: R Darlington
31	8/3	A	ROCHDALE	4,988	6 / 9	L	37	0-4	0-0	*Jenkins 57, Butler 75, 90, Buck 82* — Ref: J Thacker
32	10/3	H	ALDERSHOT	6,577	4 / 2	W	39	2-0	0-0	Hall 61, Light 73 — Ref: B Homewood
33	14/3	H	CHESTER	7,312	3 / 5	D	40	1-1	0-1	Oliver 90 / *Draper 17* — Ref: R Kirkpatrick
34	22/3	A	DONCASTER	10,799	6 / 1	L	40	0-1	0-0	*Robertson 62* — Ref: R Capey

Line-ups (Colchester / *opponent*)

No	1	2	3	4	5	6	7	8	9	10	11	12 sub used
24	Macedo / *Hardie*	Mochan / *Singleton*	Hall / *Hopkins*	Joslyn / *Atkinson*	Bickles / *Brown*	Wood / *Conley*	Simpson / *Robinson*	Oliver* / *Andrews*	Light / *Charnley**	Gibbs / *Henderson**	Dyson / *Gould*	Brown / *Hudson*
25	Macedo / *Rogan*	Mochan / *Wilson*	Hall / *Butler*	Joslyn / *Geldmintis*	Bickles / *Spencer*	Wood / *Flynn*	Simpson / *Banks*	Oliver / *Graham**	Light / *Ogilvie*	Gibbs / *Tyrer*	Dyson / *Halliday*	/ *Trail*
26	Macedo / *Godfrey*	Mochan / *Walden*	Hall / *Dawes*	Joslyn / *Walker*	Bickles / *Giles*	Wood / *Rafferty*	Simpson / *Burton*	Oliver / *Priscott**	Light / *Howarth*	Gibbs / *Melia*	Dyson / *Gowans*	/ *Newman*
27	Macedo / *Roberts*	Mochan / *Bentley*	Hall / *Lindsey*	Joslyn / *Beesley*	Bickles / *Haycock*	Wood / *Kurila*	Simpson / *Clayton*	Oliver / *Best*	Light / *Moore*	Gibbs* / *Hamilton*	Dyson* / *Chambers*	Brown
28	Macedo / *Smith*	Mochan / *Worthington*	Hall / *Oakes*	Joslyn / *Farmer*	Bickles / *Needham*	Wood / *Stubbs*	Simpson / *Bates*	Oliver / *Barker*	Light / *Butlin*	Gibbs / *Masson*	Dyson / *Pring*	
29	Macedo / *Brodie*	Mochan / *Jones*	Hall / *Renwick*	Honeywood / *Richardson*	Bickles / *Gelson*	Joslyn / *Nelmes*	Hodgson* / *Neilson*	Oliver / *Ross*	Light / *Terry !*	Gibbs / *Fenton*	Dyson / *Mansley*	Price
30	Macedo / *Smith*	Mochan / *Meagan*	Hall / *Burgin*	Brown* / *Pickering*	Bickles / *Nicholl*	Joslyn / *Wallace*	Simpson / *Massie*	Oliver / *Pearson*	Oliver / *Lawther*	Gibbs / *Shawcross*	Dyson / *McCarthy*	Price
31	Macedo / *Harker*	Joslyn / *Smith*	Hall / *Ryder*	Wood / *Leech*	Bickles / *Parry*	Honeywood / *Ashworth*	Simpson / *Whitehead*	Oliver / *Rudd*	Light / *Buck*	Gibbs* / *Jenkins*	Dyson / *Butler*	Martin
32	Macedo / *Dickie*	Mochan / *Walden*	Hall / *Lloyd*	Joslyn / *Dawes*	Wood* / *Giles*	Simpson / *Walker*	Price / *Burton*	Light / *Watson*	Gibbs / *Howarth*	Martin / *Melia*	Dyson / *Gowans*	Honeywood
33	Macedo / *Carling*	Mochan / *Cheetham*	Hall / *Sear*	Joslyn / *Ashworth*	Bickles / *Turner*	Simpson / *Brodie*	Price* / *Dearden*	Martin / *Sutton*	Gibbs / *Talbot*	Gibbs / *Draper*	Dyson / *Provan*	Oliver
34	Macedo / *Ogston*	Mochan / *Wilcockson*	Hall / *Clish*	Joslyn / *Giffillan*	Bickles / *Robertson*	Simpson / *Haselden*	Oliver / *Watson*	Martin / *Regan*	Light / *Briggs*	Gibbs / *Johnson*	Dyson* / *Usher*	Brown

Match reports

24 — Bradford PA. *Rowan returns overseas. Hall nods in Gibbs' cross, and Simpson hits the bar in one way traffic. Tommy Singleton fouls Oliver, and Dyson nets from the spot. Trevor Atkinson is booked for angrily kicking the ball way. Joslyn hits the post a minute before Oliver nods in Simpson's cross.*

25 — Workington. *Hodgson and Martin join Chelmsford (loan). U's reveal the cost of policing is one guinea per officer per hour. Brought forward to avoid the nearby RFL Cup match. U's go second overnight, courtesy of Oliver's header, his eighth in eleven, from Dyson's cross, and hits the bar (49).*

26 — Aldershot. *Bill Graver joins the board of directors. Graham is warned by the referee for 'prompting' from the touchline. Jimmy Melia schemes an opening for Jack Howarth. Hall beats Richard Walden to cross to Gibbs. Dyson nods in a perfect cross from Oliver, for United's record seventh victory.*

27 — Southend. *Southend wear lightweight boots with suction soles to combat the heavily sanded pitch. Lindsey's free-kick, wide on the left, is headed in by Gary Moore. Billy Best takes Clayton's pass, and then stabs in when Macedo drops Bickles' lobbed back-pass. Southend have two ruled out.*

28 — Notts Co. *Colchester lad Barlow joins Workington on a free. The game is not expected to go ahead because of the inclement weather, so much so that an emergency single-sheet programme is produced at the eleventh hour. U's find part-timer and Loughboro' student Graham Smith unbeatable.*

29 — Brentford. *Anglia TV Match of the Week cameras find U's at their best for the first time this term. Hodgson breaks down on his comeback match, after a year out. The referee threatens to abandon the match when a bottle is thrown onto the pitch after Light's winning goal. Pat Terry is sent off (18) for kicking Light.*

30 — Halifax. *The FL rule that clubs changing fixtures for Friday nights will have to pay £100 compensation to the Pools companies. For U's this means a 400 increase at the gate, at 5 shillings, to cover the cost. David Shawcross heads Dyson's free-kick into his own goal. Brown receives a leg wound.*

31 — Rochdale. *After going a record seven consecutive wins, U's have now managed just one win in five. Martin is recalled from his loan spell at Chelmsford because of the crippling injury list. Dale close the gap on United with a three-goal salvo in the last 15 minutes. Dennis Butler starts the rout.*

32 — Aldershot. *Bickles and Brown fail to arrive in time for the kick-off owing to a train failure. Virtually all U's players live well outside of town, giving the club a high expense bill. U's gain two valuable points to keep in the promotion hunt through Hall's free-kick goal, and a clincher from Light.*

33 — Chester. *U's come within 50 seconds of having their 13-match unbeaten home record ended. Tricky winger Billy Dearden crosses for Derek Draper. United have two ruled out for offside, but Chester are punished for their own time-wasting when Oliver thumps home after a left-wing corner.*

34 — Doncaster. *Leaders Rovers have lost just two at home in the last 18, and recently thrashed Aldershot by 7-0. Doncaster dominate the second half and are thankful for skipper Stuart Robertson's header, that keeps them ahead of the pack. United have now amassed just six points from eight games.*

35	H	LINCOLN		4	D		1-1	0-1	Joslyn 71	Macedo	Mochan	Hall	Joslyn	Bickles*	Simpson	Brown	Oliver	Gibbs	Light	Price	Honeywood
	24/3		6,787	5		41			*Harford 38*	*Tennant*	*Hubbard*	*Peden*	*Smith J*	*Harford*	*Grummett*	*Hughes*	*Lewis*	*Svarc*	*Kerrigan*	*Smith D*	
									Ref: D Lyden	Ray Harford heads in a Jim Smith free-kick. City's first-ever league goal at Layer Rd looks to have secured two points, but Price makes a great run along the goal-line, before crossing to Joslyn to prod the ball in. Bickles picks up a painful-looking shoulder injury just before the break.											
36	A	YORK		4	L		0-2	0-1		Macedo	Mochan	Hall*	Joslyn	Honeywood	Simpson	Price	Light	Brown	Gibbs	Dyson	Oliver
	29/3		*3,140*	*22*		41			*Boyer 14, 50*	*Widdowson*	*Sibbald*	*Richardson*	*Carr*	*Jackson*	*Topping*	*Taylor*	*Hodgson*	*MacDougall*	*Hewitt*	*Boyer*	
									Ref: J Quinn	Graham is ill and doesn't travel to Yorkshire, leaving trainer John Anderson in charge. The Saturday evening kick-off avoids a clash with the Grand National. A fifth consecutive away defeat is compounded when Dyson puts a penalty three yards wide (66), after Jackson fouled Gibbs.											
37	H	CHESTERFIELD		4	W		1-0	1-0	Brown 41	Macedo	Mochan	Hall	Joslyn	Bickles	Price	Simpson	Gibbs	Light*	Brown	Dyson	Oliver
	4/4		7,180	*18*		43				*Humphreys*	*Holmes*	*Lumsden*	*Pugh*	*Bell*	*Phelan*	*Moore*	*Randall*	*Wright*	*Kettleborough*	*Bishop*	
									Ref: H New	Brown nets his first senior goal for U's when he beats the grounded Alan Humphreys. Chesterfield are a poor side and this highlights United's recent stuttering form. The busy Easter schedule means that Colchester have another game tomorrow and a trip to Peterborough on Tuesday.											
38	H	EXETER		5	W		1-0	1-0	Light 36	Macedo	Mochan	Hall	Joslyn	Bickles	Simpson	Price	Light	Gibbs	Oliver	Dyson	
	5/4		5,650	*19*		45				*Shearing*	*Smyth*	*Blain*	*Parker*	*Newman*	*Balson*	*Pleat*	*Binney*	*Wingate*	*Curtis*	*Whatling*	
									Ref: M Fussey	24 hours later U's again win by the narrowest of margins, and thus gain revenge for the earlier FA Cup defeat by City that denied them a tie with Manchester U. Exeter's keeper Peter Shearing only parries Simpson's fierce shot, leaving Light the task of slotting in his 14th of the term.											
39	A	PETERBOROUGH		2	W		1-0	0-0	Brown 88	Macedo	Mochan	Hall	Joslyn	Bickles	Simpson	Price	Brown	Light	Gibbs	Dyson	
	8/4		*6,548*	*13*		47				*Drewery*	*Noble*	*Crawford*	*Ricketts*	*Wile*	*Wright*	*Price*	*Iley*	*Hall*	*Conmy*	*Robson*	
									Ref: D Corbett	United earn their first-ever six point Easter maximum, and a first-ever win at London Road. Price hits the bar for U's in the first half, but it is Brown who receives a ball to turn and crash a fine angled drive past Michael Drewery. Macedo saves well from big Jim Hall in the last minute.											
40	A	PORT VALE		2	D		0-0	0-0		Macedo	Mochan	Hall	Joslyn	Bickles	Brown	Simpson	Price	Light	Gibbs	Dyson	
	12/4		*3,774*	*14*		48				*Ball*	*Boulton*	*Wilson*	*Goodfellow*	*Sproson*	*King*	*Morris*	*James*	*Chapman**	*Green*	*Carrick*	*Gough*
									Ref: F Cowan	Both sides have punchless attacks which means United have to settle for only their third away draw of the season. Macedo again excels, saving well from Mick Morris and John Green. U's best chance comes when Keith Ball mis-punches, but Light's lob sails inches over the crossbar.											
41	H	PETERBOROUGH		2	D		2-2	1-1	Brown 25, Bickles 56	Macedo	Mochan	Hall	Joslyn	Bickles	Wood*	Simpson	Brown	Price	Gibbs	Dyson	Oliver
	14/4		6,564	*14*		49			*Price 43, Hall 48*	*Drewery*	*Noble*	*Pyatt*	*Ricketts*	*Wile*	*Wright*	*Garwood*	*Price*	*Hall*	*Conmy*	*Robson*	
									Ref: A Dimond	Posh extend their unbeaten away record to eight. Brown nods in Dyson's cross, only for Peter Price to level, despite the linesman's flag. Jim Hall gives Posh the lead just after the interval, chipping over Macedo. Price, making his 50th league appearance, crosses for Bickles to level.											
42	H	BRADFORD C		2	D		1-1	0-0	Gibbs 47	Macedo	Mochan	Hall	Price	Bickles	Joslyn	Simpson*	Oliver	Brown	Gibbs	Dyson	Light
	18/4		8,196	*5*		50			*Hall J 52*	*Liney*	*Bayliss*	*Cooper*	*Stowell*	*Hall H*	*Swallow*	*Hall J*	*Ham*	*Corner*	*Middleton*	*Bannister*	
									Ref: R Paine	Graham refuses to shake hands with City boss, Jimmy Wheeler, after a bruising battle. Bobby Ham hits the bar and has one cleared off the line by Hall. Gibbs shakes off Barry Swallow for 1-0, but John Hall nets easily from close range to maintain Bradford C's 18-match unbeaten run.											
43	H	HALIFAX		2	D		0-0	0-0		Macedo	Mochan	Hall	Honeywood	Bickles	Wood	Brown	Oliver	Light	Gibbs	Price	
	21/4		7,429	*6*		51				*Smith*	*Hampton*	*Burgin*	*Pickering*	*Nicholl*	*Robinson*	*Flower*	*Massie*	*Lawther*	*Shawcross*	*McCarthy*	
									Ref: R Spittle	Halifax, 13 unbeaten away, have a huge backlog of fixtures due to the weather and their cup run that ended against Stoke. U's have scored 22 of their 28 home goals at the Layer Rd end this season, but the negative Shaymen ensure that United suffer their third home draw in the trot.											
44	H	SWANSEA		3	L		0-1	0-1		Macedo	Mochan	Hall	Joslyn	Bickles	Wood*	Simpson	Gibbs	Light	Brown	Dyson	Oliver
	25/4		7,136	*14*		51			*Raybould 3*	*John*	*Hughes*	*Lawrence*	*Williams A*	*Slee*	*Thomas*	*Grey*	*Williams H*	*Gwyther*	*Raybould*	*Evans*	
									Ref: N Burtenshaw	United cling to a promotion spot as Bradford (played 42, 50 points), Darlington (42, 50), Bradford (42, 50), Halifax (40, 49) and Southend (41, 48) are all poised to leapfrog U's with their games in hand. Managerless Swans are the first side to win at Layer Rd since the end of August.											
45	A	DARLINGTON		4	D		1-1	0-1	Gibbs 71	Macedo	Mochan	Hall	Simpson	Bickles	Honeywood	Oliver*	Gibbs	Brown	Light	Dyson	Joslyn
	28/4		*7,505*			52			*Melling 4*	*Moor*	*Peverell*	*Felton*	*Jacques*	*Abelson*	*Robson*	*Gauden*	*O'Neill*	*Melling*	*Hale*	*Sproates*	
				5					Ref: A Gunn	United finally visit Feethams for a fixture that has been re-arranged three times. Bickles, who had a last-minute goal ruled out against Swansea, suffers again when Gibbs is adjudged to have nodded the ball out of Tony Moor's hands on the half-hour. Five draws in six may prove costly.											
46	A	NOTTS CO		6	L		0-2	0-1		Macedo	Mochan	Hall	Joslyn	Bickles*	Honeywood	Simpson	Gibbs	Brown	Light	Dyson	Oliver
	2/5		*3,576*	*19*		52			*Masson 26, 78*	*Rose*	*Ball*	*Worthington*	*Farmer*	*Needham*	*Oakes*	*Bates*	*Barker*	*Butlin*	*Masson*	*Pring*	
		Home	Away						Ref: W Castle	U' need a miracle to go up, but Don Masson, looking offside, nets County's first. His soft second is insignificant as all of the U's rivals pick up the necessary points. Adams (Crewe), Martin (Workington), Buck, Hodgson, Honeywood, Price and Perryman (all non-league) are released.											
Average		6,109	5,835																		

LEAGUE DIVISION 4 (CUP-TIES) Manager: Dick Graham SEASON 1968-69

League Cup

		F-A	H-T	Scorers, Times, and Referees	1	2	3	4	5	6	7	8	9	10	11	12 sub used
1 H READING 14/8	3,824 3:	W 2-0	1-0	Hall 41, Oliver 69p Ref: J Yates	Adams *Brown*	Moughton *Bacuzzi*	Hall *Thornhill*	Joslyn *Meldrum*	Forbes *Chapman !*	Honeywood *Yard*	Price *Allen*	Trevis *Docherty**	Oliver *Collins*	Mansfield *Sainty*	Martin *Harris*	*Dean*
2 H WORKINGTON 4/9	3,523 4:14	L 0-1	0-1	Tyrer 35 Ref: J Hunting	Adams *Rogan*	Perryman *Ogilvie*	Simpson *Butler*	Joslyn *Geidmintis*	Forbes *Spencer*	Honeywood *Middlemass*	Price *Banks*	Trevis *Griffin*	Hall *Tyrer*	Mansfield *Tinnion*	Martin *Holliday*	

Price's lob finds Hall to sweep past Brown. Martin is sent crashing by George Harris. John Chapman, booked for a foul on Price (17), is sent off (72) for 'conversing' with a linesman'. Forbes and Trevis are also booked. Stratton and Bullock refuse new deals, leaving U's short of goals.

If only U's had a deadly forward then they would have won this tie by a mile. They dominate for 95% of the game, but are beaten by Alan Tyrer's 35-yarder which sails over Adams. Forbes, in as emergency centre-forward, lobs over Mike Rogan, but also unfortunately over the top.

FA Cup

		F-A	H-T	Scorers, Times, and Referees	1	2	3	4	5	6	7	8	9	10	11	12 sub used
1 H CHESHAM 16/11	5,497 AL:	W 5-0	1-0	Light 34, 74, Hall 49, 54, Price 80 Ref: R Johnson	Macedo *O'Brien K*	Mochan *Perkins*	Hall *Smith*	Honeywood *Thackeray*	Wood *Olson*	Joslyn *O'Brien P*	Brown *Black*	O'Rourke *Bowden*	Light *Marchant*	Price *Reardon*	Dyson *Willis*	
2 H EXETER 7/12	6,180 4:19	L 0-1	0-1	Banks 10 Ref: D Smith	Macedo *Shearing*	Mochan *Smyth*	Hall *Blain*	Simpson *Kirkham*	Bickles *Harvey*	Wood *Newman*	Rowan *Carr*	Oliver *Banks*	Light* *Balson*	Gibbs *Mitten**	Dyson *Pleat*	Brown *Curtis*

Chesham make their first appearance in the first round, courtesy of an exemption for their 1967-68 FA Amateur Cup final appearance (0-1 v Leytonstone). Brown's goal is ruled offside (4). Hall springs the offside trap twice in five minutes. Light capitalises on a poor goal-kick (74).

Blain breaks away from a U's corner, before slipping a pass through for Alan Banks to leave Macedo helpless. Before City's goal, Oliver had collected a Light pass and crossed onto the upright. The floodlights fail six minutes from time, as Exeter earn a home tie with Manchester Utd.

League Table

	Team	P	W	D	L	F	A	W	D	L	F	A	Pts
				Home						**Away**			
1	Doncaster	46	13	8	2	42	16	8	9	6	23	22	59
2	Halifax	46	15	5	3	36	18	8	5	6	17	19	57
3	Rochdale	46	14	7	2	47	11	4	6	6	21	24	56
4	Bradford C	46	11	10	2	36	18	7	10	6	29	28	56
5	Darlington	46	11	6	6	40	26	6	12	5	22	19	52
6	COLCHESTER	46	12	8	3	31	17	8	4	11	26	36	52
7	Southend	46	15	3	5	51	21	4	10	9	27	40	51
8	Lincoln	46	13	6	4	38	19	4	11	8	16	33	51
9	Wrexham	46	13	7	3	41	22	5	7	11	20	30	50
10	Swansea	46	11	8	4	35	20	8	3	12	23	34	49
11	Brentford	46	12	7	4	40	24	6	5	12	24	41	48
12	Workington	46	8	11	4	24	17	7	6	10	16	26	47
13	Port Vale	46	12	8	3	33	15	4	6	13	13	31	46
14	Chester	46	12	4	7	43	24	4	9	10	33	42	45
15	Aldershot	46	13	3	7	42	23	6	4	13	24	43	45
16	Scunthorpe	46	10	5	8	28	22	8	3	12	33	38	44
17	Exeter	46	11	8	4	45	24	5	5	13	21	41	43
18	Peterborough	46	8	9	6	32	23	6	6	11	28	34	43
19	Notts Co	46	10	8	5	33	22	2	10	11	15	35	42
20	Chesterfield	46	7	7	9	24	22	6	8	9	19	28	41
21	York	46	12	8	3	36	25	2	3	18	17	50	39
22	Newport	46	9	9	5	31	26	2	5	16	18	48	36
23	Grimsby	46	5	7	11	25	31	4	8	11	22	38	33
24	Bradford PA	46	5	8	10	19	34	0	2	21	13	72	20
		1104	262	170	120	852	520	120	170	262	520	852	1104

Odds & ends

Double wins: (5) Aldershot, Chesterfield, Grimsby, Workington, Wrexham.

Double defeats: (2) Doncaster, Swansea.

Won from behind: (4) Scunthorpe (a), Grimsby (a), Aldershot (a), Brentford (h).

Lost in front: (2) Bradford PA (a), Halifax (a).

High spots: Club record seven successive wins, beating a run of six in Season 1956-57.

Dick Graham's turnaround of a relegated side into one challenging for promotion, once he had brought in his own men.

The agreement with the council to purchase Layer Road.

6,000+ average attendance.

Low spots: Failure to gain promotion, by just four points, with no wins in the last seven games.

One point from the first five games of Dick Graham's reign, leaving U's rock-bottom.

Missing out on an FA Cup home tie with Manchester United.

Player of the Year: Brian Hall.

Ever presents: (1) Brian Hall.

Hat-tricks: (0).

Leading scorer: Danny Light (14).

Appearances & Goals

Player	Lge	Sub	LC	Sub	FAC	Sub	Lge	LC	FAC	Tot
			Appearances						**Goals**	
Adams, Ernie	4		2							
Barlow, Peter	1									
Bickles, Dave	34				1		3			3
Brown, Micky	17	3			1	1	3			3
Buck, Alan	1									
Dyson, Terry	40	1			2		3			3
Forbes, Duncan	6		2							
Gibbs, Brian	37				1		11			11
Hall, Brian	46		2		2		3	2	1	6
Hodgson, Ken	1									
Honeywood, Brian	12	6	2		1					
Joslyn, Roger	37	1	2		1		3			3
Light, Danny	42	1	2		2		12		2	14
Macedo, Tony	38				2					
Mansfield, John	2	1	2		2					
Martin, John	6	1	2							
Mochan, Dennis	41				2					
Moughton, Colin	4		1							
Oliver, Jim	34	7	1		1		9		1	10
O'Rourke, Ken	1									
Perryman, Gerry	1	1	2		1					
Price, Terry	19	2	2		1		2	1		3
Rowan, Barry	2									
Simpson, Owen	41	2	1		1		4			4
Trevis, Derek	8	2					1			1
Willis, Ron	3									
Wood, Brian	28				2		1			1
(own-goals)							2			2
27 players used	506	26	22		22	1	57	3	4	64

LEAGUE DIVISION 4 — Manager: Dick Graham — SEASON 1969-70

Team line-ups (positions 1–11, with 12th man / sub used)

U's player listed first, opposition player second.

No	Date	1	2	3	4	5	6	7	8	9	10	11	12 sub used
1	A LINCOLN 9/8	Smith / Withers	Howe / Hubbard	Hall / Taylor G	Joslyn / Taylor W	Howlett / Harford	Brown / Grummett	Pitt* / Lewis	Massey / Fletcher	Light / Svarc	Gibbs / Helliwell	Whittaker / Smith D	Oliver
2	H WREXHAM 16/8	Smith / Gaskell	Howe / Bermingham	Hall / Mason	Gibbs / Davis	Bickles / May	Wood / Evans	Light / Griffiths	Massey / Park	Oliver / Smith	Brown / Purdie*	Whittaker / Kinsey	Moir
3	A NOTTS CO 23/8	Smith / Rose	Howe / Ball	Hall / Worthington	Gibbs / Jones*	Bickles / Needham	Wood / Oates	Light / Ryan	Massey / McMorran	Oliver / Bradd	Brown / Masson	Whittaker / Hobson	Butlin
4	H PETERBOROUGH 25/8	Smith / Drewery	Howe / Potts	Hall / Noble	Gibbs / Iley	Bickles / Wile	Wood / Wright	Joslyn / Moss	Massey / Conny	Oliver / Hall	Brown / Holliday	Whittaker / Robson	Joslyn
5	H PORT VALE 30/8	Smith / Ball	Howe / Boulton	Hall / Wilson	Gibbs / King	Bickles / Sproson	Wood / Green	Light* / McGhee	Massey / Gough	Oliver / Wookey	Brown / James	Whittaker / Morris	Joslyn
6	A DARLINGTON 6/9	Smith / Crampton	Howe / Peverell	Joslyn / Horner	Brown / O'Neill	Wood / Albeson	Wood / Jacques	Pitt* / Gauden	Massey / Melling	Light / Robson	Gibbs / Hale	Whittaker / Sproates	Oliver
7	H CREWE 13/9	Smith / Adams	Howe / Gater	Hall / Leig*	Joslyn / Stott	Wood / Barnes	Howlett / Turner	Oliver / Morrisey	Gibbs / Tarbuck	Massey / Hollett	Light* / Bradshaw	Whittaker / Gannon	Brown / Higgins
8	A OLDHAM 16/9	Smith / Gordine	Howe / Wood	Hall / Wilson	Joslyn / Blair	Wood / Lawson	Bickles / Bowie	Brown / Bingham	Gibbs / Colquhoun	Massey / Beardall	Oliver / Bebbington*	Whittaker / Chapman	Blore
9	A HARTLEPOOL 20/9	Smith / Bircumshaw	Howe /	Hall / Dobbing*	Joslyn / Sheridan	Bickles / Gill	Wood / Goad	Brown / Young	Gibbs / Thompson	Massey / Bell	Oliver / Wright	Whittaker / Trail	Green
10	H SWANSEA 27/9	Smith / Millington	Howe / Lawrence	Hall / Gomersall	Joslyn / Williams A	Bickles / Rosser	Wood / Slee	Oliver / Allchurch	Gibbs / Slattery	Massey / Williams H	Brown / Gwyther	Whittaker / Evans	Green
11	H SCUNTHORPE 29/9	Smith / Barnard	Howe / Foxton	Hall / Jackson	Joslyn / Deere	Bickles / Holt	Wood / Welbourne	Light / Davidson	Gibbs / Keegan	Oliver* / Cassidy	Massey / Heath	Whittaker / Kerr	Howlett

Results

No	Scorers, Times, and Referees	Att	Pos	Pt	F-A	H-T
1	Gibbs 36, 56, Massey 75 / Fletcher 20, 21, Harford 80 / Ref: G Trevett	6,761		D 1	3-3	1-2
2	Gibbs 52, Whittaker 61 / Ref: N Graham	5,292	8 / 3	W 3	2-0	0-0
3	Massey 21 / Hobson 32 / Ref: A Seeley	4,901	7 / 21	D 4	1-1	1-1
4	Hall 54, Gibbs 90 / Moss 83 / Ref: L Sinkins	7,133	5 / 16	W 6	2-1	0-0
5	Ref: J Quinn	6,323	6 / 3	D 7	0-0	0-0
6	Massey 59, 84 / Melling 21p, 70, Robson 26 / Ref: I Smith	3,767	8 / 12	L 7	2-3	0-2
7	Massey 69 / Ref: N Paget	5,084	4 / 20	W 9	1-0	0-0
8	Massey 50, Brown 64 / Beardall 15 / Ref: T Gill	3,993	5 / 18	W 11	2-1	0-1
9	Ref: H Davey	3,667	5 / 12	D 12	0-0	0-0
10	Massey 69 / Gwyther 70 / Ref: A Green	5,748	6 / 11	D 13	1-1	0-0
11	Deere 52, Heath 57p / Ref: R Paine	6,328	8 / 11	L 13	0-2	0-0

Match reports

1. LINCOLN — Bickles is suspended for a sending off in friendly at Romford. Massey (£5.5k Orient) debuts with Smith (Notts Co), Pitt (Spurs), Howe (O's). Howlett (Southend) and Whittaker (Luton) (all free). Ray Harford wrestles a point from U's, heading in D Smith's cross. Howlett is booked.

2. WREXHAM — Gaskell, U's highest paid player ever, teams up with old Fulham buddy Johnny Haynes in Durban SA (£3k). Simpson joins rivals Southend (£4k). Smith's long clearance allows Gibbs to slide under Gaskell. Whittaker smashes in Oliver's free-kick, and Gibbs later has two ruled out.

3. NOTTS CO — Brown bursts through for Mike Rose to save, but Massey pushes the rebound between keeper and post. John Hobson takes a pass from Don Masson, turns Howe inside-out before turning and slotting into the roof of the net. For Jimmy Sirrel's County it is their first goal of the season.

4. PETERBOROUGH — Hall's indirect free-kick is deflected by the Peterboro' wall past the stranded Michael Drewery, a minute after Tommy Robson had struck the underside of U's bar. Bobbie Moss grabs an offside equaliser, but justice is done as Gibbs pops up in injury-time to nod in Whittaker's cross.

5. PORT VALE — After the excitement – but disappointment of the defeat at Portman Road – it is back to more mundane duties with the search for vital points. Both clubs maintain their unbeaten record, but U's with 17 corners can't break down the Vale defence. Wookey is booked for a foul on Brown.

6. DARLINGTON — Quakers take the lead when Howlett needlessly hand-balls. Robson adds a second when Joslyn misjudges Melling's cross. Massey applies the final touch to a goalmouth melee, and has to wait for the ref to consult the flagging linesman. Melling adds his second, beating three defenders.

7. CREWE — Alex include Ernie Adams, whom they have had on a two-month trial. Adams is made captain for the day and is much the busier of the two keepers. Oliver makes ground on the right, before crossing to Massey to net. United have now avoided losing at home to Alex in four visits.

8. OLDHAM — U's get their first win in five at Boundary Park, but not before ex-Everton and England full-back Ray Wilson floats over a free-kick for Jim Beardall. Latics keeper Brian Gordine parries Gibbs effort, but only to Massey for his tenth of the term. Massey, himself, lays back for Brown.

9. HARTLEPOOL — United stretch their unbeaten run to five matches against the North-Easterners, who have only won once at home this season. Massey comes closest for Colchester in the sixth minute, only to see keeper George Smith pull off a fine save. U's sit handily-placed just below the top four.

10. SWANSEA — Massey wins possession in midfield, feeds Oliver down the right, and arrives in the box to nod the cross past Welsh international keeper Tony Millington for his eleventh. With 20 minutes left, a right-wing corner is headed back across goal by H Williams for David Gwyther to level.

11. SCUNTHORPE — Graham enquires after Norwich's Welsh international Mel Lucas. An error by Joslyn lets in Kevin Keegan to find Stephen Deere, unmarked, for Iron's first. Five minutes later Smith is one of a number to foul Terry Heath in the U's box. Gibbs is injured after U's have used their sub.

Match-by-match record (reading the rotated fixture grid, matches 12–23):

12. NEWPORT (A) — 4/10 · Att 2,996 · Pos 8 · **L 1–4 (HT 0–4)** · Pts 13
United: Smith, Howe, Hall, Joslyn, Bickles, Brown*, Howlett, Massey, Light, Whittaker, Pitt; sub Cook
Opponents: Weare, Williams, Sprague*, McLaughlin, Aizlewood, Cooper, Mabbutt, Hill, Derrick, Raybould, Young
Scorers: Whittaker 86; Derrick 3, Hill 13, 40, Raybould 33. Ref: G Jones
Albert Derrick intercepts Wood's back-pass to shoot County in front. Raybould volleys past Smith from 10 yards. Len Hill takes advantage of confusion to add the Welshmen's fourth. Pitt subs for Wood at half-time leaving hobbling Massey to finally call it a day 20 minutes from time.

13. WREXHAM (A) — 6/10 · Att 11,967 · Pos 13 · **L 2–4 (HT 1–4)** · Pts 13
United: Smith, Howe, Hall, Joslyn, Bickles, Wood, Brown, Howlett*, Light, Whittaker, Pitt; sub Cook
Opponents: Gaskell, Mason, Bermingham, Davis, May, Ingle, Park, Smith, Kinsey, Griffiths
Scorers: Brown 4, Hall 60; Smith 6, 9, 14, Park 8. Ref: D Fieldsend
Brown's great goal gives U's the lead, but the Welshmen blitz U's with four goals in eight minutes. Hall moves up front after the break and is a revelation, and nets U's consolation. Ray Smith and Bobby Park spoil it for United fans who had paid £10 for their three-day Welsh excursion.

14. BRADFORD PA (H) — 11/10 · Att 4,440 · Pos 9 · **W 2–1 (HT 0–1)** · Pts 15
United: Willis, Howe, Hall, Joslyn, Bickles, Pitt, Presland, Massey*, Light, Whittaker, Dyson; sub Hopkins
Opponents: Hardie, Atkinson, Brodie, Dolan, Brown, Carr, Saville, Massie, Charnley, Beanland, Thom*
Scorers: Whittaker 67, Brown 90; Massie 32. Ref: J Lewis
Presland loans from Palace. PA have not won away in 39 games. Willis, in for injured Smith, dives far too late to save Les Massie's neat flick. Hall's wonderful run ends with Whittaker side-footing home. Hall has a goal ruled out before finding Brown for the last kick of the game.

15. YORK (A) — 18/10 · Att 3,961 · Pos 11 · **L 2–4 (HT 0–1)** · Pts 15
United: Willis, Howe, Hall, Joslyn, Bickles*, Dyson, Brown, Hall, Light, Whittaker, Howlett
Opponents: Widdowson, Sibbald, Makin, Davidson, Jackson, Boyer, McMahon, Aimson, Hodgson, Mahon
Scorers: Brown 70, Hall 88; Hall 25 (og), Boyer 51, 84, Mahon 90. Ref: E Jolly
Already hit by injuries, U's have to sub Bickles (30) and force injured Howe to stay on. Hall makes a desperate attempt to stop Mick Mahon's header, but can only help it in. Mahon gets on the score sheet in injury-time from Paul Aimson's cross. Phil Boyer grabs City's other two.

16. CHESTER (H) — 25/10 · Att 3,754 · Pos 12 · **L 0–1 (HT 0–0)** · Pts 15
United: Smith, Presland, Mochan, Joslyn, Wood, Howlett, Gibbs, Light*, Hall, Brown, Whittaker; sub Pitt
Opponents: Carling, Cheetham, Birks, Sutton, Ashworth, Bradbury, Dearden, Tarbuck, Webber, Draper, Provan
Scorers: Bradbury 80. Ref: H Hackney
Injury-hit U's add Dyson and Mochan to the squad from the reserves. Six are listed in a bid to fund incoming transfers. Chester earn their first win in three at Layer Rd. Alan Tarbuck crosses from the left, Keith Webber turns the ball back for Terry Bradbury to shoot in off the post.

17. ALDERSHOT (A) — 1/11 · Att 5,966 · Pos 13 · **D 1–1** · Pts 16
United: Smith, Cook, Hall, Joslyn, Wood, Presland, Presland, Slater, Light, Brown*, Dyson, Whittaker
Opponents: Dixon, Walden, Walker, Giles, Dean, Newman, Burton, Brown*, Howarth, Melia, Gowans, Priscott
Scorers: Brown 40; Melia 23. Ref: W Hall
Slater loans from O's, and Pitt is released. 32nd-birthday boy Jimmy Melia is gifted the first by Wood. Wood atones by pushing a great ball through the middle and a crowd of players for Brown to run on and equalise. Fouls by Slater (Walker) and Shots' Giles (Dyson) earn bookings.

18. SOUTHEND (H) — 8/11 · Att 6,021 · Pos 14 · **L 0–2 (HT 0–1)** · Pts 16
United: Smith, Joslyn, Hall, Bickles*, Wood, Presland, Slater, Brown, Light, Whittaker, Oliver*, Dyson
Opponents: Lloyd, Lindsey, Simpson, Beesley*, Barnett, Kurila, Jacques, Best, McMillan, Clayton, Chambers, Hunt
Scorers: Clayton 20, McMillan 77. Ref: K Burns
Southend opt out of signing Oliver, as he won't move from Norwich. Instead they sign Joe Jacques (£8k Darlington). Smith parries Eddie Clayton's first effort, but can't stop him snapping up the rebound. John Chambers finds Sammy McMillan, following Joslyn's bad back-pass.

19. GRIMSBY (H) — 22/11 · Att 3,474 · Pos 13 · **W 3–2 (HT 0–1)** · Pts 18
United: Smith, Wainman, Wood, Joslyn, Wood, Bickles*, Jones, Gibbs, Light*, Brown, Dyson
Opponents: Worthington, Mobley, Kennedy, Wigginton, Ross, Oates, Marsden, Hickman, Boylen, Hickman
Scorers: Gibbs 56, Brown 59, 82; Brace 2, Hickman 84. Ref: F Bassett
Bill Graver becomes chairman as Jones signs (Millwall £5k). Player-boss Kennedy finds the unmarked Brace. Jones and Joslyn combine well to set up Gibbs' equaliser. A frantic climax sees a Hickman pair ruled out and Hall hit the post, before Brown punishes Worthington's error.

20. NORTHAMPTON (A) — 25/11 · Att 3,256 · Pos 14 · **D 1–1 (HT 1–1)** · Pts 19
United: Smith, Cook, Hall, Wood*, Wood*, Jones, Slater, Light, Brown, Gibbs, Dyson; sub Light
Opponents: Book, Fairfax, Weaver, Clarke, Rankmore, Ross, Felton, Kiernan, Hawkins, Fairbrother, Ross
Scorers: Brown 27; Kiernan 9. Ref: R Weedon
On a bitterly cold day with snow flurries, U's give away an early goal for the second match running. Joe Kiernan, on his 200th FL appearance, appears to kick out of Smith's hands. Brown, after his equaliser, is unlucky not to score the winner when his banana-shot licks the far upright.

21. CREWE (A) — 13/12 · Att 2,670 · Pos 13 · **W 1–0 (HT 1–0)** · Pts 21
United: Smith, Cook, Hall, Joslyn, Wood, Bickles, Jones, Whittaker, Brown, Jones, Dyson; sub Wallace
Opponents: Adams, Lowry, Leigh, Gater, Stott, Turner, Morrisey*, McHale, Inglis, Bradshaw, Gannon
Scorers: Jones 22. Ref: K Styles
U's hope to receive the £10.8k balance from the FA at a 3% interest rate, to secure the ground purchase. Dyson floats over a cross that Gibbs lays back for Jones, who weakly shoot his first U's goal past Ernie Adams. Crewe have enough chances to win, but resolute U's hold out.

22. DARLINGTON (H) — 20/12 · Att 2,571 · Pos 11 · **W 2–1 (HT 1–0)** · Pts 23
United: Smith, Cook, Hall, Joslyn, Wood, Bickles, Dyson, Whittaker, Gibbs, Brown, Whittaker; sub Baxter
Opponents: Moor, Peverell, Horner, Robson*, Albeson, Carr, Gauden, O'Neill, Sproates, Hale, Felton
Scorers: Jones 21, Gibbs 57; Gauden 58. Ref: K Sweet
Secretary Claude Orrin retires after 21 years. Hall wins the Gillette Sportsman of the Month for Div Four. From U's seventh free-kick, Jones hooks low into the net. Peverell 'scores' from a 40-yard free-kick (40). but Hall is impeded. Gibbs nets a picture goal from Joslyn's fine cross.

23. NOTTS CO (H) — 26/12 · Att 4,758 · Pos 10 · **W 2–1 (HT 1–1)** · Pts 25
United: Smith, Cook, Hall, Joslyn, Bickles, Wood, Whittaker, Gibbs, Brown, Jones, Dyson; sub Worthington
Opponents: Rose, Ball, Smith, Oakes, Needham, Stubbs, Ryan, Barker, Bradd*, Masson, Hobson
Scorers: Gibbs 31, 79; Ryan 42. Ref: R Sheppard
Whittaker's flag-kick finds Gibbs for U's lead. County equalise, whilst Bickles is off being treated for a cut head, when Smith only helps John Ryan's cross into the net. Mike Rose presents U's with the ultimate Christmas present, punching straight to Gibbs for U's fourth win in five.

LEAGUE DIVISION 4 — Manager: Dick Graham — SEASON 1969-70

No	Date		1	2	3	4	5	6	7	8	9	10	11	12 sub used
24	10/1	H HARTLEPOOL	Smith	Cook	Hall	Joslyn*	Bickles	Wood	Whittaker	Gibbs	Brown	Jones	Dyson	McCluskey
			Smith	Bircumshaw	Dobbing	White*	Gill	Goad	Young	Blawman	Bell	Trail	Kirk	
25	17/1	A SWANSEA	Smith	Howe	Hall	Joslyn	Wood	Wood	Cram	Massey*	Williams H	Cook	Brown	
			Millington	Slee	Gomersall	Williams A	Nurse	Thomas	Allchurch	Screen	Gwyther	Evans		
26	24/1	H WORKINGTON	Smith	Cook	Hall	Cram	Wood	Bickles	Oliver	Gibbs	Wall*	Jones	Whittaker	
			Rogan	Butler	Ogilvie	Geidmintis	Spencer	Goodfellow	Spratt	Massie	Martin	Tyer	Barlow	
27	27/1	A SCUNTHORPE	Smith	Cook	Hall	Cram	Joslyn	Wood	Brown	Gibbs	Oliver	Jones	Whittaker	
			Barnard	Foxton	Jackson	Deere	Atkin	Welbourne	Keegan	Cassidy	Kerr	Heath	Davidson	
28	31/1	H NEWPORT	Smith	Cook	Hall	Cram	Joslyn	Wood	Brown	Gibbs	Oliver	Jones	Whittaker	Young
			Weare	Williams	Ferguson	McLaughlin	Deacy	Smith	Hooper*	Radford	Jones	Derrick	Thomas	
29	7/2	A BRADFORD PA	Smith	Cook	Hall	Cram	Bickles	Wood	Brown	Gibbs	Oliver	Jones	Whittaker	
			Hardie	Brodie	Roberts	Carr	Dolan	Atkinson	Tewley	Woolmer	Charnley	Beanland*	Saville	Wright
30	21/2	A SOUTHEND	Smith	Cook	Hall	Cram	Bickles	Wood	Brown*	Gibbs	Oliver	Jones	Whittaker	Joslyn
			Roberts	Lindsey	Simpson	Beesley	Haydock	Kurila	Chisnall	Best	Garner	Moore	Clayton	
31	28/2	H YORK	Smith	Cook	Hall	Joslyn	Bickles	Wood	Cram	Gibbs	Oliver	Jones	Whittaker	
			Morritt	Mackin	Burrows	Sibbald	Swallow	Topping	Taylor*	Boyer	McMahon	Aimson	Hewitt	Davidson
32	2/3	H CHESTERFIELD	Smith	Cook	Howe	Joslyn	Bickles*	Wood	Cram	Gibbs	Oliver	Jones	Hall	Howlett
			Stevenson	Holmes	Hickton	Fenoughty	Finnigan	Phelan	Pugh	Moss	Randall	Archer	Moore	
33	11/3	A EXETER	Smith	Cook	Howe*	Joslyn	Howlett	Wood	Cram	Whittaker	Gibbs	Jones	Hall	Massey
			Wilson	Crawford	Blain	Morris	Sharples	Parker	Giles	Banks	Gadston	Wingate	Mitten	
34	14/3	H BRENTFORD	Smith	Cook	Howe	Joslyn	Bickles	Wood	Cram	Gibbs	Massey	Jones	Hall	
			Brodie	Hawley	Renwick	Nelmes	Gelson	Higginson	Tawse	Ross	Turner	Cross	Docherty	

No	Scorers, Times, and Referees	Att	Pos	Pt	F-A	H-T
24	Jones 29 / Kirk 75 / Ref: J Sier	3,200	11	26	1-1	1-0
25	Thomas 1 / Ref: A Hart	8,008	5	26	0-1	0-1
26	Whittaker 30, Gibbs 39, Jones 45 / Ref: K Wynn	4,265	24	28	3-0	3-0
27	Jones 78 / Cassidy 18 / Ref: R Judson	6,276	8	29	1-1	0-1
28	Gibbs 16 / Wood 6 (og) / Ref: H Ellis	4,679	20	30	1-1	1-1
29	Brown 5 / Ref: C Robinson	2,972	24	32	1-0	1-0
30	Oliver 31 / Best 9, Moore 76 / Ref: G Hartley	6,778	18	32	1-2	1-1
31	Jones 21, 70, Gibbs 73 / Ref: J Hunting	3,803	17	34	3-0	1-0
32	Wood 30, Jones 39, 60, Gibbs 85 / Pugh 47 / Ref: R Johnson	5,665	1	36	4-1	2-0
33	Jones 75 / Mitten 30, Banks 82 / Ref: T Reynolds	4,010	15	36	1-2	0-1
34	Jones 58 / Ross 37 / Ref: J Yates	4,878	3	37	1-1	0-1

24 Graham turns down £7k a year to succeed Vic Buckingham at Greek side Ethnikos. In pouring rain, Pool's defence only half clears Dyson's cross, leaving Joslyn's shot to be deflected in off Jones. Gibbs' 15th-minute effort was offside. Bircumshaw is booked for fouling Whittaker

25 The accounts show a loss of £19k, due mainly to high wages and the additional expenses required for players living away from the town. Cram joins from Vancouver. Veteran Welsh international Len Allchurch causes Howe problems, and supplies Thomas with a 25th-second 20-yarder.

26 Ex-U's Barlow is Workington's leading scorer with seven, but sits out on the bench. A fierce shot from Whittaker opens the scoring. Gibbs lobs over Mike Rogan, and in injury-time Cram squares for Jones to crash in. The Cumbrians finish with ten men when Butler is carried off.

27 A deal for Bournemouth's Keith East fails, as the player dwells on the move. Jones' goal is a carbon copy of his one v Workington. only this time from the left flank. Wingers Kevin Keegan and Angus Davidson give U's a torrid time, leading to Hall's first booking in twelve years.

28 The FA loan U's £5k at low interest, to secure Layer Rd. Wood, in attempting to clear Hooper's corner, can only divert into his own net. Gibbs cancels County's lead with a beautiful header from Oliver's free-kick. Wood almost scores another own-goal, but Smith pulls off a great save.

29 Graham Carr is booked for the third time this term, for dissent. Gibbs is also booked for a remark to the ref, after he was denied a second-half penalty. Earlier Jones put Whittaker away down the left and his accurate cross allowed Brown to shoot through the tangled Avenue defence.

30 Graham signs a new three-year deal. Police dogs patrol the track after crowd trouble. Billy Best gives Shrimpers the lead a minute after Brown hit the post. Bickles' free-kick is misjudged by Frank Haydock for Oliver to level. Gary Moore soars to nod in from Bill Garner's deep cross.

31 Jones diverts Oliver's shot past Gordon Morritt off the post. Shortly after, Gibbs crashes a header against the bar. Morritt is in action again: he superbly saves Jones' header, but can't stop the loose ball. U's third comes when Crams' shot falls to Gibbs at close range.

32 U's are unbeaten in seven at home to Chesterfield. Oliver breaks a small bone in his leg and will be out for a month. Woods' first U's goal puts leaders Chesterfield on the way to their first away defeat since September. Ex-boss Benny Fenton, sees U's have two more efforts disallowed.

33 U's realistically need 10 wins from their last ten to gain promotion. Despite being under the cosh, John Mitten gives Exeter the lead with a hopeful 20-yarder. A minute later Cook handles, but Smith saves Mitten's kick. Top-scorer Alan Banks nets a well-executed free-kick move.

34 Bees parade two new boys in Cross (W Ham) and Docherty (Reading). Their impressive defence had previously not conceded for 430 minutes. Bobby Ross hits a fine opportunist goal, after Bickles poor clearance. Jones pierces the Bees defence after Alan Nelmes had conceded a corner

This page is a season match-record table (Cambridge United, "U's") with per-game line-ups, scores and match reports. Each entry lists the team line-up (and, in italics, the opponents' line-up), scorers, referee, league figures and attendance.

No	Venue	Opponent	Date	HT	FT	Pos	Pts	Att
35	A	WORKINGTON	18/3	0-0	1-1	11	38	2,368 (22)
36	A	CHESTERFIELD	21/3	0-1	0-2	11	38	9,257 (1)
37	H	ALDERSHOT	27/3	2-0	3-1	10 W	40	6,163 (6)
38	H	EXETER	28/3	1-1	2-1	11 W	42	3,842 (15)
39	A	CHESTER	1/4	0-0	0-1	12 L	42	2,580 (10)
40	A	PETERBOROUGH	4/4	1-0	1-1	11 D	43	4,165 (10)
41	H	NORTHAMPTON	6/4	0-2	0-3	11 L	43	3,776 (15)
42	H	OLDHAM	13/4	2-1	3-1	11 W	45	2,921 (19)
43	A	BRENTFORD	18/4	0-1	0-2	12 L	45	4,720 (5)
44	H	LINCOLN	22/4	2-0	2-0	10 W	47	2,611 (8)
45	H	PORT VALE	25/4	0-1	1-1	10 D	48	5,626 (4)
46	A	GRIMSBY	28/4	1-2	3-5	10 L	48	2,074 (16)

Home 4,640 Away 4,902 Average 4,640

35 — WORKINGTON (A)
Scorers: Jones 60 / Spencer 47. Ref: P Baldwin
The board consider a pre-season trip to Norway, instead of Germany. U's are unbeaten in five at Borough Pk. but centre-half Tommy Spencer beats the slow defence to meet Tony Geidmintis's free-kick. Jones, U's acting skipper, nets his twelfth in 17 games, through a sea of red shirts.

36 — CHESTERFIELD (A)
Scorers: Randall 33, Moss 86. Ref: D Pugh
Wood relinquishes the captaincy to Jones. Cook is stretchered off just before the break with a suspected broken ankle. Randall had given Spererites the lead with a great turn and shot. Ernie Moss hits the post (59), but clinches the points despite Smith's courageous attempt to save.

37 — ALDERSHOT (H)
Scorers: Jones 16, 46p, Howe 44 / Brown 58. Ref: K Hawley
Recalled Dyson sends in a pin-point cross that Jones dives full-length to head in. Cram and Jones combine to set up Howe for his first U's goal. U's gain their first penalty of the term when Joe Jopling fouls Jones. Well-beaten Shots pull one back via Brown. Massey limps off (85).

38 — EXETER (H)
Scorers: Gibbs 3, Jones 72, Wingate 20. Ref: K Styles
Sharples' back-pass lets in Gibbs, and despite vain attempts, the ball spirals off Wilson's knee and over the line with Light following in. Out of the blue, John Wingate hits a 30-yarder from the right touch-line. From Cram's corner, Gibbs' flick is cleared as far as Jones, who prods home.

39 — CHESTER (A)
Scorers: Tarbuck 82. Ref: B Golightly
Hall clears off the line on six and 16 minutes. Chester sweep forward relentlessly with McMillan scorching the crossbar (81) and Alan Tarbuck crashing against the upright a minute later. The pressure finally tells when Tarbuck hooks past Smith. Wood shoots tamely at Carling (88).

40 — PETERBOROUGH (A)
Scorers: Jones 7, Hall 53. Ref: A Hart
Hall sends Gibbs down the left: he beats two before setting up Jones in front of an open goal. U's pack their defence when Bickles doesn't re-appear after the break. but Brian Wright threads a ball through U's back line for Jim Hall to score. Drewery stops Gibbs' flick on the line (88).

41 — NORTHAMPTON (H)
Scorers: McNeil 24, 43, 50. Ref: L Sinkins
Dixie McNeil ends U's 12-match unbeaten home run on his own. He hammers in his first before the break. his second when Smith, who pulled a muscle (5), reacts slowly, and holds off two challenges for a fine treble. Smith spectacularly tips Felton's (fouled by Howlett) penalty over.

42 — OLDHAM (H)
Scorers: Whittaker 5, Joslyn 24, Hall 60, Blore 23. Ref: R Challis
Latics are indebted to Brian Gordine for keeping the score down, as U's reap their third double of the season. A free-kick from Hall spins off the wall to Whittaker. Reg Blore exposes U's defence, only for Joslyn to net his first of the term. Hall cuts in from the left for U's third goal.

43 — BRENTFORD (A)
Scorers: Renwick 12, Docherty 63. Ref: G Hartley
Brentford's only home defeat came against the leaders Chesterfield. Dick Renwick nods in Gordon Neilson's flag-kick, whilst John Docherty dispossesses Joslyn. 75th-minute sub Howlett receives a broken leg (88). after a clash with Peter Gelson. United sue for Macedo's transfer fee.

44 — LINCOLN (H)
Scorers: Whittaker 13, 18. Ref: R Spittle
Whittaker destroys any hopes Lincoln had of earning a first-ever win at Layer Road by the 18th minute. His first is a great volley from a very acute angle. Bobby Svarc spurns a great opportunity to claw Imps back into the game. U's promotion hopes are typified by the small turn-out.

45 — PORT VALE (H)
Scorers: Dyson 75, McLaren 38. Ref: W Wallace
With Port Vale already promoted. U's turn out to be party-poopers as the Potteries side fail to sign off with a win. U's have only nine fit pro's and give a debut. and a contract. to 18-year-old local lad Dennis. Graham also signs Painter from Norwich as he plans for the next campaign.

46 — GRIMSBY (A)
Scorers: Light 44, 63, Gibbs 55 / Oates 20, 41, Hickman 56, 71, 82. Ref: A Bone
U's work hard and level at 2-2. only for Mike Hickman to score three passes after the restart. U's fight back to 3-3. but Hickman nods a free-kick and sticks out a foot to divert past Smith. Wood (Workington). Willis. Bickles. Dyson. Light. Oliver. Howe (all non-league) are released.

LEAGUE DIVISION 4 (CUP-TIES)

Manager: Dick Graham

League Cup

				F-A	H-T	Scorers, Times, and Referees	1	2	3	4	5	6	7	8	9	10	11	12 sub used
1	H	READING 13/8	D	1-1	1-1	Massey 9	Willis*	Howlett	Hall	Gibbs	Bickles	Wood	Light	Massey	Oliver	Brown	Whittaker	Joslyn
		5,165 3:				Harris 43p	Brown	Dixon	Thornhill	Wagstaff B	Sharpe	Sainty*	Jenkins	Allen	Silvester	Chappell	Harris	Meldrum
						Ref: H New												

Willis sustains a bad eye injury (24) in a clash with Les Chappell. He is rushed to hospital to have an emergency operation. Gibbs takes over the green jersey, but can't stop George Harris's replay-earning penalty after Harris had been impeded. Earlier Massey nets his second U's goal.

				F-A	H-T	Scorers, Times, and Referees	1	2	3	4	5	6	7	8	9	10	11	12 sub used
1R	A	READING 20/8	W	3-0	1-0	Massey 43, 72, 83	Smith	Joslyn	Hall	Gibbs	Bickles	Wood	Light	Massey	Oliver	Brown	Whittaker	
		11,065 3:3				Ref: R Challis	Brown	Dixon	Thornhill	Wagstaff B	Sharpe	Meldrum	Jenkins	Wagstaff T	Silvester	Chappell	Harris	

Massey turns on the style in a performance of the highest calibre. to earn a mouth-watering tie at Portman Rd. United's first away hat-trick for nearly ten years comes when Roy Brown drops Gibbs' cross. Massey beats Fred Sharpe to Light's cross and Brown only parries Brown's shot.

				F-A	H-T	Scorers, Times, and Referees	1	2	3	4	5	6	7	8	9	10	11	12 sub used
2	A	IPSWICH 3/9	L	0-4	0-1	Carroll 21, Mills 49, Brogan 80p, 81p	Smith	Howe	Hall	Gibbs	Joslyn	Wood	Light*	Massey	Pitt	Brown	Whittaker	Howlett
		19,012 1:22				Ref: R Paine	Best	Carroll	Mills	Viljoen	Baxter	Jefferson	Woods	Collard	Wigg*	O'Rourke	Brogan	Hunt

U's have 5,000 fans, mainly in the Churchman's Stand, although some infiltrate the North Stand. Ex-U's star Bobby Hunt comes off the bench to be rugby-tackled by Smith. Frank Brogan scores his 16th successful penalty, and adds his 17th when Wood slightly brushes Charlie Woods.

FA Cup

				F-A	H-T	Scorers, Times, and Referees	1	2	3	4	5	6	7	8	9	10	11	12 sub used
1	A	NEWPORT 15/11	L	1-2	1-1	Ferguson 24 (og)	Smith	Cook	Hall	Wood	Bickles	Presland	Brown	Gibbs	Massey*	Light	Whittaker	Oliver
		4,224 4:13				White 1, Thomas 50	Weare	Williams	McLaughlin	Ferguson	Wood	Hill	Thomas	Radford	Mabbutt	Derrick	White	Oliver
						Ref: J Sier												

U's have a glaring sun in their faces and fall to a harmless cross in the first minute from David Williams that finds Andy White. White loses control in the box, only for player-boss Bobby Ferguson to own-goal. White crosses for Thomas's winner, as Newport go ten unbeaten.

Pos	Team	P	W	D	L	F	A	W	D	L	F	A	Pts
			Home					**Away**					
1	Chesterfield	46	19	1	3	55	12	8	9	6	22	20	64
2	Wrexham	46	17	6	0	56	16	9	3	11	28	33	61
3	Swansea	46	14	8	1	43	14	9	7	10	23	31	60
4	Port Vale	46	13	9	1	39	10	7	10	6	22	23	59
5	Brentford	46	14	8	1	36	11	6	8	9	22	28	56
6	Aldershot	46	16	5	2	52	22	4	8	11	26	43	53
7	Notts Co	46	14	4	5	44	21	8	4	11	29	41	52
8	Lincoln	46	11	8	4	38	20	6	8	9	28	32	50
9	Peterborough	46	13	8	2	51	21	4	6	13	26	48	48
10	COLCHESTER	46	14	5	4	38	22	3	9	11	26	41	48
11	Chester	46	14	3	6	39	23	7	3	13	19	43	48
12	Scunthorpe	46	11	6	6	34	23	7	4	12	33	42	46
13	York	46	14	7	2	38	16	2	7	14	17	46	46
14	Northampton	46	11	7	5	41	19	5	5	13	23	36	44
15	Crewe	46	12	6	5	37	18	4	6	13	14	33	44
16	Grimsby	46	9	9	5	33	24	5	6	12	21	34	43
17	Southend	46	12	8	3	40	28	3	2	18	19	57	40
18	Exeter	46	13	5	5	48	20	1	6	16	9	39	39
19	Oldham	46	11	4	8	45	28	2	9	12	15	37	39
20	Workington	46	9	9	5	31	21	3	5	15	15	43	38
21	Newport	46	12	3	8	39	24	1	8	14	14	50	37
22	Darlington	46	8	7	8	31	27	5	3	15	22	46	36
23	Hartlepool	46	7	7	9	31	30	3	3	17	11	52	30
24	Bradford PA*	46	6	5	12	23	32	0	6	17	18	64	23
		1104	294	148	110	962	502	110	148	294	502	962	1104

* not re-elected

Odds & ends

Double wins: (3) Bradford Park Avenue, Crewe, Oldham.

Double defeat: (2) Chester, Southend.

Won from behind: (3) Oldham (a), Bradford Park Avenue (h), Grimsby (h).

Lost from in front: (1) Wrexham (a).

High spots: The successful purchase of Layer Road, for approximately £12,000.

Renewed rivalry with Ipswich after 22 years.

Roy Massey's scoring form, before injury.

Only one defeat in the first ten league games.

Thrashing leaders Chesterfield by 4-1 at Layer Road.

Low spots: The crippling injury-list that even meant that trainer Dennis Mochan had to play.

Outplayed by Ipswich in the League Cup.

Failure again to sustain a promotion bid.

Big fall of 1,500 in the average home attendance.

Player of the Year: Ken Jones.

Ever presents: (0).

Hat-tricks: (1) Roy Massey.

Leading scorer: Ken Jones (16).

Appearances / Goals

Player	Lge	Sub	LC	Sub	FAC	Sub	Goals Lge	Goals LC	Goals FAC	Tot
Bickles, Dave	33		2		1					
Brown, Micky	30	2	3		1		9			9
Cook, Micky	19	1	1		1					
Cram, Bobby	21				1					
Dennis, Alan	2	1								
Dyson, Terry	13	2					1			1
Gibbs, Brian	41		3		1		14			14
Hall, Brian	45		3		1		4			4
Howe, Bert	29		1				1			1
Howlett, Bobby	10	6	1			1				
Jones, Ken	28				1		16			16
Joslyn, Roger	38	4	2	1	1		1			1
Light, Danny	23	1	3		1		2			2
Massey, Roy	18	1	3		1		7	4		11
Mochan, Dennis	1									
Oliver, Jim	17	3	2	1			1			1
Pitt, Steve	4	2	1			1				
Presland, Eddie	5									
Slater, Malcolm	4									
Smith, Graham	43		2		1					
Whittaker, Ray	36	1	3		1		7			7
Willis, Ron	3		1							
Wood, Brian	43		3		1		1			1
(own-goals)									1	1
23 players used	506	24	33	2	11	1	64	4	1	69

LEAGUE DIVISION 4 — Manager: Dick Graham — SEASON 1970-71

Player shirt-number columns: **1 2 3 4 5 6 7 8 9 10 11 | 12 sub used**

---

1. H HARTLEPOOL — 15/8 | Att 4,866 | Pos – | Pt W 2 | 1-0 (1-0)

U's: Smith G · Cook · Gilchrist · Joslyn · Garvey · Cram · Mahon · Gibbs · Jones · Crawford · Hall

Opp: McPartland · Goad · White · Crook · Parry · Clarke · Young · Herd · Sharkey · Wright · Kirk

Scorers: Gibbs 35. Ref: D Civil

Crawford (£3k Kettering), Garvey (Watford), Gilchrist (Fulham), and Sherratt (Barnsley), join with summer signings Owen (Watford), Mahon (York), and Kurila (Southend). U's are casual in their approach, but Gibbs fires against Des McPartland's body and gobbles up the rebound.

---

2. A CHESTER — 22/8 | Att 5,447 | Pos – | Pt L 2 | 1-2 (1-2)

U's: Smith G · Cram · Gilchrist · Kurila · Garvey · Owen · Hall · Gibbs · Mahon · Crawford* · Jones | sub Massey

Opp: Carling · Cheetham* · Birks · Bradbury · Turner · Potney · Woodhall · Tarbuck · Webber · Draper · Groves | Edwards

Scorers: Owen 15, Draper 23, Cheetham 38. Ref: T Farley

Chester sold three in the summer for £30k to ease their finances. Owen heads U's in front, but is later booked, with Groves, when tempers fray. Roy Cheetham gets the winner from the tenth free-kick that U's concede. U's have now picked up only one point from five visits to Chester.

---

3. H NORTHAMPTON — 29/8 | Att 5,220 | Pos 17 / 3 | Pt D 3 | 1-1 (1-1)

U's: Smith G · Cram · Gilchrist · Owen* · Garvey · Kurila · Mahon · Gibbs · Jones · Crawford · Hall | sub Massey

Opp: Book · Fairfax · Brookes · Clarke · Rankmore · Kiernan · Felton · East · Large · Fairbrother · McNeil

Scorers: Owen 3, East 43. Ref: H Hackney

Gilchrist sends Hall away to beat the full-back and cross to unmarked Owen. John Fairbrother strikes the upright with a back-header, before Keith East shoots home from Frank Rankmore's flick. The searing heat causes players to wilt after the break, but U's miss a host of chances.

---

4. A BARROW — 31/8 | Att 2,422 | Pos 8 / 22 | Pt W 5 | 2-0 (0-0)

U's: Smith G · Gilchrist · Hall · Kurila · Garvey · Cram · Jones · Gibbs · Mahon · Crawford · Massey

Opp: Dean J · Hollis · Cooper · Hartland · Arrowsmith · Caldwell · Ellison · Harrison · Morrin · Irvine · Storf

Scorers: Gibbs 77, Crawford 87. Ref: R Armstrong

After defeats at Holker St and a goal record of 0-12, U's finally break the sequence. Barrow threaten when Harrison forces a good save from Smith, but 13 minutes from time Gibbs shoots through a ruck of players. Crawford nods in Gilchrist's cross, which Joe Dean sees late.

---

5. A SOUTHPORT — 4/9 | Att 3,792 | Pos 12 / 4 | Pt L 5 | 1-2 (0-2)

U's: Smith G · Gilchrist · Hall · Kurila · Garvey · Cram · Jones · Gibbs · Mahon* · Crawford · Massey* | subs Whittaker, Dunleavy

Opp: Armstrong · Turner · Clarke · Peat · Harrison · Calloway · Field · Russell · Redrobe · Aindow · Marsh*

Scorers: Gibbs 88, Field 15p, Redrobe 21. Ref: J Finney

Tony Field gives the Sandgrounders the lead from the spot, after Lawrie Calloway had lobbed Smith only for Hall to punch over the top from on the line. Six minutes later Eric Redrobe slides home a Kevin Marsh pass, leaving Gibbs to notch a late consolation from Massey's corner.

---

6. H NOTTS CO — 12/9 | Att 4,285 | Pos 15 / 1 | Pt L 5 | 2-3 (1-2)

U's: Smith G · Hall · Gilchrist · Worthington · Garvey · Kurila · Cram · Gibbs · Jones · Crawford · Mahon | sub Jones

Opp: Watling · Brinkley · Stocks · Oakes* · Needham · Stubbs · Bradd · Nixon · Barker · Masson · Crickmore | Jones

Scorers: Gibbs 40, Crawford 89, Stubbs 25 Barker 27, Bradd 79. Ref: R Toseland

County attacks are rare in the second half, but United have difficulty passing the impressive David Needham. Scot Don Masson is prominent in Notts' first two, crossing for Brian Stubbs and having a shot parried to Ritchie Barker. Les Bradd seals the victory eleven minutes from time.

---

7. A BOURNEMOUTH — 18/9 | Att 7,769 | Pos 19 / 3 | Pt L 5 | 1-4 (0-1)

U's: Smith G · — · Hall · Joslyn · Garvey · Kurila · Cram · Crawford* · Jones · Mahon · Cram | sub Owen

Opp: Davies · Gulliver · Stocks · Powell · Jones · Miller · Allen · MacDougall · Sainty* · Rowles · Meredith | Scott

Scorers: Crawford 47, MacDougall 26, 61, 72, 81. Ref: R Crabb

Gilchrist is missing, having been injured at Brum. Cherries' sixth successive win is courtesy of Ted MacDougall. Smith loses possession when challenged by Dennis Allen. David Stocks does the graft for his second. Substitute Tony Scott crosses for the hat-trick goal, and for the fourth.

---

8. A DARLINGTON — 21/9 | Att 4,042 | Pos 14 / 21 | Pt D 6 | 0-0 (0-0)

U's: Sherratt · Cram · Hall · Joslyn · Garvey · Kurila · Jones · Gibbs · Crawford · Massey · Whittaker

Opp: Moor · Peverell · Horner · Carr · Albeson · Graham · Gauden · Hale · Sproates · Peddeby · Harding

Scorers: — . Ref: W Johnson

Smith and Hall are dropped from the side thrashed 1-4 three days ago, giving a debut to summer signing and keeper Sherratt. Crawford twice wastes one-on-one chances with Tony Moor. After the hard-won point at unbeaten Darlington, United travel back by overnight sleeper train.

---

9. H CREWE — 25/9 | Att 5,012 | Pos 15 / 19 | Pt W 8 | 3-0 (1-0)

U's: Sherratt · Cook · Cram · Joslyn · Garvey · Kurila · Jones · Gibbs · Gilchrist · Crawford · Whittaker

Opp: Adams · Summerhill · Leigh · Lowry · Gater · Marsland · Hince · McHale · Morrisey · Wallace · Lang

Scorers: Crawford 41, 86, 90. Ref: R Challis

A dull half is dominated by Crewe's well-executed offside trap. Only Crawford's flick from a Cram free-kick botners the scorers. Marsland's poor back-pass, nine minutes from time, is intercepted by Crawford. The striker completes his treble in injury-time from Joslyn's neat centre.

---

10. A WORKINGTON — 30/9 | Att 2,350 | Pos 15 / 16 | Pt D 9 | 1-1 (0-1)

U's: Sherratt · Cook · Cram · Joslyn · Garvey · Kurila · Jones · Gibbs · Gilchrist · Crawford · Whittaker* | sub Massey

Opp: Burridge · Butler · Wilson · Spratt · Spencer · Wood · Tyrer · Massie · Wookey · Goodfellow · Martin

Scorers: Gibbs 75, Wookey 36. Ref: E Garner

Gibbs salvages a vital point for United by sliding in a cross from Massey. Earlier Jimmy Goodfellow's pass prised open U's defence for ex-U's Martin to cross to Ken Wookey. A brave save by John Burridge, at the feet of Crawford, maintains his side's 17-match unbeaten home run.

---

11. A PETERBOROUGH — 3/10 | Att 5,935 | Pos 15 / 10 | Pt W 11 | 2-1 (1-1)

U's: Sherratt · Cook · Cram · Joslyn · Garvey · Kurila · Jones · Gibbs · Massey · Crawford · Gilchrist | sub Massey

Opp: Drewery · Noble · Duncliffe · Kwiatkowski · Wile · Wright · Turpie · Sheffield* · Hall · Conny · Robson | Moss

Scorers: Gibbs 12, Massey 88, Robson 40. Ref: H Robinson

Crawford holds up Massey's cross until Gibbs arrives to cap a well-worked move. From a second successive corner, Tommy Robson equalises after a couple of Posh's shots are blocked. Massey charges down a clearance in his own half before running on for his first goal for over a year.

Colchester United — Season record (matches 12–23), Division Four

12. OLDHAM (H) — 9/10
Result: Lost 1-2 (HT 0-0) · Lge pos 17 · [6] · 11 pts · Att 5,423
Colchester: Sherratt; Cook, Joslyn, Cram, Massey*, Jones, Kurila, Garvey, Crawford, Gilcrist, Hall
Oldham: Gordine; Wood, McNeill, Whittle, Fryatt, Heath*, Bowie, Turner, Brycewood, Bebbington, Mundy
Scorers: Crawford 51 / Bebbington 50, Mundy 55
Ref: T Spencer
U's 4-3-3 system works fine away but lacks in pace for a home game Crawford curls U's level with the outside of his foot. Sub James Mundy, loaned from Man City with a £14k price tag, nets his first-ever goal, surprising the static Sherratt. Graham returns part-time after his operation.

13. HARTLEPOOL (A) — 17/10
Result: Won 2-1 (HT 0-1) · Lge pos 14 · [20] · 13 pts · Att 2,193
Colchester: Smith G; Cram, Kurila, Gilchrist, Jones, Gibbs, Owen*, Green, Crawford, Hall, Massey
Hartlepool: McPartland; Bircumshaw* (Dawes), Gill, Green, Cook, Young, Parry, Sharkey, Clarke, Kirk, Herd
Scorers: Mahon 58, Gibbs 85 / Sharkey 43
Ref: J Wrennall
Joslyn decides to join Aldershot for £8k. Des McPartland completely misjudges the flight of Mahon's corner, which hits the post, hits him and rolls in, and later parries into Gibbs' path. Pool's is a happy hunting ground for U's, who have now gone four unbeaten at the Victoria Ground.

14. YORK (H) — 19/10
Result: Won 1-0 (HT 0-0) · Lge pos 12 · [14] · 15 pts · Att 4,457
Colchester: Smith G; Cram, Kurila, Mahon, Gibbs, Crawford, Gilchrist*, Garvey, Mahon, Jones, Massey
York: Hillyard; Mackin, Burrows, Davidson, Swallow, Taylor, Topping, Bayer, Aimson, Hewitt, Owen
Scorers: Crawford 50
Ref: A Hart
Sir Alf Ramsey is present to see Ray Crawford head the winner, albeit with a slice of luck. Crawford, off-balance, gets in a looping header that teenage keeper Ron Hillyard appears to help in. Paul Aimson comes closest for Minstermen, but sees his effort go the wrong side of the post.

15. STOCKPORT (A) — 23/10
Result: Drawn 0-0 (HT 0-0) · Lge pos 13 · [9] · 16 pts · Att 5,113
Colchester: Smith G; Cram, Kurila, Hall, Cook, Garvey, Kurila, Massey, Crawford, Gibbs, Mahon
Stockport: Brown; Haydock, Elgin, Foley, Coddington, Smith, Ryden, Griffiths, Mulvaney, Price, Brookes
Ref: D Mapp
Stockport, who nearly folded last season, maintain their record of being unbeaten in five league games at home. Chairman Dragan Lukic has steadied the ship. For Colchester it is a fifth game away without defeat. The visitors manage to win the corner count by ten flag-kicks to three.

16. ALDERSHOT (A) — 30/10
Result: Won 5-2 (HT 2-1) · Lge pos 8 · [18] · 18 pts · Att 5,848
Colchester: Smith G; Cook, Gilchrist, Cram, Jones, Garvey, Mahon, Kurila, Crawford, Gibbs, Hall
Aldershot: Hollins; Walden, Walker, Giles, Dean, Walton, Howarth, Brown, Melia, Brodie
Scorers: Brodie 13 (og), Crawford 28, Hall 57 [Jones 75, 77] / Walton 44, Howarth 46
Ref: G Lewis
Shot's Walker hits the post before the goal jamboree starts. Murray Brodie heads an own goal, trying to clear Mahon's corner. Goals either side of the break draw Aldershot level. A packed box is pierced by Hall before Jones nabs a brace via Crawford's attempted shot, and a fine volley.

17. EXETER (A) — 7/11
Result: Drawn 2-2 (HT 1-1) · Lge pos 10 · [15] · 19 pts · Att 4,420
Colchester: Smith G; Cram, Kurila, Hall, Jones, Gibbs, Kurila, Garvey, Crawford, Mahon, Massey
Exeter: Wilson; Crawford, Blain, Parker, Balson, Rowan, Newman, Gadston, Banks, Mitten, Corr
Scorers: Jones 36, Massey 50 / Gadston 22, Banks 80
Ref: H Powell
A swift move between Parker and ex-U's Rowan ends with Gadston cracking home. Unsighted Wilson makes a hash of Jones' one-two with Mahon. Mahon then provides a cross that eludes Wilson's dive, giving Massey a simple tap in. Banks nets the best goal, racing fully 30 yards.

18. NEWPORT (A) — 10/11
Result: Won 3-1 (HT 2-1) · Lge pos 8 · [24] · 21 pts · Att 1,973
Colchester: Smith G; Cram, Kurila, Hall, Jones, Gibbs, Kurila, Garvey, Crawford, Mahon, Massey
Newport: Lynch; Coldrick, Williams, Mabbutt, Saunders, Harris, Hooper, Jones, Thomas*, Darrell, White (Radford)
Scorers: Jones 28, Massey 35, 55 / Jones 29
Ref: R Fennetty
County start three points adrift in 24th place, with just two wins in 17 games. P/m Bobby Ferguson drops himself for the first time this season. Roddy Jones cancels out U's opener by Ken Jones, but then on County are not in it. The win puts U's up with the promotion contenders.

19. SOUTHEND (H) — 13/11
Result: Drawn 1-1 (HT 1-1) · Lge pos 7 · [19] · 22 pts · Att 7,777
Colchester: Smith G; Cram, Kurila, Hall, Jones, Gibbs, Kurila, Garvey, Crawford, Mahon, Massey
Southend: Lloyd; Bentley, Simpson, Lumsden*, Beesley, Chisnall, Best, Garner, Moore, Chambers, Lindsay
Scorers: Crawford 36 / Moore 41
Ref: K Burns
A rain-soaked derby sees Crawford net a fine volley, via Cram's cross. Just before the break Smith fails to hold a soft shot that goes for a flag-kick. Phil Chisnall's corner is nodded in by Gary Moore. Bill Garner is booked for arguing with the ref. Crawford could well have had four.

20. BRENTFORD (H) — 28/11
Result: Won 4-0 (HT 2-0) · Lge pos 6 · [21] · 24 pts · Att 4,673
Colchester: Smith G; Cram, Gibbs, Cram*, Mahon, Jones, Kurila, Garvey, Crawford, Gilchrist, Hall
Brentford: Brodie; Hawley, Renwick, Turner, Gelson, Nelmes, Docherty, Ross, Neilson, Graham, Mahon
Scorers: Gibbs 10, Cram 14, Crawford 49, 87
Ref: R Shepherd
Leslie signs pro forms. Brentford beat Gills 2-0 in last week's FA Cup-tie. In front of the Match of the Week cameras, and with U's 2-0 up, a dog runs onto the pitch and lunges at Bees' keeper Chic Brodie. He needs lengthy treatment, whilst the dog escapes without even a booking.

21. CAMBRIDGE (A) — 5/12
Result: Lost 1-2 (HT 1-1) · Lge pos 8 · [16] · 24 pts · Att 5,183
Colchester: Smith G; Cook, Hall, Mahon, Jones, Kurila, Garvey, Slack, Crawford, Mahon, Gibbs
Cambridge: Vaspar; Thompson, Grant, Walker, Meldrum*, Hardy, Horrey, Slack, Hollett, Gregson, Harris (Cassidy)
Scorers: Crawford 16 / Harris 13, Horrey 86
Ref: R Bowling
Cambridge's offside trap means the main entertainment comes from a terrace punch-up. Ivan Hollett's header hits George Harris on the chest and in past the motionless Smith. Crawford nets a crisp header from Mahon's flag-kick. but out of the blue Roly Horrey wins it from 20 yards.

22. CHESTER (H) — 18/12
Result: Lost 0-1 (HT 0-1) · Lge pos 10 · [9] · 24 pts · Att 4,342
Colchester: Smith G; Cook, Hall, Mahon, Painter, Kurila, Garvey*, Hall, Crawford, Mahon, Gibbs
Chester: Carling; Cheetham, Birks, Bradbury, Turner, Poutney, McHale, Tarbuck, Loyden, Draper, Groves (Dennis)
Scorers: — / Draper 6
Ref: M Sinclair
Burgess trials from Plymouth. He has been out since the end of last term. helping in his father's business. The match is in some doubt due to a possible power strike. Kurila is booked for a foul. and from the resulting quickly-taken free-kick. Eddie Loyden heads back for Derek Draper.

23. LINCOLN (A) — 26/12
Result: Won 2-1 (HT 1-0) · Lge pos 9 · [16] · 26 pts · Att 5,919
Colchester: Smith G; Cook, Hall, Mahon, Simmons, Kurila, Lewis, Garvey, Crawford, Mahon, Gibbs
Lincoln: McInally; Taylor G, Peden, Hubbard, Harford, Grummett, Fletcher, Trevis, Freeman, Taylor W, Svarc
Scorers: Lewis 30, Simmons 58 / Svarc 66
Ref: K Baker
Simmons signs (Aston Villa £6k), as does Lewis (Oxford £6k). Imps had also paid the same fee for Trevis from Walsall in August. Lincoln are fresh from a 4-1 FAC 2nd replay win over Bradford United's fifth away win, and third in four at Sincil Bank, is secured by the two debutants.

LEAGUE DIVISION 4 — Manager: Dick Graham — SEASON 1970-71

Results summary

No	H/A	Opponent	Date	Att	Pos	*	Res	Pt	F-A	H-T
24	H	WORKINGTON	8/1	5,239	7	13	W	28	2-1	0-1
25	A	YORK	16/1	3,804	7	9	D	29	1-1	1-1
26	H	CAMBRIDGE	5/2	6,469	7	18	W	31	2-1	1-0
27	H	NEWPORT	20/2	6,444	8	24	W	33	4-2	2-2
28	H	GRIMSBY	22/2	7,253	6	20	W	35	1-0	0-0
29	A	ALDERSHOT	26/2	7,609	6	15	W	37	1-0	1-0
30	H	DARLINGTON	8/3	7,110	6	9	W	39	2-0	2-0
31	A	SOUTHEND	12/3	9,406	7	20	D	40	1-1	1-0
32	A	SCUNTHORPE	16/3	3,715	7	15	L	40	0-2	0-0
33	H	EXETER	20/3	5,630	6	10	D	41	1-1	0-0
34	H	SCUNTHORPE	22/3	5,592	7	15	W	43	2-0	0-0

Team line-ups list the Colchester United player (top) and the opponent (italic) in each numbered position. Scorers, times and referees, plus the match report, follow each game.

---

24. WORKINGTON (H) — Scorers: Cram 63, Crawford 71; Geidmintis 27. Ref: J Flye. 12 sub used: Garvey

1	2	3	4	5	6	7	8	9	10	11	12
Smith G	Cook	Hall	Cram	Gibbs	Kurila	Simmons	Lewis*	Mahon	Crawford	Gilchrist	Garvey
Burridge	*Wilson*	*Ogilvie*	*Geidmintis*	*Spencer*	*Wood*	*Helliwell*	*Spratt*	*Massie*	*Goodfellow*	*Martin*	

After Tony Geidmintis' goal from Jimmy Goodfellow's twice-taken free-kick, the Cumbrians shut up shop. Cram fires in a centre that deceives young John Burridge. Simmons robs John Ogilvie to square to Crawford. Workington have only two draws from their six visits to Layer Road.

---

25. YORK (A) — Scorers: Kurila 5; McMahon 17. Ref: F Hardy

1	2	3	4	5	6	7	8	9	10	11
Smith G	Cook	Hall	Cram	Garvey	Kurila	Simmons	Lewis	Crawford	Mahon	Gibbs
Hillyard	*Mackin*	*Burrows*	*Davidson*	*Swallow*	*Topping*	*Taylor*	*Hewitt*	*McMahon*	*Ainson*	*Henderson*

York are 26 unbeaten at home. Ron Hillyard only blocks Mahon's shot, the loose ball falls to Kurila to put U's one up. Tom Henderson's flag-kick ends with Kevin McMahon nodding in. John Mackin puts a penalty over (44), after Mahon trips Dick Hewitt. Crawford hits the post twice.

---

26. CAMBRIDGE (H) — Scorers: Crawford 13, 74; Horrey 58. Ref: H Robinson

1	2	3	4	5	6	7	8	9	10	11
Smith G	Gilchrist	Hall	Cram	Garvey	Kurila	Gibbs	Simmons	Lewis	Crawford	Mahon
Vaspar	*Thompson*	*Meldrum*	*Walker*	*White*	*Eades*	*Horrey*	*Collins*	*Hollett*	*Cassidy*	*Gregson*

Cambridge pull no punches with a rugged display. A shot falls to Lewis on the bye-line, his cross is put in by Crawford. Collins' cross should have been cleared, but Roly Horrey forces the equaliser. Crawford's nod from Cram's free-kick gives watching Don Revie pause for thought.

---

27. NEWPORT (H) — Scorers: Simmons 44, Mahon 45, Lewis 65p; Young 18, Brown 23 (Crawford 79). Ref: K Crabb. 12 sub used: Burgess / Saunders

1	2	3	4	5	6	7	8	9	10	11	12
Smith G	Hall*	Cram	Gibbs	Garvey	Kurila	Lewis	Simmons	Mahon	Crawford	White*	Burgess
Macey	*Williams*	*Ferguson*	*Coldrick*	*Woods*	*Aizlewood*	*Thomas*	*Jones*	*Brown*	*Young*	*White*	*Saunders*

County's boss says U's are animals and get away with it as they are everybody's darlings at the moment. U's have secured 24 points from a possible 30 against County at home, and remain unbeaten. Lewis is fouled by Alan Woods in the box, and then crosses for Crawford's winner.

---

28. GRIMSBY (H) — Scorers: Mahon 47. Ref: F Bassett

1	2	3	4	5	6	7	8	9	10	11
Smith G	Hall	Cram	Cook	Garvey	Kurila	Gibbs	Simmons	Mahon	Crawford	Lewis
Short	*Worthington*	*Kirkland*	*Kennedy*	*Rathbone*	*Gray*	*Woodward*	*Tees*	*Hickman*	*Boylen*	*Brace*

Five successive wins, ten without defeat. Cram taps a free-kick to Mahon, who explodes a 25-yard thunderbolt into the top corner past Maurice Boylen's shot is cleared to Dave Hickman, who forces a spectacular tip-over from Smith. Short for U's 72nd league and cup goal of the term.

---

29. ALDERSHOT (A) — Scorers: Cram 3. Ref: C Nicholls. 12: Burt

1	2	3	4	5	6	7	8	9	10	11	12
Smith G	Hall	Cram	Cook	Garvey	Kurila	Simmons	Gibbs	Lewis	Crawford	Mahon	
Dixon	*Walden*	*Walker*	*Joslyn*	*Dean*	*Bennett*	*Priscott**	*Brown*	*Brodie*	*Melia*	*Giles*	*Burt*

Kurila's cross reaches Lewis, who lays off for Cram's third of the term. Richard Walden is in action at both ends for Shots; he hits the bar and then trips Lewis in the box, unpunished. U's, watched by Everton manager Harry Catterick, have dropped one point in the last seven games.

---

30. DARLINGTON (H) — Scorers: Crawford 23, Simmons 35. Ref: R Johnson

1	2	3	4	5	6	7	8	9	10	11
Smith G	Hall	Cram	Cook	Garvey	Kurila	Gibbs	Simmons	Lewis	Crawford	Mahon
Moor	*Peverell*	*Horner*	*Peddelty*	*Alleson*	*Graham*	*Gauden*	*Hale*	*McDonald*	*Wright*	*Harding*

U's receive the Sunday Mirror Giant-killers cup before the kick-off, in recognition of the amazing win over Leeds. Despite the trouncing at Everton two days earlier, U's have no hangover as Mahon's wonderful run sets up Crawford's 25th, and Simmons nods in Tony Moor's parry.

---

31. SOUTHEND (A) — Scorers: Barker 23 (og); Smith 77. Ref: G Hill

1	2	3	4	5	6	7	8	9	10	11
Sherratt	Hall	Cram	Cook	Garvey	Kurila	Gibbs	Simmons	Lewis	Crawford	Mahon
Roberts	*Lindsay*	*Smith*	*Elliott*	*Barker*	*Jacques*	*Johnson*	*Best*	*Garner*	*Hunt*	*Lewis*

Kurila is captain for the day. Geoff Barker slices Crawford's header onto the bar and over the line. U's are 13 minutes away from a first win at Roots Hall in eight years, when Alex Smith takes Bill Garner's pass to shoot past Sherratt. Accounts show the Dev. Assoc. have raised £19k.

---

32. SCUNTHORPE (A) — Scorers: Woolmer 48, O'Riley 77. Ref: W Hall. 12: Whittaker

1	2	3	4	5	6	7	8	9	10	11	12
Sherratt	Hall	Cram	Cook	Garvey	Kurila	Gibbs	Simmons	Lewis*	Crawford	Jones	Whittaker
Barnard	*Davidson*	*Jackson*	*Heath*	*Deere*	*Welbourne*	*Woolmer*	*McDonald*	*O'Riley*	*Keegan*	*Kirk*	

Graham is the first Fourth Div manager to become overall Manager of the Month. Not even the return of Jones can stop the first loss since 19 December. Tenacious Scunthorpe are stronger in midfield and win via Tony Woolmer (header), and Hull loan-player Paul O'Riley (volley).

---

33. EXETER (H) — Scorers: Crawford 60; Banks 75. Ref: T Reynolds. 12: Corr

1	2	3	4	5	6	7	8	9	10	11	12
Smith G	Cook	Hall	Cram	Garvey	Cram	Gibbs	Crawford	Whittaker	Jones	Lewis	
Wilson	*Crawford*	*Blain*	*Parker*	*Balson*	*Wingate*	*Rowan*	*Banks*	*Gadston**	*Binney*	*Morris*	*Corr*

Simmons damages his cartilage warming up and is stretchered off. Hall sets up Crawford's headed goal, and clears off the line late. Hit-man Alan Banks nods in a Rowan corner. Smith is booked (88) for a remark to the ref. Exeter haven't won at Layer Road in the League since 1955.

---

34. SCUNTHORPE (H) — Scorers: Crawford 52, 55. Ref: D Biddle

1	2	3	4	5	6	7	8	9	10	11
Smith G	Cook	Hall	Cram	Garvey	Kurila	Gibbs	Crawford	Mahon	Jones	Lewis
Williams	*Davidson*	*Jackson*	*Heath*	*Deere*	*Welbourne*	*Woolmer*	*McDonald*	*O'Riley*	*Keegan*	*Kirk*

Simmons slips down his brother-in-law's stairs, putting his arm through a glass door. He is in intensive care after a huge loss of blood. Mike Williams debuts for Scunthorpe. Massey is forced to retire due to an arthritic knee. Crawford's pair denies Iron a hat-trick of Layer Road wins.

No.		Date	Opponent	Score (HT)	Score (FT)	Res	Pos		Att	Pts
35	H	27/3	SOUTHPORT	1-0	1-0	W	7	8	5,909	45
36	A	29/3	BRENTFORD	0-1	0-1	L	7	16	9,190	45
37	A	3/4	NORTHAMPTON	0-2	1-2	L	7	6	7,909	45
38	H	9/4	PETERBOROUGH	3-0	3-0	W	7	15	7,650	47
39	H	10/4	LINCOLN	1-1	1-1	D	7	21	6,430	48
40	A	12/4	NOTTS CO	0-2	0-4	L	7	1	14,084	48
41	A	17/4	OLDHAM	0-1	0-4	L	7	3	10,045	48
42	A	20/4	GRIMSBY	1-3	0-1	L	7	21	4,166	48
43	H	23/4	BOURNEMOUTH	1-1	1-1	D	7	2	4,168	49
44	H	26/4	BARROW	3-1	4-1	W	6	24	3,502	51
45	A	1/5	CREWE	3-0	3-0	W	6	14	2,708	53
46	H	7/5	STOCKPORT	1-0	1-1	D	6	11	5,471	54

Home Average 5,598 Away 5,633 Average 5,633

---

35 — H SOUTHPORT 27/3 — 1-0

U's: Smith G, Cook, Hall, Cram, Garvey, Kurila, Gibbs, Crawford, Mahon, Jones, Lewis
Opp: Wraith, Clarke, Aindow, Peat, Dunleavy, Calloway, Lee, Cocks, Marsh, Field, Hughes
Crawford 7
Ref: M Washer

Roy Chapman becomes chairman. at the same time as Graham has a row with former chairman Graver Mahon hits a long ball up the middle, where Crawford heads neatly into the net, beating the square Southport defence, and later hits the post. Clarke is booked for a foul on Lewis.

36 — A BRENTFORD 29/3 — 0-1

U's: Smith G, Cook, Hall, Cram, Garvey, Kurila, Gibbs, Crawford, Lewis, Jones, Burgess
Opp: Phillips, Hawley, Renwick, Turner, Gelson, Nelmes, Neilson, Ross, Cross, Graham, Bence
Neilson 87
Ref: A Fussey

Debut-making Burgess spurns two good openings, whilst Smith earns a standing ovation for his save from Alan Hawley. U's have now failed to win in twelve visits to Griffin Park. Brentford's hooked-in winner, by Gordon Neilson, is a very soft goal to give away at such a late stage.

37 — A NORTHAMPTON 3/4 — 1-2

U's: Smith G, Burgess*, Hall, Cram, Garvey, Kurila, Gibbs, Jones, Mahon, Crawford, Lewis / Cook
Opp: Book, Neal, Heslop, Fairfax, Large, Kiernan, McNeil, Ross, East, Gould, Fairbrother
Kurila 49, McNeil 6, 40
Ref: C Thomas

The game starts at 7 pm to avoid a clash with the Grand National. Off-key U's improve in second half, but Kurila's 30-yarder is not enough to earn a point. Dixie McNeil, who cracked a treble against U's last term, clips in Keith East's pass off the post, and heads in Eric Ross' free-kick.

38 — H PETERBOROUGH 9/4 — 3-0

U's: Smith G, Cram, Hall, Gilchrist, Garvey, Kurila, Jones, Crawford, Lewis, Gibbs, Mahon
Opp: Dighton, Noble, Duncliffe, Wright, Turner, Carmichael, Turpie*, Kwiatkowski Hall, Pleat, Robson, Iley
Gibbs 65, Gilchrist 73, Hall 90
Ref: D Corbett

Lewis ghosts past two defenders to cross for Gibbs to head in his 150th league goal. Gilchrist becomes the inaugural winner of the Players' Player of the Year award, a trophy donated by Anthony Buck MP. Hall's fine solo run gives United a third.

39 — H LINCOLN 10/4 — 1-1

U's: Smith G, McInally, Hall, Gilchrist, Garvey, Kurila, Jones, Crawford, Lewis*, Gibbs, Mahon
Opp: Brookes, Taylor G, Harford, Branston, Grummett, Meath*, Lawton, Hubbard, Smith, Taylor W, Whittaker / Meath
Gibbs 2, Hubbard 34
Ref: D Lyden

Lewis sustains a broken wrist and is out for the rest of the term, leaving Graham with 13 fit pro's to finish the season with. Hall's centre is held up by Crawford, allowing Gibbs to crash home. Hall slips trying to clear, and Smith inexplicably dives the wrong way as Phil Hubbard shoots.

40 — A NOTTS CO 12/4 — 0-4

U's: Sherratt*, Hall, Gilchrist, Garvey, Kurila, Whittaker, Crawford, Gibbs, Jones, Mahon
Opp: Waling, Brindlay, Worthington Jones, Needham, Oakes, Nixon, Barker, Hateley, Masson, Crickmore, Burgess
Hateley 2, 9, 66, Masson 72
Ref: R Challis

Sherratt receives a fractured shoulder in a clash with Tony Hateley. Gibbs goes in goal, as he did against Reading last season. Depleted United are outplayed as County add two further goals, including Hateley's hat-trick header. County gain promotion and cap it with the championship.

41 — A OLDHAM 17/4 — 0-4 [Shaw 85]

U's: Smith G, Cook, Hall, Cram, Garvey, Kurila, Gilchrist, Crawford*, Burgess, Jones, Dennis
Opp: Dowd, Wood, Whittle, McNeill, Cranston, Bowie, Heath, Shaw, Fryatt, Bryceland, Bebbington
Hall 10 (og), Bebbington 59, 86
Ref: G Hartley

Smith saves Alan McNeill's penalty (14). his fourth consecutive stop, after Garvey handles. United are well beaten by the hour. The rout starts when Hall diverts Keith Bebbington's shot into his own net. Bebbington adds a pair and David Shaw takes advantage of Cram's bad mistake.

42 — A GRIMSBY 20/4 — 0-1

U's: Smith G, Wainman, Hall, Cram, Garvey, Burgess, Gilchrist, Kurila, Leslie, Mahon, Gibbs*
Opp: Worthington, Campbell, Ross, Rathbone, Gray, Brace, Lewis, Tees, Boylen, Woodward
Burgess 63, Brace 36, Lewis 49, Ross 58p
Ref: R Raby

Chapman warns that although the season had been successful, it had been costly and that out-goings exceeded in-comings. Grimsby's win virtually ensures they won't have to apply for re-election, whilst L Smith is U's youngest debutant when he comes on after Grimsby's penalty.

43 — H BOURNEMOUTH 23/4 — 1-1

U's: Smith G, Cook, Hall, Burgess, Garvey, Kurila, Cram, Gilchrist, Crawford, Gibbs, Mahon
Opp: Davies, Benson, Stocks, Jones, Miller, Powell, Holland, MacDougall, Boyer, Sainty, Scott
Crawford 11, MacDougall 39
Ref: J Taylor

Man of the match Cook lays on Crawford's goal in an entertaining match. Ted MacDougall scores his 46th goal of the season (including nine in the 11-0 FA Cup win over Margate). York's 2-0 defeat of Scunthorpe means that United's promotion hopes are now mathematically over.

44 — H BARROW 26/4 — 4-1

U's: Smith G, Cook, Hall, Burgess, Garvey, Bloss, Cram, Gilchrist*, Leslie, Crawford, Mahon, Gibbs
Opp: Dean, Caldwell, Cooper, Arrowsmith, Russell, Noble, Garbett, Morrin, Irvine, Start, Hollis*, Rowlands
Mahon 11, Hall 16, Bloss 23, Cram 58p; Irvine 45
Ref: N Burkenshaw

Barrow are already assured of the wooden spoon. Graham experiments with youth players Bloss and Leslie. Bloss caps his debut by sliding the third under Joe Dean. Bobby Noble gives away a needless handball, when the ball was going out. Barrow haven't won in four at Layer Road.

45 — A CREWE 1/5 — 3-0

U's: Smith G, Kurila, Hall, Burgess, Cram, Gibbs, Gilchrist, Jones, Crawford, Mahon
Opp: Adams, Lowry, Leigh, Turner*, Gater, Summerhill, Tewley, Wallace, Morrisey, Bowles, Bradshaw / Osborne
Hall 4, Crawford 44, Mahon 49
Ref: K Styles

Stan Bowles is booked for a nasty foul on Gibbs, which requires lengthy treatment, just before the break. Bloss earns a pro contract. Had it not been for Adams, then U's would have run up a cricket score. Crewe introduce their 16-year-old sub Glyn Osborne (56) as they too experiment.

46 — H STOCKPORT 7/5 — 1-1

U's: Smith G, Cram, Hall, Burgess, Garvey, Kurila, Gilchrist, Crawford, Gibbs, Jones, Mahon
Opp: Brown, Haydock, Chapman, Elgin, Hart, Wilson, Ryden, Griffiths, Collier, Smith, Price
Gibbs 23; Collier 79
Ref: T Dawes

U's play end-of-season friendlies at Barnet, Chelmsford and Romford to raise funds for a club holiday in Benidorm. Brown, Painter, Whittaker and Sherratt are released into non-league. U's needed to score six to win £4k as top scorers, or one to qualify for next season's Watney Cup.

LEAGUE DIVISION 4 (CUP-TIES) Manager: Dick Graham SEASON 1970-71

League Cup

1 · H · CAMBRIDGE · 19/8 — W 5-0 (H-T 2-0) · 6,952 · 4:

1	2	3	4	5	6	7	8	9	10	11	12 sub used
Smith G	Cram	Gilchrist	Owen	Garvey	Kurila	Hall	Gibbs	Mahon	Crawford*	Jones	Massey
Roberts	*Thompson*	*Meldrum*	*Slack*	*Eades*	*Hardy*	*Leggett*	*Walker*	*Lindsay*	*Harris*	*McKinven**	*Grant*

Scorers: Hall 10, Owen 23, 80, Jones 57p, 69. Ref: A Dimond

New-boys Cambridge last visited Layer Rd in 1958, losing to U's Res by 1-10 (agg) in the Eastern Co Lge cup final. Both Owen's goals come from bursts through a static defence in a week when he is re-appointed England Youth team trainer. Smith saves George Harris's penalty (87).

2 · H · BIRMINGHAM · 9/9 — D 1-1 (H-T 0-0) · 8,085 · 2:11

1	2	3	4	5	6	7	8	9	10	11	12 sub used
Smith G	Gilchrist	Hall	Owen	Cram	Kurila	Hall	Gibbs	Mahon	Crawford	Jones	
Kelly	*Martin*	*Pendrey*	*Page*	*Hynd*	*Robinson*	*Hockey*	*Vowden*	*Latchford*	*Vincent*	*Summerhill*	

Scorers: Jones 54 / Summerhill 67. Ref: R Johnson

Hall beats Roger Hynd, who is later booked, and crosses for Jones' thundering header. A moment's hesitation by three defenders allows Phil Summerhill to level for the Midlanders. Graham goes into hospital for kidney stones treatment. Trainer Dennis Mochan takes over temporarily.

2R · A · BIRMINGHAM · 15/9 — L 1-2 (H-T 1-0) · 17,606 · 2:11

1	2	3	4	5	6	7	8	9	10	11	12 sub used
Smith G	Gilchrist	Hall	Cook	Garvey	Kurila	Cram	Gibbs	Jones	Crawford	Joslyn	
Kelly	*Thomson*	*Green*	*Robinson*	*Hynd*	*Pendrey*	*Hockey*	*Vowden*	*Summerhill*	*Francis*	*Darrell*	

Scorers: Jones 13 / Vowden 83, Summerhill 88. Ref: V Batty

U's are a goal up, through Jones' crisp drive, with just seven minutes left when Geoff Vowden punishes Smith's poor punch. Brum finally take the lead after 178 minutes to host Nottingham Forest. The three cup matches so far have boosted the coffers by £3k from the extra gate money.

FA Cup

1 · H · RINGMER · 21/11 — W 3-0 (H-T 2-0) · 6,139 · SC:1

1	2	3	4	5	6	7	8	9	10	11	12 sub used
Smith G	Cook	Hall	Cram	Garvey	Kurila	Massey	Gibbs	Jones	Crawford	Mahon*	Gilchrist
Finch	*Tasker*	*Muggeridge*	*Grimes*	*Burnett*	*Hamill*	*Jones*	*Mennham*	*Stevens G*	*Stevens J*	*Skart*	

Scorers: Crawford 7, 45, 87. Ref: R Morphew

Ringmer are unbeaten in the Sussex County League this term and their only defeat has come in the FA Amateur Cup. Most of the game is played with 19 men in the visitors' half. Crawford becomes the first player in U's history to hit a league and cup hat-trick in the same season.

2 · H · CAMBRIDGE · 12/12 — W 3-0 (H-T 2-0) · 7,348 · 4:16

1	2	3	4	5	6	7	8	9	10	11	12 sub used
Smith G	Cook	Hall	Cram	Garvey	Kurila	Jones*	Whittaker	Mahon	Crawford	Gilchrist	Owen
Vaspar	*Thompson*	*Grant*	*Slack*	*Eades*	*Hardy*	*Horrey*	*Gregson*	*Hollett*	*Cassidy*	*Howell*	

Scorers: Jones 31, Gilchrist 39, Garvey 65. Ref: J Chamberlain

U's prepare with two days at Holland-on-Sea. Owen, with his first touch, sets up Garvey for his first United goal, but collides with a defender, breaking his knee-cap. Only when U's are reduced to effectively nine and a half men for the last 25 minutes does the game become a contest.

3 · A · BARNET · 5/1 — W 1-0 (H-T 1-0) · 4,909 · SI

1	2	3	4	5	6	7	8	9	10	11	12 sub used
Smith G	Cook	Hall	Cram	Garvey	Kurila	Simmons	Lewis	Gibbs	Crawford	Mahon*	Gilchrist
McClelland	*Lye*	*Jenkins*	*Ward*	*Embury*	*King*	*Powell*	*Ferry*	*George*	*Eason*	*Adams*	

Scorers: Mahon 7. Ref: K Walker

Barnet had managed a 6-1 post-war record victory for a non-league side, v Newport in the first round. The treacherous pitch is barely playable after Saturday's postponement. McClelland slips on the icy surface, and only helps Mahon's 40-yard free-kick into the net.

4 · A · ROCHDALE · 23/1 — D 3-3 (H-T 1-1) · 12,321 · 3:23

1	2	3	4	5	6	7	8	9	10	11	12 sub used
Smith G	Hall	Cook	Cram	Garvey	Kurila	Simmons	Lewis	Gibbs*	Mahon	Crawford	Gilchrist
Tennant	*Smith*	*Ryder*	*Riley*	*Parry*	*Ashworth*	*Whitehead*	*Buck*	*Cross*	*Downes*	*Butler*	

Scorers: Crawford 3, Lewis 85, Simmons 87 / Ashworth 27, Buck 53, 61. Ref: R Capey

Dale surprisingly dispose of First Division Coventry. The Supporters' Club train... is the first to an away game since Blackpool (1948). The return fare is 45 shillings. Cram misses a penalty (68), when U's are 1-3 down, but an amazing fight-back earns United a Layer Road replay.

4R · H · ROCHDALE · 25/1 — W 5-0 (H-T 2-0) · 11,205 · 3:23

1	2	3	4	5	6	7	8	9	10	11	12 sub used
Smith G	Cram	Hall	Gibbs	Garvey	Kurila	Lewis	Simmons	Gilchrist	Mahon	Crawford	
Godfrey	*Smith*	*Ryder*	*Riley*	*Parry*	*Ashworth*	*Whitehead*	*Buck**	*Cross*	*Downes*	*Butler*	*Blair*

Scorers: Lewis 42, Simmons 44, Parry 50 (og), Crawford 70, Mahon 76. Ref: R Capey

U's are in the fifth round for the first time in 23 years, aided by the drooling prospect of a home tie with Leeds. Rochdale allowed the tie to slip on Saturday as U's hit the post twice, and have now cleared off the line. Mahon caps a superb win, skating past three to fire in from 25 yards.

5 · H · LEEDS · 13/2 — W 3-2 (H-T 2-0) · 16,000 · 1:1

1	2	3	4	5	6	7	8	9	10	11	12 sub used
Smith G	Hall	Cram	Gilchrist	Garvey	Kurila	Lewis	Simmons	Mahon	Crawford	Gibbs	
Sprake	*Reaney*	*Cooper*	*Bates*	*Charlton*	*Hunter*	*Lorimer*	*Clarke*	*Jones*	*Giles*	*Madeley*	

Scorers: Crawford 18, 24, Simmons 54. Ref: D Lyden

Graham's 'Grandad's Army' stuns the football world with a sensational win over the league leaders. Crammed with incident, Leeds are shell-shocked as U's take a 3-0 lead. Despite a late comeback, United hold on when Smith makes a magnificent world-class save from Mick Jones.

QF · A · EVERTON · 6/3 — L 0-5 (H-T 0-4) · 53,028 · 1:10

1	2	3	4	5	6	7	8	9	10	11	12 sub used
Smith G	Cram	Hall	Gilchrist	Garvey	Kurila	Lewis	Simmons	Mahon	Crawford	Gibbs	
Rankin	*Wright**	*Newton*	*Kendall*	*Kenyon*	*Harvey*	*Husband*	*Ball*	*Royle*	*Hurst*	*Morrisey*	*Brown*

Scorers: Kendall 23, 32, Royle 33, Ball 36. [Husband 46]. Ref: J Taylor

Liverpudlian Smith (22) plays the game of his life, in front of Match of the Day and 53,000 U's fans. Five goals flatter Everton. U's could have taken the lead. The midfield of Ball, Harvey and Kendall are supreme. A charter plane seat (Stansted to Speke) costs £9, the train costs £2.80.

Football League Division Four

	Team	P	Home					Away					Pts
			W	D	L	F	A	W	D	L	F	A	
1	Notts Co	46	19	4	0	59	12	11	5	7	30	24	69
2	Bournemouth	46	16	5	2	51	15	8	7	8	30	31	60
3	Oldham	46	14	6	3	57	29	10	5	8	31	34	59
4	York	46	16	6	1	45	14	7	4	12	33	40	56
5	Chester	46	17	2	4	42	18	7	5	11	27	37	55
6	COLCHESTER	46	14	6	3	44	19	6	8	9	26	35	54
7	Northampton	46	15	4	4	39	24	5	7	11	24	35	51
8	Southport	46	15	2	6	42	24	5	6	12	21	33	48
9	Exeter	46	12	7	4	40	23	7	3	13	27	45	48
10	Workington	46	13	7	3	28	13	5	3	15	20	36	48
11	Stockport	46	12	8	3	28	17	5	4	14	21	48	46
12	Darlington	46	15	3	5	42	22	2	8	13	16	35	45
13	Aldershot	46	8	10	5	32	23	7	5	11	34	48	45
14	Brentford	46	13	2	8	45	27	4	8	11	21	35	44
15	Crewe	46	13	2	8	49	35	4	8	11	26	41	44
16	Peterborough	46	14	3	6	46	23	3	6	14	24	48	43
17	Scunthorpe	46	9	7	7	36	23	6	6	11	20	38	43
18	Southend	46	8	11	4	32	24	5	6	12	21	42	43
19	Grimsby	46	13	4	6	37	26	4	5	14	20	45	43
20	Cambridge	46	9	9	5	31	27	4	8	11	20	39	43
21	Lincoln	46	11	4	8	45	33	4	5	14	25	38	39
22	Newport	46	8	3	12	32	36	2	5	16	23	49	28
23	Hartlepool	46	6	10	7	28	27	2	2	19	6	47	28
24	Barrow	46	5	5	13	25	38	3	1	19	26	52	22
		1104	295	130	127	955	572	127	130	295	572	955	1104

Appearances / Goals

Player	Appearances						Goals			
	Lge	Sub	LC	Sub	FAC	Sub	Lge	LC	FAC	Tot
Bloss, Phil	1						1			1
Burgess, Eric	8	2								
Cook, Micky	34		1	1	4					
Cram, Bobby	43		3		7		4			4
Crawford, Ray	45		3		7		24		7	31
Dennis, Alan		2								
Garvey, Brian	44		1		6		1			1
Gibbs, Brian	45		1		6		11			11
Gilchrist, John	28		1		5	2	1	1		2
Hall, Brian	41		1		7		4		1	5
Jones, Ken	32				2		4	1	4	9
Joslyn, Roger	7		1							
Kurila, John	44		3		7		2			2
Leslie, Steve	2									
Lewis, Brian	17				5		3	2		5
Mahon, Mick	37	1	2		7		5	2		7
Massey, Roy	12	3	1		1	1	4			4
Owen, Brian	4	2	2		2		2		2	4
Painter, Trevor	1									
Sherratt, Brian	9									
Simmons, Dave	10				5		2		3	5
Smith, Graham	37		3		7					
Smith, Lindsay		1								
Whittaker, Ray	5	3			1		2		1	3
(own-goals)										
24 players used	506	18	33	1	77	3	70	7	18	95

Odds & ends

Double wins: (6) Aldershot, Barrow, Crewe, Hartlepool, Newport, Peterborough.

Double defeats: (3) Chester, Notts Co, Oldham.

Won from behind: (3) Hartlepool (a), Workington (h), Newport (h).

Lost from in front: (1) Chester (a).

High spots: World-wide fame following the sensational FA Cup win over First Division leaders Leeds.

Reaching the FA Cup quarter-finals, a record for a Fourth Division club.

Ray Crawford being the highest U's scorer since Bobby Hunt in season 1961/62.

Consolation of qualification for next season's Watney Cup, as highest scoring team not securing promotion.

Dick Graham becoming the first Division Four manager to win the overall manager of the Month award.

Seven league wins and two draws from Boxing Day onwards.

Low spots: Missing out on promotion by just two points.

Only winning two points out of ten from Easter onwards.

The forced retirement of Roy Massey.

Player of the Year: Ray Crawford.

Ever presents: (0).

Hat-tricks: (2) Ray Crawford (2).

Leading scorer: Ray Crawford (31).

LEAGUE DIVISION 4

Manager: Dick Graham

SEASON 1971-72

Column key: No | Date | 1 | 2 | 3 | 4 | 5 | 6 | 7 | 8 | 9 | 10 | 11 | 12 sub used — and — Att | Pos | Pt | F-A | H-T | Scorers, Times, and Referees

---

1 — A LINCOLN — 14/8
Att 6,607 | Pos 20 | Pt 0 | L | F-A 0-2 | H-T 0-0

1	2	3	4	5	6	7	8	9	10	11	12 sub used
Smith G	Cram	Burgess	Owen	Garvey	Gilchrist	Lewis	Simmons	Gibbs	Bloss*	Mahon	Jones
Kennedy	*Bloor*	*Taylor*	*Hubbard*	*Branston*	*Meath*	*Layton*	*Worslade*	*Svarc*	*Gilliver*	*Smith*	

Scorers: Hubbard 51, Smith 63
Ref: H Powell

U's continually fall foul of the Imps' offside trap, and are somewhat hungover from last week's Watney Cup final excitement at the Hawthorns. Garvey's hesitation leads to Phil Hubbard firing a low shot past G Smith. Mahon hits the woodwork before Dave Smith seals both the points.

---

2 — H HARTLEPOOL — 20/8
Att 5,634 | Pt 2 | W | F-A 1-0 | H-T 0-0

1	2	3	4	5	6	7	8	9	10	11	12 sub used
Smith G	Burgess	Gilchrist	Jones*	Garvey	Kurila	Mahon	Gibbs	Hall	Owen	Lewis	Cram
Gadsby	*White*	*Ashurst*	*Goad*	*Green*	*Potter*	*Welsh*	*Young*	*Ellis*	*Clarke*	*Warnock*	

Scorers: Ashurst 74 (og)
Ref: T Reynolds

Four minutes after replacing Jones, sub Cram sets up Hall to beat two defenders and cross low and hard, where Hartlepool player-manager Len Ashurst turns the ball past the beleaguered Mick Gadsby. Lewis strikes the post, as does Mahon, who also rocks the crossbar from 30 yards.

---

3 — A BURY — 28/8
Att 2,557 | Pos 20 (12) | Pt 2 | L | F-A 0-3 | H-T 0-2

1	2	3	4	5	6	7	8	9	10	11	12 sub used
Smith B	Cram	Gilchrist	Kurila*	Garvey	Burgess	Mahon	Gibbs	Owen	Lewis	Hall	Jones
Hancock	*Eccleshare*	*Tinney*	*Robson*	*Lyon*	*Holt*	*McDermott*	*Rudd*	*Jones**	*White*	*Connelly*	*Hamstead*

Scorers: Jones 11, 13, White 70
Ref: P Willis

An eleventh-minute error by B Smith, mis-punching John Connelly's corner, leads to a goal off the back of George Jones' head. Jones gets another from the same source, two minutes later. White nets the third after good work by Hugh Tinney, and Jones (offside) is denied a treble.

---

4 — A NEWPORT — 31/8
Att 4,168 | Pos 20 (18) | Pt 2 | L | F-A 1-2 | H-T 1-1

1	2	3	4	5	6	7	8	9	10	11	12 sub used
Smith B	Burgess	Gilchrist*	Burgess	Cram	Cram	Mahon	Gibbs	Leslie	Owen	Lewis	Cook
Macey	*Williams*	*Sprague*	*Coldrick*	*Aizlewood*	*Harris B*	*Thomas*	*Harris P**	*Jones*	*Brown*	*White*	*Young*

Scorers: Sprague 3, Brown 88; Lewis 33
Ref: T Bosi

Lewis coolly chips over John Macey to cancel out Martin Sprague's early strike, but Willie Brown nets County's winner from a free-kick two minutes from time, nodding in past the unsighted B Smith. Jones is booked for not retreating at a free-kick, as U's fall to a third away defeat.

---

5 — H SOUTHPORT — 3/9
Att 5,439 | Pos 20 (6) | Pt 4 | W | F-A 1-0 | H-T 0-0

1	2	3	4	5	6	7	8	9	10	11	12 sub used
Smith G	Cook	Hall	Burgess	Garvey	Bloss	Owen	Lewis	Gibbs	Leslie	Mahon	Cook
Taylor	*Turner*	*Sibbald*	*McPhee*	*Dunleavy*	*Peat*	*Moore**	*Hartland*	*Redrobe*	*Field*	*Hartle*	*Lloyd*

Scorers: Mahon 57
Ref: A Grey

Lewis' centre is headed out by Bobby Sibbald straight to Mahon, who unleashes a terrific volley that sails past keeper Alan Taylor into the net. Youngsters Leslie, who celebrates his 19th birthday tomorrow and has a hand in the U's goal, and Bloss, who strikes the woodwork, excel.

---

6 — A DARLINGTON — 11/9
Att 2,683 | Pos 22 (17) | Pt 4 | L | F-A 0-2 | H-T 0-0

1	2	3	4	5	6	7	8	9	10	11	12 sub used
Smith B	Garvey	Hall	Burgess	Cram	Bloss	Lewis	Owen	Gibbs	Leslie*	Mahon	Jones
Wealands	*Peverell*	*Horner*	*Carr*	*Barker*	*Lees*	*Sproates*	*Hale*	*Gauden*	*Graham*	*Harding*	

Scorers: Harding 83, Gauden 84
Ref: H Hackney

Alan Gauden hammers a shot from the edge of the area that B Smith cannot hold, giving Alan Harding the chance to net Quakers' first home goal of the term. U's had hardly regained their composure when Gauden burst into the box, seemed to lose his footing, but recovered to slot in.

---

7 — H CREWE — 17/9
Att 6,133 | Pos 17 (21) | Pt 6 | W | F-A 4-2 | H-T 1-1

1	2	3	4	5	6	7	8	9	10	11	12 sub used
Smith G	Gilchrist	Cram	Burgess	Hall	Owen	Gibbs	Bloss	Lewis*	Leslie	Mahon	Jones
Adams	*Lowry*	*Leigh*	*Gater*	*Rosser*	*Summerhill*	*Wallace*	*Morrisey*	*East*	*Bowles*	*Bird*	

Scorers: Burgess 22, Lewis 59, Mahon 67, East 21, Morrisey 52 [Leslie 77]
Ref: P Reeves

Keith East nods in a Leigh free-kick to put Crewe in front, but within 40 seconds U's are on terms when Burgess snaps up the rebound from Leslie's shot. Stan Bowles finds Pat Morrisey for Alex, only for Lewis, Mahon, with a 30-yarder, and Leslie, with his first senior goal, to win it.

---

8 — A NORTHAMPTON — 25/9
Att 5,800 | Pos 17 (9) | Pt 7 | D | F-A 1-1 | H-T 0-0

1	2	3	4	5	6	7	8	9	10	11	12 sub used
Smith G	Gilchrist	Garvey	Burgess	Cram	Bloss	Cook	Jones*	Gibbs	Leslie	Mahon	Hall
Starling	*Neal*	*Folds*	*Clarke*	*Chatterly*	*Heslop*	*Felton**	*Kiernan*	*Large*	*McNeill*	*Hawkins*	*Ross*

Scorers: Hall 75, Hawkins 67
Ref: J Whalley

The Anglia Match of the Week cameras are in attendance to capture Graham Felton crossing for Peter Hawkins to volley first time into the net. From U's eleventh corner, Mahon finds Hall, who blasts home to level. Owen is given leave in his role as trainer to the England Youth Squad.

---

9 — A SCUNTHORPE — 28/9
Att 5,111 | Pos 18 (2) | Pt 7 | L | F-A 0-2 | H-T 0-2

1	2	3	4	5	6	7	8	9	10	11	12 sub used
Smith G	Gilchrist	Cram	Jones	Garvey	Bloss	Hall	Simmons	Gibbs*	Leslie	Mahon	Cook
Barnard	*Foxton*	*Jackson*	*McDonald*	*Deere*	*Welbourne*	*Kisby*	*Fletcher*	*Davidson*	*Heath*	*Kirk*	

Scorers: Fletcher 7, Davidson 17
Ref: T Farley

Graham, travelling with chairman Chapman, is taken ill en-route with stomach pains and turns back to Colchester. U's have Gibbs, Garvey and Gilchrist all booked, and to cap a bad day Rod Fletcher opens and G Smith fails to hold Terry Heath's shot, for Angus Davidson to gobble up.

---

10 — H CHESTER — 1/10
Att 6,048 | Pos 17 (10) | Pt 9 | W | F-A 1-0 | H-T 1-0

1	2	3	4	5	6	7	8	9	10	11	12 sub used
Smith G	Cram	Garvey	Gilchrist	Hall	Cook	Bloss	Leslie	Lewis	Simmons	Mahon	
Livesey	*Edwards*	*Birks*	*Draper*	*Turner*	*Pountney*	*Carter*	*Loydon*	*Purdie*	*Moore**	*Griffiths*	*Futcher*

Scorers: Leslie 12
Ref: M Kerkhof

G Smith saves Neil Griffiths' pen (88) to earn vital points, after Garvey had dived to punch Bernard Purdie's shot off the line. United had taken the lead when Lewis' right wing flag-kick was headed on by Leslie to Simmons, who returned the header into the path of Leslie to slide home.

---

11 — A ALDERSHOT — 9/10
Att 5,285 | Pos 14 (11) | Pt 11 | W | F-A 2-0 | H-T 2-0

1	2	3	4	5	6	7	8	9	10	11	12 sub used
Smith G	Cook	Hall	Burgess	Cram	Kurila	Lewis	Bloss	Jones	Leslie	Mahon	
Gurr	*Walden*	*Joslyn*	*Grummett*	*Dean*	*Bennett*	*Walton*	*Brown*	*Melledew*	*Pearce*	*Brodie**	*Walker*

Scorers: Lewis 22, Leslie 24
Ref: L Hayes

Graham concedes he has too many older players, but as he can't buy, the only solution is to blood the youngsters. Jones is made available, after being barracked by the crowd on several occasions. U's earn their first away win against a Shots side captained for the day by ex-U's Joslyn.

12 — H LINCOLN — 15/10

5,834 · 9 / 7 · **W 5-2** · 13

Scorers: Lewis 2, 71, 74, Bloss 45, Hall 86 / Freeman 20, 24 — Ref: J Orpin

U's: Smith G, Cook, Hall, Burgess, Cram, Kurila, Lewis, Leslie, Jones, Bloss, Mahon
Lincoln: Kennedy J, Bloor, Taylor, McMahon, Branston, Trevis, Meath, Hubbard, Freeman, Gilliver, Smith D

A seventh successive home win (ninth including Watney Cup). Ex-U's Trevis, captain for the night, concedes the free-kick for Lewis' first. His second is from Leslie's through ball, and third, via a Cram free-kick, after Hall was felled. Kurila, D Smith and Terry Branston are all booked.

13 — H SOUTHEND — 18/10

9,807 · 7 / 5 · **W 1-0** · 15

Scorers: Leslie 78 — Ref: B Homewood

U's: Smith G, Cook, Hall, Burgess, Cram, Kurila, Lewis, Leslie, Jones, Bloss, Mahon
Southend: Roberts, Tennent, Elliott, Albeson, Jacques, Duck*, Johnson, Garner, Hunt, Bernard, Barnett

Crawford returns from SA, with United still holding his FL registration until they receive the £1.5k owed from Durban City. The Essex derby seems destined for a dull draw, but discovery-of-the-season Leslie pops up with a late winner from Lewis' flick after a great cross from Cook.

14 — A CAMBRIDGE — 23/10

7,230 · 10 / 7 · **L 2-4** · 15

Scorers: Jones 61, 67 / Foote 45, Lill 50, Harris 73, 87 — Ref: J Taylor

U's: Smith G, Cook, Hall, Burgess, Cram, Kurila, Lewis, Leslie, Jones, Bloss, Mahon
Cambridge: Roberts, Thompson, Akers, Guild, Eades, Foote, Phillips, Greenhalgh, Lill, Collins, Harris

G Smith fails to hold Brian Greenhalgh's header, allowing Chris Foote to poach just on the interval. Jones' double claws U's back to 2-2, only for George Harris to nod a fine header from David Lill's cross. Trevor Roberts spectacularly denies Leslie, before Harris's second kills off U's.

15 — H GILLINGHAM — 29/10

6,622 · 11 / 13 · **D 2-2** · 16

Scorers: Lewis 63, Kurila 90 / Yeo 31, Peach 58p — Ref: T Dawes

U's: Smith G, Gibbs, Gilchrist, Cram, Kurila, Lewis, Leslie, Jones, Bloss, Mahon, Hall
Gillingham: Shearing, Parmenter, Peach, Williams, Quirke, Tydeman, Knight, Watson, Wilks, Yeo, Hall

Graham chooses to bring back older heads in place of Bloss and Cook, but U's fall 0-2 behind. Alan Wilks beats Burgess to thread through for Brian Yeo, and then sees Gilchrist palm away his shot. David Peach nets from the spot, but Kurila levels in time added for U's time-wasting.

16 — A BARROW — 6/11

1,954 · 12 / 21 · **D 2-2** · 17

Scorers: Gibbs 35, Kurila 78 / Patrick 19, Irvine 39 — Ref: C Seel

U's: Smith G, Cook, Hall, Garvey, Cram, Kurila, Lewis, Leslie, Jones, Gibbs, Mahon
Barrow: Thompson, Patrick, Storf, Clarke, Harrison, Noble, McKay, Russell, Irvine, McDonald, Hollis

United's long haul up to Cumbria makes a financial loss, as the low attendance only realises about £200 as their share of the gate money. It had cost the club £275 to get to Holker St. Kurila, as last week, spares U's blushes when he salvages a late point following a goalmouth scramble.

17 — H BRENTFORD — 13/11

6,698 · 12 / 1 · **D 1-1** · 18

Scorers: Jones 14 / O'Mara 26 — Ref: J Bent

U's: Smith G, Cook, Hall, Garvey, Cram, Kurila, Lewis, Leslie, Jones*, Bloss, Mahon (Gilchrist*)
Brentford: Phillips, Bence, Nelmes, Tom, Scales, Turner, Allen, Graham, O'Mara, Ross, Docherty

Anglia TV's first league visit of the term sees ref Bent pelted with cushions at the end after he gave a free-kick just outside, when Leslie was clearly fouled in the box, and for booking Lewis for standing in front of Gordon Phillips. John Docherty, who had fouled Hall, is also booked.

18 — H EXETER — 26/11

5,116 · 9 / 19 · **W 3-0** · 20

Scorers: Foley 20, 25, Lewis 75 — Ref: N Paget

U's: Smith B, Garvey, Hall, Cram, Foley, Woods, Lewis*, Leslie, Bloss, Gibbs, Mahon
Exeter: Wilson, Crawford, Blain, Giles, Balson, Rowan, Binney*, Gadston, Morrin, Banks, Wingate

Woods signs on loan from Watford. Lewis's pen is saved (65), after Giles' foul on Leslie, but he is on his own in the goal charts with 13 in 20 games during which he has taken a fearful ankle-battering. A dream start sees Foley become the eleventh United player to score on his debut.

19 — A STOCKPORT — 3/12

2,043 · 10 / 22 · **D 2-2** · 21

Scorers: Mahon 20, 73 / Lawther 60p, Garvey 75 (og) — Ref: P Willis

U's: Smith B, Cram, Hall, Garvey, Cook, Gibbs, Woods, Leslie, Bloss, Mahon, Simmons
Stockport: Ogley, Charter, Renwick, Hart, Wright, Chisnall, Ryden, Webber, Lawther, Griffiths, McMillan

G Smith guests in a WBA testimonial on Tuesday and signed for £10k on Thursday. Mahon scores direct from a corner, but all looks lost when Sammy McMillan backs into Hall to win a penalty. Then Garvey, booked earlier, clips in Hugh Ryden's shot. Mahon levels from Bloss's pass.

20 — A SOUTHPORT — 18/12

2,657 · 12 / 3 · **L 0-3** · 21

Scorers: Redrobe 16, Peat 43, Sibbald 62p — Ref: D Civil

U's: Smith B, Hall, Cram, Cook, Garvey, Simmons*, Woods, Lewis, Bloss, Mahon, Leslie
Southport: Gregson, Haydock, Kelley, McPhee, Sharples, Lloyd, Peat, Fryatt, Sibbald, Redrobe, Dunleavy

Jones' move to Brentford fails over personal terms, as does £1k-rated Woods' move to Layer Rd. U's struggle to contain Southport's two big men, Jim Fryatt and Eric Redrobe, who was a United trialist in 1966. The result is sealed by Bobby Sibbald when B Smith hauls down Fryatt.

21 — H PETERBOROUGH — 27/12

7,750 · 10 / 14 · **D 1-1** · 22

Scorers: Leslie 84 / Hall 59 — Ref: C Robinson

U's: Smith B, Cram, Hall, Cook, Garvey, Lewis, Bloss, Leslie, Mahon*, Simmons, Foley
Peterborough: Drewery, Carmichael, Brookes, Turner, Wright, Barker, Price, Hall, Darrell, Robson, Oates

Kurila moves to Lincoln (free), whilst Villa's third-choice keeper Geoff Crudgington trials. U's end the year of their greatest triumphs with a whimper. Their unbeaten home record is preserved when Leslie heads in from six yards, after Jim Hall nodded in Micky Darrell's corner-kick.

22 — A CREWE — 1/1

1,992 · 9 / 22 · **W 4-2** · 24

Scorers: Leslie 24, Hall 51, Lewis 52p, Cook 76 / Bradshaw 45, East 75 — Ref: E Jolly

U's: Smith B, Cram, Hall, Cook, Garvey, Lewis, Bloss, Leslie, Mahon*, Simmons, Robson
Crewe: Adams, Lowry, Leigh, Gater, Rosser, Higgins, Tewley, Turner, East, White, Bradshaw

U's kick-off 1972 with a bang. Alex are briefly in the game when Alan Bradshaw nods in Alan Tewley's cross, but two in a minute from Hall, a fizzing 30-yarder, and a handball against Tommy Lowry, put U's in command. Cook receives a booking, but notches his first-ever U's goal.

23 — H BURY — 8/1

4,942 · 9 / 12 · **D 0-0** · 25

Ref: R Baldwin

U's: Smith B, Cram, Hall, Cook, Garvey, Lewis, Bloss, Leslie, Simmons, Jones, Mahon
Bury: Hancock, Timney, Sail, Holt, Robson, McDermott, Connelly, Rudd, Jones, Murray, Hamstead

A no-holds-barred press call is told of U's financial problems. A loss of £21k in March meant that the bank reserves had been used to cover the deficit. Graham warns that it may be several years before the youngsters gel. Owen is set to quit football to become a full-time physiotherapist.

LEAGUE DIVISION 4

Manager: Dick Graham

SEASON 1971-72

No	Date		Att	Pos	Pt		F-A	H-T	Scorers, Times, and Referees	1	2	3	4	5	6	7	8	9	10	11	12 sub used
24	A	DONCASTER		11		L	0-2	0-1		Smith B	Cook	Hall	Foley	Burgess	Cram	Gibbs*	Bloss	Leslie	Simmons	Smith L	Garvey
	15/1		*3,247*	*10*	25				Elwiss 36, Haselden 90	*Johnson*	*Branfoot*	*Wilcockson*	*Irvine*	*Robertson*	*Uzelac*	*Haselden*	*Elwiss*	*Gilchrist*	*Rabjohn*	*Usher*	
									Ref: J Goggins	Dennis leaves to join Dover. Mike Elwiss heads Rovers in front from Harold Wilcockson's cross. In the last seconds, with United pressing for the equaliser, John Haselden knocks the wind out of U's sails with a second. Bolton manager Jimmy Armfield expresses an interest in Mahon.											
25	H	SCUNTHORPE		11		D	1-1	1-1	Gibbs 9	Smith B	Cook	Hall	Cram	Burgess	Gibbs	Simmons	Leslie	Foley	Mahon	Smith L	
	21/1		*4,807*	*2*	26				*Fletcher 4*	*Barnard*	*Foxton*	*Barker*	*Davidson*	*Deere*	*Atkins*	*McDonald*	*Fletcher*	*Herr*	*Jackson*	*Kirk*	
									Ref: A Teale	Owen's departure, to Wolves as player-coach, means U's are down to 15 fit pro's. Iron take the lead when Rod Fletcher picks up a long free-kick, outruns Burgess, slips a Cook tackle and fires low into the net. Leslie's defence-splitting ball helps U's back on terms five minutes later.											
26	A	SOUTHEND		10		W	4-1	2-1	Foley 22, Mahon 25, Leslie 68, 73	Smith B	Cook	Hall	Cram	Burgess	Garvey	Gilchrist	Leslie	Foley	Mahon	Gibbs	
	28/1		*8,871*	*6*	28				*Taylor 30*	*Roberts*	*Tennent*	*Smith*	*Elliott*	*Albeson*	*Jacques*	*Johnson*	*Best*	*Garner*	*Moore*	*Taylor*	
									Ref: A Hart	U's destroy Southend's ten-game unbeaten Roots Hall run. Mahon inswings a corner to Foley's head, and nets himself, direct from a flag-kick. Peter Taylor's 30-yard free-kick sails through United's wall, but Leslie twice catches Shrimpers on the break as they search for an equaliser.											
27	A	WORKINGTON		11		L	0-1	0-0		Smith B	Cook	Hall	Cram	Burgess	Garvey	Gilchrist*	Leslie	Foley	Mahon	Gibbs	Simmons
	5/2		*2,170*	*7*	28				*Ogilvie 55*	*Rogan*	*Wilson*	*Ogilvie*	*Tyler*	*Geidmintis*	*Wood*	*Helliwell*	*Spratt*	*Nicholls**	*Goodfellow*	*Martin*	*Hopkinson*
									Ref: P Baldwin	A floodlight appeal was launched at last week's AGM to raise £10k for vital repairs to the unsafe structures. Workington gain their first home win since 6 November, when the ref and linesman agree that Gilchrist had not kept out John Ogilvie's header from Tommy Spratt's cross.											
28	H	CAMBRIDGE		13		D	1-1	0-0	Lewis 66	Smith B	Cook	Hall	Cram	Burgess	Garvey	Lewis	Leslie	Bloss	Mahon	Gibbs	
	12/2		5,663	*9*	29				*Lill 87*	*Vasper*	*Thompson*	*Akers*	*Guild*	*Eades*	*Foote*	*Walton*	*Greenhalgh*	*Lill*	*Collins*	*Phillips*	
									Ref: B Homewood	Gilchrist becomes p-manager of Tonbridge, whilst Jones trials at Torquay. The power cuts affecting the country means a switch from Friday to Saturday with a 2.45 pm kick-off. Lewis livens up proceedings with a fierce drive, but B Smith tragically pushes David Lill's shot into his net.											
29	A	GILLINGHAM		10		W	2-0	0-0	Leslie 46, 57	Smith B	Cook	Hall	Cram	Burgess	Garvey	Lewis	Leslie	Gibbs	Jones*	Mahon	Smith L
	19/2		*5,313*	*9*	31					*Simpson*	*McVeigh*	*Parmenter*	*Galvin*	*Hill*	*Quirke*	*Peach*	*Knight*	*Bickle*	*Wilks*	*Yeo*	
									Ref: J Hunting	Gills surprisingly recall 38-year-old John Simpson for his 576th game. He pulls off a string of fine saves behind a suspect Gills defence. He is caught out twice however, by young prodigy Leslie, who slots a Cram pass under the keeper and then nods in from a cross by the same source.											
30	H	BARROW		11		L	0-1	0-0		Smith B	Cook	Hall	Cram	Burgess	Garvey	Lewis	Leslie	Jones	Mahon	Gibbs	
	26/2		4,618	*21*	31				*Rowlands 80*	*Thompson*	*Patrick*	*Knox*	*Clarke*	*Noble*	*Harrison*	*Garbett*	*Calvert*	*Rowlands*	*Irvine*	*Hollis*	
									Ref: G Kew	Graham signs Steve Tonsley from Ipswich as goalkeeper cover. He has only had the services of a 15-year-old schoolboy to call upon since the departure of G Smith. John Rowlands ensures that U's fail to equal the 27-match unbeaten home run, set during seasons 1956-57 and 1957-58.											
31	A	BRENTFORD		10		W	2-0	0-0	Mahon 46, 70	Smith B	Cook	Hall	Cram	Burgess	Garvey	Lewis	Leslie	Mahon	**Mills**	Smith L	
	4/3		*9,210*	*5*	33					*Phillips*	*Bence*	*Nelmes*	*Houston*	*Scales*	*Turner*	*Allen*	*Graham*	*Neilson**	*Ross*	*Docherrty*	*Gelson*
									Ref: J Yates	Ball-juggling Burnside loans from Bristol City, whilst Jones joins Margate. Brentford include Stewart Houston, signed on loan from Chelsea. Mills is the third 16-year-old to play for United, following in the footsteps of Peter Barlow, and Lindsay Smith. Leslie and Mahon are booked.											
32	H	ALDERSHOT		8		W	1-0	1-0	Lewis 12	Smith B	Cook	Hall	Cram	Burgess	Garvey	Lewis	Leslie	**Burnside**	Mahon	Smith L	
	11/3		3,776	*16*	35					*Gurr*	*Walden*	*Walker*	*Joslyn**	*Bean*	*Bennett*	*Brown*	*Storrie*	*Grummett*	*Brodie*	*Davidsbn*	*Melledew*
									Ref: R Parkin	Mahon's third inswinging corner of the term, against Brentford, brings national attention. Young L Smith signs pro forms. Rampant U's force seven corners in the first ten minutes. L Smith's dummy allows Cram to give Lewis a simple tap in, and Lewis' effort (21) is adjudged offside.											
33	H	DONCASTER		9		L	1-2	0-2	Smith L 68	Smith B	Cook	Hall	Cram	Burgess	Garvey	Burnside	Leslie	Mahon	Lewis	Smith L	
	13/3		5,004	*7*	35				*Irvine 20, Elwiss 43*	*Johnson*	*Branfoot*	*Beardsley*	*Irvine*	*Robertson*	*Uzelac*	*Hasleden*	*Elwiss*	*Briggs*	*Moore*	*Usher*	
									Ref: M Sinclair	Doncaster look the best side to visit Layer Road this season, and thank Archie Irvine, who bombs Rovers into the lead with a 25-yarder off the underside of the bar. Mike Elwiss plunders a goalmouth scramble, before L Smith celebrates his new pro status with his first-ever senior goal.											
34	A	HARTLEPOOL		10		L	2-3	1-2	Mahon 43, Garvey 83	Smith B	Cook	**McLaughlin**	Mills	Burgess	Garvey*	Mahon	Leslie	Hall	Smith L	Gibbs	**Wingate**
	18/3		*2,621*	*23*	35				*Waddell 10, Smith 28p, Young 60*	*Hillyard*	*Potter*	*Goad*	*Ashurst*	*Green*	*Dawes*	*Waddell*	*Smith*	*Veart*	*Young*	*Warnock*	
									Ref: J Wrennall	The kick-off is delayed by a sinister fog off the North Sea. When the game does start, much of the play is obscured. Robert Veart is fouled for Pool's penalty. Although Mahon repeats his party-piece, scoring direct from a corner. Ron Young seals victory with his 15th goal of the term.											

Cambridge United 1976–77 — match record (matches 35–46)

For each match the two team lines are printed stacked: the upper (roman) line is U's, the lower (italic) line is the opponents. An asterisk (*) marks a substitute. Scores are shown as half-time / full-time.

35 · A GRIMSBY · 21/3 · HT 0-1 / FT 0-3 · 12 L 5 35 · Att 13,288 (bold)
U's: Smith B, Cook, Hall, Cram, Burgess, Gibbs, Garvey, Leslie, Mahon, Simmons, Burnside, Smith L
Grimsby: Wainman, Worthington, Campbell, Chatterley*, Wigginton, Gray, Brace, Hickman, Tees, Boylen, Gauden, Lewis
Scorers: Gauden 7, Brace 85p, Tees 87
Ref: H Davey
U's struggle to raise a side through injuries and have to cancel tomorrow's reserve match. Simmons hits the post at 0-1, but U's are undone by a late burst in the last five minutes starting when Matt Tees appears to fall over B Smith for a dubious penalty, and then Tees scores himself.

36 · H DARLINGTON · 24/3 · HT 2-1 / FT 4-3 · 12 W 20 37 · Att 3,865
U's: Smith B, Cook, Hall, Cram, Burgess, Gibbs, Garvey, Leslie, Mahon, Simmons*, Burnside, Lewis
Darlington: Walters, Peverell, Carr, Horner, Barker, Hale, Wright, Harding, Graham, Peddelty, Sproates
Scorers: Burgess 11, Leslie 42, Lewis 57, Graham 33, 69, Barker 74 (Simmons 68)
Ref: D Biddle
Mahon fails to score with an inswinging corner, but Burgess prods in after it hits the bar. U's race into a 4-1 lead, but are so nearly punished for sitting back on the lead when Peter Graham adds his second, a minute after Simmons' first goal for over a year, and Geoff Barker nods in.

37 · H NORTHAMPTON · 31/3 · HT 2-0 / FT 2-0 · 10 W 16 39 · Att 5,375
U's: Smith B, Cook, Hall, Cram, Burgess, Gibbs, Garvey, Leslie, Mahon, Simmons, Burnside, Lewis
Northampton: Starling, Gould, Oman, Rioch, Townsend, Kiernan, Buchanan, Heslop, Hold, Large, Neal
Scorers: Simmons 16, Lewis 41p
Ref: N Burtenshaw
Simmons gets back into the scoring routine as he ensures that Leslie's shot goes in. Leslie is in action again when, after a great run and pass by Mahon, he is upended in the area. Lewis nets, but misses a second spot-kick (77) with a half-hearted shot that rebounds back off Alan Starling.

38 · A PETERBOROUGH · 1/4 · HT 0-3 / FT 0-4 · 10 L 13 39 · Att 4,367
U's: Smith B, Cook, Foley, Cram, Burgess, Gibbs, Garvey, Leslie, Mahon, Simmons, Burnside, Smith L
Peterborough: Drewery, Noble, Turner, Carmichael, Duncliffe, Oakes, Darrell, Barker, Price, Hall, Robson
Scorers: Price 20, Hall 33, Turner 35p, Robson 70
Ref: R Armstrong
Div Four's leading scorer Peter Price picks his spot from Jim Hall's flick. Hall adds the second following sterling work from Micky Darrell. It's all over for U's before the break, when Foley fouls Ritchie Barker for Chris Turner's pen. Tommy Robson ends it, chipping over B Smith.

39 · A CHESTER · 3/4 · HT 1-2 / FT 1-2 · 10 L 16 39 · Att 3,317
U's: Smith B, Cook, Foley, Cram, Burgess, Gibbs, Garvey, Leslie, Mahon, Mills*, Burnside, Bourne
Chester: Livesey, Edwards, Griffiths, Chartham, Turner, Pountney, Bingham, Carter*, Moore, Draper, Kennedy, Futcher G
Scorers: Lewis 79p, Moore 44, 87
Ref: E Jolly
A viral infection sweeps through the club affecting Leslie, Burgess, Simmons and worst of all, Mills. He is sick on the Sealand Rd pitch and has to be subbed by Bourne, 17, who continues the youthful trend. Neil Griffiths handles Mahon's shot, but Tony Moore's brace earns victory.

40 · H WORKINGTON · 7/4 · HT 0-0 / FT 1-0 · 10 W 8 41 · Att 3,390 (bold)
U's: Smith B, Cook, McLaughlin, Foley, Burgess, Gibbs, Garvey, Leslie, Mahon, Simmons, Burnside, Bourne
Workington: Rogan, Wilson, Ogivie, Spratt, Walker, Wood, Helliwell, Tyrer, Irving, Martin, Goodfellow
Scorers: Foley 57
Ref: R Toseland
A 7pm kick-off allows the visitors to catch their train home. Lewis joins Pompey (£9k). U's haven't spent money since Lewis and Simmons signed in December 1970. Garvey suffers a head gash and returns sporting a large bandage. Foley latches onto Leslie's pass from 25 yards out.

41 · H READING · 10/4 · HT 1-1 / FT 2-1 · 9 W 15 43 · Att 4,110
U's: Smith B, Cook, McLaughlin, Foley, Burgess, Gibbs, Garvey, Leslie, Mahon, Simmons, Burnside, Smith L
Reading: Pratt, Dixon, Morgan, Hawley, Wooler, Wagstaff B, Wagstaff T, Proudlove*, Harman, Cumming, Hetzke, Habbin
Scorers: Gibbs 35, Leslie 76, Habbin 3
Ref: T Dawes
Cook is voted player of the year, by his team-mates. Mahon takes 19 corners in the match to Reading's four, and both U's goals come from his set-pieces. B Smith slips to let in Dick Habbin on 124 seconds, and the keeper's fiancée wins the golden goal-time competition for that goal.

42 · A EXETER · 15/4 · HT 1-1 / FT 3-3 · 8 D 15 44 · Att 4,052
U's: Smith B, Cook, McLaughlin, Foley*, Burgess, Gibbs, Garvey, Leslie, Mahon, Simmons, Burnside, Smith L
Exeter: Wilson, Crawford, Stacey, Parker, Giles, Balson, Rowan, Banks, Wood, Wingate, Binney, Gibson
Scorers: Gibbs 30p, Burgess 63, Mahon 82, Binney 16, Rowan 58, Banks 71
Ref: I Jones
Fred Binney gets City off the mark, but U's draw level when Mike Balson fouls Leslie in the box. Ex-U's man Rowan blasts Grecians back in front, for Burgess to scramble home at a corner. Bogey-man Alan Banks' powerful header, is pegged back by L Smith's great ball to Mahon.

43 · H GRIMSBY · 17/4 · HT 0-1 / FT 0-1 · 10 L 7 44 · Att 5,086
U's: Smith B, Cook, McLaughlin, Smith L, Burgess, Gibbs, Garvey, Leslie, Mahon, Simmons, Burnside
Grimsby: Wainman, Worthington, Campbell, Chatterley, Wigginton, Gray, Lewis, Hickman, Tees, Boylen, Gauden*, Smith
Scorers: Chatterley 4
Ref: C Thomas
U's face an uphill battle from as early as the fourth minute, when Lew Chatterley nets for the league leaders after brilliant play by Alan Gauden and Jack Lewis. From then on Mariners are content to sit back on the points that will surely mean they will go on to win the Division Four title.

44 · H STOCKPORT · 21/4 · HT 0-2 / FT 3-2 · 9 W 23 46 · Att 4,018
U's: Smith B, Cook, McLaughlin, Hall, Burgess, Gibbs, Garvey, Leslie, Mahon, Simmons, Burnside*, Smith L
Stockport: Ogley, Ormrod, Chapman, Lawther, Hart, Charter, Ryden, Griffiths, Brennan, McMillan, Foggarty*, Webber
Scorers: Burgess 63, 83, Simmons 87, Griffiths 33, McMillan 41
Ref: R Crabb
John Griffiths opens for County after B Smith parries his first effort, as he does for Sammy McMillan's strike. U's stage a remarkable second-half comeback which culminates in Simmons' header three minutes from time, after Leslie and Man of the Match McLaughlin had combined.

45 · H NEWPORT · 24/4 · HT 2-1 / FT 2-3 · 11 L 17 46 · Att 4,311
U's: Smith B, Hall, McLaughlin, Foley*, Burgess, Gibbs, Garvey, Leslie, Mahon, Simmons, Cook, Smith L
Newport: Macey, Williams, Wood, Passey, Hill, Sprague, Young, Thomas, Jones D, Brown, Jones R, Gibbs
Scorers: Burgess 38, 40, Brown 45, Hill 54p, Jones R 72
Ref: R Challis
Skipper Cram will be released at the end of the season to become coach of Vancouver Spartans. County's penalty is a diabolical decision, as the ball clearly strikes Hall square in the stomach. Glamorgan cricketer Len Hill nets from the spot, and centres for Roddy Jones' header.

46 · A READING · 29/4 · HT 2-1 / FT 4-2 · 11 W 16 48 · Att 3,202
U's: Smith B, Cook, Hall, Foley, Burgess, Gibbs, Garvey, Leslie, Mahon, Simmons, Burnside, Smith L
Reading: Death, Butler, James, Lenarduzzi, Wooler, Wagstaff T*, Ashton, Proudlove, Harman, Chappell, Habbin, Swain
Scorers: Leslie 21, Smith L 42, 65, Burgess 61, Habbin 10, Harman 72
Ref: W Castle
The Reading side has an average age 20.5 years, with five players 18 or under. L Smith, one of U's aspiring youngsters nets a great brace, with his first from an acute angle off the bar, his second from a Mahon free-kick. U's will play Blackpool, next week, in aid of the floodlight fund.

Average attendance — Home 5,393 · Away 4,685

Watney Cup

1   H   LUTON   31/7   8,186 2:   W 1-0   H-T 0-0

Scorers: Lewis 78p   Ref: N Burtenshaw

1	2	3	4	5	6	7	8	9	10	11	12 sub used
Smith G	Cram	Owen*	Gilcrist	Garvey	Burgess	Lewis	Simmons^	Gibbs	Crawford	Mahon	Leslie/Jones
Ryan	*Slough*	*Hoy*	*Nicholl*	*Moore*	*Court*	*Busby*	*Givens**	*Keen*	*Bushy*	*Wainwright*	*Goodeve*

The experimental offside law is employed on just one occasion. Crawford plays his last game for U's before joining Durban City in S. Africa. Sub Ken Goodeve trips Lewis in front of Cup Final ref Norman Burtenshaw, who doesn't hesitate in pointing to the spot for Lewis's winner.

2   H   CARLISLE   4/8   7,871 2:   W 2-0   H-T 0-0

Scorers: Gibbs 46, Lewis 55   Ref: R Tinkler

1	2	3	4	5	6	7	8	9	10	11	12 sub used
Smith G	Cram	Owen	Gilcrist	Garvey	Burgess	Jones	Lewis	Gibbs	Simmons	Mahon	
Ross	*Hemstead*	*Gorman*	*Ternant*	*Winstanley*	*Sutton*	*Barton*	*Martin*	*Webb*	*Hatton*	*Balderstone*	

The U's board are very disappointed in the turn-outs so far in the two Watney Cup ties staged at Layer Road, but strikes from Gibbs and Lewis set U's up for a mouth-watering trip to the West Midlands for the final and the media attention that goes with it. As if they hadn't had enough!

F   A   WEST BROM   7/8   18,487 1:   W 4-4 aet   H-T 2-3

Scorers: Mahon 8, 67, Simmons 32, Lewis 86p / Cantello 16, Astle 30, 89, Hope 34   Ref: D Smith   (Colchester won 4-2 on penalties)

1	2	3	4	5	6	7	8	9	10	11	12 sub used
Smith G	Cram	Owen	Gilcrist	Garvey	Burgess	Bloss	Lewis	Simmons	Mahon	Gibbs	
Cumbes	*Hughes*	*Wilson*	*Cantello*	*Wile*	*Kaye*	*Suggett*	*Brown*	*Astle*	*Hope*	*Hartford*	

The authorities refuse to reschedule the Brum v Villa friendly, which attracts 36,000 and knocks 10,000 off the gate at the Hawthorns. Kaye is fourth booking in bringing down Mahon (88), but 18-year-old Bloss slots in the shoot-out winner after Cantello, Wilson and Cram had missed.

League Cup

1   H   BRENTFORD   18/8   6,125 4:   W 3-1   H-T 1-0

Scorers: Mahon 33, Lewis 53, 67p / Ross 87   Ref: K Baker

1	2	3	4	5	6	7	8	9	10	11	12 sub used
Smith G	Burgess	Gilcrist	Jones	Garvey	Kurila	Mahon	Gibbs	Simmons*	Owen	Lewis	Hall
Phillips	*Bence*	*Nelmes*	*Gelson*	*Scales*	*Turner*	*Ross*	*Graham*	*O'Mara*	*Cross*	*Tom**	*Neillson*

Simmons cracks an ankle bone. Mahon nets a 30-yard screamer from Gilchrist's half-cleared cross, whilst Lewis's first goal is a fine solo run, shrugging off the attention of two Bees' defenders. U's third comes when keeper Gordon Phillips up-ends Lewis, for his fifth so far this term.

2   H   SWINDON   8/9   7,437 2:14   W 4-1   H-T 1-1

Scorers: Lewis 7, 52p, 70, Mahon 60 / Horsfield 13   Ref: R Challis

1	2	3	4	5	6	7	8	9	10	11	12 sub used
Smith G	Cook	Hall	Burgess	Cram	Bloss	Lewis*	Owen	Gibbs	Leslie	Mahon	Garvey
Downsboro'	*Thomas*	*Trollope*	*Butler*	*Burrows*	*Harland*	*Porter*	*Smart*	*Horsfield*	*Noble*	*Ryan*	

Leslie has a hand in three goals. He helps Lewis to the first of his treble, riding a tackle and taking the ball wide before cleverly back-heeling into Lewis's path. U's visibly step up a gear after Rod Thomas chops Lewis, who completes his hat-trick on another memorable U's cup night.

3   A   BLACKPOOL   5/10   11,042 2:13   L 0-4   H-T 0-0

Scorers: Suddick 47, Green 63, Burns 68, 87   Ref: V Batty

1	2	3	4	5	6	7	8	9	10	11	12 sub used
Smith G	Burgess	Owen	Burgess	Cram	Garvey	Bloss	Lewis	Simmons*	Gibbs	Mahon	Leslie
Burridge	*Halton*	*Harrison*	*Booth*	*Alcock*	*Suddaby*	*Ainscow*	*Green*	*James*	*Suddick*	*Burns*	

United fans can fly on a Comet aircraft to Blackpool, from Stansted, for £11.25 inclusive of a match ticket. The players will return on the plane after the match. Scottish International Tony Green is the inspiration after the break, and scores when G Smith fails to hold onto his initial shot.

FA Cup

1   H   SHREWSBURY   20/11   5,773 3:9   L 1-4   H-T 1-2

Scorers: Hall 41 / Wood 10, Andrews 24, 67, 83   Ref: R Toseland

1	2	3	4	5	6	7	8	9	10	11	12 sub used
Smith G	Cook	Hall	Gilcrist*	Garvey	Kurila	Lewis	Cram	Gibbs	Jones	Mahon	Leslie
Mulhearn	*Brown*	*Fellows*	*Dolby*	*Holton*	*Bridgewood*	*Robertson*	*Andrews*	*Wood*	*Moir*	*Grove*	

Shrews are the first higher division team to escape from Layer Rd with a Cup victory since U's joined the league. George Andrews is the hero, netting a hat-trick. His first is a goalmouth scramble, the second from a terrible Hall back-pass and the third with just seven minutes remaining.

Home / Away League Table

Pos	Team	P	W	D	L	F	A	W	D	L	F	A	Pts
			Home					Away					
1	Grimsby	46	18	3	2	61	26	10	4	9	27	30	63
2	Southend	46	18	2	3	56	26	6	10	7	25	29	60
3	Brentford	46	16	2	5	52	21	8	9	6	24	23	59
4	Scunthorpe	46	13	8	2	34	15	9	5	9	22	22	57
5	Lincoln	46	17	5	1	46	15	4	9	10	31	44	56
6	Workington	46	12	9	2	34	7	4	10	9	16	27	51
7	Southport	46	15	5	3	48	21	3	9	11	18	25	50
8	Peterborough	46	14	6	3	51	24	3	10	10	31	40	50
9	Bury	46	16	4	3	55	22	3	8	12	18	37	50
10	Cambridge	46	11	8	4	38	22	6	6	11	24	38	48
11	COLCHESTER	46	13	6	4	38	23	6	4	13	32	46	48
12	Doncaster	46	11	8	4	35	24	5	6	12	21	39	46
13	Gillingham	46	11	5	7	33	24	5	8	10	28	43	45
14	Newport	46	13	5	5	34	20	5	6	12	26	52	44
15	Exeter	46	11	5	7	40	30	5	6	12	21	38	43
16	Reading	46	14	3	6	37	26	3	5	15	19	50	42
17	Aldershot	46	5	13	5	27	20	4	9	10	21	34	40
18	Hartlepool	46	14	2	7	39	25	3	4	16	19	44	40
19	Darlington	46	9	9	5	37	24	2	3	16	27	58	39
20	Chester	46	10	11	2	34	16	0	7	16	13	40	38
21	Northampton	46	8	9	6	43	27	4	4	15	23	52	37
22	Barrow *	46	8	8	7	23	26	5	3	15	17	45	37
23	Stockport	46	7	10	6	33	32	2	4	17	22	55	32
24	Crewe	46	9	4	10	27	25	1	5	17	16	44	29
		1104	293	150	109	955	541	109	150	293	541	955	1104

* not re-elected

Appearances / Goals

Name	Lge	Sub	LC	Sub	FAC	Sub	G Lge	G LC	G FAC	Tot
Bloss, Phil	19		1				1			1
Bourne, Richard	1	1								
Burgess, Eric	41			3			8			8
Burnside, Dave	13									
Cook, Micky	36	2	1		1		1			1
Cram, Bobby	35	1	2		1					
Foley, Steve	17						4			4
Garvey, Brian	31	1	3		1		1			1
Gibbs, Brian	30	3	3				4			4
Gilchrist, John	13	3	3		1					
Hall, Brian	36	2	1			1	3		1	4
Jones, Ken	13	4	1		1		3			3
Kurila, John	9		1		1		2			2
Leslie, Steve	40	1	1		1	1	13			13
Lewis, Brian	30		3		1		15	5		20
Mahon, Mick	41	1	3		1		8	2		10
McLaughlin, John	8	1	1							
Mills, Robert	3									
Owen, Brian	7		2							
Simmons, Dave	20	3	2		2		3			3
Smith, Barry	31									
Smith, Graham	15		3		1					
Smith, Lindsay	14	4								
Wingate, Tony		1					3			3
Woods, Charlie	3									
(own-goals)							1			1
25 players used	506	25	33	3	11	1	70	7	1	78

Odds & ends

Double wins: (4) Aldershot, Crewe, Reading, Southend.

Double defeats: (3) Doncaster, Grimsby, Newport.

Won from behind: (5) Crewe (h), Lincoln (h), Reading (h), Stockport (h), Reading (a).

Lost from in front: (1) Newport (h).

High spots: Winning the Watney Cup at the home of First Division West Bromwich Albion.

Continuation of the unbeaten run to a total of 26 matches.

Emergence of youth in Bloss, Bourne, Cook, Foley, Leslie, McLaughlin, Mills, B Smith and L Smith – the best part of a new team.

Stabilising of the club's finances by good housekeeping.

Low spots: 'Grandads' Army' succumb to tired legs after putting U's on the world-wide map.

Losing in the first round of the FA Cup, after last season's exploits.

Player of the Year: Micky Cook.

Ever presents: (0).

Hat-tricks: (2) Brian Lewis (2).

Leading scorer: Brian Lewis (23) (including 3 in Watney Cup).

LEAGUE DIVISION 4

Manager: Graham ⇨ Mochan ⇨ Smith — SEASON 1972-73

No	Date	Venue / Opponent	Att	Pos	Pt	Res	F-A	H-T	Scorers, Times, and Referees
1	12/8	H HEREFORD	6,083		2	W	1-0	0-0	Foley 47 — Ref: K Walker
2	19/8	A HARTLEPOOL	5,472	12	2	L	1-2	1-1	Green 29 (og) / Coyne 10, Smith B 70p — Ref: J Hough
3	26/8	H NEWPORT	3,639	18	2	L	1-3	0-1	Mahon 66 / Coldrick 20p, Hawkins 50, Thomas 90 — Ref: D Harwood
4	30/8	A CHESTER	4,304	20	2	L	0-4	0-3	Wallace 6p, 29p, Hollis 18, Owen 79 — Ref: J Wrennall
5	2/9	A DARLINGTON	1,251	23	2	L	1-2	1-1	Moss 23 / Sinclair 30p, Graham 69 — Ref: R Swallow
6	8/9	H CREWE	2,767	20	4	W	5-1	1-0	Simmons 8, 58, 71 Mahon 55, Nicholl 66 [McLaughlin 88] — Ref: C Smith
7	16/9	A BARNSLEY	2,297	22	4	L	0-4	0-2	Mahoney 26, 65, Greenwood 44, 69 — Ref: N Saul
8	20/9	A SOUTHPORT	2,527	22	4	L	0-1	0-0	Sibbald 57p — Ref: R Capey
9	22/9	H NORTHAMPTON	3,543	22	5	D	2-2	2-1	McLaughlin 24, Mahon 32 / Neal 2, Robertson 64 — Ref: J Bent
10	25/9	H BRADFORD C	3,474	20	6	D	0-0	0-0	Ref: T Dawes
11	30/9	A EXETER	5,005	23	6	L	0-1	0-0	Plumb 57 — Ref: D Lloyd

Line-ups (top = United, *italic = opponents*)

No	1	2	3	4	5	6	7	8	9	10	11	12 sub used
1	Smith B *Potter*	Wooldridge *Mallender*	McLaughlin *Naylor*	Foley *Jones*	Morgan *McLaughlin*	Noble *Tucker*	Leslie *Slattery*	Moss *Hollett*	Smith L *Owen*	Bloss *Radford*	Mahon *Wallace*	Simmons
2	Smith B *Watling*	Potter *Potter*	Hall *Goad*	Noble *Dawes*	Morgan *Green*	Binks *Smith R*	Thomas *Veart*	Moss* *Smith B*	Leslie *Coyne*	Bloss *Spelman*	Mahon *Ward*	Simmons
3	Smith B *Macey*	Cook *Coldrick*	McLaughlin *Sprague*	Moss *Screen*	South *Aizlewood*	Morgan *Harris*	Foley *Thomas*	Simmons *Hill*	Leslie* *Brown*	Mahon *Hawkins*	Mills *White*	Hall
4	Smith B *Eadie*	Wooldridge *Edwards*	McLaughlin *Griffiths*	Wallace *Wallace*	Morgan *Turner*	Bloss *Pountney*	Moss *Owen*	Simmons *Purdie**	Mahon *Draper*	Foley *Clapham*	Smith L *Hollis*	Davies
5	Smith B *Adams*	Cook *Nattress*	McLaughlin *Hutchinson*	Morgan *Wilson*	Morgan *Wright*	Binks *Carr*	Simmons *Holbrook*	Moss *Harding**	Leslie *Graham*	Bloss *Sinclair*	Smith L *Lees*	Leadbetter
6	Smith B *Crudgington*	Cook *Lowry*	McLaughlin *Kelley*	Foley *Peat*	Noble *Gater**	Binks *Gillett*	Thomas *Manning*	Moss *Nicholl*	Simmons *Riley*	Bloss *Humphreys*	Mahon *Bradshaw*	Tewley
7	Smith B *Stewart*	Murray *Murray*	McLaughlin* *Chambers*	Foley *Pettit*	Binks *Winstanley*	Noble *Boardman*	Thomas *Greenwood**	Simmons *Hopkinson*	Moss *Mahoney*	Mahon *Lea*	Bloss *Sharp*	Leslie *Millar*
8	Smith B *Gregson*	Cook *Sibbald*	Wooldridge *Ryder*	Foley *McPhee*	Noble *Dunleavy*	Binks *Lloyd !*	Thomas *Hughes*	Moss *Moore*	Smith L *Redrobe*	Bloss* *Provan*	Mahon *Lee*	Morgan
9	Smith B *Starling*	Cook *Tucker*	McLaughlin *Burt*	Foley *Baxter*	Noble *Robertson*	Binks *Bruck*	Thomas *Felton*	Moss *Large*	Simmons *Gould*	Mahon *Neal*	Bloss *Buchanan*	Smith L
10	Smith B *Ritchie*	Cook *Padd*	McLaughlin *Cooper*	Foley *Denton*	Morgan *Oates*	Binks* *Fretwell*	Thomas *Brown*	Moss *Hall*	Simmons *Ingram*	Bloss *Gilliver*	Mahon *Johnston*	Smith L
11	Smith B *Wilson*	Cook *Crawford*	McLaughlin *Blain*	Foley *Clapham*	Morgan *Giles*	Binks *Balson*	Thomas *Morrin*	Moss *Binney*	Simmons *Plumb*	Mahon *Scott*	Hall *Wingate**	Smith L *Stacey*

Match notes

1. United host the new-boys, who out-voted Barrow by 29-20 in a second ballot for league status, presenting them with a commemorative clock. Debutants Noble (Barrow), Wooldridge (Plym'th), Morgan (Reading) and Moss (O's) see Foley tap in, after Fred Potter parries L. Smith's shot.

2. Binks (O's) debuts. Noble (dissent) and Hall (the penalty handball) are booked. For Hall it is the second of his career, the other was an incident with a certain young Kevin Keegan. Bill Green had headed an own goal from Mahon's inswinging corner to cancel out John Coyne's header.

3. County did not arrive until 2.45 pm because of a train derailment. Trialist South (O's) debuts, but he concedes the penalty. Sub Hall is knocked out with the score at 1-2, and has to be stretchered off. Macey saves McLaughlin's late penalty after he had felled Mahon. Morgan is booked

4. Chester, who put eight past Posh on Saturday, swamp U's. L. Smith trips Bernard Purdie as he rounds B Smith, Turner's 'goal' (14) is offside, before Mick Hollis adds a second. Noble is harassed into fouling Derek Draper for a second pen, leaving Terry Owen to wrap up the points.

5. Simmons's booking at Chester was U's fifth of the term, compared with last season's seven in total. The paltry attendance earns Quakers just £40 after they pay U's £250 expenses. Cook fouls penalty-taker Colin Sinclair. 14-1 ninth favourites, U's, look set for a struggle.

6. Graham resigned yesterday, after a shareholder questions his leadership. Mochan takes over temporary charge. Simmons completes his treble with a bullet header and McLaughlin nets his first, to earn a sixth win in seven home games with Crewe. Fans chant 'we want Dick' at the end

7. Paddy Greenwood nods back to Brian Mahoney who hooks in a tremendous drive, then slides in a second just on half-time. Mahoney gets his second with a brave header, as does Greenwood, who hammers in off Noble. Home-debutant Ray Pettit is booked for a nasty foul on Foley.

8. U's suffer another away setback, beaten by a penalty that never was. Ex-Layer Rd trialist Eric Redrobe is brought down outside the box by Wooldridge, but ref Capey points to the spot. Norman Lloyd is later sent-off and Morgan picks up his third booking of the season on 85 mins.

9. Bink's back-pass falls short for Phil Neal to steal in, but U's level when McLaughlin fires in Cook's free-kick. Cook provides the cross that Billy Baxter heads straight to Mahon, 30 yards out. Cobblers level when Graham Felton's header comes back off the bar to Stuart Robertson.

10. Six points from ten games gives U's their joint worst-ever starting points haul, tieing with 1951-2 and 1964-5 Caretaker boss Mochan attempts to lure Gordon Riddick way from Brisbane Road, or Frank Saul of Millwall in an effort to afford his youngsters some experienced leadership.

11. Hall is captain as Morgan begins his suspension. United have the ball in the net (20) via a flag-kick from the skipper, but a foul on Bob Wilson rules it out. Campbell Crawford's right-wing free-kick finds Dick Plumb, a £7k close-season signing from Charlton, who glances the only goal

Match-by-match record (Colchester United — "U's"), Division Four, 1972–73

No.	V	Opponent	Date	Att.	Result	HT	Figures	U's Scorers	Opp. Scorers	Ref.
12	A	LINCOLN	7/10	6,268	L 2-3	0-2	23 · 3 · 6	Simmons 62, Moss 89	McNeil 11, 60p, Bradley 15	E White
13	H	ALDERSHOT	9/10	3,455	L 2-3	1-0	23 · 3 · 6	Moss 13, Mahon 74	Melledew 58, Stenson 60, 73	L Hart
14	H	WORKINGTON	13/10	2,997	D 1-1	1-0	24 · 12 · 7	Simmons 32	Irving 75	N Paget
15	A	CAMBRIDGE	20/10	4,465	L 0-3	0-2	24 · 5 · 7		Ross 7, Noble 28 (og), Collins 81	R Clay
16	A	PETERBOROUGH	23/10	5,648	D 2-2	2-0	24 · 23 · 8	Mahon 23, 33	Oakes 71, Heath 82	D Civil
17	H	MANSFIELD	28/10	3,789	D 1-1	1-0	24 · 1 · 9	Mahon 15p	Ellis 62p	K Crofts
18	A	BRADFORD C	4/11	3,047	L 0-3	0-2	24 · 14 · 9		Gilliver 18, Brown 44, Bairstow 89	R Boyles
19	H	SOUTHPORT	10/11	3,306	W 3-1	1-1	24 · 2 · 11	Mahon 36, Thomas 48, Foley 52	Lee 15	R Challis
20	A	READING	25/11	4,955	W 1-0	0-0	23 · 8 · 13	Foley 80		A Porter
21	A	DONCASTER	16/12	1,880	L 0-1	0-0	23 · 17 · 13		Elwiss 65	T Bosi
22	H	BURY	23/12	2,739	W 2-1	1-0	23 · 15 · 15	Morgan 29, Foley 52	Jones 50	A Robinson
23	A	NORTHAMPTON	26/12	3,298	L 0-4	0-2	23 · 22 · 15		Baxter 27p, Riddick 33, Hunt 55, 65	G Flint

Line-ups (U's XI / opponents' XI)

12 LINCOLN — U's: Smith B, Cook, McLaughlin, Foley, Noble, South, Thomas, Moss, Simmons, Mahon, Hall. Lincoln: Hulme, Bloor, Taylor, Trevis, Branston, McMahon, Cooper, Bradley, McNeil, Freeman*, Smith, Spencer.

13 ALDERSHOT — U's: Smith B, Cook, McLaughlin, Foley, Noble, South, Mahon, Simmons, Moss, Thomas, Hall*. Aldershot: Godfrey, Walden, Joslyn, Dean, Grummett, Brown, Stenson, Melledew, Travers, Brodie, Smith L.

14 WORKINGTON — U's: Smith B, Cook, McLaughlin, Foley, Noble, Hall, Morgan, Simmons, Moss, Mahon, Mahon. Workington: Ragan, Wilson, Heslop, Tyrer, Ward, Geidmintis, Helliwell, Wood, Rowlands!, Martin*, Irving.

15 CAMBRIDGE — U's: Smith B, Cook, McLaughlin, Foley, Noble, Mills, Mahon, Moss, Simmons*, Thomas, Morgan. Cambridge: Vaspar, Thompson, Akers, Guild, Eades, Watson, Ross, Lill, Foote, Phillips*, Collins.

16 PETERBOROUGH — U's: Smith B, Cook, McLaughlin, Foley, Noble, Mills, Mahon, Moss, Mahon, Hall, Noble. Peterborough: Drewery, Carmichael, Duncliffe, Oakes, Turner, Brookes, Heath, Park, Darrell*, Moss.

17 MANSFIELD — U's: Smith B, McLaughlin, Hall, Binks, Noble, Morgan, Cook, Mahon, Mahon, Simmons, Foley. Mansfield: Brown, Pate, Walker, Longhorn, Ellis, Bird, Foster, Wignall, Fairbrother, Laverick, McCaffrey.

18 BRADFORD C — U's: Kelly, McLaughlin, Hall, Binks, Noble, Morgan, Cook*, Moss, Bloss, Simmons, Hall, Thomas. Bradford C: Ritchie, Podd, Cooper, Oates, Napier, Fretwell, Hall, Brown, Bairstow, Gilliver, Johnston.

19 SOUTHPORT — U's: McInally, McLaughlin, Hall, Thomas, Noble, Morgan, Bloss*, Simmons, Morgan, Foley, Mahon, Smith J. Southport: Gregson, Brown, Ryder, McPhee, Dunleavy, Sibbald, Lloyd, Moore, Fryatt, Provan, Lee.

20 READING — U's: McInally, McLaughlin, Hall, Cook, Noble, Morgan, Foley, Simmons, Smith L, Leslie, Mahon. Reading: Death, Alleyne, Butler, Dixon, Hulme, Youlden, Cumming*, Chappell, Habbin, Carnaby, Wagstaff T, Horley.

21 DONCASTER — U's: McInally, McLaughlin, Hall, Cook, Noble, Morgan, Foley, Simmons, Smith L, Leslie, Mahon, Bloss. Doncaster: Book, Branfoot, Joy, Irvine, Brookes, Uzelac, Elwiss, Kitchen, Rabjohn, Moore, Usher.

22 BURY — U's: McInally, McLaughlin, Hall, Cook, Noble, Morgan, Foley, Thomas, Smith L, Leslie, Mahon, Tinsley. Bury: Forrest, Tinney, Saile, Heslop, Holt, Kennedy, McDermott, Rudt*, Murray, Jones, Williams.

23 NORTHAMPTON — U's: McInally, McLaughlin, Hall, Cook, Noble, Morgan, Foley, Bloss*, Smith L, Thomas, Mahon, Mills. Northampton: Roberts, Bruck*, Oman, Baxter, Robertson, Clarke, Rogers, Neal, Felton, Riddick, Hunt, Gould.

Match notes

12 Lincoln — U's bogey-man Dixie McNeil races away from a U's corner to fire the Imps in front, and four minutes later an error allows Bradley a tap-in. U's fall three behind when B Smith fouls McNeil. United stage a minor fight-back when Moss finds Simmons, and nets a second in the last minute.

13 Aldershot — Three Aldershot goals in 15 second-half minutes highlights U's defensive problems, and earn the Shots a first win at Layer Road since 1952-53 at the twelfth attempt. Mochan turns his attentions to ex-U's star Bobby Hunt of Charlton, but negotiations break down over his personal terms.

14 Workington — U's remain unbeaten in eight visits by the Cumbrians (5 wins). Simmons opens, spinning a shot off the legs of Brian Heslop. John Rowlands is sent off (69) when the linesman spots him throwing a punch at Morgan David Irving latches onto Jimmy Goodfellow's pass for the equaliser.

15 Cambridge — South is released after three-month trial. The local press suggests Graham is about to return, as six are set for interviews, incl Harry Gregg and Les Allen. Bobby Ross (ex-Bees) scores on his debut. Noble, under no pressure, heads in, and sub John Collins neatly tucks in Ross's cross.

16 Peterborough — United make a mockery of their bottom placing to earn a well-deserved point. Mahon scores from U's first attack, and then flashes a 30-yarder past Michael Drewery. Posh never look like scoring until Don Heath's free-kick finds Dennis Oakes, then Heath nods in a Bobby Moss cross.

17 Mansfield — J Smith becomes U's seventh boss since the war, and appoints Joe Hooley, manager of NP League Alfreton, as trainer when Mochan resigns. Mahon puts his first kick wide, after a Kevin Bird handball, but Graham Brown moved. Stags level when Noble hauls down John Fairbrother.

18 Bradford C — Close-season signing Kelly (Norwich) debuts. Cook is carried off (52) with a suspected fractured cheek. Allan Gilliver stabs home after Kelly parries John Napier's header, and he can't hold Brown's fierce shot. Budding cricketer David Bairstow finishes off a fine four-man City move.

19 Southport — Scunthorpe's Angus Davidson refuses a £4k move. but Lincoln loan out McInally. Frank Lee fires the Sandgrounders into the lead, but U's storm back with a Mahon 30-yarder. a long punt to Thomas, and a glancing header by Foley from Mahon's trademark curling flag-kick.

20 Reading — A £6k deal for Darlington's Peter Carr fails as J Smith loses patience with the player. McInally signs permanently. whilst Moss goes to Folkestone. Morgan wears the captain's armband against his former club Foley ghosts in on the blind side to nod Mahon's corner over Steve Death.

21 Doncaster — Mike Elwiss scores his fifth of the season. from close range. after both Archie Irvine and Peter Kitchen have efforts in the same move blocked by McInally. L Smith picks up his second successive booking in the closing stages. United's winter looks to be set for one of great discontent.

22 Bury — Wooldridge joins Moss at Folkestone. Morgan leaps to put U's in front from another Mahon 'special'. Noble sells McInally woefully short with a back-pass for George Jones to intercept. Mahon repeats his corner to find Foley. Terry McDermott is booked for a bad foul on L Smith.

23 Northampton — Svarc signs from J Smith's old club Boston (£6k). along with Brown (Fulham). Colchester-born Bobby Hunt. on-loan at Cobblers. keeps U's in trouble with a brace. Billy Baxter converts a handball decision. and six minutes later Gordon Riddick, another U's target, curls in a free-kick.

LEAGUE DIVISION 4

Manager: Graham ⇨ Mochan ⇨ Smith   SEASON 1972-73

No	Date		Att	Pos	Pt	F	A	H-T	Scorers, Times, and Referees
24	29/12	H HARTLEPOOL	3,172	14	16	1	1	1-1	Mahon 29 / *Veart 28* / Ref: D Biddle
25	6/1	A NEWPORT	3,465	5	16	0	1	0-0	*Screen 51* / Ref: K Baker
26	20/1	H DARLINGTON	3,360	24	18	1	0	0-0	Mahon 54 / Ref: M Sinclair
27	27/1	A CREWE	1,825	18	20	2	1	1-0	Thomas 36, Simmons 86 / *Gillett 87* / Ref: A Jones
28	3/2	A ALDERSHOT	3,574	5	20	0	2	0-0	*Walker 65p, Howarth 80* / Ref: A Lees
29	10/2	H BARNSLEY	3,148	11	20	1	2	0-0	Svarc 79 / *Lea 64, Mahoney 87* / Ref: R Matthewson
30	17/2	A HEREFORD	7,624	4	20	1	4	0-2	Svarc 78 / *Tucker 2, 65, Gregory 40, Redrobe 83* / Ref: J Rice
31	24/2	H DONCASTER	2,550	16	21	1	1	1-1	Foley 2 / *Briggs 18* / Ref: B Homewood
32	3/3	H LINCOLN	2,649	15	21	0	2	0-1	*McNeil 44p, 49* / Ref: P Walters
33	5/3	H TORQUAY	2,639	20	22	1	1	0-0	Leslie 60p / *Boulton 68* / Ref: J Hunting
34	10/3	A WORKINGTON	1,297	8	22	0	1	0-0	*McDonald 51* / Ref: R Perkin

Line-ups (1–11, 12 sub used; italic = opponents)

24 — HARTLEPOOL: McInally, Cook, McLaughlin, Brown, Morgan, Binks, Thomas*, Leslie, Smith L, Svarc, Mahon — Moss
Watling, Potter, Goad, Dawes, Green, Smith R, Waddell, Honour, Coyne, Young, Veart
Harford, an old pal of J Smith, loans from P Vale, whilst Binks leaves for Cambridge. Brown is made captain in a fog-shrouded match. Mahon takes 15 flag-kicks, but U's goal comes in open play. A minute earlier, Robert Veart shrugged off a half-hearted challenge from Cook to score.

25 — NEWPORT: McInally, Cook, McLaughlin, Brown, Morgan, Harford, Thomas, Leslie, Smith L, Svarc, Mahon* — Moss
Macey, Passey, Sprague, Jones R, Aizlewood, Screen, Hooper, Summerhayes, Brown, Hill, White
Hall departs to Chelmsford, as Noble begins a suspension after three bookings. Newport deserve their win, given to them by Willie Screen's solo run from Len Hill's pass, it would have been a travesty for the Welshmen if Svarc's late effort had gone in instead of hitting the upright.

26 — DARLINGTON: McInally, Cook, McLaughlin, Brown, Morgan!, Harford, Thomas, Simmons, Foley, Leslie, Mahon
Owers P, Wright, Hutchinson, Leadbetter, Barker, Sproates, Holbrook, Lees, Hopkinson, Sinclair, Harding — Graham*
Morgan is sent off (73) for punching Alan Sproates, although he leaves the field with blood streaming from his face. J Smith storms 'Morgan and Noble must learn self-control'. Sproates and Mike Wright are also booked as Mahon's inswinging corner settles the battle of the basement.

27 — CREWE: McInally, Cook, McLaughlin, Brown, Morgan, Harford, Thomas, Simmons, Smith L, Leslie, Mahon
Crudgington, Lowry, Kelley, Bradshaw, Nicholls, Peat, Robinson, Nichol, Humphreys, Manning, Gillett — Wain*
Trainer Hooley quits after a disagreement with players, and because his wife still lives in the north. U's record their fifth win in seven at Gresty Rd. Brown's cross is headed by Simmons, for Thomas to steer in. Simmons stretches U's lead, but Dave Gillett pulls one back within a minute.

28 — ALDERSHOT: McInally, Cook, McLaughlin, Harford, Noble, Brown, Thomas, Smith L, Simmons, Leslie, Mahon
Godfrey, Walden, Travers, Joslyn, Dean, Bennett, Brown, Walker, Melledew, Howarth, Brodie — Stenson*
Harford makes his move permanent. U's, who have four wins and a draw in their five visits to the Rec, are doubled by Shots for the first time at the 15th attempt. Ray Cole becomes U's first-ever dedicated physio. Shots take an unmerited lead when Noble body-checks Murray Brodie.

29 — BARNSLEY: McInally, Cook, McLaughlin, Brown, Morgan, Noble, Thomas, Simmons, Smith L*, Svarc, Mahon — Leslie
Stewart, Murphy, Chambers, Doyle, Winstanley, Greenwood, Martin, Lea, Mahoney, Brown, Sharp
Kelly is released, as Coventry youth coach Bobby Roberts, 32, turns down the chance to be J Smith's number two. Svarc, with 25 for Boston this term, nets his first for U's. Earlier Les Lea had pounced on Cook's clearance. Brian Mahoney nods in Frank Sharp's cross to deny United.

30 — HEREFORD: Smith B, McLaughlin*, Cook, Foley, Harford, Brown, Leslie, Smith L, Svarc, Simmons, Mahon — Noble
Icke, Mallender, Naylor, McLaughlin, Tucker, Tavener, Rudge, Owen, Redrobe, Gregory, Wallace
McLaughlin dislocates his shoulder, having won an England Youth cap in midweek (0-1). Mahon turns down a £6k move to Aldershot. Edgar St is shrouded in fog, but Billy Tucker puts Bulls' in front after 102 seconds. U's are down and out when Harry Gregory lobs a second.

31 — DONCASTER: McInally, Cook, McLaughlin, Brown, Morgan, Harford, Leslie, Foley, Smith L, Smith L, Mahon
Book, Brantfoot, Wignall, Uzelac, Brookes, Rabjohn, Hasleden, Irvine, Briggs, Roberts, Hunt — Elwiss*
U's take the lead on 86 seconds, when Kim Book drops Foley's cross in the path of Svarc, whose shot is cleared off the line by Steve Uzelac to Foley, who fires home. McInally only palms away Dudley Roberts' header for Steve Briggs to head. Morgan has a second-half effort ruled out.

32 — LINCOLN: McInally, Noble, Cook, Brown, Morgan, Harford, Leslie*, Mahon, Svarc, Smith L, Foley — Simmons
Kennedy, Leigh, Peden, Symm, Branston, Cooper, Worsdale, Bradley, McNeil, Heath, Walls — Trevis
U's loan Mick Hill (Ipswich), and Roberts has a change of heart. John Kennedy is the star saving penalties from Mahon (20) and L Smith (25) after fouls by George Peden and Dennis Leigh on Leslie. Dixie McNeil shows how it's done after Morgan had tugged Brendan Bradley's shirt.

33 — TORQUAY: McInally, Noble, Brown, Smith J, Morgan, Harford, Leslie, Cook, Smith L, Mahon, Foley
Mahoney, Sandercock P Stocks, Twitchin, Harrison, Edwards, Morrall, Boulton, Roberts, Jackson, Stuckey — Pook*
Simmons joins Cambridge (£3k), as J Smith makes a tremendous comeback after being out injured since the Bognor cup-tie in Nov. Leslie puts U's in front from the spot, after he had been fouled, but Derek Harrison flicks Bruce Stuckey's corner for Clint Boulton to score off J Smith.

34 — WORKINGTON: McInally, Cook, Brown, Smith J, Morgan, Harford, Leslie, Thomas, Svarc, Smith L*, Mahon — Bloss
Rogan, Geidmintis, Ogilvie, Hall, Heslop, Wood, Helliwell, McDonald, Rowlands, Goodfellow, Martin
Leslie asks for a move and Noble returns north-west to Southport (£2k). Two ex-U's men, in Wood and Martin, line up for Workington. John Ogilvie's accurate cross is nodded in by Ian McDonald for his first goal for the club. David Helliwell has the ball in the net (80), but is offside.

Dense season match-log grid (rotated page). Matches 35–46.

No	Date	V	Opponents	Att	FT	HT	Res	Pos	Opp Pos	Pts
35	16/3	H	CAMBRIDGE	3,888	0-1	0-0	L	23	4	22
36	19/3	A	STOCKPORT	3,056	0-2	0-0	L	23	8	22
37	24/3	A	MANSFIELD	4,664	1-1	0-0	D	23	3	23
38	30/3	H	READING	3,092	2-2	2-1	D	23	8	24
39	6/4	A	GILLINGHAM	3,072	1-2	0-1	L	23	12	24
40	9/4	H	PETERBOROUGH	2,437	1-0	0-0	W	23	16	26
41	13/4	H	STOCKPORT	2,772	3-0	1-0	W	23	10	28
42	16/4	H	EXETER	3,489	1-2	1-1	L	23	7	28
43	20/4	A	TORQUAY	4,081	0-3	0-0	L	23	20	29
44	23/4	A	BURY	3,079	0-4	0-3	L	23	12	29
45	27/4	H	CHESTER	2,689	2-3	0-3	L	23	15	29
46	30/4	H	GILLINGHAM	2,590	4-0	3-0	W	22	9	31

Home Average 3,232 Away Average 3,763

---

35. CAMBRIDGE (H) 16/3 — Ref: A Grey
Scorers: Ross 46
United: McNally; McLaughlin, Brown, Smith J, Morgan; Harford, Leslie, Cook, Svarc; Smith L, Thomas*; (sub) Roberts
Cambridge: Smith; Thompson, Akers, Guild, Simmons; Waison, Foote, Greenhalgh, Lill*; Ross, Collins; Phillips
Report: Hill, with personal problems, is shown the door after constantly failing to turn up when selected. Bobby Ross puts Cambridge in front from David Lill's pass. J Smith heads onto the bar (46), but U's best spell comes when Roberts arrives on 77 minutes and Harford pushes up front.

36. STOCKPORT (A) 19/3 — Ref: D Laing
Scorers: Griffiths 47, Garbett 80
United: McNally; McLaughlin, Brown, Smith J, Morgan*; Harford*, Leslie, Cook, Svarc; Smith L, Thomas; (sub) Roberts
Stockport: Ogley; Collier, Ormrod, Spratt, Nart*; Fogarty, Garbett, Lawther, Griffiths; Davidson, Charter; Keys
Report: United's tale of woe continues with a 16th away defeat, and they finish the match with ten men after Harford is replaced by Roberts, and then Leslie limps off after Eddie Garbett's second for County. John Griffiths had fired Stockport in front with an absolute beauty from 30 yards.

37. MANSFIELD (A) 24/3 — Ref: D Richardson
Scorers: Foley 65; Ellis 74
United: McNally; Thomas, McLaughlin, Smith J, Morgan; Harford, Foley, Svarc, Cook; Brown*, Mahon; (sub) Smith L
Mansfield: Arnold; Pate, Foster, Matthews, Ellis; Bird, Thompson, Roberts, Fairbrother*; Longhorn, McCaffrey; Laverick
Report: Mansfield start with an unbeaten run stretching back 32 games. Harford is captain for the day as Foley puts U's in front via a deflection off a Mahon corner. United look set for a shock win, but Sam Ellis pops up 16 minutes from time to thunder a 20-yarder into the roof of the net.

38. READING (H) 30/3 — Ref: T Spencer
Scorers: Svarc 25, Leslie 41p; Cumming 29, Hunt 50
United: McNally; Thomas, McLaughlin, Smith J, Brown; Morgan, Foley, Svarc, Cook; Leslie*, Mahon; (sub) Smith L
Reading: Death; Alleyne, Butler, Wagstaff T, Youlden*; Cumming, Hulme, Hunt, Freeman; Carnaby, Habbin; Wagstaff B
Report: Svarc gets United off to a good start when he nods in Leslie's cross, then Gordon Cumming latches onto a Tony Wagstaff pass to easily beat McNally. U's go back in front when Tommy Youlden pulls Foley over at a throw. Bobby Hunt nets his third against his old club this season.

39. GILLINGHAM (A) 6/4 — Ref: M Davey
Scorers: Svarc 48p; Yeo 45, Jacques 75
United: McNally; Thomas, McLaughlin, Smith J, Harford; Cook, Foley, Svarc, Brown; Leslie*, Mahon*; (sub) Roberts
Gillingham: Gibson; Lindsey, Peach, Quirke, Hill; Jacques, Tydeman, Jacks, Richardson; Yeo, Rogers; Leslie
Report: Gordon Parker and Stanley Firth join the board. Brian Yeo gives Gills, six without a win, the lead, but Gibson's foul on Svarc draws U's level. Joe Jacques punishes McNally for taking too many steps by netting the free-kick, leaving United 13 points from safety and win-less in eleven.

40. PETERBOROUGH (H) 9/4 — Ref: T Dawes
Scorers: Foley 83
United: McNally; Thomas, McLaughlin, Smith J, Morgan; Cook, Foley, Svarc, Brown; Leslie, Mahon
Peterborough: Drewery; Bradley, Duncliffe, Oates, Turner; Carmichael, Heath, Cozens, Hall; Young, Robson
Report: After twelve without a win, U's fans at last see a win. Unfortunately U's record their lowest-ever league crowd. Mahon's cross, seven minutes from time sees Svarc miss with the first shot, but Foley follows up. United stay off the bottom despite Darlington's 2-1 win over Workington.

41. STOCKPORT (H) 13/4 — Ref: G Hill
Scorers: Mahon 28, 60, Svarc 84
United: McNally; Thomas, McLaughlin, Smith J, Morgan; Harford, Cook, Svarc, Leslie; Brown, Mahon
Stockport: Ogley; Collier, Ormrod, Spratt, Hart; Fogarty, Garbett, Lawther, Davidson; Russell, Bingham; Ingham
Report: U's fifth home win over County. The gap reduces to nine points with a second win in a week. Mahon intercepts a pass by Malcolm Russell and unleashes a 30-yarder, then stabs home when Alan Ogley drops Foley's shot. Svarc finishes the rout by skilfully lifting the ball over Ogley.

42. EXETER (H) 16/4 — Ref: K Burns
Scorers: Svarc 43; Binney 36, 46
United: McNally; Thomas, McLaughlin, Smith J, Morgan; Harford, Cook, Svarc, Foley; Brown, Mahon; (sub) Leslie
Exeter: Clarke; Crawford, Balson, Morrin, Giles; Chapman, Neale, Binney, Plumb; Wingate, Gibson
Report: Exeter record their first win at Layer Rd since 1953-4 at the tenth attempt. U's are brought down to earth, after two wins, by the division's top scorer Fred Binney, who takes his tally to 28 for the season. He robs Morgan on halfway for his first, and then nods in John Neale's cross.

43. TORQUAY (A) 20/4 — Ref: J Homewood
United: McNally; Thomas, McLaughlin, Smith J, Morgan; Harford, Cook, Svarc, Foley; Brown, Mahon; (sub) Leslie
Torquay: Mahoney; Sandercock P, Sandercock K, Twitchin, Harrison; Edwards, Jackson, Wright, Thompson*; Stuckey, Jones
Report: Results elsewhere means that United will have to go cap-in-hand to the League members to seek re-election for the first time since 1955. Try as they might U's cannot break down the Gulls' resolute defence. Harford picks up a booking on 36 minutes for a blatantly deliberate handball.

44. BURY (A) 23/4 — Ref: P Baldwin
Scorers: Connelly 17, Murray 28, Warburton 30, Tinsley 64
United: McNally; Thomas, Brown, Harford, Smith L; Cook, Svarc, Warburton, Spence; Mahon, Leslie
Bury: Forrest; Tinney, Kennedy, Holt, Heslop; Connelly, Jackson, Wright, Murray; Stuckey, Jones
Report: J Smith blasts the FL, who forced his side to travel 1,300 miles for their Easter fixtures. Facing a strong wind, United trail by three at the break. Hopes of a comeback are dashed when Alan Tinsley nets. J Smith watches Doncaster's Dudley Roberts grab three in a 5-0 win over Mansfield.

45. CHESTER (H) 27/4 — Ref: W Gow
Scorers: Harford 59, Svarc 75; James 4, 35, Davies 18
United: McNally; Thomas*, McLaughlin, Brown, Harford; Smith L, Bourne, Cook, Foley; Leslie, Mahon; (sub) Smith L
Chester: Taylor; Edwards, Relish, Carter, Matthewson; Pountney, Owen, James, Davies; Kennedy, Purdie
Report: Chester break a sequence of six defeats and a draw at Layer Rd. John James's job leaves McNally wanting yet again when he flaps at a right wing cross that James slots in for 0-3. Bourne in a chase before hammering home. McNally is found wanting home.

46. GILLINGHAM (H) 30/4 — Ref: D Nippard
Scorers: Svarc 5, Foley 12, Leslie 37, Smith L 90
United: McNally; McLaughlin, Brown, Cook, Harford; Leslie*, Smith J, Bourne, Svarc; Foley, Mahon; (sub) Smith L
Gillingham: Gibson; Lindsey, Peach, Quirke, Hill; Jacques, Knight, Aitken, Richardson; Jacks, Yeo; Mills
Report: Confident U's blitz Gills, but are already condemned to seek re-election. L Smith grabs his first of the season with just 19 seconds left. United obtain a maximum 48 votes, whilst Northampton (43), Crewe (36) and Darlington (26) stave off the highest non-league vote by Yeovil (14).

LEAGUE DIVISION 4 (CUP-TIES)

Manager: Graham ⇨ Mochan ⇨ Smith   **SEASON 1972-73**

League Cup

			F-A	H-T	1	2	3	4	5	6	7	8	9	10	11	12 sub used
1	A GILLINGHAM 16/8	3,966 4: L	0-1	0-1	Smith B	Wooldridge	McLaughlin	Foley	Morgan	Noble	Leslie	Moss	Smith L*	Thomas	Mahon	Simmons
					Gibson	*Galvin*	*Peach*	*Tydeman*	*Hill*	*Quirke*	*Knight*	*Jacques*	*Bickle*	*Wilks*	*Yeo**	*Housden*

Scorers, Times, and Referees: Noble 13 (og). Ref: D Nippard

Only Mahon and Hall in U's 17-man squad are over 23 years old. New skipper Noble nets an own goal under the Priestfield lights. U's can't wait to try out their own new floodlights which, after the successful appeal fund, were switched on in pre-season friendly against St Mirren.

FA Cup

			F-A	H-T	1	2	3	4	5	6	7	8	9	10	11	12 sub used
1	H BOGNOR 18/11	4,321 St:21 24 W	6-0	4-0	Kelly	McLaughlin*	Hall	Smith J	Noble	Morgan	Foley	Simmons	Smith L	Thomas	Mahon	Bloss
					Minto	*Hedley*	*McIntosh*	*Croney*	*Sheppard*	*Turnill*	*Pearce*	*Horfield*	*Holmes*	*Knight*	*Bennett*	
2	A BOURNEMOUTH 9/12	11,164 3:2 23 D	0-0	0-0	McInally	McLaughlin	Hall	Cook	Noble	Morgan	Foley	Leslie	Simmons	Smith L	Mahon	Bloss
					Davies	*Machin*	*Powell*	*Gabriel*	*Jones*	*Howe*	*Gibson*	*Clark*	*Boyer*	*Miller*	*Groves*	
2R	H BOURNEMOUTH 11/12	7,419 3:2 23 L	0-2	0-2	McInally	McLaughlin	Hall	Cook	Noble	Morgan	Foley*	Leslie	Simmons	Smith L	Mahon	Bloss
					Davies	*Machin*	*Powell*	*Gabriel*	*Benson*	*Howe*	*Cave*	*Clark*	*Boyer*	*Miller*	*Groves*	

Scorers, Times, and Referees:

BOGNOR — Simmons 9, 23, 54, Morgan 43, Hall 45, [Foley 52]. Ref: C Smith

U's outclass a Bognor side that have reached this stage for the first time in their 77-year history. United are in complete control, and Simmons grabs his second hat-trick of the season; heading in a Mahon corner, stabbing in after Minto fails to hold a Foley shot, then a Mahon free-kick.

BOURNEMOUTH (9/12) — Ref: M Sinclair

J Smith is Fourth Div Manager of the Month, for his first month in charge, as Mills signs as a full-time pro. David Jones comes closest in the second half with a shot that hits the post. L Smith is booked, for fouling Alan Groves, as are Jimmy Gabriel (Leslie) and Ian Gibson (dissent).

BOURNEMOUTH (11/12) — Clark 8, Boyer 35. Ref: M Sinclair

U's miss out on a trip to eighth-placed Div One Newcastle, despite a second-half onslaught on Cherries goal with 17 corners. Simmons has one ruled out for pushing, but Brian Clark nods a corner through U's tangled defence, and Noble is barged by Keith Miller, who sets up Phil Boyer.

Pos	Team	P	Home					Away					Pts

Pos	Team	P	W	D	L	F	A	W	D	L	F	A	Pts
1	Southport	46	17	4	2	40	19	9	6	8	31	29	62
2	Hereford	46	18	4	1	39	12	5	8	10	17	26	58
3	Cambridge	46	15	6	2	40	23	5	11	7	27	34	57
4	Aldershot	46	14	6	3	33	14	8	6	9	27	24	56
5	Newport	46	14	6	3	37	18	8	6	9	27	26	56
6	Mansfield	46	15	7	1	52	17	5	7	11	26	34	54
7	Reading	46	14	7	2	33	7	3	11	9	18	31	52
8	Exeter	46	13	8	2	40	18	5	6	12	17	33	50
9	Gillingham	46	15	4	4	44	20	4	7	12	19	38	49
1	Lincoln	46	12	7	4	38	27	4	9	10	26	30	48
11	Stockport	46	14	7	2	38	18	4	5	14	15	35	48
12	Bury	46	11	7	5	37	19	3	11	9	21	32	46
13	Workington	46	15	7	1	44	20	2	5	16	15	41	46
14	Barnsley	46	9	8	6	32	24	5	5	13	26	36	44
15	Chester	46	11	6	6	40	19	3	9	11	21	33	43
16	Bradford C	46	12	6	5	42	25	4	5	14	19	40	43
17	Doncaster	46	10	8	5	28	19	5	4	14	21	39	42
18	Torquay	46	8	10	5	23	17	4	7	12	21	30	41
19	Peterborough	46	10	8	5	42	29	4	5	14	29	47	41
20	Hartlepool	46	8	10	5	17	15	4	7	12	17	34	41
21	Crewe	46	7	8	8	18	23	2	10	11	20	38	36
22	COLCHESTER	46	8	8	7	36	28	2	3	18	12	48	31
23	Northampton	46	7	6	10	24	30	3	5	15	16	43	31
24	Darlington	46	5	9	9	28	41	2	6	15	14	44	29
		1104	282	167	103	845	502	103	167	282	502	845	1104

Odds & ends

Double wins: (1) Crewe.
Double defeats: (7) Aldershot, Barnsley, Cambridge, Chester, Exeter, Lincoln, Newport.

Won from behind: (1) Southport.
Lost from in front: (2) Darlington (a), Aldershot (h).

High spots: Every voter at the Football League's AGM considered U's to be worthy of retaining league status.
The installation of new floodlights, hopefully signalling a bright future.
Mick Mahon's incredible inswinging corner kicks, which reaped direct goals as well as chances for team mates.
Jim Smith's Manager of the Month, in his first month in charge.

Low spots: The ignominy of applying for re-election, after the heady exploits of the early seventies.
Graham's sad departure because of the criticism of one shareholder.
Just six points from the first 13 games, creating a worst-ever start record.
Twelve league games without a win from September.
Twelve league games without a win from February.

Player of the Year: Mick Mahon.
Ever presents: (0).
Hat-tricks: (2) Dave Simmons (2).
Leading scorer: Mick Mahon (12).

Appearances and Goals

Player	Lge	Sub	LC	Sub	FAC	Sub	Lge	LC	FAC	Tot
Binks, Martin	10									
Bloss, Phil	12	2				2				
Bourne, Richard	2									
Brown, Stan	23									
Cook, Micky	43				2					
Foley, Steve	36		1		3		8	1		9
Hall, Brian	14			1	3				1	1
Harford, Ray	21						1			1
Kelly, Des	1									
Leslie, Steve	27	3	1		2		3			3
McInally, John	27				2					
McLaughlin, John	40		1		3					
Mahon, Mick	44		1		3		12			12
Mills, Robert	3	2								
Morgan, Stuart	3	2	1		3		1	1		2
Moss, Bobby	16	2	1				3			3
Noble, Bobby	25	2	1		3		2			2
Roberts, Bobby	2	2								
Simmons, Dave	22	2	1		1	3	6		3	9
Smith, Barry	18			1						
Smith, Jim	7	1								
Smith, Lindsay	26	5	1		3		1			1
South, John	4									
Svarc, Bobby	20						8			8
Thomas, Phil	32	1			1		2			2
Wooldridge, Steve	3	1								
(own-goals)							1			1
26 players used	506	25	11	1	33	2	48		6	54

LEAGUE DIVISION 4

Manager: Jim Smith

SEASON 1973-74

No	Date	Att	Pos	Pt	F–A	H–T	1	2	3	4	5	6	7	8	9	10	11	12 (sub used)
1	A BARNSLEY 25/8	2,500	—	2	W 1–0	1–0	**Walker**	**McLaughlin**	**Packer**	**Dyson**	**Harford**	**Morgan**	**Cook**	**Svarc**	**Aimson***	**Foley**	**Mahon**	**Thomas**
							Athlaster	*Murphy*	*Chambers*	*Petitt*	*Cole*	*Greenwood*	*Doyle*	*Mahoney*	*Butler*	*Millar*	*Lea*	
2	H CREWE 1/9	4,078	1	4	W 3–2	0–0	**Walker**	**McLaughlin**	**Packer**	**Dyson**	**Harford**	**Morgan**	**Cook**	**Svarc**	**Aimson***	**Foley**	**Mahon**	**Thomas**
							Crudgington	*Lowry*	*Kelley*	*Peat*	*Gillett*	*Bennett*	*Humphreys*	*Purdie*	*Kinsey*	*Lugg*	*Duffey*	
3	A NORTHAMPTON 7/9	4,916	3	5	D 0–0	0–0	**Walker**	**McLaughlin**	**Packer**	**Dyson**	**Harford**	**Morgan**	**Cook**	**Svarc**	**Thomas**	**Foley**	**Mahon**	
							Starling	*Bruck*	*Oman*	*Riddick*	*Robertson*	*Gregory*	*Felton*	*Neal*	*Buchanan*	*Park**	*Stratford*	*Buck*
4	H READING 11/9	4,565	3	6	D 0–0	0–0	**Walker**	**Henderson**	**Packer**	**Dyson**	**Morgan**	**Harford**	**Cook**	**Svarc**	**Thomas**	**Foley**	**Mahon**	
							Death	*Butler*	*Wagstaff B*	*Hulme*		*Youlden*	*Cumming*	*Chappell*	*Hunt*	*Carnaby*	*Habbin*	
5	H NEWPORT 15/9	3,523	3	8	W 4–1	3–1	**Walker**	**McLaughlin**	**Packer**	**Dyson**	**Morgan**	**Harford**	**Cook**	**Svarc**	**Thomas**	**Foley**	**Smith L**	
							Macey	*Coldrick*	*Aizlewood*	*Harris*	*Passey*	*Godfrey*	*Jarman*	*Screen*	*Jones R**	*Hill*	*Brown*	*White*
6	A TORQUAY 19/9	3,428	2	10	W 4–0	3–0	**Walker**	**McLaughlin**	**Packer**	**Dyson**	**Morgan**	**Harford**	**Cook**	**Svarc***	**Thomas**	**Myers**	**Mahon**	
							Mahoney	*Twitchin*	*Sandercock P / Sandercock K / Harrison*	*K Harrison*	*Morgan*	*Stocks*	*Morrall*	*Fairbrother*	*Boulton*	*Stuckey !*		
7	A SWANSEA 22/9	1,981	4	10	L 0–2	0–1	**Walker**	**McLaughlin**	**Packer**	**Dyson**	**Morgan**	**Harford**	**Cook**	**Svarc**	**Thomas**	**Screen**	**Leslie***	
							Millington	*Bevan*	*Evans M*	*Moore*	*Bruton*	*Thomas*	*Curtis*	*Lally*	*McLaughlin*	*Bartley*	*Leslie**	
8	H EXETER 28/9	5,466	1	12	W 1–0	0–0	**Walker**	**McLaughlin**	**Packer**	**Cook**	**Morgan***	**Harford**	**Cook**	**Svarc**	**Foley**	**Thomas**	**Leslie**	
							Wilson	*Crawford*	*Balson*	*Parker*	*Giles*	*Chapman*	*Scott*	*Binney*	*Plumb*	*Joy*	*Wingate*	
9	H TORQUAY 2/10	5,291	2	13	D 2–2	1–2	**Walker**	**McLaughlin**	**Packer**	**Cook**	**Harford**	**Dyson**	**Leslie**	**Svarc**	**Thomas**	**Foley***	**Mahon**	
							Mahoney	*Twitchin*	*Sandercock P / Sandercock K / Harrison*	*K Harrison*	*Harrison*	*Stocks*	*Myers*	*Rowles*	*Boulton*	*Kennedy*	*Morrall*	
10	A HARTLEPOOL 6/10	1,910	4	14	D 0–0	0–0	**Walker**	**Cook**	**McLaughlin**	**Dyson**	**Harford**	**Packer**	**Thomas**	**Svarc**	**Silvester**	**Smith L**	**Mahon**	
							Watling	*Potter*	*Goad*	*Dawes*	*Conlan*	*Smith*	*Honour*	*Shoulder*	*McMahon K / Moore*	*Moore*	*Gauden**	*Coyne*
11	H DARLINGTON 12/10	5,089	1	16	W 3–0	1–0	**Walker**	**McLaughlin**	**Packer***	**Dyson**	**Morgan**	**Harford**	**Leslie**	**Svarc**	**Silvester**	**Foley**	**Thomas**	
							Morritt	*Ingle*	*Jones*	*Cattrell*	*Barker*	*Horner*	*Burluraux*	*Mattress*	*Yeats*	*Atkins*	*Sproates*	*Smith L*

Scorers, Times, and Referees

1. Svarc 1 — Ref: M Smith
   Walker (£4k). Packer (both Watford). Dyson (O's) and Aimson (£11k Bournemouth) all debut. Chapman resigns as chairman and is replaced by Robert Jackson, as a £1m stadium is planned for Colne Bank Ave. Svarc's goal after 45 seconds earns a first-ever opening-day away win.

2. Aimson 46, Svarc 48, Morgan 76 / Lugg 52, Purdie 80 — Ref: M Veith
   The Evening Gazette are the first-ever commercial match sponsors in the UK. McLaughlin receives his England Youth cap as U's secure a sixth home win in seven against Crewe. Svarc nets for his fifth match in a row, whilst new skipper Morgan nods in a McLaughlin's free-kick.

3. Ref: R Marshall
   It is revealed that record signing Aimson suffered a cartilage injury last week and will be out for most of the term. A tight East Anglian derby sees bookings for Packer and John Buchanan. U's are closest to breaking the deadlock when Mahon (twice) and Dyson (90) hit the upright.

4. Ref: R Robinson
   The match is delayed when a fuse blows in the switchroom. U's sorely miss Aimson, when play does get under way, as Tommy Youlden and John Hulme gobble up everything U's can throw at them. When they do break through, United are thwarted by the impressive Steve Death.

5. Thomas 6, Svarc 11, Leslie 24, Morgan 57 / Hill 33 — Ref: D Civil
   Secretary David Havell quits after a disagreement with the board. Thomas runs onto a McLaughlin pass, and heads in the rebound after his shot hits the post. United are firmly in control when Dyson's short free-kick is saved by John Macey, and Morgan snaps up the loose ball.

6. Thomas 35, Svarc 40, Dyson 44, Leslie 80 — Ref: A Glasgow
   Dyson's great 35-yard free-kick goal on the stroke of half-time owes much to Svarc, whose dummy run completely distracts Gulls keeper Mike Mahoney. Bruce Stuckey receives his marching orders for a foul on Cook, before Leslie wraps up U's equal highest-ever League away win.

7. Screen 37, Thomas 67 — Ref: R Brandon
   United fall to a fourth successive defeat at the Vetch, where they have yet to score. Alan Curtis's long corner is headed powerfully in by Tony Screen. Cook and Micky Evans, for fisticuffs, are booked as is John Moore later, before Geoff Thomas seals it via a square pass from Curtis.

8. Leslie 83 — Ref: B Homewood
   Wilf Dixon, after three months' trial from Reading, joins Swindon. The match erupts when Graham Parker ploughs into Morgan (27), who is carried off with a suspected broken leg. J Smith storms on to confront the referee, and there are bookings for Parker, Scott, Joy and Dyson.

9. Svarc 37, 50 / Myers 9, Morrall 31 — Ref: T Page
   On a still night, the huge blaze at the Woolworth's store in the High St leaves a cloud of smoke lingering over Layer Road. Dyson, standing in again at centre-half, is kept busy by the prominent Eddie Rowles. Cliff Myers and Steve Morrall 'fire' Torquay in front, but Svarc saves U's.

10. Ref: R Clay
    Silvester, who has not played for two years after three operations, loans from Norwich. He had featured against U's previously for Southend, but has a quiet game in the North-East as U's slide a couple of rungs down the ladder. L Smith asks for a move, as he wants first-team football.

11. Foley 34, 55, Svarc 78 — Ref: T Dawes
    Quakers' keeper Gordon Morritt has an absolute nightmare as he mis-punches or drops everything United throw at him. Foley stabs in Cook's deflected cross, then capitalises on one of Morritt's poor clearances. Foley is there again to flick on Dyson's flag-kick for Svarc to turn home.

12 — H SCUNTHORPE — 19/10 — W 2-0
Att 4,862 | Pos 2 | Pts 18
Morgan 19, Svarc 42
Ref: K Salmon

United: Walker, McLaughlin, Cook, Dyson, Morgan, Harford, Thomas, Svarc, Silvester*, Foley, Smith L, Leslie
Scunthorpe: Barnard, Lynch, Welbourne, Simpkin, Barker, Money, Houghton, Pilling, Woods, Keeley*, Warnock, Charnley

Despite the win, United slip a place to second. The unmarked Morgan heads Dyson's corner into the far corner of the net, then seventeen minutes later Silvester powers L. Smith's corner against the underside of the bar. It is left to Svarc to wrap things up via Dyson's fine deep cross.

13 — A READING — 24/10 — D 1-1
Att 12,310 | Pos 1 | Pts 19
Svarc 70 | Chappell 3
Ref: K Baker

United: Walker, McLaughlin, Cook, Dyson, Morgan!, Harford, Thomas, Svarc, Leslie, Foley, Smith L, Mills
Reading: Death, Henderson, Butler, Bromley, Hulme, Lenarduzzi, Cumming, Chappell, Freeman, Habbin, Wagstaff T*, Carnaby

Aimson is to undergo a cartilage operation. A week after England's dismal elimination by Poland, from World Cup 1974, U's trail to a goal by Les Chappell, and look doomed when Morgan is sent off (66) for scything Percy Freeman. Ten-man United level with a fantastic Svarc volley.

14 — A ROTHERHAM — 27/10 — D 0-0
Att 4,594 | Pos 3 | Pts 20
Ref: R Walmsley

United: Walker, McLaughlin, Smith L, Dyson, Morgan, Harford, Cook, Svarc, Mills, Foley, Thomas
Rotherham: Tunks, Houghton, Breckin, Wilkinson, Mielczarek, Swift, Crawford, Womble, Phillips, Johnson, Bentley

U's have only twelve fit pros and adopt a 4-4-2 formation. The Millers are unbeaten at home and host representatives from Liverpool, who are running the eye over striker Trevor Phillips. A dour game is only punctuated by bookings for L Smith and Harford, both for handball offences.

15 — H WORKINGTON — 2/11 — W 3-0
Att 5,342 | Pos 2 | Pts 22
Morgan 33, Cook 57, Harford 77
Ref: A Hamil

United: Walker, McLaughlin, Smith L, Dyson, Morgan, Harford, Thomas, Svarc, Silvester*, Foley, Cook, Walker
Workington: Rogan, Geidmintis, Heslop, Kisby, Wilson, Wood, Murphy, Skillen, Rowlands*, Goodfellow, McDonald, Walker

The game starts at 7.15 to help the Cumbrians, as usual, catch their train. Silvester, yet to score, has his loan extended as Mike Rogan keeps the score down to a respectable level for his side. Morgan nets a diving header, Cook a short free-kick and Foley sets up Harford to nod home.

16 — A MANSFIELD — 10/11 — D 2-2
Att 3,033 | Pos 2 | Pts 23
Foley 61, 72 | Longhorn 8, Eccles 9
Ref: J Butcher

United: Walker, McLaughlin, Smith L, Dyson, Morgan, Harford, Thomas, Svarc, **Smith A**, Foley, Cook, Mahon
Mansfield: Arnold, Pate, Walker, Laverick*, Edwards, Bird, Thompson, Roberts, Eccles, Longhorn, McCaffrey, Jones

A Smith is loaned from Southend, whilst Silvester returns to Norfolk. U's give Stags a two-goal start, including one for former U's target Terry Eccles. Foley's double leaves Mansfield hanging onto their unbeaten home record, especially when Svarc scrapes the bar from Dyson's centre.

17 — A CHESTER — 14/11 — W 4-0
Att 1,973 | Pos 1 | Pts 25
Svarc 25, 34, 62, 71
Ref: D Richardson

United: Walker, McLaughlin, Smith L, Dyson, Morgan, Harford, Thomas, Svarc, Smith A, Foley, Cook, Mahon
Chester: Taylor, Mason, Griffiths, Grummett, Dunleavy, Futcher P, Seddon, Home*, Draper, James, Redfern, Edwards

After a draw and six defeats at Chester, U's create a host of records. Svarc equals the individual League scoring record; ten games unbeaten is a U's record in the Fourth Division. Only Martyn King, Bobby Hunt (both 1961) and Neil Langman (1958) had hit four in a single U's game.

18 — H STOCKPORT — 17/11 — W 3-1
Att 4,966 | Pos 1 | Pts 27
Dyson 49p, 51p, Foley 71 | Kirk 67
Ref: T Bone

United: Walker, McLaughlin*, Packer, Dyson, Morgan*, Harford, Thomas, Svarc, Smith A, Foley, Cook, Mahon, Smith L
Stockport: Ogley, Crowther, Ormrod, Spratt, Wilson, Fogarty, Griffiths*, Trevis, Hollis, Davidson, Kirk, Garbett

Svarc's scoring feat took his tally to 14 in 13 matches. The game is moved to Saturday (2.15 pm) as the power crisis forces a floodlighting ban. J Smith fined and warned by the FA over his outburst in the Exeter game. Wilson handballs, and Spratt fells Thomas for Dyson's penalties.

19 — H BRADFORD C — 1/12 — W 4-0
Att 3,460 | Pos 1 | Pts 29
Svarc 26, 80, Morgan 45, Dyson 60
Ref: K Dodd

United: Walker, Smith A, Packer, Dyson, Morgan, Harford, Mills, Foley, Svarc, Cook, Smith L, **Bunkell**
Bradford C: Ritchie, Watson, Denton, Oates, Napier, Cooper, Brown*, Johnson, Ingram, Gilliver, Johnston, Baker

McLaughlin joins Swindon (£25k) in part exchange with Bunkell (valued at £5k). Twenty matches are called off, as Anglia TV visit frost-bound Layer Rd. U's skate their way to an easy victory, but spare a thought for Mills, who was denied his first goal by L Smith being offside.

20 — A GILLINGHAM — 8/12 — L 1-4
Att 8,411 | Pos 2 | Pts 29
Smith L 30 | Richardson 6, Wilks 9, 60, Jacks 70
Ref: C Newsome

United: Walker, Smith A, Packer, Dyson, Morgan*, Harford, Thomas, Svarc, Foley, Cook, Smith L, **Bunkell**
Gillingham: Gibson, Knight, Peach, Coxhill, Galvin, Jacques, Tydeman, Jacks, Richardson, Wilks, Yeo

A Smith extends his loan, but he is determined to move back up north. Morgan and Cook are both found wanting for Gills' first two. L Smith smashes in Foley's cross, but a fine solo run by Alan Wilks, with Walker letting the ball slip from his grasp, condemn United to a heavy defeat.

21 — A STOCKPORT — 15/12 — W 3-0
Att 1,472 | Pos 1 | Pts 31
Svarc 15, Foley 35, 80
Ref: G Hill

United: Walker, Smith A, Packer, Bunkell, Morgan, Harford, Cook, Dyson, Svarc, Foley, Thomas, Smith L
Stockport: Ogley, Crowther, Ormrod*, Trevis, Lowther, Fogarty, Charter, Davidson, Broomfield, Smith, Hollis, Griffiths

U's 31-point haul before Christmas equals the total gained last season! Ex-U's Trevis is a forlorn figure as Svarc nets his 16th of the season, from Dyson's free-kick. A deft header from Alan Ogley's parry, and a scorching 35-yard drive from Foley earn a first double of the campaign.

22 — A EXETER — 22/12 — L 0-1
Att 3,638 | Pos 2 | Pts 31
Binney 55
Ref: H Powell

United: Walker, Cook, Packer, Dyson, Smith A, Harford, Thomas, Svarc, Foley, Bunkell, Smith L, Mills*
Exeter: Wilson, Joy, Bowker, Morrin, Giles, Clapham, Wingate, Binney, Plumb, Devlin, Parker

The directors pay for U's 'supremos' supporters travel costs in recognition of their support. City had gone seven without a win, but bogey-man Fred Binney nods in Keith Bowker's flick from Brian Joy's free-kick. Dyson, A Smith and Tony Morrin find their way into the ref's notebook.

23 — H PETERBOROUGH — 26/12 — D 0-0
Att 7,960 | Pos 2 | Pts 32
Svarc 90 | Hall 80
Ref: M Taylor

United: Walker, Cook, Packer, Dyson, Smith A, Harford, Thomas, Svarc, Foley, Bunkell, Smith L
Peterborough: Drewery, Bradley, Lee, Walker*, Turner, Jones, Murray, Cozens, Hall, Hill, Robson, Carmichael

Posh refuse U's plea for a morning start and with ten minutes left look to have dented the proud home record when Jim Hall scores. In the dying seconds 18-goal man Svarc pops up to equalise. The police keep the floodlights on, as the power crisis plunges the streets into darkness.

LEAGUE DIVISION 4   Manager: Jim Smith   SEASON 1973-74

No	Date	Att	Pos	Pt	F-A	H-T	1	2	3	4	5	6	7	8	9	10	11	12 sub used	Scorers, Times, and Referees
24	H NORTHAMPTON 29/12	5,042	13	W 34	1-0	0-0	Walker / Starling	Smith A / Tucker	Packer / Neal	Dyson / Buchanan	Morgan / Robertson	Harford / Gregory	Thomas / Fenton	Svarc / Best	Foley / Krzywicki	Cook / Carlton	Bunkell* / Clarke	Smith L	Dyson 77p Ref: B Martin
25	A CREWE 1/1	2,383	19	W 36	2-1	2-0	Walker / Crudgington	Smith A / Lowry	Packer / Kelley	Dyson / Peat	Morgan / Nicholls	Harford / Gillett	Thomas / Lugg	Svarc / Purdie	Foley / Rowlands*	Bunkell* / Riley	Cook / Duffey	Mills / Bennett	Svarc 12, Foley 44, Riley 89 Ref: E Garner
26	H LINCOLN 5/1	4,398	7	W 38	4-1	3-0	Walker / Kennedy	Smith A / Branfoot	Packer / Leigh	Dyson / Spence	Morgan / Ellis	Harford / Cooper	Thomas / Worsdale	Svarc / Graham	Leslie / McNeil	Smith L / McGeough	Cook / Harding		Svarc 9, 43, Morgan 20, Leslie 49, McNeil 54 Ref: L Shapter
27	A NEWPORT 12/1	3,304	10	W 40	3-1	0-0	Walker / Macey	Mills / Coldrick*	Packer / Sprague	Dyson / Godfrey	Morgan / Aldewood	Harford / Passey	Thomas / Jarman	Svarc / Hill	Leslie / Brown	Foley / Summerhayes	Bunkell* / Hooper	Screen	Cook 48, Leslie 56, Thomas 90, Hooper 50 Ref: P Richardson
28	H BARNSLEY 19/1	5,793	17	W 42	2-0	1-0	Walker / Stewart	Mills* / Yates	Packer / Chambers	Dyson / Doyle*	Morgan / Murphy	Harford / Greenwood	Thomas / Butler	Svarc / Lea	Leslie / Mahoney	Foley / Millar	Cook / Brown	Smith L / O'Connor	Svarc 9, Dyson 82p Ref: C White
29	A DONCASTER 27/1	4,285	24	L 42	0-2	0-0	Walker / Book	Smith A / Ternent	Packer / Brookes	Dyson / Irvine	Morgan / Uzelac	Harford / Wignall	Thomas / Murray	Svarc / Kitchen	Foley / Moore	Leslie* / Elwiss	Cook / Curran	Smith L	Ternent 58, Kitchen 63 Ref: A Morrisey
30	A BURY 3/2	7,796	4	L 42	0-2	0-0	Walker / Forrest	Smith A / Hoolickin	Packer / Kennedy	Mills / Nicholson	Morgan / Swan	Harford / Holt	Thomas / Rudd	Svarc / Williams	Foley / Spence	Aimson* / Murray	Leslie / Hamstead	Rowe	Spence 74, Rudd 86p Ref: M Williams
31	H SWANSEA 8/2	5,040	10	W 44	2-0	1-0	Walker / Rimmer	Smith A / Evans W	Packer / Evans M	Mills / Bruton	Morgan / Davies D*	Harford / Bevan	Thomas / Curtis	Svarc / Lally	Leslie / James	Foley / Screen !	Anderson / Bartley	Williams	Morgan 4, Svarc 71 Ref: R Challis
32	A DARLINGTON 16/2	2,275	20	L 44	0-1	0-0	Walker / Morritt	Smith A / Nattress	Cook / Renwick	Mills* / Cattrell	Morgan / Blant	Harford / Jones	Thomas / Holbrook	Svarc / Sinclair	Foley / Atkins	Leslie / Horner	Anderson / Duffy	Smith L	Atkins 50 Ref: I Smith
33	H HARTLEPOOL 22/2	5,608	16	W 46	3-0	0-0	Walker / Watling	Smith A / Potter	Cook / Shoulder	Mills / Dawes	Morgan / Gaad	Harford / Honour	Thomas / Heath	Svarc / Gauden	Anderson / Moore	Leslie / McMahon K	Cook / Ward*	Aimson / Smith	Smith A 59, Svarc 71, Aimson 82 Ref: R Challis
34	A PETERBOROUGH 2/3	10,714	3	L 46	0-2	0-1	Walker / Steele	Smith A / Bradley	Smith L / Lee	Mills* / Walker	Morgan / Turner	Harford / Jones	Foley* / Murray	Svarc / Cozens	Anderson / Hall	Leslie / Hill	Cook / Robson	Packer	Hall 12, Cozens 83 Ref: R Capey

24 — NORTHAMPTON: U's have difficulty dealing with Cobblers' long-ball game in the opening half, and are happy to reach the interval. With time running out, Svarc weaves into the box and is sandwiched by Phil Neal, who had been booked for a foul on Thomas, and John Gregory for Dyson's winning pen.

25 — CREWE: Bunkell, in only his fifth game, breaks his leg in a tackle with Arthur Peat (15). On a skating rink of a pitch, Mills is booked just a minute after coming on. U's really like playing at Gresty Rd, securing a sixth consecutive win. U's only defeat at Crewe was in the first meeting in 1961-62.

26 — LINCOLN: Mahon, the sole survivor of the side that beat Leeds, leaves to team up with old boss Graham at Wimbledon (£3k), as he prepares to become a PE teacher. A Smith plays his last game, as U's cannot afford the £5k fee. The cash from McLaughlin's transfer will pay off the big overdraft.

27 — NEWPORT: The interval score is a fair reflection on the match, but U's come out all guns blazing after the break and take the lead when Cook races through to shoot first time. Wyn Hooper pegs back United, but Leslie hooks United back in front and Thomas finds himself unmarked in added time.

28 — BARNSLEY: Svarc, who scored early at Oakwell on the opening day, does the trick again when he stabs in after Morgan had unnerved Gerry Stewart at a Dyson flag-kick. Nigel Greenwood fouls Foley and is booked for dissent, along with Barrie Murphy, giving Dyson the chance to keep U's top.

29 — DONCASTER: U's board reverses its decision and A Smith signs. U's first-ever Sunday game is one of eight in Div Four. U's give Rovers a first-half roasting, but after the tackle by Steve Uzelac leaves Thomas in agony. This unnerves U's, who fall to strikes by Stan Ternent and Peter Kitchen.

30 — BURY: J Smith picks up manager of the month. Everton boss Billy Bingham scotches rumours that he has bid £50k for Thomas. In Aimson's first full game since 1 Sept, Derek Spence slams in, and is fouled by Harford for Billy Rudd's spot-kick. U's goal record is 1-18 from their seven visits.

31 — SWANSEA: Anderson loans from Norwich, and Watford's Jimmy Lindsay is under surveillance. The power crisis is over but, to be sure, local businessman Ron West loans his 140kW mobile generator, as Friday night football returns. Tony Screen is sent off for a wrong word to referee Alf Grey.

32 — DARLINGTON: Packer is out after three bookings, leaving Dyson (11 points) as the only player in danger of suspension. Despite losing, U's stay top as Gills lose 2-3 at Bury. Walker sees a Colin Sinclair effort squirm from his grasp but hit the post. Later, Bill Atkins heads in Billy Horner's corner.

33 — HARTLEPOOL: Accounts to March 1973 show a huge loss of £26k, with gate receipts down £7k and travelling costs up by the same amount. Aimson arrives as a 73rd-minute sub and within nine minutes heads in A Smith's free-kick, but his knee swells up and he is referred back to the specialist.

34 — PETERBOROUGH: Bert Murray puts a short corner by Tommy Robson over for Jim Hall to side-foot in. All United's attacking endeavours come to nothing when Morgan slips, with no imminent danger, allowing Murray to cross for John Cozens. Gills' 0-0 draw at Cobblers keeps U's top on goal-average.

No	Venue	Date	Opponent	Att	Opp Pos	Pts	Res	FT	HT	Scorers	Referee
35	H	8/3	ROTHERHAM	5,180	19	46	L	0-1	0-1	Goodfellow 19	Ref: A Hart
36	A	16/3	SCUNTHORPE	2,134	22	46	L	0-1	0-0	Keeley 90	Ref: I Hough
37	H	19/3	BURY	4,748	4	47	W	1-1	1-0	Moore 34 / Melledew 72	Ref: D Nippard
38	H	22/3	MANSFIELD	4,695	16	49	W	1-0	1-0	Morgan 33	Ref: M Sinclair
39	A	27/3	LINCOLN	2,638	15	51	W	1-0	0-0	Svarc 50	Ref: E Wallace
40	A	30/3	WORKINGTON	1,103	24	53	W	4-1	2-0	Thomas 5, Moore 45, Svarc 46, [Wood 88 (og)] / Heslop 82	Ref: A Porter
41	H	2/4	DONCASTER	5,124	24	55	W	3-0	0-0	Cook 47, 78, Moore 74	Ref: P Reeves
42	H	5/4	CHESTER	6,371	9	56	D	1-1	0-1	Moore 89p / Owen 23	Ref: T Spencer
43	H	12/4	BRENTFORD	8,155	17	58	W	2-1	1-0	Moore 31, 76 / Simmons 61	Ref: A Lees
44	A	16/4	BRENTFORD	7,480	18	59	D	0-0	0-0		Ref: I Jones
45	H	20/4	GILLINGHAM	10,007	3	59	L	0-2	0-1	Yeo 40, 52	Ref: R Crabb
46	A	27/4	BRADFORD C	3,702	7	60	D	1-1	1-1	Moore 28 / Fretwell 34p	Ref: G Flint

Home 5,425 — Away 4,260 — Average 5,425

35 ROTHERHAM — Walker/McDonagh, Smith A/Derrett, Packer/Breckin, Dyson/Bentley, Morgan/Delgado, Harford/Swift, Thomas/Womble, Svarc/Wigg, Leslie*/Woodall*, Foley/Goodfellow, Cook/Mullen, Smith L/Crawford.
Anderson returns to Carrow Rd, where he feels he will have a chance of being spotted by a big club. United host Rotherham for the first time in the league. Jimmy Goodfellow's goal knocks U's temporarily off the top on goal-average, before Gills' 0-2 Sunday defeat at Stockport.

36 SCUNTHORPE — Walker/Barnard, Smith A/Lynch, Smith L/Barker, Dyson/Simpkin, Morgan/Welbourne, Harford/Collier, Thomas/Money, Svarc/Piling, Leslie/Andrews*, Moore*/Roberts, Cook/Keeley, Taylor/Davidson.
U's lose out on the signing of Jim Hinch from Hereford, when his registration is lodged too late on deadline day. A third defeat on the spin sees U's drop to second for real, as Gills conjure up another Sunday special. Nolan Keeley, making his home debut, wins it with the very last kick.

37 BURY — Walker/Forrest, Smith A/Hoolickin, Smith L/Kennedy, Dyson/Nicholson, Morgan/Swan, Harford/Holt, Thomas/Rudd, Svarc/Williams*, Taylor*/Spence, Moore/Murray, Cook/Hamstead, Leslie/Melledew.
Moore, a loan capture on deadline day from Southend, is unstoppable in the air, having been a thorn in United's side in the past. Svarc, goal-less since February, has two ruled out, but U's are grateful for a point when John Murray centres for sub Steve Melledew to level.

38 MANSFIELD — Walker/Arnold, Smith A/Pate*, Smith L/Foster B, Dyson/Edwards, Morgan/Burrows, Harford/Bird, Thomas/Lathan, Svarc/Foster C, Taylor/Eccles, Moore/Walker, Cook/Laverick, Leslie/McCaffrey.
Thomas crosses a short corner by Dyson for Morgan to power home. Mansfield skipper Sandy Pate, in his 300th consecutive appearance, is injured and does not reappear after the break. Early in the second half, Moore's header thunders against the crossbar from L Smith's cross.

39 LINCOLN — Walker/Kennedy, Smith A/Branfoot, Smith L/Leigh, Taylor*/Booth*, Morgan/Ellis, Harford/Cooper, Thomas/Worslade, Svarc/Ward, Cook/McNeil, Moore/Heath, Packer/Musson, Mills/McGeough.
J Smith returns to one of his old clubs, and afterwards declares enthusiastically that United are going for the championship, not just promotion. Cook heads into the middle, where Svarc plants an unstoppable volley past John Kennedy. City's John Ward has an effort ruled out for offside.

40 WORKINGTON — Walker/Rogan, Smith A/Ogilvie, Smith L/Heslop, Dyson*/Kavanagh, Morgan/Walker, Harford/Wood, Thomas/Butler*, Svarc/Skillen, Cook/Murray, Moore/Kisby, Packer/Helliwell, Mills/Martin.
Workington's new hero Dave Murray, six goals in the last three home games, is snuffed out by U's dominant defence. Goals either side of the break confirm U's superiority, and although Brian Heslop grabs a consolation, ex-U's Brian Wood diverts a harmless centre past Mike Rogan.

41 DONCASTER — Walker/Book, Smith A/Ternent, Smith L/Carver, Dyson/Irvine, Morgan/Utelac, Harford/Reid, Thomas*/Curran, Svarc/Murray, Cook/O'Callaghan, Moore/Woods, Packer/Higgins, Leslie.
Cook grabs a neat pair of headers which puts U's in the promotion driving seat. The vital clash at Priestfield sees Gills beat Posh by 1-0 before 12,297. Reading and Northampton will have to win their five remaining matches and U's lose all of their fixtures if promotion is to be denied.

42 CHESTER — Walker/Millington, Smith A/Edwards, Smith L/Loska, Dyson*/Mason, Morgan/Dunleavy*, Harford/Futcher P, Thomas/Redfern, Svarc/Seddon, Cook/Draper, Moore/James, Leslie/Owen, Taylor/Carter.
Impressive Dominey is awarded a full-time contract, but U's get the promotion jitters. L Smith concedes a free-kick near the touchline. Derek Draper nods Stuart Mason's free-kick for Terry Owen to score. In the last minute Paul Futcher fouls Thomas, for Moore to salvage a point.

43 BRENTFORD — Walker/Sherwood, Smith A/Bence, Smith L/Allen, Mills/Gabriel, Morgan/Gelson, Harford/Nelmes, Thomas*/Graham, Svarc/Simmons, Cook/Poole, Moore/Metchick, Leslie/Salvage, Taylor.
Twelve points from a possible 14 sees U's virtually secured promotion. Morgan pressuries Bees' Steve Sherwood, who drops the ball at the feet of Moore. After ex-U's Simmons had levelled, Moore steals in to head home A Smith's right-wing cross. Only an 18-goal collapse can stop U's.

44 BRENTFORD — Walker/Sherwood, Smith A/Bence, Smith L/Allen, Mills/Harding, Morgan/Gelson, Harford/Nelmes, Thomas/Riddick, Svarc/Simmons, Cook/Poole, Moore/Metchick, Leslie/Scales, Dominey.
Cobblers' draw with Crewe confirms that U's are promoted, but the result at Griffin Park means that they will probably have to settle for third spot as Gills and Posh start to catch up their games in hand. U's are hampered by lack of experience in midfield, but Dominey shows up well.

45 GILLINGHAM — Walker/Gibson, Smith A/Lindsey, Smith L/Knight, Mills/Coxhill, Morgan/Hill, Harford/Jacques, Thomas/Tydeman, Svarc/Jacks, Cook/Ricardson, Moore/Wilks, Leslie*/Yeo, Dominey.
U's perform a lap of honour before the game perhaps anticipating a pitch invasion at the end. Gillingham, going for the title, take the lead when Brian Yeo slots in his 30th of the term. Yeo, neck and neck with Fred Binney in the goal charts, nets a second from Damian Richardson's cross.

46 BRADFORD C — Walker/Downsbro', Smith A/Podd, Smith L/Cooper, Dyson/Oates, Morgan/Napier, Harford/Fretwell, Taylor/Hall, Svarc/Ham, Cook/Gilliver, Moore/Brown, Leslie*/Johnson, Dominey.
A Smith, captain for the day against his former club, concedes a penalty when he fells Rod Johnson. David Fretwell drives home to cancel out Moore's seventh goal since his loan began. Peterborough secure the title five days later, beating Gills by 4-2 at London Rd in front of 17,569.

LEAGUE DIVISION 4 (CUP-TIES) Manager: Jim Smith

League Cup

		F-A	H-T	Scorers, Times, and Referees	1	2	3	4	5	6	7	8	9	10	11	12 sub used
1 A GILLINGHAM	L	2-4	2-1	Cook 16, Svarc 42	Walker	McLaughlin	Packer	Dyson*	Morgan	Harford	Cook	Svarc	Aimson	Foley	Mahon	Thomas
29/8	3,991 4:			Peach 40, Wilks 69, Quirke 76, Yeo 88 Gibson		Lindsey	Peach	Quirke	Hill	Jacques	Tydeman	Jacks	Richardson	Wilks	Yeo	
				Ref: G Kew												

U's net first, but David Peach levels when he swaps passes with two colleagues. Svarc claws U's back in front, but once again Gills draw level when Alan Wilks' shot deflects off McLaughlin's shoulder. Brian Yeo swoops two minutes from time to put the issue beyond any doubt.

FA Cup

		F-A	H-T	Scorers, Times, and Referees	1	2	3	4	5	6	7	8	9	10	11	12 sub used
1 H PETERBOROUGH	L	2-3	1-0	Mahon 22, Harford 90	Walker	McLaughlin	Packer	Dyson	Morgan*	Harford	Thomas	Svarc	Foley	Cook	Mahon	Smith L.
24/11	9,664 4:2			Cozens 71, 77, Murray 73	Drewery	Bradley	Lee	Walker*	Turner	Jones	Murray	Cozens	Hall	Hill	Robson	Carmichael
				Ref: P Reeves												

J Smith brands his United 'pathetic' as they collapse in four minutes. John Cozens is allowed in by a Morgan blunder; Tommy Robson holds up Paul Walker's cross until Bert Murray arrives and then the Cozens ends any hopes of a cup run with Posh's third. Harford nets deep in injury-time

League Table

	Team	P	Home					Away					Pts
			W	D	L	F	A	W	D	L	F	A	
1	Peterborough	46	19	4	0	49	10	8	7	8	26	28	65
2	Gillingham	46	16	5	2	51	16	9	7	7	39	33	62
3	COLCHESTER	46	16	5	2	46	14	8	7	8	27	22	60
4	Bury	46	18	3	2	51	14	6	8	9	30	35	59
5	Northampton	46	14	7	2	39	14	6	6	11	24	34	53
6	Reading	46	11	9	3	37	13	5	10	8	21	24	51
7	Chester	46	13	6	4	31	19	4	9	10	23	36	49
8	Bradford C	46	14	7	2	45	20	3	7	13	13	32	48
9	Newport *	46	13	6	4	39	23	3	8	12	17	42	45
10	Exeter	45	12	5	6	37	20	6	3	13	21	35	44
11	Hartlepool	46	11	4	8	29	16	5	8	10	19	31	44
12	Lincoln	46	10	8	5	40	30	6	4	13	23	37	44
13	Barnsley	46	15	5	3	42	16	2	5	16	16	48	44
14	Swansea	46	11	6	6	28	15	5	5	13	17	31	43
15	Rotherham	46	10	9	4	33	22	5	4	14	23	36	43
16	Torquay	46	11	7	5	37	23	2	10	11	15	34	43
17	Mansfield	46	13	8	2	47	24	0	9	14	15	45	43
18	Scunthorpe	45	12	7	3	33	17	2	5	16	14	47	42
19	Brentford	46	9	7	7	31	20	3	9	11	17	30	40
20	Darlington	46	9	8	6	29	24	4	5	14	11	38	39
21	Crewe	46	11	5	7	28	30	3	5	15	15	41	38
22	Doncaster	46	10	7	6	32	22	2	4	17	15	58	35
23	Workington	46	10	8	5	33	26	1	5	17	10	48	33
24	Stockport	46	4	12	7	22	25	3	8	12	22	44	34
		1102	292	158	101	889	473	101	158	292	473	889	1101

* deducted one point

Injuries meant that Exeter refused to play at Scunthorpe, who were awarded both points.

Odds & ends

Double wins: (6) Barnsley, Crewe, Lincoln, Newport, Stockport, Workington.

Double defeats: (1) Gillingham.

Won from behind: (0).

Lost from in front: (0).

High spots: Promotion with a club record number of points, beating the 58 point total of 1956-57.

The dramatic turnaround in fortunes after having to apply for re-election just twelve months earlier.

Gary Moore's seven goals in eleven loan games.

Svarc's record-breaking four-goal haul at Chester.

Five successive wins at the turn of the New Year.

Five successive wins in March to secure promotion.

Low spots: Missing out on the championship, after a stuttering run of six defeats in eight games from the end of January.

Knocked out of both cups in the first round.

Loss of record signing Paul Aimson with a career-ending cartilage injury.

Player of the Year: Ray Harford.

Ever presents: (3) Ray Harford, Bobby Svarc, Mike Walker.

Hat-tricks: (1) Bobby Svarc (four goals).

Leading scorer: Bobby Svarc (25).

Appearances and Goals

Player	Appearances Lge	Sub	LC	Sub	FAC	Sub	Goals Lge	LC	FAC	Tot
Aimson, Paul	3	1	1				2			2
Anderson, Terry	4									
Bunkell, Ray	5	1								
Cook, Micky	44		1		1		4		1	5
Dominey, Barry	1	2								
Dyson, Barry	36		1				6			6
Foley, Steve	32		1		1		8			8
Harford, Ray	46		1		1		1		1	2
Leslie, Steve	21	3					5			5
Mahon, Mick	9	3			1				1	1
McLaughlin, John	18		1							
Mills, Robert	14	3								
Moore, Gary	11						7			7
Morgan, Stuart	38		1		1		8			8
Packer, Mick	32	1			1					
Rowe, Colwyn						1				
Silvester, Peter	4									
Smith, Alex	29									
Smith, Lindsay	23	11								
Svarc, Bobby	46		1		1	1	25			25
Taylor, Paul	6	3								
Thomas, Phil	38	2			1	1	4			4
Walker, Mike	46				1		1			1
(own-goals)										
24 players used	506	37	11	1	11	1	73	1	2	76

LEAGUE DIVISION 3 — Manager: Jim Smith — SEASON 1974-75

No	Venue	Date	Opponent	Att	Pos	Pt	Res	F-A	H-T	Scorers, Times, and Referees
1	H	17/8	WATFORD	5,715	—	1	D	1-1	1-0	Leslie 37 / Scullion 56 — Ref: L Shapter
2	A	24/8	BLACKBURN	8,390	18	1	L	2-3	1-1	Cook 43, Froggatt 51 / Martin 29, Oates 46, Hawkins 53 — Ref: G Nolan
3	H	31/8	BOURNEMOUTH	4,930	10	3	W	1-0	1-0	Cook 44 — Ref: R Toseland
4	A	7/9	CHESTERFIELD	3,474	12	4	D	1-1	1-0	Svarc 7 / Moss 83 — Ref: N Ashley
5	H	14/9	CHARLTON	5,527	7	6	W	3-0	2-0	Leslie 23p, Thomas 31, Svarc 67 — Ref: R Kirkpatrick
6	H	17/9	PLYMOUTH	5,389	4	8	W	1-0	0-0	Packer 90 — Ref: T Spencer
7	A	21/9	ALDERSHOT	3,539	3	10	W	1-0	0-0	Svarc 79 — Ref: K Salmon
8	A	24/9	BURY	5,223	3	11	D	0-0	0-0	— Ref: L Douglas
9	H	28/9	WALSALL	4,877	5	11	L	1-2	0-1	Svarc 56 / Buckley 8, 80 — Ref: R Lewis
10	A	30/9	PORT VALE	3,722	5	12	D	2-2	1-0	Froggatt 9, Lindsay 47 / Williams 64, Bailey 72 — Ref: J Cross
11	H	5/10	GILLINGHAM	4,684	3	14	W	4-2	2-2	Froggatt 20, 40, Svarc 46, 79 / Feeley 18, 31 — Ref: R Clay

Match details (U's XI · Opposition XI · sub used)

1. WATFORD (H) 17/8
U's: Walker, Smith A, Smith L*, Cook, Harford, Craker, Thomas, Leslie, Svarc, Lindsay, Froggatt; 12 Dominey
Watford: Rankin, Butler, Williams, Keen, Goodeve, Bond, Bond, Scullion, Jennings, Morrisey, Downes; 12 Endean
Back in Div Three after a five year break, U's include Lindsay (Watford) and Froggatt (Boston). Harford switches play to Leslie, who times his run to ram home. Harford, in for suspended Morgan, fouls Billy Jennings, and Dennis Bond's free-kick is nodded home by Stewart Scullion.

2. BLACKBURN (A) 24/8
U's: Walker, Smith A, Smith L*, Cook, Harford, Packer, Thomas, Svarc, Froggatt, Lindsay, Cook; 12 Dominey
Blackburn: Jones, Heaton, Wood*, Metcalfe, Hawkins, Waddington, Beamish, Oates, Martin, Parkes, Hilton
In the sides' first-ever meeting, Froggatt takes advantage of Mick Wood's arm injury to equalise, but when Rovers finally re-organise. Graham Hawkins grabs the winner with a powerful header from Tony Parkes' free-kick. J Smith warns he will have to sell if crowds do not improve.

3. BOURNEMOUTH (H) 31/8
U's: Walker, Smith A, Smith L, Smith L, Harford, Morgan, Thomas, Froggatt, Froggatt, Lindsay, Cook
Bournemouth: Baker, Payne, Parodi, Goddard, Delaney, Hague, Nightingale, Miller, Wingate, Howard, Buttle
Morgan returns to add aggression, as Villa take up their regular seat to watch Leslie. Svarc, head and shoulders above the other 21 players on view, crosses, forcing Keiron Baker to push Froggatt's header onto the bar. Cook stoops to nod the rebound in front of the Anglia TV cameras.

4. CHESTERFIELD (A) 7/9
U's: Walker, Smith A, Smith L, Leslie, Harford, Morgan, Thomas, Svarc, Froggatt, Lindsay, Cook
Chesterfield: Tingay, Tiler, Burton, McHale, Winstanley, Holmes, Darling, Moss, Kowalski, Bellamy, O'Neill
Walker is the star in abysmal conditions at Saltergate. Lindsay's free-kick finds Froggatt and Svarc nets his cross. L Smith trips Andy Kowalski (67), but Walker saves Ray McHale's spot-kick. The hero-keeper is finally beaten when Malcolm Darling's cross drops nicely for Ernie Moss.

5. CHARLTON (H) 14/9
U's: Walker, Smith A, Smith L, Leslie, Harford, Morgan, Thomas, Svarc, Froggatt, Packer, Cook
Charlton: Dunn, Curtis, Warman, Bowman, Horsfield, Young, Powell, Hales, Hunt, Dunphy*, Peacock; 12 Goldthorpe
United urge fans to turn up in droves, highlighting the 5p return bus fare from the town centre to the ground. Froggatt is felled by David Young; fleet-footed Thomas evades Phil Warman to lob over John Dunn, and Svarc taps in U's third, after Dunn parried Froggatt's header.

6. PLYMOUTH (H) 17/9
U's: Walker, Smith A, Smith L, Leslie, Packer, Morgan, Thomas, Svarc, Froggatt, Lindsay, Cook
Plymouth: Furnell, Darke!, Provan, Hardcastle, Griffiths, Green, Hore, Mariner, Rafferty*, Saxton, Randell; 12 Davey
United equal their best-ever start of 1958-59, with eight points from six games. The match is turned by Peter Darke's dismissal (41) who, in obstructing Cook, earns a second booking. As U's fans are streaming home, Packer latches onto the ball 40 yards out to net his first U's goal.

7. ALDERSHOT (A) 21/9
U's: Walker, Smith A, Packer, Leslie, Harford, Morgan, Thomas*, Svarc, Froggatt, Lindsay, Cook
Aldershot: Johnson, Walden, Walker, Richardson, Dean, Harley*, Walton, Brown, Howarth, Joslyn, Brodie; 12 Wallace
Ref Ken Salmon books Johnson, Harley and Harford (his third booking of the season), but Svarc keeps U's on course for the Second Division with a volley from six yards. U's fans chant for the introduction of L Smith, and within 60 seconds of his arrival he crosses for Svarc to score.

8. BURY (A) 24/9
U's: Walker, Smith A, Packer, Leslie !, Harford, Morgan, Thomas, Svarc, Froggatt, Lindsay, Cook
Bury: Forrest, Hoolickin, Kennedy, Williams, Hulme, Holt, Buchan, Rowland, Spence, Rudd, Hamstead
U's set a club record six games without conceding, beating the record of four set in 1968-69. Leslie is dismissed in a case of mistaken identity (78). Svarc scores in the move, but the linesman draws attention to the scuffling Morgan and Derek Spence and the goal is ruled out as well.

9. WALSALL (H) 28/9
U's: Walker, Smith A, Packer, Leslie*, Harford, Morgan, Thomas, Svarc, Froggatt, Lindsay, Cook
Walsall: Kearns, Harrison, Fry, Robinson, Saunders, Athey, Caswell*, Sloan, Andrews, Wright, Buckley; 12 Bennett
U's, who haven't conceded in the last four league games, have an off-day against a side that had won just two points away from home. Packer dallies and is robbed by George Andrews, who supplies Alan Buckley. Buckley wins it with an exquisite chip, with U's defence caught dozing.

10. PORT VALE (A) 30/9
U's: Walker, Smith A, Smith L, Thomas, Harford, Morgan, Rowe*, Svarc, Froggatt, Lindsay, Cook
Port Vale: Connaughton Brodie, Griffiths, Chadwick, Harris, Horton, Lacey*, Woodward, Williams, Bailey, Sharp; 12 Ridley
U's change from striped shirts to red at half-time, but it is not enough to confuse Vale. They throw away a two-goal lead after Lindsay scores from a free-kick. Ray Williams finds the net to drag Vale back, then Brian Horton's overhead kick cracks the bar and falls to Terry Bailey.

11. GILLINGHAM (H) 5/10
U's: Walker, Smith A*, Smith L, Leslie, Harford, Morgan, Thomas, Svarc, Froggatt, Lindsay, Cook
Gillingham: Hillyard, Lindsey, Ley, Jacques, Hill, Tydeman, Chadwick, Jacks, Richardson, Wilks, Feeley; 12 Bunkell
Six feet two Peter Feeley, on loan from Fulham, scores twice on his debut, but U's double-act Svarc and Froggatt each net a brace to move U's into a promotion place. Bunkell makes a welcome return as sub, after recovering from a broken leg sustained at Crewe last New Year's Day.

Match-by-match record

#	V	Opponent	Date	HT	FT	Res	Pos (U)	Pos (Opp)	Pts	Att	U Scorers	Opp Scorers	Referee
12	A	PRESTON	12/10	1-0	2-0	W	4	5	16	10,259	Harford 11, 84	—	Ref: J Hough
13	H	PORT VALE	15/10	2-0	2-0	W	3	14	18	5,184	Svarc 11, 30	—	Ref: R Tinkler
14	A	HEREFORD	23/10	0-2	1-3	L	4	11	18	6,390	Thomas 88	McNeil 7, Redrobe 30, Lee P 70	Ref: K Baker
15	A	HALIFAX	26/10	0-1	1-1	D	4	20	19	1,935	Svarc 60	Blair 31	Ref: I Smith
16	H	SOUTHEND	29/10	0-1	1-1	D	3	10	20	6,547	Lindsay 73p	Guthrie 26	Ref: P Richardson
17	H	WREXHAM	2/11	1-0	1-1	D	3	14	21	4,432	Svarc 20	Davies 78	Ref: T Page
18	H	HEREFORD	6/11	0-1	1-2	L	3	10	21	5,131	Svarc 69	McNeil 41, Tyler 49	Ref: R Robinson
19	H	HUDDERSFIELD	9/11	1-2	2-3	L	4	17	21	5,233	Froggatt 38, Svarc 75	Gowling 17p, Gray 24, Dolan 57	Ref: D Richardson
20	H	GRIMSBY	15/11	3-0	5-0	W	3	17	23	4,489	Froggatt 4, 12, 62, Svarc 16, 87	—	Ref: R Challis
21	A	SWINDON	30/11	1-2	1-4	L	5	2	23	10,072	Svarc 23	Moss 20p, 54, 84p, Eastoe 22	Ref: C Thomas
22	H	TRANMERE	6/12	1-1	2-1	W	4	23	25	4,554	Smith L 32, Froggatt 49	Tynan 34	Ref: A Glasson
23	H	CRYSTAL PALACE	20/12	0-1	1-1	D	5	2	26	6,914	Leslie 63	Evans 28	Ref: A Robinson

Line-ups and match reports

12 — PRESTON (A)
U's: Walker, Smith A, Smith L, Leslie, Harford, Packer, Thomas, Svarc, Froggatt, Lindsay, Cook*, Bunkell
Opp: Brown, Fielding, Burns, Charlton, Bird, Sadler, Lamb, Morley, Elwiss, Holden, Williams*, Treacy
John Brown drops Lindsay's corner at the feet of Harford. The centre-half has the simplest of tasks to tap home. Player-boss Bobby Charlton flashes a shot narrowly wide, but it is Brown again who presents United with a second when he parries a shot that flies in off Harford's knee.

13 — PORT VALE (H)
U's: Walker, Smith A, Smith L, Leslie, Harford, Packer, Thomas, Svarc, Froggatt, Lindsay, Cook
Opp: Connaughton, Brodie, Dulson, Chadwick, Summerscales, Horton, Lacey*, McLaren, Woodward, Bailey, Sharp, Ridley
United show their intentions by forcing six corners in the first seven minutes, so it is no surprise when Svarc scores after Thomas unnerves two Vale defenders. On the half-hour Froggatt, with time himself to shoot, unselfishly squares for the even-better placed Svarc to add U's second

14 — HEREFORD (A)
U's: Walker, Bunkell, Smith L, Leslie, Harford, Smith A, Thomas, Svarc, Froggatt, Lindsay, Cook
Opp: Hughes, Emery, Byrne, Tucker, Rylands, Rudge, Paine*, Tyler, Redrobe, McNeil, Lee P, Silkman
U's bid to go top fails when L Smith and Dominey get in a tangle, allowing Dixie McNeil to slot in his tenth of the term. Three minutes later. Svarc's goal is ruled offside. Eric Redrobe adds a second from 12 yards, and Paul Lee gets a third as U's push forward in search of a reward.

15 — HALIFAX (A)
U's: Walker, Smith A, Smith L, Leslie, Dominey, Harford, Svarc, Froggatt, Lindsay, Cook*, Bunkell
Opp: Smith A, Luckett, Collins*, McHale, Rhodes, Phelan, Jones, Blair, Ford, Moir, Gwyther, Downes
The Shay's fifth sub-2,000 crowd sees David Ford's cross destined for Walker's hands, but he collides with a defender and drops at the feet of Kenny Blair, on loan from Derby. Svarc fires in a Thomas cross. Whilst U's sit fourth, they are 18th in terms of average home attendances.

16 — SOUTHEND (H)
U's: Walker, Smith A, Packer, Smith L, Harford, Dominey, Thomas, Svarc, Froggatt, Lindsay, Cook
Opp: Webster, Dyer, Ford, Elliott, Townsend, Moody, Thomas*, Cunningham, Brace, Taylor, Love, Sutton
Shrimpers, still smarting from the League Cup defeat by U's, take the lead when Andy Ford and Dave Cunningham work a neat one-two to find Chris Guthrie's head. Southend lose Neil Townsend for ten minutes with a gashed head, and then Dave Elliott nudges Cook for U's pen.

17 — WREXHAM (H)
U's: Walker, Smith A, Smith L, Leslie, Harford, Packer, Thomas, Svarc, Froggatt, Lindsay, Cook
Opp: Lloyd, Jones, Fogg, Evans, Davis, Thomas*, Tinnion, Whittle, Davies, Smallman, Griffiths, Sutton
Anglia TV capture Gareth Davis spectacularly clearing Froggatt's header from under the bar. Micky Evans misses Walker's long punt for Svarc to pounce, but Alan Whittle finds David Smallman, who centres for Geoff Davies.

18 — HEREFORD (H)
U's: Walker, Smith A, Smith L, Leslie, Harford, Packer, Thomas, Svarc, Froggatt, Lindsay, Cook
Opp: Hughes, Emery, Byrne, Tucker, Rylands, Rudge, Paine, Tyler, Redrobe, McNeil, Lee P, Silkman
Hereford midfielder David Rudge breaks his right leg (20) for the second time in three years, following a collision with Froggatt, who is guilty of missing four good chances. The visitors take their chances to extend their unbeaten run to nine. Saints' boss Lawrie McMenemy observes.

19 — HUDDERSFIELD (H)
U's: Walker, Smith A, Cook, Leslie, Harford, Bunkell, Lindsay, Froggatt, Svarc, Thomas
Opp: Poole, Hutt, Garner, Dolan, Saunders, Ellam, Hoy, O'Neill, Gowling, Gray, Chapman
Alan Gowling is felled by Lindsay, and nets the resultant spot-kick. Terry Gray fires Terriers further in front after a goalmouth melee. Svarc hits the post for Froggatt to tap in, then heads home Lindsay's cross. In between U's goals Terry Dolan raced away to slide in Gowling's pass

20 — GRIMSBY (H)
U's: Walker, Smith A, Packer, Bunkell*, Leslie, Harford, Smith L, Svarc, Froggatt, Lindsay, Cook
Opp: Wainman, Czuczman, Cummings, Hickman, Wigginton, Gray, Barton, Hubbard, Lewis, Boylen, Brown, Rowe
Ex-Boston pair Svarc and Froggatt blitz lacklustre Mariners as chairman Robert Jackson resigns, bemoaning a lack of hands-in-pockets by his fellow directors. Froggatt's hat-trick comes via a downward header from Leslie's cross. Svarc's 15th strike of the season completes the rout.

21 — SWINDON (A)
U's: Walker, Dominey, Barron, Packer, Leslie, Harford, Bunkell*, Thomas, Svarc, Froggatt, Lindsay, Cook
Opp: Allan, Dixon, Trollope, Hubbard, Burrows, Prophett, Moss, McLaughlin, Eastoe, Butler, Anderson
Second-placed Robins swamp U's, courtesy of a David Moss hat-trick. Harford fouls him for his first penalty, he embarks on an individual run for the second, before Harford fouls Trevor Anderson for Moss's third. The striker also hits the post and provides Peter Eastoe for the fourth.

22 — TRANMERE (H)
U's: Walker, Dominey, Packer, Leslie, Morgan, Harford, Cook, Svarc, Froggatt, Lindsay, Smith L
Opp: Johnson, Parry, Flood, Moore, Philpotts, Palios, Coppell, Tynan, Young, Veitch, Crossley*, Allen
J Smith warns 'the day I have to sell looms ever closer', as attendances fail to meet the 7,000 target. L Smith gets his first of the season to cap an impressive couple of weeks. Nine minutes earlier, the usually reliable Leslie had fired a spot-kick over after being felled by Paul Crossley.

23 — CRYSTAL PALACE (H)
U's: Walker, Thomas, Smith L, Packer, Leslie, Harford, Dominey, Svarc, Froggatt, Lindsay, Cook
Opp: Burns, Mulligan, Cannon, Venables, Jeffries, Evans, Chatterton, Whittle, Swindlehurst, Hinshelwood, P Taylor, Cook
U's pursue Pompey's midfielder Billy Kellard, and recover somewhat from the cup disappointments. The energetic Ian Evans tears through U's static defence to shoot Palace in front, but keeper Tony Burns fails to hold a L Smith hot-shot allowing Leslie to swoop in for U's leveller.

LEAGUE DIVISION 3

Manager: Jim Smith

SEASON 1974-75

No	Date	Team	Att	Pos	Pt	F-A	H-T	1	2	3	4	5	6	7	8	9	10	11	12 sub used	Scorers, Times, and Referees
24	28/12	H PETERBOROUGH	7,790	5	W 28	4-1	3-0	Walker	Thomas*	Packer	Smith L	Harford	Dominey	Bunkell	Svarc	Froggatt	Lindsay	Cook	Dyson	Froggatt 2, Dominey 4, Cook 36, Turner 75 [Bradley 51 (og)] Ref T Reynolds
								Steele	*Bradley*	*Oates*	*Walker*	*Turner*	*Jones*	*Murray**	*Gregory*	*Nixon*	*Carmichael*	*Llewellyn*	*Hobson*	
25	1/1	A CHARLTON	15,246	6	L 28	1-4	1-2	Walker	Morgan	Smith L	Packer	Harford	Dominey	Bunkell	Dyson	Froggatt	Lindsay*	Cook	**Rowe**	Dyson 16 · Horsfield 12, 76, Powell 39, Warman 70 Ref: A Hamil
								Tutt	*Curtis*	*Warman*	*Bowman*	*Goldthorpe*	*Young*	*Powell*	*Hales*	*Horsfield*	*Hunt*	*Peacock*		
26	4/1	H ALDERSHOT	5,096	4	D 29	0-0	0-0	Walker	Dominey	Packer	Dyson*	Harford	Morgan	Rowe	Sims	Froggatt	Lindsay	Cook	Smith L	Ref: T Bune
								Johnson	*Walden*	*Joplin*	*Crosby*	*Dean*	*Richardson*	*Walton*	*Walker*	*Marrisey*	*Sainty*	*Bradie*		
27	10/1	A TRANMERE	2,819	8	L 29	0-2	0-0	Walker	Smith A	Packer	Dyson	Harford	Dominey	Foley*	Sims	Froggatt	Lindsay	Cook	Bunkell	Crossley 70p, Coppell 82 Ref: H Davey
								Johnson	*Webb*	*Flood*	*Mathias*	*Moore*	*Palios*	*Coppell*	*Peplow*	*Allen*	*Young*	*Crossley*		
28	25/1	A BRIGHTON	9,937	9	L 29	0-2	0-1	Walker	Smith A	Packer*	Bunkell	Morgan!	Dominey	Cook	Svarc	Froggatt	Lindsay	Cook	Smith L	Binney 28, 64 Ref: B Newsome
								Grummitt	*Tiler*	*Lewis*	*Machin*	*Piper*	*Winstanley*	*Towner*	*O'Sullivan*	*Binney*	*Fell*	*Walker*		
29	1/2	H HUDDERSFIELD	3,921	8	W 31	3-2	2-0	Walker	Smith A	Cook	Smith A	Harford	Dominey	Smith L	Svarc	Froggatt	Lindsay	Foley*	Rowe	Froggatt 23, 32, Dominey 75 Gowling 59p, 73p Ref: J Bent
								Taylor	*Hutt*	*Garner**	*Smith*	*Saunders*	*Dolan*	*Gray*	*O'Neil*	*Gowing*	*Lawson*	*Fowler*		
30	8/2	A WREXHAM	3,433	11	L 31	1-2	0-1	Walker	Cameron	Smith L	Bunkell	Harford	Dominey	Cook	Svarc*	Froggatt	Lindsay	Cook	Foley	Lindsay 85 Whittle 38, Smallman 60 Ref: W Johnson
								Lloyd	*Hill*	*Jones*	*Evans*	*Davis*	*Whittle*	*Tinnion*	*Sutton*	*Ashcroft*	*Smallman*	*Griffiths*		
31	15/2	H BRIGHTON	4,161	12	D 32	2-2	2-1	Walker	Cameron	Smith L	Bunkell	Harford	Dominey	McDonald	Svarc	Froggatt	Lindsay*	Cook	Foley	Svarc 5, McDonald 6 Binney 14, Towner 68 Ref: M Taylor
								Grummitt	*Tiler*	*Wilson*	*Machin*	*Piper*	*Winstanley*	*Towner*	*O'Sullivan*	*Binney*	*Fell*	*Walker*		
32	22/2	A GRIMSBY	5,608	11	D 33	1-1	1-0	Walker	Cameron	Cook	Bunkell	Harford	Smith L	McDonald*	Svarc	Froggatt	Lindsay	Cook	Leslie	McDonald 41 Lewis 61 Ref: G Trevett
								Wainman	*Cruzcman*	*Booth*	*Coyle**	*Wigginton*	*Govier*	*Barton*	*Hubbard*	*Wigg*	*Boylen*	*Lewis*	*Brown*	
33	1/3	A BOURNEMOUTH	4,578	8	W 35	2-0	1-0	Walker	Cameron	Cook	Bunkell	Harford	Smith L	McDonald*	Svarc	Froggatt	Lindsay	Foley	Leslie	Froggatt 22, Foley 61 Ref: M Sinclair
								Baker	*Payne*	*Parodi*	*Rickard**	*Hague*	*Benson*	*Redknapp*	*Welsh*	*Wingate*	*Greenhalgh*	*Buttle*	*O'Rourke*	
34	4/3	H SWINDON	4,041	8	W 37	2-0	1-0	Walker	Cameron	Cook	Bunkell	Harford	Smith L	McDonald	Svarc	Froggatt	Lindsay	Foley	Foley	Svarc 14, 55 Ref: L Shapter
								Barron	*Dixon*	*Trollope*	*Jenkins*	*Stroud*	*Prophett*	*Moss*	*McLaughlin*	*Eastoe*	*Butler*	*Anderson*		

24 · H PETERBOROUGH — Peterboro never recover from U's blistering start Cook and Dominey fire United in front as the Anglia TV cameras had hardly started rolling. Froggatt's shot deflects off Keith Bradley, but Chris Turner pulls one back against ten-man U's after Thomas and Svarc both pick up injuries.

25 · A CHARLTON — Before the Valley's biggest crowd for three years, Charlton, inspired by Ritchie Bowman, take the lead when Arthur Horsfield nods in Colin Powell's corner. Phil Warman back-heads a Bob Curtis free-kick and Horsfield adds his second to keep the Valiants on course for promotion.

26 · H ALDERSHOT — New loan-signing John Sims, who had been on a similar spell at Oxford, arrives from Derby for whom he had made a European Cup substitute appearance against Juventus a couple of seasons ago. He fails to impress, having one shot saved, as U's sorely miss Svarc, Leslie and Thomas.

27 · A TRANMERE — United pay for their cautious approach, keeping eight men behind the ball for much of the game. Cook pulls down Paul Crossley, who picks himself up to give Rovers the lead. U's press for an equaliser, but Steve Coppell secures the points with a header from Eddie Flood's free-kick.

28 · A BRIGHTON — Last week's game v Swindon was washed out on 57 mins with the U's leading by 3-0. Peter Taylor's Albion were also 'giant-killed', at home, by Leatherhead in the FA Cup (0-1) in front of 20,491. Morgan is sent off for not giving his name quickly enough, when about to be booked.

29 · H HUDDERSFIELD — Froggatt's opener appears to be stopped on the line by Terry Dolan, but is awarded by the linesman. The striker then nods in Bunkell's cross. Colin Garwood earns Alan Gowling two penalties for fouls by Walker and Cook, but justice is done when Dominey heads home Foley's cross.

30 · A WREXHAM — U's sign 21-year-olds McDonald (Liverpool) and Cameron (Sheffield Wed), each on a month's loan. A Smith joins Halifax to be nearer his Heckmondwike home. Brian Tinnion's cross is helped on by Arfon Griffiths to Alan Whittle, and David Smallman nods in Alan Hill's centre.

31 · H BRIGHTON — The FL refuse U's request to switch the game to Friday night, to avoid Ipswich v Villa, because of the pools coupons. J Smith puts the whole of the first team, bar Svarc, through a hastily arranged midweek game with Norwich, as punishment for throwing away a scintillating 2-0 start.

32 · A GRIMSBY — Aimson's career is ended by his cartilage injury. Manager-less Grimsby (Ron Ashman was sacked three weeks ago) fall behind to McDonald, who wishes to forge his way in at Liverpool, but Cameron expresses a desire to stay. Speedy Jack Lewis beats Walker to the ball to equalise.

33 · A BOURNEMOUTH — Cherries are under the wings of new player-manager, John Benson, who had rejoined the South coast club from John Bond's Norwich. United take the lead when Foley nods back McDonald's flag-kick for Froggatt. Harford almost slices an own-goal, before Foley volleys a fine second.

34 · H SWINDON — U's get the points that they had stolen by the January wash-out against a Swindon side that cost £200k to assemble. Foley's inch-perfect centre finds Svarc, who launches himself to head in. Then ex-U's trialist Wilf Dixon makes a hash of clearing Cook's pass, allowing Svarc to pounce.

Match-by-Match Record (Games 35–46)

No	Date	V	Opponent	Att	Pos	(2)	Res	Pts	FT	HT	Scorers / Opponents' scorers — Ref
35	15/3	A	WALSALL	4,914	10	6	L	37	2-5	1-1	Foley 25, Lindsay 64, [Buckley 76] | Athey 40, Ben' 48, Andrews 70, H'son 73. Ref: J Williams
36	19/3	A	WATFORD	3,941	9	18	W	39	2-1	1-1	Froggatt 4, Svarc 59 | Scullion 19. Ref: D Nippard
37	22/3	H	CHESTERFIELD	4,152	10	15	L	39	1-2	0-2	Lindsay 62 | Shanahan 5, Moss 17. Ref: R Crabb
38	25/3	A	CRYSTAL PALACE	16,851	10	4	L	39	1-2	0-0	Froggatt 54 | Evans 67, Cannon 78. Ref: E Read
39	28/3	A	PETERBOROUGH	7,559	13	9	L	39	0-1	0-0	Gregory 79. Ref: G Nolan
40	4/4	H	HALIFAX	3,501	11	19	W	41	2-0	2-0	Svarc 4, Rowe 29. Ref: R Tinkler
41	12/4	A	GILLINGHAM	6,504	13	11	L	41	1-2	0-1	Rowe 50 | Yeo 32, Richardson 62p. Ref: D Biddle
42	15/4	A	PLYMOUTH	23,551	13	1	L	41	0-1	0-0	Mariner 50. Ref: A Lees
43	19/4	H	PRESTON	5,228	14	9	D	42	2-2	1-1	Bunkell 34, Svarc 62 | Smith 24, Morley 77. Ref: R Challis
44	22/4	H	BLACKBURN	4,183	10	2	W	44	2-0	1-0	Lindsay 6, Svarc 82. Ref: B Homewood
45	25/4	A	SOUTHEND	5,924	12	18	D	45	1-1	0-1	Foley 78 | Dominey 44 (og). Ref: C White (J Dance)
46	2/5	H	BURY	3,202	11	14	W	47	3-1	3-1	Froggatt 1, Svarc 3, 5 | Hamstead 41, Bailey 82. Ref: K Salmon

Home Average 4,941 — Away 7,352

Line-ups & notes

35 WALSALL — Walker, Dominey*, Cook, Bunkell, Harford, Smith L, Leslie, Svarc, Froggatt, Lindsay, Foley, Thomas. *(opp.)* Kearns, Fry, Harrison, Robinson, Bennett, Athey, Taylor, Andrews, Wright, Buckley, Birch, Thomas.
Cameron and McDonald return to their clubs. Morgan joins Bournemouth (£4k), whilst Norwich boss John Bond opts for experience in Spurs Martin Peters after considering a 'substantial' bid for Foley. Walsall have sensationally beaten Man United and Newcastle in the FA Cup.

36 WATFORD — Walker, Thomas, Cook, Bunkell, Smith L, Leslie, Svarc, Froggatt, Lindsay*, Foley, Dominey. *(opp.)* Rankin, Butler, Walsh*, Joslyn, Goodeve, Garner, Bond, Greenhalgh, Mayes, Downes, Mercer.
Injury-hit Dyson was also released on deadline day. Froggatt was also released on deadline day. Froggatt has enjoyed his trips to Vicarage Rd this term, in November he dumped Hornets out of the FA Cup, now he rises to meet Lindsay's free-kick. Stewart Scullion levels, but Svarc wins it after Froggatt does all the spadework.

37 CHESTERFIELD — Walker, Thomas, Cook, Smith L, Harford, Leslie*, Svarc, Froggatt, Lindsay, Foley*, Rowe. *(opp.)* Tingay, O'Neill, Burton, McEwan, Winstanley, Barlow, Moss, Darling, Kowalski, Bellamy, Shanahan.
United wave goodbye to any lingering hopes of catching the leading pack. Ipswich reject Terry Shanahan and the prolific Ernie Moss set Chesterfield on their way, and they could have had four by the half-hour. Rowe courageously wins possession to set up Lindsay's consolation.

38 CRYSTAL PALACE — Walker, Thomas, Cook, Bunkell*, Harford, Smith L, Leslie, Svarc, Froggatt, Lindsay, Foley, Dominey. *(opp.)* Burns, Wall, Cannon, Johnson, Jeffries, Evans, Whittle, Hinshelw'd, Swindlehurst, M Hill, Taylor.
U's are undone by set-pieces after Froggatt gives them the lead with his 17th of the term, tapping in after Tony Burns had blocked Lindsay's shot. Walker misses a punch on Peter Taylor's corner, which drops for Ian Evans. Then Jim Cannon nods in a Martin Hinshelwood's free-kick.

39 PETERBOROUGH — Walker, Thomas*, Cook, Bunkell, Smith L, Leslie, Packer, Froggatt, Lindsay, Foley, Rowe. *(opp.)* Steele, Bradley, Winfield, Walker, Carmichael, Murray, Gregory, Hall*, Nixon, Robson, Hobson.
After nearly beating Palace into submission on Tuesday, U's dish out the same to Posh at London Road but fail to take chances. Rising starlet David Gregory catches United's defence on the back foot to drive in low past Walker. Tommy Robson clears Froggatt's late effort off the line.

40 HALIFAX — Walker, Packer, Cook, Bunkell, Smith L*, Leslie, Svarc, Froggatt, Lindsay, Rowe, Harford. *(opp.)* Smith A, Smith A, Collins, McHale, Rhodes*, Jones, Phelan, Ford, Downes, Campbell, Blair, Pugh.
After three dismal defeats on the trot, U's host their lowest attendance of the term so far. 18-year-old Rowe, on his full debut, crosses for Svarc to notch his 21st goal of the season, and then caps a memorable display by being quickest to the ball when his shot rebounds off John Collins.

41 GILLINGHAM — Walker, Cook, Packer, Bunkell, Harford, Smith L, Rowe*, Svarc, Froggatt, Lindsay, Leslie, Dominey. *(opp.)* Hillyard, Wiltshire, Ley, Hill, Shipperley, Tydeman, Jacks, Gauden, Richardson, O'Donnell, Yeo.
Travelling U's are sunk for the third consecutive match, by a ludicrous penalty. Brian Yeo swallow-dives after rounding Cook, realising that Walker will gather the ball. Yeo, on his 31st birthday, had nodded in Dave Shipperley's cross, and tiny Rowe grabs his second in two games.

42 PLYMOUTH — Walker, Dominey*, Packer, Packer, Harford*, Smith L, Leslie, Svarc, Froggatt, Lindsay, Foley, Bunkell. *(opp.)* Furnell, Hore, Burrows, Saxton, Green, Debre, Randell, Johnson, Mariner, Rafferty, McAuley.
Walker, after a great first half-season, is in a run of bad luck. He foils 27-goal striker Billy Rafferty on a number of occasions, but drop-kicks the ball onto the striker's back and the ball runs invitingly to Paul Mariner. The goal secures Argyle's promotion to Division Two next term.

43 PRESTON — Walker, Cook, Bunkell, Harford, Smith L, Foley, Svarc, Froggatt, Lindsay*, Leslie, Allinson. *(opp.)* Tunks, Fielding, Doyle, Bird, Baxter, Thomson*, Burns, Elwiss, Smith, Morley, Coleman.
Allinson is presented with the Young Player of the Year by North End boss Bobby Charlton, and earns a sub appearance. A larger than average crowd is disappointed that Charlton and his World Cup colleague Nobby Stiles do not play. Svarc nets his 22nd goal, but Tony Morley levels.

44 BLACKBURN — Walker, Cook, Smith L, Leslie, Harford, Packer, Svarc, Froggatt, Lindsay, Cook, Rowe. *(opp.)* Jones, Heaton, Burgin, Metcalfe, Hawkins, Fazackerley, Oates, Hickman, Parkes, Hoy, Kenyon.
U's complete a remarkable set of home wins against the division's top-dogs. They have despatched Plymouth, Charlton, Port Vale, Posh and now Blackburn at fortress Layer Road. Cook's throw-in bounces over a pack of players to Lindsay, and Derek Fazackerley is harried by Svarc.

45 SOUTHEND — Walker, Dominey*, Packer, Leslie, Harford*, Smith L, Foley, Svarc, Froggatt, Lindsay, Cook, Rowe. *(opp.)* Webster, Worthington, D Taylor, Dyer, Townsend, Moody, Little, Brace, Lamb, Cunningham, Pountney.
United complete their away programme in an uninspiring Essex derby. Foley earns U's a share of the spoils with a great diving header after Dominey had whipped the ball off the foot of Ron Pountney, only to see it sail over Walker into his own net. The ref sustains a sprained ankle.

46 BURY — Walker, Dominey, Packer, Leslie, Harford*, Smith L, Foley, Svarc, Froggatt, Lindsay, Cook, Rowe. *(opp.)* Forrest, Hoolickin, Kennedy, Nicholson, Thomson, Bailey, Buchan*, Riley, Rowland, Williams, Hamstead, Woofall.
Harford, Rowe and Dominey are to be released. United start on course to beat their record victory with an astonishing three goals in the first five minutes, via Froggatt's first-time shot and Svarc's blaster, both from Cook crosses, and then the Svarc after Lindsay's corner was not cleared.

LEAGUE DIVISION 3 (CUP-TIES)　　Manager: Jim Smith　　SEASON 1974-75

League Cup

	1	2	3	4	5	6	7	8	9	10	11	12 sub used
1 H OXFORD 20/8 4,609 2: W 1-0 H-T 1-0 — Lindsay 27p — Ref: M Taylor	Walker	Smith A	Smith L*	Leslie	Harford	Packer	Thomas	Svarc	Froggatt	Lindsay	Cook	Dyson
	Milkins	*Lucas*	*Shuker*	*Roberts*	*Clarke C*	*Briggs*	*Jeffrey*	*Fleming**	*McCulloch*	*Curran*	*Heron*	*Aylott*

U's brush aside their Second Div opponents with a brand of football that bodes well for the coming season. Oxford have £100k's worth of new talent in John Milkins, Andy McCulloch and Brian Heron, but Billy Jeffrey desperately hauls down Leslie and Lindsay scores after a re-take.

	1	2	3	4	5	6	7	8	9	10	11	12 sub used
2 A SOUTHEND 11/9 7,856 3:1 W 2-0 H-T 0-0 — Leslie 64p, 67p — Ref: J Bent	Walker	Smith A	Smith L	Leslie	Morgan	Harford	Thomas	Svarc	Froggatt	Packer	Cook	Smith L
	Webster	*Worthington D*	*Worthington R Elliott*	*Townsend*	*Moody*	*Johnson*	*Brace*	*Guthrie*	*Taylor*	*Silvester*		

Norwich bid £12k for ice-cool Leslie, who steers United through to the next round. Southend boss Arthur Rowley fumes at his sides long-ball game that plays into U's hands, and at the double penalty decisions when Malcolm Webster fouls Froggatt, and Peter Silvester pushes Morgan.

	1	2	3	4	5	6	7	8	9	10	11	12 sub used
3 H CARLISLE 9/10 7,842 1:13 W 2-0 H-T 0-0 — Svarc 75, Leslie 78p — Ref: P Reeves	Walker	Smith A	Packer	Leslie	Morgan*	Harford	Thomas	Svarc	Froggatt	Lindsay	Cook	Smith L
	Clarke T	*Carr*	*Gorman*	*Winstanley*	*Green*	*Parker*	*Martin*	*Train*	*Clarke F*	*Owen*	*Spearritt*	

Carlisle had led the Div One table in August. Morgan breaks his collar-bone in a first-half goalmouth scramble. before Svarc intercepts a bad back-pass from Dennis Martin. Ref Reeves needs a police escort after awarding a penalty. when Peter Carr floored Froggatt in the Carlisle wall.

	1	2	3	4	5	6	7	8	9	10	11	12 sub used
4 H SOUTHAMPTON 13/11 9,515 2:17 D 0-0 H-T 0-0 — Ref: D Turner	Walker	Smith A	Bunkell	Leslie	Harford	Dominey	Thomas	Svarc	Froggatt	Lindsay	Cook	
	Turner	*McCarthy*	*Mills*	*Fisher*	*Bennett*	*Steele*	*Stokes*	*Channon*	*Osgood*	*Peach*	*Gilchrist*	

Southampton's Peter Osgood is the subject of a £275k bid by Chelsea. to lure him back to Stamford Bridge. Osgood remains unbroken. For U's it is a disappointing seventh game without a win. U's force twelve corners to Saints' miserly two, but the deadlock remains unbroken.

	1	2	3	4	5	6	7	8	9	10	11	12 sub used
4R A SOUTHAMPTON 25/11 11,492 2:18 W 1-0 H-T 0-0 — Dominey 58 — Ref: D Turner	Walker	Dominey	Packer	Leslie	Harford	Bunkell	Thomas	Svarc	Froggatt*	Lindsay	Cook	Smith L
	Turner	*McCarthy*	*Mills*	*Fisher*	*Bennett*	*Steele*	*Stokes*	*Channon*	*MacLeod*	*Peach*	*Gilchrist*	

18-year-old Dominey, making only his sixth appearance, gives United victory. He leaps brilliantly to nod in Leslie's free-kick. Walker makes a fine one-handed save from Mick Channon (80). Saints have to pick themselves up to face Newcastle in the Texaco Cup final on Wednesday.

	1	2	3	4	5	6	7	8	9	10	11	12 sub used
QF H ASTON VILLA 3/12 11,812 1:6 L 1-2 H-T 0-1 — Froggatt 84, Little A 28, Graydon 60 — Ref: J Hunting	Walker	Cook	Packer	Leslie	Harford*	Dominey	Thomas	Svarc	Froggatt	Lindsay	Bunkell	Smith L
	Cumbes	*Robson*	*Aitken*	*Ross*	*Nicholl*	*Lower*	*Graydon*	*Little B*	*Little A*	*Hamilton*	*Carrodous*	

Villa overcome Hartlepool 6-1 in a replay to earn a trip to Layer Rd. Brothers Brian and Alan Little combine for Villa's first, the first conceded by United in the cup run. Ray Graydon's 20-yarder is pegged back by Froggatt, but Villa hang on to face Chester in the two-legged semi-final.

FA Cup

	1	2	3	4	5	6	7	8	9	10	11	12 sub used
1 A WATFORD 23/11 8,228 3:11 W 1-0 H-T 0-0 — Froggatt 75 — Ref: J Hunting	Walker	Cook	Packer	Leslie	Harford	Dominey	Thomas	Svarc	Froggatt	Lindsay	Bunkell	
	Rankin	*Craker*	*Williams*	*Keen*	*Goodwe*	*Lees*	*Bond*	*Mayes*	*Jenkins**	*Downes*	*McGettigan Markham*	

A superbly-taken goal by Froggatt puts United into the next round. Svarc back-heels into Froggatt's path, who sidesteps Ken Goodeve before planting a shot past Andy Rankin. Worried Southampton watch United for the sixth time, in preparation for the forthcoming League Cup-tie.

	1	2	3	4	5	6	7	8	9	10	11	12 sub used
2 A LEATHERHEAD 14/12 3,500 11:4 L 0-1 H-T 0-1 — Doyle 20 — Ref: A Hart	Walker	Cook	Packer	Leslie*	Harford	Dominey	Thomas	Svarc	Froggatt	Lindsay	Smith L	Bunkell
	Swannell	*Sargeant*	*Webb*	*Cooper*	*Read*	*Wells*	*Woffinden*	*Lavers*	*McGillicuddy Smith*	*Doyle*		

Walker's save from Peter Lavers' snap-shot gives the minnows a corner. Barry Webb floats the kick over for John Doyle to hammer in from a half-clearance. The Isthmian-leaguers fully deserve their giant-killing act, as the United bow out of both cups in the space of just eleven days.

League Table

			Home					Away					
		P	W	D	L	F	A	W	D	L	F	A	Pts
1	Blackburn	46	15	7	1	40	16	7	9	7	28	29	60
2	Plymouth	46	16	5	2	38	19	8	6	9	41	39	59
3	Charlton	46	15	5	3	51	29	7	6	10	25	32	55
4	Swindon	46	18	3	2	43	17	3	8	12	21	41	53
5	Crystal Pal	46	14	8	1	48	22	4	7	12	18	35	51
6	Port Vale	46	15	6	2	37	19	3	9	11	24	35	51
7	Peterborough	46	10	9	4	24	17	9	3	11	23	36	50
8	Walsall	46	15	5	3	46	13	3	8	12	21	39	49
9	Preston	46	16	5	2	42	19	3	6	14	21	37	49
10	Gillingham	46	14	6	3	43	23	3	8	12	22	37	48
11	COLCHESTER	46	13	7	3	45	22	4	6	13	25	41	47
12	Hereford	46	14	6	3	42	21	2	8	13	22	45	46
13	Wrexham	46	10	8	5	41	23	5	7	11	24	32	45
14	Bury	46	13	6	4	38	17	3	6	14	15	33	44
15	Chesterfield	46	11	7	5	37	25	5	5	13	25	41	44
16	Grimsby	46	12	8	3	35	19	3	5	15	20	45	43
17	Halifax	46	11	10	2	33	20	2	7	14	16	45	43
18	Southend	46	11	9	3	32	17	2	7	14	14	34	42
19	Brighton	46	14	7	2	38	21	2	3	18	18	43	42
20	Aldershot *	46	13	5	5	40	21	1	6	16	13	42	38
21	Bournemouth	46	9	6	8	27	25	4	6	13	17	33	38
22	Tranmere	46	12	4	7	39	21	2	5	16	16	36	37
23	Watford	46	9	7	7	30	31	1	10	12	22	44	37
24	Huddersfield	46	9	6	8	32	29	2	4	17	15	47	32
		1104	309	155	88	921	506	88	155	309	506	921	1103

* deducted one point

Odds & ends

Double wins: (1) Bournemouth.

Double defeats: (2) Hereford, Walsall.

Won from behind: (1) Gillingham (h).

Lost from in front:: (2) Walsall (a), Crystal Palace (a).

High spots: Consolidation in the Third Division after an early promotion challenge.

A magnificent run to the League Cup quarter-finals.

Beating Southampton, against the odds, at The Dell.

The 43-goal twin strike-force of Bobby Svarc and John Froggatt.

Interest in Foley and Leslie by higher division clubs.

Low spots: Humiliation of FA Cup defeat at non-league Leatherhead.

The summer departure of Jim Smith to Blackburn.

Seven games without a win from late October.

Missing out on a League Cup semi-final with Chester, with a better than ever chance of getting to Wembley.

The poor response of the Colchester public in attending U's games.

Player of the Year: John Froggatt.

Ever-presents: (3) Micky Cook, John Froggatt, Mick Walker.

Hat-tricks: (1) John Froggatt.

Leading scorer: Bobby Svarc (25).

Appearances and Goals

	Appearances						Goals			
	Lge	Sub	LC	Sub	FAC	Sub	Lge	LC	FAC	Tot
Allinson, Ian		1				1				1
Bunkell, Ray	23	5	3			1	1			1
Cameron, Danny	5									
Cook, Micky	46		6		2		3			3
Dominey, Barry	22	4	3		2		2	1		3
Dyson, Barry	5	1		1			1			1
Foley, Steve	16	2					3			3
Froggatt, John	46		6		2		16	1	1	18
Harford, Ray	40	1	6		2		2			2
Leslie, Steve	32	2	6		2		3	3		6
Lindsay, Jimmy	45		5		2		6	1		7
McDonald, Ian	5						2			2
Morgan, Stuart	11		2							
Packer, Mick	30	5			2		1			1
Rowe, Colwyn	4	7					2			2
Sims, John	2									
Smith, Alex	22		4							
Smith, Lindsay	38	5	2	3	1		1			1
Svarc, Bobby	42		6		2		24	1		25
Thomas, Phil	26	1	6		2		2			2
Walker, Mike	46		6		2					
(own-goals)							1			1
21 players used	506	29	66	4	22	1	70	7	1	78

LEAGUE DIVISION 3

Manager: Bobby Roberts

SEASON 1975-76

No	Date	V	Opponents	Att	Pos	Result	Pt	F-A	H-T	Scorers, Times, and Referees
1	16/8	A	PRESTON	6,324	—	L	0	1-2	1-0	Svarc 16 / Treacy 58, 70 / Ref: R Lee
2	23/8	H	MANSFIELD	3,333	24	L	0	0-2	0-2	Bird 40, Clarke 42 / Ref: B James
3	30/8	A	CRYSTAL PALACE	13,713	24	L	0	2-3	2-2	Svarc 15, Bunkell 16 / Evans 11, 27, 60 / Ref: R Kirkpatrick
4	6/9	H	HALIFAX	2,819	24	L	0	0-1	0-0	McHale 46p / Ref: R Lewis
5	13/9	A	HEREFORD	5,577	24	D	1	0-0	0-0	Ref: A Hamil
6	20/9	H	BRIGHTON	3,176	21	W	3	2-0	0-0	Froggatt 49, Svarc 90 / Ref: E Read
7	24/9	A	CHESTER	3,954	24	L	3	0-1	0-1	Owen 5 / Ref: G Flint
8	27/9	A	SWINDON	5,750	21	W	5	1-0	0-0	Packer 82 / Ref: A Lees
9	4/10	H	BURY	3,035	21	D	6	0-0	0-0	Ref: L Shapter
10	11/10	H	WALSALL	2,980	18	W	8	2-0	1-0	Froggatt 8, Dominey 56 / Ref: L Burdon
11	18/10	A	ALDERSHOT	3,586	19	D	9	2-2	1-2	Foley 23, 60 / Howarth 7, Bell 22 / Ref: D Reeves

Line-ups (U's players above, opponents in italics)

Match	Team	1	2	3	4	5	6	7	8	9	10	11	12 sub used
1	U's	Walker	O'Donnell	Cook	Bunkell	Packer	Harrison	Thomas	Svarc	Froggatt	Smith L	Dyer*	Dominey
1	Preston	*Tunks*	*McMahon*	*Williams*	*Doyle*	*Bird*	*Spark*	*Lamb*	*Burns*	*Treacy*	*Elwiss*	*Morley*	
2	U's	Walker	Thomas	Williams	Bunkell	Dominey*	Packer	Cook	Svarc	Froggatt	Smith L	Anderson	Dyer
2	Mansfield	*Arnold*	*Bird*	*Foster B*	*O'Brien*	*MacKenzie**	*Foster C*	*MacDonald*	*Laverick*	*Clarke*	*Hodgson*	*McCaffrey*	*Eccles*
3	U's	Walker	Thomas	Williams	Bunkell	Harrison	Dominey	Cook	Svarc	Froggatt	Packer	Smith L*	Leslie
3	Crystal Palace	*Burns*	*Wall*	*Cannon*	*Hinshelwood M*	*Jeffries*	*Evans*	*Hill*	*Holder*	*Kemp*	*Swindlehurst*	*Taylor*	
4	U's	Walker	Thomas	Williams	Bunkell	Harrison*	Dominey	Cook	Svarc	Froggatt	Leslie	Anderson	Dyer
4	Halifax	*Gennoe*	*Smith A*	*Collins*	*McHale*	*Rhodes*	*Phelan*	*Jones*	*Bell*	*Ford*	*Gwyther*	*Pugh*	
5	U's	Walker	Thomas	Williams	Dyer	Dominey*	Dominey	Cook*	Svarc	Froggatt	Leslie	Anderson	Foley
5	Hereford	*Charlton*	*Emery*	*Ritchie*	*Galley*	*Tucker*	*Lindsay*	*Rudge*	*Paine*	*Redrobe**	*McNeil*	*Silkman*	*Davey*
6	U's	Walker	Dyer	Williams	Leslie*	Dominey	Packer	Cook	Svarc	Froggatt	Thomas	Anderson	Foley
6	Brighton	*Grummitt*	*Tiler*	*Wilson*	*Machin*	*Piper*	*Burnett*	*Fell*	*O'Sullivan*	*Binney*	*Butlin*	*Martin*	*Towner*
7	U's	Walker	Dyer	Williams	Leslie	Dominey	Packer	Cook	Svarc	Froggatt	Thomas*	Anderson	Foley
7	Chester	*Watling*	*Edwards*	*Loska*	*Storton*	*Dunleavy*	*Mason*	*Redfern*	*Pugh*	*Daniels*	*Owen*	*Lennard*	
8	U's	Walker	Dyer	Williams	Leslie	Dominey	Packer	Cook	Svarc	Froggatt	Foley	Anderson*	Bunkell
8	Swindon	*Allan*	*Dixon*	*Trollope*	*Hubbard**	*Burrows*	*Stroud*	*Moss*	*McLaughlin*	*Eastoe*	*Butler*	*Anderson*	*Jenkins*
9	U's	Walker	Dyer	Williams	Bunkell	Dominey	Dominey	Cook	Leslie	Froggatt	Foley	Smith L	
9	Bury	*Forrest*	*Hoolickin*	*Kennedy*	*Nicholson*	*Hulme*	*Bailey*	*Phillips*	*Spence*	*Rowland*	*Riley*	*Williams*	
10	U's	Walker	Dyer	Williams	Leslie	Dominey	Packer	Cook	Leslie	Froggatt	Foley	Smith L	Foley
10	Walsall	*Kearns*	*Caswell*	*Fry*	*Robinson*	*Serella*	*Harrison*	*Dennehy*	*Spinner**	*Wright*	*Buckley*	*Taylor*	*Birch*
11	U's	Walker	Dyer	Williams	Bunkell	Dominey	Packer	Cook	Leslie	Froggatt	Foley	Smith L	Smith L
11	Aldershot	*Johnson*	*Howitt*	*Wallace*	*Crosby*	*Richardson*	*Walker*	*Walton*	*Morrisey*	*Howarth*	*Bell*	*Brodie*	*Birch*

Match reports

1 — Preston (A): Bobby Charlton's side falls behind when L. Smith's cross finds unmarked Svarc. Ray Treacy, goal-less since 1973, ends new manager Roberts' first game as boss in defeat. Lindsay joins Hereford (£13k), whilst 537 'earlybird' ground season tickets are sold, compared with 44 last term.

2 — Mansfield (H): U's host the division's new-boys. Jim McCaffrey's floated cross finds Kevin Bird, who nets a simple header. 80 seconds later Ray Clarke dives to head Gordon Hodgson's free-kick. U's press, but the nearest they come is when Williams (ex-Watford) and Anderson (twice) strike wood.

3 — Crystal Palace (A): U's gain heart from the League Cup near-miss, six days ago. Palace steal both points with a hat-trick of set-piece goals by Welsh U-23 star Ian Evans. U's remain pointless and rock bottom. O'Donnell, loaned from Cambridge on the eve of the new season, returns injured to the Abbey.

4 — Halifax (H): Harford returns as coach, having been at Romford. Four straight league defeats cements United to bottom place in the Football League. Sub Dyer (ex-Notts Co) bundles Derek Bell for Ray McHale to net the only goal of the game, and leave U's the only win-less side in the land.

5 — Hereford (A): U's enquire about QPR's Don Rogers, as an emergency board meeting makes some of the Lindsay transfer money available. Walker is watched by a member of the Welsh national set-up. A welcome first point could have been two, but for Svarc's curling effort off the bar (90).

6 — Brighton (H): Rogers turns down U's advances, because he lives in Swindon. United end their depressing win-less start when Froggatt brilliantly heads in Dyer's free-kick, then in the last minute Thomas comically dives looking for a penalty, allowing Svarc to plant past the static Albion defence.

7 — Chester (A): Walker's early slip lets in Terry Owen to prod home Stuart Mason's cross. Foley receives a nasty high-kick to the face in the penalty area on 85 minutes, but ref Flint only gives an indirect free-kick. He also takes the names of Williams and Chester's Graham Pugh, as U's stay bottom.

8 — Swindon (A): How times have changed for struggling Swindon. Last season they thrashed U's 4-1, but this time out United rarely let them settle. Ex-U's star McLaughlin strikes the upright with a first-half free-kick, but Packer's long punt eludes the chasing Foley and keeper Kenny Allan to sail in.

9 — Bury (H): Svarc joins old boss J Smith, for the third time, at Blackburn (£20k). Roberts is refused Rover's Ken Beamish in part-exchange. Svarc's last task in Colchester sees him become a Jehovah's Witness. A £12k deal for Ipswich's Ian Collard is put on ice, due to the player's thigh strain.

10 — Walsall (H): Revitalised United take the lead when Mick Kearns can only parry L. Smith's shot into the path of Froggatt. Froggatt then hits the bar in the 20th minute. Dominey, who was married this morning, fittingly seals the win, heading home Bunkell's free-kick for a great wedding present.

11 — Aldershot (A): When Terry Bell puts Shots 2-0 up in just 22 minutes, it seems that United are on their way to a walloping. Foley strikes back for U's within 60 seconds from 25 yards, and the pops up to slide in Packer's free-kick on the hour, to maintain U's record of just one defeat in the last seven.

No	Venue	Opponent	Date	Att.	Pos	Res	FT	HT	Scorers	Ref
12	H	ROTHERHAM	21/10	3,468	17 12 10	D	0-0	0-0		Ref: D Lloyd
13	H	PORT VALE	25/10	3,053	14 16 12	W	1-0	1-0	Foley 17	Ref: A Turvey
14	A	MILLWALL	1/11	7,492	14 7 13	D	1-1	0-1	Smith L 63, Hill 34	Ref: A Robinson
15	A	CHESTERFIELD	5/11	2,906	17 13 13	L	1-6	1-3	Smith L 43, Darling 36, 78, Moss 42, Shan '45, 87, 90	Ref: J Worrall
16	H	SHREWSBURY	8/11	3,088	18 7 14	D	1-1	0-1	Smith L 54, Bates 5	Ref: R Tinkler
17	A	CARDIFF	15/11	6,781	20 10 14	L	0-2	0-1	Evans 2, Alston 83	Ref: T Bosi
18	A	GILLINGHAM	29/11	5,402	18 19 16	W	1-0	0-0	Foley 84	Ref: D Civil
19	H	SHEFFIELD WED	6/12	3,534	14 21 18	W	2-1	0-0	Smith L 69, Cook 71, Potts 51	Ref: K Salmon
20	A	WREXHAM	13/12	2,143	12 14 19	D	1-1	0-1	Froggatt 80, Lee 9	Ref: I Smith
21	H	WREXHAM	20/12	2,608	18 11 19	L	0-2	0-2	Lee 36, Lyons 43	Ref: J Roost
22	A	SOUTHEND	26/12	6,167	19 22 19	L	0-2	0-1	Brace 40, 49	Ref: T Bune
23	H	GRIMSBY	27/12	3,136	18 17 21	W	1-0	0-0	Foley 62	Ref: M Taylor

12 — Rotherham (H)

U's: Walker, Dyer, Williams, Bunkell, Dominey, Packer, Cook, Leslie, Froggatt, Foley*, Smith L, Anderson
Rotherham: McDonagh, Derrett, Breckin, Phillips, Stancliffe, Spencer, Leng, Finney, Habbin, Goodfellow, Crawford

U's average attendances are at an all-time low, so Roberts sets his sights on Southport's top scorer Bobby Gough, who has notched five for the basement side. Foley is carried off on 38 minutes, after a drop-ball clash with Trevor Phillips, which is feared to be a cartilage injury.

13 — Port Vale (H)

U's: Walker, Dyer, Williams*, Bunkell, Dominey, Packer, Cook, Leslie, Froggatt, Foley, Smith L, Anderson
Port Vale: Connaughton, Tartt, Dulson, Riley, Harris, Horton, McLaren, Lees*, Williams, Bailey, Cullerton, Brownhill

Action man Foley is at it again. He collected two goals last week, was stretchered off in midweek, and then gives U's their fifth game without defeat against Vale. L. Smith has an effort ruled out for offside (70), as U's keep a record fifth clean sheet at home, beating a 1959-60 record.

14 — Millwall (A)

U's: Walker, Dyer, Williams, Bunkell, Dominey, Packer, Cook, Leslie, Froggatt, Foley*, Smith L, Anderson
Millwall: Goddard, Evans, Jones, Brisley, Kitchener, Hazell, Lee, Saul, Summerill, Walker, Hill

Foley limps off with a hamstring strain (30), then four minutes later Walker gifts Gordon Hill, who side-foots home. Millwall are in a run of five home wins on the trot, but L. Smith collects the ball wide on the left wing, cuts inside and unleashes a 30-yard scorcher into the top corner.

15 — Chesterfield (A)

U's: Walker, Dyer, Williams, Bunkell, Dominey, Packer, Cook, Leslie, Froggatt, Anderson, Smith L, Bright
Chesterfield: Tingay, Holmes, O'Neill, Hunter, Winstanley, Barlow, McEwan, Moss, Darling, Kowalski, Shanahan

U's incredibly deserved a point as their seven-match unbeaten run comes to an end. Sharp-shooting Spiverites punish every mistake, with Terry Shanahan completing his hat-trick in the third minute of added time. For U's it is the heaviest defeat since the Everton cup-tie in March 1971.

16 — Shrewsbury (H)

U's: Walker, Dyer, Williams, Bunkell, Dominey, Packer, Cook, Leslie, Froggatt*, Anderson, Smith L, Bright
Shrewsbury: Mulhearn, Collier, Roberts, Durban, Kearney, Turner, Irvine, King, Haywood, Bates, Tarbuck

U's face two body-blows in the first ten minutes, when ex-Stourbridge striker Phil Bates finishes off Alan Tarbuck's pass and then Froggatt limps off with ligament damage. Shrews sit on the lead, but a U's corner count of 19-2 pays off when L. Smith nets his third in three games.

17 — Cardiff (A)

U's: Walker, Dyer, Williams, Bunkell, Dominey, Packer, Cook, Bright, Leslie, Smith L, Anderson*, Harrison
Cardiff: Irwin, Dwyer, Charles, Livermore, England, Larmour, Reece, Giles*, Alston, Evans, Anderson, Buchanan

Close season signing Harrison (Torquay) returns after a nine week lay-off. U's fall behind after 68 seconds when Gil Reece pokes a superb ball through to Tony Evans. Australian World Cup '74 star Adrian Alston snaps up a Willie Anderson pass to slot in the second from 20 yards out.

18 — Gillingham (A)

U's: Walker, Dyer, Williams, Bunkell, Dominey, Packer, Cook, Leslie, Froggatt, Smith L*, Anderson, Wilks
Gillingham: Hillyard, Davies, Ley, Knight, Shipperley, Tydeman, Jacks, Gauden, Richardson, Westwood, Hilton*

Roberts turns his attentions to Joe Waters. Leicester's FA Cup hero of two years ago. After the midweek debacle at Dover. U's make a quick return to Kent and restore some pride when Foley's curling effort beats Ron Hillyard all ends up. U's are now gradually creeping up the table.

19 — Sheffield Wed (H)

U's: Walker, Dyer, Williams, Bunkell, Dominey, Packer*, Cook, Leslie, Froggatt, Foley, Smith L*, Anderson, Harrison
Sheffield Wed: Ramsbottom, Shaw, Quinn, Thompson, Cusack, O'Donnell, Knighton, Mullen, Joicey*, Prendergast, Potts, Proudlove

The Owl's, under new boss Len Ashurst, make their first-ever visit to Layer Road. Walker drops Brian Joicey's cross at the feet of Eric Potts, who fires once-mighty Wednesday 1-0 up. Cook provides a side-foot for L. Smith's sixth of the term, and then crashes in a Packer free-kick.

20 — Wrexham (A)

U's: Walker, Dyer, Williams, Bunkell, Dominey, Packer, Cook, Leslie, Froggatt, Foley, Smith L*, Thomas, Ashcroft
Wrexham: Lloyd, Evans, Fogg, Davis, May, Thomas, Timmon, Sutton, Lee, Dwyer*, Griffiths

United fail to lure Rochdale's Bobby Mountford, despite a record £15k bid, because Dale require a lump sum rather than instalments. The fixture is re-arranged as both clubs are out of this term's FA Cup. Wrexham lost 1-2 to Mansfield in a second replay at Villa Park last Monday.

21 — Wrexham (H)

U's: Walker, Dyer, Williams, Bunkell, Dominey, Packer, Cook, Leslie, Froggatt, Foley, Smith L, Thomas
Wrexham: Lloyd, Evans, Fogg, Davis, May, Thomas, Timmon, Sutton, Lee, Dwyer*, Lyons, Griffiths

U's and Dale compromise over Mountford, with U's paying 50% of the £17.5k. After all the bargaining Mountford fails his medical. John Lyons adds a cheeky goal from Gareth Davis's free-kick. Only Pompey (8) have fewer home goals, as United are score-less for the fifth time.

22 — Southend (A)

U's: Walker, Dyer*, Williams, Bright, Dominey, Packer, Cook, Leslie, Anderson, Foley, Smith L, Nicholl
Southend: Webster, Worthington, Ford, Little, Hadley, Moody, Fogg, Brace, Parker, Silvester, Nicholl, Allinson

Two goals by Stuart Brace, either side of the interval, sink U's in the Essex derby relegation battle. The busiest man was referee Tom Bune, who gives an astonishing 78 free-kicks and books six (three from each side). Stuart Parker and Peter Silvester provide the chances for Brace.

23 — Grimsby (H)

U's: Walker, Bright, Williams, Bunkell, Dominey, Packer, Cook, Leslie, Froggatt, Foley, Smith L, Anderson
Grimsby: Wainman, Cruczman, Booth, Walton, Young, Govier, Partridge, Hubbard, Lewis, Boylen, Wigg

U's keep out of the bottom four against the side with the worst away record in the section. U's beleaguered fans get a late Christmas present when Foley strikes a ground-hogging shot past Harry Wainman, who had saved Packer's penalty (28) after Martin Young had chopped Leslie.

LEAGUE DIVISION 3 — Manager: Bobby Roberts — SEASON 1975-76

No	Date		Scorers, Times, and Referees	Att	Pos		Pt	F-A	H-T
24	H 10/1	CRYSTAL PALACE	Taylor 7p, Swindlehurst 26, Whittle 69 Hammand — Ref: D Biddle	6.240	19	1 / L	21	0-3	0-2
25	A 14/1	PETERBOROUGH	Packer 88 / Gregory 5, Turner 58, Hughes 81 — Ref: A Grey	7,453	19	5 / L	21	1-3	0-1
26	A 17/1	BRIGHTON	[Fell 66, 75] Mellor 16, Rollings 37, Binney 45, 64. — Ref: T Reynolds	16,302	19	2 / L	21	0-6	0-3
27	H 24/1	HEREFORD	Telford 3 / McNeil 2, 38, Dominey 22 (og), Davey 87 — Ref: D Richardson	2,626	19	3 / L	21	1-4	1-3
28	A 31/1	ROTHERHAM	Spencer 30, Leng 89 — Ref: E Garner	3,943	21	14 / L	21	0-2	0-1
29	H 7/2	CHESTERFIELD	Bunkell 64p, Leslie 66 / Cammack 20, Fern 27 Darling 57 — Ref: R Crabb	2,245	23	18 / L	21	2-3	0-2
30	A 14/2	SHREWSBURY	Kearney 82 — Ref: T Spencer	4,485	23	3 / L	21	0-1	0-0
31	H 21/2	CARDIFF	Garwood 64, 80, Froggatt 60 / Dwyer 18, Anderson 86p — Ref: B Martin	3,248	22	6 / W	23	3-2	0-1
32	H 24/2	CHESTER	Gough 54 — Ref: E Read	3,534	19	15 / W	25	1-0	0-0
33	A 28/2	PORT VALE	Dyer 20, 63 / Cullerton 8, Brownbill 75, Bailey 90 — Ref: C Seel	3,803	19	10 / L	25	2-3	1-1
34	A 13/3	WALSALL	Leslie 64 / Andrews 3 — Ref: K Styles	5,371	24	6 / D	26	1-1	0-1

Line-ups (U's players, with opposition in italics)

No	1	2	3	4	5	6	7	8	9	10	11	12 sub used
24	Walker *Hammand*	Dyer* *Wall*	Williams *Cannon*	Bunkell *Johnson*	Dominey *Jump*	Packer *Evans*	Cook *Chatterton*	Gough *Hinshelw'd M Whittle*	Froggatt *Swindlehurst Taylor*	Foley	Smith L	Leslie *Smith L*
25	Walker *Steele*	Dyer* *Murray*	Williams *Walker*	Bunkell *Eustace*	Dominey *Turner*	Packer *Carmichael*	Cook *Rogers*	Gough *Gregory*	Anderson *Cozens*	Foley *Hughes*	Froggatt *Robson*	Smith L
26	Walker *Grummitt*	Dyer *Tiler*	Smith L *Wilson*	Leslie *Machin*	Dominey *Rollings*	Cook *Burnett*	Cook *Fell*	Gough *O'Sullivan*	Anderson *Binney*	Foley *Morgan*	Froggatt *Mellor*	
27	Bond *Hughes*	Bright *Emery*	Williams *Ritchie*	Bunkell *Galley*	Dominey *Layton*	Packer *Lindsay*	Cook* *Paine**	Gough *Tyler*	Telford *Davey*	Foley *McNeil*	Froggatt *Carter*	Smith L *Silkman*
28	Bond *McAllister*	Bright *Green*	Williams *Breckin*	Bunkell *Rhodes*	Harrison *Stancliffe*	Packer *Spencer*	Leslie *Leng*	Gough* *Finney*	Froggatt *Habbin*	Smith L *Goodfellow*	Dyer *Crawford*	Dominey
29	Walker *Tingay*	Bright *Badger**	Williams *Burton*	Bunkell *Kowalski*	Harrison* *Hunter*	Dominey *O'Neill*	Cook *McIntosh*	Gough *Cammack*	Froggatt *Shanahan*	Leslie *Fern*	Smith L *Bentley*	Telford *Darling*
30	Bond *Mulhearn*	Bright *King*	Cook *Leonard*	Bunkell *Tarbuck*	Dominey *Griffin*	Packer *Turner*	Dyer *Irvine*	Gough *Atkins*	Froggatt *Kearney*	Leslie *Bates*	Smith L *McGregor*	
31	Walker *Healey*	Bright *Dwyer*	Cook *Charles**	Bunkell *Pethard*	Packer *Morgan*	Dyer *Larmour*	Dyer *Livermore*	Gough *Giles*	Froggatt *Evans*	Garwood *Alston*	Foley *Anderson*	Sayer
32	Walker *Millington*	Bright *Edwards*	Cook *Loska*	Bunkell *Dunleavy*	Smith L *Delgado*	Packer *Draper*	Garwood *Redfern*	Gough* *Pugh*	Froggatt *Owen*	Williams *Lennard*	Dyer *Dearden*	Dominey
33	Walker *Connaughton Tartt*	Bright *Griffiths*	Cook *Ridley*	Bunkell *Lees*	Smith L *Dolson**	Cook *Williams*	Garwood* *Beech*	Gough *Cullerton*	Froggatt *Bailey*	Dominey *Brownbill*	Froggatt *Horton*	Smith L
34	Walker *Kearns*	Bright *Saunders*	Cook *Harrison*	Bunkell *Robinson*	Packer *Hynd*	Smith L *Taylor*	Garwood *Dennehy*	Gough *Andrews*	Froggatt *Evans*	Dominey *Buckley*	Leslie *Caswell**	Dominey *Wright*

Match notes

24 Nine-goal Gough signs (£7k), but U's fail to impress the stay-at-homes who turn up for the big match. Dominey punches Alan Whittle's lob after Walker drops Jim Cannon's cross. England U-23 Peter Taylor makes no mistake. Nick Chatterton provides Swindlehurst with the second

25 Arsenal reserve keeper Geoff Barnett turns down a move to United. Dyer and Dominey look shell-shocked at the end as Chris Turner exposes poor marking to nod in Tommy Robson's corner. Dominey fails to deal with a simple clearance, giving Lyndon Hughes the easiest of tap-ins.

26 Promotion-chasing Albion give U's their second six-goal drubbing of the term. Just as at Chesterfield, poor finishing and gift defending means that United have leaked twelve goals in the last three games. A familiar name, in Fred Binney, grabs a pair to take his tally to 19 for the season.

27 Thomas, 23, is forced to quit with a knee injury. Bond loans from Bristol C to play for his fifth club this season, but his first task is to pick the ball out of the net. Telford, on loan from Posh, reduces the arrears within 60 seconds, but U's collapse having let in 16 goals in just four games.

28 Roberts resists the fans pleas to recall Harford to shore up his shoddy defence. U's 'Supremos' travel club arrives with twenty minutes left after their coach broke down near Derby, where they had to wait for a replacement. They travel back with the players on the team coach.

29 U's problems stem from the fact that they have conceded 43 goals in the last 17 games. In front of a new lowest-attendance, United stage a comeback at 0-3 when Les Hunter is alleged to have brought down Telford, and two minutes later Leslie crashes in from Cook's throw-in.

30 U's take Garwood on loan from Huddersfield, whilst Blackburn hand over another £3k instalment as part of the J Smith compensation. Mike Kearney snatches the points of defiant U's, stretching Shrews' unbeaten run to nine, as he heads in Phil Bates' cross past the helpless Bond.

31 Hull's ex-Scunthorpe centre-half Steven Deere turns down a move to U's. United finally win after 630 minutes football, and in front of Anglia TV too. Garwood impresses and seals it with a second when Ron Healey parries Gough's shot. Packer fouls Tony Evans for a late consolation.

32 Gough grabs his first goal for the club to earn a quick-fire four-point boost to the fight against relegation. Gough thunders Packer's free-kick against the bar, but reacts quicker than Gren Millington to prod home the rebound. U's are further boosted by the £5k signing of Garwood.

33 U's are holding a deserved 2-1 lead, given to them by Dyer's first-ever league strikes, when the tide turns in the last 15 minutes. Derek Brownbill poaches a headed equaliser, and then in the dying seconds Terry Bailey meets a speculative cross to plunge U's deep into trouble.

34 U's first game for two weeks as a flu bug wiped out the games with Millwall and Bury. The players still seem a bit groggy as George Andrews loops in an early header, after good work by Brian Caswell and Brian Taylor. Cook, booked earlier, crosses low for Leslie to half-volley home.

35 H 16/3 ALDERSHOT 3,040 · 23 · W · 2-0 · 15 · 28 · 1-0
Gough 32, Leslie 70 — Ref: P Reeves
Walker · Bright · Cook · Bunkell · Smith L · Packer · Garwood · Gough · Froggatt · Foley · Leslie
Johnson · Howitt · Wallace · Walker · Goldthorpe* · Richardson · Crosby · Morrisey · Howarth · Bell · Warnock Brown
U's look to have found their best starting eleven, and get a slice of luck when Garwood's corner goes in off Gough's thigh. Walker makes a telling save from Terry Bell, before Leslie picks his spot from Cook's free-kick. Halifax's shock 2-1 win at Hereford maintains the pressure.

36 H 20/3 GILLINGHAM 3,981 · 21 · D · 2-2 · 12 · 29 · 0-0
Bunkell 62p, Leslie 65 / Richardson 74p, Durrell 84 — Ref: C White
Walker · Bright · Cook · Bunkell · Dominey · Packer · Garwood · Gough · Froggatt · Smith L · Leslie
Hillyard · Wiltshire · Ley · Galvin · Shipperley · Tydeman · Knight · Fogarty · Richardson · Westwood · Weatherley* Durrell
Bunkell slots home after Duck Tydeman handles, and Leslie finishes off a sparkling solo run. Bright trips Damian Richardson to reduce the arrears, and Dominey's season-long torment continues, when he allows Joe Durrell to steal in and nick an undeserved point for Gillingham.

37 H 23/3 MILLWALL 4,573 · 22 · L · 0-1 · 4 · 29 · 0-1
Brisley 27 — Ref: A Robinson
Walker · Bright · Cook · Bunkell · Smith L · Packer · Garwood · Gough · Froggatt · Foley · Leslie
Goddard · Donaldson · Moore · Brisley · Kitchener · Hazell · McGrath · Seasman · Summerill · Walker · Lee
U's insist they should have a penalty (7) when Dave Donaldson fouls Garwood, which only brings an indirect free-kick. Terry Brisley meets a left-wing corner. It would have been so different had U's taken the lead. Exciting coloured duo, Trevor Lee and Phil Walker, look sharp.

38 A 27/3 SHEFFIELD WED 6,905 · 23 · L · 0-1 · 21 · 29 · 0-0
Henson 72 — Ref: R Perkin
Walker · Bright · Cook · Bunkell · Smith L · Packer · Garwood · Gough* · Froggatt · Foley · Leslie
Fox · Hull · Quinn · McIver* · Cusack · Mullen · Potts · Wylde · Prendergast · Henson · Bell · Nimmo
Roberts is disappointed to be beaten by a poor Wednesday side. A goalmouth scramble sees L. Smith deflect Phil Henson's shot past keeper Walker. The sparsely populated Hillsborough will be house 55,000 next week, as Man Utd take on Derby in one of the FA Cup semi-finals.

39 H 3/4 PRESTON 2,657 · 24 · D · 1-1 · 10 · 30 · 1-1
Leslie 34 / Elwiss 17 — Ref: M Taylor
Walker · Bright · Williams · Bunkell · Smith L · Packer · Garwood · Gough · Froggatt · Foley · Leslie
Tunks · McMahon* · Williams! · Doyle · Sadler · Lawrenson · Coleman · Elwiss · Smith · Brown · Spark
U's start a crucial 72 hours without Gough, who twisted his knee last week. Roberts sets a target of eleven points from eight games, and U's have Preston at their mercy once Gary Williams is sent off (37) for an off-the-ball, which lets United down.

40 H 6/4 SWINDON 2,694 · 24 · L · 1-2 · 20 · 30 · 1-2
Leslie 23 / Anderson 17p, Syrett 26 — Ref: B James
Walker · Bright · Williams · Bunkell · Smith L · Packer · Garwood · Gough · Froggatt · Dyer · Leslie
Barron · McLaughlin · Trollope · Rogan · Burrows · Prophett · Moss · Dixon · Syrett · O'Brien · Anderson
The club announces a loss for the sixth time in the last seven years, this time £12.5k. Williams is adjudged to handle for Trevor Anderson's penalty, and although Leslie notches his sixth from Garwood's cross. A headed goal from Dave Syrett has U's fans chanting for Roberts' head.

41 A 12/4 BURY 4,505 · 24 · D · 0-0 · 14 · 31 · 0-0
— Ref: J Yates
Walker · Bright · Williams · Bunkell · Smith L · Packer · Garwood · Gough* · Froggatt! · Foley · Leslie
Forrest · Hoolickin · Kennedy · McIlwraith · Hulme · Bailey · Buchan · Phillips · Rowland* · Spence · Williams · Dominey · Woolfall
A point at Gigg Lane means U's still realistically need eight points from their remaining games. Walker hints he will leave at the end of the season, after being rested for Bond earlier in the season. Froggatt, who had taken a pounding from Shakers' defence, is sent off (65) for dissent.

42 H 16/4 PETERBOROUGH 3,887 · 24 · D · 1-1 · 9 · 32 · 1-0
Bunkell 2 / Leslie 48 (og) — Ref: R Lewis
Walker · Dyer · Williams · Bunkell · Smith L · Packer · Garwood · Gough · Allinson* · Foley! · Leslie
Steele · Hodson · Walker · Eustace · Turner · Carmichael* · Gregory · Cozens · Moss · Hughes! · Jones · Lee
U's are so much on top, it is frustrating that they are in the bottom four. Bunkell rifles in a 30-yarder on 72 seconds. U's luck is summed up when L. Smith's clearance cannons off Leslie into the net. Foley and Lyndon Hughes are sent off (70), when fighting for the ball at a free-kick.

43 H 17/4 SOUTHEND 4,260 · 23 · W · 2-1 · 24 · 34 · 0-1
Gough 60, Froggatt 69 / Moody 44p — Ref: A Glasson
Walker · Dyer · Williams · Bunkell · Smith L · Packer · Allinson · Gough · Froggatt · Cook* · Leslie
Webster · Worthington · Ford · Little · Hadley · Moody · Taylor · Brace · Parker · Silvester · Cunningham · Bright
The Essex-derby crowd saves the average attendance from being the lowest ever, with the record set in 1972-73. Gough and Froggatt both nod in Allinson crosses to ensure U's end the home campaign on a high. Alan Moody's penalty comes when Dave Cunningham falls over Leslie.

44 A 19/4 GRIMSBY 4,862 · 22 · W · 1-0 · 18 · 36 · 1-0
Gough 18 — Ref: G Nolan
Walker · Dyer · Williams · Bunkell · Smith L · Packer · Garwood · Gough · Froggatt · Foley · Leslie
Freeman · Marley · Booth · Barton · Young · Gray · Ford · Waters · Hubbard · Lewis · Cumming* · Wigg
A great goal from Gough gives U's an excellent Easter and keeps alive the hope of avoiding the drop after five points out of six. Foley lofts in a free-kick for Gough to whip first time past Neil Freeman. Young hits the bar for Mariners, but they can hardly string two passes together.

45 A 24/4 MANSFIELD 7,407 · 22 · D · 0-0 · 11 · 37 · 0-0
— Ref: A Hughes
Walker · Dyer · Williams · Bunkell · Smith L · Packer · Garwood · Gough · Froggatt · Foley · Leslie
Arnold · Pate* · Foster B · Laverick · MacKenzie · Foster C · Mathews · Eccles · Clarke · Hodgson · McCaffrey · Bird
U's determined defence stops the Stags from scoring for the first time in 13 outings. Walker pulls off a stunning save to deny 29-goal striker Ray Clarke, but this result, coupled with events elsewhere, means that United must win their last game by 9-0, and then sink deep into prayer.

46 A 26/4 HALIFAX 856 · 22 · D · 1-1 · 24 · 38 · 1-0
Gough 25 / Smith L 74 (og) — Ref: A Hamill
Walker · Bright · Williams · Bunkell · Smith L · Packer · Allinson · Gough · Froggatt · Foley · Leslie
Gennoe · Smith A · Favell · Pugh · Rhodes · Overton · Harris · McHale · Downes · Bell · Blair
Leslie finishes as U's lowest-ever top marksman with just six goals. After Gough had fired U's in front, L Smith scoops Geoff Harris' low shot into his own net. The attendance is already-doomed Halifax's lowest in their 85-year history. Anderson and Harrison are not retained by U's.

Average 3,345 · Home 3,348 · Away 5,899

League Cup

		F-A	H-T	Scorers, Times, and Referees	1	2	3	4	5	6	7	8	9	10	11	12 sub used
1:1 A CRYSTAL PALACE	L	0-3	0-2	Swindlehurst 2, Kemp 26, 49	Walker	Thomas	Cook	Bunkell	Dominey	Packer	Roberts	Svarc	Froggatt	Dyer	Smith L	
10,006 3:				Ref: R Robinson	*Burns*	*Wall*	*Johnson*	*Hinshelw'd M Jeffries*		*Evans*	*Hill*	*Chatterton*	*Kemp*	*Swindlehurst Taylor*		

Palace are 7-1 joint favourites with Millwall for the Third Div. whilst U's are 25-1. Roberts has to draft himself in to play his first game since May 1972. He fumes when Nick Chatterton and Martin Hinshelwood set up Dave Swindlehurst for the early goal that he had warned against.

		F-A	H-T	Scorers, Times, and Referees	1	2	3	4	5	6	7	8	9	10	11	12 sub used
1:2 H CRYSTAL PALACE 24	W	3-1	1-1	Svarc 40, 68, Smith L 66	Walker	Thomas	Williams	Bunkell	Dominey	Packer	Cook	Svarc	Froggatt	Dyer	Smith L	
3,912 3:1				Chatterton 16	*Burns*	*Wall*	*Johnson*	*Hinshelw'd M Cannon*		*Evans*	*Hill*	*Chatterton**	*Kemp*	*Swindlehurst Taylor*		Holder
				Ref: R Robinson												
				(Colchester lost 3-4 on aggregate)												

Colchester stage a dramatic fight-back to almost snatch an aggregate draw. Shell-shocked Palace survive a frantic last 20 minutes as Svarc reduces the arrears, powering home L. Smith's flag-kick, but try as they might United can't force extra-time, as Palace earn a trip to Doncaster.

FA Cup

		F-A	H-T	Scorers, Times, and Referees	1	2	3	4	5	6	7	8	9	10	11	12 sub used
1 H DOVER 20	D	3-3	2-2	Leslie 24, Dominey 40, Smith L 75	Walker	Dyer	Williams	Bunkell	Dominey	Packer	Cook	Leslie	Foley	Anderson	Smith L	
22/11 3,705 SL:17				Coupland 16, Waite 45, Rogers 82	*Raine*	*Hamshire*	*Keeley*	*Reynolds*	*Waite*	*Fursdon*	*Coxhill*	*Coupland*	*Housden*	*Light*	*Rogers*	
				Ref: B James												

Dover have won only one Southern League game so far. A match of six goals and six bookings sees U's take the lead when L. Smith has a free header from Anderson's corner. A bobbling ball in the box allows Rogers to earn the Kent side a replay, when United surely can't be so poor.

		F-A	H-T	Scorers, Times, and Referees	1	2	3	4	5	6	7	8	9	10	11	12 sub used
1R A DOVER 20	L	1-4	0-0	Packer 60p [Coupland 108, 120]	Walker	Dyer	Williams	Bunkell	Dominey	Packer	Cook	Leslie	Froggatt	Harrison*	Smith L	Anderson
26/11 3,779 SL:17		aet		Hamshire 52, Coxhill 102p.	*Raine*	*Reynolds*	*Keeley*	*Fursdon*	*Waite*	*Coupland*	*Hamshire*	*Coxhill*	*Housden*	*Light*	*Rogers*	
				Ref: B James												

The lights go out on U's cup campaign, and not only during the five-minute power-loss in the first half. United are denied two penalties before Waite handles a Dominey header. Dover earn a penalty when Leslie trips Coupland. Cook has one ruled out, before late goals flatter Dover.

		P	Home					Away					Pts
			W	D	L	F	A	W	D	L	F	A	
1	Hereford	46	14	6	3	45	24	12	5	6	41	31	63
2	Cardiff	46	14	7	2	38	13	8	6	9	31	35	57
3	Millwall	46	16	6	1	35	14	4	10	9	19	29	56
4	Brighton	46	18	3	2	58	15	4	6	13	20	38	53
5	Crystal Pal	46	7	12	4	30	20	11	5	7	31	26	53
6	Wrexham	46	13	6	4	38	21	7	6	10	28	34	52
7	Walsall	46	11	8	4	43	22	7	6	10	31	39	50
8	Preston	46	15	4	4	45	23	4	6	13	17	34	48
9	Shrewsbury	46	14	2	7	36	25	5	8	10	25	34	48
10	Peterborough	46	12	7	4	37	23	3	11	9	26	40	48
11	Mansfield	46	8	11	4	31	22	8	4	11	27	30	47
12	Port Vale	46	10	10	3	33	21	5	6	12	22	33	46
13	Bury	46	11	7	5	33	16	3	9	11	18	30	44
14	Gillingham	46	10	8	5	38	27	2	11	10	20	41	43
15	Chesterfield	46	11	5	7	45	30	6	4	13	24	39	42
16	Rotherham	46	11	6	6	35	22	5	6	13	19	43	42
17	Chester	46	13	7	3	34	19	2	5	16	9	43	42
18	Grimsby	46	13	7	3	39	21	2	3	18	23	53	40
19	Swindon	46	11	4	8	42	31	5	4	14	20	44	40
20	Sheffield Wed	46	12	6	5	34	25	0	10	13	14	34	40
21	Aldershot *	46	10	8	5	34	26	3	5	15	25	49	39
22	COLCHESTER	46	9	6	8	25	27	3	8	12	16	38	38
23	Southend	46	9	7	7	40	31	3	6	14	25	44	37
24	Halifax	46	6	6	12	22	32	5	8	10	19	29	35
		1104	278	158	116	890	550	116	158	278	550	890	1103

* deducted one point

Odds & ends

Double wins: (1) Grimsby.

Double defeats: (2) Crystal Palace, Chesterfield.

Won from behind: (3) Sheffield Wednesday (h), Cardiff (h), Southend (h).

Lost from in front: (3) Preston (a), Crystal Palace (a), Port Vale (a).

High spots: The late-season striking partnership of Bobby Gough and Colin Garwood.

One defeat in the last eight, albeit not enough to stave off the drop.

Low spots: The season-long fight against relegation.

21 goals conceded in a six-match New Year spell (followed by just 17 in the next 17 games).

Two six-goal hammerings on their travels (at Chesterfield and Brighton).

A crushing 1-4 FA Cup replay defeat at the hands of Southern League Dover Athletic.

Player of the Year: Lindsay Smith.

Ever presents: (0).

Hat-tricks: (0).

Leading scorer: Steve Leslie (7).

Appearances and Goals

Player	Appearances						Goals			
	Lge	Sub	LC	Sub	FAC	Sub	Lge	LC	FAC	Tot
Allinson, Ian	3	2								
Anderson, Terry	13	3			1	1				
Bond, Len	3									
Bright, Stewart	18	2								
Bunkell, Ray	40	1	2		2		4			4
Cook, Micky	39		2		2		1			1
Dominey, Barry	32	6	2		2		1		1	2
Dyer, Paul	34	2	2		2		2			2
Foley, Steve	26	3			1		5			5
Froggatt, John	41		2		1		5			5
Garwood, Colin	15		2				2			2
Gough, Bobby	22						5			5
Harrison, Derek	5	2			1					
Leslie, Steve	36	3			2		6		1	7
O'Donnell, John	1									
Packer, Mick	44		2		2		2		1	3
Roberts, Bobby			1							
Smith, Lindsay	39	2	2		2		4	1	1	6
Svarc, Bobby	8	2	2				3	2		5
Telford, Billy	1	1					1			1
Thomas, Phil	7	1	2							
Walker, Mick	43		2		2					
Williams, John	36		1		2					
23 players used	506	28	22		22	1	41	3	4	48

LEAGUE DIVISION 4 — Manager: Bobby Roberts — SEASON 1976-77

Results

No	Venue	Opponent	Date	Att	Pos	Pt	F-A	H-T	Scorers, Times, and Referees
1	A	CAMBRIDGE	21/8	3,056	—	L 0	0-2	0-2	*Biley 8, 38*; Ref J Homewood
2	H	HALIFAX	24/8	2,489	—	W 2	3-0	0-0	Allinson 74, 75 Gough 89; Ref D Reeves
3	A	ROCHDALE	28/8	1,440	13 / 3	L 2	0-1	0-0	*Hanvey 65*; Ref T Mills
4	H	EXETER	4/9	2,516	9 / 17	W 4	3-1	1-1	Froggatt 25, Cook 54, Garwood 59; *Smith L 30 (og)*; Ref C Downey
5	A	WATFORD	11/9	5,386	14 / 6	L 4	1-2	0-0	Dowman 65; *Garner 76, Mayes 78*; Ref A Turvey
6	H	CREWE	18/9	2,519	8 / 17	W 6	3-2	1-2	Froggatt 11, Garwood 46, Allinson 65; *Abbott 2, 20*; Ref T Bune
7	A	BOURNEMOUTH	25/9	3,881	10 / 6	D 7	0-0	0-0	Ref D Biddle
8	H	WORKINGTON	1/10	2,957	9 / 22	W 9	3-1	2-0	Garwood 10, 20, Gough 82; *Lowry 70*; Ref A Gunn
9	A	SOUTHEND	8/10	6,690	9 / 7	D 10	0-0	0-0	Ref K Salmon
10	H	HARTLEPOOL	16/10	3,180	6 / 24	W 12	6-2	4-2	Gough 2, 34, Garwood 8, 17, 67, [Allinson 57]; *Bielby 12, 25*; Ref R Robinson
11	A	SCUNTHORPE	23/10	3,157	9 / 10	L 12	0-2	0-1	*Pilling 40, Keeley 61*; Ref R Horner

Line-ups (United in roman, opponents in italics)

No	1	2	3	4	5	6	7	8	9	10	11	12 sub used
1	Walker	Dyer	Williams	Bunkell	Smith L	Packer	Garwood	Gough	Allinson	Leslie	Cook	Dowman
1	*Webster*	*Tuddenham*	*Baldry*	*Batson*	*Fallon*	*Howard*	*Horsfall*	*Spriggs*	*Biley*	*Bowker*	*Watson*	*Bullock*
2	Walker	Dyer	Williams*	Bunkell	Smith L	Packer	Garwood	Gough	Allinson	Leslie	Cook	
2	*Gennoe*	*Flavell*	*Kent*	*McHale*	*Trainer*	*Rylands*	*Jones A*	*McGill**	*Jones G*	*Lawson*	*Bell*	
3	Walker	Dyer	Williams	Bunkell	Smith L	Packer	Garwood*	Gough	Froggatt	Leslie	Cook	Allinson
3	*Poole*	*Hallows*	*Lacey*	*Hanvey*	*Summerscales*	*O'Loughton*	*Halliwell*	*Melledew*	*Whelan*	*Mullington**	*Tarbuck*	*Mulvaney*
4	Walker	Dyer	Williams	Bunkell	Smith L	Packer	Garwood	Gough	Froggatt	Allinson	Cook	
4	*Key*	*Templeman*	*Hooker*	*Hore*	*Clapham*	*Hatch*	*Jordan**	*Kellow*	*Morrin*	*Beer*	*Jennings*	
5	Walker	Dyer	Williams	Leslie	Smith L	Packer!	Garwood	Gough	Froggatt	Allinson*	Cook	Dowman
5	*Rankin*	*How*	*Walsh*	*Bond**	*Walley*	*Garner*	*Coffill*	*Joslyn*	*Mercer*	*Mayes*	*Downes*	*Poole*
6	Walker	Dyer	Williams	Bunkell	Smith L	Packer	Garwood	Gough	Froggatt	Allinson	Cook	
6	*Crudgington*	*Lowry*	*Evans*	*Lugg*	*Nicholls*	*Purdie*	*Davies D*	*Abbott*	*Davies W*	*Mayman*	*Tully**	*Rimmer*
7	Walker	Bright	Williams	Bunkell	Smith L	Packer	Foley	Gough	Froggatt	Allinson*	Cook	Leslie
7	*Baker*	*Butler*	*Miller*	*Benson*	*Impey*	*Barton*	*Johnson*	*Paterson*	*Riley*	*Reeves*	*McAllinden**	*Morgan*
8	Walker	Bright	Williams	Bunkell	Smith L	Packer	Garwood	Gough	Froggatt	Allinson*	Cook	
8	*Rogan*	*Kisby*	*Ellison*	*Kavanagh*	*Dawes*	*Ashworth*	*Honour*	*Lowrey*	*Moore*	*Harris*	*Donaghy*	*Bunkell*
9	Walker	Bright	Williams	Bunkell	Smith L*	Packer	Foley	Gough	Froggatt	Allinson*	Cook	Garwood
9	*Freeman*	*Moody*	*Ford*	*Clark**	*Hadley*	*Young*	*Nicholl*	*Goodwin*	*Pountney*	*Parker S*	*Cunningham*	*Denny*
10	Walker	Bright	Williams	Foley	Smith L	Packer	Garwood	Gough	Froggatt	Allinson	Cook	
10	*Edgar*	*Goad*	*Luckett*	*Veitch*	*Scott*	*Wiggett*	*Spelman*	*Rowlands*	*Reed*	*Scaife*	*Bielby*	
11	Walker	Bright	Williams	Foley	Smith L*	Packer	Garwood	Leslie	Froggatt	Allinson	Cook	Dyer
11	*Letheran*	*Markham*	*Peacock*	*Oates**	*Wigginton*	*Money*	*Collier*	*Pilling*	*Davidson*	*Green*	*Keeley*	*Wadsworth*

Match notes

1. Ron Atkinson's Cambridge have never dropped a point at home to Colchester and keep up the record with an Alan Biley brace. The Cambridge striker is yards offside for his opener. Colchester miss the services of John Froggatt, who is seeing out a suspension held over from last season.

2. Allinson, 18, has a night to remember, lifting a drab match with a 160-second pair. Cook, on his 300th game, crosses to Bunkell but Allinson arrives first. Giant Terry Gennoe fails to keep his headed second out, and only Gough's toe on Garwood's cross denies him a first hat-trick.

3. Rochdale leave out forward Bobby Mountford, whom Colchester had trailed last season. The introduction of substitute Mulvaney allows Keith Hanvey to move upfield. He duly obliges with the winner. Gough grazes the crossbar late on, but Dale hold on to go third in the league table.

4. The U's keep close tabs on 24-year-old Cornishman, Tony Kellow. He has scored in four consecutive games. After taking the lead, the U's are jolted when Jennings gets Dyer into a tangle, crosses and sees Smith turn the ball into his own net. Goals on the hour-mark secure the points.

5. United take three gallons of orange juice to Vicarage Road to instill a half-time energy boost. But after taking a deserved lead, Packer's rash challenge on Keith Mercer leads to a sending off. Within three minutes a Hornets double strike turns the game.

6. Alex's Peter Abbott grabs the lead on 80 seconds from Packer's dire back-pass, but the impressive Allinson lays on Froggatt's equaliser The experienced Wyn Davies turns L Smith to set up Abbott again, but Allinson has the last say as United average three goals per game at home.

7. Colchester gain their first point of the season away from Layer Road. Garwood is dropped and despite Foley's 87th-minute effort against the bar, the visitors are happy to settle for a point and thus stop the rot. Bright's blatant 28th-minute push on Frank Barton goes unpunished.

8. Struggling Workington become United's fourth straight victim at Layer Road, and could have been five down by the break. Lowry reduces the arrears Team-mate Ashworth, taking goal-kicks for the injured Rogan, slices the ball to Gough, who volleys first time back into the net.

9. In the Essex derby at Roots Hall, the visitors once again leave out potential goalscorer Garwood. This despite only scoring one away goal all season. Parker has a second-half effort ruled out for a foul. Both sides introduce substitutes for the last 20 minutes but the deadlock remains.

10. Garwood's second hat-trick of the season takes his tally to eleven in just eight games. Pool have no manager and no cash. Froggatt does not get on the scoresheet but excels as a provider. Ex-Man Utd trainee Paul Bielby nets twice. The North-Easterners are lucky to keep single figures.

11. At the Old Show Ground, Angus Davidson's shot takes a fortunate deflection off Stuart Pilling to give The Iron a first-half lead Davidson then produces the killer second as U's press for the equaliser. His own shot is blocked but only as far as Nolan Keeley, who rams in the rebound.

12. A 25/10 DONCASTER 3,856 — 10 L 17 12 — 2-3 (2-2)
Packer 26p, Cook 28
Taylor 5, Kitchen 20, Laidlaw 80
Ref: T Morris

Walker · Cook · Williams · Dominey · Smith L · Packer · Garwood · Foley · Froggatt · Allinson* · Leslie · Dyer
Peacock · Brookes · Robinson · Laidlaw · Wignall S · Taylor · Miller · Murray · O'Callaghan · Kitchen · Woodcock · Dyer

U's stay up in the North after the Scunthorpe game Rovers hit two early goals. Froggatt falls in the area after a heavy challenge by Robinson. Two minutes later, Cook, atoning for his assist in Doncaster's second, fires the U's level. Man-of-the-match Miller lays on the late winner.

13. H 30/10 BRENTFORD 3,607 — 10 W 20 14 — 2-1 (2-1)
Garwood 18, Cook 24
Cross 19
Ref: R Challis

Walker · Dyer · Williams · Cook · Smith L · Packer* · Garwood · Gough · Foley · Allinson · Leslie · Dowman
Priddy · Fraser · Allen · Riddick · Goldthorpe · McCulloch · Johnson · Glover · Cross · Graham · Sweetzer · Carlton*

Brentford have only won once in the last 13 games and can't stop home-kings Colchester. Garwood notches his twelfth of the season. Immediately from the restart, McCulloch crosses to Roger Cross, in acres of space, to level. Cook's second successive 25-yarder wins the day.

14. H 1/11 TORQUAY 3,102 — 6 W 16 16 — 4-0 (4-0)
Gough 15, Garwood 25, 30, Dowman 43
Ref: M Taylor

Walker · Dyer · Williams · Cook · Smith L · Dowman · Garwood · Gough · Froggatt · Allinson · Leslie · Dyer
Lee T · Lynch · Sandercock · Kruse · Forbes · Dunne · Morrall · Provan · Foster · Brown · Kennedy · Rudge*

The highest home scorers in the country continue their goal spree. On-loan Duncan Forbes in the Gulls defence is a U's target, along with ex-Leicester man Len Glover. Both deals collapse. Norwich refuse to release Forbes and Glover can't get international clearance from the USA.

15. H 12/11 STOCKPORT 3,948 — 7 W 9 18 — 1-0 (0-0)
Dowman 85
Ref: B Daniels

Walker · Dyer · Williams · Cook · Smith L · Dowman · Garwood · Gough · Froggatt · Allinson · Leslie · Smith
Holbrook · Loadwick · Rutter · Thompson · Lennard · Fagarty · McBeth · McNeill · Daniels · Sutcliffe · Johnson · Smith*

Following last week's wasted journey to South Wales and Newport's waterlogged pitch. Colchester maintain their 100% home record with a late strike against the men from Manchester. Dyer's low cross is helped on by Froggatt. Starlet Dowman scores for the second game in a row.

16. A 27/11 BARNSLEY 5,662 — 3 W 4 20 — 1-0 (1-0)
Garwood 8
Ref: J Rice

Walker · Dyer · Williams · Cook · Smith L · Dowman · Garwood · Gough · Froggatt · Packer · Leslie* · Allinson
Springett · Murphy · Chambers · Brown · Saunders · Pickering · Felton · Joicey · Peachey · Millar · Warnock · Price*

High-Flying Barnsley are undone by Garwood's 16th goal of the season. The Essex side leap-frog their Yorkshire promotion rivals. Froggatt robs a Tykes defender before finding Garwood, who slots under the advancing Peter Springett. He then has another effort ruled out for offside.

17. H 4/12 DARLINGTON 2,951 — 3 W 13 22 — 4-0 (2-0)
Gough 8, Dowman 36, 75, Smith L 80
Ref: P Reeves

Walker · Cook · Williams · Leslie · Smith L · Dowman · Garwood · Gough · Froggatt · Packer · Allinson
Ogley · Nattrass · Cochrane · Stone · Craig · Noble · Crosson · Rawles · Seal · Holbrook · Wann

Ipswich v Liverpool just up the road accounts for a depleted crowd. Unhappy Bunkell is linked to a move to Mansfield. Youngster Dowman takes his tally to five goals in the last six matches. On a bone-hard frozen pitch, the last three goals all come from well-worked set-pieces.

18. A 18/12 BRADFORD C 4,173 — 4 L 1 22 — 0-1 (0-1)
Cooke 39
Ref: A Saunders

Walker · Cook · Williams · Leslie · Smith L · Dowman · Garwood · Gough · Froggatt · Packer · Dyer* · Allinson
Downsboro' · Hardcastle · Podd · Johnson · Ratcliffe · Fretwell · Ingram · Dolan · Cooke · Hall · Hutchins

Manager of the Month, Bobby Roberts, watches his side succumb to the new league leaders. Joe Cooke's fine one-two with Johnson gives City victory. Froggatt sees an effort flash past the post and another cleared off the line. Packer's second-half booking could lead to a suspension.

19. H 27/12 ALDERSHOT 6,007 — 3 W 14 24 — 1-0 (1-0)
Smith L 43
Ref: C Maskell

Walker · Cook · Williams* · Leslie · Smith L · Dowman · Garwood · Gough · Froggatt · Packer · Leslie · Dyer
Johnson · Howitt · Wooler · Crosby · Mancini · Jopling · Walton · Howarth · Morrisey · Earls · McGregor · Butler*

Spurs manager Keith Burkinshaw and advisor Bill Nicholson checked out both L Smith and Dowman in the Brentford cup-tie. The national press value each at £100k. U's earn a proud tenth successive home win when Froggatt nods down a quickly-taken Leslie free-kick to L. Smith.

20. A 28/12 SWANSEA 5,666 — 4 W 10 24 — 5-0 (0-0)
Bunkell 49
Ref: B James

Walker · Cook · Williams · Leslie · Smith L · Dowman · Bunkell · Gough · Froggatt · Packer · Allinson · Dyer
Potter · Evans · Bartley · May · Lally · Chappell · James · Curtis · Charles · Conway

Croydon ref James refuses Roberts' plea to postpone due to the frozen pitch, and then ignores U's claims that Jeremy Charles' goal is offside. Earlier Bunkell, whose loan move to Mansfield is off, fired U's in front only for Eddie May to hook home, after he had headed against the bar.

21. H 1/1 NEWPORT 4,614 — 4 L 22 26 — 1-2 (2-0)
Gough 6, 63, Smith L 25, Dowman 52, [Garwood 64]
May 77, Charles 87
Ref: A Grey

Walker · Cook · Williams · Dyer · Smith L · Dowman · Bunkell · Gough · Froggatt · Bunkell · Allinson · Allinson
Plumley · Derrett · Bell · Emanuel · Walker · Murray · Villars · Relish · Clark · Woods · Jones R

Crisis-torn County are demolished by Colchester's ability to score from both the front line and the back. Garwood ends a five-match lean spell with his 18th of the campaign, whilst strike-partner Gough has 12 to his credit. County are staring bankruptcy and expulsion square in the face.

22. A 3/1 BRENTFORD 4,610 — 3 W 23 28 — 4-1 (0-1)
Garwood 57, Gough 67 85, Dowman 80
McCulloch 25
Ref: T Bune

Walker · Cox · Leslie · Dyer · Smith L · Dowman · Garwood · Gough · Froggatt · Bunkell · Allinson · Dominey
Salman · Smith · Riddick · Allen · Walker · Fraser · Graham · McCulloch · Walker · Rolph · Scrivens · Sweetzer*

Brentford field three 16-year olds in Scrivens, Walker and Rolph. Mike Walker spectacularly denies McCulloch a second on 50 minutes. The floodgates then open as Graham Cox in the home goal fumbles for Garwood's equaliser. For Cox, it is only his second appearance this season.

23. H 18/1 SOUTHPORT 5,634 — 2 W 21 30 — 4-1 (1-0)
Bunkell 18, Garwood 48, Packer 76p, [Allinson 84]
Dewsnip 88
Ref: R Lewis

Walker · Cook · Williams · Leslie · Smith L · Dowman · Garwood · Gough · Froggatt* · Bunkell · Allinson · Packer
Ryan · Hughes · Snookes · O'Neil · Higham · Taylor · Sibbald · Wilkinson · Jones · Gough · Wilson · Dewsnip · Rhodes*

The attendance is boosted by the provision of vouchers for the forthcoming FA Cup-tie with Derby. U's reach a half-century of goals in just 16 home league and cup games. The record, however, stands at 14 games in 1961-62, which included the club record 9-1 win over Bradford City.

LEAGUE DIVISION 4

Manager: Bobby Roberts

No	Date		1	2	3	4	5	6	7	8	9	10	11	12 sub used	Scorers, Times, and Referees	Att	Pos	Pt	F-A	H-T
24	H 21/1	CAMBRIDGE	Walker *Webster*	Cook *Batson*	Williams *Howard*	Packer *Striger*	Smith L *Fallon*	Dowman *Seddon*	Garwood *Watson*	Gough *Spriggs*	Froggatt *Hall*	Allinson* *Finney*	Dyer *Biley*	Dominey	Spriggs 24 — Ref: T Spencer	7,639	2	L 30	0-1	0-1
25	H 5/2	ROCHDALE	Walker *Poole*	Cook *Hallows*	Williams *Whelan*	Leslie *Harvey*	Smith L *Summerscales Bannon*	Dowman	Garwood *Melledew*	Gough *O'Loughton*	Froggatt *Mountford*	Bunkell *Mullington**	Packer *Hanstead Helliwell*		Dowman 27 — Ref: K Salmon	4,943	13	W 32	1-0	1-0
26	A 12/2	EXETER	Walker *Key*	Williams *Templeman Hore*	Cook	Leslie *Weeks*	Smith L *Saxton*	Dowman *Hatch*	Garwood *Hodge*	Gough *Kellow*	Froggatt *Robertson*	Bunkell *Beer*	Packer *Jennings*		Hodge 6 — Ref: M Sinclair	6,132	5	L 32	0-1	0-1
27	H 19/2	WATFORD	Ellis *Rankin*	Cook *Geidmintis*	Williams *Pritchett*	Leslie *Bind*	Smith L *Horsfield*	Dowman *Garner*	Garwood *Downes*	Gough *Joslyn*	Froggatt *Mercer*	Bunkell* *Mayes*	Packer *Coffill**	Allinson *Jenkins*	Packer 13p — Ref: D Smith	5,678	3	W 34	1-0	1-0
28	A 22/2	NEWPORT	Ellis *Plumley*	Cook *Derrett*	Williams *Bell*	Leslie *Emanuel*	Smith L *Walker*	Dowman *Murray**	Garwood *Williams*	Gough *Woods*	Froggatt *Jones R*	Allinson *Clark*	Packer *White*	Villars	Gough 44, 55, Emanuel 49 — Ref: W Harvey	1,575	2	W 36	2-1	1-0
29	A 26/2	CREWE	Walker *Brand*	Cook *Lowry*	Williams *Roberts*	Leslie *Lugg*	Smith L *Bowles*	Dowman *Bevan*	Garwood *Humphreys*	Gough *Mayman*	Froggatt *Davies W*	Allinson* *Purdie**	Packer *Tully*	Dyer *Davies D*	Smith L 31 (og) — Ref: K Hackett	2,410	4	L 36	0-1	0-1
30	H 4/3	BOURNEMOUTH	Walker *Baker*	Cook *Butler*	Williams *Miller*	Leslie *Benson*	Smith L *Impey*	Dowman *Cunningham*	Garwood *Howarth*	Gough *Paterson*	Froggatt *Cave*	Allinson *Riley*	Packer *Johnson*		Froggatt 14 — Ref: M Taylor	4,948	3	W 38	1-0	1-0
31	A 8/3	HALIFAX	Walker *Leonard*	Cook *Trainer*	Williams *Loska*	Leslie *Flavell*	Smith L *Dunleavy*	Dowman *Phelan*	Foley *Hoy*	Gough *Carroll*	Froggatt *Bullock*	Allinson* *Lawson*	Packer *Johnston*	Dyer	Packer 35, Leslie 88, Lawson 44p — Ref: N Glover	2,097	2	W 40	2-1	1-1
32	A 12/3	WORKINGTON	Walker *Rogan*	Cook *Leng*	Williams *Ashworth*	Leslie *Kavanagh*	Smith L *Brown*	Dowman *Blant*	Foley *Harris**	Gough *Kisby*	Froggatt *Prudham*	Packer *Coleman*	Dyer *Honour*	Higgins	Froggatt 37, Gough 53, Dowman 66, (Packer 83p); Kavanagh 39, Prudham 44 — Ref: B Matthewson	1,223	2	W 42	4-2	1-2
33	H 19/3	SOUTHEND	Walker *Freeman*	Cook *Banks*	Williams *Ford*	Leslie *Laverick*	Packer *Moody*	Dowman *Townsend*	Foley* *Morris*	Gough *Hadley*	Froggatt *Parker D*	Bunkell *Clark*	Dyer *Little*	Garwood	Morris 87 — Ref: J Hunting	6,637	3	L 42	0-1	0-0
34	A 21/3	HUDDERSFIELD	Walker *Taylor**	Cook *Sweeney*	Williams *Oliver*	Leslie *Gray*	Smith L *Baines*	Dowman *Hart*	Garwood *Eccles*	Gough* *Smith*	Froggatt *Campbell*	Packer *Johnston*	Dyer *McCaffrey*	Bunkell *Fowler*	Ref: J Butcher	7,508	2	D 43	0-0	0-0

24 — CAMBRIDGE: Leaders Cambridge are the team which finally dent U's proud 100% home record at the 13th time of asking. Trevor Howard finds big Jim Hall on the left. Finney dummies his cross and little Steve Spriggs is free to side-foot home to complete the double for the side from the Abbey.

25 — ROCHDALE: Back to league action after the drama of two cup-ties against Derby, witnessed by over 36,000 fans Dowman's eighth in 12 games, hauling himself in front of Harvey to meet Garwood's cross, wins it. The TV cameras are present for the third consecutive Colchester United match.

26 — EXETER: Bobby Roberts, Manager of the Month for the second time, takes his side to in-form Exeter. The Grecians have not lost since 4 December and continue their run with Bobby Hodge's third goal in four games. Player-manager Bobby Saxton chops Leslie in the box but play is waved on.

27 — WATFORD: 19-year old Ipswich trainee, Glen Ellis, has a nerveless debut. He pulls off a stunning save from Alan Mayes. With his back to goal. Gough is pushed by Alan Garner. Packer makes no mistake. It's the U's 50th league goal of the season. In the last minutes Downes hits the upright.

28 — NEWPORT: Newport have the worst scoring record in the entire country. Garwood strikes the upright in the dying moments of the first half before Gough hooks in Ex-Welsh international John Emanuel slots under Ellis, before Gary Plumley parries Allinson's shot for Gough's 13th of the term.

29 — CREWE: Crewe have not beaten Colchester for 15 years and have suffered eleven defeats in the process. This disastrous run is ended when Smith, who was under pressure from Paul Mayman, sends his downward back-pass header up over the advancing Walker. U's goal machine has dried up.

30 — BOURNEMOUTH: Garwood's corner is headed goalwards by Smith. Froggatt re-directs the ball in the net for his first league goal since September. Roberts is out of luck in the transfer market. His signed and sealed deal for a Walsall midfielder is scuppered by the resignation of Saddlers' boss Doug Fry.

31 — HALIFAX: Walker races out of his area and chops Johnny Johnston as the forward chased a hopeful ball from Albert Phelan. Jimmy Lawson makes no mistake to send the side in level. Leslie, who had cleverly stepped over the ball for Packer's goal, wins the game. U's stay over in Derbyshire.

32 — WORKINGTON: Dowman's header is the youngster's eighth of the season. Froggatt had already plundered his first away goal of the season, but a shock double saw U's trailing at the break. After Gough's equaliser, Dowman did his bit, and then Packer netted a handball decision for his sixth penalty.

33 — SOUTHEND: The Shrimpers, grateful to be heading for an away point from a certain goalless draw, gain a surprise victory. Frank Banks finds Colin Morris in a blatantly offside position. Morris picks his spot past Walker as these promotion rivals vie for a top-four spot come the end of the campaign.

34 — HUDDERSFIELD: Dick Taylor, Huddersfield's England Youth team goalkeeper, injures his back as early as the fifth minute but hobbles on in severe pain until just before the break. He is finally replaced by full-back Oliver, who makes a splendid save to deny Lindsay Smith's effort in the 65th minute.

Match-by-match record (matches 35–46), Cambridge United ("U's")

35 · A · 26/3 · HARTLEPOOL — D 2-2 (HT 1-2) · Att 1,822 · Opp pos 21 · Pos 2 · Pts 44 · Ref: A Porter
Goals: Allinson 44, Dowman 52; Poskett 27p, 29
U's: Walker, Cook, Williams, Leslie, Smith L, Dowman, Garwood, Allinson, Froggatt, Bunkell, Dyer
Hartlepool: Edgar, Creamer, Wiggett, Goad, Scott, Simpkin, Scarfe, McMordie, Turnball, Poskett, Cunningham
Foley is out with damaged ankle ligaments. Dowman handles a shot from Malcolm Poskett, who sends Walker the wrong way. Two minutes later, Poskett bags the rebound after Cunningham hits the bar. Dowman, with a suspected broken arm, levels with his tenth of the season.

36 · H · 2/4 · SCUNTHORPE — D 1-1 (HT 1-1) · Att 3,799 · Opp pos 17 · Pos 3 · Pts 45 · Ref: B James
Goals: Leslie 2; Lumby 34
U's: Walker, Cook, Williams, Leslie, Smith L, Dowman, Garwood, Allinson, Froggatt, Packer, Dyer
Scunthorpe: O'Meara, Peacock, Pilling, Oates!, Wigginton, Money, Czuczman, Kilmore*, Keeley, Lumby, Lee, Davidson
Grand National Day gives the lowest gate since 1 November: 3,799. U's are first out the stalls. Leslie taps home Allinson's effort, which clips the bar. Czuczman, free on the right, supplies Lumby's header. Bob Oates is sent off on the hour for retaliation on Froggatt, who is booked and subbed.

37 · A · 5/4 · ALDERSHOT — D 1-1 (HT 0-1) · Att 2,586 · Opp pos 15 · Pos 3 · Pts 46 · Ref: C White
Goals: Gough 85; Bell 1
U's: Walker, Cook, Williams, Leslie, Smith L, Dowman, Garwood, Gough, Froggatt, Dyer, Packer*, Allinson
Aldershot: Johnson, Howitt, Butler, Crosby, Earls, Wooler, Walton, Morrisey, Bell, Bambridge, McGregor
Shots' early goal is their first in four games. Terry Bell back-heads a Joe Butler free-kick over the embarrassed Walker. With just five minutes remaining, Gough preserves U's five-match unbeaten away run by tapping in, after Garwood's cross deflects off Mike Earls and onto the bar.

38 · H · 8/4 · SWANSEA — D 1-1 (HT 0-0) · Att 5,184 · Opp pos 11 · Pos 3 · Pts 47 · Ref: R Lewis
Goals: Dowman 83; Williams 58 (og)
U's: Walker, Cook, Williams, Leslie, Smith L, Dowman, Garwood, Gough, Froggatt, Dyer, Packer*, Allinson
Swansea: Potter, Evans, Bartley, Smith, May, Bruton, Lally!, James, Curtis, Charles, Chappell
Dowman saves the U's on a night of drama. His last-gasp equaliser spares Williams's blushes for the fifth successive draw. Williams' mis-timed back-pass leaves Walker stranded. Swans' Pat Lally, booked earlier for a foul on Leslie, is sent off on 70 mins for axing sub Allinson.

39 · A · 11/4 · TORQUAY — D 2-2 (HT 1-1) · Att 3,189 · Opp pos 19 · Pos 3 · Pts 48 · Ref: B Stevens
Goals: Dowman 24, Gough 82; Rudge 5, Lee C 81
U's: Walker, Cook, Williams, Leslie, Smith L, Dowman, Garwood, Gough, Froggatt, Bunkell*, Dyer, Allinson
Torquay: Robbins, Twitchin, Sandercock, Vassallo, Green, Boulton, Morrall, Lee C, Rudge, Brown, Dunne
An incredible sixth draw on the spin. David Rudge unleashes a 20-yard effort, which flies past Walker. Dowman nods Garwood's corner, but is at fault for the Gulls' equaliser with a poor clearance. Gough grabs a vital promotion point in this morning kick-off down in the South-West.

40 · H · 15/4 · DONCASTER — W 1-0 (HT 0-0) · Att 4,668 · Opp pos 9 · Pos 3 · Pts 50 · Ref: D Smith
Goals: Gough 79
U's: Walker, Cook, Williams, Leslie, Smith L, Dowman, Garwood, Gough, Froggatt, Allinson*, Dyer, Packer
Doncaster: Peacock, Brookes, Reed, Robinson, Wignall D, Taylor, Miller, Murray, O'Callaghan, Kitchen, Laidlaw
Gough's 18th of the term keeps U's on course for promotion and extends the run to seven without defeat. If Peter Kitchen had taken just one of his many chances then it might have been different. Garwood's corner is headed on by 19th birthday-boy Dowman, and Gough does the rest.

41 · H · 19/4 · HUDDERSFIELD — W 3-1 (HT 2-1) · Att 5,051 · Opp pos 10 · Pos 3 · Pts 52 · Ref: J Homewood
Goals: Smith L 9, 63, Garwood 39; Dowman 3 (og)
U's: Walker, Cook, Williams, Leslie, Smith L, Dowman, Garwood, Gough, Froggatt, Allinson, Dyer
Huddersfield: Starling, Sweeney, Oliver, Fowler, Sidebottom, Hart, Gray, Smith, Eccles, Johnson, Butler
U's give their promotion rivals a head start, in L Smith's 200th game, when Dowman diverts a cross by Yorkshire cricketer Arnie Sidebottom past Walker. He atones six minutes later by flicking Garwood's cross to L Smith. The latter pair reverse roles for the winner from Cook's cross.

42 · A · 22/4 · STOCKPORT — D 1-1 (HT 1-1) · Att 2,826 · Opp pos 14 · Pos 3 · Pts 53 · Ref: D Richardson
Goals: Garwood 18; Daniels 40
U's: Walker, Cook, Williams, Dyer, Smith L, Dowman, Garwood, Gough*, Froggatt, Packer, Marrin*, Allinson
Stockport: Holbrook, Loadwick, Rutter, Thompson, Smith, Jackson, Daniels, Darling, Fletcher, Buckley, McNeill
Garwood keeps ahead of Gough with his 24th of the term. With the wind at their backs in the first half, U's ruled the roost. After the break it is County in the ascendancy, spurred by their new player-boss Alan Thompson. Barney Daniels, perhaps offside, levels with his 19th of the term.

43 · H · 29/4 · BARNSLEY — W 1-0 (HT 0-0) · Att 5,802 · Opp pos 6 · Pos 4 · Pts 55 · Ref: T Bune
Goals: Smith L 83
U's: Walker, Williams, Cook, Dyer*, Smith L, Dowman, Garwood, Gough, Froggatt, Allinson, Packer
Barnsley: Springett, Collins, Pugh, Murphy, Saunders, Pickering, Felton, Joicey, Peachey, Millar, Brown
Barnsley's defeat, to a seemingly offside L Smith goal, leaves a straight fight for five clubs to win the four promotion places. Cambridge are certain to go up, so it is ex-U's loanee Gary Moore-inspired Swansea, with eight straight wins, who pose the biggest threat to U's aspirations.

44 · A · 3/5 · SOUTHPORT — W 3-1 (HT 0-1) · Att 867 · Opp pos 23 · Pos 3 · Pts 57 · Ref: C Newsome
Goals: Froggatt 85, 78, Gough 76; Walker 15 (og)
U's: Walker, Dyer, Williams, Cook, Smith L, Dowman, Garwood, Gough, Froggatt, Allinson*, Packer
Southport: Harrison, Brown, Snookes, O'Neil, Brooks, Higham, Dewsnip, Fisher, Wilson, Smith, Galley
Walker gifts struggling Southport the lead when he pushes George Dewsnip's corner into his own net. Garwood crosses for Froggatt at the far post, then Gough edges U's in front with a dipping shot. Two minutes later Williams sends Froggatt racing away to hammer in a decisive third.

45 · A · 7/5 · DARLINGTON — L 0-2 (HT 0-1) · Att 1,964 · Opp pos 11 · Pos 4 · Pts 57 · Ref: M Lowe
Goals: — ; Rowles 21, 48
U's: Walker, Dyer*, Williams, Cook, Smith L, Dowman, Garwood, Gough, Froggatt, Leslie, Allinson
Darlington: Owers, Crosson, Cochrane, Natrass, Craig, Walker, Lyons, Rowles, Seal, Young
A shock defeat in the North-East leaves a nail-biting final fixture where a United win, or a Swansea defeat at Cambridge, will earn promotion. Eddie Rowles does the damage when his shot takes a wicked deflection off Dowman, and looks suspiciously offside to give the second.

46 · H · 14/5 · BRADFORD C — W 2-1 (HT 2-1) · Att 8,912 · Opp pos 4 · Pos 3 · Pts 59 · Ref: M Sinclair
Goals: Ratcliffe 1 (og), Allinson 41; Watson 5
U's: Walker, Cook, Williams, Leslie, Smith L, Dowman, Garwood, Gough, Froggatt, Packer, Allinson
Bradford C: Downsboro', Hardcastle, Podd, Johnson, Ratcliffe, Fretwell, Watson, Dolan, Cooke*, Wright, Hutchins, Spark
City, already promoted and backed by 1,000 fans, need the U's to deny Swansea defeat at Cambridge. David Ratcliffe heads past his own keeper. Garry Watson quickly levels. Allinson gives the home side the points they need to deny Swansea, 3-2 winners at Cambridge, the last promotion spot.

Home — · Away 3,555 · Average 4,645

League Cup

1:1 A MILLWALL 14/8 — L 1-2 (H-T 1-2) — 4,599 2:
Scorers: Smith L 2; Seasman 22, Shanahan 38. Ref: C Maskell

	1	2	3	4	5	6	7	8	9	10	11	12 sub used
Colchester	Walker	Dyer	Williams	Bunkell	Smith L	Packer	Garwood	Gough	Froggatt	Leslie	Cook	Allinson
Millwall	*Goddard*	*Evans*	*Donaldson*	*Brisley*	*Kitchener*	*Hazell*	*Lee*	*Seasman*	*Shanahan*	*Walker*	*Salvage*	*Fairbrother*

In heatwave conditions, Colchester take the lead on just 2 minutes and 14 seconds. Walker parries a Trevor Lee shot: Terry Brisley crosses for John Seasman to score. Seasman has just joined the Lions from Chesterfield. Terry Shanahan ensures a first-leg lead slotting home a loose ball.

1:2 H MILLWALL 17/8 — W 2-1 (H-T 2-0) — 3,155 2:
Scorers: Gough 35, Garwood 41 / Evans 60. Ref: B Daniels (3-3 draw on aggregate)

	1	2	3	4	5	6	7	8	9	10	11	12 sub used
Colchester	Walker	Dyer	Williams	Bunkell	Smith L	Packer*	Garwood	Gough	Froggatt	Leslie	Cook	Allinson
Millwall	*Goddard*	*Evans*	*Donaldson*	*Brisley*	*Kitchener*	*Hazell*	*Lee*	*Seasman*	*Shanahan*	*Walker*	*Salvage**	*Fairbrother*

United banish last season's relegation blues with a display of controlled aggression. Garwood pushes Packer's long ball to Gough, and the pair combine six minutes later: Tony Hazell touches a free-kick to Ray Evans, who smashes past the unsighted Walker, earning a Layer Rd replay.

1R H MILLWALL 30/8 — 13 — L 4-4 (H-T 0-2) aet — 3,695 2:13
Scorers: Garwood 62, 82, 118, Bunkell 72p / Lee 34, 39, Salvage 70p, Fairbrother 119. Ref: A Grey (Colchester lost 2-4 on penalties)

	1	2	3	4	5	6	7	8	9	10	11	12 sub used
Colchester	Walker	Dyer	Williams	Bunkell	Smith L	Packer	Garwood	Gough	Froggatt	Leslie*	Cook	Allinson
Millwall	*Johnsd*	*Evans*	*Donaldson*	*Brisley*	*Kitchener*	*Hazell*	*Lee*	*Seasman*	*Fairbrother*	*Walker*	*Salvage*	

After five hours and 14 goals this tie is cruelly settled. Packer handles to give Millwall a 3-1 lead. Within a flash, Kitchener handles to drag the U's back in. Garwood's extra-time effort seems to win it, but Fairbrother has other ideas. Gough misses and Cook fires over in the shoot-out.

FA Cup

1 A CAMBRIDGE 20/11 — 7 — D 1-1 (H-T 0-0) — 5,090 4:1
Scorers: Packer 72p / Fallon 89. Ref: R Toseland

	1	2	3	4	5	6	7	8	9	10	11	12 sub used
Colchester	Walker	Dyer	Williams	Cook	Smith L	Dowman	Garwood	Gough	Froggatt	Packer	Leslie	
Cambridge	*Webster*	*Batson*	*Baldry**	*Stringer*	*Fallon*	*Howard*	*Horsfall*	*Spriggs*	*Bowker*	*Finney*	*Seddon*	*O'Neill*

Packer is concussed and needs three stitches in the first minute. He puts Colchester in the lead, after Leslie is brought down by Steve Fallon. Cambridge earn a Layer Road replay. From a long-hoisted free-kick, for a visitors' offside. Fallon redeems himself.

1R H CAMBRIDGE 24/11 — 7 — W 2-0 (H-T 2-0) — 6,041 4:1
Scorers: Garwood 3, Leslie 16. Ref: R Toseland

	1	2	3	4	5	6	7	8	9	10	11	12 sub used
Colchester	Walker	Dyer	Williams	Cook	Smith L	Dowman	Garwood	Gough	Froggatt	Packer	Leslie	
Cambridge	*Webster*	*Batson*	*Baldry**	*Stringer*	*Fallon*	*Howard*	*Horsfall*	*Spriggs*	*Biley*	*Finney*	*Seddon*	*Murray*

Ron Atkinson's side suffer their first defeat in ten, but had only saved themselves in the dying moments on Saturday. Garwood nets his 15th from Dyer's cross, then Dave Stringer, admired by Roberts, nodded down for Leslie to steal in between Steve Spriggs and Brendan Batson.

2 H BRENTFORD 20/12 — 4 — W 3-2 (H-T 2-0) — 4,730 4:21
Scorers: Gough 6, Froggatt 7, Packer 88p / Rolph 49, Fraser 74. Ref: J Sewell

	1	2	3	4	5	6	7	8	9	10	11	12 sub used
Colchester	Walker	Cook	Williams	Leslie	Smith L	Dowman	Garwood*	Gough	Froggatt	Packer	Allinson	Dyer
Brentford	*Priddy*	*Salman*	*Scales*	*Riddick*	*Allen*	*Carlton**	*Fraser*	*Graham*	*Cross*	*Rolph*	*French*	*Goldthorpe*

Re-staged, after a 62-minute abandonment, due to a frozen pitch and Terry Johnson's broken arm. Teenager Rolph shines on his debut for the Bees, but ice-cool Packer wins the tie when a Griffin Park replay seems inevitable. Bobby Goldthorpe chops Leslie in the box near time.

3 A KETTERING 8/1 — 2 — W 3-2 (H-T 2-0) — 7,176 SL:1
Scorers: Froggatt 7, Garwood 30, 60 / Clayton 80, Kellock 81. Ref: B Homewood

	1	2	3	4	5	6	7	8	9	10	11	12 sub used
Colchester	Walker	Cook	Williams	Leslie	Smith L*	Dowman	Garwood	Gough	Froggatt	Bunkell	Dyer	Allinson
Kettering	*Livsey*	*Lucas*	*Merrick*	*Mortimer*	*Dixey*	*Ashby*	*Faulkner*	*Glover*	*Kellock*	*Clayton*	*Phipps**	*Wood*

The U's who lost to Dover last term, ride a storm. Trailing 0-2, the home side have Phipps and Kellock efforts ruled out for offside. United increase the lead but lose Smith, who limps off. Revived Poppies score two quick goals. U's earn a home tie with Blackpool or Derby County.

4 H DERBY 29/1 — 2 — D 1-1 (H-T 0-1) — 14,030 1:15
Scorers: Garwood 90 / Hales 23. Ref: R Crabb

	1	2	3	4	5	6	7	8	9	10	11	12 sub used
Colchester	Walker	Cook	Williams	Leslie	Smith L	Dowman	Garwood	Gough	Froggatt	Bunkell	Dyer*	Packer
Derby	*Boulton*	*Webster*	*Daniel*	*Macken*	*McFarland*	*Todd*	*Powell*	*Gemmill*	*Hales*	*Hector*	*James*	

Derek Hales, recent £300,000 buy from Charlton, hits his fourth goal in three games. Littered with stoppages and time-wasting, Garwood levels in the fifth minute of injury-time. Cook, Garwood and Leighton James have a running battle. U's have never lost at home to a top-flight club.

4R A DERBY 2/2 — 2 — L 0-1 (H-T 0-1) — 22,155 1:15
Scorers: James 44. Ref: R Crabb

	1	2	3	4	5	6	7	8	9	10	11	12 sub used
Colchester	Walker	Cook	Williams	Leslie	Smith L	Dowman	Garwood*	Gough	Froggatt	Bunkell	Packer	Dyer
Derby	*Boulton*	*Thomas*	*Daniel*	*Macken*	*McFarland*	*Todd*	*Powell*	*Newton*	*Hector*	*Hales**	*James*	*Bourne*

Backed by 700 fans and the BBC cameras, as in the first match. U's fall behind on the stroke of half-time to a mazy run by James. He slots in the rebound after his shot strikes the post. Leslie robs Colin Todd and feeds Gough. The striker's well-placed effort hits the bar and goes over.

League Table

		P		Home						Away					Pts
			W	D	L	F	A	W	D	L	F	A			
1	Cambridge	46	16	5	2	57	18	10	8	5	30	22			65
2	Exeter	46	17	5	1	40	13	8	7	8	30	33			62
3	COLCHESTER	46	19	2	2	51	14	6	7	10	26	29			59
4	Bradford C	46	16	7	0	51	18	6	6	10	27	33			59
5	Swansea	46	18	3	2	60	30	7	5	11	32	38			58
6	Barnsley	46	16	5	2	45	18	7	4	12	17	21			55
7	Watford	46	15	7	1	46	13	3	8	12	21	37			51
8	Doncaster	46	16	2	5	47	25	5	7	11	24	40			51
9	Huddersfield	46	15	5	3	36	15	4	7	12	24	34			50
10	Southend	46	11	9	3	35	19	4	10	9	17	26			49
11	Darlington	46	13	5	5	37	25	5	8	10	22	39			49
12	Crewe	46	16	6	1	36	15	3	5	15	11	45			49
13	Bournemouth	46	13	8	2	39	13	2	10	11	15	31			48
14	Stockport	46	10	10	3	29	19	4	9	11	24	38			45
15	Brentford	46	14	3	6	48	27	4	4	15	29	49			43
16	Torquay	46	12	5	6	33	22	5	4	14	26	45			43
17	Aldershot	46	10	8	5	29	19	6	3	14	20	40			43
18	Rochdale	46	8	7	8	32	25	5	5	13	18	34			38
19	Newport	46	11	4	8	33	21	4	3	16	9	37			38
20	Scunthorpe	46	11	6	6	32	24	2	5	16	17	49			37
21	Halifax	46	11	6	6	36	18	0	8	15	11	40			36
22	Hartlepool	46	8	9	6	30	20	2	0	7	17	53			32
23	Southport	46	3	12	8	17	28	0	7	16	16	49			25
24	Workington	46	3	7	13	23	42	1	4	18	18	60			19
		1104	302	148	102	922	501	102	148	302	501	922			1104

Odds & ends

Double wins: (6) Barnsley, Brentford, Halifax, Newport, Southport, Workington.

Double defeats: (1) Cambridge.

Won from behind: (5) Crewe (h), Brentford (a), Workington (a), Huddersfield (h) Southport (a).

Lost from in front: (2) Watford (a), Swansea (a).

High spots: Record number of points in a season.

Settled side: four of the squad played just 18 games between them.

Clinching promotion at first attempt.

Two manager-of-the-month awards for Bobby Roberts.

Holding First Division Derby to a draw in the FA Cup.

Twelve straight home league wins.

Steve Dowman and Lindsay Smith's incredible 19 goals from defence.

Low spots: Six consecutive draws as promotion nerves set in.

Loss of goalscoring form in second half of season.

Narrowly losing to Derby at the Baseball Ground.

Only two points from first seven away games

Player of the Year: Steve Dowman.

Ever presents: (1) Micky Cook.

Hat-tricks: (2) Colin Garwood (2).

Leading scorer: Colin Garwood (24).

Appearances and Goals

	Appearances						Goals			
	Lge	Sub	LC	Sub	FAC	Sub	Lge	LC	FAC	Tot
Allinson, Ian	31	9			2	1	7			7
Bright, Stewart	5									
Bunkell, Ray	16	2			3		2	1		3
Cook, Micky	46		3		6		3			3
Dominey, Barry	1	2								
Dowman, Steve	33	3	3		6		12			12
Dyer, Paul	29	5	3		4	2				
Ellis, Glen	2									
Foley, Steve	10									
Froggatt, John	43		3		6		6		2	8
Garwood, Colin	40	2	3		6		16	4	4	24
Gough, Bobby	43		3		6		17	1	1	19
Leslie, Steve	40	1	3		6		2	1		3
Packer, Mick	35	4	3	1	4	1	5		2	7
Smith, Lindsay	45		3		6		6		1	7
Walker, Mick	44		3		6					
Williams, John	43		3		6		1			1
(own-goals)										1
17 players used	506	28	33	2	66	4	77	7	10	94

LEAGUE DIVISION 3 — Manager: Bobby Roberts — SEASON 1977-78

No	Date	Match	1	2	3	4	5	6	7	8	9	10	11	12 sub used	Scorers, Times, and Referees	Att	Pos	Pt	F-A	H-T
1	20/8	A GILLINGHAM	Walker	Cook	Williams	Leslie	Packer	Dowman	Garwood	Gough	Froggatt	Foley	Allinson	Hughes	Foley 22, Packer 50, Gough 75 / Westwood 27 / Ref: K Salmon	3,450		W 2	3-1	1-1
		opponents	*Hillyard*	*Williams*	*Armstrong*	*Overton*	*Shipperley*	*Knight*	*Nicholl*	*Weatherley*	*Price**	*Westwood*	*Richardson*							
2	23/8	H BRADFORD C	Walker	Cook	Williams	Leslie	Packer	Dowman	Garwood	Gough	Froggatt	Bunkell	Allinson	Middleton	Froggatt 26, Gough 38, Leslie 77 / Ref: R Challis	4,371	8	W 4	3-0	2-0
		opponents	*Downsboro*	*Podd*	*Spark*	*Dolan*	*Nicholls*	*Fretwell*	*Martinez**	*Watson*	*Cooke*	*Wright*	*Hutchins*							
3	27/8	H CHESTER	Walker	Cook	Williams	Leslie	Dowman	Packer	Garwood	Gough	Froggatt	Bunkell	Allinson	Jones	Gough 81, 85 / Ref: A Gunn	4,169	10	W 6	2-0	0-0
		opponents	*Millington**	*Raynor*	*Walker*	*Delgado*	*Storton*	*Oakes*	*Mason*	*Edwards I*	*Kearney*	*Jeffries*	*Burns*							
4	2/9	A TRANMERE	Walker	Cook	Williams	Leslie	Packer	Dowman	Garwood	Gough	Froggatt	Bunkell	Allinson	James	Moore 82 / Ref: R Chadwick	3,263	2	L 6	0-1	0-0
		opponents	*Johnson*	*Mathias*	*Flood*	*Parry*	*Philpotts*	*Evans*	*Peplow**	*Palios*	*Moore*	*Tynan*	*Allen*							
5	9/9	H PLYMOUTH	Walker	Cook	Williams	Leslie*	Packer	Dowman	Garwood	Gough	Froggatt	Bunkell	Allinson	Dyer	Williams 48, Gough 73, Dowman 83 / Hall 58 / Ref: C Downey	5,719	14	W 8	3-1	0-0
		opponents	*Barton*	*Smart*	*Uzzell*	*Horswill*	*Foster*	*Craven*	*Johnson**	*Delve*	*Austin*	*Trusson*	*Hall*	*Peddelty*						
6	13/9	A PORTSMOUTH	Walker	Cook*	Williams	Foley	Dyer	Dowman	Garwood	Gough	Froggatt	Bunkell	Allinson	Wignall	Ref: M Sinclair	11,757	17	D 9	0-0	0-0
		opponents	*Middleton*	*Roberts*	*Wilson*	*Ellis*	*Foster*	*Cahill*	*Pollock*	*Kemp*	*Stokes*	*Green*	*Mellows*							
7	17/9	A ROTHERHAM	Walker	Dyer	Williams	Foley	Packer	Dowman	Garwood	Gough	Froggatt	Bunkell*	Allinson	Wignall	Womble 71 / Ref: N Glover	4,906	5	L 9	0-1	0-0
		opponents	*McAllister*	*Forrest*	*Breckin*	*Rhodes*	*Stancliffe*	*Spencer*	*Finney*	*Gwyther*	*Womble*	*Goodfellow*	*Crawford*							
8	24/9	H PRESTON	Walker	Cook	Williams	Leslie*	Packer	Dowman	Garwood	Gough	Froggatt	Foley	Allinson	Bruce	Ref: T Bune	4,978	19	D 10	0-0	0-0
		opponents	*Tunks*	*McMahon*	*Wilson*	*Doyle*	*Baxter*	*Cross*	*Coleman*	*Burns*	*Smith*	*Elwiss*	*Bruce*							
9	27/9	H PORT VALE	Walker	Cook	Williams	Dyer	Packer	Dowman	Garwood	Gough	Froggatt	Bunkell*	Allinson		Gough 17, Garwood 90 / Beech 10, Beamish 55, 85 / Ref: M Taylor	4,820	17	L 10	2-3	1-1
		opponents	*Dance*	*McGifford*	*Griffiths*	*Ridley*	*Harris*	*Bentley*	*Sutcliffe*	*Lamb*	*Beech*	*Beamish*	*Hemmerman*							
10	1/10	A CARLISLE	Walker	Cook	Wignall	Dyer	Packer	Dowman	Garwood	Gough	Froggatt	Bunkell	Allinson		Garwood 37, 85, Gough 83 / McVitie 86 / Ref: K Redfern	4,611	17	W 12	3-1	1-0
		opponents	*Swinburne*	*Hoolickin*	*McCartney*	*Carr*	*MacDonald*	*Parker*	*McVitie*	*Ludlam*	*Tait**	*Rafferty*	*Lathan*	*Martin*						
11	5/10	A CHESTERFIELD	Walker	Cook	Wignall	Dyer	Packer	Dowman	Garwood	Gough	Froggatt	Bunkell	Allinson		Ref: D Webb	4,575	8	D 13	0-0	0-0
		opponents	*Ogrizovic*	*Tartt*	*Burton*	*Kowalski*	*Cottam*	*O'Neill*	*Cammack*	*Fern*	*Green*	*Parker**	*Hepplolette*	*Dearden*						

1 — A GILLINGHAM: Returning to the ground where they had made their league bow exactly 27 years earlier, Colchester gained an emphatic away win, which last season took them until November to achieve. Gills' ex-QPR dangerman, Westwood, is kept at bay. Packer's ingenious free-kick seals the win.

2 — H BRADFORD C: Depleted Colchester, with twelve fit professionals, maintain their winning start. Four corners in the first ten minutes put the Yorkshiremen in their place. Downsborough in the City goal is kept busy. Froggatt rattles the crossbar on the hour as the U's go top of the third division table.

3 — H CHESTER: Superbly marshalled by player-manager Alan Oakes, Chester fall to a late opportunist strike where keeper Gren Millington is injured trying to prevent. Centre-half Delgado takes over and is beaten by a downward header which appears to stay out, but the goal is given by the linesman.

4 — A TRANMERE: In the battle of the top two, visitors Colchester play for a point but are undone by a late Ronnie Moore header. Despite winning, Rovers fail to knock the visitors off the top perch of the top two. Strikers Tynan (offside) and Moore (foul) both have goals disallowed.

5 — H PLYMOUTH: Williams scores only his third goal in over 400 appearances. It could have been different but for Walker's wonderful save from Terry Austin's powerful 38th-minute header. Manager Roberts declares he would have settled for a point with 20 minutes remaining, as Argyle step up a gear.

6 — A PORTSMOUTH: A bad-tempered affair. Cook is stretchered off on 40 minutes with a kick to the chest in a penalty-box brawl. Middleton's fine one-handed save from Froggatt on 11 minutes is the only chance. Colchester's wall – Gough, Garwood, Allinson – are booked for failing to retreat at a free-kick.

7 — A ROTHERHAM: Packer's over-hit backpass concedes an unnecessary corner. Only half cleared, Millers' captain, Jimmy Goodfellow's pin-point cross is nodded home past the stranded Walker. A three-match goal drought on their travels sees Colchester surrender top spot for the first time this campaign.

8 — H PRESTON: Furious North End feel they should have a penalty when Alex Bruce is unceremoniously bundled to the ground by Packer, but despite United's crippling injury situation, Colchester are denied victory when Burns, who had been booked, clears off the line during a late goalmouth melee.

9 — H PORT VALE: Vale have not scored on their last six visits, but become the first side to score three league goals at Layer Road since Chesterfield did likewise in February 1976. Packer contrives to have his re-taken penalty-kick saved both times by Trevor Dance in the 69th minute after Harris handled.

10 — A CARLISLE: Carlisle defenders Carr and Hoolickin give 20th-birthday boy Allinson a hard time, but the youngster replies in the best possible way in setting up all three goals for the visitors after Billy Rafferty struck the post for the Cumbrians early on. New signing Wignall, from Doncaster, shines.

11 — A CHESTERFIELD: The Spireites have failed to score in four consecutive home matches. The visitors, keen to keep up with the leading pack, don't offer any help to end the tedium with 23 backpasses in the first half. Sub Dearden hits the corner flag with his first shot and the foot of the post on 79 minutes.

No	Date	Venue	Opponent	Att	Pos	Res	Opp Pos	Pts	HT	FT
12	8/10	H	HEREFORD	4,586	3	D	15	14	0-0	0-0
13	14/10	H	OXFORD	4,893	3	D	9	15	1-0	1-1
14	22/10	A	CAMBRIDGE	5,423	10	L	12	15	0-2	0-2
15	28/10	H	PETERBOROUGH	4,827	6	W	5	17	2-0	3-0
16	5/11	A	WALSALL	4,231	8	L	10	17	0-1	2-4
17	11/11	H	SWINDON	4,788	7	W	14	19	1-0	2-0
18	19/11	A	WREXHAM	9,198	8	L	1	19	1-2	1-2
19	3/12	A	SHEFFIELD WED	9,000	7	W	24	21	1-0	2-1
20	9/12	H	EXETER	4,267	5	W	15	23	1-0	3-1
21	26/12	H	LINCOLN	5,840	7	D	22	24	1-0	1-1
22	27/12	A	BURY	5,409	8	D	10	25	0-0	1-1
23	31/12	A	SHREWSBURY	4,336	8	L	7	25	0-0	0-1

12 — HEREFORD (H) 8/10

Goals: none

Colchester: Walker, Cook, Williams, Leslie, Packer, Dowman, Garwood, Gough, Froggatt, Bunkell, Allinson
Hereford: Mellor, Emery, Ritchie, Layton, Marshall, Briley, Spring, Crompton*, Sinclair, Fear, Carter

Ref: C White

Despite 'winning' 21-5 on corners in a one-sided match, Colchester couldn't pierce a Hereford defence which has now only conceded one goal in their last five games. Old stager Peter Mellor excels, but is indebted to defender Ritchie who brilliantly clears Froggatt's header off the line

13 — OXFORD (H) 14/10

Goals: Foley S 29 / Foley P 51

Colchester: Walker, Cook, Williams, Leslie, Packer, Dowman, Garwood, Gough, Froggatt, Bunkell, Allinson — Dyer*
Oxford: Burton, Kingston, Fogg, Bodel, Clarke, Jeffrey, Berry, Taylor, Foley P, Curran, Duncan — Garwood

Ref: A Grey

A third draw in the last four dents U's promotion bid. Garwood is dropped in favour of Steve Foley who responds with the opener. Namesake Peter draws Oxford level and is desperately unlucky as his match-winning effort is deflected up onto the crossbar by Dowman to save a point.

14 — CAMBRIDGE (A) 22/10

Goals: Spriggs 43, 45

Colchester: Walker, Cook, Williams, Leslie!, Packer, Dowman, Garwood, Gough, Froggatt, Bunkell, Allinson*
Cambridge: Webster, Batson, Howard, Stringer*, Fallon, Smith, Watson, Spriggs, Morgan, Finney, Biley — Dyer, Murray

Ref: J Sewell

With only one win in the last nine, Colchester plummet down the table in this Anglia Television Match of the Week. Leslie is sent off for two bookable tackles on first, Watson, then Batson. Cambridge defend stoutly, with ex-Colchester defender, £12,000 Lindsay Smith, unbeatable.

15 — PETERBOROUGH (H) 28/10

Goals: Allinson 38, Packer 40, Gough 65

Colchester: Walker, Cook, Wignall, Leslie, Packer, Dowman, Garwood, Gough, Froggatt, Bunkell, Allinson
Peterborough: Barron, Hindley, Lee, Doyle, Turner, Ross, Slough, Butlin, Cliss, Carmichael, Robson

Ref: B Daniels

Midweek defeat at Leeds empowers Colchester. Barron in the Posh goal twice carries the ball out of his area. From the second, Packer crashes home a delightful free-kick. Wignall on his home debut sees a 60th-minute header acrobatically cleared off the line by Peterborough's Lee.

16 — WALSALL (A) 5/11

Goals: Allinson 51, Garwood 87 / Serella 17, Dennehy 55, Buckley 56, 80

Colchester: Walker, Cook, Wignall, Leslie, Packer, Dowman, Garwood, Gough, Froggatt, Bunkell, Allinson
Walsall: Kearns, Macken, Harrison, Serella, Shelton, Dennehy, Wood, Bates, King

Ref: C Thomas

The Saddlers spring the biggest defeat of the season so far on their Essex visitors. Boss Dave Mackay applauds his side's best display so far, despite being pegged back. Ex-Eire international Miah Dennehy sparks two goals in a minute with prolific scorer Alan Buckley adding a brace.

17 — SWINDON (H) 11/11

Goals: Garwood 35, Bunkell 60

Colchester: Walker, Cook, Wignall, Leslie, Packer, Dowman, Garwood, Gough, Froggatt, Bunkell, Allinson
Swindon: Allan, Ford*, Trollope, McLaughlin, Aizlewood, Prophett, Moss, Stroud, Kamara, McHale, Anderson — Guthrie

Ref: D Reeves

20-year-old Town keeper Jimmy Allan plays a blinder and saves his team from a hiding. Swindon haven't won away all season, although Garwood appears to handle on scoring and Bunkell's second is clearly wind assisted. The gale-force conditions spoil the match as a spectacle.

18 — WREXHAM (A) 19/11

Goals: Wignall 30 / Shinton 7, Whittle 9

Colchester: Walker, Cook, Wignall, Leslie, Packer, Dowman, Garwood, Gough, Froggatt, Bunkell, Allinson
Wrexham: Davies, Evans, Dwyer, Davis, Roberts, Thomas, Shinton, Sutton, McNeil, Whittle, Cartwright — Foley

Ref: G Owen

League leaders Wrexham maintain their momentum at the top in front of the BBC Match of the Day cameras. Commentator John Motson is highly complimentary of both sides' endeavours, in particular United's shackling of £60,000 target man Dixie McNeil. Wignall nets his first.

19 — SHEFFIELD WED (A) 3/12

Goals: Cook 26, Garwood 53 / Wylde 63

Colchester: Walker, Cook, Wignall, Leslie, Packer, Dowman, Garwood, Gough, Froggatt, Williams, Allinson
Sheffield Wed: Turner, Walden, Dowd, Cusack, Mullen, Wylde, Bradshaw, Tynan, Porterfield*, Hope, Prendergast

Ref: J Worrall

Walker saves Tynan's eighth-minute spot-kick after Leslie brings down Roger Wylde. Wednesday's boss, Jack Charlton, says Colchester are a tidy team but is annoyed that his defender Dave Cusack picks up his sixth booking of the season. Colchester earn the third win on their travels.

20 — EXETER (H) 9/12

Goals: Dowman 13, Gough 64, Garwood 66 / Holman 61

Colchester: Walker, Cook, Wignall, Leslie, Packer, Dowman, Garwood, Gough, Froggatt, Williams, Allinson
Exeter: Key, Templeman, Hore, Bowker, Roberts, Hatch*, Weeks, Kellow, Randell, Heale, Holman — Jennings

Ref: C Maskell

Unsettled Garwood notches his 100th career league goal. Grecians defender Peter Hatch is stretched off on the hour with a serious ankle injury, sparking a five-minute goal frenzy in which Randell strikes the bar. City draw level, before the U's seal the victory with a double strike.

21 — LINCOLN (H) 26/12

Goals: Froggatt 18 / Graham 69

Colchester: Walker, Cook, Wignall, Leslie, Packer, Dowman, Garwood, Gough, Froggatt, Williams, Allinson
Lincoln: Grotier, Hubbard, Neale, Leigh, Wigginton, Cooper, Fleming, Graham, Harford, Smith, Harding

Ref: B Hill

Lincoln, under the new leadership of Willy Bell, have in striker Mick Harford the most promising young striker in the division. Bottom of the league Lincoln look to have gifted the U's a Christmas present of a third win on the trot until Graham pops up with an unexpected leveller.

22 — BURY (A) 27/12

Goals: Foley 79 / Tucker 53

Colchester: Walker, Cook, Wignall, Leslie, Dyer, Dowman, Garwood*, Gough, Rowles, Bunkell, Allinson — Foley
Bury: Forrest, Hatton, Kennedy, Thomson, Tucker, Whitehead, Stanton, Suddick, Johnson, Robins, Wilson

Ref: R Bridges

Just 11 minutes remain and a home victory looks secured when Shakers' keeper John Forrest allows a tame backpass to bounce off his body into the path of sub Foley, who gleefully accepts the opportunity. Even then Wignall dramatically clears off the line on 85 mins from Johnson.

23 — SHREWSBURY (A) 31/12

Goals: Irvine 74

Colchester: Walker, Cook, Wignall, Leslie, Packer, Dowman, Garwood, Gough, Froggatt, Bunkell, Allinson
Shrewsbury: Wardle, Leonard, Griffin, Hornsby, Turner, Atkins, Irvine, Nixon, Lindsay, Bates, Loughnane

Ref: N Ashley

A sixth away defeat and the fourth time by a single goal. Ex-Shrews keeper Walker is cheekily caught off his line by the Scot, Sammy Irvine. Both Garwood and Peter Loughnane have goals ruled out for offside. In the dying moments Chic Bates thunders a header against the crossbar

No	Date		Scorers, Times, and Referees	Att	Pos	Pt	F-A	H-T	1	2	3	4	5	6	7	8	9	10	11	12 sub used
24	H 2/1	WALSALL	Gough 67 / Buckley 38 — Ref: T Cox	6,039	8 / 13	26	D 1-1	0-1	Walker	Cook	Wignall*	Leslie	Packer	Dowman	Foley	Gough	Rowles	Williams	Allinson	Garwood
									Kearns	*Macken*	*Caswell*	*Harrison*	*Serella*	*Shelton*	*Dennehy*	*Bates*	*Wood*	*Buckley*	*King*	*Cooke*
25	A 7/1	BRADFORD C	Gough 3, Dowman 13 / Wright 20 — Ref: P Richardson	3,266	7 / 21	28	W 2-1	2-1	Walker	Cook	Wignall	Leslie	Packer	Dowman	Garwood	Gough	Froggatt	Dyer	Allinson	Cooke
									Downsbro'	*Fretwell**	*Hardcastle*	*Dolan*	*Middleton*	*Ratcliffe*	*Watson*	*Martinez*	*Wright*	*Grimes*	*Hutchins*	
26	H 13/1	GILLINGHAM	Gough 39 / Walker 82 — Ref: A Turvey	6,447	7 / 3	29	D 1-1	1-0	Walker	Cook	Wignall*	Leslie	Packer	Dowman	Foley	Gough*	Froggatt	Allinson	Garwood	Dyer
									Hillyard	*Williams*	*Armstrong**	*Overton*	*Knight*	*Crabbe*	*Hunt*	*Weatherley*	*Hughes*	*Westwood*	*Richardson*	*Walker*
27	A 21/1	CHESTER	Rowles 28 / Crossley 45p, Edwards I 58 — Ref: D Richardson	2,855	8 / 11	29	L 1-2	1-1	Walker	Cook	Wignall*	Leslie	Packer	Dowman	Foley	Rowles	Froggatt	Allinson	Garwood*	Williams
									Lloyd	*Edwards N*	*Raynor*	*Delgado*	*Storton*	*Oakes*	*Crossley*	*Livermore*	*Edwards I*	*Jones*	*Phillips*	
28	H 27/1	TRANMERE	Ref: A Robinson	4,465	7 / 1	30	D 0-0	0-0	Walker	Cook	Wignall	Leslie	Packer	Dowman	Foley	Rowles	Froggatt	Allinson	Garwood*	Dyer
									Johnson	*Mathias*	*Flood*	*Parry*	*Philpotts*	*Evans*	*Cuff*	*Bramhall*	*Moore*	*Tynan*	*Allen*	
29	A 4/2	PLYMOUTH	Rowles 28 / Taylor 5 — Ref: W Gow	4,639	6 / 19	31	D 1-1	1-1	Walker	Cook	Wignall	Leslie	Packer	Dowman	Foley	Gough	Rowles	Allinson	Dyer	Horswill
									Baron	*Harrison*	*Uzzell*	*Bason**	*Banton*	*Foster*	*Taylor*	*Megson*	*Austin*	*Craven*	*Delve*	
30	H 25/2	CARLISLE	Carr 3(og), Dowman 7 / Rafferty 51, Lathan 89 — Ref: R Lewis	3,867	7 / 14	32	D 2-2	2-0	Walker	Cook	Wignall	Leslie	Packer	Dowman	Foley	Garwood	Rowles	Allinson	Dyer	Horswill
									Swinburne	*Collins*	*McCartney*	*Carr*	*Lathan*	*Parker*	*McVitie*	*Bonnyman*	*Tait*	*Rafferty*	*Hamilton*	
31	A 28/2	PRESTON	Bruce 60p, 75, 79p, 85p — Ref: P Willis	9,225	8 / 3	32	L 0-4	0-0	Walker	Cook	Wignall	Leslie	Packer	Dowman	Foley	Garwood	Rowles	Allinson*	Bunkell	Dyer
									Tunks	*Coleman*	*Cameron*	*Burns*	*Baxter*	*Cross*	*Doyle*	*Haselgrave*	*Thomson*	*Elwiss*	*Bruce*	
32	A 4/3	HEREFORD	Barton 44p — Ref: A McDonald	3,831	13 / 23	32	L 0-1	0-1	Walker	Cook	Wignall	Leslie	Packer	Dowman	Foley	Garwood	Rowles	Allinson	Dyer	Evans
									Mellor	*Emery*	*Burrows*	*Cornes*	*Layton*	*Sheedy*	*Stephens*	*Marshall*	*Davey*	*Crompton*	*Barton**	*Spiring*
33	H 7/3	PORTSMOUTH	Foley 17, Rowles 28, Taylor 55 (og), [Allinson 67] — Ref: B Daniels	3,570	12 / 24	34	W 4-0	2-0	Walker	Cook	Wignall	Leslie	Packer	Dowman	Foley	Gough	Rowles*	Allinson	Bunkell	Dyer
									Figgins	*Roberts*	*Taylor*	*Denyer**	*Piper N*	*Cahill*	*Piper S*	*Kemp*	*Pullar*	*Mellows*	*McCaffrey*	*Barnard*
34	A 11/3	OXFORD	Curran 47, 71, Jeffrey 86 — Ref: K Baker	4,060	11 / 16	34	L 0-3	0-0	Walker	Cook	Wignall	Leslie	Packer	Dowman	Foley S	Gough	Williams	Allinson	Dyer	McGrogan
									Burton	*Kingston*	*Fagg*	*Briggs*	*Bodel*	*Jeffrey*	*Seacole*	*Taylor*	*Foley P*	*Curran**	*Duncan*	

Match notes

24 — £25,000 Alan Buckley, one of the hottest properties outside the top two divisions, hits his thirteenth league goal. Recent £15,000 signing from Bournemouth, Eddie Rowles, makes his home debut, but Gough salvages a point with his fourteenth league and cup goal of the campaign.

25 — Bradford officials praise U's as the best team seen at Valley Parade so far this season. Gough shoots United ahead after 2 minutes 40 seconds from Dyer's centre, and Dowman heads a second from a Garwood corner. Bernie Wright pulls one back, but United are always in command.

26 — Promotion chasing rivals Gillingham and Colchester produce the third successive 1-1 draw at Layer Road. Debut-making substitute Pat Walker hits a stunning equaliser just 20 minutes after entering the fray. The Kent side's large following cannot spur their team on to a late victory.

27 — Rowles nets his first goal in Colchester colours, but Packer's rash injury-time challenge on Ian Edwards gives Paul Crossley a spot-kick equaliser. Welsh international Edwards bags the winner as Colchester's shot-shy forward line miss the injured 'G' men, Gough and Garwood.

28 — Top of the table Rovers have just one intention, and that is to hold on to a point at all costs. On a bog of a pitch which makes flowing play impossible. Colchester employ a rigid offside trap to stifle Moore and Tynan. The game peters out to a nervous stalemate, keeping Rovers top.

29 — In front of Home Park's lowest gathering since the War, Argyle take the lead with a blistering 30-yard free-kick from Brian Taylor. Ex-Chelsea player Brian Bason suffers a bad knock before Rowles stabs home his second for the club from close in. Froggatt joins Port Vale for £10,000.

30 — Transfer seeking Garwood gets the U's off to a great start when his 30-yarder is deflected off the shoulder of Peter Carr into his own net, but as the home side's fans began to leave content with a points double. up popped Wearsider John Lathan to score only his third goal of the season.

31 — Boss Roberts is left fuming by ref Willis's decision on 60 mins to award a spot-kick after a goalmouth scramble in which Bruce falls to the ground. The Scot picks himself up to score and then completes his hat-trick when Wignall hauls down Ricky Thomson before adding a fourth.

32 — Garwood joins Pompey for £25k, a record fee received by U's. The promotion bid suffers a second successive defeat on its travels. Hereford end a four month run of 15 league and cup home games when Packer scythes Kevin Sheedy. Skipper Frank Barton blasts home from the spot.

33 — Beleaguered, bottom-of-the-pile Pompey succumb to United's first home win since 9 December last year. Rowles breaks his ankle just seven minutes after scoring the second, which will keep him out for the rest of the season. Tony Taylor soars brilliantly to head past his own keeper.

34 — After Allinson skimmed the bar on 20 mins. former Scottish international Hugh Curran steals the show. putting the other U's in front and then stabbing home the rebound when Walker saves his penalty. harshly awarded against Dowman for hands. Garwood gets away. to Portsmouth.

No.		Date	Opponent	Att.	Pos.			Res.		HT	Scorers	Referee
35	A	14/3	PETERBOROUGH	4,468	8	34	11	L	0:1	0-0	Camp 83	Ref: R Perkin
36	H	17/3	CAMBRIDGE	5,260	2	36	10	W	2:1	1-0	Allinson 24, Wignall 80 / Streete 51	Ref: D Lloyd
37	H	25/3	BURY	3,661	11	38	9	W	1:0	0-0	Allinson 77	Ref: D Hutchinson
38	A	27/3	LINCOLN	4,709	14	39	8	D	0:0	0-0		Ref: P Reeves
39	H	1/4	SHREWSBURY	2,910	13	39	12	L	1:2	0-1	Leslie 54 / Loughnane 38, Biggins 52	Ref: D Reeves
40	H	4/4	CHESTERFIELD	3,303	12	41	10	W	2:0	0-0	Gough 60, Leslie 64	Ref: J Bent
41	A	8/4	SWINDON	4,596	8	42	12	D	0:0	0-0		Ref: C White
42	H	15/4	WREXHAM	5,385	7	43	11	D	1:1	1-1	Foley 12 / Thomas 13	Ref: T Spencer
43	A	22/4	EXETER	3,853	17	44	11	D	0:0	0-0		Ref: L Burden
44	A	24/4	PORT VALE	3,684	20	46	11	W	3:0	1-0	Allinson 37, Foley 54, 60	Ref: T Morris
45	H	29/4	SHEFFIELD WED	4,337	16	47	9	D	1:1	1-0	Dowman 3 / Rushbury 69	Ref: B Homewood
46	H	3/5	ROTHERHAM	2,554	20	48	8	D	0:0	0-0		Ref: H Robinson

Home Average 4,568 — Away 5,189

---

35 — PETERBOROUGH (A)
Colchester: Walker, Cook, Packer, Leslie, Wignall, Dowman, Foley, Gough, Evans, Bunkell, Allinson
Peterborough: *Waugh, Hindley, Hughes, Doyle, Turner, Ross, Slough, McEwan, Camp, Robson*, Anderson, Oakes*
Local lad and 18th-birthday debutant Evans shines against Boro centre-half Chris Turner, subject of a failed midweek £80,000 transfer bid from Wolverhampton. Only Hereford have scored fewer goals than Posh but part-timer Steve Camp's effort slips under Walker's grasp.

36 — CAMBRIDGE (H)
Colchester: Walker, Cook, Packer, Leslie, Wignall, Dowman, Foley, Gough, Evans, Bunkell, Allinson
Cambridge: *Webster, Howard, Smith, Stringer, Fallon, Watson, Buckley, Spriggs, Streete*, Finney !, Sweetzer, Cozens*
Fiery Irish international, Tom Finney is sent off for scything Leslie, who himself was sent off at the Abbey earlier. Finney has already been booked for dissent. The dismissal is just 60 seconds after Floyd Streete's equaliser. Wignall hits the bar and Dowman has his effort disallowed.

37 — BURY (H)
Colchester: Walker, Cook, Packer, Leslie, Wignall, Williams, Foley, Gough, Evans*, Bunkell, Allinson
Bury: *Forrest, Thomson, Kennedy, Hatton, Bailey, Wilson, Stanton, Suddick, Rowland, Robins, Darling*, Madden*
Bob Stokoe's Bury, like Colchester, have rather thrown their promotion aspirations by the wayside of late. Referee Hutchinson takes the teams off the field for seven second-half minutes during a freak monsoon-like rainstorm. Allinson's fifth goal of the season bags both the points.

38 — LINCOLN (A)
Colchester: Walker, Cook, Wignall, Leslie, Packer, Dowman, Foley, Gough, Evans, Bunkell, Allinson
Lincoln: *Grotier, Guest, Leigh, Neale, Wigginton, Cooper, Jones, Graham, Harford, Hubbard, Dyer, Hoult*
The home side give an early warning when Mick Harford sees his header cannon off the bar after just 30 seconds. Just as in the first half, the Imps strike early in the second but Clive Wigginton's headed 'goal' from Cooper's cross is ruled out for offside with 47 minutes on the clock.

39 — SHREWSBURY (H)
Colchester: Walker, Cook, Wignall, Leslie, Packer, Williams, Foley, Gough, Evans*, Bunkell, Allinson
Shrewsbury: *Mulhearn, King, Bowers, Turner, Keay, Hayes, Irvine, Maguire, Atkins, Biggins*, Loughnane, Griffin*
Part-time footballer and local schoolteacher Steve Biggins sets up the Shrews first goal for Peter Loughnane, and notches the second himself. Colchester manager Bobby Roberts stays in bed under the weather, and is given little to cheer when listening to the match on his bedside radio.

40 — CHESTERFIELD (H)
Colchester: Walker, Williams, Packer, Leslie, Packer, Dowman, Foley, Gough, Dyer, Allinson, Evans
Chesterfield: *Letheran, Tartt, Burton, Chamberlain, Cotton, Colbatch, Cammack, Fern, Simpson, Walker, Kowalski, Evans*
New skipper Gough, taking over from Cook, celebrates his new responsibility by notching his first goal for 14 matches. Chesterfield, who have only won once during the same 14-match period are lucky not to end up further adrift as Glan Letheran smothers Leslie's well-placed effort.

41 — SWINDON (A)
Colchester: Walker, Cook, Williams, Leslie, Packer, Dowman, Foley, Gough, Dyer, Allinson, Evans
Swindon: *Allan, McLaughlin, Ford, Trollope, Carter, Prophett, Moss, Kamara, Bates, McHale*, Wright, Cunningham, Stroud*
This mid-table clash is brought briefly to life when home keeper Allan almost throws the ball into his own net on 38 minutes. It takes until 88 minutes for the first strike, but Cunningham's effort for the Robins hits the bar. Steve Wright, son of ex-U's star Peter, makes his league bow.

42 — WREXHAM (H)
Colchester: Walker, Cook, Williams, Leslie, Wignall, Dowman, Packer, Gough, Dyer, Allinson, Evans
Wrexham: *Davies, Evans, Dwyer, Davis, Roberts, Thomas, Shinton, Sutton, Lyons*, Whittle, Cartwright, Hill*
Aspiring champions, Wrexham earn a deserved point to keep themselves on course. Wrexham, who have reached the quarter-finals of both cup competitions, have lost just once in the last eleven league games and man-of-the-match Mickey Thomas cancels U's lead in under 60 seconds.

43 — EXETER (A)
Colchester: Walker, Cook, Williams, Leslie, Packer, Dowman, Foley, Gough, Dyer, Allinson, Wignall
Exeter: *Key, Templeman, Hore, Delve, Giles, Bowker, Hodge, Kellow, Randell, Ingham, Holman*
City defender John Delve has the ball in the net in the first half, but referee Burden spots, as do the majority of the crowd, that he played the ball with his hand. For the 17th time this season the goal-shy Devon men fail to score and must fight on to retain their third division status.

44 — PORT VALE (A)
Colchester: Walker, Cook, Williams, Leslie, Wignall, Dowman, Dyer, Packer*, Gough, Allinson, Evans
Port Vale: *Connaughton, Beech, Griffiths*, Ridley, Hawkins, Bentley, Moore, Lamb, Froggatt, Beamish, Bailey, Sutcliffe*
Vale sink nearer the fourth division as Colchester avenge the early season defeat at Layer Road. Vale, who include ex-Colchester centre-forward, John Froggatt, play like they know their destiny. The visitors blood another of their promising youngsters, homegrown Russell Cotton.

45 — SHEFFIELD WED (H)
Colchester: Walker, Cotton*, Williams, Leslie, Wignall, Dowman, Dyer, Packer, Gough, Allinson, Evans
Sheffield Wed: *Turner, Walden, Grant, Rushbury, Dowd*, Smith, Nimmo, Porterfield, Owen, Leman, Hornsby, McKeown*
Cook misses his first game of the season because of flu. Wednesday's young talent, Chris Turner, saves Leslie's waist high spot-kick although he appears to move well before the kick is taken. Another of the Owls' young prodigies, Lindsay McKeown, just fails to snatch the winner.

46 — ROTHERHAM (H)
Colchester: Walker, Cook, Wignall, Leslie, Packer, Dowman, Foley, Gough, Williams, Allinson, Dyer
Rotherham: *McAllister, Pugh, Breckin, Forrest, Stancliffe*, Green, Finney, Phillips, Gwyther, Goodfellow, Crawford, Young*
Player of the year Leslie has the only chance, but visiting keeper Tom McAllister pushes his effort around the post. For the home side it ends the most successful season, albeit disappointing, for eighteen years. The Millers ensure themselves a place in the division for another season.

LEAGUE DIVISION 3 (CUP-TIES) Manager: Bobby Roberts SEASON 1977-78

League Cup

				1	2	3	4	5	6	7	8	9	10	11	12 sub used
1:1	A	ALDERSHOT	13/8	Walker	Cook	Williams	Leslie	Packer	Dowman	Garwood	Gough	Froggatt	Foley	Allinson	
				Johnson	*Howitt*	*Wooler*	*Dixon*	*Youlden*	*Jopling*	*Crosby*	*Hooper*	*Bell**	*Dungworth*	*McGregor*	*Needham*

D F-A 1-1 H-T 1-1 2,574 4: Scorers: Gough 15, Crosby 25. Ref: J Bent

Unsettled Walker pulls off a string of fine saves in the season's opener at the Recreation Ground. Garwood's arrowed shot spins off the post but eludes the onrushing Allinson. Despite this, Colchester are content to finish the game all square for next week's return leg at Layer Road.

				1	2	3	4	5	6	7	8	9	10	11	12 sub used
1:2	H	ALDERSHOT	16/8	Walker	Cook	Williams	Leslie	Packer	Dowman	Garwood	Gough	Froggatt	Foley	Allinson	
				Johnson	*Howitt**	*Wooler*	*Dixon*	*Youlden*	*Jopling*	*Crosby*	*Hooper*	*Needham*	*Dungworth*	*McGregor*	*Brodie*

W 4-1 2-1 3,360 4: Scorers: Howitt 35 (og), Dowman 41, Needham 11 [Froggatt 62, 69]. Ref: C Maskell
(Colchester won 5-2 on aggregate)

After the shock of fourth division Shots cancelling out the home side's away-goal advantage Howett's deflection of Garwood's shot opens the floodgates. Froggatt, who had scored just 8 goals in 52 appearances last term, bagged a brace in a match watched by Chelsea boss Ken Shellito.

				1	2	3	4	5	6	7	8	9	10	11	12 sub used
2	A	BLACKBURN	31/8	Walker	Cook	Williams	Leslie	Packer	Dowman	Garwood	Gough	Froggatt	Bunkell	Allinson	
				Bradshaw	*Curtis*	*Bailey*	*Metcalfe*	*Fazackerley*	*Hawkins*	*Brotherston*	*Hird*	*Lewis*	*Parkes*	*Wagstaffe**	*Waddington*

D 1-1 1-1 6,193 2:5 Scorers: Garwood 38, Metcalfe 8. Ref: G Flint

Ex-U's boss Jim Smith warned his second division outfit against complacency, but United's offside trap failed to prevent Wagstaffe's pass reaching Parkes, who flicked on to Metcalfe to put Rovers in front. Colchester fight back magnificently to earn a second bite at the cherry.

				1	2	3	4	5	6	7	8	9	10	11	12 sub used
2R	H	BLACKBURN	7/9	Walker	Cook	Williams	Leslie	Packer	Dowman	Garwood	Gough	Froggatt	Bunkell	Allinson	
				Bradshaw	*Curtis*	*Bailey*	*Metcalfe*	*Fazackerley*	*Hawkins*	*Brotherston*	*Svarc*	*Lewis**	*Parkes*	*Keeley*	*Hird*

W 4-0 1-0 5,843 2:5 Scorers: Gough 22, 76, Allinson 50, Garwood 83. Ref: B Homewood

Colchester storm through this second-round replay in the knowledge that a crack at first division Leeds awaits the winners. Rovers, who include Bobby Svarc in their line up, have a disastrous off night. England Under-21 custodian, Paul Bradshaw, is the busiest player on view.

				1	2	3	4	5	6	7	8	9	10	11	12 sub used
3	A	LEEDS	26/10	Walker	Cook	Williams	Bunkell	Packer	Dowman	Garwood	Gough	Froggatt	Dyer	Allinson	
				Harvey	*Cherry*	*Gray F*	*Lorimer*	*Parkinson*	*Madeley*	*Graham*	*Hankin*	*Jordan*	*Gray E*	*Harris*	*[Hankin 83]*

L 0-4 0-2 17,713 1:14 Scorers: Jordan 12, Graham 21, Lorimer 53. Ref: J Butcher

Leeds, with Paul Madeley and Peter Lorimer remaining from the side humiliated by the U's 'Grandads' Army' five and a half years ago, are too strong for Colchester. Wingers Harris and Graham destroy the U's, who cannot contend with Scottish international Jordan's aerial power.

FA Cup

				1	2	3	4	5	6	7	8	9	10	11	12 sub used
1	H	BOURNEMOUTH	26/11	Walker	Cook	Wignall	Leslie	Packer	Dowman	Garwood	Gough	Froggatt	Bunkell	Allinson	
				Baker	*Butler*	*Miller*	*Cunningham*	*Impey*	*Cave*	*Johnson*	*Showers*	*Howarth*	*Lennard*	*Barton**	*Riley*

D 1-1 0-1 4,465 4:16 Scorers: Gough 83, Howarth 29. Ref: C White

Old stager Jack Howarth shoots the Cherries into the lead, only for colleague Geoff Butler to handle Dowman's header on the line. Butler is booked for his misdemeanour, but Bunkell's 39th-minute spot-kick is brilliantly saved by Kieron Baker. Gough earns a Dean Court replay.

				1	2	3	4	5	6	7	8	9	10	11	12 sub used
1R	A	BOURNEMOUTH	29/11	Walker	Cook	Wignall	Leslie	Packer	Dowman	Garwood	Gough	Froggatt	Williams	Allinson	
				Baker	*Butler*	*Miller*	*Cunningham*	*Impey*	*Cave*	*Johnson*	*Showers*	*Howarth*	*Lennard*	*Riley*	

D 0-0 0-0 3,838 4:16 aet Ref: C White

After 210 minutes of this tie and the deadlock still to be broken, the clubs argue on a venue for a second replay. Bournemouth are happy with the toss of a coin, but U's disagree. The Football Association decide on a neutral venue with Watford awaiting a visit from the eventual victors.

				1	2	3	4	5	6	7	8	9	10	11	12 sub used
1 RR	N	BOURNEMOUTH	5/12	Walker	Cook	Wignall	Leslie	Packer	Dowman	Garwood	Gough	Froggatt	Williams	Allinson	
	(at Watford)			*Baker*	*Butler*	*Miller*	*Cunningham*	*Impey*	*Cave*	*Johnson*	*Showers*	*Howarth*	*Lennard**	*Barton*	*Paterson*

W 4-1 3-1 2,230 4:14 Scorers: Dowman 26, Garwood 32, 39, 89, Barton 8. Ref: R Challis

Ironically, the FA arrange for the second replay to be played at Vicarage Road. A sparse Monday night crowd witness a scintillating hat-trick from Colin Garwood. Despite falling behind, three goals in 13 minutes seals Colchester's visit back to Hertfordshire in twelve days time.

				1	2	3	4	5	6	7	8	9	10	11	12 sub used
2	A	WATFORD	17/12	Walker	Cook	Wignall	Leslie*	Foley	Dowman	Garwood	Gough	Froggatt	Williams	Allinson	Dyer
				Rankin	*Geidmintis*	*Pritchett*	*Booth*	*Bolton*	*Garner*	*Downes*	*Mercer**	*Jenkins*	*Joslyn*	*Pollard*	*Mayes*

L 0-2 0-1 11,907 4:1 Scorers: Jenkins 31, Mercer 59. Ref: T Bune

This bad-tempered tie boils over when Roger Joslyn, formerly with the visitors, hacks down Leslie under the nose of the official in charge. Joslyn escapes punishment. The Hornets win through to draw West Ham at Upton Park. Leslie ends up in hospital for precautionary X-rays, Joslyn being back to draw West Ham at Upton Park.

		P	Home					Away					Pts	Odds & ends
			W	D	L	F	A	W	D	L	F	A		
1	Wrexham	46	14	8	1	48	19	9	7	7	30	26	61	Double wins: (1) Bradford.
2	Cambridge	46	19	3	1	49	11	4	9	10	23	40	58	Double defeats: (1) Shrewsbury.
3	Preston	46	16	5	2	48	19	4	11	8	15	19	56	
4	Peterborough	46	15	7	1	32	11	5	9	9	15	22	56	Won from behind: (0).
5	Chester	46	14	8	1	41	24	6	9	8	18	32	54	Lost from in front: (1) Chester (a).
6	Walsall	46	12	8	3	35	17	6	9	8	26	33	53	
7	Gillingham	46	11	10	2	36	21	4	10	9	31	39	50	High spots: Thumping second division Blackburn in the League Cup.
8	COLCHESTER	46	10	11	2	36	16	5	7	11	19	28	48	Topping the table for the first six matches.
9	Chesterfield	46	14	6	3	40	16	3	8	12	18	33	48	Only two home defeats.
10	Swindon	46	12	7	4	40	22	4	9	10	27	38	48	First Colchester league match featured on Match of the Day.
11	Shrewsbury	46	11	7	5	42	23	5	8	10	21	34	47	
12	Tranmere	46	13	7	3	39	19	3	8	12	18	33	47	Low spots: eleven home draws.
13	Carlisle	46	10	9	4	32	26	4	10	9	27	33	47	Only one win in nine after leading table.
14	Sheffield Wed	46	13	7	3	34	22	2	6	11	22	38	46	Only one win in ten from the end of January.
15	Bury	46	7	13	3	34	22	6	6	11	28	34	45	Froggatt's replacement, Rowles, season-ending, broken ankle.
16	Lincoln	46	10	8	5	35	26	5	7	11	18	35	45	
17	Exeter	46	11	8	4	30	18	4	6	13	19	41	44	
18	Oxford	46	11	10	2	38	21	2	4	17	26	46	40	
19	Plymouth	46	7	8	8	33	28	4	9	10	28	40	39	
20	Rotherham	46	11	5	7	26	19	2	8	13	25	49	39	
21	Port Vale	46	7	11	5	28	23	1	9	13	18	44	36	Player of the Year: Steve Leslie.
22	Bradford C	46	11	6	6	40	29	1	4	18	16	57	34	Ever Presents: (1) Mike Walker.
23	Hereford	46	9	9	5	28	22	0	5	18	6	38	32	Hat-tricks: (1) Colin Garwood.
24	Portsmouth	46	4	11	8	31	38	3	6	14	10	37	31	Leading Scorer: Bobby Gough 17.
		1104	272	192	88	869	504	88	192	272	504	869	1104	

	Appearances						Goals			Tot
	Lge	Sub	LC	Sub	FAC	Sub	Lge	LC	FAC	
Allinson, Ian	45		5		4		6	1		7
Bunkell, Ray	22		3		1		1			1
Cook, Micky	44		5		4		1			1
Cotton, Russell	1	1								
Dowman, Steve	43		5		4		5	1	1	7
Dyer, Paul	21	9	1			1				
Evans, Tony	5	2								
Foley, Steve	29	3	2				7			7
Froggatt, John	25		5		4		2	2		4
Garwood, Colin	28	2	5		4		7	2	3	12
Gough, Bobby	42		5		4		13	3	1	17
Leslie, Steve	41		4		4		3			3
Packer, Mick	44		5		4		2			2
Rowles, Eddie	9						3			3
Walker, Mick	46		5		4					
Wignall, Steve	32	2			4		2			2
Williams, John	28	1	5		3		1			1
Wright, Steve	1									
(own-goals)							2	1		3
18 players used	506	20	55		44	1	55	10	5	70

LEAGUE DIVISION 3

SEASON 1978-79

Manager: Bobby Roberts

No	V	Date	Team	Att	Pos	Pt	F-A	H-T	1	2	3	4	5	6	7	8	9	10	11	12 sub used
1	H	19/8	SWANSEA	2,918	—	D 1	2-2	1-0	Walker	Cook	Packer	Leslie	Wignall	Dowman	Foley	Gough	Sharkey	Rowles	Allinson	Dyer
									Crudgington	*Evans*	*Bartley*	*Toshack*	*Bruton*	*Reeves*	*Lally*	*James R*	*Curtis*	*Waddle*	*Moore*	*Smith N*
2	A	21/8	BRENTFORD	6,800	—	L 1	0-1	0-1	Walker	Cook	Packer	Leslie	Wignall	Dowman	Foley	Gough	Sharkey*	Rowles	Allinson	Dyer
									*Porter**	*Tucker*	*Allen*	*Shrubb*	*Kruse*	*Graham W*	*Carlton*	*Graham J*	*Alder*	*McCulloch*	*Phillips*	*Smith N*
3	H	26/8	SHEFFIELD WED	10,685	16 / 20	D 2	0-0	0-0	Walker	Cook	Packer	Leslie*	Wignall	Dowman	Foley	Gough	Dyer	Rowles	Allinson	Wright
									Bolder	*Blackhall*	*Grant*	*Rushbury*	*Dowd*	*Smith*	*Mullen*	*Johnson*	*Tynan*	*Portefield**	*Owen*	*Leman*
4	H	2/9	ROTHERHAM	2,448	15 / 10	D 3	0-0	0-0	Walker	Cook	Packer	Wright	Wignall	Dowman	Foley	Gough	Dyer	Rowles	Allinson	
									McAllister	*Forrest*	*Breckin*	*Rhodes*	*Green*	*Flynn*	*Finney*	*Phillips*	*Gwyther*	*Crawford*	*Smith*	
5	A	8/9	CARLISLE	4,430	21 / 7	L 3	0-4	0-4	Walker [Tait 44]	Cook	Packer	Wright*	Wignall	Dowman	Foley	Gough	Evans	Rowles	Allinson	Sharkey
									Swinburne	*Hoolickin*	*McCartney*	*MacDonald*	*Tait*	*Parker*	*McVitie*	*Bonnyman*	*Kemp*	*Lumby*	*Hamilton*	
6	H	12/9	CHESTER	2,311	18 / 9	W 5	2-1	0-0	Walker	Cook	Packer	Wright*	Wignall	Dowman	Foley	Gough	Dyer	Rowles	Allinson	Sharkey
									Lloyd	*Raynor*	*Walker*	*Storton*	*Jeffries*	*Oakes*	*Delgado*	*Livermore*	*Edwards*	*Mellor*	*Phillips*	
7	A	15/9	SHREWSBURY	2,788	15 / 5	W 7	1-0	0-0	Walker	Cook	Packer	Sharkey	Wignall	Dowman	Foley	Gough	Dyer	Rowles	Allinson	
									Mulhearn	*King*	*Leonard**	*Turner*	*Griffin*	*Hayes*	*Chapman!*	*Atkins*	*Lindsay*	*Biggins*	*Maguire*	*Cross*
8	A	23/9	WALSALL	4,052	15 / 20	D 8	2-2	0-2	Walker	Cook	Packer	Sharkey	Wignall	Dowman	Foley	Gough	Dyer	Rowles	Allinson	
									O'Keefe	*Macken*	*Caswell*	*Harrison*	*Serella*	*King*	*Birch*	*McDonough*	*Austin*	*Buckley*	*Kelly*	
9	H	27/9	EXETER	3,421	17 / 16	L 8	1-2	1-1	Walker	Cook	Packer	Sharkey	Wignall	Dowman	Foley*	Gough	Dyer	Hodge	Allinson	Rowles
									Templeman	*Hore*	*Randell*	*Giles*	*Roberts L*		*Holman*	*Kellow*	*Bowker*	*Delve*	*Hatch*	
10	A	30/9	BLACKPOOL	3,007	14 / 10	W 10	3-1	0-0	Walker	Cook	Packer	Hodge	Wignall	Dowman	Evans	Gough	Dyer	Rowles	Allinson	
									Hesford	*Gardner*	*Pashley*	*McEwan*	*Suddaby*	*Thompson*	*Ranson*	*Chandler*	*Spence*	*Bissell**	*Hockaday*	*Sermanni*
11	H	6/10	SWINDON	3,324	11 / 16	W 12	3-2	0-2	Walker	Cook	Packer	Hodge	Wignall	Bunkell	Evans	Gough	Dyer	Rowles	Allinson	
									Ogden	*Trollope*	*Ford*	*McHale*	*Lewis*	*Stroud*	*Gilchrist*	*Carter*	*Rowland**	*Bates*	*Kamara*	*Aizlewood*

Scorers, Times, and Referees

1. Foley 28, Rowles 75 — *James R 55, 61* — Ref: R Challis
2. *Kruse 15* — Ref: T Spencer
3. Ref: D Owen
4. Ref: B Homewood
5. *McCartney 5p, Bonnym'n 12, Hamilton 32* — Ref: R Chadwick
6. Gough 63, Cook 85 — *Phillips 62* — Ref: A Grey
7. Foley 67 — Ref: T Cox
8. Gough 51, Foley 53 — *King 22, Buckley 73* — Ref: E Read
9. Gough 24 — *Kellow 5p, Bowker 75* — Ref: L Burden
10. Rowles 48, Gough 78, 89 — *Hockaday 87* — Ref: K Salmon
11. Rowles 53, Evans 77, Gough 89 — *Gilchrist 14, Bates 43* — Ref: C Maskell

Match notes

1. A glorious sunny day. Swansea, back in Division Three after an absence of five years, sport yellow jerseys with a red and blue sash. Foley hits the post on seven minutes, before opening the scoring. Robbie James bags a brace, but the industrious Leslie sets up Rowles for the equaliser.
2. Brentford's boss, Bill Dodgin, is sent off on 40 minutes after racing 50 yards to protest at Wignall's tackle on Dave Carlton. Teenage keeper, Porter, is stretchered off with a broken leg. Paul Shrubb takes over between the sticks. England manager, Ron Greenwood, watches the game.
3. Wednesday have new signing, Ray Blackhall, at right-back. A dour game sees unfortunate Leslie stretchered off on 65 minutes with a broken leg. A midweek £15,000 bid for Sammy Morgan of Cambridge fails. Out-of-form Pat Sharkey is dropped 'to sort out his personal problems'.
4. The U's fail to score against the Millers for the seventh consecutive meeting. Rotherham, League Cup conquerors of Arsenal, are rocked on 33 minutes, when Allinson rattles the crossbar. Packer finds Foley on 83 minutes, but the latter's effort cannons back off the underside of the bar.
5. The Cumbrians get a great start with a handball decision. Mick Tait's 25-yarder on the stroke of half-time sets the U's up for a half-time ear-bashing. Young Tony Evans clips the bar late on.
6. The U's finally get their first win of the season. Falling behind to Ron Phillips, the response is immediate. Gough nets his first of the campaign. Five minutes from time, Rowles helps on Dyer's chip and Cook hooks home. Drama in the last minute when Walker saves Mellor's spot-kick.
7. Foley secures United's second win in four days, heading in Dyer's right-wing curling cross. Young Paul Maguire gives Cook a torrid time. His 31st-minute cross is headed in by Biggins, who is clearly offside. Sammy Chapman is dismissed on 82 minutes for aiming a kick at Allinson.
8. Saddlers keeper, Mick Kearns, has a nightmare. Twice he sticks to his line and is beaten by well-placed U's headers. Alan Birch has an effort ruled out for offside. Prolific striker Alan Buckley saves the Midlanders a point. Big Roy McDonough has a hand in both the home goals.
9. Kellow gives Exeter an early lead, picking himself up after Dowman brings him down in the box. Colchester introduce new signing, Bobby Hodge. Midfielder Hodge was ironically signed from the Devonians last week for a record fee of £15,000 and has a quiet, but confident, start.
10. The Seasiders are making their first visit to Layer Road. Keeper Iain Hesford pulls off a string of fine saves. Home-debutant, Hodge, denies the visitors a 74th-minute equaliser, clearing Derek Spence's header off the line. The highest gate of the season is really nothing to boast about.
11. The U's turn around a two-goal half-time deficit in a real Roy-of-the-Rovers showing. It is the fourth home win on the trot. In the last minute, Gough gleefully slams home to the joy of the ecstatic home fans. Evans's neat chip finds Allinson. Allinson sends in a pin-point cross, which Gough...

12 | A | LINCOLN | 13/10 | 3,541 | 9 | D | 24 | 13 | 0-0 | 0-0

Walker · Cook · Packer · Hodge · Dowman · Evans · Wignall · Dyer · Gough · Wright · Allinson
Turner · Guest · Leigh · Cockerill · Wigginton · Cooper · McCalling · Sunley · Tynan · Watson · Harding · Hobson*

Ref: P Scott

The basement-club, Lincoln, parade new £33,000 signing, Tommy Tynan, ex-Sheffield Wednesday, is well shackled by Wignall. In the 35th minute, when Dyer's shot comes back off the underside of the bar, Gough's attempt at the rebound is cleared off the line by Dennis Leigh.

---

13 | A | CHESTERFIELD | 18/10 | 4,394 | 12 | L | 7 | 13 | 1-2 | 0-0
Burton 48, Walker 68

Walker · Cook · Packer* · Hodge · Wright · Evans · Wignall · Dyer · Gough · Bunkell · Allinson
Lethran · Flavell · Burton · Hunter · Cattam · Prophett · Tartt · Kowalski · Fern · Salmons · Walker · Cammack*

Ref: B Hill

Roberts' ex-Leicester team-mate Rod Fern turns defence into attack, hitting the bar, only for Kenny Burton to stab in his first of the season from the rebound. Dyer levels via a neat one-two with Gough, but Fern sets up Phil Walker to breeze past Packer and slot past his namesake, Mick.

---

14 | H | SOUTHEND | 20/10 | 5,881 | 14 | D | 15 | 14 | 1-1 | 0-1
Evans 70, Laverick 41

Walker · Cook · Packer · Hodge · Rowles · Evans · Wignall · Dyer · Gough · Wright · Allinson
Cawston · Stead · Yates · Laverick · Cusack · Moody · Green · Pountney · Polycarpou · Dudley · Fell · Hadley · Bunkell*

Ref: A Glasson

Recent £50,000 capture, Dave Cusack, makes a glaring error to allow youngster Tony Evans the chance to preserve Colchester's unbeaten home record. Walker parries Mickey Laverick's first effort, but the Shrimpers striker is quickest to react to give the visitors a first-half lead.

---

15 | A | MANSFIELD | 28/10 | 4,515 | 13 | D | 21 | 15 | 1-1 | 0-0
Wignall 48, Moss 82

Walker · Cook · Packer · Hodge · Dowman · Evans · Wignall · Dyer · Gough · Bunkell · Allinson
Arnold · McClelland · Bird · Goodwin · Foster B · Miller · Saxby · Moss · Syrett · Martin · Phillips · Allen*

Ref: R Perkin

The Stags call on all of manager Billy Bingham's Irish luck to grab a fortunate point. Walker rolls over to Packer, who is unaware of his keeper's intentions. Packer's hurried clearance strikes Ernie Moss on his backside and flies into the net. Earlier, Wignall headed home Hodge's corner.

---

16 | H | PLYMOUTH | 3/11 | 4,564 | 10 | W | 13 | 17 | 2-1 | 0-1
Bunkell 75, Gough 90, Binney 45

Walker · Cook · Packer* · Hodge · Wignall · Foley · Wignall · Bunkell · Gough · Lee · Dyer
Hodge · Hodges · Rogers · Silkman · Foster · Fear · Smith · Megson · Perrin · Binney · Johnson · Trusson*

Ref: J Martin

Trevor Lee (£15,000 from Millwall) makes his U's bow, but it is old-stager Fred Binney who puts Malcolm Allison's side in front. New-boy Lee plays a wall-pass with Bunkell, who beats Martin Hodge from eight yards. In the closing seconds Gough nets from an Allinson flag-kick.

---

17 | A | ROTHERHAM | 11/11 | 3,777 | 14 | L | 10 | 17 | 0-1 | 0-1
Finney 40

Walker · Cook · Packer! · Hodge · Dowman · Foley · Wignall · Dyer* · Gough · Lee · Allinson
McAllister · Forrest · Breckin · Gwyther · Flynn · Finney · Green · Wynn · Phillips · Smith · Crawford · Wright · Dawson!

Ref: E Morrisey

A defensive foul-up by Walker and Packer paves the way for Richard Finney to lob in and earn Rotherham's second away win, after 30 failed attempts. Packer and Richard Dawson are sent off in the tunnel for a scuffle. Dawson and Wignall had earlier been booked for an off-the-ball.

---

18 | H | SHEFFIELD WED | 18/11 | 4,346 | 12 | W | 13 | 19 | 1-0 | 0-0
Wignall 83

Walker · Cook · Packer · Hodge · Dowman · Foley · Wignall · Bunkell · Gough · Lee · Allinson
Turner · Blackhall · Rushbury · Pickering · Mullen · Wylde · Smith · Porterfield · Leman · Owen · Hornsby · Lowey*

Ref: A Gunn

Owls welcome back skipper Jimmy Mullen after an eight-game absence, and include former Sunderland FA Cup-winning hero Ian Porterfield. Allinson is sent crashing by Mike Pickering. From the resulting free-kick, Gough crosses for Wignall, on his 50th league appearance, to score.

---

19 | H | BURY | 9/12 | 2,732 | 11 | D | 21 | 20 | 0-0 | 0-0

Walker · Cook · Packer · Hodge · Dowman · Foley · Wignall · Bunkell* · Gough · Evans · Allinson
Forrest · Ritson · Kennedy · Lugg · Tucker · Bailey · Stanton · Wilson · Beamish · Gregory · Taylor · Dyer

Ref: D Reeves

U's are unbeaten for a club record (Third Div) ten home games. After last week's postponement at Tranmere, those U's fans who chose to go Christmas shopping will have gained more entertainment from traipsing up and down the High Street. Packer is fined £25 for his sending off.

---

20 | A | WATFORD | 23/12 | 5,424 | 12 | L | 1 | 20 | 0-1 | 0-1
Jenkins 43

Walker · Cook · Packer · Hodge · Wright · Rowles · Wright · Dyer · Gough · Lee · Allinson
Sherwood · Strik · Harrison · Booth · Sims · Garner · Joslyn · Mercer · Jenkins · Train · Downes

Ref: A Grey

U's dish out presents to the crowd before kick-off, but Hornets' chairman Elton John goes one better, smashing the Third Div transfer record in signing Leicester's Steve Sims (£200k, four times the cost of U's squad). Ross Jenkins, the league's top scorer, notches his 24th for the leaders.

---

21 | A | OXFORD | 26/12 | 4,892 | 14 | L | 15 | 20 | 0-2 | 0-0
Foley P 75, Graydon 80p

Walker · Cook · Packer · Hodge · Wignall · Foley · Wignall · Bunkell · Gough · Wright · Allinson
Burton · Taylor · Fogg · Briggs · Bodel · Jeffrey · Graydon · Duncan · Jeffries · Seacole · Hodgson · Rowles

Ref: T Bune

Worryingly, U's are three points off the relegation zone, after failing to win away again. On the other hand they are four points off sixth place. Five minutes after Peter Foley had fired Oxford in front, Packer fouls Jason Seacole in the box and is booked for the second time in four days.

---

22 | A | CHESTER | 17/1 | 2,339 | 14 | D | 8 | 21 | 2-2 | 1-1
Foley 32, 65, Henderson 24, Phillips 75

Walker · Cook · Wright · Hodge · Wignall · Foley · Wignall · Bunkell · Gough · Dyer · Allinson
Lloyd · Nickeas · Walker · Storton · Jeffries · Phillips · Sutcliffe · Livermore · Edwards · Felix · Henderson

Ref: K Butcher

A vital away point is gained, but U's think they have done enough, only to be undone late on when winger Ronnie Phillips wins a point for Seals. Peter Henderson had opened via a flick by Welsh International Ian Edwards, but a Foley brace so nearly brings a United away victory.

---

23 | A | SHREWSBURY | 19/1 | 2,119 | 16 | L | 2 | 21 | 0-2 | 0-1
Biggins 22, Chapman 59

Walker · Cook · Packer* · Hodge · Wignall · Foley · Wignall · Dyer · Gough · Wright · Allinson
Wardle · King · Larkin · Turner · Griffin · Chapman · Keay · Atkins · Tong · Biggins · Maguire · Bunkell

Ref: D Shaw

Experienced Sammy Chapman exposes U's, as high-flying Shrews keep the pressure on Watford at the top. Chapman flicks on Paul Maguire's corner to Steve Biggins, and then nods in from the same source. By the time the 80-minute snow blizzard ends, U's have already lost their way.

LEAGUE DIVISION 3

Manager: Bobby Roberts

SEASON 1978-79

No	Date	V	Opponent	Att	Pos	Res	Pt	F-A	H-T	Scorers, Times, and Referees	1	2	3	4	5	6	7	8	9	10	11	12 sub used
24	2/2	H	EXETER	2,767	16	D	22	2-2	1-0	Roberts 1,39 (og), Allinson 50p; Neville 64, 65; Ref: B Hill	Walker	Cook	Wright	Hodge	Wignall	Dowman	Foley	Gough	Dyer	Lee*	Allinson	Packer
											O'Keefe	*Templeman*	*Hore*	*Randell*	*Giles*	*Roberts L*	*Neville*	*Pearson*	*Main*	*Delve*	*Hatch*	
25	10/2	A	BLACKPOOL	3,446	18	L	22	1-2	0-1	Allinson 54; Spence 21, 86; Ref: D Owen	Walker	Cook	Wright	Hodge	Wignall	Dowman	Packer	Bunkell	Dyer	Lee	Allinson	Jones
											Hesford	*Malone*	*Pashley*	*Wilson*	*Suddaby*	*McEwan*	*Kellow*	*Ronson*	*Spence*	*Davidson*	*Wagstaffe**	
26	23/2	H	LINCOLN	2,861	16	W	24	2-0	0-0	Lee 60, Hodge 80; Ref: C Downey	Walker	Cook	Wright	Hodge	Wignall	Dowman	Packer	Foley	Dyer	Lee	Allinson	Jones
											Gratier	*Hubbard*	*Leigh*	*Harding*	*Wigginton*	*Smith*	*Guest**	*Ward*	*Harford*	*Cockerill*	*Hobson*	
27	27/2	H	WALSALL	3,135	15	W	26	2-0	1-0	Hodge 15, Wignall 74; Ref: T Cox	Walker	Cook	Wright	Hodge	Wignall	Dowman	Packer	Foley	Dyer	Lee	Allinson	King
											Turner	*Harrison*	*Caswell*	*Jones*	*Serella*	*Stragia*	*Birch*	*Waddington S Austin**	*McDonough*	*Macken*		
28	2/3	A	SOUTHEND	6,957	12	D	27	1-1	0-0	Lee 75; Parker 63; Ref: A Gunn	Walker	Cook	Wright	Hodge	Wignall	Dowman	Packer	Foley	Dyer	Lee	Allinson	Laverick
											Cawston	*Moody*	*Yates*	*Stead*	*Hadley*	*Cusack*	*Morris*	*Pountney*	*Parker*	*Dudley*		
29	9/3	H	MANSFIELD	2,866	14	W	29	1-0	1-0	Gough 18; Ref: M Sinclair	Walker	Cook	Wright	Hodge	Wignall	Gough	Packer	Foley	Dyer	Lee	Allinson	Allen
											New	*Dawkins*	*Foster B*	*Curtis*	*Saxby*	*Bird*	*Hamilton*	*Carter*	*McClelland*	*Martin*	*Miller**	
30	13/3	A	HULL	4,201	15	L	29	0-1	0-0	Stewart 87; Ref: P Partridge	Walker	Cook	Wright	Hodge	Wignall	Dowman	Packer	Foley	Dyer	Lee	Allinson	Dowman
											Blackburn	*Nisbet*	*Skipper*	*Hawker*	*Croft*	*Haigh*	*Roberts*	*Horswill*	*Edwards*	*Bannister*	*Stewart*	
31	17/3	A	PLYMOUTH	5,342	14	D	30	1-1	1-0	Dyer 2; Binney 82; Ref: E Hughes	Walker	Cook	Wright	Hodge	Wignall	Gough	Packer	Foley	Dyer	Lee	Allinson	Fear
											Hodge	*McNeill*	*Uzzell*	*James*	*Clarke*	*Johnson*	*Megson*	*Harrison**	*Binney*	*Trusson*	*Rogers*	
32	20/3	A	SWINDON	6,678	11	W	32	2-1	0-0	Lee 63, 77; Rowland 57; Ref: A Hamill	Walker	Cook	Wright	Hodge	Dowman	Gough	Packer	Foley	Dyer	Lee	Allinson	Bates
											Allan	*Mayes*	*Ford*	*McHale*	*Aizlewood*	*Stroud*	*Miller**	*Carter*	*Rowland*	*Dornan*	*Williams*	
33	24/3	H	BRENTFORD	3,528	11	D	33	1-1	0-0	Hodge 73p; Shrubb 66; Ref: J Bray	Walker	Cook	Wright	Hodge	Dowman	Gough	Packer	Foley	Dyer	Lee	Allinson	Allder
											Bond	*Salman*	*Tucker*	*McNichol*	*Kruse*	*Graham J*	*Carlton*	*Shrubb*	*Glover*	*Smith D*	*Phillips**	
34	27/3	A	SWANSEA	11,645	11	L	33	1-4	0-1	Lee 90; Waddle 8, 48, James R 83, Attley 90; Ref: W Brombroff	Walker	Cook	Packer	Wright	Dowman	Foley	Dyer	Allinson	Gough	Hodge	Hodge	Boersma
											Crudgington	*Phillips*	*Bartley*	*Smith*	*Stevenson*	*Charles**	*Attley*	*James R*	*Curtis*	*Waddle*	*Callaghan*	

24 — Roberts slams his players for having their minds on the cup replay, and Man Utd. Ex-Grecian Hodge's cross appears bread and butter for Lee Roberts, but he diverts the ball in. John Hore pulls down Cook for Allinson's pen, but a pair of tap-ins by Steve Neville denies U's the victory.

25 — Before the lowest home gate in their history, the Tangerines are barracked throughout by the thin crowd. All is temporarily forgotten when Irish international Derek Spence pops up with a late winner to add to his first-half effort. Colchester have their minds on the Man Utd cup-tie.

26 — Hodge and Lee choose the ideal time to notch their first league goals for U's. Allinson, who smashes a pen against the bar after Alan Harding's foul, finds Lee unmarked at the near post via a corner. Dowman's cross finds Dyer, who strikes the crossbar, but Hodge prods in the rebound.

27 — Long-serving Cook is presented with a silver salver before kick-off to commemorate his 50th cup-tie, against Man Utd. Wignall takes all the plaudits with a sterling defensive display and caps a great performance by nodding in United's second from Hodge's right-wing free-kick.

28 — Alan Moody blazes wide from the spot (34), after Packer was adjudged to have handled. Walker fails to hold Ron Pountney's shot, allowing Derrick Parker to score. Lee throws himself at Hodge's cross to level, and afterwards Roberts brandishes the penalty award 'an absolute joke'.

29 — Sharkey joins Posh for £8k, having never shown the form that had won him N Ireland international caps. Stags debutant keeper Martin New keeps his side in the game with a string of noteworthy saves, but has no chance as Gough dummies three defenders to find room to shoot home.

30 — Roberts says he won't be happy until U's reach the 43-point mark. as they start to look over their shoulders. A 15th away game without a win is only four short of the worst-ever run, in 1950-51. Dave Stewart scrambles the winner after Walker had saved Bruce Bannister's penalty (42).

31 — The squad are stranded at Heston services for six hours after their coach breaks down. They had left Friday mid-day, and so arrive, wearily, at 1 am Saturday morning. Dyer punishes Gary Megson's error to put U's 1-0 up in just 66 seconds. Cruelly, Fred Binney levels as fatigue sets in.

32 — U's return from a successful westward sojourn with three points in the bag. Lee's pair, his fourth league goals, begins to repay his transfer fee. Despite Andy Rowlands' opener, questions are raised about Swindon's promotion credentials as they had also lost 3-5 to Southend in midweek.

33 — Bees, with ex-Layer Road loanee Len Bond between the sticks, take the lead when Paul Shrubb volleys home a great pass from Steve Phillips. Phillips is booked for a 33rd-minute kick at Wright, and is the victim of Dyer's 44th-minute card. Danis Salman fouls Lee for U's equaliser.

34 — Walker denies Alan Waddle a first-half hat-trick, but can't prevent the striker from adding his, and Swans', second just after the interval. Lee notches a consolation, but Brian Attley adds a fourth in injury-time for Tommy Smith-inspired Swans. Roberts has no funds for deadline day.

Match log (rows 35–46)

35. A PETERBOROUGH — 31/3 — Att 3,559 — Pos 12 / 22 — W 2-1 (1-0)
Scorers: Gough 42, Allinson 52 / Robson 82 — Ref: M Peck
United: Walker, Cook, Wright, Hodge, Wignall, Packer, Foley, Gough, Dyer, Lee, Allinson
Peterborough: Waugh, Carmichael, Styles, Doyle, Smith, Ross, Sharkey, Guy, Cooke, Anderson*, Robson, Cliss
U's gain their first win at London Rd since 1970-71. Posh spurn an early lead when N Ireland International Trevor Anderson shoots well wide. after Wignall had up-ended Joe Cooke in the box (16). Gough curls a beauty past Keith Waugh, and Allinson plunders his from Foley's cross.

36. H CARLISLE — 2/4 — Att 2,608 — Pos 9 / 5 — W 2-1 (0-1)
Scorers: Lee 85, Wignall 87 / Lumby 30 — Ref: C White
United: Walker, Cook, Wright, Hodge, Wignall, Packer, Foley, Gough, Dyer, Lee, Allinson
Carlisle: Swinburne, Hoolickin, McCartney, MacDonald, Tait, Parker, McVitie, Bonnyman, Lumby, Kemp, Ludlam
United once again perform a great escape. after failing to capitalise on a host of chances early on. Slick Carlisle forge their way in front on the half-hour via Jim Lumby. but Allinson's inch-perfect free-kicks find Lee, for his seventh of the campaign, and Wignall, who nets his fourth.

37. H TRANMERE — 6/4 — Att 2,578 — Pos 9 / 23 — W 1-0 (1-0)
Scorers: Lee 18 — Ref: D Hutchinson
United: Walker, Cook, Wright, Hodge, Wignall, Packer, Foley, Gough, Dyer, Lee, Allinson
Tranmere: Johnson, Flood, Mathias, Parry, Postlewhite, Evans, O'Neil, Bramhall, Kerr, Thomas, McAuley, Rowles
A bad-tempered game played out on a glue-pot pitch. Packer joins five Rovers' players in the referee's notebook. Les Parry's foul on Lee leads to United's winner. Packer's free-kick is dummied by Foley and Lee. in oceans of space, has time to curl a header out of Dick Johnson's reach.

38. A WATFORD — 13/4 — Att 17,903 — Pos 9 / 1 — W 3-0 (1-0)
Scorers: Lee 43, 57, Gough 84 — Ref: R Challis
United: Walker, Cook, Wright, Hodge, Wignall, Packer, Foley, Gough, Dowman, Lee, Allinson
Watford: Rankin, Strik, Pritchett, Booth*, Bolton, Garner, Pollard, Blissett, Jenkins, Joslyn, Train, Downes
U's have their own Good Friday as leaders Watford, unbeaten at home since 9 September, fall to a Lee double-strike. Lee takes his tally to nine goals in 13 appearances. United manager Roberts says after that promotion is not out of reach, but maximum points will have to be obtained.

39. H OXFORD — 14/4 — Att 3,892 — Pos 9 / 13 — D 1-1 (1-0)
Scorers: Gough 16 / Taylor 76 — Ref: C Maskell
United: Walker, Cook, Wright, Hodge, Wignall, Packer, Dowman, Gough, Dyer, Lee, Allinson
Oxford: Burton, Taylor, Fogg, Briggs, Badel, Duncan, Graydon, Jeffrey, Berry*, Seacole, Hodgson, Evans, McGrogan
United let Oxford off the hook and virtually kiss goodbye to any slim hopes of promotion. Hodge is forced off (7) with a fractured cheekbone, from a clash with Gordon Hodgson. Despite this, Gough heads in Cook's free-kick, but Les Taylor salvages a point via Ray Graydon's centre.

40. A GILLINGHAM — 16/4 — Att 12,030 — Pos 9 / 3 — L 0-3 (0-1)
Scorers: Price 17, Westwood 64, Funnell 75 — Ref: A Robinson
United: Hillyard, Cook, Wright, Dowman, Wignall, Packer, Cotton, Gough, Dyer, Lee, Allinson
Gillingham: Sharpe, Barker, Overton, Weatherley, Hughes, Nichol, White, Price, Westwood, Funnell
Promotion-chasing Gills brush U's aside. for whom only Cotton impresses. A programme of three matches in four days takes its toll. Danny Westwood seals the win when Walker allows his shot to squirm from his grasp. Tony Funnell grabs his first since signing from Southampton.

41. H HULL — 21/4 — Att 2,762 — Pos 8 / 12 — W 2-1 (0-0)
Scorers: Rowles 74, Gough 84 / Edwards 56 — Ref: R Lewis
United: Walker, Cook, Wright, Dowman, Wignall, Bunkell, Rowles, Gough, Dyer, Lee, Allinson
Hull: Wealands, Nisbet, Skipper, Roberts, Croft, Haigh, Hawker, Horswill, Edwards, Bannister, Farley
Bunkell starts his first full game for ten weeks. Keith Edwards 21st of the term puts Tigers in front. Rowles, and Gough, who turns down the chance to play in the US in the summer, perform another late show. Cleveland Cobras makes the approach, but he opts for a close-season rest.

42. H CHESTERFIELD — 24/4 — Att 2,762 — Pos 8 / 19 — D 0-0 (0-0)
Ref: D Reeves
United: Walker, Cook, Wright, Dowman, Wignall, Bunkell, Rowles, Gough, Dyer, Lee, Allinson
Chesterfield: Tingay, Tartt, Burton, Hunter, O'Neill, Prophett, Kowalski, Moss, Simpson, Walker, Heppolette
U's move a point nearer their Third Div points record of 52 set in 1958-59. but this is the only highlight. One of U's recent late goalscoring feats does not materialise at Saltergate. Gough's effort is hacked off the line by Colin Tartt, and Dyer sees a shot turned away by Phil Tingay.

43. A BURY — 28/4 — Att 2,905 — Pos 8 / 17 — D 2-2 (1-1)
Scorers: Gough 6, Wright 75 / Hilton 23, Wilson 46 — Ref: B Martin
United: Walker, Cook, Wright, Dowman, Wignall, Foley, Rowles, Gough, Dyer, Lee, Allinson
Bury: Forest, Ritson, Constantine, Lugg, Tucker, Bailey*, Stanton, Wilson, Beamish, Gregory, Taylor, Hilton
Gough grabs his ninth of the term. but goals by Paul Hilton and Danny Wilson, after a bad blunder by Dowman, look to have given relegation-threatened Bury the points. U's earn a point when Wright, like his father Peter in the 1950's and 1960's, gets his name on United's scoresheet.

44. H PETERBOROUGH — 4/5 — Att 2,662 — Pos 8 / 21 — W 4-2 (1-2)
Scorers: Foley 11, Allinson 61, Dowman 77, 87 / Guy 36, Cooke 38 — Ref: A Glasson
United: Waugh, Cook, Wright, Dowman, Wignall, Foley, Rowles, Gough, Dyer*, Lee, Allinson
Peterborough: Waugh, Gynn, Collins, Chard, Carmichael, Ross, Sharkey, McEwan, Cooke, Robson, Guy, Packer
Proud Posh are made to look toothless by U's. Foley strikes a low left-foot drive, although Billy McEwan nods down for Alan Guy and then Joe Cooke nets from a weak header. Rowles punishes Ian Ross' error to set up Allinson, who later provides two pin-point corners for Dowman.

45. H GILLINGHAM — 7/5 — Att 6,317 — Pos 8 / 5 — D 2-2 (2-2)
Scorers: Allinson 54, Gough 78 / Armstrong 9, Westwood 53 — Ref: B Homewood
United: Walker, Cook, Wright, Dowman, Wignall, Foley, Rowles, Gough, Packer, Lee, Allinson
Gillingham: Hillyard, Young, Barker, Overton, Weatherley, Hughes, Armstrong, White, Price, Westwood, Funnell
For the ninth home game this season, U's stage a late fight-back. A huge Gills following expects to cheer their side into Div Two. Allinson crashes U's back in it, just 50 seconds after Westwood scored Gills second. Gough taps in when Ron Hillyard only parries Dowman's header.

46. A TRANMERE — 9/5 — Att 1,016 — Pos 7 / 23 — W 5-1 (1-0)
Scorers: Gough 20, 80, Lee 66, 74, Packer 46 / Peplow 71 — Ref: D Clarke
United: Johnson, Cook, Wright, Dowman, Wignall, Packer, Rowles, Gough, Packer, Lee, Allinson
Tranmere: Johnson, Mathias, Flood, Parry, Postlewhite, Bramhall, Peplow, Craven, Kerr, Evans, Griffiths
United set a new club-record highest away win at relegation-doomed Tranmere. Gough's brace takes him past 50 goals for the club on Foley's 200th appearance. Packer's goal means that only Walker, Cotton, Leslie and Sharkey failed to score as U's finish just four wins off promotion.

Home Average 3,410
Away 5,680

LEAGUE DIVISION 3 (CUP-TIES)

Manager: Bobby Roberts

SEASON 1978-79

Pos	1	2	3	4	5	6	7	8	9	10	11	12 sub used

League Cup

1:1 H CHARLTON 12/8 — L 2-3 (H-T 1-1) — 3,016 2:
Scorers, Times, and Referees: Rowles 30, Dowman 90 / Hales 8, Brisley 78, Robinson 82 / Ref: R Toseland

	1	2	3	4	5	6	7	8	9	10	11	12 sub used
	Walker	Cook*	Packer	Bunkell	Wignall	Dowman	Foley	Gough	Dyer	Rowles	Allinson	**Sharkey**
	Wood	Berry	Warman	Tydeman	Shipperley	Dugdale	Brisley	Peacock*	Hales	Robinson	Gritt	Madden

The season kicks-off with five goals, a missed penalty, six bookings (five to Charlton) and a hospital trip. Alan Dugdale tackle puts Cook on a stretcher and is booked. Dugdale hauls down Allinson at 1-1 but escapes dismissal. Debutant Sharkey's feeble penalty is saved by Jeff Wood.

1:2 A CHARLTON 15/8 — D 0-0 (H-T 0-0) — 7,205 2:
Ref: M Sinclair
(Colchester lost 2-3 on aggregate)

	1	2	3	4	5	6	7	8	9	10	11
	Walker	Sharkey	Packer	Leslie	Wignall	Dowman	Foley	Gough	Dyer	Rowles	Allinson
	Wood	Campbell	Warman	Tydeman	Shipperley	Dugdale	Brisley	Hales	Robinson	Flanagan	Gritt

Charlton, leading from Saturday's first leg, are let off the hook by referee Malcolm Sinclair of Guildford. Steve Leslie's 29th-minute goal, deflected off Alan Dugdale, is incredibly ruled out for an offside offence. Valiants hold on their lead to earn a second-round outing to Walsall.

FA Cup

1 H OXFORD 25/11 — W 4-2 (H-T 1-1) — 4,170 3:19
Scorers, Times, and Referees: Gough 30, 74, 87, Foley S 46 / Foley P 22, Seacole 53 / Ref: C Maskell

	1	2	3	4	5	6	7	8	9	10	11
	Walker	Cook	Packer	Hodge	Wignall	Dowman	Foley S	Gough	Bunkell	Lee*	Allinson
	Burton	Taylor	Fogg	Briggs	Badel	Jeffrey	Graydon	Duncan	Foley P	Seacole	Hodgson / Wright

A harmless Peter Foley cross eludes Walker to secure a shock lead for Oxford. Ray Graydon, who had scored Villa's League Cup winner four years earlier, stars. Gough capitalises on Billy Jeffrey's suicidal back-pass, and completes his hat-trick when Foley flicks on Allinson's corner.

2 A LEATHERHEAD 16/12 — D 1-1 (H-T 1-0) — 2,250 11:2
Scorers, Times, and Referees: Gough 30 / Kelly 73 / Ref: P Reeves

	1	2	3	4	5	6	7	8	9	10	11
	Walker	Cook	Packer	Hodge	Wignall	Dowman	Foley	Gough	Dyer	Wright	Allinson
	Swannell	Cooper	Eaton	Davies	Reid	Malley	Cook	Sakeld	Kelly	Baker	Camp* / Doyle

Looking to avenge the embarrassment of defeat to the non-leaguers just four years earlier, Colchester take the lead at Fetcham Grove but fail to capitalise. Outspoken Leatherhead player, Chris Kelly, known nationally as 'The Leatherhead Lip' wipes out the lead with just 17 minutes left.

2R H LEATHERHEAD 19/12 — W 4-0 (H-T 1-0) — 3,920 11:2
Scorers, Times, and Referees: Lee 40, Gough 67 D'm'n 68, Coop'r 71 (og) / Ref: P Reeves

	1	2	3	4	5	6	7	8	9	10	11
	Walker	Cook	Packer	Hodge	Wignall	Dowman	Wright	Gough	Dyer	Lee	Allinson
	Swannell	Cooper	Eaton	Davies	Reid	Malley	Cook	Sakeld	Kelly	Baker	Doyle

On a bone-hard frozen surface Trevor Lee scores his first goal for the club. Colchester finally prove their superiority with three more goals in a four-minute spell. Dowman's header, from a Lee pass, is deflected in by Cooper. At the final whistle Chris Kelly's lip is seen to visibly droop.

3 A DARLINGTON 9/1 — W 1-0 (H-T 1-0) — 3,465 4:20
Scorers, Times, and Referees: Hodge 8 / Ref: D Mills

	1	2	3	4	5	6	7	8	9	10	11
	Walker	Cook	Wright	Hodge	Wignall	Dowman	Foley	Gough	Dyer	Bunkell	Allinson
	Burleigh	Nattrass	Cochrane	Hague	Craig	Stone	Probert	Patterson	Seal*	Wann	Walsh / Maitland

Hodge earns U's a trip to South Wales and Somerton Park, rifling in a stunning 25-yarder on a frozen Feethams pitch after good build-up play by Gough and Bunkell. Saturday's game at the Fourth Division strugglers had been called off, but the win is U's first on their travels this term.

4 A NEWPORT 30/1 — D 0-0 (H-T 0-0) — 10,329 4:8
Ref: D Turner

	1	2	3	4	5	6	7	8	9	10	11
	Walker	Cook	Wright	Hodge	Wignall	Dowman	Foley	Gough	Dyer	Lee	Allinson
	Plumley	Walden	Byrne	Thompson	Davies	Bruton	Oakes	Lowndes	Goddard	Woods	Vaughan

Newport, who had beaten 2nd Division West Ham in the last round are confident of beating 'another Essex side'. Against the roar of 10,000 Welshmen, U's are excellent in forcing a replay, typified when Walker races out of his goal to head clear of the on-rushing Howard Goddard.

4R H NEWPORT 5/2 — W 1-0 (H-T 1-0) — 7,025 4:8
Scorers, Times, and Referees: Gough 26 / Ref: D Turner

	1	2	3	4	5	6	7	8	9	10	11
	Walker	Cook	Wright	Hodge	Wignall	Dowman	Foley	Gough	Dyer	Lee	Allinson
	Plumley	Walden	Byrne	Thompson	Davies	Lowndes	Thompson	Sinclair*	Goddard	Bruton	Vaughan / Relish

A home tie against the winners of the Man Utd v Fulham replay awaits the victors. The gallant Welshmen put up a stern fight, but lose out to Gough's powerful close-range effort. U's fans must now wait for the delayed replay at Old Trafford, as the winter weather continues to bite.

5 H MANCHESTER U 20/2 — L 0-1 (H-T 0-0) — 13,171 1:9
Scorers, Times, and Referees: Greenhoff J 85 / Ref: R Challis

	1	2	3	4	5	6	7	8	9	10	11	12 sub used
	Walker	Cook	Wright	Hodge	Wignall	Dowman	Packer	Foley	Dyer	Lee	Allinson	
	Bailey	Greenhoff B*	Albiston	McIlroy	McQueen	Buchan	Coppell	Greenhoff J	Ritchie	Macari	Thomas	Nicholl

A dominant and composed Colchester defence is cruelly beaten, when Mickey Thomas's left-wing cross is flicked on by Andy Ritchie to Greenhoff. Heartbreak, as just five minutes earlier the U's spring the offside trap, only for Arthur Albiston to clear Lee's attempt off the line.

League Table

	Team	P	Home W	D	L	F	A	Away W	D	L	F	A	Pts
1	Shrewsbury	46	14	9	0	36	11	7	10	6	25	30	61
2	Watford	46	15	5	3	47	22	9	7	7	36	30	60
3	Swansea	46	16	6	1	57	32	8	6	9	26	29	60
4	Gillingham	46	15	7	1	39	15	6	10	7	26	27	59
5	Swindon	46	17	2	4	44	14	8	5	10	30	38	57
6	Carlisle	46	11	10	2	31	13	4	12	7	22	29	52
7	COLCHESTER	46	13	9	1	35	19	4	8	11	25	36	51
8	Hull	46	12	9	2	36	14	7	2	14	30	47	49
9	Exeter	46	14	6	3	38	18	3	9	11	23	38	49
10	Brentford	46	14	4	5	35	19	5	5	13	18	30	47
11	Oxford	46	10	8	5	27	20	4	10	9	17	30	46
12	Blackpool	46	12	5	6	38	19	6	4	13	23	40	45
13	Southend	46	11	6	6	30	17	4	10	10	21	32	45
14	Sheffield Wed	46	9	8	6	30	22	4	11	8	23	31	45
15	Plymouth	46	9	9	3	40	27	4	5	14	27	41	44
16	Chester	46	11	9	3	42	21	3	7	13	15	40	44
17	Rotherham	46	13	3	7	30	23	4	7	12	19	32	44
18	Mansfield	46	7	11	5	30	24	5	8	10	21	28	43
19	Bury	46	6	11	6	35	32	5	9	9	24	33	42
20	Chesterfield	46	10	5	8	35	34	3	9	11	16	31	40
21	Peterborough	46	8	7	8	26	24	3	7	13	18	39	36
22	Walsall	46	7	6	10	34	32	3	6	14	22	39	32
23	Tranmere	46	4	12	7	26	31	2	4	17	19	47	28
24	Lincoln	46	5	7	11	26	38	2	4	17	15	50	25
		1104	265	174	113	847	541	113	174	265	541	847	1104

Appearances & Goals

	Appearances Lge	Sub	LC	Sub	FAC	Sub	Goals Lge	LC	FAC	Tot
Allinson, Ian	45	1	2		7		5			5
Bunkell, Ray	10	2	1		2		1			1
Cook, Micky	46		1		7		1			1
Cotton, Russell	1									
Dowman, Steve	37	1	2		7		2	1	2	5
Dyer, Paul	37	3	2		5		2			2
Evans, Tony	8	1					2			2
Foley, Steve	34		2		6		6		1	7
Gough, Bobby	42		2		6		16		6	22
Hodge, Bobby	31				7		3		1	4
Lee, Trevor	27				5		11		1	12
Leslie, Steve	3		1							
Packer, Mick	40	2	2		5		1			1
Rowles, Eddie	19	2	1				4		1	5
Sharkey, Pat	5	1	1	1						
Walker, Mick	46		2		7					
Wignall, Steve	42	2	2		7		4			4
Wright, Steve	33	2			6	1	1			1
(own-goals)							1			1
18 players used	506	15	22	1	77	1	60	2	11	73

Odds & ends

Double wins: (3) Peterborough, Swindon, Tranmere.
Double defeats: (0).

Won from behind: (7) Chester (h), Swindon (h & a), Plymouth (h).
Carlisle (h), Hull (h), Peterborough (h).
Lost from in front: (0).

High spots: Four home league wins on the trot from September.
Club (Third Division) record ten home games unbeaten from September.
Ten times at home, U's net a late goal to earn vital wins or draws.
Club record highest away win (Tranmere 5-1).
A great FA Cup run, culminating in a home tie with mighty Man Utd.

Low spots: Promotion failure yet again.
Lack of resources to sustain a promotion bid.
Five minutes from earning an Old Trafford FA Cup replay.

Player of the year: Steve Wignall.
Ever presents: (2) Micky Cook, Mike Walker.
Hat-tricks: (1) Bobby Gough.
Leading scorer: Bobby Gough (22).

LEAGUE DIVISION 3 — Manager: Bobby Roberts — SEASON 1979-80

12 sub used

No		Date	Att	Pos	Pt	F-A	H-T	Scorers, Times, and Referees	1	2	3	4	5	6	7	8	9	10	11	12
1	A HULL	18/8	4,463		W 2	2-0	1-0	Allinson 35, Hodge 81. Ref: P Willis	Walker	Cook	Wright	Leslie	Wignall	Packer	Hodge	Gough	Foley	Lee	Allinson	
									Blackburn	*Nisbet*	*McDonald*	*Hawker**	*Croft*	*Haigh*	*Roberts*	*Horswill*	*Edwards*	*Bannister*	*Phillips*	*Skipper*
2	H SHEFFIELD UTD	21/8	4,191	12	W 4	1-0	0-0	Lee 83. Ref: T Bune	Walker	Cook	Wright	Leslie	Wignall	Dowman	Hodge	Gough	Foley	Lee	Allinson	
									Conroy	*Cutbush!*	*Tibbott*	*Kenworthy*	*McPhail*	*Matthews*	*Flood*	*De Goey*	*Butlin*	*Brown*	*Benjamin*	
3	A ROTHERHAM	25/8	3,278	7	L 4	0-3	0-2	Finney 9, Fern 38, Gwyther 46. Ref: R Toseland	Walker	Cook*	Wright	Leslie	Packer	Dowman	Hodge	Gough	Foley	Lee	Allinson	
									Mountford	*Forrest*	*Tiler*	*Rhodes*	*Green*	*Breckin*	*Gooding*	*McEwan*	*Gwyther*	*Fern*	*Finney*	
4	H SWINDON	31/8	2,794	14	L 4	2-3	1-2	Gough 32, Hodge 66, Mayes 26, Rowland 42, 90. Ref: R Lewis	Walker	Packer	Rowles	Leslie	Wignall	Bunkell	Hodge	Gough	Foley	Mayes	Allinson	
									Allan	*Templeman*	*Ford**	*McHale*	*Tucker*	*Stroud*	*Miller*	*Carter*	*Rowland*	*Mayes*	*Williams*	*Lewis*
5	A CHESTERFIELD	8/9	4,206	5	L 4	0-3	0-1	Hunter 8, Birch 73, Moss 83. Ref: J Sewell	Walker	Dowman	Rowles	Hodge	Wignall	Wright	Leslie	Gough!	Foley	Lee	Allinson	
									Letheran	*Tartt*	*O'Neill*	*Ridley*	*Green*	*Hunter*	*Birch*	*Moss*	*Walker*	*Salmons*	*Crawford*	
6	H SHEFFIELD WED	15/9	3,473	14	D 5	0-0	0-0	Ref: D Reeves	Walker	Cook	Wright	Leslie	Wignall	Dowman	Hodge	Rowles	Foley	Lee	Allinson	
									Cox	*Blackhall*	*Grant*	*Smith*	*Mullen*	*Hornsby*	*Owen*	*Porterfield*	*King*	*Fleming*	*Wylde*	
7	H MANSFIELD	18/9	2,346	21	W 7	2-1	1-0	Gough 23, Lee 78, Bird 47. Ref: K Salmon	Walker	Arnold	Wright	Leslie	Wignall	Dowman	Hodge	Gough	Packer	Lee	Allinson	
									Cox	*Dawkins*	*Foster*	*Curtis*	*Bird*	*McClelland*	*Lathan*	*Taylor*	*Austin*	*Hamilton*	*Allen*	
8	A GRIMSBY	22/9	6,962	12	W 9	2-1	0-1	Lee 66, 77, Kilmore 27. Ref: T Mills	Walker	Batch	Wright	Leslie	Wignall	Packer	Hodge	Gough	Dyer*	Lee	Allinson	
									Moore D	*Moore K*	*Waters*	*Wigginton*	*Stone**	*Brolly*	*Kilmore*	*Liddelll*	*Mitchell*	*Cumming*	*Crombie*	
9	H BARNSLEY	29/9	3,376	14	D 10	0-0	0-0	Ref: J Martin	Walker	Pierce	Wright	Leslie	Wignall	Packer	Hodge	Gough	Foley	Lee	Allinson	
										Flavell	*Chambers*	*Glavin*	*Collins*	*McCarthy*	*Pugh*	*Riley*	*Banks*	*Millar*	*Bell*	
10	A MANSFIELD	1/10	3,500	24	W 12	1-0	0-0	Lee 75. Ref: J Hough	Walker	Arnold	Packer	Leslie	Wignall	Dowman	Hodge	Gough	Foley	Lee	Allinson	
									Arnold	*Dawkins*	*Foster**	*Wood*	*Bird*	*McClelland*	*Lathan*	*Goodwin*	*Austin*	*Hamilton*	*Allen*	*Caldwell*
11	H READING	5/10	3,330	15	D 13	1-1	1-0	Rowles 54, Heale 54. Ref: H Robinson	Walker	Packer	Packer	Leslie	Wignall	Dowman	Hodge	Gough	Foley	Rowles	Allinson	
									Death	*Hetzke*	*White*	*Bowman*	*Shipperley**	*Moreline*	*Earles*	*Kearney*	*Heale*	*Sanchez*	*Wanklyn*	*Kearns*

Match commentary

1. 16-year-old Tony Adcock signs as apprentice, after a pre-season three-match tour to W Germany. A healthy 632 season tickets are sold, as U's kick-off with a first-ever win at Boothferry Pk. Allinson embarks on a fine solo run, and Hodge's cross-cum-shot deceives Eddie Blackburn.

2. The gate falls woefully short of the 8,000 break-even target. Leslie's return after last season's broken leg has already added a new dimension to the midfield. Blades' John Cutbush is sent off (61) for two fouls, leaving Lee to take advantage when Dowman glances on Hodge's flag-kick.

3. Cook equals Peter Wright's U's League appearance record, but is booked and subbed at half-time with a knee injury. Richard Finney cracks the Millers' first, Rod Fern looks offside for the second, and David Gwyther intercepts Foley's back-pass twelve seconds after the interval.

4. Several times last season U's secured late points, but they are on the receiving end as defensive slackness allows Andy Rowland to swoop in injury time. Twice United had clawed back with Gough's header and Hodge's out-of-the-blue angled volley, but Rowland has the final word.

5. Gough faces a club fine after he is cautioned for dissent (27), and retaliates a couple of minutes later when he is clattered by centre-half Les Hunter. After the glory of Villa Park, U's come down to earth with a bump. Ex-chairman Jackson, who quit in March 1974, rejoins the board.

6. Bookings for Leslie and Foley mean that U's are dangerously close to reaching the 50-point mark when they would be called before an FA disciplinary commission. Cook returns from injury to finally beat Wright's record, and helps United earn a precious first point in four matches.

7. Roberts suggests that some players don't like playing at home, as they are subjected to barracking and slow hand-clapping by sections of the crowd. Gough breaks the tedium with a free-kick off Rod Arnold's shoulder, and Lee deservedly scores in a one-on-one with the Stags keeper.

8. U's are without the injured Dowman and Foley, but welcome back Dyer after his summer cartilage operation. Lee, who could well have had a hat-trick, takes his tally to five in cancelling out a first half strike from Kevin Kilmore, Mariner's £60k buy from Scunthorpe just a week ago.

9. Play is held up for three minutes when fighting breaks out in the Barnsley section of the crowd. John Collins and Ronnie Glavin find their way into the referee's note-book, before Packer slams the upright with a 35-yarder. Mick McCarthy is also booked and Leslie strikes the bar (78).

10. United earn a third away win of the season, and a quick-fire early season double over Stags. Mansfield do have the ball in the net (41), but an offside had already been given. Lee blasts in U's only real shot on target for a win that keeps Roberts and Harford's former club rock bottom.

11. Roberts has high hopes of providing entertainment with his new brand of home football, but most of the crowd is confused by his style. Rowles opens at the best psychological moment, but Canvey Island lad Gary Heale takes advantage of defensive confusion to equalise for the Royals.

#	V	Opponent	Date	Att	U-Pos	Opp-Pos	Pts	Res	Score	HT	Scorers / Referee
12	A	SHEFFIELD UTD	9/10	18,712	4	1	15	W	2-1	0-0	Foley 73, Gough 77 / Bourne 63 — Ref: L. Robinson
13	A	SOUTHEND	12/10	5,944	3	22	17	W	1-0	1-0	Walker 23 (og) — Ref: T Cox
14	H	BLACKPOOL	19/10	4,383	2	12	19	W	3-1	2-0	Gough 16, Lee 30, Hodge 75 / Weston 90 — Ref: C Maskell
15	H	WIMBLEDON	23/10	4,396	2	21	21	W	4-0	2-0	Hodge 17p, Lee 19, Gough 77, Wignall 86 — Ref: A Gunn
16	A	BLACKBURN	27/10	6,436	3	16	21	L	0-3	0-1	Crawford 18, Keeley 55, Brotherston 85 — Ref: J Lovatt
17	H	HULL	2/11	4,510	3	10	22	D	1-1	0-1	Gough 86 / Moss 36 — Ref: D Hutchinson
18	A	WIMBLEDON	6/11	2,465	3	21	23	D	3-3	0-2	Wignall 57, Lee 64, Gough 80 / Parsons 12, 18p, Leslie J 70 — Ref: J Bray
19	A	BRENTFORD	10/11	9,060	4	2	23	L	0-1	0-1	McNichol 2 — Ref: T Spencer
20	H	PLYMOUTH	16/11	3,520	3	21	25	W	5-2	3-1	Lee 5, Packer 7, 58, Hodge 23, Gough 55 / Kemp 42, Cook 69 (og) — Ref: A Grey
21	A	MILLWALL	1/12	7,563	2	3	27	W	2-1	2-0	Lee 8, Foley 29 / Mehmet 56 — Ref: D Letts
22	H	CARLISLE	7/12	4,104	2	13	28	D	1-1	1-0	Lee 16 / Beardsley 76 — Ref: C Downey
23	A	EXETER	21/12	2,648	3	15	28	L	1-3	1-1	Wright 17 / Roberts L 5, Dowman 68 (og), Pullar 73 — Ref: W Bombroff

12 — SHEFFIELD UTD (A), 9/10
United: Walker, Cook, Packer, Leslie, Wignall, Gough, Hodge*, Dowman, Foley, Rowles, Allinson (Dyer)
Sheffield Utd: Conroy, Cutbush, Garner, Kenworthy, McPhail, Matthews, De Goey, Bourne, Butlin, Speight, Sabella
Roberts gauges U's form by the fact they have doubled the 'best side in the division'. U's prevent Blades' previously stainless home record from stretching to eight successes. Steve Conroy parries Leslie's free-kick to Foley, and Gough, who gives Foley the captaincy, nets the other.

13 — SOUTHEND (A), 12/10
United: Walker, Cook, Packer, Leslie, Wignall, Gough, Hodge, Dowman, Foley, Rowles, Allinson (Nelson)
Southend: Keeley, Dudley, Moody, Cusack, Walker, Morris, Otulakowski, Stead, Hull*, Parker, Gray
United continue to miss Lee, who injured his back in training just hours before the Reading game. Southend, knocked out of the League Cup by West Ham at the third attempt, draft in 18-year-old John Keeley. John Walker slices Gough's prodded cross home, for U's fourth away win.

14 — BLACKPOOL (H), 19/10
United: Walker, Cook, Packer, Leslie, Wignall, Gough, Hodge, Dowman, Foley, Lee, Allinson (Weston)
Blackpool: McAllister, Gardner, Pashley*, Kerr, Suddaby, Jones, Thompson, McEwan, Spence, Smith, Malone
Cook enjoys a well-deserved testimonial in midweek against WBA, watched by 2,882. Money-bags Blackpool complete the £110k signing of Sunderland defender Jack Ashurst, although he is ineligible for this match. How they could have done with him as United rip Tangerines apart.

15 — WIMBLEDON (H), 23/10
United: Walker, Cook, Packer, Leslie, Wignall, Gough, Hodge, Dowman, Foley, Lee, Allinson (Ketteridge)
Wimbledon: Goddard, Perkins, Jones, Eames, Bowgett, Cunningham, Dziadulewicz, Parsons*, Leslie J, Cork, Lewington
Unhappy Bunkell is listed after failing to break into the side. U's unbeaten ten-match run has yield 17 points. The tide turns when Terry Eames fires straight at Walker's legs (16). Allinson takes the rebound and runs the entire length, before being hauled over in the area by Steve Jones.

16 — BLACKBURN (A), 27/10
United: Walker, Cook, Packer*, Leslie, Wignall, Gough, Hodge, Dowman, Foley, Lee, Allinson (Rowles)
Blackburn: Arnold, Branagan, Morley, Kendall, Keeley, Fazackerley, Brotherston, Parkes*, Craig, Crawford, MacKenzie, Garner
Struggling Blackburn are expected to crumble to the impressive travelling U's. Lee, being watched by Villa, has a wretched day as he fails to finish two good opportunities (30 and 33). Veteran player-boss Howard Kendall 'pulls Rovers' strings, and supplies for Glenn Keeley's header.

17 — HULL (H), 2/11
United: Walker, Cook, Packer*, Leslie, Wignall, Gough, Hodge*, Dowman, Foley, Lee, Allinson (Rowles)
Hull: Blackburn, Nisbet, Devries, Croft, Kendall, Roberts, Moss, Edwards, Tait, Phillips, Hawker
Hull spent £275k in the summer, whilst U's announce a staggering loss of £73k after last years £29k profit. Free-kick maestro Gough strikes from 35 yards to cancel out Paul Moss's first-half opener. Moss had not been found wanting either, curling a great set-piece beyond Walker.

18 — WIMBLEDON (A), 6/11
United: Walker, Cook, Wright*, Leslie, Wignall, Gough, Hodge*, Dowman, Foley, Lee, Allinson (Rowles)
Wimbledon: Goddard, Eames, Jones, Galliers, Bowgett, Downes, Dziadulewicz, Parsons, Leslie J, Cork, Lewington
Plough Lane hosts United for the first time in a league fixture. Roberts out-foxes Dario Gradi by pulling off youngster Wright in favour of Rowles. Within ten minutes U's are back on terms at 2-2. Although John Leslie nets for Dons, Gough's leveller maintains the promotion push.

19 — BRENTFORD (A), 10/11
United: Walker, Cook, Packer, Leslie, Wignall, Gough, Hodge, Dowman, Foley, Lee, Allinson* (Rowles)
Brentford: Bond, Salman, Tucker, McNichol, Kruse, Fraser, Carlton !, Graham, Smith, Alder, Phillips, Strubb
Wignall gets his fifth booking of the term, for a late tackle on Jackie Graham, and faces suspension. Early in the second half Dave Carlton is sent off for a fierce foul on Leslie, but U's can't capitalize down ten-man Brentford who had led since the second minute through Jim McNichol.

20 — PLYMOUTH (H), 16/11
United: Walker, Cook, Packer, Leslie, Wignall, Gough, Hodge, Dowman, Foley, Lee, Allinson (Rowles)
Plymouth: Crudgington, Hodges, McNeill, Randall, Foster, Phil* Masters, Trusson, Kemp*, Sims, Bason, Harrison (James)
A great U's rehearsal for next week's FA Cup first round tie between the clubs. United hit five for the first time since November 1974 when they beat Grimsby 5-0. Lee slots in his tenth of the season and Packer's double takes his tally to 16 in almost 300 league and cup appearances.

21 — MILLWALL (A), 1/12
United: Walker, Cook, Packer, Leslie, Wright, Gough*, Hodge, Dowman, Foley, Lee, Allinson (Rowles)
Millwall: Jackson, Donaldson, Kinsella, Chatterton, Tagg, Blyth, Towner, Seasman, Mehmet, Lyons, Mitchell
Martyn Bennett succeeds Betty Scott as secretary. United achieve a fantastic win at the Den against the leaders in a match reported upon by BBC national radio. Lee, plucked by Lions from Epsom and Ewell, gets the first, and Foley the second, both from rebounds off John Jackson.

22 — CARLISLE (H), 7/12
United: Walker, Cook, Packer, Leslie, Wignall, Gough, Hodge, Dowman, Foley, Lee, Allinson* (Rowles)
Carlisle: Swinburne, Hoolickin, Winstanley, MacDonald, Ludlam, Parker, McVitie, Bonnyman, Bannon*, Hamilton, Staniforth (Beardsley)
Bunkell talks to Lincoln over an £8k transfer. U's offer 'half' season tickets at £11 standing or £20 seating, and sit nicely in joint top position with Sheffield Utd after an outlay of only £60k. Peter Beardsley's neat one-two with Gordon Staniforth (£125k from York) levels the score.

23 — EXETER (A), 21/12
United: Walker, Cook, Packer, Leslie, Wignall, Gough, Hodge*, Dyer, Foley, Lee, Wright (Rowles)
Exeter: Main, Mitchell, Hatch, Hore, Roberts L, Roberts P, Neville, Pearson*, Rogers P, Delve, Pullar, Bowker (Evans)
Bunkell's move breaks down as he spends five days in hospital after a training ground injury. Lee Roberts stabs in after Walker miss-punches John Delve's centre, Dowman own-goals a cross and Dave Pullar has a free header. U's haven't won at Exeter since December 1961.

LEAGUE DIVISION 3 — Manager: Bobby Roberts — SEASON 1979-80

No	Date	1	2	3	4	5	6	7	8	9	10	11	12 sub used	Att	Pos	Pt	F-A	H-T
24	H GILLINGHAM 26/12	Walker	Cook	Packer	Leslie	Wignall	Dowman	Dyer	Wright	Foley	Lee	Allinson	Wright	5,145	15	D 29	2-2	2-0
		Hillyard	*Bruce*	*Barker*	*Overton*	*Weatherley*	*Crabbe*	*Nicholl*	*Hughes*	*Price*	*Westwood*	*Funnell*						
25	H ROTHERHAM 29/12	Walker	Cook	Packer	Leslie	Wignall	Dowman	Hodge	Rowles*	Foley	Lee	Allinson	Wright	3,375	11	D 30	1-1	1-1
		Mountford	*Forrest*	*Breckin*	*Rhodes*	*Stancliffe*	*Green*	*Gooding*	*Dawson*	*Fern*	*Tiler*	*Finney*						
26	H CHESTER 8/1	Walker	Cook	Packer	Leslie	Wignall	Dowman	Hodge	Gough	Foley	Lee	Allinson*	Rowles	3,251	4	D 31	1-1	0-0
		Millington	*Jeffries*	*Walker*	*Storton*	*Oakes*	*Cottam*	*Ruggiero*	*Jones*	*Rush*	*Phillips R*	*Henderson*						
27	A OXFORD 12/1	Walker	Cook	Packer	Leslie	Wignall	Dowman	Hodge	Gough	Foley S	Lee	Allinson	White	3,857	15	W 33	2-0	1-0
		Brown	*Bodel*	*McIntosh*	*Briggs*	*O'Dowd*	*Jeffrey*	*Taylor*	*Duncan*	*Foley P*	*Berry*	*Watson**						
28	H CHESTERFIELD 18/1	Walker	Cook	Packer	Leslie	Wignall	Dowman	Hodge*	Gough	Foley	Lee	Allinson	Wright	3,763	4	L 33	0-1	0-0
		Kendall	*Tartt*	*O'Neill*	*Ridley*	*Green*	*Kowalski*	*Birch*	*Moss*	*Walker*	*Salmons*	*Crawford*						
29	A BURY 29/1	Walker	Cook	Packer	Leslie	Wignall	Dowman	Hodge	Rowles	Foley	Lee	Allinson	Madden	3,551	22	W 35	1-0	1-0
		Forrest	*Constantine*	*Kennedy*	*McIlwraith*	*Whitehead*	*Waddington*	*Mullen*	*Wilson*	*Johnson*	*Hilton*	*Halford**						
30	A SHEFFIELD WED 2/2	Walker	Cook	Packer	Leslie	Wignall	Dowman	Hodge*	Rowles	Foley	Lee	Allinson	Evans	11,958	5	L 35	0-3	0-2
		Bolder	*Blackhall*	*Grant*	*Smith*	*Pickering*	*Hornsby*	*Taylor*	*Johnson*	*Mellor*	*McCulloch*	*Curran*						
31	H GRIMSBY 8/2	Walker	Cook	Packer	Leslie	Wignall	Dowman	Rowles	Gough	Foley	Lee	Wright		5,149	1	W 37	2-1	0-1
		Batch	*Stone*	*Moore K*	*Waters*	*Wigginton*	*Crombie*	*Ford*	*Kilmore*	*Drinkell*	*Mitchell*	*Brolly*						
32	A BARNSLEY 16/2	Walker	Cook	Packer	Leslie	Wignall	Dowman	Hodge	Rowles	Foley	Lee	Allinson	Speedie	11,309	18	W 39	2-1	2-0
		Pierce	*Joyce*	*Chambers*	*Glavin*	*Hunter*	*McCarthy*	*Parker*	*Downes*	*Aylot*	*Lester**	*Banks*						
33	H SOUTHEND 22/2	Walker	Cook	Packer	Leslie	Wignall	Dowman	Rowles	Gough*	Foley	Lee	Allinson	Walker	6,135	18	W 41	2-1	1-1
		Cawston	*Moody*	*Yates*	*Nelson**	*Dudley*	*Cusack*	*Gray*	*Pountney*	*Spence*	*Mercer*	*Otulakowski*						
34	A BLACKPOOL 29/2	Walker	Cook	Packer	Leslie	Hodge	Dowman	Rowles*	Gough*	Foley	Lee	Wright	Gough	5,594	19	L 41	0-1	0-1
		Hesford	*Gardner*	*Pashley*	*Ashurst*	*Thompson*	*Doyle*	*Morris*	*Kellow*	*MacDougall**	*Harrison*	*Brockbank*	*McEwan*						

Scorers, Times, and Referees

24 — Packer 7, Allinson 16 / Overton 50, Westwood 75 — Ref: B Hill
U's have now dropped nine points at Layer Rd. They slice through Gills defence when Allinson's corner is swivelled in by Packer, and then he makes the most of Dyer's quick-thinking free-kick. Walker, in his 500th league appearance, has no chance with Danny Westwood's equaliser.

25 — Lee 42 / Gooding 13 — Ref: M Bidmead
An amazing 49,309 watched the Sheffield derby on Boxing Day. U's match, which had kicked-off in bright sunshine, is turned into a lottery as rain and snow lash Layer Rd. Lee pounces on John Forrest's poor back-pass to score U's first-ever against Rotherham in ten league meetings.

26 — Wignall 76 / Phillips R 54p — Ref: R Challis
Wignall saves U's bacon when he nods in Gough's flick from Packer's free-kick. It is U's fifth home draw in six. Three days earlier Chester had knocked Newcastle out of the FA Cup at St James'. Dowman's trip on young Jamie Phillips his penalty.

27 — Foley S 32, Lee 81 — Ref: A Gunn
Cook beats Peter Wright's U's appearance record. A seventh away win sees U's catch up with leaders Sheffield Utd with a game in hand. Foley makes the most of Gary Briggs' error, and Lee gets the second when David Brown tips his original effort over for an Allinson flag-kick.

28 — Birch 79p — Ref: D Reeves
Arthur Cox's Chesterfield put a further dent in U's desperate home form when Alan Birch, a £40k buy from Walsall, is scythed by Packer and gets up to spot the winner. Cook appears to have saved U's, but the linesman rules that Spurs loanee Mark Kendall had kept out his cannonball.

29 — Rowles 30 — Ref: P Richardson
U's return to action after missing out on Saturday owing to Swindon's FA Cup commitments. Rowles has only scored four times this term, but each one has been of momentous importance. An eighth away win keeps U's neck and neck with Sheffield U. and Leslie's goal is ruled offside (75).

30 — Smith 9p, 73p, Curran 25 — Ref: G Courtney
U's spend the week at Lilleshall. The Yorkshire TV camera show a thick blanket of snow at Hillsborough, but United are well-tanned by sun-tanned Owls, who have just returned from a break in Spain. Terry Curran uses the conditions to earn penalties against Dowman and Wignall.

31 — Gough 50, Foley 82 / Dowman 10 (og) — Ref: A Robinson
United finally get it right at home, and most impressively against the league leaders Grimsby. Mariners' late run has come as they had been pre-occupied with runs in both cups, losing to Wolves in a League Cup quarter-final third replay, and to Liverpool in the FA Cup third round.

32 — Dowman 25, Rowles 30 / Glavin 83p — Ref: J Sewell
U's stay joint top of the table with Grimsby with this ninth away win. Dowman, shirt bloodied from a Trevor Aylot clash, heads United in front. Barnsley, taken down a local mine in midweek by boss Allan Clarke, finally pull a goal back when Packer bundles over Ronnie Glavin.

33 — Rowles 44, Leslie 79 / Spence 38 — Ref: D Vickers
Derek Spence capitalises on Friday night indecision between Walker and Wignall to put the Shrimpers ahead. On the stroke of half-time Gough's cross finds Rowles to go in all-square at the break. Lee heads down to Leslie who squeezes in at the far post to put U's top overnight.

34 — Kellow 40 — Ref: M Ashley
Alan Ball returned to Blackpool yesterday in a three-year deal as player-manager, bringing with him Ted MacDougall as player-coach. Old adversary, Tony Kellow, collects a Harrison knockdown to drill a left-footed shot into the corner, denying the U's a record tenth away win.

Season match-by-match log (matches 35–46)

#	V	Opponent	Date	Pos	Res	FT	HT	Att		Pts
35	H	BLACKBURN	8/3	5	L	0-1	0-1	4,957	4	41
36	A	READING	14/3	6	L	0-2	0-2	5,444	10	41
37	H	BRENTFORD	22/3	5	W	6-1	1-0	3,818	18	43
38	A	PLYMOUTH	29/3	5	L	0-2	0-2	4,330	16	43
39	H	EXETER	2/4	5	D	0-0	0-0	2,780	8	44
40	A	GILLINGHAM	5/4	5	D	2-2	1-1	6,561	12	45
41	H	BURY	7/4	5	W	2-1	1-1	3,190	23	47
42	A	CHESTER	12/4	5	L	1-2	1-1	2,282	10	47
43	H	MILLWALL	19/4	5	D	0-0	0-0	3,296	12	48
44	A	SWINDON	22/4	5	W	3-2	3-1	7,985	11	50
45	A	CARLISLE	26/4	5	L	0-2	0-2	3,702	7	50
46	H	OXFORD	2/5	5	W	3-0	1-0	2,535	17	52

Home · Away 6,166 · Average 3,818

---

35 — H BLACKBURN, 8/3 (L 0-1)
U's: Walker, Cook, Packer, Leslie, Wright, Dowman, Rowles, Gough, Foley, Lee, Allinson
Opp: Arnold, Rathbone, Branagan, Kendall, Keeley, Fazackerley, Brotherston, Crawford, Garner, MacKenzie, Parkes
Crawford 24 — Ref: D Hedges

Howard Kendall's Rovers arrive with four straight away wins. Referee Hedges, in his first season, allows Duncan MacKenzie to hold down Walker after a goalmouth melee. Andy Crawford nets the loose ball. At the final whistle, cushions and missiles rain down on the official.

36 — A READING, 14/3 (L 0-2)
U's: Walker, Cook, Packer, Leslie, Wright, Dowman, Rowles, Gough, Foley, Lee, Allinson
Opp: Death, Joslyn, White, Bowman, Hetzke, Moreline, Earles, Williams, Heale, Sanchez, Wanklyn
Joslyn 34, Sanchez 39 — Ref: G Napthine

Reported to the FA by last weeks ref, U's promotion hopes fade with a third successive defeat. Reading repeat January's cup-tie score. Ex-U's player, Roger Joslyn, nets his first for the Royals. Steve Death plays his 100th consecutive game. Lawrie Sanchez side-foots in a Heale pass.

37 — H BRENTFORD, 22/3 (W 6-1)
U's: Walker, Cook, Packer, Leslie, Wright, Dowman, Rowles, Hodge, Foley, Lee, Allinson
Opp: Porter, Fraser, Tucker*, McNichol, Kruse, Salman, Carlton, Parkinson, Holmes, Funnell, Shrubb
Foley 6, 67, Lee 48, 78, Dowman 70, [Rowles 87]; Funnell 60 — Ref: P Reeve

Packer makes his 300th club appearance. The U's previously shot-shy forwards answer the critics to claim the first home Saturday win this season. The first half offered only Foley's interception of McNichol's backpass. Match of the Week's cameras enjoy a second-half goal glut.

38 — A PLYMOUTH, 29/3 (L 0-2)
U's: Walker, Cook, Packer, Leslie, Wright, Dowman, Hodge, Rowles, Wright, Lee, Allinson
Opp: Crudgington, James, Harrison, Randall, Foster, Phil Masters, Trusson, Kemp, Sims, Bason*, Johnson; Hodges
Trusson 2, 35 — Ref: M Robinson

Walker spares U's blushes slightly when he makes a stunning second-half penalty from Mike Trusson. The miss denies Trusson a hat-trick. An humiliating afternoon sees Roberts booked along with five of his players. A fourth defeat in five looks set to keep U's in Div Three next term.

39 — H EXETER, 2/4 (D 0-0)
U's: Walker, Cook, Packer, Leslie, Wright, Dowman, Hodge, Rowles, Foley, Lee, Allinson
Opp: Main, Rogers M, Hatch, Hore, Giles, Roberts P, Pratt, Rogers P, Ireland, Delve, Neville
Ref: R Toseland

Reserve team manager, lottery agent and former United star Bobby Hunt is sacked from his jobs when he refuses to work under the new lottery administrators. Brian Godfrey's Exeter have been on the fringe of the race all season, so the shared point does neither them nor U's any good.

40 — A GILLINGHAM, 5/4 (D 2-2)
U's: Walker, Cook, Packer, Leslie, Wignall, Wright, Rowles, Gough, Foley, Lee, Allinson
Opp: Hillyard, Sharpe, Barker, Overton, Weatherley, Crabbe, Bruce, Duncan, Price, Westwood, Richardson
Lee 44, Foley 79; Price 1, Bruce 65 — Ref: T Spencer

United return to something like the form they exhibited earlier in the season, after falling behind to Ken Price's early strike. Lee grabs his 17th of the season, but U's are well and truly out of the race despite holding fifth position. Steve Bruce beat Cook to Sharpe's cross to net for Gills.

41 — H BURY, 7/4 (W 2-1)
U's: Walker, Cook, Packer, Leslie*, Wignall, Dowman, Rowles, Gough, Foley, Lee, Allinson (sub Hodge)
Opp: Forrest, Howard, Bradley, McIlwraith, Waddington, Waldron, Whitehead, Wilson, Johnson, Hilton, Madden
Gough 34, Lee 88; Madden 31 — Ref: M Taylor

Craig Madden nets out-of-the-blue when he stabs in Steve Johnson's cross. A horrendous back-pass by ex-Newcastle Pat Howard four minutes later lets in Gough. Alan Whitehead's failed clearance, from Packer's free-kick, falls invitingly at the feet of Lee who notches United's winner.

42 — A CHESTER, 12/4 (L 1-2)
U's: Walker, Cook, Packer, Leslie, Wignall, Dowman*, Rowles, Gough, Foley, Lee, Evans (sub Phillips T / Henderson)
Opp: Millington, Raynor, Walker, Jeffries, Cottam, Oakes*, Sutcliffe, Fear, Rush, Phillips R, Henderson
Foley 6; Rush 10, 49 — Ref: J Heath

Chester's teenage scoring sensation, Ian Rush, set to join Liverpool for £300,000, took his tally to 17 for the season. Two minutes before his second he clashes with defender Dowman. The United player receives a broken nose and is subbed causing a defensive re-shuffle.

43 — H MILLWALL, 19/4 (D 0-0)
U's: Walker, Cook, Packer, Leslie, Wignall, Wright, Evans*, Harvey, Foley, Lee, Cotton (sub Rowles)
Opp: Jackson, Sitton, Gregory, Chatterton, Tagg, Blyth, Towner, Mehmet, Mitchell, Lyons, Coleman
Ref: K Baker

With Steve Dowman ruled out for the rest of the season, youth is given a chance. Colchester lad Gary Harvey makes his debut. Ian Allinson puts in a written transfer request. Despite 16 corners in the second period, the U's cannot break down a resolute, determined Lions back line.

44 — A SWINDON, 22/4 (W 3-2)
U's: Walker, Cook, Packer, Leslie, Wignall, Wright, Rowles, Harvey*, Foley, Lee, Cotton
Opp: Allan, Lewis, Ford, Carter, McHale, Stroud, Miller, Kamara, Rowland, Mayes, Williams
Rowles 4, Harvey 18, 33; McHale 24, Mayes 57 — Ref: T Bune

19-year old Gary Harvey nets his first ever League goals. Ray McHale blasts a 40th-minute penalty against the bar, after Wignall brings down Alan Mayes. Mayes's goal is his 28th of the campaign. Lee is involved in all U's goals. This is the third successive win at the County Ground.

45 — A CARLISLE, 26/4 (L 0-2)
U's: Walker, Cook, Rowles, Leslie, Wignall, Packer, Evans, Harvey*, Foley, Lee, Cotton
Opp: Swinburne, Collins, McCartney, Parker, Ludlam, Winstanley, McVitie, Houghton, Bannon, Hamilton, Beardsley
Bannon 35, 88 — Ref: P Tydesley

Allinson asks for a transfer after being dropped to the reserves, for whom he refuses to play 'because of illness'. The shirt-sleeved crowd see Carlisle top-scorer Paul Bannon unlock the U's defence in the first half and then take his season's tally to 21 with just two minutes remaining.

46 — H OXFORD, 2/5 (W 3-0)
U's: Walker, Cook, Packer, Leslie, Wignall, Rowles, Harvey*, Rowles, Foley S, Lee, Cotton
Opp: Brown, Bodel, Fogg, Briggs, Jeffrey, Cooke, Rowles, Taylor, Foley P, Hodgson, Brock
Packer, Rowles (2) — Ref: D Richardson

U's finish the season 10 points behind champions Grimsby, and six points off Div Two Gough (who thinks he can't displace Rowles and Lee). Dyer and Bunkell are freed. U's season of promise ends in a USA holiday, and a 0-1 defeat against Miami Dolphins at the Flamingo 'Stadium'.

LEAGUE DIVISION 3 (CUP-TIES)

Manager: Bobby Roberts

SEASON 1979-80

League Cup

		F-A	H-T	Scorers, Times, and Referees	1	2	3	4	5	6	7	8	9	10	11	12 sub used
1:1 H WATFORD 11/8 4,368 2:		W 2-0	2-0	Hodge 39p, Gough 44 Ref: B Martin	Walker	Cook	Wright	Leslie	Wignall	Dowman !	Hodge	Gough	Foley	Lee	Allinson	
					Rankin	Stirk	Harrison	Booth	Sims	Garner	Joslyn	Blissett	Jenkins	Bolton	Downes *	Mercer

Last season's League Cup semi-finalists. Watford, suffer a crazy five minutes just before the break. Dennis Booth handles Allinson's drive. Hodge makes no mistake from the spot. Gough increases the lead before Dowman is sent off in 84th minute for a tackle on Luther Blissett.

		F-A	H-T	Scorers, Times, and Referees	1	2	3	4	5	6	7	8	9	10	11	12 sub used
1:2 A WATFORD 14/8 10,051 2:		L 1-2	1-0	Allinson 29 Bolton 74p, 78 Ref: A Grey (Colchester won 3-2 on aggregate)	Walker	Cook	Wright	Leslie	Wignall	Dowman	Hodge	Gough	Foley	Lee	Allinson	
					Sherwood	Stirk	Harrison	Booth*	Sims	Garner	Joslyn	Blissett	Jenkins	Bolton	Downes	Pollard

Allinson's 35-yard volley flies past Sherwood. The U's take command. Cook trips Ross Jenkins in the box. Up steps Ian Bolton to level on the night. A few anxious minutes follow as Bolton reduces the arrears. Graham Taylor threatens to resign if he sees another performance like this.

		F-A	H-T	Scorers, Times, and Referees	1	2	3	4	5	6	7	8	9	10	11	12 sub used
2:1 H ASTON VILLA 28/8 6,221 1:13 8		L 0-2	0-1	Shaw 35, 73 Ref: B Hill	Walker	Packer	Rowles	Leslie	Wignall	Dowman	Hodge	Gough	Foley	Lee	Allinson	
					Rimmer	Gidman	Gibson	Evans	McNaught	Mortimer	Morley	Deehan	Shaw	Cowans	Swain	

England Youth star. Gary Shaw. steps out of reserve team football to give Colchester a mountain to climb in the second leg at Villa Park. He strikes first from Colin Gibson's low cross, has another effort ruled out for offside, then heads home a cross from flying winger Tony Morley.

		F-A	H-T	Scorers, Times, and Referees	1	2	3	4	5	6	7	8	9	10	11	12 sub used
2:2 A ASTON VILLA 5/9 19,475 1:17 14		W 2-0 aet	1-0	Lee 19, Gough 79 Ref: L Shapter (Colchester lost 8-9 on penalties)	Walker	Packer*	Rowles	Leslie	Wignall	Wright	Hodge	Gough	Foley	Lee	Allinson	
					Rimmer	Gidman	Gibson*	Evans	McNaught	Mortimer	Morley	Shaw	Deehan	Cowans	Swain	Shelton

Tony Morley. Aston Villa's £220,000 signing from Burnley, settles this thrilling penalty shoot-out. With nominees running out, U's keeper, Mike Walker, blasts over his sides ninth penalty. Morley does the rest. The U's had sensationally levelled on aggregate during normal time

FA Cup

		F-A	H-T	Scorers, Times, and Referees	1	2	3	4	5	6	7	8	9	10	11	12 sub used
1 H PLYMOUTH 24/11 4,064 3:21 3		D 1-1	1-0	Rowles 28 Hodges 85 Ref: M Baker	Walker	Cook	Packer	Leslie	Wright	Dowman	Hodge	Gough	Foley	Lee	Rowles*	Allinson
					Crudgington	James	McNeill	Randell	Foster	Phill'. Masters Hodges		Cooper	Sims	Bason	Graves	

United find Argyle a different prospect, eight days after beating them in the league at Layer Road by 5-2. Eddie Rowles's opener appears to have the U's cruising to another victory, but resolute Plymouth level with just five minutes to go through Kevin Hodges to earn a replay.

		F-A	H-T	Scorers, Times, and Referees	1	2	3	4	5	6	7	8	9	10	11	12 sub used
1R A PLYMOUTH 27/11 6,926 3:21 3		W 1-0 aet	0-0	Allinson 100 Ref: M Baker	Walker	Cook	Packer	Leslie	Wright	Dowman	Hodge	Gough	Foley	Lee	Allinson	
					Crudgington	James	McNeill	Randell	Foster	Phill'. Masters Hodges		Cooper*	Sims	Bason	Graves	Harrison

A home tie with Fourth Division Bournemouth, and a golden opportunity to draw the big boys awaits. Ian Allinson, who has been missing recently due to a family illness, blasts a shot that deflects off Tyrone James, out of the reach of despairing home keeper, Geoff Crudgington.

		F-A	H-T	Scorers, Times, and Referees	1	2	3	4	5	6	7	8	9	10	11	12 sub used
2 H BOURNEMOUTH 15/12 3,693 4:12 2		W 1-0	1-0	Rowles 28 Ref: R Bridges	Walker	Cook	Packer	Leslie	Wignall	Dowman	Hodge	Rowles	Foley*	Lee	Allinson	
					Allen	Cunningham	Ferns	Impey	Townsend	Chambers	Holder	MacDougall	Butler	Evanson	Miller	Wright

Rowles, playing against his old colleagues, seals the win. The U's have Walker to thank for a string of fine saves. Ted MacDougall sends a second-half header against the bar. which sticks in the mud on the line. MacDougall has the ball in the net on 89 minutes but is ruled offside.

		F-A	H-T	Scorers, Times, and Referees	1	2	3	4	5	6	7	8	9	10	11	12 sub used
3 A READING 5/1 7,780 3:13 3		L 0-2	0-1	Earles 1, Heale 86 Ref: A Glasson	Walker	Cook	Packer	Leslie	Wignall	Dowman	Wright	Gough*	Foley	Lee	Allinson	
					Death	Joslyn	White	Bowman	Hetzke	Moreline	Earles	Kearney	Heale	Sanchez	Lewis	Rowles

Cock-a-hoop Reading, who scored seven without reply against Barnsley last week, get off to the best possible start with Pat Earles' opener on 81 seconds. The U's press for the remainder, but are caught on the break by Gary Heale four minutes from time. Reading now visit Swansea.

League Table

	P	Home W	Home D	Home L	Home F	Home A	Away W	Away D	Away L	Away F	Away A	Pts
1 Grimsby	46	18	2	3	46	16	8	8	7	27	26	62
2 Blackburn	46	13	5	5	34	17	12	7	4	24	19	59
3 Sheffield Wed	46	12	6	5	44	20	9	10	4	37	27	58
4 Chesterfield	46	16	5	2	46	16	7	6	10	25	30	57
5 COLCHESTER	46	10	10	3	39	20	10	2	11	25	36	52
6 Carlisle	46	13	6	4	45	26	5	6	12	21	30	48
7 Reading	46	14	6	3	43	19	2	10	11	23	46	48
8 Exeter	46	14	5	4	38	22	5	5	13	22	46	48
9 Chester	46	14	6	3	29	18	3	7	13	20	39	47
10 Swindon	46	15	4	4	50	20	4	4	15	21	43	46
11 Barnsley	46	10	7	6	29	20	6	7	10	24	36	46
12 Sheffield Utd	46	13	5	5	35	21	5	5	13	25	45	46
13 Rotherham	46	13	4	6	38	24	5	6	12	20	42	46
14 Millwall	46	14	6	3	49	23	2	7	14	16	36	45
15 Plymouth	46	13	7	3	39	17	3	5	15	20	38	44
16 Gillingham	46	8	9	6	26	18	6	5	12	23	33	42
17 Oxford	46	10	4	9	34	24	4	9	10	23	38	41
18 Blackpool	46	10	7	6	39	34	5	4	14	23	40	41
19 Brentford	46	10	6	7	33	26	5	9	13	26	47	41
20 Hull	46	11	7	5	29	21	1	9	13	22	48	40
21 Bury	46	10	4	9	30	23	6	3	14	15	36	39
22 Southend	46	11	6	6	33	23	3	4	16	14	35	38
23 Mansfield	46	9	9	5	31	24	1	7	15	16	34	36
24 Wimbledon	46	6	8	9	34	38	4	6	13	18	43	34
	1104	287	144	121	893	530	121	144	287	530	893	1104

Appearances and Goals

	App Lge	Sub	LC	Sub	FA	Sub	Goals Lge	LC	FA	Tot
Allinson, Ian	37		4		3	1	2	1	1	4
Bunkell, Ray	1									
Cook, Micky	44		2		4		2			2
Cotton, Russell	4									
Dowman, Steve	37		3	1	4		2			2
Dyer, Paul	3	1								
Evans, Tony	2	4								
Foley, Steve	42		4		4		8			8
Gough, Bobby	31	1	4		3		8	2	2	12
Harvey, Gary	4	3					2			2
Hodge, Bobby	34		4		3		5	1		6
Lee, Trevor	43		4		4		17	1		18
Leslie, Steve	46		4		4		1			1
Packer, Mick	43		2		4		4			4
Rowles, Eddie	26	8	2		2	1	8			8
Walker, Mick	46		4		4					
Wignall, Steve	40		4		2		3			3
Wright, Steve	23	3	3		3	1	1			1
(own-goals)							1			1
18 players used	**506**	**21**	**44**	**1**	**44**	**3**	**64**	**5**	**3**	**72**

Odds & ends

Double wins: (6) Bury, Grimsby, Mansfield, Oxford, Sheffield Wed, Southend.

Double defeats: (2) Blackburn, Chesterfield.

Won from behind: (5) Grimsby (a), Sheffield United (a), Grimsby (h), Southend (h), Bury (h).

Lost from in front: (1) Chester (a).

High spots: A real challenge for Second Division status. A brilliant 2-0 League Cup win at Villa Park, forcing extra-time. Ten league victories away from Layer Road. Joint top of the league in December and February. Trevor Lee repays his transfer fee with 18 goals.

Low spots: Three consecutive defeats from the end of February that ruined U's chances. Tragic penalty shoot-out defeat, after 17 spot-kicks, at Villa Park. Ten home draws that also contributed to the six point gap to promotion.

Player of the Year: Mike Walker.

Ever presents: (2) Steve Leslie, Mike Walker.

Hat-tricks: (0).

Leading scorer: Trevor Lee 18.

LEAGUE DIVISION 3

Manager: Bobby Roberts

SEASON 1980-81

Player positions 1–11 shown as United player (bold) / opponent (italic). Column 12 = sub used.

No	Date	1	2	3	4	5	6	7	8	9	10	11	12 sub used	Att	Pos	Pt	F-A	H-T	Scorers, Times, and Referees
1	H PLYMOUTH 16/8	Walker / Crudgington	Cook / Harrison	Cotton / Uzzell	Gough / Cooper	Wignall / Foster	Packer / Phil' Masters Hodges	Hodge /	Rowles* / Kemp*	Foley / Graves	Lee / Bason	Allinson / Murphy	Leslie / Peachey	2,061		D 1	2 2	0-1	Hodge 53, Gough 90 / Kemp 18, Murphy 46 Ref: D Letts. Dowman joins Wrexham for £75,000. Before the lowest gate for two years, ref Letts looks long and hard at David Kemp's suspiciously offside opener. Leslie returns from injury to lead the fight-back. Argyle are loudly backed by a number of West country soldiers, serving in the town.
2	A FULHAM 20/8	Walker / Peyton	Cook / Peters	Allinson / Strong	Leslie / Beck	Wignall / Brown	Packer / Gale	Harvey* / Greenaway	Gough / Wilson	Foley / O'Driscoll	Evans / Davies	Cotton / Lock	Lee	4,250		L 1	0-1	0-0	Lock 59p Ref: R Toseland. Fulham have entered a team into the Rugby Football League. Packer hauls down Gordon Davies in a tackle akin to the oval-ball game, trying to atone for his poor backpass. Ex-West Ham star, Kevin Lock, gives the Cottagers both points in the U's first ever visit to Craven Cottage.
3	H WALSALL 23/8	Walker / Freeman	Cook / Macken	Leslie / Mower	Gough* / Serella	Wignall / Baines	Packer / Hart	Hodge / Penn	Rowles / O'Kelly	Foley / McDonough	Lee / Buckley	Allinson / Caswell*	Evans / Waddington S	1,979	23 15	D 2	1-1	0-1	Rowles 74, O'Kelly 23 Ref: R Challis. Hodge, left out at Fulham, asks for a move but provides the cross for Rowles' equaliser. Brian Caswell had centered for Richard O'Kelly. signed from Alvechurch, to net his first Saddler's goal. Essex County cricket at Castle Park contributes to U's lowest-ever home attendance.
4	A EXETER 30/8	Walker / Main	Evans / Ireland	Allinson / Hatch	Leslie / Prince	Wignall / Giles	Packer / Roberts P	Hodge / Pearson	Harvey / Neville	Foley / Kellow*	Lee / Delve	Cotton / Pullar	Rogers P	3,918	22 2	L 2	0-4	0-1	Neville 45, Giles 64, Delve 72, Kellow 82p Ref: T Spencer. Injury-hit U's are still seeking their first win of the new campaign. Stand-in centre-half Foley makes a hash of a back-pass, allowing Tony Kellow to find Steve Neville. That blow right on half-time knocks the stuffing out of United and the Grecians add a trio of second-half strikes.
5	A BURNLEY 6/9	Walker / Stevenson	Cook / Laws	Allinson / Holt	Leslie / Robertson	Wignall / Overson	Packer / Dobson	Hodge / Cassidy	Evans* / Young	Foley / Hamilton	Lee / Taylor	Rowles / Cavener	Crouch	4,391	22 18	L 2	0-1	0-1	Hamilton 27 Ref: T Farley. For the second game running the score does not reflect U's performance. Last week at St James' Park, they were unlucky to be on the end of a four-goal hiding, but at Turf Moor they are lucky not to get a hiding. Still weakened by Dowman's departure, Billy Hamilton easily heads in.
6	H MILLWALL 13/9	Walker / Gleasure	Cook / Sitton	Crouch / Gregory	Leslie / Chatterton	Wignall / Tagg	Packer / Blyth	Cotton / Roberts	Allinson / Massey	Foley / Mitchell	Lee / Lyons	Rowles / Kinsella	Rowles	2,724	21 18	W 4	3-0	1-0	Foley 23, Lee 51, Rowles 74 Ref: H Taylor. Allinson switches from full-back to midfield to engineer the first win of the season. The victory is overshadowed by Police Sgt Frank Ruggles, who comes onto the pitch on 70 mins to question Lions' Mel Blyth for three minutes about his swearing. The incident makes the national news.
7	H CHESTERFIELD 16/9	Walker / Turner	Cook / Tartt	Allinson / O'Neill	Leslie / Wilson	Wignall / Green	Packer / Hunter	Hodge / Birch	Rowles / Moss	Foley / Bonnyman	Lee / Ridley	Crouch / Walker		2,171	17 5	D 5	1-1	0-1	Lee 60, Green 39 Ref: J Deakin. John Turner. £60,000 from Torquay, saves Hodge's weak 67th-minute penalty, after Foley is scythed by Hunter. Foley leads the line but faces an Achilles operation on 27 September. He will miss five weeks. Bill Green's goal takes a lucky deflection. Rowles 'scores' an offside goal.
8	A CHARLTON 20/9	Walker / Wood	Cook / Gritt	Crouch / Warman	Leslie / Shaw	Wignall / Berry	Packer / Tydeman	Hodge / Powell	Rowles / Walsh	Foley / Hales	Lee / Smith*	Allinson / Robinson	Walker	4,323	15 10	W 7	2-1	1-1	Foley 43, Hodge 88, Hales 35p Ref: L Burden. Charlton parade 17-year-old sensation Paul Walsh and are unbeaten at the Valley. Hodge puts the worry of his mother's illness and last week's penalty miss behind him as he capitalises on Phil Warman's error to earn U's first away victory. Wignall had earlier shoved Walsh in the area.
9	H CHESTER 27/9	Walker / Millington	Cook / Raynor	Crouch / Walker	Leslie / Storton	Wignall / Cottam	Packer / Fear	Hodge / Birch	Rowles / Howatt	Foley / Kearney	Lee / Jones	Allinson / Ludlam		2,147	15 20	D 8	1-1	0-0	Lee 90, Jones 77 Ref: J Martin. Last week's hero, Hodge, has his transfer request refused and Foley delays his operation. The U's fall behind to a speculative effort from Bryn Jones. Just when it looks as if all the points are destined for the visitors, up pops Trevor Lee, deep into injury-time, to secure a home point.
10	A CHESTERFIELD 30/9	Walker / Turner	Cook / Tartt	Allinson / O'Neill	Leslie / Wilson	Wignall / Green	Packer / Ridley	Hodge / Birch	Rowles / Moss	Foley / Bonnyman	Lee / Salmons	Crouch / Walker		6,674	19 2	L 8	0-3	0-3	Moss 4, Walker 43, Birch 44 Ref: G Courtney. Cotton, finishing a three-match suspension. is sent off for the reserves at Layer Road. Formidable Chesterfield take the lead when Ernie Moss heads in a left-wing Phil Walker cross. Walker is fed clear by Geoff Salmons for number two. Moss leaves Packer in pain and supplies Birch.
11	A HUDDERSFIELD 4/10	Walker / Rankin	Cook / Brown	Allinson / Robinson	Leslie / Stanton	Wignall / Topping	Packer / Hanvey	Hodge / Laverick	Longhorn* / Kennedy	Foley / Kindon	Lee / Robins	Cotton / Cowling	Evans	8,400	20 8	L 8	0-2	0-0	Kindon 50p, Brown 64 Ref: K McNally. U's make a record bid for Highland League Keith's 22-year-old striker, Kevin Bremner. Missing three key regulars, Packer pushes Ian Robins in the back. Steve Kindon obliges. Full-back Malcolm Brown scores an out-of-this-world goal from 25 yards over on the right touchline.

No.	Venue	Opponent	Date	Att.			Pos.	Res.	Score	HT
12	H	PORTSMOUTH	7/10	2,702	8	10	17	W	1-0	0-0
13	H	BARNSLEY	11/10	2,749	12	11	17	D	2-2	2-2
14	A	BLACKPOOL	18/10	6,997	8	12	17	D	1-1	0-1
15	A	READING	22/10	3,955	8	12	20	L	0-1	0-1
16	H	ROTHERHAM	25/10	2,623	5	13	19	D	0-0	0-0
17	H	HULL	28/10	2,239	24	15	16	W	2-0	1-0
18	A	SHEFFIELD UTD	1/11	12,810	6	15	18	L	0-3	0-2
19	A	PORTSMOUTH	4/11	10,895	7	15	19	L	1-2	1-2
20	H	SWINDON	8/11	2,153	23	17	18	W	1-0	0-0
21	H	FULHAM	11/11	2,543	19	19	16	W	3-2	2-1
22	A	PLYMOUTH	15/11	4,905	8	20	15	D	1-1	1-1
23	H	OXFORD	29/11	2,114	20	22	13	W	3-0	3-0

---

12. PORTSMOUTH (H) — 7/10
Team: Walker, Cook, Crouch, Leslie, Wignall, Hodge, Gough, Rowles, Lee, Allinson
Opponents: *Mellor, McLaughlin, Viney, Brisley, Aizlewood, Gregory, Laidlaw, Perrin, Bryant, Rogers*
Lee 86
Ref: A Ward
Foley finally checks in for his op. Lee's fourth of the season is a simple side-foot past Peter Mellor. A draw looks inevitable against a sturdy Pompey defence until the coloured striker's effort just four minutes from time. Gough returns after a five-week lay-off for two broken toes.

13. BARNSLEY (H) — 11/10
Team: Walker, Cook*, Crouch*, Leslie, Wignall, Hodge, Gough, Rowles, Lee, Allinson
Opponents: *New, Cooper, Chambers*, Glavin*, Banks, Evans, McCarthy, Parker, Aylot, Lester, Riley, Hunter*
Gough 20, Hodge 87 / Parker 30, Glavin 37
Ref: M Dimblebee
Bremner, signed in midweek, is denied a sensational last-minute debut winner when ref Dimblebee awards a foul for a push on Ian Evans. Bremner, who looks a bargain, comes on at half-time and might well have had a hat-trick but for the heroics of visiting keeper Martin New.

14. BLACKPOOL (A) — 18/10
Team: Walker, Cook, Evans, Leslie, Wignall, Cotton, Gough, Rowles, Bremner, Allinson
Opponents: *Hesford, Simmonite, Williams, Ball, Stragia*, McEwan, Morgan, Hockaday, Ashurst, Marris, Deary, Thompson*
Allinson 57 / Williams 24
Ref: G Owen
Blackpool, winners in the midweek Anglo-Scottish Cup v. Kilmarnock, omit Eamonn Collins, who just days before his 15th birthday appeared in the match. Gary Williams is unmarked from a corner-kick. Gough goal is offside on 48 minutes. Allinson latches onto Wignall's clearance.

15. READING (A) — 22/10
Team: Walker, Cook, Rowles, Leslie, Wignall, Cotton, Gough, Bremner, Lee, Allinson
Opponents: *Death, Joslyn, Lewis, Webb, Hicks, Earles, Williams, Dixon, Sanchez, Beavon*
Williams 37
Ref: A Hamil
The Elm Park jinx continues. The Royals have eight players injured or suspended. Transfer-listed Jerry Williams swivels to hook the ball past Walker. Bremner is visibly shaken by a third-minute challenge by Martin Hicks. Wignall blocks a 75th-minute Kerry Dixon effort on the line.

16. ROTHERHAM (H) — 25/10
Team: Walker, Cook, Rowles, Leslie, Longhorn, Cotton, Gough, Lee, Longhorn, Allinson
Opponents: *Mountford, Forrest*, Breckin, Rhodes, Stancliffe, Mullen, Tiler, Gooding, Moore, Seasman, Henson, Winn*
Ref: B Hill
Scrooge-like Rotherham have now let in one goal to the U's in the past ten meetings. Longhorn replaces stomach-bug victim, Wignall. The Millers' keeper, Ray Mountford, is drafted from the reserves at the eleventh hour, after usual keeper Graham Brown fell ill at the team's hotel.

17. HULL (H) — 28/10
Team: Walker, Norman, Longhorn, Leslie, Wignall, Packer, Gough, Lee, Bremner, Allinson
Opponents: *Nisbet, Haigh, Swann, Roberts J, Mullen, Roberts D, Marwood, Moss, Edwards, Whitehurst*, Deacy, Norrie*
Allinson 16, Lee 89
Ref: D Reeves
Hull, under the leadership of ex-Wales manager, Mike Smith and Cyril Lea, have lost their last six matches and have not won away for 31 games. The Tigers stay rooted to the foot, as Allinson (volley) and Lee (solo run), add to their misery. Wignall's 40th-minute effort is offside.

18. SHEFFIELD UTD (A) — 1/11
Team: Walker, Richardson, Longhorn, Leslie, Wignall, Packer, Evans, Bremner, Lee, Allinson
Opponents: *Moore, Garner, Kenworthy, McPhail, Trusson, Ryan, Neville, Charles, Hatton, Peters*
Kenworthy 1p, Trusson 44, Charles 68
Ref: G Nolan
Packer handles a John Ryan cross in the very first minute, for Tony Kenworthy to hammer an unstoppable spot-kick. Walker fails to hold Steve Neville's powerful header, leaving Mike Trusson to stab in. Neville then sends Steve Charles away to score for the fourth consecutive game.

19. PORTSMOUTH (A) — 4/11
Team: Walker, Mellor, Longhorn, Leslie, Wignall, Evans, Cotton, Bremner, Lee, Allinson
Opponents: *McLaughlin, Viney, Laidlaw, Daveyd, Garner, Gregory, Tait, Showers, Bryant, Rogers*
Lee 38 / Gregory 34, 65
Ref: E Read
Portsmouth's lowest home crowd of the season, a little under 11,000 (!!), sees David Gregory strikes ninth of the season to set the Pompey chimes ringing. Tony Evans finds Lee with a wonderful ball to level. Gregory has the last laugh when he steers home a Derek Showers cross.

20. SWINDON (H) — 8/11
Team: Walker, Allan, Rowles, Leslie, Wignall, Hodge, Gough*, Bremner, Lee, Allinson
Opponents: *Trollope, Peach, Kamara, Lewis, Stroud, Miller, Carter, Rowland, Mayes, Williams, Longhorn*
Lee 76p
Ref: B Martin
A light covering of snow does not warrant a pitch inspection. Bill Trollope makes his 770th appearance. Lee's cross strikes David Peach on the arm. Hodge, who missed against Chesterfield, restores his confidence. Mayes and Rowland have yet to re-discover last season's goal touch.

21. FULHAM (H) — 11/11
Team: Walker, Peyton, Rowles, Leslie, Wignall, Hodge, Longhorn*, Bremner, Lee, Allinson
Opponents: *Peyton, Strong, Beck*, Kamara, Lewis, Brown, Hatter, O'Driscoll, Davies, Gale, Wilson, Goodlass, Foley, Corner*
Wignall 16, Allinson 17, 70 / Beck 24, Davies 53
Ref: D Lloyd
The Cottagers, with new manager Malcolm MacDonald, make their first league visit to Layer Road. A topsy-turvy match begins with Wignall coolly chipping the entire defence. Foley returns after his op. Allinson's 30-yard match-winner is in the net before Gerry Peyton even sees it.

22. PLYMOUTH (A) — 15/11
Team: Walker, Crudgington, Rowles, Leslie, Wignall, Hodge, Foley, Bremner, Lee, Allinson
Opponents: *Nisbet, Harrison, Garner, Hodges, Foster, Cooper, Kemp, Sims, Bason, Murphy*
Bremner 38 / Kemp 78
Ref: D Hutchinson
An unusual choice for Match of the Day, but the TV cameras show clearly that Geoff Crudgington did get back to stop Bremner's last-minute effort from going over the line. Walker, John Motson's man of the match, is finally beaten by David Kemp's header from Kevin Hodges' cross.

23. OXFORD (H) — 29/11
Team: Walker, Burton, Rowles, Leslie, Wignall, Hodge, Foley S, Bremner, Lee, Allinson
Opponents: *Kingston, Fogg, Jeffrey, Briggs, McIntosh, Brock, Cassells, Jones, Foley P, Lythgoe*, Smithers*
Hodge 73p, Bremner 75, 78
Ref: C Downey
Fans clear two inches of snow, helped by ref Colin Downey. Packer's 300th league appearance. Packer's spot-kick. Lee for the spot-kick. (Ipswich v Boro is off.) Gary Briggs fouls Lee for the spot-kick. Bremner rifles in Foley's cross and then heads home Packer's free-kick.

LEAGUE DIVISION 3   Manager: Bobby Roberts   SEASON 1980-81

No	Date		Team	Att	Pos	Pt	F-A	H-T	1	2	3	4	5	6	7	8	9	10	11	12 sub used
24	6/12	A	CARLISLE	3,196	15 21	L 22	0-4	0-2	Walker	Cook	Rowles	Leslie	Wignall	Packer	Hodge	Foley	Bremner	Lee	Allinson	
									Harrison	*Haigh*	*Coady*	*MacDonal*	*Campbell*	*Parker*	*Coughlin*	*Metcalfe*	*Brown*	*Beardsley*	*Staniforth*	

Scorers: [Staniforth 75/ Brown 34, Beardsley 43, 46. Ref: J Hough
Youngsters Evans and Harvey are put on the transfer list for not pushing hard enough for a place. Colchester visited Cumbria with seven points from the last eight. Carlisle have not won in six matches Starlet Peter Beardsley turns it on for the watching Newcastle manager. Arthur Cox.

No	Date		Team	Att	Pos	Pt	F-A	H-T	1	2	3	4	5	6	7	8	9	10	11	12 sub used
25	20/12	H	NEWPORT	2,160	13 6	W 24	1-0	1-0	Walker	Cook	Rowles	Leslie	Wignall	Longhorn	Hodge	Gough	Bremner	Lee	Allinson	
									Plumley	*Warriner*	*Relish*	*Davies*	*Oakes*	*Tynan*	*Vaughan*	*Lowndes*	*Gwyther*	*Elsey*	*Moore*	

Scorers: Hodge 43p. Ref: A Grey
The European Cup-Winners' Cup quarter-finalists recall transfer-listed Welsh U-21 star, Steve Lowndes. Ultra-defensive County gift-wrap the points for the U's. Nigel Vaughan inexplicably handles whilst lying on the by-line. Hodge places the penalty-kick to the right of Gary Plumley.

No	Date		Team	Att	Pos	Pt	F-A	H-T	1	2	3	4	5	6	7	8	9	10	11	12 sub used
26	26/12	A	BRENTFORD	6,240	14 13	L 24	1-2	1-1	Walker	Cook	Rowles	Leslie	Wignall	Packer	Hodge*	Longhorn	Bremner	Lee	Allinson	Cotton
									McKellar	*Hill*	*Tucker*	*Salman*	*Kruse*	*Hurlock*	*Roberts*	*Frost*	*Johnson G*	*Walker*	*Crown*	

Scorers: Bremner 43 / Kruse 18, Hurlock 71. Ref: G Napthine
The U's announce the signing of Nuneaton centre-half John Glover for £30,000. His registration is not completed in time for the trip to Griffin Park. U's may regret these two dropped points, as speedy David Crown, signed from non-league in the summer, provides both of Bees' goals.

No	Date		Team	Att	Pos	Pt	F-A	H-T	1	2	3	4	5	6	7	8	9	10	11	12 sub used
27	27/12	H	GILLINGHAM	3,879	12 21	W 26	2-1	1-1	Walker	Cook	Wright*	Leslie	Wignall	Packer	Longhorn	Gough	Bremner	Lee	Allinson	Hodge
									Sutton	*Sharpe*	*Ford*	*Bruce*	*Weatherley*	*Crabbe*	*Nicholl*	*Duncan*	*Price*	*Richardson*	*White*	

Scorers: Packer 27p, Lee 90 / Price 37. Ref: C White
18-year old debutant Gary Sutton is beaten from the spot, after Steve Bruce pushes Bremner John Sharpe's cross finds the unmarked Ken Price to level. Just as the fans were streaming away, Sharpe slips and Allinson finds Lee. The Gills lost to Maidstone in a cup replay. midweek.

No	Date		Team	Att	Pos	Pt	F-A	H-T	1	2	3	4	5	6	7	8	9	10	11	12 sub used
28	10/1	H	BLACKPOOL	2,378	12 22	W 28	3-2	1-1	Walker	Cook	Longhorn	Leslie	Wignall	Packer	Wright	Foley	Bremner	Gough	Allinson	Brockbank
									Hesford	*Gardner*	*Pashley*	*Ball*	*Stragia*	*Ashurst*	*Morgan*	*Hockaday*	*Harrison**	*Morris*	*Simmonite*	

Scorers: Foley 12, Gough 56, 74 / Morris 37, Ball 68. Ref: M Bidmead
Gough is recalled after last weeks' record £90,000 sale of Lee to Gillingham. Player-manager Alan Ball equalises. Iain Hesford, in fine form. stands five yards outside his area whenever his side are on the attack. Gough catches him out, lobbing from fully 40 yards into an empty net.

No	Date		Team	Att	Pos	Pt	F-A	H-T	1	2	3	4	5	6	7	8	9	10	11	12 sub used
29	17/1	A	OXFORD	3,498	15 18	L 28	1-2	0-1	Walker	Cook	Longhorn	Leslie	Wignall	Packer	Wright*	Foley S	Bremner	Gough	Allinson	Hodge
									Burton	*Doyle*	*Fogg*	*Jeffrey*	*Briggs*	*Shotton*	*Jones*	*Foley P*	*Thomas*	*Berry*	*Smithers*	

Scorers: Foley 89 / Shotton 18, Jeffrey 68. Ref: M Baker
Computer operator Glover decides, belatedly, to stick to his day job. He turns down a move to the U's, but has already resigned from his employers. U's dismal away record continues against the side with the worst home record. Malcolm Shotton and Billy Jeffrey win the points.

No	Date		Team	Att	Pos	Pt	F-A	H-T	1	2	3	4	5	6	7	8	9	10	11	12 sub used
30	31/1	A	WALSALL	3,195	15 12	L 28	1-3	0-2	Walker	Cook	Packer	Leslie	Wignall	Wright	Longhorn	Cotton	Bremner	Foley	Allinson	
									Green	*Caswell*	*Mower*	*Serella*	*Baines*	*Hart*	*Waddington S*	*Preece*	*Smith*	*Buckley*	*Waddington P*	

Scorers: Allinson 78 / Waddington S 8, Mower 25, Smith 90. Ref: D Owen
On the eve of the trip to Fellows Park, Gough, Packer and Hodge are transfer-listed, and a new stadium at North Station is announced. Walsall. 30 goals in 15 home matches, lead 2-0. Bremner hits the post on 75 mins, then feeds Allinson. The Saddlers snatch a breakaway third goal.

No	Date		Team	Att	Pos	Pt	F-A	H-T	1	2	3	4	5	6	7	8	9	10	11	12 sub used
31	3/2	H	EXETER	2,357	15 18	L 28	1-2	1-2	Walker	Cook	Longhorn	Leslie	Wignall	Wright	Hodge	Foley	Bremner	Foley	Allinson	
									Main	*Rogers M*	*Hatch*	*Forbes*	*Giles*	*Roberts P*	*Pearson*	*Rogers P*	*Kellow*	*Delve*	*Pullar*	

Scorers: Forbes 11, Pullar 29 / Bremner 33. Ref: J Bray
Cup giant-killers City, who beat Leicester with a Tony Kellow hat-trick, inflict the first home defeat for the U's since last March. Kellow is the country's leading scorer with 25 to his credit Bremner nets his seventh of the season, but the U's are now just four points above relegation.

No	Date		Team	Att	Pos	Pt	F-A	H-T	1	2	3	4	5	6	7	8	9	10	11	12 sub used
32	7/2	A	MILLWALL	4,565	16 15	L 28	1-3	1-1	Walker	Cook	Longhorn	Leslie	Wignall	Wright	Cotton	Hodge	Bremner	Foley	Allinson	
									Jackson	*Martin*	*Roberts*	*Anderson*	*Tagg*	*Coleman*	*Kinsella*	*Mehmet*	*Harrix*	*Bartley*	*Massey*	

Scorers: Bremner 44 / Bartley 18, Martin 57, Horrix 66. Ref: L Shapter
Bad-boy Cotton is back to bolster the defence. but Cook makes two critical errors. First he lets in John Bartley for the opener, and then caps an unusually poor performance. gifting 17-year-old debutant Dean Horrix, who nets the third. Millwall include seven teenagers in their line-up.

No	Date		Team	Att	Pos	Pt	F-A	H-T	1	2	3	4	5	6	7	8	9	10	11	12 sub used
33	14/2	H	BURNLEY	3,082	15 7	W 30	2-1	1-0	Walker	Cook	Longhorn	Cotton	Wright	Packer	Osborne	Foley	Bremner	McDonough	Allinson	Taylor
									Stevenson	*Wharton*	*Holt*	*Phelan*	*Overson*	*Dobson*	*Young*	*Laws*	*Hamilton*	*Robertson**	*Cavener*	

Scorers: McDonough 25, Bremner 63 / Hamilton 78. Ref: T Bune
U's parade 22-year old McDonough (£15,000 ex-Chelsea) and Osborne (£25,000 ex-Ipswich). Gough talks with Port Vale. The Clarets, rebuilding. field six teenagers. Osborne sets up both goals. crossing for McDonough to head in. and then plants a free-kick on Bremner's head.

No	Date		Team	Att	Pos	Pt	F-A	H-T	1	2	3	4	5	6	7	8	9	10	11	12 sub used
34	21/2	A	CHESTER	1,778	14 12	D 31	0-0	0-0	Walker	Cook	Coleman	Cotton	Wright	Packer	Osborne	McDonough	Bremner	Foley	Allinson	Ludlam
									Millington	*Raynor*	*Walker**	*Storton*	*Cattam*	*Jeffries*	*Satcliffe*	*Jones*	*Howatt*	*Phillips T*	*Burns*	

Scorers: Ref: A Challinor
U's take their season's spending to £80k, signing Millwall youngster Phil Coleman. crossing field five games and first away clean sheet of the season. Osborne clears Trevor Storton's powerful header off the line in the 89th minute.

Colchester United — Match-by-match record (season continued)

---

35 · H · CHARLTON · 28/2 — Att 4,864 · 12 / 1 · W · 33 · 2-0 (2-0)
Colchester: Walker, Cook, Coleman, Leslie, Wright, Packer, Osborne, Foley, Bremner, McDonough, Allinson
Charlton: Johns, Naylor, Warman, Shaw, Berry, Tydeman!, Powell, Walsh*, Hales, Walker, Robinson, Madden
Scorers: Foley 6, Packer 10p · Ref: D Richardson
Colchester complete a surprise double over the league leaders, in a mud-bath. Foley's 35-yarder skids off the surface and is helped on by Peter Shaw. Nicky Johns trips Bremner for a penalty. Dick Tydeman, booked earlier, is sent off ten minutes from time for hauling down Allinson.

---

36 · H · HUDDERSFIELD · 7/3 — Att 3,644 · 14 / 3 · L · 33 · 1-2 (1-1)
Colchester: Walker, Cook, Coleman, Leslie, Wignall, Packer, Osborne, Foley, Bremner, McDonough, Allinson
Huddersfield: Freeman, Brown, Purdie, Stanton, Sutton, Hanvey, Lillis, Kennedy, Austin, Robins, Cowling
Scorers: Packer 45; Robins 39, Lillis 67 · Ref: J Deakin
Wignall returns after a three-game suspension. Hanvey's shot is deflected and falls kindly for Ian Robins to tap into the empty net. In the third minute of injury time, Packer equalises. Lillis ghosts in to meet Malcolm Brown's low cross. Osborne, agonisingly, grazes the bar late on.

---

37 · A · HULL · 17/3 — Att 3,586 · 14 / 24 · W · 35 · 1-0 (1-0)
Colchester: Walker, Cook, Wignall, Leslie, Wright, Packer, Osborne, Foley, Bremner, McDonough, Cotton*
Hull: Norman, Hoolickin, Booth, Richards, Roberts G, Roberts D, Whitehurst, Ferguson, Edwards, Mutrie, Deacy, Allinson
Scorers: Cotton 4 · Ref: R Chadwick
United's relegation worries ease slightly, whilst Hull sink ever nearer the drop and stay firmly rooted to the foot of the table. Cotton strikes his first senior goal. Three minutes later there is a two-minute delay for a hoax bomb scare. The U's hold out to secure only their second away win.

---

38 · H · READING · 22/3 — Att 3,705 · 14 / 9 · L · 35 · 1-2 (1-2)
Colchester: Walker, Cook, Wignall, Leslie, Wright, Packer, Osborne, Foley*, Bremner, McDonough, Cotton
Reading: Death, Williams, Joslyn, Bowman, Hicks, Hetzke, Earles, Kearney, Heale, Beavon, Sanchez, Allinson
Scorers: Bremner 27; Heale 8, 35 · Ref: R Challis
Colchester stage their first ever home game on a Sunday. No recorded music over the tannoy and admission by membership are just two of the by-laws to be complied with. Reading's prayers are answered as the U's concede two goals at Layer Road for the eighth time this season.

---

39 · A · ROTHERHAM · 28/3 — Att 7,956 · 17 / 2 · L · 35 · 0-2 (0-1)
Colchester: Walker, Cook, Wright, Leslie, Wignall, Packer, Osborne, Foley, Bremner, McDonough, Cotton*
Rotherham: Mountford, Forrest, Breckin, Rhodes, Stancliffe, Mullen, Towner, Seasman, Moore, Fern, Henson, Allinson
Scorers: Moore 7, 76 · Ref: P Willis
After Sunday's defeat, more bad news when the Borough Council reject plans for the Colne River Centre Stadium. The U's never threaten to dent a home record which has conceded only six goals. Ronnie Moore, off the pitch for five minutes with an elbow injury, bags a brace.

---

40 · H · SHEFFIELD UTD · 4/4 — Att 2,439 · 19 / 16 · D · 36 · 1-1 (1-0)
Colchester: Walker, Cook, Wright, Leslie, Wignall, Packer, Osborne, Longhorn, Bremner, McDonough, Allinson
Sheffield Utd: Conroy, Casey, Garner, Houston, McPhail, Kenworthy, Wiggan, Givens, Charles, Hatton, Ryan
Scorers: Allinson 13; Wiggan 52 · Ref: K Salmon
Stalemate ends this relegation four-pointer. Allinson collects in midfield, strides forward and unleashes a superb drive. Packer nets a free-kick on 29 minutes but the kick is indirect. Big Trenton Wiggan runs onto John Ryan's pass to give Walker no chance to give the Blades a point.

---

41 · A · BARNSLEY · 7/4 — Att 13,283 · 20 / 4 · L · 36 · 0-3 (0-2)
Colchester: Walker, Cook, Wright*, Leslie, Wignall, Packer, Cotton, Longhorn, Bremner, Foley, Allinson
Barnsley: Pierce, Joyce, Riley, Glavin, Banks, McCarthy, Cooper, Parker, Aylot, McHale, Lester, McDonough
Scorers: McHale 30, Parker 37, 84 · Ref: P Richardson
Ray McHale, the recent £60,000 signing from Brighton, scores his first goal for the Tykes. Walker drops Neil Cooper's cross for ex-Southend-man, Derrick Parker's, easy tap-in second. Colchester slip nearer the drop zone after this fixture which was postponed three weeks previously.

---

42 · A · SWINDON · 11/4 — Att 6,120 · 21 / 18 · L · · 0-3 (0-1)
Colchester: Walker, Cook, Foley, Leslie, Wignall, Packer, Osborne, Longhorn, Bremner, McDonough, Allinson
Swindon: Allan, Henry, Peach, Kamara, Lewis, Stroud, Miller, Carter, Rowland, Rideout, Williams
Scorers: Rideout 33, 77, Rowland 74 · Ref: R Lewis
United slide into the bottom four for the first time, after defeat at one of their relegation rivals. Swindon's rising England Youth starlet, Paul Rideout, sinks the U's. The Robins time their drop-zone escape perfectly, swopping places with the team from Essex with a game in hand.

---

43 · A · GILLINGHAM · 18/4 — Att 4,408 · 21 / 18 · D · 37 · 0-0 (0-0)
Colchester: Walker, Cook, Crouch, Leslie, Wignall, Packer, Wright, Longhorn, Bremner, Foley, Allinson
Gillingham: Hillyard, Young, Overton*, Bruce, Weatherley, Crabbe, Nicholl, Duncan, Price, Lee, White, Adams
Ref: A Robinson
Ex-U's striker Trevor Lee rarely troubles his old colleagues. The visitors gain a vital point in a dull, nervous performance. Foley puts an effort into the side-netting after the break. Manager Bobby Roberts believes two home wins and an away point will suffice for 3rd Division salvation.

---

44 · H · BRENTFORD · 20/4 — Att 2,609 · 22 / 10 · L · 37 · 0-2 (0-2)
Colchester: Walker, Cook, Coleman, Leslie, Wignall, Packer*, Foley, Longhorn, Bremner, McDonough, Allinson
Brentford: McKellar, Tucker, Johnson R, McNichol, Kruse, Hurlock, Shrubb, Booker, Johnson G, Harris, Roberts, Osborne
Scorers: Shrubb 22, Booker 43 · Ref: B Hill
Colchester now need a miracle to survive the drop. Gary Johnson bursts down the left and crosses for Paul Shrubb to flick a header high into the net. Bob Booker then slots home a side-foot from the edge of the box. Anxiety sets in and United squander second-half chances to pull back.

---

45 · A · NEWPORT · 25/4 — Att 4,619 · 22 / 15 · L · 37 · 0-1 (0-1)
Colchester: Walker, Cook, Wright, Cotton, Wignall, Packer, Osborne, Foley, Bremner, Osborne, Allinson
Newport: Kendall, Walden, Relish, Davies, Oakes, Bailey, Vaughan, Tynan, Waddle, Aldridge, Moore
Scorers: Aldridge 24 · Ref: T Spencer
Walker sets a new consecutive appearance record for the club, playing his 238th game on the trot. John Aldridge's goal, coupled with results elsewhere, determines the U's fate. Eleven points from a possible 38 since the turn of the year sends the U's back down to the 4th Division.

---

46 · H · CARLISLE · 2/5 — Att 1,430 · 22 / 19 · W · 39 · 1-0 (1-0)
Colchester: Walker, Wright, Osborne, Leslie, Wignall, Packer, Osborne, Foley, Bremner, McDonough, Allinson
Carlisle: Swinburne, Haigh, Coady, Hamilton, MacDonald, Parker, Coughlin, Campbell*, Bannon, Mossop, Staniforth, Collins
Scorers: McDonough 24 · Ref: A Ward
Tony Adcock, 18, makes his bow in this low-key end of season affair. The smallest crowd in the club's 30-year history sees Walker set a new goalkeeper appearance record for the club, his 423rd game. The squad retreat for a reflective Spanish holiday, relegated by a two-point margin.

Home Average 2,641 · Away 5,824

LEAGUE DIVISION 3 (CUP-TIES)

Manager: Bobby Roberts

League Cup

#			F-A	H-T								Scorers, Times, and Referees	1	2	3	4	5	6	7	8	9	10	11	12 sub used
1:1	H	GILLINGHAM	D 0-2	0-1	2,514	3:						Price 13, Bruce 60 Ref: K Salmon	Walker *Hillyard*	Crouch ! *Sharpe*	Cusenza *Ford*	Longhorn* *Overton*	Wignall *Weatherley*	Packer *Hughes*	Hodge *Donn*	Rowles *Duncan*	Foley *Price*	Lee *Henderson*	Allinson *Bruce*	Evans

For the second successive season, U's have a player sent off in the League Cup. Steve Bruce chops debutant Nigel Crouch on the by-line. The ref only sees his retaliation. Crouch is in as Dowman has left for Wrexham, Wright has jaundice, and Cook ricks his back getting out of his car.

#			F-A	H-T			Scorers, Times, and Referees	1	2	3	4	5	6	7	8	9	10	11	12 sub used
1:2	A	GILLINGHAM	L 1-2	0-0	5,220	3:	Gough 52 Ford 88, Bruce 90 Ref: T Bune	Walker *Hillyard*	Cook* *Sharpe*	Cotton *Ford*	Gough *Overton*	Wignall *Weatherley*	Packer *Crabbe*	Hodge *Donn*	Rowles *Duncan*	Foley *Price*	Lee *Henderson*	Allinson *Bruce*	Evans

Injury-plagued United, hoping to emulate last season's comeback at Villa Park, are boosted by Gough's goal. U's press forward for the vital (Colchester lost 1-4 on aggregate) leveller, but the Gills hit two late goals on the break. Bruce, booked on Saturday, and Foley, both find their way into the referee's notebook.

FA Cup

#			F-A	H-T			Scorers, Times, and Referees	1	2	3	4	5	6	7	8	9	10	11	12 sub used
1	H	PORTSMOUTH	W 3-0	1-0	5,387 15	3:7	Lee 26, Allinson 81, Bremner 87 Ref: C Maskell	Walker *Mellor*	Cook *McLaughlin*	Rowles *Viney*	Leslie *Barnard*	Wignall *Aizlewood*	Packer *Garner*	Hodge *Perrin*	Foley *Tait*	Bremner *Showers*	Lee *Bryant*	Allinson *Rogers*	Longhorn

Pompey start without leading scorer David Gregory. He gashes his knee stumbling down the Fratton Park terrace during midweek training. Pompey search for the equaliser but succumb to a late double sucker-punch. The Colchester board celebrate with local oysters and champagne.

#			F-A	H-T			Scorers, Times, and Referees	1	2	3	4	5	6	7	8	9	10	11	12 sub used
2	H	YEOVIL	D 1-1	0-1	3,394 15	AP:13	Wignall 86 Green 14 Ref: K Salmon	Walker *Parker*	Cook *Ryan*	Rowles *Ritchie*	Leslie *Borthwick*	Wignall *Payne*	Packer *Broom !*	Hodge* *Broom !*	Gough *Bell*	Bremner *Green*	Lee *Durbin*	Allinson *Brown*	Longhorn

Foley is suspended for the battle of the Cup's famed giant-killers. The Match of the Day cameras catch Borthwick's free-kick, which the unmarked Bell helps on to Green, who slips past Walker. Sweeper. Broom is sent off for a body-check on Allinson. Wignall saves U's blushes.

#			F-A	H-T			Scorers, Times, and Referees	1	2	3	4	5	6	7	8	9	10	11	12 sub used
2R	A	YEOVIL	W 2-0	0-0	5,803 15	AP:13	Lee 58, Bremner 67 Ref: K Salmon	Walker *Parker*	Cook *Ryan*	Rowles *Ritchie*	Leslie *Borthwick*	Wignall *Payne*	Packer *Broom*	Longhorn *Morrall*	Foley *Bell**	Bremner *Green*	Lee *Durbin*	Allinson *Brown*	Williams

The U's make no mistake this time, despite the Huish slope. Bell is brought down on 17 mins, but the ref gives a free-kick just inches outside the box. Lee's calmness in a tight spot gives U's the lead. Bremner takes a square pass from Cook to make up for hitting the bar on 50 minutes.

#			F-A	H-T			Scorers, Times, and Referees	1	2	3	4	5	6	7	8	9	10	11	12 sub used
3	H	WATFORD	L 0-1	0-1	7,769 14	2:15	Poskett 19 Ref: J Martin	Walker *Sherwood*	Cook *Rice*	Longhorn *Harrison*	Leslie *Taylor*	Wignall *Sims*	Packett *Jackett*	Hodge* *Callaghan*	Foley *Armstrong*	Bremner *Blissett*	Lee *Train*	Allinson *Poskett*	Gough

Foley returns after suspension. Malcolm Poskett chases a long ball. Cook should have cut out the danger but the Hornets man gets there first to give Walker no chance. Watford fans feel they should have a penalty and shower ref Martin with coins. Watford host Wolves in the next round.

League Table

	Team	P	W	D	L	F	A	W	D	L	F	A	Pts	Odds & ends
				Home					Away					
1	Rotherham	46	17	6	0	43	8	7	7	9	19	24	61	Double wins: (2) Charlton, Hull.
2	Barnsley	46	15	5	3	46	19	6	12	5	26	26	59	Double defeats: (4) Brentford, Exeter, Huddersfield, Reading.
3	Charlton	46	14	6	3	36	17	11	3	9	27	27	59	
4	Huddrsfield	46	14	6	3	40	11	7	8	8	31	29	56	
5	Chesterfield	46	17	4	2	42	16	6	6	11	30	32	56	Won from behind: (1) Charlton (a).
6	Portsmouth	46	14	5	4	35	19	8	4	11	20	28	53	Lost from in front: (0).
7	Plymouth	46	13	5	5	35	18	5	9	9	21	26	52	
8	Burnley	46	13	5	5	37	21	5	9	9	23	27	50	High Spots: A surprising double over promoted Charlton.
9	Brentford	46	7	9	7	30	25	7	10	6	22	24	47	The signing of Kevin Bremner from Scottish non-league.
10	Reading	46	13	5	5	39	22	5	5	13	23	40	46	The emergence of 18-year-old Tony Adcock.
11	Exeter	46	9	9	5	36	30	7	4	12	26	36	45	
12	Newport	46	11	6	6	38	22	4	7	12	26	39	43	Low spots: Only one win in the last nine games, resulting in relegation.
13	Fulham	46	8	7	8	28	29	7	6	10	29	35	43	A record lowest attendance for the last game of the season (1,430).
14	Oxford	46	7	8	8	20	24	6	9	8	19	23	43	The loss of Trevor Lee, albeit in a record £90,000 transfer, to Gillingham.
15	Gillingham	46	9	8	6	23	19	3	10	10	25	39	42	An unhappy sojourn, due to restrictive bye-laws, into staging Sunday
16	Millwall	46	10	9	4	30	21	4	5	14	13	39	42	football.
17	Swindon	46	10	6	7	35	27	3	9	11	16	29	41	
18	Chester	46	11	5	7	25	17	4	6	13	13	31	41	
19	Carlisle	46	8	9	6	32	29	6	4	13	24	41	41	
20	Walsall	46	8	9	6	43	43	5	6	12	16	31	41	
21	Sheffield Utd	46	12	6	5	38	20	2	6	15	27	43	40	Player of the Year: Mike Walker.
22	COLCHESTER	46	12	7	4	35	22	2	4	17	10	43	39	Ever presents: (1) Mike Walker.
23	Blackpool	46	5	9	9	19	28	4	5	14	26	47	32	Hat-tricks: (0).
24	Hull	46	7	8	8	23	22	1	8	14	17	49	32	Leading scorer: Trevor Lee (9).
		1104	265	162	125	808	529	125	162	265	529	808	1104	

Appearances and Goals

Player	Lge	Sub	LC	Sub	FAC	Sub	Lge	LC	FAC	Tot
	Appearances						Goals			
Adcock, Tony	1									
Allinson, Ian	43	3	2		4		6	1		7
Bremner, Kevin	33	1			4		8		2	10
Coleman, Phil	4									
Cook, Micky	45				4		1			1
Cotton, Russell	18		1		1					
Crouch, Nigel	9		1		1					
Cusenza, Leo						2				
Evans, Tony	6	2			2					
Foley, Steve	30	1	2		3		5			5
Gough, Bobby	15		1		1	1	4		1	5
Harvey, Gary	2									
Hodge, Bobby	22	2	2		3		6			6
Lee, Trevor	25	1	2		4		7		2	9
Leslie, Steve	41		2		4					
Longhorn, Dennis	21	1	1		2	1	2			2
McDonough, Roy	11		1							
Osborne, Roger	11		1							
Packer, Mick	43		2		4		3			3
Rowles, Eddie	21		2		3		2			2
Walker, Mick	46		2		4					
Wignall, Steve	42		2		4		1		1	2
Wright, Steve	17									
23 players used	506	17	22	2	44	2	45	1	6	52

LEAGUE DIVISION 4

Manager: Roberts → Allan Hunter — SEASON 1981-82

Match results

No	Date	Opponent (venue)	Att	Pos	Pt	Res	F-A	H-T	Scorers, Times, and Referees
1	29/8	A HARTLEPOOL	2,007		3	W	3-1	2-0	Bremner 34, 59, Packer 39p / Harding 81 / Ref: N Wilson
2	4/9	H TRANMERE	2,474	1	6	W	4-0	2-0	Allinson 9, 36p, Cook 58, Bremner 90 / Ref: A Ward
3	12/9	A SHEFFIELD UTD	11,293	6	6	L	0-1	0-1	Hatton 43 / Ref: A Robinson
4	18/9	H TORQUAY	2,820	2	9	W	3-0	1-0	Adcock 18, 77, Cook 51 / Ref: K Salmon
5	22/9	H ALDERSHOT	2,719	4	10	D	1-1	1-0	Coleman 39 / Crosby 46 / Ref: B Hill
6	26/9	A BRADFORD C	4,772	7	10	L	1-2	0-1	Leslie 63 / Gallagher 5, Staniforth 88 / Ref: M Heath
7	28/9	A PORT VALE	3,351	7	10	L	1-2	0-0	McDonough 52 / Sproson 80, Moss 88 / Ref: N Glover
8	2/10	H NORTHAMPTON	2,760	8	13	W	5-1	2-0	Coleman 5, Allinson 7p, Bremner 72, 86, [McDonough 83] / Denyer 50p / Ref: D Reeves
9	11/10	A ROCHDALE	1,366	10	16	W	2-1	0-0	Allinson 66, McDonough 84 / Wellings 51 / Ref: N Ashley
10	16/10	H YORK	3,139	6	19	W	4-0	2-0	McDonough 8, Bremner 38, Leslie 70, [Allinson 76] / Ref: A Gunn
11	20/10	H HEREFORD	3,064	5	22	W	4-0	2-0	Allinson 20, Bremner 40, Osborne 56, 61 / Ref: J Deakin

Line-ups

No	1	2	3	4	5	6	7	8	9	10	11	12 sub used
1	Walker	Cook	Packer	Leslie	Wignall	Wright	Osborne*	Bremner	Longhorn	McDonough	Allinson	Adcock
	Burleigh	*Brown*	*Simpson*	*Hogan*	*Bird*	*Linighan A*	*Kerr**	*Sweeney*	*Staff*	*Houchen*	*Harding*	*Hampton*
2	Walker	Cook	Coleman	Leslie	Wignall	Wright	Adcock	Bremner	Longhorn*	McDonough	Allinson	Foley
	Johnson	*Burgess*	*Morley**	*Parry*	*Bramhall*	*Williams*	*Hutchinson*	*Kelly*	*Brown*	*Griffiths*	*Hamilton*	
3	Walker	Cook	Coleman	Leslie	Wignall	Wright	Osborne	Bremner	Foley*	McDonough	Allinson	Adcock
	Waugh	*Ryan*	*Kenworthy*	*Tibbott*	*McPhail*	*McAlle*	*Wiggan*	*Trusson*	*Neville*	*Hatton*	*Charles*	
4	Walker	Cook	Coleman	Leslie	Wignall	Wright	Osborne	Bremner	Foley*	McDonough	Allinson	
	O'Keefe	*Jones*	*Pendrey*	*Bowker*	*Wilson*	*Larmour*	*Fell*	*Lawrence*	*Cooper*	*Rioch*	*Pethard*	
5	Walker	Cook	Coleman	Leslie	Wignall	Wright	Adcock	Bremner	Osborne	McDonough	Allinson	
	Johnson	*Edwards*	*Wooler*	*Briley*	*Bennett*	*Jopling*	*Wanklyn*	*Crosby*	*Garwood*	*Sanford*	*Brodie*	
6	Walker	Cook	Coleman	Leslie	Wignall	Wright	Adcock	Bremner	Osborne	McDonough	Allinson	
	Smith	*Podd*	*Watson*	*Ingham*	*Jackson*	*McFarland*	*Gallagher*	*Staniforth*	*Campbell*	*McNiven*	*Chapman*	
7	Walker	Cook	Coleman	Leslie	Wignall	Wright	Adcock	Bremner	Osborne	McDonough	Allinson	
	Harrison	*Keenan*	*Deakin*	*Hunter*	*Sproson*	*Bowles*	*Brissett**	*Moss*	*Greenhoff*	*Chamberlain N / Chamberlain M*	*Bromage*	
8	Walker	Cook	Coleman	Leslie*	Wignall	Wright	Adcock	Bremner	Osborne	McDonough	Allinson	Longhorn
	Poole	*Taylor*	*Carlton*	*Brady*	*Gage*	*Coffill*	*Denyer*	*Sandy*	*Buchanan*	*Phillips*	*Alexander*	
9	Walker	Cook	Coleman	Leslie	Wignall	Wright	Adcock	Bremner	Osborne	McDonough	Allinson	
	Poole	*Cooper*	*Snookes*	*Dolan*	*Burke*	*Taylor*	*Hamilton**	*O'Laughlin*	*Hiditch*	*Wellings*	*Martinez*	*Goodwin*
10	Walker	Cook	Coleman	Leslie	Wignall	Wright!	Adcock*	Bremner	Osborne	McDonough	Allinson	Longhorn
	Blackburn	*Hood*	*Flood*	*Hedley*	*Croft*	*Dawson*	*Pollard*	*Byrne*	*Walwyn !*	*McDonald*	*Bentham*	
11	Walker	Cook	Coleman	Leslie	Wignall	Wright	Adcock	Bremner	Osborne	McDonough	Allinson	White
	Hughes	*Price*	*Bray*	*Hicks*	*Cornes*	*Dobson*	*Harvey*	*Laidlaw*	*Phillips*	*Dungworth*	*White*	

Match notes

1. A Hartlepool — Osborne suffers an eye injury in only the second minute. He plays on until half-time with a sponge for company. He still manages a left-wing cross for Bremner's first. Full-back Phil Brown punches a Bremner shot over. In the closing stages, Alan Harding pulls one back for Pool.

2. H Tranmere — Allinson fires in a low, skidding shot and adds a second from the spot when John Bramhall trips Wignall off the ball. For Rovers' boss, Bryan Hamilton, it appears to be another long hard campaign after the ignomy of last season's re-election victory. Bremner wraps it up in injury-time.

3. A Sheffield Utd — Colchester's storming start to the season comes to an abrupt halt as veteran Bob Hatton strikes just before the half-time interval. A minute after Hatton's goal, defender Wignall sees his effort cleared off the line by his opposite number, John McPhail. Foley suffers a serious knock.

4. H Torquay — U's return to winning ways, ending league leaders, Torquay's, 100% start. Adcock bags a brace and provides the other for adventurous Cook. Adcock crowns his performance when Allinson waltzes past the groggy, Gary Pendrey, to provide a pin-point cross for the red-haired striker.

5. H Aldershot — In the battle of the Garrison towns, it is Aldershot who finish on top. Coleman scores the tenth United goal in four home games, a soft header. Malcolm Crosby spoils the party with a sniper-like finish, seconds after the break. Colin Garwood is unable to inflict defeat on his old team.

6. A Bradford C — Roy McFarland's City have scored 13 in their last three games. Walker has no chance with Barry Gallagher's 25-yard free-kick. Leslie plays his 350th league game (in his eleventh season) and levels a minute before Campbell blasts over a penalty. David Staniforth hits the late winner

7. A Port Vale — The U's are coasting to victory, but are hit by two late goals. McDonough scores the first goal conceded at Vale Park this term. Paul Bowles's free-kick is headed past the diving Walker. John Deakin's cross is met by a bullet header from Ernie Moss. Allinson hits the bar on full time.

8. H Northampton — Having outplayed both Vale and Bradford, U's blitz the Cobblers. Coleman notches a simple header. Wakeley Gage then tangles with Bremner in the box. Pegged back by Wright's clumsy challenge on Steve Phillips, a late goal-surge gives the U's the superiority their play deserves.

9. A Rochdale — The switch to Sunday does nothing to swell the Spotland attendance. Barry Wellings plays a neat one-two with Eugene Martinez. U's take the initiative after Allinson's equaliser. Mike Poole races out of his area, but misses the ball in the air. McDonough gleefully prods the ball home.

10. H York — Cook appears for the 500th time in the league. McDonough scores his sixth in five games. Bremner heads in Wright's free-kick, but a minute later the young defender is involved in a scuffle with the Minstermen's Keith Walwyn. Both see red. Allinson and Leslie supply each other.

11. H Hereford — The U's dismiss the visitors' unbeaten four-match away run. The goal tally rises to 26 in just eight home games. Midfield workhorse Osborne nets his first goals for the club. Two minutes before Allinson's opener, Shrewsbury loanee John Dungworth grazes the top of the crossbar.

No.	V	Opponent	Date	Att	Pos	Result	Pts	Score	HT
12	A	HALIFAX	24/10	1,374	22	3 W	25	2-0	1-0
13	H	WIGAN	30/10	3,882	8	6 L	25	1-2	0-2
14	A	MANSFIELD	2/11	2,294	21	2 W	28	3-1	1-0
15	A	HULL	7/11	3,040	19	4 W	31	3-2	1-1
16	H	SCUNTHORPE	13/11	3,838	24	4 W	34	2-1	1-1
17	A	DARLINGTON	28/11	1,456	17	1 W	37	2-1	1-1
18	H	BLACKPOOL	4/12	3,875	10	1 W	40	2-1	1-1
19	A	BOURNEMOUTH	26/12	8,829	4	1 D	41	1-1	0-1
20	H	BURY	16/1	3,504	5	2 D	42	1-1	1-1
21	H	HARTLEPOOL	23/1	2,862	15	2 D	43	3-3	1-3
22	A	TORQUAY	30/1	2,037	10	3 L	43	0-1	0-0
23	H	SHEFFIELD UTD	6/2	5,194	4	3 W	46	5-2	4-1

12. A HALIFAX 24/10 — Allinson 2p, McDonough 50. Ref: D Webb
U's: Walker, Cook, Coleman, Leslie, Wignall, Wright, Adcock*, Bremner, Osborne, McDonough, Allinson, Longhorn
Halifax: Smelt, O'Neil, Carr, Evans, Ayre, Hendrie, Ward, Dawson, Allatt, Chamberlain, Graham
U's headed north, disappointed at the League Cup draw, which sees them travel to Fourth Division side Tranmere. Halifax are deep in the mire and the paltry attendance does not aid their precarious financial situation. Allinson grabs his eighth of the term, and McDonough his seventh

13. H WIGAN 30/10 — Coleman 86; McMahon 11, Houghton 42. Ref: M James
U's: Walker, Brown, Coleman, Leslie, Wignall, Longhorn*, Adcock, Bremner, Osborne, McDonough, Allinson, Rowles
Wigan: McMahon, Cribley, Wignall, Methven, Glenn, Barrow, Bradd, Houghton, Weston
Wright's suspension means the first change in twelve John McMahon drives a free-kick through the defensive wall. Peter Houghton has a solo run. Two mins after Coleman's goal. U's waste a free-kick opportunity after goalkeeper John Brown is penalised for handling outside the area.

14. A MANSFIELD 2/11 — Allinson 42, 57, 81p; Morgan 84. Ref: J Worrall
U's: Walker, Cook, Coleman, Leslie, Wignall, Rowles, Cotton*, Bremner, Osborne, McDonough, Allinson, Adcock
Mansfield: Arnold, McClelland, Wood*, Bell, Burrows, Bird, Thomson, Morgan, Mann, Caldwell, Nicholson, Parkinson
Mansfield's new signing, Trevor Morgan (£10,000 from Bournemouth), scores on his debut. The day belongs to tricky winger, Allinson, who scores his first ever hat-trick for the seniors. The third comes from the spot after Kevin Bird fells Bremner. This is the first treble since Nov 78

15. A HULL 7/11 — Bremner 12, McDonough 61, 77; Mutrie 15, Roberts G 48. Ref: T Fitzharris
U's: Walker, Davies, Coleman, Leslie*, Wignall, Wright, Adcock, Bremner, Osborne, McDonough, Allinson, Deacy
Hull: McNeil, Horswill*, Richards, Eccleston, Roberts G, Marwood, McClaren, Whitehurst, Mutrie, Booth
Coleman and Allinson are the key figures. Allinson has a hand in all three goals. Coleman makes a last-minute clearance off the line from marauding Les Mutrie. Hull fans spend the match berating manager Mike Smith, who has taken the Tigers from the 3rd to the foot of the 4th.

16. H SCUNTHORPE 13/11 — Allinson 38, Cook 65; Stewart 36. Ref: D Letts
U's: Walker, Neenan, Coleman, Leslie*, Wignall, Wright, Adcock, Bremner, Osborne, McDonough, Allinson, Longhorn
Scunthorpe: Gowling, Pilling, Keeley, Partridge, Oates, Grimes, O'Berg, Green*, Moss, Stewart, Lambert
Scunthorpe, without a goal in the previous three, frustrate the U's when Dave Stewart collects Paul O'Berg's through ball. Allinson's 13th, a 20-yarder from Osborne's pass, comes two minutes later. Cook continues his scoring spree with his fourth of the term from Osborne's corner.

17. A DARLINGTON 28/11 — Bremner 5, Osborne 53; Speedie 25. Ref: T Mills
U's: Walker, Cuff, Coleman, Leslie, Wignall, Wright, Adcock, Bremner, Osborne, Rowles, Allinson, Stalker
Darlington: Kamara, Mitchell, Smith, Skipper, Speedie, Hawker, McLean, Wicks, Hamilton*, Walsh
U's sit proudly on top of the Division after this sixth away win. They are the country's leading scorers with 41 goals. Leslie flicks Adcock's corner for Bremner's 12th. Alan Walsh's right-wing cross is headed home by David Speedie. Osborne finishes off Cook's long throw-in.

18. H BLACKPOOL 4/12 — Allinson 14, Noble 84(og); Bamber 31. Ref: A Robinson
U's: Walker, Hesford, Coleman*, Leslie*, Wignall, Wright, Adcock*, Bremner, Osborne, McDonough, Allinson, Rowles
Blackpool: Simmonite, Pashley, Blair, Hart, Wann, Morris, Bamber, Noble, Hockaday, Harrison
Christmas arrives three weeks early for the U's when Peter Noble heads Coleman's throw past England U-21 keeper, Iain Hesford. Noble also concedes the free-kick for the U's first goal Dave Bamber back-heads a Colin Morris corner, then clashes with Cook, who needs four stitches.

19. A BOURNEMOUTH 26/12 — McDonough 78; Goddard 20. Ref: S Bates
U's: Walker, Leigh, Coleman*, Leslie*, Wignall, Wright, Adcock*, Bremner, Osborne, McDonough, Allinson, Dawkins
Bournemouth: Heffernan, Sulley, Smith, Brignull, Impey, Dawtry*, Crawford, Funnell, Goddard, Williams
Manager of the month, Roberts takes his side to the south-coast, which has escaped the severe winter weather. At the start of the campaign he had set his side a target of being top of the division at the turn of the year, and in the third round of the FA Cup. The squad has truly delivered!

20. H BURY 16/1 — Adcock 14; Hilton P 18. Ref: T Bune
U's: Walker, Brown, Coleman*, Leslie, Wignall, Wright, Adcock, Bremner, Osborne, McDonough, Allinson, Longhorn
Bury: Constantine, Kennedy, Gore, Hilton P, Baines!, Madden, Butler, Johnson, Jakub, Cruikshank
The first televised game at Layer Road this season. Allinson's shot rebounds off the post for Adcock. Walker parries a Bury free-kick as far as Paul Hilton to steer a quick-fire reply. Steve Baines, on loan from Walsall, is sent off on 29 mins for hauling down both Allinson and Osborne.

21. H HARTLEPOOL 23/1 — McDonough 10, Bird 58 (og), Allinson 64p; Houchen 14p, 16, Bird 38. Ref: M Bodenham
U's: Walker, Burleigh, Coleman, Leslie*, Wignall, Wright, Adcock, Bremner, Osborne, McDonough, Allinson, Longhorn
Hartlepool: Sweeney, Linacre P, Brown, Bird, Fagan, Linacre J, Madden, Hogan, Newton, Houchen, Staff
U's are weary from the Newcastle game. After McDonough's eleventh, Coleman trips Keith Houchen, whose double puts Pool in front. Walker punches John Linacre's corner onto the bar John Bird nets the rebound. Bird heads Allinson's drive into his own net. Houchen trips Wignall.

22. A TORQUAY 30/1 — Sermanni 83. Ref: B Stevens
U's: Walker, O'Keefe, Coleman, Packer*, Wignall, Wright, Cotton, Bremner, Osborne, McDonough, Allinson, Adcock
Torquay: Pethard, Wilson, Brown, Lawrence, Larmour, Sermanni, Cooper, Butler*, Young, Cox
Rowles picks up a training injury. Walker and Osborne deserve better. The keeper makes fine saves, whilst Osborne gets an unlucky bounce off his shin when clean through. Tommy Sermanni's low drive gives Torquay their first win in ten. U's drop to third after four without a win.

23. H SHEFFIELD UTD 6/2 — Lyons 4, McD 8, Aln 9, 36, Bremner 59; Kenworthy 38p, Edwards 62. Ref: C White
U's: Walker, Waugh, Longhorn*, Lyons, Wignall, Wright, Adcock, Bremner, Osborne, McDonough, Allinson, Coleman
Sheffield Utd: Richardson*, Garner, Matthews, Houston, Kenworthy, Neville, Trusson, Edwards, Hatton, King, Charles
New boy Lyons (£25,000 from Cambridge) takes just four minutes to open his account in front of the Match of the Day cameras. The Blades have to wear U's away strip for clarity. McDonough scores U's 50th league goal. Wright fells Jeff King. Bremner's first goal since November.

LEAGUE DIVISION 4

Manager: Roberts ⇨ Allan Hunter — SEASON 1981-82

Results

No	V	Team	Date	Att	Pos	OppPos	Res	Pt	F-A	H-T	Scorers, Times, and Referees
24	A	ALDERSHOT	9/2	2,324	6	12	D	47	1-1	1-1	Lyons 44 / Jopling 33 / Ref: H King
25	A	NORTHAMPTON	14/2	3,102	6	24	W	50	2-1	1-0	Allinson 19, Bremner 75 / Coffill 56 / Ref: P Richardson
26	H	BRADFORD C	19/2	3,975	6	4	L	50	1-2	0-1	Cook 73 / Jackson 41, McNiven 58 / Ref: A Ward
27	H	ROCHDALE	26/2	2,760	7	22	W	53	3-2	2-1	Bremner 29, Adcock 38, 88 / O'Laughlin 28, Hilditch 75 / Ref: M Dimblebee
28	A	TRANMERE	2/3	1,252	7	13	L	53	1-2	0-2	Bremner 75 / Craven 12, Kerr 34 / Ref: P Willis
29	A	YORK	5/3	1,854	7	20	L	53	0-3	0-1	Hood 35p, Walwyn 77, 90 / Ref: R Chadwick
30	A	HEREFORD	10/3	2,060	6	16	D	54	2-2	0-1	Allinson 48p, Osborne 54 / Phillips 23, 82 / Ref: A Hamil
31	H	HALIFAX	12/3	2,464	7	21	D	55	1-1	1-1	Bremner 8 / Ayre 28 / Ref: D Reeves
32	H	MANSFIELD	16/3	2,000	7	17	L	55	0-1	0-0	Lumby 81 / Ref: A Grey
33	A	WIGAN	20/3	6,747	7	1	L	55	2-3	0-2	Bremner 62, Osborne 88 / Barrow 1, 60, Bradd 27 / Ref: J Hough
34	A	STOCKPORT	22/3	1,740	7	18	D	56	0-0	0-0	Ref: G Flint

Line-ups (1–11, 12 sub used)

U's side (top line) and opponents (lower line, in italics):

No	Team	1	2	3	4	5	6	7	8	9	10	11	12 sub used
24	U's	Walker	Cook	Longhorn	Lyons	Wignall	Wright	Adcock	Bremner	Osborne*	McDonough	Allinson	Leslie
24	*Aldershot*	*Johnson*	*Edwards*	*Scott*	*Briley*	*Bennett*	*Jopling*	*Lucas*	*McDonald*	*Garwood*	*French*	*Robinson*	
25	U's	Walker	Cook	Longhorn	Lyons	Wignall	Wright	Adcock	Bremner	Osborne	McDonough	Allinson	Adcock
25	*Northampton*	*Poole*	*Carlton*	*Saunders*	*Saxby*	*Gage*	*Denyer*	*Coffill*	*Sandy*	*Phillips*	*Perrin*	*Alexander*	
26	U's	Walker	Cook	Longhorn	Lyons	Wignall	Wright	Adcock	Bremner	Osborne	McDonough	Allinson	Cotton
26	*Bradford C*	*Ramsbottom*	*Podd*	*Watson*	*Ingham*	*Jackson*	*McFarland*	*Gallagher*	*Staniforth*	*Campbell*	*McNiven*	*Ellis*	
27	U's	Walker	Cook	Longhorn	Lyons	Coleman	Wright	Adcock	Bremner	Osborne	McDonough	Allinson*	Cotton
27	*Rochdale*	*Poole*	*Weir*	*Snooks*	*Dolan*	*Cooper*	*Taylor*	*Goodwin*	*O'Laughlin*	*Hilditch*	*Wellings*	*Esser*	
28	U's	Walker	Cook	Longhorn	Lyons	Coleman	Wright	Adcock*	Bremner	Osborne	McDonough	Allinson	Cotton
28	*Tranmere*	*Enderby*	*Mungall*	*Burgess*	*Mountfield*	*Bramhall*	*Williams*	*Hamilton*	*Powell*	*Kerr*	*Craven*	*Griffiths*	
29	U's	Walker	Cook	Longhorn	Packer*	Coleman	Wright	Cotton	Bremner	Osborne	McDonough	Allinson	Lyons
29	*York*	*Blackburn*	*Sweeney*	*Dawson*	*Hood*	*Cruzcman*	*Aitken*	*Fell*	*Crosby*	*Walwyn*	*Ford*	*Laverick*	
30	U's	Walker	Cook	Coleman	Cotton	Wignall	Wright	Lyons	Bremner*	Osborne	McDonough	Allinson*	Adcock
30	*Hereford*	*Brand*	*Price*	*Pejic*	*Hicks*	*Dobson*	*Musial*	*Harvey*	*Laidlaw*	*Phillips*	*Showers*	*White*	
31	U's	Walker	Cook	Coleman	Lyons	Wignall	Wright	Cotton*	Bremner	Osborne	McDonough	Allinson	Adcock
31	*Halifax*	*Smelt*	*Chamberlain*	*Carr*	*Evans*	*Ayre*	*Hendrie*	*Ward*	*Davison*	*Allatt*	*Spooner*	*Firth*	
32	U's	Walker	Cook	Coleman	Leslie	Wignall	Wright	Adcock	Bremner	Osborne	McDonough	Allinson	Lyons
32	*Mansfield*	*Arnold*	*McClelland*	*Foster*	*Bell*	*Burrows*	*Wood*	*Mann*	*Cannell*	*Lumby*	*Nicholson*	*Thomson*	
33	U's	Walker	Cook	Coleman	Leslie	Wignall	Wright	Cotton	Bremner	Osborne	McDonough	Allinson	Longhorn
33	*Wigan*	*Tunks*	*McMahon*	*Glenn*	*Lloyd*	*Cribley*	*Methven*	*O'Keefe*	*Barrow*	*Bradd*	*Packer**	*Evans*	
34	U's	Walker	Cook	Coleman	Leslie	Wignall	Wright	Cotton	Bremner	Osborne	Longhorn	Allinson	Longhorn
34	*Stockport*	*Lloyd*	*Rutter*	*Sherlock*	*Emerson*	*Thorpe*	*Smith*	*Williams*	*Phillips*	*Coyle*	*Park*	*Stafford*	

Match notes

24 Joe Jopling hooks in a loose ball. Adcock's is only half-cleared to Lyons, who scores his second goal in two games. Walker, in his 262nd consecutive game, appears to be knocked out on 79 mins after a clash with Mickey French, who takes a heavy knock.

25 U's Sunday service resumes at managerless bottom-club Northampton. Andy Poole punches out Osborne's corner to Allinson, who finishes. Peter Coffill nets his first for the Cobblers, but Bremner nets his 14th. Leslie, back from a right knee injury, suffers a knock to his left knee.

26 To boost income, Layer Road admission prices go up 20p throughout. It now costs £1.50/£1.00 to stand. Longhorn replaces Leslie in midfield. City's eighth away win doubles the U's. Player-manager. Roy McFarland's, bold game plan, to stifle the United's creative midfield, works.

27 Injuries, coupled with Wignall starting a three-match ban for five bookings, leaves the U's down to just twelve fit pros. McDonough at centre-half, has two errors, luckily, wiped out for offside. Adcock's screaming left-foot volley beats Mike Poole with two minutes left on the clock.

28 Tranmere, without a win in nine, complete the league and cup double over the U's at Prenton Park. Next week's (Liverpool versus Tottenham) League Cup Final referee, Peter Willis, notes down the names of Wright and McDonough, the former for hauling down winger Ian Griffiths.

29 York include two of the 'Ashton Gate Eight' free agents in Gerry Sweeney and Peter Aitken. The U's slip further behind the promotion pack. Cook fouls Micky Laverick for the penalty. Keith Walwyn's double flatters managerless City, who pack their defence for the whole game.

30 Wignall returns with Lyons, on the bench at York. The U's gain their only point from their three-match travels. Winston White's corner is headed in by Stewart Phillips. Allinson is tripped by a posse of defenders. Osborne finishes off Bremner's rebound, but Phillips saves a point.

31 Halifax, who are up for sale, score their ninth away draw. Roberts has the U's squad in on the Saturday morning for an extra training session. All seems well when Bremner bags his 18th, heading in Wright's free-kick, but Billy Ayre earns the re-election threatened Shaymen a point.

32 The U's have won just three in twelve. Jim Lumby scores his 100th league and cup goal to stun the paltry gathering. United fans have certainly voted with their feet regarding their thoughts on United's promotion aspirations. Lumby's goal comes from Shane Nicholson's fine deep cross.

33 The U's miss McDonough and Lyons through injury. The League's newest team, Wigan, are twelve points ahead of the U's in top slot. The Latics complete a win double. Graham Barrow scores after 47 seconds. Les Bradd fends off Wright. After Barrow's second the fightback is too late.

34 U's slim promotion hopes take another knock at Edgeley Park, although they keep a first clean-sheet in the league since 24 October. Walker pushes Chester loanee Trevor Phillips' shot past the post (16). Hardworking Bremner sets up Leslie (59). but his shot cannons off Brian Lloyd.

35 H HULL 26/3 — 6 · 10 · 59 · 2-0 · 0-0
Walker · Cook · Coleman · Leslie · Wignall · Wright · Adcock* · Osborne · Bremner · Cotton · Longhorn · Allinson
Norman · Richards · Booth · Roberts D · Thompson · Davis · Marwood · Whitehurst · McClaren · Flounders · Deacy · Ferguson*
Bremner 54, Coleman 78
Ref: C Downey
Hull, after sacking managers Smith and Lea, have lost only two in ten. U's have no wins in seven during mad March. Allinson, subdued of late by a chest infection, is on the bench. Bremner's 20th comes from Osborne's corner. Allinson sets up Coleman and then hits the bar on 82 mins.

36 H CREWE 30/3 — 6 · 24 · 60 · 1-1 · 1-1
Walker · Cook · Coleman · Leslie · Wignall · Wright · Cotton · Osborne · Bremner · Longhorn · Allinson
Mulhearn · Lewis · Griffiths · Salathiel · Scott · Palios · Haselgrave · Entwistle · Keighley · Chesters · Williams
Allinson 35
Palios 41
Ref: K Baker
Adcock misses out after his ricked back v Hull, as U's say goodbye to promotion with a draw against the league's bottom club. Allinson races onto Wright's long pass to tuck in his 23rd.

37 A SCUNTHORPE 2/4 — 6 · 23 · 60 · 1-2 · 0-1
Walker · Cook · Coleman · Leslie · Wignall · Wright · Adcock · Osborne · Bremner · McDonough · Allinson
Neenan · Arins · Keeley · Boyd · Thompson · Oates · Grimes · Telfer · Cammack · Moss · Goodlass
Bremner 65
Moss 19, Telfer 60
Ref: D Allison
Fading promotion hopes are further dented at re-election haunted Scunthorpe. Paul Moss plays a neat one-two with Steve Cammack to put Iron in front. George Telfer scrambles a second goal on the hour. Colchester are now a disappointing 13 points behind the fourth promotion place.

38 H BOURNEMOUTH 10/4 — 6 · 5 · 60 · 1-2 · 0-2
Walker · Cook · Longhorn* · Leslie · Wignall · Packer · Adcock* · Osborne · Bremner · Groves · Allinson
Leigh · Heffernan · Sulley · Spackman · Brignall · Carter · Williams · Crawford · Morgan · Funnell · O'Donnell*
Allinson 76
Funnell 30, Crawford 34
Ref: I Borrett
Roberts is asked to resign by the board two days before this clash. Tony Funnell appears to 'handle' the first, but the ref ignores the linesman's flag. Four minutes later Nigel Spackman's shot is parried and Andy Crawford nets the rebound. Allinson slides his 24th goal under Ian Leigh.

39 A PETERBOROUGH 13/4 — 6 · 3 · 61 · 2-2 · 0-0
Walker · Cook · Coleman · Lyons · Wignall · Packer · Groves* · McDonough · Bremner · Osborne · Allinson
Freeman · Butler · Phillips · Gynn · Smith T · Rodaway · Clarke · Cooke · Kellock · Hodgson · Chard · Leslie
Allinson 58, McDonough 79
Smith T 56, Kellock 60
Ref: A Challinor
The U's produce their best display since the demolition of Sheffield Utd in February. Tony Smith heads in Billy Kellock's corner. After Ian Allinson's low drive, Kellock finishes off a neat set-piece. Sub Leslie crosses from the left for McDonough to outjump the home defence.

40 A BLACKPOOL 17/4 — 6 · 12 · 62 · 0-0 · 0-0
Walker · Cook · Coleman · Lyons · Wignall · Packer · Groves* · Osborne* · Bremner · McDonough · Allinson
Hesford · Simmonite · Brockbank · Deary · Greenall · Noble · Morgan · Stewart · Harrison · McAvoy · Pashley · Leslie
Ref: K Redfern
Gordon Simmonite takes the heart out of the U's engine-room by nonchalantly lacerating Osborne's thigh on 33 minutes. The midfielder requires ten stitches. The local press believe that, on this display, the U's will be a force to be reckoned with next season's promotion race.

41 H DARLINGTON 24/4 — 6 · 11 · 65 · 1-0 · 0-0
Walker · Cook · Ward · Leslie · Wignall · Packer · Lyons · Groves · Bremner · McDonough · Allinson* · Adcock
Cuff · Kamara · Liddle · Smith · Skipper · Speedie · McFadden · McLean · Hawker · Wicks · Walsh · Staiker*
Bremner 77
Ref: R Lewis
Ward joins Groves in gaining a call-up to the seniors. Darlington include £100,000-rated David Speedie, who is being watched by many, including Ipswich. Manager Roberts is reported to want £45,000 compensation to pay off the remaining three-and-a-half years of his contract.

42 H PETERBOROUGH 27/4 — 6 · 4 · 66 · 1-1 · 1-0
Walker · Cook · Wright! · Leslie · Wignall · Packer · Lyons* · McDonough · Bremner · Osborne · Allinson · Ward
Freeman · Butler · Phillips · Gynn · Smith T! · Rodaway · Syrett · Kellock · Cooke · Hodgson · Chard
Bremner 34
Syrett 76
Ref: M Taylor
Speculation mounts as Martin Peters (ex-Sheff Utd boss) watches. Wright is sent off on 52 mins for kicking away a free-kick. Tony Smith, already booked, joins him, bringing down McDonough. Ian Phillips offers himself as guilty. The crowd chant 'five, five' to aid the official.

43 A BURY 1/5 — 6 · 7 · 66 · 3-4 · 1-3
Walker · Cook · Wright · Leslie · Wignall · Packer · Lyons* · Groves · Bremner · McDonough · Adcock · Coleman
Platt · Bradley · Kennedy · Gore · Bramhall · Howard · Madden · Butler · Hilton P · Jakub · Cruikshank
Lyons 40, Bremner 68, McDonough 86
Butler 18, Madden 41, 60, Hilton P 44
Ref: C Seel
Ref Seel gives Bury a corner that never was. Mick Butler heads home. Lyons levels. The ball strikes Packer's arm, play continues until the ref pulls play back for a penalty. Packer was not even in the area! Walker saves but Craig Madden follows in. His second is his 33rd of the season.

44 H PORT VALE 3/5 — 6 · 8 · 69 · 1-0 · 1-0
Walker · Cook · Ward · Wright · Wignall · Packer · Lyons · Bremner · Groves · McDonough · Adcock
Harrison · Tartt · Bromage · Hunter · Sproson · Bowles · Chamberlain N Moss · Deakin · Armstrong · Chamberlain M
McDonough 6
Ref: K Salmon
Roberts is sacked afterwards as the U's board, apparently, cannot raise the compensation. McDonough receives from Adcock and weaves past Colin Tartt before firing a ferocious shot into the roof of the net. Old-stager Ernie Moss clips the bar on 62 mins. Roberts bows out with a win.

45 H STOCKPORT 7/5 — 6 · 19 · 69 · 0-1 · 0-0
Walker · Cook · Ward · Wright · Wignall* · Packer · Lyons* · Bremner · Groves · McDonough · Adcock
Lloyd · Butter · Sherlock · Emerson · Thorpe · Smith · Williams · Coyle · Park · Power · Coleman
Phillips 83
Ref: D Letts
Allan Hunter takes over the helm after twelve years at Ipswich. U's fans blame chairman Maurice Cadman for hounding Roberts out. Cadman claims he needs to rekindle fading interest. Trevor Phillips's late goal for County goes almost unnoticed after the upheavals of the past week.

46 A CREWE 15/5 — 6 · 24 · 72 · 3-1 · 3-1
Walker · Cook · Hunter · Allinson · Wignall · Packer · Lyons · Bremner · Groves · McDonough · Adcock* · Ward
Longley · Lewis · Heath! · Salathiel · Scott · Palios · Haseglrave · Keighley · Chesters · Entwistle · Williams · Cook*
Bremner 1, Allinson 39, McDonough 41
Scott 44
Ref: K Hackett
Bremner's 24th sets the ball rolling from McDonough's knockdown with Hunter the provider. Allinson, one on one with Nick Longley, nets his 26th. McDonough completes U's scoring for the campaign. Crewe, just six wins and 29 goals, have Duncan Heath sent off on 67 minutes.

Attendances: 2,195 · 1,904 · 1,762 · 2,662 · 5,402 · 2,298 · 1,764 · 2,212 · 1,720 · 1,470 · 2,132 · 1,226
Average — Home 2,855 · Away 3,187

LEAGUE DIVISION 4 (CUP-TIES) Manager: Roberts ⇨ Allan Hunter SEASON 1981-82

League Cup

				F-A	H-T		Scorers, Times, and Referees
1:1	H	GILLINGHAM	1/9	W 2-0	1-0	2,431 3:	Bremner 11, Allinson 60p — Ref J Bray

1	2	3	4	5	6	7	8	9	10	11	12 sub used
Walker	Cook	Packer*	Leslie	Wignall	Wright	Adcock	Bremner	Longhorn	McDonough	Allinson	Coleman
Sutton	*Shape*	*Ford*	*Bruce*	*Weatherley*	*Bowman*	*Powell*	*Duncan*	*Tydeman*	*Lee*	*Price*	

A burst blood vessel in his eye keeps Osborne out. The U's prove the travesty of their relegation. Bremner leaves Mark Weatherley standing for the first. Wignall, venturing upfield, shapes to score but is hauled down by Colin Duncan. Allinson gives the U's a healthy first-leg lead.

1:2	A	GILLINGHAM	15/9	D 1-1	0-0	3,260 3:15	Bremner 52 / Price 53 — Ref C Downey (Colchester won 3-1 on aggregate)

1	2	3	4	5	6	7	8	9	10	11	12 sub used
Walker	Cook	Ford*	Leslie	Wignall	Wright	Adcock	Bremner	Osborne	McDonough	Allinson	White
Hillyard	*Sharpe*		*Bruce*	*Weatherley*	*Bowman*	*Powell*	*Duncan*	*Tydeman*	*Lee*	*Price*	

Bremner puts the tie beyond doubt, only for Ken Price to reduce the arrears within 60 seconds. Gillingham never threaten and Colchester could have won the game when Bowman fouls the tricky Adcock in the 79th minute. Allinson's spot-kick is superbly saved by veteran Ron Hillyard.

2:1	H	CAMBRIDGE	6/10	W 3-1	1-0	3,844 2:18	Cook 27, McDonough 82, 88 / Gibbins 87 — Ref J Martin

1	2	3	4	5	6	7	8	9	10	11	12 sub used
Walker	Cook	Coleman	Leslie	Wignall	Wright	Adcock	Bremner	Osborne	McDonough	Allinson	
Webster	*Christie*	*Murray*	*Reilly*	*Fallon*	*O'Neill*	*Streete*	*Spriggs*	*Goldsmith*	*Gibbins*	*Finney*	

The U's keep up their three-goals-per-game home average. The struggling 2nd division side, have lost their last eight aways. Roger Gibbins narrows the margin. McDonough's goal is the signal for 100 Cambridge 'fans' to invade the pitch in a vain attempt for an abandonment.

2:2	A	CAMBRIDGE	27/10	L 2-3 aet	1-1	4,762 2:14	Allinson 17, Bremner 110 / Gibbins 20, 54, Reilly 65 — Ref R Lewis (Colchester won 5-4 on aggregate)

1	2	3	4	5	6	7	8	9	10	11	12 sub used
Walker	Webster	Coleman	Leslie	Wignall	Wright	Adcock*	Bremner	Osborne	McDonough	Allinson	Longhorn
	Donaldson!	*Murray*	*Turner*	*Fallon*	*O'Neill*	*Streete**	*Spriggs*	*Reilly*	*Gibbins*	*Christie*	*Lyons*

Bremner wins this pulsating tie. Dave Donaldson is sent off on 34 mins for kicking the Scotsman. George Reilly takes the game into extra-time, scoring directly after receiving five minutes treatment for a gash. Allinson's 118th-minute penalty, after Jaimie Murray's trip, is saved

3	A	TRANMERE	10/11	L 0-1	0-1	2,502 4:16	Hutchinson 1 — Ref M Baker

1	2	3	4	5	6	7	8	9	10	11	12 sub used
Walker	Cook	Coleman	Leslie*	Wignall	Wright	Rowles	Bremner	Osborne	McDonough	Allinson	Adcock
Enderby	*Mungall*	*Burgess*	*Craven*	*Bramhall*	*Williams*	*Hamilton*	*Morley*	*Hutchinson*	*Brown*	*Griffiths*	

Merseyside-born Wignall plays a weak back-pass. Bobby Hutchinson intercepts to score the only goal. Adcock comes on as a second-half substitute to revive the U's, but Rovers' packed defence cannot be undone. Tranmere earn a trip to Nottingham Forest in the next round.

FA Cup

1	H	NEWPORT	21/11	W 4-0	0-0	3,535 3:18	Leslie 50, Adcock 74 — Ref B Hill

1	2	3	4	5	6	7	8	9	10	11	12 sub used
Walker	Cook	Coleman	Rowles	Wignall	Wright	Adcock	Bremner	Osborne	McDonough*	Allinson	Leslie
Kendall	*Lees*	*Relish*	*Davies*	*Oakes*	*Bailey*	*Vaughan*	*Lowndes*	*Waddle*	*Aldridge**	*Elsey*	*Tynan*

County, with just one win in 15, are lucky to finish with eleven players. Gareth Davies hacks down Wignall and McDonough. Big Roy suffers an ankle injury and is replaced by Leslie. The midfielder scores within three minutes. Adcock seals it after Rowles chests down to Bremner.

2	A	BRENTFORD	16/12	D 1-1	1-1	5,550 3:13	Allinson 15 / Roberts 33 — Ref D Hutchinson

1	2	3	4	5	6	7	8	9	10	11	12 sub used
Walker	Cook	Coleman	Leslie	Wignall	Wright	Rowles	Bremner	Osborne	McDonough	Allinson	
McKellar	*Salman*	*Tucker*	*McNichol*	*Whitehead*	*Hurlock*	*Kamara*	*Bowen*	*Johnson*	*Bowles*	*Roberts*	

Twice postponed. Wignall appears to have won the tie on 72 minutes. A linesman flags for an obstruction on David McKellar. The silky skills of Stan Bowles are stifled on a frozen pitch. Allinson thunders in another free-kick goal, but Gary Roberts steers home a Bowles flick to level.

2R	H	BRENTFORD	30/12	W 1-0	1-0	5,532 3:7	McNichol 37 (og) — Ref J Deakin

1	2	3	4	5	6	7	8	9	10	11	12 sub used
Walker	Cook	Coleman	Leslie	Wignall	Wright	Rowles	Bremner	Osborne	McDonough	Allinson	
McKellar	*Salman*	*Tucker*	*McNichol*	*Whitehead*	*Hurlock*	*Kamara*	*Bowen*	*Johnson*	*Bowles*	*Booker*	

Layer Road stages its first match for four weeks, after the heavy snow. Volunteers clear the pitch once again. As in the last home game against Blackpool. U's win with a freak own-goal. Jim McNichol's backward header, from Wignall's free-kick, is out of the reach of keeper McKellar.

3	A	NEWCASTLE	4/1	D 1-1	0-1	16,977 2:12	Wignall 83 / Varadi 31 — Ref T Mills

1	2	3	4	5	6	7	8	9	10	11	12 sub used
Walker	Cook	Coleman*	Leslie*	Wignall	Wright	Rowles	Bremner	Osborne	McDonough	Allinson	Todd
Carr	*Brownlie*	*Saunders*	*Trewick**	*Carney*	*Haddick*	*Shoulder*	*Martin*	*Varadi*	*Wharton*	*Waddle*	

Allinson shaves the post on three minutes. Eager Colchester are caught out by Alan Shoulder's cross. Imre Varadi steals in to tuck home. Division Four leaders, Colchester, deservedly draw level. 28-year-old Wignall abandons his defensive duties to nod in Allinson's free-kick.

3R	H	NEWCASTLE	18/1	L 3-4 aet	1-2	7,505 2:11	Cook 44, Allinson 67p, 116p [Varadi 115] / Waddle 12, Saunders 42, Brownlie 94, [Varadi 94] — Ref T Mills

1	2	3	4	5	6	7	8	9	10	11	12 sub used
Walker	Carr	Rowles	Leslie*	Wignall	Wright	Adcock	Bremner	Osborne	McDonough	Allinson	Coleman
Carr	*Brownlie*	*Saunders*	*Trewick*	*Carney*	*Haddick*	*Martin*	*Todd*	*Varadi*	*Wharton*	*Waddle*	

Geordies threaten to overrun U's with ex-sausage factory employee, Chris Waddle, the main tormentor. Twice U's trail in an absorbing cup-tie. Wes Saunders scores a stupendous goal before the break. Steve Carney's needless handball gives Allinson the chance to force extra-time.

League Table

			Home					Away					
	Team	P	W	D	L	F	A	W	D	L	F	A	Pts
1	Sheffield Utd	46	15	8	0	53	15	12	7	4	41	26	96
2	Bradford	46	14	7	2	52	23	12	6	5	36	22	91
3	Wigan	46	17	5	1	47	18	9	8	6	33	28	91
4	Bournemouth	46	12	10	1	37	15	11	9	3	25	15	88
5	Peterborough	46	16	3	4	46	22	8	7	8	25	35	82
6	COLCHESTER	46	12	6	5	47	23	8	6	9	35	34	72
7	Port Vale	46	9	12	2	26	17	9	4	10	30	32	70
8	Hull	46	14	3	6	36	23	5	9	9	34	38	69
9	Bury	46	13	7	3	53	26	4	10	9	27	33	68
10	Hereford	46	10	9	4	36	25	6	10	7	28	33	67
11	Tranmere	46	7	9	7	27	25	7	9	7	24	31	60
12	Blackpool	46	11	5	7	40	26	4	8	11	26	34	58
13	Darlington	46	10	5	8	36	28	5	8	10	25	34	58
14	Hartlepool	46	9	8	6	39	34	4	8	11	34	50	55
15	Torquay	46	9	8	6	30	25	5	8	10	17	34	55
16	Aldershot	46	8	7	8	34	29	5	3	15	23	39	54
17	York	46	9	5	9	45	37	5	5	13	24	54	50
18	Stockport	46	10	5	8	34	28	2	8	13	14	39	49
19	Halifax	46	6	11	6	28	30	3	11	9	23	42	49
20	Mansfield *	46	8	6	9	39	39	5	4	14	24	42	47
21	Rochdale	46	7	9	7	26	22	3	7	13	24	40	46
22	Northampton	46	9	5	9	32	27	2	4	17	25	57	42
23	Scunthorpe	46	7	9	7	26	35	2	6	15	17	44	42
24	Crewe	46	3	6	14	19	32	3	3	17	10	52	27
		1104	245	168	139	888	624	139	168	245	624	888	1486

* deducted two points

Odds & ends

Double wins: (4) Darlington, Hull, Northampton, Rochdale.

Double defeats: (2) Bradford, Wigan.

Won from behind: (4) Rochdale (a), Hull (a), Scunthorpe (h), Rochdale (h).

Lost from in front: (1) Port Vale.

High spots: Ten league wins from eleven games from October

Ian Allinson and Kevin Bremner, the half-century strike force.

Leading the table before Christmas.

Thrashing Sheffield United 5-2 in front of Match of the Day.

A fantastic draw at Newcastle in the FA Cup, followed by a pulsating replay at Layer Road.

Low spots: Promotion failure, after a bright start.

The League Cup run which disappointingly ends at the hands of Fourth Division Tranmere.

The situation when the board ask Roberts to quit, but he stands his ground.

Just failing to score a century of league and cup goals.

Player of the Year: Kevin Bremner.

Ever presents: (3) Kevin Bremner, Micky Cook, Mike Walker.

Hat-tricks: (0).

Leading scorer: Ian Allinson (26).

Appearances and Goals

	Appearances						Goals			
	Lge	Sub	LC	Sub	FAC	Sub	Lge	LC	FAC	Tot
Adcock, Tony	31	9	4	1	2	1	5	1		6
Allinson, Ian	41	1	5		5		21	2	3	26
Bremner, Kevin	46		5		5		21	3		24
Coleman, Phil	34	3	4	1	4	1				
Cook, Micky	46		5		5		4			4
Cotton, Russell	9	2								
Foley, Steve	1	1								
Groves, Perry	9						4	1	1	6
Hunter, Alan	1									
Leslie, Steve	31	3	5		4	1	2		1	3
Longhorn, Dennis	14	1	7	1						
Lyons, John	16	2	2				3			3
McDonough, Roy	40		5		5		14		2	16
Osborne, Roger	39	4	5		5		5			5
Packer, Mick	14	1	1				1			1
Rowles, Eddie	4	2								
Walker, Mick	46		5		5					
Ward, Wayne	3	2								
Wignall, Steve	43		5		5			1		1
Wright, Steve	38		5		5					
(own-goals)							2		1	3
20 players used	506	32	55	3	55	3	82	8	8	98

LEAGUE DIVISION 4

Manager: Allan Hunter ⇨ Cyril Lea — SEASON 1982-83

Each match is shown on two lines: the upper (regular) line is the Colchester United side, the lower (italic) line is the opponents.

No	Date	Att	Pos	Pt	Res	F-A	H-T	1	2	3	4	5	6	7	8	9	10	11	12 sub used	Scorers, Times, and Referees
1	H HALIFAX 28/8	2,610		3	W	1-0	0-0	Walker	Cook	Coleman	Groves	Wignall	Hunter	Allinson	Osborne	Lyons	McDonough*	Leslie	Bremner	McDonough 47. Ref: R Lewis — Roberts takes over at Wrexham during the summer. Allan Hunter, U's new boss, brings in his old Ipswich team-mate Beattie. The centre-half misses his U's debut after the broken nose he suffered in the FL Trophy game at Orient. McDonough touches in Groves' cross for the winner.
								Smelt	*Nobbs*	*Carr*	*Evans*	*Goodman*	*Wood*	*Hallybone*	*Davison*	*Staniforth*	*Spooner*	*Ward*		
2	A HEREFORD 4/9	2,465	7	4	D	0-0	0-0	Walker	Cook	Coleman	Groves	Wignall	Hunter	Allinson	Osborne	Lyons	McDonough	Leslie		Ref: L Robinson — Hereford have 40-year-old John Jackson (ex-Palace) in goal. The attendance is Edgar Street's lowest opening-match crowd since they joined the league ten years ago. The home side lose the services of midfielder John Crabbe, who is sent off on 65 minutes for a foul on John Lyons.
								Jackson	*Price*	*Bartley*	*Pejic*	*Hicks*	*Spiring*	*Crabbe !*	*Harvey*	*Phillips*	*Showers*	*White*		
3	A PORT VALE 6/9	2,877	5	5	D	0-0	0-0	Walker	Cook	Coleman	Groves	Wignall	Hunter	Allinson	Osborne	Lyons	McDonough	Leslie		Ref: V Callow — Bremner has transfer talks with Reading. Walker makes a magnificent save, pushing Neville Chamberlain's shot onto the post. The game is destined for a bore draw as the U's mean defence comes up against a Vale side who have only scored once in their opening four games.
								Siddall	*Tartt*	*Bromage*	*Hunter*	*Sproson*	*Cegielski*	*Chamberlain*	*Moss*	*Armstrong*	*Ridley*	*Sheldon*		
4	H ROCHDALE 10/9	2,638	3	8	W	4-1	2-1	Walker	Cook	Coleman	Groves	Wignall	Hunter	Allinson	Osborne	Lyons	McDonough*	Leslie	Bremner	Allinson 44p, Wignall 45, Lyons 49, 90, Wellings 17p. Ref: D Brazier — United are denied a club record sixth game without conceding, when Barry Wellings falls under a challenge from Wignall. Eric Snookes trips Allinson a minute before Wignall stoops to head in Osborne's corner. Groves feeds Lyons, who also adds the fourth three mins into injury-time.
								Pearce	*Warriner*	*Snookes*	*Weir**	*Trainer*	*Williams*	*Hamilton*	*Farrell*	*French*	*Hilditch*	*Wellings*	*Thompson D*	
5	A CREWE 17/9	2,539	2	11	W	1-0	1-0	Walker	Cook	Coleman	Groves	Wignall	Hunter	Allinson	Osborne	Lyons	McDonough*	Leslie	Bremner	Lyons 33. Ref: D Allison — U's draw Southampton in the Milk Cup, whilst Bremner speaks with Huddersfield. U's top the table for the second Friday night running. Wignall's long clearance catches Neil Salathiel in two minds, hits his back and rolls invitingly into the path of striker John Lyons to score.
								Smith	*Moore*	*Bowers*	*Salathiel*	*Scott*	*Sutton*	*Haselgrave*	*Palios*	*James**	*Evans*	*Craven*	*Purdie*	
6	H BLACKPOOL 25/9	2,918	1	14	W	4-1	2-1	Walker	Cook	Coleman	Groves	Wignall	Hunter*	Allinson	Osborne	Lyons	Bremner	Leslie	Beattie	Lyons 27, Leslie 37, Groves 63, Pashley 36p. [Allinson 85]. Ref: I Borrett — Match of the Week cameras catch Beattie's return to league action after an absence of 19 months. Lyons intercepts Peter Nobles's weak back-pass. Cook trips Dave Bamber. Leslie nips past a static defence within a minute to restore the lead and U's never look back and lead the table.
								Hesford	*Simmonite*	*Brockbank*	*Deary*	*Hetzke*	*Serella*	*Noble*	*Stewart*	*Bamber*	*Pashley*	*Hockaday*		
7	H HULL 28/9	3,071	2	15	D	0-0	0-0	Walker	Cook	Coleman	Groves	Wignall	Hunter	Allinson	Osborne	Lyons	Bremner	Leslie	McDonough	Ref: C Downey — Fans observe a minute's silence in memory of ex-chairman Bill Graver, who died last week. The U's drop their first home points. Allinson narrowly misses with a triangle free-kick routine. Midway through the first half, Gareth Roberts smashes a thunderous volley against the bar.
								Norman	*McNeil*	*Askew*	*Roberts D*	*Skipper*	*Booth*	*Marwood*	*McClaren*	*Whitehurst*	*Flaunders*	*Roberts G*		
8	A SCUNTHORPE 2/10	2,616	5	15	L	1-2	0-1	Walker	Cook	Coleman	Groves*	Wignall	Hunter	Allinson	Osborne	Lyons	Bremner	Leslie*	McDonough	Osborne 50, O'Berg 32, Angus 48. Ref: A Robinson — U's concede their first goal in open play this season to Paul O'Berg. Mike Angus nets on his a home debut. Osborne replies with a solo goal.
								Neenan	*Keeley*	*Pointon*	*Fowler*	*Boxall*	*Hunter*	*O'Berg*	*Cammack*	*Cowling*	*Angus*	*Leman*		
9	A SWINDON 10/10	4,473	7	15	L	0-3	0-2	Walker	Cook	Coleman	Adcock	Wignall	Beattie*	Allinson*	Osborne	Lyons	Bremner	Leslie*	McDonough	Rideout 36p, Rowland 44, 53. Ref: L Burden — Bremner joins Brum on loan. U's play second fiddle to promotion rivals Swindon in this Sunday game. Coleman and Howard Pritchard jostle shoulder-to-shoulder for a crazy penalty. Andy Rowland rises to head in Leigh Barnard's cross. The same duo combine for the Robin's third.
								Allan	*Henry*	*Baddeley*	*Emmanuel*	*Lewis*	*Graham*	*Pritchard**	*Batty*	*Rideout*	*Rowland*	*Barnard*	*Hughes*	
10	H DARLINGTON 15/10	2,547	9	16	D	2-2	1-0	Walker	Cook	Coleman	Adcock	Wignall	Beattie*	Allinson	Osborne	Lyons	McDonough	Leslie	Hunter	Allinson 14, McDonough 65, Walsh 50, 56. Ref: D Letts — Darlington arrive at Layer Road without a win in the last six. McDonough knocks down a floated cross from Cook for Allinson. Beattie is replaced by Longhorn and while the U's are readjusting, Alan Walsh puts the Quakers in front. McDonough levels before Walsh skims the bar.
								Cuff	*Liddle*	*Wilson H*	*Smith*	*Halliday*	*Kamara*	*Hawker*	*McLean*	*Honour*	*Walsh*	*Stalker*	*Longhorn*	
11	A NORTHAMPTON 19/10	1,955	12	16	L	1-2	0-0	Walker	Cook	Coleman	Hunter	Wignall	Beattie	Allinson	Osborne	Lyons	McDonough	Leslie		Allinson 85, Denyer 46, Burrows 88. Ref: T Spencer — Injury-hit Cobblers, who last month beat Bristol C 7-1, have no wins in five. Peter Denyer pokes in Ian Phillips's cross. Allinson looks to have salvaged a point but Adrian Burrow's header from Peter Coffill's corner strikes two U's defenders and goes in off the underside of the bar.
								Freeman	*Tucker*	*Phillips*	*Burrows*	*Gage*	*Saunders*	*Denyer*	*Buchanan J**	*Heeley*	*Massey*	*Perrin*	*Coffill*	

No		Opponent	Date	Pos	Res	Pld	Pts	Score	HT
12	A	BURY	30/10	13	L	16	1	0-1	0-0
13	H	WIMBLEDON	2/11	10	W	19	3	3-0	1-0
14	H	MANSFIELD	6/11	9	W	22	10	2-0	2-0
15	H	CHESTER	9/11	8	W	25	15	1-0	0-0
16	A	TRANMERE	13/11	7	W	28	24	4-2	3-1
17	A	BRISTOL CITY	27/11	6	W	31	23	2-0	1-0
18	H	YORK	3/12	5	D	32	??	0-0	0-0
19	A	HULL	11/12	7	L	32	4	0-3	0-0
20	H	STOCKPORT	17/12	6	W	35	16	3-0	1-0
21	A	PETERBOROUGH	27/12	7	L	35	16	1-2	1-1
22	H	ALDERSHOT	28/12	7	D	36	16	0-0	0-0
23	A	TORQUAY	1/1	8	L	36	7	0-2	0-1

12. A BURY — 30/10 — Att. 2,653
Colchester: Walker, Cook, Coleman, Longhorn, Wignall, Hunter, Allinson, Osborne, Lyons, McDonough, Leslie
Bury: Brown, Gardner, Hilton P, Bramhall, Kenworthy* Gore, Cruikshank, Jakub, Madden, Johnson, Firth, Parker
Bury boss, Jim Iley, claims the U's are 'animals' and 'kickers' after they receive six bookings. Steve Kenworthy suffers a broken leg in U's fifth successive defeat on the road. Kenworthy's replacement, Stuart Parker, hits the only goal, ghosting in to meet a cross from Tommy Gore.
Parker 63, Ref: G Tyson

13. H WIMBLEDON — 2/11 — Att. 2,219
Colchester: Walker, Cook, Coleman, Longhorn, Wignall, Hunter, Allinson, Osborne, Lyons, McDonough, Leslie S
Wimbledon: Beasant, Peters, Thomas, Galliers, Tagg, Morris*, Entwistle, Ketteridge, Leslie J, Downes, Hodges, Gage
An orange ball is used for the last 15 minutes because of the thick fog that descends on Layer Road. Dave Bassett's Dons suffer only their second defeat. McDonough sets up Allinson, then unnerves Tony Tagg for U's second. He claims his second, tapping in a rebound off the post.
Allinson 31, McDonough 52, 70, Ref: H Taylor

14. H MANSFIELD — 6/11 — Att. 2,009
Colchester: Walker, Cook!, Coleman, Longhorn, Wignall, Hunter, Allinson, Osborne, Lyons, McDonough*, Leslie, Bremner
Mansfield: Arnold, Blackhall, Reynolds, Woodhead, Ayre, Sindall, Matthews, Dungworth, Waddle, Caldwell, Nicholson
A punter puts a £10,000 bet on the Stags, pre-season, at 50-1. Cook is sent off at 50 minutes for 'saving' Alan Waddle's header, on his 550th appearance. Walker, making his 300th consecutive appearance, going back to February 1977, saves Simon Woodhead's resultant penalty-kick.
Lyons 9, 44, Ref: J Martin

15. H CHESTER — 9/11 — Att. 2,362
Colchester: Walker, Cook, Coleman, Longhorn, Wignall, Hunter, Allinson, Osborne, Lyons, McDonough*, Leslie*, Bremner
Chester: Salmon, Dean, Needham, Storton, Zelem, Blackwell, Sloan, Johnson, Thomas, Ludlam, Cooke
Wignall heads in a Longhorn corner to secure a third successive home win in this re-arranged fixture. Osborne has a perfectly good goal ruled out on nine minutes for offside. Chester, defending en masse, have the ball in the net through John Thomas who fouls a U's man in the process.
Wignall 84, Ref: T Ward

16. A TRANMERE — 13/11 — Att. 1,410
Colchester: Walker, Cook, Coleman, Longhorn, Wignall, Hunter, Allinson, Osborne, Lyons, McDonough*, Leslie, Adcock
Tranmere: Adkins, Burgess, Brown A, Mathias, Mungall, Williams J, Powell, Aspinall, Kerr, Brown 0*, Griffiths, Ferguson
Tragedy strikes as John Lyons (26) commits suicide at his new Colchester home. The League refuse U's request for a postponement. Tranmere are set to fold on 27 November. McDonough, the last player to see Lyons alive, dedicates his first-minute strike to the memory of his good pal.
McDonough 1, Allinson 3, 20, Adcock 82, Mungall 43, Kerr 74, Ref: D Lloyd

17. A BRISTOL CITY — 27/11 — Att. 4,310
Colchester: Walker, Ward, Coleman*, Longhorn, Wignall, Hunter, Allinson, Osborne, McDonough, Bremner, Adcock
Bristol City: Shaw, Stevens, Johnson I, Nicholls, Phil·Masters Riley, Newman, Thompson, Cooper, Chandler*, Crawford, Kelly N
Struggling City were in the first division only three years ago. Wignall meets a corner, which the bald John Shaw cannot hold. Kevin Bremner, returning from his loan spell, taps in his first U's goal. Osborne sends Allinson racing away for the winger's twelfth of the term.
Bremner 12, Allinson 85, Ref: T Bune

18. H YORK — 3/12 — Att. 2,214
Colchester: Walker, Ward, Coleman, Longhorn, Wignall!, Hunter, Allinson, Osborne, McDonough, Bremner, Leslie
York: Jones, Evans, Hay, Straghia, Smith, Hood, Ford, Crosby, Walwyn, Byrne!, Pollard
For the second season in succession both sides have a player sent off. On 20 minutes Wignall chases John Byrne, whose shot is saved by Mike Walker. Whilst on the ground Byrne lashes out at Wignall, who uncharacteristically retaliates. The incident upsets the tempo of the match.
Ref: A Gunn

19. A HULL — 11/12 — Att. 4,323
Colchester: Walker, Ward, Coleman, Longhorn, Wignall, Hunter, Allinson, Osborne, McDonough, Bremner, Leslie*, Adcock
Hull: Norman, McNeil, Askew, Roberts D, Skipper, Booth, Marwood, McClaren, Flounders, Hawley, Roberts G
The Tigers have four goals on four occasions, but with a stalemate looming Osborne's clearance cannons off the back of Andy Flounders into the net. John Hawley, on loan from Arsenal, shrugs off Wignall to unleash a fierce shot. Brian Marwood is the supplier of the third goal.
Flounders 69, 81, Hawley 77, Ref: D Hutchinson

20. H STOCKPORT — 17/12 — Att. 1,625
Colchester: Walker, Ward, Packer, Longhorn, Emerson, Hull, Allinson, Osborne, McDonough, Bremner, Leslie, Wardrobe
Stockport: Lloyd, Rutter, Sherlock, Emerson, Bowles, Thorpe, Smith, Phillips, Quinn, Leigh*, Coyle
Wignall serves his suspension and Packer replaces Coleman, who is having a knee op. After Mike Quinn misses two clear first-half chances, Allinson scores a picture-book third U's goal, racing onto an Osborne pass, side-stepping Steve Sherlock before chipping over Brian Lloyd.
Allinson 24, 70, McDonough 51, Ref: A Grey

21. A PETERBOROUGH — 27/12 — Att. 4,235
Colchester: Walker, Ward, Packer!, Longhorn, Wignall, Hull, Allinson, Osborne, McDonough!, Bremner, Leslie
Peterborough: Seaman, Winters, Collins, Gynn, Firm, Slack, Rodaway, Clarke, Cooke, Benjamin*, Quow, Chard
Hunter's knee injury may end his playing career. John Winter's bizarre cross-cum-shot gives Posh the lead. McDonough is red-carded on 34 minutes for a flare-up with Neil Firm. Packer follows him on 69 minutes for a soft challenge on Micky Gynn. Firm wins it a minute later.
Bremner 44, Winters 6, Firm 70, Ref: J Key

22. H ALDERSHOT — 28/12 — Att. 2,463
Colchester: Walker, Cook, Ward, Longhorn, Packer, Wignall, Allinson, Osborne, McDonough, Bremner, Hull*, Adcock
Aldershot: Johnson, Shrubb, Gillard, Goddard, Wooler, Jopling, Lucas, Banton, Sanford, McDonald, Robinson
U's lose more ground on the leading pack against a Shots side which they have already beaten twice this season. Two games in two days takes its toll. Wignall returns from suspension to see Alan Wooler slice a clearance against the bar on 13 minutes. Hull has a shot blocked on the line.
Ref: J Deakin

23. A TORQUAY — 1/1 — Att. 2,758
Colchester: Walker, Cook, Ward, Longhorn, Packer, Wignall, Keith, Allinson, Osborne, McDonough, Bremner, Hull
Torquay: Horn, Doyle, Wilson, Sheridan, Little, Hughes, Grapes, O'Donnell, Cooper, Anderson, Gallagher
Bremner joins old boss Roberts at Wrexham on loan. Torquay, with nine home wins, make it ten. Walker picks up a groin strain in his 310th consecutive appearance and is at fault for the Gulls' clincher. Mark Hughes slots home after Ward blocks on the line.
Cooper 16, Hughes 85, Ref: A Glasson

Match Summary

No	Date	H/A	Opponent	Att	Pos	Pt	F-A	H-T	Scorers, Times, and Referees
24	3/1	H	HARTLEPOOL	2,239	W 7	39	4-1	3-1	Allinson 14, Adcock 22, 85, Wignall 44 / Brown 20. Ref: M James
25	7/1	H	HEREFORD	2,216	W 7	42	3-2	2-1	Allinson 22p, 34, Adcock 59 / Harvey 4, Bartley 52. Ref: D Reeves
26	14/1	A	HALIFAX	1,863	L 7	42	0-4	0-2	Nuttall 31, Staniforth 34, 83, 86. Ref: R Guy
27	21/1	H	CREWE	2,221	W 7	45	4-3	3-1	Adcock 8, 37, 86, Allinson 11p / Cliss 9, 69, Bancroft 90. Ref: K Salmon
28	5/2	A	BLACKPOOL	1,747	W 7	48	2-1	0-0	Adcock 50, Hull 61 / Hetzke 75. Ref: P Tyldesley
29	15/2	A	WIMBLEDON	1,753	L 7	48	1-2	1-0	Adcock 20 / Smith 70, Hodges 72. Ref: L Shapter
30	18/2	A	SWINDON	2,386	W 5	51	1-0	0-0	Cook 71. Ref: M Bodenham
31	26/2	A	DARLINGTON	1,089	W 5	54	3-1	2-0	McDonough 9, Adcock 41, 57 / McLean 72p. Ref: A Challinor
32	1/3	H	NORTHAMPTON	2,501	W 5	57	3-1	1-1	Allinson 25p, Hull 56, Adcock 66 / Massey 2. Ref: M Taylor
33	5/3	A	CHESTER	1,136	D 5	58	1-1	0-0	Adcock 56 / Simpson 61. Ref: K Cooper
34	12/3	H	BURY	3,357	W 5	61	2-1	2-0	Allinson 38, Bowen 44 / Potts 83. Ref: M Dimblebee

Line-ups (Cambridge United / Opposition)

No	1	2	3	4	5	6	7	8	9	10	11	12 sub used
24	Chamberlain / Wright	Cook / Smithers	Ward / Simpson	Longhorn* / Brown	Wignall / Barker	Keith / Linighan A	Allinson / Staff	Osborne / Smith*	McDonough / Linacre	Adcock / Lawrence	Hull / Johnson	Groves / Borthwick
25	Chamberlain / Rose	Cook / Price*	Ward / Bray	Longhorn / Ross	Wignall / Pejic	Keith / Crabbe	Allinson / Harvey	Osborne / Bartley	McDonough / Phillips	Adcock / Showers	Hull / White	Musial
26	Chamberlain / Smelt	Cook / Nobbs	Ward / Wood	Longhorn / Evans	Wignall / Smith	Coleman / Hendrie	Allinson / Ward	Osborne / Spooner	Linford / Allatt	Adcock / Nuttall	Hull / Staniforth	
27	Walker / Smith	Ward / Moore	Keith / Bowers	Longhorn / Metcalfe	Wignall / Scott	Coleman / Hart*	Allinson / Haselgrave	Osborne / Bancroft	Linford / Waller	Adcock / Evans	Hull / Cliss	Craven
28	Packer / Hesford	Ward / Bardsley	Ward / Pritchett	McDonough / Deary*	Wignall / Hetzke	Coleman / Greenall	Allinson / Hockaday	Osborne / Richardson / Stewart	Adcock / Pashley	Adcock / Pashley	Hull / Downes / Noble	
29	Cook / Beasant	Packer / Peters	Packer / Sparrow	McDonough / Galliers	Wignall / Smith	Coleman / Hatter	Allinson / Evans	Osborne / Ketteridge	Linford / Leslie J	Adcock / Hodges	Hull / Fishenden	
30	Cook / Allan	Cook / Baverstock	Longhorn / Baille	Longhorn / Emmanuel	Wignall / Lewis	Coleman / Graham	Allinson / Hughes	Osborne / Batty	Linford / Rideout	Adcock / Quinn	Hull / Barnard	
31	Cook / Cuff	Cook / Honour*	Longhorn / Wilson H	McDonough / Smith	Wignall / Barton	Coleman / Kamara	Allinson / Gilbert	Osborne / McLean	Linford / Todd	Adcock / Walsh	Hull / McFadden / Wicks	
32	Walker / Kendall	Cook / Tucker	Longhorn / Phillips	McDonough / Gage	Wignall / Burrows	Coleman / Corfill	Allinson / Saxby	Leslie / Denyer	Linford / Syrett	Adcock / Saunders	Hull / Massey	
33	Walker / Harrington	Cook / Needham	Longhorn / Lane	McDonough / Storton	Wignall / Zelem*	Coleman / Blackwell	Allinson / Sloan	Osborne* / Simpson	Ward / Thomas	Adcock / Williams	Hull / Bulmer	Leslie / Bradley
34	Cook / Brown	Cook / Gardner	Longhorn / Breckin	Gore / Gore	Wignall / Bramhall	Coleman / Halliday	Allinson / Firth*	Osborne / Parker	Bowen / Johnson	Adcock / Jakub	Hull / Potts	Cutler

Match Notes

24 HARTLEPOOL — Walker's appearances run finally comes to an end. U's field non-contract players, Hull and Keith Chamberlain has a quiet debut in the U's goal. Groves, unlucky not to be on the scoresheet, takes McDonough's pass wide on the right flank and chips to Adcock for the fourth goal.

25 HEREFORD — Hereford have one point from their last eleven games and, in Kevin Rose, field their seventh keeper this season. Jimmy Harvey chips in a free-kick. Longhorn is tripped in the box and Allinson also adds a second. John Bartley finishes off a five-man move. Adcock secures the points.

26 HALIFAX — Halifax inflict U's heaviest defeat since Dec 1980 with their fourth successive win. Player-coach David Staniforth notches his first hat-trick in a 17-year playing career. His third takes a deflection off Coleman, that leaves Chamberlain flat-footed. Linford debuts, on loan from Ipswich.

27 CREWE — Allan Hunter resigns after eight months in charge, citing his inability to adapt to the pressures of management and the disappointing end of his playing career. Bob Scott fouls Linford in the box. Adcock completes his treble by racing onto a good ball by Hull to slot past Steve Smith.

28 BLACKPOOL — The Tangerines lose two points, deducted for fielding an ineligible player. Adcock scores his seventh goal in the last six games, whilst Hull bags his first for the U's. Blackpool's lowest ever crowd sees Steve Hetzke steal in to intercept Walker's throw to the sleeping McDonough.

29 WIMBLEDON — Snow puts paid to last week's game with Port Vale. The Dons kill off the U's game with Port Vale. The Dons kill off the U's with a two-minute double strike. Glyn Hodges' corner floats onto Mick Smith's head. Cook fails to cut out Gary Peters' cross. Hodges obliges with the finish. Adcock puts U's into the lead from Wignall's pass.

30 SWINDON — The first game at Layer Road for almost a month. The club receive a petition letter from Port Vale supporters upset at the late postponement and their wasted journey. Cook picks an ideal time to score his first of the season to make up for his error at Plough Lane on Tuesday night.

31 DARLINGTON — The Bremner saga ends when he signs permanently for Millwall. John Wile, John Hollins and Lea are the leading contenders for the top job. Adcock's second is pure genius. He heads down Osborne's pass and scores in his stride. Hull needlessly handles in the box for Quakers' pen.

32 NORTHAMPTON — Six wins in the last eight ties catapulted U's back into the leading pack. The Cobblers take a shock 95-second lead via the divisional leading scorer, Steve Massey. Goalkeeper Mark Kendall fouls on-loan striker Linford. Hull's cross-shot and Adcock's header keeps U's on course.

33 CHESTER — Linford returns to Suffolk. Lea's record of five wins in six makes him the leading contender. Walker's punt is headed on by McDonough for Adcock's 13th. A John Thomas cross is prodded home by Gary Simpson, who 'scores' in the second half, only for three players to be offside.

34 BURY — Bowen (23) joins on loan from Brentford and scores the important winner. U's gain sweet revenge for Jim Iley's taunts earlier in the season. John Breckin's long ball finds Eric Potts. Six minutes earlier, Allinson had worked the famous 'triangle' free-kick with Longhorn and Adcock.

35 A MANSFIELD 19/3 — Att 2,371 · 5 · 11 · 62 · **D 1-1**
Hull 48 · Nicholson 81 · Ref: R Bridges
U's: Walker, Cook, Longhorn, McDonough, Wignall, Coleman, Allinson*, Osborne, Bowen, Adcock, Hull, Groves
Mansfield: Arnold, Blackhall, Kearney, Bell, Bird, Calderwood, Woodhead, Rhodes, Dungworth, Caldwell, Nicholson
Lea is appointed as caretaker until the end of the season Hollins stays at Arsenal until after the Cup Final. The Stags, under new manager Ian Greaves, have lost only one in seven. Gary Nicholson cancels Hull's opportunist strike, firing home from 12 yards after Dungworth's corner.

36 H TRANMERE 25/4 — Att 2,547 · 5 · 16 · 63 · **D 3-3**
Osborne 4, Bowen 47, Adcock 60 · Griffiths 12, Aspinall 44, Brown O 75 · Ref: E Scales
U's: Walker, Cook, Longhorn, McDonough, Wignall, Coleman, Allinson, Osborne*, Bowen, Adcock, Hull, Leslie
Tranmere: Adkins, Burgess, Williams G, Oliver, Hamilton, Williams J, Ferguson, Aspinall, Wellings, Brown O, Griffiths
U's take on John Taylor and Craig Oldfield as full-time pro's. Bowen celebrates signing permanently with the second. In windy conditions Tranmere, who have to borrow U's away kit, earn a well-deserved point via Owen Brown after twice taking the lead in a topsy-turvy clash.

37 H PETERBOROUGH 1/4 — Att 3,759 · 5 · 10 · 66 · **W 1-0**
Allinson 9 · Ref: R Lewis
U's: Walker, Cook, Longhorn, McDonough, Wignall, Coleman, Allinson, Osborne, Bowen, Adcock*, Hull, Groves
Peterborough: Naylor, Winters, Collins, Gynn, Firm, Slack, Clarke, Radaway, Chard*, Benjamin, Linton, Carmichael
Sir Norman Chester's report on the state of the game suggests that the U's would be one of the clubs that would have to leave a re-organised structure based on historical performance. United slip and slide to victory in a mud bath. Allinson whacks his returned corner into the net.

38 A ALDERSHOT 2/4 — Att 1,670 · 5 · 19 · 69 · **W 1-0**
Hull 34 · Ref: M Robinson
U's: Walker, Cook, Longhorn, McDonough, Wignall, Coleman, Allinson*, Osborne, Bowen, Adcock, Hull, Groves
Aldershot: Johnson, Scott, Gillard, Briley, Whitlock, Jopling, Shrubb, Banton, Senior, McDonald, Brodie*, Lucas
Colchester complete a cracking Easter, at the Recreation ground, with a second win in two days. Hull capitalises on Les Briley's mistake to score his fourth U's goal. Twice in the closing stages Bowen comes near to increasing the advantage, but tired legs won the day and the points.

39 A YORK 9/4 — Att 2,538 · 5 · 7 · 69 · **L 0-3**
Busby 37, Pollard 48p, Senior 89 · Ref: R Nixon
U's: Walker, Cook, Longhorn*, McDonough*, Wignall, Coleman, Allinson, Osborne, Bowen, Adcock, Hull, Groves
York: Jones, Evans, Hay, Stragia, McPhail, Hood, Ford, Senior, Busby, Byrne, Pollard
A 650th league appearance for 37-year-old Walker. York have won 14 of 18 home fixtures so far. Adcock is denied a penalty when held back by John McPhail. Player-coach Viv Busby opens the scoring. McDonough hauls down John Byrne and Steve Senior volleys from 12 yards.

40 H PORT VALE 12/4 — Att 3,275 · 5 · 2 · 69 · **L 1-2**
Adcock 2 · Newton 18, Fox 76 · Ref: D Hedges
U's: Walker, Cook, Longhorn*, McDonough, Wignall, Coleman, Allinson, Osborne, Bowen, Adcock, Hull, Groves
Port Vale: Siddall, Tartt, Bromage, Hunter, Ridley, Cegielski, Fox, Steel, Newton, Lawrence M, Armstrong
Packer replaces the suspended McDonough. Vale's tenth away success is U's first home defeat. Adcock scores his 15th on 80 seconds. Winger Steve Fox turns the game for Vale, crossing for Bob Newton's leveller and virtually ensures Vales promotion, netting Jim Steel's low cross.

41 H SCUNTHORPE 15/4 — Att 3,155 · 5 · 6 · 72 · **W 5-1**
Adcock 9, 54, All'n 10, 81p, Keeley 89 (og) · Cammack 17 · Ref: I Borrett
U's: Walker, Cook, Longhorn*, Packer, Wignall, Coleman, Allinson, Osborne, Bowen, Adcock, Hull, Groves
Scunthorpe: Neenan, Keeley, Pointon, Boxall, Baines, Hunter, Graham, Cammack, Cowling, Lester, Leman
U's matchday programme is voted the best in the division. A vital win. Scunthorpe were two points behind with two games in hand at the start. U's penalty comes when Chris Cowling trips Allinson. In the last minute visiting defender Glenn Keeley heads spectacularly into his own net.

42 A STOCKPORT 22/4 — Att 1,733 · 5 · 12 · 72 · **L 0-3**
Smith 16, Coyle 63, Quinn 64 · Ref: H Wilson
U's: Walker, Cook, Longhorn*, McDonough, Wignall, Coleman, Allinson, Osborne, Bowen, Adcock, Hull, Groves
Stockport: Lloyd, Rutter, Thorpe, Emerson, Sword, Bowles, Williams, Smith, Quinn, Power, Coyle
The proposed merger of Reading and Oxford, by Robert Maxwell, as Thames Valley Royals means that a fifth promotion slot could be up for grabs. Stockport face the High Court with debts of £120,000. Nearest rivals Bury lose 1-2 at Ashton Gate to offset this disappointing defeat.

43 A ROCHDALE 26/4 — Att 1,219 · 6 · 18 · 72 · **L 0-2**
Higgins 80, French 32 · Ref: M Peck
U's: Walker, Cook, Longhorn*, McDonough, Wignall, Coleman, Allinson, Osborne, Bowen, Adcock*, Hull, Groves
Rochdale: Rawford, Greenhoff B, Keenan, Farrell, Higgins, Taylor, Thompson D, Thompson S, French, Greenhoff J, Martinez
Rochdale, 4-6 losers at Aldershot on Saturday, finally end U's slim promotion hopes after this fourth defeat in five. Twice postponed because of the weather. Player-manager Jimmy Greenhoff's free-kick finds Andy Higgins. Micky French chips the U's defensive wall from 20 yards.

44 H BRISTOL CITY 29/4 — Att 2,196 · 5 · 15 · 75 · **W 3-1**
Allinson 35p, Bowen 39, McDonough 87 · Ritchie 41p · Ref: T Ward
U's: Walker, Cook*, Longhorn, Leslie, Wignall, Coleman, Allinson, Osborne, Bowen, Adcock, Hull, McDonough
Bristol City: Shaw, Newman, Williams G, Nicholls, Phil? Masters Riley, Ritchie, Williams P, Williams E*, Kelly E*, Economou, Crawford, Palmer
Leslie returns after a twisted knee. Allinson is sent sprawling by John Shaw. Bowen pokes Hull's pass into the net. Packer brings down Glyn Riley. Tom Ritchie pulls a goal back from the spot. McDonough, filling in at right-back, solo-runs two-thirds of the length of the pitch to score.

45 A HARTLEPOOL 2/5 — Att 804 · 5 · 22 · 78 · **W 4-1**
Allinson 32, Coleman 65, 66, Groves 80 · Linacre 74 · Ref: D Shaw
U's: Walker, Cook, Packer, Leslie, Wignall, Coleman, Allinson, Osborne, Bowen, Adcock, Hull*, Groves
Hartlepool: Blackburn, Smithers, Simpson, Brown, Bird, Linghan A, Hogan*, Stewart, Staff, Dobson, Robinson, Linacre
Allinson scores his 51st goal in their 65 year history. The attendance is Pool's lowest in two seasons and leads the divisional scoring charts. The conditions are more suited to water polo. Coleman nets a two-minute double. Groves comes off the bench for the fourth in a morning kick-off.

46 H TORQUAY 13/5 — Att 2,181 · 6 · 12 · 81 · **W 1-0**
Wignall 71 · Ref: A Gunn
U's: Walker, Cook*, Packer, Leslie, Wignall, McDonough, Allinson, Osborne, Bowen, Adcock, Hull*, Groves
Torquay: Chamberlain, Ward, Doyle, James, Little, Jones, Sheridan, Carter, Gallagher, Anderson, Bishop, Horn, Holmes
Walker deservedly picks up all the various player of the year awards. Wignall's stunning 35-yard shot comes completely out of the blue after he gathers the ball in midfield. U's must now appoint a full-time manager during the close season break for another tilt at promotion.

Home 2,552 · Away 2,371 · Average 2,552

LEAGUE DIVISION 4 (CUP-TIES)

Manager: Allan Hunter ⇨ Cyril Lea   SEASON 1982-83

Football League Trophy

		F-A	H-T	Scorers, Times, and Referees	1	2	3	4	5	6	7	8	9	10	11	subs used
1 H SOUTHEND 13/8	W	3-1	1-1	Coleman 36, Lyons 85, Allinson 46 / Cusack 34 / Ref: K Salmon	Walker	Cook	Coleman	Groves	Wignall	Hunter	Allinson	Osborne	Lyons	McDonough	Adcock	Hadley
1,662 3:					*Keeley*	*Stead*	*Yates*	*Pountney*	*Clark*	*Cusack**	*Pennyfather*	*Phillips*	*Mercer*	*Nelson*	*Greaves*	

U's are installed as second favourites for the Fourth Division title. Dave Cusack knocks Walker's fisted clearance back into the net. Coleman levels from a well-worked triangle with Osborne and Allinson. Allinson weaves past Paul Clark and Walker makes a last-minute penalty save

		F-A	H-T	Scorers, Times, and Referees	1	2	3	4	5	6	7	8	9	10	11	subs used
1 A WATFORD 17/8	L	1-2	0-0	Allinson 80 / Blissett 72, Jenkins 79 / Ref: D Hedges	Walker	Cook	Coleman	Groves	Wignall	Beattie*	Allinson	Osborne	Lyons*	Bremner	Leslie	Hunter/McD', Patch/Armst
3,837 1:					*Sherwood*	*Rice**	*Rostron*	*Lohman*	*Terry**	*Sims*	*Callaghan*	*Blissett*	*Jenkins*	*Jackett*	*Barnes*	

Watford are in Division One for the first time in their history. England U-21 star Luther Blissett opens the scoring two minutes after Kevin Beattie is subbed. Ross Jenkins finishes off a John Barnes effort before Allinson's 20-yarder whistles past Steve Sherwood in the Hornets goal.

		F-A	H-T	Scorers, Times, and Referees	1	2	3	4	5	6	7	8	9	10	11	subs used
1 A ORIENT 21/8	W	2-0	0-0	Lyons 60, 89 / Ref: K Baker	Walker	Cook	Coleman	Groves	Wignall	Beattie*	Allinson	Osborne	Lyons	McDonough	Adcock*	Hunter/Leslie, McNeil/Bl'kah
1,384 3:					*Day*	*Fisher**	*Peach*	*Foster*	*Gray*	*Sussex*	*Godfrey**	*Donn*	*Houchen*	*Silkman*	*Taylor*	

Despite U's victory, Watford's win at Roots Hall is enough to take the Hornets through. Injury-plagued Beattie suffers a broken nose in the 80th minute, coming out second best from an attempted overhead kick by Keith Houchen. Colchester finish second in the final group table.

Milk Cup

		F-A	H-T	Scorers, Times, and Referees	1	2	3	4	5	6	7	8	9	10	11	subs used
1:1 H ALDERSHOT 31/8	W	2-0	2-0	Wignall 12, Groves 35 / Ref: M Dimbledee	Walker	Cook	Coleman	Groves	Wignall	Hunter	Allinson	Osborne	Lyons*	McDonough	Leslie	Bremner
1,665 4:					*Johnson*	*Andruszewski Gillard*		*Briley*	*Wood*	*Jopling*	*Shrubb*	*Barnton*	*Goddard*	*McDonald*	*Brodie*	

United's third successive game without conceding. McDonough flicks on Allinson's corner for centre-half Wignall's opener. Youngster, Perry Groves, scores a spectacular first senior goal from all of 35 yards. Howard Goddard forces a fine save out of Walker. U's are worthy winners

		F-A	H-T	Scorers, Times, and Referees	1	2	3	4	5	6	7	8	9	10	11	subs used
1:2 A ALDERSHOT 14/9	W	1-0	0-0	Allinson 85 / Ref: M Taylor / (Colchester won 3-0 on aggregate)	Walker	Cook	Coleman	Groves	Wignall	Hunter	Allinson	Osborne	Lyons	McDonough	Leslie	Lucas
1,680 4:6					*Johnson*	*Andruszewski Gillard*		*Briley**	*Wood*	*Jopling*	*Shrubb*	*Barnton*	*Sanford*	*McDonald*	*Brodie*	

Aldershot exert plenty of first-half pressure and enjoy the bulk of possession. Joe Jopling shaves the crossbar in only the seventh minute. U's defence is resolute, and capitalise with a breakaway winner when Osborne pushes the ball back to Allinson, unmarked on the edge of the box.

		F-A	H-T	Scorers, Times, and Referees	1	2	3	4	5	6	7	8	9	10	11	subs used
2:1 H SOUTHAMPTON 6/10	D	0-0	0-0	Ref: B Hill	Walker	Cook	Coleman	Adcock	Wignall	Beattie*	Allinson	Osborne	Lyons	McDonough	Leslie	Bremner
7,679 1:20					*Shilton*	*Baker*	*Rofe*	*Williams*	*Nichol*	*Agboola*	*Ball*	*Cassells*	*Wallace*	*Armstrong*	*Lawrence*	

Saints players Steve Moran (21) and Mark Wright (18) are held in a Swedish jail after an alleged offence before their UEFA Cup defeat in Norkopping. Keith Cassells' goal is ruled out for offside. Peter Shilton makes a string of world-class saves to deny Colchester a first-leg lead.

		F-A	H-T	Scorers, Times, and Referees	1	2	3	4	5	6	7	8	9	10	11	subs used
2:2 A SOUTHAMPTON 26/10	L	2-4	1-2	Allinson 14p, Lyons 50 / Wallace 28, Cassells 40, Armstrong 73, [Moran 90] / Ref: E Read / (Colchester lost 2-4 on aggregate)	Walker	Cook	Coleman	Hunter	Wignall	Ward	Allinson	Osborne	Lyons	McDonough	Wallace	Puckett
9,676 1:21					*Shilton*	*Rofe**	*Holmes*	*Williams*	*Nichol*	*Wright*	*Ball*	*Moran*	*Cassells*	*Armstrong*	*Wallace*	

Shilton passes a late fitness test. Mark Wright fells Lyons and U's fans hark back to the victory at the Dell eight years earlier. Shilton pushes Hunter's header onto the bar on 20 mins. David Armstrong regains the lead before Moran's goal gives Southampton a flattering two-goal win.

FA Cup

		F-A	H-T	Scorers, Times, and Referees	1	2	3	4	5	6	7	8	9	10	11	subs used
1 H TORQUAY 20/11	L	0-2	0-1	Little 34, Cooper 62 / Ref: D Reeves	Walker	Ward	Coleman*	Hunter	Longhorn	Wignall	Allinson	Osborne	McDonough	Bremner	Leslie	Adcock
2,913 4:8					*Horn*	*Doyle*	*Wilson*	*Rioch*	*Little*	*Bould*	*Grapes !*	*O'Donnell*	*Cooper*	*Anderson*	*Gallagher*	

U's bow out of the FA Cup at the first hurdle for the first time in six years. Alan Little latches onto McDonough's half clearance. Steve Grapes is sent off on 40 mins for a bad tackle on Leslie, his second booking. Player-manager Bruce Rioch keeps the U's at bay to host Carshalton.

				Home					Away					
		P	W	D	L	F	A	W	D	L	F	A	Pts
1	Wimbledon	46	17	4	2	57	23	12	7	4	39	22	98
2	Hull	46	14	8	1	48	14	11	7	5	27	20	90
3	Port Vale	46	15	4	4	37	16	11	6	6	30	18	88
4	Scunthorpe	46	13	7	3	41	17	10	7	6	30	25	83
5	Bury	46	15	4	4	43	20	8	8	7	31	26	81
6	COLCHESTER	46	17	5	1	51	19	7	4	12	24	36	81
7	York	46	18	4	1	59	19	4	9	10	29	39	79
8	Swindon	46	14	3	6	45	27	5	8	10	16	27	68
9	Peterborough	46	13	6	4	38	23	4	7	12	20	29	64
10	Mansfield	46	11	6	6	32	26	5	7	11	29	44	61
11	Halifax	46	9	8	6	31	23	7	4	12	28	43	60
12	Torquay	46	12	3	8	38	30	5	4	14	18	35	58
13	Chester	46	8	6	9	28	24	7	5	11	27	36	56
14	Bristol City	46	10	8	5	32	25	3	9	11	27	45	56
15	Northampton	46	10	8	5	43	29	4	4	15	22	46	54
16	Stockport	46	11	8	4	41	31	3	4	16	19	48	54
17	Darlington	46	8	5	10	27	30	5	8	10	34	41	52
18	Aldershot	46	11	5	7	40	35	3	3	15	21	47	51
19	Tranmere	46	8	8	7	30	29	5	3	15	19	42	50
20	Rochdale	46	11	8	4	38	25	0	8	15	17	48	49
21	Blackpool	46	10	8	5	32	23	3	4	16	23	51	49
22	Hartlepool	46	11	5	7	30	24	2	4	17	16	52	48
23	Crewe	46	9	5	9	35	32	3	3	18	18	39	41
24	Hereford	46	8	6	9	19	23	3	2	18	23	56	41
		1104	283	142	127	915	587	127	142	283	587	915	1512

Odds & ends

Double wins: (4) Blackpool, Bristol City, Crewe, Hartlepool.

Double defeats: (0).

Won from behind: (3) Rochdale (h), Hereford (h), Northampton (h).

Lost from in front: (2) Wimbledon (a), Port Vale (h).

High spots: Adaptable Ian Allinson forms a new partnership with Tony Adcock.

A sterling display against Southampton in the Milk Cup.

The total honesty of Allan Hunter, although disappointing, when he realised that he was not cut out for football management.

Low spots: Promotion failure by just two points.

The tragic suicide of striker John Lyons.

The determination of the talented Kevin Bremner to leave the club.

Player of the Year: Mike Walker.

Ever presents: (1) Ian Allinson.

Hat-tricks: (1) Tony Adcock.

Leading scorer: Ian Allinson (26) (including 2 in Football League Trophy).

	Appearances						Goals			
	Lge	Sub	LC	Sub	FAC	Sub	Lge	LC	FAC	Tot
Adcock, Tony	26	4			1	1	17			17
Allinson, Ian	46		4		1		22		2	24
Beattie, Kevin	3	1			1					
Bowen, Keith	13						4			4
Bremner, Kevin	10	5			2	1	2			2
Chamberlain, Alec	4									
Coleman, Phil	37		4		1		2			2
Cook, Micky	41		4				1			1
Groves, Perry	8	9	2				2		1	3
Hull, Jeff	27						4			4
Hunter, Allan	17	1	3		1					
Keith, Adrian	4									
Leslie, Steve	26	3	4				1			1
Linford, John	7									
Longhorn, Dennis	27	1								
Lyons, John	15		4				6		1	7
McDonough, Roy	38	3	4		1		8			8
Osborne, Roger	45		4		1		2			2
Packer, Mick	12									
Walker, Mick	42		4		1					
Ward, Wayne	14		1		1					
Wignall, Steve	44		4		1		4		1	5
22 players used	506	27	44	2	11	1	75		5	80

Player position columns: 1, 2, 3, 4, 5, 6, 7, 8, 9, 10, 11, 12 sub used. Stats columns: Att, Pos, Pt, F-A, H-T, Scorers Times and Referees.

1 — A DARLINGTON — 27/8 — Att 1,441 · Pos 3 · W · 2-0 · H-T 0-0
Scorers: Adcock 74, Houston 86. Ref: R Dilkes

1	2	3	4	5	6	7	8	9	10	11	12
Chamberlain	Cook	Farrell	Hadley	Wignall	Houston	Groves	Osborne	Bowen	Adcock	Hull	Hull
Barber	Craggs	Gilbert	McLean	Smith	Barton	Johnson*	Ross	Lee	Walsh	Honour	Wakefield

U's are a good bet as second favourites at 6-1. McDonough and Allinson leave during the summer, and Walker becomes reserve boss. Allinson secures a controversial free-transfer to Arsenal, when he and the Gunners make the most of a contract typing error, denying U's a record fee.

2 — H BLACKPOOL — 3/9 — Att 2,169 · Pos 11 · W · 2-1 · H-T 1-0
Scorers: Adcock 14p, Serella 87 (og). Serella 46. Ref: J Ashworth

1	2	3	4	5	6	7	8	9	10	11	12
Chamberlain	Cook	Farrell	Hadley	Wignall	Houston	Groves*	Osborne	Bowen	Adcock	Hull	Oldfield
O'Rourke	Bardsley	Pritchett	Rodaway	Hetzke	Serella	Windridge	Mercer	Deary	Ferns	McNiven*	Stewart

Adcock's fourth goal in three games from the spot, after his shot strikes John Deary's hand. Dave Serella side-foots Steve Hetzke's knockdown to level and then, inexplicably, deflects Hull's cross into his own net for Blackpool's sixth consecutive defeat at Layer Road. Oldfield debuts.

3 — H BRISTOL CITY — 6/9 — Att 2,120 · Pos 8 · D · 0-0 · H-T 0-0
Ref: M James

1	2	3	4	5	6	7	8	9	10	11
Chamberlain	Cook	Farrell	Hadley	Wignall	Houston	Groves	Osborne	Bowen	Adcock	Hull
Shaw	Newman	Williams G	Phill* Masters Halliday	Riley*	Pritchard	Ritchie	Kerr	Stevens	Crawford	Williams P

Colchester introduce new signing Ian Phillips (24 from Northampton) to the crowd before kick-off. He is the natural left-back manager Lea has been looking for. Neither John Shaw nor Chamberlain have a shot to save in the match which maintains United's unbeaten start to the season.

4 — A STOCKPORT — 9/9 — Att 2,077 · Pos 19 · D · 0-0 · H-T 0-0
Ref: V Callow

1	2	3	4	5	6	7	8	9	10	11
Chamberlain	Cook	Phillips	Hadley	Wignall	Houston	Groves	Osborne	Bowen	Adcock	Hull
Salmon	Jones	Rutter	Emerson	Sword	Thorpe	Williams	Smith	Quinn	Power*	Coyle	Ryan

Mike Quinn, County's leading scorer from last term, forces a magnificent save out of Chamberlain on 22 minutes. Stockport sub John Ryan, formerly with Luton and Norwich, has the ball in the net but Quinn is ruled to have fouled Cook in the build-up. A second goal-less bore-draw.

5 — H ROCHDALE — 17/9 — Att 1,955 · Pos 17 · W · 4-0 · H-T 2-0
Scorers: Bowen 30, Adcock 38, 51, Wignall 53. Ref: C Downey

1	2	3	4	5	6	7	8	9	10	11	12
Chamberlain	Cook	Phillips	Hadley	Wignall	Houston	Groves	Osborne	Bowen	Adcock	Hull*	Oldfield
Conroy	Oates	Chapman	Farrell	Higgins	Doyle	Thompson D	Hamilton	Johnson	Allatt	Griffiths	

Andy Higgins' error lets in midweek Milk Cup hero Bowen, who earlier had a shot pushed against the bar. Dale's defence collapses like a pack of cards. U's could easily have double figures. Adcock spurns a hat-trick, hitting the post with an 85th-min penalty after Higgins fouls Bowen.

6 — A CHESTERFIELD — 24/9 — Att 4,106 · Pos 10 · D · 1-1 · H-T 0-0
Scorers: Wignall 73. Birch 66. Ref: D Scott

1	2	3	4	5	6	7	8	9	10	11
Chamberlain	Cook	Phillips	Hadley	Wignall	Houston	Groves	Osborne	Bowen	Adcock	Hull
Brown J	Kendal	O'Neill	Scrimgeour	Baines	Bellamy	Birch	Spooner	Clayton	Bell	Waddington

U's take their unbeaten run to six against John Duncan's Spireites. Alan Birch heads in a misjudged punch by Chamberlain for the first goal conceded in the league for 380 minutes. Wignall plants Hull's corner firmly in the net. Adcock is denied by the bar in the closing stages.

7 — A TRANMERE — 26/9 — Att 1,866 · Pos 17 · L · 1-2 · H-T 0-1
Scorers: Adcock 60p. Williams G 18, Ferguson 89. Ref: M Heath

1	2	3	4	5	6	7	8	9	10	11	12
Chamberlain	Cook	Phillips	Hadley	Wignall	Houston	Groves*	Osborne	Bowen	Adcock	Hull	Oldfield
Davies	McMahon	Burgess	Parry	Hamilton*	Williams J	Ferguson	Aspinall	Hilditch	Allen	Williams G	Mungall

A goal just 90 seconds from time ends U's unbeaten run and the chance to go top. Gary Williams curls in a great free-kick after Houston fouls Mark Hildith. Hull rises to meet a cross but is barged by Player-boss Bryan Hamilton. Mark Ferguson stabs home after a goalmouth melee.

8 — H CHESTER — 1/10 — Att 1,976 · Pos 24 · W · 1-0 · H-T 0-0
Scorers: Adcock 55. Ref: M Bodenham

1	2	3	4	5	6	7	8	9	10	11	12
Chamberlain	Cook	Phillips	Hadley	Leslie	Houston	Groves	Osborne	Bowen	Adcock	Hull	Hull
Harrington	Williams M	Lane	Elliott	Zelem	Holden	Ryan	Allen	Parker	Blackwell*	Williams P	Bulmer

Wignall misses out due to a chest infection and is replaced by the injury-hit Leslie. Adcock's ninth in ten games earns the points. Hadley flicks on Hull's cross and the copper-topped striker is on hand to prod into the net. Chester are in crisis and remain rooted to the foot of the table.

9 — A YORK — 7/10 — Att 6,207 · Pos 1 · L · 0-3 · H-T 0-1
Scorers: McPhail 41, Pollard 72p, Walwyn 85. Ref: R Guy

1	2	3	4	5	6	7	8	9	10	11
Chamberlain	Cook	Phillips	Hadley	Leslie	Houston	Groves	Osborne	Bowen	Adcock	Hull
Jones	Senior	Hay	Sbragia	McPhail	Haselgrave	Ford	Crosby	Walwyn	Byrne	Pollard

York, the runaway leaders, complete a full year undefeated at home in a match brought forward to avoid tomorrow's big race meeting. After John McPhail's header, Hadley's foul on Gary Ford seems to be out of the box. Keith Walwyn makes it U's third 0-3 defeat on the trot at York.

10 — H NORTHAMPTON — 15/10 — Att 1,964 · Pos 12 · D · 2-2 · H-T 1-1
Scorers: Houston 16, Cook 78. Austin 11, O'Neill 81. Ref: D Letts

1	2	3	4	5	6	7	8	9	10	11	12
Chamberlain	Cook	Phillips	Hadley	Leslie	Houston	Groves*	Osborne	Bowen	Adcock	Hull	Hubbick
Gleasure	Forster	Tucker	Gage	Lewis	Burrows*	Jeffrey	O'Neill	Belfon	Mundee	Austin	Hayes

Unbeaten Cobblers, albeit with five draws on the spin, take the lead with Terry Austin's fourth of the term. Houston levels from a deep corner. Leslie rolls a free-kick for Cook to unleash a thunderbolt. Sub Austin Hayes punishes Houston's indecision to cross for Tommy O'Neill.

11 — H BURY — 18/10 — Att 1,969 · Pos 8 · W · 1-0 · H-T 1-0
Scorers: Adcock 20. Ref: I Borrett

1	2	3	4	5	6	7	8	9	10	11	12
Chamberlain	Cook	Phillips	Hadley	Wignall	Leslie	Groves*	Osborne	Bowen	Adcock	Hull	Nicholls
Brown	Gardner	Pashley	Carrodbus	Hilton P	Bramball	Potts*	Madden	Spence	Jakub	Deacy	Coleman

Adcock's eleventh goal of the campaign takes United back into a promotion spot, as they prepare for next weeks Milk Cup challenge at Swansea. David Brown parries Hull's shot, and from his resulting flag-kick, Bowen flicks on to the unmarked Adcock to coolly pick his spot.

Cambridge United 1984–85 match-by-match records (fixtures 12–23). Each entry lists the Cambridge United line-up (first name in each pair) against the opponent (second, italic name), with attendance and league data, scorers, referee and a match report.

---

12 · A · SWINDON · 22/10
3,079 | 4 | *13* | L | 19 | 1-2 | 1-0

Chamberlain / *Endersby* · Cook / *Henry* · Phillips / *Baillie* · Hadley / *Batty* · Wignall* / *Gibson* · Leslie / *Graham* · Groves / *Hockaday* · Osborne / *Emmanuel* · Bowen / *Rowland* · Adcock / *Mayes* · Hull / *Barnard* · Nicholls

Adcock 44p / *Rowland 52, Hockaday 77*
Ref: A Crickmore

Swindon include Simon Gibson, a new capture from Chelsea. Wignall suffers a groin strain on 62 minutes. Andy Rowland heads in Gary Emmanuel's flag-kick. Dave Hockaday fires home Alan Mayes' chip. Groves skins Colin Baillie, who makes a despairing lunge in the box.

---

13 · H · CREWE · 29/10
3,402 | 4 | *18* | W | 22 | 2-0 | 0-0

Chamberlain / *Naylor* · Cook / *Edwards* · Phillips / *Brady* · Hadley / *King* · Nicholls / *Scott* · Groves / *Cliss* · Osborne / *Crabbe* · Bowen / *Waller* · Adcock / *Blissett* · Hull* / *Pollar* · Hubbick

Adcock 50, 89p
Ref: M Taylor

Chaos as U's put tickets on sale for the Man Utd cup-tie prior to kick-off. Many fans are still queuing behind the main stand as Adcock picks up Groves' pass to curl past Stuart Naylor. Hull is stretchered off on 14 mins. In the last minute John Crabbe is harshly penalised for handball.

---

14 · A · DONCASTER · 1/11
3,491 | 4 | *3* | D | 23 | 3-3 | 2-1

Chamberlain / *Boyd* · Farrell / *Russell* · Phillips / *Breckin* · Hadley / *Snodin I* · Nicholls / *Lister* · Groves* / *Miller* · Osborne / *Moss* · Bowen / *Douglas* · Adcock / *Kowalski* · Leslie / *Snodin G* · Hubbick

Bowen 6, Humphries 13 (og), Adcock 62p / *Douglas 21, Miller 50, Snodin 87p*
Ref: I Hendrick

Lea praises non-contract players Nicholls and Hubbick. Bowen outpaces Glen Humphries for the first, then Humphries heads an own-goal past Willie Boyd from a Bowen cross. Humphries floors Bowen and has to walk. Three minutes from time Osborne fouls Billy Russell in the box.

---

15 · H · READING · 5/11
2,433 | 2 | *12* | W | 26 | 3-0 | 2-0

Chamberlain / *Judge* · Cook / *Richardson* · Phillips / *White !* · Hadley / *Beavon* · Wignall / *Hicks* · Hubbick / *Duncan* · Osborne* / *Harix* · Bowen / *Senior* · Adcock / *Sanchez* · Leslie / *Crown* · Groves

Houston 15, Leslie 17, Adcock 62
Ref: E Scales

Adcock wins the battle of the division's top scorers although Trevor Senior has 21 to his credit. Houston heads in a Leslie corner. Two minutes later Leslie cracks in a volley, his first goal for 14 months. Mark White gets his marching orders on 74 minutes for swearing at the linesman.

---

16 · A · MANSFIELD · 12/11
3,042 | 4 | *18* | D | 27 | 0-0 | 0-0

Chamberlain / *Daines* · Cook / *Whitworth* · Phillips / *Woodhead* · Hadley / *Lowery* · Wignall / *Foster* · Hubbick / *Matthews* · Houston / *Calderwood* · Farrell / *Keegan* · Bowen / *Galloway* · Adcock / *Dungworth* · Leslie / *Nicholson*

Ref: J Hough

U's face reality after the Man Utd defeat. Mansfield dominate the possession in the opening half but U's force ten corners after the interval. Despite the pressure and Adcock's effort against the crossbar, the game ends in deadlock. Lea bids £15,000 for Torquay striker Steve Cooper.

---

17 · A · TORQUAY · 26/11
1,364 | 7 | *13* | L | 27 | 1-2 | 1-2

Chamberlain / *Turner* · Cook / *Pugh* · Phillips / *Wharton* · Hadley / *Impey* · Wignall / *Hughes* · Hubbick / *Young* · Houston / *Carr* · Farrell / *Curle* · Bowen / *Cooper* · Adcock / *Sims* · Leslie / *Barnes*

Cook 32 / *Curle 38p, 45p*
Ref: J Deakin

The Gulls gain revenge for last week's cup defeat by the U's. Phillips' low skimming cross is only half-cleared to Cook to notch his second of the season. Keith Curle's penalties come when Wignall fouls U's target Steve Cooper, and Houston, in his 400th league game, trips John Sims.

---

18 · H · HARTLEPOOL · 3/12
1,935 | 4 | *24* | W | 30 | 6-0 | 1-0

Chamberlain / *Blackburn* · Cook / *Ray* · Phillips / *Wilson* · Nicholls / *Linghan D* · Wignall / *Linghan A* · Groves / *Brown* · Osborne / *Robinson** · Bowen / *Dixon K* · Adcock / *Staff* · Leslie / *Johnson* · Malley

Wignall 14, 82, Phillips 63, 89, Nicholls 58, [Groves 79]
Ref: A Gunn

Five of Colchester's six goals are scored by defenders. Nicholls scores his first senior goal via an Adcock pass. Not to be outdone, Phillips too score his first goal since signing. Pool's defence is pulled apart from set-pieces and look set for a long hard winter battle against re-election.

---

19 · H · HALIFAX · 17/12
1,866 | 3 | *21* | W | 33 | 4-1 | 2-0

Chamberlain / *Smelt* · Cook ! / *Nobbs* · Phillips / *Woods* · Hadley / *Evans* · Wignall / *Smith* · Groves / *Greenway** · Osborne / *Little* · Bowen / *Nuttall* · Adcock* / *Kendall* · Leslie / *Ward* · Hubbick / *Cook*

Houston 5, Adcock 34, Bowen 67, 88 / *Greenway 54*
Ref: A Buksh

U's fail by one to equal the club record for the number of goals in three consecutive games. The record of 15 was set in 1961 but did not include the record 9-1 win over Bradford. Lea opts not to sign Trevor Whymark. Cook is sent off for clashes with Mark Greenway (50 & 67 minutes).

---

20 · A · PETERBOROUGH · 26/12
6,527 | 6 | *2* | L | 33 | 0-2 | 0-0

Chamberlain / *Seaman* · Cook / *Chard* · Phillips / *Holmes* · Hadley / *Beech* · Wignall / *Wile* · Groves* / *Benjamin** · Osborne* / *Tydeman* · Bowen / *Hankin* · Adcock / *Quow* · Leslie / *Waddle* · Hubbick / *Pike*

Beech 75, Waddle 89
Ref: H Taylor

U's have still not signed the two players promised following the Milk Cup win over Swansea. Kenny Beech scores his first for Peterborough since arriving from Walsall. In the dying moments ex-Liverpool and Leicester striker Alan Waddle secures the Boxing Day points for Posh.

---

21 · H · ALDERSHOT · 27/12
3,123 | 4 | *10* | W | 36 | 4-1 | 3-1

Chamberlain / *Coles* · Cook / *Day* · Phillips / *Wooler* · Hadley / *Briley* · Wignall / *Compton* · Groves / *Shrubb* · Osborne / *Banton* · Bowen / *Lawrence* · Adcock / *McDonald* · Leslie / *Mazzon* · Hubbick

Adcock 1p, 23, Wignall 20, Bowen 51 / *McDonald 22*
Ref: J Bray

The Layer Road goals tally rises to 18 in the last four games. Adcock's penalty comes after Les Lawrence handles after just twelve seconds. Wignall nods in a Phillips corner before ex-U's loanee Ian McDonald rifles in a free-kick. Bowen hits his eighth goal in the last seven games.

---

22 · H · WREXHAM · 2/1
3,182 | 6 | *19* | D | 37 | 1-1 | 1-0

Chamberlain / *Millington* · Farrell / *King* · Phillips / *Cunnington* · Hadley / *Hunt* · Wignall / *Heath* · Groves / *Wright* · Osborne / *Arkwright* · Bowen / *Muldoon* · Adcock / *Gregory* · Leslie / *Salathiel* · Nicholls* / *Hubbick*

Adcock 43 / *Muldoon 60*
Ref: D Hedges

Cook is suspended following his sending off. Bobby Roberts returns after 20 months away from Layer Road remaining tight-lipped about his ignominious departure. The Welshmen become only the third side to escape with a point so far this season after John Muldoon's equaliser.

---

23 · H · DARLINGTON · 14/1
2,151 | 7 | *19* | W | 40 | 2-1 | 0-0

Chamberlain / *Barber* · Cook / *Craggs* · Phillips / *Johnson* · Hadley / *Gilbert* · Wignall / *Smith* · Hubbick / *Cartwright* · Osborne / *Davies** · Bowen / *Todd* · Adcock / *Walsh* · Leslie / *McLean* · Hubbick / *Honour*

Adcock 63p, 65 / *Walsh 66*
Ref: J Martin

Leslie plays his 400th game for the club. Darlington striker Alan Walsh, a target for Lea, trips Wignall in the box whilst defending a corner. Wignall flicks on Hadley's free-kick for Adcock's second and 23rd of the season. Walsh pulls a goal back after good work by Dave McLean.

CANON LEAGUE DIVISION 4   Manager: Cyril Lea   SEASON 1983-84

No	Date	1	2	3	4	5	6	7	8	9	10	11	12 sub used
24	H STOCKPORT 28/1	Chamberlain	Cook	Phillips	Hadley	Farrell	Houston	Mutrie*	Hull	Bowen	Adcock	Leslie	Groves
		Salmon	Jones	Rutter	Emerson	Bowles	Thorpe	Williams	Evans	Kerr	Sword	Coyle	
25	A CHESTER 4/2	Chamberlain	Cook	Phillips	Hadley	Wignall	Houston	Mutrie	Hull	Bowen	Adcock*	Leslie	Groves
		Harrington	Blackwell	Lane	Storton	Zelem	Hildersley	Sutcliffe	Sanderson	Phillips*	Holden	Allen	Williams M
26	H CHESTERFIELD 11/2	Chamberlain	Cook	Phillips	Hadley	Wignall	Houston	Groves	Hull	Bowen	Adcock	Leslie	Leslie
		Gregory	O'Neill	Simpson	Kendal	Baines	Hunter	Birch	Scrimgeour	Newton	Clayton	Waddington*	Klug
27	H DONCASTER 14/2	Chamberlain	Cook	Phillips	Hadley	Wignall	Houston	Groves	Hull	Bowen	Adcock	Leslie	Leslie
		Peacock	Russell	Yates	Snodin I	Lister	Humphries	Harle	Moss	Douglas	Kowalski	Snodin G	
28	A CREWE 18/2	Chamberlain	Cook	Phillips	Hadley	Wignall	Houston	Mutrie	Hull	Bowen	Adcock*	Leslie	Osborne
		Naylor	Davies	Edwards	King*	Scott	Hart	Pullar	Crabbe	Waller	Leonard	Cliss	Williams
29	A SWINDON 25/2	Chamberlain	Cook	Phillips	Hadley	Wignall	Houston	Mutrie*	Hull	Bowen	Adcock	Leslie	Groves
		Endersby	Baille	Baddeley	Batty	Gray	Rowland	Hockaday	Mayes	Quinn	Nelson	Barnard	
30	A BURY 4/3	Chamberlain	Cook	Phillips	Hadley	Wignall	Houston	Mutrie	Hull	Bowen	Adcock*	Leslie	Hedman
		Brown	Gardner	Coleman	Carradous	Bramhall	Deacy	White	Madden	Cutler	Jakub	Park	
31	A READING 7/3	Chamberlain	Cook	Phillips	Hadley	Wignall	Houston	Groves	Hull	Bowen*	Mutrie	Leslie	Osborne
		Judge	Williams	Richardson	Price	Hicks	White	Duncan	Horrix	Senior	Sanchez	Crown	
32	H MANSFIELD 10/3	Chamberlain	Cook	Phillips	Hadley	Wignall	Houston	Groves	Hull	Bowen	Mutrie	Leslie	Osborne
		Hitchcock	Woodhead	Taylor	Lowery	Ayre	Calderwood	Keegan	Matthews	Barrowclough	Caldwell	Nicholson	
33	H YORK 17/3	Chamberlain	Cook	Phillips	Hadley	Wignall	Houston	Groves	Osborne	Bowen	Adcock*	Leslie	Mutrie
		Jones	Senior	Hay	Stragia	McPhail	Hood	Ford	Haselgrave	Walwyn	Byrne	Pearce	
34	A NORTHAMPTON 24/3	Chamberlain	Cook	Phillips	Hadley*	Coleman	Houston	Groves	Osborne	Bowen	Mutrie	Leslie	Mutrie
		Gleasure	Forster	Lewis	Gage	Burrows	Hayes	Jeffrey	O'Neill	Austin	Belton	Martinez	

No | Scorers, Times, and Referees | Att | Pos | Pt | F-A | H-T

No	Scorers, Times, and Referees	Att	Pos	Pt	F-A	H-T
24	Adcock 43 / Sword 9 — Ref: D Reeves	2,213	7 / 8	41	1-1	1-1
25	Bowen 10, 66, Phillips 32, Mutrie 50 / Blackwell 82 — Ref: J Key	1,179	7 / 24	44	4-1	2-0
26	Adcock 28, Wignall 29 — Ref: R Lewis	2,358	5 / 16	47	2-0	2-0
27	Bowen 21 / Snodin G 48 — Ref: A Ward	2,821	6 / 2	48	1-1	1-0
28	Bowen 12 / Crabbe 86p — Ref: M Scott	2,532	6 / 9	49	1-1	1-0
29	— Ref: I Borrett	2,448	6 / 15	50	0-0	0-0
30	Adcock 54p / Madden 72 — Ref: D Hutchinson	1,576	6 / 11	51	1-1	0-0
31	Senior 67 — Ref: M Bodenham	3,360	6 / 4	51	0-1	0-0
32	Bowen 66 — Ref: M James	2,007	6 / 22	54	1-0	0-0
33	Bowen 86 / McPhail 30, Walwyn 32, Pearce 84 — Ref: T Spencer	3,032	6 / 1	54	1-3	0-2
34	Phillips 14 / Austin 2, Gage 59, Belton 64 — Ref: N Ashley	1,499	7 / 15	54	1-3	1-1

Match notes

24. U's sign ex-England semi-pro international Les Mutrie from Lea's old club Hull for £10,000. Hull returns following his knee ligament injury sustained in the Crewe match. County's Tommy Sword opens but Adcock's 24th shares the spoils. Last week's game at Rochdale was off.

25. Mr Consistency. Micky Cook makes his 600th league appearance spanning 15 seasons at an average of 41 games per season. U's end their ten-match run without an away win. Mutrie scores his first goal for the U's after Hull finds him unmarked in the box with a pin-point long ball.

26. 20-year old Adcock scores his 25th of the season, capitalising on hesitancy by full-back Shaun O'Neill. Colchester's eleventh home win of the season is secured a minute later, when Wignall hooks in his eighth goal to put U's back on the fringe of the promotion contenders in fifth place.

27. Mutrie is absent because of flu. Billy Bremner's second-placed Rovers, just like the U's, are unbeaten since December. Birthday boy Glyn Snodin levels just after the break. Bowen had scored his 15th, taking a curled pass from Hull in his stride before planting past Dennis Peacock.

28. 19-year-old reserve defender Rudi Hedman signs on non-contract forms. Alex provide U's with a hard test, having lost only two in their last 13 games. Hull's cross gives Bowen a close-range header, then Tony Cliss crashes to the ground. The home crowd's howls persuade Mr Scott.

29. Adcock scores just three minutes into his 100th league appearance but the goal is unfortunately ruled out for offside. Wignall sums up U's bad luck in front of goal when, with three minutes on the clock, his shot from a Groves pass strikes the inside of both posts and rolls out to safety.

30. Bury sacked manager Jim Iley two weeks ago and are now led by Wilf McGuinness. United gain a generous penalty when Gordon Coleman knocks over Adcock. Justice is done for the Shakers when Winston White finds Craig Madden. Phillips clears off the line on 87 minutes.

31. U's are without Adcock, who has a hamstring strain. Reading are under new manager Ian Branfoot, replacing Maurice Evans. They maintain their unbeaten home record. Trevor Senior's 32nd goal of the season, from a Lawrie Sanchez pass, is enough to keep the Royals above the U's.

32. Colchester manufacture a string of chances and force 20 corners, but only have Bowen's interception of Billy Ayre's weak back-pass to show for their efforts. 18-year-old Kevin Hitchcock, on loan from Nottingham Forest, excels for the Stags. Mutrie is homesick after his move south.

33. Table-toppers York become the first team to win at Layer Road in almost a year. John McPhail nods in a corner. Keith Walwyn beats Wignall's offside trap attempt. Alan Pearce completes the rout with a neat three-man move. Bowen's strike is merely a consolation for well-beaten U's.

34. Transfer deadline day passes. After their 1-5 midweek home defeat by Blackpool, the Cobblers are up for sale. Phillips, ex-skipper of Cobblers thunders in a free-kick. Wakeley Gage, ex-schoolmate of Bowen, prods in number two. Frankie Belfon intercepts Hadley's poor back-pass.

Colchester United — Match Results (matches 35–46)

No	Venue	Date	Opponent	Att	Pos	—	Pts	Result	FT	HT
35	A	31/3	BRISTOL CITY	6,504	9	2	54	L	1-4	0-1
36	A	4/4	HEREFORD	2,501	9	15	55	D	1-1	1-0
37	H	7/4	TRANMERE	1,679	9	7	55	L	0-1	0-1
38	A	14/4	HARTLEPOOL	1,001	9	23	56	D	0-0	0-0
39	A	17/4	ROCHDALE	1,020	9	20	57	D	0-0	0-0
40	H	21/4	PETERBOROUGH	1,746	9	8	58	D	1-1	1-0
41	A	23/4	ALDERSHOT	2,443	10	5	58	L	1-5	1-3
42	H	28/4	TORQUAY	1,226	9	13	61	W	3-0	2-0
43	A	1/5	BLACKPOOL	3,111	9	6	61	L	2-3	2-2
44	A	5/5	WREXHAM	1,016	8	22	64	W	2-0	0-0
45	H	7/5	HEREFORD	1,286	7	13	67	W	3-0	1-0
46	A	11/5	HALIFAX	1,248	8	21	67	L	1-4	0-2

Home Average 2,220 · Away Average 2,704

---

35 — A 31/3 Bristol City (L 1-4)
Colchester: Chamberlain, Cook, Phillips*, Hedman, Wignall, Houston, Groves, Osborne, Bowen, Adcock, Leslie; Hadley
Bristol City: Shaw, Stevens, Newman, Halliday, Phill* Masters, Stroud, Pritchard, Ritchie, Riley, Morgan, Hirst, Hadley
Scorers: Wignall 78; Ritchie 26p, 65, Riley 67, 81. Ref: M Heath

Terry Cooper, City's player-manager and the season's oldest registered league player at 39 years, remains on the bench. Houston gives City the opportunity to gain a first-half lead when he pushes Glyn Riley in the area. Wignall pulls one back, nodding in Cook's overhead-kick cross.

36 — A 4/4 Hereford (D 1-1)
Colchester: Chamberlain, Cook, Phillips, Hedman, Wignall, Houston, Groves, Osborne, Bowen, Adcock, Hull; Hadley
Hereford: Rose, Price, Bray, Hicks, Maddy, Pejic, Harvey, Delve, Phillips, Kearns, Butler
Scorers: Wignall 35; Phillips 50. Ref: J Worrall

The spoils are shared in this match, re-staged after the New Year's Eve 68th-minute floodlight failure at Edgar Street, where Colchester trailed 0-1. Wignall plants Groves's corner firmly home but within five minutes Stewart Phillips taps in the rebound from Paul Maddy's initial effort.

37 — H 7/4 Tranmere (L 0-1)
Colchester: Chamberlain, Cook, Phillips, Hedman, Wignall, Houston, Groves*, Osborne, Bowen, Adcock, Hull; Mutrie
Tranmere: Davies, Mungall, Burgess, Philpotts*, Williams G, Palios, Powell, Aspinall, Williams J, Hutchinson, Goodlass, McMahon
Scorers: Palios 47. Ref: L Burden

Lea continues to leave Adcock out of the side. U's are eight points behind fourth-placed Reading with a game in hand. Colchester take 64 mins to get a worthy effort on goal. Rovers hit the woodwork three times in the first half. A lob from Mark Palios catches Chamberlain off his line.

38 — A 14/4 Hartlepool (D 0-0)
Colchester: Chamberlain, Coleman, Phillips, Hadley, Wignall, Houston, Groves, Osborne, Bowen, Adcock, Hull
Hartlepool: Blackburn, Robinson D, Barker, Hogan, Linighan A, Smithers, Kennedy, Lowe, Linacre P, Dobson, Staff
Ref: A Robinson

Chamberlain is a busy man, denying Paul Dobson (twice), Kenny Lowe and Phil Linacre with spectacular saves. The re-called but out-of-form Adcock misses a gilt-edged chance with just four minutes remaining.

39 — A 17/4 Rochdale (D 0-0)
Colchester: Chamberlain, Coleman, Phillips, Hadley, Wignall, Houston, Groves, Osborne, Bowen, Adcock, Hull
Rochdale: Conroy, Oates, Chapman, Reid, McMahon, Doyle, Thompson D, Hamilton, Thompson S, Allatt!, Griffiths
Ref: P Willis

Former Man Utd striker Jimmy Greenhoff recently quit as player-manager of Dale after a disagreement with the club's board. Steve Conroy denies the U's on a number of occasions to earn an important point. Vernon Allatt takes an early bath on 64 minutes for pushing Tony Hadley.

40 — H 21/4 Peterborough (D 1-1)
Colchester: Chamberlain, Coleman, Phillips, Hadley, Wignall, Farrell, Groves, Osborne, Bowen, Adcock, Hull
Peterborough: Seaman, Chard, Holmes, Beech*, Slack, Firm, Pike, Tydeman, Waddle, Kelly, Worrall, Quow
Scorers: Adcock 26; Holmes 89p. Ref: M Dimbledee

The U's programme wins the divisional award again. Adcock gets back on the scoresheet, superbly chipping keeper David Seaman for his 29th of the season. With a first win in eight on the cards, Phillips fouls Errington Kelly in the box and Jimmy Holmes slots past Alec Chamberlain.

41 — A 23/4 Aldershot (L 1-5)
Colchester: Chamberlain, Coleman, Phillips, Hadley, Wignall, Farrell, Groves, Osborne*, Bowen, Adcock, Hull; [Lucas 74]
Aldershot: Coles, Day, Gillard, Shrubb, Souter, Jopling, Burvill, Banton, Lawrence, McDonald, Mazzon*, Lucas
Scorers: Adcock 44; Burvill 8, Banton 26, 66, Lawrence 30. Ref: K Barrett

In glorious sunshine Les Lawrence nets his 23rd of the season to give Shots an unassailable lead. U's promotion hopes are now completely dead. Groves conjures an opportunity for Adcock, then sees his spot-kick saved by David Coles, who fouls the U's leading scorer on 85 mins.

42 — H 28/4 Torquay (W 3-0)
Colchester: Chamberlain, Coleman, Phillips, Hadley, Farrell, Houston, Groves*, Osborne, Bowen, Adcock, Hull; Mutrie
Torquay: Allen, Dawkins, Anderson, Currie, Impey, Compton, Wakefield, Fowler, Cooper, Pugh, Hall
Scorers: Compton 8(og), Phillips 28p, Adcock 46. Ref: J Hunting

U's first win since 10 March in front of the lowest home league attendance in the club's 34-year history. Gulls defender Paul Compton gifts U's the lead with a headed 'og'. Phillips takes over penalty duties from Adcock, who later nets his 31st, when Kenny Allan brings down Groves.

43 — A 1/5 Blackpool (L 2-3)
Colchester: Chamberlain, Coleman, Phillips, Hadley, Farrell, Houston, Groves*, Osborne, Bowen, Adcock, Hull; Mutrie
Blackpool: Pierce, Moore, Ferns, Rodaway*, Hetzke, Walsh, Britton, Deary, Stewart, McNiven, Stonehouse, Walker
Scorers: Hull 12, Adcock 26; McNiven 10, Stonehouse 42, 86. Ref: C Seel

Blackpool field only four players from the side which met the U's back in September. David McNiven pounces on a Hadley error. Hull levels, shrugging off John Deary. Four minutes from time Paul Stewart is blocked in the box and the ball runs kindly for Kevin Stonehouse to score.

44 — A 5/5 Wrexham (W 2-0)
Colchester: Chamberlain, Coleman, Phillips, Hadley, Wignall, Houston, Groves*, Osborne, Bowen, Adcock, Hull
Wrexham: Sinclair, King, Cunnington, Hunt, Keay, Muldoon, Arkwright*, Gregory, Salathiel, Steel, Edwards
Scorers: Osborne 55, Groves 58. Ref: P Fitzharris

Chairman Cadman announces swingeing cuts, including wages and bonuses. Wignall is the first to opt for a transfer. More bad news as United stalwarts Cook and Leslie are both forced to retire through injury. Osborne heads the first and Groves finishes off Chamberlain's gigantic kick.

45 — H 7/5 Hereford (W 3-0)
Colchester: Chamberlain, Hadley, Phillips, Farrell, Wignall, Houston, Groves, Osborne, Bowen, Adcock, Hull
Hereford: Rose, Emery, Bray, Hicks, Larkin, Maddy, Harvey, Delve, Phillips, Kearns, Dalziel
Scorers: Bowen 19, Adcock 55, Hull 72. Ref: D Letts

Young Colchester lad Andy Farrell looks a promising prospect and he sets up both Adcock and Bowen for their goals either side of the break. A spectacular overhead kick by Hull is deflected off the back of Tony Larkin. No one can deny him the credit for the goal after his acrobatics.

46 — A 11/5 Halifax (L 1-4)
Colchester: Chamberlain, Hadley, Phillips, Farrell, Wignall, Houston, Groves, Osborne, Bowen, Adcock, Hull
Halifax: Smelt, Kendall, Wood, Evans, Smith, Hendrie, Nobbs, Little, Gallagher B*, Mell, Ward, Nuttall
Scorers: Mutrie 90; Ward 10, Gallagher B 44, 47, Mell 87. Ref: D Owen

Halifax's win does not save them from re-election. Paul Kendall robs Phillips to supply Steve Ward. Barry Gallagher notches headers either side of the break but Mutrie has the last say on a disappointing season. The ball even deflects into goal off Kendall. U's miss out by 15 points.

LEAGUE DIVISION 4 (CUP-TIES)　　Manager: Cyril Lea　　SEASON 1983-84

Milk Cup

	1	2	3	4	5	6	7	8	9	10	11	12 sub used
1:1 H READING 30/8 — W 3-2 (2-1) — 2,418 4:	Chamberlain	Cook	Farrell	Hadley	Wignall	Houston	Groves	Osborne	Bowen	Adcock	Hull	**Taylor**
(opponents)	*Judge*	*Williams*	*Richardson*	*Beavon*	*Hicks*	*Barnes*	*Tutty*	*Harris*	*Senior*	*Sanchez*	*Crown*	

Adcock 27, 50, Wignall 36 / Barnes 41, Senior 83 / Ref: M Scott

Reading, relegated from the third last season, look set for a big deficit after Adcock's double puts U's 3-1 in front. A bad misunderstanding between Wignall and Bowen allows Trevor Senior the opportunity to turn and shoot past Chamberlain. Coleman joins Wrexham on loan.

	1	2	3	4	5	6	7	8	9	10	11	12 sub used
1:2 A READING 14/9 — L 3-4 aet (2-1) — 3,460 4:10	Chamberlain	Cook	Farrell	Hadley	Wignall	Houston	Groves*	Osborne	Bowen	Adcock	Hull	**Taylor**
(opponents)	*Judge*	*Williams*	*Richardson*	*Beavon*	*Hicks*	*Wood*	*Tutty**	*Harris*	*Senior*	*Sanchez*	*White*	

Adcock 22, Wignall 30, Bowen 119 / Beavon 15, Senior 47, 48, 103 / Ref: A Ward
(Colchester won on away goals)

U's race into a 5-3 aggregate lead on the half hour. Trevor Senior's quick-fire double after the break turns the game on its head. Senior then completes his second hat-trick in ten days in the first period of extra-time. Bowen's dramatic last-gasp six-yard volley earns a memorable win.

	1	2	3	4	5	6	7	8	9	10	11	12 sub used
2:1 A SWANSEA 4/10 — D 3-3 (1-1) — 3,758 2:22	Chamberlain	Cook	Farrell	Hadley	Wignall	Houston	Groves	Leslie	Bowen	Adcock	Hull	
(opponents)	*Rimmer*	*Robinson*	*Marustik*	*Richards*	*Stevenson*	*Hughes*	*Gale*	*Curtis*	*Latchford*	*Lake*	*Pascoe*	

Adcock 15 / Gale 45 / Ref: A Saville

Swansea were relegated from the first division last season after finishing in sixth place the previous year. Farrell replaces the cup-tied Phillips.

	1	2	3	4	5	6	7	8	9	10	11	12 sub used
2:2 H SWANSEA 25/10 — W 1-0 (1-0) — 5,204 2:22	Chamberlain	Cook	Farrell	Hadley	Nicholls	Houston	Groves	Osborne	Hubbick	Adcock	Hull	
(opponents)	*Rimmer*	*Guard*	*Hughes*	*Charles*	*Stevenson*	*Lewis**	*Loveridge*	*Marustik*	*Gale*	*Richards*	*Saunders*	

Adcock 40 / Ref: K Salmon
(Colchester won 2-1 on aggregate)

Chairman Cadman promises two new players if the crowd exceeds 5,000. The public responds and cheer U's into the next round. Cash-strapped Swansea, with a host of internationals, lose out to a deft chip from Adcock over the advancing Jimmy Rimmer, his 13th this season.

	1	2	3	4	5	6	7	8	9	10	11	12 sub used
3 H MANCHESTER U 8/11 — L 0-2 (0-2) — 13,031 1:1	Chamberlain	Cook	Farrell	Hadley	Wignall	Houston	Leslie	Osborne	Bowen	Adcock	Hubbick*	Groves
(opponents)	*Bailey*	*Duxbury*	*Albiston*	*Wilkins*	*Moran*	*McQueen*	*Robson*	*Moses*	*Stapleton*	*Whiteside**	*Macari*	

McQueen 8, Moses 24 / Ref: T Bune

Gordon McQueen clears a Hubbick flick off the line and 60 seconds later heads in Arthur Graham's corner. Bryan Robson splits the U's left defence to find Remi Moses, who turns on a sixpence to shoot past the helpless Chamberlain. Manager Ron Atkinson is contented with the win.

FA Cup

	1	2	3	4	5	6	7	8	9	10	11	12 sub used
1 A TORQUAY 19/11 — W 2-1 (1-0) — 2,126 4:15	Chamberlain	Cook	Phillips	Hadley !	Wignall	Houston	Hubbick	Osborne	Bowen	Adcock	Leslie	Hubbick
(opponents)	*Turner*	*Pugh*	*Holmes*	*Impey*	*Little*	*Carr*	*Young*	*Curle*	*Cooper*	*Sims*	*Barnes*	

Bowen 17, 78 / Curle 55 / Ref: K Cooper

U's record their first ever FA Cup victory at Plainmoor. Bowen opens with a well-placed header. Hadley is sent off on 85 minutes for a challenge on Kevin Young. He was booked earlier for a foul on ex-U's loanee John Sims. Keith Curle intercepts Ian Phillips's poor back-pass.

	1	2	3	4	5	6	7	8	9	10	11	12 sub used
2 H WEALDSTONE 10/12 — W 4-0 (4-0) — 2,673 AP:	Chamberlain	Cook	Phillips	Hadley	Wignall	Houston	Groves	Osborne	Bowen	Adcock	Leslie	Price
(opponents)	*Iles*	*Perkins*	*Donnellan*	*Bratt*	*Bowgett*	*Wainwright*	*Greeaway*	*Dibble**	*Cordice A*	*Graves*	*Cordice N*	

Bowen 4, 23, 43, Houston 12 / Ref: M Bodenham

Liverpool pull out of negotiations for Adcock. Bowen nets the first hat-trick of his professional career to take his cup tally to six in seven games. Groves evades two challenges before providing a delicate chip for Bowen to complete his treble. The non-leaguers are outclassed.

	1	2	3	4	5	6	7	8	9	10	11	12 sub used
3 H CHARLTON 7/1 — L 0-1 (0-0) — 6,296 2:6	Chamberlain	Farrell*	Phillips	Hadley	Wignall	Houston	Groves	Osborne	Bowen	Adcock	Leslie	Hubbick
(opponents)	*Johns*	*Curtis*	*Dickenson*	*Gritt*	*Bowman*	*Berry*	*Harris*	*Westley*	*Moore*	*James*	*Aizlewood*	

Phillips 79 (og) / Ref: T Spencer

Cook has to sit out his suspension due to the abandonment of the Hereford game. Charlton are as precarious as their finances, which threaten their survival. Totally against the run of play Kevin Dickenson's poor cross hits Phillips on the shin, leaving the static Chamberlain stranded.

Associate Members Cup

	1	2	3	4	5	6	7	8	9	10	11	12 sub used
1 H WIMBLEDON 21/2 — W 2-1 (2-1) — 1,888 3:2	Chamberlain	Cook	Phillips	Hadley	Wignall	Houston	Mutrie*	Hull	Bowen	Adcock	Leslie	Oldfield
(opponents)	*Beasant*	*Peters !*	*Winterburn*	*Thomas*	*Morris*	*Hatter*	*Evans*	*Ketteridge*	*Cork**	*Downes**	*Fishenden*	*Hodges/Sayer*

Adcock 20p, 40p / Fishenden 26 / Ref: M Taylor

Dons, flying high in the third division, lose Gary Peters on 30 minutes for elbowing Adcock. Peters had tripped Hull for the first penalty. Paul Fishenden taps in the rebound after Wally Downes' free-kick hits the post. Steve Hatter trips Adcock for the second, and winning, spot-kick.

	1	2	3	4	5	6	7	8	9	10	11	12 sub used
2 H SOUTHEND 13/3 — L 0-2 (0-0) — 2,841 3:20	Chamberlain	Cook	Phillips	Hadley	Wignall	Coleman*	Groves	Hull*	Bowen	Adcock	Osborne	Mutrie/Leslie
(opponents)	*Keeley*	*Stead*	*Collins*	*Shepherd*	*Turner*	*Clark*	*Pountney*	*Kellock*	*Whymark*	*Fuccillo*	*Phillips*	

Whymark 60, Kellock 89 / Ref: K Hackett

Bobby Moore's Southend, battling against relegation, have not won in twelve. Adcock incredibly misses two penalties (61, 74), slotting wide of John Keeley's left both times with the keeper going the wrong way. Paul Clark handles for the first and Kellock fouls Groves for the other.

		Home						Away						
		P	W	D	L	F	A	W	D	L	F	A	Pts	
1	York	46	18	4	1	58	16	13	4	6	36	23	101	
2	Doncaster	46	15	6	2	46	22	9	7	7	36	32	85	
3	Reading	46	17	6	0	51	14	5	10	8	33	42	82	
4	Bristol City	46	18	3	2	51	17	6	7	10	19	27	82	
5	Aldershot	46	14	6	3	49	29	8	3	12	27	40	75	
6	Blackpool	46	15	4	4	47	19	6	5	12	23	33	72	
7	Peterborough	46	15	5	3	52	16	3	9	11	20	32	68	
8	COLCHESTER	46	14	7	2	45	14	5	9	11	24	39	67	
9	Torquay	46	13	7	3	32	18	6	6	12	27	46	67	
10	Tranmere	46	11	5	7	33	26	6	10	7	20	27	66	
11	Hereford	46	11	6	6	31	21	5	9	9	23	32	63	
12	Stockport	46	12	5	6	34	25	5	6	12	26	39	62	
13	Chesterfield	46	10	11	2	34	24	5	4	14	25	37	60	
14	Darlington	46	13	4	6	31	19	4	4	15	18	31	59	
15	Bury	46	9	7	7	34	32	6	7	10	27	32	59	
16	Crewe	46	10	8	5	35	27	6	3	14	21	40	59	
17	Swindon	46	11	7	5	34	23	4	6	13	24	33	58	
18	Northampton	46	10	8	5	32	32	3	6	14	21	46	53	
19	Mansfield	46	9	7	7	44	27	4	6	13	24	43	52	
20	Wrexham	46	7	6	10	34	33	4	9	10	25	41	48	
21	Halifax	46	11	6	6	36	25	1	6	16	19	64	48	
22	Rochdale	46	8	9	6	35	31	3	4	16	17	49	46	
23	Hartlepool	46	7	8	8	31	28	3	2	18	16	57	40	
24	Chester	46	7	5	11	23	35	0	8	15	22	47	34	
		1104	285	150	117	932	573	117	150	285	573	932	1506	

Odds & ends

Double wins: (2) Chester, Darlington.

Double defeats: (2) Tranmere, York.

Won from behind: (0)

Lost from in front: (3) Swindon (a), Torquay (a), Blackpool (a).

High spots: Glorious in defeat, U's make Manchester United sweat for their Milk Cup victory.

The 51-goal partnership of Tony Adcock and Keith Bowen.

Micky Cook passing 600 appearances for the club in February.

Low spots: The fiasco of losing Ian Allinson on a free transfer.

Just one win from fifteen League games from February.

The financial cut-backs, due to promotion failure, which inevitably resulted in a summer exodus.

A new record lowest attendance, when 1,226 gather to watch U's take on Torquay.

Player of the Year: Steve Wignall.

Ever presents: (2) Keith Bowen, Alec Chamberlain.

Hat-tricks: (1) Keith Bowen.

Leading scorer: Tony Adcock 33 (incl 2 in Associate Members Cup).

	Appearances						Goals			
	Lge	Sub	LC	Sub	FA	Sub	Lge	LC	FA	Tot
Adcock, Tony	41	2	5		3		26	5		31
Bowen, Keith	46		5		3		12	1	5	18
Chamberlain, Alec	46		5		3					
Coleman, Phil	7	1								
Cook, Micky	36		5		2		2			2
Farrell, Andy	15		5		1					
Groves, Perry	38	4	4	1	2		2			2
Hadley, Tony	44	1	5		3					
Hedman, Rudi	3	1								
Houston, Stewart	42		5		3		4			4
Hubbick, Dave	3	7	1	1	1				1	1
Hull, Jeff	33		4				1			1
Leslie, Steve	25	2	2		3		1			1
Mutrie, Les	10	4					2			2
Nicholls, Adam	4	2	1				1			1
Oldfield, Craig		3								
Osborne, Roger	34	2	4		3		1			1
Phillips, Ian	43		4		3		5			5
Taylor, John						1				
Wignall, Steve	36		4		3		8	2		10
(own-goals)							4			4
20 players used	506	27	55	2	33	1	69	8	6	83

CANON LEAGUE DIVISION 4 Manager: Cyril Lea SEASON 1984-85

No	Date	Att	Pos	Pt	F-A	H-T	Scorers, Times, and Referees	1	2	3	4	5	6	7	8	9	10	11	12 sub used
1 H SOUTHEND	25/8	2,378	1	D	3-3	3-2	Adcock 9, 32, 44 [Ferguson 80] Whymark 21, Phillips 22 Ref: B Hill	Chamberlain / *Keeley*	Godbold / *Stead*	Phillips / *Pennyfather*	Farrell / *Hadley*	**Day** / *May*	Houston / *Ferguson*	Groves / *Kellock*	Osborne / *Phillips*	Bowen / *Whymark*	Adcock* / *Fuccillo**	Hull / *Rogers*	**Irving** / *Pountney*
							Adcock accepts three simple close-range chances. Both new-look defences have an off day. New boy Godbold provides Adcock's first, but Southend score a quick double. The hat-trick is completed from Groves' long throw. Brian Ferguson finishes Ron Pountney's right-wing cross.												
2 A SCUNTHORPE	31/8	1,818	13 / 14	D	2-2 / 2	1-1	Bowen 4, Adcock 77 / Cammack 31, Cowling 90 Ref: T Curtis	Chamberlain / *Neenan*	Godbold / *Longden*	Phillips / *Pointon*	Farrell / *Matthews*	Day / *Whitehead*	Houston / *Green*	Groves / *Dey*	Osborne / *Cammack*	Bowen / *Broddle*	Adcock / *Lester*	Hull / *Cowling*	Hull / *Cowling*
							Once again United lose points through a late goal. Adcock grabs U's the lead for the second time with a fine finish to record his fourth goal of the season, but a thunderous volley from Chris Cowling denies U's a victory at the death. Godbold is booked for a late tackle on Neil Pointon.												
3 H BLACKPOOL	8/9	1,772	15 / 3	L	0-1 / 3	0-1	Adcock 83 / Deary 35p Ref: M Cotton	Chamberlain / *O'Rourke*	Godbold* / *Moore*	Phillips / *Walsh*	**Parkinson** / *Conroy*	Farrell / *Hetzke*	Houston / *Greenall*	Groves / *Britton*	Irving / *Davies*	Bowen / *Stewart*	Adcock / *Deary*	Hull / *Dyer*	Osborne / *Dyer*
							Parkinson, a close-season capture from Scunthorpe, debuts. Blackpool have four straight wins, scoring nine goals and conceding none. Alex Dyer (19), Paul Stewart (19) and Mike Davies (18) form the youngest forward line in their history. Godbold handles in challenging Hetzke.												
4 A BURY	15/9	2,145	19 / 3	L	3-4 / 3	0-1	Adcock 79, Houston 84, Hull 90 / Entwistle 15, Madden 71, 87, White 74 Ref: P Vanes	Chamberlain / *Brown*	Farrell / *Hill*	Phillips / *Young*	Parkinson / *Ross*	Day / *Bramhall*	Houston / *Dobson*	Groves / *White*	Osborne / *Madden*	Bowen / *Entwistle*	Adcock / *Jakub*	Hull / *James*	
							Bury player-manager Martin Dobson finds the head of Wayne Entwistle with a free-kick. Winston White's goal comes after Chamberlain pushes Craig Madden's penalty onto the post. A frantic last six minutes goalscoring is decided with Madden tapping in from close range.												
5 A MANSFIELD	19/9	2,094	12 / 15	W	1-0 / 6	1-0	Bowen 34 Ref: L Robinson	Chamberlain / *Hitchcock*	Farrell / *Whitworth**	Phillips / *Kearney*	Parkinson / *Calderwood*	Day / *Foster*	Houston / *Garner*	Groves* / *Lowery*	Osborne / *Luke*	Bowen / *Allen*	Adcock / *Caldwell*	Hull / *Vinter*	Irving / *Galloway*
							U's problems after six without a win stems from the 15 goals conceded against eleven scored. Mansfield's fourth successive defeat stems from John Allen's dreadful back-pass. The goal earns Colchester boys side Indesit Dynamo's £2.50 as a reward for each goal that Bowen scores.												
6 H ALDERSHOT	22/9	**1,641**	8 / 21	W	2-0 / 9	2-0	Adcock 4, 39 Ref: I Borrett	Chamberlain / *Coles*	Farrell / *Day*	Phillips / *Gillard**	Parkinson / *Gray*	Day / *Peters*	Houston / *Mazzon*	Groves / *Foley*	Osborne / *Banton*	Bowen / *Foyle*	Adcock / *McDonald*	Hull / *Shrubb*	Adcock / *Burvill*
							Prolific Adcock gets his eighth in eight games. Groves speeds down the right flank to find U's goal-getter. Newcomer Keith Day faces up to his brother Clive in the Shots line-up. The visiting Day miscues a clearance for Bowen to one-two with Adcock. United win 18-3 on corners.												
7 A NORTHAMPTON	29/9	1,595	7 / 24	W	3-1 / 12	0-1	Parkinson 70, Adcock 74, Bowen 78 / Hayes 24 Ref: J Martin	Chamberlain / *Gleasure*	Farrell / *Lewis*	Phillips / *Mundee!*	Parkinson / *Gage*	Day / *Cavener*	Houston / *Train*	Groves / *Scott*	Osborne / *Benjamin*	Bowen / *Belfon*	Adcock / *Bancroft*	Hull / *Hayes*	
							Cobblers' ex-Villa Euro Cup winning manager Tony Barton has just recovered from a heart attack. His side is bottom with just one point and one goal. Phillips misses a penalty (63), after Brian Mundee scythes Groves. Mundee is sent off a minute later for his third crunching tackle.												
8 H TORQUAY	2/10	1,813	5 / 20	W	2-1 / 15	0-0	Bowen 81, Hull 83 / Barnes 64 Ref: A Ward	Chamberlain / *Allen*	Farrell / *Dawkins*	Phillips / *Anderson*	Parkinson / *Barnes*	Day / *Compton*	Houston / *Chambers*	Groves / *Carter*	Osborne / *Fowler*	Bowen / *Larylea*	Adcock / *Pugh*	Hull / *Hall*	Hull / *Hall*
							U's pick up the Canon goalscoring award for August-September with 15 goals David Webb's Gulls take a surprise lead when a rare swoop on U's goal sees Colin Barnes touch in Benny Larylea's parried shot. A double burst from Bowen and Hull puts U's right up there after four wins.												
9 A DARLINGTON	13/10	2,021	7 / 5	L	**0-4** / 15	0-1	Forster 11, 75, McLean 61p, Airey 72 Ref: J McAulay	Chamberlain / *Barber*	Farrell / *Craggs*	Phillips / *Johnson**	Parkinson / *Forster*	Day / *Smith K*	Houston / *Young*	Groves ! / *Tupling*	Osborne / *Todd*	Bowen / *Airey*	Adcock* / *Cook*	Hull / *McLean*	Irving / *Hawker*
							Quakers stretch their record to one defeat in ten, but it's Groves' sending off (38), for swearing at a linesman that spurs them. Phillips misses his second consecutive penalty (49), when Bowen is flattened. Dave McLean shows him how to do it, when Chamberlain upends Mark Forster.												
10 H EXETER	16/10	1,846	8 / 16	L	3-4 / 15	2-1	Adcock 6, Hull 35, Groves 52 / Sims 4, Smith 51, Harrower 54, Pratt 55 Ref: M Bodenham	Chamberlain / *Wood*	Farrell* / *Kirkup*	Phillips / *Viney*	Parkinson / *O'Shea*	Day / *Marker*	Houston / *McNichol*	Groves / *Harrower*	Osborne / *Smith*	Bowen / *Sims**	Adcock / *Pratt*	Hull / *Neville*	Irving / *Ling*
							McDonough misses a Layer Rd return, joining Cambridge from City (£15k). A string of defensive errors gives Exeter their first away win of the season. Lea praises his hard-working strike-force, but lambastes his 'barn-door' defence, in a fixture that was washed out ten days ago.												
11 A CHESTER	20/10	1,400	7 / 14	W	2-1 / 18	2-0	Adcock 23, 45 / Fox 60 Ref: R Dilkes	Chamberlain / *Butcher*	Farrell / *Dixon*	Phillips / *Bulmer*	Parkinson / *Holden*	Day / *Higgins*	Houston / *Speight*	Groves / *Fox*	Osborne / *Walker*	Bowen / *Brown*	Adcock* / *Sayer*	Hull / *Blackwell*	Irving / *Blackwell*
							Adcock is in like a whippet when John Butcher fails to hold a 25-yard Parkinson free-kick. Seconds before the interval, Groves shows Peter Bulmer a clean pair of heels to provide a perfect cross for Adcock. Full-back Lee Dixon sends Steve Fox away for his deserved consolation.												

12 — H STOCKPORT — 23/10 — 6 W 3-0 — 17 21 — 2,153
Hull 27, 87, Groves 55
Ref: C Downey
Chamberlain, Farrell, Phillips, Parkinson, Day*, Houston, Groves, Osborne, Bowen, Adcock, Hull, Irving
Salmon, Evans, Byrom, Emerson, Sword, Jones, Williams, Hendrie, Kerr, Taylor, Coyle
Stockport look weary after taking Liverpool to extra-time in the Milk Cup, eventually losing 0-2. Hull notches the first brace of his career with a well executed free-kick, and by beating the offside trap via Osborne's pass. Day suffers a facial injury (74), delaying play by three minutes.

13 — A HALIFAX — 26/10 — 10 L 1-3 — 22 21 — 2,295
Adcock 9
Lowe 16, Ayre 57, Gallagher 86
Ref: T Bune
Chamberlain, Farrell, Phillips, Parkinson, Day, Houston, Groves, Osborne, Bowen, Adcock, Hull, Irving
Roche, Moyses, Kendall, Watson, Ayre, Knill, Thornber, Cook, Lowe, Gallagher, Ward
U's, six wins from eight, are certs to beat manager-less Halifax (Micky Bullock sacked midweek after seven successive defeats). Adcock grabs his 18th, after good work by Day, but Simon Lowe levels, Billy Ayres knocks in Stephen Moyses' free-kick and Barry Gallagher adds a third.

14 — A CHESTERFIELD — 3/11 — 10 D 1-1 — 2 22 — 3,614
Adcock 45
Moss 75
Ref: G Courtney
Chamberlain, Farrell, Phillips, Parkinson, Day, Houston, Groves, Osborne, Bowen*, Adcock, Hull, Godbold
Marples, Bellamy, O'Neill, Matthews, Baines, Hunter, Irving, Moss, Newton, Ferguson, Kendal
Gritty U's bounce back after last week's disappointment at second-placed Chesterfield. Bowen, ever-present since his signing last April, turns his ankle (20). Adcock coolly slots in his 14th of the term under Chris Marples, only for veteran Ernie Moss to nod in Gary Bellamy's cross.

15 — A TRANMERE — 6/11 — 11 L 1-3 — 7 22 — 1,587
Godbold 90
Clayton 34, 54, Clarke 36p
Ref: T Mills
Chamberlain, Farrell, Phillips, Parkinson, Day, Houston, Groves, Osborne, Bowen, Adcock, Hull, Godbold
Adkins, Edwards, Heath, Williams G, Sinclair, Williams J, Lee, Ferguson, Clarke, Clayton, Anderson
Rover's boss Bryan Hamilton turns down the chance to become Tommy Docherty's number two at Wolves. Chamberlain makes a breathtaking save from Gary Williams (38), and Godbold's first-ever goal is worthy of a bigger stage. Hedman handles for Colin Clarke's fierce penalty.

16 — H HARTLEPOOL — 9/11 — 10 W 1-0 — 11 25 — 2,136
Adcock 78
Ref: A Buksh
Chamberlain, Farrell, Phillips, Parkinson, Day, Houston, Groves, Osborne, Irving*, Adcock, Hull, Hedman
Stevenson, Robinson, Brownlie, Hedley, Smith, Brown, Dixon, Dobson, Wardrobe, Hogan*, Taylor, Proudlock
U's pick up a useful three points when Adcock's late goal, from Phillips' cross, is enough to end Hartlepool's nine-match unbeaten run. Irving, to be married on Monday, misses the chance of an ideal wedding present, when a former U's target Tony Smith clears his effort off the line.

17 — A ROCHDALE — 24/11 — 10 D 0-0 — 23 26 — 1,012
Groves 84
Cooke 90
Ref: R Bridges
Chamberlain, Farrell, Phillips, Parkinson, Day, Houston, Groves, Godbold, Irving, Adcock, Hull
Malcolm, Johnson, Chapman, Reid, Cooke, Cavanagh, Thompson, Diamond, Taylor, Seasman, Heaton
A English receives a stand-by call-up for England U-18's. Just when U's think that they have secured all the points, then up pops Dale skipper Joe Cooke to nod in John Seasman's cross. Groves had given U's the lead, dispossessing player-coach Les Chapman to slot past Paul Malcolm.

18 — H PETERBOROUGH — 1/12 — 8 W 3-1 — 5 29 — 2,070
Irving 22, Groves 24, Adcock 38
Kelly 42
Ref: M James
Chamberlain, Farrell, Phillips, Parkinson, Day, Houston, Groves, Osborne, Irving*, Adcock, Hull, Bowen
Turner, Chard, Pike, Beech, Wile, Slack, Johnson, Klug, Kelly, Quow, Worrall
Chamberlain recovers from a shoulder injury. Parkinson gives Posh an early warning, striking the inside of the post (14). Eight minutes later Irving nets after pin-ball in the box. Groves shrugs off Phil Chard for his third in three, and Adcock adds his 18th from Parkinson's deep cross.

19 — A SWINDON — 15/12 — 9 L 1-2 — 12 29 — 2,263
Adcock 33
Coyne 18, Gordon 41
Ref: K Cooper
Chamberlain, Farrell, Phillips, Parkinson, Day, Houston, Hedman, Osborne, Irving, Adcock, Bowen
Endersby, Ramsey, Baille, Barnard, Gray, Rowland, Hockaday, Coyne, Gordon, Batty, Nelson
Hull suffered a painful pelvis injury in the closing stage of the crushing FA Cup defeat by Gills. In Osborne's 150th league game for United, Adcock cancels out Peter Coyne's goal, but Lou Macari's side win when Colin Gordon rises unchallenged to meet Garry Nelson's free-kick.

20 — A CREWE — 21/12 — 8 W 4-1 — 10 32 — 1,529
Adcock 31, Groves 33, Bowen 59, 90
Allatt 16
Ref: J Bray
Chamberlain, Farrell, Phillips, Parkinson, Day, Houston, Groves, Osborne, Bowen, Adcock, Irving, Farrell
Parkin, Pullar, Aldridge, Thomas, Davis, Hart, Blissett*, Crabbe, Waller, Allatt, Cliss
Liverpool keep close tabs on Adcock, whilst A English signs pro forms. Amazingly, U's draw Gills again in the third cup competition of the season. A great start to the busy festive season is sealed when Farrell spreads wide to Irving, who crosses to Bowen for U's fourth away win.

21 — H HEREFORD — 26/12 — 9 D 2-2 — 4 33 — 2,525
Adcock 79, Bowen 80
Phillips 31, Phillips 89 (og)
Ref: D Reeves
Chamberlain, Farrell, Phillips, Parkinson, Day, Houston, Groves, Osborne, Bowen, Adcock, Irving
Rose, Price, Bray, Hicks, Pejic, Emery, Harvey, Dalzeil, Phillips, Kearns, Carter
League-leaders at the start. Hereford are set for an FA Cup tie with Arsenal. Three times recently, U's have let in last-minute goals. Phillips challenged by his namesake Stewart, turns Mike Carter's cross into his own net. He had earlier lost out to Chris Price, who supplied their first.

22 — H PORT VALE — 28/12 — 7 W 3-2 — 15 36 — 2,014
Groves 4, Bowen 32p, 56p
Brown 50, Smith 66
Ref: E Scales
Chamberlain, Farrell, Phillips, Parkinson, Day, Houston, Groves, Osborne, Bowen, Adcock, Irving
Siddall, Webb, Bromage, Hunter, Sproson, Cegielski, Williams, Lodge, Brown, Earle, Smith
Bowen had been eagerly awaiting a penalty, after being handed the job three months ago when Phillips contrived to miss two. His first chance comes when Alan Webb handles an Adcock shot, his second, after ex-WBA Ally Brown scores, comes when Wayne Cegielski also handles.

23 — A WREXHAM — 1/1 — 7 D 2-2 — 24 37 — 1,376
Phillips 21, Irving 75
Edwards 61, Horne 85
Ref: R Banks
Chamberlain, Farrell, Phillips, Parkinson, Day, Houston, Groves, Osborne, Bowen, Adcock, Irving
Parker, Salathiel, Cunnington, Keay, Williams, Wright, Edwards, Horne, Steel, Charles, Rogers
U's travel up to Chester to see in the New Year. Ex-U's boss Roberts, and defender Wright, are wary of U's strike-force. After Phillips' first and Irving's third, U's curse their luck when Barry Horne levels for the bottom club, who had beaten FC Porto and troubled AS Roma earlier.

CANON LEAGUE DIVISION 4

Manager: Cyril Lea

SEASON 1984-85

No		Date	1	2	3	4	5	6	7	8	9	10	11	12 sub used	Att	Pos	Pt	F-A	H-T	Scorers, Times, and Referees
24	H	BURY 26/1	Chamberlain	Farrell*	Phillips	Parkinson	Day	Hedman	Groves	Osborne	Bowen	Adcock	Irving	Houston	2,028	7	40	1-0	0-0	Osborne 46 — Ref: R Lewis
			Brown	Hill	Buckley	Ross	Bramhall	Dobson	White	Madden	Entwistle*	Jakub	James	Pashley						
25	A	SOUTHEND 29/1	Chamberlain	Hedman	Phillips*	Parkinson	Day	Houston	Groves	Osborne	Bowen	Adcock	Irving	English A	2,401	16	43	5-2	3-0	Adcock 8, Groves 11, 23, Bowen 62, 73 — Hadley 64, Pennyfather 80 — Ref: E Read
			O'Brien	Stead	Collins	Seaden	Clark	Hatter*	Pennyfather	Owers	Engwell	Phillips	Rogers	Hadley						
26	H	NORTHAMPTON 1/2	Chamberlain	Hedman	Phillips	Parkinson	Day	Houston	Groves	Osborne	Irving	Adcock	English A*	Farrell	2,314	22	46	4-1	0-0	Hedman 63, Adcock 70, Day 72, Mundee 85 [Parkinson 83pl] — Ref: A Ward
			Gleasure	Lewis	Mundee	Gage	Scott	Train	Lee	Mann	Belton	Benjamin	Cavener							
27	H	CHESTERFIELD 22/2	Chamberlain	Hedman	Phillips	Parkinson	Day	Houston	Groves	Osborne*	Bowen	Adcock	Irving	English A	2,303	7	49	3-1	1-0	Adcock 33, 60, 77, Newton 56 — Ref: N Butler
			Marples	Scrimgeour	O'Neill	Henderson	Baines	Hart	Brown P	Moss	Newton	Kendal	Ferguson*	Spooner						
28	H	MANSFIELD 26/2	Chamberlain	Hedman	Phillips	Parkinson	Day	Houston	Groves	Osborne	Bowen	Irving	English A	Jones	2,267	15	52	2-1	1-1	Day 4, Groves 82 — Vinter 38 — Ref: D Letts
			Hitchcock	Whitworth	Kearney!	Garner	Foster	Calderwood	Lowery	Vinter	Whatmore	Galloway	Jones							
29	A	HALIFAX 1/3	Chamberlain	Hedman	Phillips	Parkinson	Day	Houston	Groves	Osborne	Bowen	Irving	English A	Ward	1,022	18	53	0-0	0-0	Ref: M Peck
			Roche	Podd	Thornber	Kendall	Moyses	Knill	Sanderson	Little	Lowe	Gallagher	Ward							
30	A	STOCKPORT 4/3	Chamberlain	Hedman	Phillips	Parkinson	Day	Houston	Groves	Osborne	Bowen	Irving	English A	Coyle	1,561	15	53	0-1	0-0	Evans 88 — Ref: A Seville
			Salmon	Rutter	Sherlock	Emerson	Sword	Smith	Evans	Hendrie	Kerr	Leonard	Coyle							
31	H	CHESTER 8/3	Chamberlain	Hedman	Phillips	Parkinson	Day	Farrell	Groves	Osborne	Bowen	Irving	English A	Bulmer	2,224	20	54	1-1	0-1	Irving 75 — Rimmer 31 — Ref: K Baker
			Harrington	Blackwell	Lane	Speight	Coy	Brett	Rimmer	Walker	Greenhough	Blease	Bulmer							
32	H	DARLINGTON 15/3	Chamberlain	Hedman	Phillips	Parkinson	Day	Farrell	Groves	Osborne	Bowen	Irving	English A	Todd	1,739	1	54	1-2	1-2	Irving 40 — McLean 22, Airey 38 — Ref: A Gunn
			Barber	Atkinson	Johnson	Tupling	MacDonald	Lloyd	Haire*	Forster	Airey	Cook	McLean	Todd						
33	A	EXETER 23/3	Chamberlain	Hedman	Phillips*	Parkinson	Day	Houston	Groves	Osborne	Bowen	Irving	English A	Farrell	1,828	19	57	5-1	1-0	Bowen 32, 55, Parkinson 61, Morgan 49 [Irving 83, 87] — Ref: R Milford
			Smelt	Kirkup	King	McNichol	Marker	Viney	Ling	O'Shea	Morgan	Pratt*	Burgher	Phil-Masters						
34	A	BLACKPOOL 26/3	Chamberlain	Hedman	Phillips	Parkinson	Day	Houston	Groves	Osborne	Bowen	Irving	English A	Windridge	4,057	5	58	1-1	1-0	English A 7 — Pashley 68 — Ref: D Shaw
			O'Rourke	Moore	Price	Deary	Walsh	Greenall	Britton	Conroy	Pashley	Craine	Windridge							

Table-topping Bury visit Layer Road 13 points ahead of the U's. Straight from the restart Groves flies down the right flank in familiar style for Osborne to volley past David Brown. Colchester have 20-year-old Chamberlain, 15 years Osborne's junior, to thank with a string of fine saves.

Southend were 1-5 losers at Chester last week and fall to U's biggest away win since May 1979. The four clashes between the Essex rivals have realised 22 goals. Groves bags a pair of solo goals, whilst ex-U's player Hadley pulls one back at 0-4. 18-year-old Tony English debuts.

Royal London announce the cessation of their five-year shirt sponsorship. Three wins in seven days improves U's pre-match standing of five points behind fourth-placed Blackpool. Lea is January manager of the month. Denny Mundee handles, then pulls one back inside two minutes.

U's have suffered four postponements since 5 February. Adcock picks the perfect time to notch his second treble of the term in front of Howe (Arsenal). Ashurst (Sunderland) and Brown (Norwich). Hedman flicks back a Parkinson corner for Adcock's third, his 84th goal in 170 games.

Ex-U's player Mutrie retires due to drug problems. Adcock gets a knee injury in training. Stags have the best defence in the league, conceding only 16 in 25 games. Day crashes in a flag-kick and Groves nets after Kevin Hitchcock parries. Mark Kearney clouts Hedman (84) and walks.

U's 28-goal striker Adcock undergoes an exploratory knee operation. Irving takes his place at the Shay but only twelve players make the trip. Colchester fail to score for the first time since mid-October. Groves' rough treatment earns bookings for Paul Kendall and Barry Gallagher.

A flurry of three corners from John Rutter ends with a John Kerr flick being bundled in by Clive Evans at the death. Chamberlain appeared to be fouled in the process. National newspaper reports suggest that Sunderland have bid £100,000 for young trio Adcock, Groves and Hedman.

Adcock has a cartilage op. U's steal an undeserved point. City's outstanding Stuart Rimmer, on loan from Everton, clinically finishes a half-clearance. Caretaker boss Mickey Speight inspires his side. Hedman robs David Brett on the right for Irving to net U's first goal in 263 minutes.

League leaders Darlington have only lost three this season. The televised West Ham v Man U match affects the Friday night attendance. A pre-match sleet shower helps Mitch Cook's shot skid off Chamberlain's chest for Dave McLean to net. Carl Airey steals past Farrell and Phillips.

Exeter had a disastrous week when they also lost 1-7 at Scunthorpe. U's, with 67 goals, are the league's leading scorers ahead of division one leaders Everton's 63. The win equals the record away win. City's 19-goal striker Ray Pratt is stretchered off with a broken leg on 20 minutes.

Adcock will be out for the rest of the season. Blackpool have conceded only eight goals and have been defeated only once at Bloomfield Road. Parkinson's floated free-kick finds the head of 18-year-old Tony English. All of the first-team players have now scored, except Chamberlain.

35 | H | TRANMERE | 29/3 — Att: 2,044 — 6 / 8 — W — 61 — 2-1 (0-1)
Day 80, English A 84
Clarke 22
Ref: D Hedges
- Chamberlain, Hedman, Day, Parkinson, Phillips*, Houston, Groves, Burman, Bowen, Irving, English A, Farrell
- Adkins, Edwards, Sinclair !, Mungall, Burgess, Williams J, Palios*, Williams G, Clarke, Clayton, Anderson, Ferguson

Gills' Shinners joins on loan. Robust and physical Rovers get nothing for their spoiling tactics. Colin Clarke opens the scoring. Nick Sinclair is sent off (65) for a bad tackle on Day, who levels from Bowen's flick. Tranmere's John Clayton has overtaken Adcock in the scoring charts.

---

36 | H | SCUNTHORPE | 2/4 — Att: 2,409 — 6 / 8 — D — 62 — 1-1 (0-0)
Day 49
Braddle 51
Ref: M James
- Chamberlain, Hedman, Day, Parkinson, Farrell, English A, Groves, Osborne, Bowen, Irving, English A, Burman
- Gregory, Lees !, Whitehead, Hill, Pointon, Green, Brolly*, Cammack, Graham !, Lester, Braddle, Cowling

Phillips has broken his leg. Tommy Graham is booked for dissent and then handles for an early bath. Terry Lees joins him. Already booked for squaring up to English, he then manhandles the ref, claiming a punch from a fan. He returns with a policeman to try and identify the culprit.

---

37 | A | HEREFORD | 6/4 — Att: 3,485 — 6 / 5 — L — 62 — 1-2 (0-2)
Bowen 75p
Phillips 11, Price 25
Ref: P Tyldesley
- Chamberlain, Farrell, Day, Parkinson, English A, Groves, Osborne, Bowen, Irving, Burman*, Hubbick
- Rose, Bray, Pejic, Larkin, Price, Dalziel, Carter, Emery, Phillips, Kearns, Butler

Houston is out for the rest of the season with a dislocated shoulder suffered against Scunthorpe. Bogey-man Stewart Phillips opens the scoring, followed by a deflection off Day from a Chris Price effort. U's have never won at Hereford but pull one back when Kevin Rose chops Groves.

---

38 | H | WREXHAM | 8/4 — Att: 2,204 — 6 / 23 — W — 65 — 4-1 (2-1)
Bowen 17, Irving 32, 80, Hubbick 90
Edwards 25
Ref: I Borrett
- Chamberlain, Farrell, Day, Parkinson, English A, Groves, Osborne, Bowen, Irving, Burman*, Hubbick
- Hooper, Salathiel, Williams, Keay, Constive, Cunnington, Edwards, Horne, Steel, Charles, Gregory*, Rogers

Wrexham dismissed former U's manager Bobby Roberts two weeks previously. U's have only eleven fit senior players and include four teenagers and a part-timer on the bench. Irving takes his tally to nine, whilst Dave Hubbick comes on to score with virtually his first touch.

---

39 | A | HARTLEPOOL | 13/4 — Att: 1,512 — 6 / 15 — L — 65 — 1-2 (0-1)
Parkinson 76
Dobson 32, 77
Ref: N Glover
- Chamberlain, Farrell*, Day, Parkinson, English A, Groves, Osborne, Bowen, Irving, Burman, Hubbick
- Blackburn, Robinson, Hogan, Venus, Smith, Brown, Honour, Dixon, Dobson, Gallogly*, Gavin, Taylor

U's are twelve points adrift of leaders Chesterfield and have not won at the Victoria Ground since 1970-71. U's find a sugar daddy in the shape of marketing consultant Jonathan Crisp. In gale-force conditions Dobson nets Honour's corner. Parkinson volleys in Mark Venus's clearance.

---

40 | A | TORQUAY | 16/4 — Att: 1,191 — 6 / 21 — D — 66 — 1-1 (1-0)
Bowen 34
Walsh 54
Ref: R Groves
- Chamberlain, Farrell, Day, Parkinson, English A, Groves, Shinners, Bowen, Irving, Burman, Hubbick
- Allen, Jarvis, Dawkins, Kelly, Hall, Fowler, O'Dell, Perry, Walsh, Loram, Pugh

Crisp aims for Division Two in five years, a new stadium and entertainment centre. Shinners debuts after a leg injury. From U's third corner, Bowen heads his 17th goal. Promotion hopes end when Nigel Jarvis and Andy O'Dell work the ball into U's box for Mario Walsh to level.

---

41 | H | ROCHDALE | 19/4 — Att: 1,853 — 6 / 19 — D — 67 — 1-1 (1-1)
Parkinson 15
Diamond 13p
Ref: J Ball
- Chamberlain, Farrell, Day, Parkinson, English A, Groves, Shinners*, Bowen, Irving, Burman, Hubbick
- Redfern, Robinson, Cooke, Grant, McMahon, Dwyer, Thompson, Diamond, Taylor, Chapman, Heaton

On a bone-hard pitch busy ref Ball, a police inspector, gives 55 free-kicks and books eight. Colchester lad Farrell makes his 50th appearance. Day is penalised for handball, giving Barry Diamond a chance from the spot. Immediately Parkinson levels, latching onto an English free-kick.

---

42 | A | ALDERSHOT | 23/4 — Att: 1,624 — 7 / 12 — L — 67 — 0-1 (0-0)
McDonald 76
Ref: D Brazier
- Chamberlain, Farrell, Day, Parkinson, English A, Groves, Hubbick*, Bowen, Irving, Burman, Youngman
- Coles, Blankley, Coleman, Smith, Day, Shrubb, Staff*, Langley, Foyle, Fielder, McDonald, McNeil

Injury-plagued U's have to call up Stuart Youngman from the Youth Opportunities Programme to make up the numbers. A packed defence can't stop former Layer Road loanee Ian McDonald weaving through U's rearguard, chipping over English before simply rolling the ball in.

---

43 | A | PETERBOROUGH | 27/4 — Att: 1,500 — 6 / 11 — W — 70 — 1-0 (1-0)
Hedman 30
Ref: L Robinson
- Chamberlain, Farrell, Day, Parkinson, English A, Groves, Shinners, Bowen, Irving, Burman
- Turner, Quow, Wile, Martin, Pike, Slack, Shepherd, Chard, Kelly, Klug, Worrall

U's programme scoops the best award once again. Adcock returns to the reserves. Hedman scores from 8 yards. Chamberlain saves Martin Pike's penalty on 74 minutes after Farrell's handball. Posh fans light a small protest fire, while a flurry of snow falls during most of the game.

---

44 | H | SWINDON | 4/5 — Att: 1,867 — 6 / 7 — L — 71 — 0-1 (0-1)
English A 77
Ramsey 43
Ref: G Napthine
- Chamberlain, English A, Day, Parkinson, Phillips, Groves, Osborne, Bowen, Irving, Burman
- Endersby, Ramsey, Baille, Mayes, Cole, Rowland, Cayne, Hockaday, Gordon, Barnard, Nelson

Crisp's £150k takeover is agreed by the shareholders. Both goals are scored by full-backs. Chris Ramsey, who played for Brighton in the 1983 Cup Final against Man Utd, scores his first for the Robins. Tony English pops up to steer Day's flick from a Parkinson free-kick in for the U's.

---

45 | A | PORT VALE | 6/5 — Att: 2,526 — 8 / 12 — L — 71 — 2-3 (0-1)
Shinners 85, Groves 89
Brown 40, Kellock 65, Earle 71p
Ref: G Aplin
- Chamberlain, English A, Day, Parkinson, Phillips, Groves, Osborne, Bowen, Shinners, Irving, Hubbick
- Pearce, Webb, Sproson, Hunter, Bromage*, Ridley, Williams, Earle, Brown, Banks, Tartt, Kellock

Two goals by the U's keeps them on track for a cash prize as divisional highest scorers. Day's error lets in Ally Brown for Vale's first. Billy Kellock crashes home a 30-yard free-kick. Brown appears to hold Chamberlain down, forcing Day to punch Robbie Earle's shot over the bar.

---

46 | H | CREWE | 10/5 — Att: 1,864 — 7 / 10 — W — 74 — 4-1 (1-1)
Osborne 35, Bowen 66, Parkinson 70, [Irving 89]
Allatt 20
Ref: B Hill
- Chamberlain, English A, Day, Parkinson, Farrell, Groves, Osborne, Bowen, Shinners, Irving, Hubbick
- Longley, Pemberton, Davis, Thomas, Armstrong, Hart, Platt, Mason*, Waller, Allatt, Walker, Priddle

U's claim the £2,500 Canon goal award. Bowen's 100th appearance as 20 hours later tragedy strikes at Valley Parade, Bradford. 56 people lose their lives as fire sweeps through the wooden main stand in the championship celebration match against Lincoln City.

Away 1,963
Home 2,076
Average 2,076

CANON DIVISION 4 (CUP-TIES)　　Manager: Cyril Lea　　SEASON 1984-85

Milk Cup

		F-A	H-T	1	2	3	4	5	6	7	8	9	10	11	12 sub used	Scorers, Times, and Referees
1:1 A GILLINGHAM 28/8, 2,689 3:	L	2-3	0-1	Chamberlain	Godbold	Phillips	Farrell	Day	Houston	Groves	Osborne	Bowen	Adcock	Hull*	Parkinson	Bowen 54, Houston 87 / Weatherley 31, Mehmet 49, Leslie 90. Ref: R Lewis
				Hillyard	Higgin	Sage	Oakes	Johnson	Shaw	Cochrane	Leslie	Weatherley	Mehmet	Cascarino		U's meet Gills in the 1st round for the third time in five seasons. Mark Weatherley's cheeky back-heel opens the scoring. U's morale remains high despite Dave Mehmet making it 0-2. Houston looks to have earned a draw, only for John Leslie to pop up unmarked in the dying seconds.
1:2 H GILLINGHAM 4/9, 2,162 3:3	L	0-2	0-0 13	Chamberlain	Godbold	Phillips	Farrell*	Day	Houston	Groves	Osborne	Bowen	Adcock	Hull	Irving	Weatherley 68, 86. Ref: K Hackett
				Hillyard	Leslie	Sage	Oakes	Muster	Shaw	Cochrane	Johnson	Weatherley	Mehmet	Cascarino		(Colchester lost 2-5 on aggregate) U's dominate much of the game in the search for an aggregate equaliser but Gills score with their only two efforts on goal. Mark Weatherley clashes with Chamberlain for a high ball and reacts first to the loose ball. He bags his second, and third of the tie, from Tony Cascarino's cross.

FA Cup

		F-A	H-T	1	2	3	4	5	6	7	8	9	10	11	12 sub used	Scorers, Times, and Referees
1 A SOUTHEND 17/11, 2,935 4:17	D	2-2	2-1 10	Chamberlain	Farrell	Phillips	Parkinson	Day	Houston	Groves	Osborne	Irving*	Adcock	Hull	Hedman	Irving 3, Houston 21 / Clark 14, Phillips 51p. Ref: E Scales
				Cawston	Pennyfather	Collins	Phillips	Clark	Hadley	Kellock	Pountney*	Shepherd	Fuccillo	Rogers	Wymark	With Bowen struggling with injury, Irving cracks his first senior goal when he intercepts Billy Kellock's back-pass. Paul Clark seems to 'hand' in the equaliser, but Houston restores the lead from Parkinson's free-kick. Day's innocuous challenge on Nigel Rogers leads to the penalty.
1R H SOUTHEND 21/11, 3,907 4:17	W	3-2 aet	1-2 10	Chamberlain	Cawston	Phillips	Parkinson	Day	Houston	Groves	Godbold*	Irving	Adcock	Hull	Hedman	Adcock 29, Pennyfather 74 (og), [Groves 104] Shepherd 13, Phillips 31. Ref: E Scales
					Pennyfather	Collins	Phillips	Clark	Hadley	Kellock	Pountney	Shepherd*	Fuccillo	Rogers	Wymark	Groves volleys U's through after Mervyn Cawston fumbles a Parkinson free-kick. Extra-time comes when Glenn Pennyfather own-goaled another Parky free-kick, given when Ron Pountney impeded Groves' long throw. Steve Phillips' goal came via a great one-two with Pountney.
2 H GILLINGHAM 8/12, 4,487 3:4	L	0-5	0-2 8	Chamberlain	Farrell*	Phillips	Parkinson	Day	Hedman	Groves	Osborne	Irving	Adcock	Hull	Bowen	Robinson 30, Shearer 31, 61, 90. [Cascarino 86] Ref: C Downey
				Hillyard	Sage	Hinnigan	Oakes	Muster	Shaw	Cochrane	Shearer	Robinson	Mehmet	Cascarino		U's meet Gills for the third time in five seasons and suffer the heaviest home defeat in their 34-year Football League history. Late goals by Tony Cascarino, tapping in a Terry Cochrane cross, and David Shearer's third show Gills have the pedigree to challenge for Div Two.

Freight Rover Trophy

		F-A	H-T	1	2	3	4	5	6	7	8	9	10	11	12 sub used	Scorers, Times, and Referees
1:1 A GILLINGHAM 23/1, 962 3:3	D	2-2	2-0 7	Chamberlain	Farrell*	Phillips	Parkinson	Day	Hedman	Groves	Osborne	Bowen	Adcock*	Irving	English A/Houston	Groves 22, Adcock 29 / Oakes 62, Shinners 89. Ref: A Robinson
				Fry	Sharpe	Macowat	Oakes	Sitton	Collins	Leslie	Shinners	Robinson*	Johnson	Young*	Weatherley/Edwards	U's return to action after a three-week lay-off due to the freeze. Gills are pre-occupied with Saturday's FA Cup-tie at Ipswich and rest six regulars. Groves shows Ian Macowat a clean pair of heels and Adcock tucks in his 22nd. In the last minute Paul Shinners levels the scoring.
1:2 H GILLINGHAM 5/2, 1,762 3:2	W	2-0	2-0 6	Chamberlain	Hedman	Phillips	Parkinson	Farrell	Farrell*	Groves*	Osborne	Irving	Adcock*	English A	Hull/English T	Adcock 34, 43. Ref: C Downey
				Fry	Sharpe	Macowat	Hinnigan	Sitton	Collins	Johnson*	Shinners	Weatherley	Mehmet	Cascarino	Edwards	(Colchester won 4-2 on aggregate) U's gain revenge for defeat in both major cup competitions. Adcock's pair impresses a posse of first division managers including Howe (Arsenal), Pleat (Luton) and Ferguson (Ipswich). The English's are the first brothers to play together for the U's since the 1960s.
2 A WALSALL 12/3, 4,108 3:7	L	0-1	0-1 6	Chamberlain	Hedman	Phillips	Parkinson	Day	Farrell	Groves	Osborne	Bowen	Irving	English A	Kelly	Childs 15. Ref: K Nixon
				Cherry	Caswell	Mower	Jones	Brazier	Hart	Rees*	O'Kelly	Elliott	Childs	Handysides		Walsall, undefeated in their last seven at home, are outplayed by U's in the second half, conceding twelve corners. Adcock is sorely missed but U's could still progress as highest scoring losers. Steve Elliott and Gary Childs's one-two ends with the latter toe-poking a dipping shot home.

	Team	P			Home					Away				Pts
			W	D	L	F	A	W	D	L	F	A		
1	Chesterfield	46	16	6	1	40	13	10	7	6	24	22		91
2	Blackpool	46	15	7	1	42	15	9	7	7	31	24		86
3	Darlington	46	16	4	3	41	22	9	6	8	25	27		85
4	Bury	46	15	6	2	46	20	9	6	8	30	30		84
5	Hereford	46	16	2	5	38	21	6	9	8	27	26		77
6	Tranmere	46	17	1	5	50	21	7	2	14	33	45		75
7	COLCHESTER	46	13	7	3	49	29	7	7	9	38	36		74
8	Swindon	46	16	4	3	42	21	5	5	13	20	37		72
9	Scunthorpe	46	14	6	3	44	21	5	8	10	22	29		71
10	Crewe	46	10	7	6	32	28	8	5	10	33	41		66
11	Peterborough	46	11	7	5	29	21	5	7	11	25	32		62
12	Port Vale	46	11	8	4	39	24	3	10	10	22	35		60
13	Aldershot	46	11	6	6	33	20	6	2	15	23	43		59
14	Mansfield	46	10	8	5	25	15	5	3	15	16	23		57
15	Wrexham	46	10	6	7	39	27	5	3	15	28	43		54
16	Chester	46	11	3	9	35	30	4	6	13	25	42		54
17	Rochdale	46	8	7	8	33	30	5	7	11	22	39		53
18	Exeter	46	9	7	7	30	27	4	12	7	27	52		53
19	Hartlepool	46	10	6	7	34	29	4	15	4	20	38		52
20	Southend	46	8	8	7	30	34	5	3	15	28	49		50
21	Halifax	46	9	3	11	26	32	6	2	15	16	37		50
22	Stockport	46	11	5	7	40	26	2	3	18	18	53		47
23	Northampton	46	10	1	12	32	32	4	4	15	21	42		47
24	Torquay	46	5	11	7	18	24	4	3	16	20	39		41
		1104	282	136	134	884	594	134	136	282	594	884		1520

Odds & ends

Double wins: (4) Crewe, Mansfield, Northampton, Peterborough.

Double defeats: (1) Darlington.

Won from behind: (5) Northampton (a), Torquay (h), Crewe (a).

Lost from front: (2) Exeter (h), Halifax (h).

High Spots: Tony Adcock's 24 league goals in just 27 games.

Six league wins in eight games from September.

Ten unbeaten league games from December.

Two five-goal away performances (at Southend and Exeter).

New owner Jonathan Crisp's promise of Second Division football within five years.

Low spots: Loss of Tony Adcock, through injury, just as the big clubs were becoming interested in his services.

Flurry of late goals conceded, denying precious promotion points.

Record margin of home defeat in the 0-5 FA Cup loss to Gillingham.

Player of the Year: Alec Chamberlain.

Ever presents: (1) Alec Chamberlain.

Hat-tricks: (2) Tony Adcock.

Leading scorer: Tony Adcock (28) (including 3 in Freight Rover Trophy).

Appearances and Goals

	Appearances						Goals			
	Lge	Sub	LC	Sub	FAC	Sub	Lge	LC	FAC	Tot
Adcock, Tony	27		2		3		24		1	25
Bowen, Keith	41	1	2		1		17	1		18
Burman, Simon	8	1								
Chamberlain, Alec	46		2		3					
Day, Keith	45		2		3		4			4
English, Tony	20	2	2		3		3			3
Farrell, Andy	35	3	2		3					
Godbold, Daryl	4	2	2		1		1			1
Groves, Perry	44		2		3		11			11
Hedman, Rudi	29	1	2		1	2	2			2
Houston, Stewart	28	1			4		1	1	1	3
Hubbick, Dave	1	4					1			1
Hull, Jeff	18	2	2		3		5			5
Irving, Russell	34	7		1	3		9			9
Osborne, Roger	39	1	2		1	2	2			2
Parkinson, Noel	44		1		3	1	6			6
Phillips, Ian	37		2		3		1			1
Shinners, Paul	6				2		1			1
Youngman, Stuart					1					
(own-goals)									1	1
19 players used	506	25	22	2	33	3	87	2	5	94

CANON LEAGUE DIVISION 4

Manager: Cyril Lea ⇨ Mike Walker

SEASON 1985-86

No	Date		1	2	3	4	5	6	7	8	9	10	11	12 sub used	Scorers, Times, and Referees	Att	Pos	F-A	H-T
1	17/8	H STOCKPORT	Chamberlain	Hedman	Phillips	Reeves	Day	Houston	Groves*	Osborne	Bowen	Adcock	English A	Irving	Osborne 36, Day 71, Adcock 74	1,719	3	W 3-1	1-0
			Salmon	*Rutter*	*Chapman*	*Lodge*	*Sword**	*Smith N*	*Hodkinson*	*Thorpe*	*Leonard*	*Smith P*	*Sherlock*	*Coyle*	*Smith P 78* / Ref: E Scales				
2	24/8	A WREXHAM	Chamberlain	Hedman	Phillips	Reeves*	Day	Houston	Groves	Parkinson	Bowen	Adcock	English A	Irving	Reeves 30	2,296	3	L 1-2	1-0
			Hooper	*Salathiel*	*Cartwright*	*Williams*	*Keay*	*Emery*	*Muldoon**	*Horne*	*Steel*	*Charles*	*Gregory*	*Edwards*	*Bowen 59 (og), Steel 63* / Ref: M Reed				
3	27/8	H ALDERSHOT	Chamberlain	Hedman	Phillips	Reeves	Day	Houston	Groves	Parkinson	Bowen	Adcock	English A*	Osborne	English A 36, Adcock 73, Groves 78,	1,928	12	W 4-0	1-0
			Lange	*Blankley*	*Gillard**	*Massey*	*Smith*	*Mazzon*	*Staff*	*Johnson*	*Fielder*	*Foyle*	*McDonald*	*Shrubb*	[Hedman 82] / Ref: K Baker				
4	31/8	A TORQUAY	Chamberlain	Hedman	Phillips	Reeves	Day	Houston	Groves	Parkinson	Bowen	Adcock	English A*	Osborne	Adcock 27	1,023	23	L 1-2	1-1
			Allen	*Fowler D*	*Crowe*	*Kelly*	*Compton*	*Wright*	*Dawkins*	*Pugh*	*Lambert*	*Smith*	*Loram*		*Lambert 3, Crowe 54* / Ref: A Robinson				
5	6/9	H HALIFAX	Chamberlain	Farrell	Phillips	Reeves*	Day	Hedman	Groves	Parkinson	Bowen	Adcock	English A	Padd	Adcock 1, 20, Bowen 56	2,023	9	W 3-1	2-0
			Roche	*Brown*	*Ward*	*Shaw*	*Kendall*	*Ayre*	*Gallagher*	*Kellock*	*Lowe*	*Longhurst**	*Nicholson*		*Gallagher 60* / Ref: M Cotton				
6	14/9	A TRANMERE	Chamberlain	Hedman	Phillips	Reeves*	Day	Houston	Groves	Parkinson	Bowen	Adcock	English A	Ashcroft	English 34, Groves 38, Park'n 40, Day 46	1,362	14	W 4-3	3-2
			Adkins	*Sinclair*	*Burgess*	*Edwards*	*Mungall*	*McVicar**	*Muir*	*Train*	*Worthington*	*Miller*	*Anderson*		*Sinclair 30, Muir 41, Worthington 58p* / Ref: D Shaw				
7	17/9	H CAMBRIDGE	Chamberlain	Hedman	Phillips	Reeves*	Day	Houston	Groves	Parkinson	Bowen	Adcock	English A	Osborne	Adcock 2, 30, 57, Groves 85	2,574	15	W 4-1	2-0
			Hansbury	*Lee*	*Bennett*	*Finney*	*Moyes*	*Scott*	*Sinton*	*Spriggs*	*Pyle*	*Comfort*	*Crown*		*Crown 75* / Ref: N Butler				
8	21/9	A ORIENT	Chamberlain	Hedman	Phillips	Reeves	Day	Houston	Groves	Parkinson	Bowen	Adcock	English A	Juryeff	Parkinson 56, Bowen 88	2,577	13	W 2-1	0-1
			Wells	*Hales*	*Dickenson*	*Sussex*	*Sitton*	*Cornwell**	*Foster*	*Brooks*	*Shinners*	*Godfrey*	*Cooke*		*Shinners 33* / Ref: G Napthine				
9	27/9	H PORT VALE	Chamberlain	Hedman	Phillips	Reeves	Day	Houston	Groves*	Parkinson	Bowen	Adcock	English A	Irving	Bowen 32	3,110	13	W 1-0	1-0
			Arnold	*Webb*	*Bromage*	*Hunter*	*Sproson*	*Williams J*	*Williams O*	*Earle*	*Brown**	*Jones*	*Maguire*	*Banks*	Ref: A Gunn				
10	1/10	A BURNLEY	Chamberlain	Hedman	Phillips	Reeves	Day*	Houston	Hull	Parkinson	Bowen	Adcock	English A	Irving	Adcock 46, Bowen 60	3,375	24	W 2-0	0-0
			Peacock	*Palmer*	*Hampton*	*Chippendale**	*Deakin*	*Heggarty*	*Grewcock*	*Malley*	*Devine*	*Biggins*	*Rhodes*	*Taylor*	Ref: A Saunders				
11	4/10	H EXETER	Chamberlain	Hedman	Phillips	Reeves	Day	Houston	Groves	Parkinson	Bowen	Adcock	English A	Osborne	Day 29	3,927	17	D 1-1	1-0
			Gwinnett	*Kirkup*	*Viney*	*McNichol*	*Impey*	*Marker*	*Ling*	*Jackson*	*Kellow*	*Gale*	*Crawford*		*Gale 47* / Ref: D Reeves				

Admission prices are set at £2 - £1 for standing. In the wake of Bradford and Heysel, the U's have made several safety improvements, including an 11.30 am kick-off, the first of the day. Salmon drops Phillips' cross into the path of Osborne, who nets the country's first goal of the season.

Osborne requires five stitches in a head injury sustained at Millwall. Groves' dropping cross eludes everyone but Reeves, who nets his first U's goal. Bowen, defending at a corner, helps David Gregory's effort in. Jim Steel steals onto Hedman's woefully short back-pass throw-in.

Shots loan Tony Lange from Charlton. English meets Parkinson's corner with a bullet header and is injured in the process. Hedman one-two's with English to feed Adcock, who five minutes later combines with Reeves to set up Groves. Hedman's glancing header completes the rout.

Last season's wooden-spoonists are already occupying bottom slot. U's have not won at Plainmoor since Sept 1973. Martin Lambert side-foots Mark Crowe's miscue. Pugh's long-throw is mis-punched by Chamberlain, in his 100th league appearance, for Crowe to head firmly home.

The three league games at Layer Road have yielded twelve goals – ten to the U's. Adcock curls one past ex-Man Utd keeper Paddy Roche in 22 seconds. Playing a deeper role, he notches the second from Bowen, who fires the third after Parkinson's free-kick thunders the crossbar.

The division's leading scorers don't disappoint in a game riddled with defensive errors. United twice hold two-goal leads, scoring three in six minutes. Rovers' player-manager Frank Worthington's penalty, after Hedman fouled Ian Muir, causes an anxious last half hour for Colchester.

Ken Shellito's Cambridge have suffered successive relegation from the second to the fourth and are languishing in the bottom four. Adcock's fourth career hat-trick comes from a Hedman flick, Bowen's miscued shot and a cheeky far post chip by Groves. Irving asks for a transfer.

O's, the wind at their backs, take the lead via a third in three from Shinners. Parkinson picks up a half-clearance and volleys magnificently past Peter Wells. He then provides a diving header opportunity for Bowen, his fifth goal of the campaign. First U's league win at Brisbane Road.

U's require a safety certificate to increase the 4,900 capacity. Phillips makes his 250th appearance before the largest crowd since the Man Utd cup tickets went on sale. Adcock hits the bar (15). Bowen outpaces Phil Sproson to plant past Jim Arnold. Osher Williams strikes the post (74).

Houston meets ex-Old Trafford buddy Martin Buchan, player-boss of the Clarets. U's eighth win in ten is the best ever start. Day dislocates his shoulder (69). Bowen's mazy run gives Adcock the chance to put U's in front, then the striker robs Geoff Palmer to slot past Dennis Peacock.

Lea is awarded manager of the month before the best crowd since Feb 1982. Day heads United in front but the onslaught never comes. Darren Gale, a recent Exeter signing from Swansea, lifts the equaliser over the advancing Alec Chamberlain after Houston's poorly judged back-pass.

No	Venue/Date	Opponent / Att.	Pos	P	Res	HT	Team (starting XI)	Opposition / scorers	Score details & Ref	Report

12 — A MANSFIELD 12/10
Att 3,364 · 1 · 6 · L · 1-2 · 0-0

Chamberlain · Hedman · Phillips · Reeves* · Day · Houston · Groves · Parkinson · Bowen · Adcock · English A · Osborne
Hitchcock · Graham · Logan · Lowery · Foster · Pollard · Chamberlain · Whatmore · Cassells · Kent · Luke · McKernan*

English A 51
Luke 56, Chamberlain 62
Ref K Brean

Stags manager Ian Greaves is wanted by WBA. Around 50 fans stage a centre-circle sit-in protest. Second division Grimsby chase Lea. Bowen has three disallowed for offside and a 78th-minute penalty, after a push on Adcock, saved by Kevin Hitchcock's seemingly premature dive.

13 — H SCUNTHORPE 18/10
Att 3,462 · 1 · 24 · D · 1-1 · 0-0

Chamberlain · Hedman · Phillips · Reeves · Day · Houston · Groves · Parkinson* · Bowen · Adcock · English A · Osborne
Gregory · Russell · Pointon · Lister · Whitehead · Money · Brolly · Cammack · Broddle · Cooper · Hill

Reeves 78
Broddle 67
Ref B Hill

Scunthorpe, on their travels, have no points and two of their three goals have come from penalties. Lea subs Parkinson to 'protect him from the boo-boys' after his misplaced pass gives Iron the lead. Bowen's penalty is saved (60) after Money trips Adcock. U's, however, stay top.

14 — A SOUTHEND 22/10
Att 8,120 · 1 · 6 · W · 4-2 · 1-0

Chamberlain · Hedman · Farrell · Reeves · Day* · Houston · Groves · Parkinson · Bowen · Adcock · English A · Hull
Stannard · Stead · O'Shea · Westley · Hatter · Pennyfather · Silkman · Cadette · McDonough · Rogers · Gymer*

Bowen 16, Groves 49, 63, 85
Gymer 74, McDonough 77
Ref D Vickers

A pulsating derby with a second half hat-trick from 20-year-old Groves, who also provides Bowen. Day dislocates his shoulder twice in the first 20 mins. Parkinson and McDonough both have efforts disallowed. Groves's hat-trick arrives when Farrell forces Shane Westley's error.

15 — H NORTHAMPTON 26/10
Att 2,872 · 2 · 12 · L · 0-2 · 0-2

Chamberlain · Farrell · English A · Reeves · Hedman · Houston · Groves · Parkinson · Bowen · Adcock · Hull* · Osborne
Gleasure · Reed · Mundee · Chard · Lewis · Nebbeling · Donald · Benjamin · Hill · Morley · Mann

Chard 2, Mann 23
Ref M James

An 11 am start to avoid Ipswich v W Ham. U's recent bad home form continues in a third successive match against yellow-shirted opposition. This is the first blank in 21 league and cup-ties. Trevor Morley's left-wing cross is fired in by Phil Chard, who feeds 18-year-old Adrian Mann.

16 — A HEREFORD 2/11
Att 3,081 · 5 · 9 · L · 0-2 · 0-2

Chamberlain · Farrell* · English A · Reeves · Hedman · Houston · Groves · Parkinson · Osborne · Adcock · Hull · Irving
Rose · Price · Dalziel · Halliday · Pejic · Deke · Harvey · Carter · Phillips · Wells · Butler

Phillips 7, 37
Ref R Groves

Bowen suffers a broken leg and head injuries after last week's game, crashing his car into iron railings. Lea misses the game scouting. Stewart Phillips is denied a hat-trick by a fine save from Chamberlain, who drops the ball for the opening goal. Hereford are unbeaten at home in ten.

17 — A CHESTER 6/11
Att 2,809 · 7 · 2 · L · 0-4 · 0-1

Chamberlain · English A · Farrell · Reeves · Hedman · Houston · Groves · Parkinson · Osborne · Adcock · Hull · Irving
Castley · Abel · Lane · Greenhough · Gage · Coy · Kelly · Graham · Rimmer · Bennett · Houghton

Greenhough 16, Rimmer 53, 70, Abel 75
Ref D Allison

Whymark and T English are signed on non-contract, whilst Robin Turner is loaned from Swansea. Stuart Rimmer, who impressed against the U's last term, has since signed permanently from Everton for £10,000. Rimmer's double helps to inflict U's heaviest defeat for 13 months.

18 — H ROCHDALE 8/11
Att 2,624 · 8 · 10 · L · 0-1 · 0-0

Chamberlain · Hedman · Farrell · Reeves · Game · Houston · Groves · Parkinson · Turner* · Adcock · English A · Game
Redfern · Heaton · Grant · McMahon · Cooke · Hicks · Diamond · Taylor · Moore · Seasman · Gamble

McMahon 70
Ref I Hemley

U's are in the middle of their worst goal drought since February 1981 with four blanks. A far cry from winning the race to score 25 league goals at the beginning of the campaign. Dale have never won at Layer Road until Dave McMahon's shot takes a wicked deflection off Game.

19 — A PRESTON 23/11
Att 2,793 · 9 · 20 · L · 2-3 · 0-2

Chamberlain · Hedman · Farrell* · Turner · Day · Houston · Groves · Parkinson · Whymark · Adcock · English A · Game
Platt · Rudge · McAteer · Atkins · Twentyman · Martin · Stevens · Gray · Thomas · Allatt · Brazil

Parkinson 68p, Adcock 80
Thomas 16, Gray 38, Stevens 47
Ref F Roberts

U's finally score, but still lose, after five 'dry' games. Cash-strapped Preston, 3-7 FA Cup losers at Walsall, can't afford floodlight repairs so the game kicks off at 2 pm. Despite the poor run, U's are only six points adrift of second-placed Southend. Dale Rudge brings down Adcock.

20 — A HARTLEPOOL 14/12
Att 2,507 · 12 · 3 · L · 1-4 · 1-2

Chamberlain · Hedman · Farrell · Game · Day · Houston · Groves · Parkinson · Whymark · Adcock · English A · Burman
Blackburn · Nobbs · Chambers · Robinson · Smith · Linighan · Honour · Shoulder · Dixon · Walker · Gallogly

Hedman 36
Shoulder 2, 43p, Dixon 74, Robinson 78
Ref A Banks

Hull quits with a back injury. Inactive for three weeks and no new faces. Alan Shoulder, the smallest man on the pitch at 5'5", scores in 80 seconds and then takes a theatrical dive over Chamberlain. Edwin Blackburn saves Parkinson's shot on the line and admits later that it was in.

21 — H WREXHAM 20/12
Att 1,683 · 12 · 17 · W · 5-2 · 2-0

Chamberlain · Hedman · Farrell · Osborne · Day · Houston · Groves · Parkinson · Burman* · Adcock · English A · English T
Keen · Salathiel · Comstive · Brignull · Keay · Cunnington · Edwards · Horne · Mooney · Hencher · Gregory

Comstive 9 (og), Adc'k 17, 84, Groves 77
Cunnington 55, Gregory 77 [Hedman 79]
Ref A Robinson

Lea chases Les Berry of Charlton. Turner signs permanently from Swansea, who face expulsion for failing to show at Walsall. Recalled 35-year-old Osborne is the star. Paul Comstive, under pressure from A English, chips over his keeper. Three goals in seven minutes seals the win.

22 — A ALDERSHOT 28/12
Att 1,757 · 11 · 15 · D · 1-1 · 1-1

Chamberlain · Hedman · Phillips · Osborne · Day · Houston · Groves* · Parkinson · Burman · Adcock · English A · English T
Coles · Blankley · Ferns · Massey · Smith · Coleman · Fielder · Johnson · Butler · Mazzon · McDonald · Brazil

Day 4
Coleman 35
Ref K Cooper

U's throw the points away after Houston neatly heads on a corner from Parkinson for Day to score. Ex-U's defender Phil Coleman clears a Hedman effort off the line and then pops up unmarked to nod in a well taken free-kick, almost on the corner flag, for the Aldershot leveller.

23 — A SWINDON 1/1
Att 8,802 · 13 · 1 · L · 1-2 · 0-2

Chamberlain · Hedman · Phillips · Osborne · Day* · Houston · Burman · Parkinson · English T · Adcock · English A · Irving
Allen · Ramsey · Roberts · Barnard · Cole · Calderwood · Bamber · Henry · Gordon · Wade · Hockaday

Parkinson 55
Cole 4, Wade 45
Ref R Lewis

Swindon, under Lou Macari, move to the top of the table for the first time this term after last week's win at Torquay. They sit 13 points ahead of the U's. Day dislocates his shoulder for the fourth time. Bryan Wade secures the Robins' twelfth successive win at the County Ground.

CANON LEAGUE DIVISION 4

Manager: Cyril Lea ⇨ Mike Walker

SEASON 1985-86

No	Date		1	2	3	4	5	6	7	8	9	10	11	12 sub used	Att	Pos	Pt	F-A	H-T	Scorers, Times, and Referees
24	H 3/1	HEREFORD	Chamberlain *Rose*	Hedman *Price*	Phillips *Dalziel*	Osborne *Pejic*	Day* *Ceglelski*	Houston *Devine*	Burman *Harvey*	Parkinson *Delve*	English T *Wells*	Adcock *Kearns*	English A *Butler**	Irving *Maddy*	2,214 *12*	11	W 36	4-1	1-0	Parkinson 43, 83, English T 77, Phillips 80 / Delve 84. Ref: A Ward — A madcap four goals in six minutes breaks the tedium. Parkinson, relishing in his role behind the front two, takes his tally to six. Day sustains his fifth dislocated shoulder of the season on 24 minutes. Irving, his replacement, sets up Parkinson's second. T English gets his first U's goal.
25	H 11/1	TORQUAY	Chamberlain *Fry*	Hedman *Dawkins*	Phillips *Pugh**	Osborne *Wright*	Baker *Compton*	Houston *Crowe*	Turner* *Crabbe*	Parkinson *Walsh*	English T *Phillips*	Adcock *Fowler D*	English A *Dreyer*	Groves *Smith*	2,063 *24*	11	D 37	0-0	0-0	Ref D Hedges — Day reluctantly goes under the surgeon's knife just as the deal for Les Berry fails. Baker debuts in this 11.30 start. Torquay, bossed by ex-U's player Stuart Morgan, are eight points adrift at the foot. The only highlight is the eleven-year-old girl who wins the half-time penalty shoot-out.
26	A 17/1	STOCKPORT	Chamberlain *Walker*	Hedman *Evans*	Phillips *Matthewson*	Osborne *Chapman*	Baker *Sword*	Houston *Williams*	Turner *Hodkinson*	Parkinson *Hendrie*	Groves *Leonard*	Adcock *Diamond*	English A *Coyle*		2,336 *7*	10	D 38	1-1	1-1	Groves 30 / Hodkinson 9. Ref: T Mills — A lifetime has passed since these two met on the opening day of the season. U's fail to clear a second successive corner and Tommy Sword heads down for Andy Hodkinson to smash home. Groves finishes off the triangle free-kick for his fourth of the week and eleventh of the term.
27	H 24/1	TRANMERE	Chamberlain *Adkins*	Hedman *Mungall*	Phillips *Burgess*	Osborne *Hughes*	Baker *Rodaway*	Houston* *Edwards*	Turner *Morrisey*	Parkinson *Train*	Groves *Hildtch*	Adcock *Worthington*	English A *Anderson*	English T	2,013 *14*	12	L 38	1-2	0-2	Parkinson 78 / Hildtch 30, Mungall 41. Ref: C Downey — Ipswich's Kevin Steggles could join the U's, who are now closer, points wise, to re-election than promotion. 37-year-old Frank Worthington assists both Rovers' goals and has an effort disallowed (23), for pushing Houston, who suffers a broken nose in a clash of heads on 65 minutes.
28	A 31/1	HALIFAX	Chamberlain *Roche*	Hedman *Brown*	English A *Ward*	Osborne *Thornber*	Baker *Knill*	Game *Galloway*	Burman *Sanderson*	Parkinson *Kellock*	Groves *Lowe*	Adcock *Longhurst*	Irving *Nicholson*		989 *21*	12	D 39	2-2	1-0	Baker 36, Adcock 60 / Sanderson 70, Kellock 73. Ref: G Aplin — Angry Lea was set to play the first team in the reserves v Tiptree, but the game was called off due to icy weather. Inexperienced Baker and Game partner at the back on a pitch where a three-inch covering of snow had melted. A English makes his 50th league appearance.
29	H 4/2	SOUTHEND	Chamberlain *Stannard*	Hedman *Pennyfather*	Phillips *Lock*	Osborne *Silkman**	Baker *Westley*	Houston *McDonough*	Burman *Clark*	Parkinson *Stebbing*	Groves *Cadette*	Adcock *Neal*	English A *Rogers*	May	1,915 *8*	10	W 42	2-0	2-0	Adcock 4, Clark 22 (og) / Ref: E Scales — U's lead Southend by 21-12 on goals scored in the last six meetings. Adcock's seventh is U's first double of the season and only the fifth clean sheet. Burman is tireless in midfield. Paul Clark heads in Parkinson's cross. Roy McDonough keeps close tabs on Perry Groves.
30	A 1/3	PORT VALE	Chamberlain *Arnold*	Hedman *Webb*	Phillips *Bromage*	Osborne *Hunter*	Baker *Sproson*	Houston *Williams J*	Burman* *Griffiths**	Parkinson *Earle*	Groves *Jones*	Adcock *Bowden*	English A *Maguire*	Turner *Brown*	2,726 *6*	9	D 43	1-1	0-0	Groves 68 / Jones 77. Ref: P Willis — U's turn a £50k loss into a £11k profit and return to action after a month of heavy snow. Phillips and Houston play their 100th U's league game. Vale Park is devoid of grass. Osborne beats the offside trap for Groves to chip over Jim Arnold. Andy Jones hits a left-footed equaliser.
31	A 8/3	EXETER	Chamberlain *Shaw*	Hedman *Harrower*	Phillips *Viney*	Osborne *McNichol*	Baker* *McCaffrey*	Houston *Marker*	Burman *Ling*	Parkinson *Pratt**	Groves *Ward*	Adcock *Keough*	English A *Crawford*	Turner *Kellow*	1,520 *16*	12	D 44	2-2	1-0	Adcock 42, Burman 85 / Ward 49, Crawford 67. Ref: K Cooper — Bowen is fined £500 and ten points for reckless driving last October. Depleted U's earn a fourth successive away draw. Adcock's 16th gives U's the lead. Against the run of play, Ling crosses for Ward and Harrower's blocked shot runs kindly for Crawford. Burman's first U's goal.
32	H 14/3	MANSFIELD	Chamberlain *Hitchcock*	Farrell *Graham*	Phillips *Garner*	Osborne *Lowery*	Hedman *Foster*	Houston *Pollard*	Burman* *Kent**	Parkinson *Kenworthy*	Groves *Cassells*	Adcock *McKernon*	English A *Chamberlain*	Turner *Collins*	1,956 *3*	13	D 45	0-0	0-0	Ref: L Shapter — After five weeks without a game U's fans are disappointed by the lack of incident. Tony Kenworthy clips the bar on four minutes but the Stags are content to sit deep. Elsewhere, 683 spectators see Northampton beat Southend 3-1, thus eliminating the U's from the Freight Rover Trophy.
33	A 22/3	NORTHAMPTON	Chamberlain *Gleasure*	Farrell *Reed*	Phillips *Friar*	Osborne *Donald*	Baker *Lewis*	Houston *McPherson*	Burman *Schiavi**	Parkinson *Benjamin*	Groves *Chard*	Adcock* *Morley*	English A *Hill*	Turner *Sugrue*	2,035 *8*	15	L 45	0-1	0-1	Donald 13 / Ref: P Tyldesley — Reeves is transfer-listed whilst Groves, seeking pastures new, asks to be put in the shop window. Northampton beat the Colchester for the third time this season, through Warren Donald's direct free-kick. awarded after Chamberlain had carried a Tony Morley ball out of his penalty area.
34	H 25/3	CREWE	Chamberlain *Parkin*	Hedman *Pemberton*	Phillips *Booth*	Osborne *Thomas*	Baker *Davis*	Houston *Hart*	Farrell *Platt*	Parkinson *Cutler*	Groves *Waller*	English T *Handford**	English A *Blissett*	Groves *Power*	1,356 *11*	15	L 45	1-2	0-2	English A 62 / Cutler 20, Phillips 31 (og). Ref: I Hemsley — Adcock is out with a throat infection for the third attempt in as many weeks. Crewe acquire their first win at Layer Road for 25 years. Fans unfurl a 'Lea must go' banner. Phillips passes straight to Dave Waller who, via David Platt, finds Chris Cutler. Phillips then own-goals a Platt corner.

Match-by-match records (matches 35–46)

35 — H SWINDON — 28/3
Att 2,997 · Pos 14 (7) · D · 1-1 · HT 0-0 · Pts 46
Scorers: English A 54 / Bamber 62
Ref: A Gunn

U's	Chamberlain	Hedman	Phillips	Osborne	Baker	Houston	Farrell	Parkinson	Groves	English T	English A	Ferguson
Opp	Allen	Ramsey	Roberts	Barnard	Cole	Calderwood	Bamber	Henry	Gordon	Wade	Kamara	

U's sign Ferguson (31) from Brighton on deadline day to fill in for Bowen. Champions-elect Swindon have their six away-match winning streak ended by United. A English's powerful shot deflects off Paul Roberts. Chamberlain can only palm a good save towards Dave Bamber.

36 — A PETERBOROUGH — 31/3
Att 2,316 · Pos 13 (19) · W · 2-1 · HT 1-1 · Pts 49
Scorers: English A 6, Baker 84 / Fuccillo 29
Ref: M Reed

U's	Chamberlain	Hedman	Phillips	Osborne	Baker	Houston	Farrell	Parkinson*	Groves	English T	English A	Ferguson
Opp	McManus	Parris	Pike	Collins	Slack	Gage	Kowalski	Fuccillo	Shepherd	Gallagher	Kelly	

Eric McManus's attempt to punch a cross lands at the feet of A English to score. Steve Collins gets the better of Hedman and drills a low cross to Lil Fuccillo. Martin Pike hits the post (44) before Ferguson and Houston cause consternation in the Posh defence allowing Baker to ghost in.

37 — H CHESTER — 4/4
Att 2,281 · Pos 14 (2) · L · 2-3 · HT 0-2 · Pts 49
Scorers: English T 57, 62p / Johnson 3, Glenn 30, Greenhough 62
Ref: D Reeves

U's	Chamberlain	Day	Phillips	Osborne*	Baker	Houston	Farrell	Ferguson	Groves	English T	English A	Houghton
Opp	Butcher	Glenn	Barrett	Greenhough	Butler	Coy	Kelly	Graham	Richardson	Johnson	Bennett*	

73-year-old Vera Webster is the U's mascot for this game. Day returns after 15 weeks out through injury. City throw away a two-goal lead and then get an undeserved winner. Barry Butler fouls A English for the penalty, but outwits Day eight mins from time to feed Ricky Greenhough.

38 — H ORIENT — 8/4
Att 1,771 · Pos 13 (8) · W · 4-0 · HT 2-0 · Pts 52
Scorers: Ferguson 17, Day 33, Phillips 66, [English A 78]
Ref: T Holbrook

U's	Chamberlain	Day	Phillips	Osborne*	Baker	Houston	Farrell	Ferguson	Groves	English T	English A	Turner
Opp	Wells	Hales	Dickenson	Juryeff	Foster	Sitton	Cornwell	Harvey*	Shinners	Sussex	Castle	

Ferguson notches his first U's goal, steering home a cross from Day. Phillips strikes a tremendous free-kick with his weaker right foot, and when Peter Wells can only parry a Baker shot, A English steals in first to stab home the loose ball.

39 — A ROCHDALE — 12/4
Att 1,182 · Pos 12 (15) · D · 3-3 · HT 1-1 · Pts 53
Scorers: Ferguson 20, Farrell 76, English T 83p / Baker 32 (og), Taylor 50, 74p
Ref: P Vanes

U's	Chamberlain	Hedman	Phillips	Osborne*	Baker	Day	Groves	Ferguson	Farrell	English T	English A	Bradtle
Opp	Redfern	Johnson !	Grant	Heaton	Cooke	Hicks	Thompson	Taylor	McCluskie	Hildersley	Measham	

Lea was sacked on Thursday. Reserve-team coach Walker becomes caretaker. Director Nigel Fitch quits in protest. U's, 1-3 down with 14 mins left, earn a great point. Steve Taylor forces Baker's own goal and grabs his 28th when Farrell pushes Grant. Measham fouls Groves in the area.

40 — A SCUNTHORPE — 15/4
Att 1,238 · Pos 12 (19) · D · 1-1 · HT 1-1 · Pts 54
Scorers: Dixon 21 / Ferguson 7
Ref: G Tyson

U's	Chamberlain	Hedman	Phillips	Osborne*	Baker	Day	Groves	Ferguson	Farrell	English T	English A	Turner
Opp	Johnson	Russell	Longden	Lister	Whitehead	Hunter	Dixon*	Cammack	Houchen	Hill	Measham	

Impressive T English signs full-time. Walker's new resilient team withstands the onslaught after Ferguson's fine diving header off a Groves cross. A huge clearance finds Kevin Dixon in the last match of his three-month loan from Hartlepool. U's borrow Brightlingsea's all-white kit.

41 — H PRESTON — 18/4
Att 2,046 · Pos 12 (23) · W · 4-0 · HT 1-0 · Pts 57
Scorers: English T 30p, 75, 83p, Ferguson 78
Ref: A Ward

U's	Chamberlain	Hedman	Phillips	Osborne	Baker	Day	Groves	Ferguson*	Farrell	English T	English A	Turner
Opp	Kelly	Atkins !	Jones	McAteer	Gibson !	Martin	Foster	Gray	Thomas	Greenwood	Brazil	

Jon Clark with five wins in six, is in charge after Brian Kidd's sacking. Simon Gibson is sent off (27) for flooring Ferguson. His positional replacement. Wayne Foster. and Alan Kelly, foul T English and Groves. The woe is complete when Bob Atkins walks for dissent on 85 mins.

42 — H PETERBOROUGH — 22/4
Att 1,863 · Pos 9 (21) · W · 5-0 · HT 1-0 · Pts 60
Scorers: Reeves 26, English T 64, [English A 66, 88, 89]
Ref: M Bodenham

U's	Chamberlain	English A	Phillips	Osborne	Baker	Day	Farrell*	Turner	Groves	English T	Reeves	Hedman / Johnson
Opp	McManus	Parris	Pike	Collins	Slack	Gage	Kowalski	Fuccillo	Nuttell*	Gallagher	Cavener	

In his first game since Christmas, Reeves gets the lead Tony English emulates brother Tom by firing in a treble. Groves chases a lost cause for the first. A English rattles in the second after confusion at an Osborne corner and completes his hat-trick, taking a pass-in-stride from Baker.

43 — A CREWE — 26/4
Att 1,555 · Pos 8 (11) · W · 2-0 · HT 2-0 · Pts 63
Scorers: Groves 25, 39
Ref: N Glover

U's	Chamberlain	English A !	Phillips	Osborne	Baker	Day	Farrell	Ferguson	Groves	English T !	Reeves	Pemberton
Opp	Powner	Pullar	McCarrick	Thomas	Davis	Booth	Platt	Cutler	Waller	Power*	Blissett !	

Rock-star David Essex is rumoured to have an interest in buying into the U's. The English brothers headline again. Gary Blissett kicks Tony to the ground. Tom floors the Crewe player and all are sent off (66). First three clean-sheets since Walker was in goal during November 1982.

44 — A CAMBRIDGE — 29/4
Att 3,115 · Pos 6 (22) · W · 3-1 · HT 3-0 · Pts 66
Scorers: Reeves 7, Ferguson 14, 35 / Crown 69p
Ref: G Napthine

U's	Chamberlain	English A	Phillips	Osborne	Baker	Day	Farrell	Ferguson	Groves	English T	Reeves	Cooper
Opp	Branagan	Clark	Mundee	Beattie	Dowman	Finney	Richards S	Richards G	Crown	Towner		

Despite being in the bottom four. Cambridge are unbeaten in the last nine. Walker is pressing hard to be full-time manager. Reeves robs Gary Richards. Ferguson back-heads a corner and stoops to nod in T English's low cross. The linesman awards Cambridge a contentious hand-ball.

45 — H HARTLEPOOL — 2/5
Att 2,410 · Pos 6 (5) · W · 3-1 · HT 1-1 · Pts 69
Scorers: Ferguson 25, English T 89, English A 90 / Hogan 7p
Ref: H Taylor

U's	Chamberlain	English A	Phillips	Osborne	Baker	Day	Farrell	Ferguson	Groves !	English T	Reeves	Kelly
Opp	Blackburn	Taylor	Chambers	Hogan	Smith	Robinson	Dixon	Honour	Borthwick*	Walker	Little	

T English hits his ninth in twelve after signing contracts on the pitch along with Hedman and Farrell. Day bowls over Kevin Dixon for Pool's lead before Ferguson's perfect header. Groves is sent-off (79) for two body-checks on Mark Taylor. The English brothers give U's a late win.

46 — H BURNLEY — 6/5
Att 2,726 · Pos 6 (14) · D · 2-2 · HT 1-0 · Pts 70
Scorers: Groves 41, English T 80 / Lawrence 62, Devine 84
Ref: M Cotton

U's	Chamberlain	English A	Phillips	Osborne	Day	Farrell	Ferguson	Groves	English T	Reeves*	Turner
Opp	Meenan	Hird	Hampton	Malley	Heggarty	Deakin	Greecock	Devine	Taylor	Lawrence	Hoskin

United finish the highest divisional scorers with 88. John Devine's 30-yarder denies U's a final placing of fifth. Groves gives U's the lead with his 15th from an Osborne free-kick. Les Lawrence pops up after Chamberlain drops Jim Hoskin's cross. Osborne's penetration finds T English

Average — Home 2,328 · Away 2,734

CANON DIVISION 4 (CUP-TIES)

Manager: Cyril Lea ⇨ Mike Walker

SEASON 1985-86

Milk Cup

			F-A	H-T	Scorers, Times, and Referees	1	2	3	4	5	6	7	8	9	10	11	12 sub used
1:1	H MILLWALL 21/8 1,430 2:	L	2-3	1-3	Bowen 12, 89	Chamberlain	Hedman	Phillips	Osborne*	Day	Houston	Groves	Reeves	Bowen	Adcock	English A	Parkinson
					Lovell 7p, 10p, Fashanu 14 Ref: I Borrett	Sansome	Hinshelwood	Roffey	Briley	McLeary	Nutton	Lowndes	Wilson	Fashanu	Lovell	Kinsella	

An unusual 6.30 pm kick-off and a large police presence greets Millwall's notorious fans. The Lions gain two penalties, following Hedman's lunge at John Fashanu and Les Briley's cross, which hits Reeves on the hand. Bowen's last-gasp second gives U's hope for the second leg.

			F-A	H-T	Scorers, Times, and Referees	1	2	3	4	5	6	7	8	9	10	11	12 [Leslie 80]
1:2	A MILLWALL 2/9 3,330 2:10	L	1-4	0-2	Bowen 78p	Chamberlain	Hedman	Phillips	Reeves	Day	Houston	Irving*	Parkinson	Bowen	Adcock	English A	Osborne
					Lovell 9, Lowndes 35, Fashanu 72, Ref: J Bray	Sansome	Hinshelwood	Roffey	Briley	McLeary	Nutton	Lowndes	Wilson	Fashanu	Lovell*	Kinsella	Leslie

(Colchester lost 3-7 on aggregate) U's dominate but in truth Millwall are better in every department. Welsh international Steve Lovell and Bowen both record three goals over the tie. Lovell is happiest as Lions go on to meet Southampton. Bowen's late penalty comes when John Fashanu palms away Reeve's flag-kick.

FA Cup

			F-A	H-T	Scorers, Times, and Referees	1	2	3	4	5	6	7	8	9	10	11
1	A WYCOMBE 16/11 3,089 GL:13	L	0-2	0-2	West 3, Read 40	Chamberlain	Hedman	Farrell	Reeves	Game	Houston	Groves	Parkinson	Turner	Adcock	English A
					Ref: E Scales	Lester	Collins	Riley	Burgess	Vircavs	McMahon	West	Read	Dell	Link	Stanley

The re-organisation plans being discussed could mean these sides meeting in a new third division south-east. The Loakes Park slope, eleven feet from side to side, aids Mark West's header from a corner. Farrell's slip lets in Simon Read. Wycombe now host Chelmsford in round two.

Freight Rover Trophy

			F-A	H-T	Scorers, Times, and Referees	1	2	3	4	5	6	7	8	9	10	11	12
1	H SOUTHEND 14/1 1,364 4:7	W	4-1	4-0	Groves 12, 38, 39, Adcock 29	Chamberlain	Hedman	Phillips	Osborne	Baker	Houston	Turner	Parkinson	Groves*	Adcock	English A	English T
					Clark 47 Ref: J Moules	Stannard	May*	Lampard	Lock	Westley	Hatter	Clark	Stebbing	Cadette	McDonough	Gymer*	McNeil/Rogers

All-action Groves nets his second treble against Southend this term. His first is a 20-yard solo run, rounding Jim Stannard before providing a long throw-in for Adcock. Adcock returns the compliment via a cross. Groves hits a low drive for his third before being replaced on 55 mins.

			F-A	H-T	Scorers, Times, and Referees	1	2	3	4	5	6	7	8	9	10	11	12
1	A NORTHAMPTON 21/1 1,958 4:13	L	1-2	1-1	Baker 36	Chamberlain	Hedman	Phillips	Osborne	Baker	Houston	Turner	Parkinson*	Groves	Adcock	English A	Game
					Schiavi 4, Benjamin 82 Ref: G Ashby	Gleasure	Reed	Mundee	Lewis	Nebbeling	Chard	Donald	Hill*	Benjamin	Morley	Schiavi	Mann

Defeat means that U's must hope that Southend defeat the Cobblers by five clear goals. A clanger from Chamberlain gifts Northampton the win. He tangles with Phillips for a Mark Schiavi cross, and drops it at the feet of Ian Benjamin. Baker scores his first senior goal for United.

League Table

Pos	Team	P	W	D	L	F	A	W	D	L	F	A	Pts
				Home					Away				
1	Swindon	46	20	2	1	52	19	12	4	7	30	24	102
2	Chester	46	15	5	3	44	16	8	10	5	39	34	84
3	Mansfield	46	13	8	2	43	17	10	4	9	31	30	81
4	Port Vale	46	13	9	1	42	11	8	7	8	25	26	79
5	Orient	46	11	6	6	39	21	9	6	8	40	43	72
6	COLCHESTER	46	12	6	5	51	22	7	7	9	37	41	70
7	Hartlepool	46	15	6	2	41	20	5	4	14	27	47	70
8	Northampton	46	9	7	7	44	29	9	3	11	35	29	64
9	Southend	46	13	4	6	43	27	5	6	12	26	40	64
10	Hereford	46	15	6	2	55	30	3	4	16	19	43	64
11	Stockport	46	9	9	5	35	28	8	3	12	28	43	63
12	Crewe	46	10	6	7	35	26	6	6	11	19	35	60
13	Wrexham	46	11	5	7	34	24	5	6	12	34	56	59
14	Burnley	46	11	3	9	35	30	5	8	10	25	35	59
15	Scunthorpe	46	11	7	5	33	23	4	6	13	17	32	58
16	Aldershot	46	12	5	6	45	25	4	3	16	21	49	56
17	Peterborough	46	9	11	3	31	19	3	8	12	21	45	55
18	Rochdale	46	12	7	4	41	29	2	5	16	16	48	54
19	Tranmere	46	9	1	13	46	41	8	2	13	28	32	54
20	Halifax	46	10	8	5	35	27	4	4	15	25	44	54
21	Exeter	46	10	4	9	26	25	5	5	13	21	34	54
22	Cambridge	46	12	2	9	45	38	4	4	15	20	42	54
23	Preston	46	7	4	12	32	41	4	6	13	22	48	43
24	Torquay	46	8	5	10	29	32	1	5	17	14	56	37
		1104	277	136	139	956	620	139	136	277	620	956	1520

Odds & ends

Double wins: (3) Cambridge, Orient, Southend.

Double defeats: (2) Chester, Northampton.

Won from behind: (3) Tranmere (a), Orient (a), Hartlepool (h).

Lost from in front: (2) Wrexham (a), Mansfield (a).

High spots: Topping the table in October.

Groves' two hat-tricks against Southend in league and cup.

The English brothers each score hat-tricks in successive matches.

A late rally of just one defeat in the last twelve matches, eight of them under caretaker boss Mike Walker.

Low spots: Missing out on promotion again, despite being top scorers.

Six straight league defeats after being in top spot in November.

Keith Bowen's road accident, which probably turned U's season.

The English brothers being sent off in the same match.

FA Cup defeat at Gola League Wycombe.

Player of the year: Roger Osborne.

Ever presents: (1) Alec Chamberlain.

Hat-tricks: (5) Groves (2), Adcock, English A, English T.

Leading scorer: Tony Adcock 16 (including 1 in Freight Rover Trophy).

Appearances and Goals

Player	Appearances Lge	Sub	LC	Sub	FAC	Sub	Goals Lge	LC	FAC	Tot
Adcock, Tony	33		2		1		15			15
Baker, Terry	21				1		2			2
Bowen, Keith	15			2			5		3	8
Burman, Simon	10	1					1			1
Chamberlain, Alec	46		2		1					
Day, Keith	30		2		1		5			5
English, Tony	45		2		1		13			13
English, Tom	16	7	2				8			8
Farrell, Andy	24			1			1			1
Ferguson, Mike	9	1					7			7
Game, Kirk	3	1								
Groves, Perry	42	1	1	1	1		12			12
Hedman, Rudi	38	1	2		1		3			3
Houston, Stewart	36		2		1					
Hull, Jeff	4	1		1						
Irving, Russell	2	7		1						
Osborne, Roger	28	6	1	1	1	1	1			1
Parkinson, Noel	35		1	1	1		7			7
Phillips, Ian	37		2		1		2			2
Reeves, John	24		2		1		4			4
Turner, Robin	6	5				1				
Whymark, Trevor	2	5					2			2
(own-goals)										
22 players used	506	37	22	2	11		88		3	91

TODAY LEAGUE DIVISION 4

Manager: Mike Walker

SEASON 1986-87

No	Date	Att	Pos	Pt	F-A	H-T	Scorers, Times, and Referees	1	2	3	4	5	6	7	8	9	10	11	12 sub used
1	A LINCOLN 23/8	2,303	21	L 0	1-3	0-3	Adcock 75 / McInnes 10, Lund 26, Cooper 36 / Ref: M Bailey	Chamberlain	Game (Hodson)	Phillips (Buckley)	Hedman (Daniel)	Baker (West)	Day* (Stradder)	Burman (McInnes)	Farrell (Cooper)	Ferguson (Lund*)	Adcock (Kilmore)	Reeves (McGinlay)	Norman (Gamble)
2	H EXETER 29/8	1,633	7	D 1	1-1	0-0	English A 75 / Kellow 89 / Ref: G Napthine	Chamberlain	Hedman (Shaw)	Phillips (Pugh)	English A (Viney)	Baker (Marker)	Day (McCaffrey)	Farrell (Watson)	Ferguson (Batty)	Groves (Gale)	Adcock* (O'Connell*)	Reeves (Priddle)	English T (Kellow)
3	A TRANMERE 5/9	1,281	13	W 4	4-3	2-2	Reeves 9, Adcock 27, English T 70, 90 / Muir 28, Anderson 36, Hughes 77 / Ref: P Harrison	Chamberlain	Hedman (McManus)	Phillips (Bullock)	English A (Mungall)	Baker (Thorpe)	Game (Moore)	Adcock (Morrisey)	English T (Vickers)	Ferguson (Worthington)	English T (Muir)	Reeves (Anderson)	Reeves
4	H TORQUAY 12/9	2,476	5	W 7	3-0	2-0	English A 5, 27, 61 / Ref: D Elleray	Chamberlain	Hinshelwood (Smeulders)	Hedman (McNichol)	Chatterton (King)	Baker (Richards)	Game (Crowe)	Adcock (Musker)	English A (Kelly*)	Ferguson (Pyle)	English T* (Nardiello)	Farrell (Dobson)	Farrell (Walsh)
5	H HARTLEPOOL 16/9	2,326	3	W 10	2-1	0-1	Adcock 60, 87 / Hogan 36p / Ref: K Morton	Chamberlain	Hinshelwood (Blackburn)	Hedman (Gallogly)	Chatterton (McKinnon)	Baker (Smith)	Game (Sword)	Adcock (Gibb)	English A (Shoulder)	Ferguson (Lowe)	Farrell (Walker)	Reeves (Dixon)	Burman
6	A ROCHDALE 20/9	1,240	5	L 10	0-1	0-0	Taylor 60 / Ref: R Hart	Chamberlain	Hinshelwood (Redfern)	Hedman (Johnson)	Chatterton (Grant)	Baker (Smart)	Game (Bramhall)	Adcock (Reid)	English A (Taylor)	Ferguson* (Young)	Farrell (Wakenshaw)	Reeves (Seasman)	Burman
7	H PETERBOROUGH 27/9	2,343	11	L 10	1-3	0-0	Day 86 / Gregory 46, Lawrence 57, Gunn 63p / Ref: D Reeves	Chamberlain	Hinshelwood (Beasley)	Hedman (Nightingale)	Chatterton (Gunn)	Baker (Price)	Game (Gage)	Farrell (Gregory)	Day (Fuccillo)	Ferguson* (Lawrence)	English A (Gallagher)	Reeves (Nuttell)	Burman
8	A HEREFORD 1/10	2,144	7	W 13	3-2	2-0	Burman 7, Hedman 18, Ferguson 47 / Wells 49, Halliday 66 / Ref: F Roberts	Chamberlain	Hinshelwood (Rose)	Hedman (Rodgerson)	Chatterton (Halliday)	Game (Cegielski)	Day (Devine)	Burman (Harvey)	English A (Spooner)	Ferguson (Phillips)	Hedman (Wells)	Leadbitter* (Devine)	Gorman
9	H WREXHAM 3/10	2,633	4	W 16	2-1	1-1	Ferguson 15, Williams 50 (og) / Massey 30 / Ref: P Don	Chamberlain	Hinshelwood (Pearce)	Phillips (Salathiel)	Chatterton* (Cumnington / Williams)	Game (Cooke)	Day (Conroy)	Burman (Massey)	Ferguson (Horne)	Steel	English A (Charles)	Farrell (Emson)	Gorman
10	A SOUTHEND 10/10	4,004	4	D 17	1-1	0-1	Hedman 47 / Cadette 23 / Ref: R Wiseman	Chamberlain	Hinshelwood (Stannard)	Phillips (O'Shea)	Farrell (Martin)	Day (McDonough)	Game (Hall)	Burman (Clark)	Ferguson (Pennyfather)	Ferguson (Cadette)	English A (Neal)	Farrell (Gymer*)	Short
11	H CARDIFF 17/10	3,160	3	W 20	3-1	1-0	Reeves 18, English A 55, Burman 81 / Wheeler 83 / Ref: A Buksh	Chamberlain	Hinshelwood (Rees)	Phillips (Kerr)	Farrell (Wimbleton*)	Day (Brignull)	Game (Boyle)	Burman (Marustik)	English A (Curtis)	Ferguson (Wheeler)	Hedman (Vaughan)	Hedman (Rogers)	Platnauer

Match notes

1. U's have no close season additions. ex-Arsenal boss Bertie Mee is appointed part-time consultant. Colchester are quoted at 7-1 favourites for the fourth division title. Suspensions held over from last season mean that Groves and the English brothers are missing. Lincoln blitz the U's.

2. Despite welcoming back the suspendee's, Walker is 'disgusted' by this lacklustre performance. A English puts U's ahead via the inside of the post, but Exeter hit back with a last-gasp equaliser from substitute Tony Kellow, who loops a shot on the run over the advancing Chamberlain.

3. Colchester claim a 4-3 win at Prenton Park for the second season in a row. Reeves' opener for the U's comes direct from a corner. When Ian English nods down from a corner. When T. English volleys into the roof of the net. Muir and Mark Hughes combine, it looks as if Rovers have saved a point until deep into injury-time.

4. Walker raids Millwall for Hinshelwood and Chatterton. Groves is new Arsenal manager, George Graham's first signing. Ferguson nods down for A English to bundle in his first, brother Tom provides the second, whilst Adcock moves upfield to put in a low centre for Tony's third.

5. Pool were denied a Layer Road draw last season by two very late goals, and with just three minutes remaining this time round Adcock dished out a repeat, chipping over Eddie Blackburn. Simon Lowe is sandwiched by Hedman and Baker, but it is Game's handball that is penalised.

6. Rochdale rely on the long-ball game to supply Rob Wakenshaw, a new signing from Carlisle. Only three shots on target are registered in the opening 45 minutes. The goal comes as a U's attack breaks down and a quick interchange sees Steve Taylor's shot deflecting off Hinshelwood.

7. Adcock breaks his arm in training when struck by a shot from A English. Walker locks the team in the changing room after to hammer out the reason for his first home defeat. Les Lawrence's shot strikes Day's hand and ex-Nottingham Forest defender, Bryan Gunn, makes no mistake.

8. Club captain Phillips returns after a hernia op in Chamberlain's 150th league game. Hereford's first team were demoted to the reserves during midweek, beating Torquay's second's 9-0. Hedman answers the striker crisis with a man-of-the-match showing. U's first win at Edgar Street.

9. Comedian Frank Carson joins the board, he is a friend of Crisp. Wrexham have beaten Maltese side Zurrieq in the Cup-Winners' Cup. On his 32nd birthday and 200th league game, Ferguson gives U's the lead. Chatterton dislocates his shoulder. Mike Williams turns in a Phillips cross.

10. Roots Hall has been a happy hunting ground for the U's in recent years. Dean Neal's cross receives a cheeky flick from the much sought-after Richard Cadette. Just after the break, Hedman harasses Dave Martin and manages to get a toe to divert past Jim Stannard to level.

11. Tom English returns to the bench after five matches out with a thigh strain. Cardiff make only their second visit to Layer Road. Day is immaculate at the heart of U's defence. Burman shrugs off the challenge of Steve Sherlock for the third after having a goal disallowed (44).

12   A   CREWE   21/10 — Pos 2, D, Att 1,812, (opp 12), Pts 21, 0-1 (FT 1-1)
English T 57, Thomas 45
Ref: W Flood
U's: Chamberlain, Hinshelwood, Phillips, Farrell, Day, Game, Burman, English A, Ferguson, Hedman, Reeves*, English T
Opp: Parkin, Goodison, Pemberton, Thomas, Davis*, Hart, Platt, McGuinness, Cutler, Milligan, Blissett, Pullar
Report: Reeves dislocates his shoulder. Chamberlain makes a splendid point-blank save from David Platt on 39 mins. Alex take the lead in the second minute of first-half injury-time through Geoff Thomas. T English, jeered throughout after of last season's sending off, nods in Burman's cross.

13   A   STOCKPORT   24/10 — Pos 4, D, Att 1,278, (opp 24), Pts 22, 0-1 (FT 1-1)
English T 77, Entwistle 9
Ref: T Ashby
U's: Chamberlain, Hinshelwood, Phillips, Farrell, Day, Game, Burman, English A, Ferguson, Hedman, English T
Opp: Farnworth, Evans, McKenzie, Lester, Matthewson, Hodkinson, Wilkes, Entwistle, Allatt, Bailey, Mossman
Report: The squad stays over at Keele University after the Crewe game. County, under Jimmy Melia, have only won once this term and that was against Halifax, the side immediately above them. U's hit wood three times, Ferguson (handball) and T English (offside) have efforts ruled out.

14   H   WOLVES   31/10 — Pos 3, W, Att 4,741, (opp 11), Pts 25, 3-0 (HT 0-0)
Ferguson 49, Streete 74 (og), English A 82
Ref: M Scott
U's: Chamberlain, Hinshelwood, Phillips, Farrell, Day, Game, Burman, English A, Ferguson, Hedman, Grenfell
Opp: Nixon, Oldroyd, Stoutt, Streete, Forman, Zelem, Purdie, Holmes, Mutch, Handysides, Edwards D
Report: Grenfell (20) joins on loan from Spurs. Once-proud Wolves find themselves mid-table in the fourth division. A near safety-designated capacity crowd is the best since the visit of Sheffield Utd in February 1982. Man City-loanee Nixon comically misjudges Floyde Streete's back-pass

15   A   BURNLEY   4/11 — Pos 4, L, Att 1,692, (opp 15), Pts 25, 1-2 (HT 0-2)
Ferguson 85, Grewcock 28, Hoskin 45
Ref: J Key
U's: Chamberlain, Hinshelwood, Phillips, Farrell, Day, Game, Burman*, English A, Ferguson, Hedman, Grenfell
Opp: Neenan, Malley, Hampton, Rodaway, Gallagher, Deakin, Britton, Regis, Grewcock, James, Hoskin
Report: The seven-match unbeaten run comes to an end at Burnley, with only one win in the last seven. 18-year-old Ashley Hoskins, who later scores, has a shot parried by Chamberlain for Neil Grewcock, looking suspiciously offside, to tap in. Turf Moor hosts its lowest post-war attendance.

16   H   LEYTON ORIENT   7/11 — Pos 4, D, Att 3,924, (opp 13), Pts 26, 0-0 (HT 0-0)
Ref: D Hedges
U's: Chamberlain, Hinshelwood, Phillips, Farrell, Day, Game, Burman*, English A, Ferguson, Hedman, Grenfell
Opp: Wells, Sitton, Dickenson, Foster, Mountford, Cornwell, Castle, Brooks, Fishenden*, Comfort, Harvey
Report: Turner quits due to a knee injury. U's sign Wilkins (21) from Eastern League. Haverhill. Ref Hedges courts controversy. when, with eight minutes left, Farrell's corner is nodded down by Ferguson for T English to score. Afterwards the ref doesn't know why he disallowed the goal.

17   A   SCUNTHORPE   21/11 — Pos 6, L, Att 1,725, (opp 12), Pts 26, 2-5 (HT 1-2)
Hedman 25, Grenfell 70 (McLean 83p)
Lister 4, Braddle 45, Johnson 63, 66
Ref: A Robinson
U's: Chamberlain, Hinshelwood, Phillips, Farrell, Day, Game, Burman*, English A, Ferguson, Hedman, Reeves
Opp: Green, Atkins, Longden, Money, Lister, Hunter, Russell, McLean, Johnson, Broddle, Hill
Report: Ferguson is banished to the reserves. U's concede five for the first time since April 1984. Mike Walker is not unhappy with the performance, claiming Scunthorpe have a lucky day. Dave McLean completes the nap-hand after Day is forced to handle a Billy Russell shot on the line.

18   H   HALIFAX   28/11 — Pos 4, W, Att 2,567, (opp 21), Pts 29, 3-1 (HT 1-0)
Farrell 37, Adcock 75, Phillips 89, Longhurst 84
Ref: I Hemley
U's: Chamberlain, Hinshelwood, Phillips, Grenfell, Day, Game, Farrell, Adcock, Hedman, Hedman, English A
Opp: Roche, Brown, Shaw*, Matthews M / Krill, Galloway, Sanderson, Matthews N / Black, Longhurst, Holden, Thornber
Report: Halifax are set to fold with debts of £440,000. Grenfell signs for £15,000. David Essex is spotted in the directors' box. Farrell gets his second career goal in which he has worn every shirt from two to twelve. Halifax's consolation comes via David Longhurst's close-range header.

19   H   PRESTON   13/12 — Pos 8, L, Att 2,240, (opp 6), Pts 29, 0-2 (HT 0-0)
Williams 63, Hildersley 90
Ref: J Martin
U's: Chamberlain, Hinshelwood, Phillips, Grenfell, Day, Game, Farrell, Adcock, Hedman*, English A
Opp: Brown, McNeil, Bennett, Atkins, Jones, Alladyce, Williams O, Brazil, Thomas, Swann, Hildersley
Report: Chairman Cadman hands over control to majority shareholder Crisp. Walker bemoans the injury crisis and the poor form of his forwards. Against the run of play, Osher William appears to hand-in Ronnie Hildersley's flag-kick. Hildersley then wraps up the points in injury-time.

20   A   SWANSEA   20/12 — Pos 5, W, Att 4,515, (opp 3), Pts 32, 2-1 (HT 0-1)
English T 47, Farrell 76, McCarthy 7p
Ref: K Baker
U's: Chamberlain, Hinshelwood, Phillips, Grenfell, Day, Game, Farrell, Adcock, Lowe*, Hedman*, English A*
Opp: Hughes, Harrison, Phelan, Lewic, Melville, Emmanuel, Williams, McCarthy, Love, Pascoe, Hough* / French
Report: Lowe of Hartlepool signs on a month's loan. Bowen returns to training after 14 months and 61 games out. Baker's tussle with Ian Love gives Swans an early penalty. Adcock robs Terry Phelan to give T English a simple tap in. Adcock sets up Farrell, who curls out of reach of Hughes.

21   H   CAMBRIDGE   26/12 — Pos 6, L, Att 3,376, (opp 12), Pts 32, 1-2 (HT 0-2)
Lowe 51, Crown 12, Spriggs 19
Ref: I Borrett
U's: Chamberlain, Hinshelwood, Phillips, Grenfell, Day, Game, Farrell, Adcock, Lowe*, Hedman, English A*
Opp: Branagan, Measham, Kimble A, Downman, Smith, Beck, Butler, Spriggs, Cooper, Crown, Kimble G
Report: Boxing Day morning sees A English make his 100th appearance. Cambridge are well marshalled in defence by ex-United duo. Smith and Downman. Linesman Saunders flags for handball by Lindsay Smith but is ignored by ref Borrett. Birthday boy Lowe nets his first U's goal.

22   A   ALDERSHOT   27/12 — Pos 8, L, Att 2,594, (opp 6), Pts 32, 0-1 (HT 0-0)
Langley 67
Ref: A Ward
U's: Chamberlain, Hinshelwood, Phillips, Grenfell*, Day, Game, Farrell, Adcock, Lowe, Hedman, Wilkins*
Opp: Lange, Blankley, Friar, Burvill, Smith, Wignall, Ring, Mazzon, Foyle, McDonald, Langley
Report: U's receive a third defeat within the month at the Recreation Ground to end a very poor Christmas. Hinshelwood replaces A English in midfield after his ankle injury yesterday. Ex-QPR and Chelsea marksman, Tommy Langley, capitalises on a bad defensive error to slot home

23   A   NORTHAMPTON   1/1 — Pos 8, L, Att 8,215, (opp 1), Pts 32, 2-3 (HT 0-0)
Adcock 52, 63, Benjamin 50, Morley 56, Gilbert 86p
Ref: D Vickers
U's: Chamberlain, Hedman, Phillips, Grenfell*, Day, Game, Farrell, Adcock, Lowe, Hedman, Wilkins*
Opp: Gleasure, Chard, Gernon, Donald, Wilcox, McPherson, McGoldrick, Benjamin, Gilbert, Morley, Hill
Report: Table-toppers Northampton are an impressive 17 points clear of second-placed Southend and 25 ahead of fifth-placed United. Colchester are denied a deserved point when Eddie McGoldrick's goal is pulled back for hitting a U's hand. Ice-cool Dave Gilbert obliges from the spot.

TODAY LEAGUE DIVISION 4 — Manager: Mike Walker — SEASON 1986-87

Match results

No		Team	Date	Att	Pos	Pt	Res	F-A	H-T	Scorers, Times, and Referees
24	H	SCUNTHORPE	3/1	2,100	6 / 7	35	W	1-0	1-0	Adcock 45; Ref: N Butler
25	H	LINCOLN	10/1	1,768	5 / 7	38	W	2-0	1-0	Farrell 39, 68; Ref: V Callow
26	A	EXETER	17/1	2,553	5 / 7	38	L	0-2	0-1	Baker 4 (og), Robson 80; Ref: D Reeves
27	H	TRANMERE	23/1	2,167	6 / 15	39	D	1-1	0-0	Norman 79, Worthington 53; Ref: M Cotton
28	A	TORQUAY	31/1	1,034	6 / 23	39	L	1-3	0-1	Adcock 51; McNichol 41, Dobson 48, Nardiello 64; Ref: J Deakin
29	A	HARTLEPOOL	6/2	1,235	7 / 19	39	L	0-1	0-0	Walker 90; Ref: C Seel
30	H	ROCHDALE	13/2	2,020	5 / 24	42	W	2-0	1-0	English T 13, Wilkins 82; Ref: B Hill
31	A	PETERBOROUGH	21/2	3,474	7 / 6	42	L	0-2	0-2	Phillips 7p, Gallagher 15; Ref: D Scott
32	H	HEREFORD	27/2	1,999	6 / 16	45	W	2-0	0-0	English T 52p, Phillips 54; Ref: A Buksh
33	A	WOLVES	3/3	5,715	6 / 7	45	L	0-2	0-1	Holmes 41, Bull 86; Ref: D Shaw
34	H	STOCKPORT	6/3	2,001	6 / 22	48	W	5-1	4-0	Lowe 4, 14, 30, English T 17, Day 46; Edwards 78; Ref: N Butler

Line-ups (U's top; opponents in italics)

Match	Team	1	2	3	4	5	6	7	8	9	10	11	12 sub used
24	U's	Chamberlain	Game	Hedman	Hinshelwood	Day	Baker	Farrell	Adcock	Lowe	Grenfell	Norman	
24	*Scunthorpe*	*Green*	*Money*	*Longden**	*DeMange*	*Lister*	*Hunter*	*Russell*	*Reeves*	*Johnson*	*Broddle*	*Hill*	*Atkins*
25	U's	Chamberlain	Game	Hedman	Hinshelwood	Day	Baker	Farrell	Adcock	Lowe	Grenfell	Norman	
25	*Lincoln*	*Swinburne*	*Franklin*	*Buckley*	*Hodson*	*West*	*Strodder*	*McInnes*	*Kilmore*	*Lund*	*Cooper*	*Mitchell**	*Simmons*
26	U's	Chamberlain	Game	Hedman	Hinshelwood	Day	Baker	Farrell	Adcock	Lowe	Grenfell	Norman	
26	*Exeter*	*Shaw*	*Harrower*	*Viney*	*Marker*	*McCaffrey*	*Taylor*	*Batty**	*O'Connell*	*Biggins*	*Keough*	*Robson*	*Kellow*
27	U's	Chamberlain	Hedman	Phillips	Hinshelwood	Day	Game	Farrell*	Adcock	Lowe	Grenfell	Norman	Wilkins
27	*Tranmere*	*Farnworth*	*Mungall*	*Hay*	*Hughes*	*Vickers*	*Moore*	*Morrisey*	*Bell*	*Worthington*	*Muir*	*Anderson*	
28	U's	Chamberlain	Hedman	Phillips	Hinshelwood	Day	Game	Wilkins	Grenfell	Lowe	Adcock	Norman*	Farrell
28	*Torquay*	*Allen*	*Richards*	*King*	*Impey*	*Cole*	*McNichol*	*Dobson*	*Musker*	*Walsh*	*Nardiello*	*Holloway*	
29	U's	Chamberlain	English A	Phillips	Hinshelwood	Day	Game	Chatterton	Adcock	Lowe	Grenfell	Wilkins	
29	*Hartlepool*	*Blackburn*	*Nobbs*	*McKinnon**	*Hogan*	*Smith*	*Sword*	*Barrett*	*Hewitt*	*Dixon*	*Toman*	*Walker*	*Honour*
30	U's	Chamberlain	English A	Phillips	Chatterton	Game	Baker	Adcock*	English T	Lowe	Grenfell	Wilkins	
30	*Rochdale*	*Welch*	*Conning*	*Grant*	*Seasman*	*Bramhall*	*Smart*	*Stanton**	*Wakenshaw*	*Parlane*	*Reid*	*Hudson J*	*Holden*
31	U's	Chamberlain	English A	Phillips	Chatterton	Game	Baker	Adcock	English T	Lowe	Grenfell*	Norman	Hedman
31	*Peterborough*	*Shoemake*	*Paris*	*Gunn*	*Nightingale*	*Price*	*Gage*	*Luke*	*Fuccillo*	*Gallagher*	*Phillips*	*Kelly*	
32	U's	Chamberlain	Hinshelwood	Phillips	Chatterton	Hedman	Baker	Adcock	English T	Lowe	Grenfell	Wilkins	
32	*Hereford*	*Rose*	*Rodgerson*	*Leadbitter*	*Pejic*	*Cegielski*	*Devine*	*Harvey*	*Spooner*	*Phillips**	*Kearns*	*Butler*	*Carter*
33	U's	Chamberlain	English A	Phillips	Chatterton	Hedman	Baker	White*	English T	Lowe	Grenfell		Adcock
33	*Wolves*	*Kendall*	*Stoutt*	*Thompson*	*Streete*	*Brindley*	*Robertson*	*Purdie**	*Forman*	*Bull*	*Mutch*	*Holmes*	*Kelly*
34	U's	Chamberlain	Hinshelwood	Phillips	Chatterton	Day	Hedman	White	English T*	Lowe	Grenfell	Wilkins	Edwards
34	*Stockport*	*Garton*	*Evans*	*Stokes*	*Hendrie*	*Matthewson*	*Williams*	*Hodkinson**	*Moss*	*Allatt !*	*Robinson*	*Brown*	

Match notes

24 — Scunthorpe: U's walking wounded are back on course, and so is Adcock, who nets his third in two games after scoring only ten during the whole of 1986. He bursts through the Scunthorpe defence to unleash a 25-yard curler that leaves Ron Green helpless. It is Adcock's 95th goal for Colchester.

25 — Lincoln: Youth-teamer Lee Hunter is selected for N Ireland. Lee Hunter signs for a fee of £5,000. The treacherous frozen pitch looks doomed to providing an abandonment, but Farrell taps in when Trevor Swinburne drops a cross and curls a second. City are said to be pricing Gary Lund at £1m.

26 — Exeter: St James Park escapes the worst of the countrywide freeze-up. Ref Reeves, however, orders the open terraces to remain closed for spectator safety. City are in a run of 13 without loss. Baker, in attempting to clear, lobs over Chamberlain. Adcock's goal is ruled out for offside (71).

27 — Tranmere: U's have played more than most during the cold snap. Volunteers clear the pitch of snow. John Morrisey, one of six bookings, lifts a corner to Mark Hughes, who finds the wily Frank Worthington. Lowe holds up and lays the ball off to Norman to register his first senior goal for U's.

28 — Torquay: Torquay, with one win in sixteen, are favourites to suffer demotion out of the league, but are far more committed than the U's. Chamberlain carries the ball out, Jim McNichol whacks in the resultant free-kick. Mario Walsh appears to palm the ball to Donato Nardiello for the third.

29 — Hartlepool: U's are beaten for the tenth time in eleven outings. Chatterton returns after a long lay-off. Keith Nobbs' hand knocks the ball out of Adcock's path in the box but goes unpunished. Right on time, closing in on goal, Nigel Walker lifts the ball over the advancing Chamberlain into the net.

30 — Rochdale: Chamberlain's 200th consecutive appearance, against Eddie Gray's Dale. Walker warns T English to start giving 100%. Adcock shapes to shoot and fools everyone by planting the ball on T English's head. Hedman comes on, allowing Wilkins to move upfield and clinch the second.

31 — Peterborough: T English reacts angrily to Walker's newspaper jibes and demands a transfer. U's meet Posh for the fifth time this term. Baker's error forces Phillips to chop down Errington Kelly. Namesake, Steve, mis-hits the penalty in. Kelly then produces the opportunity for Jackie Gallagher.

32 — Hereford: After last season's £11k profit, the U's are faced with a £132K loss. Bowen is forced to quit, T English is granted his transfer request and U's sign White from Bury (free). United gain their first penalty of the season when Mel Pejic handles. Phillips starts and finishes the second goal.

33 — Wolves: Walker hopes White will fill Groves' boots in Colchester's first ever visit to Molineux. Chamberlain is booked for protesting about Steve Bull's seemingly offside goal. Micky Holmes had earlier given Wolves the lead.

34 — Stockport: Lowe's second career hat-trick keeps U's on course for the play-offs. Stockport arrive only 35 minutes before kick-off and fore-go a pre-match meal. Vernon Allatt is dismissed (10) for throwing the ball at the ref. Lowe's third stems from Wilkins. Sub Levi Edwards comes on back.

Match Results (35–46)

No	H/A	Opponent	Date	Att.	Pos		Res	Pts	FT	HT	Scorers	Ref
35	A	CARDIFF	14/3	2,222	6	14	W	51	2-0	0-0	Lowe 49, 51	V Callow
36	H	CREWE	17/3	2,249	5	13	W	54	2-1	1-0	Day 13, Lowe 84; Blissett 47	C Downey
37	H	SOUTHEND	20/3	3,357	6	3	L	54	1-2	1-0	White 43; Johnson 59, Cadette 88	R Lewis
38	A	WREXHAM	28/3	1,320	6	12	W	57	1-0	0-0	English T 80	J Worrall
39	A	LEYTON ORIENT	3/4	3,105	7	9	L	57	0-1	0-1	Jones 38	K Cooper
40	H	BURNLEY	10/4	2,635	7	23	W	60	1-0	1-0	Adcock 29	M Dimblebee
41	H	NORTHAMPTON	17/4	3,676	5	1	W	63	3-1	1-1	Wilkins 39, Chatterton 57p, Hedman 76; Logan 15	C Downey
42	A	CAMBRIDGE	21/4	2,946	5	11	W	66	1-0	0-0	English A 63	P Vanes
43	H	SWANSEA	24/4	3,323	5	9	W	69	2-1	0-1	Hinshelwood 58, Adcock 59; Atkinson 11	J Ashworth
44	H	HALIFAX	29/4	911	5	15	D	70	0-0	0-0		M Heath
45	H	ALDERSHOT	4/5	4,310	5	6	L	70	0-1	0-1	Ring 26	I Borrett
46	A	PRESTON	9/5	8,757	5	2	L	70	0-1	0-0	Swann 90	M Scott

Home Average 2,740 · Away 2,873

35 — Cardiff
Line-up: Chamberlain, Hinshelwood, Phillips*, Chatterton, Day, Hedman, White, Adcock, Lowe, Grenfell, Wilkins
Cardiff: Moseley, Kerr*, Ford, Wimbleton, Brignull, Boyle, Platnauer, Wheeler, Horrix, Curtis, Marustik, Gummer

Cardiff have only three home wins, so U's first away win in nine is welcomed, so Lowe follows up his hat-trick with two more. Adcock split the absent defence for Lowe's low drive. Andy Kerr forgets to move up for offside. Lowe takes the ball on to slip past keeper Graham Moseley.

36 — Crewe
Line-up: Chamberlain, Hinshelwood, Phillips, Chatterton, Day, Hedman, White, Adcock, Lowe, Grenfell, Wilkins*
Crewe: Parkin, Goodison, Pemberton, Thomas, Wright, Gannon, Platt, Badak*, Pullar, Milligan, Blissett, Billinge

Crewe have gone six without defeat and in keeper Brian Parkin possess the man of the match. He makes five stunning saves. Day wades in to a packed area to thump home. Parkins sends Adcock tumbling on 39 mins but saves Hinshelwood's kick. In-form Lowe gets his sixth in three.

37 — Southend
Line-up: Chamberlain, Hinshelwood, Phillips, Chatterton, Day, Hedman, White, Adcock, Lowe, Grenfell, Wilkins
Southend: Stannard, Roberts, Johnson, O'Shea, Westley, Hall, Clark, Pennyfather, Cadette, McDonough, Rogers

Southend are still reeling from Dave Webb's resignation four games ago, but are five points ahead of U's at the start. White gives U's the lead. A long-range effort from Peter Johnson and Richard Cadette's winner, 90 secs from time, gives them a first win at Layer Road for ten years.

38 — Wrexham
Line-up: Chamberlain, English A, Phillips, Chatterton, Day, Hedman, White, Adcock, English T, Hinshelwood, Wilkins
Wrexham: Salmon, Salathiel, Cunnington, Williams, Cooke, Constive, Oghani, Horne*, Steel, Conroy, Emson, Buxton

United's injury list is beginning to shorten in their 22-man squad. Colchester complete an unusual 100% set of wins in Wales after previous successes at Cardiff and Swansea. In doing so they shatter Wrexham's unbeaten home record. T English heads in a deep cross from Phillips.

39 — Leyton Orient
Line-up: Chamberlain, English A, Phillips !, Chatterton, Day, Hedman, White, Adcock, English T*, Hinshelwood, Wilkins*
Orient: Wells, Cunningham* Dickenson, Smalley, Cass, Cornwell, Sussex, Brooks, Jones, Godfrey, Comfort, Hales

Frank Clark's O's are snapping at the heels of the U's. U's battle on despite having Phillips sent off on 21 minutes for a scuffle with sub Kevin Hales. The match was delayed for 45 minutes owing to a power failure. Former Tottenham striker Chris Jones produces a fine diving header.

40 — Burnley
Line-up: Chamberlain, English A, Phillips, Chatterton, Day, Hedman, White, Adcock, Lowe, Hinshelwood, Wilkins
Burnley: Neenan, Leebrook, Hampton, Rodaway, Gallagher, Deakin, Grewcock*, Malley, Parker, Britton, James, Hoskins

Once-proud Clarets are in serious danger of losing their league status by dropping into the GM Vauxhall Conference. Boss Walker praises the defensive pairing of Day and Hedman. Adcock's eleventh of the season is the copper-haired striker's first goal at Layer Road for three months.

41 — Northampton
Line-up: Chamberlain, English A, Norman, Chatterton, Day, Hedman, White, Adcock, Lowe, Hinshelwood, Wilkins
Northampton: Gleasure, Reed*, Logan, Donald, Wilcox, McPherson, McGoldrick, Benjamin, Gilbert, Morley, Hill, Chard

Runaway leaders Northampton are already promoted to the third division, but get a rare come-uppance. Chatterton's goal, given when Russ Wilcox fouls Adcock, creates a new record as the 16th different player to find the net in a single season. David Logan had secured the lead.

42 — Cambridge
Line-up: Chamberlain, English A, Norman, Reeves, Day, Hedman, White, Adcock, Lowe, Hinshelwood, Wilkins
Cambridge: Branagan, Measham, Kimble A, Smith, Crowe, Beck, Butler, Cowling, Kimble G, Crown, Schiavi

United open up a six-point gap over their nearest rivals. A. English notches his first goal for almost six months when Lowe holds the ball up before releasing in to A English's path. Colchester have now won seven of the last nine and look set to at least reach the first ever play-offs.

43 — Swansea
Line-up: Chamberlain, English A, Norman, Reeves, Day, Hedman, White, Adcock, Lowe, Hinshelwood, Wilkins
Swansea: Hughes, Harrison, Phelan, Melville, Stevenson, Atkinson, Emmanuel, McCarthy, Raynor, Pascoe*, Hutchison, Hough

Rivals Swansea, having had three points deducted for failing to shake at Rochdale, have the points dramatically re-instated and therefore close in on the U's. Paul Atkinson shoots Swans in to the lead. U's notch two in a minute but Day is lucky to stay on when he floors Sean McCarthy.

44 — Halifax
Line-up: Chamberlain, English A, Norman, Reeves, Day, Hedman, White, Adcock, Lowe, Hinshelwood, Wilkins*
Halifax: Roche, Brown, Harrison, Matthews M Knill, Galloway, Sanderson*, Martin, Black, Allison, Holden, Nicholson

The game is brought forward to allow the townsfolk of Halifax to follow their Rugby League team to Wembley on Saturday. The attendance is the league's lowest of the term. Thankfully, linesman Kirkby's flag stays aloft for a throw-in during the build up to Russell Black's 'goal' (82).

45 — Aldershot
Line-up: Chamberlain, English A, Norman, Chatterton, Day, Hedman, White, Adcock, Lowe*, Hinshelwood, Wilkins
Aldershot: Lange, Mazzon, Friar, King, Smith, Wignall, Barnes, Burvill, Langley, McDonald, Ring, Reeves

Nervous U's need a win to ensure a place in the play-offs. Andy King sets up the chance for Mike Ring with a bobbling cross which centre-half Day cannot deal with. Colchester must now win on the plastic pitch at Deepdale, otherwise they will have to rely on others slipping up.

46 — Preston
Line-up: Chamberlain, English A, Norman, Wilkins, Day, Hedman, White, Adcock, Lowe, Hinshelwood, Reeves*
Preston: Brown, Miller, Bennett, Atkins, Jones, Allardyce, Chapman, Swann, Thomas, Brazil, Hildersley, Farrell

Burnley's defeat of Orient to retain league status and Aldershot's surprise loss at home to Cardiff ensures U's place in the play-offs. Lowe has the ball in the net on 55 mins but is ruled offside. Gary Swann's last minute header could have been so costly to the U's, who now face Wolves.

TODAY DIVISION 4 (CUP-TIES)

Manager: Mike Walker

SEASON 1986-87

							1	2	3	4	5	6	7	8	9	10	11	12 sub used

Play-offs

SF 1 · 14/5 · H WOLVES · 4,829 · 4 · L · F-A 0-2 · H-T 0-2

1	2	3	4	5	6	7	8	9	10	11	12 sub used
Chamberlain	English A	Norman	Hinshelwood	Day	Hedman	White	Adcock	Lowe	Grenfell	Wilkins	
Kendall	*Stoutt*	*Barnes*	*Streete*	*Kelly*	*Robertson*	*Purdie*	*Thompson*	*Bull*	*Mutch*	*Holmes*	

Scorers: Kelly 28, Bull 32. Ref: R Lewis

Heavy rain causes puddles to appear on the pitch Steve Bull's cross loops off Day's foot for Robert Kelly to stoop and head over Chamberlain at bay. Bull then claims his 18th when Andy Thompson's shot bounces back off the post. Mark Kendall performs heroics to keep Colchester at bay.

SF 2 · 17/5 · A WOLVES · 16,330 · 4 · D · F-A 0-0 · H-T 0-0

1	2	3	4	5	6	7	8	9	10	11	12 sub used
Chamberlain	English A	Norman	Chatterton	Baker	Hedman	White	Adcock	Lowe	Hinshelwood	Wilkins	
Kendall	*Stoutt*	*Barnes*	*Streete*	*Kelly*	*Robertson*	*Dennison**	*Thompson*	*Bull*	*Mutch*	*Holmes*	*Purdie*

Ref: A Buksh

The high-noon showdown at Molineux is delayed 15 mins to allow Wolves' biggest crowd since the opening day of 1984-5 to take their places Andy Mutch is closest to breaking the deadlock with an offside goal (19) and then skims the crossbar (69). Wolves face Aldershot in the final.

(Colchester lost 0-2 on aggregate)

Littlewoods Cup

1:1 · 26/8 · H PETERBOROUGH · 1,551 · 4: · D · F-A 0-0 · H-T 0-0

1	2	3	4	5	6	7	8	9	10	11	12 sub used
Chamberlain	Hedman	Phillips	Burman	Baker	Game	Farrell	Ferguson	Adcock	Norman	Reeves	
Beasley	*Paris*	*Collins*	*Gunn*	*Price*	*Gage*	*Nightingale*	*Fuccillo*	*Lawrence*	*Shepherd**	*Luke**	*Christie/Gregory*

Ref: M Bodenham

Posh have recruited heavily during the close season, with a string of free transfers. U's have only eight fully-fit professionals and are also hit by suspensions held over from last season. Posh defend in depth and are only troubled when Burman and Hedman combine to set up Adcock.

1:2 · 3/9 · A PETERBOROUGH · 2,648 · 4:9 · L · F-A 0-2 · H-T 0-0

1	2	3	4	5	6	7	8	9	10	11	12 sub used
Chamberlain	Hedman	Phillips	English A	Baker	Game	Farrell	Ferguson	Adcock	English T	Reeves	
Beasley	*Paris*	*Collins*	*Gunn*	*Price*	*Gage*	*Christie*	*Fuccillo*	*Lawrence*	*Shepherd**	*Luke**	*Game/Burman, Gallagher*

Scorers: Gallagher 70, Luke 86. Ref: K Barrett

Adcock is still struggling to shrug off the virus that forced him to miss the last 13 games of last season. but he scored two for the reserves on Saturday. Sub Jackie Gallagher's cross-cum-shot deflects off Phillips. Noel Luke punishes a defensive error to earn a tie with Norwich City.

(Colchester lost 0-2 on aggregate)

FA Cup

1 · 15/11 · H BISHOPS STORTF'D · 2,413 · VO:10 · D · F-A 1-1 · H-T 1-1

1	2	3	4	5	6	7	8	9	10	11	12 sub used
Chamberlain	Hinshelwood	Phillips	Farrell	Day	Game	Adcock	English A	Ferguson*	English T	Grenfell	
Taylor	*Hopkins*	*Goodchild*	*Glazier*	*Hull*	*Cassidy*	*Templeton*	*Fergusson*	*Hardy*	*Johnson*	*Newbury**	*Hedman, Weddell*

Scorers: English T 20; Ferguson 45. Ref: C Downey

The game is delayed two minutes after a pitch invasion United followers cause trouble in the town centre before the match. Tom English puts United in the lead with a firm header but slack marking allows Ian Fergusson to earn a Layer Road replay, stroking in on the half-time whistle.

1R · 18/11 · H BISHOPS STORTF'D · 3,516 · VO:10 · W · F-A 2-0 · H-T 1-0

1	2	3	4	5	6	7	8	9	10	11	12 sub used
Chamberlain	Hinshelwood	Phillips	Farrell*	Day	Game	Adcock	English A	Ferguson	Hedman*	Grenfell	
Taylor	*Wickenden*	*Goodchild*	*Glazier*	*Hopkins*	*Cassidy*	*Numn*	*Fergusson*	*Hardy**	*Johnson*	*Newbury**	*Reeves/Wilkins, Weddell*

Scorers: English T 2, Adcock 77. Ref: C Downey

Rain-lashed Layer Road sees Day break up a Stortford attack to feed Adcock on the right. Defender Wickenden slips in dealing with the cross, allowing T English to score. Adcock twice strikes wood before Hedman's cross from Grenfell's ball gives U's a second. Wilkins debuts (88).

2 · 6/12 · A ALDERSHOT · 2,997 · 4:10 · L · F-A 2-3 · H-T 1-2

1	2	3	4	5	6	7	8	9	10	11	12 sub used
Chamberlain	Hinshelwood	Phillips	Grenfell	Day	Game	Farrell	Adcock	Hedman*	English T	English A	
Lange	*Blankley*	*Friar*	*King*	*Smith*	*Wignall*	*Barnes*	*Mazzon*	*Foyle*	*McDonald*	*Langley*	*Wilkins*

Scorers: English T 1, Grenfell 90; Wignall 2, Foyle 17, 77. Ref: A Gunn

T English nets a tap-in after 50 seconds, ex-U's favourite Wignall levels in a minute after Game failed to pick him up. Martin Foyle's pair puts Shots through to a host first division Oxford. Grenfell curls a great free-kick around the defensive wall just before the whistle for full-time.

Sherpa Van Trophy

Q · 25/11 · H PETERBOROUGH · 1,404 · 6 · W · F-A 2-1 · H-T 1-0

1	2	3	4	5	6	7	8	9	10	11	12 sub used
Chamberlain	Hinshelwood	Phillips	Grenfell	Day	Game	Adcock	Farrell	Hedman	English T	Wilkins	
Shoemake	*Paris*	*Collins*	*Nightingale*	*Price*	*Gage*	*Gregory*	*Phillips*	*Gallagher*	*Gunn*	*Doyle**	*Luke*

Scorers: Hedman 25, Gage 73 (og); Phillips 56. Ref: C Downey

Hedman diverts in A English's cross. Farrell's clearance (12) hits Jeff Doyle's shin and rebounds past Chamberlain. who scoops the ball away. Despite the ball clearly crossing the line, the officials are unsighted. Huge Wakeley Gage stumbles into T English's shot to score an own-goal.

Q · 9/12 · A ALDERSHOT · 993 · 4:10 · L · F-A 2-4 · H-T 1-2

1	2	3	4	5	6	7	8	9	10	11	12 sub used
Chamberlain	Hinshelwood	Phillips	Grenfell	Day	Smith	Farrell	Adcock*	English T-	Wilkins	English A*	
Lange	*Fielder*	*Friar*	*King*	*Smith*	*Wignall*	*Barnes*	*Mazzon**	*Foyle*	*McDonald*	*Ring*	*Young/Hedman, Burvill*

Scorers: Wilkins 34, 85; King 8, Fielder 15, Mazzon 48, Ring 70. Ref: M James

U's have already qualified for the next stage as a result of the 3-3 draw between Posh and Shots, and so experiment. Wilkins. on his full debut, notches an impressive double, heading in two Steve Grenfell flag-kicks. Saturday's FA Cup-tie between the sides.

Sherpa Van Trophy

1 · 26/1 · A GILLINGHAM · 1,984 · 3:3 · L · F-A 0-2 · H-T 0-0

1	2	3	4	5	6	7	8	9	10	11	12 sub used
Chamberlain	Hinshelwood	Phillips	Grenfell	Day*	Game	Farrell	Wilkins	Adcock	Grenfell	Norman	
Hillyard	*Haylock*	*Elsey*	*Pearce*	*Wetherley*	*Greenall**	*Pritchard*	*Quow*	*Smith*	*Robinson*	*Cascarino*	*Radford, Jacobs*

Scorers: Smith 66, Cascarino 77. Ref: I Borrett

Speedy winger David Smith causes U's all kind of problems and notches his first goal for Gills since his move from GM Vauxhall Conference side Welling United. Tony Cascarino. who had supplied Smith's goal, gets the compliment returned via a neat cross to end United's interest.

League Table

		P	W	D	L	F	A	W	D	L	F	A	Pts
				Home					Away				
1	Northampton	46	20	2	1	56	20	10	7	6	47	33	99
2	Preston	46	16	4	3	36	18	10	8	5	36	29	90
3	Southend	46	14	4	5	43	27	11	1	11	25	28	80
4	Wolves	46	12	3	8	36	24	12	4	7	33	26	79
5	COLCHESTER	46	15	3	5	41	20	6	4	13	23	36	70
6	Aldershot*	46	13	5	5	40	22	7	5	11	24	35	70
7	Leyton Orient	46	15	2	6	40	25	5	7	11	24	36	69
8	Scunthorpe	46	15	3	5	52	27	3	9	11	21	30	66
9	Wrexham	46	8	13	2	38	24	7	7	9	32	27	65
10	Peterborough	46	10	7	6	29	21	7	7	9	28	29	65
11	Cambridge	46	12	6	5	37	23	5	5	13	23	39	62
12	Swansea	46	13	3	7	31	21	4	8	11	25	40	62
13	Cardiff	46	6	12	5	24	18	9	4	10	24	32	61
14	Exeter	46	11	10	2	37	17	0	13	10	16	32	56
15	Halifax	46	10	5	8	32	32	5	5	13	27	42	55
16	Hereford	46	10	6	7	33	23	5	5	14	27	38	53
17	Crewe	46	8	9	6	38	35	5	5	13	32	37	53
18	Hartlepool	46	6	11	6	24	30	5	7	11	20	35	51
19	Stockport	46	9	6	8	25	27	4	6	13	15	42	51
20	Tranmere	46	6	10	7	32	37	3	5	11	22	35	50
21	Rochdale	46	8	8	7	31	30	3	9	11	23	43	50
22	Burnley	46	9	7	7	31	35	3	6	14	22	39	49
23	Torquay	46	8	8	7	28	29	2	10	11	28	43	48
24	Lincoln	46	8	7	8	30	27	4	5	14	15	38	48
		1104	262	154	136	844	612	136	154	262	612	844	1502

* promoted after play-offs

Odds & ends

Double wins: (4) Cardiff, Hereford, Swansea, Wrexham.

Double defeats: (3) Aldershot, Peterborough, Preston.

Won from behind: (4) Hartlepool (h), Swansea (a), Northampton (h), Swansea (h).

Lost from in front: (1) Southend (h).

High spots: Ten wins from fourteen from February onwards. 100% record against the three Welsh clubs. Comprehensively beating champions Northampton, 3-1 at Layer Road. A record 17 individual goalscorers hit the net. Reaching the inaugural play-off promotion deciders.

Low spots: Crippling injuries throughout the season. Only 64 league goals. Five scoring blanks in the last five matches of the season. Seven away defeats from December. Defeat in two cup competitions by Aldershot within four days.

Player of the Year: Rudi Hedman.

Ever presents: Alec Chamberlain.

Hat-tricks: (2) Tony English, Simon Lowe.

Leading scorers: Tom English, Tony Adcock (12).

Appearances and Goals

Player	Lge	Sub	LC	Sub	FAC	Sub	Goals Lge	LC	FAC	Tot
Adcock, Tony	33	2	2		3		11		1	12
Baker, Terry	19		2				2			2
Burman, Simon	10	2	1			1				
Chamberlain, Alec	46		2		3					
Chatterton, Nicky	20	1					1			1
Day, Keith	38		1		3		3			3
English, Tony	32		1		3		3			3
English, Tom	18	6	1		3		9		3	12
Farrell, Andy	24	4	2		1		4			4
Ferguson, Mike	16		2		2		4			4
Game, Kirk	25		1	1	3					
Gorman, Keith					1					
Grenfell, Steve	23				3		1		1	2
Groves, Perry	1									
Hedman, Rudi	38	6	2		2	1	4			4
Hinshelwood, Paul	41				3		1			1
Lowe, Simon	25	1	1				7			7
Norman, Sean	12	1	1				1			1
Phillips, Ian	33		2		3		2			2
Reeves, John	16	1	2				2			2
White, Winston	14				1		1			1
Wilkins, Richard	22	1				2	2			2
(own-goals)										
22 players used	**506**	**26**	**22**	**2**	**33**	**4**	**64**		**5**	**69**

BARCLAYS LEAGUE DIVISION 4 Manager: Walker ⇨ Foley ⇨ Brown SEASON 1987-88

No		Date	Opponent	Att	Pos	Pt	F-A	H-T	Scorers, Times, and Referees	1	2	3	4	5	6	7	8	9	10	11	subs used
1	A	15/8	BURNLEY	5,369		W / 3	3-0	2-0	Walsh 25, English 27, Lowe 75 — Ref: J Penrose	Benstead / *Pearce*	Hinshelwood / *Leebrook*	Norman* / *McGrory*	Chatterton / *Daniel*	Baker / *Zelem*	Hedman / *Deakin*	White / *Grewcock*	English / *Farrell*	**Walsh** / *Oghani*	Lowe / *Comstive*	Britton / *Britton*	Gardner/Hoskin
2	H	21/8	TORQUAY	1,372	8 / 1	L / 3	0-1	0-0	Dobson 66 — Ref: M Bodenham	Benstead / *Allen*	Hinshelwood / *McNichol*	Norman / *Kelly*	Chatterton / *Haselgrave*	Baker / *Cole*	Hedman / *Impey*	White / *Gardiner*	English / *Lloyd*	Walsh* / *McLoughlin*, Loram*	Lowe / *Dobson*	Wilkins / *Wilkins*	Reeves, Musker
3	A	29/8	SCUNTHORPE	2,003	9 / 10	D / 4	2-2	0-1	Wilkins 61, White 83 — Johnson 23, Flounders 65 — Ref: S Lodge	Benstead / *Green*	Hinshelwood / *Russell*	Norman* / *Longden*	Chatterton / *McLean*	Baker / *Brown*	Hedman / *Nicol*	White / *Dixon* *	English / *Harle*	Tempest / *Johnson*	Lowe / *Flounders*	Wilkins / *Hill*	Grenfell, Broddle
4	H	31/8	SCARBOROUGH	1,525	18 / 4	L / 4	1-3	1-0	Tempest 18 — Thompson 68p, Mell 70, Moss 72 — Ref: A Ward	Benstead / *Blackwell*	Hinshelwood / *McJannet*	Grenfell / *Thompson*	Chatterton / *Bennyworth*	Baker / *Richards*	Hedman / *Kendall*	White / *Hamill*	English / *Moss*	Tempest / *McHale* *	Lowe / *Mell*	Wilkins / *Graham*	Walsh, Cork
5	A	4/9	CREWE	1,843	20 / 17	D / 5	0-0	0-0	Ref: G Aplin	Benstead / *Greygoose*	Hinshelwood / *Pemberton*	Grenfell / *Macowat*	Chatterton / *Milligan*	English / *Wright*	Hedman / *Gage*	White / *Platt*	Wilkins / *Bodak* *	Tempest* / *Cutler*	Lowe / *Goodison*	Reeves / *Wakenshaw, Gymer/Davis*	Walsh/Norman
6	H	12/9	PETERBOROUGH	1,164	9 / 18	W / 8	4-1	1-0	White 35, Tempest 51, Chatterton 74p, [Walsh 83] — Lawrence 54 — Ref: R Wiseman	Benstead / *Neenan*	Hinshelwood / *Paris*	Grenfell / *Gunn*	Chatterton / *Gooding*	English / *Pollard*	Hedman / *Price*	White / *Lawrence*	Reeves / *Phillips*	Tempest* / *Riley*	Lowe* / *Halsall*	Radford / *Luke*	Radford, Walsh
7	A	16/9	HEREFORD	1,951	9 / 19	L / 8	0-1	0-0	Stant 90 — Ref: G Ashby	Benstead / *Rose*	Hinshelwood / *Jones*	Grenfell / *Devine*	Chatterton / *Stevens*	English / *Pejic*	Hedman / *Spooner*	White / *Rodgerson*	Wilkins / *Bowyer*	Tempest / *Phillips*	Walsh / *Stant*	Radford / *Leadbitter*	
8	A	19/9	HARTLEPOOL	1,698	19 / 14	L / 8	1-3	0-1	Hinshelwood 71 — Baker 41p, 51, 80p — Ref: I Hendrick	Benstead / *Prudhoe*	Hinshelwood / *Nobbs*	Grenfell / *McKinnon*	Chatterton / *Haigh*	English / *Smith*	Hedman / *Stokes*	White / *Honour*	Wilkins / *Toman*	Tempest / *Baker*	Walsh* / *Borthwick*	Reeves / *Barratt*	Lowe
9	H	25/9	EXETER	1,443	22 / 1	L / 8	0-2	0-1	Batty 32, Edwards 58 — Ref: A Buksh	Benstead / *Shaw*	Hinshelwood / *Nisbet*	Grenfell / *Viney*	Chatterton / *Marker*	English / *Massey*	Hedman / *Carter*	White* / *Batty*	Reeves / *Edwards*	Tempest / *Phillips*	Lowe* / *Olsson*	Reeves / *Harrower*	Walsh/Norman
10	H	29/9	SWANSEA	1,140	18 / 22	W / 11	2-1	1-0	Tempest 3, Hinshelwood 47 — Raynor 90p — Ref: R Lewis	Benstead / *Hughes*	Hinshelwood / *Harrison*	Grenfell / *Coleman*	Chatterton / *Melville*	English / *Knill*	Hedman / *Emmanuel*	White / *Williams*	Wilkins* / *McCarthy* *	Tempest / *Raynor*	Norman / *Pascoe* *	Reeves / *Lewis D*	Reeves, Hough/Andrews
11	A	3/10	NEWPORT	1,200	17 / 24	W / 14	2-1	1-0	Wilkins 22, Chatterton 51 — Thompson 87 — Ref: N Butler	Benstead / *Dillon*	Hinshelwood / *Hodson*	Grenfell / *Preece*	Chatterton / *Thackeray*	Baker / *Williams*	Hedman / *Holtham* *	White / *Giles*	Wilkins* / *Tupling*	Tempest / *Taylor*	Norman / *Gibbins*	Reeves / *Lewis*	Walsh, Thompson

Match notes

1. Adcock joins Man City (£80k), turning down Sheffield United and Dundee Utd. after scoring 96 goals in 211 league games. Crisp introduces a controversial 100% members-only ground entry. New signing Walsh, from Torquay (£15,000 by tribunal), turns in a simple cross from Lowe.

2. Torquay, fresh from an opening day 6-1 victory over Wrexham, become the first visitors to have their fans banned from Layer Road under the membership scheme, which has attracted just 1,600 applicants. A swift counter-attack brings Paul Dobson's goal from Mark Gardiner's cross.

3. U's sign Tempest, (£40,000) from Belgian club Lokeren, in a club record deal. Steve Johnson, at the far post, taps in the rebound from Andy Flounders shot. Wilkins heads in White's corner, who salvages a point seven minutes from time, slotting past Ron Green via a Chatterton pass.

4. U's tumble to their third home defeat of the season. Tempest gets his first U's goal on his home debut against the league new-boys. Hamill pulls down Stuart Hamill, enabling Neil Thompson to score the club's first ever league penalty. Hamill shell-shocks U's by creating two more.

5. U's players are forced to train on their day off. Alex include ex-U's man, Steve Wright. Walker demands a good defensive display and a clean sheet. In the last minute, U's spots Dean Greygoose off his line, but his cheeky chip clips Wakeley Gage's shoulder and sails over the bar.

6. Reeves faces suspension for a reserve dismissal. English continues at centre-back in front of the lowest home attendance in history as United gain their first home win for almost five months. Mick Gooding blatantly handles White's flag-kick for Chatterton to easily beat Joe Neenan.

7. U's unbeaten away start ends when ex-SAS man Phil Stant grabs a dramatic winner in the second minute of injury time, after Steve Spooner's shot is blocked. Stant finishes the rebound with a diving header. Seven minutes from time Walsh misses a great opportunity, firing well wide.

8. Paul Baker hits a hat-trick including two penalties. The first is awarded when Hinshelwood pushes Tony Smith at a free-kick. John Borthwick then supplies Baker with a flick. Hinshelwood levels with the goal of the game. Chatterton pulls down Andy Toman for the second spot-kick.

9. U's, after three successive home defeats, occupy their lowest league position for more than a decade. Paul Batty stabs the first home from an acute angle, out-pacing Grenfell. Walker deems the goal a fluke. Dean Edwards adds the second completing a breakaway from a U's corner.

10. A new lowest home attendance record is set as Walker experiments with Wilkins and Tempest up front. United win with goals in each half. Skipper Hinshelwood earns a booking for his protestations over Swansea's last-minute penalty, awarded for a trip on Paul Raynor by Hedman.

11. Newport are bottom of the table with just five points. U's winning Welsh streak continues with an ninth successive victory. Tempest knocks on Hedman's free-kick to Wilkins, who is also involved in U's second, when Dean Holtham's hand prevents him from getting a strike on target.

12 · H · 9/10 · LEYTON ORIENT — Att. 1,665 · 15/3 · **D 0-0** (HT 0-0) · Pts 15

U's: Benstead, Hinshelwood, Grenfell, Chatterton, Baker, Hedman, White, Wilkins, Tempest, Norman, Reeves
Orient: Wells, Hales, Dickenson, Smalley, Day, Nugent, Ketteridge, Castle, Shinners, Godfrey*, Comfort, Harvey

Ref: M James

U's proposed new stadium at Turner Rise gathers momentum as the council allow Layer Road to be sold to developers. Orient are denied top spot by the draw. Some of their fans are the first to beat the Members' Rule, accompanying U's fans as guests. The first 0-0 since O's last visit.

---

13 · A · 17/10 · WREXHAM — Att. 1,493 · 15/17 · **W 1-0** (HT 1-0) · Pts 18

U's: Benstead, Hinshelwood, Grenfell, Chatterton, Baker, Hedman, White, Wilkins, Tempest, English, Reeves, Lowe
Wrexham: Salmon, Preece, Jones, Hinnigan, Williams, Cunnington, Buxton, Hunter, Steel, Carter', Emson*, Hencher/Wright

Reeves 26 · Ref: P Harrison

Colchester's fourth win in five and tenth successive 'Welsh' win. Baker plays on with a cut eye for the last 20 minutes. Wrexham defender Joe Hinnigan, in attempting to head out a cross from Tempest, only succeeds in dragging the ball across the area where Reeves provides the finish.

---

14 · H · 20/10 · CARLISLE — Att. 1,328 · 12/19 · **W 1-0** (HT 0-0) · Pts 21

U's: Benstead, Hinshelwood, Grenfell, Chatterton, Baker, Hedman, White, Wilkins, Tempest, English, Reeves, Hill
Carlisle: Crompton, Patterson, Gorman, Robinson, Wright, Houston', Clark, Cooke, Poskett, Tynan*, Hetherington, Harrison/Harbach

Tempest 75 · Ref: D Reeves

U's are seven points behind leaders Scarborough at the start. Carlisle were thrashed 0-5 at Bolton on Saturday and their goal is under constant pressure throughout. Wilkins has three efforts cleared off the line. The inevitable goal comes via Wilkins' dazzling left-flank run and dribble.

---

15 · A · 24/10 · CAMBRIDGE — Att. 2,450 · 9/15 · **W 1-0** (HT 0-0) · Pts 24

U's: Benstead, Hinshelwood, Grenfell, Chatterton, Baker, Hedman, White*, Wilkins, Tempest, English, Reeves, Lowe
Cambridge: Branagan, Poole, Murray, Beattie, Smith, Brattan, Butler, Clayton, Rigby*, Crown, Purdie, Horwood

Chatterton 64p · Ref: D Phillips

Walker awaits international clearance for Hill, signed from Portuguese side Maritimo. U's have not conceded for more than six hours. Only Bolton have a better record. Chatterton's kick, after ex-U's star Lindsay Smith fouls Wilkins, gives U's a third successive win at the Abbey.

---

16 · H · 30/10 · DARLINGTON — Att. 1,659 · 7/12 · **W 2-1** (HT 0-0) · Pts 27

U's: Benstead, Hinshelwood, Grenfell, Chatterton, Baker, Hedman, White*, Wilkins, Tempest, English, Reeves', Hill
Darlington: Roberts', Outterside, Morgan, Hine, Robinson, Bonnyman !, Bell, Ward, MacDonald* Currie, Stonehouse, Worthington

Wilkins 56, Chatterton 68; Worthington 87 · Ref: I Hemley

Incredibly, after seven wins in eight, Walker and coach Hunter are reported by Crisp to have quit 'on a matter of principle'. Wilkins looks offside for the first, and Chatterton's spot-kick rebounds back to him off Jerry Roberts. Phil Bonnyman is sent-off for protesting his handball.

---

17 · A · 3/11 · ROCHDALE — Att. 1,399 · 5/23 · **W 4-1** (HT 2-1) · Pts 30

U's: Benstead, Hinshelwood, Grenfell, Chatterton*, Baker, Smith, White, Wilkins, Tempest, English, Reeves, Hill
Rochdale: Welch, Lomax, Hampton, Reid, Bramhall, Smart*, Parker, Simmonds, Parlane, Coyle, Warren, Seasman

Wilkins 34, 42, Chatterton 58p, Simmonds 45 [Hinshelwood 72] · Ref: K Hackett

Walker claims he was sacked and Crisp already had someone in mind. Youth coach Foley takes over as caretaker, and steers U's to a ninth game without defeat, a point behind leaders Wolves. Rochdale fans protest against boss Eddie Gray and chairman Tommy Cannon (and Ball).

---

18 · A · 6/11 · HALIFAX — Att. 1,432 · 2/12 · **W 2-1** (HT 1-1) · Pts 33

U's: Benstead, Hinshelwood, Grenfell, Chatterton, Baker, Smith, White, Wilkins, Tempest, English, Reeves, Hill
Halifax: Roche, Brown, Harrison*, Matthews M, Shaw, Galloway, Martin, Thornber, Matthews N, Holden, Allison, Ferebee

Wilkins 14, Chatterton 83p; Galloway 42 · Ref: M Dimblebee

Brown becomes U's 16th manager since joining the league. Previously in charge at Poole Town, the local press ask 'Roger who?'. Benstead returns to Norwich even though Walker has agreed a fee. A seventh win on the trot and five wins on their travels both set new club records.

---

19 · H · 21/11 · WOLVES — Att. 2,413 · 5/1 · **L 0-1** (HT 0-0) · Pts 33

U's: Walton, Hinshelwood, Grenfell, Chatterton, Baker, Smith, White, Wilkins, Tempest, English, Reeves !
Wolves: Kendall, Stoutt, Thompson, Streete, Clarke, Gallagher, Dennison, Vaughan, Bull !, Mutch, Downing*, Robinson

Thompson 76p · Ref: M Bailey

Walker is awarded manager of the month, after his dismissal! Director Frank Carson appears at Layer Road for the first time. Reeves and Steve Bull, the league's leading scorer with 20, are dismissed for a 65th-minute flare-up. Chatterton handles for Andy Thompson's penalty.

---

20 · A · 27/11 · STOCKPORT — Att. 1,703 · 5/20 · **D 1-1** (HT 0-1) · Pts 34

U's: Walton, Hinshelwood, Grenfell*, Chatterton, Baker, Smith, White, Wilkins, Tempest, English, Reeves
Stockport: Marples, Bullock, Bailey, Robinson, Scott, Williams, Hodkinson, Colville, Worthington, Farnaby, Birch, Walsh/Hill

Chatterton 50p; Farnaby 43 · Ref: J Lloyd

Lowe asks for a move back north and joins Scarborough on loan. Reading-based property developers Norcross become shirt sponsors. County include 39-year-old Frank Worthington. Craig Farnaby, unmarked, nets the first, but Bill Williams, under no pressure, handles a Reeves cross.

---

21 · H · 11/12 · BOLTON — Att. 1,725 · 3/8 · **W 3-0** (HT 1-0) · Pts 37

U's: Walton, Hinshelwood, Hedman, Chatterton, Hill, Williams, White, Wilkins, Tempest, English, Grenfell
Bolton: Felgate, Scott, Neal, Savage, Came, Sutton, Brookman*, Callaghan', Thomas, Elliott, Darby, Henshaw/Morgan

Wilkins 29, White 68, 81 · Ref: B Hill

New player-coach Williams (ex-Bournemouth) debuts. Bolton, under Phil Neal, have dramatically fallen over recent years. White's second-half double added to Wilkins' ninth of the term, gives hard-working U's a fine victory. Walton has only a Steve Elliott shot (34) to deal with.

---

22 · A · 18/12 · TRANMERE — Att. 2,642 · 2/22 · **W 2-0** (HT 1-0) · Pts 40

U's: Walton, Hinshelwood, Hedman, Chatterton, Hill, Williams, White, Wilkins, Tempest, English, Grenfell
Tranmere: Chamberlain, Higgins, McCarrick, Martindale, Moore, Vickers, Mungall, Harvey, Steel, McKenzie*, Murray', Morrisey/Craven

White 45, 70 · Ref: F Roberts

Crisp reveals that he has received death threats during the course of the season. Brown signs Keane from Bournemouth (£10k) and Angell, on loan, from Pompey. The young centre-half limps off with serious ankle ligament damage on 35 mins. White cracks a second successive brace.

---

23 · A · 26/12 · EXETER — Att. 2,675 · 1/18 · **W 2-0** (HT 0-0) · Pts 43

U's: Walton, Hinshelwood, Hedman, Chatterton, Hill, Williams, White, Wilkins, Tempest, English, Grenfell
Exeter: Shaw, Harrower, Viney, Carter, Taylor, Watson, Batty, Cooper, Edwards, O'Connell, Rowbotham* Harris

Wilkins 62, Tempest 75 · Ref: R Gifford

Lowe joins Scarborough permanently, whilst Walton signs for £17,500. U's win their first Boxing Day fixture since 1970, at Lincoln City. Tempest dummies Grenfell's cross for Wilkins to ghost in. The same trio were involved in Tempest's match-winner, 15 minutes from time.

BARCLAYS LEAGUE DIVISION 4 Manager: Walker ⇨ Foley ⇨ Brown SEASON 1987-88

No	Date		Att	Pos	Pt	F-A	H-T	Scorers, Times, and Referees	1	2	3	4	5	6	7	8	9	10	11	subs used
24	H 28/12	CARDIFF	2,599	1	46	W 2-1	1-1	Tempest 40, English 75 / Kelly 24 / Ref: P Don	Walton	Hinshelwood	Hedman	Chatterton	Hill	Williams	White	Wilkins	Tempest	English	Grenfell	
									Endersby	Bater	Platnauer	Wimbleton	Stevenson	Boyle	Curtis*	Ford	Gilligan	McDermott*	Kelly	Wheeler/Sanderson Keane

U's hit top spot for the first time with an eleventh successive win over a Welsh club. Walton, disastrously, punches straight to Mark Kelly to chip his first of the season. Tempest joins Wilkins and Chatterton on nine goals. English adds the second with Scott Endersby in no-man's land

No	Date		Att	Pos	Pt	F-A	H-T	Scorers, Times, and Referees	1	2	3	4	5	6	7	8	9	10	11	subs used
25	H 1/1	SCUNTHORPE	2,287	2	46	L 0-3	0-0	Daws 53, 77, Lister 61 / Ref: D Allison	Walton	Hinshelwood	Hedman	Chatterton	Hill	Williams	White	Wilkins	Tempest	English	Grenfell*	Keane
									Taylor M	Russell	Longden	Taylor K	Lister	Money	Dixon	Harle	Nicol	Flounders	Daws	

Brown becomes manager of the month, whilst Walker is appointed reserve manager at Norwich. Scunthorpe's late change to a yellow kit, after an apprentice had washed reds and whites together, dazzles hapless U's. Walton hesitates as Tony Daws approaches, who finds an empty net.

No	Date		Att	Pos	Pt	F-A	H-T	Scorers, Times, and Referees	1	2	3	4	5	6	7	8	9	10	11	subs used
26	A 2/1	PETERBOROUGH	3,666	3	46	L 0-2	0-0	White 56, Luke 81 / Ref: N Butler	Walton	Hinshelwood	Hedman	Chatterton	Baker	Williams	White*	Wilkins	Tempest	Grenfell	Williams	Keane
									Neenan	Paris	Collins	Gooding	Gunn	Price	Nightingale	Halsall	White	Kerr	Luke	

U's happy Christmas turns into a sour New Year at rain-lashed London Road. Walton deflects Mick Gooding's shot onto the bar, Dean White reacts first. Mark Nightingale's free-kick off the post ends United's proud unbeaten away run when Noel Luke wins the race for the rebound.

No	Date		Att	Pos	Pt	F-A	H-T	Scorers, Times, and Referees	1	2	3	4	5	6	7	8	9	10	11	subs used
27	H 15/1	HARTLEPOOL	1,768	3	47	D 0-0	0-0	Ref: A Ward	Walton	Hinshelwood	Hedman	Williams	Hill	English	White	Wilkins	Tempest	Keane	Grenfell	
									Carr	Barratt	McKinnon	Nobbs	Smith	Haigh	Danskin*	Toman	Baker	Whellans	Borthwick	Tinkler

United revoke the 100% Members scheme, claiming that it had been a six-month trial. Cautious U's, anxious to stop the run of three defeats, force only one of four corners in the match. Andy Toman strikes the bar on the hour. The only cheer comes when referee Ward takes a tumble.

No	Date		Att	Pos	Pt	F-A	H-T	Scorers, Times, and Referees	1	2	3	4	5	6	7	8	9	10	11	subs used
28	A 30/1	SCARBOROUGH	2,155	4	47	L 1-3	0-0	Hinshelwood 84p / Graham 47, Cook 56, 64p / Ref: A Robinson	Walton	Hedman	Grenfell	Radford	Hill	English*	White	Wilkins	Tempest	Keane*	Grenfell	Ray/Walsh Mell
									Neenan	Podd	Kamara	Short	Bennyworth	Kendall	Russell !	Moss	Cook	Love K*	Graham	

Keeley (33) joins on loan from Oldham. Scarborough beat the U's 3-1 for the second time this season. Colin Russell's sending off (41) for aiming a kick at Walton, fires up Boro. 18-year-olds Walton and Ray, who needlessly handles an Ernie Moss cross, show their inexperience.

No	Date		Att	Pos	Pt	F-A	H-T	Scorers, Times, and Referees	1	2	3	4	5	6	7	8	9	10	11	subs used
29	H 5/2	CREWE	1,822	5	47	L 1-4	0-2	Tempest 47 / Goulet 15, 62, Fish 18p 22, English 88 (og) / Ref: J Moules	Greygoose	Hinshelwood	Hedman	Radford*	Keeley	English*	White	Wilkins	Tempest	English	Grenfell	Keane Morton
									Goodison	Pemberton	Murphy	Billing	Gage	Fishenden	Bodak*	Goulet	Milligan	Cutler		

Crisp is roundly booed as he presents Foley, who is joining Watford, with a memento. Non-members are allowed in for the first time. Wayne Goodison's second-minute drive clearly hits the stanchion and rebounds out. Yank Brent Goulet hassles English into lobbing over Walton.

No	Date		Att	Pos	Pt	F-A	H-T	Scorers, Times, and Referees	1	2	3	4	5	6	7	8	9	10	11	subs used
30	A 13/2	CARDIFF	5,458	6	47	L 0-1	0-0	Ford 49 / Ref: D Hutchinson	Walton	Hinshelwood	Hedman	Wilkins	Keeley	Hill	White	Keane	Tempest	English	Grenfell*	Bartlett
									Wood	Bater	Platnauer	Wimbleton	Stevenson	Boyle	Curtis*	Ford	Gilligan	McDermott	Bartlett	Mardenborough

Baker asks for a move. U's look into ground sharing at one of the local sides whilst the new Turner Rise stadium is built. In-form Cardiff beat Wolves 4-1 last week. U's lack of fire-power costs them dearly. Grenfell has an opportunity to level on 84 minutes, but contrives to miss.

No	Date		Att	Pos	Pt	F-A	H-T	Scorers, Times, and Referees	1	2	3	4	5	6	7	8	9	10	11	subs used
31	H 19/2	BURNLEY	2,520	10	47	L 0-1	0-1	Reeves 32 / Ref: R Lewis	Walton	Smith	Coleman	Coleman	Keeley	Hill	White	Wilkins	Tempest	English	Grenfell*	Keane/Hedman Grewcock
									Pearce	Daniel*	Deakin	Britton	Davis	Gardner	Farrell	Reeves	Taylor	Comstive	Hostin	

Brown moves swiftly after Chatterton breaks his leg in the reserves, signing Coleman, (20), from Bournemouth. When asked about promotion, Brown vows 'we are going up as champions', but blames Walton and Smith for the Clarets' goal by Sheffield Wed loanee, David Reeves.

No	Date		Att	Pos	Pt	F-A	H-T	Scorers, Times, and Referees	1	2	3	4	5	6	7	8	9	10	11	subs used
32	H 26/2	NEWPORT	1,784	12	48	D 0-0	0-0	Ref: K Barratt	Walton	Smith	Coleman	Hinshelwood	Keeley	Hill	White !	Wilkins	Tempest	English	Grenfell	
									Coles	Hodson	Sherlock	Carr	Williams	Osborne	Jones	Gibbins	Brook	Mann	Bodin	

Brown personally takes Walton for shooting practice. U's have slumped since the turn of the year with one point from the last 21. Newport are virtually certain to drop out of the league. White is dismissed (86) for striking Adrian Mann. Coleman comes closest to breaking the deadlock.

No	Date		Att	Pos	Pt	F-A	H-T	Scorers, Times, and Referees	1	2	3	4	5	6	7	8	9	10	11	subs used
33	A 1/3	SWANSEA	4,011	7	51	W 2-1	0-0	Tempest 63, White 74 / Love 90 / Ref: B Stevens	Walton	Smith	Coleman	Hinshelwood	Hetzke	Hill	White	Wilkins*	Tempest	English	Grenfell	Keane
									Guthrie	Harrison	Lewis J	Lewis D	Knill	James	Davies	Raynor	McCarthy*	Pascoe	Love	Andrews

Hetzke, £10,000 from Chester, replaces Keeley who returns to Oldham. Forrest is loaned from Ipswich to help Walton. United pick St David's Day to get back on the winning track. Hetzke is dominant and equals a record as the fourteenth player to make his U's debut in any one season.

No	Date		Att	Pos	Pt	F-A	H-T	Scorers, Times, and Referees	1	2	3	4	5	6	7	8	9	10	11	subs used
34	H 4/3	WREXHAM	1,797	12	51	L 1-2	1-2	Coleman 18 / Burton 7, Carter 38 / Ref: A Buksh	Forrest	Smith	Coleman	Hinshelwood	Hetzke	Hill	White	Wilkins	Tempest	English	Grenfell	Keane
									Salmon	Salathiel	Wright	Jones	Williams	Flynn	Preece	Hunter	Burton !	Russell	Carter	

U's seek council permission to increase the safe capacity to 6,500. Canadian U-21 international Forrest is a record fifth different United keeper in a League season. Steve Buxton is sent off for kicking White. Coleman grabs his first United goal, clipping a 20-yarder into the top corner.

35   A   LEYTON ORIENT   12/3   3,125 | 12   D   0-0 | 7   52 | 0-0

Forrest   Hedman   Coleman   Hinshelwood   Hetzke   Hill   Keane   Wilkins   Tempest   English   Grenfell
Wells   Howard   Day   Sitton   Smalley   Conroy   Hales   Castle   Hull   Jurpett   Comfort

The third goal-less draw between these sides in the past four meetings. Keane, replacing the suspended White, creates most of U's openings. The draw hinders both sides' promotion hopes, a win would have put United a point behind their east London rivals, but U's remain mid-table.
Ref: H King

---

36   A   DARLINGTON   19/3   2,034 | 12   L   0-2 | 4   52 | 0-0

Forrest   Hedman   Coleman   Hinshelwood   Hetzke   Hill   Keane   Wilkins   Tempest   English   Grenfell
Granger   Outterside   Morgan   Hine   Robinson   Bonnyman   Roberts A   Ward   MacDonald   Clayton   Stonehouse

Bonnyman 60, MacDonald 79
Ref: J Ireland

White asks for a transfer. The sodden pitch passes an early morning inspection and despite creating plenty of chances, U's fall to two second-half strikes. Phil Bonnyman arrives on the end of Mark Hine's cross. Clayton's header slips from Forrest's grasp into Gary MacDonald's path.

---

37   H   CAMBRIDGE   25/3   2,146 | 12   D   0-0 | 15   53 | 0-0

Forrest   Hedman   Radford   Hinshelwood   Hetzke   English   Keane*   Wilkins   Tempest   Hill   Grenfell   —   Farrell
Bastock   Poole   Kimble A   Crowe   Smith   Beck   Rigby   Clayton   Lawrence   Fuccillo   Hollis   —   Benjamin*

Ref: P Don

The re-arranged game with Hereford was called off last Tuesday due to power failure in the main stand that plunged the changing rooms into darkness forty mins prior to kick-off. Brown fails to sign Paul Mariner on deadline day, whilst Coleman returns, unsigned, to Bournemouth.

---

38   H   HALIFAX   1/4   1,992 | 11   W   2-1 | 20   56 | 0-1

Forrest   Hedman   Radford   Hinshelwood*   Williams*   Hill   White   Wilkins   Tempest   English   Grenfell   —   Kendall/Farrell
Roche   Brown   Matthews N   Matthews M   Robinson   Shaw   Martin   Thornber   Duffield   Allison   Richardson   —   Kendall*/Farrell*

Hinshelwood 62, Farrell 80 | Matthews N 12
Ref: K Cooper

Defensive lynch-pin Hetzke is ruled out for the season with an Achilles problem. Brown makes the players watch the 'video nasty' of the Cambridge bore. Banners appear calling for Brown's head. U's secure a first home win in three months via 19-year-old Luton loanee Farrell.

---

39   A   WOLVES   4/4   13,433 | 13   L   0-2 | 1   56 | 0-1

Forrest   Hedman   Radford   Hinshelwood*   Williams   Hill   White   Wilkins   Tempest   English   Grenfell   —   Kendall/Vaughan
Kendall   Bellamy   Venus   Streete   Robertson   Robinson   Dennison   Chard   Bull   Mutch   Holmes   —   Vaughan*

Bull 10, 75
Ref: K Walmsley

Steve Bull's double takes his season's tally to 44, creating a new Wolves scoring record. Andy Mutch flicks on a Phil Chard throw for his first. The killer second comes when Holmes lays back Nigel Vaughan's cross into the path of the burly striker. Sub Farrell twice tests Mark Kendall.

---

40   H   ROCHDALE   8/4   1,864 | 12   W   1-0 | 20   59 | 0-0

Forrest   Hedman*   Radford   Smith   Hicks   Hill   Farrell   Wilkins   Tempest   English   Grenfell*   —   Keane*/Williams / Holden
Welch   Smart   Stanton   Mellish   Bramhall   Lomax   Seasman   Simmonds   Moss   Warren   Harris   —   Holden*

Tempest 51
Ref: P Danson

Trialist Hicks, from Wisbech, makes a surprise debut at the heart of U's defence as the injury crisis deepens. Dale include 39-year-old Ernie Moss, who has already played against U's twice this season with Scarborough. Wilkins' cross flies past Keith Welch via the head of Tempest.

---

41   A   TORQUAY   15/4   3,508 | 12   D   0-0 | 5   60 | 0-0

Forrest   Hedman   Radford*   Smith   Hicks   Hill   Farrell   Wilkins   Tempest   English   Hinshelwood*   —   Keane/White / Dawkins/Dobson
Allen   McNichol   Kelly   Dobson   Coles   Impey   Sharpe   Lloyd   Caldwell   Loram   Gibbins

Ref: K Cooper

Crisp considers building a stadium that will house both U's and the Colchester Gladiators American football team. Plainmoor. operates its own 100% Members scheme following regular trouble in the resort. Torquay bad-boy, Dave Caldwell, has been red-carded five times this season.

---

42   H   HEREFORD   19/4   1,367 | 8   W   1-0 | 20   63 | 0-0

Forrest   Hedman   Radford   Smith   Hicks   Hill   Farrell*   Wilkins   Tempest   English   Reeves   —   Keane / Maddy
Rose   Rodgerson   Devine   Stevens   Pejic   Spooner   McLoughlin   Dalziel   Stant   Benbow   Leonard   —   Maddy*

Tempest 55
Ref: M Dimblebee

U's faint play-off hopes continue. due mainly to the shortcomings of their rivals. This third successive home win means that U's are level on points with L Orient, who occupy the last play-off berth. Tempest dummies a cross-field ball by Reeves and collects the return from Radford.

---

43   A   CARLISLE   23/4   1,496 | 10   L   0-4 | 23   63 | 0-2

Forrest   Hedman   Radford*   Smith   Radford*   English   White   Wilkins   Tempest   Keane*   Reeves   —   Farrell/Daniels
Prudhoe   Clark   Gorman   Saddington   Wright   Robinson   Bishop   Fyfe   Poskett   Halpin   Rowell   —   Castle*

Fyfe 11, 90, Saddington 20, Halpin 80
Ref: G Courtney

Crisp has preliminary talks with Ipswich about a temporary ground-share. Hill breaks his arm in training. Youngster Daniels becomes the 18th debutant. Ex-supermarket shelf-stacker Tony Fyfe comes out of Sunday football to kill off any lingering promotion hopes with a smart pair.

---

44   H   STOCKPORT   29/4   1,607 | 10   W   2-0 | 20   66 | 0-0

Forrest   Smith   Grenfell   Hedman   Hicks   Hill   Farrell   Wilkins*   Tempest   English   Reeves   —   Keane/White / Radford
Marples   Scott   McKenzie   Thorpe   Bullock   Cronin   Hodkinson   Colville   Entwistle   Hartford   Hendrie

Tempest 59, Wilkins 60
Ref: A Gunn

This pair takes U's home total to eight goals this year. Grenfell escapes down the left and his cross gives unmarked Tempest ample time to pick his spot. Sixty seconds later, Keane's low cross was met at the far post by Wilkins, carrying a dislocated shoulder, for his eleventh of the term.

---

45   A   BOLTON   2/5   5,540 | 10   L   0-4 | 4   66 | 0-2

Walton   Hedman   Grenfell   Hedman   Hunter   English   White*   Wilkins   Tempest   Keane   Reeves*   —   Farrell/Daniels [Chandler 82] / Radford/Farrell
Felgate   Scott   Neal   Savage   Came   Winstanley   May   Thompson   Thomas   Morgan   Darby   —   Chandler*

Savage 6, Thomas 37, Came 57, [Chandler 82]
Ref: T Simpson

Ipswich recall Forrest. Walton. producing heroics to keep the score in single figures as Wanderers press for promotion. is fouled at a free-kick, dropping the ball to Jeff Chandler for the fourth. Trevor Morgan fouls Keane (89). Tempest blasts the spot-kick. like U's hopes, over and out.

---

46   H   TRANMERE   6/5   1,704 | 9   D   0-0 | 14   67 | 0-0

Walton   Hedman   Radford   Hunter   Hicks   English   White   Wilkins   Tempest   Farrell   Grenfell   —   Murray
Gorton   Higgins   McCarrick   Martindale   Hughes   Vickers   Morrisey   Bishop   Steel   Muir   Mungall   —   Murray*

Ref: D Elleray

The game is rumoured to be U's last at Layer Road. if all the speculation concerning the new stadium comes to fruition. Hunter gets a call up as a reward for his selection in the Northern Irish youth team. The season ends in uncertainty with fans calling for the head of Crisp and Brown.

Home Average 1,769   Away 3,143

BARCLAYS DIVISION 4 (CUP-TIES)

Manager: Walker ⇨ Foley ⇨ Brown

SEASON 1987-88

Littlewoods Cup

1:1 A FULHAM 18/8 — L F-A 1-3 H-T 1-0 — Att 2,782 (3:)
Scorers, Times, and Referees: Walsh 45. Davies 49, Marshall 68, Rosenior 70. Ref: B Stevens

1	2	3	4	5	6	7	8	9	10	11	subs used
Lake*	Hinshelwood	Norman	Chatterton	Baker	Hedman	White	English	Walsh	Lowe	Wilkins	Reeves
Stannard	*Langley*	*Thomas*	*Lewington*	*Hopkins*	*Oakes*	*Marshall*	*Skinner*	*Rosenior*	*Davies*	*Barnett*	*Grenfell/Reeves*

Norwich refuse to let loan keeper Benstead become cup-tied. His replacement, Lake, hobbles off on 32 minutes with a career-ending knee injury. English goes in goal but is helpless to prevent any of the Cottagers' goals. U's take the lead during six minutes of first-half injury-time.

1:2 H FULHAM 25/8 — L 0-2 0-0 — Att 1,554 (3:1)
Scorers: Barnett 48p, Davies 59. Ref: K Morton
(Colchester lost 1-5 on aggregate)

1	2	3	4	5	6	7	8	9	10	11	subs used
Walton	Hinshelwood	Norman*	Chatterton	Baker	Hedman	White	English	Walsh*	Lowe	Wilkins	
Stannard	*Langley*	*Thomas*	*Lewington*	*Hopkins*	*Oakes*	*Marshall*	*Skinner*	*Rosenior*	*Davies*	*Barnett*	*Kerrins/Donnellan*

Welshman Walton (18) becomes U's fourth keeper in less than a week, joining on loan from Luton. U's bow out of the League Cup at the first stage for the fourth year in a row. Experienced Gordon Davies 'wins' a penalty by diving over Walton to put the tie out of Colchester's reach.

Freight Rover/Sherpa Van Trophy

0 H PETERBOROUGH 13/10 — W 3-2 2-0 — Att 912 (4:12)
Scorers: Tempest 3, 52, Norman 35. Nuttell 70, Gooding 84. Ref: K Morton

1	2	3	4	5	6	7	8	9	10	11	subs used
Walton	Hinshelwood	Grenfell	Chatterton	Baker	Hedman	White	Wilkins	Tempest	Norman	Reeves	
Neenan	*Paris*	*Gunn*	*Gooding*	*Nightingale*	*Price*	*Luke*	*Halsall !*	*Lawrence*	*Nuttell*	*Collins*	*Carr/Butterworth*

U's are thankful that this tie is not two-legged, as they surrender a three-goal lead. Tempest heads Reeves's free-kick for U's third. Teenager Micky Nuttell gets free of Hedman to head his first senior goal. Mick Gooding adds a second. Mick Halsall is sent-off in the tunnel afterwards.

0 A CAMBRIDGE 24/11 — D 0-0 0-0 — Att 857 (4:13)
Ref: D Vickers

1	2	3	4	5	6	7	8	9	10	11	subs used
Benstead	Hinshelwood	Grenfell	Chatterton	Baker	Hedman	White	Wilkins	Tempest	English	Reeves*	
Branagan	*Poole*	*Murray*	*Crowe*	*Beattie*	*Turner*	*Butler*	*Clayton*	*Rigby*	*Purdie*	*Kimble*	*Hill/Horwood*

Having already beaten Posh, the result of their clash with Cambridge is immaterial to the U's as they qualify for the area quarter-finals with this bore-draw. Hill's international clearance comes through and he recovers from a knock to make his debut Wilkins strikes the post (88).

1 H LEYTON ORIENT 19/1 — D 1-1 1-1 aet — Att 1,351 (4:2)
Scorers: White 26. Juryeff 18. Ref: D Hedges
(Colchester won 6-5 on penalties)

1	2	3	4	5	6	7	8	9	10	11	subs used
Walton	Hinshelwood	Hedman	Radford	Hill	English	White	Wilkins	Tempest	Keane	Grenfell	
Wells	*Howard*	*Dickenson*	*Sitton*	*Day*	*Harvey*	*Hales*	*Ketteridge**	*Nugent*	*Juryeff*	*Comfort*	*Hull/Conroy*

U's progress through English's sudden-death kick after O's Ian Harvey had struck the bar. English's was the 14th kick. Hedman had saved following John Sitton's effort against the bar. Tempest, earlier, missed a 17th-minute penalty, striking the post after Peter Well's foul on him.

2 H NOTTS CO 9/2 — L 2-3 0-1 — Att 1,564 (3:2)
Scorers: White 51, 59. McParland 2, Thorpe 60, Lund 71. Ref: J Martin

1	2	3	4	5	6	7	8	9	10	11	subs used
Walton	Smith	Hedman	Chatterton	Keeley	Hill	White	Keane	Tempest	English	Reeves	
Leonard	*Smalley*	*With*	*Kevan*	*Yates*	*Mills*	*Birtles*	*McParland*	*Lund*	*Pike*	*Thorpe*	*Thorpe*

County boss John Barnwell employs ex-Man Utd and Notts F striker Gary Birtles as a centre-back. U's bow out of the cup having yet to win in 1988. Notts open on 70 seconds with Ian McParland's wind-assisted effort. Walton's legs save from Gary Mills, only for Gary Lund to net.

FA Cup

1 H TAMWORTH 14/11 — W 3-0 0-0 — Att 3,215 (BB:1)
Scorers: Wilkins 55, Tempest 56, Chatterton 87p. Ref: J Ashworth

1	2	3	4	5	6	7	8	9	10	11	subs used
Walton	Hinshelwood	Grenfell	Chatterton	Baker	Hedman	White	Wilkins	Tempest	English	Reeves	
Hemming	*Lockett*	*Brown B*	*McCormack*	*Poole*	*Cartwright**	*Myers*	*Stanton*	*Maddocks*	*Rathbone*	*Gilmour*	*Brown G/Haynes*

Walton returns on loan. 'The Banks' Brewery' Midland League side are followed by 800 fans. U's winning run is stretched to eight. Chatterton scores a record-setting fifth penalty in five consecutive matches. Boss Brown's brother, Gary, is involved in fouling Wilkins for the spot-kick.

2 H HEREFORD 5/12 — W 3-2 2-1 — Att 2,216 (4:19)
Scorers: Chatterton 2p, Wilkins 37, Hill 76. Stant 9, Phillips 89. Ref: A Gunn

1	2	3	4	5	6	7	8	9	10	11	subs used
Walton	Hinshelwood	Hedman	Chatterton	Baker	Hill	White	Wilkins*	Tempest	English	Reeves	
Rose	*Jones*	*Devine*	*Stevens*	*Pejic*	*Spooner*	*Dalziel*	*Bowyer*	*Phillips*	*Stant*	*Leadbitter*	*Walsh*

Hill on his full debut scores the important third goal, glancing home a brave diving-header from Hinshelwood's cross. Chatterton scores his seventh penalty in nine games, when Gary Stevens hauls down Tempest. Wilkins 'scores' fractionally after Referee Gunn's half-time whistle.

3 A PLYMOUTH 11/1 — L 0-2 0-2 — Att 10,351 (2:13)
Scorers: Cooper S 41, Matthews 44. Ref: I Hemley

1	2	3	4	5	6	7	8	9	10	11	subs used
Walton	Hinshelwood	Hedman	Chatterton*	Hill	White	Keane	Tempest	English	Grenfell	Walsh	
Cherry	*Brimacombe*	*Cooper I*	*Burrows*	*Marker*	*Smith*	*Hodges*	*Matthews*	*Tynan*	*Cooper S*	*Anderson*	*Walsh*

U's are in the third round for the first time in four years. Plans to provide a supporters train fail through lack of interest. The game is postponed through rain anyway. In the re-staged game, Steve Cooper completely mis-hits the first. John Matthews controls with his hand for the second.

League Table

	Team	P	Home W	D	L	F	A	Away W	D	L	F	A	Pts
1	Wolves	46	15	3	5	47	19	12	6	5	35	24	90
2	Cardiff	46	15	6	2	39	14	9	7	7	27	27	85
3	Bolton	46	15	6	2	42	12	7	6	10	24	30	78
4	Scunthorpe	46	14	5	4	42	20	6	12	5	34	31	77
5	Torquay	46	10	6	7	34	16	11	7	5	32	25	77
6	Swansea *	46	9	7	7	35	28	11	3	9	27	28	70
7	Peterborough	46	10	5	8	28	26	10	5	8	24	27	70
8	Leyton Orient	46	13	4	6	55	27	6	8	9	30	36	69
9	COLCHESTER	46	10	5	8	23	22	9	5	9	24	29	67
10	Burnley	46	12	5	6	31	22	8	2	13	26	40	67
11	Wrexham	46	13	3	7	46	26	7	6	13	23	32	66
12	Scarborough	46	12	8	3	38	19	6	12	5	18	29	65
13	Darlington	46	13	6	4	39	25	5	5	13	32	44	65
14	Tranmere **	46	14	2	7	43	20	5	7	11	18	33	64
15	Cambridge	46	10	6	7	32	24	6	7	10	18	28	61
16	Hartlepool	46	9	7	7	25	25	6	7	10	25	32	59
17	Crewe	46	7	11	5	25	19	6	8	9	32	34	58
18	Halifax ***	46	11	7	5	37	25	3	7	13	17	34	55
19	Hereford	46	8	7	8	25	27	6	5	12	16	32	54
20	Stockport	46	7	7	9	26	26	5	8	10	18	32	51
21	Rochdale	46	5	9	9	28	34	6	6	11	19	42	48
22	Exeter	46	8	6	9	33	29	3	7	13	20	39	46
23	Carlisle	46	9	5	9	38	33	3	3	17	19	53	44
24	Newport	46	4	5	14	19	36	2	2	19	16	69	25
		1104	253	142	157	830	574	157	142	253	574	830	1511

* promoted after play-offs
** deducted 2 points
*** deducted 1 point

Odds & ends

Double wins: (3) Halifax, Rochdale, Swansea.
Double defeats: (2) Scarborough, Wolves.
Won from behind: (2) Cardiff (h), Halifax (h).
Lost from in front: (1) Scarborough (h).
High spots: Nine games without defeat from September.
Topping the table at the turn of the New Year.
Low spots: The controversial Members Only ground entry scheme.
Walker's departure, did he resign or was he pushed?
Uncertainty over the new stadium and sale of Layer Road.
Sale of Adcock, Chamberlain, Farrell and Day – the squad's backbone.
The crippling injury crisis.
Instability due to the record-breaking need to blood 19 debutants.

Player of the Year: Colin Hill.
Ever presents: (1) Richard Wilkins.
Hat-tricks: (0).
Leading scorer: Dale Tempest 13 (incl. 1 in Freight Rover Trophy).

Appearances and Goals

Player	Lge	Sub	LC	Sub	FA	Sub	Goals Lge	LC	FA	Tot
Angell, Darren	1									
Baker, Terry	15		2		2					
Benstead, Graham	18									
Chatterton, Nicky	26		2		3		7		2	9
Coleman, David	6						1			1
Daniels, Scott		1								
English, Tony	43		2		3		2			2
Farrell, Sean	4	5					1			1
Forrest, Craig	11									
Grenfell, Steve	39	2		1	3					
Hedman, Rudi	41	1	2		3					
Hetzke, Steve	5									
Hicks, Stuart	7									
Hill, Colin	22	3	2		2				1	1
Hinshelwood, Paul	40		2		3		5			5
Hunter, Lee	1									
Keane, Tommy	9	7								
Keeley, Glenn	4									
Lake, Trevor			1							
Lowe, Simon	7	3	2				1			1
Norman, Sean	6	2	2							
Radford, Mark	12	2	2							
Ray, John		1								
Reeves, John	18	2	2		1		1			1
Smith, Gary	11									
Tempest, Dale	44				3		11		1	12
Walsh, Mario	4	7	2			2	2			2
Walton, Mark	17		1		3					
White, Winston	40	1	2		3		7	1		8
Wilkins, Richard	46		2		3		9		2	11
Williams, Keith	9	1								
31 players used	506	38	22	3	33	2	47	1	6	54

BARCLAYS LEAGUE DIVISION 4 — Manager: Brown ⇨ Foley ⇨ Wallace — SEASON 1988-89

No	Date	Att	Pos	Pt	F-A	H-T	1	2	3	4	5	6	7	8	9	10	11	subs used
1	H York 27/8	1,664	3	W	1-0	0-0	Walton	Hedman	Cartwright	Barnett!	Hetzke	Hill	White	Wilkins	Tempest	Swindleh'rst	Grenfell	Canham
							Marples	Bradshaw	Johnson	Wilson*	Fazackerley	Smith	Howlett	Spooner	Hellewell	Banton	Himsworth	
2	A Tranmere 2/9	3,401	4	D	0-0	0-0	Walton	English	Cartwright	Barnett	Hetzke	Hill	Wilkins	White	Tempest	Swindlehurst	Grenfell*	Bedford
							Nixon	Higgins	Williams	Martindale	Moore	Vickers	Morrisey	Harvey	Steel	Muir	Mungall	
3	H Doncaster 9/9	1,726	12	L 4	0-1	0-0	Walton	English	Cartwright	Radford	Hicks	Hill*	Wilkins	White	Tempest	Swindleh'st*	Grenfell	Bedford/Hunter
							Malcolm	Douglas	Robinson R	Raffell	Beattie	Raven	Robinson L	Gaughan	Rankine	Dobson	Kimble	
4	A Wrexham 16/9	2,873	13	D 5	2-2	1-0	Walton	Hedman	Cartwright	Radford	Hicks	Hill	Wilkins	White*	Tempest	Swindlehurst	Bedford	Hunter
							Salmon	Salathiel	Wright*	Bowden*	Beaumont	Jones J	Flynn	Thackeray	Buxton	Russell	Cooper	Preece/Hunter
5	H Scarborough 20/9	1,420	12	W 8	3-1	1-0	Walton	Hedman	Cartwright	Barnett*	Hicks	Hill	Wilkins	White	Tempest	Swindlehurst	Bedford	Radford
							Blackwell	Kamara	Thompson N	Short Crg	Richards	Bennyworth	Morris	Cook*	Norris	Brook*	Graham	Mell
6	A Burnley 24/9	7,177	12 3	L 8	0-2	0-1	Walton	Hedman	Cartwright	Barnett	Hicks	Hill	Wilkins	White	Tempest	Swindlehurst	Bedford*	Radford
							Pearce	Daniel	Deakin*	Farrell	Davis	Gardner	Britton	Oghani	O'Connell	Comstive	Atkinson	Rowell
7	H Lincoln 1/10	1,529	16 10	L 8	1-3	1-1	Walton	Hedman	Cartwright	Barnett	Hicks	Hill	White	Hunter	Tempest	Swindlehurst	Wilkins*	Radford
							Wallington	Evans	Nicholson*	Brown	Bressington	Matthewson	Davis	Cumming	Hobson	Clarke	Sertori	James
8	A Carlisle 4/10	2,193	16 24	W 11	2-1	0-0	Walton	Hedman	Cartwright	Barnett	Hicks	Hill	White	Hunter	Tempest	Swindlehurst	Wilkins	Radford
							Prudhoe	Graham	Walsh	Saddington	Ogley	Clark	Hetherington	Gorman	Daws	Fitzpatrick	Marshall	
9	H Scunthorpe 8/10	1,299	17 12	L 11	1-2	1-1	Walton	Hedman	Cartwright	Barnett!	Hicks	Hill	Hunter	White	Tempest	Swindlehurst	Wilkins*	Radford
							Musselwhite	Smalley	Rumble*	Taylor	Lister	Stevenson	Hodkinson	Harle	Daws	Flounders*	Brown	Longden/Richardson
10	A Leyton Orient 15/10	3,421	21 17	L 11	0-8	0-4	Walton	Hedman	Cartwright	Barnett*	Hicks	Hill	Hunter	White	Tempest	Juryeff	Comfort	Radford
							Wells	Howard	Dickenson	Hales	Day	Sitton	Baker	Ward	Hull	Juryeff	Comfort	
11	H Cambridge 21/10	2,138	22 7	L 11	1-2	0-0	Walton	Hedman	Bedford	Cartwright	Hicks	Hill	Wilkins	English	Tempest	Walsh	Grenfell!	Radford/Bennett
							Vaughan	Baillie	Kimble	Smith	Chapple	Beck	Clayton	Taylor	Reilly	Hamilton	Anderson	

Scorers, Times, and Referees

1. Tempest 58. Ref: R Pawley.
During the summer the club announces a loss of £151k. Referee Pawley, new to the league list, sends off debutant Barnett. The 21-year-old, signed from Windsor, was booked seven minutes earlier. Tempest finishes off a smart move involving Swindlehurst to fire past Chris Marples.

2. Ref: K Cooper.
Rovers' success in last season's Mercantile Credit Centenary Cup at Wembley makes them one of the favourites for the title. Eric Nixon, a £60k buy from Man C, makes three reaction saves in the same attack. U's have now kept three successive clean sheets, but have a solitary goal.

3. Rankine 80. Ref: J Moules.
Hetzke and Barnett are injured, giving a recall to Hicks. Dave Mackay includes six of last year's FA Youth Cup final side. Rovers' enterprise is rewarded ten minutes from time. Gary Kimble reaches the by-line and crosses to Mark Rankine, who scores from the narrowest of angles.

4. Hunter 55, Cooper 68. Ref: R Hamer.
Grenfell joins White and Walsh on the list. Skipper Swindlehurst nets his first for the club, only for the Welshmen to roar back after the break. Sub Geoff Hunter levels, followed by Graham Cooper's fifth in six games. Radford nutmegs Neil Salathiel, and crosses to unmarked Tempest.

5. Swindlehurst 23p, Tempest 88, Wilkins 90, Cook 50p. Ref: K Morton.
Steve Richards fouls Hicks for U's penalty. Mitch Cook levels the scores following Barnett's foul on Tommy Graham. With two minutes left, Radford sends Tempest bursting in to score, followed two minutes later, by Wilkins' goal after Tempest had created the opportunity.

6. Rowell 43, O'Connell 55. Ref: A Wilkie.
Ex-U's player Andy Farrell is involved in the build-up to Brendan O'Connell's clincher. Tempest nods wide from six yards to spurn hope of an equaliser, after Gary Rowell had given Clarets the lead. Hicks hauls down O'Connell late on, but Walton blocks Paul Comstive's penalty-kick.

7. Swindlehurst 14, Hobson 5, 90, Hill 51 (og). Ref: M James.
U's score three times in the first half, but efforts from Tempest (8) and Barnett (33) are ruled out for fouls. Gordon Hobson, Imps record buy from Southampton (£70k), provides a cross that Hill turns into his own net. Hobson's second goal wraps it up in the second min of added time.

8. Tempest 47, Swindlehurst 61, Sendall 48. Ref: A Simmons.
Mark Prudhoe fumbles Swindlehurst's feeble shot for Tempest to easily slot his fourth goal of the season. Walton joins the circus by sending a drop-kick direct to Richard Sendall, who steers a diagonal shot past the keeper. Swindlehurst, nursing an earlier head wound, grabs the winner.

9. Hedman 28, Flounders 13, Richardson 86. Ref: I Borrett.
Barnett, dubbed Psycho by fans, receives his second red card of the season twelve minutes from time after stamping on Kevin Taylor. U's are beaten by a late goal from sub Ian Richardson, who turns in a neat pass from Tony Daws. Hedman had cancelled out Andy Flounders' strike.

10. [Comfort 41, Hales 85p, Day 90] Hull 9, 53, 74, Sitton 11, Baker 20. Ref: P Durkin.
Yesterday, Brown predicted 'sooner or later one of our opponents is going to get a hiding. Let's hope it's Orient'. Barnett starts a three-match ban. United slip into the bottom four, suffering the heaviest defeat in their league history. U's fans cheer O's goals to hide their embarrassment.

11. English 88, Anderson 65, 79. Ref: G Pooley.
Brown, on three months board-designated trial in order to prove himself, resigns. U's have won 15 of 47 games played under Brown. Foley becomes caretaker. Colin Anderson's long-range effort takes a deflection off a divot, whilst his second comes via a George Reilly knockdown.

12 | A ROTHERHAM | 25/10 — 23 L 0-2 — Att: 4,066 (1 / 11)
Green 48, Williamson 90
Ref: J.Lloyd

United: Walton, Hedman, Bedford, **Kelly**, Hicks, Hill, Wilkins, English, Tempest*, Swindlehurst, Grenfell, Radford/Walsh
Rotherham: *O'Hanlon, Russell, Heald, Goodwin, Green, Crosby, Williams, Williamson, Haycock, Hazel*, Grealish*

Cartwright returns to Tamworth, as 24-year-old Scouser Tony Kelly arrives from West Brom. Swindlehurst has a hip injury. John Green volleys in a loose ball from a corner and Bobby Williamson strikes the bar twice, before forcing the ball from Walton's grasp in injury-time.

---

13 | H STOCKPORT | 28/10 — 23 D 1-1 — Att: 1,643 (17 / 12)
Tempest 37
Hill 48 (og)
Ref: P.Alcock

United: Walton, Hedman, Bedford, Kelly, Hicks, Hill, Wilkins, English, Tempest, Swindlehurst, Radford*, Hunter
Stockport: *Gorton, Butler, Hart, Logan, Thorpe, Scott, Wylde*, Angell, Coyle, Hartford`, Howard, Colville/Payne*

U's halt a run of three defeats at home. County, having lost on their last four visits, grab a lucky draw. Bedford, with a new lease of life under Foley, crosses for Tempest. A defensive lapse lets Mark Howard put in a cross that Hill, for the second time this term, puts into his own goal.

---

14 | A CREWE | 4/11 — 23 L 1-3 — Att: 2,787 (3 / 12)
Walsh 9
Gardiner 13, Edwards 63, Callaghan 76
Ref: D.Allison

United: Walton, Hedman, Bedford, Kelly, Hicks*, Hill, Wilkins, English, Tempest, Swindlehurst, Radford*, Grenfell/Daniels
Crewe: *Greygoose, Swain, Edwards, Billing, Macowat, Callaghan, Jasper, Murphy, Cronin, Gardiner, Fishenden*

Alex move to the top overnight, after giving United a one-goal start. Radford's deep cross gives Walsh his first of the season. Mark Gardiner quickly equalises as Walton stays rooted to his line. Paul Edwards (volley) and Aaron Callaghan (header) score from Dennis Cronin crosses.

---

15 | A HALIFAX | 8/11 — 23 L 2-3 — Att: 2,176 (7 / 12)
Kelly 13, Wilkins 84
Martin 42, McPhillips 45p, 87
Ref: J.Timmons

United: Walton, Hedman, Bedford, Kelly, Hicks, Hill*, Wilkins, English, Tempest, Swindlehurst, Barnett, Daniels
Halifax: *Roche, Richardson I, Barr W, Matthews M, Robinson, Bramall, Martin, Watson, McPhillips, Allison, Matthews N*

Northampton chase Hedman as U's face the divisions top scorers, with 34 to their credit. Five win-less games leaves U's just five points clear of bottom club Darlington. Kelly's first U's goal is cancelled out by a Terry McPhillips double, including a penalty for hands against Bedford.

---

16 | H TORQUAY | 11/11 — 22 D 2-2 — Att: 1,926 (9 / 13)
English 13, Kelly 85
Loram 62, Thompson 90
Ref: D.Elleray

United: **Coombe**, Hedman, Bedford, Kelly, Hicks, Hill, Wilkins*, English, Tempest, Swindlehurst, Barnett*, Radford/Daniels
Torquay: *Veysey, Holmes, Kelly, McNichol, Cole, Joyce, Smith J, Lloyd, Edwards*, Loram, Weston*, Thompson/Dawkins*

U's are heading for their first win in eight through Kelly's curling free-kick, but in the third minute of injury-time Richard Thompson nets to steal an equaliser. The time is added for Wilkins' serious injury. Darlington's first win in 16, at Carlisle, puts them three points behind the U's.

---

17 | H DARLINGTON | 25/11 — 24 L 1-2 — Att: 1,550 (23 / 13)
Radford 72
Worthington 26p, 62
Ref: A.Ward

United: **Coombe**, Hedman, Bedford, Kelly, Hicks, Bennett*, Radford, English*, Tempest, Swindlehurst, Barnett, Chatterton/Daniels
Darlington: *Batch, Robinson N, Morgan, McAndrew, Moore, Willis, McAughtrie, Hyde*, Clayton, Worthington, Emson, Bonnyman*

U's occupy 92nd spot in the league for the first time since 1972. Crisp returns from abroad to watch a game shrouded in fog, which makes it impossible to see the whole pitch. Hicks pulls down Paul Clayton, Gary Worthington nets the spot-kick and later gets on the end of a free-kick.

---

18 | A EXETER | 3/12 — 24 L 2-4 — Att: 2,132 (14 / 13)
Swindlehurst 25, Tempest 79
Taylor 18, Neville 30, Hiley 53, Row'm 88
Ref: K.Cooper

United: **Coombe**, Hedman, Bedford, Kelly, Hicks, Hedman, Radford*, English, Tempest, Swindlehurst Walsh, Tempest/Hetzke
Exeter: *Walter, Banks, Jones*, Rogers, Taylor, Cooper, Rowbotham, Hiley, Vinnicombe, Neville, Harrow`, Harris J*

City's £300k-rated defender Shaun Taylor, a target for Norwich, scores when Coombe drops a corner. By the time Scott Hiley makes it 1-3 the game looks over, but a double substitution and Tempest's goal gives the U's hope, only for Darren Rowbotham to catch them on the break.

---

19 | A ROCHDALE | 16/12 — 24 D 1-1 — Att: 1,258 (10 / 14)
Walsh 58
O'Shaughnessy 29
Ref: J.Key

United: Walton, Hedman, Bedford, Kelly*, Daniels, Hill, Barnett, English, Wilkins*, Walsh, Allinson, Tempest/Hetzke
Rochdale: *Welch, Lomax, Armitage, Reid, Sutton, Copeland, O'Shaughn'sy Smith, Beaumont*, Edmonds, Frain, Walling*

Tempest and Radford join Grenfell on the list. Allison re-joins on a free from Luton. Steve O'Shaughnessy slams a free-kick past U's two-man wall for Dale's goal. United gain a deserved point when Daniels' cross eludes Dale's defence but not Walsh, who sneaks in at the far post.

---

20 | H PETERBOROUGH | 26/12 — 24 L 1-2 — Att: 2,828 (14 / 14)
Walsh 65
Gunn 44p, McElhinney 87
Ref: I.Hemley

United: Walton, Hill, Bedford, Kelly, Daniels*, Hetzke, Barnett, English*, Tempest, Swindlehurst Walsh, Allinson, Tempest/Hicks
Peterborough: *Crichton, Collins, Gunn, Luke, McElhinney, Oakes, Langan, Halsall*, Cusack, Longhurst, Goldsmith, Philpott*

Hedman joins C Palace for a reported £100k fee. U's haven't won a home Boxing Day fixture since 1969. Kelly, normally the provider, fouls David Longhurst in the box. Walsh, guilty of glaring misses, levels, but a defensive lapse lets Irish international Gerry McElhinney nod home.

---

21 | H HARTLEPOOL | 30/12 — 24 L 1-2 — Att: 2,359 (16 / 14)
English 45
Borthwick 67, Stokes 78
Ref: V.Callow

United: Walton, Hill*, Bedford, Kelly, Daniels, Hetzke, Barnett, English, Tempest, Wilkins Walsh, Allinson*, Tempest/Radford
Hartlepool: *Moverley, Nobbs, McKinnon, Tinkler, Stokes, Baker, Honour, Toman, Borthwick, Grayson, Barratt*

Swindlehurst joins Posh on loan and Coombe is released Kelly, in the second min of injury-time, plays a super ball to English who beats Rob Moverley off Paul Baker. Baker makes amends heading Brian Honour's corner to John Borthwick and then finds Dave Stokes with a free-kick.

---

22 | A GRIMSBY | 2/1 — 24 D 2-2 — Att: 4,472 (20 / 15)
Wilkins 32, Allinson 76
O'Kelly 14, Alexander 26
Ref: S.Lodge

United: Walton, English, Bedford, Kelly*, Hetzke, Hill, Daniels, Barnett, Wilkins*, Walsh, Allinson*, Tempest/Radford
Grimsby: *Reece, McDermott, Agnew, Tillson, Lever, Cunnington, Watson, Saunders, O'Kelly, Jobling*, Alexander*, North/Cockerill*

Foley is full of praise for gutsy U's, who fight back from two down. Hetzke inadvertently nods down into Richard O'Kelly's path, then Kevin Jobling's cross finds Keith Alexander. Kelly's pass finds Wilkins for his fifth of the term. Allinson pokes past Reece for a deserved equaliser.

---

23 | H TRANMERE | 13/1 — 24 L 2-3 — Att: 3,458 (5 / 15)
Walsh 16, 50
McCarrick 53, Harvey 61, Vickers 89
Ref: M.James

United: Walton, English, Bedford, Kelly, Hicks*, Hetzke, Daniels, Barnett*, Tempest, Wilkins Walsh, Allinson, Hill/**Taylor**
Tranmere: *Nixon, Higgins, McCarrick, Martindale, Hughes*, Vickers, Malkin, Harvey, Steel, Muir, Mungall, Bishop*

The Evening Gazette starts a 'Save Our Soccer' campaign, recognising United could drop to non-league. Jock Wallace, (53), is U's new boss. It was Friday the 13th! prompting the match to be featured on ITV's Saint & Greavsie. Steve Vickers spoils the party, slamming in a loose ball.

BARCLAYS LEAGUE DIVISION 4 — Manager: Brown ⇨ Foley ⇨ Wallace — SEASON 1988-89

No	Date	Att	Pos	Pt	F A	H-T	Scorers, Times, and Referees	1	2	3	4	5	6	7	8	9	10	11	subs used
24	A YORK 21/1	2,219	24 18	L 15	0 2	0-1	Dixon 33, Howlett 66 — Ref R Dilkes	Walton / Marples	Coleman / Bradshaw	Bedford / Johnson	Kelly* / Reid	Hicks / Greenough	Hetzke / Smith	Daniels / Dunn*	English / Spooner	Tempest* / Helliwell	Walsh / Dixon	Allinson / Canham	Taylor/Hill / Howlett
25	A SCARBOROUGH 4/2	1,913	24 5	D 16	0 0	0-0	Ref: K Hackett	McAllister / Ironside	Hicks / Kamara	Bedford / Thompson N Short Crg	Taylor / Richards	Hetzke / Bennyworth* Morris	Hill / Cook	Barnett / Olsson	English / Brook	Wilkins / Graham	Walsh	Allinson	Adams
26	H BURNLEY 10/2	3,809	24 8	D 17	2 2	0-2	Allinson 62, Walsh 74 / White 14, 16p — Ref M Bailey	McAllister / Pearce	Hicks / Measham	Bedford / Farrell*	Taylor / Britton	Hetzke / Davis	Hill / Gardner	Allinson / White	English / Oghani	Wilkins / O'Connell	Walsh / Comstive	McGee* / Deakin	Barnett / Rowell
27	A SCUNTHORPE 18/2	4,286	24 3	W 20	3 2	2-0	Wilkins 10, English 23, Warner 84 / Lister 57, Nicol 75 — Ref K Redfern	McAllister / Mussewhite Smalley	Hicks / Stevenson*	Bedford / Taylor	Taylor* / Nicol	Hetzke / Brown	Hill / Lister	Allinson / Cowling	English / Daws	Wilkins / Flounders*	Walsh* / Hamilton	McGee*	Daniels/Warner / Hodkinson/Cork
28	H LEYTON ORIENT 24/2	4,269	24 12	W 23	1 0	1-0	Allinson 20 — Ref I Borrett	McAllister / Heald	Hicks / Howard	Bedford / Dickenson	Taylor / Castle	Hetzke / Day	Hill / Sitton	Barnett / Baker	English / Ward	Warner* / Cooper*	Walsh* / Campbell	McGee* / Comfort	Bennett / Hull
29	H ROTHERHAM 28/2	3,671	24 4	D 24	1 1	0-1	Allinson 81 / Grealish 27 — Ref D Hedges	McAllister / O'Hanlon	Hicks / Russell	Bedford / Scott	Taylor* / Grealish	Hetzke / Barnsley	Hill / Crosby	Allinson / Dempsey	English / Goodwin*	Tempest / Williamson	Warner / Haycock	Wilkins / Hazel	Bennett / Buckley
30	A CAMBRIDGE 5/3	4,205	24 9	L 24	1 3	1-2	Taylor 32, Leadbitter 42, Ryan 53 — Ref J Moules	McAllister / Vaughan*	Hicks / Clayton	Stafford* / Kimble	Taylor / Turner	Hetzke* / Chapple	Hill / Daish	Barnett / Dennis	English / Beck	Warner / Ryan	Tempest / Taylor	Wilkins / Leadbitter	Daniels/Radford / Croft
31	H CREWE 10/3	3,088	24 1	W 27	2 1	1-1	English 19, 82 / Murphy 43 — Ref A Seville	McAllister / Edwards P Swain	Coleman / Edwards P R Billing	Stafford / Callaghan	Radford / Walters	Daniels / Jasper	Hill / Murphy	Bennett / Clayton*	English / Gardner	Warner* / Fishenden	Hicks	Wilkins	Tempest / Sussex/Gage
32	A STOCKPORT 13/3	2,027	24 11	L 27	0 1	0-0	Cooke 49 — Ref G Courtney	McAllister / Gorton	Coleman / McKenzie	Stafford / Logan	Tempest / Matthews	Daniels / Hart	Hill / Williams	English / Coyle	Hicks / Colville	Warner / Hancock*	Walsh / Caldwell	Radford / Cooke*	Angell/Hartford
33	A DONCASTER 18/3	1,237	24 17	L 27	1 3	1-2	Walsh 16 / Rankine 22, 38, Jones 89 — Ref R Pawley	McAllister / Malcolm	Coleman / Douglas	Stafford / Gaughan	Taylor / Brockle	Hetzke / Ashurst	Hill / Raven	English / Robinson L Daly*	Wilkins / Rankine	Allinson / Turnbull	Walsh! / Kimble	Radford* / Jones	Warner
34	H GRIMSBY 24/3	4,507	24 12	D 28	0 0	0-0	Ref: A Gunn	McAllister / Sherwood	English / McDermott	Stafford / Agnew	Taylor / Tillson	Hetzke / Lever	Hill / Cunnington	Allinson / Jobling	Hicks / Saunders	Scott / O'Kelly	Walsh / Cockerill	Bedford* / Alexander	Warner

Match commentaries:

24 — Kelly can't agree terms, despite an agreed £20k fee, and storms off and away without a good-bye after being subbed. York, who have conceded only five in seven, take the lead when Steve Spooner's ball beats the offside trap to find Kevin Dixon. Gary Howlett nets Walton's poor punch.

25 — West Ham's McAllister becomes Wallace's first signing. Walton will attend Upton Park for training. A valuable point puts U's three points behind Darlington, who contrive to lead Exeter with a minute left but still lose by 1-2. A nearby chimney fire shrouds Seamer Road in smoke.

26 — McGee signs for £35k from Irish side Bohemians. Clarets include two U's old-boys in Farrell and White, who nets his first Burnley goals. The run extends to a club record 18 without a win. McAllister fouls George Oghani. Walsh earns resolute U's a share, nodding in Allinson's cross.

27 — Barnett, two reds and eight yellows in 28 games, is listed. Glandford Park is expected to be the first of a new generation of stadia. Sub Warner, a security guard at Ford's Dagenham plant, joins from Burnham Ramblers to shoot U's to their first victory in 19 games with an angled drive.

28 — Allinson's fifth goal, from good work by Warner and McGee, coupled by an immense display by Hetzke that earns a first clean sheet since the opening day of the season, gives United a first win at home in five months. They now sit just a point behind Darlington, who only get a draw.

29 — McGee, after just four games, joins Bobby Gould's Wimbledon for an eventual £150k. Rotherham boss Billy McEwan is dismissed for touch-line coaching. Irishman Tony Grealish gives Millers the lead, but Allinson is only the second U's player to score against them in 14 meetings.

30 — Stafford, from Diss Town, is the 29th player this term. Ex-U's apprentice John Taylor cancels out Wilkins' opener and then plays the final ten minutes in the sticks after John Vaughan tears shoulder ligaments in a collision with Phil Chapple. Taylor has little to deal with.

31 — Wallace gives Hicks the task of man-marking Crewe's play-maker Mark Gardiner. Neutrals in the crowd would be forgiven for thinking that it was U's who were top and not Alex. Stafford's cultured left foot has a hand in both of skipper English's strikes. Aiden Murphy had levelled.

32 — Jaded U's miss the opportunity to lift themselves off the bottom. Daniels, under pressure from two County forwards, mis-hits a back-pass to McAllister. John Cooke slips in to notch the only goal of the game. U's could fall further behind tomorrow when their rivals are all in action.

33 — Ipswich boss John Duncan offers any of his reserves to aid U's fight for league status. Walsh, who gave U's the lead is sent off on 84 mins for punching Paul Raven. Dave Mackay had resigned yesterday over the sale of his young protegees. Gary Jones bundles home a late killer goal.

34 — Wallace makes the first team play for the reserves against Enfield. 25-year-old triallist Robert Scott nets a hat-trick. He is signed on deadline day from Edinburgh side Whitburn Jnrs. Grimsby fans have taken to carrying inflatable Harry the Haddocks in their impressive FA Cup run.

Match log (matches 35–46)

---

35. A — 27/3 — PETERBOROUGH — 3,529 — 24 / 23 / L / 28 — **0-3** (HT 0-1)
Scorers: *Hetzke 34 (og), Longhurst 85, 90*
Ref: D Reeves
Line-up: McAllister, Coleman˜ *Crichton / Luke*, Stafford˜ *Gunn*, Hicks *Harle*, Hetzke! *McElhinney* (Oakes), English *Sterling*, Scott *Halsall*, Allinson *Cusack**, Walsh *Longhurst*, Bedford* *Goldsmith*, subs Daniels/Warner *Osborne*
> Hetzke has a day to forget as he heads Worrall Sterling's free-kick into his own net and then receives a red card for an horrific tackle on Craig Goldsmith, two minutes from time. On a positive note, he struck the bar twice. David Longhurst's double pulls Peterboro' away from trouble.

---

36. H — 31/3 — ROCHDALE — 3,631 — 24 / 20 / W / 31 — **3-0** (HT 0-0)
Scorers: Scott 50, Bennett 67, Wilkins 75
Ref: D Axcell
Line-up: McAllister, Daniels *Welch*, Coleman˜ *Brown*, Stafford *Armitage*, Radford *Smart*, Hetzke *Jones*, English *Beaumont*, Scott* *Taylor*, Walsh *Waling*, Wilkins* *Edmonds*, Bedford* *Frain*, subs Allinson/Hicks
> U's remain unbeaten at home in six. Radford has a hand in all three. Keith Welch parries Walsh's volley to Scott. Bennett puts U's two up from 15 yards. Both enjoy their first goals in the seniors, whilst Wilkins grabs his seventh when Welch drops Radford's corner at Wilkins' feet.

---

37. H — 4/4 — HEREFORD — 2,862 — 24 / 16 / D / 32 — **1-1** (HT 1-1)
Scorers: English 35; *Bradley 27*
Ref: I Hemley
Line-up: McAllister, Daniels *Elliott*, Elliott *Jones M*, Stafford *Crane˜*, Radford *Bradley*, Hetzke˜ *Devine*, English *Jones R*, Scott* *Narbett*, Allinson *Lamb*, Walsh *McLoughlin* / Tester*, Bedford *Wilkins*, subs Warner/Hicks *Mardenboro/Peacock*
> Walsh starts a four-match ban, whilst Hereford miss the division's 28-goal top scorer, Phil Stant. These clubs' previous meetings have seen a floodlight failure and a power cut. Phil Bradley, on loan from Forest, nods in Paul Tester's corner. English firmly heads in Allinson's corner.

---

38. A — 8/4 — HARTLEPOOL — 1,501 — 24 / 21 / L / 32 — **1-2** (HT 0-0)
Scorers: Scott 66; *Tinkler 47, Baker 69*
Ref: I Hendrick
Line-up: McAllister, Hicks *Moverley*, Hicks* *Plaskett*, Stafford *McKinnon*, Radford *Tinkler*, Daniels *Stokes*, English *Nobbs*, Scott *Allon*, Warner* *Baker*, Allinson *Grayson**, Bedford *Dalton*, subs Wilkins/Coleman *Atkinson*
> Newport, last season's relegated club, have been expelled from the GMVC. Wallace appoints Alan Ball as first team coach until the end of the season. Scott fires in an Allinson cross after John Tinkler had opened. Three minutes later, Paul Baker was left in acres of space to slot home.

---

39. A — 12/4 — HEREFORD — 2,015 — 24 / 16 / D / 33 — **1-1** (HT 1-0)
Scorers: Scott 44; *McLoughlin 85*
Ref: R Gifford
Line-up: McAllister, Hicks *Elliott*, Hicks *Jones M*, Stafford *Devine*, Radford *Stevens**, Daniels *Bradley*, English *Jones R*, Scott* *Tester*, Warner* *Lamb*, Tempest *Stant*, Allinson *McLoughlin*, subs Radford/Coleman *Maddy*
> U's surrender one of their games in hand over Darlington and still can't get off the bottom. Scott nets his third goal in six, turning in a good cross from Allinson. With just five minutes left, Stafford tries a suicidal back-pass that Stant intercepts to lay off for Paul McLoughlin to level.

---

40. A — 15/4 — LINCOLN — 3,519 — 24 / 9 / D / 34 — **1-1** (HT 0-0)
Scorers: Wilkins 83; *McGinley 62*
Ref: T West
Line-up: McAllister, Hicks *Bowling*, Hicks* *Evans**, Stafford *Davis*, Taylor *Nicholson*, Daniels *James*, English *Matthewson / Gamble*, Scott* *Cumming*, Tempest˜ *McGinley*, Warner* *Smith*, Allinson *Clarke*, subs Radford/Coleman *Brown*
> Wilkins, who has a 41st-minute effort ruled out for offside, nets a vital equaliser, side-footing in from Taylor. John McGinley had put the Imps in front but all is overshadowed as news filters through that 95 fans have been crushed to death during the FA Cup semi-final at Hillsborough.

---

41. H — 21/4 — CARLISLE — 3,906 — 24 / 14 / D / 35 — **1-1** (HT 0-1)
Scorers: Scott 90; *Proudlock 44*
Ref: B Hill
Line-up: McAllister, Hicks* *McKellar*, Stafford* *Graham*, Taylor *Dalziel*, Daniels *Ogley*, Hill *Jeffries*, Wilkins *Walsh*, English *Gorman*, Tempest *Sendall*, Walsh *Proudlock*, Allinson *Halpin*, subs Tempest/Hunter
> U's struggle to gain a point, and with Darlington securing their second successive victory, U's trail by four points with a game in hand and are indebted to Scott's last-minute saver. John Gorman's fierce free-kick appears to strike Hill's arm, but Paul Proudlock is on hand to stab home.

---

42. H — 25/4 — WREXHAM — 2,918 — 24 / 7 / W / 38 — **2-1** (HT 1-1)
Scorers: Allinson 26, Hetzke 88; *Russell 40*
Ref: K Morton
Line-up: McAllister, Coleman* *Salmon*, English *Thackeray*, Taylor *Wright*, Hetzke *Williams*, Hill *Beaumont*, Wilkins˜ *Preece*, Radford *Flynn*, Tempest* *Buxton !*, Allinson *Bowden !*, Walsh *Russell*, subs Daniels/Walsh *Cooper*
> Wallace stays for next season. Hetzke's goal is a lifesaver, winning uncharacteristically a one-on-one with keeper Mike Salmon. Steve Buxton sees off Hetzke (73), tussling with Hetzke. Both earlier goals were rebounds from missed penalties. Scott's shirt is pulled. Hill wrestles Kevin Russell.

---

43. A — 29/4 — DARLINGTON — 7,126 — 23 / 24 / W / 41 — **2-1** (HT 1-1)
Scorers: Walsh 39, Scott 66; *Bonnyman 21p*
Ref: K Hackett
Line-up: McAllister, Daniels *Prudhoe*, Coleman* *McJannet*, Stafford *Morgan*, Taylor *Gidman˜*, Hetzke *Dyson*, Wilkins˜ *Willis*, English *Robinson N˜ / Bonnyman*, Scott* *Stephens*, Allinson *Worthington / MacDonald*, Walsh *Bowden˜*, subs Warner/Radford *Hine/Moore*
> U's are off the bottom for the first time since 26 November 800 U's fans cause a twelve-minute delay due to late arrival. Gary MacDonald races through and is up-ended by McAllister. Radford switches the ball back to Walsh to score at close range. Scott volleys the vital winner.

---

44. H — 1/5 — HALIFAX — 5,065 — 23 / 21 / W / 44 — **3-2** (HT 0-1)
Scorers: Wilkins 61, Warner 74, Allinson 79p; *Hill 27 (og), McPhillips 54*
Ref: P Don
Line-up: McAllister, Radford *Roche**, Radford *Fleming P*, Stafford *Harrison*, Taylor* *Horner*, Hetzke *Richardson N / Bramhall*, Wilkins *Barr W*, English *Watson*, Scott* *Broadbent*, Allinson *Allison*, Walsh *Matthews N / McPhillips*, subs Warner/Coleman
> Hill, unluckily, deflects Andy Watson's shot past McAllister. It all looks over when Terry McPhillips makes it two. Paddy Roche is replaced by Graham Broadbent, after clashing with Walsh (34). U's comeback is complete when John Bramhall handles Walsh's powerful header.

---

45. H — 5/5 — EXETER — 5,256 — 23 / 12 / W / 47 — **4-0** (HT 2-0)
Scorers: Walsh 5, Allinson 40, Pollard 83, [English 90]
Ref: J Ashworth
Line-up: Walton, Daniels *Vinnicombe˜ / Dryden*, Stafford *Rogers*, Radford˜ *Taylor*, Hetzke *McDermott* / Rowbotham / Benjamin*, Wilkins *Richardson N / Bramhall*, Wilkins *Barr W*, English *Rowbotham / Benjamin*, Scott* *Young*, Allinson *Broadbent / Allison*, Walsh *Neville*, subs Warner/Pollard *Harris C/Banks*
> Two wins will guarantee survival after Darlington's 3-1 win at Cambridge. The first is completed in emphatic style in front of the biggest league attendance for nine years. 17-year-old John Pollard nets six minutes into his debut. Walton saves Rowbotham's penalty on 87 minutes.

---

46. A — 13/5 — TORQUAY — 2,066 — 22 / 14 / W / 50 — **3-1** (HT 0-0)
Scorers: Warner 52, Hetzke 88, Tempest 90; *Allinson 46 (og)*
Ref: J Deakin
Line-up: Walton, Daniels *Coombe*, Stafford *Pugh*, Radford˜ *Kelly*, Hetzke *McNichol*, Wilkins *Elliott*, Wilkins *Loram*, English *Smith J**, Scott* *Lloyd*, Allinson *Edwards*, Warner *Weston*, subs Tempest/Pollard *Morrison˜ / Smith P/Joyce*
> Darlington's 1-5 defeat at Scunthorpe ensures that U's go into this game in safety. Torquay's minds are set on the Sherpa Van Trophy final meeting with Bolton, at Wembley. Their membership scheme is still in operation. United recover well after Allinson sliced into his own net.

Home 2,892 Average Away 3,113

BARCLAYS DIVISION 4 (CUP-TIES) Manager: Brown ⇨ Foley ⇨ Wallace SEASON 1988-89

Littlewoods Cup

1:1 H NORTHAMPTON — 29/8 — 1,678 — 3: — D 0-0 (0-0) — Ref: P Don

1	2	3	4	5	6	7	8	9	10	11	subs used
Walton	Hedman	Cartwright	Barnett	Hetzke	Hill	Wilkins	White	Tempest	Swindlehurst	Grenfell	
Gleasure	*McGoldrick*	*Thomas*	*Donald*	*Flexney*	*Reed*	*Singleton*	*Culpin*	*Gilbert*	*Adcock*	*Donegal*	

Adcock returns to Layer Road 13 months after joining Man C., albeit wearing a Cobblers' shirt. It's five years since United won a League Cup-tie. Glenville Donegal hits the post after the ball squirms from Walton's grasp. Cobbler's wear U's red away shorts to avoid a colour clash.

1:2 A NORTHAMPTON — 6/9 — 3,957 — 3: — L 0-5 (0-3) — Scorers: [Gilbert 68p]; Singleton 9, Culpin 27, Adcock 43, 81 — Ref: D Hutchinson — (Colchester lost 0-5 on aggregate)

1	2	3	4	5	6	7	8	9	10	11	subs used
Walton	English	Cartwright	Barnett	Hetzke*	Hill	Wilkins	White	Tempest	Swindlehurst	Grenfell*	Bedford/Radford
Gleasure	*McGoldrick*	*Thomas*	*Donald*	*Flexney*	*Reed*	*Singleton* *	*Culpin*	*Gilbert*	*Adcock*	*Wilson*	*Slack*

Adcock overcomes a groin strain to plot the downfall of his old team. His first is a header from David Gilbert's free-kick, and he completes the rout heading in a corner from the same provider. Barnett nudges Eddie McGoldrick, after the winger makes a brilliant 50-yard goalwards run.

FA Cup

1 A FULHAM — 19/11 — 4,481 — 3:7 — W 1-0 (1-0) — Scorers: Walsh 10 — Ref: J Moules

1	2	3	4	5	6	7	8	9	10	11	subs used
Coombe	Hedman	Bedford	Kelly	Hicks	Hill	Radford	English	Tempest	Walsh	Barnett	
Stannard	*Marshall*	*Thomas*	*Wilson*	*Peters* *	*Eckhardt*	*Barnett*	*Scott*	*Sayer*	*Gordon* *	*Walker*	*Gore/Davies*

U's gain a memorable first FA Cup away win in five years. Kelly, still negotiating a permanent move, plays a neat one-two with Radford to put Walsh clear to slot past the advancing Jim Stannard. Fulham's 90th-minute free-kick in the area, beats the wall, but is saved by Coombe's legs.

2 H SWANSEA — 10/12 — 2,697 — 3:6 — D 2-2 (1-1) — Scorers: Hedman 13, Wilkins 66; Coleman 38, Melville 63 — Ref: K Cooper

1	2	3	4	5	6	7	8	9	10	11	subs used
Walton	Hedman	Bedford	Kelly	Hicks	Hill	Daniels	English	Swindlehurst*	Walsh	Wilkins	Radford
Bracey	*Melville*	*Coleman*	*Hough*	*Knill*	*Davies*	*Thornber*	*James*	*Hutchison* *	*Wade*	*Lewis*	*Bodak*

Walton returns after a five-match ligament injury. Swansea include the league's oldest player in 41-year-old Tommy Hutchison. Foley's bold approach in playing wing-backs results in Hedman's goal. Coleman's equaliser comes from a bizarre free-kick for Walton's time-wasting.

2R A SWANSEA — 13/12 — 4,045 — 3:6 — W 3-1 (2-0) — Scorers: Hedman 9, Walsh 39, Wilkins 65; Wade 55 — Ref: K Cooper

1	2	3	4	5	6	7	8	9	10	11	subs used
Walton	Hedman	Bedford	Kelly	Daniels	Hill	English	Barnett	Wilkins*	Walsh	Radford	Tempest
Bracey	*Melville*	*Coleman*	*Hough*	*Knill*	*Davies*	*Thornber* *	*James*	*Hutchison*	*Wade*	*Lewis* *	*Bodak/Puckett*

Hedman nods U's in front after Kelly makes the chance. Walsh puts U's two up, powering a header into the roof of the net after Kelly taps a short corner to Radford. Bryan Wade, aided by a deflection, pulls one back before Wilkins secures a fantastic win with a screaming 20-yarder.

3 A SHREWSBURY — 7/1 — 3,982 — 2:22 — W 3-0 (1-0) — Scorers: Walsh 17, Pratley 47 (og), Allinson 85p — Ref: R Nixon

1	2	3	4	5	6	7	8	9	10	11	subs used
Walton	English	Bedford	Kelly	Hicks	Hetzke	Daniels	Barnett*	Tempest	Walsh	Allinson	
Hughes	*Green*	*Rougvie*	*Williams W*	*Pratley*	*Finley*	*Brown*	*Bell* *	*Griffiths* *	*Irvine*	*Thomas*	*Priest/Kasule*

Foley signs Taylor from Reading (£20k). A third away win in the same FA Cup campaign creates a club record. Walsh fires U's in front from close in. The aptly-named Dick Pratley diverts English's bullet-header past Ken Hughes. Tempest is then up-ended, in full flight, in the box.

4 A SHEFFIELD UTD — 28/1 — 14,406 — 3:4 — D 3-3 (2-1) — Scorers: Hicks 27, Hill 37, Hetzke 81; Todd 40, Deane 58, Bryson 72 — Ref: A Gunn

1	2	3	4	5	6	7	8	9	10	11	subs used
Walton	Coleman	Bedford	Hill	Hicks*	Hetzke	Daniels	English	Tempest	Walsh*	Allinson	Barnett/Radford
Benstead	*Smith*	*Pike*	*Booker*	*Stancliffe*	*Carr*	*Duffield*	*Todd*	*Agana*	*Deane*	*Bryson*	

Hicks, surprisingly playing right midfield, nets his first U's goal. Hill joins him to the delight of U's 1,000-strong army. Bassett's interval roasting spurs Brian Deane and Ian Bryson to put Blades in front. Allinson lifts a free-kick into the box and a third 'H', Hetzke, nets his first.

4R H SHEFFIELD UTD — 31/1 — 7,588 — 3:4 — L 0-2 (0-1) — Scorers: Deane 3, 76 — Ref: A Gunn

1	2	3	4	5	6	7	8	9	10	11	subs used
Walton	Coleman	Bedford	Hill	Hicks	Hetzke	Daniels	English	Swindlehurst*	Walsh*	Allinson	Wilkins/Barnett
Benstead	*Smith*	*Pike*	*Thompson*	*Stancliffe*	*Carr*	*Duffield*	*Roberts*	*Agana*	*Deane*	*Bryson*	

A trip to Norwich awaits the victors. Deane, who with Tony Agana has struck 37 times so far this campaign, kills off U's cup dreams. Alan Roberts' cross is touched on by Agana for Deane's 20th of the campaign. A mistake by Hetzke gives the lanky striker a chance in off the post.

Sherpa Van Trophy

Q A LINCOLN — 30/11 — 1,448 — 4:5 — W 2-1 (0-0) — Scorers: Walsh 55, 85; Gamble 57p — Ref: G Stones

1	2	3	4	5	6	7	8	9	10	11	subs used
Coombe	Hedman	Bedford	Kelly	Hicks	Daniels	Barnett	Chatterton	Swindlehurst	Walsh	Radford	
Wallington	*Evans*	*Clarke*	*Schofield*	*Bressington*	*Matthewson*	*Davis*	*Nicholson*	*McGinley* *	*Brown*	*Sertori*	*Gamble*

Lincoln, mysteriously, appear in the southern part of the competition. U's win, however, means that City are eliminated. Tempest misses his first U's game. His replacement Swindlehurst, back after injury, sets up both of Walsh's goals. Hicks puts his hand to a Darren Davis header.

Q H SOUTHEND — 20/12 — 993 — 3:17 — W 2-1 (1-1) — Scorers: Tempest 23, Swindlehurst 90; Young 29 — Ref: D Vickers

1	2	3	4	5	6	7	8	9	10	11	subs used
Walton	Coleman	Rooke	Kelly	Hicks	Hetzke	Allinson	Barnett*	Swindlehurst	Tempest	Grenfell	Chatterton
Sansome	*O'Shea*	*Johnson*	*Butler*	*McDonough*	*Brush* *	*Smith*	*Hall*	*Young*	*Matthews* *	*Ling*	*Edinburgh/Jones*

Hard on the heels of old-boy Allinson rejoining U's, another in the shape of Phil Coleman returns. Already through, Colchester earn a home tie courtesy of Swindlehurst's injury-time clincher. Rooke, one of seven changes, does well on his senior debut and has a hand in Tempest's goal.

1	H	LEYTON ORIENT	24	W	3-1	Walsh 27 Allinson 58, Wilkins 77			
17/1			1,736	4:14		Hull 66	Ref R Wiseman		1-0
QF	H	HEREFORD	24	L	0-1				0 1
S	14/2		2,059	4:21		Stant 18	Ref: A Buksh		

Leyton Orient: Walton, Coleman, Bedford, Kelly, Hicks, Hetzke, Daniels, English, Tempest*, Walsh, Allinson, Wilkins
Subs/opp: Heald, Howard, Dickenson, O'Shea*, Day, Sitton, Hull, Ward, Baker, Juryeff, Comfort, Castle — Stant 18 — Ref: A Buksh

Hereford: McAllister, Elliott, Hicks, Barnett*, Hetzke, Hill, Allinson, English, Wilkins, Walsh, Allinson, Daniels
Subs/opp: Elliott, Jones M, Devine, Stevens, Pejic, Jones R, Benbow, Narbett, Stant, Tester, McGee, McLoughlin

U's avenge the Brisbane Rd mauling. Walsh rises majestically to head in Kelly's free-kick. his eleventh so far. Allinson picks up the ball in U's half, fends off ex-U's star Day, to unleash a 20-yarder Alan Hull pulls one back, only for Wilkins, five minutes after coming on. to score.

U's fail again at home for the tenth time this season. Being just three steps from Wembley does not inspire the team. McAllister fails to hold on to a Paul Tester shot, which Phil Stant gobbles up for his 23rd of the season. Allinson is fouled on the box-edge (85), Buksh gives a free-kick.

		P		Home						Away					Pts
			W	D	L	F	A		W	D	L	F	A		
1	Rotherham	46	13	6	4	44	18		9	10	4	32	17		82
2	Tranmere	46	15	6	2	34	13		6	11	6	28	30		80
3	Crewe	46	13	7	3	42	24		8	8	7	25	24		78
4	Scunthorpe	46	11	9	3	40	22		10	5	8	37	35		77
5	Scarborough	46	12	7	4	33	23		9	7	7	34	29		77
6	Leyt' Orient*	46	16	5	2	61	19		5	10	8	25	31		75
7	Wrexham	46	12	7	4	44	28		7	7	9	33	35		71
8	Cambridge	46	13	7	3	45	25		5	7	11	26	37		68
9	Grimsby	46	11	9	3	33	18		6	6	11	32	41		66
10	Lincoln	46	12	6	5	39	26		6	4	13	25	34		64
11	York	46	10	8	5	43	27		7	5	11	19	36		64
12	Carlisle	46	9	6	8	26	25		6	8	9	27	27		60
13	Exeter	46	14	4	5	46	23		2	2	17	19	45		60
14	Torquay	46	15	2	6	32	23		2	6	15	13	37		59
15	Hereford	46	11	8	4	40	27		3	8	12	26	45		58
16	Burnley	46	12	6	5	35	20		2	7	14	17	41		55
17	Peterborough	46	10	7	6	29	32		4	9	10	23	42		54
18	Rochdale	46	10	10	3	32	26		3	4	16	24	56		53
19	Hartlepool	46	10	6	7	33	33		4	4	15	17	45		52
20	Stockport	46	8	10	5	31	20		2	11	10	23	32		51
21	Halifax	46	10	7	6	42	27		3	4	16	27	48		50
22	COLCHESTER	46	8	7	8	35	30		4	7	12	25	48		50
23	Doncaster	46	9	6	8	32	32		4	4	15	17	46		49
24	Darlington	46	3	12	8	28	38		5	6	12	25	38		42
		1104	267	161	124	899	599		124	161	267	599	899		1495

* promoted after play-offs

Odds & ends

Double wins: (0)
Double defeats: (4) Cambridge, Doncaster, Hartlepool, Rotherham.
Won from behind: (3) Darlington (a), Halifax (h), Torquay (a).
Lost from in front: (6) Crewe (a), Halifax (a), Tranmere (h), Hartlepool (h). Cambridge (a), Doncaster (a).
High spots: Successful season-long fight against the drop to non-league.
Great cup run, including a record three away victories.
Large transfer fees from the sale of McGee and Hedman.
Appointment of 'big' names in Wallace and Ball.
Five consecutive wins to end the season.
Eight games unbeaten to save demotion.
'Pressure-cooker' win over demotion rivals Darlington, at Feethams.
Low spots: From top spot to bottom in exactly twelve months.
Humiliating record defeat at Brisbane Road.
18 games without a win from October.
Instability of 14 more debutants, following on from 19 last season.

Player of the year: Colin Hill.
Ever presents: (0).
Hat-tricks: (0).
Leading scorer: Dale Tempest (14) (including 2 in Sherpa Van Trophy).

	Appearances						Goals			
	Lge	Sub	LC	Sub	FA	Sub	Lge	LC	FA	Tot
Allinson, Ian	24	1	2		3		7		1	8
Barnett, Dave	19	1	2		3	2				
Bedford, Kevin	24	2	1		6				1	1
Bennett, Gary	6	3								
Cartwright, Steve	10		2				1			1
Chatterton, Nicky	1	1								
Coleman, Phil	6	4			2					
Coombe, Mark	3				1					
Daniels, Scott	18	8			1					
English, Tony	36		1		6		8			8
Grenfell, Steve	5	1	2		2					
Hedman, Rudi	17		1		3		1		2	3
Hetzke, Steve	22	2	2		3		2		1	3
Hicks, Stuart	34	3			5				1	1
Hill, Colin	42		2		5					
Hunter, Lee	4	4								
Kelly, Tony	13				4		2			2
McAllister, Tom	20									
McGee, Paul	3									
Pollard, John		2					1			1
Radford, Mark	16	14	1		2	2	1			1
Scott, Robert	12				5		5			5
Stafford, Clive	16									
Swindlehurst, Dave	12				2		5			5
Taylor, Les	14	2	2		2					
Tempest, Dale	25	8	2		3	1	7			7
Walsh, Mario	25	2			6		9		3	12
Walton, Mark	23		2		5					
Warner, John	7	8					3			3
White, Winston	10	2								
Wilkins, Richard	39	1	2		2	1	8		2	10
(own-goals)									1	1
31 players used	506	69	22	2	66	6	60		12	72

BARCLAYS LEAGUE DIVISION 4 — Manager: Wallace ⇨ Foley ⇨ Mills — SEASON 1989-90

No		Team	Date	Att	Pos	Pt	F-A	H-T	Scorers, Times, and Referees	1	2	3	4	5	6	7	8	9	10	11	subs used
1	A	CHESTERFIELD	18/8	3,161		D 1	1-1	1-1	Radford 9 / Thompson 38 / Ref: A Smith	Grace	Hicks	Rooke	English A	Daniels	Radford	Bennett	Collins	Wilkins	Scott	Allinson	Hoole
									Leonard, Gunn, Ryan, Arnott, Brien, Slack, Plummer*, Shaw, Waller, Thompson, Morris												
2	H	HALIFAX	26/8	2,404	13	D 2	2-2	0-0	Bennett 64, Radford 90p / Hicks 51 (og), Watson 69 / Ref: R Pawley	Hansbury	Hicks	Rooke*	English A	Daniels	Radford	Bennett	Collins	Wilkins	Scott	Allinson^	Taylor/Kinsella
									Whitehead, Barr, Cook, Hedworth, Bramhall, Horner, Martin, Watson, Juryeff, Butler, Hall												
3	A	GRIMSBY	2/9	4,678	19	L 2	1-4	0-2	Allinson 48 / Rees 11, 75, Watson 45, Daniels 59 (og) / Ref: J Kirkby	Hansbury	Hicks	Rooke	English A	Daniels	Radford*	Bennett	Collins	Wilkins	Scott*	Allinson	Taylor/Pollard, Alexander
									Reece, McDermott, Agnew, Tillson, Lever, Cunnington, Childs, Gilbert, Rees, Watson, Birtles*												
4	H	HEREFORD	8/9	3,269	19	D 3	1-1	1-0	Allinson 35p / Pejic 90 / Ref: P Jones	Hansbury	Hicks	Stafford	English A	Daniels	Blake	Bennett	Collins	Wilkins	Taylor	Allinson	
									Phillips, Jones MA, Williams, Pejic, Peacock, Bradley, Jones R, Narbett, Benbow, Robinson, Tester												
5	A	ROCHDALE	16/9	1,466	19	D 4	2-2	1-1	Collins 23, Blake 68 / Whellans 25, Walling 66 / Ref: A Dawson	Hansbury	Hicks	Stafford	English A	Daniels	Blake	Bennett*	Collins	Whellans	Taylor	Radford	Stonehouse* Burns
									Welch, Goodison, Hill, Brown, Cole, O'Shaughn'sy, Ainscow, Holmes, Whellans, Walling												
6	H	SCARBOROUGH	23/9	2,420	20	D 5	0-0	0-0	Ref: R Bigger	Grace	Hicks	English A	Radford*	Daniels	Blake	Bennett	Collins	Wilkins	Taylor	Allinson	Stafford, Saunders/Brook
									Blackwell, Kamara, Clarke, Short, Richards, Bennyworth, Olsson*, Graham, Morris, Robinson^, Russell												
7	H	MAIDSTONE	26/9	2,946	15	W 8	4-1	1-0	Radford 2 Allinson 57p, Taylor 64, Cooper 70p [Bennett 69] / Ref: K Morton	Grace	Hicks	English A	Taylor	Daniels	Blake	Bennett*	Collins	Wilkins	Radford	Allinson	Lillis
									Beeney, Barton, Rumble*, Pamphlett, Golley, Pearce, Cooper, Elsey, Sorrell, Butler, Gall												
8	A	CARLISLE	30/9	3,979	16	L 8	0-1	0-1	Fyfe 17 / Ref: P Harrison	Grace	Hicks	English A	Taylor	Daniels	Blake	Bennett	Collins	Wilkins	Radford*	Allinson	Scott, Shepherd
									McKellar, Graham, Dalziel, Saddington, Jones, Fitzpatrick, Miller, Proudlock*, Walwyn, Fyfe, Halpin												
9	A	ALDERSHOT	7/10	2,092	18	L 8	0-4	0-2	Puckett 6, 17p, Wignall 77, Burvill 90 / Ref: G Pooley	Grace	Hicks	English A	Taylor	Daniels	Blake	Allinson*	Collins	Wilkins	Scott	Radford*	Bennett/Pollard, Stewart
									Sheffield, Brown, Phillips, Burvill, Smith, Wignall, Claridge, Puckett, Banton, Williams*, Russell												
10	H	YORK	13/10	3,274	21	L 8	0-2	0-2	Himsworth 8, 28 / Ref: M James	Grace	Hicks	Radford	Taylor	Daniels	English A	Bennett*	Collins	Scott	Wilkins	Allinson	Devereux, Canham
									Marples, McMillan, Kelly, Barratt, Tutill, Warburton, Howlett, Spooner, Helliwell, Dixon, Canham												
11	H	WREXHAM	17/10	2,564	23	L 8	1-3	1-1	Scott 33 / Reck 41, Worthington 53, 79p / Ref: A Buksh	Grace	Hicks	Radford	Taylor	Daniels	English A	Bennett*	Collins	Scott*	Wilkins	Allinson	Kinsella/Pollard, Flynn
									O'Keefe, Barnes, Beaumont, Reck, Williams, Jones J, Cooper, Hunter*, Kearns, Worthington, Bowden												

Match notes:

1. Tribunals set deals for Hill, £85k + 30%, to Sheffield U and Walton, £75k + £75k after 50 games, to Norwich. U's are seventh favourites at 14-1. Hicks wins possession in midfield, feeding Radford to slot in. Nigel Thompson shrugs off three challenges to plant a low drive past Grace.

2. Hansbury, loaned from Brum, is the seventh keeper in two years. U's leave it late to dent Halifax's 100% start. Hicks own-goals Dean Martin's innocuous-looking cross. Andy Watson catches United napping at a free-kick. Radford scores a re-taken penalty after Brian Butler handles.

3. United suffer their first defeat in eleven league games. Scott Daniels puts the ball into his own net to restore the Mariner's two-goal advantage. Tony Rees's spectacular overhead kick. is the icing on the cake as U's are outclassed. Gary Childs, in Grimsby's midfield, dictates the game.

4. Wallace bolsters the defence, signing Blake on loan from Southampton. Wilkins weaves his way into the box and, as he shapes to shoot, his legs are pulled from under by Russell Bradley. Second-half pressure pays off 30 seconds from time, when veteran Mel Pejic nods in a corner.

5. Collins gives U's the lead against the run of play from a Bennett cross. Mick Holmes' long throw is knocked home by Robbie Whellans within two mins. A Dean Walling header gives Dale the lead, but new-boy Blake gets his first for U's via a double deflection, deceiving Keith Welch.

6. Wallace slams the handful of U's fans who spoil the minute's silence for the victims of the Deal bombing. Injury-hit Brum recall Hansbury but Grace excels, making great saves from Tommy Graham, Alan Kamara and Steve Saunders. Eight without a win is U's worst start to a season.

7. A twelve-minute threesome gives U's their first win of the season. Radford heads an early opener. Graham Pearce tugs Wilkins' shirt for the penalty. Taylor nets his first U's in 20 yards. Bennett stabs home Mark Beeney's parry before Hicks fouls Tony Pamphlett for a corner.

8. A fifth in six games for Tony Fyfe is enough to give the Cumbrians a record eighth game unbeaten. David McKellar's long punt is flicked on by Keith Walwyn to Fyfe. Daniels hauls down John Halpin on 62 minutes, but Ian Dalziel's penalty is well saved by Grace diving to his left.

9. Shots, still reeling from an 0-8 League Cup mauling by first division Sheff Wed, give Wallace his self-declared worst-ever performance during his 25 years in football. U's are three points clear of bottom side Hartlepool. Ex-U's star Wignall nets as does Glen Burvill, who rounds Grace.

10. U's suffer their first home league defeat under Wallace since his first game in charge last January, despite winning by 15-2 on corners. Gary Himsworth's double both arrive via the lanky Ian Helliwell. English slides away from a twelve-man brawl after already having been booked.

11. Wallace signs Gilbert from Pompey on a free. Ball leaves to join second division Stoke. Scott meets Taylor's cross, but Gary Worthington's shot is deflected in by Shaun Reck. Radford trips Worthington, whilst Vince O'Keefe saves Ian Allinson's penalty (90) after a foul on Wilkins.

| 12 | A | SCUNTHORPE | 21/10 | 3,254 | 23 9 | L 8 | 0-4 |

[Taylor 88]
Stevenson 20, Daws 41, Hamilton 63,
Ref: P Danson

| Grace | Litchfield | Pollard *Smalley* | **Gilbert** *Longden* | Taylor *Taylor* | Daniels *Lister* | English A! *Stevenson Cowing* | Devereux *Hamilton* | Collins` | Hicks *Lillis* | English T *Daws* | Radford* *Marshall* | Allinson/Stafford |

T English re-signs, but Chesterfield's Andy Morris refuses. United's latest setback is marred by the 38th-minute sending off of A English, for an off-the-ball incident. Collins (knee) and Radford (foot) are carried off Kevin Taylor's 88th-minute 35-yarder puts United deep into trouble.

| 13 | H | PETERBOROUGH | 28/10 | 3,460 | 23 3 | L 8 | 0-1 |

Osborne 88
Ref: J Carter

| Grace | Barber | Hicks *Luke* | Stafford *Crosby* | Taylor *Halsall* | Daniels *Robinson* | English A *McElhinney Sterling* | Gilbert* *Culpin*` | Collins *Morgan* Longhurst | English T *Harle* | Wilkins *Butterworth Osborne* | Bennett |

Morgan signs from Bolton for £8k, as Hetzke quits with a knee injury. The high winds that spoil the game lift the giant inflatable football, used as half-time entertainment, up and over the stand into adjoining gardens. Steve Osborne, lucky to still be on the pitch, breaks free to score.

| 14 | A | EXETER | 1/11 | 3,905 | 23 8 | L 8 | 1-2 |

English A 30
Neville 39, 79
Ref: J Martin

| Grace | Walter | Hicks *Hiley* | Stafford *Vinnicombe McNichol* | Taylor | Daniels *Taylor* | English A *Batty* | Gilbert *Rowbotham Bailey*` | Collins *Morgan* McDermott | English T *Neville* | Wilkins *Dryden* | Bennett *Young* |

Exeter have five wins from six at home. G Rangers scouts are in attendance to watch Chris Vinnicombe. Morgan chests down for A English's left-foot volley. Steve Neville's double comes either side of Dave Walter's penalty save from Collins (72). given for a Hiley foul on Wilkins.

| 15 | A | BURNLEY | 4/11 | 6,145 | 23 8 | D 9 | 0-0 |

Ref: S Lodge

| Grace | Pearce | Hicks *Measham* | Stafford *Hardy* | Taylor *Deary* | Daniels *Eli* | English A *Daws* | Bennett *White*` | Collins *Murphy* O'Connell | Morgan^ *White*` | English T* *Jakub* | Wilkins *Farrell* | Kinsella/Pollard Hancock |

A English starts a three-match ban, for his sending off at Scunthorpe. The Clarets, under the leadership of ex-Turf Moor star Frank Casper, are attempting to rebuild after coming so close to losing their league status. United play neat football to earn a first point in seven league outings.

| 16 | H | CAMBRIDGE | 10/11 | 3,771 | 23 10 | L 9 | 1-2 |

English T 32p
Dennis 36, Dublin 74
Ref: D Wiseman

| Grace | Vaughan | **Bruce** *Clayton* | Stafford *Kimble* | Taylor *Cheetham* | Daniels *Chapple* | Gilbert* *Daish* | Bennett *Dennis* | Collins` *Leadbitter* | Morgan *Dublin* | English T *Taylor* | Wilkins *Philpott* | Pollard/Kinsella |

Cambridge have 16 points from 18. Bruce, only 18. is a surprise debutant. Gary Clayton trips Collins for T English to score, but John Vaughan saves his second penalty (40) when Phil Chapple handles. Tony Dennis meets a Lee Philpott cross and Dion Dublin finishes off a long punt.

| 17 | A | GILLINGHAM | 24/11 | 3,816 | 23 7 | D 10 | 3-3 |

English T 50p, Bennett 56, Morgan 63
Heritage 15, Lovell 26p, O'Shea 87
Ref: M Bailey

| Grace | Hillyard | Haylock *Johnson* | Stafford *Walker* | Taylor *Place* | Daniels *Palmer* | Gilbert *Trusson*` | Bennett *O'Shea* | Collins *Lovell* | Morgan* *Heritage* | English T *Manuel*` | Wilkins *Gavin/Docker* |

Gills lose. midweek, to Conference side Welling in the FA Cup. Gilbert's handball puts them 2-0 up. Morgan is pushed over by Alan Walker. who then mis-judges a Bruce cross to give Bennett his fifth of the term. Morgan's first for U's is cancelled by a stunning 35-yarder from Tim O'Shea.

| 18 | H | LINCOLN | 2/12 | 2,517 | 23 5 | L 10 | 0-1 |

Nicholson 29
Ref: M Pierce

| Grace | Wallington | Hagan *Williams P* | Stafford *Clarke* | English A *Nicholson* | Daniels *Thompson* | Gilbert *Davis* | Bennett *Schofield* | Collins ! *Bressington Sertori* | Morgan^ | English T* *Carmichael Hobson* | Wilkins* *Taylor/Scott* |

Hagan, 1987-8 Spanish Overseas Player of the Year. joins having played for Celta Vigo. United short-change the fans again with a record sixth successive home loss. Shane Nicholson looks offside as he takes a Matt Carmichael pass. Collins is sent-off (74) for kicking Gordon Hobson.

| 19 | H | TORQUAY | 16/12 | 1,720 | 23 18 | L 10 | 0-3 |

Loram 26, Caldwell 71, Smith P 87
Ref: P Alcock

| Grace | Veysey | Bruce *Holmes* | **Grainger** *Lloyd* | English A *Elliott* | Daniels *Matthews*` | Gilbert *Joyce* | Bennett *Loram* | Collins* *Edwards* | Hagan *Smith P* | Taylor *Caldwell* | Allinson* *Morrison* | English T *Bastow* |

Wallace bloods another youngster. Grainger. Allinson returns after an ankle injury. Fans turn on Wallace after a dismal showing, calling for his head. Speculation mounts after Wallace is made a director and Mick Mills, John Deehan and Ian Atkins are spotted in the stands with Crisp.

| 20 | A | SOUTHEND | 26/12 | 5,563 | 23 4 | W 13 | 2-0 |

Grainger 65, English T 69
Ref: R Lewis

| Grace | Sansome | Bruce *Roberts* | Stafford *Edinburgh* | English A *Martin* | Daniels *Edwards* | Gilbert* *Brush* | Bennett *Cook* | Collins *Smith N/Walsh*` | Wilkins *Taylor* | English T *McDonough Ling* | Scott` *Bennett* | Grainger/Warner |

Rooke and Allinson are released. Wallace quits to move upstairs. Foley is caretaker for the third time in 26 months. T English dummies for Grainger's first U's goal, then slots home Paul Sansome's parry from Bennett. The win is dampened as Hartlepool beat Scarborough by 4-1.

| 21 | A | DONCASTER | 30/12 | 2,942 | 24 19 | L 13 | 0-2 |

Robinson 41p, Turnbull 51
Ref: K Breen

| Grace | Samways | Bruce *Robinson* | Stafford *Brevett* | English A *Rankine* | Daniels *Ashurst* | Radford* *Douglas* | Bennett *Adams* | Collins *Stiles* | Wilkins* *Turnbull* | English T* *Jones D!* | Morgan* *Nateman*` | Grainger/Pollard Gaughan |

U's win the Performance of the Week award for the Southend win, but enter the new decade rock bottom. Rovers have won seven of the last nine. David Jones is sent-off (26) for elbowing Daniels. Bruce chops Mark Rankine for Les Robinson's penalty. Lee Turnbull gets the second.

| 22 | H | HARTLEPOOL | 1/1 | 3,826 | 23 24 | W 16 | 3-1 |

Morgan 60, Grainger 63, Radford 86
Dalton 20
Ref: A Gunn

| Grace | Priestley | Bruce *Olsson* | Stafford *McKinnon* | English A *Tinkler* | Daniels *Smith M*` | Radford *Bennyworth Alton* | Bennett *Kinsella* | Taylor* *Tupling* | Morgan *Baker* | English T` *Nobbs* | Grainger *Dalton* | Ball/Scott MacDonald |

The battle of the bottom two opens with Paul Dalton cutting inside Bruce for the 18th goal against at Layer Rd. U's seventh corner is nodded in by Morgan, whose shot is fumbled by Jason Priestley to Grainger. T English lays a ball back to Radford. Local lad Ball, joins from Arsenal.

| 23 | H | STOCKPORT | 5/1 | 3,609 | 23 3 | L 16 | 0-0 |

Frain 89
Ref: I Hemley

| Grace | Redfern | Bruce *Bullock* | Stafford *Logan* | Collins *Frain* | Daniels *Williams B* | English A *Jones* | Bennett *Payne* | Radford *Downes* | Morgan *Edwards* | Warner *Cooke* | Grainger *Angell* |

Mills takes over the hot seat, just 50 weeks after Wallace had been installed. He inherits a crippling injury list, but appoints ex-Wolves boss Sammy Chung as his assistant. He gets a first-hand view of the enormity of the task as Daniels' error lets in David Frain in the dying moments.

BARCLAYS LEAGUE DIVISION 4 — Manager: Wallace ⇨ Foley ⇨ Mills — SEASON 1989-90

No	Date	1	2	3	4	5	6	7	8	9	10	11	subs used
24	A HALIFAX 12/1	Barrett	Bruce	Stafford	Taylor	Daniels	English A	Collins	Ball	Wilkins	Bennett`	Radford*	Morgan/Scott
		Brown	*Fleming P*	*Harrison*	*Hedworth*	*Bramhall*	*Horner*	*Hall*	*Broadbent**	*Richardson*	*Butler*	*Matthews*	*McPhillips/Cook*
25	H CHESTERFIELD 20/1	Barrett	Bruce	English A	Taylor	Daniels	Marmon	Collins	Ball*	Morgan	Wilkins	Radford	Scott
		Leonard	*Rogers*	*Hart*	*Shaw*	*Brien*	*Gunn*	*Plummer*	*Hewitt*	*Waller*	*Ryan*	*Morris*	
26	A YORK 27/1	Barrett	Bruce	English A	Taylor	Daniels	Marmon	Collins	Ball*	Morgan	Wilkins	Radford*	Hicks/Bennett, Hall
		Marples	*Heathcote*	*Kelly*	*Reid**	*Tutill*	*Warburton*	*Howlett*	*Barratt*	*Helliwell*	*Longhurst*	*Canham*	
27	A SCARBOROUGH 3/2	Barrett	Bruce	Goddard	Taylor	Daniels	Marmon	Collins	English A	Morgan	Wilkins	Radford*	Bennett
		Richardson	*Short*	*Kamara*	*Matthews*	*Richards*	*Meyer*	*Dixon*	*Russell*	*Clarke*	*Dobson*	*MacDonald*	
28	H ROCHDALE 10/2	Barrett	Bruce	Goddard	Gilbert	Daniels	Marmon	Collins	English A	Morgan	Wilkins	Radford*	Bennett/Gilbert
		Welch	*Goodison*	*Burns*	*Brown*	*Cole*	*Ward*	*Duxbury*	*Johnson*	*Dawson*	*O'Shaughn'sy*	*Hill*	
29	A LINCOLN 17/2	Barrett	Bruce	Goddard	Gilbert	Daniels	Marmon	Collins	English A	Morgan	Wilkins	Bennett*	Scott, Nicholson
		Wallington	*Stoutt*	*Clarke*	*Conforth*	*Brown G*	*Davis*	*Smith P*	*Bressington*	*Hobson*	*Lormor*	*Puttnam**	
30	A GRIMSBY 20/2	Barrett	Bruce	Goddard	Gilbert	Daniels	Marmon	Collins	English A	Morgan	Wilkins	Scott*	Taylor, Alexander/Agnew
		Sherwood	*McDermott*	*Jobling*	*Tillson*	*Knight**	*Cunnington*	*Childs*	*Gilbert*	*Rees*	*Cockerill**	*Birtles*	
31	H GILLINGHAM 23/2	Barrett	Bruce	Goddard	Gilbert	Daniels	Marmon	Collins	English A	Morgan	Wilkins	Scott*	Bennett, Trusson/Eeles
		Hillyard	*Haylock*	*Johnson*	*Manuel*	*Walker*	*Haines*	*Docker*	*O'Shea*	*Gavin**	*Heritage*	*O'Conner**	
32	A STOCKPORT 2/3	Barrett	Bruce	Goddard	Gilbert	Daniels	Marmon	Collins	English A	Morgan	Wilkins	Scott*	Bennett, Cook
		Muggleton	*Brown*	*Bullock*	*Downes*	*Thorpe*	*Jones*	*Beaumont**	*Frain*	*Edwards*	*McInerney*	*Angell*	
33	H CARLISLE 6/3	Barrett	Bruce	Goddard	Gilbert	Daniels	Marmon	Collins	English A	Morgan	Wilkins*	Scott*	Taylor, Morris
		McKellar	*Walsh*	*Edwards*	*Saddington*	*Graham*	*Fitzpatrick*	*Shepherd*	*Miller*	*Sendall*	*Proudlock*	*Goldsmith**	
34	A MAIDSTONE 10/3	Barrett	Bruce	Goddard	Gilbert	Daniels	Marmon	Collins	English A	Morgan	Wilkins	Scott*	Hicks
		Beeney	*Barton*	*Cooper*	*Berry*	*Rumble*	*Golley*	*Lillis*	*Elsey*	*Charlery*	*Butler*	*Sorrell*	

No	Scorers, Times, and Referees	H-T	F-A	Pt	Pos	Att
24	Scott 79, Hall 17 — Ref: P Jones	0-1	D 1-1	20	23	1,397
25	Wilkins 35 — Ref: D Hedges	1-0	W 1-0	20	22	3,016
26	Wilkins 9, Longhurst 30, 36, Reid 58 — Ref: G Aplin	1-2	L 1-3	20	22	2,311
27	English A 67, Morgan 85, Dobson 59, Russell 70p — Ref: T West	0-0	D 2-2	21	19	1,786
28	Morgan 26, Cole 39, Johnson 45 — Ref: G Pooley	1-2	L 1-2	21	21	2,744
29	Wilkins 88, Lormor 6, Smith P 23 — Ref: D Scott	0-2	L 1-2	21	24	3,284
30	Bruce 31 — Ref: M James	1-0	W 1-0	24	23	3,026
31	Morgan 38p, Scott 70 — Ref: P Vanes	1-0	W 2-0	27	23	4,456
32	Goddard 51, Angell 47 — Ref: K Barratt	0-0	D 1-1	28	23	3,452
33	Wilkins 2, Marmon 31, Morgan 52p, 64p — Ref: K Morton	2-0	W 4-0	31	22	3,752
34	Morgan 68p, Lillis 15, 42, 43, Butler 86 — Ref: R Hamer	0-3	L 1-4	31	23	2,856

24. Mills signs Barrett (26) on loan and sets up a £35k fee for Nicky Morgan, both from his old club Stoke. Halifax keeper David Brown performs heroics to keep U's at bay. Derek Hall turns smartly to prod home Phil Horner's flag-kick. Subs Scott and Morgan combine for the equaliser.

25. English-born Marmon (28) signs for a small fee from German side Hanover 96. Wilkins gets his first goal for 30 games to give U's a third win in six fixtures. U's move above Wrexham, who lose 0-2 to Scarborough. Wilkins' goal comes from a quickly-taken free-kick by Collins.

26. York could easily have notched six or seven as David Longhurst (thrice) and Tony Canham miss one-on-one's with Barrett. U's actually take the lead via hesitancy in the York defence. Longhurst's double and a third from Shaun Reid, brother of Man City's Peter, wrap up the points.

27. Goddard (22, from Bradford) is U's fourth loan of the season. Boro's Paul Dobson is left unmarked to shoot into an empty net. A English levels when Barry Richardson parries Bennett's shot. Martin Russell scores after Daniels trips Dobson. Morgan runs through a square defence.

28. Dale, who face Palace in the FAC 5th round, inflict U's eleventh home loss. Wrexham, with a game in hand, trail U's by two points. Goddard crosses for Morgan's fourth. U's goal. Wayne Goodison's free-kick is fluffed by Barrett and falls to David Cole. Steve Johnson lobs Barrett.

29. Stafford joins Exeter on loan. Last week's postponement saw U's go bottom. Mark Wallington's wind-assisted kick finds Tony Lormor, who nets from an acute angle. Barrett dives in vain at Paul Smith's glancing header. Wilkins pounces on Graham Bressington's poor back-pass.

30. A crucial second win in nine games under Mills' leadership comes via the unlikely source of 19-year-old Bruce, timing his run to perfection to meet Goddard's cross with a glancing header. Gilbert gets out of his sick bed to run a new sweeper system that Mills has been toying with.

31. U's earn a second home win in a week. Scott heads a Gilbert free-kick across the face of goal, that Alan Walker handles. The loudest cheer comes via an announcement over the tannoy, that if a suspicious car is not moved from the nearby Army property, then it would be blown up.

32. Wallace makes public the fact that he is suffering from Parkinson's Disease and retires to his Spanish home. U's bid to win at Edgeley Park for the first time since 1973-4. Goddard's first league goal is cancelled by Brett Angell, but is enough to take U's six points clear of Wrexham.

33. Wilkins' fourth in nine games. Marmon nets his first British goal. Morgan's penalties make him the first double scorer since A English at Crewe, last season. The first, a handball in a crowded goalmouth, the second a David McKellar foul on Marmon at a Collins corner.

34. U's make a loss of £317k, putting the club £1.01m in the red. Stand-in striker Jason Lillis grabs a first-half treble. his third via a wind-assisted Tony Sorrell throw for the homeless Stones, who play at Dartford. Mark Beeney's lunge at Wilkins gives U's a spot-kick, that Morgan fires in.

Match 35 — HEREFORD (A) 14/3

Barrett	Bruce	Stafford*	Gilbert	Daniels	Marmon	Collins	English I	Morgan	Wilkins	English T	Hicks
Elliott	Jones MA	Devine	Hemming	Peacock	Pejic	Jones M	Narbett	Wheeler	Starbuck	Juryeff	Bennett/Hicks

2,253 · 17 · 31 · 0-2 · L · 0-0

Wheeler 49, 73
Ref: T Mills

Defeat, and Wrexham's third successive win, puts U's to 24th position. The visit to Wrexham takes on increasing importance.

Match 36 — ALDERSHOT (H) 17/3

Barrett	Bruce	English A	Gilbert	Daniels	Marmon	Collins	Taylor	Morgan	Wilkins	Scott*	Bennett/Hicks
Coles	Ogley	Phillips	Powell	Smith	Wignall	Williams	Puckett	Stewart	Henry	Randall	

2,682 · 20 · 34 · 1-0 · W · 0-0

Morgan 87
Ref: D Vickers

Barrett plays the last game of his loan spell. Aldershot become the fourth successive team to fail to score, or gain points, at Layer Rd. Mark Ogley back-headers a Barrett punt across his own box for Morgan to stab home an unusual open-play goal after his recent run of penalty goals.

Match 37 — WREXHAM (A) 24/3

Marriott	Bruce	Goddard	Gilbert	Daniels	Marmon	Collins	English A	Morgan	Wilkins	Taylor	Armstrong
O'Keefe	Salathiel	Wright	Thackeray	Beaumont	Youds	Preece R*	Owen	Sertori	Worthington	Bowden	

4,653 · 23 · 34 · 2-3 · L · 1-0

Marmon 27, Wilkins 72
Worthington 69, 89, Thackeray 76
Ref: J Kirkby

Marriott joins from Notts F. U's twice hold the lead in this vital bottom-of-the-table clash. A freak five-minute hailstorm after Wilkins' goal and the storm clouds that gather are ominous for U's as Andy Thackeray nets the greasy ball, and Gary Worthington stuns U's faithful late on.

Match 38 — SCUNTHORPE (H) 31/3

Marriott	Bruce	Goddard	Gilbert	Daniels	Marmon	Bennett	English A	Morgan	Wilkins	Taylor	Daws/Marshall
Musselwhite	Smalley	Longden	Ward	Bramhall	Taylor	Lillis	Cowling*	Cotton`	Flounders	Hamilton	

2,920 · 12 · 37 · 1-0 · W · 1-0

Morgan 45
Ref: J Carter

Away from the relegation battle, U's announce plans for a stadium at Wick Farm. Ardleigh. Morgan's eighth in ten and twelfth of the season, gives U's a much needed victory, but all of their rivals pick up points as well. Wilkins and Bennett create room for Bruce to cross for the goal.

Match 39 — PETERBOROUGH (A) 7/4

Marriott	Bruce	Goddard	Gilbert	Daniels	Marmon	Bennett	English A	Morgan	Wilkins*	Taylor	Restarick
Godden	Luke	Crosby	Halsall	Robinson	McElhinney	Sterling	Hine	Jepson*	Riley	Oakes	Osborne

4,025 · 9 · 37 · 0-1 · L · 0-1

Sterling 30
Ref: N Midgley

Goddard's 62nd-min free-kick curls round Tony Godden but comes back off the inside of the post. U's press and waste four real chances, but they are unable to cancel out Posh's goal on the half-hour. Ronnie Jepson, on loan from P Vale, knocks Phil Crosby's cross to Worrell Sterling.

Match 40 — EXETER (H) 10/4

Marriott	Bruce	Goddard	Gilbert	Daniels	Marmon	Bennett	English T*	Morgan	Wilkins	Taylor	Scott
Miller	Hiley	McPherson	McNichol	Taylor	Whitehead	Kelly	Bailey	McDermott	Neville	Young	

3,369 · 1 · 37 · 0-1 · L · 0-0

McNichol 60
Ref: D Reed

Exeter arrive as favourites for the title, but curiously have lost more away games than the U's T English has a great chance on 48 minutes but misses from 10 yards. Shaun Taylor touches on a free-kick to Jim McNichol to fire in the first goal conceded for two months, or 555 minutes.

Match 41 — HARTLEPOOL (A) 14/4

Marriott	English A	Goddard	Gilbert	Daniels	Marmon	Bennett	Taylor	Morgan	Wilkins	Scott*	Bennett
Siddall	Olsson	McKinnon	Tinkler	MacDonald	Bennyworth	Allon	Tupling	Baler	Dalton	Atkinson P*	Wilson

3,397 · 21 · 40 · 2-0 · W · 0-0

Bennett 76, Collins 83
Ref: W Burns

U's start seven points adrift of Halifax. Doncaster and Wrexham haven't lost at home since Cyril Knowles took over in December. The writing is on the wall by the time Gilbert, under pressure from Steve Cookson, lobs over Marriott. Morgan's goal comes when Ken Veysey fouls English.

Match 42 — SOUTHEND (H) 16/4

Marriott	English A	Goddard	Gilbert*	Daniels	Marmon	Bennett*	Collins	Morgan	Wilkins	Taylor	Bruce/Scott
Sansome	Austin	Edinburgh	Martin	McDonough	Clark	Ansah	Smith P*	Crown	Benjamin	Cooper	Daley

5,283 · 3 · 40 · 0-2 · L · 0-1

Benjamin 42, Daley 82
Ref: I Borrett

U's throw away the lifeline given to them by the win at Hartlepool with a dismal display in the Essex derby. A long throw-in reaches Andy Ansah, whose shot hits the post and rebounds to Ian Benjamin. Sub Peter Daley adds a stunning second, leaving Goddard trailing in his wake.

Match 43 — TORQUAY (A) 21/4

Marriott	Bruce	Goddard	Gilbert	Daniels*	Marmon	Collins	English A	Morgan	Wilkins	Grainger*	Bennett/Scott
Veysey	Holmes	Lloyd	Whiston	Matthews	Hannigan	Hall	Elliott*	Loram`	Cookson	Hay	Edwards/Hirons

1,531 · 15 · 40 · 1-4 · L · 0-3

Morgan 78p [Loram 59]
Cookson 11, Gilbert 24 [og], Elliott 43.
Ref: H King

Crisp and businessman Ray Hollingsworth foot the bill for U's travelling fans as Torquay abandon their Members Scheme. The writing is on the wall by the time Gilbert, under pressure from Steve Cookson, lobs over Marriott. Morgan's goal comes when Ken Veysey fouls English.

Match 44 — DONCASTER (H) 24/4

Marriott	English A	Goddard	Gilbert	Daniels	Marmon	Collins	English A	Morgan	Wilkins	Taylor	Bennett
Samways	Adans*	Raffell	Harle !	Ashurst	Douglas	Muir`	Stiles	Turnbull	Jones D	Noteman	Brackle/Reddish

2,631 · 23 · 43 · 2-0 · W · 2-0

Marmon 31, 38
Ref: D Elleray

U' prolong the inevitable with a too-late win. They need maximum points and a rival to slip up. David Harle is booked for a foul on Collins, remonstrates and is red-carded (45). Marmon doubles his U's goal tally with two firmly-placed headers. Wilkins hits the bar on 89 minutes.

Match 45 — CAMBRIDGE (A) 29/4

Marriott	Bruce	Radford	Gilbert*	Daniels	Marmon	Collins	English A	Morgan	Wilkins	Bennett*	Scott/Taylor
Vaughan	Fensome	Kimble`	Leadbitter	Chapple	Daish	Cheetham	Baillie	Dublin*	Claridge	Philpott	Taylor/Cook

4,558 · 6 · 43 · 0-4 · L · 0-2

Cheetham 25, 67p, 70p, Claridge 35
Ref: G Pooley

With Doncaster and Hartlepool both winning yesterday. U's already know their fate in this Sunday noon clash at the Abbey Stadium. Michael Cheetham completes his first hat-trick after English fouls him, and when Daniels trips John Taylor. ex U's, who had just replaced Dion Dublin.

Match 46 — BURNLEY (H) 5/5

Marriott	English B	Hicks*	Daniels	Marmon	Bennett	Collins*	Morgan	Wilkins	Jakub	Atkinson*	Grainger/Kinsella
Williams	Measham	Deakin	Deary	Farrell	Davis S	White	Smith*	Francis	Jakub	McGrory/Howarth	

2,786 · 16 · 43 · 1-2 · L · 1-1
Away 3,326

Morgan 17p
Taylor 39 [og], White 65p
Ref: J Ashworth

Only the possible winding up of Aldershot can save U's. Steve Davis pushes Morgan in the back, and he despatches his twelfth of the season. Taylor rifles Joe Jakub's low cross into his own net. Winston White scores the last league goal at Layer Road after Bruce fells John Francis.

Home 3,150 · Average 3,150

BARCLAYS DIVISION 4 (CUP-TIES) Manager: Wallace ⇨ Foley ⇨ Mills SEASON 1989-90

Littlewoods Cup

			1	2	3	4	5	6	7	8	9	10	11	subs used
			Grace	Hicks	Rooke	English A	Daniels	Radford*	Bennett	Collins	Wilkins	Scott	Allinson	Taylor
			Sansome	*Dixon*	*Roberts*	*Martin*	*Prior*	*Brush*	*Cook*	*Butler*	*Crown*	*Walsh*	*Bennett*	

1:1 H SOUTHEND 22/8: F-A 3-4, H-T 2-1, L

Scott 27, 78, Bennett 34
Bennett 15, Crown 53, 80, Martin 55
Ref: T Ward

Newly-relegated Southend signed Walsh for £30k in the summer. U's young side is punished for every error. Wilkins shrugs off the attention of Spencer Prior to set up Scott. Gary Bennett, in two guises, scores for both sides. David Crown settles the game via a deflection off English.

			1	2	3	4	5	6	7	8	9	10	11	subs used
			Grace	Hicks	Rooke	English A	Daniels	Radford*	Bennett	Collins	Wilkins	Scott*	Allinson	Taylor/Kinsella
			Sansome	*Dixon*	*Roberts*	*Martin*	*Prior*	*Brush*	*Cook*	*Butler*	*Crown*	*Walsh*	*Bennett*	*Smith*

1:2 A SOUTHEND 29/8: F-A 1-2, H-T 0-1, L

Collins 79
Crown 3p, Bennett 78
Ref: M Bailey

(Colchester lost 4-6 on aggregate)

U's are eliminated because of six errors during the tie. Hicks pushes Mario Walsh, as they jump to meet Andy Dixon's cross. The defence is caught again when Walsh flicks on Paul Roberts' long throw. Collins, the only star, deservedly nets his first U's goal with a low drilled shot.

Leyland DAF Trophy

			1	2	3	4	5	6	7	8	9	10	11	subs used
			Grace	Hicks*	Stafford	Kinsella	Daniels	Gilbert	Bennett	Collins	Morgan	English T*	Wilkins	Pollard/Scott
			Gleasure	*Chard*	*Gernon*	*Thomas*	*Wilcox*	*McPherson*	*Berry*	*Singleton*	*Sandeman**	*Barnes*	*Scope*	*Collins*

1 H NORTHAMPTON 7/11: 23 F-A 0-3, H-T 0-1, L 1,780 3:17

Barnes 26, Chard 76, Collins 88
Ref: D Vickers

17-year-old Kinsella makes his full debut. Bobby Barnes, Cobblers' replacement for Adcock, who has joined Bradford, runs the show and opens the scoring despite a lunge from Hicks. His free-kick finds Phil Chard and late on he provides the cross for Steve Collins to hammer in.

			1	2	3	4	5	6	7	8	9	10	11	subs used
			Grace	Taylor	Radford	Collins	Daniels	English A	Bennett	Ball	Morgan*	Scott	Grainger*	Kinsella/Wilkins
			Beeney	*Barton*	*Cooper*	*Berry*	*Oxbrow*	*Golley*	*Gall*	*Elsey**	*Pritchard*	*Butler**	*Sorrell*	*Rumble/Charlery*

1 A MAIDSTONE 10/1: 23 F-A 1-2, H-T 0-2, L 1,176 4:6

Ball 88
Gall 8, Butler 29
Ref: P Don

U's must beat the Stones by three clean goals to progress, but two in the first half-hour eliminates them from the competition. Mark Gall's 17th of the campaign and an eleventh for Steve Butler seal the win. United's consolation comes when Scott's cross is nodded on by Daniels to Ball.

FA Cup

			1	2	3	4	5	6	7	8	9	10	11	subs used
			Grace	Bruce	Stafford	English A	Daniels	Gilbert	Bennett	Collins	Morgan	English T*	Wilkins	Taylor
			Parks	*Perryman**	*Peters*	*Millen*	*Evans*	*Ratcliffe*	*Jones*	*May*	*Holdsworth**	*Blissett*	*Smillie*	*Godfrey/Haag*

1 A BRENTFORD 18/11: 23 F-A 1-0, H-T 0-0, W 4,171 3:24

Bennett 46
Ref: B Hill

The Bees, like U's, are struggling near the foot. Despite this the U's gain a magnificent win, only their second in 20 games. Terry Evans strikes the underside of the bar. Morgan pushes a ball wide to Collins: his cross is diverted past the despairing dive of Tony Parks by Gary Bennett.

			1	2	3	4	5	6	7	8	9	10	11	subs used
			Grace	Bruce	Hagan	English A	Daniels	Gilbert	Bennett	Collins*	Morgan*	English T	Wilkins	Taylor/Scott
			Thomas	*Ashley*	*Frain*	*Atkins*	*Overson*	*Matthewson*	*Bell*	*Bailey*	*Sturridge**	*Gleghorn*	*Langley*	*Hopkins*

2 H BIRMINGHAM 9/12: 23 F-A 0-2, H-T 0-1, L 3,858 3:8

Gleghorn 4, 90
Ref: A Ward

Dave Mackay's Brum are facing up to life in the third division for the first time. A disappointing all-ticket crowd and the Match of the Day cameras sees Simon Sturridge have two efforts disallowed. Nigel Gleghorn's double come via an Ian Atkins free-kick and a Dougie Bell cross.

League Table

		P		Home					Away				Pts
			W	D	L	F	A	W	D	L	F	A	
1	Exeter	46	20	3	0	50	14	8	9	13	33	34	89
2	Grimsby	46	14	4	5	41	20	8	9	6	29	27	79
3	Southend	46	15	3	5	35	14	7	6	10	26	34	75
4	Stockport	46	13	6	4	45	27	8	5	10	23	35	74
5	Maidstone	46	14	4	5	49	21	8	3	12	28	40	73
6	Cambridge *	46	14	3	6	45	30	7	7	9	31	36	73
7	Chesterfield	46	12	9	2	41	19	7	5	11	22	31	71
8	Carlisle	46	15	4	4	38	20	6	4	13	23	40	71
9	Peterborough	46	10	8	5	35	23	7	9	7	24	23	68
10	Lincoln	46	11	6	6	30	27	7	8	8	18	21	68
11	Scunthorpe	46	9	9	5	42	25	8	6	9	27	29	66
12	Rochdale	46	11	4	8	28	23	9	2	12	24	32	66
13	York	46	10	5	8	29	24	6	11	6	26	29	64
14	Gillingham	46	9	8	6	28	21	8	3	12	18	27	62
15	Torquay	46	12	2	9	33	29	3	10	10	20	37	57
16	Burnley	46	6	10	7	19	18	6	4	11	26	37	56
17	Hereford	46	7	4	12	31	32	8	6	9	25	30	55
18	Scarborough	46	10	5	8	35	28	5	5	13	25	45	55
19	Hartlepool	46	12	4	7	45	33	3	6	14	21	55	55
20	Doncaster	46	7	7	9	29	29	5	4	14	24	31	51
21	Wrexham	46	8	8	7	28	28	5	4	14	23	39	51
22	Aldershot	46	8	7	8	28	26	4	7	12	21	43	50
23	Halifax	46	5	9	9	31	29	7	4	12	26	36	49
24	COLCHESTER	46	9	3	11	26	25	2	7	14	22	50	43
		1104	261	135	156	841	585	156	135	261	585	841	1521

* promoted
after play-offs

Odds & ends

Double wins: (1) Hartlepool.

Double defeats: (6) Cambridge, Exeter, Lincoln, Peterborough, Wrexham, York.

Won from behind: (1) Hartlepool (h).

Lost from in front: (7) Wrexham (h). Exeter (a). Cambridge (h), York (a). Rochdale (h), Wrexham (a), Burnley (h).

High spots: Emergence of youth players in Bennett, Bruce, Grainger, Kinsella, Pollard and Radford.

Five consecutive home wins from February, without conceding a goal.

Low spots: Relegation to the GM Vauxhall Conference after 40 seasons in the league.

Relegation fate decided, in advance by others, whilst U's not in action.

Retirement of the inspirational Jock Wallace due to illness.

Defection of coach, Alan Ball to greener pastures.

A further 17 debutants, maintaining team instability.

Eight-game non-winning start to the season.

Only one cup win in six ties played.

Continuing uncertainty over the location of the new stadium.

Player of the Year: Neale Marmon.

Ever presents: (1) Scott Daniels.

Hat-tricks: (0).

Leading scorer: Trevor Morgan (12).

Appearances and Goals

	Appearances						Goals			
	Lge	Sub	LC	Sub	FAC	Sub	Lge	LC	FAC	Tot
Allinson, Ian	12	1	2				3			3
Ball, Steve	3	1								
Barrett, Scott	13									
Bennett, Gary	26	10	2		2		4	1	1	6
Blake, Mark	4						1			1
Bruce, Marcelle	28	1			2	2	1			1
Collins, Eamonn	39		2	2	2	2	2	1		3
Daniels, Scott	46		2	2	2	2				
Devereux, Robert	1	1			1					
English, Tony	44		2	2	2	2	2			2
English, Tom	12	1			2	2	3			3
Gilbert, Billy	26	1			2	2				
Goddard, Karl	16						1			1
Grace, John	19	3	2		2		2			2
Grainger, Martin	4	3								
Hagan, Jim	2			1						
Hansbury, Roger	4									
Hicks, Stuart	16	4	2			1				
Kinsella, Mark	1	5		1						
Marmon, Neale	22						4			4
Marriott, Andy	10									
Morgan, Trevor	31	1			2	2	12			12
Pollard, John	1	6								
Radford, Mark	19	1	2		1		4			4
Restarick, Steve		1			1					
Rooke, Rodney	4		2			1				
Scott, Robert	14	11	2		1		3	2		5
Stafford, Clive	15	2		1						
Taylor, Les	30	6	2	2	2		1			1
Warner, John	1	1								
Wilkins, Richard	43		2	2	2	3	5			5
31 players used	506	57	22	3	22	3	48	4	1	53

GM VAUXHALL CONFERENCE

Player Manager: Ian Atkins

SEASON 1990-91

No	Date	Att	Pos	Pt	F-A	H-T	1	2	3	4	5	6	7	8	9	10	11	subs used	Scorers, Times, and Referees
1	A YEOVIL 18/8	4,169	L	0	0-2	0-1	Barrett	English	Atkins	Collins	Daniels	Marmon	Kinsella*	Bennett	**Scott**	Yates	Smith	Radford	Spencer 20, Conning 74 Ref: G Cain
							Bond	*Sherwood*	*Lowe*	*Shail*	*Rutter*	*Dawkins*	*Carroll*	*Wallace*	*Wilson*	*Spencer*	*Conning*		

Atkins becomes player-boss on a two-year contract. Aldershot's survival sees U's as the first competitive visitors to the plush £3.2m Huish Pk. Wilkins joins Cambridge for £65k. Micky Spencer's effort appears not to cross the line. Peter Conning volleys home Robbie Carroll's cross.

No	Date	Att	Pos	Pt	F-A	H-T	1	2	3	4	5	6	7	8	9	10	11	subs used	Scorers, Times, and Referees
2	A WELLING 22/8	1,828	D	1	1-1	0-1	Barrett	English	Atkins	Collins	Daniels	Marmon	Radford*	Bennett*	Yates	Kinsella	Smith	Bruce/Scott	Yates 76 Clemmence 38 Ref: M Daughtery
							Humphries	*Hone*	*Horton*	*Glover*	*Ransom*	*Clemmence*	*White*	*Handford**	*Abbott*	*Robbins*	*Reynolds*	*Francis*	

United are clearly the better side, but have to wait until 14 minutes from the end for Bruce to cross to Yates, who is on loan from Brum. U's had fallen behind when Stuart White put Terry Robbins away on the left, and his cross was headed in from close range by Neil Clemmence.

No	Date	Att	Pos	Pt	F-A	H-T	1	2	3	4	5	6	7	8	9	10	11	subs used	Scorers, Times, and Referees
3	H MERTHYR 25/8	2,008	W	4	3-1	2-1	Barrett	English	Atkins	Collins	Daniels	Marmon	Bruce*	Bennett	Yates	Kinsella	Smith	Radford	Yates 9, Bennett 45, Collins 56 Boyle 10 Ref: D Madgewick
							Wager	*Tucker*	*Stevenson*	*Boyle*	*Lewis*	*Rogers*	*Lissaman*	*Webley*	*Thompson*	*Beattie*	*Evans**	*Sanderson*	

U's take the lead when Collins' shot clips Yates' heel and flies into the net. Ex-C Palace man Terry Boyle levels within a minute. In the fourth minute of injury-time, Smith's cross finds Bennett to curl past Gary Wager. Collins' celebrations after his goal are straight out of Italia '90.

No	Date	Att	Pos	Pt	F-A	H-T	1	2	3	4	5	6	7	8	9	10	11	subs used	Scorers, Times, and Referees
4	A FISHER 27/8	1,395	D	5	0-0	0-0	Barrett	English	Atkins	Collins	Daniels	Marmon	Bruce*	Bennett*	Yates	Kinsella	Smith	Donald/Scott	Ref: D Orr
							Jolly	*Blackford*	*Bright*	*Little*	*Smart P*	*Collins*	*Dryden*	*Mehmet*	*Gorman*	*Mann**	*Docker*	*Kellcher*	

U's face up to the realities of life in the Conference at the tiny Surrey Docks ground in London's Docklands. The bulk of the crowd follow the green and yellow-striped U's, who create only two chances via Bennett. He shoots wide (33), and tamely into Simon Jolly's hands on 49 mins.

No	Date	Att	Pos	Pt	F-A	H-T	1	2	3	4	5	6	7	8	9	10	11	subs used	Scorers, Times, and Referees
5	H NORTHWICH 1/9	**1,966**	W	8	**4-0**	2-0	Barrett	English	Atkins	Collins*	Daniels	Marmon	Kinsella*	Bennett	Yates	Walsh	Smith	Donald/Radford	Walsh 8, 73, Yates 15, English 48 Ref: P Vosper
							Ball	*Blain*	*Clarke*	*Maguire*	*Parker J*	*Hancock**	*O'Connor*	*Jones*	*Parker D*	*Callaghan*	*Stringer**	*Morton/Shaw*	

Walsh returns from Southend for £25k, the same fee set by a tribunal for Barrett, who poaches two goals. He becomes the first U's player to score on two club debuts, having scored at Burnley in 1987. Atkins hopes to sign Yates, after the loanee notches his third goal in five games.

No	Date	Att	Pos	Pt	F-A	H-T	1	2	3	4	5	6	7	8	9	10	11	subs used	Scorers, Times, and Referees
6	A BARROW 8/9	1,441	D	9	2-2	1-2	Barrett	English	Atkins	Collins	Daniels	Marmon	Kinsella*	Bennett*	Yates	Walsh	Smith	Grainger/Donald	Walsh 5, Yates 76 Cowperthwaite 18, 21 Ref: J Parker
							McDonnell	*Marsh*	*Chilton*	*Skivington*	*Messenger*	*Farrell*	*Doherty*	*Gilmour*	*Comp'thw'te*	*Lowe*	*Butler*		

U's take the lead from an unstoppable shot by Walsh, via Collins' corner. Colin Cowperthwaite, Barrow's all-time leading scorer, flicks in a Gary Messenger nod, and follows up with a spectacular overhead kick from 18 yards. Yates exploits their aerial weakness with a firm header.

No	Date	Att	Pos	Pt	F-A	H-T	1	2	3	4	5	6	7	8	9	10	11	subs used	Scorers, Times, and Referees
7	H TELFORD 15/9	2,164	W	12	2-0	2-0	Barrett	English	Atkins	Collins	Daniels	Marmon	Donald*	Bennett*	Yates	Walsh*	Smith	Grainger/Scott	Daniels 3, Walsh 25 Ref: B Foreman
							Charlton	*Salathiel*	*Brindley*	*Humphreys*	*Dyson P*	*Grainger*	*Davison**	*Myers*	*Osbourne*	*Richards*	*Nelson*	*Crawley*	

Wallace receives stab wounds in an attack near his Spanish home. Yates' loan spell is extended indefinitely. Walsh, carrying a thigh injury, nets his fourth in three, after Bennett's shot rebounds off Kevin Charlton. Earlier, Daniels scored his first U's goal, chipping in a loose ball.

No	Date	Att	Pos	Pt	F-A	H-T	1	2	3	4	5	6	7	8	9	10	11	subs used	Scorers, Times, and Referees
8	A BOSTON 19/9	1,620	W	15	3-1	2-0	Barrett	English*	Atkins	Collins	Daniels	Marmon	Donald	Bennett*	Yates	Walsh	Smith	Ryan/Kinsella	Walsh 15, 87, Bennett 38 Cavell 60 Ref: M Swift
							McKenna	*Shirtliff*	*Stephenson*	*Beech*	*Hardy*	*Raffell*	*Tomlinson*	*Cook C*	*Cavell*	*Richardson*	*Campbell*		

Boston, 7-0 winners v Lowestoft in Saturday's FA Cup-tie, fall to U's first away win. On a windy night, Walsh's tally rises to six in four. 83rd-minute sub Ryan, loaned from Cambridge Utd, provides the pinpoint cross for Walsh after Boston had threatened with the wind at their backs.

No	Date	Att	Pos	Pt	F-A	H-T	1	2	3	4	5	6	7	8	9	10	11	subs used	Scorers, Times, and Referees
9	H CHELTENHAM 22/9	2,527	W	18	3-1	1-1	Barrett	English	Atkins	Collins	Daniels	Marmon	Donald	Bennett*	Yates*	Walsh	Smith	Rees/Ryan	Atkins 23p, Bennett 49, Walsh 90 Buckland 10 Ref: M Alexander
							Barron	*Jordan*	*Willets*	*Brogan**	*Vircavs*	*Williams*	*Crouch*	*Burns*!	*Nuttall*	*Buckland*	*Brain**	*Tuohy/Bloomfield*	

U's sit neatly behind Kettering and Barnet. Mark Buckland, top scorer in the last two seasons, meets Kevin Willets' cross. Walsh is hauled down by Nick Jordan in the box for Atkins' first U's goal. Chris Burns aims a kick at Collins on the hour and receives a red card for his pains.

No	Date	Att	Pos	Pt	F-A	H-T	1	2	3	4	5	6	7	8	9	10	11	subs used	Scorers, Times, and Referees
10	A RUNCORN 29/9	861	W	21	3-0	2-0	Barrett	Williams	Atkins	Collins	Daniels	Marmon	Donald	Bennett*	Yates*	Walsh	Smith	Ryan	Atkins 7, 88p, Marmon 16 Ref: A Davies
							Edwards	*Sang*	*Carroll*	*Hawtin*	*Harold*	*Rudge*	*Saunders*	*Carter*	*Highdale**	*Willis**	*Brady/Withers*		

Walsh trails Runcorn's Mark Carter, with nine, by two goals in the scoring charts. Ex-Everton star Atkins returns to Merseyside to hit a great double-strike. His first, from 20 yards, takes the slightest deflection past Arthur Williams; the second, a harsh handball against Tony Edwards.

11. A — MACCLESFIELD — 6/10
- Div 3 | L | 21 | 0-1 (0-0) | Att 1,100 | Pos 14
- Heesom 80
- Ref: J Winter
- U's: Barrett, English, Atkins, Collins, Daniels, Marmon, Donald, Bennett*, Yates, Walsh, Smith, Kinsella
- Macclesfield: Zelem, Shepherd, Heesom, Edwards, Tobin, Hanlon, Askey, Kendall, Lambert, Burr, Imrie
- Macclesfield's full-back. Darren Heesom's third corner in as many minutes is caught in the wind and creeps through a melee of players, past Barrett into the net for a bizarre winner. Collins spurns three glorious chances from Bennett, who has two efforts saved by Alan Zelem's legs.

12. H — SUTTON — 13/10
- Div 3 | W | 24 | 1-0 (1-0) | Att 2,716 | Pos 11
- Bennett 35
- Ref: C Proud
- U's: Barrett, English, Atkins, Collins, Daniels, Marmon, Donald*, Bennett, Yates, Walsh*, Smith, McDonough/Kinsella
- Sutton: Sullivan*, Rains, Dawson, Berry, Golley, Rogers, Massey, Gill, Newman^, McKinnon, Gates, Dack/Seagroat
- Atkins signs McDonough from Southend in a straight swap with Morrys Scott. Tending Council raise objections to the Ardleigh Stadium project. U's extend their 100% home record, after Nicky Sullivan is stretchered off with a broken jaw from a clash with Walsh on just 15 secs.

13. A — BATH — 20/10
- Div 3 | W | 27 | 2-1 (2-0) | Att 1,078 | Pos 22
- Atkins 1p, Yates 16 | Randall 78
- Ref: B Baker
- U's: Barrett, English, Atkins, Collins, Daniels, Marmon, Donald, Bennett*, Yates, Walsh, Smith, McDonough
- Bath: Churchwood/Underhill, Singleton, Ricketts, Crowley, Brown, Cowins*, Banks, Freegard, Randall, Mings^, Smith C/Payne
- Walsh is fouled by Tony Ricketts, for Atkins to net his fourth of the season. Walsh then chases an English ball that should have been a goal back up by Crowley, and crosses to Yates to sidefoot in. U's toy with the home side, but have an anxious end when Paul Randall pulls a goal back.

14. H — BARROW — 27/10
- Div 3 | W | 30 | 1-0 (1-0) | Att 2,650 | Pos 14
- Walsh 35
- Ref: L Short
- U's: Barrett, English, Atkins, Collins, Daniels, Marmon, Donald, Bennett, Yates*, Walsh, Smith, McDonough
- Barrow: McDonnell, Marsh, Chilton^, Skivington, Stimpson, Proctor, Doherty, Gilmour*, Messenger, Lowe, Butler, Todhunter/Burgess
- Barrow visit for the first time since February 1972, the season in which they were not re-elected. Walsh rises to plant Bennett's accurate cross into the net for his eighth goal in ten. U's now possess one of three 100% home records with Liverpool and third division leaders Southend.

15. H — STAFFORD — 3/11
- Div 3 | W | 33 | 2-0 (2-0) | Att 2,403 | Pos 20
- Walsh 2, English 32
- Ref: C Finch
- U's: Barrett, English, Atkins, Collins, Daniels, Marmon, Donald, Bennett, Yates, Walsh*, Smith, McDonough
- Stafford: Price, Turley, Wood, Simpson, Essex, Bremner, Anastasi*, Merchant, Palgrave, Collymore, Shelley, Khan
- Stafford's Changez Khan is reputed to be the longest throw-in in soccer. His run up, and handstand on the ball catapults the throw up to 60 yards and has been on national TV. Walsh receives a head injury scoring the opener. Stan Collymore comes closest for the visitors on 20 mins.

16. A — KETTERING — 10/11
- Div 3 | L | 33 | 0-1 (0-1) | Att 5,020 | Pos 7
- Keast 10
- Ref: G Poll
- U's: Barrett, English, Atkins, Collins, Daniels, Marmon, Donald, Bennett, Yates*, Walsh, Smith, McDonough
- Kettering: Blackwell, Keast, Phillips, Nicol, Slack, Goodwin, Huxford, Bancroft, Brown, Hunt^, Cooke*, Jones/Graham
- After a great start, Kettering have lost to Chelmsford in the FA Cup and Wycombe, 1-5, in the league. Backed by 1,500 fans U's are class up to the box, but an inability to finish allows the Poppies to win courtesy of Dougie Keast's stunning 25-yarder. Kevin Blackwell performs heroics.

17. H — WYCOMBE — 24/11
- Div 3 | D | 34 | 2-2 (0-1) | Att 2,970 | Pos 7
- Yates 69, Walsh 80 | Ryan 32, 77
- Ref: W Norbury
- U's: Barrett, English, Atkins, Collins, Daniels, Marmon, Donald, Bennett*, Yates*, Walsh, Smith, McDon'gh/Masters
- Wycombe: Granville, Crossley, Walford, Kerr, Creaser, Smith G, Blackler*, Stapleton, West, Ryan^, Hutchinson, Robinson
- Giant Yank Masters begins a trial. Uproar as the Orient FA Cup-tie is fixed, by BSB, for a first-ever UK Sunday night (8 pm) kick-off. In-form Wycombe end U's 100% record. The introduction of McDonough spurs U's to two goals, but Keith Ryan heads in a Simon Hutchinson cross.

18. A — STAFFORD — 1/12
- Div 3 | W | 37 | 2-0 (2-0) | Att 1,304 | Pos 20
- Marmon 7, McDonough 8
- Ref: B Rudkin
- U's: Barrett, English, Atkins, Collins, Daniels, Marmon, Donald, Yates, McDon'gh!, Walsh*, Smith, Bennett
- Stafford: Price, Pearson, Wood R*, Wood F, Essex, Bremner, Turley, Anastasi, Palgrave, Tuohy, Shelley, Khan/Devlin
- McDonough marks the first full game of his second spell with a goal and a red card. Marmon nods in Smith's swinging cross, and 60 secs later runs 40 yards to find Big Roy in space to lob Ryan Price. McDonough, tussling with Steve Essex (43), is booked and kicks Mick Tuohy (80).

19. A — MERTHYR — 15/12
- Div 3 | L | 37 | 0-3 (0-2) | Att 710 | Pos 15
- Green 8, 12, 77
- Ref: A Danskin
- U's: Barrett, English, Atkins, Elliott, Collins, Marmon, Donald, Ryan*, Yates, Walsh, Smith*, Masters/Bruce
- Merthyr: Wager, Mullen, Williams, Boyle, Lewis, Rogers, Giles, Green, Sanderson, Tucker, Lissaman
- U's include former England-B defender Elliott, along with Ryan, who rejoins from Cambridge. Pacey Paul Sanderson leaves Marmon for dead to cross to Phil Green. Four minutes later Green finds himself unmarked at a corner, then completes his treble after good work by Paul Giles.

20. A — CHELTENHAM — 22/12
- Div 3 | W | 40 | 2-1 (2-1) | Att 1,397 | Pos 20
- English 7, Walsh 39 | Casey 2
- Ref: R Harris
- U's: Barrett M, English, Atkins, Collins, Daniels, Marmon, Donald*, Masters*, Yates, Walsh, Smith, Bennett/Elliott
- Cheltenham: Bloomfield, Willetts, Brogan, Stuart, Kennard*, Burns, Payne, Casey, Buckland, Williams, Brooks
- Barrett produces two stunning saves from Kim Casey to gain the two points. Casey gave Town the lead, pouncing on a rebound off Marmon. Collins' pass allows English to cut inside and slot a left-footer home. Masters' shot skids off Mike Barrett, leaving Walsh with a simple tap in.

21. H — BARNET — 26/12
- Div 3 | D | 41 | 0-0 (0-0) | Att 3,946 | Pos 2
- Ref: J Moore
- U's: Barrett, English, Atkins, Collins, Daniels, Marmon, Donald, Masters*, Yates*, Walsh, Smith, Elliott/McDonough
- Barnet: Phillips, Poole, Cooper, Bodley, Nugent, Richardson^, Stein, Clarke^, Bull, Willis, Durham, Hayrettin/Lynch
- This goal-less draw leaves U's a massive 13 points behind runaway leaders Kettering. Barnet boss Barry Fry concedes that United provide a bigger threat to his club than that of Kettering. Marmon sweeps Roger Willis' 23rd-minute effort off the line after Barrett had only half-saved.

No	Date	Team	Att	Pos	Res	Pt	F-A	H-T	Scorers, Times, and Referees	1	2	3	4	5	6	7	8	9	10	11	subs used
22	29/12	H BOSTON	2,416	3 *(14)*	W	44	3-1	2-0	Collins 39, English 45, Walsh 71 / Beech 50 — Ref: D Orr	Barrett / *McKenna*	English / *Shirtliff*	Atkins / *Vaughan*	Collins / *Beech*	Daniels / *Raffell*	Marmon / *Cusack*	Donald / *Nesbitt*	Bennett / *Wharton*	McDon'gh* / *Cavell*	Walsh / *McGinlay*	Smith / *Campbell*	Elliott/Masters
23	1/1	A BARNET	5,105	2 *(3)*	W	47	3-1	1-0	Bennett 9, Walsh 57, Masters 87 / Poole 64p — Ref: D Gallagher	Barrett / *Phillips*	Elliott / *Poole*	Atkins / *Stein*	Collins / *Bodley*	Daniels / *Howell*	Marmon / *Richardson*	Donald / *Tomlinson*^	Bennett* / *Clarke*	McDon'gh* / *Bull^*	Walsh / *Willis*	Smith / *Durham*	Masters/Yates, Hayrettin/Lynch
24	5/1	H SLOUGH	2,175	2 *(8)*	W	50	2-1	2-1	Bennett 16, Walsh 22 / Donnellan 41 — Ref: H Brown	Barrett / *Lahill*	Elliott / *How*	Atkins / *Mallinson*	Collins* / *Stacey*	Daniels / *Anderson*	Marmon / *Knight*	Donald / *Dell*	Bennett / *Stanley*	McDon'gh* / *Sissons*^	Walsh / *Thompson*	Smith / *Donnellan*	Masters/Yates, Langley
25	19/1	A ALTRINCHAM	1,388	2 *(4)*	D	51	2-2	0-2	English 68, McDonough 90 / McKenna 14, Shaw 32 — Ref: R Shepherd	Barrett / *Wealands*	Elliott / *Reid*	Atkins / *Wiggins*	Collins* / *Rowlands*	Daniels / *Rooney*	Marmon* / *Anderson*	Donald / *Shaw*	Bennett / *Daws*	McDonough / *Brady*	Walsh / *McKenna*	Smith / *Showler*	Yates/English
26	26/1	A SUTTON	1,496	2 *(17)*	W	54	1-0	1-0	McDonough 9 — Ref: S Tomlin	Barrett / *McCann*	English / *Hopkins*^	Atkins / *Golley*	Collins* / *Berry*	Daniels / *Rains*	Elliott / *Rogers*	Donald / *Evans*	Bennett / *Barnes*	McDonough / *Dennis*	Yates / *McKinnon*	Smith / *Gates^*	Masters, Elliott/Massey
27	2/3	H BATH	2,277	4 *(21)*	W	57	2-0	1-0	Atkins 23p, Walsh 72 — Ref: R Tye	Barrett / *Churchward/Gill*^	English / *Pratt*^	Atkins / *Palmer*	Collins / *Lowe*	Daniels / *Crowley*	Elliott / *Clark*	Donald / *Banks*	Bennett* / *Lundon*	McDonough / *Singleton^*	Walsh* / *Randall*	Smith / *Mings*	Masters/Ryan, Underhill/Townsend
28	5/3	A SLOUGH	1,120	3 *(11)*	W	60	2-0	1-0	McDonough 38, 79 — Ref: G Bargery	Barrett / *Bunting*	English / *Stacey*	Atkins / *Pratt^*	Collins* / *How*	Daniels / *Anderson*	Marmon / *Dell*	Donald / *Knight*	Bennett* / *Stanley^*	McDonough / *Thompson*	Walsh^ / *Sissons*	Smith / *Donnellan*	Elliott/Ryan, Bashir/Turkington
29	9/3	H MACCLESFIELD	2,735	3 *(7)*	W	63	1-0	1-0	Atkins 33p — Ref: D Madgewick	Barrett / *Zelem*	English / *Sheppard*	Atkins / *Johnson*	Collins / *Edwards*	Daniels / *Tobin*	Marmon / *Hanlon*	Donald / *Askey*	Bennett* / *Lambert*	McDon'gh* / *Ellis^*	Walsh / *Imrie*	Smith / *Timmons^*	Masters/Ryan, Tomlinson/Burr
30	12/3	H RUNCORN	2,969	3 *(7)*	D	64	2-2	0-1	Ryan 55, Bennett 60 / Saunders 36, Byrne 69 — Ref: I Mitchell	Barrett / *Williams*	English / *Edwards*	Atkins / *Byrne*	Collins / *Wilson*	Daniels / *Brady*	Marmon / *Harold*	Donald / *Henshaw*	Bennett / *Rudge*^	McDonough / *Shaugh'sy*^	Walsh* / *Saunders*	Smith / *Withers*	Ryan, King/Dooner
31	23/3	H FISHER	2,493	3 *(22)*	W	67	2-1	1-0	McDonough 26, Walsh 79 / Martin 72 — Ref: C Proud	Barrett / *Bastock*	English / *Little*	Atkins / *Ward*	Collins / *Quinn*	Daniels / *Pearson*	Elliott / *Collins P*	Donald* / *Roberts*	Bennett* / *Parry^*	McDonough / *Gorman*	Walsh / *Victor*	Smith / *Martin*	Marmon/Ryan, Mitchell

Match notes:

22 — Boston, who had drawn 1-1 with Kettering on Boxing Day, are made to look very ordinary by impressive U's. Walsh holds up well to lay off to Collins, who strikes from 18 yards. McDonough does the same for English. Walsh gets a header after Glenn Beech had reduced the arrears.

23 — U's close the gap on Kettering to ten points and a game in hand with three wins and a draw from the holiday programme. Bennett scores a 25-yarder past the sleeping Gary Phillips. Walsh's 13th and Masters' second U's goals are matched only by Atkins' supposed foul on Tony Lynch.

24 — Orient's Frank Clark reports Atkins to the FA after comments following the FA Cup-tie. U's power into an early lead but are unable to produce the goal-feast that their overall play deserves. Collins' perfect pass frees Bennett for his sixth. Six minutes later Atkins' long cross finds Walsh.

25 — The Ardleigh 'Stadium Park' development is officially presented to Tendring Council. A 90th-minute goal from McDonough gives rocky U's an undeserved point. Altrincham race into a two-goal lead via Nigel Shaw's deflection off Marmon's heel. English nods in a Smith cross.

26 — The FA reject Frank Clark's accusations. Birmingham, who have sacked Dave Mackay, are said to be interested in the U's boss. Kettering's last-minute defeat at Altrincham means that United are six points behind the Poppies, with a game in hand and await their visit to Layer Road.

27 — U's fans launch a rival petition against the objectors to Stadium Park, a Sheffield developer seeks planning for a 'sports stadium' at Frating. Brum appoint Lou Macari, ending Atkins' interest. U's slip to fourth after five weeks without a league game due to cup-ties and cancellations.

28 — Kinsella is selected for the Eire U-19 squad. U's 18th league win, and sixth double, puts U's back into third spot, a point behind Kettering and Barnet. All-white U's enjoy the mudbath, that passed a late inspection, especially McDonough who heads in crosses from Bennett and Ryan.

29 — Osbourne joins on trial from Telford. Atkins' penalty gives U's victory in their toughest test so far. Dave Tomlinson, on loan from Barnet, loses aginst the U' for his third different club this season after a similar spell at Boston. Elfyn Edwards, grounded, handles in challenging Bennett.

30 — U's blow the opportunity to go top as Kettering lose at home to Wycombe. Marmon gifts Steve Saunders with a reckless under-hit back-pass. Ryan and Bennett put U's in the ascendancy, only for full-back Steve Byrne to blast a long-range equaliser which the visitors richly deserved.

31 — The Council buys Layer Rd for £1m and leases the ground back for three years. Fisher's Dean Martin, set to join the U's on trial, cancels out McDonough's opener after Barrett only half saves. Walsh apologises for his recent antics, and fittingly gets the winner with an overhead kick.

Season results grid (matches 32–42)

---

32. A WYCOMBE — 25/3
3,200 · 2 L 5 67 · 0-1

U's: Barrett · English · Atkins · Collins · Daniels · Elliott · Marmon · Ryan^ · McDonough · Smith · Masters/Donald
Opp.: Granville · Hutchinson* Cash · Crossley · Creaser · Carroll · Robinson · Stapilton · Ryan · Scott · Guppy · Scope
Scorers: Scott 37
Ref: A Murphy

Defeat leaves Barnet ahead of U's and Kettering on goal-difference. All have 67 points from 32 games, although Altrincham in fourth have 65 from 30 games. Steve Guppy bursts down the left flank and provides the cross for Keith Scott, on loan from Lincoln, to net his fourth in four.

---

33. H YEOVIL — 30/3
3,115 · 2 L 19 67 · 0-0

U's: Barrett · English · Atkins · Collins · Daniels · Marmon · Elliott · Bennett^ · McDonough · Smith · Walsh/Donald
Opp.: Fry · De Souza · Harrower · Shail · Batty · Rutter · McDermott Cooper · Wilson · Carroll · Conning
Scorers: Batty 67
Ref: G Pearson

U's pay £3k for McGavin (22) from Sudbury, and borrows Leworthy (Reading) and Hedman (Palace). The re-shuffled side looks out of sorts as Yeovil complete U's first double defeat. Paul Batty's opportunist 25-yarder takes a deflection off Daniels, who later clears off the line (73).

---

34. A GATESHEAD — 1/4
753 · 3 W 20 70 · 2-1 · 1-1

U's: Barrett · Smith S · English · Atkins · Donald · Daniels · Elliott · Leworthy · McDonough · Walsh* · Smith*/Osbourne/McGavin
Opp.: Farrey · O'Brien · Hall · Halliday · Granycombe Atkinson* · Bell · Butler · Nicholson^ · Allen · Dixon/Sharkey
Scorers: Leworthy 6, McDonough 77; Granycombe 38
Ref: D Oliver

Atkins accepts the blame for changing the side on Saturday and re-calls Donald. Donald's cross is flicked on by McGavin to McDonough after Simon Smith parries. Leworthy had scored his first U's goal, but Neil Granycombe out-witted Smith to level. Altrincham take over as leaders

---

35. A NORTHWICH — 5/4
1,094 · 2 D 18 71 · 2-2 · 1-1

U's: Barrett · Ball · English · Atkins · Donald · Daniels · Elliott · Hedman · Leworthy · McDonough · Osbourne
Opp.: Salathiel · Jones · Atkinson* · Hancock · Wrench · Maguire^ · Blain · Graham · O'Connor · Hemmings · Cutler/Callaghan
Scorers: Walsh 23, McDonough 58; O'Connor 43, Blain 90p
Ref: K Whittaker

Elliott, who has his transfer set at £7k, 48 hours earlier, is slated by Atkins for 'two schoolboy errors' which cost United top spot in front of the Sportscast cameras. In the dying seconds he chops Tony Hemmings, who is going nowhere. U's have now blown three opportunities to go top.

---

36. H WELLING — 9/4
2,889 · 1 W 10 74 · 2-1 · 1-0

U's: Barrett · Barron · English · Atkins · Collins · Daniels · Elliott · Hedman · Leworthy* · McDonough · Osbourne
Opp.: Hone · Robinson · Glover · Ransome · Booker · White · Handford · Abbott · Robbins · Reynolds
Scorers: Atkins 14p, English 62; Hone 65p
Ref: C Finch

Having dropped ten points in the last six games, U's finally hit top spot as Altrincham draw 0-0 with Fisher. Collins, about to shoot, is tugged by Stuart White, giving Atkins his fifth successful kick. Three minutes after English puts U's two up, Hedman fouls Trevor Booker in the box.

---

37. H KETTERING — 17/4
5,048 · 1 W 3 77 · 3-1 · 0-1

U's: Barrett · Blackwell · English · Atkins · Donald · Daniels · Elliott · Hedman · Leworthy* · Walsh* · Osbourne
Opp.: Collins · Huxford · Nicol · Slack* · Goodwin · Keast · Bancroft · Graham^ · Cooke · Brown · Phillips/Emson
Scorers: Bennett 52, English 60, Donald 62; Brown 7
Ref: P Taylor

Another Sportscast broadcast to pubs and clubs. U's had slipped to fourth due to the vagaries of the fixture list. Falling behind to an early Phil Brown stunner, and the loss of Walsh with a head gash, United respond with Bennett's eleventh and a first ever for man-of-the-match Donald.

---

38. H ALTRINCHAM — 20/4
7,221 · 1 D 3 78 · 1-1 · 1-1

U's: Barrett · Wealands · English · Atkins · Donald · Daniels · Marmon · Hedman · Leworthy · McDon'gh* · Osbourne
Opp.: Miller · Wiggins · Rowlands · McCarrick · Shaw · Reid · Daws · Brady* · McKenna · Showler^ · Hughes/Kelly
Scorers: Leworthy 6; Daws 19
Ref: G Willard

The best Conference crowd of the term sees U's lose McDonough (gashed ankle) after 14 mins. He joins Walsh in being out for the rest of the season. The visitors, unbeaten in 27, level Leworthy's early strike when Micky Daws has time to pick his spot from Paul Showler's cross.

---

39. A KIDDERMINSTER — 22/4
1,721 · 2 D 15 79 · 0-0 · 0-0

U's: Barrett · Jones · English · Atkins · Doanld · Daniels · Marmon · Hedman · Leworthy · Bennett · Collins*/Osbourne
Opp.: Wilcox · McGrath · Weir · Benton · Forsyth · Joseph · Whitehouse · Hadley · Lilwall · Humphreys · Elliott/McGavin
Ref: B Millership

U's face an almost impossible task after this and Altrincham's 4-1 win over Sutton. The Robins are a point ahead but have two games in hand. Leworthy has claims for a last-minute penalty turned down, whilst English misses a simple header from two yards. Crisp freezes his money.

---

40. A TELFORD — 26/4
1,592 · 3 L 6 79 · 0-2 · 0-0

U's: Barrett · Humphreys · English · Elliott · Donald · Daniels* · Marmon · Hedman · Leworthy · Bennett* · Grainger
Opp.: McGinty · Nelson · Dyson · Brindley · Humphreys Myers · Forsyth · Langford · Clarke · Benbow* · Worrall · Ryan/McGavin Hurst
Scorers: Hurst 84, Langford 90
Ref: J Everton

The door to the league remains ajar due to Altrincham's defeat at lowly Barrow. U's trail by a point, but have played a game more going into their second Sportscast broadcast of the week. Two late goals see U's drop to third, with Barry Fry's Barnet now emerging as new favourites.

---

41. H GATESHEAD — 30/4
2,667 · 2 W 18 82 · 3-0 · 2-0

U's: Barrett · Smith S · English · Atkins · Donald · Elliott · Marmon · Bennett* · Leworthy · McGavin* · Grainger
Opp.: Farrey · O'Brien · Hall · Brabin · Granycombe Vell · Dixon · Langford · Butler · Sharkey · Atkinson* · Ryan/Kinsella Robinson
Scorers: Bennett 38, Leworthy 45, 78
Ref: G Poll

Despite their poor form of late, this win means that U's can still win the title as Altrincham succumb to a late equaliser at Slough. Gateshead could have been routed but U's have to settle for Leworthy's brace and his assist in Bennett's opener.

---

42. H KIDDERMINSTER — 4/5
3,481 · 2 W 13 85 · 2-0 · 2-0

U's: Barrett · Jones · English · Atkins · Donald · Marmon · Elliott · Hedman · Bennett* · Ryan · McGavin
Opp.: Kurila · McGrath · Weir · Barnett · Forsyth* · Joseph · Howell · Lilwall · Whitehouse · Hadley/Wilcox · Grainger Kinsella
Scorers: Ryan 22, 42
Ref: D Gallagher

Altrincham's 0-2 defeat by Northwich on Thursday leaves a two-horse race. U's must win and Barnet lose at lowly Fisher. As late as the 65th minute, Fisher led 2-1, but eventually lost 2-4. As the last seconds were played out, U's win the trophy they didn't want, the Runners-Up bowl

---

Average 2,992 (Home) · Away 1,876

VAUXHALL CONFERENCE (CUP-TIES) Player Manager: Ian Atkins SEASON 1990-91

FA Cup

	Venue/Opp	Date	F-A		H-T	Att.	1	2	3	4	5	6	7	8	9	10	11	subs used
1	H READING	17/11	2-1 W 3		0-1	3,761 3:14	Barrett Francis	English Jones	Atkins Gilkes	Collins McPherson	Daniels Hicks	Marmon Williams	Donald Friel*	Bennett Taylor	Yates Senior	Walsh Conroy	Smith Moran	Maskell
2	H LEYTON ORIENT	12/12	0-0 D 3		0-0	6,150 3:4	Barrett Heald	English Baker	Atkins Howard	Collins Zorich	Daniels Whitbread	Marmon Pike	Donald Carter	Yates* Castle	McDonough Walsh	Walsh Sitton	Smith Berry	Bennett
2R	A LEYTON ORIENT	17/12	1-4 L 3		1-2	4,615 3:3	Barrett Heald	English Baker	Atkins Howard	Collins Sitton	Daniels* Whitbread	Marmon Pike	Donald Carter*	Masters* Castle	Yates Nugent	Walsh Achampong	Grainger Berry	Bruce/Bennett Hull

Scorers, Times and Referees:
- 1 READING: Atkins 46p, Marmon 60 / Hicks 25 / Ref: A Buksh
- 2 LEYTON ORIENT: Ref: R Wiseman
- 2R LEYTON ORIENT: Masters 22 [Castle 72] / Carter 31, Howard 45, Pike 51, / Ref: R Wiseman

U's continue their great Cup record against third division sides over recent years. A long throw from Adrian Williams is only partially cleared by Atkins, for Martin Hicks to fire home. Straight from the restart, Williams tugs Collins. On the hour Marmon firmly heads Collins' free-kick

The hullabaloo concerning the 8 pm Sunday kick-off is forgotten when the original tie is snowed off. BSB keep to their obligations and show the re-arranged match live. United have to install brighter floodlights for the TV cameras. The strong icy wind spoils the game as a spectacle.

Atkins accuses O's players of getting Grainger sent off after his 80th-minute tackle on Steve Castle causes a dozen-player fracas. Collins is booked for vociferously protesting a clear 11th-minute handball of Walsh's shot. O's second-half supremacy earns a home tie with Swindon.

FA Trophy

	Venue/Opp	Date	F-A		H-T	Att.	1	2	3	4	5	6	7	8	9	10	11	subs used
1	A WINDSOR & ETON	15/1	1-0 W 2		1-0	727 VP:10	Barrett Mitchell	Elliott Gould*	Atkins Walters	Collins Merriman	Daniels Richards	Marmon Woods	Donald Bates	Bennett* White	McDonough Evans	Walsh* Gilman	Smith Creighton	English/Masters Chapman/Dodds
2	H RUNCORN	2/2	2-0 W 2		1-0	2,348 GM:8	Barrett Williams	Elliott Edwards	Atkins Wilson	Collins Carroll	Daniels Brady	Elliott ! Harold	Donald Byrne*	Bennett* Rudge	McDonough Carter	Walsh Saunders	Smith* Hawtin	Yates/Marmon Withers
3	H WIVENHOE	23/2	3-0 W 2		1-0	4,923 VP:6	Barrett Godden	English Hunter	Atkins Fuccillo	Collins Price	Daniels Wright	Marmon Leslie	Donald Bain	Bennett* Edwards*	McDonough Gittings	Walsh* Clark	Smith King	Grainger/Ryan Thompson
QF	H WITTON	16/3	0-2 L 3		0-0	3,079 HFS:1	Barrett Mason	English Lee	Atkins Stewart	Collins McNellis	Daniels Ellis	Elliott Anderson	Donald Thomas	Bennett Lodge	McDonough McCluskie	Walsh Ryan*	Smith Connor	Masters Edwards

Scorers, Times and Referees:
- 1 WINDSOR & ETON: Bennett 42 / Ref: G Poll
- 2 RUNCORN: Walsh 33, Marmon 81 / Ref: J Moore
- 3 WIVENHOE: McDonough 25, Bennett 57, 68 / Ref: M Bailey
- QF WITTON: Connor 86, 88 / Ref: P Jones

Saturday's waterlogged pitch allows United's injuries to clear up. An atrocious Stag Meadow pitch, in the flight path of nearby Heathrow, is frozen on one flank and saturated on the other. Bennett's third in three sees U's through, despite a suspected broken ankle for striker Walsh.

Runcorn have lost just one in eleven. but Walsh's 15th of the term is a simple goal, heading in an English flick from Collins' free-kick. It takes centre-half Marmon to settle the tie with a bullet header, although Elliott, already booked. is red-carded (86) for retaliation on John Carroll.

The first ever north Essex derby sees up-and-coming Wivenhoe, fielding three ex-U's players and bossed by Micky Cook, well-beaten by U's. McDonough opens the scoring with a sweet diving header from Bennett's cross. The youngster adds two, after a Dragons rally after the break.

Walsh goes AWOL after being subbed in the draw with Runcorn. The aggressive runaway HFS Loans League leaders win when Joe Connor taps in Andy Grimshaw's shot against the post, and shrugs off Elliott, who has signed pending a fee to be set by tribunal, for his second goal.

Bob Lord Trophy

	Venue/Opp	Date	F-A		H-T	Att.	1	2	3	4	5	6	7	8	9	10	11	subs used
1	A FISHER	21/1	3-2 W aet 2		1-1	293 VC:22 aet	Barrett Bastock	Bruce Blackford	Atkins Friar	Yates Roberts	Pollard Smart	Marmon Collins	Brooke* Martin	English Mehmet	Masters Gorman	Ryan Little	Smith* Quinn	Restarick/Radford
2	A SUTTON	26/2	0-2 L 3		0-1	582 VC:14	Barrett Sullivan	Bruce Adams	Atkins Hopkins	Yates Taylor	Pollard Costello	Marmon Rogers	Donald* Evans	Radford Barnes	Masters Dennis	Ryan* Massey	Smith* Golley*	Restarick/Hannigan McKinnon

Scorers, Times and Referees:
- 1 FISHER: Marmon 2, Restarick 99, 117 / Gorman 7, Mehmet 106 / Ref: G Pearson
- 2 SUTTON: Dennis 13, Massey 73 / Ref: D Orr

This tie, four times postponed, finally takes place. In only his second senior outing, 18-year-old Restarick cracks the winner, three minutes from the end of extra-time. U's include ex-Spurs and Norwich trialist, Brooke. The attendance is the lowest to assemble for a senior U's match.

With the FA Trophy and league title in sight. Atkins fields only three of the side that beat Wivenhoe. Stuart Massey's flag-kick is cleared only as far as Paul Rogers, whose firm header is diverted in by Lenny Dennis. Peter Evans' floated free-kick is met by Massey's glancing header.

League Table

Pos	Team	P	Home W	Home D	Home L	Home F	Home A	Away W	Away D	Away L	Away F	Away A	Pts
1	Barnet	42	16	4	1	50	23	13	5	3	53	29	87
2	COLCHESTER	42	12	6	3	48	22	11	7	3	39	24	85
3	Altrincham	42	12	6	3	38	19	11	7	5	29	26	82
4	Kettering	42	15	3	3	46	17	6	5	7	29	29	80
5	Wycombe	42	11	3	7	30	21	9	8	4	32	31	74
6	Telford	42	11	4	6	38	22	6	8	8	25	30	67
7	Macclesfield	42	12	4	5	44	29	4	8	11	25	38	63
8	Runcorn	42	9	5	7	37	24	7	4	10	25	37	58
9	Merthyr	42	10	8	3	34	24	5	7	12	25	41	57
10	Barrow	42	7	10	4	33	27	6	10	5	22	30	57
11	Welling	42	8	7	6	33	30	5	6	10	32	45	54
12	Northwich	42	8	5	8	38	29	6	5	10	23	37	52
13	Kidderminster	42	9	5	7	30	26	4	6	11	18	29	52
14	Yeovil	42	7	9	5	29	25	5	11	5	20	47	50
15	Stafford	42	8	6	7	32	38	4	6	11	25	47	50
16	Cheltenham	42	10	6	5	40	31	4	6	11	20	38	48
17	Gateshead	42	9	3	8	31	29	3	7	11	20	54	48
18	Boston	42	9	4	8	40	31	4	7	11	15	38	47
19	Slough	42	9	4	8	31	29	2	15	16	51	45	
20	Bath	42	9	4	8	39	27	1	8	12	16	34	42
21	Sutton	42	6	6	9	29	33	4	3	14	33	49	39
22	Fisher	42	3	9	9	22	30	2	6	13	16	49	30
		924	214	119	129	795	569	129	119	214	569	795	1267

Appearances / Goals

Player	Lge	Sub	FAT	Sub	FAC	Sub	Goals Lge	FAT	FAC	Tot
Atkins, Ian	41		4		3		7		1	8
Barrett, Scott	42		4		3					
Bennett, Gary	34	2	4	1	1	2	9	3		12
Bruce, Marcelle	2	2				1				
Collins, Eamonn	35		4		3		2			2
Daniels, Scott	40		4		3		1			1
Donald, Warren	33	5	4		3		1			1
Elliott, Shaun	14	5	3							
English, Tony	39	1	3	1	3		7			7
Grainger, Martin	3	2		1	1					
Hedman, Rudi	10									
Kinsella, Mark	6	3								
Leworthy, David	9					1	4			4
McDonough, Roy	17	7	4			1	8	1		9
McGavin, Steve	2	6								
Marmon, Neale	36	1	2	1	3		2	1	1	4
Masters, Mike	2	9		2	1		1	1		2
Osbourne, Garry	5	1								
Radford, Mark	1		3							
Rees, Mark		1								
Ryan, Laurie	3	10	1	1	1		3			3
Scott, Morrys	1	3								
Smith, Nicky	34		4		2					
Walsh, Mario	31	1	3		3		17	1		18
Yates, Mark	22	3	3		1		6			6
25 players used	**462**	**65**	**44**	**7**	**33**	**3**	**68**	**6**	**3**	**77**

Odds & ends

Double wins: (7) Bath, Boston, Cheltenham, Gateshead, Slough, Stafford, Sutton.

Double defeats: (1) Yeovil.

Won from behind: (3) Cheltenham (h), Cheltenham (a), Kettering (h).

Lost from in front: (0).

High spots: Seven consecutive home wins from the start of the season. FA Cup win over third division Reading. First ever live satellite TV broadcast. Tremendous travelling support. Biggest Conference attendance of the entire season v Altrincham. Highest average crowd in the Conference.

Low spots: Only five points from the first four league games. Failure, unlike Lincoln and Darlington, to regain League status at the first attempt. Home defeat by Witton in the FA Trophy. Three without a win after going top in March.

Player of the Year: Scott Barrett.

Ever presents: (1) Scott Barrett.

Hat-tricks: (0).

Leading scorer: Mario Walsh (18).

GM VAUXHALL CONFERENCE

Player Manager: Roy McDonough

SEASON 1991-92

No	Date	Att	Pos	Pt	F-A	H-T	Scorers, Times, and Referees	1	2	3	4	5	6	7	8	9	10	11	subs used
1	H MACCLESFIELD 17/8	2,233	W	3	2-0	2-0	Bennett 10, McGavin 45 — Ref: C Proud	Barrett	Donald	Grainger	Kinsella	English	Elliott	Collins	Bennett	McDonough	McGavin*	Smith	Walsh
								Farrelly S	*Shepherd*	*Johnson**	*Edwards*	*Tobin*	*Hanlon*	*Askey*	*Dempsey*	*Lambert*	*Clayton*	*Imrie^*	*Farrelly M/Dawson*

Crisp stands down, and Atkins goes to Brum as Terry Cooper's assistant. Daniels joins Ball at Exeter for £50k. Second-favourites. U's, get off to a great start. A long ball from Collins finds McDonough, who nods into Bennett's path. On half-time, McGavin springs Maccs' offside trap.

No	Date	Att	Pos	Pt	F-A	H-T	Scorers, Times, and Referees	1	2	3	4	5	6	7	8	9	10	11	subs used
2	A BARROW 24/8	1,480	D	4	1-1	1-0	Kinsella 5, Cowperthwaite 49 — Ref: R Poulain	Barrett	Donald	Grainger	Kinsella	English	Elliott	Collins	Bennett	McDonough	McGavin	Smith	Smith
								McDonnell	*Doolan*	*Chilton*	*Skivington*	*Messenger*	*Slater*	*Ballantyne*	*McNall*	*Cowp'thw'te*	*Proctor*	*Doherty*	

U's gain a point from the long trip to Holker St, with Kinsella's first-ever senior goal. He drills a 20-yarder past the despairing dive of Peter McDonnell. The joy is short-lived as Colin Cowperthwaite adds to his pair from last season, deflecting Neil Doherty's fine effort off his shin.

No	Date	Att	Pos	Pt	F-A	H-T	Scorers, Times, and Referees	1	2	3	4	5	6	7	8	9	10	11	subs used
3	A SLOUGH 26/8	2,226	2 / W	7	4-2	4-2	McDonough 4, 24, 28, 41, O'Connor 6, Thompson 12 — Ref: P Taylor	Barrett	Donald	Grainger	Kinsella	English	Elliott*	Collins	Bennett	McDonough	McGavin*	Smith	Phillips/Abrahams
								Bunting	*Stacey*	*Pluckrose*	*Hill*	*Putman*	*Turkington*	*Fielder*	*McKinnon*	*Donnellan*	*Thompson*	*O'Connor*	*Stanley*

McDonough becomes the ninth U's player to score four, with three headers and a tap-in – all in the first half. He is somewhat upset that a second-half lob over Trevor Bunting goes narrowly wide, but enthuses over U's dominance. The third comes after McGavin hits the crossbar.

No	Date	Att	Pos	Pt	F-A	H-T	Scorers, Times, and Referees	1	2	3	4	5	6	7	8	9	10	11	subs used
4	H BATH 31/8	2,416	2 / W	10	5-0	3-0	McGavin 28, 51, Bennett 32, 39, 87 — Ref: M Hair	Barrett	Donald	Grainger	Kinsella	English	Elliott	Collins	Bennett	McDon'gh*	McGavin	Smith	Abrahams
								Churchward/Hedges	*Payne*	*Singleton*	*Crowley**	*Radford*	*Banks*	*Brown*	*Withey*	*Randall**	*Boyle*	*Ricketts/Painter*	

Walsh asks for a move and Luton eye English. Bennett emulates his boss, with the first Layer Rd hat-trick since Lowe in March 87. McGavin scores the best goal pulling down, and striking a Collins pass in one movement (51). Bennett latches onto Barrett's long punt for his third.

No	Date	Att	Pos	Pt	F-A	H-T	Scorers, Times, and Referees	1	2	3	4	5	6	7	8	9	10	11	subs used
5	A WITTON 7/9	1,045	2 / D	11	2-2	1-1	Collins 27, McDonough 47, Thomas 19, Ellis 60 — Ref: K Whittaker	Barrett	Donald	Grainger*	Kinsella	English	Elliott	Collins	Bennett	McDonough	McGavin	Smith	Goodwin McCluskie/Edwards
								Mason	*Stewart*	*Coathup*	*McNellis*	*Ellis**	*Anderson*	*Thomas^*	*Lodge*	*Lutkevitch*	*Cuddy*	*Connor*	

Second-placed U's trail Wycombe by seven points. Paul Lodge's free-kick is won in the air by Steve Ellis, for Karl Thomas to side-foot home. Collins equalises from the edge of the box, and McDonough finishes off Bennett's shot against the bar. Ellis levels with a towering header.

No	Date	Att	Pos	Pt	F-A	H-T	Scorers, Times, and Referees	1	2	3	4	5	6	7	8	9	10	11	subs used
6	H FARNBOROUGH 10/9	2,954	1 / L	11	2-3	1-2	McGavin 21, Collins 86, Coombs 25, Read 45, 67 — Ref: W Norbury	Barrett	Donald	Grainger	Kinsella	English	Elliott	Collins	Bennett	McDonough	McGavin	Smith	Goodwin
								Power	*Holmes*	*Baker*	*Broome*	*Bye*	*Wigmore*	*Rogers*	*Doherty*	*Coombs**	*Read*	*Horton*	*Lovell*

Farnboro' move above U's with a fourth successive away win. For U's, it's only the second Layer Road defeat in 24 Conference games. Simon Read puts Famboro' into an unassailable 3-1 lead after a slip by Elliott. A Collins goal from the edge of the box is too late to salvage a point.

No	Date	Att	Pos	Pt	F-A	H-T	Scorers, Times, and Referees	1	2	3	4	5	6	7	8	9	10	11	subs used
7	H YEOVIL 13/9	2,979	2 / W	14	4-0	1-0	English 41, Bennett 51, 90, [McGavin 56] — Ref: I Mitchell	Barrett	Donald	Grainger	Kinsella	English	Elliott	Collins	Bennett	McDonough	McGavin	Smith	McDermott/McEvoy
								Fry	*Harrower**	*Ferns*	*Shail*	*Rutter*	*Cooper*	*Carroll*	*Batty*	*Pritchard^*	*Spencer*	*Conning*	

U's respond to McDonough's criticism of the recent leak of five goals, with a clean sheet. The Layer Road tally increases to 13 in four games. Ex-C Palace keeper, David Fry, is kept very busy. McDonough warns the fans not to expect a goal-feast every time. Stadium Park is killed off.

No	Date	Att	Pos	Pt	F-A	H-T	Scorers, Times, and Referees	1	2	3	4	5	6	7	8	9	10	11	subs used
8	A CHELTENHAM 21/9	1,157	3 / D	15	1-1	1-1	McDonough 15, Owen 40 — Ref: K Leach	Barrett S	Donald	Grainger	Kinsella	English	Elliott	Collins	Bennett	McDonough	Gray	Smith	Reck
								*Barrett M**	*Butler*	*Willets*	*Owen*	*Vircavs*	*Brogan*	*Brooks**	*Stobart*	*Buckland*	*Casey*	*Purdie*	*Reck*

Holimarine, of the Mowat Group that planned to build Stadium Pk, pulls out of shirt sponsorship. McGavin is sorely missed. McDonough fires a half-volley across the face of Mike Barrett. Steve Owen levels from six yards, and Barrett is relieved to see Jon Purdie's strike hit the post.

No	Date	Att	Pos	Pt	F-A	H-T	Scorers, Times, and Referees	1	2	3	4	5	6	7	8	9	10	11	subs used
9	A WYCOMBE 28/9	5,186	3 / W	18	2-1	0-0	Smith 49, Barrett 90, Guppy 57 — Ref: C Wilkes	Barrett	Donald	Roberts	Kinsella*	English	Elliott	Collins	Bennett	McDonough	McGavin	Smith	Cook
								Hyde	*Cousins*	*Crossley*	*Kerr*	*Creaser*	*Smith*	*Carroll*	*Stapleton**	*West^*	*Nuttell*	*Guppy*	*Scott/Hutchinson*

New-boys Roberts, from Fisher, and Cook, loaned from Southend, debut. 28-year-old Barrett becomes the first United keeper to score in open play. His last-minute punt bounces off the rain-soaked surface and straight over the bemused and stunned Paul Hyde in the Wanderer's goal.

No	Date	Att	Pos	Pt	F-A	H-T	Scorers, Times, and Referees	1	2	3	4	5	6	7	8	9	10	11	subs used
10	H ALTRINCHAM 5/10	2,853	4 / D	19	3-3	2-1	And'n 16(og), McG'n 35, McD'gh 70p, McKenna 19, Anderson 50, Brady 78p — Ref: G Poll	Barrett	Donald	Roberts	Kinsella	English	Elliott	Collins	Bennett	McDonough	McGavin	Smith	Lewis
								Wealands	*Edwards*	*Densmore*	*Rowlands*	*Reid*	*Anderson*	*Rudge*	*Daws*	*Brady*	*Hughes**	*McKenna*	*Lewis*

Six goals, five bookings, two penalties and an own-goal entertain the crowd. McDonough pressures Gary Anderson into a handball, but fouls Paul Rowlands in the box six minutes later for Altrincham's third equaliser. Anderson had put Rowlands' cross into his own net for U's first.

11 H RUNCORN 12/10 — 2,617 — 4 18 22 — W 2-1 — 0-0
Bennett 52, McDonough 86p / Redmond 69
Ref: A Danskin
Barrett / Palladino, Donald / Hughes, Roberts / Redmond, Cook / Carroll, English / Hill, Elliott / Hagan*, Collins / Brabin, Bennett* / Harold, McDonough / Shaughn'sy Saunders, Smith / Withers, Kinsella / Hawtin

Free-scoring U's have netted 30 in eleven games. McDonough and Bennett keep at the top of the GMVC scoring charts, as 'Benno' nets his seventh and the boss gets his eighth, past boxer-keeper Joe Palladino. With McGavin also on seven goals, U's boast a fearsome strike-force.

---

12 A TELFORD 19/10 — 1,109 — 3 4 25 — W 3-0 — 3-0
McDonough 9, 23p, Smith 38
Ref: T Atkinson
Barrett / Acton, Donald / Humphreys Nelson, Roberts / Dyson, Cook* /, English / Brindley*, Elliott / Whittington Myers, Collins /, Bennett* / Grainger Langford, McDon'gh* / Benbow, Smith / Parrish, Kinsella / Phillips Worrall

McDonough moves to the top of the Conference goal chart, one ahead of nine-goal Gary Abbott of Welling. Superbly marshalled by Elliott, U's rip Gerry Daly's Telford to shreds in the first half. Paul Dyson flattens McGavin in the box for the penalty, as the striker shapes to shoot.

---

13 A YEOVIL 30/10 — 2,385 — 3 20 28 — W 1-0 — 0-0
McGavin 90
Ref: R Budden
Barrett / Fry, Donald / Harrower, Roberts / Rowbotham Shail, Cook / Batty, English /, Elliott / Cooper, Collins / Carroll, Bennett* / Wallace, McDonough / Rowlands Spencer, Smith / Conning, Kinsella / Goodwin

U's fall short of the six goals required to take the goalscorers of the month award. McGavin's last-gasp winner puts the U's three points behind leaders Famboro'. Smith's cross sees McGavin's first attempt hit the post, but he reacts quickest to the rebound to settle an uninspiring game.

---

14 H STAFFORD 2/11 — 2,139 — 2 19 31 — W 2-0 — 2-0
Smith 35, McDonough 41
Ref: G Pearson
Barrett / Price, Donald / Lindsey Palgrave, Roberts / Simpson, Cook / Kinsella, English / Wood, Elliott / Berks, Collins / Wilson, Bennett / Pare*, McDon'gh* / Tuohy Newman, Smith / Devlin, Kinsella / Restarick Goodwin, Bradshaw

U's consider a ground-share with Wivenhoe. Bassett (Sheff Utd) offers a derisory £40k for Kinsella. A ninth league win puts U's second, one point behind Famboro'. Barrett earns the plaudits with three stunning saves from Paul Devlin (twice) and a 25-yard thunderbolt by Palgrave.

---

15 A FARNBOROUGH 9/11 — 3,069 — 1 3 34 — W 2-0 — 0-0
Bennett 67, Elliott 80
Ref: S Tomlin
Barrett / Thompson Stemp, Donald /, Roberts / Baker, Cook / Broome*, English / Bye, Elliott / Wigmore*, Collins / Hobson, Bennett* / Doherty, McDon'gh* / Horton Read, Smith / Holmes, Kinsella / Restarick Cook, Rogers/Fleming

Table-toppers Famboro' have eight wins out of eight way, but are not so hot at home. Before a record crowd for the Cherrywood Road ground, swelled by 1,500 U's fans, Smith's corner is flicked on by McDonough for Bennett to net, and then a first in U's colours for lynch-pin Elliott.

---

16 H WELLING 23/11 — 2,933 — 1 11 37 — W 3-1 — 0-0
Bennett 51, Cook 60, English 73 / Robbins 62
Ref: D Orr
Barrett / Barron, Donald / Hone, Roberts / Clemmence Brown, Cook /, English / Ransom, Elliott* / Berry, Collins / White, Bennett* / Francis, McDonough / Abbott Robbins, Smith / Reynolds*, Kinsella / Cook Robinson

Pint-sized Cook's contender for goal-of-the-season is a venomous 30-yarder, that Welling's ex-goalie, Paul Barron, only sees as it re-bounds out off the stanchion. Two mins later GMVC leading scorer, Terry Robbins, nets his twelfth. The first conceded for a record 623 mins.

---

17 A NORTHWICH 30/11 — 1,042 — 1 10 38 — D 1-1 — 0-1
McDonough 64 / Butler 44p
Ref: J McGrath
Barrett / Bullock, Donald / Locke, Roberts / Butler, Cook / Phillips Jones, English / Hancock, Elliott / Stringer, Collins / Ainsworth, Cook / Feeley, McDonough / Easter O'Connor* Blain, Smith* / Kinsella Graham

McDonough's sixth booking brings an automatic suspension, and the draw means he is pipped for Manager of the Month by Telford's Gerry Daly. Roberts 'handles' protecting his face from an Andy Feeley thunderbolt. McDonough forces in Grainger's cross at the second attempt.

---

18 A STAFFORD 3/12 — 961 — 1 19 39 — D 3-3 — 1-0
Bennett 41, 77, McGavin 66, Wolv'son 59, Simpson 69p, Brad'w 86
Ref: R Andrews
Barrett / Price, Donald / Pearson, Roberts / Bradshaw* Simpson, Cook / Kinsella, English / Essex, Elliott / Wood, Collins / Wolverson Hemming, Bennett / Hope Berks, McDonough / Devlin, Smith / Baker

Bennett's opener is U's 50th in all competitions this season, and after putting U's in front for the third time with just 13 minutes left, cavalier attack play loses two points, when sloppy play by Bennett allows Mark Bradshaw to level. McDonough fouls Tony Hemming for the penalty.

---

19 H WYCOMBE 7/12 — 5,086 — 1 2 42 — W 3-0 — 1-0
Bennett 33, McGavin 62, 86
Ref: P Taylor
Barrett / Hyde, Donald / Cousins*, Roberts / Stapleton Crossley, Cook / Creaser, English / Smith, Elliott / Hutchinson Carroll, Collins / West Scott, Bennett / Guppy*, McDonough / Cooper/Deakin, Smith /

U's complete a notable double, to move four points ahead of the Chairboys. Paul Hyde, who had been beaten by Barrett at Adams Park, has a stinker. First he lets a long-range Bennett shot slip under his body, then McGavin's second, and 13th, bounces through his outstretched arms.

---

20 A GATESHEAD 14/12 — 542 — 1 19 45 — W 2-0 — 2-0
Bennett 5, McDonough 30
Ref: G Bradbury
Barrett / Smith S, Donald / Forrest, Roberts / Faddington Lowery, Cook / Corner, English / Halliday, Elliott / Chambers Bell, Collins / Farrey, Bennett* / Restarick* Lamb, McDonough / Veart*, Smith / Dixon, Kinsella / Abrahams

The game kicks-off at 1.30 pm, because the International Stadium has no lights. McDonough escapes suspension, for now, by one point. U's unbeaten league run stretches to 14. Tyneside's boss Tommy Cassidy says 'quite simply they (U's) are the best organised side in the league.'

---

21 H WITTON 21/12 — 2,842 — 1 18 48 — W 3-2 — 2-1
McGavin 3, Bennett 9, English 79, Thomas 42, 63
Ref: C Finch
Barrett / Mason, Donald / Cuddy, Roberts / Coathup, Cook / McNellis, English / Morgan, Elliott / Anderson Thomas, Collins / Wilson*, Bennett* / McCluskie Stewart*, McDonough / Connor Joe Connor Jim/Alford, Smith / English/Restarick

U's race into the lead via McGavin, who nets a McDonough flick from Collins' corner and Bennett, after Keith Mason had blocked his first effort. Witton hit cocky U's with a Karl Thomas double, assisted by the swirling wind. English wins it with a firm header via Smith's corner.

GM VAUXHALL CONFERENCE

Player Manager: Roy McDonough — **SEASON 1991-92**

No	Date	Att	Pos	Pt	Res	F-A	H-T	Scorers, Times, and Referees
22	A 26/12 REDBRIDGE (3)	2,327	1	48	L	1-2	1-1	McDonough 15; *Pamphlett 20, Walsh 81*; Ref: J Smyth
23	A 28/12 RUNCORN (20)	883	1	51	W	3-1	1-1	Bennett 15, Cook 69, McGavin 88; *Saunders 8*; Ref: E Wolstenholme
24	H 1/1 REDBRIDGE (4)	4,773	1	54	W	1-0	1-0	McGavin 17; Ref: K Bullivant
25	A 4/1 MERTHYR (8)	1,032	1	54	L	0-2	0-0	*Coates 54, D'Auria 83*; Ref: D Colwell
26	H 18/1 CHELTENHAM (22)	2,643	1	57	W	4-0	0-0	McGavin 46, 86, McDonough 75, [Kinsella 90]; Ref: A Danskin
27	A 24/1 KETTERING (6)	4,100	1	58	D	2-2	2-2	McGavin 5, Smith 11; *Hill 15, 20p*; Ref: D Shadwell
28	A 7/2 KIDDERMINSTER (14)	1,828	1	59	D	2-2	0-2	Bennett 60, Smith 61; *Davies 4, Humphreys 25*; Ref: D Mansfield
29	H 11/2 BOSTON (15)	3,229	1	62	W	1-0	0-0	McGavin 52; Ref: J Moore
30	A 15/2 WELLING (11)	1,837	1	62	L	1-4	1-2	McDonough 10p; *Robbins 5, 75, Ransom 24, White 89*; Ref: I Mitchell
31	A 28/2 ALTRINCHAM (9)	905	1	65	W	2-1	2-1	McGavin 15, McDonough 35; *McKenna 23*; Ref: T Heilbron

Line-ups

22 — REDBRIDGE (A)

Team	1	2	3	4	5	6	7	8	9	10	11	subs used
U's	Barrett	Donald	Roberts	Kinsella	English	Elliott	Cook*	Bennett*	McDonough	McGavin	Smith	Collins/Restarick
Redbridge	Bennett	Jacques	Watts	Pamphlett	Connor	Ebdon	Mayes	Richardson*	Cavell	Walsh	Blackford	Broom

Barrett rocks U's with a transfer request ahead of his summer contract renewal. Walsh, who joined Redbridge in October for £15k, sinks his old mates, and U's twelve-match unbeaten away run. He taunts the huge U's army, after netting good work by Paul Cavell and David Jacques.

23 — RUNCORN (A)

Team	1	2	3	4	5	6	7	8	9	10	11	subs used
U's	Barrett	Donald	Roberts	Cook*	English	Elliott	Collins	Bennett	McDonough	McGavin	Smith	Kinsella
Runcorn	Williams	Bates	Mullen	Redman	Hill	Hughes*	Brabin	Withers	Shaugh'sy Saunders	McCarty	Richards	

U's maintain a seven-point cushion over Wycombe. Steve Saunders accepts a Gary Brabin pass, shrugs off Roberts and drives across Barrett. Bennett's 15th goal levels. Cook, with his second of the season, and McGavin, his 16th, settle it. McGavin cleverly rounds Arthur Williams.

24 — REDBRIDGE (H)

Team	1	2	3	4	5	6	7	8	9	10	11	subs used
U's	Barrett	Donald	Roberts	Cook*	English	Elliott	Collins	Bennett*	McDonough	McGavin	Smith	Kinsella/Restarick
Redbridge	Bennett	Jacques	Watts	Barrett*	Connor	Broom	Mayes	Richardson	Cavell	Walsh	Blackford	Garvey

Masters still awaits international clearance after returning from the States. Atkins, of Brum, enquires about signing McGavin, who scores his 17th goal. Collins' quick free-kick finds Smith, who supplies the cross. Earlier Barrett prevented Walsh scoring with a fine one-handed save.

25 — MERTHYR (A)

Team	1	2	3	4	5	6	7	8	9	10	11	subs used
U's	Barrett	Cook*	Roberts	Kinsella	English	Elliott	Collins	Bennett*	McDonough	McGavin	Smith	Restarick/Grainger
Merthyr	Wager	Williams M	James	Boyle*	Lewis	Rogers	Beattie	Coates	D'Auria	Hutchison	Williams C	Tucker

Donald misses out with a hamstring. McGavin and Grainger are ordered to sweat a few pounds off as punishment for being too fancy on the ball, and sluggish, respectively. Veteran Tommy Hutchison inspires the Welshmen to beat the U's, by nil, for the second season in succession.

26 — CHELTENHAM (H)

Team	1	2	3	4	5	6	7	8	9	10	11	subs used
U's	Barrett	Donald	Roberts	Kinsella	English	Elliott*	Cook	Bennett*	McDonough	McGavin	Smith	Masters/Grainger
Cheltenham	Livingstone	Masefield	Willets	Smith	Vircavs	Howells	Brooks*	Owen	Evans	Buckland*	Purdie	Turnbull/Perrett

Bennett picks up the Mail on Sunday goal award for December with six, one more than McGavin. McGavin takes his tally to 20 for the season, stabbing home Bennett's lob over Glen Livingstone, and finishing off a fine pass from the inspirational Kinsella, who finishes the rout himself.

27 — KETTERING (A)

Team	1	2	3	4	5	6	7	8	9	10	11	subs used
U's	Barrett	Donald	Roberts	Kinsella	English	Elliott	Cook	Bennett*	McDonough	McGavin	Smith	Masters
Kettering	Shoemake	Huxford	Jones	Nicol	Price*	Slack	Keast	Brown	Christie	Culpin	Hill*	Graham/Bancroft

Concern mounts over a rule that clubs must have a minimum ten-year stadium tenure to enter the league. U's, who have less than three years left, acquire astro-boots to contend with the frozen pitch, and are furious at a harsh handball against Roberts in front of Sportscast cameras.

28 — KIDDERMINSTER (A)

Team	1	2	3	4	5	6	7	8	9	10	11	subs used
U's	Barrett	Cook*	Roberts	Kinsella	English	Elliott	Collins	Bennett*	McDonough	McGavin	Smith	Donald/Masters
Kidderminster	Green	Benton	Joseph	Weir	Gillett	Forsyth	Lilwall*	Howell	Hadley	Davies	Humphreys	Wolsey

U's second Sportscast airing of the term, and annoying fixture changes, will only result in a £3k equal share of sponsorship. Paul Davies seems to 'handle' in the first and Delwyn Humphreys celebrates his goal with a series of somersaults. Smith's sixth of the season earns a vital point.

29 — BOSTON (H)

Team	1	2	3	4	5	6	7	8	9	10	11	subs used
U's	Barrett	Cook	Roberts	Kinsella	English	Elliott	Collins*	Bennett	McDonough	McGavin	Smith	Stewart/Donald
Boston	McKenna	Shirtliff	Raffell	Hardy	Swailes	Moore*	Nesbitt	Stoutt	Jones	Nuttell!	Adams*	Retallick/Collins

U's move eleven points clear of Wycombe, who have four games in hand. Norfolk official Moore sends off already-booked Micky Nuttell, for the striker's injurious play-acting after a clash with Roberts. Coach Phillips leaves 20 mins from the end to attend the birth of his daughter.

30 — WELLING (A)

Team	1	2	3	4	5	6	7	8	9	10	11	subs used
U's	Barrett	Cook*	Roberts	Kinsella	English	Elliott	Collins	Bennett*	McDonough	McGavin	Smith	Stewart/Donald
Welling	Harrison	Golley	Robinson	Glover	Ransom	Berry	White	Francis	Hone	Robbins	Reynolds	

U's suffer their heaviest GMVC defeat against a team that McDonough 'would not cross the road to watch'. All seems well after Joe Francis hauls down Smith for the penalty, but Barrett has a hesitant afternoon and is at fault for three goals. Stuart White catches United on the break.

31 — ALTRINCHAM (A)

Team	1	2	3	4	5	6	7	8	9	10	11	subs used
U's		Donald	Roberts	Kinsella	English	Cook	Collins	Stewart	McDon'gh*	McGavin*	Smith	Bennett/Masters
Altrincham	Wealands	Edwards*	Chilton	Wiggins	Reid	Rudge	Shaw	Daws	McDonald*	McKenna	Lee	Worrall/Kilshaw

McDonough's tenth booking of the term is through play-acting by Jeff Wealands. A first win in front of Sportscast keeps the eleven-point gap. McGavin heads his 24th via Smith's cross. McDonough loses possession for Ken McKenna's 20th strike, but atones with a near-post header.

Wycombe Wanderers — match-by-match record (matches 32–42)

32. GATESHEAD — H — 7/3 — W 2-0 (Pos 19, Pts 68) — Att 2,897

Team: Barrett · Donald · Roberts · Kinsella · English · Cook · Collins · Stewart* · McDon'gh* · McGavin · Smith · Bennett/Masters
Opposition: Smith S · Farrey · Veart* · Forrest · Corner · Halliday · Granycombe Healey · Cuthbert* · Grayson · Lamb · Butler/Bell
Scorers: Roberts 45, Masters 90
Ref: D Madgewick

Good news as the Council extends the lease on Layer Rd for seven years. McDonough faces another suspension after his 11th booking. Roberts scores his first goal for seven years, rising to meet a Stewart corner. Masters curls his first of the season, and Wycombe lose by 0-1 at Yeovil.

33. NORTHWICH — H — 21/3 — W 1-0 (Pos 11, Pts 71) — Att 3,218

Team: Barrett · Donald · Roberts · Kinsella · English · Elliott · Cook* · Bennett* · Masters · McGavin · Smith · Collins/Stewart
Opposition: Berryman · Locke · Blundell · Jones · Hancock · Vaughan · McIlroy · Butler* · Hemmings · O'Connor · O'Gorman
Scorer: Smith 83
Ref: M Hair

Chairman Bowtidge kicks off the 'Back To The League' campaign in order to raise funds to bring Layer Road up to current Football League standard. Sportscast pulls out of non-league coverage. Nicky Smith's stunning angled drive leaves Steve Berryman, in the Vics' goal, helpless.

34. BATH — A — 24/3 — D 0-0 (Pos 8, Pts 72) — Att 1,101

Team: Barrett · Donald · Roberts · Kinsella · English · Elliott · Cook · Bennett* · Masters · McGavin* · Smith · Martin
Opposition: Churchward/Hedges · Dicks · Crowley · Singleton · Cousins · Banks · Weston · Withey · Randall · Boyle* · Gill
Ref: B Priest

Kinsella withdraws from the Eire U-21 squad to face the Swiss in order to play at Twerton Park. Barrett makes a second appearance on BBC's Question of Sport. 'What happened next?' slot. Wycombe's 2-0 win at Northwich puts them three points behind, but with two games in hand.

35. KIDDERMINSTER — H — 28/3 — W 3-0 (Pos 20, Pts 75) — Att 3,073

Team: Barrett · Donald · Roberts* · Kinsella · English · Cook · Stewart · McDon'gh* · McGavin · Smith · Collins/Masters
Opposition: Green · Benton · McGrath · Weir · Joseph · Wilcox* · MacKenzie Grainger · Hanson · Davies · Humphreys Lilwall/Howell
Scorers: English 42, Benton 45(og), Stewart 90
Ref: P Taylor

U's goal tally rises to an incredible 98, with eleven consecutive home wins and none against in the last five. On 35 mins, Weir goes off with a head cut, and returns to see David Benton own-goal under pressure from Martin. Ian Stewart jinks inside to fire past Ron Green in injury-time.

36. SLOUGH — H — 14/4 — W 4-0 (Pos 15, Pts 78) — Att 3,197

Team: Barrett · Donald* · Roberts · Kinsella · English · Martin · Cook · Stewart · McDon'gh* · McGavin* · Smith · Masters/Bennett
Opposition: Watkiss · Knight · Pluckrose · Stacey · Anderson · Mallinson · Fielder · McKinnon · Scott · Donnellan · Hickey
Scorers: McDonough 38, Masters 83, [Stewart 87, Kinsella 90]
Ref: J Moore

Whilst U's have been on Trophy duty, Wycombe move three points clear at the top. This win and Wycombe's 1-3 defeat at Macclesfield sees U's back on top. The goal of the match comes from substitute Masters, who sprints the length of the pitch before thumping in from 15 yards.

37. TELFORD — H — 18/4 — W 2-0 (Pos 4, Pts 81) — Att 3,964

Team: Barrett · Donald* · Roberts · Kinsella · English · Martin · Cook* · Stewart · McDonough · McGavin* · Smith · Bennett/Masters
Opposition: Acton · Humphreys Clarke · Dyson · Brindley · Forsyth · Garratt · Ferguson · Benbow · Gilman* · Alleyne* · Cooke/Withe
Scorers: McDonough 67, 89
Ref: C Finch

Elliott (sent-off in the reserves) and Collins (failed to follow instructions) continue to sit out. A double-substitution just after the hour inspires jaded-looking U's. Stewart finds McDonough for a powerful header, and the player-boss repeats the trick in the last minute via Bennett's pass.

38. MERTHYR — H — 20/4 — W 2-0 (Pos 7, Pts 84) — Att 4,148

Team: Barrett · Donald · Roberts · Kinsella · English · Martin · Cook* · Masters · McDon'gh* · McGavin · Smith · Bennett/Elliott
Opposition: Wager · Williams M James · Boyle · Abraham · Webley · Davey · Tucker · D'Auria · Hutchison* Williams C · Beattie
Scorers: Smith 25, Masters 64
Ref: M Hair

A psychological war of words starts between McDonough and Wycombe boss Martin O'Neill as the sides remain neck and neck at the top. U's despatch bogey side Merthyr. Masters heads in a Martin flick from Roberts free-kick, after being beaten in a race, by Smith, to prod in the first.

39. BOSTON — A — 22/4 — W 4-0 (Pos 8, Pts 87) — Att 2,305

Team: Barrett · Donald · Roberts · Kinsella · English · Martin* · Cook · Masters · McDonough · McGavin* · Smith · Elliott/Bennett
Opposition: McKenna · Shirtliff · Ciollins · Hardy · Moore · Raffell · Casey* · Stoutt · Nuttell! · Jones · Adams · Retallick
Scorers: McGavin 14, McDonough 70, 74p, McD' 60 [Masters 88]
Ref: A Streets

U's open up a two point lead, as Wycombe draw 1-1 at Kettering, with the biggest away win for seven years and a 28th clean sheet. Micky Nuttell, who had been sent off at Layer Rd in February, collects another red card for a foul on English (50). Raffell fouls Masters for the pen.

40. MACCLESFIELD — A — 25/4 — D 4-4 (Pos 14, Pts 88) — Att 886

Team: Barrett · Donald · Roberts · Kinsella* · English · Cook* · Martin · Masters* · McDonough · McGavin · Smith · Elliott/Bennett
Opposition: Bastock · Bimson · Shepherd · Edwards · Kendall · Johnson · Askey · Green · Lambert · Doherty · Dempsey* Ellis
Scorers: Kend'3(og), Eng'22,76, Doherty 47, L'bert 27, 62, Doherty 47, Edw's 49 Farrelly S, Roberts
Ref: P Roberts

Maccs are fired up to avenge their Trophy defeat. A vital equaliser from English keeps U's on top as Wycombe beat Gateshead 3-2 in the last four mins. Paul Kendall intercepts McGavin, but only side-foots into his own net. Two minutes from time, Farrelly denies Kinsella the winner.

41. KETTERING — H — 28/4 — W 3-1 (Pos 3, Pts 91) — Att 6,303

Team: Barrett · Donald · Roberts · Kinsella* · English · Cook · Martin · Masters* · McDonough · McGavin · Smith · Elliott/Bennett
Opposition: Bastock · Huxford · Keast · Nicol* · Slack · Graham* · Brown · Gavin · Barker · Hill · North/Price
Scorers: McDonough 27, 57, McGavin 61, North 90
Ref: W Norbury

Boss McDonough takes his season's tally to 28 and McGavin, his, to 27. McGavin hits the bar on 13 mins, beating Paul Bastock, who then fouls English in the box and saves McDonough's pen, but can't stop the rebound. Marc North scores the first visitors' goal since 21 December.

42. BARROW — H — 2/5 — W 5-0 (Pos 22, Pts 94) — Att 7,193

Team: Barrett · Donald · Roberts · Kinsella* · English · Cook · Martin · Masters* · Bennett · Smith · Elliott/Stewart
Opposition: McDonnell · Slater · Messenger · Rowlands* · Knox · Atkinson · Kelly · Skivington · Brady · Power! · Doherty* · Nolan/Rutter
Scorers: Masters 8, 15, 77, Smith 47, [McDonough 65]
Ref: G Poll

Wycombe have to beat Witton by EIGHT more than U's beat Barrow. A 16th home win on the trot seals the championship, with a magnificent hat-trick from Masters, who won't get a work permit for the Football League. Phil Power is red-carded on 17 minutes for punching Cook.

Home Average 3,509 · Away 1,781

VAUXHALL CONFERENCE (CUP-TIES)

Player Manager: Roy McDonough

SEASON 1991-92

Bob Lord Trophy

1 — H KETTERING — 8/10 — W 4-0 (H-T 2-0) — 1,289 VC:10

Scorers, Times, and Referees: McGavin 16, Collins 45, Kinsella 74, 84. Ref: G Monk

1	2	3	4	5	6	7	8	9	10	11	subs used
Barratt	Donald	Grainger	Cook	English	Roberts	Collins*	Brown	**Duffett**	McGavin	Smith	Kinsella/Abrahams
Bastock	*Price*	*Jones*	*Nicol*	*Slack**	*Bloodworth*	*Graham*	*Catton*	*Bancroft*	*Appleby*	*Christie*	

McDonough orders all of the first team. apart from himself, to play in this match after the disappointing result against Altrincham. Big Roy's place is taken by trialist and local parks prospect, Shaun Duffett. Collins calls the tune and nets the second before giving way to a leg injury.

2 — H WYCOMBE — 16/12 — L 2-6 (H-T 1-1) — 919 VC:2

Scorers, Times, and Referees: Restarick 34, McGavin 86 [Creaser 76], West 27, 51, 90, Hutchinson 61, 65. Ref: J Moore

1	2	3	4	5	6	7	8	9	10	11	subs used
Barratt	Donald	Grainger	Cook	Roberts*	English	Goodwin	Restarick	McDonough*	McGavin	Abrahams	Hannigan/Gray
Hyde	*Cousins^*	*Stapleton*	*Crossley*	*Creaser*	*Smith*	*Hutchinson*	*Carroll*	*West*	*Scott**	*Guppy*	*Cooper/Deakin*

Only once have U's let in six at home. against Southend (3-6) in 1955. McDonough wishes Wycombe a good run as the psychology sets in. Unfortunately for Mark West, no one witnesses his hat-trick in a farcical game which normally would have been abandoned. due to thick fog.

FA Cup

4Q — H BURTON — 26/10 — W 5-0 (H-T 1-0) — 2,147 BH:22

Scorers, Times, and Referees: McDonough 1p, McGavin 51, 80p, [Restarick 85 Kinsella 89]. Ref: R Biggar

1	2	3	4	5	6	7	8	9	10	11	subs used
Barratt	Donald	Phillips	Kinsella	English	Elliott	Collins^	Bennett	McDonough*	McGavin*	Smith	Restarick/Abrahams
Goodwin	*Bottomley*	*Foster*	*Straw*	*Gelan*	*Simms*	*Davies*	*Redfern S*	*Lycett*	*Redfern D**	*Hall^*	*Cordner/Sallis*

Rampant United nap the visitors, who are propping up the Beazer Homes League. U's are in the qualifiers for the first time since 1950-51. The writing is on the wall from the moment 'silky' McGavin is hauled down by Mark Bottomley on just 34 seconds, and then later by S Redfern.

1 — H EXETER — 16/11 — D 0-0 (H-T 0-0) — 4,965 3:6

Ref: G Pooley

1	2	3	4	5	6	7	8	9	10	11	subs used
Barratt	Donald	Cook	Kinsella	English	Elliott	Collins	Bennett	McDonough	McGavin	Smith*	Grainger
Miller	*Hiley*	*Cook*	*Williams!*	*Daniels*	*Whiston*	*Hilaire*	*Brown*	*Moran*	*Chapman*	*Kelly*	

Collins, who played nine games on loan at Exeter, meets up with his football 'father' in ex-U's coach and City boss Alan Ball. Local night-club sponsors. The Hippodrome steps in as shirt sponsors. Steve Williams is sent off (18) for a second booking, and in front of the Match of the Day cameras.

1R — A EXETER — 27/11 — D 0-0 (aet) — 4,066 3:9

Ref: G Pooley
(Colchester lost 2-4 on penalties)

1	2	3	4	5	6	7	8	9	10	11	subs used
Barratt	Donald	Cook	Kinsella	English	Goodwin*	Collins	Bennett	McDonough	McGavin	Smith	Grainger/Restarick
Miller	*Brown*	*Cook*	*Williams*	*Daniels*	*Whiston*	*Hilaire**	*Wimbleton^*	*Marshall*	*Kelly*	*Chapman*	*Redwood/Cole*

U's become the first team to be knocked out of the FA Cup without conceding a goal. The FA's new ruling is that ties can go to one replay. Kevin Miller saves two of the U's spot-kicks after 210 goalless minutes. City proceed to host Swansea, but Ball agrees that the rule is wrong.

Vauxhall FA Trophy

1 — H KINGSTONIAN — 11/1 — D 2-2 (H-T 1-2) — 2,724 DP:6

Scorers, Times, and Referees: Restarick 9, English 90. Cherry 5, Tutt 10. Ref: P Taylor

1	2	3	4	5	6	7	8	9	10	11	subs used
Barratt	Donald*	Roberts	Cook	English	Elliott	Collins^	Bennett	Restarick	McGavin	Smith	Kinsella/Grainger
Blake	*Barnett*	*Kempton*	*Eriemo*	*Dear*	*Braithwaite*	*Harlow*	*Tutt*	*Vines*	*Cherry*	*Smart**	*Davidson*

K's are led by ex-'Leatherhead Lip'. Chris Kelly. Ex-U's trainee Richard Cherry finishes off a long punt from Adrian Blake. Suspended. McDonough sees replacement Restarick level. only for Elliott to let in Steve Tutt. Barrett goes up for a last-minute corner and flicks on to English.

1R — A KINGSTONIAN — 14/1 — W 3-2 (H-T 1-0) — 1,642 DP:6

Scorers, Times, and Referees: Smith 39, Bennett 72, McGavin 79. Cherry 51p, 84p. Ref: P Taylor

1	2	3	4	5	6	7	8	9	10	11	subs used
Barratt	Donald	Roberts	Kinsella*	English	Elliott	Cook	Bennett	Restarick^	McGavin	Smith*	Grainger/**Dart**
Blake	*Barnett*	*Kempton*	*Eriemo*	*Dear*	*Braithwaite*	*Harlow*	*Tutt*	*Vines*	*Cherry*	*Smart^*	*Pearce*

After Saturday's late show. U's suffer another bumpy ride when Roberts is penalised twice. first for pushing Solomon Eriemo and then. after McGavin had coolly drilled past Blake to make it 3-1. handling Francis Vines's shot. Cherry's second penalty leaves desperate U's hanging on.

2 — A MERTHYR — 2/2 — D 0-0 (H-T 0-0) — 1,211 VC:12

Ref: D Gallagher

1	2	3	4	5	6	7	8	9	10	11	subs used
Barratt	Donald	Roberts	Kinsella	English	Elliott	Cook	Masters*	McDonough	McGavin	Smith	Bennett/Webley
Wager	*Williams M*	*James*	*Boyle*	*Lewis*	*Rogers**	*Beattie*	*Coates**	*D'Auria*	*Hutchison*	*Williams C*	*Webley*

The tie is switched to Sunday to avoid the Five-Nations Rugby match in Cardiff between Wales and France. United have Barrett to thank for a stupendous 53rd-minute point-blank save from Marc Coates. Again. the Welsh side are inspired by 44-year-old Hutchison, but United hold on.

2R — H MERTHYR — 4/2 — W 1-0 (H-T 0-0) — 2,746 VC:12

Scorers, Times, and Referees: McDonough 86. Ref: D Gallagher

1	2	3	4	5	6	7	8	9	10	11	subs used
Barratt	Cook	Roberts	Kinsella	English	Elliott	Cook	Bennett	McDonough*	McGavin	Smith	Webley/Tucker
Wager	*Williams M*	*James*	*Boyle*	*Lewis*	*Rogers**	*Beattie*	*Coates*	*D'Auria*	*Hutchison*	*Williams C*	*Pearce*

Barrett clocks up his 100th U's appearance. 87 of them consecutive. Stewart joins from debt-ridden Aldershot. A 17th clean sheet in 36 games aided by McDonough's 17th of the term. after Gary Wager parries McGavin's shot. Wycombe losing to Cheltenham makes for a perfect night.

3 — H MORECAMBE — 22/2 — W 3-1 (H-T 2-1) — 3,206 HFS:7

Scorers, Times, and Referees: Stewart 12, Collins 32, McGavin 65. Cain 26. Ref: P Vanes

1	2	3	4	5	6	7	8	9	10	11	subs used
Barratt	Donald	Roberts*	Kinsella	English	Elliott	Cook	Stewart	McDonough^	McGavin	Smith	Masters/Dart
Allison	*Tomlinson*	*Armstrong*	*Parillon*	*Dullaghan*	*Lodge*	*Brown*	*Lavell**	*Coleman^*	*McMahon*	*Cain*	*McInerney/Holden*

A second-half floodlight failure can't prevent debutant Stewart from lighting up U's Wembley chances. The 1974 Trophy winners rally briefly through lively Ian Cain. McGavin's 22nd goal puts U's through, after McDonough blasts a pen over the top when Bruce Lavelle handled (57).

Match results

No		Opponent	Date		Pos	Result	Score
4	H	TELFORD	14/3		1 W	4-0	
SF 1	H	MACCLESFIELD	4/4		1 W	3-0	
SF 2	A	MACCLESFIELD	10/4		1 D	1-1	
F	N	WITTON (at Wembley)	10/5		1 W	2-0	

4 — Telford (H), 14/3 — 4-0. 3,894 VC:5
McGavin 19, Kinsella 50, Bennett 53, [Smith 67]
Ref: M Pierce
Lineups — Colchester: Barrett, Donald, Roberts, Kinsella*, English, Elliott, Cook, Bennett, McDonough*, McGavin, Smith / Stewart/Collins.
Telford: Acton, Humphreys, Nelson, Dyson, Brindley, Whittington* Myers, Ferguson, Benbow, Langford, Grainger, Clarke.
Telford, six times Trophy semi-finalists, are no match for rampant U's. Roberts' long throw is flicked on by McDonough for McGavin's 25th. Kinsella rifles a drive into the roof of the net, followed moments later by Bennett's 18th. A left-footed angled drive from Smith wraps it up.

SF 1 — Macclesfield (H), 4/4 — 3-0. 5,443 VC:14
Stewart 23, English 25, McDon'gh 70p
Ref: A Ward
Lineups — Colchester: Barrett, Donald, Roberts, Kinsella, English, Elliott, Cook*, Stewart*, McDonough, McGavin, Smith / Collins/Bennett.
Macclesfield: Farrelly S, Shepherd, Johnson, Edwards, Farrelly M, Hanlon, Askey, Green, Lambert, Timmons, Dempsey.
U's near a first Wembley appearance. Referee Ward inadvertently plays a one-two with Stewart to set the winger in the clear. Appropriately, Skipper English gets U's 100th of the term, two mins later. John Askey misses two sitters for Maccs, before Elfyn Edwards fouls McDonough.

SF 2 — Macclesfield (A), 10/4 — 1-1. 1,650 VC:14
Cook 45 / Timmons 20
Ref: K Redfern
(Colchester won 4-1 on aggregate)
Lineups — Colchester: Barrett, Donald, Roberts, Kinsella, English, Elliott, Cook, Stewart, McDonough*, McGavin*, Smith / Masters/Bennett.
Macclesfield: Farrelly S, Shepherd, Johnson, Edwards, Farrelly M*, Hanlon, Askey, Green, Lambert, Timmons, Ellis*, Boughey/Clayton.
800 U's fans stream on to the Moss Rose pitch at the whistle to salute their Wembley-bound heroes. Maccs counter-attack, after McGavin's unsuccessful penalty appeal, and John Timmons nods in Askey's cross. Smith's corner is only half-cleared for a sweet volley from Cook.

F — Witton (N, at Wembley), 10/5 — 2-0. 27,806 VC:10
Masters 5, Smith 19, McGavin 89 / Lutkevich 57
Ref: K Barratt
Lineups — Colchester: Barrett, Donald, Roberts, Kinsella, English, Martin, Cook!, Masters, McDonough*, McGavin, Smith / Bennett.
Witton: Mason, Halliday, Coathup, McNellis, Connor Jim, Anderson, Thomas, Rose, Alford, Grimshaw*, Lutkevich*, Connor Joe/McCluskie.
Backed by over 20,000 fans, U's complete the league and cup double on their first visit to Wembley. Masters is the first American to score at the stadium, but the FA bar Jason Cook from receiving a medal after he throws a punch (81). Non-playing sub Collins hands him his medal.

League table

Pos	Team	P	W	D	L	F	A	W	D	L	F	A	Pts
			Home					Away					
1	COLCHESTER	42	19	1	1	57	11	11	3	7	35	29	94
2	Wycombe	42	18	1	2	49	13	12	3	6	35	22	94
3	Kettering	42	12	6	3	44	23	8	7	6	28	27	73
4	Merthyr	42	14	4	3	40	24	4	10	7	19	32	68
5	Farnborough	42	8	7	6	36	27	10	5	6	32	26	66
6	Telford	42	10	4	7	32	31	9	3	9	30	35	64
7	Redbridge	42	12	4	5	42	27	6	5	10	27	29	63
8	Boston	42	10	4	7	40	35	8	5	8	31	31	63
9	Bath	42	8	6	7	27	22	8	6	7	27	31	60
10	Witton	42	11	6	4	41	26	5	4	12	22	34	58
11	Northwich	42	10	4	7	40	25	6	2	13	23	33	54
12	Welling	42	8	6	7	40	38	6	6	9	29	41	54
13	Macclesfield	42	7	7	7	25	21	8	7	6	25	29	52
14	Gateshead	42	8	5	8	22	22	4	7	10	27	35	48
15	Yeovil	42	8	6	7	22	21	3	8	10	18	27	47
16	Runcorn	42	5	11	5	26	26	6	2	13	24	37	46
17	Stafford	42	7	8	6	25	24	3	8	10	16	35	46
18	Altrincham	42	5	8	8	33	39	6	4	11	28	43	45
19	Kidderminster	42	8	6	7	35	32	4	3	14	21	45	45
20	Slough	42	7	3	11	26	39	6	3	12	30	43	45
21	Cheltenham	42	8	5	8	28	35	2	8	11	28	47	43
22	Barrow	42	5	8	8	29	23	3	6	12	23	49	38
		924	208	120	134	759	584	134	120	208	584	759	1266

Appearances and goals

Player		Appearances						Goals			
	Lge	Sub	FAT	Sub	FAC	Sub		Lge	FAT	FAC	Tot
Abrahams, Paul											1
Barrett, Scott	42		9		3						1
Bennett, Gary	31	8	4		3			16	2		18
Collins, Eamonn	29	3	3		3			2	1		3
Cook, Jason	28	3	9		2			2	1		3
Dart(Hazel), Julian					2						
Donald, Warren	38	3	8		3			1			1
Elliott, Shaun	32	5	5		2						
English, Tony	37	1	9		3			6	2		8
Goodwin, James		3			1						
Grainger, Martin	8	2	2			2					
Gray, Simon	1										
Kinsella, Mark	37	5	8	1	3			3	1	1	5
Martin, Dave	8	1	3								
Masters, Mike	7	8	2		3			7	1		8
McDonough, Roy	40		7		3			26	2	1	29
McGavin, Steve	39		9		3			20	4	2	26
Phillips, Ian	1	2									
Restarick, Steve	1	6	2			2			1		2
Roberts, Paul	35		9					1			1
Smith, Nicky	42		9		3			8	3		11
Stewart, Ian	6	4	3		1			2	2		4
Walsh, Mario		1									
(own-goals)								3			3
23 players used	462	58	99	14	33	5		98	20	5	123

Odds & ends

Double wins: (7) Boston, Gateshead, Runcorn, Telford, Slough, Wycombe, Yeovil.
Double defeats: (0).
Won from behind: (2) Slough (a), Runcorn (a).
Lost from in front: (2) Farnborough (h), Redbridge (a).
High spots: Regaining League status.
Champions with a GMVC record number of points.
First-ever appearance at Wembley.
Completing the non-league double.
Only one home league defeat.
19 home wins, including a record 16 on the trot.
123 goals scored in total.
Doubling close rivals, Wycombe.
Goalkeeper Scott Barrett's winner against Wycombe.
Low spots: Defeat in the FA Cup without conceding a goal, to Exeter.
Concern over Layer Road's suitability to meet Football League requirements.
Player of the Year: Nicky Smith.
Ever presents: (2) Scott Barrett, Nicky Smith.
Hat-tricks: (3) Roy McDonough (4 goals), Gary Bennett, Mike Masters.
Leading scorer: Roy McDonough (29).

BARCLAYS LEAGUE DIVISION 3 — Player Manager: Roy McDonough — SEASON 1992-93

No	Date	Att	Pos	Pt	F-A	H-T	Scorers, Times, and Referees	1	2	3	4	5	6	7	8	9	10	11	subs used
1	H LINCOLN 15/8	4,131		3	W 2-1	2-1	McDonough 3, Oxbrow 7 / West 1 / Ref: G Poll	Newell / *Bowling*	Donald* / *West**	Roberts / *Clarke*	Kinsella / *Bressington Carmichael Brown*	English	Oxbrow	Devereux* / *Schofield*	Bennett	McDonough / *Lee Kabia*	Grainger	Smith / *Puttnam**	Abrahams / *Finney/Alexander*
2	A BARNET 21/8	3,600		3	L 1-3	1-0	Kinsella 16 / Willis 72, Bull 73, Hoddle 81 / Ref: A Smith	Newell / *Phillips*	Donald / *Hurford*	Roberts / *Cooper*	Kinsella / *Badley*	English / *Barnett*	Oxbrow / *Horton*	Devereux* / *Willis*	Bennett / *Carter**	McDonough Grainger* / *Bull*	Grainger / *Payne**	Smith / *Showler*	Abrahams/Phillips / *Hoddle/Stein*
3	H DARLINGTON 29/8	3,524	18 / 8	3	L 0-3	0-1	Shaw 10, Juryeff 75, Dobson 90 / Ref: G Willard	Newell / *Prudhoe*	Donald* / *Hinchley*	Roberts / *Ball*	Kinsella / *Gaughan*	English / *Parkin*	Oxbrow / *O'Shaugn'sy Mardenbor'**	Cook* / *Toman^*	Bennett	McDonough Hazel* / *Juryeff*	Grainger / *Shaw*	Smith / *Dowson*	Abrahams/Donald / *Dobson/Tupling*
4	H SHREWSBURY 1/9	3,530	22 / 5	3	L 0-2	0-1	Griffiths 44, Brough 76 / Ref: P Taylor	Edwards / *Worsley*	Donald / *Lynch*	Roberts / *Taylor*	Kinsella / *Spink*	English	Oxbrow / *Blake*	Cook^ / *Brough*	Hazel* / *Summerfield Williams*	McDon'gh ! McGavin / *Griffiths*	Grainger	Smith / *Lyne*	Bennett
5	A BURY 5/9	2,072	22 / 6	3	L 2-3	0-1	Bennett 85, McDonough 90p / Lyons 44, Robinson 79, Scott 87 / Ref: K Leach	Newell / *Kelly*	Donald / *Anderson*	Roberts / *Reid*	Kinsella / *Daws*	English* / *Valentine*	Oxbrow / *Knill^*	Cook / *Mauge*	Bennett / *Robinson*	McDonough McGavin / *Stevens^*	Grainger / *Kearney*	Smith / *Kilner*	Grainger/Abrahams / *Scott/Lyons*
6	H WALSALL 12/9	3,218	18 / 6	6	W 3-1	2-0	Bennett 15, Smith 35, McDon'gh 84p / Ntamark 64 / Ref: P Alcock	Newell / *Gayle*	Donald^ / *Williams*	Roberts / *Statham*	Kinsella / *MacDonald West*	English / *West*	Oxbrow / *Smith*	Cook / *Ntamark*	Bennett / *Clarke*	McDonough Grainger / *Marsh*	Grainger / *Okenshaw* McDonald*	Smith / *Blackstone*	Edwards / *Edwards*
7	A DONCASTER 15/9	1,719	20 / 16	6	L 0-1	0-1	Jeffrey 24 / Ref: R. Dikes	Newell / *Crichton*	Donald / *Rowe*	Roberts / *Prindiville*	Kinsella / *Crosby*	English / *Richards*	Oxbrow / *Hicks*	Cook / *Hewitt*	Bennett / *Hine**	McGavin / *Heritage*	Grainger / *Jeffrey*	Smith / *Gormley*	Quinlan
8	A YORK 19/9	3,820	20 / 1	6	L 0-2	0-1	Blackstone 14, 46 / Ref: J Winter	Newell / *Kelly*	Donald* / *McMillan*	Roberts / *Hall*	Kinsella* / *Pepper*	English / *Stancliffe*	Oxbrow / *Warburton*	Cook / *McCarthy*	Bennett / *Borthwick*	McGavin / *Barnes*	Grainger / *Swann*	Smith / *Blackstone*	Ball/Devereux
9	H CHESTERFIELD 26/9	3,436	14 / 8	9	W 3-0	1-0	Bennett 45, 56, Kinsella 90 / Ref: M Bailey	Newell / *Leonard*	Donald / *Leman*	Roberts / *Carr*	Kinsella / *Williams*	English / *Brien*	Oxbrow / *Rogers*	Cook / *Cash*	Bennett / *Morris**	Ball / *Morris^*	McGavin / *Lancaster*	Smith / *Hebberd*	Turnbull/Kennedy
10	A HALIFAX 10/10	2,445	15 / 17	12	W 4-2	2-0	Kinsella 13, Oxbrow 35, McDon'gh 46, Matthews 74, German 85 [Bennett 82] / Ref: A Wilkie	Newell / *Bracey*	Grainger / *Barr*	Roberts / *Wilson*	Kinsella / *Lucketti*	English / *Cawley*	Oxbrow / *Thompstone Griffiths*	Ball^ / *Case^*	Bennett / *Matthews Case^*	McDon'gh* McGavin / *Lewis*	McGavin / *Greenwood Peake*	Smith / *German*	Devereux/Donald / *German*

Match notes:

1. Bowdidge stands down, due to business commitments Barrett (Gills) and Collins (Exeter) are freed. Poll, who refereed U's last GMVC, is in charge for the first game back in the league, after U's meet stringent provisos. Oxbrow, freed by Maidstone, nods in Roberts' long throw-in.

2. Barnet increase their ground limit from 1,075 to 4,900, with some late repair work. McDonough remains injured after a holiday stunt goes wrong. Kinsella strikes a low drive. Paul Showler provides two crosses in a minute to put the Bees in front, then Carl Hoddle hits a stunning 30-yarder

3. Darlington, with only one goal scored this season, romp to victory. Steve Mardenborough crosses from the right to Simon Shaw. The Quakers increase their lead when Ian Juryeff heads in Andy Toman's cross. Roberts falls foul of the new back-pass rule, allowing Paul Dobson to score.

4. Red-carded McDonough will have an operation, whilst unmarked, after elbowing Mark Williams (15). A match of six cautions and 60+ fouls, Ref Taylor struggles with the back-pass rule. On half-time Carl Griffiths nods in Mark Taylor's corner, and later finds John Brough, unmarked

5. Pleat (Luton) offers Chamberlain or Jurgen Sommer on loan, whilst Big Roy chases Saints' reserve, Paul Moody. A frantic late fight-back still leaves U's bottom. Bennett slides in to reduce the deficit, only for Ian Scott to chip in from 20 yards. Lee Anderson handles Abrahams' shot.

6. Gayle chases QPR's Garry Thompson, and warns that the GMVC honeymoon is definitely over. Kinsella is clearly offside as Bennett scores, but referee Alcock overrules his linesman, and then, with six nail-biting minutes left, spots Wayne Williams handle under pressure from Smith.

7. The U's boss turns his attentions to Watford's Luther Blissett and Steve Butler Rovers' Mike Jeffrey, son of Doncaster's England U-23 star of the 50's – Alick, nets his sixth goal in seven games following his £20k move from Bolton. He nods in Brian Rowe's superb right-wing cross.

8. McDonough agrees terms with Spurs to sign 20-year-old Peter Beadle, who cost £250k from Gills. United suffer their ninth defeat in eleven visits to York. A Paul Barnes cross and a Nigel Pepper free-kick both pick out Ian Blackstone. The team coach breaks down on the way home.

9. Plymouth's Micky Evans and Dave Regis join the growing list of strikers NOT joining the U's. Chesterfield pulled off a magnificent 4-4 at Anfield on Tuesday in the Coca-Cola Cup. The match ball is dropped by the Red Devils Parachute team, despite Chesterfield arriving late.

10. Masters has problems obtaining a work permit, despite his summer appearance for USA against Ukraine. Halifax fans are given a three-match ultimatum to support the team, or the club will fold. Man-of-the-match Kinsella jets off to Denmark on Tuesday to earn his second U-21 cap.

11 — H CREWE — 16/10

Attendance 4,524 — Pos 12 (5 / 15) — W 3-2 (HT 2-1)

Goals: Bennett 4, McDon'gh 40, Oxbrow 75 / McCauley 7, Naylor 77
Ref: D Elleray

U's	Opp
Newell	*Greygoose*
Grainger	*McKearney*
Roberts	*Whalley*
Kinsella	*Wilson*
Cawley	*Carr*
Oxbrow	*McCauley*
Cook^	*Hignett*
Bennett	*Naylor*
McDonough	*Clarkson*^
Ball*	*Gardiner*
Smith	*Walters*
Subs: English/McGavin	*Garvey*

Bor Dortmund are said to have bid £500k for Kinsella, and Middlesbro' also enquire. The stand is full of scouts, who are also watching Craig Hignett. McDonough celebrates his 34th birthday with a bullet header. Oxbrow's header is deemed by the linesman to have crossed the line.

12 — A SCUNTHORPE — 24/10

Attendance 2,473 — Pos 13 (15 / 15) — L 1-3 (HT 1-2)

Goals: McGavin 38 / Daws 34, Martin 36, Helliwell 61
Ref: P Jones

U's	Opp
Newell	*Whitehead*
Grainger	*Joyce*
Roberts	*Longden*
Kinsella	*Martin*
Cawley	*Elliott*
Oxbrow*	*Stevenson*
Cook	*Daws*
Bennett	*Alexander*
McDonough	*White*
McGavin	*Buckley*
Smith	*Helliwell*
Subs: Devereux/English	

U's are brought back down to earth after three wins and collect five bookings, making a total of 30 yellows and a red from 15 games. McGavin gets his long-awaited first league goal, after Iron take a two-goal lead. The giant Ian Helliwell heads the third from Graham Alexander's cross.

13 — H WREXHAM — 30/10

Attendance 4,423 — Pos 14 (11 / 15) — L 2-4 (HT 1-2)

Goals: Ball 40, Kinsella 58 [Connolly 77] / Bennett 23, 67, Jones B 45,
Ref: R Bigger

U's	Opp
Newell	*Morris*
Grainger*	*Jones K*
Roberts	*Phillips*
Kinsella	*Esdaille*^
Cawley	*Jones B*
English	*Sertori*
Cook^	*Bennett*
Bennett	*Owen*
McDonough	*Connolly*
Ball	*Thomas*
Smith	*Taylor*
Subs: Oxbrow/McGavin	*Flynn*

The Kinsella bid rumours are dispelled as a cruel hoax. U's employ an offside trap that neither they, nor linesman Pettit are in tune with McDonough (Bennett offside) appears to have levelled at 3-3 on 75 minutes, only for Karl Connolly to break away and score. Cawley signs full-time.

14 — H CARLISLE — 3/11

Attendance 3,263 — Pos 13 (19 / 18) — W 2-1 (HT 1-0)

Goals: Roberts 20, Cawley 90 / Barnsley 49p
Ref: I Borrett

U's	Opp
Newell	*O'Hanlon*
Grainger	*Williams*
Roberts	*Dalziel*
Kinsella	*Holden*
Cawley	*McCreery*
English	*Holmes*
Cook	*Gabbiadini*
Bennett	*Barnsley*
McDonough	*Hawke*
Ball*	*Oghani*^
Smith	*Arnold*
Subs: McDonough	*Sendall*

Newell plays the last game of his loan spell as U's and O's can't agree a fee. A dramatic injury-time winner from Cawley, heading in a Smith free-kick via the underside of the bar, is his first for U's Earlier Roberts had done likewise, only for Cawley to foul George Oghani in the box.

15 — A CARDIFF — 7/11

Attendance 5,505 — Pos 13 (10 / 18) — L 0-3 (HT 0-0)

Goals: Kinsella 90 / Dale 46, Blake 77, English 78 (og)
Ref: K Leach

U's	Opp
Green	*Ward*
Cook	*Gibbins*
Roberts	*Searle*
Kinsella	*James*
Cawley	*Matthews*
English	*Brazil*
Ball	*Ramsey*
Bennett^	*Kelly*
Sorrell	*Blake*
McGavin	*Dale*
Smith*	*Millar*
Subs: Oxbrow/McDon'gh	

Following a stalemate half, all U's effort goes to waste 30 seconds after the break. A lapse in concentration allows Nathan Blake to score Carl Dale. Blake heads from close range, as does English, albeit into his own net. Kinsella blasts McGavin's short free-kick past Gavin Ward.

16 — H ROCHDALE — 21/11

Attendance 3,172 — Pos 14 (8 / 19) — D 4-4 (HT 2-2)

Goals: Caw 24, Ball 27, Sorrell 71, McD 79 / Payne 15p, Milner 36, F'ders 76p, 88 (og), Jones 45
Ref: P Scobie

U's	Opp
Green	*Rose*
Sorrell	*Thackeray*
Roberts	*Graham*
Kinsella*	*Reid*
Cawley	*Reeves*
English	*Ryan*
Ball	*Bowden*
Bennett^	*Payne*
McDonough	*Flounders*
McGavin	*Whitehall*
Smith*	*Milner*^
Subs: Cook/Oxbrow	*Anders*

Green's attempt to clear a back-pass cannons off Andy Flounders, whom he fouls. He stays on despite hauling down Steve Whitehall, only for Flounders to catch him off his line with a late looping header. Kevin Rose saves McD's pen (63), after the boss is pulled over by John Bowden.

17 — A HEREFORD — 28/11

Attendance 1,671 — Pos 16 (19 / 19) — L 1-3 (HT 0-3)

Goals: Oxbrow 58 / Pickard 9, Donald 16 (og), Jones 45
Ref: R Groves

U's	Opp
Green	*Judge*
Donald	*Fry*
Roberts	*Downs*
Sorrell	*Davies*^
Cawley*	*Theodosiou*
English	*Titterton*
Ball	*Hall^*
Bennett	*Jones*
McDon'gh*	*Pickard*
Anderson	*Anderson*
Smith	*Cousins*
Subs: Oxbrow/Cook	*Rowboth'm/Nich'son*

U's have the worst defensive record in the division, and are just five points clear of bottom-club Northampton. Donald deflects a Derek Hall corner into U's goal, and in the third minute of added time Richard Jones strikes from Hall's free-kick. Oxbrow stabs in a loose ball in the box.

18 — H TORQUAY — 11/12

Attendance 2,774 — Pos 14 (20 / 22) — W 2-0 (HT 2-0)

Goals: McDonough 6, Smith 33
Ref: G Willard

U's	Opp
Green	*Sommer*
Grainger	*Lewis*
Roberts	*Davis*
Kinsella	*Johnson*
Cawley	*Moore*
English	*Hodges*^
Cook	*Joyce*
Bennett	*Foster*
McDon'gh*	*Darby*
Sorrell	*Myers*
Smith	*Salman*
Subs: Bennett/Ball	*Herd*

U's discipline is cause for concern with 47 yellow and 2 red cards. McGavin, rated at £250k, is superbly shackled by Ian Johnson, who cost six match balls from Whitley Bay. McGavin dummies Kinsella's pass for McD's seventh. Kinsella crosses for Smith, sliding in at the far post.

19 — A GILLINGHAM — 18/12

Attendance 2,331 — Pos 14 (22 / 25) — W 1-0 (HT 0-0)

Goals: McGavin 86
Ref: R Pawley

U's	Opp
Emberson	*Barrett*
Grainger*	*Henry*
Roberts	*Martin*
Kinsella	*Butler*
Cawley	*Breen*
Betts	*Smith*
Cook	*Clark*
Bennett	*Houghton*
McDonough	*Arnott*^
McGavin	*O'Connor*
Smith	*Stephenson*
Subs: Barrett	*Ayllott/Sorrell*

McD attempts to stop the flood of goals, signing 19-year-old Emberson from Millwall on loan. The Walker/Crisp incident surfaces again as the ex-U's boss takes Norwich eight points clear at the top of the Premiership. McGavin gains revenge for the Cup exit, via Barrett and the post.

20 — A NORTHAMPTON — 26/12

Attendance 4,861 — Pos 12 (21 / 25) — L 0-1 (HT 0-1)

Goals: McParland 23
Ref: K Morton

U's	Opp
Emberson	*Richardson*
Grainger	*Curtis*
Roberts	*Chard*
Kinsella	*Harmon*
Betts	*Angus*
English	*Terry*
Cook	*Burnham*
Bennett*	*Wilkin*
McDonough	*Bell*
McGavin	*Brown*
Smith	
Subs: Abrahams	*McParland*

Oxbrow (Barnet) and Devereux are released. Emberson saves well from Micky Bell and Paul Curtis. U's go in at the break trailing by a slick strike from Ian McParland for lowly Cobblers. McDonough blasts the players for their poor final ball and fumes 'get better or get out'.

21 — H SCARBOROUGH — 29/12

Attendance 3,640 — Pos 11 (8 / 28) — W 1-0 (HT 1-0)

Goals: McGavin 14
Ref: G Pooley

U's	Opp
Emberson	*Ford*
Grainger	*Thompson*
Roberts	*Mudd*
Kinsella	*Lee*
Betts	*Hirst*
English	*Curran*
Cook	*Ashdjian*^
Bennett	*Himsworth*
McDonough	*Mooney*
McGavin	*Foreman*
Smith	*Jones^*
	McGee/Lightbourne

Martin, whom Atkins had tried to sign from Fisher, joins on loan from West Ham. He had moved to Upton Park for £50,000. Scarborough are looking forward to their Coca-Cola home tie with Arsenal. McGavin takes the ball in his stride, from Kinsella, to sweep home from 18 yards.

BARCLAYS LEAGUE DIVISION 3 Player Manager: Roy McDonough SEASON 1992-93

No	Date		Att	Pos		Pt	F-A	H-T	Scorers, Times, and Referees	1	2	3	4	5	6	7	8	9	10	11	subs used
22	A WALSALL		3,669	10 *4*	W	31	3-1	2-0	Martin 17, McGavin 44, Cawley 62 / Clarke 81 / Ref: J Kirby	Emberson	Grainger	Roberts	Kinsella	Cawley	Betts	Cook	Bennett	**Martin**	McGavin	Smith	Smith
									Gayle *Cecere* *Reece* *Methven* *Knight* *Smith* *Ntamark** *Clarke* *Marsh* *MacDonald McDonald* *Statham*												

Martin's debut goal is only bettered by a spectacular Hugo Sanchez-style celebratory somersault. McGavin's angled drive leads to the Saddlers being booed off at the break. A linesman awards Cawley's goal, despite Mike Cecere's apparent clearance off the line. U's fourth win in five.

No	Date		Att	Pos		Pt	F-A	H-T	Scorers, Times, and Referees	1	2	3	4	5	6	7	8	9	10	11	subs used
23	H DONCASTER		4,402	6 *16*	W	34	2-0	0-0	Grainger 81, McGavin 88 / Ref: P Taylor	Emberson	Grainger	Roberts	Kinsella	Cawley	Betts	Cook*	Bennett*	Martin	McGavin	Smith	Ball/Abrahams
									Crichton *Rowe* *Prindiville** *Douglas* *Richards* *Hicks* *Hewitt* *Crosby* *Morrow* *Jeffrey* *Gormley* *Reddish*												

Masters is denied a work permit through not having 20 USA caps. McDonough enthuses 'if Jeffrey (Rovers) is worth £390k, then what price McGavin?' as the striker hits his sixth of the term. Grainger nets his first league goal for three years after sterling work on the flank, by Smith.

No	Date		Att	Pos		Pt	F-A	H-T	Scorers, Times, and Referees	1	2	3	4	5	6	7	8	9	10	11	subs used
24	A CHESTERFIELD		3,016	7 *8*	L	34	0-4	0-0	Williams 66, 76, Leman 75, [Lancaster 88] / Ref: T Fitzharris	Emberson	Grainger	Roberts	Kinsella	Cawley	Betts	Cook	Williams*	Martin	McGavin	Smith	
									Marples *Leman* *Carr* *Hebberd* *Rogers* *Brien* *Cash* *Lancaster* *Dyche* *Kennedy* *Turnbull*												

Kinsella signs a new two-and-a-half year deal. U's capitulate in eleven minutes after the interval, playing into a gale. Emberson, deceived by the high winds, is at fault for two of them. The score-line flatters Chesterfield, even more so when Dave Lancaster taps in a series of ricochets.

No	Date		Att	Pos		Pt	F-A	H-T	Scorers, Times, and Referees	1	2	3	4	5	6	7	8	9	10	11	subs used
25	H YORK		4,528	9 *3*	D	35	0-0	0-0	Ref: M.James	Emberson	Grainger	Roberts	Kinsella	Cawley	Betts	Cook*	Bennett*	Martin	McGavin	Smith	Ball/Abrahams
									Kiely *McMillan* *Hall* *Pepper* *Stancliffe* *Tutill* *McCarthy* *Borthwick** *Barnes* *Swann* *Canham* *Naylor*												

McDonough declares 'if I had £50k to spend now, I'd guarantee promotion'. Dean Kiely is lucky not to be sent off (20), spreading himself at the feet of Kinsella, but sliding out of his area. McGavin spurns the best chance, glancing Smith's 84th-minute cross the wrong side of the post.

No	Date		Att	Pos		Pt	F-A	H-T	Scorers, Times, and Referees	1	2	3	4	5	6	7	8	9	10	11	subs used
26	H BARNET		**5,609**	9 *1*	L	35	1-2	0-0	Bennett 53 / Bull 63 Payne 69 / Ref: D Shadwell	Emberson	Ball	Roberts	Kinsella	Cawley	Betts	Cook	Bennett	Martin*	McGavin	Smith	Abrahams
									Phillips *Huxford* *Naylor* *Bodley* *Barnett* *Wilson* *Payne* *Carter** *Bull* *Lowe** *Shoulder* *Stein/Evans*												

Tuesday's match at Darlington was called off because a mechanical digger cut through the water main at the cricket ground next to Feethams. The stiff test continues, after facing second-placed York last week, leaders Barnet visit. The Bees start three points clear of the Yorkshire side.

No	Date		Att	Pos		Pt	F-A	H-T	Scorers, Times, and Referees	1	2	3	4	5	6	7	8	9	10	11	subs used
27	A LINCOLN		3,380	11 *8*	D	36	1-1	0-0	Martin 75 / Bressington 81 / Ref: J Rushton	Emberson	Grainger	Roberts	Kinsella	Cawley	English	Betts	Bennett	Martin*	McGavin	Smith	Lee
									Pollitt *Smith* *Clarke* *Barraclough Carmichael* *Brown* *West** *Bressington Matthews* *Costello* *Puttnam* *Lee*												

Sorrell's contract is ended for 'unacceptable behaviour', whilst Hopkins, back from Hong Kong, joins on trial. Ref Rushden, 20 yards behind play, awards a penalty for Roberts' lunge at Peter Costello. Emberson saves from Graham Bressington, but can't get to his feet quick enough.

No	Date		Att	Pos		Pt	F-A	H-T	Scorers, Times, and Referees	1	2	3	4	5	6	7	8	9	10	11	subs used
28	H BURY		3,264	12 *10*	D	37	0-0	0-0	Ref: D Axcell	Emberson	Grainger	Roberts	Ball	Cawley*	English	Betts	Bennett	Martin*	McGavin	Smith	Cook/Abrahams
									Kelly *Kearney* *Stanislaus* *Daws** *Valentine* *Knill* *Adekola* *Rigby* *Hulme* *Stevens* *Ward* *Esdaille*												

Bury visit on the back of six straight wins. U's haven't won in four, but have two cleared off the line. Martin rounds Gary Kelly, only to be thwarted by Roger Stanislaus. Ball, in injury-time, sees his goal-bound header cleared by Nicky Daws. Shaker's Kevin Hulme had hit the bar.

No	Date		Att	Pos		Pt	F-A	H-T	Scorers, Times, and Referees	1	2	3	4	5	6	7	8	9	10	11	subs used
29	A SHREWSBURY		2,653	12 *5*	L	37	3-4	0-1	Hopkins 52, Grainger 74p, McG'n 82 / Grif's 8, 88, Smith M 60, Engl' 66 (og) / Ref: R Hamer	Emberson	Grainger	Roberts	Ball*	Cawley	English	Betts	Hopkins*	Martin	McGavin	Smith	Abrahams/Kinsella
									Edwards *Worsley !* *Lynch* *Taylor** *Williams M* *Blake* *Kinnaird* *Summerfield Brough** *Griffiths* *Smith M* *Clarke/O'Toole*												

A game of six bookings and a red card for Graeme Worsley (84). for a reckless challenge on Grainger. Debutant and ex-Shrew, Hopkins nets. English own-goals Paul Kinnaird's hopeful cross. McGavin is tripped by Kevin Summerfield, but Carl Griffith's catches U's chasing a winner.

No	Date		Att	Pos		Pt	F-A	H-T	Scorers, Times, and Referees	1	2	3	4	5	6	7	8	9	10	11	subs used
30	H HALIFAX		3,007	12 *18*	W	40	2-1	1-1	McGavin 31, Grainger 57 / Thompstone 10 / Ref: P Alcock	Emberson	Grainger	Roberts	Kinsella	Cawley	English	Betts	Hopkins	McDon'gh*	McGavin	Smith	Abrahams
									Bracey ! *German* *Hardy* *Matthews* *Lucketti* *Bradley* *Megson* *Ridings* *Thompstone Greenwood* *Everingham*												

McDonough returns after eight games, with a new club disciplinary code installed, after 68 bookings. Emberson mis-hits a free-kick to Ian Thompstone, to roll in the empty net. McGavin slides in his eighth, and Grainger nets, three mins after Lee Bracey is sent-off for fouling McD.

No	Date		Att	Pos		Pt	F-A	H-T	Scorers, Times, and Referees	1	2	3	4	5	6	7	8	9	10	11	subs used
31	H CARDIFF		4,538	13 *1*	L	40	2-4	1-3	McDonough 17p, McGavin 57 / Pike 21, 33, Rich'son 23, Matthews 63 / Ref: G Pooley	Emberson	Betts	Roberts	Kinsella	Flowers*	Hopkins*	Cook	Bennett	McDonough	McGavin	Smith	Partner/Abrahams
									Ward *James* *Searle* *Brazil* *Perry* *Ratcliffe* *Matthews* *Richardson* *Stant* *Pike* *Griffiths*												

Flowers gets his chance with English, Cawley and Grainger suspended. Jason Perry handles McD's shot. Cardiff fans twice invade the pitch to celebrate. Roberts, in his 400th league game, takes his young side off for four minutes. Cardiff players are said to be on £40k to win the league.

No		Opponent	Date	Att	Pos	Pld	Pts	Res	FT	HT
32	A	CARLISLE	20/3	3,003	13	16	43	W	2-0	2-0
33	H	HEREFORD	23/3	3,024	13	19	46	W	3-1	1-0
34	A	ROCHDALE	27/3	1,783	13	11	46	L	2-5	2-2
35	A	TORQUAY	6/4	2,915	13	21	47	D	2-2	1-0
36	A	SCARBOROUGH	13/4	1,803	11	14	50	W	1-0	1-0
37	H	GILLINGHAM	16/4	4,695	11	20	53	W	3-0	2-0
38	H	NORTHAMPTON	20/4	3,519	11	20	56	W	2-0	0-0
39	A	CREWE	24/3	3,250	10	5	56	L	1-7	1-4
40	H	SCUNTHORPE	1/5	3,421	10	13	59	W	1-0	1-0
41	A	DARLINGTON	4/5	2,007	10	15	59	L	0-1	0-1
42	A	WREXHAM	8/5	**9,705**	10	2	59	L	3-4	0-2

Home Average 3,792 · Away 3,223

---

32. CARLISLE (A) 20/3 — W 2-0
Cook 23, Edmondson 38 (og). Ref: K Redfearn
United: Barber, Betts, Roberts, Kinsella, Flowers, Hopkins, Cook*, Bennett, McDon'gh*, McGavin, Smith
Opponents: O'Hanlon, Burgess, Thorpe, Walling, McCreery*, Edmondson, Oghani, Davey, Arnold, Proudlock, White
Subs: Ball/Abrahams, Gabbiadini
O'Hanlon tips Betts' 30-yarder over. From the corner, Cook volleys his first league goal. Darren Edmondson diverts in McGavin's cross-shot. Emberson returns to Millwall, and is replaced by yet another loanee in Posh's Barber. U's complete only their second ever win at Carlisle. Kel...

33. HEREFORD (H) 23/3 — W 3-1
Titterton 7 (og), McDonough 78, Fry 86 [Abrahams 88]. Ref: M Bailey
United: Barber, Grainger, Roberts, Hopkins, Cawley, Betts, Cook*, Bennett*, McDonough, McGavin, Smith
Opponents: Judge, Downs*, Titterton, Davies, Abraham, Jones, Hall, Devine, Pickard*, May, Nicholson
Subs: English/Abrahams, Morris/Fry
Barber makes his trademark entry, wearing an 'old man' mask and bowing to the U's fans. Abrahams has played the equivalent of three games in his sub appearances, and gets his first league goal after Chris Fry had pulled one back. David Titterton's own-goal thunders past Alan Judge.

34. ROCHDALE (A) 27/3 — L 2-5
Smith 28, Abrahams 41 [Bowden 73]; Jon 36, How'd 33, Wh'al 46, Th'k 50. Ref: M Peck
United: Barber, Grainger, Roberts, Kinsella, Cawley, Betts*, Hopkins*, McDon'gh!, Abrahams, McGavin, Smith
Opponents: Rose, Thackeray, Graham, Butler, Reeves, Jones, Howard, Luke*, Whitehall, Doyle
Subs: Bennett/Cook, Bowden/Anders
Kinsella completes his miserable week, after losing 0-8 to Germany in an Eire U-21 game on Tuesday. McDonough is sent off (66), a minute after being booked, for an off-the-ball. Abrahams finally gets a start and caps a man-of-the-match display with a goal from McDonough's flick.

35. TORQUAY (A) 6/4 — D 2-2
McGavin 41, Ball 66; Barrow 54, Hodges 60. Ref: G Ashby
United: Barber, Grainger, Roberts, Kinsella, Cawley, English, Ball, Hopkins*, Sale*, McGavin, Smith
Opponents: Blackwell, Barrow, Colcombe, O'Riordan, Moore, Kelly, Trollope, Curran, Hodges, Hancock*
Subs: Muir/Darby
Amid the disciplinary controversy, McDonough retires as a player. Abrahams' left-wing cross gives McGavin his tenth goal. Smith's clearance ricochets off Lee Barrow into the net. Deadline signing Mark Sale (£20k from Brum) misses a sitter after Ball's 25-yard thunderbolt levels.

36. SCARBOROUGH (A) 13/4 — W 1-0
Abrahams 33. Ref: J Kirkby
United: Barber, Betts, Roberts, Kinsella, Cook, English, Ball, Hopkins*, Abrahams, McGavin, Smith
Opponents: Ford, McGee, Mudd, Himsworth, Curran, Hirst, Charles, Ashdjian, Thompson*, Foreman, Horsfield*
Subs: Lightbourne/James
Abrahams, 19, gets his third in four, pouncing on a loose ball after McGavin's shot is blocked. Betts, who had spent a spell as a non-contract player at Scarborough, clears Chris Curran's effort off the line. Scarborough's only other chance comes when Lutel James hits the side-netting.

37. GILLINGHAM (H) 16/4 — W 3-0
Clark 19 (og), Smith 26, Abrahams 56. Ref: J Martin
United: Barber, Betts, Roberts, Kinsella, Cook, English, Ball, Hopkins*, Abrahams, McGavin, Smith
Opponents: Barrett, Green, Martin, Butler, Carpenter, Smith, Clark, Crown*, Baker, Forster, Dempsey*
Subs: Crane/Eeles
West Ham attempt to take McGavin on loan until the end of the season, with a view to a £200k deal, but the deal fails. Barrett returns, having gathered three red cards so far for professional fouls, with Gills just four points off the bottom. Paul Clark own-goals Ball's vicious free-kick.

38. NORTHAMPTON (H) 20/4 — W 2-0
Ball 62p, Abrahams 90. Ref: R Wiseman
United: Barber, Betts, Roberts, Kinsella, Cook, English, Ball, Hopkins*, Abrahams, McGavin, Smith
Opponents: Richardson, Parsons, Gillard, Harman, Chard, Terry, Wilkin, Hawke*, Gavin, Brown!, Bell
Subs: Grainger/Bennett, Aldridge
Steve Brown is sent off (83) for a terrible challenge on Kinsella. Ball picks himself up, after being chopped by Ken Gillard, to give U's the lead. Abrahams' fifth in six comes after Barry Richardson parries Grainger's shot. Cobblers join Gills, Halifax and Torquay to fight the drop.

39. CREWE (A) 24/3 — L 1-7
English 22; Naylor 2, 39, 63, 77, 86, McKearney 23, [Clarkson 45]. Ref: J Watson
United: Barber, Betts, Roberts, Kinsella, Cook*, English, Ball, Hopkins*, Abrahams*, McGavin, Smith
Opponents: Smith M, McKearney, Smith S, Evans, Whalley, Carr*, Ward*, Naylor, Clarkson, Walters, Jackson
Subs: Woodward/Edwards
U's slim play-off chances end with 'The Tony Naylor Show'. 1: Robs injured Roberts to slot under Barber. 2: Outpaces Roberts to slide under Barber. 3: Whalley knocks down McKearney's cross. 4: Unmarked, knocks in McKearney's corner. 5: Races on to Whalley's through ball...

40. SCUNTHORPE (H) 1/5 — W 1-0
Abrahams 29. Ref: R Bigger
United: Barber, Betts, Roberts, Kinsella, Cook*, English, Ball, Hopkins*, Abrahams, McGavin, Smith
Opponents: Samways, Joyce, Platnauer, Martin, Elliott, Greaves*, Alexander, Helliwell, White, Thompstone, Constable*
Subs: Grainger/McDonoug, Foy/Maxwell
McDonough comes out of retirement to beef up the attack. U's reserve side will be re-instated next season in the Capital League. Hopkins lays a ball back to Betts, and his low cross is met by the prolific Abrahams. Two wins in the last two will put U's in the play-offs on goals scored.

41. DARLINGTON (A) 4/5 — L 0-1
Reed 36. Ref: T West
United: Barber, Grainger*, Roberts, Betts, Cook, English, Ball, Hopkins*, Abrahams*, McGavin, Smith
Opponents: Prudhoe, Shaw, Dowson, Parkin, O'Shaugn's, Reed, Isaacs*, Mardenboro, Dobie, Gaughan, Ball
Subs: Cawley/McDon'gh, Ball
U's rekindled hopes are finally dashed when Abrahams' shot is handled on the line (87), but no penalty is awarded. John Reed, on loan from Sheff Utd, nets one of a host of Quakers' chances. Several of the U's players, young and old alike, sink tearfully to the ground at the whistle.

42. WREXHAM (A) 8/5 — L 3-4
Hardy 54 (og), Bennett 68, Kinsella 79; Con' 10, Betts 43 (og), Watkin 63, 89. Ref: D Allison
United: Munson, Betts, Roberts*, Kinsella, Grainger, Cawley, Ball, Hopkins*, Abrahams*, McGavin, Smith
Opponents: Morris, Jones, Hardy, Owen*, Humes, Pejic, Bennett, Lake, Connolly, Watkin, Cross
Subs: Flowers/Hopkins, Case
Munson is U's fifth keeper of the term. Despite the win, Cardiff pip their Welsh rivals for the title at Scunthorpe. Betts heads Jon Cross' corner into his own net, whilst Phil Hardy does the same off Ball's shot. Kinsella seems to secure a point, only for Steve Watkins to net from close in.

BARCLAYS DIVISION 3 (CUP-TIES)

Player Manager: Roy McDonough   SEASON 1992-93

Coca-Cola League Cup

		F-A	H-T	Scorers, Times, and Referees	1	2	3	4	5	6	7	8	9	10	11	subs used
1:1 H BRIGHTON 18/8	D	1-1	0-0	English 74 / Wilkins 64 / Ref: I Borrett	Newell / *Beeney*	Donald / *Chivers*	Roberts / *Chapman*	Kinsella / *Wilkins*	English / *Bissett*	Oxbrow / *Foster*	Devereux / *Robinson*	Bennett / *Funnell*	McDonough / *Edwards*	Grainger / *Codner*	Smith / *Walker*	Smith
	3,814 2:															
1:2 A BRIGHTON 26/8	L	0-1	0-0	Wilkins 61 / Ref: A Buksh / (Colchester lost 2-1 on aggregate)	Newell / *Beeney*	Donald* / *Chivers*	Roberts / *Chapman*	Kinsella / *Wilkins*	English / *Crumplin*	Oxbrow / *Foster*	Cook / *Robinson*	Bennett / *Funnell*	McDonough / *Edwards `*	Hazel / *Codner `*	Smith / *Walker*	Abrahams / *Washalo/Wilkinson*
	4,125 2:10															

English earns U's a draw. volleying in from close range via Bennett's lob. Dean Wilkins had given the Seagulls the lead from 20 yards after Roberts had half-cleared. McDonough seems to seal it three minutes later, lobbing Mark Beeney from 35 yards, but Bennett is ruled offside.

Wilkins nets his second goal of the tie, after a half-clearance from Roberts, to earn a money-spinning two-legged tie against Man Utd. Hazel, who nets his full debut, forces a good 34th-minute save from Beeney. McDonough has a towering header cleared off the line by Simon Funnell (70).

FA Cup

		F-A	H-T	Scorers, Times, and Referees	1	2	3	4	5	6	7	8	9	10	11	subs used
1 H SLOUGH 14/11	W	4-0	2-0	Sorrell 16, Bennett 42, 90, Ball 85 / Ref: P Alcock	Green / *Bunting*	Sorrell / *Whitby*	Roberts / *Pluckrose*	Kinsella / *Briley*	Cawley / *Folan*	English / *Anderson !*	Ball / *Hazel*	Bennett / *Scott*	McDonough* / *Sayer*	McGavin / *McKinnon*	Smith / *Fiore*	Oxbrow
	3,858 VC:2															
2 A GILLINGHAM 5/12	D	1-1	0-1	McGavin 65 / Crown 15 / Ref: K Morton	Green / *Barrett*	Grainger / *Green*	Roberts / *Martin*	Kinsella / *Butler*	Cawley / *Breen*	English / *Smith*	Ball / *Clark*	Sorrell ! / *Crown*	McDonough / *Forster `*	McGavin / *Forster `*	Smith / *Dempsey `*	O'Connor/Henry
	5,319 21															
2R H GILLINGHAM 16/12	L	2-3	0-3	Ball 88, 90 / Forster 7, Arnott 17, Henry 45p / Ref: K Morton	Green / *Barrett*	Grainger / *Henry*	Roberts / *Martin*	Kinsella / *Butler*	Ball / *Breen*	English / *Smith*	Cook* / *Clark*	Sorrell* / *Forster `*	McDonough / *Arnott*	McGavin / *O'Connor*	Smith / *Dempsey `*	Bennett/Betts
	4,440 21															

Green makes his home debut. after joining on loan from Kidderminster. Slough defender Darren Anderson is sent off (35) for pole-axing McDonough. Sorrell, also on his home debut, scores with a header from Smith's corner, and cracks the inside of the post (64), and the bar (70).

McD and Barrett are at each other's throats. McD says 'put a high ball in the box and it won't be the goalie there first'. Barrett retorts 'with a pensioner in goal (Green). Colchester will have an old man up front as well. I wanted to stay'. Sorrell is sent off (90) for a second booking.

Nicky Forster gives leaden-footed U's a torrid time. He shrugs off Kinsella and English to put Gills in front, then finds Liburd Henry to cross to Andy Arnott for the second. On half-time Roberts fouls Arnott in the box. Ball's late double, and seven minutes added. is too little, too late.

Autoglass Trophy

		F-A	H-T	Scorers, Times, and Referees	1	2	3	4	5	6	7	8	9	10	11	subs used
1 H NORTHAMPTON 1/12	L	1-2	1-1	Grainger 27p / Beavon 45p, Brown 63 / Ref: D Axcell	Green / *Richardson*	Donald / *Curtis*	Grainger / *Beavon*	Devereux / *Harmon !*	Oxbrow / *Angus*	English / *Terry*	Hazel* / *Burnham*	Roberts* / *Wilkin*	McDonough / *Bell`*	McGavin / *Brown*	Smith / *McParland*	Bennett/Kinsella
	1,454 21															
1 A BARNET 21/12	L	2-4	0-3	Ball 57, Cook 58 / Evans 3, Carter 13, Stein 34, Hunt 54 / Ref: D Gallagher	Monk / *Phillips*	Betts / *Huxford*	Phillips* / *Cooper*	Roberts / *Bodley*	**Partner** / *Barnett `*	Ball / *Horton `*	Cook / *Payne*	Bennett / *Carter*	Abrahams / *Stein*	McGavin / *Evans*	Smith / *Hunt*	Donald / *Hayrettin/Wilson*
	1,193 1															

In U's first attack. Micky Curtis fouls McGavin in the box. Oxbrow's scuffed clearance gifts Kevin Wilkin, who is felled by Green. Hazel is stretchered off with cartilage damage before Micky Bell provides Steve Brown's winner. Darren Harmon is sent off (90) for fouling McGavin.

U's need a win or minimum 2-2 draw to progress, hopes of a 4-4 draw are dashed when Roberts and Abrahams hit the woodwork in a make-shift side. Monk tries to dribble a back-pass and clear, only for it to bounce off Mark Carter and in. 19-year-old trialist Betts again impresses.

GMVC Championship Shield

		F-A	H-T	Scorers, Times, and Referees	1	2	3	4	5	6	7	8	9	10	11	subs used
F A WYCOMBE 6/10	L	0-3	0-1	Scott 34p, Casey 57, 79 / Ref: P Scobie	**Monk** / *Hyde*	Abrahams / *Cousins*	Roberts / *Crossley*	Kinsella / *Kerr*	**Cawley** / *Creaser*	Oxbrow / *Hutchinson*	Cook* / *Carroll`*	Bennett / *Casey*	Ball* / *Stapleton`*	McGavin / *Scott*	Smith / *Guppy*	Partner/Donald / *Greene/Ryan*
	3,309 VC:1															

U's include trialists Alistair Monk (Norwich) and Cawley (Barnet). Disinterested U's lose the match for the JC Thompson Shield, played for by the GMVC champions and FA Trophy winners. Wycombe, as runners-up. compete. and currently lead the GMVC table by a clear margin.

		Home					Away						
	P	W	D	L	F	A	W	D	L	F	A	Pts	
1 Cardiff	42	13	7	1	42	20	12	1	8	35	27	83	
2 Wrexham	42	14	3	4	48	26	9	8	4	27	26	80	
3 Barnet	42	16	4	1	45	19	7	6	8	21	29	79	
4 York*	42	13	6	2	41	15	8	6	7	31	30	75	
5 Walsall	42	11	6	4	42	31	11	1	9	34	30	73	
6 Crewe	42	13	3	5	47	23	8	4	9	28	33	70	
7 Bury	42	10	7	4	36	19	8	2	11	27	36	63	
8 Lincoln	42	10	6	5	31	20	8	3	10	26	33	63	
9 Shrewsbury	42	11	3	7	36	30	8	2	11	21	22	62	
10 COLCHESTER	42	13	3	5	38	26	5	2	14	29	50	59	
11 Rochdale	42	10	3	8	38	29	6	7	8	32	41	58	
12 Chesterfield	42	11	3	7	32	28	4	8	9	27	35	56	
13 Scarborough	42	7	7	7	32	30	8	2	11	34	41	54	
14 Scunthorpe	42	8	7	6	38	25	6	5	10	19	29	54	
15 Darlington	42	5	6	10	23	31	7	8	6	25	22	50	
16 Doncaster	42	6	5	10	22	28	5	9	7	16	29	47	
17 Hereford	42	7	9	5	31	27	3	6	12	16	33	45	
18 Carlisle	42	7	5	9	29	27	4	6	11	22	38	44	
19 Torquay	42	6	4	11	18	26	6	3	12	27	41	43	
20 Northampton	42	6	5	10	19	28	5	3	13	29	46	41	
21 Gillingham	42	9	4	8	32	28	0	9	12	16	36	40	
22 Halifax	42	3	5	13	20	35	6	4	11	25	33	36	
	924	209	111	142	740	571	142	111	209	571	740	1275	

* promoted after play-offs

Odds & ends

- Double wins: (5) Carlisle, Gillingham, Halifax, Scarborough, Walsall.
- Double defeats: (5) Barnet, Cardiff, Darlington, Shrewsbury, Wrexham.
- Won from behind: (2) Lincoln (h), Halifax (h).
- Lost from in front: (4) Barnet (a), Cardiff (h), Rochdale (a), Barnet (h).
- High spots: Back to the league.
- Mark Kinsella selected for the Republic of Ireland Under-21s.
- Dean Martin's goal celebrations – somersaults and head-stands.
- Fred Barber's crowd-pleasing mask and pre-match ritual.
- Late surge for the play-offs, with four wins in five.
- Emergence of Abrahams, six goals in nine full appearances.
- Low spots: Four defeats in the first five league games.
- Inability to persuade a big-name striker to sign.
- Work permit refusal for GMVC-hero, Masters.
- Crushing 1-7 defeat at fellow contenders, Crewe.
- Not having a permanent recognised goalkeeper all season.
- Missing out on the play-offs by four points, despite having scored
- enough goals to secure seventh place if level on points.

Player of the Year: Paul Roberts.
Ever presents: (2) Paul Roberts, Nicky Smith.
Hat-tricks: (0).
Leading scorer: Roy McDonough (9).

Appearances / Goals

	Appearances						Goals			
	Lge	Sub	LC	Sub	FAC	Sub	Lge	LC	FAC	Tot
Abrahams, Paul	9	14					6			6
Ball, Steve	19	5	1		2		4		3	7
Barber, Fred	10									
Bennett, Gary	30	8	2		1	1	8		2	10
Betts, Simon	23					1				
Cawley, Peter	22	2			2		3			3
Cook, Jason	30	4			2		1			1
Devereux, Robert	3	3			1					
Donald, Warren	8	2		2						
Emberson, Carl	13									
English, Tony	30	3	2		3		1	1		2
Flowers, Paul	2	1								
Grainger, Martin	28	3	1		2		3			3
Green, Ron	4				3					
Hazel, Julian	2		1							
Hopkins, Robert	13	1	2		3		1			1
Kinsella, Mark	37	1	2		3		6			6
McDonough, Roy	21	4	2		3		9			9
McGavin, Steve	35	2	2		3		9			9
Martin, Dean	8									
Munson, Nathan	1									
Newell, Paul	14		2							
Oxbrow, Darren	12	4	2		1	1	4			4
Partner, Andy		1			3					
Phillips, Ian		1								
Roberts, Paul	42				3		1			1
Smith, Nicky	42	2	2		3		4			4
Sorrell, Tony	4	1			3		1		1	2
(own-goals)										4
28 players used	462	60	22	1	33	3	67	1	7	75

ENDSLEIGH LEAGUE DIVISION 3

Player Manager: Roy McDonough

SEASON 1993-94

No	Date		Att	Pos	Pt	Res	F-A	H-T	1	2	3	4	5	6	7	8	9	10	11	subs used
1	14/8	H LINCOLN	3,198		3	W	1-0	0-0	Keeley	Betts*	Roberts	Kinsella	English	Grainger	Ball	Bennett	McDon'gh*	McGavin	Smith	**Abrahams/Cook J**
									Pollitt	Smith P	Clarke	Hill	Smith M	Brown*	Schofield	Mardenboro	Baraclough	Costello*	Puttnam	Dunphy/Dixon
2	21/8	A CREWE	2,700	2	3	L	1-2	0-1	Keeley	Betts*	Roberts	Kinsella	English	Grainger	Ball	Bennett*	McDonough	McGavin	Smith	**Allpress/Campbell**
									Smith	Collins^	Gardiner	Evans	Wilson	Hughes	Rowbotham	Clarkson	Ward	Whalley*	Walton*	Lennon/Lyons
3	28/8	H NORTHAMPTON	2,874	19	6	W	3-2	2-2	Keeley	Allpress	Roberts	Kinsella	English	Grainger	Ball	Bennett*	McDon'gh*	McGavin	Smith	**Morrow/Brown S**
									Richardson	Parsons	Gillard	Phillips	Terry	Chard	Fleming	Colkin	Gilzean	Brown	Bell	
4	31/8	H SHREWSBURY	2,723	22	7	D	3-3	3-1	Keeley	Allpress	Roberts	Kinsella	English	Grainger	Ball	Brown S	McDonough	McGavin	Smith	
									Edwards	Hockaday	Lynch	Taylor	Williams	Blake	Brown	Clark	Donaldson*	Summerfield	Evans^	Patterson/Spink
5	4/9	A TORQUAY	2,989	5	8	D	3-3	2-0	Keeley	Allpress*	Roberts	Kinsella	English	Cawley	Ball	Brown S	McDon'gh*	McGavin	Smith	**Grainger/Dickens**
									Lowe	Burton	OToole^	O'Riordan	Moore	Curran	Trollope	Kelly	Darby^	Hodges	Hathaway	Foster/Loram
6	11/9	H ROCHDALE	2,776	2	8	L	2-5	2-2	Keeley	Allpress	Roberts	Kinsella	English	Grainger	Ball*	Brown S*	McDonough	McGavin	Smith	**Bennett/Dickens**
									Hodge	Thackeray*	Graham	Reid	Reeves	Butler	Stuart	Bowden	Flounders^	Whitehall	Lancaster	Ryan/Milner
7	18/9	A WYCOMBE	6,025	6	11	W	5-2	1-1	Keeley	Betts	Roberts	Kinsella*	English	Cawley	Dickens	Brown S	McDonough	McGavin	Smith	**Grainger**
									Hyde	Cousins!	Crossley	Kerr	Evans*	Ryan	Carroll	Langford	Hayrettin^	Scott	Guppy	Potter/Hemmings
8	25/9	H BURY	2,702	20	14	W	4-1	2-0	Keeley	Betts	Roberts	Kinsella*	English	Cawley	Dickens	Brown S	McDon'gh*	McGavin	Smith	**Grainger/Richards'n**
									Bracey	Wood	Stanislaus	Daws	Anderson	Jackson	Rigby	Kearney	Kelly	Blissett	Carter	
9	2/10	A PRESTON	6,412	1	14	L	0-1	0-0	Keeley	Betts*	Roberts	Kinsella*	English	Cawley	Dickens	Brown S	McDonough	McGavin	Smith	**Richardson**
									O'Hanlon	Masefield	Sulley	Lucas*	Nebbeling	Matthewson	Ainsworth	Cartwright	Conroy^	Ellis	Raynor	Challender/Norbury
10	9/10	H SCUNTHORPE	3,405	10	17	W	2-1	1-1	Keeley	Locke	Roberts	Kinsella	English	Cawley	Dickens	Brown S	McDonough	McGavin	Smith	**White/Trebble**
									Samways	Alexander	Mudd*	Carmichael	Elliott	Bradley	Thompstone	Martin	Smith	Hope	Toman^	

Scorers, Times, and Referees

1. Kinsella 55 — Ref M Reid
The league block United's Friday night fixtures, to appease the Pools companies Keeley signs for two years on a free from Oldham. To end the keeper crisis. U's have a suspended £7.5k fine imposed for last season's indiscipline United win with a 25-yard free-kick. put in by Kinsella.

2. Ball 68 / Ward 41, 59 — Ref T Holbrook
Crewe, who thrashed U's 7-1 last term, lost to York in the play-off final. Alex's opener comes when Ashley Ward's shot delicately flicks Keeley with a wicked deflection. A lapse leads to Gareth Whalley's cross finding Ward, unmarked. Ball rifles home a loose ball, following McD's cross.

3. Grainger 34p, English 41, Kinsella 71 / Brown 5, Gilzean 35 — Ref M Bailey
Cobblers lead with a Steve Brown lob. Steve Terry's clearance hits Lee Colkin and goes in, but a penalty is given for Barry Richardson's lunge at English. A minute later, Ian Gilzean, son of ex-Spurs ace Alan, puts the visitors ahead Kinsella's 20-yard dipping shot wins U's the points.

4. McGavin 3, 23, Brown S 45 / Lynch 1, Summerfield 79, Spink 88 — Ref G Poll
U's sign Dickens on a free. whilst Shrews were hammered 1-6 at Preston on Saturday Brown, signed from Southend, scores on his first full game. U's are coasting to a 3-1 win with eleven minutes left, but slack defending lets in Kevin Summerfield (header) and Dean Spink (volley).

5. Brown S 35, McG' 36, Curran 47 (og) / Foster 58, 78, 82 — Ref S Dunn
McDonough vows to carry on attacking, despite surrendering a three-goal lead. Enter Gulls' subs. Adrian Foster and Mark Loram, at the break. Foster turns Cawley to shoot past Keeley, heads in Tom Kelly's free-kick. and finds himself in acres of space to complete a remarkable treble.

6. McD' 8, Brown S 37 [Whitehall 78] / Lancaster 10,74, Butler 16, Reeves 67 [Hodge] — Ref G Pooley
Bennett's free transfer to Kettering falls through. McDonough seeks revenge on Dale boss. Mick Docherty, after his sending-off at Spotlands last term. U's second-half nightmare strikes for the fifth time. Grainger's blunder leads to Alan Reeves heading in for 2-3, as U's are booed off.

7. Kins' 43, McG' 59, McD' 65, G'ger 75, Scott 19p, Langford 49 [Brown S 89] — Ref C Wilkes
After a week of criticism. McDonough hopes for a clean sheet at Wycombe. who follow U's up from the GMVC. He milks the applause from U's travelling army with the third, after Paul Hyde parries Dickens' shot. Jason Cousins is sent off (30). handling a through ball to Kinsella.

8. Brown S 8, 48, 53, McGavin 38 / Kearney 55 — Ref P Alcock
Richardson joins from Chesham. Brown nets his first-ever hat-trick to take his tally to seven in six starts. United sit five points behind leaders Rochdale. Roberts finds Brown with a pin-point ball. he then half-volleys a McGavin lay-off. before prodding in Grainger's left-wing cross.

9. Ellis 73 — Ref J Watson
U's don't just have a 'plastic' pitch to contend with, but also Preston boss John Beck, notorious for gamesmanship. Paul Raynor's long-throw zips up off the surface. eluding English and Roberts for Tony Ellis. on seven with Brown, to win the battle of the divisional leading scorers.

10. Kinsella 32, Brown S 78 / Carmichael 5 — Ref K Morton
Locke. 23, joins on loan from Southend. Scunthorpe have conceded only one in five away matches. Brown. who spent an unhappy time at Iron, gives the best retort to his chief tormentor, manager Richard Money. gleefully blasting in McDonough's knockdown from Cawley's long ball.

11 · A · HEREFORD · 16/10 — Att. 1,848 — Pos 7 · L · 17 17 — **0-5** (HT 0-2)

Scorers: Pike 29, 43p, 51, Fry 65, Hall 88
Ref: R Groves

U's: Keeley! · Locke · Roberts · Kinsella* · Dickens · Cawley · English · Brown S* · McDonough · McGavin · Smith · Ball/Munson!
Hereford: Judge · Davies · Downs · Abraham · Hall · Morris · Smith · Fry · Pike · Nicholson* · Anderson

Chris Pike's hat-trick is overshadowed by U's having two keepers sent off. Keeley is the first on 43 mins for up-ending Chris Fry. McDonough takes over until the break. Munson, on 68 minutes also goes, colliding with Derek Hall. Pike's goals each come against a different goalkeeper.

---

12 · H · WIGAN · 23/10 — Att. 2,814 — Pos 4 · W · 17 20 — **3-1** (HT 1-1)

Scorers: McDonough 4, 51, Kinsella 65 / Gillespie 27
Ref: I Hemley

U's: Keeley · Allpress · Roberts · Kinsella · English · Cawley · Dickens* · Brown S · McDonough · McGavin · Smith · Ball
Wigan: Farnworth · Carragher · McKearney · Robertson · Strong* · Kennedy^ · Gillespie · Rimmer · Daley · Gavin · Lyons · Duffy/Langley

Keeley gets a one-match ban, whilst Munson, incredibly, gets three. Ex-U's loanee Keith Gillespie returns to the area. for Newbury at Witham (Diadora Lge) with a great solo run and shot. Kinsella nets his seventh. McDonough nods in Dickens' cross, only for Man Utd loanee Keith Gillespie to level with a great solo run and shot. Kinsella nets his seventh.

---

13 · A · GILLINGHAM · 30/10 — Att. 3,964 — Pos 6 · L · 14 20 — **0-3** (HT 0-2)

Scorers: Green 17, Forster 40, Reinelt 90
Ref: G Willard

U's: Desborough · Locke · Roberts · Kinsella · English · Cawley · Ball · Dickens · McDonough · McGavin* · Smith · Richardson
Gillingham: Barrett · Dunne · Palmer · Butler · Green · Carpenter · Micklewhite · Forster · Arnott* · Smith · Smillie · Reinelt

An amazing blunder leaves U's without a keeper for the visit to Priestfield, until the eleventh-hour signing of Desborough from Chelmsford reserves. It was discovered that 41-year-old Mervyn Cawston had received insurance payments and so could no longer play in a league match.

---

14 · A · DARLINGTON · 2/11 — Att. 1,299 — Pos 9 · L · 22 20 — **3-7** (HT 1-3)

Scorers: Dick' 9, McG' 59, Kins' 75 [H'th 71] / Ellison 1, 80, P'ter 20, 58, Chap' 33, 84
Ref: P Harrison

U's: Keeley · Locke · Roberts · Kinsella · English · Cawley · Dickens · Ball* · McDonough · McGavin · Smith · Richardson
Darlington: Collier · Reed · Pearson · Himsworth · Sunley · Gregan · Isaacs · Painter · Ellison* · Chapman · Kirkham^ · Shaw/Ball

Winless Quakers start five points adrift of Northampton at the bottom. and have a new boss in Alan Murray. Keeley, back after suspension, is the star-man and prevents double figures. Roberts has a stinker against a side with eight players under 20. Dickens scores his first United goal

---

15 · H · WALSALL · 6/11 — Att. 2,736 — Pos 12 · L · 4 20 — **0-1** (HT 0-1)

Scorer: Peer 9
Ref: D Orr

U's: Keeley · Betts · Roberts · Kinsella · English · Cawley · Dickens · Richardson* · McDonough · McGavin · Smith · Abrahams
Walsall: Walker · Evans · Marsh · Watkiss · Keister · Ryder · Ntamark · Lillis · Lightbourne · Peer · McDonald* · Wright

Still wounded from the midweek mauling, U's welcome Walsall, fresh from a 2-0 win over leaders Preston. There appears little danger as Rod McDonald chips into United's box, until Dean Peer ghosts in late to wrong-foot Keeley. Colchester's second-half onslaught counts for nothing.

---

16 · A · DONCASTER · 20/11 — Att. 2,034 — Pos 15 · D · 6 20 — **1-2** (HT 0-0)

Scorers: McGavin 62 / Yates 54, Page 67
Ref: B Hill

U's: Keeley · Betts · Roberts · Kinsella · Basham · Cawley · Dickens* · Brown S · McDon'gh* · McGavin · Smith · Ball/Richardson
Doncaster: Ford · Measham · Freeman · Harper · Wilcox · Page · Roche · Yates · Jones · Turnbull · Williamson

Basham (West Ham), 20, is loaned to help a defence that has leaked 47 goals. Keeley excels, but can't stop a fifth successive defeat. Ex-U's star, Mark Yates, opens for Rovers, but McGavin sweeps in Kinsella's defence-splitting pass. Don Page heads in Clive Freeman's flag-kick.

---

17 · H · CARLISLE · 27/11 — Att. 2,316 — Pos 12 · W · 17 23 — **2-1** (HT 1-1)

Scorers: English 43, 88 / Thomas 5
Ref: P Danson

U's: Munson · Betts* · Roberts* · Kinsella · English · Cawley · Ball · Brown S · McDonough · McGavin · Smith · Abrahams/Rich'rds'n
Carlisle: Day · Burgess · Gallimore · Walling · Joyce · Edmondson · Thomas · Flounders* · Reeves · Davey · Reddish · McCreery

Southend's Barry Fry, having failed with a £150k bid for McGavin, offers £50k plus Steve Tilson and John Cornwell. Keeley falls down his stairs before the match. Rod Thomas's goal is cancelled by English, who steers McGavin's free-kick past Mervyn Day two minutes from time.

---

18 · H · CREWE · 11/12 — Att. 2,647 — Pos 14 · L · 1 23 — **2-4** (HT 1-2)

Scorers: English 44, Brown S 64 [Whalley 90] / Rowbotham 2, 17, Gardiner 64
Ref: B Coddington

U's: Munson · Betts · Roberts · Kinsella · English · Cawley · Ball* · Brown S · McDonough · Abrahams · Smith* · Dickens/Richardson
Crewe: Smith · Booty* · Gardiner · Evans · Abel · Wilson · Whalley · Naylor · Collins · Walters^ · Rowbotham · Smith S/Murphy

Cornwell pulls out of the McGavin deal. Basham (groin) returns to Upton Park. Injury-ravaged U's fight back magnificently to level at 2-2, but Mark Gardiner chips over stranded Munson, and Gareth Whalley seizes onto a Tony Naylor pass to round the U's keeper and send Crewe top.

---

19 · H · MANSFIELD · 27/12 — Att. 3,478 — Pos 16 · D · 12 24 — **0-0** (HT 0-0)

Ref: M Bailey

U's: Sheffield · Betts · Roberts · Kinsella · English · Cawley · Ball* · Brown S · McDonough · McGavin* · Smith · Fry/Dickens
Mansfield: Ward · Fleming · Platnauer · Holland · Gray · Rees · Noteman* · McLoughlin · Wilkinson · Parkin · Boothroyd · Wilson

The postponement of the Lincoln game allows U's without any injuries to heal. and McDonough to recruit yet another keeper in Sheffield of Cambridge and Fry from Hereford on Christmas Eve. McDonough can't win: he abandons the cavalier attack to concentrate on defence.

---

20 · A · SCARBOROUGH · 28/12 — Att. 1,226 — Pos 12 · W · 20 27 — **2-0** (HT 0-0)

Scorers: McDonough 65, McGavin 88
Ref: N Barry

U's: Sheffield · Betts · Roberts · Kinsella · English · Cawley · Dickens · Brown S* · McDonough · Fry* · Smith · McGavin/Ball
Scarborough: Evans · Knowles · Swailes · Calvert · Davis* · Meyer · Charles · Murray · White · Whitington · Toman^ · Young/Thompson

Sheffield is the first U's keeper for 31 games to keep two successive clean sheets. Fry goes close, shooting just wide on a mud-bath of a pitch. Smith's corner finds McDonough to out-jump Adie Meyer with a downward header. Sub McGavin seals victory, sliding under Mark Evans.

---

21 · H · CHESTER · 1/1 — Att. 3,170 — Pos 11 · D · 4 28 — **0-0** (HT 0-0)

Ref: G Willard

U's: Sheffield · Betts · Roberts · Kinsella · English · Cawley · Dickens · Brown S · McDonough · McGavin* · Smith · Fry
Chester: Felgate · Preece · Jakub · Jenkins · Came · Greenall · Thompson · Lightfoot · Wheeler^ · Leonard · Pugh · Rimmer

McDonough reveals he has been chasing Michael Meaker (QPR). Lee Howey (Sunderland) and John Hartson (Luton). without success. City have just one defeat in 16. McGavin misses an easy chance on 16 seconds, shooting tamely at David Felgate. Flu-ridden U's settle for a point.

ENDSLEIGH LEAGUE DIVISION 3 — Player Manager: Roy McDonough — SEASON 1993-94

No	Date		Att	Pos	Pt	F-A	H-T	Scorers, Times, and Referees	1	2	3	4	5	6	7	8	9	10	11	subs used
22	3/1	A SHREWSBURY	4,245	12 / 2	28	L 1-2	1-0	Ball 40 / Walton 55, Spink 80 / Ref: R Milford	Sheffield / Edwards	Betts / Hockaday	Roberts* / Withe	Kinsella / Taylor	English / Williams	Cawley / Patterson*	Dickens / Brown	Brown S / Clarke	McDon'gh* / Spink	McGavin / Walton	Smith / Smith*	Ball/Allpress Summerfield/Lynch
23	15/1	H HEREFORD	2,439	11 / 20	31	W 1-0	0-0	Dickens 75 / Ref: G Pooley	Sheffield / Judge	Betts / Clark	Allpress / Anderson	Kinsella / Davies!	English / Abraham	Cawley / Reece	Dickens / Hall	Watts* / Steele	McDonough Fry / Pike	Fry / Pickard	Ball / Nicholson	Booty
24	22/1	A SCUNTHORPE	2,854	11 / 9	32	D 1-1	0-0	Cawley 67 / Carmichael 54 / Ref: I Cruickshanks	Sheffield / Samways	Betts / Alexander	Allpress / Mudd	Kinsella / Hope	English / Knill	Cawley / Bradley	Dickens / Thompstone Henderson	Brown S* / Carmichael Bullimore	McDonough Fry* / Smith*		Ball / Sansom	Smith/Watts
25	29/1	H GILLINGHAM	3,436	13 / 15	32	L 1-2	0-0	Watts 67 / Smith 51, Forster 89 / Ref: J Key	Ch'sewright / Banks	Betts / Dunne	Allpress / Palmer	Kinsella / Butler	English / Green	Cawley / Reinelt	Dickens / Smillie	Ball* / Baker	McDonough Fry* / Henry*	Smith / Smith	Brown S* / Micklewhite Forster	Watts/Smith Cheesewright
26	5/2	A WIGAN	1,695	12 / 20	35	W 1-0	0-0	Dickens 80 / Ref: G Singh	Ch'sewright / Farnworth	Betts / Carragher	Allpress / Johnson	Kinsella / Robertson	English / Skipper*	Cawley / Kennedy*	Dickens / Langley	Ball / Duffy	McDonough Fry* / Gavin	Fry / Morton	Watts / Lyons	Campbell Rennie/Connelly
27	12/2	H CHESTERFIELD	2,783	12 / 10	35	L 0-2	0-1	/ Morris 6, 58 / Ref: R Bigger	Ch'sewright / Leonard	Betts / Hewitt	Allpress / Rogers	Kinsella / Trotter	English / Madden	Cawley / Law	Dickens / Curtis	Ball* / Davies	McDonough Campbell* / Morris Moss*	Watts /	Brown S* / Jules	Fry/Smith Dennis
28	19/12	A NORTHAMPTON	3,185	13 / 22	36	D 1-1	1-1	McDonough 24 / Wilkin 19 / Ref: T Lunt	Ch'sewright / Richardson	Betts / Fleming	Allpress / Gillard	Kinsella / Harman	English / Warburton	Cawley / Chard	Dickens / Wilkin	Brown S* / Elad	McDonough Hyslop! / Gitzean*	Hyslop / Cornwall	Watts* / Bell	Fry/Smith Patmore
29	25/2	H TORQUAY	2,573	14 / 3	36	L 1-2	0-0	Betts 73 / Hathaway 56, Hodges 77 / Ref: M Pierce	Ch'sewright / Bayes	Betts / Hodges	Allpress / Colcombe	Kinsella / O'Riordan	English / Moore	Cawley / Curran	Dickens / Trollope	Brown S / Buckle	McDon'gh* / Foster	Hyslop / Darby	Smith / Hathaway	Fry
30	5/3	A ROCHDALE	2,202	15 / 8	37	D 1-1	1-0	Watts 6 / Stuart 73 / Ref: K Lupton	Ch'sewright / Hodge	Hyslop / Thackeray	Allpress / Graham	Kinsella / Reid	English / Reeves	Cawley / Butler*	Dickens / Stuart	Brown S / Doyle	Ball* / Lancaster	Watts* / Whitehall*	Fry / Milner	Betts/Smith Williams/Bowden
31	12/3	H WYCOMBE	3,932	15 / 4	37	L 0-2	0-0	Stapleton 58, Titterton 89 / Ref: P Alcock	Ch'sewright / Hyde	Hyslop / Cousins	Allpress / Stapleton	Kinsella / Crossley	English / Creaser	Cawley / Ryan	Dickens / Carroll	Brown S / Langford*	McDon'gh* / Reid	Fry* / Garner	Ball / Guppy	Smith/Betts Titterton/Thompson

22 — High-flying Shrews are rocked at rain-drenched Gay Meadow by sub Ball's first goal since August. He stoops to nod in Brown's low cross. Dave Walton thunders in Mickey Brown's corner, and Dean Spink nets his 14th from the same source. Allpress returns after a cartilage op.

23 — Barry Fry, now at Brum with a larger wallet, captures McGavin for £150k, but U's board rejects the boss's attempts to take Ian Atkins, sacked by Sunderland with boss Terry Butcher, on an expense-only deal. Gareth Davies is sent off (11) for a pro foul on Watts, loaned from Palace.

24 — Sheffield is poached by Premier League Swindon, on loan, as he was about to extend his stay. Cawley keeps up his four-game record of never losing when scoring. He hits a blistering 25-yard free-kick after Russell Bradley fouled Fry. Matt Carmicael had poached his 18th of the term.

25 — An uninspiring match is transformed by Gills' opener. Richard Green's header is pushed home by Neil Smith. Brown suffers a suspected foot fracture in a tackle by Paul Butler. His replacement, Watts, slots in Fry's corner. Two minutes from time Nicky Forster rounds Cheesewright.

26 — Ipswich's Steve Whitton may join U's, whilst Kinsella is invited to train at Portman Rd. A stray back-pass by Kevin Langley lands straight at the feet of Dickens to net his third U's goal. McDonough apologises, later, for the negative tactics that ensure a league double over the Latics.

27 — Frustrated U's can't break down the Spireites, who keep nine men behind the ball. Cawley only half-clears a David Moss cross to Lee Rogers, who puts the ball back into Andy Morris to sweep past Cheesewright. Betts' poor back-pass leads to a Rogers corner that Morris nods home.

28 — Hyslop, who had been on loan at Cobblers, signs midweek for free from Southend. He is sent off after seven minutes for a body check on Efon Elad. He is one of nine players to have been sent off on their debuts, two of whom, Crouch (1980) and Barnett (1988) were also U's players.

29 — U's can virtually kiss goodbye to promotion, despite having 13 games left. Ian Hathaway scores with a deflection, only for Betts to get his first of the term with a vicious left-foot drive. Kevin Hodges nets the winner four minutes later. U's have only nine points from the last nine games.

30 — The board agrees to buy £25k Mick Danzey (Cambridge), but Big Roy wants £30k Whitton. Hyslop's red at Cobblers is reduced to yellow on video evidence. Watts extending his loan, lashes the ball past veteran Martin Hodge. Mark Stuart levels after Shaun Reid's shot is parried.

31 — Norwich bid £110k, and a player for Kinsella. Tempers fray as U's fail to win for the tenth time in the last 17 home league games. The game is ended sixty seconds early, after David Titterton's goal from Steve Guppy's cross, prompts a pitch invasion and sit-in protest against the board.

32. LINCOLN — A — 15/3 — 17 — L — 14 — 37 — 0-2 — 1,631

Mardenborough 75, Matthews 84
Ref: R Poulain

| Ch'sewright | Betts | Allpress* | Kinsella | English | Cawley | Dickens | Brown S | Watts | Hyslop | Ball | Smith |
| Pollitt | Smith P | Platnauer | Schofield | Mardenboro' | Matthews | Smith M | Baraclough | Johnson D | Daws* | Johnson A | Coughlin |

The alarm bells are ringing as U's are just seven points off the drop. Leading scorer Brown has gone ten without a goal. Cheesewright has no chance with Steve Mardenborough's 18-yard drive, but the keeper fumbles Alan Johnson's cross for Neil Matthews to stab into the net.

---

33. BURY — A — 19/3 — 15 — W — 9 — 40 — 1-0 — 2,108

McDonough 57
Ref: P Wright

| Ch'sewright | Betts | Allpress | Kinsella | English | Hyslop | Dickens | Brown S* | McDonough | Watts* | Ball | Smith/Campbell |
| Bracey | Cross | Stanislaus* | Lucketti | Jackson | Hughes | Kelly | Mauge | Rigby | Carter | Stevens | Johnrose |

Short of form, Keeley quits to joins Chelmsford. U's sign Ian Brown on loan from Bristol C. Big Roy nets his 97th league goal with a header, from Ball's free-kick, that whistles off the post past Lee Bracey. Disappointed Bury fans call for the head of boss Mike Walsh on the whistle.

---

34. PRESTON — H — 26/3 — 14 — D — 5 — 41 — 0-1 — 2,950

Brown l 76, Norbury 16
Ref: P Jones

| Ch'sewright | Betts | Hyslop | Kinsella | English | Cawley | Dickens | Brown S | McDonough | Ball* | Brown l | Smith |
| O'Hanlon | Fensome | Sulley | Cartwright | Kidd | Mayes | Ainsworth | Bryson | Norbury | Challender | Magee* | Raynor |

U's snap up Whitton on deadline day, but he is suspended Ian Brown, who would have signed for United in 1988 had Roger Brown not been sacked, finally starts and grabs an important equaliser, after namesake Steve loses control. Micky Norbury had earlier notched a diving header.

---

35. CHESTERFIELD — A — 29/3 — 15 — D — 7 — 42 — 0-0 — 3,089

Ref: J Worrall

| Ch'sewright | Betts | Hyslop* | Kinsella | English | Cawley | Dickens | Whitton | McDonough | Brown l | Ball* | Smith/Brown S |
| Leonard | Hewitt | Rogers | Dawes | Carr D | Law | Curtis | Norris | Lyne* | Moss | Jules | Gregory |

Keeley dramatically joins Stockport, after saying he was quitting the pro game. New player-coach Whitton teams up with his old West Ham team-mate Dickens. Cawley is a rock at the back. On the rare occasions that 20-goal Steve Norris gets through, Cheesewright stands resolute.

---

36. MANSFIELD — A — 2/4 — 16 — D — 13 — 43 — 1-1 — 2,117

Gray 34 (og), Holland 5
Ref: S Dunn

| Ch'sewright | Betts | Smith | Kinsella | English | Cawley | Dickens* | Whitton | Brown S | Brown l* | Ball | McDonough/Watts |
| Ward | Lampkin* | Boothroyd | Holland | Gray | Noteman | Timons | Castledine | Wilkinson | Hadley | Ireland | Fairclough |

Ian Brown is guilty of a glaring first-minute miss, with only Darren Ward to beat. Paul Holland gives the home side the lead, with a speculative overhead kick that loops over Cheesewright. United's neat football is rewarded when Kevin Gray glances Smith's free-kick into his own net.

---

37. SCARBOROUGH — H — 4/4 — 18 — L — 14 — 43 — 0-2 — 2,501

Meyer 72 (og), Thompson 6, Young 41
Ref: G Willard

| Ch'sewright | Betts | Smith | Kinsella | English | Cawley | Dickens | Whitton | McDonough | Brown l* | Ball* | Watts/Brown S |
| Sheppard | Knowles | Thompson | Calvert | Meyer | Rockett | Charles | Murray | White | Whitington | Davis* | Young |

Cheesewright misses a wind-assisted punt, that Jason White retrieves His cross-shot is set to be cleared by Betts or English, who collide and watch Stuart Young prod home. Earlier Simon Thompson scored a long-range free-kick. Adie Meyer's header pulls one back for sorry United.

---

38. CHESTER — A — 9/4 — 18 — L — 1 — 43 — 1-2 — 3,394

Brown S 34, Lightfoot 30, 89
Ref: R Shepherd

| Ch'sewright | Betts | Smith | Kinsella | English | Cawley | Allpress | Whitton | McDonough | Brown l* | Ball | Smith/Brown S |
| Felgate | Preece | Jakub | Wheeler* | Came | Greenall | Thompson | Lightfoot | Leonard | Lancashire | Pugh | Rimmer |

Chester boast the best goals-against record in the division, with just 14 conceded at the new Deva Stadium. Chris Lightfoot heads in David Pugh's knock-back. Cawley's ferocious free-kick smashes off the bar to S Brown. Lightfoot climbs high to head in Pugh's last-minute corner

---

39. DARLINGTON — H — 16/4 — 18 — L — 22 — 43 — 1-2 — 2,337

Kinsella 45, Shaw 8, Chapman 78
Ref: K Leach

| Ch'sewright | Betts | Allpress* | Kinsella | English | Cawley | Dickens | Whitton | Brown S | Fry | Ball | McDonough |
| Collier | Reed | Switzer | Gaughan | Crosby | Cross | Slaven | Painter | Chapman | Shaw | O'Shaughn's | |

U's seventh failure to win at home on the trot. Cheesewright, pressured by Paul Cross, drops the ball at the feet of Simon Shaw. Kinsella levels with his ninth of the term, only for Gary Chapman to grab a vital Quakers win. U's lie eight points ahead of Darlington, with three games left.

---

40. WALSALL — A — 23/4 — 17 — W — 9 — 46 — 1-0 — 2,980

Watkiss 19 (og), Kinsella 74, Watkiss 80
Ref: J Key

| Ch'sewright | Betts | Allpress | Kinsella | English | Cawley | Ball | Whitton | McDonough | Fry | Smith | Smith |
| Walker* | Evans | Marsh | Watkiss | O'Hara^ | Smith | Lightbourne | O'Connor | Butler | Pearce | McDonald | Livingstone/Ntamark |

U's reserves beat St Albans's 19-0 in the Capital League. Stuart Watkiss sends a great header past James Walker, via Betts' cross. Walker breaks his leg, colliding with Whitton. Kinsella strikes a superb second, before Watkiss slightly atones. Three points secures U's league status.

---

41. DONCASTER — H — 30/4 — 16 — W — 17 — 49 — 3-1 — 2,378

Whitton 79, 81, Brown S 83
Wilcox 43
Ref: P Alcock

| Ch'sewright | Betts | Allpress | Kinsella | English | Cawley | Cook T* | Whitton | McDon'gh* | Fry | Smith | Gentle/Brown S |
| Ford | Kitchen | Limber | Marquis | Yates | Swailes | Lawrence* | Roche | Wilcox | Worthington | Harper | Page |

Ian Atkins' Doncaster are safe from the drop and look to be heading for all their points. Up steps Whitton to score his first U's goals. for a first home win in eight. He strikes a poor Chris Swailes back-pass into the corner of the net, and then taps in the rebound, after first hitting the bar

---

42. CARLISLE — A — 7/5 — 17 — L — 7 — 49 — 0-1 — 9,305

Kinsella 3 (og), Conway 61
Ref: J Kirkby

| Ch'sewright | Betts | Allpress | Kinsella | English | Cawley | Ball* | Whitton | McDon'gh* | Fry | Brown S | Cook T/Gentle |
| Caig | Joyce | Gallimore | Walling | Reddish | Robinson | Thomas* | Conway | Reeves | Davey | Arnold | Burgess |

McDonough is presented with a silver salver in recognition of this 500th league game. As with last season, United gate-crash a party, as the Cumbrians qualify for the play-offs. Kinsella wrong-foots his keeper, under pressure from Ian Arnold. American Paul Conway seals the win.

Average Home 2,865 — Away 3,205

ENDSLEIGH DIVISION 3 (CUP-TIES) Player Manager: Roy McDonough SEASON 1993-94

Coca-Cola Cup

1:1 A FULHAM 17/8 — L 1:2, H-T 1-0 — 2,820 3:
Scorers: Kinsella 35 / Betts 59 (og), Farrell 60
Ref: A Smith

1	2	3	4	5	6	7	8	9	10	11	subs used
Keeley	Betts	Roberts	Kinsella	English	Grainger	Ball	Bennett*	McDonough	McGavin	Smith	Abrahams/Allpress
Stannard	*Morgan*	*Pike*	*Ferney*	*Jupp*	*Thomas*	*Hails*	*Cooper*	*Farrell*	*Brazil*	*Marshall*	*Angus*

Fulham boss Don Mackay's half-time tongue-lashing does the trick, after Kinsella strikes a carbon copy of his goal on Saturday. The turning-point comes when Betts hammers Julian Hails' cross into his own net. A minute later Hails crosses for ex-U's loanee Sean Farrell, to nod in.

1:2 H FULHAM 24/8 — L 1:2, H-T 1-0 — 3,360 3:14
Scorers: McDonough 5 / Brazil 55, Farrell 63
Ref: R Bigger

1	2	3	4	5	6	7	8	9	10	11	subs used
Keeley	Allpress	Roberts	Kinsella	English	Grainger	Ball	Bennett*	McDonough	McGavin	Smith	Abrahams
Stannard	*Morgan*	*Pike*	*Ferney*	*Jupp*	*Thomas*	*Hails*	*Cooper*	*Farrell*	*Brazil*	*Marshall*	*Baah/Onwere*

It is now 17 games since U's last won a League Cup-tie, (v Swansea in 1983). A virtual repeat of the first leg sees U's level on aggregate via McD. from Ball's corner. Keeley, a virtual spectator, is at fault for Gary Brazil's opener, and makes a half-hearted attempt at Farrell's drive. (Colchester lost 2-4 on aggregate)

Autoglass Trophy

1 A GILLINGHAM 28/9 — D 0:0, H-T 0-0 — 1,091 3:16
Ref: A Gunn

1	2	3	4	5	6	7	8	9	10	11	subs used
Keeley	Betts	Roberts	Grainger	English	Cawley	Dickens	Brown S	Richardson*	McGavin	Ball	McDonough
Barrett	*Martin*	*Watson*	*Clark*	*Hague*	*Breen*	*Eeles*	*Reinelt*	*Baker*	*Crane*	*Dempsey*	*Trott*

U's rest eight, ahead of the table-top clash at Deepdale on Saturday. Gills include Barrett and ex-Wivenhoe striker, Robbie Reinelt. Brown forces a great save from Barrett on four minutes. Keeley restores lost confidence with equally fine saves from Elliott Martin and Paul Baker.

1 H CAMBRIDGE 19/10 — D 2:2, H-T 1-0 — 1,489 2:14
Scorers: Kinsella 12, Brown S 56 / Clayton 47, Heathcote 90
Ref: R Bigger

1	2	3	4	5	6	7	8	9	10	11	subs used
Keeley	Locke*	Allpress	Kinsella	English	Cawley	Dickens	Brown S	McDonough*	McGavin	Smith	Ball/Richardson
Sheffield	*Powett*	*Barrick*	*O'Shea*	*Heathcote*	*Daish*	*Livett*	*Claridge*	*Jeffrey*	*Clayton*	*Nyamah*	*Hunter*

Grainger joins Brentford for £60k. Mick Heathcote's last-gasp equaliser means that U's must hope that Gills get only a 1-1 draw, or worse, at Cambridge. Classy Dickens picks out Brown for a 2-1 second-half lead, but Steve Claridge finds Heathcote, to out-jump Smith at the far post.

2 A WREXHAM 4/12 — W 1:0, H-T 0-0 — 1,860 2:13
Scorers: McDonough 87
Ref: J Brandwood

1	2	3	4	5	6	7	8	9	10	11	subs used
Munson	Betts	Roberts	Kinsella	English	Cawley	Ball	Brown S	McDonough	McGavin	Smith	
Marriott	*Pepic*	*Hardy*	*Brammer*	*Humes*	*Hunter*	*Bennett*	*Lake*	*Connolly*	*Watkin*	*Taylor*	

Kinsella is outstanding at sweeper, as U's meet the Welshmen in a cup-tie for the first time since 1948. Curiously Wrexham are in the southern half of the competition. Kinsella caps his all-round performance by laying on a tap-in for McDonough, with extra-time and penalties looming.

3 H WYCOMBE 11/1 — L 0:1, H-T 0-0 — 2,751 3:4
Scorers: Guppy 86
Ref: P Jones

1	2	3	4	5	6	7	8	9	10	11	subs used
Ch'sewright	Betts	Allpress	Kinsella	English	Cawley	Dickens	Ball	McDonough	Booty*	Campbell*	Watts/Cook T
Hyde	*Cousins*	*Horton*	*Kerr*	*Evans*	*Ryan*	*Carroll*	*Thompson*	*Stapleton*	*Hodges*	*Guppy*	*Shepstone*

Cheesewright is signed on an 18-month contract from Braintree. Martin O'Neill rekindles the GMVC war of words by declaring, 'Roy will say that this comp 'is unimportant' if we (Wycombe) win'. Cawley dallies over a clearance that strikes Steve Guppy on the back and goes in.

FA Cup

1 H SUTTON 13/11 — L 3:4, H-T 1:2 — 3,051 VP:6
Scorers: McGavin 40, Brown S 52, English 86 / Quail 18, Smart 30, N'man 84, Morah 88
Ref: N Barry

1	2	3	4	5	6	7	8	9	10	11	subs used
Keeley	Betts	Roberts	Kinsella	English	Cawley	Dickens	Brown S	McDonough	McGavin	Smith	
McCaulsky	*Gates*	*Smart*	*Golley*	*Costello*	*Jones*	*Anderson*	*Newman*	*Morah*	*Quail*	*Byrne*	*McKinnon*

McDonough is 'not afraid of Sutton's cup record'. Kinsella awaits a call-up to the injury-hit Eire squad. U's calamitous defence is torn to shreds once again. Failure to settle for a draw, after English's late goal, allows ex-Spurs apprentice Ollie Morah to race clear for the winner.

		P	Home					Away					Pts
			W	D	L	F	A	W	D	L	F	A	
1	Shrewsbury	42	10	8	3	28	17	12	5	4	35	22	79
2	Chester	42	13	5	3	35	18	8	6	6	34	28	74
3	Crewe	42	12	4	5	45	30	9	6	6	35	31	73
4	Wycombe *	42	11	6	4	34	21	8	7	6	33	32	70
5	Preston	42	13	5	3	46	23	5	8	8	33	37	67
6	Torquay	42	8	10	3	30	24	9	6	6	34	32	67
7	Carlisle	42	10	4	7	35	23	8	6	7	22	19	64
8	Chesterfield	42	8	8	5	32	22	8	6	7	23	26	62
9	Rochdale	42	10	5	6	38	22	6	7	8	25	29	60
10	Walsall	42	7	5	9	28	26	10	4	7	20	27	60
11	Scunthorpe	42	9	7	5	28	30	6	7	8	24	30	59
12	Mansfield	42	9	6	6	28	22	6	7	8	25	32	55
13	Bury	42	9	6	6	33	22	5	5	11	22	34	53
14	Scarborough	42	8	4	9	29	28	7	4	10	26	33	53
15	Doncaster	42	8	6	7	24	26	6	4	11	20	31	52
16	Gillingham	42	8	8	5	27	23	5	6	10	17	28	51
17	COLCHESTER	42	8	4	9	31	31	5	6	10	25	38	49
18	Lincoln	42	7	4	10	26	29	5	7	9	26	34	47
19	Wigan	42	6	7	8	33	33	5	5	11	18	37	45
20	Hereford	42	6	4	11	34	33	2	13	6	26	46	42
21	Darlington	42	7	5	9	24	28	3	6	12	18	36	41
22	Northampton	42	6	7	8	25	23	3	4	14	19	43	38
		924	193	125	144	705	560	144	125	193	560	705	1261

* promoted after play-offs

Odds & ends

Double wins: (2) Bury, Wigan.

Double defeats: (3) Crewe, Darlington, Gillingham.

Won from behind: (5) Northampton (h), Wycombe (h), Scunthorpe (h). Carlisle (h), Doncaster (h).

Lost from in front: (2) Rochdale (h), Shrewsbury (a).

High spots: Steve Brown's early scoring firm, including a first U's hat-trick in the league since 1987.

First cash signing since the Crisp era, in Chris Fry.

Low spots: Denial, by order of the Football League, of the traditional Friday night home fixtures.

Heavy defeats against Rochdale (h), Hereford (a) and Darlington (a).

Desperately poor defending, due to the cavalier attacking style.

Loss of 'silky' Steve McGavin, albeit for a huge profit.

Two keepers sent off in one match, at Hereford.

Defeat in the FA Cup, at home to Vauxhall Premier side Sutton Utd.

A record 35 players used during the season.

Seven home games without a win from January.

No further news on any new stadium development.

Player of the Year: Mark Kinsella.

Ever presents: (2) Tony English, Mark Kinsella.

Hat-tricks: (1) Steve Brown.

Leading scorer: Steve Brown (13) (including 1 in Auroglass Trophy).

Appearances and Goals

	Appearances						Goals			
	Lge	Sub	LC	Sub	FAC	Sub	Lge	LC	FAC	Tot
Abrahams, Paul	1	3		2						
Allpress, Tim	21	2	1	1						
Ball, Steve	27	5	2				2			2
Barada, Taylor	1									
Basham, Michael	1									
Bennett, Gary	3	1	2							
Betts, Simon	31	2	1		1		1			1
Booty, Justin		1					1			1
Brown, Ian	4									
Brown, Steve	30	4			1		11		1	12
Campbell, Sean	1	3								
Cawley, Peter	36						1			1
Cheesewright, John	17									
Cook, Jason		1								
Cook, Tony	1	1								
Desborough, Mike	1									
Dickens, Alan	28	4			1		3			3
English, Tony	42		2		1		4		1	5
Fry, Chris	12	5								
Gentle, Justin		2								
Grainger, Martin	5	3	2		1		2			2
Hyslop, Christian	8									
Keeley, John	15		2		1					
Kinsella, Mark	42		2		1		8	1		9
Locke, Adam	4									
McDonough, Roy	36	2	2		1		8	1		9
McGavin, Steve	20	1	2		1		7		1	8
Morrow, Grant		1								
Munson, Nathan	2	1								
Richardson, John	1	7								
Roberts, Paul	21		2		1					
Sheffield, John	6									
Smith, Nicky	29	10	2		1					
Watts, Grant	8	4					2			2
Whitton, Steve	8						2			2
(own-goals)							4			4
35 players used	462	63	22	3	11		56	2	3	61

No	Date		Att	Pos	Pt	F-A	H-T	Scorers, Times, and Referees	1	2	3	4	5	6	7	8	9	10	11	subs used
1	13/8	H TORQUAY	3,175		0	L 1-3	1-2	Kinsella 12 / Okorie 13, Buckle 42, Trollope 51 / Ref: G Barber	Ch'sewright	Culling	Dalli*	English	**Caesar**	**Dennis**	Fry	Brown	Whitton	Kinsella	Abrahams	Allpress
		(opp XI)		*13*					*Bayes*	*Hodges*	*Stamps*	*O'Riordan*	*Barrow*	*Curran*	*Trollope**	*Buckle*	*Hancox**	*Okorie*	*Goodridge*	*Hathaway/Darby*
2	20/8	A MANSFIELD	2,247	18	0	L 0-2	0-0	Holland 80, Hadley 90 / Ref: N Barry	Ch'sewright	Culling	Davis	Allpress	Caesar	English	Dennis	Brown	Whitton	Kinsella*	Abrahams	Fry
		(opp XI)							*Ward*	*Boothroyd*	*Baraclough*	*Holland*	*Howarth*	*Aspinall*	*Ireland*	*Parkin*	*Wilkinson*	*Hadley*	*Fleming**	*Noteman*
3	27/8	H DONCASTER	2,320	21	0	L 0-3	0-2	Jones 12, Donaldson 35, 75 / Ref: I Hemley	Ch'sewright	Burley	Davis	Allpress	Caesar	Dennis	**Putney**	Brown	Whitton	Kinsella	Abrahams	
		(opp XI)		*1*					*Suckling**	*Kirby*	*Hackett*	*Meara*	*Wilcox*	*Swailes*	*Lawrence*	*Thew*	*Jones**	*Donaldson*	*Parrish*	*Torfason/Williams*
4	30/8	A EXETER	1,804	21	0	L 0-1	0-1	Bailey 18 / Ref: S Dunn	Ch'sewright	Burley	Davis	Allpress	Caesar*	Dennis*	Putney	Brown	Whitton	Kinsella	Abrahams	Fry/Partner
		(opp XI)		*22*					*Fox*	*Minett*	*Anderson*	*Bailey*	*Came*	*Richardson*	*Storer*	*Thirlby*	*Cooper*	*Coughlin**	*Gavin*	*Brown*
5	3/9	A SCARBOROUGH	1,494	20	3	W 1-0	0-0	Dennis 70 / Ref: E Lomas	Ch'sewright	English	Davis	Cawley	Caesar	Dennis	Putney	Brown*	Whitton	Kinsella	Abrahams	Fry
		(opp XI)		*13*					*Kelly*	*Knowles*	*Charles*	*D'Auria*	*Dunphy*	*Rockett*	*Rowe*	*Swann*	*Foreman**	*White**	*Blackstone*	*Young/Calvert*
6	10/9	H HARTLEPOOL	2,428	18	6	W 1-0	0-0	Whitton 53 / Ref: G Pooley	Ch'sewright	Burley	English	Cawley	Caesar	Dennis	Putney	Brown	Whitton	Kinsella	Abrahams*	Allen
		(opp XI)		*20*					*Horne*	*Ingram*	*Skedd**	*Gilchrist*	*Tait*	*Oliver*	*Thompson*	*Ainsley*	*Houchen*	*Lynch**	*Sloan*	*Hyson/Garnett*
7	13/9	H WALSALL	**2,239**	15	9	W 3-2	0-1	Kinsella 87, 90, Whitton 89 / Lightbourne 23, Houghton 90 / Ref: B Harris	Ch'sewright	Burley	English	Cawley	Caesar	Dennis	Putney*	Brown	Whitton	Kinsella	Abrahams	Betts
		(opp XI)		*13*					*Walker*	*Ryder*	*Rogers*	*Gibson*	*Marsh*	*Palmer*	*Peer*	*Ntamark*	*Lightbourne*	*Wilson*	*Houghton*	
8	17/9	A TORQUAY	3,390	12	10	D 3-3	0-1	Whitton 63, Brown 71, Dennis 89 / Trollope 3, Hancox 67, Darby 88 / Ref: J Holbrook	Ch'sewright	Betts	English	Cawley	Caesar	Dennis	Putney*	Brown	Whitton	Kinsella	Abrahams*	Burley
		(opp XI)		*4*					*Davis*	*Hodges*	*Stamps**	*Hathaway*	*Moore*	*Barrow*	*Trollope*	*Buckle*	*Hancox*	*Okorie**	*Goodridge*	*Darby/Burton*
9	24/9	A DARLINGTON	2,260	11	13	W 3-2	2-1	Whitton 27, 76, Brown 36 / Chapman 45, Himsworth 47 / Ref: B Burns	Ch'sewright	Betts	English	Cawley	Caesar	Dennis	Putney	Brown*	Whitton	Kinsella	Fry*	Locke/Allen
		(opp XI)		*9*					*Pollitt*	*Appleby*	*Cross*	*Banks*	*Crosby*	*Reed*	*Himsworth*	*Painter**	*Gaughan*	*Olsson*	*Chapman*	*Slaven*
10	1/10	H BURY	3,286	8	16	W 1-0	0-0	Cawley 79 / Ref: P Alcock	Ch'sewright	Betts	English	Cawley	Caesar	Dennis	Locke	Brown	Whitton	Kinsella	Abrahams	Fry
		(opp XI)		*2*					*Kelly*	*Jackson*	*Stanislaus*	*Daws*	*Lucketti*	*Matth'ws'n**	*Paskin*	*Carter*	*Hulme*	*Johnose*	*Pugh*	*Rigby*

1. Burley, 38, is appointed boss after a spell as player-coach at Motherwell. Favourites Torquay inflict U's first home opening defeat since 1966 (2-3 Middlesbrough). Paul Buckle scores direct from a free-kick, and Ashley Bayes saves Whitton's penalty (69) after Paul Trollope fouls Fry.

2. English plays his 300th league game and Davis (Plymouth) joins on trial. Paul Holland nets a brave near-post header. Caesar steers a poor kick back to Cheesewright, only for Stuart Hadley to intercept and score. Kinsella blasts a free-kick over after Darren Ward picks up a back-pass.

3. U's sign Putney on loan from L.Orient. Rovers, under ex-U's coach Sammy Chung, made eleven signings in the close season. James Meara finds Graham Jones in space, and O'Neill Donaldson chips and then drives past Cheesewright. Perry Suckling goes off with a torn hamstring.

4. United occupy bottom spot for the first time since 1990, after six straight defeats. Substitute Andy Partner is seriously injured in a clash with Peter Fox. U's worst-ever start is confirmed when Danny Bailey hits a 30-yarder to hoist striker-less City off the bottom at United's expense.

5. Burley appoints Dale Roberts as his assistant. A richly deserved win, secured by Dennis, signed from Chesterfield, lifts U's off the foot at the first attempt. United continue the improvement with a Monday night 3-3 draw against a full-strength Ipswich, in English's testimonial match.

6. Burley hopes to re-sign Mark Walton, who played for U's against Ipswich, as Emberson does not fit in his plans. Pool, who haven't won away in a year, sacked boss John McPhail yesterday. Abrahams bursts down the wing to supply Whitton's first of the term, past flailing Brian Horne.

7. Kinsella buries an equaliser that appears to have settled the game. In a frantic last three minutes Whitton bundles United in front, only for Scott Houghton to level with a simple tap-in. Astonishingly, Kinsella bags a deflected winner via a loose ball, from Abrahams' injury-time corner.

8. Betts returns after a pre-season broken jaw as U's trail on three occasions. Abrahams suffers a bad injury in setting up Dennis for the last-gasp equaliser. After a shaky start, three wins and a draw have seen U's recover to occupy a healthy mid-table position. Burley tries to retain Putney.

9. Ex-Palace apprentice Locke signs on loan from Southend. U's lead 2-1 when Cheesewright hauls down Robbie Painter in the box. He gets up and strikes the post, but Gary Himsworth follows up to score. Whitton wins it with a stunning 40-yard half-volley over stranded Mike Pollitt.

10. A best crowd of the season see U's stretch their unbeaten run to seven against table-toppers Bury. Gary Kelly makes five stunning saves, but when Whitton crosses, Kinsella dummies and Cawley nets his first of the term. Shakers' Mike Walsh pips Burley for Manager-of-the-Month.

11. H CHESTERFIELD — 8/10 — L 0-3 — Att 3,476 — (9 / 8) — Pts 16
Davies 22, Moss 67, Morris 90
Ref: S Dunn

Ch'sewright	Betts	English	Cawley*	Caesar	Dennis	Locke	Brown	Whitton	Kinsella	Abrahams*
Marples	*Fairclough*	*Rogers*	*Spooner**	*Madden*	*Laws**	*Curtis*	*Davies*	*Morris*	*Moss*	*Reddish*

Fry/Burley — Jules/Roberts

Sloppy defending lets in Kevin Davies for a one-on-one, which he slots in with ease. U's are restricted to long-range shots and it is Davies who sets up David Moss for the second. Two minutes into injury-time Andy Morris runs unchallenged half the length of the pitch to notch the third.

12. A CARLISLE — 15/10 — D 0-0 — Att 5,817 — (11 / 2) — Pts 17
Ref: G Cain

Ch'sewright	Betts	English	Cawley	Caesar	Dennis	Locke	Brown	Whitton	Kinsella	Fry*
Caig	*Joyce*	*Gallimore*	*Walling*	*Valentine*	*Edmondson**	*Thomas*	*Arnold*	*Reeves*	*Davey*	*Prokas*

Abrahams/Locke — Lowe/Peacock

Putney's loan is extended by two months. The draw dents Carlisle's 100% home record. A number of stiff Carlisle challenges go unpunished. A last-ditch tackle by Tony Caig prevents Abrahams scoring at the near post.

13. H PRESTON — 22/10 — W 3-1 — Att 3,015 — (9 / 16) — Pts 20
Brown 11, 78, Whitton 49 — Treble 46
Ref: K Leach

Ch'sewright	Betts	English	Cawley	Caesar	Locke	Putney	Brown	Whitton	Kinsella	Fry*
Vaughan	*Fensome*	*Sharp*	*Whalley*	*Hicks*	*Moyes*	*Cartwright**	*Bryson*	*Treble*	*Conroy**	*Atkinson*

Abrahams — Sale/Fleming

Brown scores his first home goal of the season, only for Neil Treble to level after the restart. John Beck's Lancastrians have the smile wiped off their faces when Whitton beats the advancing John Vaughan. Twelve minutes from time, the unselfish Whitton lays on Brown's second.

14. A WIGAN — 29/10 — W 2-1 — Att 1,621 — (6 / 22) — Pts 23
Kinsella 31, Fry 39 — Robertson 76
Ref: K Lynch

Ch'sewright	Betts	English	Cawley	Caesar	Locke*	Putney	Brown	Whitton	Kinsella	Fry*
Farnworth	*Carragher**	*Jakub**	*Strong*	*Robertson*	*Farrell*	*Kilford*	*Benjamin*	*Leonard*	*Miller*	*Lyons*

Dennis/Abrahams — Rennie/Adekola

United sit in their best league position for six years after seeing off the bottom club. Kinsella nets the first, despite the attention of Greg Strong. Betts shrugs off Matt Carragher to provide Fry with a cross. Simon Farnworth saves Kinsella's penalty (89), after Andy Lyons fouls Putney.

15. H GILLINGHAM — 5/11 — D 2-2 — Att 3,817 — (6 / 17) — Pts 24
Fry 29, Kinsella 53 — Reinelt 8, Pike 27
Ref: M Pierce

Ch'sewright	Betts	English	Cawley	Caesar	Locke	Putney	Brown	Whitton	Kinsella	Fry*
Banks	*Dunne**	*Watson*	*Carpenter*	*Green*	*Butler*	*Micklewhite*	*Arnott*	*Pike*	*Reinelt*	*Smillie*

Abrahams — Hutchinson

Chris Pike provides ex-Wivenhoe striker, Robbie Reinelt with the first for Gills. Pike grabs the second, before his ex-Hereford mate, Fry, pulls one back. Whitton is felled by Tony Butler (37), but Cawley's miss is U's fourth spot-kick failure. Kinsella salvages a point via a deflection.

16. A ROCHDALE — 19/11 — D 0-0 — Att 1,903 — (6 / 10) — Pts 25
Ref: U Rennie

Ch'sewright	Betts	English	Cawley	Caesar	Dennis*	Locke	Brown	Whitton	Kinsella	Abrahams*
Gray	*Thackeray*	*Formby*	*Reid*	*Matthews*	*Butler*	*Doyle*	*Valentine*	*Williams**	*Whitehall*	*Stuart*

Fry — Taylor

Neither side is impressed by Referee Rennie's performance, which takes U's bookings to 33, compared with 18 and two reds at the same stage last season, when a suspended fine hung over the club. Whitton hits the bar (11) and Cheesewright excels after being dropped against Yeading.

17. H SCUNTHORPE — 26/11 — W 4-2 — Att 2,904 — (6 / 9) — Pts 28
Brown 26, Ab'ms 45, 87, Whitton 79 — Thornber 54, Knill 85
Ref: K Cooper

Ch'sewright	Betts	English	Cawley	Caesar	Locke	Putney	Brown	Whitton	Kinsella	Abrahams
Samways	*Ford*	*Mudd*	*Thornber*	*Knill*	*Carmichael*	*Alexander*	*Bullimore*	*Juryeff*	*Sansam**	*Nicholson**

Thompstone/Hope

U's fans have not witnessed so many goals in such a short space of time since 1956 in Division Three (South), when they beat Exeter 4-0 and Shrewsbury 6-0 in the space of five days. The Anglia TV Kick-Off cameras see U's add to the seven they scored in the midweek FAC replay.

18. H MANSFIELD — 10/12 — D 1-1 — Att 3,016 — (6 / 14) — Pts 29
Fry 8 — Wilkinson 48
Ref: G Barber

Ch'sewright	Betts	Dennis	Cawley	Caesar	Locke	Fry	Brown	Whitton	Kinsella	Abrahams
Ward"	*Boothroyd*	*Baraclough*	*Holland*	*Timons*	*Aspinall*	*Ireland*	*Doolan**	*Wilkinson*	*Campbell*	*Noteman**

C'dine/P'rson/Trinder

Ref Barber has given U's eleven yellow cards in four matches. Darren Ward parries Brown's shot for Fry to snap up from six yards out. Jamie Campbell's effort is ruled offside (31) and Ward clashes with Whitton. Jason Trinder, his replacement, finds Steve Wilkinson with a long punt.

19. A DONCASTER — 16/12 — W 2-1 — Att 2,460 — (5 / 3) — Pts 32
Cawley 60, Brown 84 — Brabin 79
Ref: I Cruickshanks

Ch'sewright	Burley	Betts	Cawley	Caesar*	Locke	Fry	Brown	Whitton	Kinsella*	Dennis
Williams	*Kirby*	*Hackett*	*Brabin*	*Wilcox*	*Swailes*	*Bryan**	*Schofield*	*Harper*	*Norbury*	*Meara*

Abrahams/Allpress — Thew

Cawley seizes on Warren Hackett's back-pass to let fly from 20 yards. James Meara's shot deflects in off Gary Brabin. Burley, rumoured to be joining Ipswich, crosses for Brown's eighth of the term on a rapidly freezing pitch. A £100k Clock End stand is planned to meet FL criteria.

20. H NORTHAMPTON — 26/12 — L 0-1 — Att 5,064 — (6 / 20) — Pts 32
Harmon 35p
Ref: P Alcock

Ch'sewright	Betts	Dennis	Cawley	Caesar	Locke*	Putney*	Brown*	Whitton	Kinsella	Abrahams
Stewart	*Norton*	*Colkin*	*Sampson*	*Curtis*	*Sedgemore**	*Harmon*	*Brown*	*Grayson*	*Flounders**	*Williams*

Pascoe/Patmore

Burley signs Stoneman from Blackpool, and then walks out on U's on Christmas Eve. Stunned U's fans find out just before this morning kick-off. The news affects U's performance so badly that Cobblers earn their first away win, when Betts manhandles ex-U's loanee Ian Brown.

21. A FULHAM — 27/12 — W 2-1 — Att 4,243 — (6 / 13) — Pts 35
Kinsella 31, Blake 90 (log) — Hamill 5
Ref: S Dunn

Stoneman	Betts	Dennis	Cawley	Stannard	Locke!	Putney*	Brown*	Whitton	Kinsella	Fry
Stannard	*Jupp*	*Angus*	*Hurlock*	*Moore*	*Blake*	*Finnigan*	*Morgan*	*Cusack*	*Brazil*	*Hamill*

Abrahams/Allpress — Hamill

Adam Locke is sent off on 40 minutes for a professional foul on Simon Morgan. Managerless United gain a surprise win when Cheesewright's long clearance is back-headed by ex-Colchester loanee Mark Blake over the stranded and bemused Jim Stannard in the Cottager's goal area.

ENDSLEIGH LEAGUE DIVISION 3

Manager: Burley ⇨ Roberts ⇨ Wignall SEASON 1994-95

Match summary

No	Venue	Opponents	Date	Att	Pos	Pt	Opp	Res	F-A	H-T	Scorers, Times, and Referees
22	H	HEREFORD	31/12	3,322	7	36	18	D	2-2	0-2	Stoneman 76, Whitton 89 / Brough 12, Whitton 38 (og) / Ref: G Pooley
23	A	PRESTON	10/1	6,377	8	36	10	L	1-2	0-1	Fry 81 / Smart 44, Trebble 85 / Ref: N Barry
24	H	BARNET	14/1	3,706	8	37	6	D	1-1	0-1	Putney 49 / Hodges 44 / Ref: J Rushton
25	H	WIGAN	28/1	3,067	11	37	16	L	0-1	0-0	Doolan 71 / Ref: A D'Urso
26	A	SCUNTHORPE	4/2	2,748	9	40	6	W	4-3	2-3	Locke 25, English 28, Thompson 82, Betts 85 / Eyre 4, 18, Bullimore 16 / Ref: R Fernandiz
27	H	ROCHDALE	11/2	3,080	7	41	13	D	0-0	0-0	Ref: M Pierce
28	A	BARNET	18/2	2,242	5	44	11	W	1-0	1-0	Asaba 18 / Ref: R Harris
29	A	LINCOLN	21/2	1,969	7	44	15	L	0-2	0-0	Bannister 78, Johnson 90 / Ref: M Bailey
30	A	BURY	25/2	2,484	9	44	7	L	1-4	0-1	Fry 78 (Lucketti 68!) / Stant 32, Hughes 47, Betts 57 (og) / Ref: J Winter
31	H	DARLINGTON	4/3	6,055	7	47	16	W	1-0	1-0	Asaba 3 / Ref: A Butler

Line-ups (Colchester / *opponent*)

No	1	2	3	4	5	6	7	8	9	10	11	subs used
22	Ch'sewright / *MacKenzie*	Betts / *Warner*	English / *Lloyd*	Cawley / *Reece*	Stoneman / *Smith*	Locke / *Browning*	Putney* / *Davies*	Brown / *Cross**	Whitton / *Brough*	Kinsella / *Lyne*	Fry* / *Pick*	Abrahams/Allpress / *Pounder*
23	Ch'sewright / *Vaughan*	Betts / *Fensome*	English! / *Finning*	Cawley / *Cartwright*	Caesar / *Kidd*	Dennis / *Moyes*	Putney / *Magee*	Brown / *Bryson*	Whitton / *Smart*	Kinsella / *Lancashire**	Abrahams* / *Raynor*	Fry/Emberson / *Trebble/Atkinson*
24	Emberson / *Newell*	Betts / *Hamlet*	English / *Mitchell*	Cawley / *Hoddle*	Caesar / *Walker*	Locke / *Primus*	Putney / *Tomlinson*	Dennis / *Freedman*	Thompson* / *Hodges*	Kinsella / *Smith*	Abrahams / *Wilson*	Fry
25	Emberson / *Farnworth*	Betts / *Carragher*	Stoneman / *Wright*	Cawley / *Miller*	Caesar / *Robertson*	Locke / *Farrell*	Putney* / *Rodwell*	Dennis / *McKearney*	Thompson* / *Leonard*	Kinsella / *Doolan*	Abrahams / *Lyons*	Brown/Lock
26	Emberson / *Samways*	English / *Ford*	Betts / *Mudd*	Cawley / *Thornber*	Caesar / *Knill*	Locke* / *Carmichael*	Fry / *Alexander*	Dennis / *Bullimore*	Whitton / *Young*	Kinsella / *Eyre**	Brown / *Nicholson*^	Thompson / *Thompstone/Smith*
27	Emberson / *Gray*	English / *Thackeray*	Betts / *Formby**	Cawley / *Reid*	Caesar / *Valentine*	Dennis^ / *Butler*	Fry / *Thompson*	Brown / *Peake*	Whitton^ / *Deary*	Kinsella / *Whitehall*	Thompson / *Sharpe*^	Allpress/Abrahams / *Martini/Stuart*
28	Emberson / *Phillips*	Locke / *McDonald*	English / *Newson*	Cawley / *Watson*	Caesar / *Walker!*	Dennis / *Primus*	Fry / *Tomlinson*^	Asaba / *Freedman*	Whitton* / *Hodges*	Kinsella / *Cooper*	Abrahams* / *Scott*^	Allpress/Thompson / *Gibson/Gale*
29	Emberson / *Leaning*	Locke / *West*	English / *Johnson*	Cawley / *Smith*	Caesar / *Greenall*	Dennis / *Brown*	Fry / *Johnson*	Asaba / *Carbon*	Thompson* / *Williams*^	Kinsella / *Hebberd*	Abrahams / *Hill*	Lock / *Bannister*
30	Emberson / *Kelly G*	Locke / *Stanislaus*	English / *Bimson*	Cawley / *Rigby*	Caesar / *Lucketti*	Dennis / *Hughes*	Fry / *Kelly T**	Putney! / *Paskin*	Asaba / *Stant*	Kinsella / *Daws*	Abrahams* / *Pugh*	Allpress / *Hulme*
31	Emberson / *Pollitt*	Locke / *Appleby*	English / *Himsworth*	Cawley / *Banks*	Caesar / *Gregan*	Dennis / *Shaw*^	Fry / *Slaven*	Putney / *Painter*	Whitton* / *Chapman*	Kinsella / *Olsson*	Asaba / *Gaughan*	Brown / *Blake*

Match reports

22 – Hereford. U's are aggrieved that Ipswich didn't agree a compensation package before speaking to Burley, as agreed. Roberts takes over as caretaker boss. Stoneman bundles in his first U's goal. Whitton had steered Andy Reece's effort into his own net, but atoned with a great volleyed equaliser.

23 – Preston. Rain-lashed Deepdale is only passed fit 40 minutes before kick-off. Whitton misses his third penalty of the season, but Fry is on hand to net the rebound. English is sent off (89) for a second spot. Ex-Bournemouth boss Tony Pulis emerges as a U's manager candidate.

24 – Barnet. Ex-U's star Wignall, from the resurgent Diadora League side Aldershot, is named U's 20th boss. Cawley loses out to Micky Tomlinson, who squares to Lee Hodges. Putney nets his first for U's before the Anglia Kick-Off cameras. Ray Clemence's Barnet had lost their last three away.

25 – Wigan. Wignall fails to sign Paul Reed (Arsenal) and David Gregory (Ipswich). Cheesewright, who was replaced at half-time at Preston, faces a spell on the sidelines after dizziness is pin-pointed to a mystery virus. Colchester have picked up just five points out of 18 since Burley's departure.

26 – Scunthorpe. U's produce their greatest escape. Trailing by 0-3 after 18 minutes. Locke adds his first of the season and English reduces the arrears further by the break. Enter Canadian trialist Thompson (68) to flick home after Brown hits the post, and score a sensational winner from Betts' cross.

27 – Rochdale. Thompson earns an 18-month contract. This draw means that U's have not won at home since November. Dale keeper Ian Gray keeps United at bay in his last game of a loan period from first division Oldham. Whitton is forced to leave the action on the half-hour with a bad rib injury.

28 – Barnet. Brown is left out for Asaba, 22, signed on loan from Brentford. Barnet, too, have a loanee in Spurs' Kevin Watson. Asaba runs in U's goal and is the victim of two vicious tackles by Bees' Alan Walker. The first earns a booking, and the second sees the defender sent off on 81 minutes.

29 – Lincoln. Flu-ridden U's have not won at Sincil Bank since 1968 (3-0). Colin Greenall scythes through Thompson (65), but stays on. Gary Bannister is offside as he tucks in the first. Caesar hauls down David Johnson (88). Emberson saves Johnson's penalty, but not his effort two minutes later.

30 – Bury. Culling is released back to Braintree. Putney is red-carded on 42 minutes for uncharacteristically swearing at the ref. The game is over when Betts runs Ian Hughes's pass into his own net. Gigg Lane is in an atrocious condition, through rental to Man Utd Reserves and Swinton RLFC.

31 – Darlington. U's make history by letting all fans in for free to increase the fan base. Quakers boss Alan Murray was sacked yesterday and replaced by Paul Futcher. Asaba scores on his home debut to match one on his away debut. Bernie Slaven's 'goal' (52) is offside. Gibbs signs from Diss Town.

U's season match-by-match record (continued)

Average — Home 3,277 · Away 2,962

---

32 · A · HARTLEPOOL · 11/3
Pos 9 · L · 20 · Pts 47 · 1-2 · Att **1,371**
Fry 17 / Southall 13p, 35, 85p · Ref: J Kirkby
U's: Emberson, Betts, **Gibbs**, Cawley*, Caesar, Dennis, Fry, Brown^, Asaba, Kinsella, **Williams** · Subs: Allpress/Thompson
Hartlepool: Horne, Reddish, Cook, Holmes, McGuckin, Tait, Halliday, Oliver, Houchen, Henderson, Southall
Gibbs and loanee Williams (Luton) debut at Victoria Park in driving rain. First Emberson hauls down Keith Houchen, then Cawley handles on the edge of the box for Southall to score a direct free-kick. Caesar then fouls Southall for his second penalty

---

33 · H · EXETER · 18/3
Pos 8 · W · 19 · Pts 50 · 3-1 · Att 2,375
Thompson 4, Betts 78p, Lock 87 / Cecere 82 · Ref: J Holbrook
U's: Emberson, Betts, Gibbs, English, **McCarthy**, Dennis, Fry, Thompson, Asaba, Kinsella, Williams* · Sub: Lock
Exeter: Fox, Minett, Cooper, Anderson, Came, Brown, Phillips, Cecere, Peats*, Thirlby, Gavin · Sub: Cooper
Abrahams joins division two leaders Brentford for £30k. McCarthy arrives on a free from Millwall. Asaba is brought down in the box by Mark Cooper, for Betts to banish the U's penalty hoodoo. Mike Cecere pulls one back before Lock scores his first goal in his first full appearance

---

34 · H · SCARBOROUGH · 25/3
Pos 8 · L · 22 · Pts 50 · 0-2 · Att 3,025
Charles 46, Trebble 52 · Ref: D Orr
U's: Emberson, Betts, Gibbs, English, McCarthy, Caesar, Putney*, Asaba, Whitton, Kinsella, Williams^ · Subs: Thomps'n/Cheeth'm
Scarborough: Ironside, Love, Swales, Charles, Meyer*, Rockett, Scott, D'Auria, White, Trebble, Calvert · Sub: Wells
Boro', bottom and six points adrift at the start, embarrass U's with a first win in nine. McGavin joins Wycombe from Brum, for £175k, giving U's 25% of the profit. Steve Charles hits a left-foot volley. Trebble, who had netted for Preston against U's, intercepts McCarthy's back-pass

---

35 · A · WALSALL · 1/4
Pos 9 · L · 3 · Pts 50 · 0-2 · Att 3,622
Lightbourne 71, O'Connor 82p · Ref: P Harrison
U's: Emberson, Betts, English, McCarthy, Caesar, Dennis, Cheetham, Locke, Whitton, Kinsella, Asaba
Walsall: Wood, Evans, Gibson, Ryder, Marsh*, Palmer, O'Connor, Keister, Lightbourne, Wilson, Houghton · Sub: Ntamark
Brown is swapped for Gills' Reinelt, following Cheetham's move from Chesterfield. Allpress leaves for Hitchin. Whitton and Kinsella both have to go off with head wounds. Kyle Lightbourne nets his 22nd of the season, followed eleven minutes later by Betts' trip on Scott Houghton.

---

36 · A · HEREFORD · 8/4
Pos 11 · L · 16 · Pts 50 · 0-3 · Att 1,669
White 4, 34, Smith 57 · Ref: S Mathieson
U's: Emberson, Betts, English, McCarthy, Caesar, Dennis*, Cheetham, Putney, Asaba*, Kinsella, Whitton · Sub: Fry
Hereford: MacKenzie, Stoker, Fishlock*, Pick, Smith, Lloyd, Wilkins, Davies, White, Lyne, Pounder · Sub: Warner
U's reached the play-offs last time they won at Edgar St (1987). Steve White catches McCarthy sleeping, three mins before Asaba has an effort ruled out for offside. White adds his 17th of the season via a rebound off the post. Dean Smith adds the third. Ex-U's star Wilkins dominates.

---

37 · A · GILLINGHAM · 11/4
Pos 9 · W · 20 · Pts 53 · 3-1 · Att 3,328
Betts 58p, Thompson 87, 90 / Watson 15 · Ref: P Rejer
U's: Emberson, Kinsella, Betts, McCarthy, Caesar, Putney, Fry^, English, Whitton, Cheetham, **Gibbs*** · Subs: Reinelt/Thompson
Gillingham: Banks, Dunne, Martin, Smith, Green, Arnott, Carpenter, Micklewhite, Brown, Forster, Watson
Thompson comes off the bench to inspire U's second great escape of the campaign. Paul Watson strikes a cracking free-kick, that Betts cancels after Joe Dunne trips Cheetham. Thompson's first is a simple tap-in, his second a stunning 50-yard run. U's are five points off the play-offs.

---

38 · H · FULHAM · 15/4
Pos 8 · W · 11 · Pts 56 · 5-2 · Att 3,448
Cheetham 8, English 11, Caesar 18, Fry 36, 56 / Morgan 4, Mison 80 · Ref: K Leach
U's: Emberson, Kinsella, Betts, McCarthy, Caesar, Putney, Fry, English, Gibbs, Cheetham^, Whitton* · Subs: Reinelt/Thompson
Fulham: Harrison, Jupp!, Herrera, Hurlock^, Moore, Blake, Marshall, Morgan, Cusack, Adams, Brazil* · Subs: Cork/Mison
Fulham take an early lead through Simon Morgan, but rampant U's hit four in reply before the break. Scottish U-21 international Duncan Jupp is red-carded after two bookable offences. English heads in a Gibbs cross, whilst Caesar scores his first goal for U's since joining from Airdrie.

---

39 · A · NORTHAMPTON · 17/4
Pos 8 · D · 17 · Pts 57 · 1-1 · Att 5,011
Whitton 66 / Brown 8 · Ref: U Rennie
U's: Emberson, Kinsella, Betts, McCarthy, Caesar*, Putney, Fry, English, Gibbs*, Cheetham, Whitton · Subs: Asaba/Thompson
Northampton: Woodman, Daniels*, Hughes, Sampson, Warburton, O'Shea, Colkin, Brown, Thompson, Burns, Grayson · Sub: Norton
Ex-Layer Rd loanee Ian Brown thumps the Cobblers in front, after Emberson blocked Neil Grayson's effort. Whitton levels with a goal of pure class, volleying in off the underside of the bar from 20 yards. Wignall pushes four up in search of an elusive winner, but two points are lost.

---

40 · H · LINCOLN · 22/4
Pos 9 · L · 12 · Pts 57 · 1-2 · Att 2,654
McCarthy 38 / Bannister 22, Huckerby 72 · Ref: M Bailey
U's: Emberson, Kinsella, Betts^, McCarthy, Caesar, Putney, Fry*, English, Gibbs, Cheetham^, Whitton · Subs: Asaba/Reinelt
Lincoln: Sherwood, Huckerby, Dixon, Platnauer, Greenall, Williams, Matthews, Daws, Carbon, Bannister, Hill
U's play-off failure is official after this defeat. Ex-Forest star Gary Bannister strikes a low-angled drive. McCarthy levels with his first United goal, but City, marshalled by reserve's Nicky Platnauer, win when Darren Huckerby breaks on the left to beat the advancing Emberson

---

41 · H · CARLISLE · 29/4
Pos 10 · L · 7 · Pts 57 · 0-1 · Att 3,333
Walling 58 · Ref: S Dunn
U's: Emberson, Kinsella, Gibbs, McCarthy, Caesar, Dennis, Putney, Fry*, Reinelt*, Cheetham, Whitton · Sub: Asaba
Carlisle: Caig, Edmondson, Gallimore, Walling, Robinson, Conway, Thomas^, Currie*, Reeves, Hayward, Prokas · Subs: Joyce/Thorpe
Carlisle lost to Brum in last Sunday's Autowindscreen Shield final, but wrap up the championship courtesy of Dean Walling's bundled effort. Carlisle, eight points clear of Chesterfield, only needed one point for promotion and two for the title. Their 800 fans celebrate on the pitch.

---

42 · A · CHESTERFIELD · 6/5
Pos 10 · D · 3 · Pts 58 · 2-2 · Att 4,133
Whitton 38, Putney 65p / Lormor 7p, 73 · Ref: A Dawson
U's: Emberson, Kinsella, Betts, McCarthy, Caesar, Dennis, Fry, Putney*, Reinelt, Cheetham, Whitton · Subs: Asaba / Gibbs
Chesterfield: Beasley, Hewitt, Rogers, Curtis, Carr, Fairclough, Robinson, Davies*, Lormor, Morris^, Perkins · Subs: Moss/Howard
Putney retires to a job in the City, and bows out with a penalty after Lee Rogers fouls Whitton. Earlier Darren Carr had fouled the same player, but Betts' kick was saved by Andy Beasley (27). Despite Lormor's leveller, Chesterfield will lose second place to Walsall at the eleventh hour.

ENDSLEIGH DIVISION 3 (CUP-TIES) Manager: Burley ⇨ Roberts ⇨ Wignall SEASON 1994-95

Coca-Cola Cup

1:1 H BRENTFORD 16/8 — L 0-2 H-T 0-1 — 2,521 2:
Scorers, Times, and Referees: Stephenson 26, Taylor 55
Ref: A D'Urso

1	2	3	4	5	6	7	8	9	10	11	subs used
Ch'sewright	Culling	English	Allpress	Caesar	Dennis	Fry*	Brown	Whitton	Kinsella	Abrahams	Roberts
Dearden	*Hurdle*	*Westley*	*Hutchings*	*Harvey*	*Smith*	*Forster**	*Taylor*	*Bates*	*Stephenson*	*Parris*	*Benjamin*

The Bees open the scoring when the impressive Gus Hurdle drives in a low cross for Paul Stephenson. A long clearance by Jamie Bates is touched on by Nicky Forster to Robert Taylor, 18 yards out. Whitton misses his second penalty in four days, blasting over in the second half.

1:2 A BRENTFORD 23/8 — L 0-2 H-T 0-1 — 2,315 2:11
Parris 33, Smith 61
Ref: D Orr
(Colchester lost 0-4 on aggregate)

1	2	3	4	5	6	7	8	9	10	11	subs used
Emberson	English*	Davis	Allpress	Caesar	Dennis	Roberts	Brown	Whitton	Kinsella	Abrahams	Burley
Dearden	*Hurdle*	*Hutchings*	*Bates*	*Ashby*	*Smith*	*Parris*	*Harvey*	*Taylor**	*Forster**	*Stephenson*	*Ratcliffe/Mundee*

Burley debuts and Emberson starts, after the board pay £20k for his services. George Parris drives in a shot to settle the tie, and Paul Smith stabs in after a goalmouth melee. English is taken to hospital, following a kick from Taylor. U's have not won a League Cup-tie since 1983.

Autowindscreen Shield

1 H LEYTON ORIENT 27/9 — W 1-0 H-T 0-0 — 1,486 2:19
Abrahams 63
Ref: M Bailey

1	2	3	4	5	6	7	8	9	10	11	subs used
Ch'sewright	Betts	English	Cawley	Caesar	Dennis	Locke	Brown	Whitton	Kinsella	Abrahams	
Heald	*Warren**	*Austin*	*Purse*	*Howard*	*Hague !*	*Putney*	*Cockerill*	*Carter*	*West*	*Martin**	*Barnett/Lakin*

Putney returns after his loan spell ends, but in an O's shirt. Abrahams bags his first of the season with a diving header. Three minutes later, O's are reduced to ten men when Paul Hague is sent off for a second booking. Burley is in line be U's first manager-of-the-month for five years.

1 A FULHAM 8/11 — L 2-3 H-T 0-1 — 1,451 3:12
Abrahams 62, Kinsella 66
Hallworth 3, Adams 75, Cusack 90
Ref: G Pooley

1	2	3	4	5	6	7	8	9	10	11	subs used
Ch'sewright	Betts	English	Cawley	Caesar	Dennis	Locke	Brown*	Whitton	Kinsella	Abrahams*	Fry/Burley
Harrison	*Finnigan**	*Herrera*	*Marshall*	*Angus*	*Blake*	*Mison*	*Morgan*	*Cusack*	*Hallworth**	*Adams*	*Jupp/Williams*

U's only need a draw to progress, as Fulham lost 2-5 to L Orient. Behind to an early goal, U's are on the Wembley trail with a four-minute double. Micky Adams levels, and then in the last minute provides the cross for Nicky Cusack, on loan from Oxford U, to nod in unchallenged.

FA Cup

1 A YEADING 12/11 — D 2-2 H-T 1-1 — 1,780 DP:12
Whitton 9, Abrahams 56
Hippolyte 45, Dicker 64
Ref: G Barber

1	2	3	4	5	6	7	8	9	10	11	subs used
Emberson	Betts	English	Cawley	Caesar	Dennis	Locke	Brown	Whitton	Kinsella	Abrahams	
MacKenzie	*Dicker*	*Cuffie*	*Bruce*	*McGrath*	*Hoon Park*	*Graham*	*Bowder*	*Hippolyte*	*McKinnon*	*Cordery*	

Emberson is brought in to combat the threat from crosses, but is beaten to the ball on the stroke of half-time, by Johnson Hippolyte. The home side include 1986 S Korean World Cup star Kyong Hoon Park. Play is stopped for four minutes (83), when a barrier in the U's end collapses.

1R H YEADING 22/11 — W 7-1 H-T 3-1 — 4,016 DP:12
Ab'ms 3, 56, Wh't'n 28, 53, Brown 33,53, [Kinsella 82]
McKinnon 27p
Ref: G Barber

1	2	3	4	5	6	7	8	9	10	11	subs used
Ch'sewright	Betts	English	Cawley	Caesar	Dennis	Fry	Brown	Whitton*	Kinsella	Abrahams	Dennis/Thompson
MacKenzie	*Dicker*	*Cuffie*	*Woods*	*McGrath*	*Hoon Park*	*Graham*	*Bowder*	*Hippolyte*	*McKinnon*	*Cordery*	

U's biggest cup win for 22 years, emulating victories over Woodford (1950) and Yeovil (1958). Yeading threaten briefly when Cheesewright fouls McKinnon. United fans sing 'Is that all you take away?' The small band of Yeading fans reply rather smartly 'this is all we get at home!'

2 A EXETER 3/12 — W 2-1 H-T 0-1 — 3,528 3:19
Whitton 47, English 87
Morgan 22
Ref: P Durkin

1	2	3	4	5	6	7	8	9	10	11	subs used
Ch'sewright	Betts	English	Cawley	Caesar	Dennis	Locke	Brown*	Whitton	Kinsella	Abrahams	Dennis/Fry
Woodman !	*Minett*	*Brown*	*Bailey*	*Daniels*	*Richardson*	*Storer*	*Coughlin**	*Cooper**	*Morgan"*	*Gavin*	*Thirlby/Robins'n'Belotti*

City include two ex-U's stars in Trevor Morgan and Scott Daniels. Morgan's last touch puts City in front. as moments later he makes way for sub keeper Ross Bellotti, after Andy Woodman handles outside the area. English ghosts in late to meet Whitton's flick from Abrahams' corner.

3 A WIMBLEDON 7/1 — L 0-1 H-T 0-1 — 6,903 P:9
Harford 9
Ref: P Danson

1	2	3	4	5	6	7	8	9	10	11	subs used
Ch'sewright	Betts	English	Cawley	Caesar	Dennis	Putney	Brown	Whitton	Kinsella	Abrahams*	Abrahams*
Segers	*Cunningham*	*Thorn*	*Reeves*	*Kimble*	*Fear*	*Jones*	*Earle*	*Clarke*	*Harford*	*Holdsworth*	*Dennis*

U's last played Wimbledon in the FA Cup 33 years earlier when the Dons were non-league. Cheesewright fails to come for a cross and gets fouled by Dean Holdsworth, allowing Mick Harford to nod in. Backed by 3,000 fans. U's keep Han Segers busy, but can't force an equaliser.

* promoted after play-offs

		P	Home W	D	L	F	A	Away W	D	L	F	A	Pts
1	Carlisle	42	14	5	2	34	14	13	5	3	33	17	91
2	Walsall	42	15	3	3	42	18	9	8	4	33	22	83
3	Chesterfield*	42	11	7	3	26	10	12	5	4	36	27	81
4	Bury	42	13	7	1	39	13	10	4	7	34	23	80
5	Preston	42	13	3	5	37	17	6	7	8	21	24	67
6	Mansfield	42	10	5	6	45	27	8	6	7	39	32	65
7	Scunthorpe	42	12	2	7	40	30	6	6	9	28	33	62
8	Fulham	42	11	5	5	39	22	5	9	7	21	32	62
9	Doncaster	42	9	5	7	28	20	8	5	8	30	23	61
10	COLCHESTER	42	8	5	8	29	30	7	4	10	27	34	58
11	Barnet	42	7	7	7	37	27	7	4	10	19	36	56
12	Lincoln	42	10	7	4	34	22	5	4	12	22	33	56
13	Torquay	42	10	8	3	35	25	4	5	12	19	32	55
14	Wigan	42	7	6	8	28	30	7	4	10	25	30	52
15	Rochdale	42	8	6	7	25	23	4	8	9	19	44	50
16	Hereford	42	9	6	6	22	19	3	7	11	19	43	49
17	Northampton	42	8	5	8	25	29	2	9	10	20	38	44
18	Hartlepool	42	9	5	7	33	32	2	5	14	10	37	43
19	Gillingham	42	8	7	6	31	25	2	4	15	15	39	41
20	Darlington	42	7	5	9	25	24	4	3	14	18	33	41
21	Scarborough	42	4	7	10	26	31	4	3	14	23	39	34
22	Exeter	42	5	5	11	25	36	3	5	13	11	34	34
		924	209	121	132	705	524	132	121	209	524	705	1265

Odds & ends

- Double wins: (3) Darlington, Fulham, Scunthorpe.
- Double defeats: (0).
- Won from behind: (5) Walsall (h), Fulham (a), Scunthorpe (a), Gillingham (a), Fulham (h).
- Lost from in front: (1) Torquay (h).
- High spots: Burley's record of just one defeat in 20 league and cup-ties prior to his departure.
- Crushing 7-1 win over Yeading in the FA Cup.
- First-ever game against a Premiership side, in Wimbledon, since its inception.
- Tremendous comebacks at Scunthorpe (4-3) and Gillingham (3-1), both inspired by Canadian Niall Thompson.
- Low spots: Six straight defeats at the beginning of the season.
- A plethora of penalty misses., six in total.
- Last minute defeat in the Autowindscreen Shield.
- The departure of Burley, and the way it was handled by Ipswich.
- Only two points from the last four games, and play-off failure again.

Appearances and Goals

	Appearances Lge	Sub	LC	Sub	FAC	Sub	Goals Lge	LC	FAC	Tot
Abrahams, Paul	20	8	2		4		2		3	5
Allen, Leighton		2								
Allpress, Tim	3		2							
Asaba, Carl	9	8	3				2			2
Betts, Simon	34	1			4		2			2
Brown, Steve	26	2	2		4		6		2	8
Burley, George	5	2				1				
Caesar, Gus	39						2			2
Cawley, Peter	23		2		4		1			1
Cheesewright, John	23		1		3					
Cheetham, Michael	8	1					1			1
Culling, Gary	2		1							
Dalli, Jean	1									
Davis, Aaron	4	1								
Dennis, Tony	32	1	2		1	3	2			2
Emberson, Carl	19	1	1		1					
English, Tony	33	2	2		4		2		1	3
Fry, Chris	24	9	1		1	1	8			8
Gibbs, Paul	8	1								
Kinsella, Mark	42		2		4		6		2	8
Lock, Tony		3								
Locke, Adam	20	2			4		1			1
McCarthy, Tony	10									
Partner, Andy		1								
Putney, Trevor	28	3			2		2			2
Reinelt, Robbie	2	3								
Roberts, Danny					1	1				
Stoneman, Paul	3						1			1
Thompson, Niall	5	8					5			5
Whitton, Steve	36		2		4		10		3	13
Williams, Martin	3						1			1
(own-goals)										
31 players used	462	56	22	2	44	5	56		11	67

Player of the Year: Steve Whitton.

Ever presents: (1) Mark Kinsella.

Hat-tricks: (0).

Leading scorer: Steve Whitton (13).

ENDSLEIGH LEAGUE DIVISION 3 Manager: Steve Wignall SEASON 1995-96

No	Date		Att	Pos	Pt	F-A	H-T	Scorers, Times, and Referees	1	2	3	4	5	6	7	8	9	10	11	subs used
1	H 12/8	PLYMOUTH	3,585		3	2-1	1-0	Betts 15, Locke 59 / Littlejohn 54 / Ref: A D'Urso	Emberson	Locke	Betts	McCarthy	Caesar	Cawley	Kinsella	English !	Whitton	Adcock	Cheetham*	Dennis
								Hammond / Patterson" / Williams / Burnett / Heathcote / Hill / Billy / Mauge / Littlejohn / Nugent / Leadbitter* / Hodg'n/Twiddy/Evans*												
								Walton rejects U's for Barry Town and Adcock returns via Luton. Locke rolls a free-kick to Betts to hammer home from 20 yards. Argyle level when Adrian Littlejohn finishes a rebound off the post, three mins after English was sent off for a second booking. Locke wins it from 25 yards.												
2	A 19/8	BARNET	1,966	9 / 18	D 4	1-1	0-0	Adcock 81 / Freedman 69 / Ref: S Bennett	Emberson	Locke	Betts	McCarthy	Caesar	Cawley	Kinsella	English	Whitton	Adcock*	Cheetham	Reinelt
								Taylor / McDonald / Campbell / Pardew / Primus / Thomas / Gale / Freedman / Hodges / Robbins / Scott / Tomlinson/Cooper*												
								Kinsella signs a new 12-month deal. Linvoy Primus hauls down Cheetham (71), but Adcock crashes the kick against the bar. U's rue the miss when Peter Scott finds Dougie Freedman. who lobs Emberson. Whitton hits the crossbar. but then provides the cross for Adcock's redemption.												
3	H 26/8	LINCOLN	2,939	6 / 17	W 7	3-0	2-0	Dennis 2, 8, Mardenborough 74 / Ref: B Harris	Emberson	Locke	Betts	McCarthy	Caesar^	Cawley	Kinsella	Dennis	Whitton	Adcock	Cheetham*	Fry/Mardenborough
								Key / Minett / Dixon / Mudd^ / Greenall / Brightwell / West / Onwere / Dyer / Huckerby / Carbon / Daws/Johnson*												
								Dennis finishes off a fine three-man move and then taps in a well-weighted pass from Whitton. The pair equalled his tally for the whole of last season. Caesar picks up a first-half injury. Mardenborough. his replacement. strikes a low angled drive against one of his many former clubs.												
4	A 29/8	CAMBRIDGE	3,476	8 / 9	L 7	1-3	0-2	Adcock 49 / Palmer 15, Joseph 23, Corazzin 60 / Ref: A Butler	Emberson	Locke	Betts	McCarthy	Caesar^	Cawley !	Kinsella	Dennis^	English '	Adcock	Cheetham*	English/Mardenboro'
								Barrett / Jeffrey / Palmer / Thompson / Craddock / Joseph Matt Stock / Middleton / Butler / Corazzin / Barrick												
								U's fail to secure the win to go top. despite Adcock's 100th U's goal. a brilliant diving header. United are run ragged in the first half and trail to goals by Lee Palmer and Matt Joseph. Carlo Corazzin poaches a third and is then elbowed by Cawley (74). who receives a second booking.												
5	A 2/9	GILLINGHAM	7,667	5 / 1	W 10	1-0	0-0	Adcock 75 / / Ref: M Pierce	Emberson	Locke	Betts	McCarthy	English	Cawley	Kinsella	Dennis	Whitton	Adcock	Cheetham*	Mardenborough
								Stannard / Smith^ / Naylor / Butler / Harris / Green / Rattray / Ratcliffe / Fortune-West Bailey / O'Connor / Martini/Carpenter*												
								Gills start as the only team in the country with a 100% record. Adcock. who has scored 187 goals in all four divisions. puts paid to that record. Tony Butler's poor back-pass is intercepted by the 'Red Rooster'. Although Jim Stannard smothers his first attempt. Adcock reacts quickest.												
6	H 9/9	CHESTER	3,422	8 / 2	L 10	1-2	0-0	Whitton 82 / Priest 54, Regis 81 / Ref: B Knight	Emberson	Locke*	Betts	McCarthy	English	Cawley	Kinsella	Dennis	Whitton	Adcock	Cheetham*	Fry/Reinelt
								Stewart / Jenkins / Burnham / Fisher / Jackson / Whelan^ / Richardson / Priest / Regis^ / Milner* / Noteman / Alst'd/Rimmer/Flitcroft*												
								Chester include new signing Nick Richardson. £40k from Cardiff. and ex-England striker Cyrille Regis. Chris Priest scores with a bouncing volley. Spencer Whelan receives a second booking (65). but Regis loops a header over the stranded Emberson. Whitton nets a left-foot volley.												
7	H 12/9	PRESTON	2,869	8 / 12	D 11	2-2	1-0	Fry 25, Whitton 50 / Cartwright 57, Bryson 87 / Ref: D Orr	Emberson	Locke*	Betts	McCarthy	English	Fry	Kinsella	Dennis	Whitton	Adcock	Cheetham*	Reinelt
								Richardson / Fensome / Kidd ! / Atkinson / Squires / Johnson / Cartwright / Bryson / Saville / Wilkinson / Brown												
								Danish keeper Henrik Jorgensen doesn't sign. but Caldwell arrives on trial. Ryan Kidd is dismissed for rugby-tackling Cheetham (43). When Whitton beats Jamie Squires to the ball. U's seem set. Defensive errors let in Lee Cartwright and Ian Bryson.												
8	A 16/9	DARLINGTON	1,685	9 / 18	D 12	2-2	2-0	Dennis 10, Cheetham 20 / Muir 46, Bannister 78 / Ref: D Allison	Emberson	Fry	Betts	McCarthy	English	Cawley	Kinsella	Dennis*	Whitton*	Adcock	Cheetham	Mardenborough/Gibbs
								Stephens / Appleby / Himsworth / Gaughan^ / Crosby / Gregan / Muir / Olsson / Worboys^ / Bannister / Carss / Blake/Shaw												
								Dennis strikes a 25-yard drive and Cheetham puts U's two up. a minute after Whitton is carried off following a vicious knee-high scything tackle by Sean Gregan. McCarthy slips from the restart. letting in ex-Tranmere star Ian Muir. Gary Bannister (Whit' was his best man) levels.												
9	H 23/9	HEREFORD	2,596	7 / 17	W 15	2-0	1-0	Reinelt 22, 65 / / Ref: G Pooley	Emberson	Locke*	Betts	McCarthy	English	Cawley	Kinsella	Fry	Reinelt*	Adcock	Cheetham*	Mardenborough/Gibbs
								MacKenzie / Evans / Lloyd / Smith / Blatherwick Downing / Pounder / Wilkins / Lyne / Cross / Stoker* / Pick/Preedy*												
								Whitton joins Tony's Cook and Lock with cruciate ligament damage. Fry makes his 200th appearance. hampers his former club. Betts makes his 100th league appearance. Reinelt hooks in McCarthy's flick. but has to leave the field with concussion. four minutes after adding his second.												
10	A 30/9	SCUNTHORPE	2,051	9 / 19	L 15	0-1	0-1	Eyre 15 / / Ref: B Burns	Emberson	Locke*	Betts	McCarthy	Lewis	Cawley	Kinsella	Fry^	Reinelt*	Adcock	Cheetham	Mard'boro/Gibbs/Ball
								Samways / Hope / Wilson / Ford / Knill / Bradley / Housham / Thornber / Young / Eyre^ / Sansam^ / N'lson/McFarl'n/Varadi*												
								Scunthorpe receive a much-needed cash injection when their former player Mark Atkins joins Wolves from Blackburn. Local Tollesbury lad Lewis is called up on the morning of the game after English pulls out with a severe migraine. John Eyre takes advantage of McCarthy's slip.												
11	H 7/10	HARTLEPOOL	2,618	7 / 21	W 18	4-1	3-0	Locke 9, 54, Adcock 20, Reinelt 26 / Howard 88 / Ref: J Brandwood	Emberson	Locke	Betts	McCarthy	Lewis	Cawley	Kinsella	Fry	Reinelt	Adcock	Cheetham	Hamer
								Jones / Ingram / McAuley / Billing / McGuckin / Lowe / Oliver / Tait / Henderson / Halliday / Howard*												
								Whitton receives support from Alan Shearer in his rehabilitation. Pool had lost 0-5 at Highbury in midweek. Locke arrives late. courtesy of British Rail. but is first to respond to Fry's low cross. Reinelt retrieves a deflection and chips in from an impossible angle for his fourth in four.												

Colchester United — Match Record (games 12–23)

No	Venue	Opponent	Date	Att	Pos	Res	Pts	FT	HT
12	A	ROCHDALE	14/10	2,193	7 / 5	D	19	1-1	1-0
13	H	NORTHAMPTON	21/10	3,823	6 / 10	W	22	1-0	0-0
14	A	CARDIFF	28/10	3,207	4 / 19	W	25	2-1	2-1
15	A	FULHAM	31/10	2,870	4 / 18	D	26	1-1	1-0
16	H	EXETER	4/11	3,377	5 / 14	D	27	1-1	1-0
17	A	DONCASTER	18/11	1,603	5 / 7	L	27	2-3	1-2
18	H	MANSFIELD	25/11	2,819	6 / 15	L	27	1-3	1-1
19	A	HEREFORD	9/12	3,324	8 / 17	D	28	1-1	0-0
20	H	SCUNTHORPE	16/12	2,138	7 / 15	W	31	2-1	2-0
21	A	BURY	23/12	3,559	7 / 9	D	32	0-0	0-0
22	H	LEYTON ORIENT	26/12	4,965	5 / 15	D	33	0-0	0-0
23	A	TORQUAY	1/1	2,425	5 / 24	W	36	3-2	1-1

---

12 — ROCHDALE (A), 14/10
Scorers: Reinelt 29 / Stuart 67. Ref: G Frankland

U's: Emberson, Locke", Betts, McCarthy, English, Cawley, Kinsella', Fry!, Reinelt, Adcock, Cheetham*. Subs: M'boro/Gibbs/Dennis
Rochdale: Gray, Thackeray, Formby, Deary, Bayliss', Butler, Thompson, Shaw*, Stuart, Whitehall, Peake. Subs: Thompstone/Taylor

Boyce joins on trial from Stevenage as work begins on the new £150k Clock End stand Reinelt makes it five goals in as many games, only for Mark Stuart to level. Both scorers strike the bar and Cheetham and Dennis are denied penalties. Fry gets his first-ever red card, for dissent (79)

13 — NORTHAMPTON (H), 21/10
Scorer: Kinsella 60. Ref: G Pooley

U's: Emberson, Fry, Betts, McCarthy, Caesar*, Cawley, Kinsella, English, Reinelt, Adcock, Cheetham. Subs: Dennis
Northampton: Woodman, Norton", Maddison, Pear, Warburton, Hartfield, Gibb, Grayson, Sampson", Burns, Colkin*. Subs: Williams/Hunter/White

Wignall thinks about signing Clive Allen, once of Spurs. Cobblers arrive at 2.30 pm due to A12 roadworks, with Wignall warning of a trench battle. Uncompromising Cobblers keep nine men at bay, but Adcock lays off to on-rushing Kinsella, who plants past Andy Woodman.

14 — CARDIFF (A), 28/10
Scorers: Adcock 13, 14 / Adams 30. Ref: J Rushton

U's: Emberson, Williams, Betts, McCarthy, Caesar, Cawley, Kinsella*, Dennis, Mardenboro'', Adcock, Cheetham. Subs: English, Gibbs/Boyce
Cardiff: Gray, Brazil, Searle, Harding, Baddeley, Young, Wigg", Adams, Oatway*, Dale, Gardner. Subs: Ingram/Haworth

Suspended Fry misses the chance to play against his home-town club. Adcock nets two goals of outstanding quality. Both are cheeky chips that Bluebird's keeper Dave Williams is powerless to stop. Darren Adams' shot takes a deflection off Betts to completely wrong-foot Emberson.

15 — FULHAM (A), 31/10
Scorers: Mardenborough 26 / Cusack 61. Ref: G Singh

U's: Emberson, Gibbs, Betts, McCarthy, English, Cawley, Kinsella, Dennis!, Mardenboro'*, Adcock, Cheetham*. Subs: Lewis
Fulham: Lange, Brazil, Jupp, Gray, Herrera, Moore, Thomas, Morgan, Brazil, Hamill", Cusack. Subs: Brooker/Conroy

U's start three points behind leaders Gills. Mardenborough executes a well-worked move. Dennis is sent off for kicking the ball away (43), after earlier tussling with Michael Mison. McCarthy's ball falls short of Emberson, allowing Rory Hamill to cross to unmarked Nick Cusack.

16 — EXETER (H), 4/11
Scorers: Kinsella 20 / Pears 82. Ref: M Bailey

U's: Emberson, Fry, Betts, McCarthy, English, Cawley, Kinsella, Dennis, Mardenboro'*, Adcock, Cheetham. Subs: Reinelt
Exeter: Fox, Parsley, Anderson, Buckle, Blake, Richardson, Medlin*, Bailey, Pears, Came, Phillips. Subs: Hughes

Wignall is pipped for Manager-of-the-Month by David Hodgson (Darlington). Kinsella latches onto Adcock's ball, but Richard Pears levels. At half-time several Barsiders break into the City end, steal a flag and set light to it, apparently, retribution for an ambush at last year's cup-tie.

17 — DONCASTER (A), 18/11
Scorers: Cheetham 45, Adcock 85 / Colcombe 18, Jones 25, 75. Ref: G Cain

U's: Emberson, Fry, Betts, McCarthy, Caesar, Cawley, Kinsella, English, Mardenboro'*, Adcock, Cheetham*. Subs: Boyce
Doncaster: Sucking, Kirby, Maxfield*, Colcombe, Carmichael, Murphy, Clark', Brabin, Jones, Warren, Robertson. Subs: Darby/Measham

U's fail to clear allowing Scott Colcombe to net. Seven mins later Graeme Jones' hopeful chase is rewarded with the second. Cheetham latches onto Matt Carmichael's short back-header, only for Jones to meet Duane Darby's cross. Adcock glances, close in, on his 500th league game.

18 — MANSFIELD (H), 25/11
Scorers: Adcock 46p / Hadley 41, Boothroyd 50p, Ireland 70. Ref: K Leach

U's: Emberson, Fry, Betts*, McCarthy, Greene, Cawley, Kinsella, English, Reinelt*, Adcock, Cheetham. Subs: Gibbs/Mardenborough
Mansfield: Bowling, Boothroyd, Hackett, Sherlock, Howarth, Peters, Ireland, Parkin, Sale, Hadley, Barber

Mardenborough completes his three-month trial, and is replaced by Luton's Greene. Stags, with the worst defence in the division, take the lead via top scorer Hadley. Cheetham is tripped by Steve Sherlock and Betts handles (50). Simon Ireland sweeps in the winner with U's all at sea.

19 — HEREFORD (A), 9/12
Scorers: Betts 77 / Smith D 62. Ref: R Poulain

U's: Emberson, Fry, Betts*, McCarthy, Greene, Cawley, Kinsella, English, Ball*, Adcock, Cheetham*. Subs: Duguid
Hereford: MacKenzie, Evans, Lloyd, Smith D, Stoker, Brough, Lyne, Wilkins, Cross, White*, Downing. Subs: Fishlock

Peter Beadle opts to join Bristol R. instead of U's, from Watford after a £30k deal is agreed. Gregory, 25, joins on a free from Ipswich. United have not won at Edgar St for ten years and fall behind to Duane Smith's goal. Betts hits a cracking 30-yarder to earn U's a share of the points.

20 — SCUNTHORPE (H), 16/12
Scorers: Ball 19, Kinsella 40 / Young 62. Ref: I Hemley

U's: Emberson, Fry, Betts*, McCarthy, Greene, Cawley, Kinsella, English, Ball', Adcock, Cheetham.
Scunthorpe: Samways, Wilson*, Ford, Hope, Bradley, D'Auria, Turnbull, McFarlane, Young, Patterson, Nicholson.

Wignall's latest target. Mansfield's Mark Sale, is amongst the crowd. Ball, in his second game of the season, slots into an empty net. Kinsella delivers a delightful chip over Mark Samways before the break. Shaun Young pulls a goal back when Emberson flaps at Paul Wilson's cross.

21 — BURY (A), 23/12
Ref: R Furnandiz

U's: Emberson, Fry, Betts, McCarthy, Greene, Cawley, Kinsella, English, Ball*, Adcock, Cheetham.
Bury: Kelly, West, Hughes, Daws, Jackson, Matthewson, Rigby, Johnson, Stant, Johnrose, Pugh.

Bury complete an amazing ten hours at Gigg Lane without conceding. The deal to bring Sale to Layer Rd is put on ice when the giant striker breaks his toe in a Mansfield reserve match. United's best chance comes when Gary Kelly pushes Ball's thumping 20-yard effort past the post.

22 — LEYTON ORIENT (H), 26/12
Ref: A D'Urso

U's: Emberson, Fry, Betts, McCarthy, Greene, Cawley, Kinsella, English, Ball', Adcock, Cheetham'. Subs: Dennis/Locke
Leyton Orient: Fearon, Purse, Stanislaus, Brooks', Bellamy, McCarthy, Kelly, Cockerill, Inglethorpe, West, Austin*. Subs: Gray/Hanson

U's have only won six at home on Boxing Day in 45 league years. Two mid-morning inspections allow the game to go ahead, despite the pitch being frozen. The temperature is only raised when Ron Fearon dives full length to deny Cheetham. The difficult conditions spoil the spectacle.

23 — TORQUAY (A), 1/1
Scorers: Kinsella 1, Duguid 77, Betts 90 / Jack 35, Newhouse 50. Ref: G Barber

U's: Emberson, Fry, Betts, McCarthy, Greene, Cawley, Kinsella, English, Ball', Adcock, Cheetham'. Subs: Dennis", Duguid, Abrahams
Torquay: Bayes, Winter, Kelly, Gore, Watson, Ramsey, Hall, Oatway*, Newhouse, Jack, Hathaway. Subs: Stamps

U's re-sign Abrahams to aid their striker crisis. Kinsella opens the scoring after 15 seconds. Torquay fight back via Rodney Jack and Aiden Newhouse, before sub Duguid strikes his first-ever goal. Betts' fourth of the term, is the third time that the defender has notched the winner.

ENDSLEIGH LEAGUE DIVISION 3 — Manager: Steve Wignall — SEASON 1995-96

No	Date		Att	Pos	Pt		F-A	H-T	Scorers, Times, and Referees
24	13/1	H BARNET	3,252	4	39	W	3-2	3-2	Betts 5p, Abrahams 10,16 / Primus 22, Devine 36 / Ref: S Bennett
25	20/1	A PLYMOUTH	5,800	5	40	D	1-1	0-1	Greene 89 / Baird 30 / Ref: D Orr
26	30/1	A WIGAN	2,101	5	40	L	0-2	0-2	Johnson 14, 37 / Ref: T Heilbron
27	3/2	A LINCOLN	2,531	6	40	D	0-0	0-0	Ref: G Frankland
28	6/2	H SCARBOROUGH	2,299	4	42	D	1-1	1-0	Cawley 5 / Treble 66 / Ref: B Knight
29	10/2	H WIGAN	3,082	6	42	L	1-2	0-0	Adcock 52 / Lancashire 64, 86 / Ref: J Kirkby
30	17/2	A PRESTON	9,335	9	42	L	0-2	0-2	Saville 13, 39 / Ref: R Pearson
31	24/2	H DARLINGTON	2,653	9	43	D	1-1	1-0	Adcock 38 / Blake 72 / Ref: D Orr
32	27/2	A CHESTER	2,001	9	44	D	1-1	0-0	Gibbs 72 / Richardson 77 / Ref: J Brandwood
33	2/3	A LEYTON ORIENT	4,049	8	47	W	1-0	1-0	Adcock 41p / Ref: S Baines
34	9/3	H BURY	2,832	8	50	W	1-0	0-0	Caesar 75 / Ref: M Bailey

Line-ups (1–11 and subs used)

No	1	2	3	4	5	6	7	8	9	10	11	subs used
24	Emberson	Fry	Betts	McCarthy	Greene	Cawley	Kinsella	Locke*	Abrahams*	Gregory	Cheetham	Duguid/Dennis
25	Emberson	Fry	Betts	McCarthy	Greene	Cawley	Kinsella	Dennis	Abrahams	Adcock	Gregory*	Duguid
26	Farnworth	Fry*	Betts	McCarthy	Greene	Cawley	Kinsella	Dennis*	Abrahams	Adcock	Gregory	Cheetham/Duguid
27	Richardson	Locke	Betts	McCarthy	Greene	Cawley	Kinsella	Ball*	Abrahams	Adcock	Gregory	Fry
28	Emberson	Locke	Betts	McCarthy	Greene	Cawley	Kinsella	Cheetham*	Abrahams	Adcock	Gregory	Reinelt/Ball
29	Emberson	Betts*	Betts	McCarthy	Greene	Cawley	Kinsella	Cheetham*	Abrahams	Adcock	Gregory*	Reinelt/Ball
30	Emberson	Fry	Betts*	Caesar	Greene	Ball*	Kinsella	Dennis	Abrahams	Adcock	Gregory*	Cheeth'm/Dug'd/Gibbs
31	Emberson	Fry	Betts	Caesar	Greene	Locke*	Kinsella	Dennis	Duguid	Adcock	Gibbs	McGleish
32	Emberson	Fry	Betts	McCarthy	Caesar	Cawley	Kinsella	Dennis	Duguid*	Adcock	Gibbs	Cheetham
33	Emberson	Fry*	Betts	McCarthy	Caesar	Cawley	Kinsella	Dennis	Duguid	Adcock	Gibbs*	McGleish/Gregory
34	Petterson	Fry	Betts	McCarthy	Caesar	Cawley	Kinsella	Dennis	Duguid*	Adcock	Gibbs*	McGleish/Reinelt

Opposition line-ups (1–11 and subs)

No	1	2	3	4	5	6	7	8	9	10	11	subs used
24	Taylor	Gale	Thomas*	Pardew	Primus	McDonald	Hodges	Scott	Cooper	Devine !	Wilson	Mills
25	Petterson	Billy	Williams	Logan	Heathcote	Curran	Baird	Mauge	Littlejohn*	Evans	Leadbitter*	Saunders/Hill
26	Fearon	Carragher	Johnson	Greenall	Pender	Sharp	Diaz	Martinez	Leonard	Lancashire*	Rimmer	Biggins
27	Ironside	Fleming	Knowles	Minett	Robertson	Brown G	Ainsworth	Barnett	Alcide	Brown S	Carbon	
28	Ironside	Knowles	Johnson	Toman	Hicks	Rockett	Midgley	Charles	Treble	Page*	Magee	Ritchie
29	Farnworth	Carragher	Johnson	Greenall	Pender	Sharp	Farrell	Martinez	Lancashire	Biggins*	Rimmer	Barnwell
30	Vaughan	Holmes	Barrick	Atkinson	Kidd	Moyes	Davey	Bryson	Saville	Wilkinson	Cartwright	
31	Newell	Shaw	Barnard	Appleby	Crosby	Brumwell*	Bannister	Gaughan	Painter*	Blake	Olsson	Carss/Fr'son/Mattison
32	Stewart	Davidson	Rogers	Fisher	Jackson	Whelan	Richardson	Priest	Rimmer*	Milner	Burnham*	Murphy/Noteman
33	Fearon	Hendon	Austin	Arnott	Bellamy	McCarthy*	Kelly*	Cockerill	Brooks	West	Chapman	Warren
34	Kelly	West	Reid*	Daws	Lucketti	Jackson	Rigby*	Matthews*	Carter	Johnrose	Pugh	Johnson/Rigby/Paskin

24 BARNET — A goal-crazy game is spoilt by Ref Bennett, who books seven and dismisses Sean Devine, for a scuffle with Kinsella. Abrahams accepts a long punt from Emberson, and a pass from Fry. Devine, whose flick gives Linvoy Primus his first-ever goal, scores after Mark Cooper hits the bar

25 PLYMOUTH — Despite England v France rugby, the attendance is the division's highest of the day. Ian Baird puts Argyle ahead with a deflected free-kick. On-loan keeper Andy Petterson fouls Abrahams, but saves Betts' spot-kick (23). Greene is pushed up front and side-foots a late U's equaliser

26 WIGAN — Cawley inspires the Latics by declaring 'Wigan is the dustbin of the world and I never want to play here again [by gaining promotion]'. The comments are pasted in the home dressing room. Gavin Johnson, on-loan from Luton, bags a brace for Colchester's first defeat in eight games.

27 LINCOLN — U's board ask Cawley to explain his Wigan comments. Lincoln include ex-U's favourite Steve Brown after he played just eight for Gills. Imps boss John Beck is up to old tricks: overheated dressing room, scalding hot and icy cold showers, undrinkable tea and rock-hard practice balls.

28 SCARBOROUGH — U's still haven't beaten Boro' at home since they entered the league in 1987. Cawley gets U's off to a good start, side-footing in after Adcock unsights Ian Ironside; Neil Treble bundles in a flag-kick from his fellow ex-Preston colleague. Kevin Magee United are booed off at the end

29 WIGAN — U's have just three wins in the last 15. Adcock ends his drought, stabbing in Abrahams' cross-shot. Graham Lancashire, on loan from Preston, sweeps in after Emberson parries Roberto Martinez's shot. The keeper can only watch as his half-save trickles over the line for the winner.

30 PRESTON — Kinsella is appointed captain against money-bags Preston, who cost a combined £500k compared to U's £40k. Leading scorer Andy Saville, with 21 this term, nets another pair. First he meets Ian Bryson's quickly-taken corner, and he then intercepts Greene's weak backward header.

31 DARLINGTON — Haydon (England U-16) and Caldwell (Canada Olympic) receive call-ups. McGleish, 21, is loaned from Posh when Abrahams is recalled by Brentford. Adcock nods in Betts' 40-yard cross. Robbie Blake levels, direct from a free-kick, after Caesar fouled 16-year-old Paul Robinson

32 CHESTER — Greene's loan ends, as Gibbs nets his first-ever league goal after recovering from a hernia op. Gibbs had just struck the bar with a tremendous 40-yard effort (70). High-flying City equalise when Nick Richardson turns in a loose ball following a corner. their 50th league goal of the term.

33 LEYTON ORIENT — The Sale deal collapses. Andy Arnott fouls Dennis, four minutes before the break, for Adcock to send Ron Fearon the wrong way and register his 16th of the season. The win was sweet revenge for United's last league visit to Brisbane Road when they were thrashed 0-8 back in 1987.

34 BURY — Emberson fractures his thumb in training, colliding with Cawley. Petterson, who had played against United for Plymouth, signs on loan from Charlton. Caesar's second-ever United goal secures a great win against promotion rivals Bury. He meets Gibbs free-kick with a bullet header.

No	Date	H/A	Opponent	Goals / Ref	Att	Pos	Pts	Res	Score	HT
35	16/3	A	SCARBOROUGH	Ref: T West	1,201	22	51	8	D	0-0	0-0
36	19/3	H	CAMBRIDGE	Adcock 9, McGleish 51 / Middleton 31 — Ref: M Pierce (S Clingo)	2,995	23	54	8	W	2-1	1-1
37	23/3	H	TORQUAY	Fry 6, McGleish 47, Betts 74p / Laight 86 — Ref: G Pooley	2,888	24	57	7	W	3-1	1-0
38	30/3	A	HARTLEPOOL	Gibbs 45 / Halliday 17, Howard 73 — Ref: K Lynch	1,364	16	57	8	L	1-2	1-1
39	2/4	H	ROCHDALE	Reinelt 54 — Ref: R Furnandiz	3,021	14	60	8	W	1-0	0-0
40	6/4	H	CARDIFF	Kinsella 56 — Ref: G Singh	3,345	22	63	8	W	1-0	0-0
41	8/4	A	NORTHAMPTON	Reinelt 90 / Grayson 65, Gibb 81 — Ref: S Bennett	5,021	11	63	9	L	1-2	0-0
42	13/4	H	FULHAM	McGleish 43, 76 / Morgan 30, Conroy 46 — Ref: U Rennie	3,795	16	64	8	D	2-2	1-1
43	16/4	H	GILLINGHAM	McGleish 64 / Gayle 58 — Ref: P Richards	4,952	1	65	8	D	1-1	0-0
44	20/4	A	EXETER	Caesar 6, McGleish 65 / Braithwaite 10, Chamberlain 25 — Ref: E Wolstenholme	2,788	12	66	9	D	2-2	1-2
45	27/4	A	MANSFIELD	Reinelt 68, Dunne 90 / Eustace 49 — Ref: M Fletcher	2,073	17	69	7	W	2-1	0-0
46	4/5	H	DONCASTER	Gibbs 45 — Ref: C Wilkes	5,038	13	72	7	W	1-0	1-0

Average 3,274 · Home 3,274 · Away 3,230

35 — SCARBOROUGH
Petterson, Fry, Betts, McCarthy, Caesar, Cawley, Kinsella, Dennis*, Duguid*, Adcock, Gibbs*, McGsh/Reinelt/Greg'y
Ironside, Knowles, Wells, Toman, Charles, Rackett, Ritchie', Myers, Trebble, Partridge, Magee, Willgrass/Page*
15 months on. Colchester are still trying to obtain compensation from Ipswich, over Burley's ignominious departure. U's fans are forced to pay £9.50, whereas Hartlepool fans had paid £7 in Boro's last home game. The point leaves Torquay ten points adrift of the Seadogs at the bottom.

36 — CAMBRIDGE
Petterson, Fry, Betts, McCarthy, Caesar, Cawley, Kinsella!, Locke, Duguid*, Adcock, Gibbs, McGleish/Gregory
Barrett, Wanless, Granville, Vowden, Craddock, Raynor, Joseph Matt Middleton, Richards, Corrazin, Beall', Jeffrey/Robinson*
Senior linesman Clingo replaces Pierce at half-time through injury. Clingo books Kinsella, unaware that Pierce had already given the Irishman a yellow. Adcock heads U's in front, only for Craig Middleton to crack a stunner. McGleish wins it and celebrates with a double somersault.

37 — TORQUAY
Petterson, Fry, Betts, McCarthy, Caesar, Cawley, Kinsella, Locke, McGleish, Adcock*, Gibbs*, Duguid/Whitton
Bayes, Monk, Stamps, Barrow, Watson, Coughlin, Hall, Oatway, Baker, Thomas', Hathaway, Hawthorne/Laight*
The only saviour for Torquay's league status will be if Stevenage win the GMVC. Their ground does not meet FL criteria. U's lead 2-0 when Scott Stamps fouls Fry in the area. Betts sends Ashley Bayes the wrong way. Wignall sets his side a target of 68 points to reach the play-offs.

38 — HARTLEPOOL
Petterson, Fry, Betts, McCarthy, Caesar, Cawley, Kinsella, Locke!, McGleish*, Whitton*, Gibbs", Reinelt/Duguid/Dunne
Home, Ingram', McAuley, Henderson, McGuckin, Howard, Conlon, Tait, Houchen, Halliday, Canham", Allinson/Billing/Walton*
U's pocket £40k as Martin Grainger moves from Brentford to Brum. Dunne signs from Gills until the end of the term. On Betts' 150th game, Ref Lynch loses control and sends off Locke for retaliation (50). Kinsella is forced off the field for 13 minutes, for treatment to a head wound.

39 — ROCHDALE
Emberson, Fry, Betts, McCarthy, Caesar, Cawley, Dennis, Locke, McGleish*, Whitton*, Gibbs, Reinelt
Key, Thackeray, Hardy, Deary, Martin, Hall, Thompson, Taylor', Peake, Whitehall*, Stuart, Danci/Maulden/Proct'r*
Emberson returns to the side after Charlton recall Petterson. Fears that Whitton has aggravated his ligament injury are unfounded, as the diagnosis is a pulled calf muscle Reinelt, his replacement just before the break, volleys the winner via a delightful left-wing cross from Gibbs.

40 — CARDIFF
Emberson, Betts, McCarthy, Caesar, Cawley, Kinsella, Locke, McGleish, Whitton*, Adcock*, Gibbs*, Reinelt
Williams, Rodgerson', Searle, Harding, Jarman, Young, Osman, McGorry, Philliskirk, Dale, Gardner, Johnson/Fleming*
Adcock signs a one-year extension. Kinsella strikes a vicious 20-yard screamer, that Cardiff keeper Dave Williams has no hope of stopping. Moments earlier, Carl Dale had struck the crossbar with a spectacular diving header. U's hold out to complete their second double of the term.

41 — NORTHAMPTON
Emberson, Fry, Betts, McCarthy, Caesar, Cawley*, Kinsella, Dennis, McGleish*, Adcock, Gibbs/Dennis/Dunne
Woodman, Sampson', Grayson', Peer, Warburton, O'Shea, Williams, Hunter, Thompson, White, Burns, Doherty/Gibb*
Cobblers boss Atkins laid the foundations for U's return to the league five years ago, but his side dent U's div two aspirations. Gary Thompson heads sub Ali Gibb's cross back to Neil Grayson, then Gibb lashes home a loose ball from 18 yards. Reinelt nets Gibbs' shot against the post.

42 — FULHAM
Emberson, Fry, Betts, McCarthy, Caesar, Dennis, Kinsella, Fry, McGleish, Adcock!, Reinelt
Lange, Marshall, Herrera, Morgan, Angus!, Blake, Thomas, Brooker, Conroy, Scott, Simpson, Hamill*
Adcock and Terry Angus both see red, and continue the argument down the tunnel. Emberson's mistake is in Simon Morgan. only for McGleish to level with a terrific angled drive. 30 secs after the break, Mike Conroy beats the on-rushing Emberson. McGleish nods U's level.

43 — GILLINGHAM
Emberson, Fry, Betts, McCarthy, Caesar, Cawley, Kinsella, Dennis, McGleish, Adcock*, Gibbs
Stannard, Thomas, Manuel, Smith!, Harris, Butler, Martin, Ratcliffe, Gayle, Fortune-West Bailey, Micklewhite*
Gills start joint top with Preston on 77 points, and include ex-U's FA Trophy hero, Dave Martin. Giant John Gayle puts the Kent side in front, but McGleish nets his third in four days. Preston fall to a 1-2 defeat at Cambridge. Neil Smith hacks down Adcock for a red card on 70 minutes.

44 — EXETER
Emberson, Fry*, Betts, McCarthy, Caesar*, Cawley, Kinsella, Dennis, McGleish, Adcock, Reinelt*, Dunne/Gibbs/Duguid
Fox, Chamberlain, Rice, Myers, Blake, Richardson, Butler, Bailey, Gayle, Sharpe, Came, Foster
Steven Gage, former Wigan chairman, joins as an associate director. Despite the draw, results go U's way. Caesar forces in the first, but Leon Braithwaite nets a one-on-one. 15 minutes later, Mark Chamberlain puts City in front, but McGleish's fourth in three games rescues a point.

45 — MANSFIELD
Emberson, Fry*, Betts, McCarthy, Dunne, Cawley, Kinsella, Dennis, McGleish, Reinelt, Duguid*, Locke/Gibbs
Bowling, Boothroyd, Hackett, Doolan, Timons, Eustace, Ireland, Wood, Onoura, Williams, Hadley, Lampkin*
Scott Eustace puts the Stags in front, just after the interval. with a header. Reinelt, the only player booked, puts United back on terms. Dunne, replacing the injured Caesar, who had limped off at Exeter, sends U's fans wild with delight by heading in a late winner in the 93rd minute.

46 — DONCASTER
Emberson, Fry', Betts, McCarthy, Caesar*, Cawley, Kinsella, Dennis, McGleish, Reinelt, Gibbs, Locke/Whitton
O'Connor, Kirby, Robertson', Murphy, Moore, Marquis, Schofield, Warren, Colcombe, Cramb, Parrish, Jones/Smith*
Last week's hero Dunne is missing through a burst blood vessel in his knee. Gibbs' speculative left-wing cross-cum-shot puts United in the play-offs as one of their rivals, Wigan, slip up as required. Jason White gives Northampton an unexpected 86th-minute win at Springfield Park.

ENDSLEIGH DIVISION 3 (CUP-TIES)

Manager: Steve Wignall

SEASON 1995-96

Play-offs

			F-A	H-T	
SF 1	H	PLYMOUTH 7	W 1-0	1-0	6,511 4

1	2	3	4	5	6	7	8	9	10	11	subs used
Emerson	Fry	Betts	McCarthy	Caesar	Cawley	Kinsella	Dennis	McGleish	Reinelt*	Gibbs*	Locke/Whitton
Cherry	*Patterson*	*Williams*	*Billy*	*Heathcote*	*Barlow**	*Leadbitter*	*Logan*	*Littlejohn*	*Evans**	*Curran*	*Corazzin/Mauge*

Scorers: **Kinsella 44**
Ref: M Pierce

Warnock jibes 'little teams like Colchester shouldn't even be on the same pitch as us'. Argyle's 'little teams' have been assembled at a cost of £1.03m. whilst United's cost a measly £2k. Kinsella rams Warnock's words down his throat with a thunderbolt from 25 yards just before the break.

			F-A	H-T	
SF 2	A	PLYMOUTH 7	L 1-3	0-2	14,525 4

1	2	3	4	5	6	7	8	9	10	11	subs used
Emerson	Fry	Betts	McCarthy	Caesar*	Cawley	Kinsella	Dennis	McGleish	Reinelt*	Gibbs*	Adcock/Whitton/Locke
Cherry	*Patterson*	*Williams*	*Mauge*	*Heathcote*	*Barlow*	*Leadbitter*	*Logan*	*Littlejohn*	*Evans*	*Curran*	

Scorers: **Kinsella 66** / Evans 3, Leadbitter 41, Williams 85
Ref: J Kirkby

(Colchester lost 2-3 on aggregate) kick. Kinsella levels the scores in an intimidating atmosphere, and Chris Leadbitter puts the Devon side in front with a curling 20-yard free-kick. Kinsella seems to have it settled on away goals, but with five minutes to go, Martin Barlow crosses for Paul Williams to net the winner.

Coca-Cola Cup

			F-A	H-T	
1:1	H	BRISTOL CITY 9	W 2-1	2-1	2,831 2:

1	2	3	4	5	6	7	8	9	10	11	subs used
Emerson	Locke	Betts	McCarthy	Caesar	Cawley	Kinsella	English	Whitton	Adcock	Cheetham	
Welch	*Hansen*	*Munro**	*McLeary*	*Dryden*	*Kuhl*	*Bent*	*Partridge**	*Seal*	*Agostino*	*Barber*	*Shail/Kite*

Scorers: **Adcock 15, Kinsella 16** / Seal 3
Ref: P Taylor

U's notch their first win in the competition for 12 years. Joe Jordan's City take the lead through Australian David Seal's 20-yard looping volley over the top of Emerson. Adcock curls in past Keith Welch, followed 30 seconds later by a Kinsella shot that deflects in off Stuart Munro.

			F-A	H-T	
1:2	A	BRISTOL CITY 9	L 1-2	0-1	3,648 2:13 aet

1	2	3	4	5	6	7	8	9	10	11	subs used
Emerson	Locke	Betts	McCarthy	Caesar	Cawley	Kinsella	English	Whitton	Adcock*	Cheetham*	Reinelt/Fry
Welch	*Hanson**	*Shail*	*McLeary*	*Dryden*	*Kuhl*	*Bent*	*Fowler*	*Seal*	*Agostino**	*Barber**	*Pridge/Plum'r/Bryant*

Scorers: **Cheetham 61** / Seal 20, 81
Ref: G Barber

United miss out on a money-spinning two-legged tie with Newcastle in a tense penalty shoot-out. Betts misses at 2-2 and all the remaining (Colchester lost 4-5 on penalties) penalties are scored. Earlier, Cheetham's equaliser on the night had put U's in the driving seat, only for Seal to head in with nine minutes left.

Autowindscreen Shield

			F-A	H-T	
1	H	TORQUAY 7	W 5-2	2-0	1,121 3:16

1	2	3	4	5	6	7	8	9	10	11	subs used
Emerson	Locke*	Betts	McCarthy	English	Cawley	Kinsella	Fry	Reinelt	Adcock	Cheetham	Ball
Bayes	*Winter*	*Barrow*	*O'Riordan*	*Gore**	*Curran*	*Hawthorne*	*Kaasikmae*	*Hancox**	*Hathaway*	*Mateu**	*Laight/Hall/Stamps*

Scorers: **Adcock 2, 57, 68, Reinelt 35, Cawley 55** / Hathaway 67, Stamps 78
Ref: P Taylor

Adcock hits his first U's hat-trick since 1985 (v Cambridge). His first comes when Ashley Bayes parries Kinsella's shot. Reinelt flicks on Emerson's punt. for 'Adcock's punt. for Adcock's audacious 25-yard lob. The third is another stunning 22-yard chip. Scott Stamps pulls one back after U's relax.

			F-A	H-T	
1	A	SWINDON 5	L 0-2	0-0	6,222 2:1

1	2	3	4	5	6	7	8	9	10	11	subs used
Caldwell	Betts	Gibbs	McCarthy	Lewis	Caesar*	Kinsella	Dennis	Mardenboro	Adcock	Cheetham	English
Digby	*Hooper*	*Drysdale**	*Gooden*	*Thorne G*	*Taylor*	*Robinson*	*Ling**	*Finney*	*Allison**	*Horlock*	*McMn'O'Sul/Th'ne P*

Scorers: Thorne P 82, Finney 89
Ref: P Taylor

Caldwell makes his debut at runaway division two leaders Swindon. Player-coach Steve McMahon comes on to stop U's controlling the game. Peter Thorne and top scorer Steve Finney put Town top of the group. after their 1-1 draw at Torquay. U's qualify for a second-round away tie.

			F-A	H-T	
2	A	OXFORD 6	W 2-1	1-1	1,943 2:13

1	2	3	4	5	6	7	8	9	10	11	subs used
Emerson	Betts	Gibbs	McCarthy	Greene	Cawley	Kinsella	English	Ball*	Adcock	Cheetham	Dennis
Whitehead	*Wood**	*Ford M*	*Smith**	*Elliott*	*Rush**	*Massey*	*Moody*	*Ford B*	*Angel*	*Murphy/Powell/Beau'p*	

Scorers: **Adcock 26, Betts 88p** / Angel 41
Ref: D Orr

Adcock headed U's in front before Oxford drew level with a long-range Darren Angel shot David Rush had a goal disallowed before Adcock is felled by Massey. Betts scored easily to send the damp U's supporters into ecstasy. The fans are moved from the open terrace to the seats.

			F-A	H-T	
3	A	PETERBOROUGH 5	L 2-3	0-1	2,460 2:17

1	2	3	4	5	6	7	8	9	10	11	subs used
Emerson	Betts	Gibbs	McCarthy	Greene	Cawley	Kinsella	English	Fry	Abrahams*	Cheetham	Duguid
Sheffield	*Williams*	*Spearing*	*Le Bihan*	*Breen*	*Heald*	*Carter*	*Shaw*	*Martindale*	*Farrell**	*Morrison**	*Rioch/McGleish*

Scorers: **Betts 71, Kinsella 75** / Martindale 44, 78, McGleish 66
Ref: R Furnandiz

Gary Martindale is guilty of missing an open goal. but makes amends by pouncing at the far post. Sub Scott McGleish puts Posh two up with his first touch. Betts, with his fourth goal in seven games, and Kinsella level the score. Martindale heads Posh into the southern area semi-final.

FA Cup

			F-A	H-T	
1	A	GRAVESEND 5	L 0-2	0-1	3,218 BH:13

1	2	3	4	5	6	7	8	9	10	11	subs used
Emerson	Fry	Betts	McCarthy	Caesar*	Cawley	Kinsella	English	Mardenboro	Adcock	Cheetham	Gibbs
Turner	*Walker*	*Lamb*	*Gubbins*	*Mortley*	*Jackson*	*Best**	*Cotter**	*Blewden*	*Munday*	*Powell*	*Bourne/Gooding*

Scorers: Jackson 35, Mortley 70
Ref: G Pooley

Fleets ground is sold out as they advance into the second round, and a trip to Cinderford, for only the second time. Dire U's can't muster a shot on target. Jimmy Jackson fires a 40-yard free-kick past Emerson. and Peter Mortley volleys in from 20 yards. Wignall brands U's 'cowards'.

League Table

	P	W	D	L	F	A	W	D	L	F	A	Pts
		Home					Away					
1 Preston	46	11	8	4	44	22	12	9	2	34	16	86
2 Gillingham	46	16	6	1	33	6	6	11	6	16	14	83
3 Bury	46	11	6	6	33	21	11	7	5	33	27	79
4 Plymouth*	46	14	5	4	41	20	8	7	8	27	29	78
5 Darlington	46	10	6	7	30	21	10	12	1	30	21	78
6 Hereford	46	13	5	5	40	22	7	9	7	25	25	74
7 COLCHESTER	46	13	7	3	37	22	5	11	7	24	29	72
8 Chester	46	11	9	3	45	22	7	7	9	27	31	70
9 Barnet	46	13	6	4	40	19	5	10	8	25	26	70
10 Wigan	46	15	3	5	36	21	5	7	11	26	35	70
11 Northampton	46	9	10	4	32	22	9	3	11	19	22	67
12 Scunthorpe	46	8	8	7	36	30	7	7	9	31	31	60
13 Doncaster	46	11	6	6	25	19	5	5	13	24	41	59
14 Exeter	46	9	9	5	25	22	4	9	10	21	31	57
15 Rochdale	46	7	8	8	32	33	7	5	11	25	28	55
16 Cambridge	46	8	8	7	34	30	6	4	13	27	41	54
17 Fulham	46	10	9	4	39	26	2	8	13	18	37	53
18 Lincoln	46	8	7	8	32	26	5	7	11	25	47	53
19 Mansfield	46	6	10	7	25	29	5	10	8	29	35	53
20 Hartlepool	46	8	9	6	30	24	4	4	15	17	43	49
21 Leyton Orient	46	11	4	8	29	22	1	7	15	17	41	47
22 Cardiff	46	8	6	9	24	22	3	6	14	17	42	45
23 Scarborough	46	5	5	13	22	28	6	2	15	17	41	40
24 Torquay	46	4	9	10	17	36	1	5	17	13	48	29
	1104	239	175	138	781	565	138	175	239	565	781	1481

* promoted
after play-offs

Appearances and Goals

	Appearances						Goals			
	Lge	Sub	LC	Sub	FAC	Sub	Lge	LC	FAC	Tot
Abrahams, Paul	8						2			2
Adcock, Tony	41		2		1		12		1	13
Ball, Steve	6	2					1			1
Betts, Simon	45		2		1		5			5
Boyce, Robert		2								
Caesar, Gus	23		2				2			2
Cawley, Peter	42		2				1			1
Cheetham, Michael	25	3	2		1		2		1	3
Dennis, Tony	24	8					3			3
Duguid, Karl	7	9					1			1
Dunne, Joe	2	3					1			1
Emberson, Carl	41		2		1					
English, Tony	20	1	2		1					
Fry, Chris	35	3			1	1	2			2
Gibbs, Paul	13	11				1	3			3
Greene, David	14				1		1			1
Gregory, David	7	3								
Kinsella, Mark	45		2		1		5		1	6
Lewis, Ben	1	1								
Locke, Adam	22	3	2				3			3
Mardenboro', Steve	4	8			1		2			2
McCarthy, Tony	44		2		1					
McGleish, Scott	10	5					6			6
Petterson, Andy	5									
Reinelt, Robbie	12	10	1				7			7
Whitton, Steve	10	2	2				2			2
26 players used	506	74	22	2	11	1	61		3	64

Odds & ends

Double wins: (2) Cardiff, Torquay.

Double defeats (1) Wigan.

Won from behind: (2) Mansfield (a), Torquay (a).

Lost from in front: (1) Wigan (h).

High spots: Reaching the play-offs on the last day of the season.

Success achieved on a shoe-string budget.

Just two defeats in the last 16 league games.

Autowindscreen Shield victory at second division Oxford.

Mark Kinsella's spectacular long-range goals.

Scott McGleish's goal-scoring celebratory somersaults.

Low spots: Five minutes from a Wembley play-off appearance.

Five league games without a win from October.

Eight league games without a win from January.

Suspensions and crippling injury list.

Loss of the influential Steve Whitton.

League Cup penalty shoot-out defeat at Bristol City.

FA Cup defeat at Beazer Homes League Gravesend and Northfleet.

Player of the Year: Mark Kinsella.

Ever presents: (0).

Hat-tricks: (1) Tony Adcock in Autowindscreen Shield.

Leading scorer: Tony Adcock (17) (including 4 in Autowindscreen Shield).

NATIONWIDE LEAGUE DIVISION 3 — Manager: Steve Wignall — SEASON 1996-97

No	Date	1	2	3	4	5	6	7	8	9	10	11	subs used	Att	Pos	Pt	F-A	H-T	Scorers, Times, and Referees
1	H HARTLEPOOL 17/8	Caldwell	Betts	Barnes	McCarthy!	Greene	Cawley	Kinsella	Locke	Whitton	Adcock	Fry*	Reinelt	2,942		0	L 0-2	0-0	Allon 52, McAuley 60
		Pears	*Ingram*	*McAuley*	*Beech*	*Davies*	*McDonald*	*Alton*	*Cooper*	*Howard*	*Halliday*	*Clegg**	*Tait*						Ref: P Robinson
2	A ROCHDALE 24/8	Caldwell	Dunne	Barnes	McCarthy	Greene	Cawley	Kinsella	Locke	Whitton	Adcock	Reinelt*	Fry	1,816	21	1	D 0-0	0-0	Ref: D Laws
		Gray	*Fensome*	*Formby**	*Johnson*	*Hill*	*Farrell*	*Russell"*	*Deary*	*Leonard*	*Whitehall*	*Stuart"*	*Th'mpson/Bayliss/Lancaste*						
3	A DARLINGTON 27/8	Caldwell	Dunne	Barnes	McCarthy	Greene	Cawley	Kinsella	Locke	Whitton	Adcock*	Wilkins	Reinelt	2,906	20	2	D 1-1	1-1	Locke 44, Atkinson 1p
		Newell	*Shaw*	*Barnard*	*Crosby*	*Gregan*	*Oliver**	*Atkinson*	*Roberts*	*Blake*	*Twynham"*	*Innes/Carss*							Ref: R Furmandiz
4	H HEREFORD 31/8	Caldwell	Betts	Betts	Gregory	Greene	Cawley	Kinsella	Locke*	Whitton	Adcock*	Wilkins	Reinelt/Fry	2,723	22	3	D 1-1	0-0	Reinelt 79, Smith 63
		DeBont	*Norton*	*Fishlock*	*Smith*	*Brough*	*Townsend*	*Stoker*	*Downing*	*Foster*	*Hargreaves*	*Mahon*							Ref: M Fletcher
5	A FULHAM 7/9	Emberson	Dunne	Betts	Gregory*	Greene	Cawley	Kinsella	Locke*	Fry	Reinelt	Wilkins	Fry/Duguid/Adcock	5,189	23	3	L 1-3	0-1	Conroy 5, 51, Morgan 79
		Lange	*Watson*	*Herrera*	*Cullip*	*Cusack*	*Blake*	*Freeman*	*Angus*	*Conroy*	*Morgan*	*Scott*							Ref: A D'Urso
6	H BRIGHTON 10/9	Emberson	Dunne	Betts	McCarthy	Greene*	Cawley	Kinsella	Reinelt	Fry	Adcock	Wilkins	Wilkins	2,540	18	6	W 2-0	1-0	Kinsella 24, Reinelt 53
		Rust	*Johnson*	*Storer*	*Parris*	*Allan*	*Hobson*	*Minton*	*Peake*	*Baird*	*Marshall*	*McDonald**	*Smith*						Ref: B Knight
7	H HULL 14/9	Emberson	Dunne	Betts	McCarthy	Greene*	Cawley	Kinsella	Reinelt	Fry	Adcock	Wilkins	Duguid	3,073	17	7	D 1-1	0-0	Kinsella 50, Gordon 52
		Carroll	*Trevitt*	*Rioch*	*Allison*	*Wright*	*Brien*	*Joyce*	*Doncel*	*Darby**	*Peacock*	*Gordon*	*Maxfield*						Ref: R Styles
8	A LEYTON ORIENT 21/9	Emberson	Dunne	Betts	McCarthy	Greene	Cawley!	Locke	Reinelt*	Fry	Adcock*	Wilkins	Duguid/Gregory	5,254	17	8	D 1-1	0-0	Fry 52
		Sealey	*Hendon*	*Naylor*	*Chapman*	*Martin A*	*Arnott*	*Martin D**	*Ling*	*Hanson*	*West*	*Channing*	*Kelly*						Channing 69; Ref: M Halsey
9	H DONCASTER 28/9	Emberson	Dunne	Barnes"	McCarthy	Greene	Cawley	Locke	Reinelt	Fry*	Adcock	Wilkins*	Whitton/Duguid/Gregory	2,672	19	9	D 2-2	2-2	Cawley 26, Adcock 40
		Williams	*Murphy*	*Ryan*	*Moore*	*Gore*	*Bullimore*	*Schofield*	*Colcombe*	*Lester**	*Cramb*	*Birch*	*Pearce*						Colcombe 29, Schofield 39p; Ref: P.Taylor
10	A CARLISLE 1/10	Emberson	Dunne	Barnes*	McCarthy	Greene	Cawley	Locke	Reinelt*	Fry	Adcock*	Wilkins	Whitton/Duguid/Gregory	4,089	21	9	L 0-3	0-1	Currie 43, Reeves 57, Archdeacon 58
		Caig	*Delap**	*Archdeacon*	*Walling*	*Robinson*	*Pounew'tchy*	*Thomas"*	*Peacock*	*Reeves*	*Hayward*	*Aspinall"*	*Currie/Heath/Prokas*						Ref: T Heilbron
11	A SWANSEA 4/10	Emberson	Dunne	Barnes	Gregory	Greene*	Cawley	Locke	Fry*	Whitton	Duguid	Wilkins	Reinelt	2,531	22	10	D 1-1	1-1	Greene 4, Torpey 39
		Freestone	*Casey*	*Lacey*	*Walker*	*O'Leary*	*Jones*	*Jenkins*	*Penney*	*Torpey*	*Molby*	*Thomas*						Ref: F Stretton

1. U's sign Wilkins (Hereford) and Greene (Luton) for £30k apiece. Jock Wallace, 60, dies. The new Clock End stand is opened and witnesses six bookings and a red card for McCarthy. He is adjudged to elbow Steven Howard (40). Barnes debuts, having joined on a free from Watford.

2. Six of the previous seven meetings at Spotlands have been drawn. Both managers are pleased to get their first point of the season. Kinsella's move to Charlton falls through over the size and schedule of instalments. Only a fine finger-tip save by Ian Gray denies McCarthy the winner.

3. Whitton returns to the ground where his career was almost ended. Caldwell hauls down Darren Roberts, for Brian Atkinson to score an early penalty. Locke slips in an equaliser, on the stroke of half-time, under the body of ex-U's loanee Paul Newell. Locke could have had a hat-trick.

4. Bulls defender Dean Smith gobbles up everything that U's can throw at him. He puts the visitors in front, direct from a 20-yard free-kick. An injection of pace on 70 mins, via Fry and Reinelt, leads to the latter turning in Wilkins' knock-back, after Andy DeBont flaps at Dunne's cross.

5. Emberson replaces Caldwell, injured at WBA. Cawley misses Simon Morgan's cross, giving Mike Conroy the first. Another error leads to Conroy's seventh of the term, when Gregory misjudges Rob Scott's cross. Whitton heads U's back in it, only for Morgan to net a breakaway.

6. Brighton visit for the first time in 21 years, when Brian Clough and Peter Taylor were in charge. U's move off the bottom of the table against a side that has lost it's last ten away. Kinsella strikes a loose ball from 22 yards and Reinelt nips in to intercept Peter Johnson's poor back-pass.

7. Fulham lead the table with six wins from seven. Hull, with three wins, maintain their unbeaten start but haven't won at Layer Rd for 32 years. Kinsella curls a fine 20-yard free-kick, after a foul by Spaniard Antonio Doncel. Gavin Gordon nods in Duane Darby's cross two minutes later.

8. Charlton sign Kinsella for an eventual £300k. O's Colin West blows a chance when Cawley handles (44). He scores, but is ordered to re-take the kick. He inexplicably chips the ball into Emberson's hands from the re-take. Cawley's second yellow is for a foul on Dave Hanson (61).

9. Adcock has a tame 85th-minute penalty saved by Dean Williams, who felled Reinelt. Scott Colcombe's drive puts Kerry Dixon's Rovers in front. Cawley rises to meet Fry's corner, only for McCarthy to pull back Ian Gore in the box. Adcock levels within 60 seconds with a miscue.

10. Greene fouls Lee Peacock outside the box. Steve Hayward's free-kick falls to David Currie, who had only been on two minutes. Another Hayward free-kick finds David Reeves. Carlisle take over at the top when Owen Archdeacon strides through United's defence to plant into the net.

11. Whitton makes his 400th league appearance. Steve Jones handles outside the box. The resulting Wilkins free-kick sees Greene head in. Steve Torpey levels after good work from Kris O'Leary and David Thomas. United have the most draws in the country, with seven in eleven games.

12 · H 12/10 · WIGAN · W 3-1 · (17/4/13) · 2,700
Adcock 69, Gregory 76, Duguid 80 / Sharp 41 — Ref: C Finch

Emberson	Butler	Dunne*	Betts	McCarthy	Greene	Locke	Gregory	Kelly*	Whitton	Duguid*	Wilkins	Adcock/Reinelt/Fry
Carragher	Johnson	Greenall	Pender	Lowe	Martinez	Kilford!	Jones*	Biggins^	Sharp		Love/Diaz^/Butler	

Kelly is loaned from L Orient. Ian Kilford is sent off for a second yellow, after clattering Locke. Adcock's snap-shot creeps in, then Gregory blasts in John Pender's poor clearance from 25 yards. Bleached-blond Duguid finishes off Gregory's cross.

13 · H 15/10 · BARNET · W 1-0 · (13/10/16) · 2,732
Fry 81 — Ref: R Poulain

Emberson	Taylor	Dunne	Betts	McCarthy	Greene	Locke	Gregory	Kelly*	Whitton	Duguid*	Wilkins	Reinelt/Fry
Taylor	Gale	McDonald	Campbell	Primus	Howarth	Brazil*	Devine	Pardew	Codner			

Barnet are looking to impress their new director of football. Alan Mullery. Fry, on a 68th-minute sub, unleashes a 25-yarder that dips over Mark Taylor. Duguid faces the wrath of Wignall for his dissension at being subbed. Sean Devine and Robert Codner force Emberson to save.

14 · A 19/10 · NORTHAMPTON · L 1-2 · (15/14/16) · 4,119
Fry 41 / Parrish 45, Grayson 55 — Ref: S Baines

Emberson	Woodman	Dunne	Betts	McCarthy*	Greene	Gregory	Fry*	Whitton	Duguid*	Wilkins	Adcock/Reinelt/Kelly
Clarkson	Maddison	Sampson	Warburton	Rennie	Parrish	Hunter*	Cooper	White^	O'Shea	Grayson/Lee	

Abrahams re-signs from Brentford for £20k. Fry scores another pile-driver, but Sean Parrish cancels it in injury-time. McCarthy fails to cut out a Mark Cooper through-ball that half-time sub Neil Grayson races onto to score. U's have recorded just three wins at Northampton since 1950.

15 · A 26/10 · LINCOLN · L 2-3 · (18/14/16) · 2,768
Betts 26p, Duguid 43p / Ainsworth 32, Martin 59, Greene 62 (og) — Ref: A Butler

Emberson	Dunne	Betts*	McCarthy	Greene	Greene^	Fry	Wilkins	Whitton!	Duguid	Abrahams	Locke/Reinelt
Richardson	Barnett	Whitney	Hone	Brown^	Austin	Ainsworth	Fleming	Bos!	Martin	Alcide	

A stormy match with two red cards. Whitton is first, retaliating to a two-footed tackle by Jon Whitney (68). Grijsbert Bos's elbow (86) gives Greene ten stitches in a face wound. Whitney fouls Fry (Betts is injured scoring), and then Wilkins too. Greene nods the third into his own net.

16 · H 29/10 · EXETER · W 1-0 · (16/19/19) · 2,384
Myers 61(og) — Ref: G Pooley

Emberson	Bayes	Dunne	Gibbs	McCarthy	Greene	Locke	Fry	Wilkins	Whitton	Duguid	Abrahams*	Adcock/Reinelt/Gregory
Richardson	Hughes	Myers	Blake	Chamberlain	Hodges	Flack*	Dale	Philliskirk	Baddeley/Bennett			

Everyone in the crowd receives a free programme on entry and see U's record their ninth 1-0 victory over the Grecians. Whitton raps the cross-bar, but it is City defender Chris Myers who gets in the way of Duguid's shot to deflect the teenager's effort past wrong-footed Ashley Bayes.

17 · H 2/11 · CARDIFF · D 1-1 · (16/8/20) · 3,226
Duguid 18 / White 57p — Ref: B Harris

Emberson	Dunne	Gibbs	McCarthy*	Greene	Locke	Fry	Wilkins	Whitton*	Duguid	Abrahams*	Adcock/Reinelt/Gregory
Elliott	Fleming	Gardiner	Eckhardt	Jarman*	Young	Middleton	Fowler^	White	Dale	McConnell	

Betts tore a groin muscle in scoring last week. U's and City play out the first-ever draw between the clubs. Gibbs puts Duguid through: he out-paces Tony Philliskirk before slotting under Tony Elliott. Carl Dale's dive is worthy of an Oscar, giving Steve White the chance from the spot.

18 · A 9/11 · TORQUAY · W 2-0 · (13/6/23) · 2,251
Reinelt 62, Abrahams 90 — Ref: M Pierce

Emberson	Wilmot	Dunne	Locke	Greene	Locke	Fry	Wilkins	Reinelt	Taylor	Abrahams*	Hancox
Winter	Barrow	McCall	Wright	Watson	Oatway	Neeson	Laight	Hathaway*	Stamps		

Wignall rules out a move for Posh's McGleish, instead signing 32-year-old, ex-U's, Taylor from Luton on loan. Gulls' boss Kevin Hodges is named Manager-of-the-Month. Wilkins sends Reinelt through to shrug off a couple of challenges, then Abrahams repeats, courtesy of Locke.

19 · H 19/11 · SCUNTHORPE · D 1-1 · (12/18/24) · 1,842
Sertori 71(og), Clarkson 59 — Ref: C Wilkes

Emberson	Samways	Barnes	Gregory	Locke	Cawley	Abrahams	Taylor	Adcock*	Duguid*	Fry/Reinelt
Walsh	Wilson	Sertori	Hope	Patterson	Housham	D'Auria	Baker	Eyre^	Clarkson	McFarlane

Barnes returns after seven weeks out, in front of the lowest Layer Road attendance since 1989. Andy McFarlane's low cross skids off Cawley invitingly into the path of Ian Clarkson, who sends a looping header over Emberson. Mark Sertori guides Fry's cross past Mark Samways.

20 · A 22/11 · CHESTER · W 2-1 · (12/13/27) · 2,028
Taylor 7, 19, Whelan 53 — Ref: G Laws

Emberson	Sinclair	Barnes	Locke	Greene	Fry	Wilkins	Taylor	Whitton	Abrahams*	Gibbs
Davidson	Fisher	Woods*	Jackson	Watson	Flitcroft	Milner	Helliwell	Rimmer	Noteman	Priest

Taylor scores his first-ever goal for United. 13 years after his debut. From Fry's neat lay-off Taylor doubles the lead after good play by Fry and Locke gives the tall striker time to control, turn and rifle a shot into the roof of the net. Spencer Whelan pulls one back for City from a corner.

21 · H 30/11 · LINCOLN · W 7-1 · (7/9/30) · 2,738
Abms 19, Taylor 42p, 45p, Whitton 61, [Adcock 83, Fry 86, 90], Martin 64 — Ref: D Ott

Emberson	Richardson	Barnes	Gregory	Locke	Fry	Wilkins	Whitton*	Taylor	Abrahams	Adcock
Barnett	Austin	Hone	Brown G	Robertson	Ainsworth	Dennis	Bos	Martin	Alcide	

Buckle joins on a week-to-week, having been released by Torquay. Wignall is in seventh heaven in his 100th match as manager. Taylor's two penalties are awarded when Jason Barnett trips Abrahams and Kevin Austin does likewise on Wilkins. Fry completes the rout in injury-time.

22 · A 3/12 · SCARBOROUGH · D 1-1 · (8/11/31) · 1,605
Locke 24 / Mitchell 52 — Ref: R Furmandiz

Emberson	Ironside	Gregory	Locke	Greene	Fry*	Wilkins	Whitton	Taylor	Abrahams*	Dunne
Kay	Wells	Bennett	Hicks	Lucas	McElhatton	Thompstone	Mitchell	Ritchie	Williams*	Daws

U's, with just two league defeats in twelve, are set to sign Taylor after his four goals in five games. Locke gives U's the lead. crashing home Cawley's knock-back from Fry's flag-kick. Andy Ritchie flicks on Ian Ironside's long kick for Jamie Mitchell to beat U's flat-footed defence.

23 · A 14/12 · MANSFIELD · D 1-1 · (8/19/32) · 1,653
Abrahams 73 / Sale 90 — Ref: T Heilbron

Emberson	Bowling	Gregory	Barnes	Buckle*	Greene*	Fry	Whitton	Taylor	Abrahams*	Dunne
Ford	Harper	Kilcline	Eustace	Hackett	Sedgemore	Walker	Wood^	Hadley*	Doolan^	Hurst/Sale

Fry picks out Abrahams in oceans of space. He surges forward before slotting under the advancing Ian Bowling. Ex-transfer target Mark Sale comes off the bench to head in Steve Harper's cross in the dying moments. Dunne replaces Greene, who has blood streaming from his face.

NATIONWIDE LEAGUE DIVISION 3 — Manager: Steve Wignall — SEASON 1996-97

No	Date	Venue/Opponent	Att	Pos		Pt	F-A	H-T	Scorers, Times, and Referees	1	2	3	4	5	6	7	8	9	10	11	subs used
24	20/12	H CAMBRIDGE	3,707	11	3	33	2-2	0-1	Taylor 60, Adcock 90; Beall 39, Raynor 63; Ref: N Barry	Emberson / *Barrett*	Gregory / *Joseph*	Gibbs / *Granville*	Buckle / *Preece*	Greene / *Craddock*	Cawley" / *Raynor*	Fry / *Hayes*	Wilkins / *Hyde*	Whitton* / *Kyd*	Taylor / *Bil-Edinboro Beall*	Abrahams" / *Richards*	Adcock/Duguid/Dunne
25	26/12	A BRIGHTON	4,839	9	24	34	1-1	1-1	Whitton 15; Mundee 34p; Ref: A Wiley	Emberson / *Rust*	Gregory / *Smith*	Gibbs" / *Tuck*	McCarthy / *Mundee*	Greene / *Allan*	Buckle / *Johnson*	Fry / *Starer*	Wilkins / *Peake**	Whitton / *Baird*	Taylor* / *Fox'*	Duguid" / *McDonald*	Adcock/Dunne/Reinelt, *Maya/Andrews*
26	11/1	A DONCASTER	1,458	11	21	35	0-0	0-0	Ref: U Rennie	Emberson / *O'Connor*	Gregory / *Murphy*	Gibbs" / *Ryan*	McCarthy / *Moore*	Greene / *Gore*	Buckle / *McDonald*	Fry / *Schofield*	Wilkins / *Warren*	Whitton / *Larmour*	Adcock / *Cramb*	Abrahams* / *Birch"*	Locke/Dunne, *Doling*
27	14/1	H FULHAM	3,820	7	1	38	2-1	1-0	Abrahams 43, Fry 71; Morgan 65; Ref: M Bailey	Emberson / *Lange*	Gregory / *Watson'*	Gibbs / *Herrera*	McCarthy / *Parker*	Greene! / *Angus*	Buckle / *Cullip*	Fry / *Carpenter**	Wilkins* / *Cockerill"*	Whitton" / *Conroy*	Adcock / *Morgan*	Abrahams / *Scott*	Locke, *Cusack/Freeman/Brooker*
28	18/1	H CARLISLE	3,588	8	2	39	1-1	1-1	Adcock 4p; Archdeacon 34; Ref: P Taylor	Emberson / *Caig*	Gregory / *Edmondson*	Gibbs / *Archdeacon*	McCarthy / *Walling*	Greene / *Varty*	Buckle / *Pounewtchy*	Fry / *Peacock*	Wilkins / *Conway*	Whitton* / *Smart"*	Adcock / *Hayward*	Abrahams* / *Aspinall'*	Locke/Reinelt, *Delap/Thomas*
29	25/1	A EXETER	2,666	7	20	42	3-0	2-0	Abrahams 15, Locke 28, 55; Ref: J Brandwood	Emberson / *Bayes*	Gregory / *Chamberlain/Rice*	Gibbs / *Minett**	McCarthy / *Blake*	Greene / *Richardson N*	Buckle / *Rowbotham*	Fry / *Richardson J*	Wilkins / *Braithwaite*	Locke / *Bailey*	Adcock* / *McConnell*	Abrahams" / —	Lock/Dunne, *Hughes/Flack*
30	31/1	H TORQUAY	3,895	7	11	45	2-0	1-0	Adcock 44, 56; Ref: S Baines	Caldwell / *Wilmot*	Gregory / *Mitchell'*	Gibbs / *Barrow'*	McCarthy / *Hawthorne*	Cawley" / *Gittens*	Buckle / *Watson*	Locke / *Winter*	Wilkins / *Nelson*	Whitton* / *Jack*	Adcock / *McFarlane*	Abrahams / *Stamps*	Reinelt/Dunne, *Oatway/Hathaway*
31	4/2	H LEYTON ORIENT	3,689	6	17	48	2-1	1-1	Wilkins 11, 75; Channing 33; Ref: S Bennett	Vaughan / *Hyde*	Gregory / *Winston*	Gibbs / *Clapham*	McCarthy / *Chapman*	Cawley / *Warren*	Buckle / *Castle*	Locke* / *Channing*	Wilkins / *Ling*	Whitton / *McGleish*	Adcock / *Joseph*	Abrahams / *Baker*	Lock/Locke, *Fry*
32	8/2	A CARDIFF	3,912	6	8	51	2-1	2-0	Adcock 6, Whitton 20; Haworth 90; Ref: G Singh	Vaughan / *Elliott*	Gregory / *Jarman*	Gibbs / *Lloyd*	McCarthy / *Eckhardt*	Greene / *Fowler*	Buckle / *Young**	Locke* / *Watson*	Wilkins / *Middleton'*	Whitton / *White*	Adcock / *Haworth*	Abrahams* / *Ware*	Lock/Locke, *Rodgerson/Gardner*
33	14/2	H CHESTER	3,855	6	10	52	0-0	0-0	Ref: J Kirkby	Vaughan / *Sinclair*	Gregory / *Davidson*	Gibbs / *Jenkins*	McCarthy / *Clapham*	Greene / *Reid*	Buckle / *Alsford*	Locke* / *Flitcroft*	Wilkins / *Priest*	Whitton / *McDonald*	Adcock / *Milner'*	Abrahams / *Noteman*	Lock/Locke, *Whelan*
34	22/2	A SCUNTHORPE	2,738	6	15	52	1-2	0-0	Whitton 89; D'Auria 50, Jones 61; Ref: D Laws	Vaughan / *Clarke*	Gregory / *Walsh*	Gibbs* / *Wilson*	McCarthy / *Sertori*	Greene / *Knill*	Buckle / *Hope*	Fry / *Housham*	Wilkins / *D'Auria*	Locke / *Baker'*	Adcock* / *Jones*	Abrahams* / *Turnbull*	Dunne/Lock/Whitton, *Eyre*

Match reports

24 — v Cambridge: Billy Beall taps into the empty net after Gregory and Emberson make a hash of a clearance. Ex-Cambridge Taylor, gives ex-U's Scott Barrett no chance with a header from Fry's cross. Paul Raynor's drive slips through Emberson's fingers, before Adcock nets his 200th United goal.

25 — v Brighton: The frost-bound Goldstone is staging its last season of football, before being demolished. U's have not won here in 14 attempts. Whitton opens the scoring with a well-executed 25-yard free-kick. Buckle is adjudged to have tripped Ian Baird, giving Denny Mundee the chance to level.

26 — v Doncaster: U's first league game for 14 days, due to postponements. Taylor opts to join Cambridge after U's drag their heels over a deal. Greene has U's best chance when he heads a Fry corner, but sees Gary O'Connor tip it onto the crossbar. Emberson saves well from Darren Moore's header.

27 — v Fulham: Fulham start four points clear at the top. Simon Morgan lashes in a loose ball, off McCarthy. Greene clashes with Rob Scott and sees red (67). A coach-load of Fulham supporters are taken to Cambridge by mistake. Fry gets a sensational winner, running from the halfway line to score.

28 — v Carlisle: Adcock chests down Abrahams' cross, but is felled by Darren Edmondson. Adcock nets goal 201 for U's. Owen Archdeacon is free to run past U's defenders to notch his eighth of the campaign. Sub (45) Reinelt is sent off for lunging at Will Varty (67) and Stephane Pounewatchy (70).

29 — v Exeter: Locke returns from injury to sink the Devonians. Abrahams scores when Ashley Bayes can only parry Adcock's close-range effort. Excellent approach play by Buckle and Abrahams sets up Locke for a 25-yarder. The midfielder gets his second with a volley from Gibbs' corner-kick.

30 — v Torquay: Greene starts his suspension, whilst Caldwell returns after injury. Adcock puts U's in front on the stroke of half-time with a point-blank header from Gibbs' corner. Adcock is on hand, eleven minutes into the second period, to meet Locke's knee-high cross and volley past Rhys Wilmot.

31 — v Leyton Orient: Wignall picks up Manager-of-the-Month for January, and loans Vaughan, 32, from Lincoln. Orient have loanee Paul Hyde (Leicester) in goal. Adcock blazes over, late, after Mark Warren fouls Abrahams in the box. Wilkins' double takes U's unbeaten run to 16 league and cup games.

32 — v Cardiff: Cardiff are fresh from a 4-1 win at leaders Fulham. Adcock scores early from a Gibbs corner and then Whitton puts United further ahead by turning in Gregory's low cross from 18 yards. Deep into injury-time, Jason Fowler feeds Simon Haworth to slot a consolation under Vaughan.

33 — v Chester: U's run puts them eleven points behind Fulham. Fiery Reinelt joins Brighton for £15k, after falling out with Wignall, who denies he is off to Southend after Ronnie Whelan is sacked for a sending off at Man City. U's haven't lost at home since the opening day but have now drawn 16.

34 — v Scunthorpe: Locke asks for a move. Irons Tim Clarke, loaned from York, makes a string of fine saves. David D'Auria fires in a low shot and Gary Jones, also on loan (Notts Co), nods D'Auria's cross. Mark Sertori's poor clearance falls to Whitton. Iron have now drawn 16 clean sheets for a record 20 games.

35	H	28/2	SCARBOROUGH	9	L	1-1	Adcock 24
			3,719	8	52		Williams G 36, 70, Rigby 74
							Ref: D Crick

Lineup: Vaughan, Gregory, Gibbs, McCarthy, Greene, Buckle, Fry, Wilkins", Whitton, Adcock, Abrahams*
Subs: Martin, Kay, Wells, Bennett*, Hicks, Rackett, McElhatton Rigby, Currie`, Williams G, Brodie", Duguid/Locke, Sutherland/Ritchie/Knowles

Wignall pleads 'don't panic' after a dismal defeat. Adcock prods in the loose ball after Kevin Martin had saved from Fry. Gary Williams nets a Gary Bennett pass and an 18-yard volley. Wilkins is hospitalised by a stray elbow, and Tony Rigby returns Vaughan's poor kick into the net.

36	A	7/3	CAMBRIDGE	10	L	0-1	Wanless 6
			3,485	6	52		Ref: C Wilkes

Lineup: Emberson, Gregory, Dunne, McCarthy, Greene, Buckle, Fry*, Locke!, Whitton, Adcock, Abrahams
Subs: Barrett, Joseph, Granville, Preece*, Craddock, Raynor, Wanless, Hyde, Taylor, B"/Edinboro Hayes, Beall, Duguid

Cambridge have secured just seven points from the last 30, whilst U's welcome back Emberson, playing his 100th game, following Vaughan's return to Lincoln. Paul Wanless cracks a low drive from 25 yards. Unsettled Locke is sent off for a high two-footed tackle on Micah Hyde (38).

37	H	14/3	MANSFIELD	10	W	2-0	Greene 37, Adcock 42
			3,064	14	55		Dunne 82 (og)
							Ref: A D'Urso

Lineup: Emberson, Gregory*, Gibbs, McCarthy, Greene, Buckle", Fry*, Wilkins, Whitton, Adcock, Abrahams*
Subs: Bowling, Ford, Harper!, Kilcline, Eustace, Hackett, Clark, Walker`, Hadley, Christie, Doolan!, Sale, Dunne/Pitcher/Locke, Watkiss

Sale makes his league debut against his old club. Barnes is forced to quit, but Forbes signs for free from Millwall. Buckle creates both United's goals. John Doolan (46) and Steve Harper (82) see red for two bookings. Dunne, who had just arrived as sub, heads in Isyeden Christie's cross.

38	H	21/3	ROCHDALE	7	W	1-0	Abrahams 59
			3,211	15	58		Ref: A Wiley

Lineup: Emberson, Gregory, Gibbs, McCarthy, Greene, Buckle, Fry, Wilkins", Whitton", Adcock*, Sale
Subs: Gray, Fensome`, Farrell, Johnson, Hill, Gouck, Russell, Deary, Leonard, Formby`, Stuart, Abrahams/Duguid/Dunne, Robson/Bailey

Wignall warns the players to forget Wembley and concentrate on promotion. Emberson's free-kick is flicked on by Sale for Abrahams to put the ball out of the reach of Ian Gray. Emberson makes a great save from Keith Hill's late downward header to secure vital promotion points.

39	A	29/3	HARTLEPOOL	7	L	0-0	Beech 78
			2,725	22	58		Ref: T Leake

Lineup: Emberson, Gregory`, Gibbs`, McCarthy!, Greene, Buckle, Fry*, Wilkins, Whitton, Adcock", Abrahams*
Subs: O'Connor, Knowles`, Lucas, Beech, Bradley, Davies, Cullen`, Proctor, Baker, Brown, Hislop, Adcock/Stamps/Dunne, Lee/Halliday

Torquay defender Scott Stamps signs for £15k, whilst Pool signed six players on deadline day. McCarthy is sent off for a professional foul on one of the new boys. Michael Brown (Man City). Chris Beech wins the game, heading in from a corner. Stamps debuts as a 58th-minute sub.

40	H	31/3	DARLINGTON	10	L	0-3	Naylor 2, 13, 73p
			3,604	19	58		Ref: G Pooley

Lineup: Emberson, Gregory, Stamps*, McCarthy, Greene, Buckle, Fry, Wilkins, Whitton*, Sale, Abrahams/Gibbs
Subs: Moilanen, Shaw!, Bernard, Reed, Crosby, Hope, Twynham, Bramwell", Roberts*, Naylor, Carss, Brydon/Atkinson

U's clearly have Wembley on their minds. Glenn Naylor pops up unmarked at a free-kick to slot in off the post, then strikes a glorious second. He completes his hat-trick from the penalty spot after Buckle gives Brian Atkinson the slightest nudge. Simon Shaw gets a second yellow (82).

41	A	5/4	HEREFORD	12	L	0-1	McGorry 45
			2,535	22	58		Ref: R Styles

Lineup: Emberson, Gregory, Stamps, McCarthy, Greene, Buckle, Wilkins, Whitton, Sale*, Abrahams, Adcock`/Dunne/Fry
Subs: Wood, Norton, Fishlock, Smith*, Sandeman, Matthewson Hargreaves McGorry, Foster A", Warner, Turner, Brough/Foster I

The U's squad spend the week cutting a Wembley CD. United are down to ten men for 15 minutes whilst Sale receives stitches to his 'nether' region. Brian McGorry's 25-yard free-kick wins it. Buckle is distraught. His booking will mean he's suspended, like McCarthy, for Wembley.

42	A	8/4	WIGAN	13	L	0-1	McGibbon 44
			4,571	1	58		Ref: K Lynch

Lineup: Emberson, Dunne, Stamps, McCarthy, Greene, Buckle, Duguid", Whitton, Sale*, Abrahams*, Fry/Gregory
Subs: Butler, McGibbon, Johnson, Greenall, Bishop, Martinez, Diaz*, Jones, Saville, Rogers, Kilford, Lowe

A left-sided corner gives Manchester United loanee Pat McGibbon the opportunity to confirm Wigan will be second division for next season. Wignall sets his side a target of 70 points to rescue a play-off spot, after the disastrous run of four defeats since winning through to Wembley.

43	H	11/4	SWANSEA	9	W	3-1	Whitton 22, Sale 56, Abrahams 66
			3,162	4	61		Molby 58
							Ref: R Furnandiz

Lineup: Emberson, Stamps, McCarthy, Greene, Buckle, Sale, Duguid", Whitton, Adcock*, Abrahams*, Fry/Duguid
Subs: Freestone, Thomas, Ampadu, Willer, Edwards, Jenkins*, Penney, Molby, Torpey, Quigley, Coates, Heggs

The FA confirm Buckle's suspension. Whitton blasts in Greene's lay-off for U's first goal in 413 minutes. Sale nets his first for United, rising highest to Buckle's corner. Player-boss Jan Molby pulls one back in a crowded box, but Abrahams regains the advantage at the second attempt.

44	A	15/4	HULL	9	W	2-1	Adcock 22, Sale 27
			2,035	15	64		Darby 19
							Ref: R Pearson

Lineup: Emberson, Dunne, Stamps, McCarthy, Greene, Cawley, Sale, Whitton, Adcock*, Abrahams*, Locke/Fry
Subs: Wilson, Trevitt, Rioch, Doncel*, Brien, Wright`, Gordon`, Darby!, Quigley, Peacock, Mann/Greaves/Fewings

Duane Darby is a hero-turned-villain for Tigers. The 20-goal striker races on to a Michael Quigley pass to put Hull in front. United are level when Adcock heads home, then Sale finishes Adcock's flick from 15 yards. Darby is sent off for fouls on Cawley (36) and Emberson (49).

45	H	26/4	NORTHAMPTON	9	D	0-0	Ref: P Rejer
			5,956	6	65		

Lineup: Emberson, Dunne`, Stamps, McCarthy*, Greene, Cawley, Sale, Whitton, Adcock*, Abrahams*, Locke/Gregory/Lock
Subs: Woodman, Clarkson, Maddison, Sampson, Warburton, Rennie, Frain, Cooper, Gayle", White`, Hunter, Grayson/Gibb

Last season Atkins' side opened the door for U's to win through to the play-offs with a last-day victory at Wigan. This result closes the door firmly shut for United. Cobblers needed a win to ensure their own play-off place, but fail when Cawley clears Jason White's effort off the line.

46	A	3/5	BARNET	8	W	4-2	Lock 14, Sale 35, Forbes 56, Haydon 86
			1,909	15	68		Campbell 6, Hodges 58
							Ref: B Harris

Lineup: Emberson, Dunne, Stamps, Forbes*, Greene, Cawley, Sale, Whitton, Adcock*, Abrahams*, McCarthy/Haydon
Subs: Harrison, Stackley, Gale, Goodhild, Primus, Howarth, Hodges", Adams`, Wilson, Gayle`, White`, Campbell, Simpson/Brady

U's look at the University of Essex as a possible stadium site. Stamps crosses to Lock to score at the second attempt. Sale turns and strikes a low shot past Lee Harrison. Forbes scores a great goal on his debut, as does sub Haydon. U's agonisingly miss the play-offs by a single point.

Home 3,254 Away 3,003 Average 3,254

NATIONWIDE DIVISION 3 (CUP-TIES) Manager: Steve Wignall SEASON 1996-97

Coca-Cola Cup

1:1 H WEST BROM 20/8 — 2,466 — L 2-3 (H-T 1-1)
Scorers: Kinsella 1, Fry 76 / Hunt 22, Hamilton 71, Donovan 85 — Ref: D Orr

1	2	3	4	5	6	7	8	9	10	11	subs used
Caldwell	Betts*	Barnes	McCarthy	Greene	Cawley	Kinsella	Locke	Whitton	Adcock	Reinelt	Fry
Spink	*Holmes*	*Nicholson*	*Sneekes*	*Marden*	*Raven*	*Hamilton*	*Gilbert*	*Taylor*	*Hunt**	*Groves**	*Donovan/Cunnington*

Kinsella justifies his price-tag with a stunning 20-yarder on 48 seconds. Jonathan Hunt heads in Dave Gilbert's cross, then Ian Hamilton does likewise. Fry slides in to meet Reinelt's cross for 2-2, but Kevin Donovan has the last say to give Baggies a rather undeserved first-leg lead.

1:2 A WEST BROM 3/9 — 9,809 (1:18) — W 3-1 (H-T 1-0)
Scorers: Reinelt 22, 49, Dunne 53 / Groves 83 — Ref: A Leake — (Colchester won 5-4 on aggregate)

1	2	3	4	5	6	7	8	9	10	11	subs used
Caldwell*	Dunne	Betts	Gregory	Greene	Cawley	Kinsella	Locke	Whitton	Reinelt*	Wilkins	Adcock/Fry
Spink	*Holmes*	*Marden*	*Burgess*	*Nicholson**	*Hamilton*	*Sneekes**	*Groves*	*Gilbert**	*Taylor*	—	*Peschisolido/Cunnington/Donovan/Ashcroft*

Reinelt cracks a superb 20-yarder, via a great Gregory pass. Caldwell fails to come out for the second half, and is replaced between the sticks by Whitton. Reinelt and Dunne both strike tremendous drives, before Whitton is finally beaten by Paul Groves. Baggies fans applaud U's off.

2:1 A HUDDERSFIELD 17/9 — 5,112 (1:10) — D 1-1 (H-T 0-1)
Scorers: Adcock 46 / Cowan 45 — Ref: S Baines

1	2	3	4	5	6	7	8	9	10	11	subs used
Emberson	Dunne	Betts	McCarthy	Greene	Cawley	Kinsella	Locke	Fry*	Adcock	Wilkins	Duguid
Francis	*Jenkins*	*Cowan*	*Bullock*	*Collins Sam Gray*	*Reid**	*Burnett*	*Stewart*	*Payton*	*Edwards**	—	*Lawson/Collins Simon*

Birthday-boy Wignall is delighted with a draw at the impressive McAlpine Stadium. Town parade £150k Wayne Burnett. He had joined hours earlier from Bolton. Tom Cowan nets from Paul Reid's corner. Town's tackle on Fry sees the ball run to Adcock just 35 seconds into the half.

2:2 H HUDDERSFIELD 24/9 — 4,095 (1:14) — L 0-2 (H-T 0-0) aet
Scorers: Stewart 98, Collins Simon 110 — Ref: M Pierce — (Colchester lost 1-3 on aggregate)

1	2	3	4	5	6	7	8	9	10	11	subs used
Emberson	Dunne*	Betts*	McCarthy	Greene	Cawley	Locke	Reinelt	Fry*	Adcock	Wilkins	Whitton/Duguid/Gregory
Francis	*Jenkins*	*Cowan**	*Bullock*	*Makel**	*Gray*	*Reid*	*Burnett*	*Stewart*	*Payton*	*Edwards**	*Col's Sam/Col's Sim/Law'n*

Marcus Stewart, £1.2m from Bristol Rovers, breaks the deadlock eight minutes into extra-time. Betts fails to cut out a cross-field ball, leaving Stewart with a clear run on goal. U's hopes are dashed when Andy Payton plays a square ball through to Simon Collins, to slot past Emberson.

Autowindscreen Shield

1 A CAMBRIDGE 10/12 — 1,108 (3:3) — W 1-0 (H-T 0-0)
Scorers: Whitton 89 — Ref: S Mathieson

1	2	3	4	5	6	7	8	9	10	11	subs used
Emberson	Gregory	Barnes	Locke*	Greene	Cawley	Fry	Wilkins	Whitton	Taylor	Abrahams	Dunne
Barrett	*Joseph Matt Granville*	*Wanless*	*Craddock*	*Raynor**	*Hayes*	*Hyde*	*Turner*	*Richards**	*Beall*	—	*Joseph Marci/B'ell-Edinboro*

Roy McFarland's Cambridge lost 0-2 at home to GMVC Woking in the FA Cup on Saturday. With just 60 seconds left and extra-time and the new 'golden goal' rule looming, Taylor knocks a Dunne cross into the path of Whitton to strike a sweet left-foot shot past keeper Scott Barrett.

2 A MILLWALL 7/1 — 2,759 (2:3) — W 3-2 (H-T 0-1)
Scorers: Adcock 53, 88, Buckle 93 / Crawford 10, Savage 76 — Ref: R Harris — (Colchester won on golden goal)

1	2	3	4	5	6	7	8	9	10	11	subs used
Emberson	Gregory	Barnes	McCarthy	Greene	Buckle	Fry*	Wilkins	Whitton	Adcock	Abrahams	Locke
Iga	*Newman*	*Harie*	*Savage*	*Webber*	*Rogan**	*Hartley*	*Wilkins*	*Crawford**	*Bright*	*Dolby*	*Sinclair/Doyle/Van Blerk*

Lions include Ray Wilkins, on a match-to-match basis. Paul Hartley's cross is headed goalwards by Mark Bright, for Jimmy Crawford to beat Emberson. Adcock levelled at 2-2 with a delicate chip over nervy Andrew Iga. Buckle volleys a 'golden goal', 140 seconds into added time.

3 A BRENTFORD 28/1 — 2,253 (2:1) — W 1-0 (H-T 1-0)
Scorers: Abrahams 35 — Ref: K Leach

1	2	3	4	5	6	7	8	9	10	11	subs used
Emberson	Gregory	Barnes	Gibbs	McCarthy	Cawley	Fry	Wilkins	Locke	Adcock	Abrahams*	Taylor
Dearden	*Hutchings*	*Statham*	*Ashby*	*Bates*	*McGhee*	*Asaba*	*Smith**	*Dennis*	*Bent*	*Taylor*	*McPherson/Omigie*

Wignall returns to Griffin Pk, home of the second division leaders, where he once was club skipper. U's stun the home side when Adcock finds Abrahams in space. The ex-Bees striker spots Kevin Dearden off his line and plants a great shot over the keeper into the top corner of the net.

4 H NORTHAMPTON 18/2 — 3,978 (3:8) — W 2-1 (H-T 0-0)
Scorers: Greene 66, Buckle 75 / Martin 67 — Ref: N Barry

1	2	3	4	5	6	7	8	9	10	11	subs used
Vaughan!	Gregory	Barnes	Locke*	Greene	Buckle	Fry	Wilkins	Whitton	Adcock	Abrahams*	Cawley/Lock
Woodman	*Clarkson*	*Maddison**	*Hunter*	*Warburton*	*Sampson*	*Martin**	*Rennie*	*Gayle*	*Lee*	*Frain*	*Colkin/White*

U's are up against it when Vaughan is sent off (22) for racing out of his area and colliding with Chris Lee. Cawley takes over in goal. Greene rises to head in Locke's cross, only for Dave Martin to level within a minute. Buckle side-foots the winner after Adcock beats two defenders.

SF 1 A PETERBOROUGH 11/3 — 4,556 (2:22) — L 0-2 (H-T 0-1)
Scorers: Otto 14, Charlery 55 — Ref: B Burns

1	2	3	4	5	6	7	8	9	10	11	subs used
Emberson	Gregory	Dunne	McCarthy	Greene	Buckle	Fry*	Locke	Whitton	Adcock	Duguid*	Sale/Gibbs
Tyler	*Boothroyd*	*Spearing*	*Edwards*	*Bodley*	*Ramage**	*Donowa**	*Payne*	*Willis*	*Charlery*	*Otto*	*Morrison/Le Bihan*

Sale debuts on the hour as U's already trail to Ricky Otto's mazy run past Gregory and McCarthy. Andy Edwards hits a 60-yard pass for Ken Charlery to outpace Greene. Barry Fry praises U's noisy 700-strong following, but warns his Peterborough side that the tie is far from finished.

SF 2 H PETERBOROUGH 18/3 — 5,000 (2:22) — W 3-0 (H-T 1-0)
Scorers: Fry 38, Buckle 80, Abrahams 100 — Ref: U Rennie — (Colchester won on golden goal)

1	2	3	4	5	6	7	8	9	10	11	subs used
Emberson	Gregory	Gibbs*	McCarthy	Greene	Buckle	Fry	Locke	Whitton	Adcock	Sale	Abrahams/Locke
Griemink	*Boothroyd*	*Spearing*	*Edwards*	*Heald*	*Bodley*	*Le Bihan**	*Payne*	*Willis*	*Charlery*	*Cleaver**	*Donowa/Houghton*

Gregory's free-kick is deflected by Andy Edwards for Fry to stick out his boot and divert over the line. Buckle takes the game into extra-time. Sub Abrahams sends United to Wembley for the second time with a majestic 'golden goal' winner.

F N CARLISLE 20/4 — 45,077 (3:3) — L 0-0 (H-T 0-0) aet — (at Wembley)
Scorers: Ref: J Kirkby — (Colchester lost 3-4 on pens)

1	2	3	4	5	6	7	8	9	10	11	subs used
Emberson	Dunne	Gregory*	McCarthy	Greene	Cawley	Wilkins	Sale	Whitton	Adcock	Abrahams*	Fry/Locke/Duguid
Caig	*Delap*	*Archdeacon Whalley*	*Varty*	*Conway*	*Pounew'tchy*	*Conway*	*Peacock*	*Smart**	*Hayward*	*Aspinall*	*Thomas/Jansen*

The biggest attendance of the weekend in England, only bettered by 46,989 at Celtic v Aberdeen, watch a nervy final with very few clear-cut chances. Owen Archdeacon, Cawley and Duguid miss spot-kicks, enabling Skipper Steve Hayward to grab the winner and collect the trophy.

FA Cup

	H							
1	WYCOMBE	13	L	1:2	0:1	Wilkins 69		
16/11	4,376	2:24				De Souza 43, Williams 65		
						Ref: J Winter		

Emberson Dunne Gibbs Greene Gregory* Fry Wilkins
Chesewright Cousins Bell Evans Crossley McCarthy Carroll Brown*
Reinelt^ Locke Abrahams Adcock/Duguid
Williams McGavin De Souza Paterson

Wignall has to make do without Taylor, who is ineligible. Excellent work down the right flank by John Williams sets up Miguel De Souza. Williams is at least five yards offside for the second. Wilkins reduces the arrears, even though a hooligan United fan is on the loose in the area.

		P	W	D	L	F	A	W	D	L	F	A	Pts
				Home					Away				
1	Wigan	46	17	3	3	53	21	9	6	8	31	30	87
2	Fulham	46	13	5	5	41	20	12	7	4	31	18	87
3	Carlisle	46	16	3	4	41	21	8	9	6	26	23	84
4	Northampton*	46	14	4	5	43	17	6	8	9	24	27	72
5	Swansea	46	13	5	5	37	20	8	3	12	25	38	71
6	Chester	46	11	8	4	30	16	7	8	8	25	27	70
7	Cardiff	46	11	4	8	30	23	9	5	9	26	31	69
8	COLCHESTER	46	11	9	3	36	23	6	8	9	26	28	68
9	Lincoln	46	10	8	5	35	25	8	4	11	35	44	66
10	Cambridge	46	11	5	7	30	27	7	6	10	23	32	65
11	Mansfield	46	9	8	6	21	17	7	8	8	26	28	64
12	Scarborough	46	9	9	5	36	31	7	6	10	29	37	63
13	Scunthorpe	46	11	3	9	36	33	4	6	10	23	29	63
14	Rochdale	46	10	6	7	34	24	4	10	9	24	34	58
15	Barnet	46	9	9	5	32	23	5	7	11	14	28	58
16	Leyton Orient	46	11	6	6	28	20	4	6	13	22	38	57
17	Hull	46	9	8	6	29	26	4	10	9	15	24	57
18	Darlington	46	11	5	7	37	28	3	5	15	27	50	52
19	Doncaster	46	9	7	7	29	23	5	3	15	23	43	52
20	Hartlepool	46	9	6	9	33	32	6	3	14	20	34	51
21	Torquay	46	9	4	10	24	24	4	7	12	22	38	50
22	Exeter	46	6	9	8	25	30	6	3	14	23	43	48
23	Brighton**	46	12	6	5	41	27	1	4	18	12	43	47
24	Hereford	46	6	8	9	26	25	5	6	12	24	40	47
		1104	256	148	148	807	576	148	148	256	576	807	1506

* promoted after play-offs
** deducted 2 points

Odds & ends

Double wins: (3) Barnet, Exeter, Torquay.
Double defeats: (1) Hartlepool.

Won from behind: (3) Wigan (h), Hull (a), Barnet (a).
Lost from in front: (3) Northampton (a), Lincoln (a), Scarborough (h).

High spots: Reaching Wembley for the second time in the club's history. Fine cup performances against division one sides Huddersfield and West Brom, and division two Brentford and Millwall. Crushing 7-1 Layer Road victory over Lincoln. Just one defeat in 22 league and cup games from October. The progression of Mark Kinsella from Youth team to Charlton.

Low spots: Failure to reach the play-offs by just one point. Punishing four straight defeats after qualifying for the Wembley final. Losing at Wembley on penalties, without conceding a goal. Only one win in the first eleven league games. Nine home draws. Eight red cards in all competitions.

Player of the Year: Chris Fry.
Ever presents: (0).
Hat-tricks: (0).
Leading scorer: Tony Adcock (14) (including 2 in Autowindscrn Shield).

Appearances / Goals

	Lge	Sub	LC	Sub	FAC	Sub	Lge	LC	FAC	Tot
	Appearances						Goals			
Abrahams, Paul	27	2		1	1		7			7
Adcock, Tony	26	10	3	1	1		11	1		12
Barnes, David	11	1								
Betts, Simon	10	4					1			1
Buckle, Paul	24		2							
Caldwell, Garrett	6									
Cawley, Peter	28		4				1			1
Duguid, Karl	10	10		2		1	3			3
Dunne, Joe	23	12	3		1			1		1
Emberson, Carl	35		2		2					
Forbes, Steve	1						1			1
Fry, Chris	31	11	2	2	2		6		1	7
Gibbs, Paul	18	2			1					
Greene, David	44		4		1		2			2
Gregory, David	32	6	1	1	1	1	1			1
Haydon, Nicky		1					1			1
Kelly, Tony	2	1								
Kinsella, Mark	7		3				2			2
Lock, Tony	1	5					1			1
Locke, Adam	22	10	3	1	1		4			4
McCarthy, Tony	34	1	3							
Pitcher, Geoff		1								
Reinelt, Robbie	8	13	4		1		3	2		5
Sale, Mark	10						3			3
Stamps, Scott	7	1								
Taylor, John	8						5			5
Vaughan, John	5									
Whitton, Steve	36	3	3	2	1		6			6
Wilkins, Richard	40		3		1		2	1		3
(own-goals)							2			2
29 players used	506	89	44	8	11	2	62	5	1	68

NATIONWIDE LEAGUE DIVISION 3

Manager: Steve Wignall — SEASON 1997-98

No	H/A	Date	Opponent	Att	Res	Pos	Pt	F-A	H-T	U's Scorers	Opp Scorers	Referee
1	H	9/8	DARLINGTON	2,958	W	3	3	2-1	1-0	Abrahams 32, Buckle 59p	Oliver 74p	B Knight
2	A	16/8	HARTLEPOOL	2,174	L	8	3	2-3	1-1	Buckle 38p, Abrahams 60	Baker 38p, Allon 56, 63	P Robinson
3	H	22/8	BARNET	3,286	D	12	4	1-1	0-0	Wilkins 72	Howarth 59	M Bailey
4	A	30/8	TORQUAY	2,081	D	14	5	1-1	0-0	Wilkins 65	Gittens 85	D Crick
5	A	2/9	CAMBRIDGE	3,254	L	17	5	1-4	1-1	Gregory D 36	Butler 6, 46, Taylor 61, 68	F Stretton
6	H	8/9	BRIGHTON	3,081	W	12	8	3-1	1-0	Greene 4, 57, Abrahams 49	Baird 47	J Kirkby
7	H	12/9	SCARBOROUGH	2,756	W	10	11	1-0	0-0	Lock 87		A Wiley
8	A	20/9	SWANSEA	3,414	W	7	14	1-0	0-0	Greene 49		S Mathieson
9	H	27/9	EXETER	3,175	L	9	14	1-2	0-1	Abrahams 52	Rowbotham 28, Flack 56	A Butler
10	A	4/10	MANSFIELD	2,341	D	9	15	1-1	1-1	Greene 12	Whitehall 6	K Lynch
11	A	11/10	PETERBOROUGH	6,277	L	11	15	2-3	1-0	Rankin 32, Adcock 82	Carruthers 55, Houghton 58, Quinn 78	P Taylor

Line-ups (1–11 and subs used)

1. DARLINGTON
U's: Emberson; Gregory D; Stamps; Devas; Greene; Cawley; Wilkins; Buckle; Sale*; Abrahams; Hathaway. Subs: Adcock/Forbes
Darlington: Preece; Shaw; Barnard; Devos*; Crosby; Hope*; Oliver; Lowe; Roberts*; Shutt; Naylor*. Subs: Turnbull/Robinson/Brydon!
U's get a £55k shirt sponsor and £100k three-year kit deal. Fry (Exeter) and McCarthy (Shelbourne) move on, whilst Hathaway (Torquay) and Skelton (Luton) join. Jason Devos impedes Abrahams and Gregory trips Mark Barnard. Sub Lee Brydon is sent off (81) for a two-footed foul.

2. HARTLEPOOL
U's: Emberson; Gregory D; Stamps; Skelton*; Greene; Cawley; Wilkins; Buckle*; Sale*; Abrahams; Hathaway. Subs: Adcock/Lock/Forbes
Hartlepool: Davis; Knowles; Lucas; Ingram; Davies; Bradley; Allon*; Cullen; Baker; Barron; Halliday.
U's net £300k from the Burley saga. Wignall fumes 'If Pool finish above us, then I'm on my bike' Wilkins is shoved by Denny Ingram. but U's allow Joe Allon too much space on two occasions. Stingy Pool charge U's players for programmes as the needle in this fixture continues.

3. BARNET
U's: Emberson; Gregory D; Stamps; Skelton*; Greene; Cawley*; Wilkins; Buckle; Sale; Abrahams; Hathaway. Subs: Adcock/Lock/Forbes
Barnet: Harrison; Stackley*; Harle*; Heald; Howarth; Ford; Manuel*; Simpson; Charlery; Devine; Wilson. Subs: Onwere/Goodhind/Mustafa
Wilkins' mis-directed cross-field ball leads to a corner, from which Lee Howarth puts the Bees in front. Wilkins atones for his earlier error by meeting Greene's inch-perfect cross with a powerful header. Wignall is glad that he didn't have to pay to watch U's abysmal performance.

4. TORQUAY
U's: Emberson; Gregory D; Stamps; Forbes; Greene; Cawley; Wilkins; Buckle; Sale; Abrahams; Hathaway.
Torquay: Gregg; Gurney; Gibbs; Robinson; Gittens; Watson; Clayton; Mitchell*; Jack; McFarlane*; McCall*. Subs: Barrow/Hill/Bedeau
U's field four ex-Gulls players in Stamps, Buckle, Sale and Hathaway, whilst the home side have ex-U's Paul Gibbs. Matt Gregg saves Sale's header, but Wilkins taps in the loose ball. U's should be 3-0 up by the time Lee Barrow's 45-yard free-kick falls into the path of Jon Gittens.

5. CAMBRIDGE
U's: Emberson; Gregory D; Stamps; Forbes*; Greene; Cawley; Wilkins; Buckle*; Sale; Adcock*; Abrahams. Subs: Lock/Haydon/Whitton
Cambridge: Barrett; Chenery; Wilson; Joseph Marc Foster; Campbell; Wanless; Rees; Kyd*; Butler; Taylor; Youngs
U's, who miss the reliable McCarthy, gift three of the four goals. Martin Butler knocks in Emberson's poor punch. No one picks up Butler from Paul Wilson's corner. Cawley is robbed by Jason Rees for John Taylor's first. His second comes from a glorious Michael Kyd pull-back.

6. BRIGHTON
U's: Emberson; Gregory D; Stamps*; Forbes; Greene; Cawley; Wilkins; Buckle; Sale; Adcock*; Abrahams. Subs: Lock/Haydon
Brighton: Ormrod; Smith; Hobson; Armstrong*; Morris; Johnson; Storer; Mayo; Baird; Maskell*; Reinelt. Subs: Westcott/McDonald
The game is switched due to Saturday's funeral of Diana, Princess of Wales. U's set-piece training pays off when Greene nods in Stamps' corner, and later, one from Buckle. Seagulls' goal comes when Craig Maskell finds Ian Baird in space. Caldwell walks out on U's to a job in USA.

7. SCARBOROUGH
U's: Emberson; Gregory D; Stamps; Forbes*; Greene; Cawley; Wilkins; Buckle*; Sale*; Adcock*; Abrahams. Subs: Lock/Hathaway
Scarborough: Martin; Key; Sutherland; Snodin; Bennett G; Rackett; Williams; V d Velden*; Robinson; Brodie; Bennett T*. Subs: Campbell/McElhatton
Sub Lock finds the key to Mick Wadsworth's Boro defence when Kevin Martin can only punch a cross into his path. He strikes a sweet volley from the edge of the box. Forbes had earlier struck the inside of the post, and Boro's Neil Campbell had a goal ruled out for a foul on Gregory.

8. SWANSEA
U's: Emberson; Gregory D; Stamps; Forbes*; Greene; Cawley; Wilkins; Buckle; Sale; Adcock*; Abrahams. Subs: Lock/Whitton
Swansea: Freestone; Price; Agnew; Walker; Edwards; Coates; Appleby; O'Gorman; Bird; Ampadu*; Hills*. Subs: Jones/Heggs
Abrahams (100) and Wilkins (200) reach league appearance milestones at last season's play-off semi-finalists. United rocket up the table with Greene's third of the term, a header from Wilkins' perfectly-flighted cross. Dave O'Gorman rattles the crossbar with just six minutes to go.

9. EXETER
U's: Emberson; Gregory D; Stamps; Skelton*; Greene!; Cawley; Wilkins; Buckle; Sale*; Adcock*; Rankin. Subs: Adcock/Lock
Exeter: Bayes; Gale; Fry; Blake; Curran*; Richardson; Rowbotham; Birch; Flack; Gardner; Williams*. Subs: Braithwaite/Baddeley
Arsenal's Rankin, 19, signs a three-month loan. John Williams pulls back for Darren Rowbotham to score. Sale forces Ashley Bayes to drop Skelton's shot, for Abrahams to level. Steve Flack taps in Emberson's parry, then gets Greene red-carded (62) with a theatrical 'elbowed' fall.

10. MANSFIELD
U's: Emberson; Gregory D; Stamps; Skelton*; Greene; Cawley; Wilkins*; Forbes*; Sale; Abrahams; Whitton. Subs: Adcock
Mansfield: Bowling; Ford; Harper; Hassell; Eustace; Hackett; Schofield; Sedgemore; Christie; Whitehall*; Doolan. Subs: Hadley
Sale, in his desperation to put one over his old club, misses a hat-trick of opportunities. Steve Harper's right-wing cross finds Steve Whitehall. Emberson saves Whitehall's spot-kick (23) after Greene, who had netted via Ian Bowling flapped at Buckle's corner, trips Iyseden Christie.

11. PETERBOROUGH
U's: Emberson; Gregory D; Stamps; Skelton; Whitton; Cawley; Wilkins; Forbes*; Sale*; Adcock; Rankin. Subs: Abrahams/Duguid
Peterborough: Tyler; McMenamin; Lewis; Bullimore; Bodley; Edwards; Farrell; Castle; Carruthers; Quinn*; Houghton; DeSouza
Greene is suspended through lack of video evidence. Rankin opens his account via Forbes' flick. Mick Bodley fouls Sale (46), but Mark Tyler saves Adcock's kick. Posh reply with three, including Jimmy Quinn's eleventh of the term. Adcock gets a diving header from Duguid's cross.

Colchester United — match-by-match record (matches 12–23)

No	H/A	Date	Opponent	Att	U's Pos	Opp Pos	Res	Score	HT	Pts
12	H	18/10	SHREWSBURY	2,977	13	19	D	1-1	0-1	16
13	H	21/10	DONCASTER		10	24	W	2-1	2-1	19
14	A	25/10	LEYTON ORIENT	4,592	7	17	W	2-0	1-0	22
15	H	31/10	SCUNTHORPE	3,134	9	7	D	3-3	3-0	23
16	A	4/11	MACCLESFIELD	1,577	7	12	D	0-0	0-0	24
17	A	8/11	ROCHDALE	1,702	12	17	L	1-2	0-1	24
18	H	18/11	NOTTS CO	2,643	10	3	W	2-0	0-0	27
19	H	22/11	LINCOLN	2,932	12	1	L	0-1	0-0	27
20	A	29/11	ROTHERHAM	3,259	13	7	L	2-3	0-1	27
21	A	13/12	HULL	3,895	16	20	L	1-3	0-0	27
22	H	19/12	CHESTER	1,867	14	9	W	2-0	1-0	30
23	A	26/12	BRIGHTON (at Gillingham)	2,647	14	23	D	4-4	3-0	31

12 — SHREWSBURY (H) 1-1
U's: Emberson, Gall, Haydon, Stamps, Skelton, Whitton*, Cawley, Buckle, Forbes", Sale*, Adcock, Rankin. Subs: Brown/Abrahams/Duguid.
Shrewsbury: Blaney, Hammer, White, Herbert, Wilding, Berkley*, Brown M, White, Seabury, Currie, Preece. Sub: Dempsey.
Scorers: Skelton 51; Seabury 25. Ref: B Harris
Brown, 20, is loaned from Ipswich. Whitton limps out of his 100th U's league appearance. Buckle's corner is half-cleared by Peter Wilding to Skelton, who scores a stunning first-ever goal from 30 yards. Kevin Seabury had earlier also netted his first, via Haydon's unlucky knock-on.

13 — DONCASTER (H) 2-1
U's: Emberson, Gregory D*, Stamps, Skelton, Haydon, Cawley, Buckle, Forbes, Sale, Adcock, Abrahams. Sub: Duguid.
Doncaster: Williams, Sanders, Pemberton, Warren, Gore, Dobbin, Cunningham, McDonald, Mike, Ireland, Hawes". Sub: Moncrieffe.
Scorers: Sale 6, Skelton 8, McDonald 31. Ref: A D'Urso
U's are expected to whip four-point Rovers, who like W Ham have no shirt sponsors. All looks well when Sale nets after good work by Forbes and Haydon, followed by another Skelton piledriver. From then on, U's play degenerates, allowing Rovers to score through Mike McDonald.

14 — LEYTON ORIENT (A) 2-0
U's: Emberson, Gregory D, Stamps, Skelton, Greene, Cawley, Buckle, Forbes, Sale, Adcock*, Lock*. Subs: Haydon/Abrahams.
Leyton Orient: Hyde, Warren, Naylor, Smith, Hicks, Channing`, Ling, Inglethorpe, Griffiths, Baker, Colkin`. Subs: West/Linger.
Scorers: Adcock 4, Forbes 78. Ref: A Bates
Adcock gets the faintest of touches to Greene's low cross. Stamps clearly fouls Joe Baker in the box, but amazingly stays on as O's are only awarded a free-kick. Forbes gets his first of the term, ignoring the calls of well-placed Sale, to drive past Paul Hyde into the corner of the net.

15 — SCUNTHORPE (H) 3-3
U's: Emberson, Gregory D*, Stamps*, Skelton, Greene, Cawley`, Buckle, Forbes, Sale, Adcock*, Rankin. Subs: Lock/Brown/Whitton.
Scunthorpe: Clarke, Walsh, McAuley, Sertori, Laws, Hope, Walker, D'Auria`, Eyre, Forrester, Marshall*. Sub: Calvo-Garcia.
Scorers: Rankin 2, Buckle 35, Sale 40, Hope 52, D'Auria 61, 63. Ref: R Furmandiz
Rankin returns, in Adcock's 300th league game, to intercept David D'Auria's back-pass. Cawley, playing with pain-killing foot injections, is subbed at half-time. Iron blitz sorry U's with three goals, and only Emberson's acrobatic save from Jamie Forrester (86) prevents a defeat.

16 — MACCLESFIELD (A) 0-0
U's: Emberson, Gregory D, Stamps, Skelton, Greene, Cawley, Whitton, Forbes, Sale, Adcock*, Rankin`. Subs: Buckle/Duguid.
Macclesfield: Price, Timson, Gardiner, Payne, Whittaker, Sodje, Cooper, Wood, Landon*, Irving`, Sorvel. Subs: Peel/Power.
Ref: C Foy
Last season's GMVC champions Macclesfield had started the season like a train, but have faltered of late. Emberson makes up for the faux-pas against Scunthorpe with good saves from Steve Wood (twice) and Neil Sorvel. Ex-Grecian Mark Cooper 'scores' on 88 minutes, but is offside.

17 — ROCHDALE (A) 1-2
U's: Emberson, Gregory D*, Stamps, Skelton, Greene, Cawley, Whitton, Forbes, Sale, Adcock`, Duguid. Subs: Dunne/Lock.
Rochdale: Edwards, Fensome, Barlow, Hill, Farrell, Gouck, Bryson, Painter, Leonard, Russell, Stuart.
Scorers: Duguid 60, Stuart 44, Painter 65p. Ref: T Heilbron
Greene gifts Dale the points. His half-clearance falls to Mark Stuart, who lets fly past Emerson. Duguid levels from the angle of the box, only for Greene to inexplicably handle Robbie Painter's cross, that Dunne, returning from a pre-season broken shin, would have easily cleared up.

18 — NOTTS CO (H) 2-0
U's: Emberson, Dunne, Stamps", Skelton, Gregory D, Cawley, Abrahams, Rankin, Sale, Whitton, Duguid*. Subs: Hathaway/Forbes.
Notts Co: Ward, Hendon, Pearce, Redmile, Strodder, Hogg*, Finnan, Derry, Jones, Jackson`, Baraclough. Subs: Richardson/Robson.
Scorers: Sale 67, Rankin 86. Ref: R Styles
County start level at the top with free-scoring Posh, on 33 points, and had beaten Colwyn Bay in the Cup on Sunday. Sale finds his goal touch to volley Abrahams' cross for his fourth in seven. Rankin notches his third, charging onto Greene's clearance to slot past keeper Darren Ward.

19 — LINCOLN (H) 0-1
U's: Emberson, Dunne, Betts*, Skelton, Gregory D, Cawley !, Abrahams, Rankin, Sale, Whitton, Duguid`. Subs: Adcock/Hathaway.
Lincoln: Richardson, Barnett, Whitney, Fleming, Holmes, Austin, Walling, Thorpe, Gordon, Smith, Hone.
Scorers: Gordon 61. Ref: R Pearson
Imps have put together a 14-match unbeaten run to go top of the table. Cawley is booked protesting Gavin Gordon's goal is offside, after Mark Hone's shot rebounds. Dean Walling thunders the bar (30) from Hone's cross. Cawley gets a second yellow in the 90th minute for a late tackle.

20 — ROTHERHAM (A) 2-3
U's: Emberson, Dunne, Betts, Skelton, Gregory D*, Cawley, Hathaway, Skelton*, Sale, Whitton, Duguid. Sub: Rankin.
Rotherham: Mimms, Clark, Hurst, Garner, Knill, Richardson, Berry, Thompson, White*, Glover, Roscoe. Sub: Hayward.
Scorers: Skelton 47, Sale 61, Glover 11, 62, Knill 73. Ref: B Burns
U's have still to beat the Millers after 17 league and cup meetings. Skelton cracks U's first-ever league goal at Millmoor. Sale, head bandaged after a clash with Alan Knill, nods in Gregory's cross. Rotherham fight back and win it via Lee Glover and Knill's finish, in a crowded area.

21 — HULL (A) 1-3
U's: Emberson, Dunne, Gregory D, Skelton, Greene, Cawley, Wilkins, Haydon, Forbes*, Whitton, Forbes*. Subs: Stamps*/Lock/Buckle/Hathaway.
Hull: Wilson, Lowthorpe, Rioch, Dewhurst, Hocking, Joyce, Bettney, Rocastle, Darby, Hodges, Mann.
Scorers: Adcock 88, Dewhurst 54, Rioch 57p, Darby 82. Ref: M Jones
Hull manager Mark Hateley has recently recruited ex-Gunner David Rocastle. Wignall slams calls for his head, after a terrible show. Duane Darby misses five easy chances before actually scoring. Greg Rioch, son of Bruce, takes a dubious fall when tussling with Forbes in the area.

22 — CHESTER (H) 2-0
U's: Emberson, Dunne*, Gregory D, Skelton, Greene, Cawley, Wilkins, Haydon, Forbes, Adcock, Stamps. Sub: Duguid.
Chester: Sinclair, Davidson, Jenkins, Richardson, Whelan, Johnson, Bennett, McDonald, Alsford, Rimmer, Flitcroft, Thomas*. Sub: Woods.
Scorers: Adcock 13, Duguid 75. Ref: M Pierce
Wignall chases £25k Gills striker Dennis Bailey. Despite only two wins in twelve, United are just seven points behind Chester, who occupy seventh place. Adcock gets his 125th U's goal, volleying in Stamps' corner. Sub Duguid instinctively fires back Rod McDonald's clearance.

23 — BRIGHTON (A, at Gillingham) 4-4
U's: Emberson, Dunne, Gregory D, Skelton", Greene, Cawley, Wilkins, Rankin, Forbes*, Adcock, Stamps. Subs: Duguid/Buckle.
Brighton: Rust, Smith, Tuck`, Minton, Hobson, Johnson, Storer, Mayo, Barker, Emblem, Linger. Subs: Westcott.
Scorers: Rankin 15, 29, Adcock 23, Stamps 75, Emblem 47, 61, 67, Minton 86p. Ref: M Halsey
Rankin grabs a double in his last loan game. U's concede a three-goal lead for the second time this season when Charlton loanee Paul Emblem completes a quick treble after Emberson drops Jeff Minton's cross. Cawley pushes Emblem in the box, after Stamps had restored U's lead.

NATIONWIDE LEAGUE DIVISION 3   Manager: Steve Wignall   SEASON 1997-98

No	Date		Scorers, Times, and Referees	Att	Pos	Pt	F-A	H-T	1	2	3	4	5	6	7	8	9	10	11	subs used
24	H 29/12	CAMBRIDGE	Wilkins 45, 48, Skelton 67 / Barnwell-Edinboro 6, 69 / Ref: P Rejer	4,518	13 15	W 34	3-2	1-1	Emberson / *Barrett*	Dunne / *Chenery*	Gregory D / *Wilson*	Skelton / *Ashbee*	Greene / *Foster**	Cawley / *Campbell*	Wilkins / *Rees**	Whitton / *Kyd*	Sale* / *Taylor**	Adcock / *B'll-Edinbro*	Duguid* / *Beall*	Lock/Haydon *Benjamin/Joseph/Radosth's*
25	H 3/1	HARTLEPOOL	Buckle 81 / Clarke 13, Howard 75 / Ref: A Wiley	2,885	13 6	L 34	1-2	0-1	Emberson / *Hollund*	Dunne / *Knowles*	Gregory D" / *Lucas**	Skelton / *Barron*	Greene / *Lee*	Cawley / *Bradley*	Wilkins / *Beech*	Whitton* / *Cullen*	Sale / *Pederson*	Adcock* / *Clark*	Gregory N / *Howard*	Buckle/Lock/Haydon *Larsen*
26	A 10/1	DARLINGTON	Gregory N 69, 78 [Dorner 86] / Gaughan 40, Roberts 59, Haydon 84 (og) / Ref: S Mathieson	2,170	13 19	L 34	2-4	0-1	Emberson / *Preece*	Haydon / *Shaw*	Stamps* / *Barnard*	Skelton* / *Hope*	Greene / *Crosby*	Cawley / *Atkinson**	Wilkins / *Oliver*	Whitton* / *Bramwell*	Gregory N / *Roberts*	Sale / *Dorner**	Buckle / *Gaughan**	Gregory D/Lock/Forbes *Resch/Robinson Naylor*
27	H 16/1	TORQUAY	Lock 86 / Ref: F Stretton	2,776	13 10	W 37	1-0	0-0	Emberson / *Veysey*	Haydon / *Gurney*	Stamps* / *Gibbs*	Skelton / *Robinson*	Greene / *Gittens*	Cawley* / *Watson*	Wilkins / *Clayton**	Forbes / *Leadbitter*	Gregory N / *Jack*	Sale / *Roberts*	Buckle / *Mitchell**	Gregory D/Lock *Thomas/Hapgood*
28	H 20/1	CARDIFF	Gregory N 69, Buckle 79 / Dale 85 / Ref: M Bailey	1,929	12 17	W 40	2-1	0-0	Emberson / *Hallworth*	Haydon* / *Eckhardt**	Stamps / *Beech*	Skelton" / *Young*	Greene / *Harris**	Gregory D / *Fowler*	Wilkins / *O'Sullivan*	Forbes / *Penney*	Gregory N / *Nugent*	Sale* / *Dale*	Buckle / *Carss**	Dunne/Lock/Whitton *Saville/Partridge/Jarman*
29	A 24/1	BARNET	Skelton 4, Wilkins 83 / Devine 44, 65, McGleish 59 / Ref: P Danson	2,471	13 3	L 40	2-3	1-1	Emberson / *Harrison*	Dunne / *Goodhind*	Stamps* / *Harle*	Skelton / *Heald*	Greene / *Howarth*	Gregory D / *Stockley*	Wilkins / *Doolan*	Forbes* / *Wilson*	Gregory N / *Devine*	Sale / *McGleish*	Buckle* / *Simpson*	Haydon/Lock/Whitton
30	A 31/1	SCARBOROUGH	Whitton 46 / Campbell 83 / Ref: G Laws	2,219	13 4	D 41	1-1	0-0	Emberson / *Burton*	Dunne / *Kay*	Haydon / *Heck'bot'm**	Skelton / *Bennett T*	Greene / *Bennett G*	Cawley / *Sutherland**	Wilkins / *Williams*	Forbes* / *Mitchell"*	Gregory N / *Campbell*	Sale / *Brodie*	Whitton / *Robinson*	Atkin/Worrall/Tate
31	H 6/2	SWANSEA	Gregory N 27 / Coates 52, Price 78 / Ref: J Kirkby	2,789	13 18	L 41	1-2	1-0	Emberson / *Freestone*	Dunne / *Hartfield*	Haydon* / *Coates*	Skelton / *Edwards*	Greene / *Walker*	Gregory D / *Bound*	Wilkins / *Cusack*	Forbes / *Price*	Gregory N / *Bird"*	Sale* / *Alsop*	Whitton* / *Appleby**	Buckle/Lock/Duguid *Jenkins/Watkin*
32	H 13/2	MANSFIELD	Lock 30, Gregory D 68 / Ref: J Robinson	2,320	12 15	W 44	2-0	1-0	Emberson / *Bowling*	Dunne / *Clarke*	Branston / *Harper*	Skelton / *Peters*	Greene* / *Eustace*	Buckle / *Ford*	Wilkins / *Schofield*	Forbes" / *Sedgemore**	Gregory N / *Christie*	Lock / *Milner**	Whitton / *Tallon**	Duguid/Skelton *Kerr/Sissons/Williams*
33	A 21/2	EXETER	Lock 68 / Ref: A Bates	3,346	11 12	W 47	1-0	0-0	Emberson / *Bayes*	Gregory D / *Gale*	Betts / *Cyrus*	Skelton / *Blake*	Branston / *Clark*	Buckle / *Hare*	Wilkins / *Rowbotham**	Forbes / *Devin*	Gregory N / *Flack**	Lock / *Birch*	Whitton / *Medlin**	Williams/Ghazghazi/McConnell
34	A 24/2	SHREWSBURY	Gregory N 7, Gregory D 68 / Ref: C Wilkes	1,972	11 18	W 50	2-0	1-0	Emberson / *Edwards*	Gregory D / *Seabury*	Betts / *Hanmer*	Skelton / *Scott**	Branston / *Tretton*	Buckle / *Gayle*	Wilkins / *Berkley*	Forbes / *White*	Gregory N / *Steele**	Lock* / *Evans*	Whitton / *Preece*	Adcock *Jagielka/Williams*

24 CAMBRIDGE — Cawley and Greene have a nervy half, allowing Jamie B-Edinboro to tuck in Taylor's pass. Sale nods down crosses from Dunne and Gregory for Wilkins, and Skelton nets his customary 30-yarder B-Edinboro causes anxious final moments when he gets a knee to Ben Chenery's cross.

25 HARTLEPOOL — N Gregory is loaned from Ipswich, after a similar spell at Posh. U's are put off by Carlisle's £75k valuation of Dean Walling, but invite Hearts' Jeremy Goss for a trial. Wignall may rue his early-season comments about Pool when Steven Howard nets his eleventh goal of the campaign.

26 DARLINGTON — Andy Crosby fails to clear, giving N Gregory his first U's goal His second, via Stamps' through-ball, levels at 2-2. Tragically Haydon own-goals in attempting to clear Austrian Mario Dorner's shot. Dorner rubs it in two minutes later. Quakers prepare to face Wolves in the FA Cup.

27 TORQUAY — Dunne asks for a move, after being dropped last week, and is granted a free. Wignall sets a target of 72 points to reach the play-offs. Super-sub Lock comes off the bench to grab his second late winner of the season. He jinks past two defenders before slotting past keeper Ken Veysey.

28 CARDIFF — A second win in five days puts United in the top half for the first time since November. Lock again comes off the bench to set up N Gregory within two minutes Lock then feeds Buckle who stumbles, but scores. Wilkins' back-pass deceives Emberson, allowing Carl Dale to nip in.

29 BARNET — Defeat leaves U's five points off the play-offs. Emberson races off his line to miss Wilkins' back-pass – again! Sean Devine levels Skelton's early strike. Having failed to make use of the slope and wind, U's are up against it after the break and let in Devine and Scott McGleish efforts.

30 SCARBOROUGH — U's fail to sign Fulham's Mark Blake, but capture Fernandes from Brentford Neil Campbell robs U's of two vital points when he pops up to head in a corner seven minutes from time. Whitton had put U's in front just 30 seconds after the restart, nodding in Haydon's precision cross.

31 SWANSEA — Branston is loaned from Leicester. Swansea win at Layer Rd for the first time in 35 years. Sale's pass finds N Gregory whose loan is extended, on the left. He cuts inside and scores with his right. Jonathan Coates nods in Matthew Bound's long throw and Jason Price helps Coates' shot in.

32 MANSFIELD — Dunne talks with Brighton Branston has his kit sponsored by Crosse & Blackwell. N Gregory flicks on Branston's headed clearance for Lock to score. D Gregory shrugs off a challenge to net United's 3,000th league goal since Bob Curry scored the first. v Swindon almost 48 years ago.

33 EXETER — Kirklees McAlpine Stadia are appointed to manage the new stadium plan. Greene is out with a knee injury, just as Norwich show an interest. Lock finishes off great work by Branston and N Gregory. Ref Bates fails to give U's two penalties, or send off Matthew Hare for a pro foul.

34 SHREWSBURY — Cawley's contract will not be renewed. A third successive clean sheet is highlighted by the Gregorys joining the Hunts (1961) and Englishs (1986) as brothers to score in the same U's match. Neil gets his fifth in ten games, whilst David's is a left-footed shot off the inside of the post.

35 · H · 27/2 · PETERBOROUGH — 9 · 6 · 53 · W 1-0 (0-0) · Att 4,117

U's: Emberson, Gregory D*, Betts, Skelton, Branston, Buckle, Wilkins, Forbes*, Adcock, Lock, Whitton, Duguid/Dunne
Peterborough: Tyler, McMenamin Drury, Payne, Bodley, Edwards, Farrell, Castle, De Souza, Cleaver`, Houghton*, Lewis/Davies
Branston 61
Ref: D Crick

U's great run sees them close to within three points of the previously unassailable Peterborough. Branston picks a great moment to score his first U's goal and secure a fourth win on the trot 'Posh are unrecognisable from the free-scoring side that took the division by storm early on.

---

36 · H · 3/3 · ROCHDALE — 9 · 21 · 54 · D 0-0 (0-0) · Att 2,112

U's: Emberson, Dunne, Betts, Skelton, Branston, Buckle, Wilkins, Forbes, Adcock, Lock, Sale*, Hathaway
Rochdale: Edwards, Fensome, Bayliss*, Hill, Leonard, Gouck, Jones, Painter, Farrell, Russell, Stuart, Barlow
Ref: S Baines

U's fans chant 'we've only got ten grand' at the club's failure to sign N Gregory. Emberson creates a personal record with his fifth consecutive clean sheet Adcock helps Wilkins volley onto the post (12), and Hathaway lands a shot on top of the bar (67), a minute after coming on as sub.

---

37 · A · 7/3 · SCUNTHORPE — 10 · 12 · 54 · L 0-1 (0-1) · Att 2,143

U's: Emberson, Dunne, Betts, Skelton, Branston, Buckle, Wilkins, Haydon, Adcock*, Lock, Gregory D*, Sale/Hathaway
Scunthorpe: Clarke, Walsh, McAuley, Sertori*, Wilcox, Hope, Walker, Harsley, Eyre, Marshall*, Calco-Garcia, Ormondroyd/Forrester
McAuley 17
Ref: K Lynch

Scunthorpe start six points behind the U's, and have a game in hand. In midweek Scunthorpe became the first side to win at Hartlepool (1-0). Branston's foul on Sertori, near the corner, leads to Sean McAuley's free-kick being diverted in by Skelton. U's first against for 489 minutes.

---

38 · H · 14/3 · MACCLESFIELD — 7 · 5 · 57 · W 5-1 (1-1) · Att 2,760

U's: Emberson, Dunne, Betts, Skelton, Greene*, Gregory D, Wilkins, Buckle, Sale*, Lock*, Duguid*, Haydon/Abrahams/Hathaway
Macclesfield: Price, Tinson, McDonald, Payne, Howarth, Edy, Askey, Wood, Chambers*, Sorvel, Whittaker*!, Power !/Phillskirk
Sale 36, 57, Skelton 76, Abrahams 79, Whittaker 38 [Lock 88]
Ref: S Bennett

Branston's loan is extended, although he has a two-match suspension. U's move into a play-off spot by hammering one of their rivals. Sale's great double is outshone by Skelton's 35-yarder that is still rising as it hit the net. Sub Phil Power is sent off (82) for a scuffle with Abrahams.

---

39 · A · 21/3 · NOTTS CO — 8 · 1 · 58 · D 0-0 (0-0) · Att 6,284

U's: Emberson, Dunne, Betts, Skelton*, Greene, Gregory D, Wilkins, Buckle, Sale*, Lock*, Abrahams*, Forbes/Duguid/Haydon
Notts Co: Ward, Hendon, Pearce, Hughes*, Holmes, Dyer, Finnan, Robinson, Farrell, Jones, Sorvel, Cunnington/Lormor/Jackson
Ref: E Lomas

United are one of only four sides to beat leaders County this term. County's 16-point lead means that they need one win to secure promotion, and still they have seven games left. U's travelling fans are magnificently noisy, and Sale could easily have won it, but for two missed chances.

---

40 · A · 28/3 · LINCOLN — 7 · 6 · 61 · W 1-0 (1-0) · Att 4,040

U's: Emberson, Dunne*, Betts, Skelton, Greene, Branston, Wilkins, Buckle, Sale, Lock*, Gregory D, Forbes/Abrahams
Lincoln: Richardson, Brown G, Whitney, Fleming, Holmes, Austin, Walling, Miller, Hone*, Thorpe, Alcide, Bailey/Martin
Dunne 28
Ref: J Brandwood

N Gregory signs for a record £50k fee. Kinsella wins his first Eire cap in the Czech Rep. Lincoln are fined for fielding three suspended players. Sale finds Dunne lurking for an angled drive. L Orient are fined for fielding three suspended players.

---

41 · H · 3/4 · ROTHERHAM — 6 · 9 · 64 · W 2-1 (1-1) · Att 3,824

U's: Emberson, Dunne, Betts, Skelton, Branston, Wilkins, Buckle, Sale*, Lock*, Gregory N/Abrahams
Rotherham: Mimms, Richardson, Dillon, Roscoe, Warner*, Knill, Berry*, White, Glover, Martindale*, Thompson/Hurst/Druce
Skelton 11, Sale 55, Martindale 12
Ref: R Styles

Branston is valued at £500k by Leicester, ruling out a move to U's. Rotherham request that the kick-off is brought forward to 7.30 pm. Anyone turning up for normal time will have missed Skelton's thunderbolt and Gary Martindale's leveller. Sale deftly lobs his eighth of the campaign.

---

42 · A · 11/4 · CARDIFF — 6 · 20 · 67 · W 2-0 (0-0) · Att 2,809

U's: Emberson, Dunne, Betts, Skelton*, Greene, Branston*, Wilkins, Buckle, Sale*, Lock*, Gregory D, Gregory N/Duguid/Abrahams
Cardiff: Hallworth, Jarman, Beech, Phillips*, Young, Middleton, Carss, Fowler, Saville, Dale*, O'Sullivan, Cadette/Earnshaw/Roberts
Abrahams 48, Gregory D 60
Ref: M Fletcher

Whitton quits playing after 532 (+45 sub) games and 118 goals. The FA bow 'to pressure from rival contenders to deduct L Orient three points. Lock pulls back from the by-line for Abrahams' goal. Abrahams repeats the move for D Gregory to earn U's third successive win at Ninian Pk.

---

43 · H · 13/4 · HULL — 4 · 22 · 70 · W 4-3 (2-1) · Att 4,700

U's: Emberson, Dunne, Betts, Skelton, Greene, Branston, Wilkins, Buckle, Sale*, Lock*, Gregory D*, Gregory N/Duguid/Abrahams
Hull: Wilson, Lowthorpe*, Rioch, Edwards, Doncel, Joyce, Peacock, McGinty, Brown, Darby*, Boyack, Mann/Wright
Gregory D 6, Lock 13, Dunne 79, D'd 90; Boyack 24, McGinty 48, Darby 70
Ref: P Taylor

U's move tantalisingly into fourth spot, courtesy of Duguid's 93rd-minute winner from Emberson's goal-kick. Steven Boyack, on loan from G Rangers curls a great 20-yarder. Dunne's equaliser at 3-3 is adjudged to have crossed the line by the alert assistant referee, setting up the finale.

---

44 · A · 18/4 · CHESTER — 4 · 13 · 70 · L 1-3 (0-3) · Att 1,780

U's: Emberson, Dunne, Betts, Skelton*, Greene, Branston, Wilkins, Buckle, Sale*, Lock*, Gregory D*, Forbes/Duguid/Abrahams
Chester: Brown, Dobson*, Fisher, Richardson, Whelan, Woods, Bennett, Priest, Wright, Fitcroft, Rimmer, Shelton/Giles
Abrahams 75, Whelan 19, Fisher 35, Rimmer 36
Ref: P Richards

On the back of nine wins from twelve, against two wins in fourteen for Chester, United are obvious favourites. Spencer Whelan's halfway-line clearance beats Emberson, who claims a foul by Gary Bennett. Two goals in a minute, including a spectacular curler from Neil Fisher, win it.

---

45 · H · 25/4 · LEYTON ORIENT — 5 · 11 · 71 · D 1-1 (1-1) · Att 6,220

U's: Emberson, Dunne, Betts, Greene*, Gregory D, Wilkins, Buckle, Sale*, Lock*, Gregory N/Abrahams
Leyton Orient: MacKenzie, Joseph R, Raynor*, Smith, Warren, Ling, Joseph M, Harris, Maskell*, Inglethorpe, Simpson/Baker
Gregory N 45, Inglethorpe 44
Ref: A Hall

O's believe U's instigated their points deduction. The point secures U's play-off place, thanks to Emberson's 88th-minute save from Martin Ling. That made up for the error at Chester. Alex Inglethorpe heads in Jason Harris's cross, but N Gregory levels via Greene's return header.

---

46 · A · 2/5 · DONCASTER — 4 · 24 · 74 · W 1-0 (0-0) · Att 3,572

U's: Emberson, Dunne, Betts, Skelton, Greene, Gregory D, Wilkins, Buckle, Sale*, Lock*, Gregory N, Abrahams*/Lock/Duguid/Forbes
Doncaster: Davis, Donnelly*, Hilton, Warren, George, Hawthorne, Cunningham, Moncrieffe, Mike, Wilson, Helliwell, Pell
Gregory N 56
Ref: T Heilbron

Doncaster, long since relegated to the GMVC, are slowly dying as a club. Their fans stage a mock funeral, and invade the pitch twice to protest against the board. N Gregory's goal is not enough to secure automatic promotion as Lincoln beat Brighton 2-1 at home to secure third position.

Home Average 3,132 · Away Average 3,058

NATIONWIDE DIVISION 3 (CUP-TIES)

Manager: Steve Wignall — SEASON 1997-98

Play-offs

					F-A	H-T		
SF 1	A	BARNET	4	L	0:1	0:0	3,858	7

Colchester: 1 Emberson, 2 Dunne, 3 Betts, 4 Skelton, 5 Greene, 6 Branston!, 7 Forbes, 8 Buckle, 9 Sale, 10 Gregory N*, 11 Gregory D — subs used: Lock
Barnet: Harrison, Stockley, Harle, Forbes, Heald, Basham, Goodhind, Searle, Devine!, McGleish*, Simpson^ — subs used: Charley/Manuel*

Scorers, Times: Heald 48. Ref: E Wolstenholme
Branston, already booked, and in the last game of his loan, is sent off (82) along with Sean Devine. Devine appeared to elbow Branston, who gets up and chases the striker. Dunne intervenes and is clattered by Devine. Emberson's mis-punch falls to Greg Heald, just eight yards out.

					F-A	H-T		
SF 2	H	BARNET	4	W	3:1 (aet)	1:1	5,863	7

Colchester: Emberson, Dunne, Betts, Forbes*, Greene, Howarth!, Wilkins, Buckle, Sale, Gregory N*, Abrahams^ — subs used: Skelton/Duguid/Lock
Barnet: Harrison, Stockley, Harle^, Heald, Howarth!, Basham, Goodhind, Searle, Charley, McGleish, Wilson^ — subs used: Manuel/Samuels/Simpson*

Scorers, Times: Gregory D 12p, 95, Greene 65, Goodhind 41. Ref: T Heilbron
(Colchester won 3-2 on aggregate)
Lee Howarth needlessly handles for D Gregory to level on aggregate. Howarth is sent off (60) for a brutal tackle on N Gregory. Warren Goodhind meets Sam Stockley's cross, but Dunne's deep free-kick drops to Greene, then Forbes lays off for D Gregory to shoot U's to Wembley.

					F-A	H-T		
F	N	TORQUAY	4	W	1:0	1:0	19,486	5

(at Wembley)
Colchester: Emberson, Dunne, Betts, Skelton*, Greene, Gregory D, Wilkins, Buckle, Sale, Gregory N*, Forbes — subs used: Duguid/Lock
Torquay: Gregg, Gurney, Gibbs, Robinson, Gittens, Watson, Clayton, Leadbitter, Jack, McFarlane, McCall^ — subs used: Thomas/Bedeau*

Scorers, Times: Gregory D 22p. Ref: M Fletcher
U's and Torquay sue for compensation, after the final is moved to Friday night to accommodate a meaningless England v S Arabia friendly. D Gregory fires U's into the second division from the spot, after Jon Gittens was harshly adjudged to have handled, under pressure from Sale.

Coca-Cola Cup

					F-A	H-T		
1:1	H	LUTON	12	D	0:1	0:0	2,840	2:

Colchester: Emberson, Gregory D, Stamps, Skelton", Greene, Cawley, Wilkins, Buckle, Sale", Abrahams*, Hathaway — subs used: Adcock/Lock/Forbes
Luton: Feuer, Douglas, Thomas, Waddock, Davis, Johnson, McLaren, Alexander, Oldfield, Thorpe, Davies" — subs used: Harvey*

Scorers, Times: Thorpe 87. Ref: S Bennett
Brentford enquire about Wignall, to replace Micky Adams, but are put off by U's £300k compensation demand. Greene makes a total hash of a late clearance to give diminutive Tony Thorpe, scorer of 30 goals last season, the chance to notch an undeserved first-leg win for the Hatters.

					F-A	H-T		
1:2	A	LUTON	12	D	1:1	0:1	2,816	2:15

Colchester: Abbey, Gregory D, Stamps, Skelton", Greene, Cawley, Wilkins, Buckle, Sale", Abrahams*, Hathaway^ — subs used: Adcock/Lock
Luton: James, Thomas, Waddock, Davis, Johnson, Davies, McLaren, Oldfield, Thorpe, Marshall, Douglas*

Scorers, Times: Hathaway 51, Thorpe 34. Ref: D Orr
(Colchester lost 1-2 on aggregate)
Ian Feuer is out and reserve Kelvin Davis is cup-tied, on loan at Hartlepool. Lennie Lawrence calls on Nathan Abbey between the sticks. David Oldfield picks out Thorpe, who turns Cawley inside out. United dominate, but only Hathaway's volley, from Abrahams' hanging cross, counts.

FA Cup

					F-A	H-T		
1	A	BRENTFORD	12	D	2:2	1:1	2,899	2:24

Colchester: Emberson, Gregory D, Stamps, Skelton", Greene, Cawley, Wilkins*, Forbes*, Sale, Whitton, Duguid — subs used: Adcock/Dunne/Abrahams
Brentford: Dearden, Hurdle, Barrowcliff, Hutchings, Bates, Oatway, McGhee, Cockerill, Bent^, Reina^, Taylor — subs used: Rapley/Canham*

Scorers, Times: Sale 38, Gregory D 88, Taylor 9, 55. Ref: B Knight
Betts asks for a transfer after Dunne returns from injury and jumps the queue. Marcus Bent swings in a cross for Robert Taylor's first. Charlie Oatway flicks on for his second in Forbes' centre. Duguid squares for Gregory to just beat Kevin Dearden to the ball.

					F-A	H-T		
1R	H	BRENTFORD	12	W	0:0 (aet)	0:0	3,694	2:22

Colchester: Emberson, Dunne, Betts, Gregory D, Greene, Cawley, Abrahams^, Adcock*, Sale, Whitton^, Duguid — subs used: Lock/Hathaway/Bryan
*Brentford: Dearden, McPherson*Townley, Hutchings, Bates, Oatway, McGhee, Cockerill, Bent, Reina^, Barrowcliff^Hurdle*

Ref: B Knight
(Colchester won 4-2 on pens)
The fans endure 120 minutes of complete boredom. Marcus Bent skies the first penalty, followed by goals for Greene, Carl Hutchings and Gregory. Jamie Bates strikes Emberson's legs, for Skelton and Oatway to score. Betts plants the winner to put United through a forgettable tie.

					F-A	H-T		
2	H	HEREFORD	13	D	1:1	1:0	3,558	VC:10

Colchester: Emberson, Dunne, Betts, Gregory D, Greene", Skelton, Duguid, Buckle, Sale, Adcock*, Hathaway" — subs used: Lock/Stamps/Haydon
Hereford: DeBont, Norton, Fishlock, Pitman, Brough, Walker, Hargreaves, McGorry, Grayson, Warner, Mahon

Scorers, Times: Gregory D 10, Grayson 61. Ref: K Lynch
U's attempt to sign Rankin until the end of the term. Hereford were dramatically relegated to the GMVC on the last day of last season instead of Brighton. A fine one-two by Buckle and Adcock sets up Gregory, but Neil Grayson (£20k from Cobblers) finishes off a 'triangle' free-kick.

					F-A	H-T		
2R	A	HEREFORD	16	L	1:1 (aet)	0:0	3,752	VC:10

Colchester: Emberson, Dunne, Gregory D, Skelton, Greene, Cawley, Wilkins*, Haydon*, Forbes, Stamps*, Mahon — subs used: Lock/Duguid/Betts
Hereford: DeBont, Raynor, Fishlock, Cook, Brough, Walker, Hargreaves, McGorry, Grayson, McCue, Pitman/Williams*

Scorers, Times: Forbes 47, Grayson 48. Ref: K Lynch
(Colchester lost 4-5 on penalties)
On a freezing night Greene flicks on Wilkins' throw for Forbes to hook in. A minute later Murray Fishlock crosses from the right to Grayson. Hereford go on to host Tranmere. The first nine penalties are scored, but Betts, the hero in the last round, sees his shot saved by Andy DeBont.

Autowindscreen Shield

1	A	LEYTON ORIENT	13	L	0-1	L 0-0
9/12	933	3:14				

Inglethorpe 51
Ref: A Hall

Team (players):

Emberson	Dunne	Gregory D	Sale	Buckle"	Cawley	Haydon	Skelton	Stamps	Gregory D	Sale	Adcock*	Rankin"	Lock/Forbes/Duguid
MacKenzie	Channing	Naylor	Smith	Inglethorpe	Clark				Warren	Griffiths*	Harris"	Baker	Simpson/Hanson

Despite being finalists last season, neither United nor Carlisle secure one of the eight byes into the second round. Rankin's pace forces Mark Warren into a 25th-minute foul. Buckle's penalty is saved by Chris MacKenzie. Dominic Naylor's inswinging corner finds Alex Inglethorpe.

League Table

		P			Home						Away				Pts
			W	D	L	F	A	W	D	L	F	A			
1	Notts Co	46	14	7	2	41	20	15	5	3	41	23			99
2	Macclesfield	46	19	4	0	40	11	4	9	10	23	33			82
3	Lincoln	46	11	7	5	32	24	9	8	6	28	27			75
4	COLCHESTR*	46	14	5	4	41	24	7	6	10	31	36			74
5	Torquay	46	14	4	5	39	22	7	9	9	29	37			74
6	Scarborough	46	14	6	3	44	23	5	9	9	23	35			72
7	Barnet	46	10	8	5	35	22	9	5	9	26	29			70
8	Scunthorpe	46	11	7	5	30	24	8	5	10	26	28			69
9	Rotherham	46	10	9	4	41	30	6	10	7	26	31			67
10	Peterborough	46	13	6	4	37	16	5	7	11	26	35			67
11	Leyt' Orient**	46	14	5	4	40	20	5	7	11	22	27			66
12	Mansfield	46	11	9	3	42	26	5	8	10	22	29			65
13	Shrewsbury	46	12	3	8	35	28	4	10	9	26	34			61
14	Chester	46	12	7	4	34	15	5	3	15	26	46			61
15	Exeter	46	10	8	5	39	25	5	7	11	29	38			60
16	Cambridge	46	11	8	4	39	27	3	10	10	24	30			60
17	Hartlepool	46	10	12	1	40	22	2	11	10	21	31			59
18	Rochdale	46	15	3	5	43	15	2	4	17	13	40			58
19	Darlington	46	13	6	4	43	28	5	3	15	13	44			54
20	Swansea	46	8	8	7	24	16	5	3	15	25	46			50
21	Cardiff	46	5	13	5	27	22	4	10	9	21	30			50
22	Hull	46	10	6	7	36	32	1	2	20	20	51			41
23	Brighton	46	3	10	10	21	34	3	7	13	17	32			35
24	Doncaster	46	3	3	17	14	48	1	5	17	16	65			20
		1104	267	164	121	857	574	121	164	267	574	857			1489

** 3 points deducted
* promoted after play-offs

Odds & ends

Double wins: (2) Cardiff, Doncaster.
Double defeats: (1) Hartlepool.

Won from behind: (2) Cambridge (h), Hull (h).
Lost from in front: (4) Peterborough (a), Barnet (a), Swansea (h), Rotherham (a).

High spots: Promotion to the second division via the play-offs.
Third Wembley appearance in six years.
Breaking the record highest transfer fee paid.
Ten wins from the last 15 league games.
Miserly defence with the addition of Guy Branston.
Missing out on automatic promotion by one point, with Wembley as the consolation.
U's prodigy Mark Kinsella wins his first full Eire cap, and captains his Charlton side to the Premiership, with a play-off win over Sunderland.
Aaron Skelton's spectacular long-range goals.
Finalisation of the Burley compensation saga.

Low spots: Record lowest play-off final attendance, due to date change.
Giving away three-goal leads against Scunthorpe (h) and at Brighton.
Defeat by GMVC side Hereford in the FA Cup.

Player of the Year: Richard Wilkins.
Ever presents: (1) Carl Emberson.
Hat-tricks: (0).
Leading scorers: Mark Sale and Neil Gregory (8).

Appearances & Goals

	Appearances						Goals			
	Lge	Sub	LC	Sub	FAC	Sub	Lge	LC	FAC	Tot
Abrahams, Paul	16	9	2			1	7			7
Adcock, Tony	19	6	2		3	1	5			5
Betts, Simon	17		2		2	1				
Branston, Guy	12								1	1
Brown, Wayne		2								
Buckle, Paul	33	5	2		1		5			5
Cawley, Peter	27		2		3					
Duguid, Karl	6	15			3	1	3			3
Dunne, Joe	22	3			3	1	2			2
Emberson, Carl	46		2		4					
Forbes, Carl	25	10	1	1	2		1		1	2
Greene, David	38		2		4		4			4
Gregory, David	42	2	2		2	4	5		2	7
Gregory, Neil	12	3					8			8
Hathaway, Ian	5	7	2					1		1
Haydon, Nicky	9	8		1	1	1				
Lock, Tony	14	18	2			3	6			6
Rankin, Isiah	10	1					4			4
Sale, Mark	38	1	2		3		7			7
Skelton, Aaron	37	2	1		3	1	7			7
Stamps, Scott	26	2	2		2	1	1			1
Whitton, Steve	15	6			2		1			1
Wilkins, Richard	37	2			2		5			5
23 players used	506	98	22	5	44	12	72	1	4	77

NATIONWIDE LEAGUE DIVISION 2 — Manager: Wignall ⇒ Wadsworth — SEASON 1998-99

No	Date	Att	Pos	Pt	Res	F-A	H-T	Scorers, Times, and Referees	1	2	3	4	5	6	7	8	9	10	11	subs used
1	H 8/8 CHESTERFIELD	4,042	3	3	W	1-0	0-0	Sale 90 — Ref: P Danson	Emberson / *Mercer*	Betts / *Hewitt*	Stamps / *Perkins*	Williams / *Curtis*	Greene / *Williams M*	Buckle / *Breckin*	Wilkins* / *Willis*	Gregory D~ / *Holland*	Sale / *Reeves*	Lock" / *Wilkinson*	Abrahams / *Howard"*	Duguid/Dunne/Gregory N / *Beaumont*
2	A 15/8 WREXHAM	4,157	2	6	W	4-2	2-0	Abrahams 16, Haydon 43, Gregory N 48, Roberts 62, Connolly 78p [Greg' D 64p] — Ref: E Lomas	Emberson / *Cartwright*	Betts / *McGregor*	Stamps / *Brace*	Williams / *Owen*	Greene / *Humes*	Buckle / *Carey*	Haydon" / *Chalk"*	Gregory D / *Russell"*	Sale / *Connolly*	Gregory N* / *Rush*	Abrahams" / *Ward*	Adcock/Dunne/Wiles / *Brammer/Roberts*
3	H 22/8 FULHAM	6,377	5	6	L	0-1	0-0	Collins 82 — Ref: S Bennett	Emberson / *Taylor*	Dunne* / *Uhlenbeek*	Stamps / *Brevett*	Williams / *Morgan*	Greene / *Coleman*	Buckle / *Symons*	Wilkins / *Beardsley"*	Gregory D~ / *Bracewell"*	Sale~ / *Lehmann"*	Gregory N / *Hayward*	Abrahams* / *Salako**	Haydon/Adcock/Forbes / *Collins/Moody/Peschisolido*
4	A 29/8 LUTON	5,005	11	6	L	0-2	0-0	Douglas 61, Davis S 81 — Ref: R Furnandiz	Emberson / *Davis K*	Dunne" / *Alexander*	Stamps / *McGowan*	Williams / *Spring*	Greene / *Davis S*	Buckle / *Johnson S*	Wilkins / *McKinnon !*	Gregory D / *Evers*	Sale" / *Douglas**	Gregory N / *Gray"*	Abrahams / *George"*	Haydon/Duguid/Forbes / *Fotiadis/Bacque/Thomas*
5	H 31/8 STOKE	4,728	12	6	L	0-1	0-0	Kavanagh 78 — Ref: P Taylor	Emberson / *Muggleton*	Haydon / *Short*	Betts / *Small*	Williams / *Sigurdsson*	Greene / *Robinson*	Buckle" / *Woods*	Wilkins / *Keen"*	Gregory D / *Kavanagh*	Sale / *Thorne*	Gregory N* / *Crowe"*	Duguid" / *Oldfield*	Abrahams/Forbes / *Lightbourne/Wallace*
6	A 5/9 YORK	2,699	9	9	W	2-1	1-0	Gregory N 2, Forbes 86 — Thompson 76p — Ref: S Baines	Emberson / *Mimms*	Haydon / *McMillan*	Stamps / *Hall"*	Williams / *Tinkler*	Greene / *Jones*	Buckle" / *Thompson*	Wilkins" / *Connelly*	Gregory D / *Poulton*	Sale / *Cresswell*	Gregory N* / *Woods"*	Lock* / *Garratt"*	Forbes/Rainford/Betts / *Reed/Jordan/Tolson*
7	A 8/9 WIGAN	2,784	12	10	D	1-1	0-0	Sale 62 — Lee 86 — Ref: T Bates	Emberson / *Carroll*	Haydon* / *Green*	Stamps / *Bradshaw*	Williams / *Griffiths*	Greene / *McGibbon**	Buckle / *Rogers*	Forbes / *Sharp*	Gregory D / *Greenall"*	Sale / *Warne"*	Gregory N / *Kilford*	Lock" / *Barlow*	Betts/Dunne / *Lee/Lowe*
8	H 12/9 GILLINGHAM	4,612	11	11	D	1-1	1-1	Gregory N 28 — Asaba 27 — Ref: G Frankland	Emberson / *Bartram*	Dunne / *Patterson*	Stamps / *Galloway*	Williams / *Smith*	Greene / *Bryant"*	Buckle / *Carr*	Forbes" / *Saunders*	Gregory D / *Hessenthaler*	Sale / *Asaba*	Gregory N / *Southall"*	Lock" / *Taylor"*	Hayden/Duguid / *Butler/Edge*
9	A 19/9 READING	9,058	12	12	D	1-1	0-1	Duguid 89 — Williams 17 — Ref: D Pugh	Emberson / *Hammond*	Dunne / *Booty*	Stamps / *McPherson*	Williams / *Brebner"*	Greene / *Primus*	Buckle / *Casper*	Forbes" / *Glasgow"*	Gregory D / *Caskey**	Sale / *Williams*	Gregory N* / *Gray"*	Lock* / *Sarr"*	Adcock/Duguid/Betts / *Reilly/Crawford/Grayson*
10	H 26/9 WYCOMBE	4,205	10	15	W	2-1	0-0	Forbes 65, Gregory D 89p — Stallard 60 — Ref: A D'Urso	Emberson / *Taylor*	Dunne / *Kavanagh*	Stamps / *Beeton*	Williams / *Cornforth*	Greene / *Cousins*	Buckle / *Mohan*	Forbes / *Vinnicombe**	Gregory D / *Brown*	Sale / *Stallard*	Gregory N* / *Bulman*	Lock* / *Emblem*	Adcock/Duguid / *Baird*
11	A 3/10 OLDHAM	4,231	13	15	L	0-1	0-1	Rickers 20 — Ref: B Coddington	Emberson / *Kelly*	Dunne / *McNiven*	Stamps / *Holt*	Williams* / *Graham*	Greene / *Sinnott*	Buckle" / *Duxbury*	Forbes / *Rickers"*	Gregory D / *Allott"*	Sale / *Tipton"*	Gregory N* / *Whitehall"*	Lock* / *Reid*	Skelton/Duguid/Branston / *Littlejohn/Ritchie/Hodgson*

Match notes

1. Emberson renews his contract at the eleventh hour, whilst Williams, 36, capped 13 times by Wales, debuts. Guy Branston delays any hopes of year-long loan by getting sent off for Leicester reserves. Dunne swings over a long looping cross for Sale in the second minute of injury-time.

2. Ex-U's loanee Isaiah Rankin (Arsenal) joins Bradford for £1.3m. Cuckoo Farm will house the new stadium, subject to a new A12 access road. Ex-Liverpool legend Ian Rush is kept quiet. Abrahams' shirt is pulled for United's penalty, whilst Greene fouls Neil Roberts for Wrexham's.

3. Star-studded Fulham, bossed by Kevin Keegan, and backed by the multi-millions of Harrods' boss Mohammed Al Fayed, gain an undeserved victory when Wayne Collins comes off the bench to knock in Paul Peschisolido's cross. Sale has a header ruled out (13) for Greene's offside.

4. Dozzell starts training after being released by Northampton. The 53rd-minute sending-off of Marvin Johnson, for a pro foul on Ray McKinnon's corner, sparks the Hatters into life. Stuart Douglas ends a neat move to slot past Emberson, then Steve Davis rises to nod in Ray McKinnon's corner.

5. U's are consoled by Stoke boss Brian Little, who says that his side were lucky to escape with their fifth straight win. Carl Muggleton makes stunning saves from both Gregorys, only for Graham Kavanagh to blast home from 25 yards after Phil Robinson's free-kick was half-cleared.

6. Branston's three-month loan goes from bad to worse when he picks up a training injury at Filbert St. U's, who have been slow starters so far, are given a pre-match rollicking. It pays off as N Gregory taps in Wilkins' flick. Greene fouls Tolson, but Betts provides Forbes' late winner.

7. U's pick up a creditable fourth point on their four-day excursion. D Gregory has his 34th-minute penalty saved, after Gareth Griffiths' foul on Sale. Sale gives U's the lead with a drilled shot from Lock's cross. Sub David Lee breaks United's hearts with a drive through a crowded area.

8. D Gregory makes his 100th league appearance. Ex-U's loanee Carl Asaba, Gills recent £600k purchase from Reading, collects the ball some 40 yards out, to stride forward and beat Emberson. Within 60 seconds, ex-Gill Dunne swings over a right wing cross for N Gregory to nod in.

9. A first visit to the very impressive new £37m Madejski Stadium. Royals give a debut to Chris Casper, signed from Man United. Liberian Mass Sarr breaks free of Greene to cross to ex-U's loanee Martin Williams. Buckle's corner is dropped by Nicky Hammond for Duguid to stab in.

10. United sit handily placed, just three points off a play-off place. With 60 seconds remaining Nicky Mohan hauls down Sale, giving penalty-king D Gregory the chance to win it. Earlier Mark Stallard was first to a one-on-one with Emberson, and Forbes ghosted in to nod in Dunne's cross.

11. Hathaway joins Aldershot. U's have only won once (1969-70) at Boundary Park in seven visits. To benchmark U's progress, Oldham were in the Premier whilst U's were in the GMVC. Paul Rickers nets after Adrian Littlejohn robs Dunne. N Gregory should have had a first-half treble.

#		Date	Pos			HT	FT	Att	Pos
12	H	9/10	17	L	15	0-4	0-2	5,532	18

BURNLEY — Payton 2, 11, Vindheim 50, Cooke 72. Ref: D Crick

Emberson, Dunne, Betts', Williams, Greene, Buckle, Forbes', Gregory D, Sale", Gregory N, Abrahams, Lock/Duguid/Skelton
Ward, Scott, Armstrong, Vindheim*, Heywood, Reid, Little, Robertson, Cooke', Payton', Smith P', Smith C/Maylett

Branston asks to end his loan, as the Leicester managerial post may change. Burnley were the last side to visit as U's slipped out of the league. A rain-drenched crowd is boosted by 'Quid-a-Kid.' Sloppy defending gives Andy Payton a quick double from which United never recover.

13	A	17/10	17	L	15	0-2	0-2	10,483	2

PRESTON — Eyres 12, Nogan 39. Ref: P Dowd

Emberson, Dunne, Stamps, Williams", Greene, Buckle, Forbes*, Gregory D, Sale, Gregory N, Abrahams', Dozzell/Duguid/Betts
Molanen, Parkinson, Ludden, Murdock, Kidd, Gregan, McKenna, Rankine, Nogan, Macken, Eyres

Dozzell signs on a monthly basis, whilst Adcock has a testimonial v Ipswich. At Deepdale, U's approach play is first-class, but the killer touch is missing. David Eyres scores when Emberson parries Jon Macken's shot. D Gregory fails to pick up Kurt Nogan, who nods in Eyres' corner.

14	A	20/10	18	D	16	0-0	1-1	3,319	4

WALSALL — Lock 87 / Platt 47. Ref: G Laws

Emberson, Dunne, Stamps, Williams, Greene, Buckle, Dozzell*, Gregory D, Sale*, Gregory N, Duguid, Forbes/Lock
Walker, Marsh, Pointon, Keates, Green, Viveash, Wrack, Porter*, Platt*, Larsson, Brissett, Lambert

U's are in a three-match goal drought. Stamps beats James Walker all ends up, but his shot comes back off the post (20). 68th-minute sub Lock lashes a left-footer into the roof of the net to level. Clive Platt had guided in Darren Wrack's cross, despite Greene's valiant attempt to clear.

15	A	31/10	20	L	16	0-0	1-2	24,820	6

MANCHESTER C — Dozzell 59 / Horlock 50p, Morrison 53. Ref: M Pike

Emberson, Dunne, Stamps, Williams, Greene, Buckle, Dozzell, Gregory D, Lock, Gregory N*, Duguid*, Sale/Abrahams
Weaver, Edghill, Vaughan, Morrison, Wiekens, Crooks, Allsopp*, Mason, Goater, Branch*, Horlock, Dickov/Bishop

After last week's wash-out, U's visit Maine Rd for the first time, backed by 1,644. United outplay City, who are booed off at the break. Michael Branch's dive, shadowed by Greene, gives Kevin Horlock the pen. Andy Morrison powers in a header, before Dozzell nods in Dunne's cross.

16	H	6/11	20	D	17	0-1	1-1	3,925	21

MACCLESFIELD — Greene 75 / Griffiths 28. Ref: R Oliver

Emberson, Dunne, Haydon, Williams*, Greene, Buckle, Dozzell, Gregory D, Lock, Gregory N*, Duguid*, Sale/Forbes/Adcock
Price, Tinson, Hitchen", Payne, McDonald', Sodje, Griffiths, Sorvel, Smith, Sedgemore, Whittaker*, Wood/Tomlinson/Howarth

Cuckoo Farm is officially named as the stadium site. U's fail to sign Posh's Andy Edwards to cover injury-plagued Wilkins. Greene is eyed by Liverpool. Peter Griffiths' shot deflects over Emberson, but Greene levels with an unusual volley. Macclesfield get the draw they came for.

17	H	10/11	19	W	20	1-0	1-0	3,598	21

NORTHAMPTON — Greene 88. Ref: R Furmandiz

Emberson, Dunne, Stamps, Williams, Greene, Buckle, Dozzell, Gregory D, Sale, Lock*, Forbes*, Gregory N/Haydon
Woodman, Wilder*, Frain, Sampson, Hodgson, Parrish*, Hunt, Corrazzin, Howey", Freestane, Hill, Gibbi/Lee/Savage

Dublin loans from Southend. Cobblers' negative approach means that they are never likely to win the contest. United have difficulty breaking them down until two minutes from time, when Greene rises highest to nod in Buckle's flag-kick. Worryingly, United have just six home goals.

18	A	21/11	14	W	23	2-0	3-1	4,598	16

NOTTS CO — Greene 10, 23, Gregory D 48 / Murray 52. Ref: M Jones

Emberson, Dunne, Betts, Williams, Greene, Buckle, Dublin, Gregory D, Sale*, Lock*, Duguid, Dozzell/Gregory N
Ward, Hendon, Pearce, Redmile, Fairclough, Richardson, Owens", Hughes", Devlin, Jones, Murray", Garcia/Jackson/Liburd

Betts asks for a move, whilst U's talk with O's Mark Warren. United wipe away last week's FA Cup disaster with a couple of goals straight off the training pitch. Greene steers in two Buckle corners, and D Gregory accepts a glorious through-ball from Williams. Shaun Murray replies.

19	H	28/11	15	D	24	0-0	0-0	4,476	11

MILLWALL — Ref: A Hall

Emberson, Dunne, Betts, Williams, Greene, Buckle, Dublin, Gregory D, Sale*, Lock*, Duguid", Adcock/Dozzell/Gregory N
Spink, Lavin, Stuart, Cahill, Nethercott ! Fitzgerald, Reid, Bircham, Harris, Shaw, Roche", Neill

United are stuck on just six home goals despite a host of chances against ten-man Lions. Ex-Spurs star Stuart Nethercott is red-carded (40) for punching the back of Lock's head. D Gregory, Greene and Dozzell all spurn good chances. N Gregory cracks the underside of the crossbar.

20	A	12/12	15	D	25	0-0	0-0	4,513	24

LINCOLN — Ref: A Wiley

Emberson, Dunne, Betts*, Williams, Greene, Buckle, Wilkins, Gregory D, Dozzell, Duguid*, Stamps, Abrahams/Lock
Grobbelaar, Barnett, Bimson, Miller, Holmes, Austin, Smith, Finnigan, Battersby* Thorpe, Alcide", Gordon/Brown/Brabin

Dublin goes back to Southend because he 'can't bear the extra driving to Colchester'. Blackpool defender Tony Butler's demands are too high. Wilkins returns after a troublesome back injury. Stamps misses U's best chance, firing into the diving body of 41-year-old Bruce Grobbelaar.

21	H	19/12	15	D	26	2-2	1-1	3,228	13

BLACKPOOL — Greene 7, Gregory D 78 / Ormerod 11, Hughes 88. Ref: S Baines

Emberson, Dunne, Betts, Williams, Greene, Abrahams*, Wilkins, Gregory D, Dozzell, Gregory N*, Stamps, Sale/Lock
Barnes, Hughes, Hills, Bardsley, Carlisle, Butler, Paterson, Clarkson, Ormerod, Bushell*, Malkin*, Nowland/Bent

Dozzell signs to the end of the campaign. Greene seizes onto Williams' pass to beat late replacement Phil Barnes. A poor clearance from David Bardsley's free-kick drops to Brett Ormerod. D Gregory restores the lead with his seventh, only for Ian Hughes to hammer in John Hills' cross.

22	A	26/12	16	L	26	0-2	0-1	11,939	1

FULHAM — Smith 26, Hayles 72p. Ref: P Walton

Emberson !, Dunne, Betts, Williams, Greene, Buckle, Wilkins, Gregory D, Dozzell", Abrahams*, Stamps*, Gregory N/Lock/Sale
Taylor, Uhlenbeek, Brevett*, Morgan, Coleman, Symons, Hayward, Bracewell, Horsfield", Peschisol'", Smith, Trollope/Lehmann/Hayles

Abrahams is transfer-listed. U's contain their wealthy hosts, after Neil Smith heads in Rufus Brevett's cross, without threatening. German sub Dirk Lehmann collides with Emberson, who is red-carded, earning his side a penalty. N Gregory takes over but can't stop Barry Hayles' kick.

23	H	28/12	16	L	26	0-3	0-2	4,609	15

BRISTOL ROV — Cureton 2, Roberts 44, Ipoua 84. Ref: K Hill

Emberson, Dunne', Betts, Williams*, Greene, Buckle, Wilkins, Gregory D, Lock, Gregory N*, Lock, Sale/Haydon/Abrahams
Jones, Leoni, Challis, Holloway, Lee, Trought, Shore !, Meaker, McKeever, Cureton, Roberts", Ipoua

Emberson has his dismissal 23 hours earlier on his mind as he slides out of his area and releases the ball, allowing Jamie Cureton a simple tap in. Jason Roberts nets before the break, but sees colleague Jamie Shore sent off (69) for retaliation on Wilkins, who is also booked for the foul.

Match summary

No	Date	V	Team	Att	Pos	Pt	F-A	H-T	Scorers, Times, and Referees
24	2/1	H	LUTON	4,694	16 (14)	27	D 2-2	1-1	Gregory D 20p, Abrahams 84 / Alexander 7p, White 72 / Ref: B Knight
25	9/1	A	CHESTERFIELD	3,761	17 (7)	27	L 1-3	0-0	Lua-Lua 75 / Wilkinson 61, Howard 68, Reeves 81 / Ref: B Burns
26	15/1	H	WREXHAM	3,491	19 (17)	27	L 1-3	1-3	Wilkins 15 / Whitley 9, Haydon 11 (og), Griffiths 24 / Ref: S Bennett
27	23/1	A	STOKE	12,507	17 (4)	28	D 3-3	2-3	Betts 9, Gregory D 44, Dozzell 80 / Gregory D 30 (og), Light 34, Sig'son 42 / Ref: T Jones
28	30/1	A	BRISTOL ROV	6,249	18 (16)	29	D 1-1	0-1	Gregory D 88p / Roberts 28 / Ref: P Richards
29	5/2	H	YORK	3,982	17 (13)	32	W 2-1	2-0	Betts 1, Greene 4 / Cresswell 74p / Ref: P Rejer
30	12/2	H	WIGAN	3,934	15 (11)	35	W 2-1	2-0	Wilkins 22, Gregory D 28 / Sharp 70 / Ref: M Fletcher
31	20/2	A	GILLINGHAM	7,276	16 (4)	36	D 1-1	0-1	Duguid 64 / Asaba 22 / Ref: J Kirkby
32	27/2	H	READING	4,696	15 (11)	37	W 1-0	1-0	Gregory N 8 / Parkinson 81 / Ref: A Bates
33	6/3	A	WYCOMBE	4,670	16 (23)	38	D 2-2	1-0	Dozzell 18, Gregory D 90p / Baird 57, Scott 75 / Ref: F Stretton
34	9/3	H	OLDHAM	3,616	16 (19)	39	D 2-2	1-0	Allen 40, Gregory D 67p / Whitehall 56, Duxbury 75 / Ref: K Hill

Line-ups and reports

24 — LUTON (H)
Colchester (1–11): Fernandes, Dunne, Betts, Williams", Greene, Buckle, Wilkins, Gregory D, Sale*, Abrahams, Duguid". Subs used: Gregory N/Lock/Haydon.
Luton: Davis, Alexander, Thomas, Spring, White, Johnson, McLaren, Harrison, Douglas", Gray, Evers, Docherty.
Out-of-sorts Emberson is rested. Betts bundles over Phil Gray to give Graham Alexander a penalty. Marvin Johnson hauls down Sale for U's leveller. Alan White. replacing Steve Davis, sold to Burnley (£800k), volleys Hatters in front, but Abrahams drives out of Kelvin Davis' reach.

25 — CHESTERFIELD (A)
Colchester (1–11): Fernandes, Haydon, Betts, Williams, Greene, Buckle, Wilkins, Gregory D*, Sale, Abrahams", Duguid. Subs used: Lock/Lua-Lua.
Chesterfield: Mercer, Hewitt, Nicholson, Curtis, Williams, Breckin, Howard", Beaumont, Lenagh", Ebdon, Wilkinson, Perkins/Reeves.
U's set up a £110k deal for Scarboro's Neil Campbell. Spireites have 22 points from 27 at home. It's nine games since a U's striker scored. Lua Lua, scorer of twelve goals in 17 reserve and youth games, nets four minutes into his debut. Errors by Greene and Fernandes lose the points.

26 — WREXHAM (H)
Colchester (1–11): Fernandes, Dunne, Haydon, Williams, Greene, Lock*, Wilkins, Gregory D, Sale, Abrahams, Duguid. Subs used: Lua-Lua.
Wrexham: Cartwright, McGregor, Hardy, Brammer, Spink, Carey, Chalk, Whitley, Connolly, Griffiths, Ward.
Campbell's agent turns down U's, as does Lincoln's Colin Alcide. United receive £56k compensation for the Wembley date change. Wrexham kill off U's with goals from loanees Jeff Whitley (Man City) and Carl Griffiths (L Orient). Haydon dives to own-goal Peter Ward's free-kick.

27 — STOKE (A)
Colchester (1–11): Emberson, Dunne, Betts, Williams", Greene, Buckle, Wilkins, Gregory D, Skelton, Gregory N*, Duguid". Subs used: Abrahams/Dozzell.
Stoke: Muggleton, Wallace*, Small", Sigurdsson, Robinson, Woods, Keen, Kavanagh, Thorne, Lightbourne, Forsyth, Oldfield/Crowe/Petty.
Wignall quits as he 'has taken the squad as far as he can'. Whitton and Cook become caretakers for the trip to the Britannia. Betts opens with a cracker, but a deflection by D Gregory and two further goals put U's 1-3 down. D Gregory atones, and then Dozzell nods in from close range.

28 — BRISTOL ROV (A)
Colchester (1–11): Emberson, Dunne, Betts, Williams", Greene, Buckle, Wilkins, Gregory D, Skelton, Gregory N*, Duguid". Subs used: Dozzell/Lua-Lua/Abrahams.
Bristol Rov: Jones, Pritchard*, Challis, Trees, Foster, Thomson, Holloway, McKeever", Lee, Cureton, Roberts, Trought/Penrice.
Whitton attempts to bring back McGavin. Wadsworth, 46, leaves his post at Scarborough to become U's 21st manager. He watches from the stands. Jason Roberts nets his 13th in 13 games. U's salvage a point when Andy Thomson obstructs D Gregory, who coolly nets from the spot.

29 — YORK (H)
Colchester (1–11): Emberson, Dunne, Betts, Williams, Greene, Skelton, Wilkins, Gregory D, Dozzell, Gregory N*, Duguid. Subs used: Lua-Lua.
York: Mimms, McMillan", Hall, Tinkler, Jones, Barras*, Garrett, Poulton, Cresswell, Rowe, Hinsworth, Agnew/Carruthers.
Whitton agrees to stay on as Wadsworth's number two. Betts catches Bobby Mimms slightly off his line with a 35-yard chip. Greene flicks in a second. Wilkins long throw. Richard Cresswell, capped midweek by England U-21, reduces the arrears with his 17th of the term, after Greene's foul.

30 — WIGAN (H)
Colchester (1–11): Emberson, Dunne, Betts, Williams, Greene, Skelton, Wilkins, Gregory D, Dozzell, Gregory N*, Duguid". Subs used: Lua Lua/Buckle.
Wigan: Carroll, Green, Sharp, McGibbon, Balmer, Rogers, Liddell, Greenall", Lee, Bradshaw, Barlow", Lowe/Porter.
Wadsworth makes his first signing, bringing in Aspinall on a month's loan from Brentford. Latics lose their first game since 7 November as the Wadsworth reign goes from strength to strength. Midfielders Wilkins and D Gregory score to continue the goal drought by United's strikers.

31 — GILLINGHAM (A)
Colchester (1–11): Emberson, Dunne, Betts, Aspinall, Greene!, Skelton, Wilkins", Gregory D", Dozzell!, Buckle, Duguid. Subs used: Gregory N/Abrahams/Sale.
Gillingham: Bartram, Southall, Carr, Smith, Butters, Pennock, Patterson, Hessenthaler, Asaba!, Galloway*, Taylor, Hodges.
Frenchman Pounewatchy signs until the end of the season. Asaba cuts in from the left to notch his 18th of the season. He then gets involved in a 41st-minute head-butting incident with Greene. Both are sent off. Duguid salvages a point when his 25-yard shot deflects in off Guy Butters.

32 — READING (H)
Colchester (1–11): Emberson, Dunne, Betts, Williams", Greene, Skelton, Aspinall, Buckle, Gregory N*, Dozzell, Allen*. Subs used: Forbes/Abrahams/Sale.
Reading: Howie, Glasgow", Polston, Parkinson, Primus, Casper*, Murty, Cskey, McIntyre, Thorpe, Brebner, Bernal/Brayson"/Gray.
Lack of video evidence lets Greene a suspension. Allen joins on loan from Charlton. Sale attracts the interest of Hartlepool. N Gregory nets his first for six months, slotting past Scott Howie. Man-of-the-match Phil Parkinson, head bandaged over ten stitches, curls a great equaliser.

33 — WYCOMBE (A)
Colchester (1–11): Emberson, Dunne, Aspinall, Williams, Betts, Lawrence, Carroll, Brown, Allen*, Dozzell", Gregory N. Subs used: Buckle/Emblem/McCarthy.
Wycombe: Taylor, Wright, Vinnicombe, Ryan, Cousins, Carroll, Baird, McSporran", Scott, Baird".
Macclesfield chase Sale, whilst Forbes (Posh) and Haydon (Kettering) are loaned out. Asaba has his ban lifted by Gills' fans verbal evidence. N Gregory (4) and Allen (22) have goals wiped out. D Gregory levels in the 97th minute, after his brother was hauled down by Martin Taylor.

34 — OLDHAM (H)
Colchester (1–11): Emberson, Dunne, Betts, Williams, P'newatchy, Buckle, Aspinall, Mardon", Allen, Gregory N*, Dozzell". Subs used: Lua Lua/Abrahams/Sale.
Oldham: Kelly, Orlygsson, Garnett, Rickers, Duxbury, Mardon", Sheridan, Tipton", Whitehall, Reid, Thom/McNiven.
Allen nets whilst grounded by Shaun Garnett's challenge. Lee Duxbury's long throw is smacked in by Steve Whitehall. Sub Sale. set to depart. is felled by Stuart Thom a minute after coming on. Duxbury scores via another long throw. Andy Holt is sent off (81) for two yellow cards.

35 · A · MACCLESFIELD · 13/3 · 16 · L · 2,796 / 23 · 39 · 0–2

Emberson / *Price* | Abrahams / *Tinson* | Duguid / *Hitchen* | Aspinall* / *Payne* | P'newatchy / *Sedgeme* | Buckle / *Sodje* | Wilkins / *Askey** | Gregory D* / *Sorvel* | Allen* / *Landon* | Gregory N / *Matias** | Sale / *Durkan* | subs: Dozzell/Dunne/Williams · *Wood/Bailey*

Pounewatchy's ex-Martigues team-mate Richard joins on trial. Wilkins returns to bolster a defence that has conceded 27 in the last 14 games. The terrible state of the Moss Rose pitch gives Wilkins a further injury, and U's no points via Richard Landon and Man C loanee Alan Bailey.

Landon 65, Bailey 90 — Ref: B Coddington

---

36 · H · MANCHESTER C · 20/3 · 17 · L · 6,544 / 6 · 39 · 0–1

Emberson / *Weaver* | Abrahams / *Crooks* | Duguid / *Edgehill* | P'newatchy / *Wiekens* | Greene / *Morrison* | Buckle / *Vaughan* | Aspinall / *Brown* | Gregory D / *Bishop* | Dozzell / *Taylor* | Gregory N* / *Goater* | Fumaca* / *Cooke** | subs: Sale*/Stamps · *Whitley*

U's host the second ever pay-per-view match in Britain. Brazilian Jose Antunes <Fumaca> debuts and excites in a brief 14-minute spell, before being knocked unconscious in a challenge with Andy Morrison. Shaun Goater capitalises on Emberson's poor kick. Aspinall later hits the post.

Goater 55 — Ref: R Styles

---

37 · A · BOURNEMOUTH · 27/3 · 18 · L · 6,442 / 5 · 39 · 1–2

Emberson / *Ovendale* | Dunne / *Rawlinson* | Richard* / *Warren* | Williams / *Howe* | Greene / *O'Neill* | Buckle" / *Bailey* | Aspinall / *Cox* | Gregory D / *Huck** | Launders / *Stein* | Gregory N* / *Hayter* | P'newatchy / *Hughes* | subs: Betts/Abrahams/Lua Lua · *Dean*

U's lose Fumaca to Barnsley, as he had an option to join a bigger club. The match kicks off at noon as England face Poland at Wembley later. Greene gets U's off to the best possible start, but U's fall to two set pieces that Wadsworth had warmed, and trained his men against, all week.

Greene 20; Warren 35, Hughes 40 — Ref: M Pierce

---

38 · H · PRESTON · 2/4 · 16 · W · 5,644 / 2 · 42 · 1–0

Emberson / *Lucas* | Richard / *Alexander* | Dunne / *Clement !* | Williams / *Murdock* | Greene / *Jackson* | P'newatchy / *Gregan* | Aspinall* / *Macken* | Gregory D / *Rankine* | Dozzell* / *Nogan* | Lua Lua* / *Basham* | Duguid / *Appleton** | subs: Gregory N/Germain/Buckle · *McKenna/Eyers*

Launders, out for the rest of the term, returns to Derby. Another Frenchman, Germain, joins from AS Cannes. Meanwhile, Sale joins Plymouth on loan. U's pull away from the relegation zone when Aspinall heads in Lua Lua's cross. Neil Clement is red-carded (51) for two bookings.

Aspinall 78 — Ref: J Robinson

---

39 · A · BURNLEY · 5/4 · 18 · L · 10,747 / 17 · 42 · 1–3

Emberson / *Crichton* | Richard / *Pickering'* | Wilkins" / *Cowan* | Williams" / *Mellon* | Greene / *Davis* | P'newatchy / *Brass** | Aspinall" / *Little* | Gregory D / *Armstrong* | Dozzell / *Cook"* | Lua Lua ! / *Payton* | Duguid / *Johnson* | subs: Buckle/Germain/Betts · *Branch/Jepson/Reid*

United's stadium plan will go before the planners 'by the end of May'. Lua Lua expresses remorse when his petulant kick at Tom Cowan (54) earns a red card. United, leading through D Gregory's 25-yarder, fall to pieces after the dismissal, and succumb to a late Andy Payton brace.

Gregory D 26; Johnson 57, Payton 82, 89 — Ref: G Cain

---

40 · H · WALSALL · 10/4 · 17 · W · 4,082 / 2 · 45 · 1–0

Emberson / *Walker* | Richard / *Marsh* | Dunne* / *Pointon"* | Williams / *Henry* | Greene / *Viveash* | P'newatchy / *Roper* | Williams" / *Wrack* | Gregory D / *Steiner* | Dozzell / *Rammell* | Lua Lua / *Larusson"* | Duguid" / *Mavrak"* | subs: Duguid"/Abrahams · *Brissett/Keates/Green*

Planners reveal that 'the first sod could be turned in early 2000'. Lua Lua keeps his place, despite angering Wadsworth. Second-placed Walsall fail to impress. Greene scores direct from a free-kick, but Richard is accused of spitting at Walsall fans, who had thrown the ball in his face.

Greene 45 — Ref: M Halsey

---

41 · A · MILLWALL · 14/4 · 18 · L · 4,696 / 9 · 45 · 0–2

Fernandes / *Spink* | Richard / *Bircham* | Dunne" / *Bull* | Williams" / *Fitzgerald* | Greene / *Stephens* | P'newatchy / *Bubb** | Wilkins / *Odunsi* | Gregory D* / *Hockton* | Dozzell / *Grant* | Lua Lua / *Cook* | Aspinall / *Hicks* | subs: Gregory N/Duguid"/Abra'ms

Wilkins' 250th appearance is against a side showing ELEVEN changes from Saturday. They have a Wembley date on Sunday. Kim Grant nets on 34 secs. Keith Stevens fouls Aspinall for Nigel Spink to save D Gregory's spot-kick (11). Greene scythes Danny Hockton for Grant's pen.

Grant 1, 16p — Ref: L Cable

---

42 · H · NOTTS CO · 16/4 · 16 · W · 4,215 / 14 · 48 · 2–1

Fernandes / *Ward* | Richard / *Owers* | Dunne* / *Pearce'* | Williams* / *Hughes* | Greene / *Redmile* | Stamps / *Warren* | Betts / *Tierney** | Wilkins / *Richardson* | Gregory D* / *Stallard* | Lua Lua / *Beadle* | Aspinall / *Murray** | subs: Abrahams · *Rapley/Holmes/Dyer*

Big spenders County have brought their way out of relegation with one defeat in eleven. Dozzell plays a penetrating ball for Buckle to take in his stride for his first of the term. Mark Stallard levels, for Aspinall and Lua Lua to fight for the ball, when sub Paul Holmes pushes Abrahams.

Buckle 37, Aspinall 86p; Stallard 78 — Ref: D Crick

---

43 · A · NORTHAMPTON · 24/4 · 18 · D · 6,136 / 21 · 49 · 3–3

Fernandes / *Francis* | Richard / *Parrish'* | P'newatchy / *Frain* | Betts" / *Sampson* | Greene / *Howey* | Wilkins / *Savage* | Buckle / *Wilson** | Aspinall / *Corazzin* | Dozzell* / *Howard* | Gregory N* / *Hunt* | Abrahams* | subs: Gregory D/Germain/Duguid · *Gibb/Spedding*

Lua Lua is suspended as U's prevent Cobblers from closing the gap. Ref Frankland has a nightmare: adjudging Pounewatchy to have pushed Steven Howard; Lee Howey to handle; Duguid not to be pushed by Ian Sampson; and disallowing a valid, perfectly good Northampton winner.

Buckle 3, Aspinall 47p, Duguid 71; Savage 18, Corazzin 41p, Howey 63 — Ref: G Frankland

---

44 · H · BOURNEMOUTH · 27/4 · 18 · W · 4,168 / 6 · 52 · 2–1

Fernandes / *Ovendale* | Richard / *Young* | P'newatchy / *Warren* | Betts* / *Howe* | Greene / *Hayter** | Wilkins / *Huck** | Buckle" / *Cox* | Gregory D / *Stein* | Dozzell / *Robinson* | Aspinall / *Fletcher* | Duguid* / *Hughes* | subs: Stamps/Germain/Lock · *Lovell/Griffin*

James Hayter bizarrely heads over keeper Mark Ovendale. Fernandes punches a knee-high William Huck corner that rebounds off Greene. Dozzell nods the winner from Duguid's cross. Justice is done, as U's led 3-1 when the October fixture was abandoned through water-logging.

Hayter 11 (og), Dozzell 67; Greene 34 (og) — Ref: L Cable

---

45 · H · LINCOLN · 1/5 · 17 · L · 4,613 / 23 · 52 · 1–3

Fernandes / *Vaughan* | Richard / *Barnett* | P'newatchy / *Bimson* | Stamps / *Phillips* | Greene / *Holmes* | Buckle / *Austin* | Wilkins* / *Thorpe* | Gregory D* / *Finnigan* | Aspinall / *Stein* | Aspinall / *Gordon** | Duguid / *Miller* | subs: Lock/Germain · *Philpott, Fleming*

U's were as good as safe, but second division status is secured by other results. City have more to play for and capitalise on errors through Gavin Gordon and Lee Thorpe. Duguid pulls one back from Aspinall's pass, but Thorpe increases the lead, and has a third harshly ruled out.

Duguid 49; Gordon 43, Thorpe 44, 75 — Ref: A Hall

---

46 · A · BLACKPOOL · 8/5 · 18 · L · 4,866 / 14 · 52 · 1–2

Walker / *Caig* | Richard / *Bardsley* | P'newatchy / *Shut'worth"/Hughes* | Duguid" / *Rogan* | Greene / *Watts* | Buckle / *Bent* | Wilkins / *Clarkson* | Gregory D* / *Malkin"* | Germain* / *Garvey** | Lua Lua / *Ormerod* | Aspinall / *Bryan/Nowland/Cold* | subs: Okafor/Opara

U's fans spend a party weekend on the coast, free from any worries. Pounewatchy nods in his first U's goal from Aspinall's free-kick. Youth-teamers Walker, Okafor and Opara earn debuts, whilst compatriot Lua Lua shows his devastating dribbling skills to the shirt-sleeved crowd.

Pounewatchy 27; Omerod 73, Clarkson 88 — Ref: D Laws

Home Average 4,479 · Away 6,714

LEAGUE DIVISION 2 (CUP-TIES) Manager: Wignall ⇨ Wadsworth SEASON 1998-99

Worthington League Cup

		F-A	H-T	Scorers, Times, and Referees	1	2	3	4	5	6	7	8	9	10	11	subs used
1:1	A BOURNEMOUTH 11/8 3,745 2:	L 0-2	0-1	Robinson 16, Howe 87 Ref: C Wilkes	Emberson *Ovendale*	Betts *Young*	Stamps *Vincent*	Williams *Howe*	Greene *Berthe`*	Buckle *Bailey*	Haydon *Cox*	Gregory D *Robinson*	Sale *Stein*	Gregory N* *Fletcher**	Abrahams^ *Hughes*	Duguid/Adcock *Tawn/Tindall*

Accountants Deloitte and Touche reveal U's are the second fastest growing club, behind Middlesbro', with a 61% increase in revenue over five years. Cherries' Steve Robinson rifles in a close-range drive. Stamps concedes a needless corner for England U-21 Eddie Howe to head home

		F-A	H-T	Scorers, Times, and Referees	1	2	3	4	5	6	7	8	9	10	11	subs used
1:2	H BOURNEMOUTH 18/8 2,550 2:4	W 3-2	1-2	Gregory D 12p, 90p, Abrahams 66 Stein 23, Fletcher 28 Ref: B Knight	Emberson *Ovendale*	Betts^ *Young*	Stamps *Vincent*	Williams *Howe*	Greene *Berthe`*	Buckle *Bailey*	Haydon *Cox*	Gregory D *Robinson**	Sale *Stein*	Gregory N* *Fletcher*	Abrahams *Hughes*	Forbes/Dunne *Tindall/O'Neill*

Arsenal refuse to switch the reserve fixture, so Forbes and Duguid have to dash back to make up the numbers. Richard Young fouls Haydon, but a Mark Stein volley and Steve Fletcher header means that Abrahams' goal from Dunne's cross and a baffling hand-ball are too late for U's.

(Colchester lost 3-4 on aggregate)

FA Cup

		F-A	H-T	Scorers, Times, and Referees	1	2	3	4	5	6	7	8	9	10	11	subs used
1	A BEDLINGTON 14/11 20 2,027 NL:1	A 1-4	0-2	Adcock 88 Ditchburn 16, Milner 23, 86p, Cross 60 O'Connor Ref: M Messias	Emberson *Sokoluk*	Dunne *O'Connor*	Stamps^ *Pike*	Williams *Teasdale*	Greene *Ditchburn*	Buckle *Melrose*	Dozzell *Cross*	Gregory D *Bond*	Sale^ *Gibb*	Lock *Milner*	Forbes* *Middleton*	Adcock/Duguid/Haydon

Many of the Terriers' squad face an uncertain future, as redundancies are announced at the town's biggest employer – Wilkinson Sword. U's pampered professionals have no such worries. John Milner collects his 26th of the term for the Geordies, after Buckle had hauled him down.

Autowindscreen Shield

		F-A	H-T	Scorers, Times, and Referees	1	2	3	4	5	6	7	8	9	10	11	subs used
1	H GILLINGHAM 5/12 15 1,742 2:5	L 1-5	1-4	Gregory D 23p [Smith 37] Asaba 22, Pennock 29, Taylor 34, 67, Ref: W Jordan	Emberson *Bartram*	Dunne *Bryant*	Betts *Butters*	Williams *Smith*	Greene *Ashby*	Buckle *Pennock*	Forbes^ *Hodge*	Gregory D *Southall*	Sale* *Asaba**	Gregory N* *Galloway*	Abrahams *Taylor*^	Dozzell/Lock/Stamps *Pinnock/Noseworthy*

Gills are picking up after poor start. Wignall slams his players and asks if they really want to play for the club. United are briefly in the game following Barry Ashby's foul on Sale, but Emberson's poor back-pass, from Greene's equally poor back-pass, falls to Robert Taylor to add the fifth.

League Table

			Home					Away					
	P	W	D	L	F	A	W	D	L	F	A	Pts
1 Fulham	46	19	3	1	50	12	12	5	6	29	20	101
2 Walsall	46	13	7	3	37	23	13	2	8	26	24	87
3 Man City*	46	13	6	4	38	14	9	10	4	31	19	82
4 Gillingham	46	15	5	3	45	17	7	9	7	30	27	80
5 Preston	46	12	6	5	46	23	10	7	6	32	27	79
6 Wigan	46	14	5	4	44	17	8	5	10	31	31	76
7 Bournemouth	46	14	7	2	37	11	7	6	10	26	30	76
8 Stoke	46	10	4	9	32	32	11	2	10	27	31	69
9 Chesterfield	46	14	5	4	34	16	3	8	12	12	28	64
10 Millwall	46	9	8	6	33	24	8	3	12	19	35	62
11 Reading	46	10	6	7	29	26	6	7	10	25	37	61
12 Luton	46	10	4	9	25	26	6	6	11	26	34	58
13 Bristol Rov	46	8	9	6	35	28	5	8	10	30	28	56
14 Blackpool	46	7	8	8	24	24	7	6	10	20	30	56
15 Burnley	46	8	7	8	23	33	5	9	9	31	40	55
16 Notts Co	46	8	6	9	29	27	6	9	11	23	34	54
17 Wrexham	46	8	8	7	21	27	5	8	10	23	34	53
18 COLCHESTER	46	9	7	7	25	30	3	9	11	27	40	52
19 Wycombe	46	8	5	10	31	26	5	7	11	21	32	51
20 Oldham	46	8	4	11	26	31	6	5	12	22	35	51
21 York	46	6	8	9	28	33	7	3	13	28	47	50
22 Northampton	46	4	12	7	26	31	6	6	11	17	26	48
23 Lincoln	46	9	4	10	27	27	4	3	16	15	47	46
24 Macclesfield	46	7	4	12	24	30	6	4	13	19	33	43
	1104	243	146	163	769	589	163	146	243	589	769	1510

* promoted after play-offs

Odds & ends

Double wins: (1) York.

Double defeats: (3) Burnley, Fulham, Manchester City.

Won from behind: (1) Wycombe (h).

Lost from in front: (2) Bournemouth (a), Burnley (a).

High spots: Retaining hard-won second division status.

Competing on the same stage as the likes of Manchester City, Stoke and Fulham.

The probability of a new stadium at Cuckoo Farm.

Increase in home attendances, giving the highest average since 1977-78.

United go continental, with Frenchmen, a Zairois, a Nigerian and a brief glimpse of a Brazilian.

A record number of penalties in a season, 11 scored, 2 missed.

Eight games without defeat post-Wignall.

Layer Road a virtual fortress in the last ten home games.

The exciting potential of Lomano Tresor Lua Lua.

Low spots: Defeat in all cup competitions at the first stage.

Tony Adcock narrowly missing out on beating Bobby Hunt's club goal-scoring record by just four goals.

Humiliation of FA Cup defeat at Northern League Bedlington Terriers.

Desperately low scoring rate of the club's strikers.

Only six clean sheets in the league.

Player of the Year: David Greene.

Ever presents: (0).

Hat-tricks: (0).

Leading scorer: David Gregory (14) (incl. one in Autowindscreen Shield).

Appearances and Goals

	Appearances						Goals			
	Lge	Sub	LC	Sub	FAC	Sub	Lge	LC	FAC	Tot
Abrahams, Paul	13	14	2				2	1		3
Allen, Bradley	4						1			1
Aspinall, Warren	15						3			3
Adcock, Tony		6		1					1	1
Betts, Simon	22	6	2		1		2			2
Branston, Guy		1								
Buckle, Paul	39	4	2			1	2			2
Dozzell, Jason	23	6			1	1	4			4
Dublin, Keith	2									
Duguid, Karl	23	10	1		1	1	4			4
Dunne, Joe	32	4	1		1					
Emberson, Carl	37		2		1					
Fernandes, Tamar	8									
Forbes, Steve	8	7			1	1	2			2
Fumaca	1									
Germain, Steve		5								
Greene, David	42	2	2				8			8
Gregory, David	43	1	2		1		11	2		13
Gregory, Neil	29	9	2		1		4			4
Haydon, Nicky	7	6	2			1	1			1
Launders, Brian	1									
Lock, Tony	14	9					1			1
Lua Lua, Lom' Tresor	6	7					1			1
Okafor, Sam		1								
Opara, KK		1								
Pounewatchy, Steph'	15						1			1
Rainford, David		1								
Richard, Fabrice	10									
Sale, Mark	21	10	2		1		2			2
Skelton, Aaron	7	2								
Stamps, Scott	19	2	2							
Walker, Andy	1									
Wiles, Ian		1								
Wilkins, Richard	25	1	2				2			2
Williams, Geraint	38	1	2		1		1			1
(own-goals)							1			1
35 players used	506	115	22	4	11	3	52	3	1	56

SUBSCRIBER	FAVOURITE PLAYER
Mr John A Baker	Mike Walker
John Barnard	Mark Kinsella
Martyn Bell	Tony Adcock
Steve Blake	Mark Kinsella
Keith Blaxall	Steve Leslie
Peter Bower	Brian Hall
Ian Bown	Tony Adcock
Mervyn Bright	David Greene
Katie Jane Brooks	Alec Chamberlain
Jane Butler	Roy Massey
Natasha Byford	Karl Duguid
Bert Cardy	Brian Hall
Robin Carter	Mike Walker
Dan Cave	Tony Adcock
Andy Chambers	Mark Kinsella
Bill Chatten	Steve Wignall
Jenny & Frank Clements	Mark Kinsella
Raymond V Cole	Bobby Svarc
M & J Collins	Tony English
The Cordell family	Richard Wilkins
Ken Craig	Tony Adcock
Mark Cutting	Mick Packer
Mr A R Daldry	Mick Mahon
Paul Darby	Mark Kinsella
Alan F J Dews	Mark Kinsella
Roger Dicker	Steve McGavin
Mrs W J Dodshon	
Tom & Jean Dowson	Ian Atkins
Jeff Dunn	Mark Kinsella
Mr M Duthie	Brian Hall
The Eley family	Simon Betts
John Elmy	Peter Wright
Jerry Everett	Trevor Lee

SUBSCRIBER	FAVOURITE PLAYER
Jeremy Fielden	Steve Leslie
Colin Foster	Micky Cook
Joe Geddis	Lindsay Smith
Peter Gibbs	Percy Ames
Phil Gladwin	Brian Hall
Jason Gunn	Tony Adcock
Robert Hadgraft	Brian Lewis
Phil Harris	Tony Adcock
Robert Jackson	Brian Lewis
Edmund Jenkinson	Tony Adcock
David Johnson	Ray Crawford
Nick Johnson	Mike Walker
Robert Kerry	Joe Dunne
Richard Lay	Graham Smith
Bernie Lewis	Brian Hall
Ray Lilley	Mark Kinsella
Lina P, CUFC Swedish Branch	Tony English
Rob Lloyd	Bobby Gough
L-O A, CUFC Swedish Branch	Nicky Smith
Martin H, CUFC Swedish Branch	Adam Locke
Stephen Martin	Mark Kinsella
Michael G Middleton.	Micky Cook
Gerald Mott	
Susie Owers	Mark Kinsella
Paul A, CUFC Swedish Branch	Mark Kinsella
Steve Peacock	Mark Kinsella
Chris Porcas	Mark Kinsella
Roger Potter	Micky Cook
Scott Robinson	Mark Kinsella
Chris Rogers	Mark Kinsella
Josephine Root	Mark Kinsella
Richard Rose	Bobby Svarc
Dale Rout	Brian Hall

SUBSCRIBER	FAVOURITE PLAYER
Bob Russell MP	Mark Kinsella
Graham Scillitoe	Roy McDonough
Alan Smith (Brightlingsea)	Ray Crawford
Brian A Smith	Duncan Forbes
David C Smith	Mark Kinsella
Duncan Stonehouse	Tony Adcock
Keith & William Stott	Mark Kinsella
Steven Streeter	Mark Kinsella
Mr P A Taylor	Mark Kinsella
Ted & Daphne (Rowhedge)	Bobby Svarc
Alf Todd	Ian Atkins
Matthew Tokley	Mark Kinsella
Graham E Tuckwell	Scott Barrett
J R B Tweed	Micky Cook
Neil Waldock	Nicky Smith
William A Ward	
Julian Wareham	Tony Adcock
Andrew Webber	Mark Kinsella
Edward Wells	Peter Cawley
Roger, Jeanette & Ben Westlake	Mark Kinsella
Simon Whiting	Tony Adcock
Daniel Whymark	Tony Adcock
J W Wolton	Colin Garwood
Christopher John Woods	Warren Aspinall
Steve Wright	Bobby Gough
Duncan Wyatt	Mark Kinsella

MOST POPULAR
U'S PLAYER 1968-1999

36 different players
received votes

1st   Mark Kinsella
2nd Tony Adcock
3rd Brian Hall

4th Micky Cook
5th Mike Walker
6th Bobby Svarc